Contents of *Contemporary Investments*
Data Disk

Chapter	File Name	Brief Description
1	stock1.xls	Data on large stocks, broken into price and income, monthly, 1991–1993.
2	rcturns1.xls	Annual returns for stocks, T-bonds, T-bills, and inflation data, 1949–1993.
4	fund1.xls	Net asset values and total cash distributions for Fidelity Magellan mutual fund (1983–1993).
6	price1.xls	Weekly values for the S&P 500, 1990–1993.
6	price2.xls	Weekly values for the S&P 500, and four industries, 1990–1993.
7	price3.xls	Weekly values for the S&P 500, 1990–1993.
10	WMT.txt	Text of Wal-Mart stock report from A.G. Edwards & Sons.
11	FINA1.xls	Data on revenue and operating profits for three companies.
11	FINA2.xls	Wal-Mart sales data and consumer spending data.
11	K-mart.xls	Selected financial data for Kmart Corporation (1990–1992).
11	SWA.xls	Analysts forecast of earnings for Southwest Airlines, variables used to make estimate.
12	stkret1.xls	Quarterly returns for 10 stocks.
13	stkret2.xls	Quarterly returns for 10 stocks; Value Line estimates for 1994 (earnings, dividends, and price).
12,13	FINA3.xls	Monthly returns for 8 stocks plus the market return.
14	mreturn.xls	Betas and 1993 returns for 40 mutual funds.
15	return2.xls	44 quarterly returns for 20 stocks, the market, and T-bills.
16	bond1.xls	Bond data (cash flows, price, yield to maturity, etc.).
17	ch17a.xls	Yields and prices for pure discount bonds with maturities of 1, 7, & 20 years (use current yields on zero coupon T-bonds).
17	ch17b.xls	Yields and prices on several different bonds to fund a known future liability.
18	option1.xls	Recent prices of S&P 100 (OEX) options. Several strike prices and delivery dates.
18	bs1.xls	Quarterly returns for the S&P 500 and G.E.
19	CTD.xls	Bonds that can be delivered against the Dec. 93 T-bond contract (prices, yields, and conversion factors as of a particular date).
19	OOF.xls	Calls and puts on Dec. 93 T-bonds futures.
20	fund2.xls	Quarterly return data for Dreyfus 3rd Century mutual fund along with the S&P 500.

CONTEMPORARY INVESTMENTS

Security and Portfolio Analysis

CONTEMPORARY INVESTMENTS

Security and Portfolio Analysis

Douglas Hearth
University of Arkansas

Janis Zaima
San Jose State University

The Dryden Press
Harcourt Brace College Publishers

Fort Worth   Philadelphia   San Diego   New York   Orlando   Austin   San Antonio
Toronto   Montreal   London   Sydney   Tokyo

Senior Acquisitions Editor Rick Hammonds
Developmental Editor Shana M. Lum
Project Editor Matt Ball
Art Director Brian Salisbury
Production Manager Ann Coburn
Photo & Permissions Editor Elizabeth Banks, Louis Karkoutli
Product Manager Craig Johnson
Marketing Coordinator Sam Stubblefield

Copy Editor David Talley
Indexer Leoni McVey
Composition GTS Graphics
Text Type 10/12 New Baskerville

Address for Editorial Correspondence
The Dryden Press, 301 Commerce Street, Suite 3700, Fort Worth, TX 76102

Address for Orders
The Dryden Press, 6277 Sea Harbor Drive, Orlando, FL 32887
1-800-782-4479, or 1-800-433-0001 (in Florida)

ISBN: 0-15-500049-7

Library of Congress Catalog Card Number: 93-74359

Printed in the United States of America

4 5 6 7 8 9 0 1 2 3 039 9 8 7 6 5 4 3 2 1

The Dryden Press
Harcourt Brace College Publishers

This book is dedicated to our spouses, Karen and Ken, and children, Alan, Eric, Jana, and Kelly.

The Dryden Press Series in Finance

The HB College Outline Series

Preface

We designed this textbook for use in the first undergraduate or MBA investments course. Our goal was to write an investments book that is primarily devoted to discussing how real investors actually make decisions and whether these decisions are right or wrong. We have integrated the traditional investments course topics such as modern portfolio theory, valuation, and market efficiency within this framework to illustrate their relevance to actual investing techniques that may be used by the individual or professional investor.

To the Instructor

With more than 30 years of combined teaching experience, we know just how difficult it can be to cover all the material you want and need to cover. It often seems like there's never enough time to cover everything. We've tried to help by structuring the text material in such a way that topics can be covered generally, or in more depth, depending on the needs and preferences of instructors and their students. For example, the breadth of the in-text examples, articles, and end-of-chapter material will easily support a two-semester (or quarter) sequence.

The chapters are designed to be read in the order they are presented; however, in designing and writing the chapters, we've allowed for some flexibility depending on instructor preferences. Other instructors tell us that they prefer to cover modern portfolio theory in class earlier than we do in the book. This presents no problem as *Contemporary Investments* isn't, after all, a novel! Students can read the chapters on modern portfolio theory (Chapters 12–15) before the chapters on security analysis (Chapters 8–11) without much loss in continuity. Other instructors who prefer to cover bonds before common stocks can read the two chapters devoted to bonds (Chapters 16 and 17) before Chapters 8–11 without becoming hopelessly confused.

Features

Contemporary Investments offers a number of unique and important features designed to capture student interest and thereby aid student learning.

- *More emphasis on common stock investing and traditional security analysis (sometimes referred to as the Graham and Dodd approach).* Not only have common stocks proven to be superior investments, they are also, in our view, the most interesting, albeit complicated investment instrument. The Graham and Dodd approach for valuing common stocks was first published more than 60 years ago, at the height of the Great Depression. It has easily withstood the test of time.
- *In-depth examination of qualitative, as well as the quantitative factors that may determine common stock values and prices—something most textbooks overlook.* While it may be difficult to define what is meant by the *quality of management,* it is too important a topic to ignore, or even downplay. A company can appear to have good-looking financial statements but still be poorly managed.
- *An intuitive approach to modern portfolio theory (MPT), presented with a minimum of mathematics.* We emphasize how MPT contributes to understanding how investment markets function. At the same time, we show how the combination of traditional security analysis and MPT can help all types of investors make better investment decisions. When students see the relationship of MPT to the real world, we believe they will take it more seriously and it will be easier to learn.

- *A more balanced treatment of how professional investors make their investment decisions (technical and fundamental analysis).* We recognize, and point out, that professionals are often wrong. However they've made more than their share of correct calls as well, and some professionals have excellent track records. Why professionals are right is as important as why they are wrong.

- *An entire chapter specifically devoted to a study of speculative bubbles and other past investment follies.* We can, after all, argue that investments is often the study of mistakes in retrospect. The mistakes serve to reinforce an important truism in investments: price and value can diverge substantially in the short run, but in the long run, investments tend to sell for their intrinsic values. Further, speculative bubbles help to illustrate the human, emotional side of investing.

- *Integration of global investment topics.* The globalization of the financial markets and investing has been one of the most significant trends in recent years. Virtually all textbooks discuss this topic but address the globalization of investing by adding a chapter at the end. The international chapter then becomes a logical candidate for omission when time runs short. We've addressed globalization by integrating it throughout the text, making international issues a natural part of the material. Where appropriate, an icon, which is illustrated in the margin, is used for quick identification of specific international examples.

- *Coverage of ethical issues.* Investing raises a number of ethical situations, such as those involving the use of inside or privileged information. Throughout the textbook we provide numerous opportunities for class discussion involving ethical issues and investing in the form of everything from boxes to end-of-chapter questions.

- *A conversational writing style throughout the book.* We realize that some instructors might feel that an informal tone means a less rigorous book. In our case, this is not true. We have found that students are more interested in the course and able to handle more difficult material if we "talk" to them in an engaging, friendly way and in terms that they can understand.

Pedagogy

- Each chapter begins with a set of learning objectives designed to guide the student's reading and ends with a summary reviewing the chapter material in terms of these objectives.

- Throughout each chapter we extensively use real companies and real investment situations to illustrate key points. We believe students will understand these concepts better if they see how real companies apply them. Students will run into such well known companies as Disney, General Electric, Sara Lee, Southwest Airlines, and Wal-Mart Stores, just to name a few.

- Each chapter includes at least one *Investment Insights* box, most contain two or three. These are current articles reprinted from the business and financial press, such as *The Wall Street Journal, Business Week,* and *Fortune.* We think it is important for students to become familiar with the publications that are often a daily part of the investment world. These articles also reinforce key points and show practical applications of the chapter material. For that reason, we actually integrate discussion about the articles within the body of the chapter.

- Most figures and graphs contain a boxed note. Because figures and graphs do not immediately follow their text explanations, students are often unaware of exactly what key concept the figure or graph shows. We use a boxed note to guide them to the important relationship illustrated by the figure.

- In selected chapters, a brief one-paragraph summary follows difficult, complicated material. These brief summaries give students a chance to catch their breath and review what was covered before pushing ahead.

- The most complicated, demanding material, whether it be mathematical or conceptual, is placed in separate sections that are indicated by asterisks. Instructors have the flexibility of omitting these sections without losing continuity.
- At the end of each chapter, we provide extensive questions and problems. Almost all the chapters have one or two mini-cases—comprehensive problems, with the solutions provided, that are designed to test student comprehension over large portions of material. All chapters have 15 to 20 discussion questions and problems to test students' knowledge over more specific points. Finally, each chapter has at least one critical thinking exercise (most have two or three). Critical thinking exercises require library research, computer work or both. Not only are these designed to see how well students comprehend the chapter material, they also give students some hands-on practice with real data in investment situations.

Supplements

A number of excellent supplements have been developed to accompany *Contemporary Investments*.

- ***Instructor's Manual.*** The instructors manual outlines each chapter, provides a list of general and specific learning objectives, shows points to emphasize in class, and indicates where students often get confused. We have included a list of possible student projects and term papers. The instructors manual provides solutions for all end-of-chapter questions, problems, and critical thinking exercises. Also included is a set of 130 transparency masters for easy adaptation into overheads.
- ***Test Bank.*** A thorough, comprehensive test bank is available, both in paper and computerized versions. The test bank contains numerous objective questions, short answer essay questions, and problems for each chapter along with several sample tests. Our test bank is also available in computerized form in PC 5.25″, 3.5″ and Mac formats. Dryden's computerized testing format, ExaMaster+, has many features which making test preparation, scoring, and recording grades easy. For example, ExaMaster+ allows you to convert multiple-choice questions and problems into free-response questions. You can also easily scramble the order of test questions for different sections of your course. In addition, the program gives you the ability to add to or edit the existing test questions. Through key-word searches and qualifier-screening, you can easily compile a test specific to your class.
- ***Data Disk.*** A data disk is available with all copies of the book. It contains the Lotus/Excel data files to accompany many critical thinking exercises along with other material referred to in the text.
- ***Investment Wizard.*** The Investment Wizard is a stand-alone software package. It is an easy to use, menu-driven program that performs common investment and statistical calculations. For their excellent work on this software, we are indebted to Dilip Kare, University of South Florida; Jim Pettijohn, Southwest Missouri State and Joe Evans.
- ***Study Guide.*** An excellent study guide written by Thomajean Johnsen of the University of Denver is available for purchase by students. The guide contains a detailed chapter outline, and additional questions and problems for student practice and mastery.

Acknowledgements

As with all books, we have many, many people to thank. At the risk of this preface sounding like an acceptance speech at the Academy Awards, we want to start by thanking the individuals who reviewed various drafts of the manuscript and participated in focus groups. Their comments and suggestions were invaluable in making *Contemporary Investments* better. They have our heartfelt thanks. These individuals are:

Jerry Boswell	*Metropolitan State College of Denver*
Larry Byerly	*University of Pittsburgh at Johnstown*
James D'Mello	*Western Michigan University*
David Dubofsky	*Seattle University*
John Emery	*California State University—Fresno*
Stevenson Hawkey	*Golden Gate University*
Jeffry Manzi	*Ohio University*
Saeed Mortazavi	*Humboldt State University*
Henry Oppenheimer	*University of Rhode Island*
Aaron Phillips	*American University*
Robert Ryan	*Ithaca College*
Patricia Smith	*University of New Hampshire*
Andrew Whitaker	*North Central College*

In addition, a number of other friends and colleagues provided a great deal of input and assistance. These include Professors Robert Kennedy, David Kurtz, and James Rimbey, all of the University of Arkansas; Professors Bill Ashley, Joe Black, and Bruce Cochran, all of San Jose State University; Professor Mier Statman of Santa Clara University; Professor Stu Rosenstein of Clemson University; Professor Ken Leong of San Francisco State University; Professor Nikihil Varaiya of San Diego State University; Professor Ronald Melicher of the University of Colorado; Professors Mac Clouse and Thomajean Johnsen of the University of Denver; Professor Jean Claude Bosch of the University of Colorado—Denver; Professor Larry Johnson of the University of Tulsa; Professor Don Nast of Florida State University; Professors Carl Schwser and J. Sa-Aadu both of the University of Iowa; and Professor Darryl Gurley of Florida A&M University. We also wish to thank our academic leaders for their support, Dean Doyle Z. Williams of the University of Arkansas, and Dean Marshall Burak and Professor Joseph Mori of San Jose University.

We received research and clerical help from a number of people at both the University of Arkansas and San Jose State University. We wish to thank Clint Aguiar, Bill Callahan, Juli Douglas, Joyce D'Amico, Shannon Hoodswain, Chad Jolly, Peck Lau, Jim Philpot, Danny Pruett, Doris Robinson, and Donna Walker.

We've worked with some great people at The Dryden Press over the last couple of years. Rick Hammonds, our acquisitions editor, who encouraged us to start the project; Shana Lum, the developmental editor; Matt Ball, the project editor; Ann Coburn, the production manager; Brian Salisbury, the art director; Elizabeth Banks and Louise Karkoutli, the permissions editors; Craig Johnson, product manager; and Sam Stubblefield, marketing coordinator. We appreciate their expertise, encouragement, and, goodness knows, their patience.

Finally, to our families, Karen, Alan and Eric, and Ken, Jana and Kelly, we acknowledge their love, encouragement, and understanding. Without their support, this project would never have gotten off the ground, much less have been completed.

Douglas Hearth
Fayetteville, Arkansas

Janis K. Zaima
San Jose, California

October 1994

Brief Contents

Contents

Part I

The World of Investments

This opening section presents an overview of the subject of investments. It introduces a number of important concepts and ideas that reappear throughout the rest of the text. We discuss the importance of investment decisions, the general investment process, the concepts of risk and return, and some apparent truisms in investments. We discuss the essential characteristics of contemporary investment alternatives ranging from Treasury bills to common stocks to real estate. We also take a look at financial markets and trading, including how securities are bought and sold and how the financial markets are regulated. Finally, we examine sources of investment information, including security market indexes. We'll see that investors can draw on a massive body of information, much of it publicly available.

Chapter 1

Prelude: The World of Investments

Chapter Objectives
1. Understand why people invest and why investment decisions are so important in today's financial environment.
2. Discuss the components or parts of the investment process.
3. Review the basic characteristics of risk and return.
4. Understand some apparent truisms in investments.
5. Outline the remainder of the text.

In the next 800 pages or so, we plan to lead you on a journey through the fascinating world of investments. We'll look carefully at investment alternatives like stocks, bonds, options, and mutual funds. We'll examine how the securities markets function and how professionals make investment decisions. We'll review some past follies of investors and develop an understanding of how investors *should* make investment decisions. We believe you'll find the journey to be rewarding intellectually, and perhaps at some point economically.

Why is the study of investments an important and interesting topic? To help answer this question, consider two stories.

On June 20, 1986, investors enthusiastically greeted the initial public offering (IPO) of Worlds of Wonder, a toy maker known for innovative products, many using state-of-the-art electronics.[1] The stock raced from an offering price of $18 per share to a high of almost $30 a share over the next few months. During the 1986 Christmas season, stores couldn't keep many of the company's products on their shelves.

Quickly, however, the company began to stumble. After posting profits of around $18.5 million for the fiscal year ending March 31, 1987, Worlds of Wonder proceeded to lose over $40 million during the next six months. Management could do nothing to stop the accelerating financial hemorrhage. Out of cash and hounded by creditors, Worlds of Wonder filed for bankruptcy protection under Chapter 11 on December 22, 1987.

The stock price sank along with company profits, and by the end of 1987, Worlds of Wonder was selling for around 32.5 cents per share. When an investor group led by Eli Jacobs acquired the assets of the company in 1988, all proceeds went to creditors; stockholders received nothing.

---

[1]An initial public offering, or going public, is the first sale of a company's stock to public investors.

Also during 1986, another company, Microsoft, sold shares to the public. The well-known maker of DOS and Windows has enjoyed better success than Worlds of Wonder. Between 1986 and 1993, Microsoft's earnings grew at a rate of over 51 percent *each year.* Its annual revenues grew from less than $200 million in 1986 to over $3 *billion* in 1993.

Needless to say, Microsoft's stock has been one of the great investment successes of recent years. An investment of $1,000 in Microsoft stock when the company went public in 1986 would have grown to be worth more than $35,500 at the end of 1993, a staggering increase of 3,500 percent! At a price of $80 per share, Microsoft has a market value of over $24 billion (calculated as the share's market price times number of shares outstanding), almost as much as the market value of venerable IBM.

Of course, few investments perform as wonderfully as Microsoft, or as miserably as Worlds of Wonder. Yet these stories illustrate that investing offers the potential for both spectacular gains and devastating losses. This text explores techniques investors can use to try to separate a future Microsoft from a future Worlds of Wonder.

This chapter introduces the subject of investments. It begins by answering a simple, initial question: Why do people invest? It also presents some reasons why, we believe, investment decisions are more important today than ever before. Next, the chapter reviews the basic investment process, discussing methods for setting goals and assessing risk tolerance. The chapter then turns to a brief overview of risk and return, examining how to measure both risk and return and how to evaluate their interrelationship. Next we discuss some apparent truisms in investments, such as the positive relationship between risk and return; these truisms will reappear throughout the text. Finally, the chapter ends by outlining the rest of the text along with some suggestions for its use by both students and instructors.

Now, let's embark on our journey!

Why Invest?

Why do people invest? This seems like a simple question, and it can be answered by defining the word *invest*. According to the dictionary, *invest* means to commit money in order to earn a financial return; to make use of for future benefits or advantages.[2] In a nutshell, this definition explains why people commit money to investments: in order to increase their future wealth. By investing money to earn financial **returns,** people have more money to spend in future years. If you invest $1,000 today and earn 10 percent over the next year, you'll have $1,100 one year from today. Had you invested $1,000 at the beginning of 1991 in a broad portfolio of common stocks of large firms, your investment would have been worth around $1,300 by the end of 1991.[3]

Some of the more specific reasons that someone might invest include accumulating funds to buy a home, send their children to college, retire comfortably, or weather an unexpected crisis in their lives (such as temporary unemployment). Also, even though investing is serious business and

---

[2] *Webster's Ninth New Collegiate Dictionary* (Springfield, Mass.: Merriam-Webster, 1984), p. 636.

[3] The total return from dividend payments plus price appreciation for large-firm stocks for 1991, before taxes and transaction costs, was 30.6 percent, as reported in *SBBI 1992 Yearbook* (Chicago: Ibbotson Associates, 1992).

should never be taken lightly, some people invest because they find that it provides a fun challenge.

Investing also benefits society and the economy as a whole. Obviously, by increasing personal wealth, investing can contribute to higher overall economic growth and prosperity. For example, if investing increases the value of an individual's pension fund, at retirement that person will have more disposable income and a higher standard of living—both benefit the economy as a whole. In addition, the process of investing helps to create financial markets where companies can raise capital. This, too, contributes to greater economic growth and prosperity.

Specific types of investments provide other benefits to society, as well. Common stocks, for example, provide a mechanism for monitoring the performance of company management by stockholders who own a corporation. Municipal bonds benefit those who pay proportionally high income tax because interest from municipal bonds is exempt from federal tax. At the same time, municipal bonds provide capital for valuable public projects such as schools and roads.

The Importance of Investment Decisions Today

Investment decisions may be more important today than ever before. There are a number of reasons for this, and the following sections discuss some of the more important ones.

Larger Menu of Investment Choices

Today's investors choose among a dizzying array of investment alternatives, many of which have only been around a few years. Consider mutual funds, for example, which divide large portfolios of investments into small shares to allow investors to commit limited funds. In 1970, 361 mutual funds operated in the United States. By the end of 1993 that number had grown tenfold to over 3,800. Even to buy something as simple as a money market mutual fund, which invests in short-term government securities, an investor has to choose from over 850.

As the number of funds has grown, so has the diversity of their investment goals. The Investment Company Institute classifies mutual funds by investment objective. In 1975, it defined seven categories of mutual funds. By 1993, the number of mutual fund categories had tripled to 21.

The larger menu of investment choices today means that an investor can probably find an investment instrument that suits personal needs. At the same time, however, the larger menu also increases the potential for confusion and poor choices. Today's investors have to do their homework extremely carefully.

Longer Life Expectancies

You probably already know that life expectancies in the United States and in most developed countries, are rising. Since 1950, the life expectancy of an American turning age 65 has increased by about one-third. A 65 year old can expect to live another 18.5 years, on average.

One effect of longer life expectancies is an increase in the duration of the average person's retirement. Accumulating funds for retirement is one major reason that people invest, and a longer retirement period means that they have to accumulate more funds, which requires more careful investing. Further, the rising cost of health care will likely require greater reserves for tomorrow's retirees, compared to today's retirees, in order to provide the same standard of living.[4]

Flat Growth in Personal Income

How much have personal incomes grown in the United States over the last 10 or 20 years? Adjusted for inflation, median per-capita U.S. income increased at an annual rate of less than 1.5 percent between 1980 and 1992. Real median per-capita income actually fell between 1989 and 1991. Experts believe that average personal income is unlikely to substantially outpace the rate of inflation over the next 10 to 15 years.[5]

These personal income data suggest that one shouldn't rely merely on increasing personal income to improve one's future standard of living. The key to improving a future standard of living may well be careful investing.

Changing Labor Market

The average person entering the workplace today will change jobs about five times over his or her lifetime. Further, one in three workers will be unemployed at some point during their working years. The old ideal of going to work for a company right out of college and staying there until retirement will likely be the exception, not the rule, in tomorrow's labor market.

These sobering trends imply that people will have to rely more on their own resources, and less on corporate paternalism, in order to meet major financial goals. If nothing else, the changing labor market means everyone should accumulate a larger cushion of resources to break an unexpected fall. You never know when your employer is going to "downsize" your job out of existence!

Changing Inflation Environment

The outlook for inflation has changed dramatically during the last ten years or so. The annual rate of inflation has fallen from over 10 percent in 1981 to less than 3 percent during 1993, and most economists expect inflation to remain low throughout the rest of the 1990s. That's good news for investors who are worried about the future cost of living, right? The answer is both yes and no. Certainly low inflation historically has been good for stocks and bonds. During the inflation-ravaged 1970s, stock and bond returns often failed to keep pace with rising prices, eroding the value of investment returns. As inflation fell during the 1980s, stock and bond returns easily outpaced the rate of inflation in most years.

Low inflation can make investment decisions more complicated, however. For example, during the 1970s and most of the 1980s, home prices soared in many parts of the country.[6] Homeowners' equity, of course, soared along with rising housing prices. Homeowners could generally count on a pretty good nest egg, if they sold their homes when they retired, and buying a home seemed like a great investment. This may no longer be true. According to a

---

[4]Today, a general rule of thumb states that one should have an annual retirement income equal to about 70 percent of one's annual preretirement income in order to have a comparable standard of living. Some experts believe that this percentage will rise to around 75 percent by the turn of the century.

[5]*U.S. News & World Report,* October 7, 1991, 61.

[6]The median sales price of a single-family home in the United States rose from $25,200 in 1971 to $131,200 in 1990, an annual increase of about 6 percent.

study published in *Money* magazine, U.S. home prices, on average, are expected to barely keep up with the rate of inflation for the rest of the 1990s; prices will likely fall in some major markets.[7] This will force many people to look elsewhere, such as investments in stocks and bonds, for their retirement nest eggs.

Another consequence of today's low inflation is low interest rates. While that's great news for those who want to buy homes, it's tough on savers, especially those who rely on interest income to boost their standards of living. The average yield on taxable money market funds fell from around 9 percent in 1989 to less than 4 percent in 1993. Investors had relied on 8 percent to 10 percent yields on very low-risk investments, such as money market funds and certificates of deposit (CDs); now they must search for yields of 3 to 4 percent. As a result, many people are forced to consider investing in stocks or longer-term bonds for the first time. Stock and bond investing is more complicated, not to mention more risky, than simple money funds and CDs, and it requires more thoughtful planning and consideration.

The Investment Process

The descriptions of why people invest and why investment decisions are so important today raise the question of how to go about investing. We now turn our attention to a general description of the investment process, beginning with several preparations that many financial experts believe people should complete before they begin investing.

Getting Ready to Invest

The first preparatory task is to inventory all of the investor's assets and liabilities (both financial and nonfinancial). Add up all current financial assets (checking and savings accounts, CDs, and so forth) and try to determine how much is already set aside for retirement (e.g., the current balance of any pension plan, individual retirement account, and such). In addition, assign rough market values to all physical, or real, assets (automobiles, home furnishings, and a home, if the investor owns one). Next, add up all liabilities, including things such as the current balances on any mortgage, auto, or credit card loans. Subtracting liabilities from assets gives the investor's current net worth and a pretty good picture of his or her current financial situation. The net worth influences appropriate investment goals and helps with investment planning and selection.

Having inventoried your assets and liabilities, the analysis should proceed by asking some questions about investment goals. What should investing accomplish? Having goals will help guide investment selection and management. These goals can be fairly specific (e.g., to accumulate sufficient funds to send two children to college starting ten years from now) or they can be more general (e.g., to fund a comfortable retirement in 20 years). Whether general or specific, investment goals should be realistic and they should bear some relationship to the investor's present and expected future situation.

The next task is to review current insurance coverage. Most people can break all their insurance policies into three general areas: life, health and disability, and property insurance. An investor needs adequate insurance in

---

[7]*Money*, March 1993, p. 151. The article doesn't imply you shouldn't buy a home today, only that it is unrealistic to expect the same substantial appreciation in home prices as has occurred in the past.

all three areas, but it should be the right kind of insurance. Many financial experts argue that few American households meet this goal; most are over-insured in some areas and underinsured in others. A number of books on personal financial planning discuss insurance in detail.

Finally, the investor should establish an **emergency fund** before investing. This fund should consist of low-risk, short-term investments like money market funds. The emergency fund has two basic purposes: to provide a financial safety net in the event of an unexpected emergency, such as a long-term illness or temporary unemployment, and to store funds to take advantage of changing financial conditions. Experts generally suggest that an adequate emergency fund should hold approximately three to six months of one's normal salary.

Risk and Return Assessment

After performing these preliminary tasks, the next step in the investment process is an assessment of risk and return priorities. This assessment involves answering three specific questions: What holding period is appropriate? What expected return is necessary? How much risk is tolerable?

What Holding Period Is Appropriate? Historically, security returns have behaved differently over short periods of time than over longer periods of time. Returns over long **holding periods** have been far less volatile than returns over short holding periods. Between 1926 and 1993, stock returns for one-year holding periods have ranged between 54 percent and −43 percent. By contrast, annualized stock returns for 25-year holding periods have ranged between 15 percent and 6 percent. The decision to invest for the short or long term could have a major impact on investment selection decisions.

What Expected Return Is Necessary? Investing offers very few guarantees, so we refer to future returns as **expected returns.** Everyone wants the highest return possible, but, as we'll see, higher expected returns come at a price. Investment choices depend, in part, on the return that's needed to achieve investment goals. For example, to accumulate $25,000 in ten years in order to send a child to college, a parent who is willing to invest $1,500 per year (starting today) will need to earn a return of about 8 percent per year. If money market funds are yielding only 3 percent, what other alternatives would allow him or her to achieve this goal? Two solutions are to invest more each year, or to find investment instruments that have expected returns higher than those of money market funds.

How Much Risk Is Tolerable? The question of willingness to accept **risk** is very difficult to answer, but it is critical. Risk tolerance is low for someone who practically suffers a nervous breakdown every time a stock drops one-eighth of a point (12.5 cents per share). On the other hand, someone who merely shrugs when a stock drops five points ($5 per share) can tolerate more risk. The point is that each investor has to be *comfortable* with his or her investment selections.

Measuring an individual's risk tolerance in any kind of objective way may be next to impossible. However, certain things appear to influence tolerance for risk. These include age, marital status, family responsibilities, and income. For example, a retiree living on a fixed income may be less tolerant of risk than a young person with a rising income.

Other Questions

In addition to current financial status and risk and return preferences, three other questions should guide preparation to invest. The first concerns tax status. An investor should always know his or her marginal tax rate (based on combined federal and state taxes). Also, an account that accommodates investment for retirement may earn **tax-deferred income.** This means that the owner pays no taxes on account income until the money is withdrawn at retirement.

Tax status can have a major impact on the selection of investments. For example, someone who is investing for retirement in a tax-deferred account has no reason to buy municipal bonds, the interest from which is exempt from federal income taxes. On the other hand, someone in a high marginal tax bracket who is not investing for retirement may find that municipal bonds provide valuable protection from taxes.

After considering tax status, the analysis should turn to preference for capital gains or income. As we'll see, investment returns can come from both capital gains (price appreciation) and income (dividend and interest payments). Someone who has a preference for income is probably better off investing in bonds than stocks. Since capital gains receive preferential tax treatment for some taxable investors, tax status may greatly influence the choice between capital gains and income.

Finally, ask yourself how much time you can afford to spend on your investments. Someone may be better off investing in mutual funds than individual securities if he or she can't spend much time selecting and managing investments, or if this work seems undesirable.

Investment Selection

With preparations completed and questions about risk/return preferences, tax effects, and other background issues resolved, the investment process proceeds with selection of the most appropriate investment instruments. This is probably the most complex and time-consuming stage in the investment process, and it includes two phases. In the first, the investor must decide on the general mix of investment instruments to include in the portfolio. Should it focus on stocks, bonds, money market instruments, or some combination of the three? If a combination of instruments is most appropriate, what proportion of each should the portfolio contain? For example, an investor's situation may dictate a mix of investment instruments in a portfolio of about 60 percent stocks, 30 percent bonds, and 10 percent money market instruments.

The second phase of investment selection is to select specific investment instruments. Remember that today's investment environment offers a wide range of choices, but, in general, an investor can take one of two approaches to the selection of investment instruments: passive or active.[8]

A **passive investor** tries to "buy the market," usually in the form of a mutual fund that tries to replicate the performance of a broad market without many changes in portfolio composition. Such funds are called *index funds.* Vanguard, a large U.S. mutual fund company, offers an index fund that attempts to replicate the performance of worldwide capital markets by mixing stocks and bonds from throughout the world. Many funds make similar efforts to track the U.S. stock or bond markets. If a portfolio should

---

[8]In reality, many investors mix the two approaches.

contain 50 percent stocks and 50 percent bonds, a passive investor might buy equal amounts of two such funds, one that replicates the broad stock market and one that replicates the broad bond market.

Active investors take a more vigorous approach to investment selection. They look for specific investment instruments that offer superior risk/return characteristics. This approach requires a decision whether to invest in individual securities, mutual funds, or both. An active investor might decide that Canadian stocks were, as a group, undervalued and invest in a mutual fund whose portfolio consisted solely of Canadian stocks. Perhaps, believing that long-term interest rates would fall in the next couple of years, someone might invest all available funds in long-term corporate bonds. Active investing is more time consuming and difficult than passive investing, but many investors believe that the payoff is worth the extra effort.

Investment Management

The last stage in the investment process involves monitoring the performance of investments and making changes, when necessary. Investment management techniques fall into two categories: active management of portfolios, and buy-and-hold management.[9]

Investors who actively manage their portfolios buy and sell more frequently than more passive investors. Active investors may shift funds between various types of instruments in anticipation of changing markets. To plan these moves, they tend to monitor the performance of their investments more closely and they may be more concerned about short-term performance than passive investors. A passive investor, on the other hand, tends to buy a portfolio of securities and keep it pretty much intact for a long period of time. This investor may be less inclined to make changes to the portfolio in response to changing market conditions.

Those that select securities passively (e.g., invest in index funds) are more likely to approach investment management passively, as well. On the other hand, an investor could actively select securities and still take a passive, buy-and-hold approach to investment management. This investor would buy a portfolio of specific securities that meet certain criteria, and then hold the portfolio for a fairly long period of time making few, if any, changes.

Financial experts agree that both active and passive investors should make changes to the contents of their investment portfolios as they go through life. What is best for a 30 year old may be inappropriate for someone who is 65. For someone just starting to invest for retirement, which may be 40 years away, most experts suggest that growth-oriented investments, such as common stocks, should make up the bulk of the portfolio. On the other hand, as this person ages and begins to approach retirement, experts suggest that the portfolio shift toward income-producing instruments such as bonds.

The Basics of Risk and Return

This first chapter has already generally introduced the concepts of risk and return. These topics dominate the subject of investments. Investors exchange current income for promised future returns. At the same time, however, all investing involves exposure to varying degrees of risk. In this section, we provide a brief overview of the basics of risk and return.

---

[9]Some investors employ both techniques. They may adopt a buy-and-hold approach for their retirement investments, but manage their nonretirement portfolio more actively.

Measuring Returns

The most common way to measure security returns is the **holding period return.** The holding period return (HPR) measures the total return from an investment over a specific period of time (such as a year, month, or day). It incorporates both price changes from the beginning to the end of the period, as well as any cash received during the period (such as dividend or interest payments). The formula for finding the holding period return, for investment i during period t, $HPR_{i,t}$, is:

$$HPR_{i,t} = \frac{P_{i,t} - P_{i,t-1} + CF_{i,t}}{P_{i,t-1}} \tag{1.1}$$

where $P_{i,t}$ is the price of the investment at the end of the period, $P_{i,t-1}$ is the price at the beginning of the period, and $CF_{i,t}$ is cash received during the period.[10] Let's look at an example of how to calculate some actual holding period returns.

Table 1.1 presents some data for the Janus Fund, a large stock mutual fund. The table shows the fund's net asset value, which is the equivalent of share price of a mutual fund, at the end of each year along with the total amount of cash distributed per share per year. These data give an HPR for 1985 of:

$$(\$13.19 - \$11.61 + \$1.27)/\$11.61 = 24.5 \text{ percent}$$

For 1991, the fund's HPR was:

$$(\$18.60 - \$13.79 + \$1.00)/\$13.79 = 42.1 \text{ percent}$$

Annualizing Holding Period Returns. There is nothing magical about a one-year holding period. To calculate HPR for a holding period shorter than one

Table 1.1

Holding Period Return for the Janus Fund: 1984–1993

	NAV	Cash Distributions	Total Return
1983	$13.34	—	—
1984	11.61	$1.65	−0.6%
1985	13.19	1.27	24.5
1986	12.47	2.20	11.2
1987	10.39	2.59	4.1
1988	11.55	0.56	16.6
1989	14.21	2.69	46.3
1990	13.79	0.32	−0.7
1991	18.60	1.00	42.1
1992	18.68	1.19	6.8
1993	19.39	1.33	10.9
Arithmetic mean			16.1
Geometric mean			15.1

Source: *1993 Annual Report,* Janus Fund.

---

[10]You can break Equation 1.1 into two components. The first, $(P_{i,t} - P_{i,t-1})/P_{i,t-1}$, is the percentage price appreciation; the second, $CF_{i,t}/P_{i,t-1}$, is the percentage return due to income from the investment.

year, it may be beneficial to annualize the holding period return since we generally think of returns on an annual basis. Annual returns are also more widely reported in the financial press. The general formula for annualizing a holding period return is:

$$(1 + HPR_{i,t})^m - 1 \qquad (1.2)$$

where m is the number of periods per year. For example, to annualize a monthly holding period return, m would equal 12.

Say, for example, that a bond has a current price of $1,025. It was purchased six months ago at a price of $1,010 and has paid $50 in interest during that time. Its holding period return is:

$$(\$1,025 - \$1,010 + \$50)/\$1,010 = 6.4 \text{ percent}$$

To annualize this six-month return, Equation 1.2 gives:

$$(1 + 0.064)^2 - 1 = 13.2 \text{ percent}$$

Expected versus Actual Returns. So far we've discussed how to calculate holding period returns based upon historical data. These historical returns are also referred to as *actual, observed,* or *ex-post returns*. To use Equation 1.1 to calculate expected future returns, sometimes referred to as *ex-ante returns,* simply substitute expected values for next period's ending price and investment income to be received during the coming period.

Suppose that an analyst expects the Janus Fund to have a net asset value at the end of 1994 of $20.50 per share and to distribute $1.25 per share in cash by that time. Given a net asset value of $18.68 at the end of 1993, the expected return for 1994 is:

$$(\$20.50 - \$18.68 + \$1.25)/\$18.68 = 16.4 \text{ percent}$$

Of course, this is only an expected return; the actual 1994 return may be quite different! We'll discuss the importance of expected returns later in Chapter 12.

Measuring Average Returns

A holding period return (whether an actual or expected return) really represents a return for a single period of time. Investors often hold securities for many periods, so they need to calculate average returns over several periods of time. Table 1.1 presents ten yearly holding period returns (for 1984 through 1993). What was the average return during that ten-year period?

One way to find an average return is to calculate an **arithmetic mean.** This is the simple average of all observations in a series. You probably know how to calculate an arithmetic mean, but as a reminder, you sum all the observations in the series (single-period returns) and divide by the number of observations (ten in Table 1.1). The arithmetic mean of annual returns for the Janus Fund between 1984 and 1993 was 16.1 percent. More formally, the general formula for finding the arithmetic mean for returns on security i is:

$$M_i = \sum_{t=1}^{T} HPR_{i,t} / T \qquad (1.3)$$

where T is the number of periods, and $HPR_{i,t}$ is the holding period return on security i for period t.

An alternative measure of an average over several periods of time is the **geometric mean.** [The geometric mean of a return series is also the average compound rate of return.] The formula for geometric mean is:

$$GM_i = \left[\prod_{t=1}^{T} (1 + \text{HPR}_{i,t}) \right]^{1/T} - 1 \qquad (1.4)$$

where Π is the product of the terms $(1 + \text{HPR}_{i,1})(1 + \text{HPR}_{i,2}) \ldots (1 + \text{HPR}_{i,T})$. Between 1984 and 1993 the return from the Janus Fund had a geometric mean of 15.1 percent. This geometric mean implies that, between 1984 and 1993, the Janus Fund produced an average compound rate of return of 15.1 percent per year.

Why does this differ from the arithmetic mean? A simple example will illustrate the differences between the arithmetic and geometric means. Assume five years' holding period returns as follows:

Year	Holding Period Return
1	+25%
2	−25
3	0
4	+25
5	−25

The arithmetic mean is 0 percent. The geometric mean, on the other hand, is −2.6 percent. If you had invested $1,000 at the beginning of Year 1, you would have had about $879 left at the end of the fifth year, a compound return of −2.6 percent per year. Thus, the geometric mean effectively measures the change in wealth produced by an investment over several periods of time. The geometric mean is backward looking, measuring the change in wealth over more than one period, including compounding effects.

On the other hand, the arithmetic mean simply represents typical or average performance over time. The typical performance in the example is 0 percent per year. The arithmetic mean also provides an indication of the expected return for an investment for use in forecasting, discounting, or estimating the cost of capital.

The arithmetic and geometric means will be equal only if an investment provides a set, equal return each period. If the returns vary, the arithmetic mean will always be higher than the geometric mean. Also, more variation in returns from period to period increases the difference between the arithmetic and geometric returns. Because of this difference, it's a good idea to calculate both means. You'll find that most historical data for security returns include both arithmetic and geometric means.

The Concept of Risk

We have said that the concepts of return and risk dominate investments. Almost all investing involves some degree of risk, and, as we'll see later, investors can be exposed to a variety of different types of risk. For now, a general definition of *risk* will suffice: risk is the possibility that the actual return from an investment will differ from the expected return when the investor purchases it. As that possibility rises, or as the difference between the expected and actual returns grows, the risk of the investment increases.

To illustrate this general definition of risk, consider three hypothetical investments, A, B, and C. There is some uncertainty concerning their

Table 1.2

Probability Distribution of Possible
Returns for Three Hypothetical
Securities

Possible Return	Probability of Possible Return		
	Security A	Security B	Security C
0%	0.00	0.00	0.10
5	0.00	0.15	0.20
10	1.00	0.70	0.40
15	0.00	0.15	0.20
20	0.00	0.00	0.10

returns, but assume that all possible returns for the next year are known for all three securities, as are the **probabilities** that these returns will occur.

Table 1.2 gives the probability distributions of next year's possible returns for all three securities. The probability distributions are shown graphically in Figure 1.1. For Security A, there is a 100 percent chance (probability = 1.00) that its return next year will be 10 percent. Security B has a 15 percent chance (probability = 0.15) that it will return 5 percent, a 70 percent chance that it will return 10 percent, and a 15 percent chance that it will return 15 percent. There is a 10 percent chance that Security C will return 0 percent, a 20 percent chance that it will return 5 percent, a 40 percent chance that it will return 10 percent, a 20 percent chance that it will return 15 percent, and a 10 percent chance that it will return 20 percent.

Recognize, initially, that all three securities have the same expected return next year, 10 percent. Next year's expected return for each security is simply the sum of the possible returns times the probability of each return occurring, as follows:[11]

$$ER_A = (10\%)1.00 = 10 \text{ percent}$$
$$ER_B = (5\%)0.15 + (10\%)0.70 + (15\%)0.15 = 10 \text{ percent}$$
$$ER_C = (0\%)0.10 + (5\%)0.20 + (10\%)0.40 + (15\%)0.20$$
$$+ (20\%)0.10 = 10 \text{ percent}$$

Given the general definition of risk, which of the three securities is the riskiest? Looking at Figure 1.1, Security C certainly appears to be the riskiest of the three securities. It has the greatest range of possible returns, 0 percent to 20 percent, and it has the highest probability that its actual return will differ from its expected return. There is only a four in ten chance (probability = 0.40) that Security C's actual return will equal its expected return. By contrast, there is a seven in ten chance that Security B's actual return will equal its expected return. Based on our definition of risk, Security A appears to be risk-free. There appears to be no possibility that its actual return can

---

[11]The general formula is:

$$ER = \sum_{s=1}^{S} R_{i,s} \Pr(R_{i,s})$$

where ER is the expected return for investment i, $R_{i,s}$ is a possible return for next period, and $\Pr(R_{i,s})$ is the probability of that return occurring. There are a total of S possible returns. As with all probability distributions, the sum of the probabilities must equal 1.0.

Figure 1.1

Return Distributions for Three Hypothetical Securities

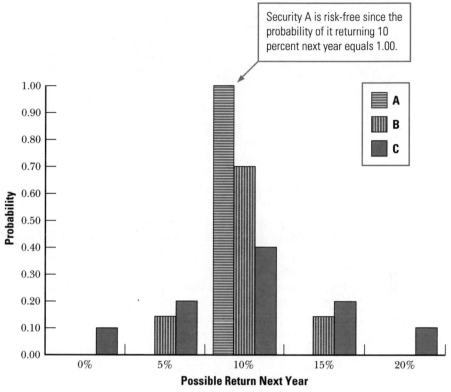

differ from its expected return. However, in order to determine that Security C certainly has the most risk of the three, and that Security A is risk-free, we need to be able to measure risk reliably.

How to Measure Risk

Our general definition of risk provides some clues as to how risk can be measured. A higher probability that the actual return will differ from the expected return, and/or a greater difference between actual and expected returns, imply a riskier investment. Two common measures of risk, range and standard deviation, both apply to our general definition.[12] **Range** is just the difference between the highest return and the lowest return. A broader range implies greater risk. **Standard deviation** is a statistical measure of risk as the dispersion around the mean, or average, return.[13] A more dispersed distribution has a higher standard deviation. A higher standard deviation of security returns means higher risk. Like return, risk can be measured using either historical data or expected future probabilities.

---

[12]The rationale behind risk measures, including range and standard deviation, will be discussed in detail in Chapter 12. That chapter will also show why standard deviation is the best measure of investment risk.

[13]The standard deviation of returns on security i equals:

$$\text{SD}_i = \sqrt{\sum_{s=1}^{S} [R_{i,s} - ER]^2 \cdot \text{Pr}(R_{i,s})}$$

Now we can restate the three hypothetical security return distributions listed in Table 1.2 to present the range and standard deviation:

Security	Range	Standard Deviation
A	10 to 10 percent = 0 percent	0.0%
B	5 to 15 percent = 10 percent	2.7
C	0 to 20 percent = 20 percent	5.5

These data confirm our initial suspicion that Security C is the riskiest of the three. It has the largest range, 20 percent, and the largest standard deviation. The data also show that Security A is indeed risk-free since it has a zero range and a standard deviation of zero.

Now let's apply these two risk measures to some historical returns from large-firm stocks and securities issued by the federal government: Treasury bonds and Treasury bills (commonly referred to as T-bonds and T-bills). Intuitively, common stocks seem like riskier investments than either T-bonds or T-bills, since the federal government is more creditworthy than any corporate issuer of common stock. Both risk measures confirm the conventional wisdom.

Figure 1.2 shows the range of annual holding period returns for stocks, T-bonds, and T-bills between 1926 and 1993. Over this 68-year period, annual stock returns climbed as high as 54 percent and fell as low as −43 percent, a range of 97 percent. By contrast, T-bond returns have ranged between 40 percent and −9 percent while T-bill returns have ranged between 15 percent and approximately zero (−0.2 percent).

Figure 1.2

Range of Annual Holding Period Returns: 1926–1992

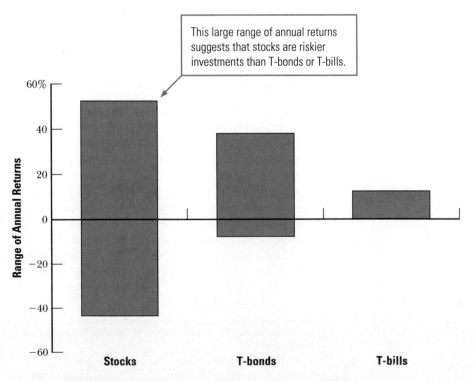

Source: *SBBI 1994 Yearbook* (Chicago: Ibbotson Associates, 1994).

Figure 1.3

Distribution of Annual Returns from Stocks, T-bonds, and T-bills: 1926−1993

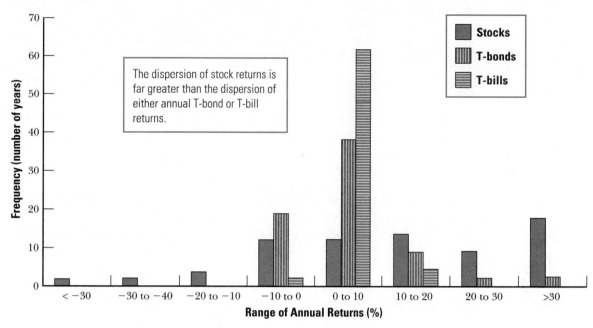

Source: *SBBI 1994 Yearbook* (Chicago: Ibbotson Associates, 1994).

Figure 1.3 shows the frequency distribution of annual returns to illustrate the dispersion of returns. As you can see, the dispersion of stock returns is far greater than the dispersion of either T-bond or T-bill returns. All 68 annual T-bill returns between 1926 and 1993 fall within a range of −10 percent to 20 percent while 64 of the 68 annual T-bond returns fall within the same range. On the other hand, only about half (35) of the 68 annual stock returns fall in this range. Since standard deviation measures dispersion, the standard deviation of historical stock returns is higher at 20.5 percent than that for T-bonds (8.7 percent) and T-bills (3.3 percent).[14] Thus, our two measures of risk, range and standard deviation, confirm the intuition that stocks have historically been riskier investments than either Treasury bonds or Treasury bills.

Determining Required Rates of Returns

As we've discussed, an investor buys a security to earn a return over some holding period. What determines this expected, or required, rate of return? Three things affect required rates of return: the time value of money, the expected rate of inflation, and the risk of the security.

One of the underlying principles of finance is that money has a time value. This means that a dollar received today is worth more than a dollar received

---

[14]The formula for calculating the standard deviation of historical returns on security i is:

$$SD_i = \sqrt{\frac{1}{T-1} \sum_{t=1}^{T} (R_{i,t} - M_i)^2}$$

where M_i is the mean return for security i.

later. Two reasons that money has time value are, of course, inflation and risk. Even with no inflation and absolutely no risk, however, required returns on securities would still be positive. We can call this required return, assuming no inflation or risk, the **real rate of return.**

Now the assumption of no inflation may seem unreasonable. To adjust the real rate of return to account for inflation, while still assuming a security that is risk-free, the required return would become:

$$RF = \text{Real rate of return} + \text{Expected rate of inflation}^{15} \qquad (1.5)$$

This risk-free return, *RF,* is often referred to as the **nominal rate of return.** Thus, a higher expected rate of inflation increases the required return, even on a risk-free security. This should make sense, since investors want to be compensated for the expected erosion of the value of their returns due to inflation over a security's holding period. In other words, if they expect the rate of inflation to be 5 percent next year, they must earn at least 5 percent on their investments just to keep pace with inflation.

Figure 1.4 compares changes in the yield on Treasury bills between 1983 and 1993 to changes in the rate of inflation. (For reasons we'll discuss in

Figure 1.4

Nominal and Real Yields on 90-Day Treasury Bills: 1983–1993

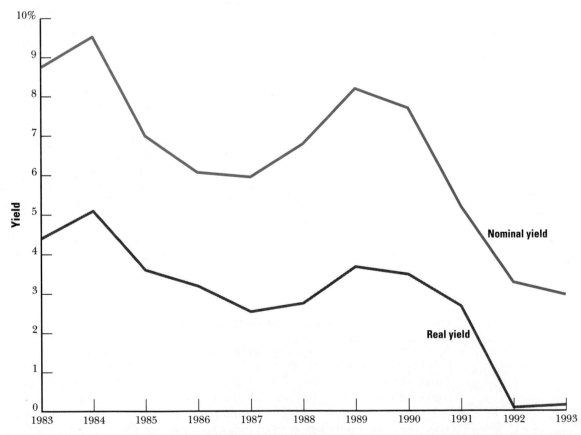

Source: *Federal Reserve Bulletin,* various issues.

[15]Technically, Equation 1.5 should be written as:

$$RF = (1 + RR)(1 + I) - 1,$$

where *RR* is the real rate of return and *I* is the expected rate of inflation.

Figure 1.5

Yields on Treasury Bills, Treasury Bonds, and Corporate Bonds: 1983–1993

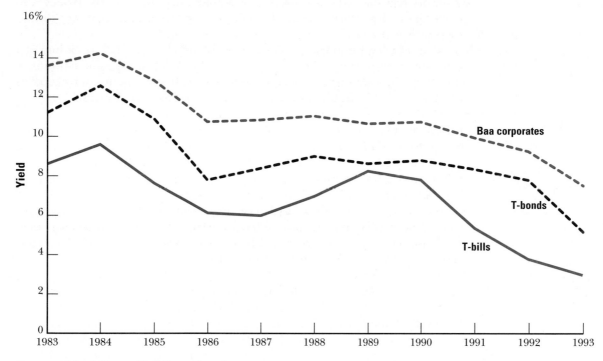

Source: *Federal Reserve Bulletin,* various issues.

later chapters, a Treasury bill is considered the closest practical approximation to a truly risk-free security.) The figure shows both the nominal and real yields on T-bills. The real yield on T-bills is a reasonable approximation of the real rate of return.[16] Nominal T-bill yields and inflation generally moved in the same direction (i.e., they rose and fell together). However, notice that the real T-bill yield fluctuated dramatically over the ten-year period, ranging from slightly more than 5 percent to about 0.2 percent.

The nominal rate of return still assumes a risk-free security. Few investors try to avoid risk entirely, however. The required return on a risky security can be written as:

$$\text{Required return} = RF + \text{Risk premium} \qquad (1.6)$$

The **risk premium** reflects compensation for the amount of risk for a particular security. More risk requires a higher risk premium, which boosts the required rate of return. As an example, look at Figure 1.5. It shows the yields on T-bills, T-bonds, and bonds issued by creditworthy corporations between 1983 and 1993. T-bill yields were consistently lower than T-bond yields, which, in turn, were lower than corporate bond yields. In 1992, for example, T-bills yielded 3.45 percent, T-bonds yielded 7.01 percent, and corporate bonds

---

[16]We measured the real rate of return in Figure 1.4 as follows: $(1 + RF)/(1 + I) - 1$, where RF is the nominal yield on 90-day Treasury bills and I is the actual rate of inflation. Note that all measures of real rates of return are only approximations since there is no way to accurately measure *expected* inflation.

yielded 8.14 percent. Using the simple relationship in Equation 1.6, investors assigned a risk premium of around 3.56 percent to T-bonds and about 4.69 percent to corporate bonds over the risk-free T-bill rate. This suggests that investors feel that T-bonds are less risky than corporate bonds. Notice also from Figure 1.5, however, that the risk premiums were not constant during the ten-year period.

Securities have many potential sources of risk and the risk premium is a function of all of them. We'll have a lot to say about the specific risks investors take when we discuss specific investment instruments in later chapters, but for now we'll simply overview several of the risks bond investors face:

- Default risk
- Interest rate risk
- Call risk
- Foreign exchange risk

Default risk is the risk of not receiving interest and principal payments when they are due. For reasons we'll discuss later, Treasury bonds have essentially no default risk; bonds issued by corporations and state and local governments have varying degrees of default risk.

Interest rate risk is the risk that a bond's price will change due to changing interest rates. As interest rates rise, bond prices fall; falling interest rates increase bond prices. All bonds, including T-bonds, carry interest rate risk. Generally, bonds with longer maturities have higher interest rate risk.

Call risk comes from provisions that allow issuers to call most long-term bonds, or redeem them prior to maturity. If interest rates are falling, issuers may call their bonds and issue new ones at the lower rates. This forces bondholders to reinvest at the lower rates, as well.

Finally, foreign exchange risk is the risk associated with changing exchange rates between currencies. If you buy a bond denominated in a foreign currency, say Japanese yen, changing exchange rates can have a dramatic affect on your actual rate of return. Obviously for U.S. investors, bonds denominated in dollars are not subject to foreign exchange risk. Therefore, the risk premium on a foreign bond must reflect this risk, along with the other kinds of risk that bond investors face.

Some Apparent Truisms in Investments

While investments may sometimes seem to be a rational, precise, almost scientific field of study, much of investing actually involves ambiguity, subjective analysis, and opinion. One investor's favored security selection technique or other method may be scorned by another. Nevertheless, five major relationships appear to characterize investments without dispute. We will briefly discuss each of these *truisms,* as we call them, in this section and throughout the entire book.

Lessons of History

As you read the pages that follow, you will confront the assumption that history teaches a number of important lessons about investments. In fact, the other four truisms we'll discuss are all based, at least in part, on historical observation. Further, investment theory and analysis often involves the application of historical relationships. For example, much of modern portfolio theory, which we discuss in Chapters 12 through 15, was developed and tested using historical data.

Consider some of the lessons that speculative bubbles teach us.[17] As detailed in Chapter 5, which discusses these investment follies, history teaches that all speculative bubbles eventually break and, when they break, prices often collapse much faster than they initially rose. History also tells us that bubbles are difficult to avoid—they are probably a permanent part of the investment landscape.

However, remember an important caveat whenever you apply historical observations or relationships to evaluate current and future investment situations. The past is no guarantee of the future; the past may repeat itself, but variations are common. This is another very important lesson from history. Go back to the history of speculative bubbles, for example. No two bubbles have been identical, either in duration or magnitude. Some periods of time have seen many bubbles, while others have seen very few. In fact, as you'll learn in Chapter 5, it may be easy to state that bubbles are inevitable, but predicting when and where they will occur is far more difficult.

As another example, consider the general history of security returns. Between 1964 and 1993, stocks have outperformed Treasury bonds by a substantial margin (10.9 percent versus 6.8 percent per year). Does that mean that stocks will outperform bonds over the next 30 years? No one can answer *yes* for certain, though most believe they probably will. The next 30 years could be quite different from the past 30 years, however.

Finally, since 1972 stocks have passed through six bull markets and six bear markets.[18] Each general market move has differed in both duration and magnitude. Whenever some "expert" claims that a system has accurately predicted every major turning point in the stock market, remember this warning: Past performance is all well and good, but the past is no guarantee of the future.

Positive Relationship between Risk and Return

While there may be some important exceptions, generally there is a positive relationship between risk and return. As Equation 1.6 implies, higher risk demands a higher risk premium, and, therefore, a higher expected rate of return. Historically at least, the positive relationship between risk and return seems pretty clear.

When we discussed how to measure risk earlier in the chapter, we examined some historical data on security returns. We found that the range and standard deviation of stock returns were far greater between 1926 and 1993 than the range and standard deviation of either Treasury bill or Treasury bond returns. On the other hand, stock returns historically have been much higher, on average, than either T-bond or T-bill returns.

Figure 1.6 graphs the **cumulative wealth indexes** of stocks and T-bills. All these indexes assume that an investor started with $1,000 in 1926 and held each investment through 1993. The indexes show how much wealth the investments in stocks or bills would have produced at the end of each subsequent year. Stocks have clearly outperformed T-bills by a wide margin. A $1,000 investment in stocks at the beginning of 1926 would have been worth more than $800,000 by the end of 1993. Similar investments in Treasury bills would have been worth around $11,700 at the end of 1993. Measuring the averages, stock returns had an arithmetic mean of 12.3 percent per year, and

---

[17]A speculative bubble is a situation where the price of some investment rises rapidly, in a short period of time, for no apparent reason other than the belief that the price will go still higher.

[18]The term *bull market* refers to a market when stock prices are generally rising, while the term *bear market* refers to a generally falling market.

Figure 1.6

Cumulative Wealth Indexes of Common Stocks and Treasury Bills: 1925–1993

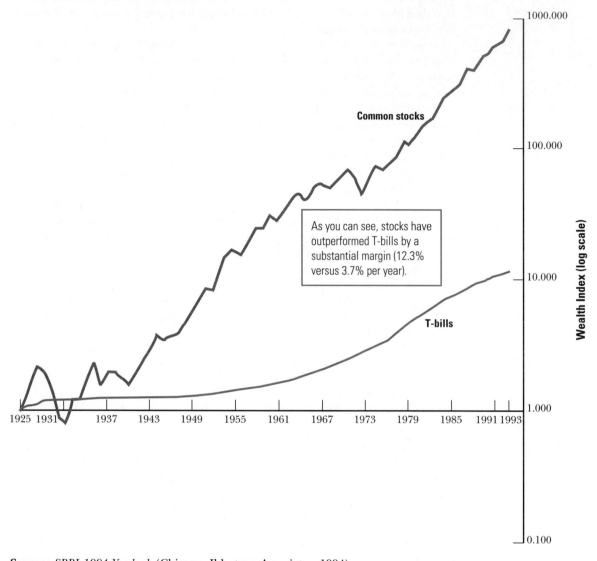

As you can see, stocks have outperformed T-bills by a substantial margin (12.3% versus 3.7% per year).

Source: *SBBI 1994 Yearbook* (Chicago: Ibbotson Associates, 1994).

a geometric mean of 10.3 percent per year over this period. By contrast, the arithmetic mean for T-bill returns was 3.7 percent per year. (Geometric mean was 3.7 percent.)

What explains the positive relationship between risk and return? The answer is **risk aversion;** all investors are risk averse to one degree or another; that is, they prefer to avoid risk without some enticement. Let's say you can play a game of chance for $100. There is a 50/50 chance that, if you play the game, you will either lose your $100 bet or double your money. Would you play the game? If you're risk averse, you probably would not. If you play the game, you're taking a risk and the total expected payoff from the game is zero.[19] This means your expected wealth will be the same regardless of whether or not you take the risk.

---

[19]The expected payoff from the game is: 0.5($100) + 0.5(−$100) = 0.

Now change the odds slightly. Suppose you have a 1-in-3 chance of losing $100 and a 2-in-3 chance of making $100. (The game still costs $100 to play.) If you're risk averse, you are more likely to play the game now since the expected payoff is now positive (it's around $34) meaning your expected wealth will increase if you play. Risk aversion leads you to demand compensation, in the form of a positive expected payoff, to voluntarily take risk.

Benefits of Diversification

The desire to avoid risk leads investors to resist putting all of their investment nest eggs in one basket. Distributing available funds among several investments reduces the risk of harm from an adverse move in any one security. This **diversification** is very beneficial to investors, as both academics and practitioners widely agree. The well-known financial advisor and writer Andrew Tobias states that the goal of investing is to:

> Buy low, sell high. Having said that, the fact remains that it's rarely possible to know with any real degree of confidence what is low or high. To know that you have to know what the future will bring—*and no one does.* As a result, the only sensible strategy for all but the most avid risk takers is to diversify.[20]

In a nutshell, diversification is beneficial because it allows investors to beat the risk/return tradeoff, up to a point. Through diversification they can expose themselves to less risk, yet at the same time maintain the same expected return. Alternatively, they can increase the expected returns on their investments without significantly increasing risk.

Does diversification really work? The answer is pretty clearly yes. For example, a standardized measure of the risk/return tradeoff is a statistic called the **coefficient of variation,** which is the standard deviation divided by the mean. Recall that common stocks had an average return between 1926 and 1993 of 12.3 percent and a standard deviation of 20.5 percent; this gives a coefficient of variation of about 1.7. A diversified portfolio holding 75 percent in stocks and 25 percent in Treasury bills over the same period would have had a lower average return, of course (10.3 percent), but its standard deviation would have dropped more, to 15.5 percent.[21] This gives a coefficient of variation of about 1.5, indicating a better risk/return tradeoff.

Not only do we know that diversification works, but perhaps more remarkably, we know why it works. Diversification works because returns on individual securities are not perfectly correlated over time. Just because one security's price rises by 10 percent this year, no one can say that all securities will perform exactly that way. Some securities' prices will rise more, some will rise less, and some will fall. For example, between July 1984 and August 1987, the S&P 500 stock index (a broad measure of stock market activity) more than doubled (up to 118 percent), yet stocks of drug companies were up more than 200 percent while oil stocks rose less than 90 percent. Between October 1990 and December 1992, the S&P 500 rose about 42 percent, but computer stocks *dropped* about 40 percent. We'll have a lot more to say about diversification in Chapter 12.

---

[20]Andrew Tobias, *The Only Other Investment Guide You'll Ever Need* (New York: Bantam Books, 1989), p. 104.

[21]At this point, unless you want to jump ahead and read Chapter 12, you'll have to trust our numbers.

Investing Knows No National Boundaries

Throughout history some investors have searched outside their own countries for investment opportunities. During the 1800s, for example, English and Scottish investment trusts provided much of the capital to build the railroads in the western United States. In the 1960s, visionaries like John Templeton started to open up foreign stock markets to U.S. investors. Nevertheless, even ten years ago few U.S. investors ever ventured beyond national boundaries.

This is no longer true. Today more and more U.S. investors are going international. For example, in August 1993, U.S. investors poured almost $5.5 billion into foreign-oriented mutual funds, nearly half of total mutual fund investments made that month. These investments are not limited to established foreign markets such as Canada, Germany, or Japan; intrepid investors have expanded to newer markets in countries such as Brazil, Malaysia, and Turkey.

Many forces are driving contemporary investing across national boundaries. Certainly the political and economic changes that swept over the world in the late 1980s and early 1990s contributed to the globalization of investments by opening up many parts of the world to foreign investment. Another factor has been the integration of security markets worldwide. Today U.S. Treasury bonds are traded in Singapore, German stocks are traded in Tokyo, and Japanese stocks are traded in New York. An investor who wants to buy or sell several thousand shares of stock in a U.S. company may be as likely to trade on the London Stock Exchange as on the New York Stock Exchange. Furthermore, most governments and large corporations raise capital by selling securities worldwide.

Arguably, perhaps, the main reason so many U.S. investors are going global is the realization that many international investments offer attractive opportunities. Between the end of 1983 and 1993, U.S. stocks produced a total return of slightly less than 200 percent. By contrast, the total return over the same period from Japanese stocks was almost 400 percent. As another example, during the first half of 1993, mutual funds that focused on international stocks had a total return of more than 13.5 percent compared to less than 5 percent for the S&P 500.

Foreign investing, however, carries special risks for U.S. investors. Many emerging markets are notoriously volatile. For example, during the first six months of 1993, Turkish stock prices soared by over 140 percent. Prices then plunged by 20 percent during a six-week period in the summer. During the late summer and fall of 1993, prices suddenly reversed direction again and rose about 60 percent on average.

Even more troubling for U.S. investors is foreign exchange risk, as mentioned earlier. Fluctuations in foreign exchange rates can augment or wipe out gains in foreign stocks. For example, as the U.S. dollar plunged in value relative to the Japanese yen during the first half of 1993, a 25 percent gain in Japanese stocks, measured in yen, became a 46 percent increase when translated into dollars. By contrast, between mid-1992 and mid-1993, stocks in Sweden rose by about 31 percent, measured in local currency. However, because the U.S. dollar became 40 percent more valuable relative to the Swedish currency, this gain became a loss of 5.9 percent when translated into U.S. dollars.

Financial Markets Function Pretty Well

Despite the risk and novelty of international investing, our fifth truism states that the financial markets function pretty well throughout most of the world, especially in the more developed countries. While not perfect, financial markets are generally fair, orderly, and very competitive with many buyers and sellers. Furthermore, while investors should always be wary, unscrupulous traders are peddling far fewer outright fraudulent securities today compared to 75 years ago.

What makes a market function well? Three characteristics of today's financial markets illuminate this question. First, security prices adjust quickly, though not always correctly, to new information. For example, on June 9, 1993, Apple Computer's stock lost more than 10 percent of its value as investors reacted to negative news about the company's earnings. Had you owned Apple it is very unlikely that you could have avoided the debacle since the stock dropped so rapidly after the announcement that day. Further, prior to the June announcement, between June 2 and June 8 Apple had lost more than 14 percent of its value. In order to have avoided the June 9 sell off, you would have had to correctly anticipate the earnings news. The issue of how security prices react to new information will be discussed extensively in Chapter 7.

A second beneficial characteristic of today's financial markets is the existence of several major equilibrium pricing relationships. If specific pricing relationships among different securities get out of line, in a well-functioning market, prices will quickly adjust to correct levels specified by the pricing relationships. Consider a simple example of an equilibrium pricing relationship. An investor might buy an option to buy 100 shares of some stock at, say, $50 per share. (This is referred to as a *call option.*) If the stock is currently trading for $60 per share, you know that the option must have a market price of *at least* $1,000 (60 minus 50, times 100). To see why, assume the option is selling for $700. Someone could buy the option, exercise it to buy the stock for $50 per share, paying $5,000 for 100 shares, and then immediately sell the stock for $60 per share. This riskless transaction would pay $300 (ignoring transaction costs). This is an example of **arbitrage.**[22] Obviously, if one person could profit from this transaction, so could everyone else, and their purchases would drive the option's price upward quickly from $700 to at least $1,000. This kind of balance between supply and demand keeps price relationships among securities near equilibrium positions.

Finally, in today's smoothly functioning financial markets there is no easy money on the table. Each investor competes with millions of other investors for great investments; many of these competitors devote substantial resources to the search. This does not mean, however, that small, individual investors can't compete with large, institutional investors, nor does this mean that investors shouldn't look. It means simply that great investments, those that are undervalued and offer substantially higher returns than the market in general, aren't easy to find. Any that occur don't stay undervalued for long.

Outline of Future Chapters

This textbook is divided into five parts. Part I, The World of Investments, reviews contemporary investment alternatives, financial markets and trading, and sources of investment information. Part II, Investment Decision Making: Past and Present, describes how investors have made investment decisions in the past, and how they make them today. Part II also discusses the concept of market efficiency and its relationship to investment decision making. Part III is devoted to common stock analysis and valuation. Both the quantitative

---

[22]*Arbitrage* is defined as the ability to earn a risk-free profit, with no real commitment of capital, from the buying and selling of securities. In the example, all the transactions could be completed within a couple of minutes without really putting up any money.

and qualitative factors that determine common stock values are discussed. Part IV is designed to help you understand modern investment and portfolio theory. It examines risk, diversification, and the capital asset pricing model in depth, as well as giving some idea of how to apply investment theory to real investment situations. The final part, The World beyond Common Stocks, discusses bonds, options, futures, and investment companies.

Some Philosophical Thoughts

Our goal in writing this book has been to emphasize three general things. First, we stress the importance of history. Even with our caveat that the past is no guarantee of the future, we believe that history can teach a great deal. After all, one can argue that the study of investments is really the study of mistakes in retrospect. We believe that by examining past investment decisions, you can better appreciate the contemporary environment and, hopefully, avoid past follies.

Second, we have tried to balance investment theory with practice. Don't get us wrong; we still believe that investment theory is important. It will help you understand how the financial markets work and why some basic relationships exist. At the same time, however, it is important to examine how investors actually make investment decisions. You need to be able to objectively and critically evaluate professional investment advice.

Third, we focus on traditional common stock valuation, sometimes referred to as the **Graham and Dodd approach.**[23] Other investment instruments, such as bonds and options, will get their fair share of coverage, but we believe that common stocks arguably are the most interesting, and in many ways the most complicated, investment alternative. Besides, common stocks have easily outperformed all other investment alternatives over the last sixty some years.

Chapter Summary

1. **Understand why people invest and why investment decisions are so important in today's financial environment.**

   People invest primarily to increase their expected future wealth. Investing allows people to increase their future standards of living, pay for major expenses (such as children's college education), or retire comfortably. Investing also benefits society as a whole. By raising people's standard of living, it accelerates economic growth. Investment decisions are important today for five reasons: the larger modern menu of investment choices, longer life expectancies, expected flat growth in personal income, the changing labor market, and the changing inflation environment.

2. **Discuss the essentials of the investment process.**

   Financial experts believe that prior to actually investing, people should complete several tasks. These include inventorying existing assets and liabilities, deciding on investment goals, reviewing insurance coverage, and establishing emergency funds. After getting ready to invest, the next task is to assess preferences for risk and return. This involves identifying an expected holding period, evaluating the expected return needed to achieve investment goals, and deciding how much risk is tolerable. Other important considerations include the investor's tax status, preference for capital gains or income, and time available for managing investments.

---

[23]The Graham and Dodd approach refers to the fathers of modern stock analysis, Benjamin Graham and David Dodd. The first edition of their classic book, *Security Analysis,* was published in 1934.

The investment process proceeds with security selection. This consists of two general parts: a decision about the general mix of investment instruments and selection of specific investment instruments. Investors can take a passive approach to investment selection, perhaps buying index funds, or they can more actively search for specific securities that they feel offer the best risk/return tradeoffs. The final stage of the investment process involves monitoring the performance of investments and making changes, when necessary. Again, investors can take a passive or active approach to investment management, but even a passive investment manager should make changes to an investment portfolio as he or she goes through life.

3. **Review the basic characteristics of risk and return.**

The concepts of risk and return dominate the subject of investments. People invest for the promise of future returns; at the same time, however, investing exposes them to varying degrees of risk. The most common method of measuring returns is the so-called *holding period return*. It measures both price appreciation and cash income from an investment over a specific period of time. The general formula for finding holding period returns can apply to either historical or expected, future data. Average returns can be measured by either the arithmetic or geometric mean. The arithmetic mean better represents typical performance over a single period, while the geometric mean better measures the change in wealth produced by an investment over several periods of time.

Next, we provided a general definition of risk: the possibility that the actual return from an investment will differ from the expected return. A greater possibility, and/or a larger difference between actual and expected returns, implies a higher risk. We looked at two ways of measuring risk, range and standard deviation, and saw that both could be applied to either historical or expected, future return data. Finally, we discussed the factors that determine the required rate of return for a security: a combination of some real rate of interest (compensation for the time value of money), the expected rate of inflation, and a security-specific risk premium. A security's risk premium reflects all the potential sources of risk to which it exposes an investor.

4. **Understand some apparent truisms in investments.**

In spite of the ambiguity, subjective analysis, and opinion that seems to dominate investments, five major relationships appear to be true. We call these relationships *truisms*. The first truism is that history can teach today's investors a number of important lessons. Further, most investment theory and analysis is based, at least in part, on historical data and observation. However, the past is no guarantee of the future. While history may repeat itself, it rarely does so in exactly the same way. The second truism is the positive relationship between risk and return. To enjoy higher expected returns, an investor must accept greater levels of risk. One reason for the positive relationship between risk and return is the fact that rational investors are, to one degree or another, risk averse. A risk averse investor will voluntarily take risk only in exchange for some compensation, that is, a higher expected payoff. The third truism is that diversification is beneficial. Up to a point, it allows an investor to beat the risk/return tradeoff and reduce risk without sacrificing expected return. Diversification works because security returns are not perfectly correlated over time. The fourth truism is that national boundaries do not contain investing today. More and more U.S. investors are going global and securities markets are becoming integrated worldwide. Even though foreign investing offers attractive opportunities, going global does expose U.S. investors to additional risks. Finally, our fifth truism is that the financial markets function pretty well through most of the developed world. Today's financial markets are generally fair, orderly, very competitive, and free of outright fraud. In today's smoothly functioning financial markets, security prices adjust quickly to new information, several major equilibrium pricing relationships exist, and no big, easy, guaranteed returns are available.

5. **Outline the remainder of the text.**

   We briefly discussed the outline the text will follow along with some of our goals in writing the book.

Key Terms

Return	Range
Holding period	Standard deviation
Risk	Real rate of return
Emergency fund	Nominal rate of return
Tax-deferred income	Risk premium
Passive investor	Cumulative wealth index
Active investor	Risk aversion
Holding period return	Diversification
Arithmetic mean	Coefficient of variation
Geometric mean	Arbitrage
Probability	Graham and Dodd approach

Discussion Questions and Problems

1. What is the general reason people invest money? Cite two or three more specific reasons.
2. How does investing benefit society as a whole? What are the societal benefits of municipal bonds?
3. Give an example of how the menu of investment choices has gotten longer. Why does this complicate investment decision making?
4. Explain how longer life expectancies and flat growth in personal income make investment decisions more critical. Are both trends likely to continue?
5. How has the inflation environment changed in recent years? Why does this make investment decisions more difficult?
6. Before you begin to invest, what preparations should you complete? What factors should influence your investment goals?
7. When you assess risk and return, what three questions should you ask yourself? What factors appear to explain differences in risk tolerance?
8. Explain the differences between active and passive investment selection. Explain how these differences relate to approaches to investment management.
9. Find the holding period return for a mutual fund with a net asset value (NAV) of $12.00 at acquisition six months ago, an NAV of $12.75 today, and cash distributions during the six months of $0.50. Annualize the six-month holding period return.
10. How would you go about computing an expected holding period return? What is the major difference between expected and actual returns?
11. What are the differences between arithmetic and geometric means? Which is a better measure of average returns?
12. Define *risk*. Given the following probability distribution of possible returns, find the expected return and standard deviation:

Probability	Possible Return
0.25	−10%
0.50	+10
0.25	+20

Given your definition, is this a risky security?

13. What is a real rate of return? For what does it compensate an investor?
14. Define the term *risk premium*. Does it compensate an investor for the expected rate of inflation?
15. When we say that the past is no guarantee of the future, what do we mean? Cite an example.
16. Historically, have risk and return had a positive or negative relationship? Why should we expect to see such a relationship?
17. Why is diversification beneficial? How does it work?
18. Define the term *equilibrium pricing relationship*. Give an example of such a relationship.

Critical Thinking Exercise

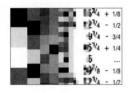

This exercise requires computer work. Open file STOCK1.XLS on the data diskette. The file contains monthly price and income data for large stocks for the period from 1991 to 1993. Using the data in the file, perform the following calculations and answer the following questions:

1. Calculate the monthly holding period return. Annualize the monthly holding period return.
2. Calculate the arithmetic and geometric means.
3. Why are the two means different? In what situations would you want to use the arithmetic mean rather than the geometric mean, and vice versa?
4. Find the range and standard deviation of monthly returns.

Chapter 2

Contemporary Investment Alternatives

Chapter Objectives

1. Understand the general categories under which today's investment alternatives fall.
2. Review the basic investment characteristics of money market instruments.
3. Outline and describe the investment characteristics of capital market instruments.
4. Understand the basic characteristics of derivative securities.
5. Describe the general features of investment companies.
6. Review the investment characteristics of real assets.
7. Summarize the historical returns produced by major investment alternatives.

Selecting between investment alternatives used to be pretty simple. For a typical individual, investing meant putting money into a savings account at a local bank, buying a home, monitoring a company-provided pension, holding a life insurance policy, and perhaps, for the very adventuresome, owning a handful of stocks and bonds. Most Americans faced limited choices, but times have changed. Today, investors choose among literally thousands of investment alternatives, many of which didn't even exist 20 years ago. Money market mutual funds, tax-exempt municipal bond funds, Ginnie Maes, stock options, financial futures, ADRs, and Eurobonds are a few relatively new possibilities. More than ever before, it has become important for any investor to have a good, thorough understanding of all available investment alternatives.

This chapter provides an overview of today's major investment alternatives. We begin with a discussion of how to categorize investment alternatives. This is followed by descriptions of the investment characteristics of each major category (money market instruments, capital market instruments, derivative securities, investment companies, and real assets). Note that this chapter is the only place where the book will discuss money market instruments in any detail. Though they fulfill very important roles, money market instruments are simple, relative to other securities. They are easy to value and fairly homogeneous. Since we devote individual chapters to stocks, bonds, derivative securities, and investment companies, this chapter's discussion of these investments will provide general background information.

After discussing the major investment alternatives, we conclude the chapter by reviewing some of the historical data on their returns. For example, we review the performance of stocks and bonds between 1926 and 1993.

Categorizing Investment Alternatives

How many alternative investments does the worldwide market offer today? Counting all the individual security issues, investment companies, and so forth, the number certainly exceeds 30,000, and it may reach 40,000 or more.[1] To make that staggering number of choices more manageable, it is useful to define some general categories in which to group investment alternatives, as illustrated in Figure 2.1.

First, we divide investment instruments into **financial assets** and **real assets.** We then divide financial assets between direct investments and **indirect investments.** A direct investment gives the buyer actual ownership of securities; indirect investment gives ownership of an entity that owns actual securities. Indirect investments include mutual funds, closed-end funds, and unit investment trusts. We divide direct investments in financial assets into nonmarketable assets (such as bank deposits and U.S. savings bonds) and **marketable securities.**[2] Marketable securities include money market instruments (e.g., Treasury bills and commercial paper), capital market instruments (e.g., Treasury bonds and common stocks), and derivative securities (e.g., options and futures contracts).

We can also divide real assets between direct and indirect investments. Direct investments in real assets give buyers actual ownership of such things as real estate (both owner-occupied housing and investment properties), gold, diamonds, art work, and so forth. Indirect investments in real assets provide ownership of entities like real estate investment trusts and limited partnerships that own real assets.

Given the rather long menu of investment alternatives, it might be interesting to take a brief look at what individuals actually own. Flow of funds data from the U.S. Federal Reserve Board for 1989 (the last year for which complete data are available) suggest the approximate distribution of household assets shown in Figure 2.2. Individual investors seem to divide their assets among bank deposits, securities, pension and life insurance reserves, equity in noncorporate business firms, and equity in owner-occupied housing.[3] The data show that the largest portions of the almost $18 *trillion* in household assets in 1989 were held as equity in owner-occupied housing (approximately $4.7 trillion or 26 percent of the total) and securities (about $4.5 trillion or 25 percent of the total).[4]

With this background established, let's take a closer look at the major investment alternatives. We begin our discussion with a subcategory of financial assets: money market instruments.

---

[1] Just to give you an idea of this range of choices, over 3,800 mutual funds operate in the United States alone today!

[2] By *marketable* we mean that an asset or security can be sold to another investor in a secondary market. The distinction between primary and secondary markets will be discussed in detail in the next chapter.

[3] Bank deposits include checking and savings deposits (including so-called *money market deposits*) and certificates of deposit. Only assets classified as investments (i.e., those likely to retain or go up in value) are included. Durable goods, such as automobiles, are not included. Also excluded are collectibles (e.g., art works), precious metals, and gems.

[4] Of the $4.5 trillion worth of securities owned by households, almost half ($2.1 trillion) were corporate common stocks. By contrast, in 1970, households owned approximately $975 billion worth of securities, 70 percent of which were corporate stocks.

Figure 2.1

Contemporary Investment Alternatives

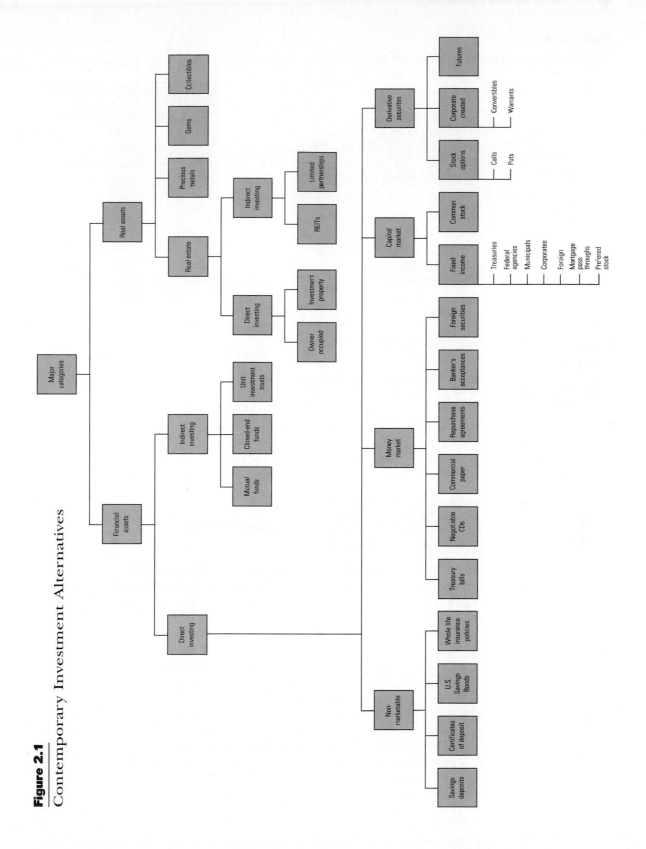

Figure 2.2

Approximate Distribution of Household Assets

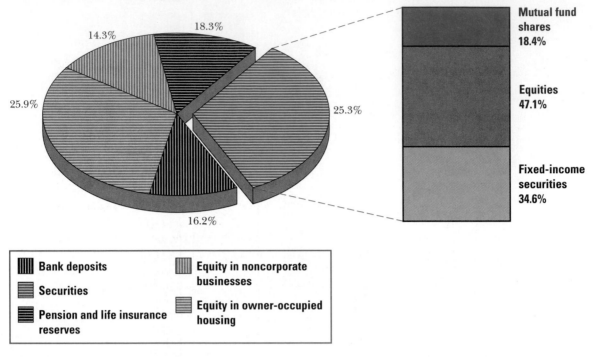

Bank deposits

Securities

Pension and life insurance reserves

Equity in noncorporate businesses

Equity in owner-occupied housing

Source: U.S. Bureau of the Census.

Money Market Instruments

Money market instruments are short-term debt securities. The category includes such securities as Treasury bills, large (or marketable) certificates of deposit, commercial paper, and banker's acceptances. Of all the major categories of investments, money market instruments are arguably the most homogeneous. All share some important features, including:

1. *Maturity.* All money market instruments mature (i.e., pay their face values) within one year of issue. Many money market instruments have maturities of only a few days.
2. *Quality.* Most, though not all, money market instruments are high-quality securities; their risk of default, or failure to repay principal, is very low. (In some cases, this risk is effectively nonexistent.)
3. *Large denominations.* Another characteristic of money market instruments is their tendency to trade in large denominations. It is not unusual to see money market instruments sell in denominations of $1 million, or more. This characteristic makes it difficult for small investors to own most money market instruments directly.[5]
4. *Discount securities.* With the exception of bank deposits such as CDs, virtually all money market instruments are **discount securities,** meaning they

---

[5]In fact, up until the early 1980s, small investors had little access (direct or indirect) to the money market. The advent of money market mutual funds changed that dramatically.

are sold for less than their face (or par) values and do not pay periodic interest payments. When such an instrument matures, the investor receives the face value. The difference between the selling price and face value is the investor's return.

Short-Term U.S. Government Securities

The best-known short-term U.S. government security, and perhaps the best-known money market instruments in the world, is the U.S. **Treasury bill** (or T-bill). Treasury bills are, in essence, IOUs issued by the United States Treasury and are backed by the **full faith and credit** of the United States government. As such, investors believe that Treasury bills have effectively no default risk.[6] Given the large number of investors willing to buy them, Treasury bills are also very liquid. Therefore, Treasury bills are often considered the closest thing to a truly risk-free security available today. Interest received from Treasury securities is taxable at the federal level, though it is exempt from state income taxes.

Treasury bills are originally issued with three standard maturities: three months, six months, and one year. The Treasury sells them to investors via an auction process. Three-month and six-month bills are auctioned weekly, while one-year bills are auctioned monthly. (We'll describe the Treasury's auction process in detail in Chapter 3.) Treasury bills are discount securities and have a minimum par value of $10,000. At the end of 1993, approximately $660 billion in Treasury bills were outstanding.

T-bill Yields and Prices. Because Treasury bills are discount securities and do not make periodic interest payments, their yields and prices are quoted differently than many securities. T-bill prices are often quoted on a **bank discount basis**. The **bank discount yield (BDY)** is computed as follows:

$$BDY = (D/F) \times (360/t)$$

where D = Discount (Face value − Price)

F = Face value

t = Number of days before the bill matures

As an example, assume that a T-bill matures in 180 days, and has a discount of $1,650 and a face value of $100,000. Its BDY equals:

$$(\$1,650/\$100,000) \times (360/180) = 3.3 \text{ percent}$$

The above formula can be rewritten to find the price of a T-bill, given its bank discount yield:

$$\text{Price} = F[1 - BDY \times (t/360)]$$

For example, if a 180-day T-bill has a bank discount yield of 3.5 percent and a face value of $100,000, its price equals:

$$\$100,000[1.000 - 0.035(180/360)] = \$98,250$$

---

[6]In reality, this perception is probably true. The Treasury has never failed to repay investors, nor, for reasons to be explained later, do we anticipate any default. However, there have been several instances where the Treasury delayed repayment of maturing Treasury bills due to technical reasons. See, for example, "Treasury Hits Delays in Mailing Checks to the Holders of Its Maturing Securities," *The Wall Street Journal*, May 9, 1979, p. 8.

Table 2.1

Federal Agency Debt Outstanding ($ millions, end of period)

Agency	1989	1990	1991	1992	1993 (August)
Federal and federally sponsored agencies	$411,805	$434,668	$442,772	$483,970	$544,642
Federal agencies	35,664	42,159	41,035	41,829	44,816
Defense Department[1]	7	7	7	7	7
Export–Import Bank[2,3]	10,985	11,376	9,809	7,208	6,258
Federal Housing Administration[4]	328	393	397	374	154
Government National Mortgage Association certificates of participation[5]	0	0	0	0	0
Postal Service[6]	6,445	6,948	8,421	10,660	10,182
Tennessee Valley Authority	17,899	23,435	22,401	23,580	28,215
United States Railway Association[6]	0	0	0	0	0
Federally sponsored agencies[7]	375,428	392,509	401,737	442,141	499,826
Federal Home Loan Banks	136,108	117,895	107,543	114,733	129,808
Federal Home Loan Mortgage Corporation	26,148	30,941	30,262	29,631	55,421
Federal National Mortgage Association	116,064	123,403	133,937	166,300	184,924
Farm Credit Banks[8]	54,864	53,590	52,199	51,910	51,406
Student Loan Marketing Association[9]	28,705	34,194	38,319	39,650	38,397
Financing Corporation[10]	8,170	8,170	8,170	8,170	8,170
Farm Credit Financial Assistance Corporation[11]	847	1,261	1,261	1,261	1,261
Resolution Funding Corporation[12]	4,522	23,055	29,996	29,996	29,996
Memo Federal Financing Bank debt[13]	134,873	179,083	185,576	154,994	128,616
Lending to federal and federally sponsored agencies					
Export–Import Bank[3]	10,979	11,370	9,803	7,202	6,252
Postal Service[6]	6,195	6,698	8,201	10,440	10,182
Student Loan Marketing Association	4,880	4,850	4,820	4,790	4,790
Tennessee Valley Authority	16,519	14,055	10,725	6,975	6,325
United States Railway Association[6]	0	0	0	0	0
Other lending[14]					
Farmers Home Administration	53,311	52,324	48,534	42,979	38,619
Rural Electrification Administration	19,265	18,890	18,562	18,172	17,897
Other	23,724	70,896	84,931	64,436	44,551

The bill's discount would be $100,000 minus $98,250, or $1,750.

The bank discount yield is obviously not a very meaningful measure of the real return an investor earns from owning a Treasury bill. For one thing, the BDY is based on a 360-day year, not 365 or 366. Also the BDY bases the return on the face value of the T-bill, not the amount actually invested. An alternative way of stating the yield on a T-bill is the **bond equivalent yield (BEY):**

$$BEY = (365 \times BDY)/[360 - (BDY \times t)]$$

A 180-day T-bill with a BDY of 3.5 percent would have a BEY of:

$$(365 \times 0.035)/[360 - (0.035 \times 180)] = 3.61 \text{ percent}$$

The bond equivalent yield is considered to be a truer estimate than the bank discount yield of the return an investor would actually earn from owning a T-bill. Because it is based on a 365-day year and the actual amount paid for

[1] Consists of mortgages assumed by the Defense Department between 1957 and 1963 under family housing and homeowners assistance programs.

[2] Includes participation certificates reclassified as debt beginning Oct. 1, 1976.

[3] On-budget since Sept. 30, 1976.

[4] Consists of debentures issued in payment of Federal Housing Administration insurance claims. Once issued, these securities may be sold privately on the securities market.

[5] Certificates of participation issued before fiscal year 1969 by the Government National Mortgage Association acting as trustee for the Farmers Home Administration; the Department of Health, Education, and Welfare; the Department of Housing and Urban Development; the Small Business Administration; and the Veterans' Administration.

[6] Off-budget.

[7] Includes outstanding, noncontingent liabilities: notes, bonds, and debentures. Some data are estimated.

[8] Excludes borrowing by the Farm Credit Financial Assistance Corporation, shown on line 17.

[9] Before late 1982, the association obtained financing through the Federal Financing Bank (FFB). Borrowing excludes that obtained from the FFB, which is shown on line 22.

[10] The Financing Corporation, established in August 1987 to recapitalize the Federal Savings and Loan Insurance Corporation, undertook its first borrowing in October 1987.

[11] The Farm Credit Financial Assistance Corporation, established in January 1988 to provide assistance to the Farm Credit System, undertook its first borrowing in July 1988.

[12] The Resolution Funding Corporation, established by the Financial Institutions Reform, Recovery and Enforcement Act of 1989, undertook its first borrowing in October 1989.

[13] The FFB, which began operations in 1974, is authorized to purchase or sell obligations issued, sold, or guaranteed by other federal agencies. Because FFB incurs debt solely for the purpose of lending to other agencies, its debt is not included in the main portion of the table in order to avoid double counting.

[14] Includes FFB purchases of agency assets and guaranteed loans; the latter are loans guaranteed by numerous agencies, with the amounts guaranteed by any one agency generally being small. The Farmers Home Administration entry consists exclusively of agency assets, whereas the Rural Electrification Administration entry consists of both agency assets and guaranteed loans.

Source: *Federal Reserve Bulletin,* November 1993.

the T-bill, the bond equivalent yield is always higher than the bank discount yield.[7]

Short-Term Federal Agency Securities.
In addition to the U.S. Treasury, several federal and quasifederal agencies are empowered to issue debt securities called **federal agency securities.** Table 2.1 lists the federal agencies that currently have securities outstanding along with the amount outstanding at the end of years 1989 to August 1993. Short-term obligations (i.e., those with

---

[7] If interest rates are low, the BDY does not dramatically understate the return from a T-bill. However, if rates are high, the difference becomes important since the difference between the BDY and BEY gets larger as the discount on the T-bill rises. For example, assuming 180 days until maturity and a face value of $100,000, if the discount is $2,000, the BDY is 4.00 percent and the BEY is 4.14 percent. If the discount is $4,000, the BDY is 8.00 percent and the BEY is 8.45 percent. Traders occasionally state T-bill yields a third way called the *CD equivalent yield,* which equals $(360 \times BDY)/(360 - t \times BDY)$. The CD equivalent yield puts T-bill yields on a basis similar to bank deposits that pay interest based on a 360-day year.

maturities of less than one year) make up approximately 20 percent of outstanding federal agency securities.

Short-term federal agency securities are very similar to T-bills. They are discount securities and typically have a minimum face value of $10,000. Unlike T-bills, however, federal agency securities are *not* backed by the full faith and credit of the U.S. government. While there is some theoretical possibility of default with federal agency securities, investment professionals see little likelihood that Congress would allow a federal agency to default on its debt.[8]

Commercial Paper

In essence, **commercial paper** is the corporate equivalent of a Treasury bill. It is a short-term IOU issued by a corporation to provide working capital. Corporations often issue commercial paper to supplement, or even as an alternative to, loans from commercial banks. Commercial paper typically has a maturity of less than 270 days; the most common maturity range is between 30 and 59 days.[9] Commercial paper is usually sold in large denominations ($100,000 or more) and is virtually always issued as a discount security. At the end of 1993, more than $540 billion in commercial paper was outstanding, up from about $239 billion at the end of 1984. Approximately 75 percent of outstanding commercial paper at the end of 1993 was issued by financial companies. General Motors Acceptance Corporation (GMAC), GM's captive finance subsidiary, is the largest single issuer of commercial paper in the world.

Corporations issue commercial paper in one of two ways: as dealer placed paper or directly placed paper. The difference is straightforward. Dealer placed paper involves a third party, the commercial paper dealer, who purchases the paper from the issuing corporation and immediately resells it, at a slightly higher price, to investors. Directly placed paper bypasses dealers; the issuing corporation sells the paper directly to investors. Approximately 60 percent of outstanding commercial paper is dealer placed. Institutional investors (such as mutual funds, pension funds, banks, etc.) purchase virtually all newly issued commercial paper. Since most of these investors plan to hold the paper until maturity, trading in previously issued commercial paper is not very active.

Traditionally, only companies with the strongest credit ratings have issued commercial paper.[10] Therefore, while defaults are not unknown, they are very rare. In recent years, some companies with lower credit ratings have been able to issue commercial paper, pledging high-quality assets as collateral or backing the paper by bank letters of credit.

Banker's Acceptances

Banker's acceptances are instruments created to facilitate commercial trade transactions, many of which are international. The name comes from the fact that banks accept ultimate responsibility for paying off all the parties. There-

---

[8]Note also that the U.S. Treasury has emergency authority to lend money to federal agencies to keep them from defaulting on their securities.

[9]There are some important reasons for this. For one, corporate security issues with maturities of 270 days or less are exempt from registration requirements of the U.S. Securities and Exchange Commission. (We'll examine SEC registration in Chapter 3.) Another reason is that banks can use commercial paper as collateral for loans from the Federal Reserve only if it has a maturity of less than 90 days.

[10]Commercial paper has been around the U.S. markets since colonial times. Ironically, commercial paper was first issued by companies that couldn't qualify for bank loans. Over the years, however, the commercial paper market has evolved to a point where only a handful of financially strong companies can issue it.

fore, the default risk of a banker's acceptance depends more on the credit-worthiness of the bank than on the financial strength of the companies that conduct the commercial transactions. Banker's acceptances are sold at discount and their maturities range from a few days up to one year. Like commercial paper, virtually all banker's acceptances are sold to institutional investors.

Banker's acceptances are less prominent today than they were 10 years ago. For example, at the end of 1993, almost $35 billion in marketable banker's acceptances was outstanding, down from almost $76 billion at the end of 1984.[11]

The easiest way to understand how banker's acceptances work is by looking at a hypothetical example. Suppose a California retail chain wants to import 1,000 "genuine Persian rugs" from the manufacturer in Hong Kong for sale in the United States. The manufacturer would like immediate payment while the U.S. retailer would rather pay for the rugs after it sells them, say in 90 days. The retailer and the manufacturer come up with the following arrangement: The retailer agrees to pay $2.5 million for the 1,000 rugs in 90 days and the manufacturer agrees to accept the present value of $2.5 million at the time the rugs are shipped. The retailer then obtains a letter of credit from its bank, First Interstate Bank of California, which guarantees that the manufacturer will be paid 90 days after the rugs are shipped. First Interstate Bank then sends the letter of credit, called a *time draft,* to the manufacturer's Hong Kong bank, Heng Sen Bank. Heng Sen Bank notifies the manufacturer which then ships the rugs to the retailer. With proof of shipment, Heng Sen Bank pays the rug manufacturer the present value of $2.5 million and the manufacturer leaves the picture. Heng Sen Bank presents the time draft and shipping documents to First Interstate which stamps *accepted* on the time draft. First Interstate has created a banker's acceptance by which it agrees to pay $2.5 million to the holder of the banker's acceptance at maturity. Heng Sen Bank, the holder of the banker's acceptance, can either keep it, turn it over to First Interstate for its present value, or sell it to another money market investor. The retailer owes First Interstate Bank $2.5 million in 90 days, plus interest.

Large Certificates of Deposit

Most of us are already familiar with **certificates of deposit (CDs).** CDs are time deposits issued by financial institutions such as banks and credit unions. CDs mature anywhere from a few weeks to a few years from the date of issue. Unlike other money market instruments, CDs are interest bearing securities; they pay interest on their principal amounts at specified annual rates.

While CDs can be issued in almost any denomination, an important distinction developed during the 1960s and 1970s between so-called *small CDs* and *large CDs.* Traditionally, all CDs were federally insured and could not be sold prior to maturity without substantial interest penalties. For a variety of historical reasons, interest rates on CDs were kept low, and were subject to ceilings set by the Federal Reserve.[12] During the 1960s and 1970s, CD rates started to fall well below rising money market rates. In an attempt to increase

---

[11]There are several explanations of the decline in marketable banker's acceptances. One is that banks are holding onto more of their banker's acceptances, instead of selling them to other investors. Another explanation is that more banks are willing to handle both ends of import/ export transactions themselves.

[12]Federal Reserve Regulation Q, which stated this requirement, was phased out starting in 1980 with the passage of the Depository Institutions and Monetary Reform Act. Today, financial institutions can offer whatever rates they wish on savings deposits and CDs.

their direct access to the money market in the face of rising short-term rates, banks offered a new type of CD. These new CDs were not federally insured, their interest rates were not subject to Federal Reserve ceilings, and they could be sold prior to maturity in a secondary market. These became known as *large CDs* since they usually had face values of at least $1 million. Today, any CD with a face value in excess of $100,000 is considered to be a large CD.[13] At the end of 1993, almost $400 billion in large CDs was outstanding, compared to more than $1 trillion in small CDs.

The credit risk associated with large CDs depends directly on the creditworthiness of the financial institutions that issue them. Since large CDs are not federally insured, loss of principal is possible if the financial institution fails. While the overall credit risk of large CDs is very low, some recent bank failures have cost large CD holders some, though rarely all, of their principal.

Repurchase Agreements

Repurchase agreements, or repos, are basically short-term loans with securities as collateral. In a repo, one party sells a package of securities (often U.S. government securities) to another party and agrees to buy back, or repurchase, the securities at a later date (ranging from overnight to months later) at a higher price. For example, suppose that a securities dealer has just purchased $10 million in U.S. government bonds to sell to customers and needs to finance the purchase for a couple of days. A city government is flush with cash from tax receipts that it must soon pay out for services, but it needs a short-term investment until that time. The securities dealer sells the bonds to the city for $9,997,777.78, agreeing to repurchase them in two days for $10 million. The discount is found as follows:

$$\text{Face value} - [\text{Repurchase rate} \times (\text{Term}/360) \times \text{Face value}]$$

The repurchase rate in this example is 4 percent per annum and the term is two days:

$$\$10,000,000 - [.04 \times (2/360) \times \$10,000,000]$$

The size of the repo market has exploded in recent years. At the end of 1993, more than $400 billion in repurchase agreements were outstanding. Since repos are collateralized, they are considered to be very safe investments.

Short-Term Municipal Securities

In addition to the federal Treasury and other federal agencies, thousands of state and local government units in the United States (states, cities, school districts, etc.) issue securities, many of which are money market instruments.[14] (In the terminology of investments, *government* refers to securities issued by the Treasury or federal agencies, while *municipal* refers to securities

---

[13]In 1982, Merrill Lynch got into the retail CD business by offering clients small CDs issued by a variety of financial institutions. Merrill Lynch also stood ready to buy back these CDs prior to maturity at prevailing market prices. Several other retail brokerage firms followed Merrill Lynch's lead and today small savers can enjoy many of the benefits once enjoyed only by large institutional investors.

[14]Approximately 19,000 government units in the United States have the authority to issue some sort of debt security.

issued by all state and local government units.) Virtually all short-term municipals are called *anticipation notes*. They are issued in anticipation of revenue from another source (e.g., property tax receipts), and are almost always discount securities.[15] They are sold in minimum denominations of at least $25,000. Short-term municipals have become increasingly popular in recent years; at the end of 1993 approximately $140 billion of them were outstanding.

The quality of short-term municipals varies, though the overall credit risk is very low. Municipal securities may have some credit risk while government securities, specifically Treasury securities, do not. While many issuers of municipal securities can levy taxes, unlike the federal government, they cannot legally print money. The Treasury could always print money to pay its bills (including the face value of maturing securities) if need be.[16] State and local governments can rely only on receipt of tax payments and other revenue.

Like all municipal securities, short-term municipals have a very important feature: the interest they pay is exempt from federal income taxes.[17] As a result, short-term municipals typically have lower yields than even Treasury bills.

Because of this tax feature, taxable investors should compute the **taxable equivalent yield (TEY)** when comparing municipals to other securities. The TEY equals:

$$TEY = \text{Yield on the tax-exempt security}/(1 - T)$$

where T is the investor's marginal tax rate.[18] For example, if a short-term municipal security yields 3 percent and the investor has a marginal tax rate of 28 percent, the TEY equals 3%/0.72, or 4.17 percent. Obviously as the investor's tax rate increases, the TEY increases, making these securities most attractive to investors in high tax brackets.

Foreign Money Market Instruments

Various money market instruments are sold in other countries. These instruments are denominated in either foreign currencies or U.S. dollars. Many foreign governments issue short-term securities similar to U.S. Treasury bills. Canada, for example, sells Treasury bills weekly with maturities of 90, 180, and 360 days. These discount securities have denominations as small as C$1,000. Foreign and U.S. corporations also issue commercial paper throughout the world. For example, most U.S. finance companies, such as GMAC, have Canadian operations and issue commercial paper in Canada to finance those operations.

Two of the most significant foreign money market instruments are **Eurodollar** deposits and Eurodollar certificates of deposit. These are simply bank deposits and CDs denominated in U.S. dollars, but issued and held outside

---

[15]Bond anticipation notes are BANs, revenue anticipation notes are RANs, and tax anticipation notes are TANs.

[16]Excessive printing of money is, of course, inflationary, but, as we explained in the prior chapter, purchasing power risk and credit risk are quite different.

[17]The interest received from municipal securities may be subject to state income taxes. Laws vary from state to state, but generally if an investor purchases a security issued by a state other than his or her own, it will be subject to state income tax. For example, if you live in California and purchase a municipal security issued by a government unit in Illinois, the interest you receive will be subject to California state income tax.

[18]If interest is also exempt from state income taxes, T should equal the investor's combined marginal state and federal income tax rate.

the United States, or in U.S. branches of foreign banks.[19] For example, a 180-day, U.S. dollar CD issued by the London branch of Citibank would be a Eurodollar CD. At the end of 1993, outstanding Eurodollar deposits and CDs exceeded $61 billion.

One of the most widely followed money market interest rates, **London Interbank Offered Rate (LIBOR),** is the rate at which five large London banks are willing to lend dollar-denominated funds to one another in the interbank market. The rates on most Eurodollar deposits and CDs are tied to the LIBOR. Many other money market rates worldwide are also tied to the LIBOR.

Many U.S. investors have been attracted to foreign money market instruments in recent years as U.S. money market rates have fallen well below rates in other countries. For example, in early September 1992 the yield on a 90-day U.S. Treasury bill was about 3 percent, compared to around 4.25 percent on a short-term British government security. Investing in any foreign security, even a government security, exposes investors to additional risks, however, and such instruments should always be considered more risky than U.S. government securities.[20]

Capital Market Instruments

Money market instruments have, by definition, maturities of one year or less. Capital market instruments include all financial assets that have maturities longer than one year. Unlike money market instruments, capital market instruments form a very diverse group that includes bonds, mortgages, preferred stocks, common stocks, and many other types of instruments. Thousands of units of government and corporations worldwide issue capital market instruments. Capital market instruments include fairly safe securities, such as Treasury bonds, as well as highly speculative securities. We begin our discussion of capital market instruments with fixed-income securities.

Fixed-Income Securities

Aside from the obvious difference, maturity, a number of other important characteristics separate money market instruments from capital market fixed-income securities (usually called *bonds*).[21] With the exception of CDs, money market instruments are typically discount securities. By contrast, fixed-income securities usually bear interest. Most of these securities pay regular interest payments at fixed rates called **coupon rates.** Interest is computed and paid at regular intervals (the most common being twice a year) as a percentage of the security's par, or face, value. Furthermore, while they vary widely in terms of credit risk, all fixed-income securities expose investors to more interest rate and purchasing power risk than money market instru-

---

[19]In addition to Eurodollars, Euroyen deposits and CDs are prominent in several major financial centers, especially in London. These are simply deposits and CDs denominated in Japanese yen, but issued and held outside Japan.

[20]Investing in any security not denominated in U.S. dollars exposes American investors to the risk of fluctuating exchange rates. For example, say someone owns an interest-bearing security denominated in German marks (face value = DM1,000) that pays 8 percent interest. If the DM/dollar exchange rate were to equal 1.75 (DM1.75 = $1.00), the owner would receive $45.71 per year in interest. If the exchange rate were to change to 2.00 (DM2.00 = $1.00), however, annual interest, in dollars, would decline to $40.00.

[21]Technically speaking, not all longer term fixed-income securities are bonds. The term *bond,* however, is often used generically to refer to any fixed-income security with a maturity in excess of one year.

ments, and these risks generally increase as time to maturity increases. Finally, many fixed-income securities have **call provisions** that allow the issuers to buy back the securities from their owners, at prespecified prices, prior to maturity. Not surprisingly, issuers are far more likely to call bonds when interest rates are falling, which allows them to issue new bonds with lower coupon rates.

Treasury Bonds and Notes. The U.S. Treasury issues a variety of fixed-income securities with maturities ranging between 2 and 30 years. Treasury securities issued with maturities between 2 and 10 years are called **notes;** those with original maturities in excess of 10 years are called **bonds.**[22] Besides their maturities, bonds and notes differ in that bonds are often callable starting five years prior to maturity; notes are generally not callable. Other than that, T-notes and T-bonds are similar securities. Both bear interest, trade in vigorous secondary markets, and are sold in denominations as small as $1,000. Like Treasury bills, T-notes and T-bonds are backed by the full faith and credit of the U.S. Treasury, so they have no default risk.

Figure 2.3 illustrates the distribution of outstanding Treasury securities between bills, notes, and bonds from 1988 to the end of 1993. As the figure shows, T-notes make up the largest portion of outstanding, marketable Treasury securities with more than $1,700 billion (60 percent of the total) outstanding at the end of 1993, compared to about $488 billion in T-bonds (about 23 percent of the total). The average maturity of outstanding Treasury securities has risen in recent years. At the end of 1975, it was approximately $2\frac{1}{2}$ years; the average maturity had risen to about six years by the end of 1993.[23]

Federal Agency Securities. Besides short-term securities, the federal agencies listed in Table 2.1 also issue a variety of longer-term fixed-income securities to finance their operations. One of the largest issuers in recent years has been the Resolution Trust Corporation (RTC), which was created by Congress in 1989 to help finance cleanups of problems associated with failed U.S. savings and loan institutions.[24] Federal agency securities are very similar to Treasury notes and bonds. Remember, though, that federal agency securities are not backed by the full faith and credit of the U.S. government, so they carry some, albeit minuscule amount of credit risk.

Municipal Securities. Across the United States, thousands of state and local government units issue longer-term fixed-income securities, in addition to the short-term securities discussed previously. The interest earned on these securities is also exempt from federal income tax. Municipal bonds fall into two categories: general obligation bonds and revenue bonds. **General obligation bonds** are backed by the full faith and credit of the government unit that issues them. Since the issuer can spend any of its tax revenues to pay interest and principal on these bonds, general obligation bonds can be issued only by government units that have independent taxing authority. By contrast, **revenue bonds** are used to finance revenue-producing projects (e.g., toll roads) and only revenues generated by the project may be used to

---

[22]The same terminology applies to municipal and corporate debt securities; securities with intermediate terms to maturity (up to 10 years) are technically notes, whereas securities with maturities in excess of 10 years are technically bonds.

[23]The average maturity of outstanding Treasury securities has been as long as $10\frac{1}{2}$ years (in June 1947). In 1993, the Treasury announced plans to significantly reduce the average maturity of outstanding Treasury debt by 1998.

[24]During 1990, the RTC issued approximately 80 percent of new federal agency securities.

Figure 2.3

Distribution of Outstanding U.S. Treasury Securities by Type

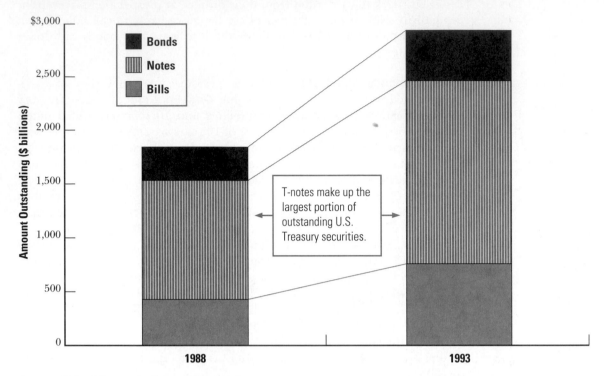

Source: *Federal Reserve Bulletin,* various issues.

pay bondholders. Revenue bonds can be issued by government units that have no taxing authority. Thus, as a *very* general rule, revenue bonds are considered to have more credit risk than general obligation bonds.

Figure 2.4 breaks down new municipal bond issues in 1988 and 1993 by type. Most new municipal bond issues were revenue bonds in both years; however, the predominance of revenue bonds has declined since 1988. Revenue bonds made up around 74 percent of all new municipal issues in 1988, but less than 63 percent of all new municipal issues in 1993.[25] Municipal bonds are often serial issues, as opposed to term issues. In a **serial bond** issue, a predetermined number of bonds mature each year until final maturity. All **term bonds** in a single issue mature on the same date.

As we discussed in the previous section, investors must realize that municipal securities are not free of credit risk, even if the securities are issued by a government unit that has taxing authority. Defaults are not unknown.[26] Credit risk varies widely from issue to issue, with some municipal bonds considered to be almost as safe as U.S. government securities while others are seen as far more speculative. In order to help investors assess credit risk, most municipal securities carry **bond ratings** assigned by agencies like Standard & Poor's and Moody's to indicate objective assessments of the issuers' credit-

[25]Part of the explanation for this may be restrictions placed on the issuance of tax-exempt industrial revenue bonds by the 1986 Tax Reform Act.

[26]The largest municipal bond default occurred in 1983 when the Washington Public Power System (known as WHOOPS) failed to repay (or defaulted) approximately $2.25 billion worth of bonds.

Figure 2.4

New Municipal Bond Issues by Type

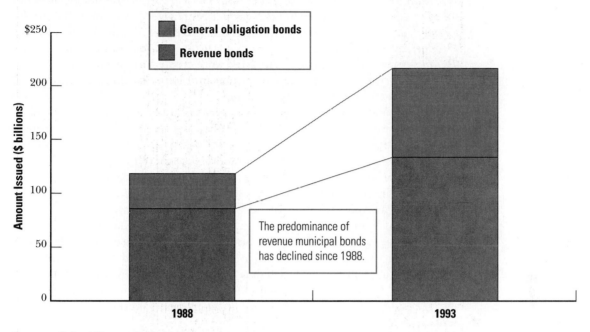

Source: *Federal Reserve Bulletin,* various issues.

worthiness. Standard & Poor's ratings, for example, range from AAA (highest quality) to D (in default). We'll examine bond ratings in more detail in Chapter 16.

To reassure risk averse investors, many municipal securities are insured by private companies, which guarantee the timely payment to investors of all interest and principal due. Insured bonds almost always carry AAA ratings.

Corporate Debt Issues. Corporations issue a wide variety of longer-term debt securities to raise capital for company projects. Most are term issues that mature after anywhere between 5 and 40 years; most have par values of $1,000. In addition, almost all corporate bond issues are callable. A large corporation may have several different debt issues outstanding at any one time. Shell Oil Company, for example, had 16 different long-term debt issues outstanding at the end of 1993.

In general, corporate bonds can be divided into categories based on their collateral provisions. Some bonds give their owners legal claims to specific assets in the event the issuers go bankrupt; these are secured bonds. A **mortgage bond** is secured by a lien on real assets, such as property or machinery. Unsecured bonds are known as **debentures.** Holders of debentures are considered to be general creditors of the issuers; if the company's assets are liquidated in bankruptcy, they have junior claims relative to mortgage bond holders. Owners of **subordinated debentures** have even lower claims to assets in the event of bankruptcy. Finally, **income bonds** are the corporate equivalent of municipal revenue bonds; they finance the purchase of income-producing assets. Unlike other corporate bonds, an income bond carries a commitment to pay interest and principal only if income from the asset is sufficient.

Mortgage Pass-through Securities. One of the most dramatic changes to occur in the financial system over the last 20 years has been the so-called *securitization* of mortgages, especially home mortgages. Three federally sponsored organizations, the Federal National Mortgage Association (known as *Fannie Mae*), the Government National Mortgage Association (known as *Ginnie Mae*), and the Federal Home Loan Mortgage Corporation (known as *Freddie Mac*), played a major role.[27] All three were created to purchase loans from primary mortgage lenders, such as savings and loan associations, in order to increase the supply of mortgage credit.

Traditionally all three organizations issued bonds to finance their mortgage purchases. However, in 1975, Ginnie Mae offered the first **mortgage pass-through** security, which pledged interest payments backed by a self-liquidating pool of mortgages, all with the same term and interest rate. As homeowners make their monthly house payments (consisting of both interest and principal), the pooled payment is *passed-through* to the security holders. Owning a mortgage pass-through security is equivalent to owning a piece of a large pool of home mortgages. Today, Fannie Mae, Freddie Mac, and several other private financial institutions also issue mortgage pass-through securities, making them extremely popular. Between 1984 and 1993, the total of outstanding mortgage pass-through securities increased by over 344 percent from $332.1 billion to $1,473 billion. During the same period, the percentage of residential mortgages held in mortgage pools increased from 16 percent to over 40 percent.

Mortgage pass-throughs are considered to be high-quality securities with minimal, if any, credit risk. All mortgages in the pool are insured, which means that the outstanding principal is paid by the insurer in the event of default. The organization that issues a mortgage pass-through security almost always guarantees timely payment of interest and principal to investors. Mortgage pass-throughs also offer attractive yields relative to Treasury securities. At the end of 1993, for example, longer-term Treasuries (those with maturities in excess of ten years) were yielding about 6.5 percent compared to an average yield of around 7.25 percent for mortgage pass-through securities. Also, many investors like the monthly income from pass-throughs. The main drawback with mortgage pass-throughs is their uncertain maturities. All the loans in the pool have the same original term (usually 30 years), however most homeowners pay off their mortgages early when they refinance, move, etc. Since the pool is liquidated as mortgages are paid off, the pass-through could mature any time between one day and 30 years from the date of issue!

Foreign Bonds. Governments and corporations throughout the world issue debt securities outside their own countries. These bonds often have colorful names. For example, foreign bonds issued in the United States are called **Yankee bonds** while foreign bonds issued in the United Kingdom are referred to as **Bulldog bonds.** Many U.S. corporations issue **Eurobonds** (bonds denominated in U.S. dollars, but issued outside the United States). Companies also issue Euroyen bonds, bonds denominated in Japanese yen issued outside Japan. As for foreign money market instruments, foreign bonds' yields can seem very attractive to U.S. investors, but they do expose investors to unique risks, such as the risk of adverse changes in foreign exchange rates.

---

[27]Fannie Mae and Freddie Mac are stockholder-owned corporations, though both retain some important links to the federal government. Ginnie Mae is part of the U.S. Department of Housing and Urban Development (HUD).

Preferred Stock. Preferred stock is another security issued by corporations. Preferred stock is a **hybrid security;** it shares characteristics of both common stock and bonds. Legally, it is a class of stock, representing an ownership or equity claim on firm assets, not a debt instrument. We include it with other fixed-income securities, such as bonds, because from an investor's standpoint, preferred stock performs much more like a bond than a stock. Preferred stock pays a set annual dividend. This fixed amount almost never changes, regardless of the issuing firm's profitability. In addition, preferred shareholders have no voting rights and they have a senior claim, relative to common shareholders, to firm assets in the event of bankruptcy. However, failure to pay preferred stock dividends cannot force the issuer into bankruptcy, as failure to make principal and interest payments on bonds can. While, in theory, preferred stock has no maturity, most issues are callable and experience suggests that most preferred issues are eventually called.

Preferred stocks run the gamut from high to low quality. Like corporate and municipal bonds, preferred stocks are often rated by Standard & Poor's and Moody's. A rating reflects experts' assessment of the issuer's ability to maintain the preferred stock dividend in the future. Preferred stock yields usually, though not always, exceed corporate bond yields.

For many reasons, preferred stock has long been viewed as an orphan security, not particularly popular with either issuers or investors. In fact, the total amount of preferred stock outstanding in the United States actually declined between 1970 and 1985. In recent years, however, preferred stock has made a modest comeback. In 1985, approximately $6.5 billion in new preferred stock was issued, representing about 2.7 percent of all long-term corporate securities issued that year. In 1993, more than $25 billion in preferred stock was issued, or about 5 percent of all long-term corporate securities issued during the year.

Common Stock

Common stock represents an ownership claim in a corporation; bondholders are creditors, but stockholders are owners. This leaves stockholders as **residual claimants.** If the company liquidates its assets, common stockholders get whatever remains after all creditors have been paid. Shares of publicly held companies (i.e., shares that can be purchased by the investing public) are traded in markets known as *stock exchanges*.

Unlike owners of sole proprietorships or partnerships, however, common stockholders have the advantage of limited liability. In the event the company goes bankrupt, stockholders can lose no more than what they paid for their stock. Stockholders are not fully liable for corporate debts.

While the primary benefit to investors of fixed-income securities is clearly current income from interest payments, investors purchase common stocks primarily for potential capital appreciation. Many common stocks do distribute some part of corporate net income as cash dividends, however, this income should be considered a secondary reason for investing in most stocks. In theory, as the company becomes more valuable (e.g., as its earnings rise), shares of its common stock should also become more valuable, creating capital appreciation.

Unlike fixed-income securities, it is difficult to categorize common stocks based on factors such as quality. Wall Street professionals use loose terms like *cyclical, defensive, growth, value, blue chip,* and so forth to categorize individual common stocks. The term **blue chip,** for example, was first introduced by *The Wall Street Journal* in 1904 to describe the stocks of the largest, most consistently profitable companies. In poker, the blue chips are always the most

The Elephant That Roared

It's as if one elephant in a herd of docile beasts deliberately turned rogue. The huge and powerful California Public Employees Retirement System, with some $65 billion under its control, has been far ahead of the pack in the movement by big public pension funds to make managements listen—and listen hard—to shareholders. CalPERS, as it is known, has fought antitakeover provisions, battled greenmail—premium-priced share buybacks from raiders—and challenged swollen executive-pay packages.

Under the whip of Dale Hanson, its aggressive chief executive, CalPERS of late has become even more combative as an enforcer of corporate accountability to shareholders. Soon Hanson plans to release a hit list of a dozen corporations he wants shaped up. And CalPERS intensified its activism by telling Chrysler in September that it didn't like the No. 3 U.S. auto maker's plans to sell 33 million shares to the public because it would water down the value of CalPERS's 1.6 million Chrysler shares.

That put Chrysler in a pickle. Its cash balances are shrinking in a slumping auto market, and the credit-rating agencies have warned the beleaguered car manufacturer to come up with new cash or face another drop in its already battered credit rating. Chrysler's ability to stay alive would suffer a major, if not lethal, blow.

CalPERS's resistance to the stock sale has raised eyebrows—and concerns. "What happens if shareholder opposition sinks the offering and then the credit-rating agencies put Chrysler on the junk-bond list?" says management consultant Peter Drucker. Moreover, he says, as CalPERS moves from challenging companies on issues like executive overcompensation to matters of business policy, Hanson may discover a distinct lack of expertise.

A New Role. The larger problem, in Drucker's view, is that once pension funds—and other institutional shareholders—amass millions of shares in a company, they can't easily sell their holdings. So their role changes: They become owners more than investors. Yet the funds obviously cannot wear the cloak of day-to-day managers. Their primary role, in Drucker's view, should be "to make sure that a company has the management it needs."

That's exactly what Hanson says he is trying to do. He insists that he has no intention of running companies but wants the people who do run corporations to heed the concerns of shareholders. "We feel it is our fiduciary obligation to speak up when something isn't going right with a company whose stock we hold," says Hanson.

valuable.[28] These terms are very general, however, and they are not mutually exclusive. Two investors often put a single stock in different categories. One of the goals of security analysis is to try to categorize individual common stocks, as we'll discuss at more length later.

Since common stockholders are legal owners of a corporation, their investments give them certain rights. Among these are **voting rights.** Each share normally gives its owner one vote in elections of the company's board of directors and on other significant issues facing the company.[29] Management retains responsibility for the day-to-day operation of the company within guidelines set by stockholders and the board of directors. The role of stockholders in corporate governance relative to the roles of the board of directors and management has become quite controversial in recent years as shareholders have asserted their will far more aggressively on issues such as management compensation and performance. The article from *U.S. News & World Report* in the Investment Insights feature discusses the new activism of one large shareholder, the $65 billion California Public Employees Retire-

---

[28]What do the other terms mean? A cyclical stock is one that tends to follow the overall economy, doing well in a good economy and poorly in a poor economy. A defensive stock tends to do well when the economy is doing poorly. A growth stock is one that seems likely to exhibit above-average price appreciation in spite of the overall economy. A value stock is one that, for some reason(s), is selling at a price lower than it should.

[29]The exception to this rule is the company that has so-called *dual classes* of common stock outstanding. For example, Coors Brewing has two classes of common stock (A and B). The A shares carry voting rights while the B shares do not. The Coors family owns all the A shares; only the B shares are available to the public.

CalPERS's gut-check approach may strike many corporate chieftains as pure meddling, but when CalPERS speaks, they tend to listen. ITT is revising its executive compensation to track its stock price more closely after criticism by Hanson, among others, of juicy bonuses when the company's shares stagnated. And Time Warner, the publishing and entertainment giant, rejiggered a huge shareholder rights offering earlier this year after objections to the vague pricing of the deal. "You were being asked to buy a pig in a poke," says Hanson. But increasingly, CalPERS is taking a look at the larger picture—"the total return provided by companies in which we have invested and whether management has some strategic plan," says Hanson.

That's why he has challenged Chrysler. The pending stock offering, he feels, will amount to a temporary Band-Aid. The company has to seek a merger mate, Hanson argues. But he discerns no long-term strategy at all at Chrysler. And he frets that the board has not yet named a successor to Chairman Lee Iacocca, scheduled to retire at the end of next year. (Chrysler said it cannot comment because of the pending offering.)

The result of such increased activism in the long run is an open question. Some worry that because of political pressures, CalPERS may stray from its bottom-line concerns. "Do we want them pursuing social agendas as well?" asks

INVESTMENT INSIGHTS

Keith Bishop, an attorney who is a member of the California Senate's Commission on Corporate Governance. The bulk that has made CalPERS under Hanson a force to reckon with has made it a magnet for politicians as well. Earlier this year, Gov. Pete Wilson tried to tap CalPERS's reserves for $1.6 billion to close California's budget deficit and sought unsuccessfully to supplant its board with one entirely made up of political appointees.

So far, at least, shareholders in the companies CalPERS has targeted seem to have little to complain about. The issues it is taking on, such as laggard management, echo broader shareholder priorities. But CalPERS and other public pension funds already own $300 billion in stock, or nearly 10 percent of the value of the New York Stock Exchange. As they increasingly become the de facto owners of corporate America, in what Drucker calls "one of the most startling power shifts in economic history," their role is bound to become much more controversial.

Jack Egan, "The Elephant That Roared," *U.S. News & World Report*, October 7, 1991, p. 95. Copyright October 7, 1991, U.S. News & World Report.

ment System (CalPERS). CalPERS has questioned decisions made by managers at such companies as Chrysler, ITT, and Time Warner. ITT, for example, revised its executive compensation system to make it track the company's stock price more closely in response to criticism by CalPERS, and other large shareholders, who objected when ITT's management received large bonuses regardless of how well the company and its stock performed.

Rights to retain a proportionate ownership in a company are known as **preemptive rights.** This concern stems from dilution of the percentage of shares controlled by existing shareholders, should a company decide to sell additional shares of common stock. For example, if a company with 1 million shares outstanding were to sell another 500,000 shares to new investors, the proportion of the company owned by existing shareholders would fall to 67 percent. Preemptive rights prevent dilution by giving existing shareholders the right to purchase any new share offerings before other investors. Preemptive rights eventually expire after set time periods, after which any remaining shares of a new issue can be sold to outside investors.

American Depository Receipts. As we'll discuss more thoroughly in the next chapter, stock exchanges are located throughout the world. Most exchanges trade primarily the shares of companies located in their home countries. For example, most of the shares traded on the Tokyo Stock Exchange are in the stocks of Japanese companies. An American investor can buy shares of Honda Motor Company (a Japanese company) or Philips Electronics (a Dutch company), of course, by making the transaction directly on the foreign stock exchange. However, a much easier way is to buy **American depository receipts (ADRs),** which represent claims to shares of foreign stocks. ADRs are denominated in U.S. dollars, however, and trade on U.S. stock exchanges, so they eliminate some of the risk and complication of foreign investing. Over 100 ADR issues are traded on the New York Stock Exchange alone.

Derivative Securities

One of the more interesting developments in recent years has been the growth of **derivative securities.** The value of any derivative security depends on the value of another asset such as an agricultural commodity, an individual common stock, a stock index, a Treasury bond, and so forth. Most derivative securities are considered to be riskier investments than traditional capital market instruments like stocks or bonds. As a result, these securities are sometimes referred to as **speculative securities.** Derivative securities can be divided into three categories: stock options, corporate-created derivative instruments, and futures contracts.

Stock Options

A stock option gives the owner the right to buy or sell an individual stock, or a stock index, at a fixed price for a fixed period of time. Most options expire within one year after their issue dates. A **call option** is an option to buy while a **put option** is an option to sell.

Investors use options in many ways. They can buy or sell options to speculate that the underlying stocks will rise or fall in value over a short period of time. Options can also be used to **hedge** various stock positions, reducing their risk by gaining the right to buy or sell at set prices, despite market movements. Options are currently available on approximately 350 individual stocks as well as several well-known stock indexes. The most actively traded options are those on the Standard & Poor's 100 stock index (OEX options). Of course you can't buy or sell an index. These options are settled in cash. How much cash depends on the index value on the settlement date. This process will be described in Chapter 18.

To illustrate how options work, consider a December call option on Microsoft at an exercise price of $90. This call option gives the holder the right to buy 100 shares of Microsoft at a price of $90 per share at any time before late December. If Microsoft's stock price were to rise above $90 per share before late December, the holder of the option could *call* the stock (i.e., exercise the option). If Microsoft were to remain at or below $90 per share before late December, the option would expire unexercised and worthless. By contrast, a December put option on Microsoft at an exercise price of $90 would give the holder the right to sell 100 shares of Microsoft at $90 per share until late December. If Microsoft's stock were to drop to $75 per share before late December, the holder of the put could buy 100 shares of Microsoft at $75 per share, then exercise the put option to sell the stock for $90 per share, making $15 per share (ignoring transaction costs). On the other hand, if Microsoft were to remain above $90 per share through late December, the put option would expire unexercised.

This simple example suggests generally how options work, and how their value is tied to the value of the underlying stock (Microsoft, in the example). It leaves a number of questions unanswered, however. For example, who sells the stock when someone exercises a call option or buys the stock when someone exercises a put? Other investors sell the same call or put option, and accept the obligation to sell or buy in exchange for a fee. We'll answer the complex questions that options raise in more depth in Chapter 18.

Corporate-Created Derivative Securities

Corporations issue two kinds of securities that resemble options. These are convertible bonds or preferred stock issues and warrants. Like all derivative instruments, the value of these securities depends, in part, on the value of the underlying securities, which is the issuers' common stocks, for these derivatives.

Convertibles. A **convertible security** is just like a regular corporate bond or preferred stock issue with the added feature that the investor has the option of exchanging the convertible for a fixed number of shares of the issuing company's common stock. For example, Home Depot has a convertible bond outstanding that can be converted into 19.35 shares of Home Depot common stock. Since it allows the investor to exchange a bond with a par value of $1,000 for 19.35 shares of common stock, this convertible has a *conversion price* of $51.68 per share. The conversion price normally remains constant, regardless of the market price of the issuer's common stock, much like the exercise price on a call option. The value of the convertible depends, in part, on the value of the issuer's common stock. If Home Depot's common stock is trading at $60 per share, the convertible bond should sell for at least $1,161, the value of 19.35 shares at the market price.

Convertibles are attractive to investors because they combine fixed-income characteristics (the Home Depot convertible pays interest at a coupon rate of $4\frac{1}{2}$ percent) with the potential to share in stock price appreciation. As a result, convertibles typically have lower coupon rates, (or preferred stock dividends) than do similar *straight* bonds or preferred stock issues (i.e., those that are not convertible).

Warrants. In essence, **warrants** are long-term call options issued by companies. The investor redeems the warrant with the issuing corporation and receives, for a preset price, a specified number of shares of common stock. Warrants are typically issued with lives of five to ten years. They are often attached to other securities (especially bonds) to make them more marketable. Since an investor can sell the warrant, and still keep the security to which it was attached, warrants trade on the major stock exchanges. Like all call options, the value of a warrant rises and falls as the price of the underlying common stock rises and falls. For example, Genzyme Corporation (a biotechnology company) currently has an issue of warrants outstanding that were sold, attached to a bond issue, in October 1990 and expire at the end of 1994. Each warrant gives the holder the right to purchase one share of Genzyme common stock at $19 per share. If Genzyme's common stock were selling for, say, $40 per share, the warrant would sell for at least $21.

Futures Contracts

A **futures contract** is a contract between parties for future delivery of a commodity at an agreed price, usually within one year. The party who agrees to deliver the commodity is said to have the *short* position while the party who agrees to accept delivery has the *long* position. Let's say you go short and we go long in December corn. You agree to deliver, and we agree to accept, a specified amount of corn in December at a price on which we agree today.[30]

---

[30]The futures contract specifies the grade of corn to be delivered and the delivery location, as well as the amount, date, and price.

In essence, the short position makes money if the price of the commodity falls between the contract date and the delivery date, while the long position makes money if the price of the commodity rises.

Futures contracts began in ancient Egypt, and have historically involved only agricultural commodities such as corn, wheat, and livestock. Today, futures contracts are available on such diverse assets as foreign currencies, Treasury bonds, stock indexes, precious metals, and petroleum products, in addition to traditional agricultural products. The most actively traded futures contracts involve long-term Treasury bonds.[31] Futures contracts are traded throughout the world with the two largest futures exchanges located in Chicago (the Chicago Board of Trade and the Chicago Mercantile Exchange).

Basically two groups of investors trade futures contracts: hedgers and speculators. A hedger owns or needs to buy the commodity that underlies the futures contract, and uses the futures to reduce price uncertainty. A wheat farmer might use futures to guarantee the price at which a wheat crop would sell, prior to its harvest. Speculators have no need to trade commodities; they trade futures contracts to try to profit from short-term movements in commodities' prices. A speculator might go long in a wheat contract, believing that wheat is likely to rise in price over a short period of time. Another speculator might go short in Treasury bonds, believing that interest rates would soon climb higher, reducing the market prices of Treasury bonds.

We'll have a lot more to say about the investment uses of and trading in futures contracts in Chapter 19. Suffice to say at this point that while futures do not suit the needs of every investor, they can be quite useful in some situations.

Indirect Investing

Up until now, we've discussed the direct ownership of investment instruments. Many investors prefer, however, to own investment instruments *indirectly* through investment companies. Investment companies work much like banks and other financial institutions, pooling funds from many investors and then using the funds to purchase investment instruments. A money market mutual fund, for example, purchases various money market instruments; a municipal bond unit investment trust purchases a group of municipal bonds. As its securities change in value, and as they pay interest or dividends, the value of the investment company changes, passing market moves and income through to the investment company's shareholders. All investment companies charge their shareholders fees and expenses, which vary widely from company to company.

There are three types of investment companies: **unit investment trusts, closed-end funds,** and **mutual funds.** Unit investment trusts and closed-end funds have fixed numbers of shares outstanding. Shares of many closed-end funds trade on the major stock exchanges. Unit investment trusts are unmanaged; they hold set portfolios over time. Closed-end funds are actively managed; their portfolio managers make changes to their portfolios to try to maximize returns, while adhering to appropriate risk guidelines.

By far the most common type of investment company is the mutual fund. (Mutual funds are also referred to as *open-end funds.*) Unlike unit investment trusts and closed-end funds, mutual funds continually issue new shares and redeem existing shares. Most mutual funds are also actively managed. Mutual

---

[31]The Treasury bond futures market is actually larger than the cash market for T-bonds, measured by trading volume.

funds can be divided into many different categories based on the types of securities they purchase and their investment objectives. For example, growth funds invest primarily in common stocks with the primary objective of generating capital gains rather than dividend income. By contrast, balanced funds have three objectives: preservation of capital, current income, and long-term growth in both principal and income. Balanced funds purchase bonds, preferred stocks, convertible securities, and common stocks, altering the percentage of their portfolios invested in each to exploit changing market conditions.

Mutual funds have been around since the 1920s, but they have grown very rapidly in recent years. The net assets of U.S. mutual funds increased from about $51 billion in 1976 to almost $2 trillion in 1993. The number of funds increased from less than 450 to over 3,800 in the same period. Mutual funds serve an estimated 70 million shareholders today, up from fewer than 10 million in 1976. Much of this growth has been attributed to the creation of money market mutual funds in the 1970s. Money market funds, for the first time, gave small savers access to competitive money market yields; small savers were no longer restricted to savings accounts paying 5 percent interest while T-bills were yielding 10 percent. Money market funds turned many savers into investors.

Investment company shareholders measure their costs and changes in wealth by looking at **net asset value (NAV).** A fund's net asset value is found by subtracting its liabilities (if any) from the market value of its assets, and then dividing this figure by the number of outstanding shares. Owners of a mutual fund can often redeem shares at the fund's NAV; in some cases, investors can purchase shares at the NAV, as well.[32]

While they don't suit everyone, investment companies offer many investors the benefits of diversification and other substantial advantages over direct investing. We'll have more to say about investment companies in Chapter 20.

Real Assets

The discussion so far has covered investing in financial assets, or paper assets. To conclude our overview of investment alternatives, we will turn our attention to real assets. Real assets can be divided into real estate, precious metals, gems, and collectibles (e.g., art). While some real assets have produced spectacular returns, real assets can expose the investor to more problems and risks than paper assets. There are three major reasons for this. First, many real assets have poor secondary markets, so liquidity can be a problem. Second, assessing the value of real assets can be quite subjective. How much would you pay for an original da Vinci painting? Its value depends on whatever someone else is willing to pay. Third, most real assets produce no income, so all of their returns must take the form of capital gains.

Real Estate

When one thinks of real assets, real estate may come to mind first. Land, developed property, houses, etc., have long been considered viable invest-

---

[32]If the mutual fund is a so-called *no-load fund,* shares are purchased at the NAV. If the fund is a *load fund,* the purchase price is a specified percentage above the fund's NAV.

ment options, and they have often provided attractive returns. Essentially, real estate investments fall into two categories: direct ownership of real estate, and indirect ownership through real estate investment trusts (REITs) or limited partnerships.

Many Americans already invest in real estate, even if they don't realize it. That's because about 55 percent of all households own their own homes. Figure 2.2 showed that equity in owner-occupied housing represents almost 26 percent of the approximately $18 trillion in household assets. Owner-occupied housing has often been an excellent investment, but not always and not in every part of the country. Other real estate investments include farm-land, rental property, and various types of commercial property.

Just as for financial assets, one can also invest in real estate indirectly. **Real estate investment trusts (REITs)** are corporations that invest in real estate in much the same way that closed-end investment companies invest in financial assets. They pool funds from many investors and use the proceeds to purchase either property, mortgages, or both. A **limited partnership** consists of a general partner and several limited partners who invest funds in return for equity in property purchased by the partnership. The partners share in the income and/or capital appreciation produced by the property. The limited partners have limited liability; like corporate stockholders, they can lose only what they initially invested. The general partner has unlimited liability for all debts of the partnership.

Precious Metals, Gems, and Collectibles

Investors have long been drawn to the glitter of gold, diamonds, and great works of art. Gold is one of the oldest investments and has long been considered a safe harbor in which money can weather economic and political storms. Other precious metals, such as silver and platinum, have their advocates, as well. Still others tout the investment potential of gems. What could be safer, they ask, than a bag full of diamonds? Some investors favor the investment potential of collectibles such as art, antiques, or even baseball cards and classic comic books.

While precious metals, gems, and collectibles have produced very impressive returns at times, these investments are even riskier than real estate. Gold and silver, for example, are selling for about half what they sold for in the early 1980s. As another example, the auction prices of many art works fell sharply in the early 1990s when Japanese investors stopped buying art.

A Brief Review of Historical Returns

Now that we've reviewed the major investment alternatives, we'd like to conclude the chapter by comparing the historical returns they have produced. Before proceeding, we must point out that our purpose in this section is to provide a summary of the major highlights rather than a comprehensive review of the historical record. Also, all returns represent holding period returns based on both price changes and income. Finally, remember one of our investment truisms: examining the past is very informative, but historical relationships do not necessarily predict future relationships.

Paper Assets: 1926–1993

Ibbotson and Associates of Chicago have documented the history of security market returns in the United States from the beginning of 1926 through the

Table 2.2

Summary of Returns from Stocks and
Bonds: 1926–1993

Instrument	Value of Portfolio, Year-End 1993[a]	Average Annual Rate of Return[b]
Small-firm stocks	$2,757,150	17.6%
Large-firm stocks	800,080	12.3
Treasury bonds	28,030	5.4
Treasury bills	11,730	3.7
U.S. inflation	8,130	3.2

Source: *SBBI 1994 Yearbook* (Chicago: Ibbotson Associates, 1994).

[a]Portfolio consists of $1,000 invested in each alternative at the end of 1925, assuming reinvestment of all dividend and interest payments.

[b]Arithmetic mean.

end of the most recent year.[33] Ibbotson's return series represent total returns (capital gains/losses plus income) on stocks (large and small), bonds (corporate and Treasury), and Treasury bills. These data reveal a great deal about the relative performance of stocks and bonds over almost 70 years.

Some of the Ibbotson data are summarized in Table 2.2 and graphed in Figure 2.5. Clearly, over the last 68 years, stocks have outperformed bonds by a huge margin. If one had invested $1,000 at the end of 1925 in large-firm stocks (essentially the stocks that make up the Standard & Poor's 500), the initial investment would have been worth more than $800,000 at the end of 1993, an annual compound rate of return of 12.3 percent.[34] The Ibbotson data also show that small-firm stocks have outperformed large-firm stocks by a wide margin.[35] The same $1,000 invested in small-firm stocks at the end of 1925 would have been worth over $2.7 million by the end of 1993, a compound annual return of 17.6 percent.

By contrast, $1,000 invested in long-term Treasury bonds (those with maturities in excess of ten years) at the end of 1925 would have grown to only $28,000 by the end of 1993, a compound annual return of about 5.4 percent.[36] Finally, a $1,000 portfolio of Treasury bills would have grown to be worth about $12,000 from the end of 1925 to the end of 1993, a compound annual return of only 3.7 percent. This barely exceeded the average annual rate of inflation between 1926 and 1993, 3.2 percent.

So far, the Ibbotson data have shown that stocks, on average, have outperformed bonds, and small-firm stocks have outperformed large-firm stocks. This does not imply, however, that stocks outperformed bonds every individual year. To elaborate on this, Figure 2.6 illustrates the range of returns (the largest minus the smallest observed returns) for one-, five-, and ten-year holding periods. These data support two general conclusions. First,

[33]See *SBBI 1994 Yearbook* (Chicago: Ibbotson Associates, 1994). Updated annually.

[34]All dollar figures and returns assume reinvestment of dividends or interest.

[35]Ibbotson Associates defines small-firm stocks as follows: all publicly traded stocks are ranked by their respective market value (price times number of outstanding shares) from highest to lowest. The rankings are then divided into deciles. Small-firm stocks are those that make up the lowest two deciles.

[36]The Ibbotson data show that corporate bonds did slightly better than Treasury bonds. Investing $1,000 in long-term, investment-grade corporate bonds (those rated in the top three quality categories) produced a portfolio worth about $40,000 at the end of 1993 (an annual compound return of 5.9 percent).

Figure 2.5

Value of $1,000 Invested at the Beginning of 1926 by the End of 1993

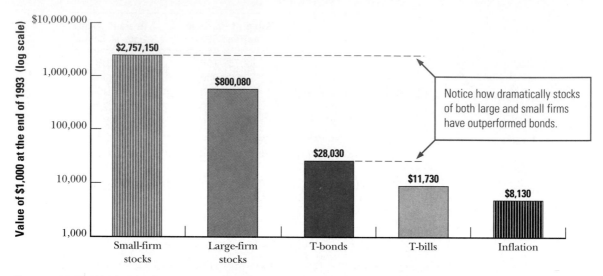

Source: *SBBI 1994 Yearbook* (Chicago: Ibbotson Associates, 1994).

the year-to-year (or period-to-period) variation in returns has been greater for stocks than for bonds. For example, looking at annual returns (those for one-year holding periods), the best year for large-firm stocks was 1933, with a total return of 54.0 percent while the worst year was 1931, with a total return of −43.3 percent. These returns produced a range of one-year returns of 97.3 percent. By contrast, annual returns for Treasury bonds have ranged from a high of 40.4 percent (1982) to a low of −9.2 percent (1967), a range of 49.6 percent.

In fact, higher average annual rates of return have always accompanied greater year-to-year variation in returns. As you may recall from Table 2.2, Treasury bills had the lowest average annual rate of return (about 3.8 percent). T-bills also have the smallest range between their best and worst years, 14.9 percent (from 14.7 percent in 1981 to −0.2 percent in 1938).

The second general conclusion that we can draw from Figure 2.6 is that the period-to-period variation decreases as the length of the holding period increases. As an example of this, take a look at small-firm stocks. The range between the highest and lowest one-year returns is over 200 percent. By contrast, the range between the highest and lowest five-year returns is about 73 percent (annualized) and the range between the highest and lowest ten-year returns is less than 36 percent (annualized). This leads to an interesting concept, diversification across time, which we'll discuss in detail in Chapter 12.

Paper Assets versus Real Assets

Having discussed historical returns from various types of paper assets, we'd like to compare their performance to those of various real assets. Salomon Brothers Inc., a large New York investment firm, has compiled data on returns from real and paper assets for about the last 20 years. Remember the earlier warning, however, that it can be quite difficult to measure and generalize returns from real assets. The returns from real estate, for example, can vary widely from location to location, and from type to type. With this in mind, some of Salomon's most recent data appear in Table 2.3.

Figure 2.6

Range of Returns for One-, Five-, and Ten-Year Holding
Periods: 1926–1993

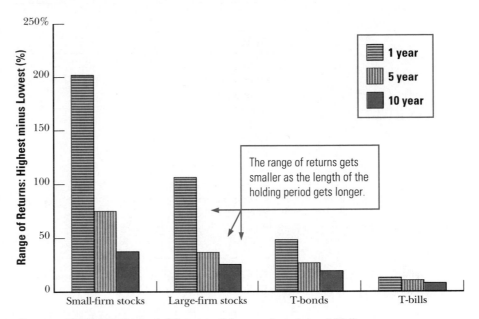

Source: *SBBI 1994 Yearbook* (Chicago: Ibbotson Associates, 1994).

During the last few years, paper assets have easily outperformed real assets. Over the year that ended June 1, 1992, Salomon Brothers found that bonds (government and corporate) posted the best performance, followed by stocks (essentially the S&P 500). Notice that none of the real assets listed in Table 2.3 even beat the general rate of inflation, and many *lost* value. Old masters paintings, for example, lost an estimated 15.8 percent of their value. For five- and ten-year periods, paper assets still dominated almost all real

Table 2.3

Returns from Paper and Real Assets
(periods ending June 1, 1992)

	Compound Annual Returns		
Asset	**One Year**	**Five Years**	**Ten Years**
Bonds	14.5%	11.5%	15.2%
Stocks	9.9	11.1	18.4
Treasury bills	4.5	6.8	7.6
U.S. inflation	3.5	4.4	4.0
Stamps	3.4	−1.1	−2.8
Single-family homes	2.2	3.6	4.4
Chinese ceramics	0.6	13.8	8.5
U.S. farmland	0.6	2.7	−1.8
Diamonds	0.0	8.8	6.4
Oil	−0.8	0.7	−5.1
Silver	−1.6	−11.3	−3.9
Gold	−6.4	−5.3	0.6
Old masters paintings	−15.8	17.2	13.3

Source: Salomon Brothers Inc.

Table 2.4

Returns from Paper and Real Assets:
1968–1979

Asset	Average Annualized Return
Gold	19.4%
Chinese ceramics	19.1
Stamps	18.9
Silver	13.7
Old masters paintings	12.5
Diamonds	11.8
U.S. farmland	11.3
Oil	11.2
Single-family homes	9.6
U.S. inflation	6.5
Treasury bills	6.2
Bonds	5.8
Stocks	3.1

Source: Salomon Brothers Inc. Reprinted from *A Walk down Wall Street* by Burton G. Malkiel, with the permission of W. W. Norton & Company, Inc. Copyright © 1990, 1985, 1981, 1975, 1973 by W. W. Norton & Company, Inc.

assets and many real assets had trouble keeping up with inflation. Gold, for example, produced an average annual return of less than 1 percent over the ten years ending June 1, 1992; silver lost an average of almost 4 percent per year during the same period.

These relationships have not always held true. If the 1980s can be described as the decade of paper assets, the 1970s were clearly the decade of real assets, as shown in Table 2.4. According to Salomon Brothers, between 1968 and 1979 the best-performing asset was gold. It achieved an annual compound return of about 19.4 percent. Paper assets, like stocks and bonds, ranked at the bottom, failing to keep pace with inflation.[37] Stocks, for example, produced an average annual return of only 3.1 percent compared to an average annual inflation rate of 6.5 percent.

What explains the difference between the 1970s and 1980s? In a word, the answer is inflation. Historically, real assets have tended to do much better than paper assets in an inflationary environment, especially if future rates of inflation are extremely uncertain. When inflation is low and future inflation is more predictable, paper assets tend to do better than real assets. Again, though, this has been true in the past, but there is no guarantee that it will be true in the future.

Chapter Summary

1. **Understand the general categories under which today's investment alternatives fall.**

   Today's investment alternatives can be divided into real assets and financial assets. Financial assets can be divided into direct investments and indirect investments. Direct investments include money market instruments, capital market instruments, and derivative securities. Indirect investments

---

[37]Remember, these data give results for stocks and bonds *in general*. Some individual stocks did very well during the 1970s, producing returns far exceeding those produced by gold and other real assets.

(also called *investment companies*) consist of unit investment trusts, closed-end funds, and mutual funds. Real assets include real estate, precious metals, gems, and collectibles. Real estate investments can be either direct or indirect investments.

2. **Review the basic investment characteristics of money market instruments.**
   Money market instruments may be the most homogeneous group of investments. All money market instruments mature (i.e., repay principal) within one year and have little, if any, credit risk. Most are discount securities (i.e., are sold for less than their face values at maturity), and most are sold in large denominations. Money market instruments include Treasury bills, short-term federal agency securities, commercial paper, banker's acceptances, large certificates of deposit, repurchase agreements, short-term municipal securities, and various money market instruments issued by foreign governments and corporations.

3. **Outline the investment characteristics of capital market instruments.**
   Capital market instruments include all financial assets that have maturities in excess of one year. This diverse group of investments includes bonds, mortgages, preferred stocks, and common stocks. Thousands of governments and corporations worldwide issue capital market instruments. They range from fairly safe securities, such as Treasury bonds, to highly speculative securities. Capital market instruments are classified as either fixed-income securities (governments, corporates, municipals, mortgage pass-throughs, and preferred stocks) or equities (common stocks).

4. **Understand the basic characteristics of derivative securities.**
   Derivative securities *derive* their values from the values of other assets such as agricultural commodities and stock indexes. Most derivative securities are considered to be riskier investments than more traditional capital market instruments. A stock option gives its owner the right to buy (call) or sell (put) an individual stock, or stock index, at a fixed price for a fixed period of time. Corporations also issue securities that resemble options: warrants and convertible bonds or preferred stocks. A warrant allows an investor to purchase a company's common stock at a fixed price for a period of several years. Futures contracts are contracts that specify the future delivery of a commodity, at a given point in time, at a stated price. Futures contracts cover exchanges of everything from corn to crude oil to Treasury bonds.

5. **Describe the general features of investment companies.**
   An owner of shares of an investment company owns a piece of a portfolio of securities. As the investment company's securities pay interest or dividends, these payments pass through to the investment company's shareholders. In addition, as the securities become more valuable, the investment company shares also become more valuable. There are three types of investment companies: unit investment trusts, closed-end funds, and mutual funds. Unit investment trusts and closed-end funds issue fixed numbers of shares which trade on securities exchanges. Unit investment trusts are also unmanaged; they hold fixed portfolios. Closed-end funds are actively managed. Mutual funds continually issue and redeem shares, and most are actively managed. Investment companies have grown in popularity in recent years. Mutual funds, however, have grown the fastest and are, by far, the most common type of investment company.

6. **Review the investment characteristics of real assets.**
   Real asset investing involves the ownership of physical assets such as real estate, precious metals, and works of art. Real estate investors can own property directly or invest indirectly through real estate investment trusts. The most common form of real estate investing is home ownership. Investors have tried to earn returns on many other physical assets including

gold, diamonds, old masters paintings, and comic books. Real asset investing has produced spectacular returns, but it exposes investors to a number of unique risks. Real assets generally have poor secondary markets (lack of liquidity), can be difficult to value objectively, and often produce no income.

7. **Summarize the historical returns produced by major investment alternatives.**

   The chapter ended with an examination of part of the historical record on the returns produced by various investment instruments. Over the past 68 years or so, stocks have outperformed both corporate and Treasury bonds by a large margin, and small-firm stocks have outperformed large-firm stocks. Year-to-year variation in returns has also been greater for stocks than bonds, and period-to-period variation in returns gets smaller as the length of the holding period increases. Finally, we examined the returns produced by real assets relative to those produced by paper assets. The decade of the 1980s was clearly the decade of paper assets, while the 1970s was the decade of real assets.

Key Terms

Financial asset	Subordinated debenture
Real asset	Income bond
Indirect investment	Mortgage pass-through
Marketable security	Yankee bond
Discount security	Bulldog bond
Treasury bill	Eurobond
Full faith and credit	Hybrid security
Bank discount yield	Residual claimant
Bond equivalent yield	Blue chip
Federal agency security	Voting right
Commercial paper	Preemptive rights
Banker's acceptance	American Depository Receipt (ADR)
Certificate of deposit	Derivative security
Repurchase agreement	Speculative security
Taxable equivalent yield	Call option
Eurodollar	Put option
London Interbank Offered Rate (LIBOR)	Hedge
	Convertible security
Coupon rate	Warrant
Call provision	Futures contract
General obligation bond	Unit investment trust
Revenue bond	Closed-end fund
Serial bond	Mutual fund
Term bond	Net asset value (NAV)
Bond rating	Real estate investment trust (REIT)
Mortgage bond	Limited partnership
Debenture	

Discussion Questions and Problems

1. What are the general characteristics of money market instruments? Give three examples of money market instruments.

2. Assume you purchased a 90-day Treasury bill for $9,910. (Its face value is $10,000.) Find the T-bill's bank discount yield and its bond equivalent yield. Which yield comes closer to measuring your true rate of return?

3. What is a repurchase agreement? Are repurchase agreements secured or unsecured?

4. Assume that a short-term municipal is yielding 2.75 percent. Find its taxable equivalent yield for an investor in a 28 percent tax bracket. When should the marginal tax rate for this calculation reflect both state and federal income taxes?

 5. Define the terms *Eurodollar* and *LIBOR*. What is the relationship between Eurodollars and LIBOR?

6. What are the practical differences between federal agency securities and Treasury securities? Give an example of a federal agency security.

7. What are the differences between U.S. Treasury bills, notes, and bonds? Which of the three exposes investors to the most risk?

8. What are the two types of municipal bonds? What are the important differences between the two?

9. List several types of corporate bonds that have different collateral provisions. Which type on your list is the safest?

10. What is a mortgage pass-through security? What are its investment advantages and drawbacks?

 11. What is a Eurobond? How does a Eurobond differ from a Yankee bond?

12. Why is preferred stock considered to be a hybrid security? Do investors consider preferred stock to be more like a bond or more like common stock?

13. What major rights does common stock give its owner? Which of these rights has received a great deal of press attention lately?

 14. What is an American depository receipt (ADR)? Why would an American investor purchase ADRs rather than buy shares directly?

15. What rights do call and put options give their owners? Why are convertible securities and warrants considered to be options?

16. What is a futures contract? List the two general categories of futures traders.

17. Compare and contrast the three types of investment companies. Which of the three is the most poppular with contemporary investors?

18. What are the general investment characteristics of real assets? List the most popular real asset investments.

19. Review the historical data on security returns between 1926 and 1993. What are three general conclusions you can draw from the data? Provide examples to support your conclusions.

Critical Thinking Exercise

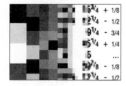

This exercise requires computer work. Open the file RETURNS1.XLS on the data disk. The file lists annual total returns from large-firm stocks, Treasury bonds, and Treasury bills, as well as annual inflation data between 1949 and 1993. Use the data in the file to answer the following questions:

a. Which were the five best years to have owned large-firm stocks?

b. Which were the five worst years to have owned large-firm stocks?

c. Answer questions a and b for U.S. Treasury bonds and bills.

d. Which five years had the highest inflation rates? Which five years had the lowest inflation rates?

e. What do your findings in questions a through d tell you about the historical performance of large-firm stocks, Treasury bonds, and Treasury bills, relative to each other and relative to inflation?

Chapter 3

Organization and Functioning of the Securities Markets

Chapter Objectives

1. Identify traits that constitute a good, well-functioning financial market.
2. Understand the organization and functioning of primary financial markets.
3. Review the importance of secondary financial markets.
4. Describe the world's major secondary markets.
5. Outline how trading is conducted in the major secondary markets.
6. Discuss the regulation of the financial markets.
7. Review the past and likely future evolution of the financial markets.

The following kinds of headlines are probably familiar to anyone who watches the evening news or reads the morning newspaper:[1]

- London shares skid on fears of Labor party win
- Bond prices rise on view of weak recovery in U.S.
- Industrial average, S&P 500 post impressive gains in the afternoon
- Investors revolt against lofty IPO prices for biotech, forcing cutbacks
- Plunge in Nikkei sends yen reeling after Japan cuts discount rate

These kinds of public comments on the world financial markets are common. Still, most individuals, indeed even many active investors, have only fragmentary knowledge of how those financial markets are organized or how they function.

Think about the following questions; how well can you answer them?

- What are the differences between the primary and secondary markets?
- Can individual investors buy T-bills directly at the weekly Treasury auction?
- What really happens when an investor places an order to buy or sell with a broker?
- Why are some stocks listed on more than one exchange?

---

[1] All of these headlines were taken from *The Wall Street Journal*, April 2, 1992.

Basic questions such as these often stump investors. That's too bad since, we believe, no one can make informed, intelligent investment decisions without a good understanding of the financial markets in which those decisions are implemented. Since the economic prosperity of any society is enhanced by smoothly functioning financial markets, some knowledge of the financial markets is important for everyone, not just active investors.

In this chapter, we review the organization and functioning of the world's major financial markets. We begin with a discussion of what markets are, and the characteristics of a good market. Next, we examine the primary financial markets, covering such topics as the U.S. Treasury auction market, investment banking, and initial public offerings. We then describe the major secondary financial markets like the New York Stock Exchange, the NASDAQ system, and the Tokyo Stock Exchange. Next, we conduct a detailed examination of how trading takes place in the financial markets. We explain, for example, the role of the NYSE specialist. Finally, we explore some of the major innovations in the financial markets in recent years, and speculate on what the markets might look like in the next century.

What Is a Financial Market?

The dictionary defines a *market* as a meeting of people, or a place, for selling and buying of a good or service. That rather broad definition suggests that a financial market exists almost any time and anywhere that anyone trades a security. The dictionary definition does not imply that trading has to take place in a physical location. It is only necessary that buyers and sellers have the ability and opportunity to communicate with one another. Nor does the definition imply that all buyers and sellers must receive the best price possible.

Rather than "what is a market," a more fundamental question would ask, what is a **good market?** We argue that a good financial market is one where trading is conducted in a fair, open, and orderly manner. In order to meet this standard, what characteristics should a good market have?

Characteristics of a Good Market

Perhaps the single most important characteristic of a good market, for both buyers and sellers, is **liquidity.** Liquidity is the ability to quickly buy or sell an asset at a price justified by its underlying supply and demand conditions. In a liquid market, a seller should be able to quickly sell an asset for a cash price close to the market price. For example, someone wants to sell a house and receives an offer of $75,000. Suppose, however, that the underlying supply and demand conditions suggest that the house should be worth around $100,000. This real estate market is not liquid. While it allows a seller to turn a house into cash, it doesn't set a price that is justified by the underlying supply and demand conditions. Of course, liquidity does not prevent an asset from falling in price, nor does it mean that an investor never has to sell an asset for a price well below the purchase price. One can lose lots of money in the most liquid of markets.

A good financial market should have the following characteristics in order to be considered fair, open, and orderly:

• Sufficient information is available to determine the underlying supply and demand conditions, and this information is available to all market participants at about the same time. This implies that all trading should take place in full view of all market participants.

- **Price continuity** exists. This means that, assuming no new information has entered the market, one can buy or sell at a price close to that of the most recent, similar trade.
- **Transaction costs** are low. All participants should have the opportunity to buy or sell at reasonable cost.
- All participants have equal access to the market. The market should not allow some participants to execute orders to buy or sell faster than others.
- Prices adjust quickly to new, public information, and this information is disclosed at the same time to all participants.

These conditions are not absolute standards, and any assessment of how well any specific financial market meets these conditions is somewhat subjective. Later in this chapter we'll see that regulation of the financial markets, in both the United States and most other countries, is designed primarily to ensure that these conditions exist.

The conditions of a good market do not demand a **perfect market**. For one thing, a perfect market would have to eliminate frictions, with no transaction costs, taxes, or constraining regulations. Obviously in the real world, market participants must pay transaction costs and taxes, and contend with other conditions that impede their trading somewhat. Furthermore, a good market need not even be an **efficient market** all the time. Market efficiency is the extent to which security prices reflect all relevant information. Chapter 7 will explore several versions of market efficiency theory, along with evidence supporting and contradicting the theory.

An Example of a Good Market

To further elaborate on the conditions a good market should satisfy, let's take a look at an actual financial market, the New York Stock Exchange (NYSE). Does the NYSE satisfy the conditions of a good market? Generally, it does.

It certainly provides adequate information on underlying supply and demand conditions of all securities it trades. A series of rules and monitoring tools are designed to maintain a fair and open market. For example, the NYSE requires that every trade be instantaneously published on its electronic ticker tape, which is broadcast worldwide, including live on CNN Headline News, CNBC, and other mass-media outlets.

There is also little question that the NYSE maintains price continuity. Approximately 96 percent of all trades during 1993 took place within one-eighth of a point ($12\frac{1}{2}$ cents per share) of the prior trades' prices. In another example of price continuity, approximately 85 percent of all quotes from NYSE specialists (whose role will be described in detail later) were within one-quarter point of the prior trades in 1993. Of course, price continuity doesn't mean that prices cannot rise or fall, but only that they do so in small increments.

The cost of buying and selling securities on the NYSE varies widely depending on the type of trade, the type of investor (institution or individual), and the type of brokerage firm used by the investor (discount or full-service broker). Generally, most NYSE traders would agree that its costs are reasonable; rarely do transaction costs exceed about 2 percent of the total value of a trade. For example, suppose that an individual investor wants to purchase 100 shares of a stock currently trading at $60 per share for a total trade value of $6,000. A discount brokerage firm would charge about $55 to process the trade, about 0.9 percent of its total value, while a full-service brokerage firm would charge around \$107, about 1.8 percent of the total value of the trade.[2]

The NYSE claims to give all investors, regardless of size, equal access to the market. As we will discuss in more detail later, the NYSE can be best described as an auction market, with competing buyers and sellers bidding against one another. The exchange argues that its auction process treats all investors equally since no trade can take place unless it reflects the highest price any buyer is willing to pay, and the lowest price any seller is willing to accept. To increase access further, computer software available from some brokerage firms (such as Quick & Reilly) can allow individual investors to use their personal computers to directly access the NYSE's electronic order system and place buy or sell orders. Members of the exchange cannot access the electronic order system faster.

Finally, we will deal with the issue of how rapidly prices adjust to new public information, and how that information is disclosed, in detail in Chapter 7. Suffice to say at this point that strong evidence suggests that prices adjust very quickly to new information on all major financial markets, including the NYSE. For example, on December 2, 1993, The Limited, a large retail chain, announced that its same-store sales had dropped 7 percent between November 1992 and November 1993. The company also indicated that its fiscal year earnings would fall as much as 12 percent. The stock was mauled during the first few hours of trading that day, dropping in price about $3\frac{3}{8}$ points, or about 15 percent, on trading volume that was six times normal for the stock.

Classification of Financial Markets

Financial markets can be distributed among several general categories. These include primary and secondary markets, debt and equity markets, money and capital markets, auction and over-the-counter markets, and so forth. We will focus our discussion on stock and bond markets for now. Options and futures markets function somewhat differently, as we'll see in Chapters 18 and 19.

Primary Financial Markets

A **primary financial market** is one where investors buy newly issued securities and security issuers (such as corporations) receive the proceeds from those sales. A popular misconception is that selling stock on the NYSE takes money away from a corporation. This isn't true—all NYSE trades involve one investor buying shares from another investor. The company received its money when it sold the stock initially in the primary market. Subsequent trades simply change the owners of the corporation and leave its financial condition unaffected.

Primary financial markets function as intermediaries between savers (investors) and borrowers (corporations and governments). Well-functioning primary markets allow borrowers to raise funds as cheaply as possible, while, at the same time, they give savers the opportunity to earn the highest possible expected rates of return. No modern economy can exist without well-functioning primary financial markets in which firms can raise capital to fund their operations.

---

[2]The differences between discount and full-service brokerage firms will be described later. Source: *Survey of Brokerage Commissions,* Charles Schwab and Co., San Francisco, 1992.

Primary financial markets vary widely in size and organizational complexity. Generally, they process sales of new security issues in one of three ways: through open auctions, through underwriting by investment bankers, or through private placement with large, institutional investors.

Open Auctions

Several types of securities are sold primarily through **open auctions,** where investors bid on the basis of price or yield. The most significant new security auctions sell U.S. Treasury securities, federal agency securities, and mortgage-backed securities.

U.S. Treasury Security Auctions.

As we discussed in Chapter 2, the U.S. Treasury issues a variety of debt instruments. The size of this market is staggering. During May 1993, for example, the Treasury sold $46.9 billion in 90-day bills, $46.7 billion in 180-day bills, $14.4 billion in one-year bills, $60.6 billion in notes, and $8.6 billion in bonds.

Virtually all Treasury securities are initially sold to the investing public via an auction process. These auctions are held regularly, usually on a Monday. Auctions for three-month and six-month bills are usually held every Monday (excluding holidays), auctions for two-year and five-year notes are held monthly, and auctions for other securities (e.g., 30-year bonds) are held quarterly. The Treasury usually announces on the Wednesday before each auction how much of what types of securities it will sell the following Monday.

As the fiscal agent for the federal government, the Federal Reserve actually conducts the auctions, with the Federal Reserve Bank of New York taking the leading role. Buyers can submit two types of bids: competitive bids and noncompetitive bids. A competitive bid must specify a face amount and a bid price while a noncompetitive bid specifies only the face amount the buyer wants to purchase, with maximums of $5 million for notes and bonds, and $1 million for bills. The Treasury accepts all noncompetitive bids, and then it reviews the competitive bids to determine the *stop-out bid,* the one with the lowest price (or highest investor yield) that it will accept. Those who submit noncompetitive bids agree to pay the average price on accepted, competitive bids.

In theory, anyone can submit a competitive bid, but in reality only the primary **government bond dealers** do so. (There are currently 40 primary government bond dealers.)[3] Despite the lack of formal restrictions, the Federal Reserve will deal directly only with primary dealers, which the Federal Reserve itself designates. The Fed verifies that any firm requesting primary dealer status has adequate capital and handles a reasonable volume of trading in Treasuries (at least 1 percent of Treasury market activity).

Primary dealers are expected to participate in every Treasury auction, and are not allowed to bid for more than 35 percent of a total issue. Primary dealers may then resell the securities to other investors, such as pension funds. To fulfill this function, primary dealers are expected to maintain inventories of Treasury securities at all times and to participate in secondary market trading.

The Treasury auction system is not without its critics. Some argue that given the size and importance of this market (more than $2 trillion annually), the Treasury's auction system is obsolete. Primary dealers, for example, still hand deliver written bids to the New York Fed! The revelation

---

[3]Noncompetitive bids can be submitted by anyone, including small, individual investors. In fact, individual investors can purchase newly issued Treasury securities directly through any Federal Reserve Bank.

in 1991 by one primary dealer, Salomon Brothers, that it had committed serious "irregularities and rule violations in connection with its submission of bids in certain auctions of Treasury securities" has focused attention on the need to modernize the auction system for U.S. government securities. The commentary by *Business Week* financial reporter Mike McNamee, in the Investment Insights feature on page 69 suggests a number of possible reforms. The Treasury and Federal Reserve are currently studying ways to improve the auction system and some changes appear likely.

Federal Agency Securities. As we discussed in Chapter 2, several federal and quasifederal agencies are empowered to issue debt. These federal agency securities are sold in essentially the same manner as Treasury securities. Auctions generate competitive and noncompetitive bids, which are accepted based upon a minimum price and funding needs. Again, the primary government bond dealers submit virtually all of the competitive bids and bid on almost every new issue. Dealers also are expected to maintain inventories of federal agency securities and to participate in secondary market trading. Since the amount of federal agency debt outstanding is much smaller than the amount of outstanding Treasury debt, sales of new federal agency issues are smaller than new Treasury issues and the auctions are held less frequently.

Mortgage-Backed Securities. Virtually all mortgage-backed securities issued by the federally sponsored mortgage agencies, GNMA, FNMA, and FHLMC (often referred to as Ginnie Mae, Fannie Mae, and Freddie Mac), are sold via auctions similar to those for Treasury and federal agency securities. The primary government bond dealers do most of the bidding and maintain inventories of mortgage-backed securities. Some mortgage-backed securities are issued by nongovernment entities like large financial institutions; these securities are usually underwritten and sold through investment bankers.

Underwriting and Investment Banking

Virtually all nongovernment security issues are sold to the investing public through investment bankers. This includes most municipal debt issues and public offerings of corporate debt and equity instruments.[4] Bonds that are issued in other countries (such as Eurobonds) are also sold through investment bankers. Some foreign governments also tap the international credit markets by issuing bonds, which are typically underwritten, as well.

The Role of the Investment Banker. The **investment banker** plays a number of important roles in the sale of new securities. These roles can be described as origination, risk-bearing, and distribution. In the origination role, the investment banker helps the issuer design the terms and set the price of the new security issue. In the risk-bearing role, the investment banker purchases the issue (called **underwriting**) and accepts responsibility for reselling it to other investors. The risks associated with mispricing the issue are borne by the investment banker, not the issuer. Finally, in the distribution role, the investment banker distributes the issue to the public. The issuer could, of course, perform these functions itself. However, most issuers (such as municipalities and corporations) find it much more efficient and less costly to sell new security issues through investment bankers.

Investment bankers don't provide their services for free. They charge **underwriting discounts,** purchasing securities from issuers below the prices

---

[4]Remember that *municipal* refers to any security issued by a state or local government unit. The term *government* refers only to U.S. Treasury and federal agency issues.

How to Keep Solly's Folly from Happening Again

The very size of the market for U.S. Treasury securities makes the notion of a squeeze seem silly. After all, who could amass the capital to corner any part of the world's biggest, deepest, and most liquid market? Plus, thousands of traders monitor Treasuries around the clock, prepared to pounce whenever rates move one-hundredth of a percentage point.

The revelation that Salomon Brothers Inc. muscled the Treasury market—controlling up to 57 percent of one issue—kills this smug assurance. The system clearly needs an overhaul, but there's a right way and a wrong way.

Upsetting as Solly's Folly is, the biggest damage to the $2.3 trillion Treasuries market might come from a congressional backlash. Congress is inclined to respond to abuses in any market by shouting: "Crack down!" Stiffened regulation mandated by Capitol Hill, however, may drive investors away, making it more difficult to finance the national debt and adding billions to the government's interest costs.

Treasury Secretary Nicholas F. Brady and New York Fed President E. Gerald Corrigan hope the punishment they've meted out to Salomon—barring it from bidding on customers' behalf—will keep traders in line. Still, that's not enough. The regulators can fix the system with powers they already have. Here's how:

Strengthen the cops. Three agencies split the chore of policing the market. Treasury sets the rules, such as the 35 percent limit on any one bidder's share of an auction, but lacks investigative powers. The New York Fed gets reports on primary dealers' bond and note holdings, although the data are too skimpy for adequate enforcement. The Securities and Exchange Commission is called in only after violations are detected. Result: The government hadn't noticed anything wrong in three of the five auctions in which Salomon admitted to violating rules.

Some say the solution is to lower the 35 percent cap. But squeezers could get around any

ceiling if the monitoring is only a joke. And the panacea is not to create a single regulator, which would take years of political wrangling to accomplish. Instead, a simple and effective step for Corrigan would be to beef up

INVESTMENT INSIGHTS

the New York Fed's weak dealer-surveillance unit into a sharper-eyed monitor of bidding and trading. The SEC would be happy to show him how to get better, more timely information from market players.

Open the market. Treasury's auctions are still paper-and-pencil affairs. Primary dealers use runners to deliver handwritten bids to the New York Fed. In theory, anyone can offer a competitive bid. In practice, only the 40 primary dealers have the information to bid successfully for themselves and their customers.

Treasury is considering requiring large customers to submit bids directly rather than buying through dealers. A better idea: set up a computerized market open to direct bids by hundreds of institutions.

Swamp the squeezers. Treasury has the power to break a squeeze by hitting the market with a special issue of notes. It hasn't done so because that would disrupt its announced borrowing schedule. Treasury should realize that a squeeze does more damage than does a minor calendar change.

If handled badly, the Salomon scandal could bring a replay of the banking credit crunch. "Lax regulation that suddenly turns tough at exactly the wrong time could choke this market," frets an official at one primary dealer. The Treasury and the Fed have the power to prevent that by shaping rules that guarantee a robust yet fair market. They shouldn't wait any longer.

Source: Mike McNamee, "How to Keep Solly's Folly from Happening Again," *Business Week*, September 2, 1991, p. 70. Reprinted from September 2, 1991 issue of *Business Week* by special permission, copyright © 1991 by McGraw-Hill, Inc.

at which they hope to resell them. Figure 3.1 shows the front page of a prospectus (a document that accompanies a new issue, as discussed later in the chapter) for a new issue of 7.65 million shares of common stock in Rawlings Sporting Goods. Notice that the underwriting discount is stated as $0.76 per share (or about 7 percent of the value of the issue).[5] The investment bankers stood to receive over $5.8 million for their role in the deal.

---

[5]The size of the underwriting discount varies widely from issue to issue. Generally, underwriting discounts are higher for equity issues than debt issues, and discounts tend to get smaller (as a percentage of the issue's value) as the size of the issue increases.

Figure 3.1

Prospectus for a New Security Issue

"The Mark of a Pro."

7,650,000 Shares

RAWLINGS SPORTING GOODS COMPANY, INC.

Common Stock

All of the 7,650,000 shares of common stock, par value $.01 per share (the "Common Stock"), of Rawlings Sporting Goods Company, Inc. (the "Company" or "Rawlings") are being offered and sold by Figgie International Inc. ("Figgie" or the "Selling Stockholder") in concurrent offerings in the United States and Canada and outside of the United States and Canada. Of such shares, 6,120,000 shares initially are being offered in the United States and Canada by the U.S. Underwriters (the "U.S. Offering") and 1,530,000 shares initially are being offered outside of the United States and Canada by the International Underwriters (the "International Offering" and, together with the U.S. Offering, the "Offerings"). The price to the public and aggregate underwriting discounts and commissions per share for the U.S. Offering and for the International Offering will be identical. See "Underwriting."

The Company will not receive any of the proceeds from the sale of shares offered hereby, other than the proceeds, if any, received as a result of the exercise of the over-allotment options granted by the Company to the U.S. Underwriters and the International Underwriters (collectively, the "Underwriters"). Any proceeds received as a result of the exercise of the over-allotment options will be used to reduce indebtedness of the Company. In the Offerings, Figgie is selling 100% of its ownership interest in the Company, which will constitute over 99%, but less than 100%, of the issued and outstanding shares of the Company's Common Stock.

Prior to the Offerings, there has been no public market for the Common Stock. For a discussion of the factors considered in determining the initial public offering price, see "Underwriting." The Common Stock has been approved for quotation through the Nasdaq National Market System under the symbol "RAWL."

See "Risk Factors" for a discussion of certain factors that should be considered by prospective purchasers of the Common Stock.

THESE SECURITIES HAVE NOT BEEN APPROVED OR DISAPPROVED BY THE SECURITIES AND EXCHANGE COMMISSION OR ANY STATE SECURITIES COMMISSION NOR HAS THE SECURITIES AND EXCHANGE COMMISSION OR ANY STATE SECURITIES COMMISSION PASSED UPON THE ACCURACY OR ADEQUACY OF THIS PROSPECTUS. ANY REPRESENTATION TO THE CONTRARY IS A CRIMINAL OFFENSE.

	Price to Public	Underwriting Discounts and Commissions*	Proceeds to the Selling Stockholder†
Per Share	$12.00	$0.76	$11.24
Total‡	$91,800,000	$5,814,000	$85,986,000

* The Company and the Selling Stockholder have agreed to indemnify the Underwriters against certain liabilities, including liabilities under the Securities Act of 1933, as amended. See "Underwriting."

† Before deducting expenses of the Offerings estimated at $2,000,000 which will be paid by the Selling Stockholder.

‡ The Company has granted the Underwriters 30-day options to purchase up to an aggregate of 1,000,000 additional shares of Common Stock at the initial public offering price per share, less the underwriting discount, solely to cover over-allotments, if any. If such options are exercised in full, the total price to public will be $103,800,000, the total underwriting discounts and commissions will be $6,574,000 and the total proceeds to the Selling Stockholder and to the Company will be $85,986,000 and $11,240,000, respectively. See "Underwriting."

The Common Stock is being offered by the Underwriters as set forth under "Underwriting" herein. It is expected that delivery of certificates therefor will be made at the offices of Dillon, Read & Co. Inc., New York, New York on or about July 8, 1994, against payment therefor in New York funds. The Underwriters include:

Dillon, Read & Co. Inc.

A.G. Edwards & Sons, Inc.

J.J.B. Hilliard, W.L. Lyons, Inc.

The date of this Prospectus is June 30, 1994.

Competitive versus Negotiated Arrangements. Issuers of securities employ investment bankers based on either competitive or negotiated arrangements. In a competitive arrangement, the issuer solicits bids from several investment bankers and then chooses the firm that offers the smallest underwriting discount, imposing the lowest cost on the issuer. In a negotiated arrangement, the issuer selects the investment banking firm and then negotiates all aspects of the issue, including the underwriting discount, with the firm. Some argue that, while competitive bidding might reduce the cost of a new security issue slightly, the extra services provided by the investment banking firm in a negotiated arrangement more than offset the extra expense to the issuer.

Most corporations issue securities by negotiated arrangements. In fact, most large corporations have ongoing business relationships with one or more investment banking firms. Public utility companies, however, are still required in many states to complete competitive bidding processes.

Many states require that municipal general obligation bonds be sold through competitive bidding as well, though this requirement seldom affects revenue bond issues. However, during the last 15 years or so a trend has increased the use of negotiated arrangements for sales of new municipal securities. The increasingly close relationship between some issuers of municipal bonds and their investment banking firms has been strongly criticized as not serving the best interests of either taxpayers or investors. Critics have accused some local officials of trading underwriting business for political contributions.[6]

Syndication. For virtually any security issue, the investment banking firm selected by the issuer, whether by negotiation or competitive bidding, forms a **syndicate** to actually sell the issue to the public. The syndicate is a group of investment banking firms, each of which purchases a portion of the issue, accepting responsibility for reselling only that portion. For example, the syndicate for the Rawlings Sporting Goods stock issue consisted of 70 firms, each of which purchased between 20,000 and 1,359,000 shares for resale to the public. Syndicates allow investment bankers to spread the risk, limit their commitment of capital, and improve the marketing of the issue.

A few corporate securities, mostly speculative equity issues, are sold by investment bankers on a best efforts basis. In this arrangement, the investment banker does not underwrite the issue. The issuing corporation retains ownership of the stock and the investment banking firm, or syndicate, merely acts as a broker to try to find buyers for the stock at the best possible price. The fees charged for a best efforts issue are less than the underwriting discount, because the investment banker takes less risk.

Initial Public Offerings. One type of primary market transaction deserves a little extra attention: **initial public offerings (IPOs).** An IPO is the company's first sale of common stock to the investing public when it initially *goes public.* Initial public offerings are usually underwritten by investment banks, though the underwriting discounts tend to be higher given the added risk of pricing IPOs without existing securities as benchmarks. The proceeds from an IPO can be used to inject equity capital into the company and/or to buy out existing owners.

Conventional wisdom holds that investment bankers intentionally underprice IPOs to reduce their own risk and to aid in the sale of the newly issued shares. However, there is also strong evidence that, despite many spectacular exceptions, IPOs generally underperform the market during their first few years of public trading.[7] Further, as we'll see in Chapter 5, IPOs appear prone to speculative bubbles.

---

[6]See for example, "The Trouble with Munis," *Business Week,* September 6, 1993, pp. 44–51.

[7]See, for example, Jay Ritter, "The Long-Run Performance of Initial Public Offerings," *The Journal of Finance,* March 1991, pp. 1–27.

Private Placements

Some new security issues may not be sold publicly, but rather only to a small, select group of large, institutional investors (e.g., pension funds and life insurance companies). These sales are referred to as **private placements.** Virtually all private placements involve corporate debt issues, though a small amount of municipal debt (less than 10 percent) is privately placed. In 1993, for example, about 30 percent of new long-term corporate debt issues were privately placed. An investment banking firm usually assists the corporation in the private placement, acting as a broker.

A private placement typically gives a company some cost savings. The issuer avoids both the underwriting discount and the various costs associated with registering the issue with the Securities and Exchange Commission. Institutions buy private placements because they typically carry slightly higher yields than publicly issued securities. In addition, the terms of the issue can be tailored to meet the specific needs of both the issuer and the institutional investor. Of course, the institutional investor gives up liquidity. Privately placed securities will not trade in any secondary market.

Secondary Financial Markets

Secondary financial markets handle trading of previously issued securities between investors. Like primary markets, secondary financial markets can be classified in a number of different ways. There are auction and negotiated markets, organized and over-the-counter markets, markets with face-to-face trading, and markets where trading takes place by computer. Before we look briefly at the world's principal financial markets, let's try to answer a basic question: why are secondary markets important?

The Importance of Secondary Markets

The importance of secondary financial markets to investors is rather obvious. Many investors want, or need, to sell securities that they acquire in the primary markets. For example, an investor might purchase a five-year Treasury note with the full expectation of holding it until maturity. However, the investor's situation might change and he or she might want to sell the note after, say, three years. The secondary market for U.S. Treasury securities provides liquidity for this investor by allowing him or her to sell the note for approximately its market value.

While it's obvious why secondary markets are important to investors, their importance to issuers may not seem as obvious. Secondary markets benefit issuers of securities in the primary markets because, if investors doubted that they could sell a newly issued security in a secondary market, they might refuse to purchase it or demand a substantially higher rate of return. By giving investors the option of selling their securities, a well-functioning secondary market lowers the cost of capital for issuers.

Aside from liquidity, secondary markets serve an important economic need for **price discovery.** Even if an investor plans to continue to hold a security, the secondary market still tells the investor what the security is currently worth. Furthermore, new issues of securities to be sold in the primary market are actually priced by the secondary market. For example, if five-year Treasury notes are yielding 5 percent in the secondary market, newly issued Treasury notes will have to yield about 5 percent to attract buyers.

Any security issue that is not privately placed has some kind of secondary market. However, some secondary markets function better than others (i.e., they provide more liquidity to investors). One way of seeing this is to look at the spread between the bid and ask price of the market makers. Every secondary market has market makers, dealers willing to buy and sell the securities traded on that market. The **bid price** is the price at which the market maker is willing to buy the security, and the **ask price** is the price at which it is willing to sell the security. Market makers make their profits by selling securities at higher prices than they pay for them. A larger bid/ask spread, however, makes a secondary market less liquid.

Why, then, do some securities develop better secondary markets than others? While there are several factors, the most important appears to be the size of the issue (e.g., how many individual bonds or shares of stock were originally issued). Larger issues, in general, have more active and liquid secondary markets. Another important factor is the number of investors who originally purchased the issue. If, for example, ten large institutions buy up an entire new security issue, it is less likely that an active secondary market will develop than if the issue had been sold to thousands of investors, any of whom may decide to sell at any time.

U.S. Secondary Bond Markets

Secondary markets trade U.S. government securities, municipal securities, corporate debt securities, and foreign debt securities. Most secondary bond markets are **over-the-counter markets.** In such a market, trading doesn't take place in a physical location, such as a trading floor, but rather through computer-based communications systems that link dealers. These systems allow dealers, who are often widely dispersed geographically (sometimes in other countries), to exchange offers and make deals without meeting at a single location.

U.S. Governments. U.S. government securities (Treasuries, federal agencies, and most mortgage-backed securities) are traded by government bond dealers, including the 40 primary dealers discussed earlier. Given the approximately $3.5 trillion in outstanding Treasury, federal agency, and mortgage-backed securities, this secondary market is predictably very large and very active; it is considered to be the largest, most liquid financial market in the world. Government bond dealers buy and sell billions of dollars' worth of government securities each day in a busy over-the-counter financial market.[8]

As you might expect, trading activity is heaviest in Treasuries and lightest in federal agencies, simply due to differences in amounts outstanding. This is reflected in the bid/ask spreads of each kind of security. For example, on December 2, 1993, the spread between the bid and ask price on a Treasury bond maturing in 2020 was $0.0625 per $100 in par value. By contrast, the bid/ask spread on a Resolution Trust Corporation bond maturing in 2020 was $0.25 per $100 in par value.

Municipal Securities. Like government securities, municipal securities are traded over the counter by municipal bond dealers. Commercial banks are large investors in municipal securities, and they often function as municipal bond dealers in some secondary market activity. As a rule, municipal bonds are not actively traded and many issues lack good secondary markets. In fact, only a handful of municipal issues are traded in any particular day. Much of this trading occurs in large trades between institutions (such as mutual funds and commercial banks). This sparse trading activity is reflected in the bid/

---

[8]Approximately 750 Treasury securities are listed on the New York Stock Exchange. However, less than 1 percent of the secondary market trading in Treasuries occurs on the NYSE.

ask spread, which can be as high as 250 basis points (2.5 percent). The reason for this lack of trading activity is simply that most municipal issues are relatively small.

Corporate Debt Securities. Some corporate debt instruments are traded over the counter. Others are listed and traded on some of the major stock exchanges. Today about 1,800 corporate debt issues of over 650 different companies are listed on the New York Stock Exchange.

As the sizes of corporate debt issues vary, so does the trading activity in the secondary market. Like most municipal issues, small corporate issues do not trade frequently. The bonds listed on the NYSE tend to be the larger issues (the average par value of these issues was less than $300 million), but even these are not as actively traded as government bonds. During 1993, for example, the average number of daily bond trades was around 2,500, representing about $50 million in par value.

Foreign Bonds. Bonds issued by foreign companies and governments trade, in the United States, over-the-counter or on the NYSE. As with U.S. corporate bonds, only the larger foreign bond issues are listed on the NYSE. Today fewer than 100 foreign corporate bonds and 44 foreign government bonds representing less than $10 billion in par value were listed on the NYSE. These bonds typically do not trade frequently.

Foreign Bond Markets

Bonds trade throughout the world.[9] After those in the United States, the largest bond markets are located in Japan and Germany. Bond trading in Japan resembles bond trading in the United States. Trading takes place on both organized exchanges such as the Tokyo Stock Exchange and over-the-counter. One difference between the U.S. and Japanese markets, however, is that a greater percentage of government bonds trade on organized exchanges in Japan than in the United States.

In Germany, banks make up the largest group of bond investors. In addition, unlike the United States and Japan, German law mandates no separation between banking and securities businesses. Banks dominate underwriting, trading, and investing in securities. As a result, secondary bond trading in Germany takes place in essentially an interbank market.

As you might expect, bonds issued in a particular country tend to trade in that country. The largest market for trading Canadian government bonds, for example, is in Toronto. However, the globalization of the financial markets extends to the bond market, as well. U.S. government bonds trade in London, as well as New York, and Eurobonds trade in Tokyo, as well as Zurich.

U.S. Secondary Stock Markets

The United States has a number of secondary stock markets, some with national, indeed international operations and others that serve more regional needs. Trading on some U.S. equity markets is over the counter, while others place trading on a trading floor. Figure 3.2 illustrates the distribution of stock trading volume among the major U.S. markets for 1993. Measured in terms of number of shares traded, the NYSE and the NASDAQ system were about the same size in 1993. However, measured in terms of the

---

[9]Global bond markets are described in more detail in Frank Fabozzi, *Bond Markets, Analysis and Strategies,* 2d ed. (Englewood Cliffs, N.J.: Prentice-Hall, 1993), pp. 162–186.

Figure 3.2

Breakdown of 1993 Trading Activity by Number of Shares Traded (Left) and by Dollar Volume of Shares Traded (Right)

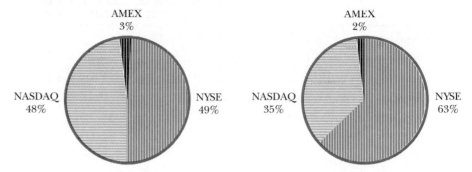

Note: NYSE figure includes trading of NYSE listed stocks on regional exchanges.
Sources: National Association of Securities Dealers and New York Stock Exchange.

dollar value of shares traded, the NYSE was clearly the largest U.S. equity market in 1993.

New York Stock Exchange. The New York Stock Exchange, founded in 1792, is arguably the most famous financial market in the world. It is also one of the largest. Today over 2,500 stock issues (common and preferred) representing about 1,900 different companies are listed on the NYSE, called the "big board" by some market participants. The total market value of the stock issues listed on the NYSE exceeds $4 trillion, most of them shares of U.S.-based companies. However, over 125 stock issues of foreign companies are also listed on the exchange.[10] Companies that wish to have their securities traded on the NYSE must apply directly to the exchange and meet certain listing requirements, as stated in Table 3.1. Companies must also meet certain requirements each year and pay annual listing fees. Why do companies choose to submit to the requirements and pay the cost to list their stocks on the NYSE? Four common reasons are given: liquidity for shareholders, access to capital, prestige, and exposure.

Today more than 250 million shares of stock worth more than $10 billion change hands each day on the exchange. Trading volume has grown steadily over the last 15 years. Between 1976 and 1993, daily trading volume grew at an annual rate of over 15 percent. The NYSE has traditionally dominated the other U.S. stock markets in terms of volume, though its share of total U.S. trading volume has declined in recent years. For example, in 1979 approximately 12.9 billion shares of stock were traded in the United States, 63 percent of them on the NYSE. By 1993, total trading volume had increased to over 100 billion shares, but the proportion traded on the NYSE had fallen to 45 percent.[11]

The NYSE is an **auction market.** Unlike the secondary market for Treasury securities, all trading on the NYSE takes place on the exchange floor. Only members of the exchange (firms that own at least one of the 1,366 **seats**)

[10]With the exception of Canadian companies, all foreign stock issues listed on the NYSE are American depository receipts (ADRs). We discussed ADRs briefly in Chapter 2. The NYSE has requested permission from the Securities and Exchange Commission to directly list shares of foreign companies, but so far the SEC has not approved this request.

[11]In terms of the dollar value of trading, the NYSE's market share has fallen from around 80 percent in the early 1980s to around 58 percent in 1993.

Table 3.1

NYSE Listing Requirements ($000 and shares)

	Effective Date					
	April 15, 1965	May 23, 1968	July 15, 1971	May 20, 1976	February 13, 1984	October 3, 1988
Net income latest year	$ 1,200	b	b	b	b	b
Net income preceding year	1,200	b	b	b	b	b
Pretax income latest year	2,000	$ 2,500	$ 2,500	$ 2,500	$ 2,500[c]	$ 2,500[c]
Pretax income preceding two years	2,000[a]	2,000	2,000	2,000	2,000[c]	2,000[c]
Net tangible assets	10,000	14,000	16,000	16,000	18,000	18,000
Aggregate market value of publicly held shares	12,000	14,000	16,000	16,000	18,000	18,000[d]
Shares outstanding	1,000	1,000	b	b	b	b
Shares not concentrated (publicly held)	700	800	1,000	1,000	1,100	1,100[e]
Number of stockholders-of-record	2,000	2,000	b	b	b	b
Number of holders of round lots (100 shares or more)	1,700	1,800	2,000	2,000	2,000[f]	2,000[g]

[a] Normally earnings yardsticks should have been exceeded for three years.

[b] No longer applicable.

[c] *Or* $6.5 million aggregate for last three fiscal years *together with* minimum of $4.5 million in most recent fiscal year.

[d] Value as of December 31, 1990.

[e] If the unit of trading is less than 100 shares, the requirement relating to number of publicly held shares shall be reduced proportionately.

[f] *Or* 2,200 total stockholders *together with* average monthly trading volume (for most recent six months) of 100,000 shares.

[g] Number of holders of 100 shares or more *or* a unit of trading if less than 100 shares.

are entitled to trade on the floor of the NYSE.[12] Customer orders are delivered to the exchange by telephone, teletype, or computer. Buyers and sellers of an issue meet, face-to-face, at one of the 42 posts where that issue is traded, and bid against each other in an auction.

Each security listed on the NYSE is assigned to one of the 42 **specialists.**[13] A specialist assumes the responsibility of maintaining an orderly and liquid market in each security assigned to it. Specifically, specialists have four roles. First, they act as auctioneers, calling out quotes throughout the trading session. Second, they act as catalysts, bringing buyers and sellers together. Third, specialists act as agents for limit orders (discussed later in the chapter). Fourth, they provide liquidity by buying or selling out of their own inven-

[12] The number of seats has remained at 1,366 since 1953. Currently, seats are owned by the 42 specialist firms along with 471 brokerage firms. Many own multiple seats; Merrill Lynch, for example, owns about 135 seats. Seats can be traded (bought and sold) as well as leased, with the approval of the NYSE. (Currently, 583 seats are leased out.) Just prior to the October 1987 market break (September 27, 1987), a seat sold for $1.15 million. Seats currently sell for around $700,000.

[13] Specialists are either firms or groups of independent specialists who join together to share their workloads and spread their risk. While each stock has only one specialist, larger specialist units handle, or *run*, several stocks. The number varies with the size of the unit and the trading volume of the issue. At the present time, the largest specialist unit, La Branche & Company, handles 89 stocks including AT&T, The Gap, and Glaxo Holdings.

tories when no other buyers or sellers are present. Specialists directly participate in only about 20 percent of all trades. A specialist must have sufficient capital to maintain an inventory of about 15,000 shares of each security assigned to it.

Like other market participants, specialists participate to make money. They earn money primarily in two ways: first, by acting as agents in limit orders, for which they receive part of the commissions, and second, by buying and selling the stocks assigned to them. As mentioned earlier, a specialist offers to buy its assigned stock at a price (the bid price) slightly below the last trade price; at the same time, it offers to sell the stock at a price (the ask price) slightly above the last trade price. Over time, specialists should end up selling their stocks at higher prices than what they pay for the shares. However, specialists are required to buy when no one else is willing to buy, and to sell when no one else is willing to sell, in order to maintain liquidity in the market. In a period when prices are rising or falling sharply, specialists put their own capital at risk. For example, during the market break on October 19, 1987, NYSE specialists lost over $100 million. Several specialist firms were forced to merge as a result.

American Stock Exchange. The American Stock Exchange (AMEX), sometimes referred to as the *curb,* was founded in New York City around 1910 to provide a market for unlisted securities. In fact, the AMEX did not have formal listing requirements until the 1930s, and it continued to trade unlisted securities until about 1946. Like the NYSE, the AMEX is considered to be a national market, and it conducts trading in much the same way as the NYSE. The AMEX began listing foreign securities and warrants before the NYSE and, since 1975, the AMEX has become a major options market. It does still trade stock issues. Today, the AMEX lists about 1,100 issues of 900 companies. Since 1985, trading volume on the AMEX has increased at an annual rate of about 10 percent. However, the AMEX's share of total stock trading volume has declined during the past 15 years.

Traditionally, the AMEX has traded the stocks of smaller, less well-known companies.[14] That is still the case, as its listing requirements reflect. While the NYSE requires that the total market value of a listed firm's publicly held shares exceed $18 million, the AMEX requires that it exceed only $3 million.

Regional Exchanges. In addition to the two national exchanges, several smaller, regional markets trade stocks in the United States. Virtually all trading on the regional exchanges (in excess of 95 percent) is in *dual-listed shares,* stocks that are listed on both a regional exchange and one of the national exchanges. For example, Disney's common stock is listed on the NYSE, along with the Boston, Cincinnati, Midwest (Chicago), Pacific (San Francisco), and Philadelphia stock exchanges. Buyers and sellers may get slightly better prices on a regional exchange, pay slightly lower transaction costs, or make trades when the NYSE is closed. Some of the smaller regional brokerage firms, which are not NYSE members, also use the regional exchanges.

The NASDAQ System. The **National Association of Securities Dealers Automated Quotation (NASDAQ) system** is a computer-based communications network that links the member firms to serve the vast over-the-counter market for stocks. Trading volume on the NASDAQ system has increased sharply in recent years. Between 1979 and 1993, NASDAQ trading volume increased at an annual rate of about 17 percent.

---

[14]Except for a short period during the 1970s, no stocks have been listed on both the AMEX and NYSE at the same time. If a company that is currently listed on the AMEX applies to the NYSE for listing, upon acceptance, it is automatically delisted from the AMEX.

Small-firm stocks, those that couldn't meet NYSE or AMEX listing requirements, have traded over-the-counter for years. Various dealers make markets in these sometimes thinly traded stocks, earning the name **market makers,** by buying and selling from their own inventories. Prior to the establishment of the NASDAQ system, to buy or sell a stock traded over-the-counter, a broker would call around to the various market makers to receive current bid and ask prices. The broker would then buy from, or sell to, the market maker offering the best apparent price. However, a customer could never tell whether a broker obtained the best price, since public trading information was incomplete.

As the over-the-counter, or OTC, market grew in size and activity, this system became more and more cumbersome. In 1971, the National Association of Securities Dealers (NASD) created the NASDAQ system to gather all market maker quotes together for immediate reference by all member firms. The association also wanted to spruce up the somewhat unsavory reputation of the OTC market.

The current NASDAQ system offers three levels of information to members. Level 1 provides a median representative quote based on bid and ask prices that changes constantly as individual market makers adjust their prices. Level 1 is designed for firms that want current OTC quotes but don't do heavy OTC trading for customers and are not OTC market makers. Level 2, designed for firms that do heavy OTC trading but are not market makers, provides a list of real-time quotes from all market makers in a particular stock. Level 3, designed for OTC market makers, resembles Level 2 except that it allows dealers to change their bid and ask prices continually throughout the day.

Today more than 4,700 issues trade on the NASDAQ system. These issues have an average market value of approximately $200 million. The most actively traded issues, about 2,700, are listed on the NASDAQ National Market System (NMS). The NMS was created in 1982 and reports trading data in much the same way as the NYSE does. A company must meet the requirements stated in Table 3.2 to be listed on the NMS.

NASDAQ has been in the forefront among U.S. markets' participation in international activity. Today more than 80 ADR issues are listed on the NASDAQ system. Further, about 200 issues are listed on both NASDAQ and foreign stock exchanges. In addition, NASDAQ has developed links with the Singapore Stock Exchange and the London Stock Exchange that accommodate round-the-clock trading.

Unlike the NYSE, all NASDAQ-listed stocks have at least two market makers, and most have many more. Recently an average of 10.5 market makers handled each NASDAQ stock (11.7 per NMS-listed stock). In addition, 189 stocks had more than 25 market makers. Any NASDAQ member can become a market maker for any NASDAQ-listed stock, subject to minimum capital requirements. Today NASDAQ has 425 qualified market makers, including all the well-known brokerage firms.

Third and Fourth Markets. During the 1970s many large, institutional investors became dissatisfied with the cost of trading stocks on the NYSE. Their objection gave birth to the **third market,** which involves trading of NYSE-listed stocks off the exchange floor. It's considered an over-the-counter market in which firms that are not NYSE members act as market makers for the institutional investors.[15] Approximately 3.5 billion shares of stocks listed on the NYSE and AMEX traded in the third market each year.

---

[15]NYSE members are prohibited, by Exchange Rule 390, from trading listed securities off the floor of the Exchange without permission.

Table 3.2

NASDAQ/NMS Listing Requirements

Standard	Initial NASDAQ/NMS Inclusion		Continued NASDAQ/NMS Inclusion
	Alternative 1	Alternative 2	
Registration under Section 12(g) of the Securities Exchange Act of 1934 or equivalent	Yes	Yes	Yes
Net tangible assets[a]	$4 million	$12 million	$2 million or $4 million[b]
Net income (in last fiscal year or two of last three fiscal years)	$400,000	—	—
Pretax income (in last fiscal year or two of last three fiscal years)	$750,000	—	—
Public float (Shares)[c]	500,000	1 million	200,000
Operating history	—	3 years	—
Market Value of float	$3 million	$15 million	$1 million
Minimum bid	$5	—	—
Shareholders	—	400	400[d]
if between 0.5 and 1 million shares publicly held	800	—	—
if more than 1 million shares publicly held	400	—	—
if more than 0.5 million shares publicly held and average daily volume in excess of 2,000 shares	400	—	—
Number of market makers	2	2	2

NASDAQ/ National Market System Qualitative Standards

To qualify for admission to NASDAQ/NMS, a company must adhere to corporate governance standards that require it to:

- Have a minimum of two independent directors on its board.
- Maintain an Audit Committee composed of a majority of independent directors.
- Provide shareholders with annual reports and make quarterly as well as other reports available to them.
- Examine all related-party trades for potential conflicts of interest.
- Hold an annual meeting of shareholders and provide notice of such meeting to the NASD.
- Specify in its bylaws a quorum of not less than $33\frac{1}{3}$ percent of the outstanding shares of the company's common stock.
- Solicit proxies and provide statements for all meetings of shareholders, as well as file such proxy solicitations with the NASD.
- Secure shareholder approval for certain transactions and increases in the amount of stock outstanding.
- Execute a NASDAQ/NMS listing agreement.

Note: Foreign issuers may be exempted if compliance would be in contravention of law or business practices in the issuers' countries of domicile.

[a]*Net tangible assets* means total assets (excluding goodwill) minus total liabilities.

[b]Continued NASDAQ/NMS inclusion requires net tangible assets of at least $2 million if the issuer has sustained losses from continuing operations and/or net losses in two of its three most recent fiscal years or $4 million if the issuer has sustained losses from the continuing operations and/or net losses in three of its four most recent fiscal years.

[c]Public float is defined as shares that are not "held directly or indirectly by any officer or director of the issuer and by any person who is the beneficial owner of more than 10 percent of the total shares outstanding. . . ."

[d]Or 300 shareholders of round lots.

Source: *1992 NASDAQ Fact Book* (Washington, D.C.: National Association of Securities Dealers), p. 43. Reprinted with Permission from the *Nasdaq Fact Book and Company Directory.* © National Association of Securities Dealers, Inc., 1994.

Figure 3.3

Dollar Volume of Stock Trading in 1992 in Major World Capital Markets

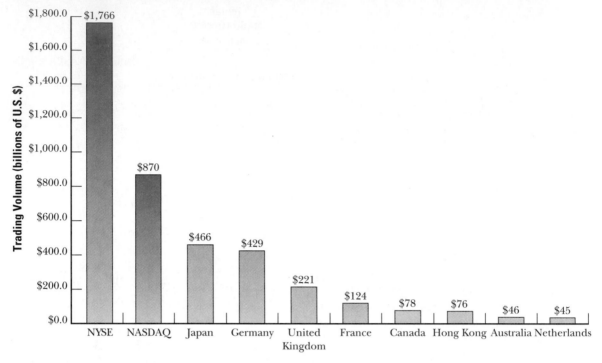

Source: *Morgan Stanley Capital International Perspective,* March 1993, p. 14.

The **fourth market** trades stocks listed on the NYSE or AMEX over the counter, between institutions without the intervention of market makers. Because the fourth market's trades are essentially private deals between buyers and sellers, it is difficult to obtain detailed data on its trading activity.

Foreign Secondary Common Stock Markets

Secondary markets trade stocks throughout the world. Virtually all industrialized countries have at least one national stock market. Shares of domestic companies typically dominate the trading activity on these markets. In other words, shares issued by Canadian companies account for much of the trading volume on the Toronto Stock Exchange. The approximate international distribution of equity trading during 1993 is shown in Figure 3.3. Out of a total worldwide dollar volume of approximately $4.5 trillion, more than half took place outside the United States; 35 percent of this trading activity took place on the Tokyo and London stock exchanges.

Tokyo Stock Exchange. The NYSE wasn't the world's largest stock exchange in 1989, measured by the dollar volume of trading. In 1989, the dollar volume of trading on the Tokyo Stock Exchange (TSE) exceeded $2.3 trillion, compared to $1.5 trillion on the NYSE. The NYSE has since regained its position as the world's largest stock market, as volume on the TSE has declined sharply during the last couple of years. For example, TSE trading volume declined about 24 percent between 1990 and 1993.

Currently, approximately 1,600 Japanese and 125 non-Japanese stock issues are listed on the TSE. It also trades bonds issued by the Japanese government and corporations, foreign bonds, options, and futures contracts. Listing requirements for both Japanese and non-Japanese stocks are shown in Table 3.3.

Only the 150 most active issues, all Japanese companies, are traded on the floor of the exchange in an auction-type market. Trading in the other issues is done by automatic computer matching of buy and sell orders. Besides this distinction, the TSE is also divided into the first section and second section. Stocks in the first section are more actively traded stocks of larger companies than second-section stocks. Approximately 1,250 stocks make up the first section.

London Stock Exchange. The London Stock Exchange (LSE) is the world's fourth-largest stock market and one of the largest in Europe. It lists approximately 2,500 issues, over 500 of which are shares of companies based outside the United Kingdom and Ireland. In addition to stocks, the LSE trades bonds (especially Eurobonds), options, and futures contracts. The London market is a very international market; over 66 percent of the world's cross-border trading (e.g., trading of U.S. stocks outside the United States) takes place in London. The figure rises to over 95 percent for cross-border trading in European issues alone.

On October 27, 1986 (known in London as the "Big Bang") member firms gained the capability to trade off the exchange floor using an automated quotation system. Trading on the exchange floor dropped so sharply that it was closed on February 28, 1991. Today, all trading on the LSE is conducted "upstairs," using a NASDAQ-type computer system.

Table 3.3

Listing Requirements for the Tokyo Stock Exchange

Application	Domestic Stock All of the following criteria must be met:	Foreign Stock All of the following criteria must be met:
Number of shares to be listed	If the issuer is based: 1. In or around Tokyo; 4 million shares or more 2. Elsewhere; 20 million shares or more	If the stock is to be traded in a unit of: 1. 1,000 shares; 20 million shares or more 2. 100 shares; 2 million shares or more 3. 50 shares; 1 million shares or more 4. 10 shares; 200,000 shares or more 5. 1 share; 20,000 shares or more
Number of Shares Held by "Special Few" (i.e., 10 largest shareholders and persons having special interest in the issuer)	Provisional Criteria: 80 percent or less of the number of shares to be listed by the time of listing, and 70 percent or less by the end of the first business year after the listing	Not applicable. The stock is instead required to have good liquidity in the home market.
Number of shareholders holding one "unit" or more (excluding "Special Few")	If the number of shares to be listed is: 1. Less than 10 million shares; 800 or more 2. 10 million shares or more, but less than 20 million shares; 1,200 or more 3. 20 million shares or more; 2,000 plus 100 per each 10 million shares in excess of 20 million shares, up to 3,000	Not applicable. The stock is instead required to have 1,000 or more shareholders in Japan.
Time elapsed after incorporation	Five years or more with continued business operation	Same.
Shareholders' equity	¥1 billion or more in total and ¥100 or more per share	¥10 billion or more in total

continued

Table 3.3

Listing Requirements for the Tokyo Stock Exchange

Application	Domestic Stock All of the following criteria must be met:	Foreign Stock All of the following criteria must be met:

Net profit before taxes	Following 1 or 2
	1. a. Annual total for each of last three business years:
	   first business year, ¥200 million or more
	   second business year, ¥300 million or more
	   Last business year, ¥400 million or more
	b. Amount per share
	   ¥15 or more for each of last three business years and ¥20 or more for last business year
	2. a. Annual total for each of last three business years:
	   ¥400 million or more
	b. Amount per share
	   ¥15 or more for either first business year or second business year and ¥15 or more for last business year
		Annual total for each of last three business years:
		¥2 billion or more

Dividends	1. Dividend record: Paid in cash for the business year ended within the latest year 2. Dividend prospect: Able to maintain ¥5 or more in cash per share after listing	1. Dividend record: Paid for each of last three business years 2. Dividend prospect: Able to pay continuously after listing

Notes: 1. The TSE also has listing regulations for straight bonds, convertible bonds, bonds with warrants, etc.

2. All numerical criteria above are for a company which provides 1,000 shares as the number of one "Unit" of shares.

Source: *TSE Fact Book*

Emerging Stock Markets. One of the most interesting developments in recent years is the emergence of new equity markets in many developing nations. New markets have opened in places as diverse as Chile, China, Malaysia, and Turkey. Investing in these markets exposes U.S. investors to extreme risk, however. These markets can be quite volatile, liquidity can be a problem, and market regulation is less strict than regulation in more established markets.

Trading in More Detail

The discussions of various markets have covered some aspects of the mechanics of trading. For example, you know that on the NYSE, trading takes place on the floor of the exchange, face-to-face, while on the NASDAQ system, trading takes place by computer through a group of market makers. In this section we'd like to take a more detailed look at how trading is actually conducted and how the investor participates. We'll concentrate primarily on the trading of stocks on secondary markets.

Setting Up an Account

Before making any trade, an investor must set up a brokerage account. This fairly simple and straightforward process does entail a few important decisions. The first decision, of course, is to choose a brokerage firm and, in many cases, a specific broker. Investors select firms and brokers on the basis of reputation, personal contact, referral, and similar criteria. All brokerage firms require each investor to fill out an application to provide minimal information regarding such characteristics as income and net worth. Many firms require that new customers have cash or cash-equivalent assets of at least $5,000.[16]

The investor must decide whether to set up an account with a full-service brokerage or a discount brokerage. **Full-service brokerage firms,** such as Merrill Lynch and Smith-Barney, offer investment advice to their customers in addition to order execution and record keeping. A full-service firm usually assigns a specific broker to each individual customer. **Discount brokerage firms,** such as Charles Schwab and Quick & Reilly, provide mainly order execution and record-keeping services, though some provide information on investment opinions from independent sources. A customer of a discount firm must likely deal with many individual brokers. Of course, full-service firms charge much higher commissions and fees than discount firms.

Which type of brokerage should an investor choose? It depends on what type of investing the account will handle and the investor's need for services. Someone who makes personal investment decisions and trades frequently would probably be better off with a discount firm. On the other hand, someone who needs help making investment selections for infrequent trades may prefer a full-service firm. Also, since the customer of a full-service firm usually deals with one specific broker, it is just as important to select an appropriate broker as it is to select the right brokerage firm. You should look for a broker that understands and accepts your personal investment objectives and risk preferences. Someone who gets nervous buying Treasury bonds should avoid a broker who constantly pushes newly issued, speculative shares of biotech companies.

Most brokerage customers set up cash accounts that require them to pay the full cost, in cash, for all securities purchased. Some customers also set up margin accounts, which allow them to finance portions of their securities purchases by borrowing from the brokerage firm. The customer repays the borrowed funds with interest. We'll talk more about buying securities on margin a little later in the chapter.

Virtually all brokerage firms belong to the **Securities Investor Protection Corporation (SIPC),** which insures brokerage accounts up to $500,000 to reimburse investors in the event the brokerage firm fails. Over the past 20 years, the SIPC has paid out approximately $200 million to customers of failed brokerage firms. Of course, it does not repay customers for losses due to adverse market moves! In addition to SIPC insurance, most large brokerage firms carry private insurance to further protect customers from financial loss in the event the firm fails. We strongly recommend using only brokerage firms that are SIPC members and carry insurance.

Once an investor establishes an account, there are three types of orders by which to buy or sell. They are market orders (the most common), limit orders, and stop (or stop-loss) orders.

---

[16]Brokerage firms may have additional requirements for customers who wish to trade futures contracts and/or options.

Market Orders

A **market order** instructs the broker to buy or sell a security at the best currently prevailing price (the lowest price for a purchase or the highest price for a sale). Market orders must be settled within five business days of the trade. This means you must pay what you owe in full, if you bought stocks, within five days of the trade date. If you sold stocks, you must wait five business days to receive the proceeds. Market orders are executed somewhat differently on the organized exchanges than on the over-the-counter markets, so let's look at an example of each.

Organized Exchange Market Order. Let's assume that an investor would like to buy 100 shares of Home Depot, which trades on the NYSE.[17] In response to this request, the broker looks up the stock's symbol, HD, on a quote machine which returns the following information: 43 bid, $43\frac{1}{8}$ ask, $43\frac{1}{8}$ last trade. HD last traded at $43\frac{1}{8}$, and the stock's specialist is currently offering to buy it at 43 or to sell it at $43\frac{1}{8}$. The investor enters a market order, which the broker transmits to the floor of the NYSE to be delivered (either physically or electronically) to the post where HD is traded. If no sellers are present when the order arrives, the HD specialist sells 100 shares from inventory at the current ask price. If sellers are present, an auction takes place and the specialist may not be involved. The broker relays confirmation of the trade back to the investor and the trade appears on the NYSE consolidated tape. How long does all this take? Over 98 percent of all market orders are filled within two minutes!

This speed is possible because the NYSE has become highly automated. An electronic system helps to match buy and sell orders entered before the market opens, and sets an opening price for each stock. The exchange has an electronic order-routing system called **SuperDot** that carries members' orders directly to the appropriate trading posts, and then returns trade confirmations. The NYSE's major automated systems are described in more detail in Table 3.4.

Over-the-Counter Markets. Now assume that another investor wants to buy 100 shares of Snapple Beverage, which trades on the NASDAQ National Market System under the symbol *SNPL*. After the broker receives instructions to enter a market order, he or she consults the NASDAQ electronic quotation machine to find out the current bid and ask prices for SNPL. A broker who has access to Level 2 of the NASDAQ system sees the bid and ask prices for each SNPL market maker (which probably number over 30).[18] Assume that the broker finds the following quotes:

Dealer	Bid	Ask
A	$23\frac{5}{8}$	$23\frac{3}{4}$
B	$23\frac{1}{2}$	$23\frac{5}{8}$
C	$23\frac{5}{8}$	$23\frac{3}{4}$
D	$23\frac{3}{4}$	24

---

[17]Any order in a multiple of 100 shares (100, 200, 300, 1,000, and so forth) is called a *round-lot* while any order not in a multiple of 100 shares is an *odd-lot*. Less than 1 percent of trading activity on the NYSE is in odd-lots.

[18]Level 2 also indicates the number of shares each market maker is willing to buy or sell at its respective bid or ask prices.

Table 3.4

NYSE Automated Systems

SuperDot

SuperDot is an electronic order-routing system that enables member firms to quickly and efficiently transmit market and limit orders in all NYSE-listed securities directly to the Specialist post where the securities are traded or to the member firm's booth. After the order has been executed in the auction market, a report of execution is returned directly to the member firm office over the same electronic circuit that brought the order to the trading floor, and the execution is submitted directly to the comparison systems.

During 1990, SuperDot processed an average of 138,000 orders per day for a year-end total of 182 subscribers. The NYSE increased the capacity of the system to provide the order processing capability to handle a 750 to 900 million share day. Below is a detailed description of the components of the system.

Opening Automated Report Service (OARS)

OARS, the opening feature of the SuperDot system, is designed to accept member firms' preopening market orders up to 30,099 shares for rapid, systematic execution and immediate reporting. OARS automatically and continuously pairs buy and sell orders and presents the imbalance to each Specialist up to the opening of a stock, thus assisting the Specialist [in determining] the opening price. OARS is floorwide in all issues.

Market Order Processing

All SuperDot service features apply to post-opening market orders of up to 2,099 shares. However, SuperDot's market order system is designed to process member firms' market orders of up to 30,099 shares. The system provides for rapid execution and reporting of market orders. In 1990, 98.5 percent were executed and reported back to the originating member firm within two minutes.

Limit Order Processing

The limit order system electronically files orders which are to be executed when and if the specific limit price is reached. The system accepts limit orders up to 99,999 shares, appends a turnaround number, and either electronically updates the Specialist's Electronic Book or delivers printed orders to the member firm's booth. Good-'til-cancelled orders not executed on the day of submission are automatically stored until executed or cancelled.

Electronic Book

The Electronic Book is a tool which greatly increases the Specialist's volume handling and processing capabilities. This data base system facilitates the recording, reporting, and researching of limit and market orders, and in the process helps eliminate paperwork and processing errors. At the end of 1990, there were approximately 2,000 stocks on Electronic Books on the NYSE Trading Floor.

Post Trade Processing

After a trade is executed, SuperDot automatically submits it to the comparison cycle on a locked-in basis. This guarantees that each member firm's systematized orders are processed virtually error free with a complete audit trail prior to settlement and delivery of securities.

The NYSE's Overnight Comparison System provides member firms with the ability to begin the comparison process earlier and to reconcile errors in an on-line environment. The effect is to reduce exposure risk as well as comparison and processing costs.

Source: *1992 NYSE Fact Book* (New York: New York Stock Exchange), p. 22.

The broker contacts Dealer B, either by telephone or electronically, because it is offering the best (i.e., lowest) price for Snapple. To sell SNPL, the broker would contact Dealer D, which currently has the highest ask price (i.e., it is willing to pay the most for SNPL).

Today, the process of entering small orders into the NASDAQ system is even simpler. In 1985, NASDAQ introduced its Small Order Execution System (or SOES) to automatically execute small market orders (usually defined as orders for fewer than 1,000 shares) at the best possible price available in the NASDAQ system. SOES returns confirmation to the broker in a matter of seconds.

Limit Orders

A **limit order** instructs a broker to buy a security for no more than a specific price, or to sell for no less than a specific price. Return to the buyer of Home Depot stock, but suppose that some analysis leads to the conclusion that the current ask price, $43\frac{1}{8}$, is a little too high. The investor tells the broker to enter an order to buy HD *limit* $42\frac{3}{4}$; the investor would willingly pay less than $42\frac{3}{4}$, but not more, for HD. The broker transmits the order to the post where HD is traded. If no one is willing to sell the stock for $42\frac{3}{4}$ (or less), the order remains with the specialist for entry into the *limit order book* (which today is an electronic data file). If HD eventually declines to $42\frac{3}{4}$, the specialist executes the order and informs the broker, who informs the customer. In return for this service, the specialist receives part of the commission.

In 1989, NASDAQ introduced a new limit order service within its Small Order Execution System. The service automatically accepts and stores limit orders for less than 1,000 shares, and it executes them when NASDAQ market maker ask quotations reach or improve on the limit prices set by the customers.

Limit orders can be valid for varying periods of time from one trading day to several trading days, one week, or longer. A limit order can also be placed on a *good until canceled (GTC)* basis, which leaves the order open-ended. Brokerage firms' policies regarding limit orders vary, and many charge slightly higher commissions for limit orders than for market orders.

Stop (or Stop-Loss) Orders

A **stop order** enters a market order that takes effect at a specified price. Stop orders are often referred to as *stop-loss orders* because they are usually used to sell stock if its value drops below some threshold. For example, an investor may have bought HD at $23 per share and watched it rise to $43 per share. The investor still likes the outlook for the stock, but worries about a temporary setback due to other stockholders selling to realize their gains (sometimes called *profit taking*). Instead of selling the stock outright for around $43 per share, the investor instructs a broker to enter a "sell order 40 stop." Should HD decline below $40, this stop order would automatically become a market order and the stock would be sold at the prevailing price, protecting most of the investor's profit. The stop order does not guarantee a sale at $40 per share, only that the stock will be sold quickly at the best price currently available should its price fall below $40. Stop orders can be valid for varying periods of time, or they can be open-ended. Like limit orders, various brokerage firms have different policies on stop orders and most charge higher commissions to execute them than to execute simple market orders.

Margin Transactions

As we noted earlier, margin trading involves borrowing money to buy securities. Banks lend funds to brokerage firms, which lend them, in turn, to customers to buy securities on margin. Customers typically pay between 1 percent and $1\frac{1}{2}$ percent over the rate the brokerage firm pays the bank.[19] The brokerage firm specifies how and when the customer repays a margin loan. Approximately $60 billion in margin debt is outstanding today.

Technically, margin is the part of the total value of the securities that the

---

[19]The interest rate charged on margin loans is relatively low, compared to the cost of other types of consumer credit (such as auto loans). Brokerage firms pay close to the prime lending rate, which banks charge their most creditworthy customers, so the cost to the investor may be only slightly above prime.

Table 3.5

Illustration of a Margin Transaction

	Disney Rises to 45	Disney Falls to 35	Disney Falls to 30
Value	$9,000	$7,000	$6,000
Margin	5,000[a]	3,000[c]	2,000[e]
Required margin	4,500[b]	2,800[d]	2,400[f]
Margin call	—	—	400[g]

[a]$200 \times (45 - 40) + \$4,000$

[b]$0.5 \times \$9,000$

[c]$\$4,000 - 200 \times (40 - 35)$

[d]$0.4 \times \$7,000$

[e]$\$4,000 - 200 \times (40 - 30)$

[f]$0.4 \times \$6,000$

[g]$\$2,400 - \$2,000$

investor pays with cash, or the investor's equity. The Federal Reserve sets minimum initial margin requirements; in other words, it specifies how much the investor must put up initially to purchase a security on margin. The current requirement of 50 percent has not changed in many years. To purchase 200 shares of JNJ at 48 on margin, an investor would have to put up at least $4,800 in cash (plus the commission),[20] borrowing the other $4,800. In addition, the NYSE requires that a margin customer maintain at least a 25 percent margin as a security's price changes; this is called the *maintenance margin requirement*. Most brokerage firms have higher maintenance requirements (30 percent to 40 percent).

Suppose, for example, that someone buys 200 shares of Disney (DIS) at 40 on margin. The broker would require an initial margin of 50 percent ($4,000 in cash) and a maintenance margin of 40 percent. Table 3.5 shows what happens to the margin at various stock prices. First, assume that Disney rises to $45 per share. This boosts the value of the shares to $9,000 and the margin rises to $5,000 (56 percent of the total). The broker may allow the stockholder to withdraw $500 from the account, bringing the margin back down to 50 percent. Assume, however, that Disney then falls to $35 per share. The margin drops to $3,000 (43 percent of the total value). Between the initial margin of 50 percent and the maintenance margin of 40 percent, most brokerage firms wouldn't require any deposits of more cash, but they wouldn't allow any additional margin transactions, either.

Assume that Disney continues its slide to $30 per share. This drops the margin to $2,000, only 33 percent of the total value of the stock. Now below the maintenance margin requirement, the investor faces the dreaded **margin call.** The broker will require another deposit of $400 in order to bring the margin back up to 40 percent. Failure to meet the margin call leads the broker to sell the Disney shares and repay the margin loan.

Why should anyone buy stock on margin and pay interest on a margin loan? The answer is simply because margin trading gives investors the potential benefit of leverage. When one margin trader purchased 200 shares of Disney at 40 on margin, putting up $4,000 and borrowing the rest, suppose that another investor bought 200 shares of Disney at 40 for $8,000 cash. Figure 3.4 illustrates the returns for both investors, at various stock prices (ignoring commissions and interest on the margin loan).

---

[20]Securities markets and brokerage firms are free to set higher initial margin requirements and many brokerage firms do so for certain customers.

Figure 3.4

Illustration of Cash versus Margin Purchases

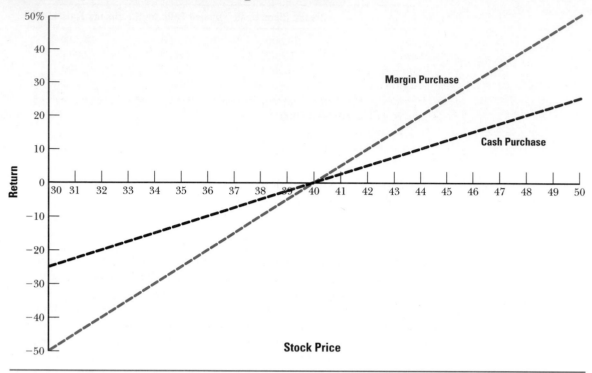

Clearly, the leverage created by the margin loan has a significant impact. If Disney were to rise from 40 to 50, the return to the margin investor would be 50 percent ($2,000/$4,000) while the return to the cash investor would be only 25 percent ($2,000/$8,000). The trouble, of course, is that leverage is a double-edged sword. If the price of Disney were to fall from 40 to 30, the return to the margin investor would be −50 percent while the return to the cash investor would be −25 percent.[21] Buying stock on margin might increase the return to the investor, but, at the same time, it increases the potential risk. Margin purchases do not suit every investor.

Short Sales

Someone who buys a security is said to be taking the *long position*. This investor purchases the stock with the expectation that it will provide a satisfactory return in the form of dividend payments plus price appreciation. What about taking the opposite position if a stock seems likely to fall in value? This is possible by executing what is known as a **short sale,** selling borrowed stock with the expectation of buying back shares at a lower price to return to the owner at some point in the future.[22] This is a perfectly legal transaction, though certain conditions have to be met. The NYSE reports that in recent years 1 share of stock is sold short for every 10 shares purchased.[23]

---

[21]These returns do not include the interest expense on the margin loan. Interest expense would reduce returns to the margin investor slightly.

[22]Simply selling currently owned stock is not the same thing as a short sale. Someone who sells stock, or any security, merely transfers ownership of the security to another investor. All rights and responsibilities associated with the security are transferred, as well.

[23]However, during 1990 about 60 percent of all short sales were done by NYSE members, many by specialists in their roles as market makers.

Table 3.6

Anatomy of a Short Sale

1. Find the stock. It can be grievously mismanaged, or simply a bit overpriced. Let's say it's Feb. 19, and the short seller notices that IBM is selling at $139—a 30 percent gain since year-end—and decides to sell it short.

2. Borrow the stock. It must be marginable—priced at $5 or more. IBM is a widely held stock, so it is easy to borrow.

3. Sell the stock. This happens simultaneously with Step 2. The short sells 2,000 in borrowed shares for $278,000—a transaction that ties up just $139,000 in collateral. Commissions are about $2,900.

4. Collect a rebate. If the broker agrees, the short seller gets a rebate on the proceeds—about a 6 percent annual rate.

5. Pay dividends. IBM's are $1.21 a share, payable May 6. That's $2,420 on 2,000 shares, to the owner of the borrowed stock.

6. Eureka! IBM shares have collapsed because of unexpectedly bad earnings. If the short sale is covered on May 23 at $104,[a] the gain is $35 a share times 2,000— $70,000—minus $2,900 in commissions and $2,420 in dividends, plus $1,390 in rebate interest. Total profit: $66,070.

[a]That is, the short seller buys 2,000 shares of IBM and returns them to the investor who loaned them initially.

Source: Reprinted from June 10, 1991 issue of *Business Week* by special permission, copyright © 1991 by McGraw-Hill, Inc.

Table 3.6 details the anatomy of a short sale. The shares sold short are borrowed from another account, and the short seller must keep at least 50 percent of the proceeds in a margin account as collateral. The short seller is free to use the balance for anything, though the brokerage firm sometimes pays the short seller interest (called a *rebate*) on the collateral. If the stock rises in price, the short seller must add to the collateral balance (much like maintaining a margin). The short seller is also responsible to the stock's owner for any cash dividends paid on the borrowed stock.

In addition to the requirements listed in Table 3.6, the NYSE will allow a short sale only on an **uptick.** A short sale can take place at the last trade price only if that price exceeds the last different price before it. The example in Table 3.6 worked out quite nicely, and the short seller earned a profit of $66,070, but short selling can involve substantial risk and is recommended only for experienced, knowledgeable investors.[24]

Block Trading

The increase in institutional investing in stocks has brought an increase in the number of giant **block trades,** which NYSE rules define as any trade of at least 10,000 shares with a minimum market value of $200,000. In 1970, NYSE member firms traded 17,217 blocks, an average of 68 per day, representing about 15 percent of total NYSE trading volume. In 1993 more than 1 million blocks were traded, about half of total NYSE volume. Today the average block consists of approximately 23,000 shares.[25] Block trading is also prominent on the NASDAQ system. In 1993, for example, over 40 percent of NASDAQ/NMS trading volume consisted of block trades.

[24]Some brokerage firms strongly discourage short selling, arguing that it contradicts the notion that stocks are good, long-term investments and encourages speculation.

[25]The largest block trade recorded by the NYSE occurred on April 10, 1986, when almost 49 million shares of Navistar changed hands. The second-largest block trade involved the sale of 42.3 million shares of Texaco on June 1, 1989.

As block trading increased during the 1970s, it began to strain the specialist system. Many specialists lacked the capital necessary to buy large blocks and accommodate the huge trades. Even when they had sufficient capital, most specialists were reluctant to take the large risks involved. The NYSE recognized this problem and started to allow member firms, with permission from the NYSE, to trade large blocks off the floor of the exchange.[26]

Here's how a block trade might work: The manager of a state pension fund has 100,000 shares of Marion Merrell Dow and would like to sell 60,000 shares. (Assume that Marion's last trade price was 32.) The fund manager contacts Lehman Brothers, a large block house. Since Lehman underwrote Marion's recent stock issue, it probably has a list of customers, most likely other institutional investors, who might be interested in the block. Assume that Lehman receives commitments from several customers to purchase 45,000 shares of the block at an average price of $31\frac{3}{4}$. Lehman returns to the pension fund manager and bids $31\frac{5}{8}$ (plus a negotiated commission) for the 60,000-share block. If the fund accepts the offer, Lehman then purchases the block and immediately resells 45,000 shares, keeping a position of 15,000 shares. The block trade appears on the NYSE ticker, since Lehman Brothers is a member of the exchange, as one trade of 60,000 at $31\frac{5}{8}$. Lehman Brothers then attempts to sell the other 15,000 shares to other customers, risking about $474,000 of its capital. The NYSE specialist for Marion might purchase some of the remaining shares to fill limit orders between $31\frac{5}{8}$ and 32.

Program Trading

Institutional investors buy and/or sell large numbers of stocks in another technique called **program trading.** Program trading involves the use of sophisticated computer programs which can make automatic decisions to buy or sell. To take advantage of an expected marketwide increase, a pension fund might execute a program trade to buy all 500 stocks that make up the Standard & Poor's 500. Program trades are usually executed directly, using the NYSE's electronic SuperDot system.[27] Program trades make up approximately 11 percent of NYSE volume.

Program trades serve a number of purposes. A pension fund manager might execute a program trade each time the fund's sponsor makes a monthly or quarterly contribution. The program trade would deploy new cash into the stock market without substantially altering the contents of the fund's portfolio. Another use of program trading, **index arbitrage,** attempts to gain risk-free returns by exploiting differences between the prices of stock index futures and prices of the underlying stocks. We'll take a closer look at index arbitrage in Chapter 19.

Program trading is controversial. Some small investors complain that program trades often get priority in execution, despite NYSE rules and policies that give priority to small orders. Critics also allege that program trading tends to exaggerate market moves (both upward and downward), making stock prices more volatile. Some have even blamed program trading for contributing to the 1987 market break. However, no conclusive evidence links program trading to market volatility.

---

[26]The problems created by block trading helped stimulate development of the third market (discussed earlier). Some have suggested that the NYSE modified its off-floor trading rules to stem the flow of orders from the NYSE to the third market.

[27]Program trades can often use the SuperDot system since, even though they involve large numbers of stocks, rarely do the buy or sell orders for individual stocks exceed the maximum number of shares SuperDot will handle (currently 30,099).

Regulation of the Financial Markets

Primary and secondary U.S. financial markets are regulated by both federal and state authorities, as well as industry self-regulation systems. In other countries, financial markets are also regulated, to a greater or lesser extent, by national government agencies. U.S. financial markets are considered to be among the best regulated, and fairest, financial markets in the world.

Government Regulation in the United States

Regulation of U.S. securities markets is primarily a function of the federal government. Federal regulation grew out of various abuses during the 1920s. During the Great Depression, in an attempt to restore confidence and stability in the financial markets after the 1929 stock market crash, Congress passed a series of landmark legislative acts that have formed the basis of federal securities regulation ever since.[28]

The U.S. Securities and Exchange Commission (SEC), created in 1934, is the principal federal regulatory overseer of the securities markets.[29] The SEC's mission is to administer securities laws and protect investors in public securities transactions. The SEC is a quasijudicial agency with broad enforcement power.[30]

Some of the best-known cases of regulatory intervention have involved **insider trading,** broadly defined as the use of material, nonpublic information to make investment profits. Names such as Ivan Boesky, Dennis Levine, and Michael Milken may be familiar; all were involved in a famous series of related insider trading cases during the 1980s.[31] Partly in response to the insider-trading cases in the 1980s, and because regulators had trouble defining insider trading, Congress passed the Insider Trading and Securities Fraud Enforcement Act in 1988 (P.L. 100–702), which attempted to tighten up the definition of insider trading and make convictions easier to obtain.

In the primary security markets, the SEC requires that virtually all new public issues of corporate securities be *registered.*[32] Before offering securities for sale, an issuer must file a registration statement with the SEC. As part of the registration process for a new security issue, the issuer must prepare a **prospectus.** Figure 3.1 reprinted the first page from a prospectus, and Figure 3.5 presents a couple more pages to give you an idea of the contents of a typical prospectus. The typical prospectus gives a fairly detailed description of the company issuing the securities, including financial data, recent developments, products, research and development projects, pending litigation,

---

[28]The major Depression-era legislation regulating the securities markets includes the Securities Act of 1933 (P.L. 73–22), the Securities Exchange Act of 1934 (P.L. 73–291), the Maloney-Eicher Act of 1936 (P.L. 75–719), and the Investment Company and Advisors Act of 1940 (P.L. 76–768).

[29]Other federal agencies play more minor roles in securities regulation, including the U.S. Department of the Treasury and the Federal Reserve Board. Futures are currently regulated by the Commodity Futures Trading Commission (CFTC). Turf battles between the SEC and the CFTC in the regulation of financial futures have led to proposals to abolish the CFTC and extend the SEC's regulatory powers to cover futures.

[30]The SEC can file only civil charges in connection with violations of securities laws. While the SEC can impose fines and other penalties, it cannot send anyone to jail. Criminal charges must be filed by the U.S. Justice Department.

[31]The exploits (real and alleged) of Boeksy, Levine, Milken, *et al.,* have been documented in detail in a number of books. See, for example, James Stewart, *Den of Thieves* (New York: Simon & Schuster, 1991).

[32]So-called *small issues,* worth under $500,000, are exempt registration requirements, as are government and municipal security issues.

Figure 3.5

Contents of Rawlings Sporting Goods Prospectus

PROSPECTUS SUMMARY

As used in this Prospectus, unless the context otherwise requires, "Rawlings" and the "Company" refer to Rawlings Sporting Goods Company, Inc., its subsidiaries and its predecessor, Rawlings Sporting Goods Company, an unincorporated operating division of Figgie, and all of the assets and liabilities relating to the Rawlings business (collectively, the "Rawlings Business"). Unless otherwise indicated or the context otherwise requires, the information contained in this Prospectus gives effect to the Organizational Transactions (as defined herein) to be consummated prior to or concurrently with the Offerings and assumes no exercise of the over-allotment options granted by the Company to the Underwriters.

The Company

Rawlings is a leading supplier of team sports equipment in North America and, through its licensee, of baseball equipment and uniforms in Japan. Rawlings, founded in 1887, is one of the oldest and most recognized names in the sporting goods industry. The Company's products have a long-standing reputation for quality and the Company believes many of its products have leading market positions.

Under the RAWLINGS® brand name, the Company provides an extensive line of equipment and team uniforms for the sports of baseball, basketball and football, including baseball gloves, baseballs, baseball bats, batter's helmets, catcher's and umpire's protective gear, bases, basketballs, footballs, football shoulder pads and other protective gear and various accessories as well as hockey gloves. In addition, licensees of the Company sell numerous products including golf equipment, athletic shoes and retail active wear using the RAWLINGS® brand name.

The Company has the exclusive right to use the logos of certain sports organizations and events on selected products, including the logos of the National and American Leagues, the All-Star Game and the World Series on baseballs and the National Collegiate Athletic Association ("NCAA") on basketballs and footballs. The Company has been the exclusive supplier of baseballs to the National and American Leagues since 1977. In addition, the Company is the leading supplier of baseball gloves to major and minor league players and annually presents the RAWLINGS GOLD GLOVE AWARD®, the most prestigious award a baseball player can receive for his fielding abilities. Rawlings' products are endorsed by more than 85 college coaches, more than 75 sports organizations and numerous athletes, including approximately 300 Major League Baseball players. These persons or entities have entered into agreements with the Company under which they are paid or provided products for endorsing the Rawlings' products or for permitting the Company to use their names or logos.

Since 1920, when Rawlings introduced the original deep pocket baseball glove, the Company has established a tradition of developing new products which have often set the standard for quality and competitive performance. In recent years, the Company has introduced the Soft Touch Football™, an improved batter's helmet which is able to withstand faster pitch speeds, an improved baseball for collegiate and high school use, the Jammer™ basketball warm-up jacket and numerous baseball gloves with improved features. The Company currently holds 44 patents on various products and designs. The Company believes its tradition of innovation as well as the quality and performance of its products, strong brand recognition and breadth of product lines are significant competitive strengths which will enable Rawlings to maintain and improve its strong market position. The Company believes it has significant opportunities for further growth through increased distribution, new product development, licensing opportunities and increased international sales.

Prior to the Offerings, the Rawlings Business has been owned by Figgie. In the Offerings, Figgie is selling 100% of its ownership interest in the Company. The Company's recent operations have been adversely affected by a significant shortage of liquidity at Figgie which forced the Company to limit production of certain products and cancel certain customer orders. The Company believes that it has received a lower level of orders in certain of its product lines as a result of the Company's delay and cancellation of certain customer orders. Although the shortage of liquidity has diminished since February 1994, the Company continues to operate under some liquidity constraints imposed by Figgie. Upon consummation of the Offerings, the Company will be independent of Figgie and it will no longer operate under the liquidity constraints imposed by Figgie. The Company believes that the liquidity constraints have not had an adverse effect on its long-term relationships with its customers, suppliers and vendors or its business.

3

---

and so forth. It also describes the security issue and underwriting agreement in detail.

The registration process seeks to guarantee **full and fair disclosure.** The SEC does not rule on the investment merits of a registered security issue. It is concerned only that an issuer gives investors enough information to make their own informed decisions.

In 1982, SEC Rule 415 introduced shelf registration to allow a large issuer to register a bundle of security issues once and then sell them piecemeal over a period as long as two years. The purpose is to reduce the time delays and expenses associated with registering individual security issues. Companies can now sell new securities on short notice to take advantage of favorable

Figure 3.5

The Offerings

Common Stock offered by the
Selling Stockholder:
    U.S. Offering . . . .   6,120,000 shares
    International Offering . . . .   1,530,000 shares
    Total . . . .   7,650,000 shares

Common Stock to be outstanding
after the Offerings[1] . . . .   7,650,081 shares

Use of Proceeds . . . .   The Company will not receive any proceeds from the Offerings other than the proceeds, if any, received as a result of the exercise of the over-allotment options granted by the Company to the U.S. Underwriters and the International Underwriters. Any proceeds received by the Company as a result of the exercise of the over-allotment options will be used to reduce indebtedness of the Company.

Nasdaq Symbol . . . .   RAWL

---

(1) Does not include 303,266 shares of Common Stock issuable upon exercise of options granted by the Company in connection with the Offerings to certain of its employees at an exercise price per share equal to the initial public offering price or an aggregate of 10,000 shares of Common Stock issuable upon exercise of options to be granted automatically to non-employee directors upon their appointment as directors. See "Management — Executive Compensation After the Offerings" and "— Compensation of Directors."

Summary Combined Financial Data

(Dollars in thousands, except per share data and footnotes)

	Year Ended December 31,						Three Months Ended March 31,		
	1989	1990	1991	1992	1993	1993[1] Pro Forma	1993	1994	1994[1] Pro Forma
Income Statement Data:									
Net revenues[2]	$101,415	$116,920	$144,912	$135,469	$139,553	$139,553	$ 45,237	$ 40,347	$ 40,347
Cost of goods sold	(74,267)	(83,869)	(98,828)	(90,647)	(95,329)	(95,464)	(29,673)	(26,419)	(26,449)
Gross profit	27,148	33,051	46,084	44,822	44,224	44,089	15,564	13,928	13,898
Selling expenses	(17,778)	(20,725)	(22,756)	(20,795)	(22,783)	(22,783)	(5,984)	(6,122)	(6,122)
General and administrative expenses	(5,585)	(5,894)	(5,637)	(6,196)	(6,001)	(6,976)	(1,406)	(1,481)	(1,726)
Environmental expenses	0	0	(766)	(85)	(1,559)[3]	(1,559)[3]	(29)	0	0
Intercompany charge[4]	(1,592)	(6,232)	(6,859)	(5,822)	(6,899)	0	(1,724)	(2,152)	0
Operating income[5]	2,193	200	10,066	11,924	6,982	12,771	6,421	4,173	6,050
Interest and other expense, net	(80)	(229)	(334)	(203)	(388)	(1,981)	(123)	(143)	(677)
Income (loss) before income taxes	2,113	(29)	9,732	11,721	6,594	10,790	6,298	4,030	5,373
Income tax benefit (provision)	(824)	11	(3,837)	(4,609)	(2,672)	(4,350)	(2,527)	(1,612)	(2,149)
Net income (loss)	$ 1,289	$ (18)	$ 5,895	$ 7,112	$ 3,922	$ 6,440	$ 3,771	$ 2,418	$ 3,224
Net income per common share	—	—	—	—	—	$ 0.84	—	—	$ 0.42
Common shares outstanding . . .	—	—	—	—	—	7,650,081	—	—	7,650,081
Balance Sheet Data:									
Working capital	$ 44,993	$ 52,499	$ 54,143	$ 55,577	$ 49,057	$ 49,057	$ 66,961	$ 33,219[6]	$ 57,379
Total assets	61,661	71,577	69,958	71,097	67,616	96,771	84,415	55,324[6]	105,475
Total long-term debt, including current maturities	2,847	2,522	2,214	1,762	1,262	36,937[7]	1,676	1,230	36,905[7]
Investment by Figgie/Stockholders' equity[8]	48,346	56,958	58,854	60,580	55,599	36,372	72,108	39,349[6]	42,510

4

---

market conditions. Companies have used shelf registrations primarily to sell new corporate bond issues.

Besides primary market registration requirements, SEC regulation extends to the secondary markets as well, keeping tabs on trading activity to make sure it is fair to all participants. Every securities exchange, including NASDAQ, must, by law, follow a set of trading rules that have been approved by the SEC. In response to the 1987 market break, Congress passed the Market Reform Act of 1990 (P.L. 101–432), giving the SEC emergency authority to halt trading and restrict practices such as program trading during periods of extreme volatility.

Securities laws also require every public corporation to file a number of reports each year with the SEC; the contents of these reports become public information. The best known, of course, is the annual report. Public corporations prepare annual reports for their shareholders, and they file another report containing essentially the same information, Form 10-K, with the SEC. The SEC requires additional reports each time certain officers and directors buy or sell a company's stock for their own accounts (Form 4), or any time an investor accumulates more than 5 percent of a company's outstanding stock (Form 13-d).

State Regulation. In addition to federal regulations, all states have laws regulating securities markets. In 1911, Kansas became the first state to enact a set of comprehensive securities laws. State securities laws, often referred to as **blue sky laws,** vary widely. Some states have fairly lax laws, deferring virtually all regulatory power to the SEC, while other states impose much stricter regulations. Unlike federal regulation, which is concerned primarily with full and fair disclosure, these states empower regulators to pass judgment on the worthiness of new security issues as investments. Some states have prohibited sales of security issues approved by registration with the SEC. In one celebrated case in 1980, Massachusetts initially refused to allow the first publicly issued shares of Apple Computer to be sold in the state.[33]

Securities Regulation in Other Countries

Securities are regulated in most countries. Generally, securities regulation throughout the world is modeled more or less closely after U.S. regulation. The main goal is to insure fair, orderly, and open securities markets. Let's briefly look at securities regulation in three other countries.

In Canada, securities regulation is more a provincial than a national responsibility. Since Toronto is Canada's largest business center and the home of the country's largest stock exchange, the Ontario Securities Commission is probably the most important regulatory body in the country. The Ontario Securities Commission is closely patterned after the U.S. Securities and Exchange Commission, often following the SEC's lead to adopt rule changes. For example, in 1993 the commission passed a series of rules concerning the disclosure of CEO pay similar to rules passed by the SEC a couple of years earlier. We'll look at these new disclosure requirements in Chapter 10.

The Ministry of Finance is the principal regulatory body for securities trading in Japan. All public security issues require the approval of the Ministry of Finance, and its reporting and public disclosure requirements are similar to the SEC's. Further, it licenses all securities firms and brokers. The ministry used to impose severe restrictions on foreign access to the Japanese capital markets, especially the bond markets. In recent years, however, the Ministry of Finance has liberalized some of these restrictions. As a result, the Japanese foreign bond market (called the *Samurai bond* market) and the Euroyen bond market have both expanded and developed.

Germany differs from Japan and the United States in that no regulatory walls separate the banking and securities businesses. As we noted earlier in this chapter, the secondary markets for both stocks and bonds in Germany are essentially interbank markets. Consequently, the German central bank,

---

[33]Massachusetts regulators relented a few days after Apple went public on December 12, 1980, and allowed the stock to be sold in-state. The regulators claimed that their actions made the public more aware of the potential risks associated with buying Apple stock.

the Bundesbank, has the major responsibility for securities regulation in Germany. It must approve all public security issues, and it is responsible for maintaining orderly secondary markets. The German capital markets are among the most open in the world to foreign (non-German) entities.

Industry Self-Regulation

In the United States and most other countries, the securities industry is heavily self-regulated by professional associations and the major financial markets. Industry participants recognize that rules and regulations designed to ensure fair and orderly markets will promote investor confidence, to the benefit of all participants. Two examples of self-regulation are the rules of conduct established by the National Association of Securities Dealers (NASD), and the market surveillance techniques used by the major securities markets.

Prodded initially by federal legislation, the NASD established, and periodically updates, rules of conduct for members (both individuals and firms). These rules try to ensure that brokers perform their basic functions honestly and fairly, under constant supervision. Failure to adhere to rules of conduct can result in a variety of disciplinary actions. The NASD also established a formal arbitration procedure through which investors can attempt to resolve disputes with brokers without litigation.

Like all major financial markets, the NYSE employs a series of market surveillance techniques. Trading activity is monitored continuously throughout the trading day. A key technical tool is Stock Watch, an electronic monitoring system that flags unusual price and volume activity. NYSE personnel then investigate to seek explanations for unusual activity from the member firms and companies involved. In addition, all market participants must keep detailed records of every aspect of every trade (called an *audit trail*). The NYSE's enforcement division acts as its prosecutorial arm and may impose a variety of penalties on members. Further, the exchange turns over evidence to the SEC for further action if it believes that violations of federal securities laws may have occurred.

Evolution of the Financial Markets

In the final section of this chapter, we discuss the evolution of the financial markets and speculate a little on their future. It should be apparent by now that the financial markets have evolved almost constantly throughout their modern history. The last 15 years have, however, seen some of the most dramatic changes. What forces have stimulated these recent changes?

Stimuli for Market Changes

One reason for market changes, of course, is new computer and communications technology. Technology makes NASDAQ-type trading systems much faster and more efficient than they were 15 years ago. The NYSE's new automated systems allow the exchange to handle far larger trading volumes than it could in the past.[34]

---

[34]The NYSE claims that its automated systems could easily handle a daily volume of up to 850 million shares. On the single trading day with the highest volume, October 20, 1987, 608.1 million shares changed hands.

Another reason for changing conditions is the rise of institutional investors. As we've noted, institutional investors are far more important today than they were 20 years ago. At the end of 1993, for example, institutional investors owned in excess of 50 percent of 21 of the 30 stocks that make up the Dow Jones Industrial Average, and they owned in excess of 65 percent of 8 of the 30 stocks. Two consequences of institutional ownership have been the dramatic increase in block trading and the creation of the third market. The financial markets simply had to evolve to keep pace with the rise of institutional trading.

One of the most important stimuli for recent market changes was the passage by Congress of the Securities Act Amendments in 1975 (P.L. 94–29), considered to be the most significant piece of securities legislation passed since the 1930s. The act called for the creation of a **national market system** to promote a fully competitive market for the trading of securities. Let's take a closer look at the possible form of a national market system.

National Market System

The 1975 act left the final form of the national market system vague. While no one knows exactly what the national market system will look like, most experts believe that it should meet five goals:

1. Fully negotiated brokerage commissions
2. Central reporting mechanism for price quotations and transaction data
3. Central order routing system
4. National processing of limit orders (central limit order book)
5. Free and open competition among all qualified market makers

How far have the markets progressed toward meeting these goals, and what will the future bring?

Until May 1, 1975, the NYSE required its members to charge fixed, minimum commissions. The 1975 act eliminated fixed commissions, and today, commissions are supposed to be fully negotiable, with each brokerage firm free to act independently. This change led to the creation of discount brokerage firms which gave small investors greater choice, and it probably slowed the growth of the third market. The end of fixed commissions has also substantially reduced the cost of trading for all investors, large and small. In 1975, for example, large investors paid an average of 25 cents per share to buy or sell; today the average is about 5.5 cents per share, or less.

The second goal of the National Market System has also been practically achieved. Beginning in June 1975, the NYSE began compiling and broadcasting a consolidated record (or *tape*) of trading activity in NYSE-listed stocks, including trades that take place on the floor of the exchange, on the regional exchanges, and in the over-the-counter market. The only body of data currently lacking from the consolidated tape is trading in NYSE-listed stocks that takes place in foreign markets (such as London and Tokyo).

The third goal, creation of a centralized order routing system, has been partially achieved. Many brokerage firms have electronic systems that search out the best price and automatically send a customer's order to that market. Eight markets (NYSE, AMEX, NASDAQ, and some of the regional exchanges) have developed and implemented an **inter market trading system** that allows brokers, specialists, and market makers to interact with their counterparts on any of the other markets. The system can, for example, allow a broker on the floor of the NYSE to search for a better price on one of the regional exchanges. It does not guarantee, however, that the order will be automatically routed to the market offering the best price.

The goal of a central limit order book has yet to be achieved, though this idea is quite simple. Someone might enter an order to buy Johnson & Johnson (JNJ), limit 45. The broker would give the limit order to the NYSE specialist that handles JNJ. Assume that the price of JNJ declined to 45 on the Boston Stock Exchange, but not on the NYSE. A national processing system for limit orders would route that order automatically to the Boston exchange for execution. Unfortunately, today's system gives no guarantee that that will happen. A limit order might continue to sit with the NYSE specialist.

The final goal, free and open competition among qualified market makers, is very controversial. To achieve it would mean an end to the NYSE specialist system, which dates back to the 1870s. (Remember, however, that the NASDAQ system already features competitive trading among all qualified market makers.) While critics contend that the specialist system is obsolete, the NYSE continues to defend it. Critics claim that the specialist system has led many institutional investors to abandon the NYSE for other markets, damaging its competitiveness in world markets.[35] On the other hand, the NYSE points out that 85 percent of all trades on the floor of the exchange do not involve specialists. The exchange also likes to point out that during the 1987 market break, most specialists stayed at their posts and continued to fill orders, despite losing millions of dollars. (Specialists that failed to perform their market-making functions were disciplined by the NYSE.) Over on NASDAQ, critics allege that many market makers simply stopped answering their phones and ceased trading as stock prices plunged on October 19, 1987.

Future Developments

It is difficult to gaze into the future to predict what the financial markets might look like in the twenty-first century; so many unknowns cloud the crystal ball. However, two current trends appear likely to continue: the globalization of the financial markets (including the accompanying move toward 24-hour trading) and continued automation.

The globalization of the financial markets is already virtually complete. Shares of more and more U.S. companies will likely be listed and traded in markets throughout the world, and shares of foreign companies will trade more widely in the United States. A trading system will likely route an order to buy an NYSE listed stock to London or Hong Kong, if one of those markets offers the best price.

As trading moves worldwide, it moves toward around-the-clock activity. Already, as we've noted, NASDAQ has developed trading links with markets in London and Singapore. Further, to handle growing volume of worldwide, around-the-clock trading, automation is bound to continue. The pace of technological innovation is likely to speed up dramatically.

Is continuous, 24-hour trading a good thing? Perhaps. For one thing, continuous trading may make the markets function even more smoothly than they do today. Say, for example, that a company makes a significant announcement after the NYSE closes. Without continuous trading, a supply/demand imbalance will likely make trading hectic when the NYSE opens the next day. Continuous trading would adjust prices to the new information as soon as announcements were made.

---

[35]Two recent, unreleased government studies were said to be very critical of the NYSE specialist system. See "Studies Criticized Big Board's System of Market Makers," *The Wall Street Journal,* January 18, 1990, p. C1. One study claimed that a significant portion of institutional trades in NYSE-listed stocks were being executed on the London Stock Exchange in order to avoid the NYSE specialist system.

Some believe that these changes will destroy the exchange floor as we know it. Will only computers trade stocks, not people? It's hard to say. Trading in many world markets has moved away from exchange floors in recent years, most notably in London, Paris, and Toronto, and trades are matched by computer, not face-to-face agreements. After the Big Bang, the London Stock Exchange tried to keep the floor open, but its trading volume vanished virtually overnight. In Tokyo, more issues are traded solely by computer each year. Could the floor trading system even cope with global, 24-hour trading? Some doubt that it could. Like all floor markets, the NYSE depends upon people who have limited stamina and cannot function beyond the current number of trading hours. To extend the trading day, some argue, would be too burdensome and too expensive.

In response, the NYSE argues that no conclusive evidence demonstrates that computerized trading systems, like NASDAQ, are any more efficient than its floor trading system, which is already quite automated. The NYSE argues that the human element is still a critical part of trading. Computers cannot "feel" a stock, "work" a sensitive order, or take necessary risk—in short, computers can't make all the decisions needed during the frenzy of trading. As evidence, the NYSE often points to a recent error by a clerk at Salomon Brothers. On March 26, 1992, a Salomon Brothers clerk incorrectly sent millions of dollars of sell orders to the floor of the exchange through SuperDot just before the closing bell. The NYSE and its supporters argue that human traders caught the error and headed off potential disaster where computers would have blindly compounded the error.[36] Nevertheless, individuals close to senior NYSE officials believe that the exchange is developing an off-the-floor automated trading system that still has a role for specialists, operating the computers. The NYSE could look quite different in 20 years. Time will tell.

Chapter Summary

1. **Identify traits that constitute a good, well-functioning financial market.**
   A good financial market should meet five basic conditions: widely available information, price continuity, low transaction costs, equal access to all participants, and rapid adjustment of prices to new information. One well-known financial market, the New York Stock Exchange, while not perfect, met all five conditions.

2. **Understand the organization and functioning of primary financial markets.**
   A primary market transaction is one where the issuer of a security receives the proceeds from the sale. New security issues can be sold in the primary market in one of three ways: through open auctions, underwriting by investment bankers, and private placement. The most significant type of securities sold via open auction are U.S. government securities (Treasury, federal agency, and mortgage-backed instruments). Most new corporate and municipal issues are underwritten and sold by investment bankers who help issuers design and originate security issues, take some risk by purchasing the securities for resale, and help distribute the securities. Finally, issuers can privately place their securities, selling them directly to institutional investors to avoid the cost and work of registration.

3. **Review the importance of secondary financial markets.**
   Secondary markets are important for a number of reasons. They provide liquidity for investors, allowing them to sell securities quickly at approxi-

---

[36]See "Clerk's Error Stirs Worry on Street," *The Wall Street Journal,* March 27, 1992, p. C1.

mate market values. Secondary markets also lower the cost of capital for issuers and allow for price discovery. If ten-year, AAA-rated corporate bonds are yielding 8.5 percent in the secondary markets, new ten-year, AAA-corporate bonds will also have to yield about 8.5 percent. Some securities develop better secondary markets than others due to differences in the sizes of the issues and the number of investors who initially purchased them in the primary market.

4. **Describe the world's major secondary markets.**

   Secondary markets fall into two rough categories. In some markets, trading is done by computer (usually referred to as *over-the-counter markets*); in others, trading is done face-to-face on the floor of an exchange (often referred to as *organized markets*). The secondary markets for government, municipal, and corporate bonds vary widely in terms of organization and activity. The secondary market for government securities, an over-the-counter market, is considered to be the largest, most liquid financial market in the world. Among the secondary stock markets, the New York Stock Exchange is an auction market where trading takes place face to face on the floor of the exchange. NYSE's market makers—the specialists—play important roles. The American Stock Exchange and the regional exchanges operate in much the same way as the NYSE. The NASDAQ system is different; it is an over-the-counter market where trading takes place via a computer system that gives traders access to a set of market makers. Unlike the NYSE, every NASDAQ stock has at least two market makers, though most have many more. The NASDAQ market has grown rapidly during the last 15 years. Institutional investors trade with one another in two special over-the-counter markets, the third and fourth markets. Finally, some of the major foreign stock markets play prominent roles in the global economy as well.

5. **Outline how trading is conducted in the major secondary markets.**

   Concentrating on trading in the secondary equity markets, an investor must first open a brokerage account and answer some basic questions. Most security trading orders are market orders, which are executed at the best currently available price on both organized exchanges (such as the NYSE) and over-the-counter markets (such as NASDAQ). Investors might place two other common types of orders: limit orders and stop (or stop-loss) orders. Buying stocks on margin increases both an investor's expected return and his or her risk. Short sales sell borrowed securities today and then buy them back at a lower price, the investor hopes, sometime in the future. Finally, block trades and program trades are increasingly common. While institutional investors are the only ones involved directly in these types of trades, both could have major impacts on small investors as well.

6. **Discuss the regulation of the financial markets.**

   In the United States, the financial markets are regulated by both federal and state government authorities, in addition to industry self-regulation systems. The federal Securities and Exchange Commission (SEC) provides most market regulation. It requires that any new public security issue be registered, including publication of a prospectus, and that all public corporations publicly report a variety of information at regular intervals. The SEC also requires that every financial market adopt an approved set of trading rules and guidelines. It is primarily concerned with providing full and fair disclosure of information and maintaining open and fair trading. The SEC also watches for insider trading. State regulations vary widely, and some state agencies actually pass judgment on the investment value of new security issues. We briefly examined securities regulation in three other countries (Canada, Japan, and Germany). Finally, industry participants operate self-regulation systems, including the rules of conduct for brokers and investment advisors established by the National Association of Securities Dealers, and the market surveillance techniques used by the New York Stock Exchange. The purpose of self-regulation is to promote investors' confidence that the markets are fair, open, and orderly.

7. **Review the past and likely future evolution of the financial markets.**

In the final section of the chapter, we identified three reasons for recent changes in the financial markets: new technology, more active institutional investors, and the 1975 Securities Act amendments, which created the objective of a national market system. Two of the five goals of a national market system (fully negotiated commissions and central reporting of prices and transaction data) have been pretty much met today. The goal of a central order routing system has been partly met, as well. The markets have made some progress toward national processing of limit orders, but free competition among all qualified market makers remains elusive. The NYSE still strongly defends its specialist system and fiercely resists meeting this final goal. Two obvious trends seem likely to shape the markets in the next 20 years: increasing automation and continuing globalization, resulting in true 24-hour trading. Whether either, or both, will eliminate the exchange floor, and the NYSE as we know it, remains to be seen.

Key Terms

Good market	Market maker
Liquidity	Third market
Price continuity	Fourth market
Transaction costs	Full-service brokerage firm
Perfect market	Discount brokerage firms
Efficient market	Securities Investor Protection
Primary financial market	Corporation (SIPC)
Open auction	Market order
Government bond dealer	SuperDot system
Investment banker	Limit order
Underwriting	Stop order
Underwriting discount	Margin call
Syndicate	Short sale
Initial public offering (IPO)	Uptick
Private placement	Block trade
Price discovery	Program trading
Bid price	Index arbitrage
Ask price	Insider trading
Over-the-counter market	Prospectus
Auction market	Full and fair disclosure
Seat	Blue sky law
Specialist	National market system
National Association of Securities	Inter market trading system
Dealers Automated Quotation	
(NASDAQ) system	

Mini Case   **OBJECTIVE**

The purpose of the mini case is to illustrate various types of orders and stock trades.

Today is Monday, December 13, 1993. You placed an order this morning to buy 300 shares of Auto Zone. Answer the following questions about the order, assuming that Auto Zone is currently trading for $65 per share and your broker charges a commission of 1.5 percent of the total trade value.

a. If you had placed a market order, how much would you have owed your broker, and when would the payment have been due?

b. Had you placed a limit order to buy (limit $62\frac{1}{2}$), and made it good until canceled, what would have happened to your order?

c. Had you bought the stock on margin, with an initial margin requirement of 50 percent and a maintenance requirement of 30 percent, how much cash would you have had to deposit initially?

d. Using the information from Question c, at what price would you have faced a margin call?

e. Compute your return on both a cash transaction and a margin transaction, assuming you had bought Auto Zone at 65 and sold it three months later for 80. Assume that your margin loan would carry an annual rate of interest of 6 percent.

Discussion Questions and Problems

1. What are the major characteristics of a good market? Pick a major financial market; does it have most of these characteristics?

2. What is the major difference between primary and secondary financial markets? Are the majority of financial market transactions conducted in the primary or secondary markets?

3. Explain the auction process for U.S. Treasury securities. Can small investors participate in Treasury auctions?

4. What is the role of the investment banker? Why do investment bankers form syndicates?

5. Explain a private placement. What are the advantages and disadvantages of an investor buying a privately placed security?

6. Why are secondary markets important? Why do some securities develop better secondary markets than other securities?

7. Explain the differences between organized and over-the-counter financial markets. Where are the various types of bonds (e.g., corporate or municipal) traded?

8. Compare and contrast the NYSE specialist with the NASDAQ market maker. How does a specialist make money?

9. List several major foreign stock exchanges. Are these markets more similar to the NYSE or the NASDAQ system in their trading practices?

10. Explain how a market order would be executed on the NYSE and on the NASDAQ system. How do limit and stop-loss orders differ from market orders?

11. What is margin? Why do investors buy stocks on margin?

12. Explain block trades and program trading. Why have both increased in recent years?

13. What U.S. federal agency has most of the regulatory responsibility over the financial markets? When was this agency created?

14. Define the term *full and fair disclosure*. Give an example of a trading practice that violates federal securities law.

15. What are the major goals of the national market system? Which have been met?

16. (CFA, 1992, Level I) This question is composed of two parts, for a total of 15 minutes.

Ann Carter, CFA, recently became a portfolio manager at Riverside Bank. She has both ERISA-qualified retirement plans and personal trust accounts. She knows she will be acting in a fiduciary capacity for both kinds of accounts and that her duties and responsibilities for both kinds of accounts are similar.

A. **Explain** what a "fiduciary" is and **describe** an investment manager's specific duties as a fiduciary under ERISA.

In reviewing all of the accounts under her management, Carter notices that several of the personal trust portfolios have substantial holdings of Riverside Bank's own stock. When she accepted her new position at Riverside, she was told in confidence that a major national bank was seeking to take over Riverside. Carter is unsure what the effect of a takeover would be on the shareholders of Riverside or on her employment at Riverside. In view of her fiduciary responsibilities, Carter is concerned about how to apply the AIMR Standards of Professional Conduct in managing the portfolios that hold Riverside stock. She is particularly concerned about Standard II C—Compliance with Governing Laws and Regulations and the Code and Standards–Prohibition against Use of Material Nonpublic Information. Standard II C prohibits a financial analyst from using material nonpublic information in a breach of duty or if the information is misappropriated. She is also concerned about Standard V—Disclosure of Conflicts. Standard V requires a financial analyst to disclose to clients material conflicts of interest that could reasonably be expected to impair her ability to render unbiased and objective advice to clients.

B. **Describe** *each* of these *two* standards. With reference to Carter's fiduciary responsibilities, **explain** how *each* standard applies to the management of her accounts in view of the information Carter possesses about the possible takeover.

The situation described above presents Carter with a dilemma in performing her fiduciary duties. **Briefly discuss** the dilemma that Carter faces. (Do not attempt to resolve the dilemma.)

17. (CFA, 1991, Level II) This question is composed of two parts, for a total of 20 minutes.

BanCo, a major public bank whose common shares tend to trade at a high yield, announced a substantial dividend cut on April 30, 1991. BanCo has had a record of steady dividend growth. The following descriptions outline how three individuals employed by investment banking firms derived information regarding BanCo.

- Karen Dawson, CFA, is an analyst in the Corporate Finance Department of DSP Ltd. On April 29, 1991, the chief financial officer (CFO) of BanCo, a longstanding client, told Dawson that the dividend was going to be cut, with an announcement planned for the next day.
- Joan Davidson, CFA, a security analyst with Equity Co., has covered the banking industry for 20 years. On April 29, 1991, she was having one of her usual quarterly management interviews with the CFO of BanCo, and the CFO told her that the dividend was going to be cut.
- Sonia Black, CFA, a senior bank analyst with Security Co., has not talked to the company specifically about the dividend for the past two months. After extensive research on the economic environ-

ment and on the company, Black concluded BanCo's dividend would be cut. On April 26, 1991, she notified all her clients over the newswire of her conclusion.

A. Define both the terms "material" and "nonpublic" as established by securities regulators and the courts. Your answer must include *two* criteria for the term "material" and *one* criterion for the term "nonpublic." **State** whether BanCo's dividend cut was "material nonpublic" information.

B. Based on AIMR's Standards of Professional Conduct, **describe** the duty of *each* of the three CFAs listed above regarding both their use of the information about the dividend cut and their required action following the receipt of this information. **Identify** the reason(s) for the differences in duty and required action among the three CFAs.

Critical Thinking Exercise

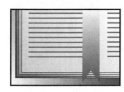

1. This exercise requires library research. Data on short interest (volume of short sales) are published monthly in *The Wall Street Journal*. Look at the most current data you can find and answer the following questions:

   a. Which five stocks had the greatest change (both up and down) in short interest for the month for which you have data?

   b. Which five stocks had the largest short interest at the end of the month?

   c. How did the prices of the stocks you identified in Questions a and b change during the month?

   d. Would you ever consider buying a stock with a large amount of short interest? Why or why not?

Mini Case   SOLUTION

a. You would have owed $19,792.50 ($65 × 300 × 1.015), due five business days following the trade. If the trade occurred on December 13, five business days later would have been December 20.

b. Auto Zone is traded on the NYSE. Since Auto Zone was trading above your limit order price, your order would have been left with the Auto Zone specialist. If Auto Zone stock had fallen until one of its market makers became willing to sell 300 shares for $62\frac{1}{2}$, or less, your order would have been executed automatically (assuming you didn't cancel it). It could take days or weeks before the order would be executed.

c. You would have had to put up, in cash, 50 percent of the initial value of the trade or $9,750 (plus commission). You would have borrowed the other $9,750.

d. Solve the following: 0.3 = (Value − Loan amount)/Value. Since Value equals 300 times the stock price, and the Loan amount equals $9,750, solve for the stock price, $46.425.

e. The value of 300 shares at $80 per share would have been $24,000 (an increase of $4,500). If you had paid cash, your return would have been $4,500/$19,500 = 23 percent. If you had bought the stock on margin, your return would have been: $4,500 − $146.25 (three months' interest, at 6 percent per annum, on $9,750) divided by $9,750 (the amount of cash you would have put up). The return would have equaled about 45 percent (rounded).

Chapter 4

Sources of Investment Information

Chapter Objectives
1. Review the sources of statistical data on the economy.
2. Identify the types of investment information provided by newspapers and periodicals.
3. Understand the types of information provided by investment advisory services.
4. Review computer-based sources of investment information.

You've probably heard the following cliché: "We live in an information age today." While it's true that information is very important in today's society and that investing is an extremely information-intensive activity, an investor may suffer not from a lack of information, but from an overabundance of information. Investors often have to sift through mountains of statistics, opinions, news announcements, and so forth, in an effort to make informed decisions. As an example, we searched three computer databases covering several major newspapers and periodicals to ask the following question: How many articles were published between January 1, 1991 and October 31, 1992 on the Walt Disney Company?[1] Quite a few; the search turned up 680 different articles on Disney![2]

The purpose of this chapter is to help you sort through the massive amount of information available to investors today. We begin by reviewing the major sources of both **objective** and **subjective** investment information sources.[3] We also examine **security market indexes** (such as the S&P 500) since they are important sources of investment information as well.

We begin the chapter with a discussion of the sources of statistical data about general economic conditions and industry trends, both domestically and internationally. For example, we'll show where to obtain data on the entire national production figures, that is, the **gross domestic products (GDPs),** of the countries that make up the European Community (EC). Next, we look through the major newspapers and general interest and trade

---

[1] We searched the following databases: ABI/Inform, CIRR, and ProQuest Periodical Abstracts. Your college library may subscribe to these common computer databases.

[2] Some articles resulted from different publications covering the same news event. For example, both the *New York Times* and *The Wall Street Journal* reported several quarterly earnings announcements for Disney.

[3] We define an objective source as one that provides information and data, but no opinions or analysis. A subjective source generally provides both data and opinions.

periodicals, starting with a pretty basic explanation of how to read stock and bond price quotations. This is followed by a discussion of investment advisory services like Value Line, Moody's, and individual brokerage companies. Following this discussion, we take a look at several computer databases and information sources like Compact Disclosure and Value Screen Plus.

Before starting, note that our discussion is not meant to be comprehensive. For one thing, we don't have the space to cover everything and, for another, we believe it's more important to cover examples of what's available as opposed to a list of sources.[4] Also, this chapter won't cover one major source of investment information, company-provided information (such as annual reports). The uses and limitations of company-provided information will be examined in detail in Part III (Equity Valuation). Finally, understand that the information needs of investors vary substantially. Sources that are very important to certain professional or institutional investors may have little or no value for small, individual investors. Many small investors can satisfy all their information needs with general-interest periodicals and newspapers.

Sources of Statistical Data

A variety of government and private organizations compiles and publishes all kinds of economic and industry data. You can find the number of housing starts in the United States between 1960 and 1992, the profits of electric and gas utilities over the past four quarters, or the current breakdown of the Canadian GDP. Most sources of such information provide objective data (e.g., historical economic statistics), rather than subjective opinions and analysis. We'll start by examining government sources of statistical data about economy-wide and industry-specific conditions and trends.

Government Publications

Several U.S. federal agencies, international organizations, and foreign governments compile and publish statistical data. Some series are reported monthly, some quarterly, and some annually. For some series, historical data going back many years may be available.[5] Let's look at several examples of government publications that contain economic and industry data.

Survey of Current Business. The U.S. Department of Commerce publishes the *Survey of Current Business* each month to review recent developments in the U.S. economy (and, to a lesser extent, the world economy) and to present data on GDP, industrial production, employment, wages, interest rates, and so forth. The *Survey* also contains detailed data on conditions in specific industries. Figure 4.1 shows an example of the type of data presented in the *Survey of Current Business*. It presents, in tabular form, the breakdown of U.S.

---

[4]There are, in fact, entire reference books devoted to sources of investment information. See, for example, Mathew Lesko, *The Investors' Information Sourcebook* (New York: Harper-Collins, 1988).

[5]We're considering only what data are available here, not the *quality* of these data. The quality of government-compiled economic data is the subject of some controversy, as we will discuss in Chapter 9.

Figure 4.1

Sample Data from the *Survey of Current Business*

NATIONAL INCOME AND PRODUCT ACCOUNTS

Selected NIPA Tables

New estimates in this issue: "Preliminary" estimates for the fourth quarter of 1993.

The selected set of national income and product accounts (NIPA) tables shown in this section presents quarterly estimates, which are updated monthly. (In most tables, the annual estimates are also shown.) These tables are available on the day of the gross domestic product (GDP) news release on printouts and diskettes on a subscription basis or from the Commerce Department's Economic Bulletin Board. For order information, write to the National Income and Wealth Division (BE-54), Bureau of Economic Analysis, Washington, DC 20230 or call (202) 606–5304.

Tables containing the estimates for 1929–87 are available in the two-volume set *National Income and Product Accounts of the United States*; see inside back cover for order information. For 1988–92, the complete official time series of NIPA estimates can be found as follows:

	1988	1989	1990–92
Most tables..................	*NIPA's*, vol. 2	July 1992 SURVEY	Aug. 1993 SURVEY
Tables 1.15, 1.16, and 7.15......	"	"	Sept. 1993 SURVEY
Tables 3.15–3.20 and 9.1–9.6...	"	Sept. 1992 SURVEY	"
Tables 7.1, 7.2, and 8.1........	Sept. 1993 SURVEY	Sept. 1993 SURVEY	"

Summary NIPA series back to 1929 are in the September 1993 SURVEY. Errata to published NIPA tables appear in the September 1992, April 1993, and October 1993 issues. NIPA tables are also available, most beginning with 1929, on diskettes or magnetic tape. For more information on the presentation of the estimates, see "A Look at How BEA Presents the NIPA's" in this issue.

NOTE.—This section of the SURVEY is prepared by the National Income and Wealth Division and the Government Division.

Table 1.1.—Gross Domestic Product

[Billions of dollars]

	1992	1993	Seasonally adjusted at annual rates					
			1992		1993			
			III	IV	I	II	III	IV
Gross domestic product	6,038.5	6,379.4	6,059.5	6,194.4	6,261.6	6,327.6	6,395.9	6,532.4
Personal consumption expenditures	4,139.9	4,391.9	4,157.1	4,256.2	4,296.2	4,359.9	4,419.1	4,492.5
Durable goods	497.3	537.9	500.9	516.6	515.3	531.6	541.9	562.6
Nondurable goods	1,300.9	1,351.0	1,305.7	1,331.7	1,335.3	1,344.8	1,352.4	1,371.5
Services	2,341.6	2,503.0	2,350.5	2,407.9	2,445.5	2,483.4	2,524.8	2,558.4
Gross private domestic investment	796.5	892.8	802.2	833.3	874.1	874.1	884.0	939.0
Fixed investment	789.1	875.8	792.5	821.3	839.5	861.0	876.3	926.4
Nonresidential	565.5	623.4	569.2	579.5	594.7	619.1	624.9	655.0
Structures	172.6	178.9	170.8	171.1	172.4	177.6	179.1	186.5
Producers' durable equipment	392.9	444.5	398.4	408.3	422.2	441.6	445.8	468.5
Residential	223.6	252.4	223.3	241.8	244.9	241.9	251.3	271.4
Change in business inventories	7.3	17.0	9.7	12.0	34.6	13.1	7.7	12.6
Nonfarm	2.3	22.5	4.4	9.5	33.0	16.8	22.6	17.6
Farm	5.0	−5.5	5.3	2.4	1.5	−3.7	−14.9	−5.1
Net exports of goods and services	−29.6	−63.2	−38.8	−38.8	−48.3	−65.1	−71.9	−67.6
Exports	640.5	661.7	641.1	654.7	651.3	660.0	653.2	682.2
Imports	670.1	724.9	679.9	693.5	699.6	725.0	725.1	749.7
Government purchases	1,131.8	1,157.9	1,139.1	1,143.8	1,139.7	1,158.6	1,164.8	1,168.5
Federal	448.8	443.6	452.8	452.4	442.7	447.5	443.6	440.5
National defense	313.8	303.6	316.7	315.7	304.8	307.6	301.9	300.1
Nondefense	135.0	140.0	136.1	136.7	137.9	140.0	141.7	140.4
State and local	683.0	714.3	686.2	691.4	697.0	711.1	721.2	728.0

NOTE.—Percent changes from preceding period for selected items in this table are shown in table 8.1.

Table 1.2.—Gross Domestic Product in Constant Dollars

[Billions of 1987 dollars]

	1992	1993	Seasonally adjusted at annual rates					
			1992		1993			
			III	IV	I	II	III	IV
Gross domestic product	4,986.3	5,137.7	4,998.2	5,068.3	5,078.2	5,102.1	5,138.3	5,232.1
Personal consumption expenditures	3,341.8	3,453.7	3,350.9	3,397.2	3,403.8	3,432.7	3,469.6	3,508.6
Durable goods	456.6	490.1	459.0	473.4	471.9	484.2	493.1	511.1
Nondurable goods	1,062.9	1,088.7	1,062.9	1,081.8	1,076.0	1,083.1	1,093.0	1,102.7
Services	1,822.3	1,874.9	1,829.0	1,842.0	1,855.9	1,865.4	1,883.5	1,894.8
Gross private domestic investment	732.9	821.4	739.6	763.0	803.0	803.6	813.4	865.5
Fixed investment	726.4	805.8	730.0	754.3	773.7	790.6	806.9	852.2
Nonresidential	529.2	591.7	533.8	543.7	562.3	584.3	594.8	625.2
Structures	150.6	151.7	148.8	148.0	148.2	151.1	151.2	156.3
Producers' durable equipment	378.6	440.0	385.1	395.7	414.1	433.2	443.6	469.0
Residential	197.1	214.2	196.2	210.6	211.4	206.2	212.1	226.9
Change in business inventories	6.5	15.5	9.6	8.7	29.3	13.0	6.5	13.4
Nonfarm	2.7	20.9	5.8	7.5	29.3	17.1	19.4	17.8
Farm	3.8	−5.3	3.8	1.2	0	−4.1	−12.9	−4.4
Net exports of goods and services	−33.6	−76.4	−42.5	−38.8	−59.9	−75.2	−86.3	−84.1
Exports	578.0	598.3	579.3	591.6	588.0	593.2	591.9	620.1
Imports	611.6	674.7	621.8	630.3	647.9	668.4	678.2	704.2
Government purchases	945.2	939.0	950.2	946.9	931.3	941.1	941.7	942.0
Federal	373.0	355.1	377.0	373.7	357.6	359.4	353.7	349.5
National defense	261.2	242.6	264.4	261.3	246.0	246.4	240.1	238.0
Nondefense	111.8	112.4	112.5	112.4	111.5	113.0	113.7	111.5
State and local	572.2	583.9	573.2	573.2	573.7	581.6	588.0	592.5

NOTE.—Percent changes from preceding period for selected items in this table are shown in table 8.1.

Source: U.S. Dept. of Commerce, *Survey of Current Business,* February 1994, p. 9.

GDP between 1992 and 1993. The *Survey* reports current data and limited historical data, typically going back a couple of years.

Besides the *Survey*, every two years the U.S. Commerce Department publishes *Business Statistics,* which provides longer-term historical, economic data. This source could provide data, for example, on the value of new construction activity in the United States between 1963 and 1991, as shown in Figure 4.2.

Figure 4.2

Sample Data from *Business Statistics*

BUSINESS STATISTICS, 1963–91

CONSTRUCTION AND REAL ESTATE—CONSTRUCTION CONTRACTS AND HOUSING STARTS

YEAR AND MONTH	Total (Millions of dollars)	Total (Index, 1987=100)	By ownership Public	By ownership Private	By type of building Nonresidential	By type of building Residential	Non-building construction	NEW CONSTRUCTION PLANNING (ENGINEERING NEWS-RECORD), (Millions of dollars)[2]	NEW HOUSING Unadjusted Total (Private and public)	NEW HOUSING Unadjusted Privately owned Total	NEW HOUSING Unadjusted Privately owned One-family structures	Seasonally adjusted Privately owned Total	Seasonally adjusted Privately owned One-family structures
1963	45,546	...	14,653	30,893	14,377	20,502	10,667	...	1,634.9	1,603.2	1,012.4	...	...
1964	47,299	...	15,371	31,928	15,495	20,561	11,244		1,561.0	1,528.8	970.5	...	...
1965	49,272		16,302	32,970	17,219	21,248	10,805		1,509.7	1,472.8	963.7		
1966	50,150		18,152	31,998	19,393	17,827	12,930		1,195.8	1,164.9	778.6		
1967	54,513		19,048	35,464	20,496	21,164	12,853		1,321.9	1,291.6	843.9		
1968	61,436		19,432	42,004	22,840	24,772	13,824		1,545.4	1,507.6	899.4		
1969	[4]67,828		[4]22,940	[4]44,888	[4]26,681	[4]25,450	[4]15,698		1,499.5	1,466.8	810.6		
1970	67,981	43	23,491	44,490	25,406	24,713	17,862		1,469.0	1,433.6	812.9		
1971	79,642	51	23,944	55,698	26,715	34,741	18,185		2,084.5	2,052.2	1,151.0		
1972	90,788	58	24,037	66,751	27,313	44,824	18,652		2,378.5	2,356.6	1,309.2		
1973	98,770	63	26,565	72,205	31,876	45,479	21,616		2,057.5	2,045.3	1,132.0		
1974	91,661	58	31,911	59,750	33,203	33,453	25,004		1,352.5	1,337.7	888.1		
1975	91,074	58	30,894	60,180	31,433	31,209	28,432		1,171.4	1,160.4	892.2		
1976	110,016	70	29,304	80,711	30,096	44,106	35,813		1,547.6	1,537.5	1,162.4		
1977	140,971	90	37,021	103,950	35,656	62,129	43,186		2,001.7	1,987.1	1,450.9		
1978	160,606	102	39,278	121,328	45,544	75,049	40,013		2,036.1	2,020.3	1,433.3		
1979	170,865	109	47,548	123,317	50,691	74,709	45,466		1,760.0	1,745.1	1,194.1		
1980	151,822	97	41,787	110,035	53,494	63,826	34,501		1,312.6	1,292.2	852.2		
1981	157,270	100	39,474	117,796	61,580	60,242	35,448		1,100.3	1,084.2	705.4		
1982	157,139	100	41,481	115,658	60,260	59,330	37,549		1,072.1	1,062.2	662.6		
1983	194,089	75	45,457	148,632	62,549	93,718	37,822		1,712.5	1,703.0	1,067.6		
1984	214,269	83	49,283	164,985	75,570	101,839	36,860		1,755.8	1,749.5	1,084.2		
1985	235,819	91	55,407	180,412	85,061	109,359	41,399		1,745.0	1,741.8	1,072.4		
1986	249,271	96	59,944	189,328	84,160	122,977	42,134	288,568	1,807.1	1,805.4	1,179.4		
1987	258,570	100	66,448	192,123	91,361	121,234	45,975	267,823	1,622.7	1,620.5	1,146.4		
1988	260,752	101	67,875	192,876	90,624	121,940	48,188	283,448	(6)	1,488.1	1,081.3		
1989	261,163	105	71,305	189,859	93,058	120,436	47,670	275,118		1,376.1	1,003.3		
1990	245,396	95	72,090	173,307	90,240	105,509	49,645	213,389		1,192.7	894.8		
1991	221,230	88	74,422	146,806	76,898	96,353	47,978			1,014.5	841.2		
1988:													
January	15,176	93	3,867	11,309	5,889	6,743	2,544	28,423	78.2	78.2	55.8	1,339	986
February	17,659	101	4,644	13,015	6,359	7,971	3,329	28,172	90.3	90.2	64.0	1,507	1,101
March	23,103	99	5,872	17,232	7,365	11,018	4,720	[5]31,547	129.0	128.8	99.9	1,541	1,188
April	22,633	99	5,788	16,846	6,994	10,735	4,905	21,094	153.4	153.2	106.1	1,570	1,070
May	24,248	103	6,668	17,580	7,341	11,671	5,237	23,321	140.3	140.2	104.0	1,414	1,011
June	26,901	106	7,944	18,958	9,162	12,404	5,335	[5]20,096	150.3	150.2	113.6	1,476	1,100
July	22,340	100	5,768	16,572	8,241	10,102	3,996	19,566	137.2	137.0	100.3	1,460	1,056
August	24,877	103	5,814	19,063	9,303	11,784	3,790	21,883	136.8	136.8	101.4	1,480	1,088
September	22,676	100	6,134	16,543	8,022	10,523	4,131	[5]20,405	131.4	131.1	97.7	1,475	1,046
October	22,223	106	5,805	16,418	7,913	10,473	3,837	23,176	135.2	135.1	97.7	1,511	1,128
November	19,762	100	4,780	14,982	7,326	9,541	2,895	25,114	113.2	113.0	81.2	1,556	1,125
December	19,198	108	4,777	14,421	6,726	9,007	3,465	[5]20,652	(6)	94.2	65.7	1,564	1,131
1989:													
January	17,536	104	3,931	13,605	6,998	8,135	2,403	23,659		100.1	69.9	1,659	1,188
February	16,450	99	4,448	12,002	5,613	7,432	3,405	22,688		85.8	59.3	1,454	1,026
March	21,945	97	6,162	15,783	7,100	10,506	4,339	[5]25,083		117.8	83.5	1,405	979
April	24,134	109	6,817	17,317	7,482	11,466	5,186	23,972		129.4	100.4	1,341	1,028
May	24,738	102	6,925	17,813	8,269	11,851	4,618	20,155		131.7	101.4	1,308	977
June	24,650	105	6,859	17,792	8,496	11,568	4,586	[5]24,319		143.2	100.3	1,414	971
July	22,330	105	6,111	16,219	7,976	10,318	4,036	21,210		134.7	98.0	1,424	1,029
August	25,884	106	7,035	18,850	9,521	11,838	4,525	[5]25,170		122.4	91.7	1,325	987
September	25,267	113	7,130	18,137	10,119	10,600	4,548	21,042		109.3	82.4	1,263	969
October	24,695	110	6,397	18,298	9,540	11,378	3,777	25,564		130.1	91.2	1,423	1,023
November	20,329	104	5,594	14,735	7,508	9,278	3,543	[5]23,182		96.6	71.9	1,347	1,010
December	18,814	108	4,810	14,004	8,006	7,442	3,365	19,075		75.0	53.4	1,273	931
1990:													
January	18,146	105	4,946	13,200	7,031	7,928	3,188	18,132		99.2	67.9	1,568	1,078
February	16,259	96	4,028	12,231	5,407	7,589	3,262	22,463		86.9	65.9	1,488	1,127
March	22,220	102	6,352	15,869	7,723	10,211	4,286	[5]22,343		108.5	83.2	1,298	988
April	21,195	93	5,668	15,527	7,238	9,932	4,025	18,230		119.0	90.0	1,217	901
May	25,052	101	7,485	17,567	8,212	11,104	5,735	[5]17,134		121.1	92.4	1,208	897
June	24,674	100	7,505	17,069	8,861	10,493	5,320	15,279		117.8	88.9	1,187	890
July	22,387	96	7,009	15,378	8,423	9,605	4,359	15,564		111.2	85.5	1,155	876
August	22,279	92	7,243	15,036	7,976	9,633	4,670	[5]19,935		102.8	75.6	1,131	835
September	19,347	90	5,725	13,622	7,435	8,164	3,748	18,901		93.1	71.9	1,106	858
October	21,454	92	6,397	15,057	8,824	8,530	4,100	16,895		94.2	75.6	1,026	839
November	18,201	93	5,213	12,988	7,079	6,837	4,285	[5]13,169		81.4	54.9	1,130	769
December	14,182	83	4,419	9,763	6,031	5,483	2,667	15,344		57.4	43.1	971	751
1991:													
January	14,092	80	5,147	8,945	6,120	4,936	3,036	[5]14,365		52.5	39.2	844	644
February	13,376	85	4,925	8,450	5,091	5,185	3,100	8,136		59.1	46.1	1,008	803
March	16,276	86	5,803	10,473	5,747	6,785	3,744	10,619		73.8	61.4	918	751
April	20,929	93	6,700	14,229	7,076	8,712	5,141	9,229		99.7	82.8	978	802
May	20,713	88	6,665	14,047	6,778	9,190	4,745	[5]17,726		97.7	84.5	983	830
June	19,552	82	6,728	12,824	6,412	8,909	4,231	9,433		103.4	86.8	1,036	870
July	21,283	88	6,881	14,402	6,940	9,695	4,648			103.5	87.4	1,053	881
August	21,558	92	7,250	14,308	7,454	9,764	4,339			94.7	78.7	1,053	881
September	19,411	86	6,498	12,913	6,218	8,941	4,252			86.6	73.7	1,020	864
October	22,738	96	7,736	15,002	8,337	9,984	4,417			101.8	80.9	1,085	887
November	15,083	81	4,240	10,843	5,103	7,427	2,552			75.6	62.6	1,085	907
December	16,277	96	5,880	10,397	5,819	6,670	3,788			65.6	56.3	1,118	972

Footnotes giving source of data and description of series appear in the section immediately following these tables.   ★Monthly data prior to 1988 are shown on pp. A-51 and A-52.

Source: U.S. Dept. of Commerce, *Business Statistics,* 1963–1991, p. 32.

Federal Reserve Bulletin. The *Federal Reserve Bulletin* is published monthly by the Board of Governors of the U.S. Federal Reserve System. It is the investor's primary source for current monetary and banking data. The *Bulletin* also presents a number of other financial data series, both domestic and international. Figure 4.3 gives an example of the type of data reported in the *Federal Reserve Bulletin.*

In addition to banking and financial data, the *Bulletin* also contains articles, written by the staff of the Board of Governors, on contemporary mon-

Figure 4.3

Sample Data from the *Federal Reserve Bulletin*

1.35 INTEREST RATES Money and Capital Markets

Averages, percent per year; figures are averages of business day data unless otherwise noted

Item	1990	1991	1992	1993 Aug.	Sept.	Oct.	Nov.	1993, week ending Oct. 29	Nov. 5	Nov. 12	Nov. 19	Nov. 26
MONEY MARKET INSTRUMENTS												
1 Federal funds[1,2,3]	8.10	5.69	3.52	3.03	3.09	2.99	3.02	2.97	3.04	2.96	3.03	2.98
2 Discount window borrowing[2,4]	6.98	5.45	3.25	3.00	3.00	3.00	3.00	3.00	3.00	3.00	3.00	3.00
Commercial paper[3,5,6]												
3 1-month	8.15	5.89	3.71	3.14	3.14	3.14	3.15	3.14	3.15	3.15	3.14	3.15
4 3-month	8.06	5.87	3.75	3.18	3.16	3.26	3.40	3.28	3.38	3.40	3.40	3.42
5 6-month	7.95	5.85	3.80	3.33	3.25	3.27	3.43	3.30	3.40	3.42	3.43	3.45
Finance paper, directly placed[3,5,7]												
6 1-month	8.00	5.73	3.62	3.08	3.07	3.08	3.08	3.07	3.09	3.09	3.08	3.06
7 3-month	7.87	5.71	3.65	3.13	3.09	3.16	3.25	3.18	3.23	3.26	3.26	3.27
8 6-month	7.53	5.60	3.63	3.16	3.11	3.13	3.19	3.14	3.19	3.19	3.19	3.20
Bankers acceptances[3,5,8]												
9 3-month	7.93	5.70	3.62	3.10	3.07	3.19	3.29	3.24	3.31	3.30	3.28	3.29
10 6-month	7.80	5.67	3.67	3.23	3.17	3.19	3.32	3.24	3.32	3.33	3.31	3.31
Certificates of deposit, secondary market[3,9]												
11 1-month	8.15	5.82	3.64	3.09	3.09	3.09	3.11	3.10	3.11	3.10	3.09	3.09
12 3-month	8.15	5.83	3.68	3.14	3.12	3.24	3.35	3.29	3.36	3.36	3.33	3.36
13 6-month	8.17	5.91	3.76	3.32	3.24	3.25	3.39	3.30	3.39	3.39	3.36	3.40
14 Eurodollar deposits, 3-month[3,10]	8.16	5.86	3.70	3.14	3.08	3.26	3.36	3.29	3.35	3.38	3.34	3.38
U.S. Treasury bills Secondary market[3,5]												
15 3-month	7.50	5.38	3.43	3.02	2.95	3.02	3.10	3.06	3.08	3.10	3.11	3.12
16 6-month	7.46	5.44	3.54	3.14	3.06	3.12	3.26	3.18	3.25	3.25	3.25	3.27
17 1-year	7.35	5.52	3.71	3.30	3.22	3.25	3.42	3.32	3.40	3.39	3.42	3.46
Auction average[3,5,11]												
18 3-month	7.51	5.42	3.45	3.05	2.96	3.04	3.12	3.08	3.11	3.11	3.11	3.14
19 6-month	7.47	5.49	3.57	3.17	3.06	3.13	3.27	3.19	3.25	3.28	3.26	3.30
20 1-year	7.36	5.54	3.75	3.30	3.27	3.25	3.43	n.a.	n.a.	n.a.	3.43	n.a.
U.S. TREASURY NOTES AND BONDS												
Constant maturities[12]												
21 1-year	7.89	5.86	3.89	3.44	3.36	3.39	3.58	3.46	3.56	3.55	3.58	3.61
22 2-year	8.16	6.49	4.77	4.00	3.85	3.87	4.16	3.97	4.15	4.13	4.13	4.20
23 3-year	8.26	6.82	5.30	4.36	4.17	4.18	4.50	4.28	4.47	4.48	4.49	4.56
24 5-year	8.37	7.37	6.19	5.03	4.73	4.71	5.06	4.82	5.03	5.04	5.04	5.13
25 7-year	8.52	7.68	6.63	5.35	5.08	5.05	5.45	5.19	5.41	5.42	5.41	5.54
26 10-year	8.55	7.86	7.01	5.68	5.36	5.33	5.72	5.44	5.66	5.68	5.71	5.83
27 20-year	n.a.	n.a.	n.a.	n.a.	n.a.	6.07	6.38	6.14	6.31	6.35	6.39	6.47
28 30-year	8.61	8.14	7.67	6.32	6.00	5.94	6.21	5.99	6.12	6.19	6.22	6.31
Composite												
29 More than 10 years (long-term)	8.74	8.16	7.52	6.18	5.94	5.90	6.25	5.99	6.17	6.21	6.25	6.34
STATE AND LOCAL NOTES AND BONDS												
Moody's series[13]												
30 Aaa	6.96	6.56	6.09	5.37	5.25	5.13	5.10	5.05	5.08	5.10	5.12	5.12
31 Baa	7.29	6.99	6.48	5.84	5.76	5.63	5.61	5.55	5.58	5.60	5.02	5.62
32 *Bond Buyer series[14]*	7.27	6.92	6.44	5.45	5.29	5.25	5.47	5.31	5.45	5.46	5.46	5.49
CORPORATE BONDS												
33 Seasoned issues, all industries[15]	9.77	9.23	8.55	7.19	6.98	6.97	7.25	7.03	7.18	7.24	7.26	7.32
Rating group												
34 Aaa	9.32	8.77	8.14	6.85	6.66	6.67	6.93	6.73	6.87	6.92	6.94	6.99
35 Aa	9.56	9.05	8.46	7.06	6.85	6.87	7.12	6.93	7.07	7.11	7.13	7.18
36 A	9.82	9.30	8.62	7.25	7.05	7.04	7.29	7.08	7.22	7.28	7.30	7.36
37 Baa	10.36	9.80	8.98	7.60	7.34	7.31	7.66	7.38	7.57	7.65	7.69	7.74
38 A-rated, recently offered utility bonds[16]	10.01	9.32	8.52	7.16	6.94	6.91	7.25	6.97	7.25	7.23	7.37	7.27
MEMO												
Dividend–price ratio[17]												
39 Preferred stocks	8.96	8.17	7.46	6.83	6.70	6.71	6.87	6.81	6.81	6.82	6.85	6.99
40 Common stocks	3.61	3.24	2.99	2.76	2.73	2.72	2.72	2.71	2.72	2.72	2.71	2.73

1. The daily effective federal funds rate is a weighted average of rates on trades through New York brokers.
2. Weekly figures are averages of seven calendar days ending on Wednesday of the current week; monthly figures include each calendar day in the month.
3. Annualized using a 360-day year or bank interest.
4. Rate for the Federal Reserve Bank of New York.
5. Quoted on a discount basis.
6. An average of offering rates on commercial paper placed by several leading dealers for firms whose bond rating is AA or the equivalent.
7. An average of offering rates on paper directly placed by finance companies.
8. Representative closing yields for acceptances of the highest-rated money center banks.
9. An average of dealer offering rates on nationally traded certificates of deposit.
10. Bid rates for Eurodollar deposits at 11:00 a.m. London time. Data are for indication purposes only.
11. Auction date for daily data; weekly and monthly averages computed on an issue-date basis.

12. Yields on actively traded issues adjusted to constant maturities. Source: U.S. Treasury.
13. General obligations based on Thursday figures; Moody's Investors Service.
14. General obligations only, with twenty years to maturity, issued by twenty state and local governmental units of mixed quality. Based on figures for Thursday.
15. Daily figures from Moody's Investors Service. Based on yields to maturity on selected long-term bonds.
16. Compilation of the Federal Reserve. This series is an estimate of the yield on recently offered, A-rated utility bonds with a thirty-year maturity and five years of call protection. Weekly data are based on Friday quotations.
17. Standard & Poor's corporate series. Preferred stock ratio is based on a sample of ten issues: four public utilities, four industrials, one financial, and one transportation. Common stock ratio is based on the 500 stocks in the price index.
NOTE. Some of the data in this table also appear in the Board's H.15 (519) weekly and G.13 (415) monthly statistical releases. For ordering address, see inside front cover.

Source: U.S. Federal Reserve System, *Federal Reserve Bulletin,* February 1994, p. A26.

etary and banking issues. Announcements, Congressional testimony by board members, and so forth, are also printed in the *Bulletin.*

Monthly Energy Review. The *Survey of Current Business* and the *Federal Reserve Bulletin* report a wide range of economic data. Other government publications concentrate on specific segments of the economy. An example of this type of specialized government publication is the *Monthly Energy Review,* published by the U.S. Department of Energy. It reports data series on

Figure 4.4

Sample Chart from the *Mutual Fund Fact Book*

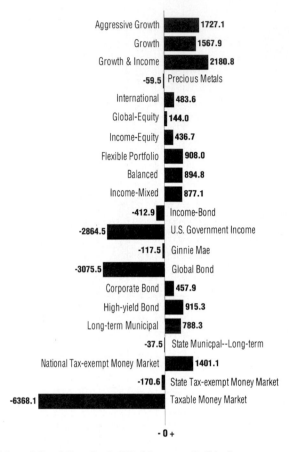

Net Exchanges by Investment Objective—1992
(millions of dollars)

Aggressive Growth	1727.1
Growth	1567.9
Growth & Income	2180.8
-59.5 Precious Metals	
International	483.6
Global-Equity	144.0
Income-Equity	436.7
Flexible Portfolio	908.0
Balanced	894.8
Income-Mixed	877.1
-412.9 Income-Bond	
-2864.5 U.S. Government Income	
-117.5 Ginnie Mae	
-3075.5 Global Bond	
Corporate Bond	457.9
High-yield Bond	915.3
Long-term Municipal	788.3
-37.5 State Municpal--Long-term	
National Tax-exempt Money Market	1401.1
-170.6 State Tax-exempt Money Market	
-6368.1 Taxable Money Market	

- 0 +

Source: *1992 Mutual Fund Fact Book* (Washington, D.C.), Investment Company Institute, 1992, p. 23. Reprinted with permission.

all types of energy consumption, prices, and production. For example, it gives detailed data on petroleum prices like that in Figure 4.4.

Many investors will need the information in specialized publications, like the *Monthly Energy Review,* less than that in more general publications, such as the *Survey of Current Business.* Someone who closely follows the petroleum industry, however, would probably find the *Monthly Energy Review* an invaluable source of detailed data and information.

International Publications. A number of international organizations can provide detailed data on world economies, including the International Monetary Fund (IMF), United Nations, and World Bank. In addition, the governments of most developed countries publish statistical data regularly. Canada, for example, publishes a statistical abstract annually. An example of this type of publication is *International Financial Statistics,* published by the International Monetary Fund. It provides data, on a country-by-country basis, on such things as inflation, industrial production, and main components of GDP.

The average investor may have little interest in these types of international data, but some professionals might be interested. For example, say an analyst for a big Wall Street investment firm follows a company that generates a high percentage of its sales in Europe. Obviously the prospects for that company, and therefore the investment potential of its stock, will be closely tied to the economic outlook in Europe.

Nongovernment Sources

Economic data are also available from nongovernment sources such as financial institutions, investment firms, securities exchanges, trade associations, and so forth. In fact, many of these private organizations provide some of the data that appear in government publications such as the *Survey of Current Business*. For example, the data excerpted in Figure 4.2 from *Business Statistics* came originally from F. W. Dodge, a unit of McGraw-Hill.[6] Private sources also publish data on their own; let's look at two examples of the many nongovernment publications available.

***Mutual Fund Fact Book* (Investment Company Institute).** The Investment Company Institute is the trade association for investment companies, of which mutual funds make up the largest group. Each year, the institute publishes the *Mutual Fund Fact Book* with articles and data pertaining to the mutual fund industry including trends in sales, assets, and performance.[7] An example of the type of data found in the *Mutual Fund Fact Book* is shown in Figure 4.4.

***Stocks, Bonds, Bills, and Inflation* (Ibbotson Associates).** One of the most widely cited sources of data on historical stock and bond returns is *Stocks, Bonds, Bills, and Inflation (SBBI)* published annually by the investment firm Ibbotson Associates. *SBBI* contains monthly data on returns from stocks of both large and small companies, corporate bonds, both intermediate and long-term government bonds, and Treasury bills, as well as inflation data, starting in 1926. In addition, it breaks down stock and bond returns into capital appreciation and income components.

Newspapers and Periodicals

Most investors probably get the bulk of their information from newspapers and periodicals. You're probably already familiar with *Barron's, The Wall Street Journal, Business Week*, and such, but hundreds of more specialized publications are published that interest certain investors. Before examining all the various types of newspapers and periodicals, let's first examine some basic information about how to read stock and bond quotations.[8]

---

[6]Other examples of data sources for the *Survey of Current Business* and *Business Statistics:* data on business failures come from Dun & Bradstreet; data on the financial operations of U.S. railroads come from the Association of American Railroads; data on electric power sales come from the Edison Electric Institute.

[7]All the major securities exchanges (e.g., the New York Stock Exchange and the Tokyo Stock Exchange) publish annual fact books full of the same general type of data as published in the *Mutual Fund Fact Book*.

[8]We'll review price quotations for options and futures contracts, respectively, in Chapters 18 and 19.

Table 4.1

Sample Price Quotations

Common Stock

52 week High	Low	Stock	Ticker	Dividend	Yield	P/E	Volume	High	Low	Close	Change
s $46\frac{5}{8}$	$32\frac{3}{4}$	Disney	DIS	0.25f	0.5	28	13520	$46\frac{1}{8}$	$44\frac{7}{8}$	46	$+\frac{1}{2}$

Disney has traded as high as $46\frac{5}{8}$ and as low as $32\frac{3}{4}$ during the previous 52 weeks; the s means that the stock split during the past year. Disney pays an annual dividend of 0.25 per share. (The f means it was raised on the latest declaration.) The $0.25 dividend translates into a dividend yield of 0.5 percent (dividend divided by price). Disney's stock currently has a price–earnings ratio of about 28. Volume is the number of shares traded on January 28, 1993, in hundreds; over 1.35 million shares of Disney changed hands that day. The high, low, and close cover trading on January 28. Disney traded as high as $46\frac{1}{8}$ and as low as $44\frac{7}{8}$ during that day; it closed at 46, an increase of $\frac{1}{2}$ point over its closing price on January 27.

Corporate Bond

Issuer	Coupon	Maturity	Yield	Volume	Close	Change
ATT	$8\frac{1}{8}\%$	2022	7.9%	508	$103\frac{3}{8}$	$-\frac{1}{4}$

This bond, issued by AT&T, carries an annual coupon rate of $8\frac{1}{8}$ percent, and matures in 2022. During trading on January 28, 508 bonds changed hands. The bond closed at $103\frac{3}{8}$ (or 103.37 percent of par), giving it a current yield of 7.9 percent. The bond's closing price was $\frac{1}{4}$ point (or 0.25 percent of par) lower on January 28 compared to its close January 27.

Treasury Note/Bond

Coupon	Maturity	Bid Price	Ask Price	Change	Yield
$7\frac{1}{2}$	May 02 n	107:13	107:15	+ :11	6.42%

This Treasury security has an annual coupon rate of $7\frac{1}{2}$ percent and matures on May 15, 2002; the n means that it was originally issued as a note. At the close of trading on January 28, government bond dealers were willing to buy this note for $107\frac{13}{32}$ (or 107.40625 percent of par value). The dealers were willing to sell this note for $107\frac{15}{32}$ (or 107.46875 percent of par value). This note's bid price increased by $\frac{11}{32}$ (or 0.34375 percent of par) over its closing bid price the prior trading day. At this bid price, the note has a current yield (coupon rate divided by price) of about 6.42 percent.

Stock and Bond Quotations

Tables of stock and bond prices appear in most large-city daily newspapers as well as *USA Today* and *The Wall Street Journal*.[9] These tables provide investors with some important information. Table 4.1 reprints three representative security price quotations from the January 29, 1993 edition of *The Wall Street Journal*. Each reports on trading activity that occurred the previous day.

The quote tells us that Disney's common stock traded as high as $46\frac{5}{8}$ and as low as $32\frac{3}{4}$ during the previous year. It split within the previous 12 months,

---

[9]Some sources, of course, publish more detailed and comprehensive price quotations than others. *The Wall Street Journal* publishes probably the most detailed and comprehensive security price quotations. Of daily city newspapers, the most comprehensive source is usually the *New York Times*.

has an annual dividend of \$0.25 per share which was raised on the latest declaration, giving the stock a **dividend yield** (dividend divided by current price) of 0.5 percent. Disney is currently selling for about 28 times its earnings, that is, it has a **price–earnings ratio** of about 28. The price quotation also tells us the number of shares traded on January 28, 1993, the highest and lowest prices at which the stock traded and its closing price on that date, and the change over the previous day's closing price.

The bond price quotations don't give quite as much detail as stock quotations, but they do provide some important information. The AT&T bond has an annual coupon rate of $8\frac{1}{8}$ percent. It matures in 2022, and has a **current yield** (coupon rate divided by price) of about 7.9 percent. The quote reveals that 508 bonds were traded on January 28 and the bond closed at a price of $103\frac{3}{8}$, down $\frac{1}{4}$ point from the prior day's closing price. This is a percentage of par value; a bond with a par value of \$1,000 was worth \$1,033.75 at the close of trading on January 28, 1993.

The price quotation for the Treasury security states the annual coupon rate ($7\frac{1}{2}$ percent), the maturity date (May 2002), and that the security was originally issued as a note. It gives the prices at which government bond dealers were willing to buy and sell the note, its change in price, and its current yield. The quotes reveal one difference between Treasury and corporate securities: prices of corporate bonds, like stock prices, change in $\frac{1}{8}$ point increments. (For a bond $\frac{1}{8}$ point equals 0.125 percent of par; for a stock $\frac{1}{8}$ point equals \$0.125 per share.) Treasury securities' prices change in $\frac{1}{32}$ point increments ($\frac{1}{32}$ of a point equals 0.03125 percent of par value, or 31.25 cents per \$1,000).

Ticker Symbols. While electronic readers have replaced ticker tape machines, all stocks, and many other securities, still have ticker symbols to save space in quotations. (Technically, ticker symbols are referred to as *trading symbols*.) All NYSE and AMEX stocks have one-, two-, or three-letter ticker symbols. NASDAQ-listed stocks have four-letter ticker symbols.[10] When a stock is first listed, the exchange assigns it a ticker symbol. Most ticker symbols are abbreviated versions of companies' names. For example, Apple Computer is APPL, Disney is DIS, Ford is F, Intel is INTC, Liz Claiborne is LIZ, Merck is MRK, and Wal-Mart is WMT. A few ticker symbols are somewhat more creative. Some examples include BUD (Anheuser-Busch), FON (Sprint), LUV (Southwest Airlines), and TOY (Toys Я Us).

Newspapers

Most daily newspapers report some business and economic news, though the quality and quantity of coverage can vary widely. Many daily papers, even in larger cities, tend to concentrate on local business news, but there are exceptions. The *New York Times,* for example, provides extensive, well-respected coverage of national business and economic news. Many investors prefer daily business newspapers for more in-depth financial information. Let's look at two examples.

The Wall Street Journal is arguably the best-known, most widely quoted business publication in the world. It is also one of the oldest. Founded in 1885, the *Journal* provides detailed coverage of business and economic news, both nationally and globally.[11] The paper carries extensive price quotations for

---

[10]NASDAQ-listed stocks that are divided between Class A and Class B shares have five-letter ticker symbols. For example, Oshkosh B'Gosh, the clothing maker, has both A and B shares listed on NASDAQ. Their respective ticker symbols are GOSHA and GOSHB.

[11]Dow Jones also publishes *The Asian Wall Street Journal* which focuses its coverage on news and information about businesses and countries in the Pacific Rim.

stocks, bonds, options, futures, and mutual funds. It also reports earnings announcements, dividend declarations, new product information, management changes, and so forth. The *Journal's* **"Heard on the Street"** column has been known to move stock prices.[12]

Barron's, like *The Wall Street Journal,* is published by Dow Jones & Company. *Barron's* is a weekly newspaper that covers a wide range of investment topics. A typical issue contains a review of the week's major business and economic developments, interviews with professional investors, recent analyst opinions on stocks, and columns on commodities, mutual funds, options, and so forth. *Barron's* also publishes thorough price quotations on all major types of investments, as well as detailed technical information. (We'll talk about technical analysis in Chapter 6.)

Periodicals

Dozens of periodicals seek to serve the information needs of investors. These include general-interest periodicals such as *Newsweek* and *Time,* business periodicals such as *Business Week* and *Fortune,* and international periodicals such as *The Economist.* All contain news and analysis of contemporary business and economic issues. The business periodicals tend to focus more narrowly on investing, providing articles on specific companies, consumer trends, economic forecasts, and so forth.

Trade periodicals may also interest certain investors. These publications of various trade associations provide in-depth coverage of specific industries and segments of the economy. Two examples of trade periodicals are *Air Transport World* and *Public Utilities Fortnightly.*

In addition to the general business press, some well-known periodicals deal more heavily with investments. *Money* magazine, published monthly, proclaims itself the magazine of personal finance. Its articles seek to explain how individuals can get better deals on such financial products as auto insurance and home mortgages, as well as the financial situations of specific families in a feature called "One Family's Finances." Each issue of *Money* also offers several articles on personal investing, covering the economic and market outlook, stocks to buy, stocks to avoid, where to put $1,000 now, etc. In each February issue, *Money* publishes extensive data on mutual fund performance. For small, individual investors, this is one of the best sources of information on mutual funds.[13]

Biweekly issues of *Forbes* contain several columns written for individual investors, often including specific investment recommendations. Of all the business- and investment-oriented periodicals, *Forbes* is perhaps the most aggressive pursuer of stories about investment rip-offs and wildly overpriced stocks. An example of this type of reporting occurred in 1987 when *Forbes* published a highly critical article about Home Shopping Network, the first of the cable TV shopping channels.[14] The article questioned not only the value of the company's stock price, which had risen from $3 to over $47 per share in less than a year, but also its accounting practices and the quality of the merchandise it sold. Soon after the article appeared, the Home Shopping bubble burst. By the end of 1987, the stock was down to about $7 per share.

---

[12]In 1985, R. Foster Winans, an author of many "Heard on the Street" columns, was charged with insider trading and subsequently convicted. He leaked information about companies to be mentioned in forthcoming columns to several stock traders, who were also convicted of insider trading. The parties split the proceeds from these trades.

[13]Most other business newspapers and periodicals also publish regular mutual fund information and analysis. *Barron's,* for example, devotes four issues per year primarily to mutual funds.

[14]See "Fabulous Fads that Fizzled?" *Forbes,* February 23, 1987, pp. 40–48.

Investment Advisory Services

To supplement published information, investors can consult private companies that specialize in providing investment information and advice. These include the large, well-known **financial information services** such as Standard & Poor's, brokerage firms like Merrill Lynch, and investment newsletters with names like *The Professional Tapereader.* The cost of these services varies. Many large public and college libraries offer at least some of these publications to patrons. Clients of brokerage firms may have access to some of this information free of charge. On the other hand, purchasing many of these services as an individual can be quite expensive. A yearly subscription to a typical newsletter costs between $200 and $300. An annual subscription to *The Outlook,* a publication of Standard & Poor's, costs $280. Any investor should carefully evaluate the cost and benefit of buying any of these publications.

Moody's and Standard & Poor's

Moody's Investors Service and Standard & Poor's (S&P) provide similar publications and information services covering a wide range of investment topics. Generally both Moody's and S&P tend to provide more objective information than subjective advice.

As one service, Moody's and S&P each publish basic reference volumes covering most public corporations. Moody's *Manuals* group company information by industry for banking, industrial, international, transportation, and public utility firms. These publications and S&P's *Corporation Reports* both provide detailed historical and current information on revenue, earnings, capitalization, major news developments, and so forth. Moody's and S&P update these reference volumes continuously throughout the year.[15] Both also publish regular reports on the economy and specific industries. S&P's two-volume *Industry Survey*s, for example, provide valuable industry information.

Moody's *Bond Survey* is another example of the many reports and publications of these advisory services. This weekly publication provides extensive information on and analysis of the bond market. A typical issue of the *Bond Survey* includes a list of new bond issues, data on interest rates, and bond ratings under review.

In addition to its *Corporation Reports,* S&P publishes *Stock Reports,* two-page summary reports on most public companies. Updated quarterly, these reports provide basic financial information (such as revenue, assets, dividends, etc.), as well as brief assessments of companies' future prospects. An S&P *Stock Report* on Disney is reprinted in Figure 4.5.

Earlier we mentioned another S&P weekly publication, *The Outlook.* Unlike *Stock Reports, The Outlook* tends to offer more subjective analysis of the financial markets and specific stocks. A typical issue might analyze conditions in the overall market ("Selective Buying Still Advised"), make changes in stock recommendations ("Stars Status"), and highlight special situations ("High Tech Favorites" and "Four Appealing Takeover Candidates").[16] Figure 4.6, on page 118, shows an example of the type of information found in *The Outlook.*

Value Line

One of best-known and most widely followed investment advisory services, Value Line, follows about 1,700 individual stocks in 98 industries. Each weekly report spotlights one or two industries, and the companies in those

---

[15]Moody's, for example, updates all but the international manual weekly.

[16]All of these articles appeared in the January 27, 1993 issue.

Figure 4.5

Sample Standard & Poor's *Stock Report*

Disney (Walt) 758M

NYSE Symbol DIS Options on ASE & CBOE (Jan-Apr-Jul-Oct) In S&P 500

Price	Range	P–E Ratio	Dividend	Yield	S&P Ranking	Beta
May 13'94	1994					
41⅝	48⅝–39⅝	29	0.30	0.7%	A	1.37

Summary

Earnings of this leading entertainment company have been hurt by losses related to the 49%-owned Euro Disney business. In addition to theme parks, DIS's businesses include filmed entertainment and consumer product operations. Long-term expansion may include a history-related theme park in Virginia.

Current Outlook

Including an adverse impact from the 49%-owned Euro Disney business, share earnings for the fiscal year ending September 30, 1994, are estimated at $2.00, up from fiscal 1993's $1.23, which included a large deficit relating to Euro Disney.

The quarterly dividend is being raised 20%, to $0.07½, effective with the May 1994 payment.

Profit from the theme park segment, which does not include Euro Disney, is expected to be restrained by relatively weak levels of international tourism. Filmed entertainment and consumer product earnings are each estimated to increase more than 15%. Expected adoption of a Euro Disney restructuring plan is viewed as favorable for long-term prospects, but is expected to reduce DIS's earnings by about $0.10 to $0.15 a share in fiscal 1994's second half.

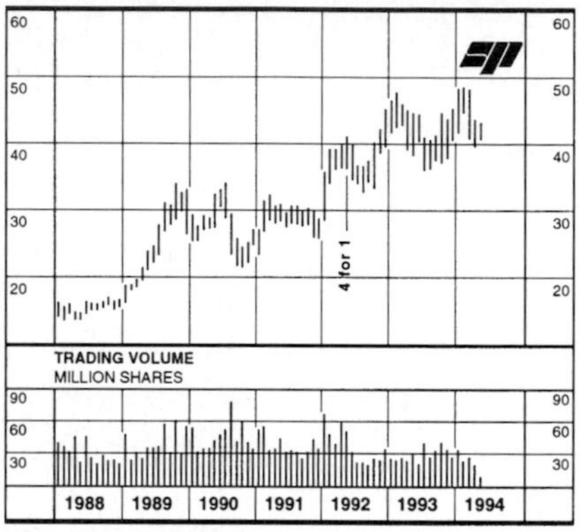

Revenues (Million $)

Quarter:	1993–94	1992–93	1991–92	1990–91
Dec.	2,727	2,391	1,916	1,492
Mar.	2,276	2,026	1,629	1,439
Jun.	---	1,937	1,883	1,512
Sep.	---	2,175	2,075	1,739
	---	8,529	7,504	6,182

Revenues in the six months ended March 31, 1994, increased 13%, year to year. Helped by a 28% rise in profit from filmed entertainment and the absence of a deficit related to the Euro Disney investment, net income rose 26% to $1.13 a share, from $0.90, which was before an unusual charge of $0.68.

Common Share Earnings ($)

Quarter:	1993–94	1992–93	1991–92	1990–91
Dec.	0.68	0.50	0.39	0.32
Mar.	0.45	0.39	0.31	0.24
Jun.	E0.40	0.48	0.41	0.31
Sep.	E0.47	d0.15	0.42	0.33
	E2.00	1.23	1.52	1.20

Important Developments

May '94— A plan to financially restructure the 49%-owned Euro Disney theme park business in France would include a large equity rights offering in which DIS would pay roughly $500 million for additional Euro Disney shares. This, and various other measures, would assist Euro Disney in easing cash flow pressure and improving profitability. The plan has been recommended by a bank committee, but had to be accepted by various lenders. If adopted, the plan is expected to have an adverse impact on DIS's earnings in the second half of fiscal 1994. Earlier, in fiscal 1993, DIS wrote down to zero the value of its earlier investment in Euro Disney. Also, Disney is planning to create a history-oriented theme park project, called Disney's America, in Prince William County, Virginia. The project could open as early as 1998.

Next earnings report expected in late July.

Per Share Data ($)

Yr. End Sep. 30	1993	1992	1991	1990	[1]1989	[1]1988	1987	1986	1985	[1]1984
Tangible Bk. Val.	**8.68**	8.24	6.80	5.96	4.95	4.21	[2]3.50	2.65	2.22	2.08
Cash Flow	**3.12**	2.94	2.69	2.48	2.12	1.57	1.40	0.97	0.66	0.32
Earnings[3]	**1.23**	1.52	1.20	1.50	1.28	0.95	0.71	0.46	0.32	0.04
Dividends[4]	**0.178**	0.193	0.160	0.133	0.110	0.095	0.080	0.079	0.075	0.075
Payout Ratio	**18%**	13%	13%	8%	8%	10%	11%	17%	23%	197%
Prices[5]—High	**48¾**	45¼	32½	34⅛	34⅛	17⅛	20⅝	13¾	7⅜	4 5/16
Low	**36**	28½	23⅜	21½	16¼	13½	10 5/16	7 1/16	3¾	2⅞
P/E Ratio—	**40–29**	39–19	27–20	23–14	27–13	18–14	29–14	30–15	23–12	NM

Data as orig. reptd. Adj. for stk. divs. of 300% in May 1992, 300% Mar. 1986. **1.** Reflects merger or acquisition. **2.** Includes intangibles. **3.** Bef. results of disc. ops. of +0.38 in 1987 and spec. item(s) of -0.68 in 1993, +0.53 in 1984. **4.** Dividends declared. **5.** Cal. yr. d-Deficit. E-Estimated. NM-Not Meaningful.

Standard NYSE Stock Reports
Vol. 61/No. 98/Sec. 14

May 20, 1994
Copyright © 1994 McGraw-Hill, Inc. All Rights Reserved

Standard & Poor's
25 Broadway, NY, NY 10004

industries. A new report is prepared on each company and industry approximately once every three months. While Value Line reports a great deal of objective information, most investors view it primarily as a source of subjective analysis.

Figure 4.7, on pages 120 and 121, reprints two Value Line reports: the industry report for the recreation industry and the company report on Disney, which Value Line places in the recreation industry.[17] The industry

[17]Value Line often classifies industries differently than Standard & Poor's, and different companies can appear in similarly named industry groupings between the two services.

Figure 4.5 continued

Sample Standard & Poor's *Stock Report*

758M   The Walt Disney Company

Income Data (Million $)

Year Ended Sep. 30	Revs.	Oper. Inc.	% Oper. Inc. of Revs.	Cap. Exp.	Depr.	Int. Exp.	[4]Net Bef. Taxes	Eff. Tax Rate	[5]Net Inc.	% Net Inc. of Revs.	Cash Flow
1993	8,529	2,589	30.4	814	1,028	184	1,074	37.5%	[3]671	7.9	1,700
1992	7,504	2,047	27.3	599	760	152	1,302	37.3%	817	10.9	1,576
1991	6,182	1,799	29.1	954	795	142	1,019	37.5%	637	10.3	1,431
1990	5,844	1,825	31.2	727	538	91	1,325	37.8%	824	14.1	1,362
[1]1989	4,594	1,573	34.2	785	464	76	1,153	39.0%	703	15.3	1,167
[1]1988	3,438	1,127	32.8	835	338	38	842	38.0%	522	15.2	860
[2]1987	2,877	1,083	37.7	319	377	53	726	46.0%	392	13.6	769
1986	2,471	784	31.7	187	281	69	462	46.5%	247	10.0	528
1985	2,015	474	23.5	189	113	88	310	44.0%	173	8.6	356
[1]1984	1,656	331	20.0	193	107	76	17	NM	22	1.3	182

Balance Sheet Data (Million $)

Sep. 30	Cash	Assets	Curr. Liab.	Ratio	Total Assets	% Ret. on Assets	Long Term Debt	Common Equity	Total Cap.	% LT Debt of Cap.	% Rct. on Equity
1993	363	NA	NA	NA	11,751	5.9	1,131	5,030	6,834	16.5	13.7
1992	765	NA	NA	NA	10,862	8.0	1,608	4,705	7,201	22.3	19.0
1991	886	NA	NA	NA	9,429	7.3	1,818	3,871	6,443	28.2	17.4
1990	820	NA	NA	NA	8,022	11.4	1,330	3,489	5,822	27.2	25.5
1989	381	NA	NA	NA	6,657	11.9	375	3,044	4,482	19.2	25.9
1988	428	NA	915	NA	5,109	11.7	424	2,359	3,371	12.6	24.7
1987	354	NA	642	NA	3,806	11.3	530	1,845	2,971	17.8	24.0
1986	70	NA	NA	NA	3,121	8.2	[6]547	1,419	2,484	22.0	18.9
1985	39	NA	NA	NA	2,897	6.3	[6]823	1,185	2,396	34.3	15.1
1984	35	NA	NA	NA	2,739	0.9	[6]862	1,155	2,296	37.5	1.7

Data as orig. reptd. **1.** Reflects merger or acquisition. **2.** Excl. disc. ops. **3.** Reflects accounting change. **4.** Incl. equity in earns. of nonconsol subs. **5.** Bef. results of disc. ops. and spec. items. **6.** Incl. current portion of long term debt. NM-Not Meaningful. NA-Not Available.

Business Summary

Walt Disney Co. (formerly Walt Disney Productions) is engaged in the ownership and operation of theme parks and related businesses, and is a major supplier of filmed entertainment. Business segment contributions in fiscal 1993 (excluding an adverse impact from the 49%-owned Euro Disney project) were:

	Revs.	Profits
Theme parks/resorts...........	40%	43%
Filmed entertainment..........	43%	36%
Consumer products............	17%	21%

Theme parks/resorts include Disneyland in Anaheim, Calif., and the Orlando, Fla.-based Walt Disney World Complex, which contains the Magic Kingdom and resort hotels, Walt Disney Village, Epcot (Environmental Prototype Community of Tomorrow) Center and the Disney-MGM Studio Theme Park (opened to the public in May 1989). In April 1992, the Euro Disney theme park complex (49% owned) opened near Paris, France. Euro Disney has been losing money, and a financial restructuring plan has been proposed. Tokyo Disneyland, which has been open since April 1983, is owned and operated by Oriental Land Co., Ltd., pursuant to a licensing agreement with the company. DIS also earns royalties on certain revenues generated by the Tokyo park.

Filmed entertainment consists of the production and distribution of motion pictures for the theatrical, television, cable and home video markets. Movie financing has come, in part, from limited partnerships. The company also creates TV programming, owns a pay cable TV service called The Disney Channel, and owns a Los Angeles television station. Consumer products include licensing of products, a growing chain of retail stores, and publishing activity. In addition, at December 31, 1993, Disney had cash and investments totaling $2.49 billion.

Dividend Data

Dividends have been paid since 1957.

Amt. of Divd. $	Date Decl.	Ex-divd. Date	Stock of Record	Payment Date
0.06¼	Jun. 28	Jul. 2	Jul. 9	Aug. 20'93
0.06¼	Sep. 27	Oct. 6	Oct. 13	Nov. 19'93
0.06¼	Nov. 22	Jan. 4	Jan. 10	Feb. 18'94
0.07½	Jan. 24	Apr. 11	Apr. 15	May 20'94

Capitalization

Total Debt: $2,654,400,000 (12/93)

Common Stock: 536,971,398 shs. ($0.025 par).
Institutions hold about 46%.
Shareholders of record: About 408,000.

Office—500 South Buena Vista St., Burbank, CA 91521. **Tel**—(818) 560-1000. **Chrmn, Pres & CEO**—M. D. Eisner. **SVP & CFO**—R. D. Nanula. **VP & Treas**—M. J. Montgomery. **Investor Contact**—W. M. Webb. **Dirs**—R. F. Bowers, R. E. Disney, M. D. Eisner, S. P. Gold, I. E. Lozano, Jr., R. A. Nunis, I. E. Russell, R. A. M. Stern, E. C. Walker, R. L. Watson, S. L. Williams, G. L. Wilson. **Transfer Agent & Registrar**—Co.'s office, North Hollywood, Cal. **Incorporated** in California in 1938; reincorporated in Delaware in 1987. **Empl**—62,000.

Information has been obtained from sources believed to be reliable, but its accuracy and completeness are not guaranteed.   Tom Graves, CFA

Source: *Stock Report,* 59, no. 187, Standard & Poor's, May 20, 1994, section 12, no. 758M. Reprinted with permission of Standard & Poor's, a division of McGraw-Hill Inc.

---

report provides some basic operating and financial data for the industry (combining historical data with Value Line's forecasts), a discussion of results from the prior year, an assessment of prospects for the next couple of years, and some investment advice. When the report on the recreation industry was written, Value Line did not rank it as especially attractive, but Value Line did like some of the stocks in the industry.

In the company report on Disney, Value Line provided 15 years of historical financial and operating statistics, along with estimates for the next few years. In addition, Value Line reports recent institutional and insider buy/

Figure 4.6

Sample from *The Outlook*

STARS: STOCK APPRECIATION RANKING SYSTEM

STARS PERFORMANCE

CHANGES FOR 4/29 THROUGH 5/5

RISING STARS

NEW RANKING	OLD RANKING
★★★★★	★★★★

Harcourt General/H—Diversified company's efforts to restructure retail store operations should boost earnings.

★★★★	★★★

Comsat/CQ—Shares of satellite communications company attractive following 20% price drop.

Gundle Environmental Systems/GUN—Maker of landfill liners well-positioned for growth in Europe as economy improves and stricter regulations take effect.

Kennametal/KMT—Maker of hard metal tools to benefit from growth in U.S. economy and recovery in Europe.

Watts Industries/WATTA—Maker of valves used in plumbing and heating to show good earnings growth this year, aided by acquisitions.

Williams Companies/WMB—LDDS Communications has offered $2 billion for this gas pipeline company's digital telecommunications network.

★★★	★★

CIGNA Corp./CI—Although insurer posted better-than-expected first-quarter earnings, shares are fairly valued now.

Eastman Kodak/EK—Planned divestitures should boost support for shares. See page 2.

Itel Corp./ITL—Although rail car lessor's shares are somewhat more attractive following price decline, they remain richly valued at more than 30 times estimated 1994 earnings.

★★★	★

Syntex Corp./SYN—Shares of pharmaceutical company now trading at close to $24 offer from Roche Holdings.

Viacom/VIA—Prospect of asset sales should provide a floor under shares of this entertainment giant.

★★	★

Alien Group/ALN—Although maker of electronics products faces higher taxes and slower growth rate, the market has already taken much of this into account.

FALLING STARS

★★★★	★★★★★

Designs, Inc./DESI—Specialty retailer's first-quarter results hurt by truckers' strike. See some near-term weakness in shares on market overreaction.

★★★	★★★★

Recognition International/REC—Although we still like the stock of this document handling company long term, near term it could be just an average performer as order delays and distribution problems slow earnings growth.

★★	★★★★

Paco Pharmaceuticals/PACO—Increased competition in store-brand over-the-counter remedies to hurt sales and profits.

Worthington Foods/WFDS—Company facing tougher competition in selling its vegetarian foods to supermarkets.

★	★★

Western Publishing/WPGI—Publisher of children's books facing continuing losses that could force additional asset sales.

STARS VS. THE MARKET 1/1/87 to 4/30/94

5-STARS	$39,442
4-STARS	$24,346
NASDAQ	$21,038
	$19,419 DOW JONES INDUS.
S&P 500	$18,620
3-STARS	$18,454
AMEX	$16,709
2-STARS	$15,802
1-STARS	$5,501

MARKET VALUE APRIL 30, 1994 OF $10,000 INVESTED ON JANUARY 1,1987

Performance results of the 5, 4, 3, 2 and 1 STARS stock groups have been calculated using standard time-weighted performance formulae. Since such results are exclusive of transaction costs, dividend income and subscription costs to The Outlook, the actual results obtained by investors may be different. Because recommendations are made with the intent of maximizing gains in the case of 5 STARS and identifying well below average performance in the case of 1 STARS, the volatility of these groups is likely to be higher than that of the 4, 3 and 2 STARS groups, as well as higher than that of the S&P 500 Index. There is no assurance that any future 5 STARS recommendations will be profitable, and you should understand that such recommendations do not take into account a subscriber's personal circumstances, such as tolerance for risk, investment goals or access to investment capital. A complete list of the recommendations set forth in The Outlook in the last year is available upon request.

FIVE-STARS STOCKS IN THE NEWS

H&R BLOCK indicated last week that it expects to report record earnings for fiscal 1994 (ended April 30). The company said that its tax services unit's worldwide fee volume increased 2.3% as it processed 4.1% more returns. U.S. tax return volume rose 0.7%, while electronic filings increased 1.8%. We are keeping our fiscal 1994 earnings estimate at $1.90 a share vs. fiscal 1993's $1.68. For the current fiscal year, we look for profits of $2.25 a share. The Master List issue (HRB, 43, NYSE) should outpace the market in the months ahead.

SOUTHWEST AIRLINES slid last week on news that the low-cost carrier would be bumped from some computer reservations systems. We think that the market overreacted, since the systems involved account for only a small part of the airline's business. Despite increasing competition, we believe Southwest will continue its strong growth and should earn $1.45 this year vs. 1993's $1.05. The company reported a 15.7% increase in traffic for April. The Master List shares (LUV, 27, NYSE) are a good choice for long-term capital appreciation.

Source: *The Outlook,* Standard & Poor's, a division of McGraw-Hill, May 11, 1994.

sell decisions and a detailed breakdown of the company's capital structure. The report also commented on Disney's current situation and future prospects.

Many users of Value Line rely on several summary measures. Two especially important numbers appear in the upper left-hand corners of its company reports: timeliness (probable price performance in the next 12 months) and safety (probable safety in the future). To develop its timeliness ranking, Value Line uses a computer model to rank each of the 1,700 or so stocks it follows, with higher ranks indicating better investment potential. The service assigns ranks of 1 and 5 to the top 100 and bottom 100 stocks, respectively. Ranks of 2 and 4 identify the next 300 stocks from the top and bottom, respectively. The remaining, middle group of about 900 stocks get timeliness ranks of 3.[18]

Brokerage Firms

In Chapter 3 we discussed the difference between full-service brokerage firms, such as Merrill Lynch, and discount firms, such as Charles Schwab. Other than their commission rates, the major difference between the two is the full-service firm's offer of investment advice and information.[19] All full-service firms, for example, maintain lists of stocks that they recommend. Brokers at full-service firms often use some of the sources we've already discussed (S&P and Value Line, for example). Often, however, they rely more on reports prepared by their firms' analysts.

Every major full-service brokerage firm employs a group of security analysts, each of whom concentrates on specific industries and/or stocks. Each major firm, for example, has at least one analyst who follows Disney. Brokerage firms also employ economists, market strategists, technical analysts, bond market analysts, and so forth, in order to fully serve their clients. The data disk includes an actual security analysis report on Wal-Mart Stores (file name WMT.TXT). We'll discuss the report in more detail in Chapters 10 and 11. Furthermore, all large full-service brokerage firms now follow international as well as domestic investment issues.

Analysts prepare periodic reports on the companies or industries they follow, and they keep constant tabs on major developments and news. For example, an analyst may obtain some new information that leads him or her to reduce earnings estimates, and/or change the recommendation on the stock from "buy" to "hold." Brokerage reports look much like the reports that come from S&P or Value Line.

Mutual Fund Rating Services

Several investment advisory services follow mutual funds almost exclusively. Three of the most firmly established mutual fund rating services are CDA/Wisenberger, Lipper Analytical Services, and Morningstar.[20] In 1993, Value Line began offering a mutual fund rating service similar to the company's well-respected stock rating service. Mutual fund rating services all present objective information and historical results for mutual funds; some also make subjective recommendations.

An example of a report from a mutual fund rating service, a report from Morningstar on the Fidelity Balanced Fund, appears in Figure 4.8 on page 122.[21] This report blends objective and subjective information. As you'd

---

[18]Value Line claims, with the support of some independent studies, that its ranking system has produced above-average returns in the past.

[19]The *quality* of this advice will be examined later, especially in Chapter 6. Remember that brokerage firms do not make their money by providing information or advice. All brokerage firms make most of their money on the commissions they charge customers to buy and sell securities, which cost the same amount, regardless of investment performance.

[20]As we mentioned earlier, *Money* magazine (along with other business publications) publishes regular mutual fund information and analysis. Organizations such as Lipper Analytical Services provide much of the data to these publications.

[21]A balanced fund owns a mix of stocks and bonds (government and corporate), which the fund manager changes in anticipation of market moves. Most balanced funds keep at least 30 percent of their total assets in bonds or stocks, regardless of the market environment.

Figure 4.7

Sample Value Line Industry and Company Reports

March 4, 1994   **RECREATION**   **1751**   3

Most companies in the Recreation Industry reported better results for 1993 than the year before. For those with problems last year, chances for recovery in 1994 are good.

Europe's recession remains a snag for the companies heavily involved there. For some, strong business in the Far East is a favorable offset.

The entertainment side of this Value Line group has been lightened by mergers with companies in other industries. But there are many providers of active diversions to replace them.

The Recreation Industry currently is a good place to look for timely investment ideas.

Accent On Activity

The composition of Value Line's Recreation Industry is changing dramatically. In keeping with the growing importance the public is placing on health and fitness, the mix of companies in this group increasingly emphasizes active forms of recreation. The shift is not altogether a matter of editorial selection, however. Rather, it largely reflects the historical attractiveness of entertainment companies, particularly film studios, to corporate empire builders. In years past, it was the fashion for domestic conglomerates to round out their horizontal expansions by adding a movie distributor. Often lacking any synergies, the mergers were not always a roaring success.

In recent years, the combinations have generally made more economic sense. Japanese giants in home electronics, for example, had sound reasons for wanting captive producers of entertainment software. Accordingly, prosperous companies like Sony and Matsushita averted any competing U.S. bids when they offered to buy Columbia Pictures and MCA, with its Universal Studios, at Japanese-type price-earnings multiples. Business considerations appeared to predominate as well in the recent acquisition of New Line Cinema by Turner Broadcasting. And, while a bidding contest may have made the payoff more distant, Viacom is arguably a stronger contender for the interactive multimedia future as a result of its move to combine with *Paramount* and Blockbuster.

Already a fully synergistic entertainment powerhouse, the route *Disney* prefers to take generally is expansion or duplication of existing operations. Even here, there is an alertness to opportunities to acquire

unusual talent, as in the absorption of the noted independent film producer, Miramax. Early in his business career as a successful animator and producer of films, Walt Disney recognized the opportunity to endow other endeavors with value based on the fame of his characters. The success of Disneyland and Walt Disney World affirm the accuracy of his foresight. The formula has worked well enough at Tokyo Disneyland to inspire the Euro Disney project in France. In the depressed European economy, however, this enterprise has encountered more than ordinary start-up problems. The parent does not lack the capability to make Euro Disney a paying venture, but a return to European prosperity seems to be a prerequisite.

In contradistinction to the passive nature of filmed entertainment, the *Disney* theme parks offer active physical involvement. The audience has to get up off the couch and go somewhere, and people are generally inclined to make the effort. If the original motivation was just to please the kids, the addition of attractions like Epcot Center plus cabaret entertainment and golf now offer adult diversion as well.

Other companies in this industry take more specific aim at fulfilling the desire for active recreation. Both *Brunswick* and *Outboard Marine*, which fell on hard times in the aftermath of an unsustainable worldwide powerboat buying binge in the late 1980s, appear to be in a recovery mode. Restructurings have lowered their break-even points and reduced their former reliance on Europe as a significant source of income. Domestic economic indicators like personal income and durable goods orders foretell much better times ahead for these boat makers, which their operating reports will confirm only after some lag.

Less volatile in recession are the recreation companies that don't sell equipment but emphasize vacation activity farther from home. New in this edition is *Royal Caribbean Cruises*, which is vying for a share of the much bigger cruise market it and *Carnival Cruise Lines* both envision in their ambitious construction plans.

Investment Advice

The recreation group stands comparatively high on the list of industries in order of Timeliness Rank. The specifics by company are on the pages that follow.

Edmund B. Swort, CFA

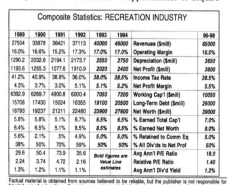

Composite Statistics: RECREATION INDUSTRY								
1989	1990	1991	1992	1993	1994			96-98
27504	33878	36421	37113	40000	46000	Revenues ($mill)		65000
16.0%	16.6%	15.2%	17.3%	17.0%	17.0%	Operating Margin		16.5%
1290.2	2032.6	2194.1	2173.7	2550	2750	Depreciation ($mill)		3650
1193.6	1255.3	1077.6	1910.9	2020	2400	Net Profit ($mill)		3600
41.2%	40.9%	38.9%	36.0%	38.0%	38.5%	Income Tax Rate		38.5%
4.3%	3.7%	3.0%	5.1%	5.1%	5.2%	Net Profit Margin		5.5%
6392.9	6269.7	4900.8	6000.4	7050	7200	Working Cap'l ($mill)		10050
15708	17430	15024	16355	19100	20500	Long-Term Debt ($mill)		26000
18793	19237	21211	22480	23900	27600	Net Worth ($mill)		39000
5.8%	5.8%	5.1%	6.7%	6.5%	6.5%	% Earned Total Cap'l		7.0%
6.4%	6.5%	5.1%	8.5%	8.5%	8.5%	% Earned Net Worth		9.0%
5.6%	2.1%	.5%	4.9%	5.0%	5.0%	% Retained to Comm Eq		5.0%
38%	50%	70%	59%	50%	50%	% All Div'ds to Net Prof		50%
29.6	50.4	73.9	35.6	*Bold figures are*		Avg Ann'l P/E Ratio		18.0
2.24	3.74	4.72	2.16	*Value Line*		Relative P/E Ratio		1.40
1.3%	1.2%	1.1%	1.1%	*estimates*		Avg Ann'l Div'd Yield		1.2%

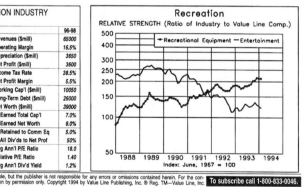

Recreation
RELATIVE STRENGTH (Ratio of Industry to Value Line Comp.)
← Recreational Equipment — Entertainment
Index: June, 1967 = 100

expect, it contains extensive information on the fund's historical performance (both in absolute terms and relative to several benchmarks, such as the S&P 500 and the average for all balanced funds). The Morningstar report also contains information on the fund's expenses, portfolio turnover, portfolio composition, and so forth. It also comments on the fund's recent performance and its prospects for the future.

Newsletters

Investors can subscribe to dozens of **investment newsletters.** Some of the better-known newsletters include *The Zweig Forecast, The Prudent Speculator, The*

Figure 4.7 continued

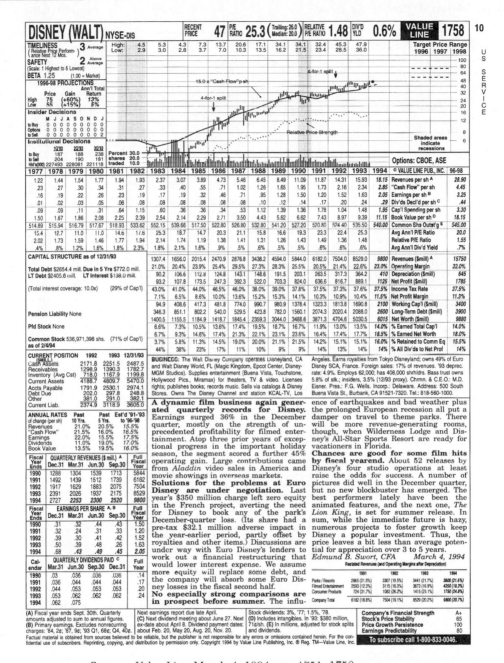

Source: *Value Line*, March 4, 1994, pp. 1751, 1758.

Chartist, and *Elliott Wave Theorist*. Newsletters provide subjective analysis and opinion rather than objective information. Newsletters tell investors what they should buy, what they should avoid (or sell), whether to hold stocks or cash, and so forth. Many, though not all, newsletters rely on technical analysis to make their investment recommendations.

One of the most famous newsletter recommendations in recent years was Joe Granville's warning on the evening of Sunday, January 6, 1981 to subscribers of his newsletter, *The Granville Market Letter*, to sell everything. The next morning, brokerage firms were swamped with sell orders and the Dow Jones Industrial Average dropped 24 points during the first couple of hours of trading, representing paper losses of over $40 billion. Unfortunately for

Figure 4.8

Sample Mutual Fund Report

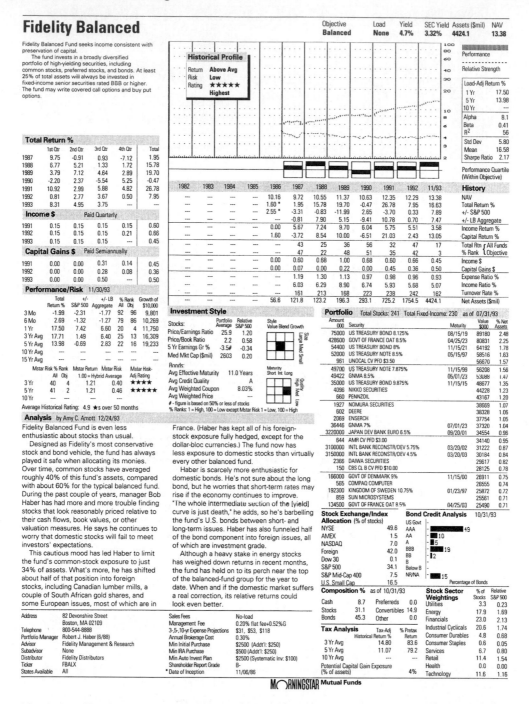

Source: *Morningstar Newsletter,* August 20, 1994, p. 774. *Morningstar Mutual Funds,* MORNINGSTAR, INC., 255 W. Wacker, Chicago, IL 60606.

followers of Granville, this probably represented the peak of his forecasting prowess. Granville was consistently pessimistic throughout the 1980s, and those who followed his advice missed the greatest bull market in history.

Mark Hulbert, editor of the *Hulbert Financial Digest* and a regular contributor to *Forbes,* follows the performance of investment newsletters. According to Hulbert, most newsletters have, at best, mediocre track records. A recent analysis showed that the investment recommendations of only 16 percent of the newsletters he follows (14 out of 88) were able to beat the performance of a broad stock market average (the Wilshire 5,000) over recent one- and five-year periods.[22]

Computer-Based Information Sources

One of the most significant developments in recent years has been the growth of computer-based sources of investment information. These allow computer users to access large information databases without having to go to the library or turn a page. Computer-based sources can be divided into two groups: on-line services and historical databases. An on-line service connects the user's computer to the service's computer to give access to its databases and information. Historical databases provide users with financial information on disks or computer tapes, updated periodically.

Traditional Computer Databases

Several computer databases have been around for a number of years. Many universities and large institutions subscribe to these databases, which require mainframe computers. COMPUSTAT, a service of Standard & Poor's, maintains a body of historical financial information on thousands of companies, as well as industry and economic data. It can provide either annual data, going back up to 20 years, or quarterly data, going back up to 20 quarters.

Another established computer database is CRSP, developed by the Center for Research in Security Prices at the University of Chicago.[23] CRSP produces computer tapes, updated annually, that report monthly and daily historical security price returns on approximately 5,000 NYSE, AMEX, and over-the-counter stocks. Dividends and closing prices are also included. Some of the series go back as far as 1926.

PC Services

Obviously few investors can afford COMPUSTAT or CRSP, since subscriptions to both cost between $5,000 and $15,000 annually, and they require access to a mainframe computer. Frankly, very few investors *need* the detailed information available from COMPUSTAT or CRSP. Today, the personal computer is an excellent alternative. Over the last few years, personal computers have become very sophisticated, employing valuable new technologies, such as CD-ROM. The growth of personal computer use has spawned a number of reasonably priced computer services that provide both on-line and historical data access for PC users. Let's look at a few examples.

Three popular on-line services, Prodigy, CompuServe, and America Online offer a number of investment services, including current stock and bond price quotations, investment news, and so forth. Both services allow users to actually trade securities through on-line brokerage services. CompuServe also offers historical price data, company financial statements, and earnings estimates. It allows users to screen companies and mutual funds on the basis of several criteria that they specify. CompuServe gives users the ability to graph technical indicators, as well.

---

[22]Source: *The Wall Street Journal,* February 3, 1993, p. C1.

[23]Many academic research articles on investments have been based on data from the COMPUSTAT or CRSP databases.

Another on-line service, the Dow Jones News Retrieval Service (DJNRS), dedicates itself to financial news. The DJNRS stores a vast amount of current and historical information; users can access articles from *The Wall Street Journal* and *Barron's,* read about breaking news, and obtain current security price quotations. Users also have access to historical economic and financial data, as well as forecasts of current earnings for over 2,400 companies. On-line services do require a modem and cost depends on usage.

In addition to the on-line services, a number of discount brokerage firms sell software that allows customers to buy and sell securities, and to access some limited news services. *The Equalizer,* from Charles Schwab's Electronic Brokerage Service, is an example of such software.

Some other PC databases are not on-line; they provide users with information and data on disk. These services include Value Screen Plus (sold by Value Line) and Compact Disclosure (sold by Standard & Poor's). Value Screen Plus contains basic Value Line variables on all 1,700 or so stocks the service follows. The software allows users to screen the Value Line database by several criteria (e.g., timeliness rankings) or to create model portfolios. Data from Value Screen Plus can also be input to several popular spreadsheet programs. Subscribers to Value Screen Plus can receive updated disks monthly, quarterly, or annually.

Compact Disclosure comes in the form of a compact disc, so a user needs a CD-ROM drive. Compact discs, of course, hold far more data than regular diskettes. Compact Disclosure provides detailed financial and company information on more than 12,000 companies, updated monthly, including annual reports, SEC filings, proxy statements, and so forth.

Financial Planning Software

In addition to all this information, a PC user can take advantage of a number of software programs to find help managing investments. An example of this type of software is *Wealthbuilder* by *Money* magazine. This program is designed to help an individual investor understand his or her current financial situation, establish realistic goals, and formulate investment strategies using a portfolio allocation model. *Wealthbuilder* also supports evaluation of investment alternatives using its database of information about mutual funds, stocks, and bonds and to track the performance of a portfolio.[24]

Other popular money and investment management programs include *Managing Your Money, Microsoft Money,* and *Quicken.* All three allow users to pay bills electronically, track investments, compile tax information, and so forth. These software programs, however, rely primarily on user-provided data.

Chapter Summary

1. **Review the sources of statistical data on the economy.**

   A variety of government and private organizations compile and publish economic data. Most of these sources provide objective data and information rather than subjective opinions and analysis. Several U.S. government publications provide extensive current and historical data on aspects of the U.S. economy like industrial production, housing starts, inflation, and interest rates; some specialized U.S. government publications concentrate on specific segments of the economy such as energy and transportation. International agencies (e.g., the United Nations) compile current and historical economic data on economies throughout the world.

---

[24]*Wealthbuilder*'s database contains historical information on approximately 1,200 mutual funds, 4,000 stocks, and 6,000 bonds. Data are updated annually by subscription.

Additional economic data are available from nongovernment sources such as financial institutions, investment firms, financial markets, trade associations, and so forth.

2. **Identify the types of investment information provided by newspapers and periodicals.**

   Many investors get most of their information, including stock and bond quotations, from newspapers and periodicals. Newspapers and periodicals can be classified as general-interest, specialized business, or trade publications. Trade publications provide detailed coverage of specific industries or segments of the economy that may interest small groups of investors. While general-interest newspapers and periodicals often contain some business and economic information, investors often read specialized business and economic publications to get more in-depth news. Investors can refer to specialized business newspapers *(The Wall Street Journal* and *Barron's)* and business periodicals *(Money* magazine and *Forbes).*

3. **Understand the types of information provided by investment advisory services.**

   Investors have access to a wealth of information from many private companies that specialize in providing investment information and advice. Some of this information can be obtained free, or at low cost, through libraries or brokerage firms. Publications from Moody's and Standard & Poor's provide information on a wide variety of investment topics such as the overall economy, specific industries, companies, and bonds. Another well-known investment advisory service, Value Line, follows about 1,700 individual stocks and 98 industries, providing historical information and forecasts. Value Line ranks stocks and industries on the basis of their expected future performance. Full-service brokerage firms provide still more investment information, along with analysis and advice, to their clients. Finally, mutual fund rating services (such as Morningstar) and investment newsletters offer information on their chosen topics. Newsletters tend to be quite expensive and should always be considered sources of subjective analysis and opinion rather than objective information.

4. **Review computer-based sources of investment information.**

   One of the most significant developments in investing in recent years has been the growth of computer-based sources of investment information. These sources can be classified as either on-line services or historical databases. On-line services connect users' computers directly to the services' computers to give access to databases and information. Historical databases provide users with tapes or computer disks, which are updated periodically. Traditional historical databases, such as COMPUSTAT and CRSP, require mainframe computers and are very expensive. As microcomputer technology has developed, PC databases (such as Compact Disclosure and Value Screen Plus) have emerged to offer excellent alternatives. Some popular on-line services include America Online CompuServe, the Dow Jones News Retrieval Service, and Prodigy. In addition, software is available that allows investors to actually buy and sell securities via communications links. Finally, we briefly examined some of the financial planning software currently available.

Key Terms

Objective information source	Price–earnings ratio
Subjective information source	Current yield
Security market index	"Heard on the Street"
Gross domestic product (GDP)	Investment advisory service
Dividend yield	Investment newsletter

Discussion Questions and Problems

1. What are the differences between objective and subjective sources of information? Do most sources of economic data provide objective or subjective information?

2. List two sources of economic data. Are these sources general or specialized in their coverage?

3. List the information you can obtain from a stock price quotation found in *The Wall Street Journal*. If *pf* follows the name of a company, what does it mean?

4. Why do many investors rely on business newspapers or magazines, in addition to general-interest publications? Give a couple of examples of business magazines.

5. What is a trade publication? Why would an investor be interested in reading a trade publication?

6. Compare and contrast Standard & Poor's and Value Line. Which of the two is considered to be more subjective?

7. What are investment newsletters? How do they differ from other sources of investment information?

8. Computer-based sources of investment information can be divided into two general categories. What are they? Give an example of each.

Critical Thinking Exercise

1. This exercise requires library research. Below is a list of ten data items. For each item, identify an information source, collect the most recent data you can find, and answer any questions asked. In addition, speculate on who might be interested in knowing more about each item.

   a. Breakdown of Canadian GDP (gross domestic product) into the four major components (private consumption, net exports, government spending, and private investment).

   b. Japanese and U.S. savings rates. Collect the most recent year's data and data for 1985. Be sure to define *savings rate*.

   c. Distribution of U.S. population by age group and projected change in each age group by 2000.

   d. Performance of the T. Rowe Price International mutual fund from 1985 through the most recent year.

   e. U.S. retail sales (seasonally adjusted and not seasonally adjusted). Obtain overall data and sales for specific types of retailers (such as discount stores).

   f. Revenue, operating expenses, and net income of U.S. electric and gas utilities (overall industry data). Collect the most recent year's data and data for 1985.

   g. Stock price index for the computer industry from 1985 through the most recent year. Be sure to specify how the computer industry is defined.

   h. Exchange rates between the U.S. dollar and the Japanese yen, and the U.S. dollar and the German mark from 1985 through the most recent year.

   i. Earnings and dividends for The Gap from 1985 through the most recent year. Could you construct a total return index using these data?

   j. Projection of earnings for The Gap for next year. Why are The Gap's earnings expected to rise or fall?

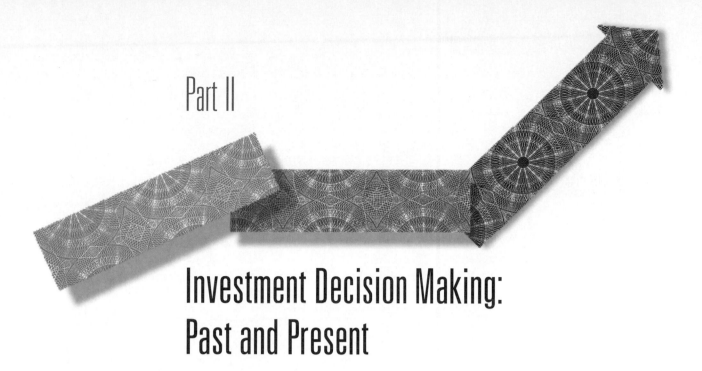

Part II

Investment Decision Making: Past and Present

Part II is devoted to a discussion of investment decision making, both past and present. We believe it is important to understand how investors make decisions, and perhaps how they *should* make these decisions. We begin by presenting a series of stories of past situations where asset prices rose almost irrationally for limited periods of time, only to come crashing back down; these are speculative bubbles. Some of these bubble stories occurred many years ago, but some are much more recent. Bubbles help illustrate the human side of investing. Next we examine technical and fundamental analysis, two techniques professional investors rely on to make investment decisions. Technical analysts believe that past market behavior repeats itself in predictable trends. Fundamental analysis is based on the notion that every security has an intrinsic value that can be estimated, and, in the long run, price will equal intrinsic value. We show how to apply these techniques, and whether they really work. Finally, we review the concept of market efficiency. We try both to determine whether the financial markets are efficient and to understand what market efficiency implies for investment selection and analysis.

Chapter 5

A Brief History of
Investment and Speculation

Chapter Objectives

1. Provide some historical background for investing and investments.
2. Examine some of Europe's most infamous speculative bubbles.
3. Review some of the speculative bubbles that occurred in the United States early in this century.
4. Examine several postwar speculative bubbles from the United States market.
5. Answer several important questions about speculative bubbles.

Writing in 1932, after witnessing an extraordinary period in American history, the legendary financier and investor Bernard Baruch wrote:

> I have always thought that if, in the lamentable era of the "New Economics," culminating in 1929, even in the very presence of dizzily spiraling prices, we had all continuously repeated, "two and two still makes four," much of evil might have been averted.[1]

Baruch was writing, of course, about the **speculative bubble** commonly referred to as the Great 1929 Stock Market Crash. After soaring between early 1928 and October 1929, the stock market proceeded to lose almost 90 percent of its value over the next three years.

We believe that contemporary investors can learn a great deal from the 1929 crash, as well as the many other speculative bubbles that have littered investment history. Much of this chapter is devoted to a series of stories and vignettes describing some of history's most spectacular speculative bubbles involving such diverse assets as tulip bulbs and biotech stocks. Some of these bubbles involved new commodities, while others involved established investments; some involved assets of questionable quality (even outright frauds), while others involved more legitimate investments; some of the assets that rode speculative bubbles eventually recovered, while others never did.

You may find many of these stories quite amusing. You may even wonder, in retrospect, how seemingly intelligent, rational people could get involved

---

[1]Bernard Baruch, foreword to the 1932 edition of Charles Mackay, *Extraordinary Popular Delusions and the Madness of Crowds* (Boston: L. C. Page, 1932).

in the madness. Certainly, *you* would have avoided these scenes of mass hysteria! Unfortunately, history teaches that speculative bubbles can be difficult to avoid, occur repeatedly, and will likely always be part of the investment landscape.

This chapter begins with some basic historical background on the development of investments. Next, we turn our attention to three of Europe's most infamous speculative bubbles that occurred before 1800. Speculative bubbles in the United States early this century receive our attention next. Then we examine some postwar bubbles from the United States. We conclude the chapter by trying to answer several important questions concerning speculative bubbles, such as what causes them and why they seem certain to reoccur.

Historical Background

Mortgage-backed bonds, the NASDAQ stock market, the SEC, and mutual funds are all very familiar to contemporary investors. Remember, however, that none of them have been around that long. The SEC wasn't founded until the early 1930s. The NASDAQ stock market and mortgage-backed bonds weren't born until the early 1970s. Mutual funds have been around since 1924, but they really didn't enter mainstream American life until the late 1970s.

In fact, investing itself, as a legitimate, organized human endeavor, doesn't have a very long history.[2] Investing is an outgrowth of economic development and the maturation of modern capitalism. About three centuries ago the world economy featured no stock exchanges or bond markets to speak of, and only a handful of banks. The Bank of England, for example, wasn't founded until 1694. It is considered to be history's first modern bank because it was the first institution empowered to accept deposits, issue notes to serve as paper money, make loans, and **discount bills.**[3]

The London Stock Exchange, the first recognizable **stock exchange,** or **bourse,** was also chartered in 1694.[4] Stock markets were established in most other economically advanced countries over the next 100 years or so. (The ancestor of the New York Stock Exchange, for example, was founded in 1792.) Both the Bank of England and the London Stock Exchange were initially distrusted, and even despised, by many in English society. As recently as the middle of the last century, the London Stock Exchange was a struggling weakling, often threatened with extinction by Parliament. (We'll discuss some possible reasons for this a little later.)

The notion of individuals pooling their capital in an organized fashion to jointly finance and own a business venture is also a fairly new concept. Though there is some evidence of **joint-stock associations** in ancient Rome, the evolution of common stock, as we know it, didn't start until the European

---

[2]Ancient history does provide examples of transactions that contemporary investors would probably recognize. The ancient Greek philosopher Thales is reported to have speculated on olive presses. Prior to one year's harvest, thinking it to be especially large, Thales is said to have cornered the market for olive presses, later selling them to olive growers at a handsome profit.

[3]To *discount a bill* meant to buy a promissory note at less than its face value. The term has survived. Recall, for example, that Treasury bills and commercial paper are sold to investors at varying discounts.

[4]Prior to the establishment of the London Stock Exchange, a number of *bourses,* or financial markets, had operated. The first was founded in Antwerp in 1531. These bourses weren't, strictly speaking, stock exchanges. Rather, they were continuous fairs where dealings in commodities, bills of exchange, and insurance took place.

commercial revolution that sprang from the Renaissance. Joint-stock companies were first organized in Europe to finance sea voyages, exploration, and trade.[5] A joint-stock company proved to be an efficient organizational form in which to provide the large capital needs, and distribute the risks, that these voyages entailed. The historical evidence suggests that the Dutch East India Company, founded in 1602, was the first corporation established with permanent capital stock.[6] The idea of transferring shares from individual to individual soon followed. However, general incorporation laws, and the notion of limited liability that protected stockholders from responsibility for all of a corporation's debts, weren't firmly established in either Europe or the United States until the mid-19th century.

Less than a century ago, stock manipulation and insider trading were neither illegal nor uncommon in the United States. During 1929, for example, more than 100 issues traded on the NYSE were subject to active pool, or syndicate, operations which involved overt manipulation of stock prices by members of the exchange.[7] Wildly overpriced, even fraudulent, securities were bought and sold openly, with little fanfare or government interference. In 1901, U.S. Steel is reported to have raised $1.4 billion in capital, including more than $500 million in common stock, supported by at least $700 million of intangible, even fictitious, assets.[8]

Prior to the 1920s, those who thought of themselves as investors generally owned bonds to assure income and safety of principal. Only a few firms' stocks qualified as investment-grade securities. These consisted mostly of bank and insurance stocks, which were unlisted, backed by real capital, and could expect to raise dividends regardless of the economic environment. The stocks traded on the NYSE were generally considered to be speculative in nature. Railroads, for example, simply carried too much debt to be considered *investments*. It wasn't until the 1920s that common stocks matured as investment vehicles.[9]

Few Americans owned any securities, however, much less any common stocks, in the early part of this century. Even in the speculative frenzy that preceded the 1929 stock market crash, probably no more than 3 million individuals out of a population of around 122 million actually owned any shares of common stock.[10] This fact contradicts the popular view that millions of ordinary Americans were playing the stock market in the late 1920s. Some historians doubt that the crash, in fact, caused, or even contributed significantly to, the Great Depression.[11]

Stock ownership, and investing in general, weren't common in American households until after the end of World War II. In 1952, 6.5 million individuals owned stocks (about 4 percent of the population). By 1970, that number

---

[5]One of the first recognizable joint-stock firms in Europe, the Mahona in northern Italy, openly engaged in piracy!

[6]Early joint-stock companies were usually formed to finance specific sea voyages and then disbanded following the ends of the voyages.

[7]See J. K. Galbraith, *The Great Crash of 1929* (Boston: Houghton-Mifflin, 1954), pp. 84–85. Today, this practice is illegal.

[8]See L. Lowenstein, *What's Wrong with Wall Street* (Reading, Mass.: Addison-Wesley, 1988), p. 16.

[9]Edgar Smith was one of the first to show that stocks had outperformed bonds over varying periods between 1866 and 1922, often by substantial margins, and were less risky than commonly believed. See Edgar Smith, *Common Stocks as Long-Term Investments* (New York: Macmillan, 1924).

[10]The estimate of 3 million shareholders was made by Joseph McCoy, chief actuary of the Treasury Department, in 1928. The number of *active* shareholders, however, was estimated to be much smaller—around 1.5 million in 1929. See Robert Sobel, *The Big Board: A History of the New York Stock Exchange* (New York: Free Press, 1965), pp. 251–254.

[11]There is evidence that the U.S. economy was weakening for several months prior to the crash. See Galbraith, *The Great Crash,* pp. 171–179.

had risen to about 31 million (around 15 percent of the population).[12] Still, the vast majority of household financial assets, about 80 percent in 1970, consisted of savings accounts and certificates of deposit from financial institutions.

During the 1970s and 1980s millions of Americans finally made the transformation from savers to investors. This trend was stimulated by the explosive growth of money market mutual funds during the late 1970s. Fed up with earning 5.5 percent interest on savings deposits in banks, savers moved billions of dollars into money market funds that yielded 10 percent, or more.[13] As interest rates began to fall during the 1980s, many of these individuals started buying stocks, bonds, and mutual fund shares; in short, they became investors. In 1990, the number of Americans who owned common stocks was estimated to be around 51.5 million, or about one in four adults. The number of mutual fund accounts grew from around 9 million in 1976 to over 70 million today.

European Speculative Bubbles: 1634–1720

In this section we review three spectacular speculative bubbles that occurred in Europe during the early commercial revolution. None of these bubbles lasted long, but all had serious repercussions for governments and societies. In retrospect, it's remarkable, not that these bubbles happened, but rather that they occurred in three of Europe's wealthiest and most financially sophisticated countries.[14]

What Is a Speculative Bubble?

Before unfolding these stories, perhaps we should first formally define the term *speculative bubble*. After you've read about the three bubbles in this section, and those that follow in the next two sections, you'll have a pretty good idea of their general characteristics. A speculative bubble is a rapid increase in the price of something, from tulips to biotech stocks, with no apparent justification other than the belief, or hope, that the price will go still higher. As such a bubble rises, trading volume normally explodes and prices often swing wildly from day to day. In the middle of a bubble, thousands of usually rational people seem gripped by mass hysteria (thus Mackay's term, *madness of crowds*). Sadly for all those involved, and for many innocent bystanders as well, all speculative bubbles eventually burst. When prices do collapse, they can do so almost instantly, with serious consequences for a nation's economy and society as a whole.

---

[12]These figures do not include the number of Americans who may have owned stocks indirectly through insurance policies or pension plans.

[13]The assets of money market funds increased from $3.7 billion in 1976 to over $186 billion only five years later in 1981. The number of shareholder accounts increased from 200,000 to over 10.3 million during the same period.

[14]These three events are chronicled in detail by Charles Mackay, *Extraordinary Popular Delusions and the Madness of Crowds* (New York: Harmony Books, 1980), originally published in 1841 by Bentley Press, London. Mackay didn't limit his treatise on mass hysteria to money mania. He also examined the madness of crowds associated with medieval alchemists, the Crusades, and witchhunts, to name a few. These events have been widely reported by a number of other authors. See, for example, Burton Malkiel, *A Random Walk Down Wall Street,* 5th edition (New York: Norton, 1990), pp. 34–43.

Speculative bubbles teach two basic lessons about investments and investing:

1. The price of an investment, in the long run, will reflect its intrinsic (or true fundamental) value. In the short run, however, a substantial difference can separate market price and intrinsic value, but eventually the market will correct its mistake.
2. Bubbles provide a context for understanding the psychological and emotional effects on investment decision making and valuation. Speculative bubbles remind us that investor emotions have affected investment performance in the past, and they will continue to affect investment performance in the future, as well.

As you read the rest of the book, remember these lessons.

Tulipomania: 1634–1637

It's hard to believe today, but the tulip bulb once sparked one of the most portentous episodes in modern financial history, in 17th-century Holland. After winning *de facto* independence from Spain in the middle 1500s, the Dutch aggressively pursued commercial ventures and trade throughout the known world. Amsterdam became the chief financial center in Europe, surpassing Antwerp, Lyons, and the Italian city states. The Dutch merchant fleet, protected by a large navy, came to dominate European trade. By 1600, Holland was arguably the most commercially advanced and prosperous country in Europe.

Supposedly, tulips were introduced to European horticulture in Vienna around 1559 when an Austrian count brought some plants back from Turkey, where they had been grown for centuries. (The word *tulip* comes from a Turkish word meaning *turban*.) The Dutch fascination with tulips started soon after. Wealthy individuals began to order tulip roots directly from Constantinople, often paying very high prices, and tulips in one's garden became a social necessity. The rage for tulips eventually caught on in the Dutch middle class, as merchants and shopkeepers began to vie with one another for the most sought-after varieties of the plants.[15] The resulting demand began to drive the prices of tulip bulbs sharply upward until, at some point, people started to view tulips as more than decorative additions to gardens, but rather as ways to make money. Tulips were seen as investments whose prices were bound to go higher and higher; the frenzy had begun.

By around 1635, **tulipomania** was in full bloom in Holland. The normal business of the nation "was neglected, and the population, even to its lowest dregs, embarked in the tulip trade. . . . [P]eople of all grades converted their property into cash, and invested it in flowers. Houses and lands were offered for sale at ruinously low prices."[16] Traders in the bourses in Amsterdam, Rotterdam, and other Dutch towns, abandoned mundane things like loans and wheat and began actively trading tulip bulbs. Even call options were available—one could have the right to buy tulips at a fixed price for a fixed period of time.

The prices of tulips reached absurd levels. One person is reported to have offered 12 acres of land in exchange for one especially glorious bulb. A *Semper Augustus* root, the most prized of all, was sold for 5,500 florins in 1636

---

[15]Of the many varieties of tulips, the most prized during this period were plants infected with a nonfatal virus, called a *mosaic,* that caused the petals to develop contrasting colors.

[16]Mackay, *Popular Delusions,* pp. 90 and 94.

though it weighed less than half an ounce. At the same time, in Amsterdam, 4,600 florins would have bought a new carriage complete with two horses!

There is a story of a visiting English botanist who happened to see a most interesting and unusual root lying in the conservatory of a Dutch acquaintance. The botanist promptly began to dissect the plant, an *Admiral Van der Eyck* bulb worth 4,000 florins. Its chagrined owner seized the astonished man of science by the collar and dragged him through the streets to the local magistrate. The botanist was jailed until he raised sufficient funds to repay the bulb's owner.

Eventually the more prudent Dutch citizens began to see that this folly couldn't last forever and they began to sell their tulip bulbs. As this conviction spread in the early part of 1637, prices started to fall faster and faster. Dealers went bankrupt and refused to honor their commitments to buy bulbs. As more and more people tried to sell their tulips, a general panic took hold and prices plunged even further. When the dust finally settled, tulips were selling for no more than common onions, and Holland's economy plunged into a severe recession. Its days as the dominant economic power in Europe had ended.

Mississippi Scheme: 1719–1720

France was on the edge of bankruptcy in the early part of the 18th century, due in large part to the extravagance and corruption associated with the long reign of Louis XIV before his death in 1715. The government had issued billions in interest-bearing notes, far more than the nation's reserves of precious metals or its annual tax revenues.[17] John Law, despite his position in a reputable Scotch family, had a somewhat dark past. (He had killed a man in a London duel and subsequently escaped from prison.) Law came upon this dire financial scene in 1716, having spent the previous 14 years on the continent learning banking, commerce, and gambling. In Paris, Law befriended the royal regent and convinced him of a plan to save the country from financial ruin. Part of Law's plan involved the establishment of a royal bank, which would collect tax revenue and issue sound paper money. Due to a number of ingenious features, Law's bank, established in May 1716, helped put French government finances back on firm ground almost immediately.

The following year, Law organized the Company of the West (known by its popular name: the **Mississippi Company**) and was granted a royal monopoly on trade with the territories of Louisiana and Canada. The company's initial capitalization was set at 100 million livres and shares could be purchased with government notes, taking more government paper off the market. Through a series of transactions between 1717 and 1719, Law's company acquired control over most of France's overseas trade, financing each expansion by issuing more stock. In addition to controlling the public debt, the mint, and the collection of taxes, Law's bank lent money for the purchase of shares.

During this time, the shares of the Mississippi Company continually rose in value and soon the madness began; shares often rose 10 or 20 percent per *hour*. Stock issued for 1,000 livres was soon worth 10,000 livres. Law was considered to be a genius who would make everyone rich. People fought for each new issue of stock, and wild scenes were enacted in the districts where the stock was traded. Stories were told of beggars turned into millionaires

---

[17]In 1715, the French national debt is reported to have been 3 billion livres. The government's annual revenue was around 145 million livres, and, since its annual expenses amounted to 142 million livres, only 3 million was available to service this massive debt.

overnight (the word *millionaire* supposedly originated during this time), and of a hunchback who grew rich renting out his back as a writing table. The government began to issue more and more bank notes, and, coupled with the false prosperity created by the Mississippi bubble, inflation soared.

The bubble finally started to break in February 1720. People began to realize, slowly at first, that the Mississippi Company could never earn enough to justify the astronomical price of its shares. The stock abruptly stopped its upward spiral and even started to fall in price. Once public confidence was shaken, prices tumbled as more and more people tried to sell their stock. People even stormed Law's bank to try to convert their bank notes into coin. Eventually Law's entire financial empire crumbled, and by the end of 1720, Law had hastily fled into exile.

The Mississippi scheme had several lasting effects in France. For one, it created a deep distrust in the public of stock companies, banks, and paper money which probably inhibited the development of the French economy for many years. Some historians have gone as far as to conclude that the Mississippi scheme contributed to the demise of the French monarchy and the beginning of the French Revolution. The Mississippi scheme shows how wild speculation can turn even a basically sound plan (Law's bank) into a disaster.

South Sea Bubble: 1720

While the Mississippi scheme was in full frenzy, a similar drama was played out in England. Like the French government, the English government was also in financial difficulty due to a large public debt in the early part of the 18th century. The concept of granting special privileges in exchange for loans had been used successfully by the English government in organizing the Bank of England and in reorganizing the East India Company. This device was applied again in 1710; a joint-stock company was chartered, known for short as the **South Sea Company.**[18] In return for assuming £10 million of government debt, the South Sea Company was given a monopoly over virtually all trade between England and the New World.

The South Sea Company began tentative trading operations, employing only a small amount of its capital, and had some limited success. As a monetary enterprise, however, the South Sea Company was far more successful. In 1719, the company took over a government loan in the amount of £1,750,000, paying the bondholders in stock. It was able to reduce the amount of interest the government had to pay and still earn the company a profit of £72,000. This worked so well that in 1720 the company offered to assume the entire government debt (around £33 million), paying bondholders and the government large bonuses in the process.

These transactions would work only if South Sea stock was selling for more than its par value (£100). A speculative frenzy had taken care of that. Since the public believed that trade promised vast riches, South Sea shares had always been viewed with favor. Peace with Spain in December 1719 only strengthened the public's belief that the South Sea Company, and its shareholders, would become very wealthy. In January 1720, South Sea shares were selling for £129; by March the price was up to £200, and by May it had climbed above £400. The price of South Sea shares finally peaked in June 1720 at over £1,000!

Unlike the mania in France, which was centered on John Law's company, the South Sea bubble spread in England. The price of East India Company

---

[18]The official name of the South Sea Company was the *Governor and Company of Merchants of Great Britain trading to the South Seas and other Parts of America and for the Encouragement of Fishing!*

shares, for example, more than doubled during the first half of 1720. Further, hundreds of wildly speculative companies were formed and sold stock to the public. Some of the more outrageous included companies that planned to trade in hair, to develop a perpetual motion wheel, to improve the art of making soap, and to extract silver from lead. Needless to say, many of these "companies" were simply scams. It didn't matter, however, as the public would buy stock in almost anything.

Two events during the summer of 1720 finally burst the South Sea bubble. The first was the **Bubble Act,** passed by Parliament, which forbade stock issues by companies that lacked royal charters. Ironically, the South Sea Company pushed for passage of the Bubble Act because it felt that these new companies were siphoning off potential buyers of newly issued South Sea shares. The passage of the Bubble Act caused stock prices, including South Sea shares, to tumble, however. The other event was the revelation during the summer that many South Sea Company insiders had quietly disposed of their shares. The insiders knew, of course, that the company could never earn enough to justify the stock price. In spite of efforts to prop up prices, South Sea shares slid to £390 on September 19, to £180 on September 29, and to £120 by the end of 1720.

The South Sea bubble had a number of important implications.[19] Until the Bubble Act was repealed in 1825, few shares of stock were available for sale in England. Even after that, however, public distrust of speculation, stock exchanges, and joint-stock companies persisted. For many years following the South Sea bubble, English ventures met great difficulty raising capital in England. English capital flowed overseas throughout the 18th and 19th centuries, much of it to the United States.

The Great Crash: Wall Street Lays an Egg[20]

The tendency toward speculative bubbles apparently crossed the Atlantic with the early European settlers and traders. Americans, it appears, were no more immune from the madness of crowds than were their European ancestors. All types of booms and busts were common features of American life during the nineteenth and early twentieth centuries.

In many respects, early bubbles were mere appetizers for the main course, the **Great 1929 Stock Market Crash.** The Great Crash is perhaps the most important speculative bubble we'll review, one with profound, long-lasting effects. For example, many of the securities laws and practices discussed in prior chapters were enacted partly as a result of the Great Crash.

The Bubble Builds

Figure 5.1 illustrates the history of the Dow Jones Industrial Average between 1920 and 1932, along with annual NYSE trading volume. Even in retrospect, it is difficult to say exactly when the speculative bubble began. After a poor year in 1920 when the Dow dropped about 33 percent, stock prices generally

---

[19]Unlike the Mississippi scheme in France, the South Sea bubble didn't bring down the Bank of England—it had stayed out of the mania. Thus, some historians argue that the permanent results of the South Sea bubble were less damaging to England than were those of the Mississippi scheme to France.

[20]The famous headline "Wall Street Lays an Egg" appeared in the show business newspaper *Variety* shortly after the October 29, 1929 stock market crash.

Figure 5.1

Dow Jones Industrial Average (high, low, close) and NYSE Trading Volume: 1920–1932

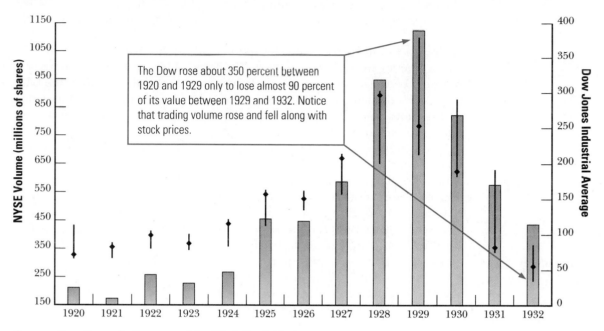

The Dow rose about 350 percent between 1920 and 1929 only to lose almost 90 percent of its value between 1929 and 1932. Notice that trading volume rose and fell along with stock prices.

Source: Dow Jones & Company, New York Stock Exchange.

rose, albeit unevenly, during the next six years. Trading volume also increased.[21] The Dow more than doubled between the end of 1920 and the end of 1926 (rising from 71.95 to 157.20), but this increase could be characterized as something of a standard bull market, rather than a speculative bubble. The increase was generally orderly, backed by some good economic reasons. The U.S. economy, for example, grew by about 30 percent between 1921 and 1926. Add strong corporate earnings, low interest rates, and very modest inflation, and you have a pretty good environment for stocks.

During 1927, stock prices increased almost daily; the Dow had only three losing months during the entire year, and finished 1927 with a gain of almost 29 percent, at 202.40, its yearly high. Trading activity also increased as yearly NYSE volume grew by 28 percent to 577 million shares. However, most of the gains in stock prices during 1927 were quite modest, at least by later standards. Stocks were still considered to be reasonably priced in terms of corporate earnings and dividend yields.

Most historians believe that sometime during early 1928 the bull market became a true speculative bubble. After a fairly quiet winter during which the Dow actually dropped about 4 percent during January and February, stock prices rose sharply during March. The Dow gained over 18.5 points, almost 10 percent, and a record 85.8 million shares changed hands on the NYSE. Stock prices came down again during April, May, and June and the Dow finished the first half of 1928 only about 8 points higher than its level at the beginning of the year.[22] Trading volume, however, remained very

---

[21]Yearly NYSE volume rose from 171 million shares in 1921 to about 450 million shares in 1926.

[22]Some market watchers became concerned during the first part of 1928 that stock prices had caught, and perhaps even passed, levels justified by corporate dividends and earnings. The market suffered several sharp sell-offs during June, leading some to conclude that the 1920s bull market was over.

heavy. During the second half of 1928, stock prices soared. The Dow gained almost 89.5 points (an increase of about 42 percent) between the beginning of July and the end of December. (The index gained over 41 points in November alone.) NYSE trading volume during the last half of 1928 exceeded 500 million shares. By the end of the year, the frenzy was in full force.

By almost any measure, 1929 is perhaps the most remarkable, and infamous, year in stock market history. The Dow added another 81 points (27 percent) between the beginning of January and September 3, when the bubble finally reached its zenith. Trading was often frantic with wild daily price swings (both upward and downward). Trading volume was very heavy, even during the normally slow summer months.[23]

Two factors appear to have contributed to the genesis of the frenzy sometime during 1928: margin buying and investment trusts. In the 1920s, stocks could often be purchased with 10 percent margin requirements, giving investors and speculators tremendous leverage. (We discussed how margin works in Chapter 3.) Today, the minimum margin for stock purchases is 50 percent.

Essentially closed-end investment companies, investment trusts, also became popular in the late stages of this bull market. By autumn 1929, investment trusts had total assets of around $8 billion, 11 times their total assets at the end of 1927. Many investment trusts used borrowed money to leverage their stock investments, producing returns to shareholders of 700 percent when the value of their holdings rose a comparatively meager 50 percent.

Table 5.1 summarizes the bull market of the 1920s. It compares the prices for several stocks, along with the Dow, at the end of 1921 to their peaks in 1929 (all of which were established on September 3). Over those 93 months, the Dow Jones Industrial Average increased more than 370 percent (from 81.1 to 381.2). Many individual stocks did even better. Wright Aeronautical soared from slightly more than $4 per share to $149.50 per share (an increase of more than 3,500 percent). Radio (now RCA) increased an astounding *23,000* percent! Even conservative stocks, such as AT&T and U.S. Steel, more than tripled in value between 1922 and September 1929.

Table 5.1

Some Examples of Security Price Increases during the 1920s

Stock/Index	Prices		Percentage Change
	December 31, 1921	September 3, 1929	
AT&T	111.50	335.00	200%
GE	35.00	396.25	1,032
Radio (RCA)	0.43	101.00	23,388
U.S. Steel	83.50	262.00	214
Wright Aeronautical	4.13	149.50	3,524
Dow	81.10	381.20	370

Note: All prices adjusted for subsequent stock splits.
Source: *The New York Times.*

---

[23]For example, almost 100 million shares were traded on the NYSE during August. By comparison, 67 million shares were traded on the NYSE during August 1928.

The Bubble Breaks

September 3, 1929 turned out to be the peak for stock prices, and trading set marks that day that wouldn't be surpassed for over a quarter of a century. A number of disturbing events cast shadows over the late summer and fall of 1929. U.S. economic growth was showing signs of slowing, interest rates were inching upward, and credit was tightening. Most significant, perhaps, was a growing recognition that the upward spiral in stock prices couldn't continue indefinitely.

On September 5, Roger Babson, a respected financial advisor, repeated a prediction he had made a year earlier that a stock market crash was coming. Stocks suffered a sharp selloff that day as the Dow declined over 10 points on very heavy volume. (September 5, 1929 is known as the **Babson Break.)** Even though stocks recovered most of their losses over the next two days, a crash suddenly looked possible to more and more investors.

Stocks drifted over the next few weeks, though there were more down days than up days. By the end of October, the Dow had dropped about 80 points from its September 3 high. As stock prices dropped, an increasing number of investors faced margin calls. Unwilling to put up more cash, many sold their holdings, further depressing prices.

The bubble finally ruptured on October 28 and 29. Stock prices dropped in an almost linear fashion. Some stocks' prices fell $5 or $10 per share on subsequent trades. The Dow lost almost 70 points (23 percent), and over 27.5 million shares were traded on the NYSE during those two days. The dreams of many, along with billions of dollars, were suddenly wiped out.

Aftermath

The 1929 crash was only the beginning of a prolonged slide in stock prices. As the U.S. economy descended into depression, stock prices continued to sink. The next three years, 1930, 1931, and 1932, were among the worst in history for stocks, as shown in Table 5.2. The Dow lost almost 90 percent of its value between September 3, 1929 and July 8, 1932. Many individual stocks did much worse. Wright Aeronautical, for example, dropped 99 percent. Even conservative AT&T, which actually raised its dividend during the period, dropped more than 78 percent.

Trading volume also evaporated as stocks were shunned. Yearly NYSE trading volume fell from 1,125 million shares in 1929 to around 425 million shares in 1932, to less than 210 million shares in 1940. It took the Dow over

Table 5.2

The Great 1929 Stock Market Crash and Its Aftermath: Some Examples

Stock/Index	Prices		Percentage Change
	September 3, 1929	1932 Low	
AT&T	335.00	72.00	−78.5%
GE	396.25	8.50	−97.9
Radio (RCA)	101.00	2.50	−97.5
U.S. Steel	262.00	22.00	−91.6
Wright Aeronautical	149.50	1.50	−99.0
Dow	381.20	41.20	−89.2

Note: All prices adjusted for stock splits.
Source: *The New York Times.*

25 years to fully recover from the Great Crash. The index didn't reach 300 again until March 11, 1954 and it didn't break the record established on September 3, 1929 until November 23, 1954.[24]

Postwar Bubbles

Each decade since the end of World War II has seen at least one speculative bubble. Before we take a look at some of these more recent fads, note two changes to the postwar investment environment. The first is the rise in importance of institutional and professional investors such as mutual funds and pension funds. Today, professionals have come to dominate the financial markets. Are these investors less likely to fall victim to speculative frenzies? The evidence suggests that professional and institutional investors are as vulnerable to current fads and the madness of crowds as individual investors.

The second notable change to the postwar investment environment has been the substantial reduction in the sale of fraudulent securities and in abusive trading practices, though these threats have not been totally eliminated. Practices that were common during the 1920s, such as price manipulation by insiders, are rare today and many are also illegal. Obviously, improved regulation hasn't prevented speculative bubbles, so today's investors usually have no one to blame but themselves.

The 1950s and 1960s: Electronics and Conglomerates

Investors finally started returning to the stock market in large numbers in the early 1950s, and stocks, in general, did quite well for a number of years. The S&P 500, for example, produced an average annual total return of 18.3 percent between the beginning of 1950 and the end of 1961. The period of the 1950s and early 1960s, however, also had its share of fads and bubbles.

One of the first fads was uranium mining companies. (This was the dawn of the atomic age, after all.) A company called Lisbon Uranium went public in January 1954 for $0.10 per share, running up to over $3.00 per share in less than six months. Investors soon lost interest and the stock sank. Lisbon Uranium never made much money and its assets were acquired in 1959 for securities worth about $0.25 per share. Next, investors liked stocks of leisure-product companies (bowling companies were especially popular). As *Forbes* has noted, some of these stocks more than doubled in the mid-1950s.[25] Like the uranium fad, the leisure-company fad didn't last long.

The first serious bubble in the postwar era occurred in the late 1950s and early 1960s. Dubbed the **'tronics boom,** it sent stocks of companies associated with glamorous new technologies such as electronics, space exploration, etc., soaring. Much of the speculative fever was concentrated in **new issues;** there were more initial public offerings between 1959 and 1962 than at any time in history. Prices often rose wildly after these companies went public. For example, a company called Geophysics Corporation of America went public on December 8, 1960 at $14 per share. By the end of its first day of trading, the stock had almost doubled. The stock peaked in 1961 at $58 per share, a

---

[24]What were popular investments in the 1930s and 1940s? Cash was king. After private ownership of gold was outlawed in 1933, investors poured money into Treasury bills at such a rate that, for brief periods in the late 1930s and early 1940s, T-bills actually had *negative* yields.

[25]See "A Brief History of Stock Fads," *Forbes,* September 14, 1992, pp. 253–268.

good price for a company that earned all of $0.10 per share in 1961. The speculative fever even infected established technology companies. Texas Instruments, for example, rose from $24 per share in 1959 to over $102 per share in late 1960. At its peak in 1960, it was selling for 66 times earnings.

The 'tronics bubble broke in 1962. For a variety of reasons, stocks suffered their first major decline in more than a decade. The S&P 500 dropped about 22 percent between the end of 1961 and June 1962. The high-flying growth and technology stocks were hammered even harder. Geophysics Corporation traded as low as $9 per share during 1962 and Texas Instruments dropped from $102 per share in 1960, to as low as $19\frac{5}{8}$ in 1962.

Conglomerates. The decline in stock prices during 1962 didn't last very long. By the end of the year the bull market was back on track—between June 1962 and the end of 1968, the S&P 500 rose almost 87 percent. During this period, the market became fascinated with **conglomerates.**

During the 1960s, a number of companies grew large through acquisitions. The buzzword **synergy** expressed the belief that a company could acquire another company, even if it operated in a different industry, and increase the earnings potential of the combined enterprise. Creative accounting helped. A conglomerate could report higher earnings merely because it had acquired another earnings stream, regardless of efficiency or profitability. Table 5.3 illustrates this technique, often referred to as the **bootstrap game,** by a hypothetical example.

Global Enterprises, a conglomerate, acquires the stock of Arkansas Catfish. Global exchanges 2 million new shares for Catfish's 5 million outstanding shares. Now, if the acquisition produces no synergy (after all, what does Global know about catfish?), the combined company's earnings should simply be the sum of the two companies' individual earnings (in our example, $125 million). Notice, however, that Global's *reported* earnings per share jumps from $5.00 to $5.68, a nice gain of over 13.5 percent. This is not real growth, of course; it is simple accounting hocus pocus. If a conglomerate continues to make these types of acquisitions, however, it can build a pretty impressive earnings record, attracting unsuspecting investors.

Two of the better-known conglomerates in the 1960s were Gulf & Western and Litton Industries. For a while, investors fell in love with both stocks. Gulf & Western rose from a low in 1965 of $9\frac{1}{8}$ to a high in 1968 of $64\frac{1}{4}$ (an increase of over 600 percent). Litton did almost as well, rising from a low of $30\frac{5}{8}$ in

Table 5.3

Hypothetical Example of the Bootstrap Game

	Before Acquisition	
	Global Enterprises	**Arkansas Catfish**
Earnings	$100 million	$25 million
Number of shares outstanding	20 million	5 million
Earnings per share	$5.00	$5.00
P/E	20 times	5 times
Price	$100 per share	$25 per share

Global issues 2 million new shares to acquire Catfish's 5 million outstanding shares.

Earnings	$125 million ($100 million plus $25 million)
Number of outstanding shares	22 million
Earnings per share	$5.68 (an increase of 13.6 percent)

1965 to a high of $104\frac{1}{4}$ in 1968. At its peak in 1968, Litton was selling for 43 times earnings.

After peaking in November 1968, stocks generally declined for the next 18 months. The S&P 500 dropped about 29 percent between December 1968 and June 1970. As usual, the high-flying stocks—this time the conglomerates—did much worse. Gulf & Western dropped from $64\frac{1}{4}$ in 1968 to as low as $9\frac{1}{2}$ in 1970. Litton lost about 87 percent of its value between 1968 and 1970, falling from $104\frac{1}{4}$ to 14, dropping its price/earnings ratio from 43 to 8.

The 1970s: The Nifty Fifty and Hi, Ho, Silver

Many stock investors would have preferred to forget the 1970s. Between the beginning of 1970 and the end of 1979, the S&P 500 had an average annual total return of 5.9 percent, less than the average rate of inflation for the period, 7.4 percent. The only major stock market fad, called the **nifty fifty,** came early in the decade.

Bounced by past bubbles, many investors, especially professional money managers and mutual fund managers, decided in the early 1970s to focus exclusively on sound, rational investments, avoiding any fads. This notion led them to buy shares of companies with established growth records and very familiar names: Disney, Hewlett-Packard, Xerox, and so forth. These stocks numbered about four dozen, thus the term *nifty fifty*. They were considered to be one-decision stocks—you bought them and held them forever. Unlike many past fads, the nifty fifty were quality stocks. Unfortunately, a bubble caused by excessive demand carried the prices of nifty fifty stocks well above values justified by their prospective growth rates.

Examples from the nifty fifty are shown in Table 5.4. Between its low in 1970 and its high in 1972 to 1973, the S&P 500 gained about 57 percent. The average price/earnings ratio of S&P 500 stocks rose from 14 to 19. Nifty fifty stocks did much better, as the examples in the table illustrate. Disney and Hewlett-Packard, for example, each more than quadrupled between 1970 and 1972 to 1973. At its peak in late 1972, McDonald's was selling for 82 times earnings. Yet again, sophisticated investors fell into the trap of believing that whatever price they paid for a nifty fifty stock, it would continue to go up. Of course, that didn't happen.

The market peaked in early 1973 and then declined sharply for most of the next two years. Between early 1973 and the end of 1974, the S&P 500 lost over 43 percent of its value. The prices of the nifty fifty held up for a while, and then collapsed. Avon Products and Disney, for example, each dropped more than 86 percent from their 1972 to 1973 highs. Polaroid lost over 90 percent of its value between 1972 and 1974 as its price/earnings ratio fell from 115 to 16.

The 1980s and 1990s: Meltdown Monday and New Issues Revisited

The 1980s and early 1990s have been generally good years for stocks. The S&P 500, for example, produced a total return of more than 460 percent between the end of 1981 and the end of 1993. This historic bull market has, however, seen a number of fads and bubbles, many of which have involved new issues. Before we get to some of these, we'd like to review another infamous event during the 1980s: the 1987 market break.

The 1987 Market Break: Meltdown Monday. On October 19, 1987, stocks suffered their worst one-day decline in history. The Dow Jones Industrial Average lost more than 500 points that day. In percentage terms, the Dow's

Table 5.4

Some Examples of the Nifty Fifty

Stock/Index	Low 1970		1972 to 1973 High		1974 Low		Percentage Change		Relative P/E		
	Price	P/E	Price	P/E	Price	P/E	70 to 72/73	72/73 to 74	70	72/73	74
Avon Products	$59\frac{1}{8}$	34	140	65	$18\frac{5}{8}$	10	136.8%	−86.7%	2.43	3.42	1.43
Disney	$19\frac{3}{8}$	24	$110\frac{5}{8}$	82	$15\frac{3}{8}$	10	471.0	−86.1	1.71	4.32	1.43
Eastman Kodak	$57\frac{5}{8}$	23	$151\frac{3}{4}$	44	$57\frac{5}{8}$	15	163.3	−62.0	1.64	2.32	2.14
Hewlett-Packard	$19\frac{3}{8}$	21	$100\frac{5}{8}$	53	52	17	419.4	−48.3	1.50	2.79	2.43
McDonald's	$9\frac{1}{8}$	19	$77\frac{3}{8}$	82	$21\frac{1}{4}$	13	747.9	−72.5	1.36	4.32	1.86
Polaroid	51	25	$149\frac{1}{2}$	115	$14\frac{1}{8}$	16	193.1	−90.6	1.79	6.05	2.29
Xerox	$65\frac{1}{4}$	27	$171\frac{7}{8}$	54	49	12	163.4	−71.5	1.93	2.84	1.71
S&P 500	75.6	14	118.4	19	67.1	7	56.6	−43.3	1.00	1.00	1.00

Notes: P/E refers to price/earnings ratio. Relative P/E is equal to an individual stock's P/E divided by the P/E for the S&P 500.

Source: Standard & Poor's.

decline on October 19, 1987 was far greater than its decline on October 29, 1929 (23 percent versus 12 percent). The S&P 500 dropped more than 50 points (a decline of 20 percent). Even relatively stable utilities dropped sharply. The S&P utilities index, for example, fell by more than 19 points (18 percent) on October 19, 1987.

Much has already been written about the causes of the 1987 market break. Some have argued that it was the result of rampant speculation in stocks; others have blamed the break on program trading; still others have blamed it on simple investor panic. In our view, all three factors probably contributed to what became known as **Meltdown Monday.**[26] Did it mark the end of a period of speculative frenzy similar to that of the 1920s? The answer is both yes and no.

Table 5.5 puts the 1987 market break into some perspective. Stocks had risen rapidly throughout 1987, prior to the break. The S&P 500 added more than 90 points (about 38 percent) between the end of 1986 and August 25, when the index peaked at 336.8. As shown in Table 5.5, many individual stocks did much better. Ford, for example, more than doubled between the end of 1986 and its high in the summer of 1987.

During the late summer and early fall of 1987, some investors began to worry that stocks were becoming overvalued. The average price/earnings ratio of the S&P 500 stocks had risen from 16.7 to 21.1. Interest rates were also rising. The yield on long-term T-bonds, for example, had risen 1.5 percent between January and August. Stocks started to drift lower throughout September and the first week of October. The S&P 500 lost about 30 points between August 25 and October 14.

Things then got serious. Several reports of bad economic news were released, fueling fears of inflation and recession. Also, interest rates continued to climb; the yield on long-term Treasury bonds crossed a psychological barrier at 10 percent several days before the market break. Friday, October 16 was a bad day for stocks. The S&P 500 lost more than 16 points (about 5 percent), and trading volume was very heavy.

---

[26]John Phelan, then chairman of the NYSE, was quoted as saying "that's the closest I want to be to a meltdown" after the conclusion of trading on Monday, October 19, 1987; thus the expression *Meltdown Monday*.

Table 5.5

Stock and Index Values around the 1987 Market Break

Stock/Index	Opening 1987	1987 High	October 19, 1987 Close	High 1989
Ford	$28\frac{1}{8}$	$56\frac{3}{8}$	$34\frac{1}{2}$	$56\frac{5}{8}$
GE	43	$66\frac{3}{8}$	$41\frac{7}{8}$	$64\frac{3}{4}$
Microsoft	$24\frac{1}{8}$	$39\frac{5}{8}$	$22\frac{5}{8}$	$44\frac{1}{8}$
Wal-Mart	$23\frac{1}{4}$	$42\frac{7}{8}$	$26\frac{5}{8}$	$44\frac{7}{8}$
S&P 500	242.2	336.8	224.8	359.8
Dow	1,895.95	2,722.42	1,738.74	2,791.41
NASDAQ Composite	348.83	455.26	291.88	485.73

Source: *The New York Times.*

Over the weekend, many investors apparently hit the panic button. By the time the U.S. markets opened Monday morning, thousands of sell orders were waiting. (Markets in Asia and Europe had already experienced sharp selloffs.) Prices tumbled from the opening bell. Falling prices triggered sell commands in computer trading programs, driving prices even lower. By the time the dust settled the S&P 500 had lost over 58 points, or about 21 percent of its value. The stocks shown in Table 5.5 all took big hits. Ford, for example, dropped $15\frac{1}{4}$ points to $34\frac{1}{2}$. NYSE trading volume on October 19, 1987 was huge, exceeding 600 million shares.

Following many anxious days after Meltdown Monday, the markets stabilized by the end of the year. The Federal Reserve quickly intervened to prevent any liquidity crisis. No major banks or brokerage firms failed. Interest rates started to fall (the yield on the long T-bond was down to about 9 percent by the end of 1987), and no recession materialized. Unlike the 1929 crash, which ushered in a prolonged bear market, the 1987 market break turned out to be only a temporary setback. The S&P 500 broke its earlier 1987 record on July 26, 1989 and crossed the 300 point mark again on April 14, 1989. The individual stocks listed in Table 5.5 had all recovered from Meltdown Monday by 1989.

Biotech Madness. As we indicated earlier, the bull market of the last 12 years has seen its share of bubbles. One group of stocks that has experienced several bubbles is **biotech** issues. Biotech companies develop new drugs through genetic engineering. Investors became so enthralled with these stocks that they sometimes forgot that, like all new technologies, it would take time and a great deal of capital for biotechs to develop their new products. It would take even longer before many of these companies would be profitable.

The first biotech company to go public, Genentech, offered its first shares on October 15, 1980 at a price of $5\frac{7}{8}$.[27] Investors went wild over the stock, bidding up its price to more than double the offering price on its first day of trading. Genentech closed that day at $11\frac{7}{8}$, after trading as high as $14\frac{3}{8}$. That gave Genentech, a company with less than $7 million in actual revenue, an instant market value of about $1 billion. Investors soon recognized that it would indeed take years for Genentech to realize its huge potential or turn a profit, and the stock dropped almost as quickly as it had risen. By 1982, it was trading as low as $4\frac{1}{2}$.

---

[27]All prices are adjusted for subsequent stock splits.

Table 5.6

Examples of the Biotech Bubble: 1990–1992

Stock	1989 to 1990 Low	1991 to 1992 High			
		Price	P/E Ratio	Market Value ($ billions)	1991 Revenues ($ millions)
Amgen	$21\frac{1}{2}$	$78\frac{1}{8}$	104	$10.2	$682.2
Biogen	$14\frac{3}{8}$	$49\frac{3}{4}$	216	1.5	61.4
Centocor	$7\frac{1}{2}$	$60\frac{1}{4}$	N/A	2.5	53.2
Genzyme	$12\frac{1}{2}$	$66\frac{1}{2}$	114	1.4	109.0
Immunex	6	68	N/A	1.0	52.7
Immune Response	$2\frac{3}{4}$	$62\frac{3}{4}$	N/A	1.0	4.3

Note: N/A = not applicable.
Source: Standard & Poor's.

Investors regained their fascination with biotechs a couple of years later, helped along by several new issues. In the meantime, Genentech was producing several blockbuster drugs and developing other promising products to generate annual revenues of around $250 million. Its stock soared from $8\frac{5}{8}$ in 1985 to $65\frac{1}{4}$ in 1987. At that price Genentech had a market value of around $5.5 billion, almost as large as the value of Warner-Lambert, an established drug company with over $3.5 billion in annual revenue. A somewhat more speculative company, Enzon, saw its stock zoom from $2\frac{3}{8}$ in 1985 to $12\frac{3}{4}$ in 1987. This increase occurred in spite of the fact that Enzon really hadn't sold anything, much less made any money, since it went public. The 1987 market break took care of this biotech bubble. By 1988, Genentech had dropped to $14\frac{3}{8}$.[28] Enzon plunged from $12\frac{3}{4}$ in 1987 to a low of $3\frac{7}{8}$ in 1988.

Action in biotech stocks was quiet for a while, and then the group took off again between 1989 and 1992. Some examples are shown in Table 5.6. Of the six stocks listed, Amgen, Biogen, and Genzyme are considered to be among the most established biotech companies. All three have successful products, as well as new drugs under development.

In some ways this most recent bubble may have been the most spectacular of all. Each of the six stocks *at least* tripled in value between 1988 to 1989 and 1991 to 1992; some rose in price more than tenfold. At their peaks, all three established biotech companies had triple-digit P/E ratios. At a price of $62\frac{3}{4}$, Immune Response had a market value of around $1 billion, even though its 1991 revenues amounted to a mere $4.3 million.

As with all bubbles, the market finally decided that, even if these companies met all their potential, and more, they could never make enough money to justify these stratospheric valuations. The selling started and soon the bubble broke. The results in Table 5.7 speak for themselves. Even industry leader Amgen lost over half its value in a matter of months.

The Tokyo Stock Exchange: 1986–1991. Figure 5.2 shows the yearly low, high, and closing values for the Tokyo Price Index (TOPIX) between 1986 and 1991. The average year-end price/earnings ratio for stocks listed on the Tokyo Stock Exchange is also shown. The Tokyo market of the late 1980s looked a little like U.S. stocks during the late 1920s: a classic speculative bubble.

---

[28]The Swiss company Roche Holdings, Ltd. acquired a controlling interest in Genentech in 1990 for about $2.1 billion.

Table 5.7

Collapse of the Biotech Bubble:
1991–1993

Stock	High Price 1991 to 1992	Low Price 1992 to 1993	Percentage Decline
Amgen	$78\frac{1}{8}$	$31\frac{3}{4}$	59.4%
Biogen	$49\frac{3}{4}$	$20\frac{3}{4}$	58.3
Centocor	$60\frac{1}{4}$	$5\frac{1}{2}$	90.9
Genzyme	$66\frac{1}{2}$	$27\frac{1}{4}$	59.0
Immunex	68	$25\frac{3}{4}$	62.1
Immune Response	$62\frac{3}{4}$	10	84.1

Source: Standard & Poor's.

For many years, the Tokyo stock market was considered to be something of an investment backwater, even though Japanese stocks had risen almost steadily throughout the 1970s and early 1980s. The Japanese economy was growing rapidly, corporate profits were high, and inflation and interest rates were low. Like the U.S. market in the 1920s, the Japanese bull market eventually became a speculative bubble, probably sometime in the mid-1980s.

Figure 5.2

Tokyo Stock Prices and Average Price/Earnings Ratio: 1985–1991

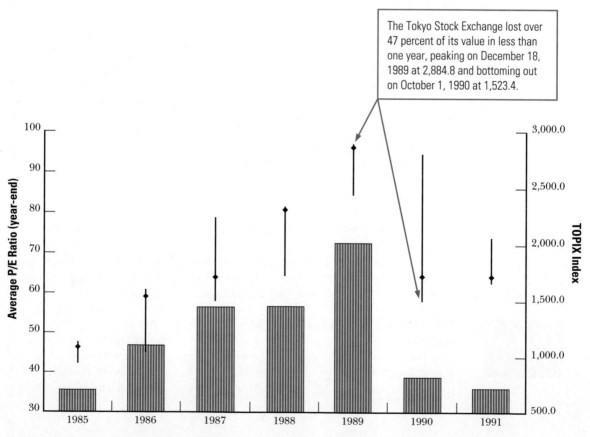

The Tokyo Stock Exchange lost over 47 percent of its value in less than one year, peaking on December 18, 1989 at 2,884.8 and bottoming out on October 1, 1990 at 1,523.4.

Source: Tokyo Stock Exchange.

D. H. Blair & Co.'s Most Recent Offering Shows How Speculative IPOs Are Getting

Anyone who doubts that a speculative frenzy is sweeping through the initial-public-offering market may want to take a look at the recently launched IPO of Advanced Mammography Systems.

This development-stage company was brought to market last week at $6 by D. H. Blair & Co., a frequent underwriter of stock offerings by very risky companies. Presto, the stock's now at $7\frac{3}{4}$, chalking up a 29 percent gain in a week.

The company sold a 26 percent stake to investors, raising $7.8 million. What did they get?

The company has no products for sale. It has no revenue. It expects operating losses "for the foreseeable future."

Auditors have expressed "substantial doubt about the company's ability to continue as a going concern."

The company did the IPO to finance "an initial prototype" of a new device to detect breast cancer. A real product won't emerge for "several years, if at all."

The underwriter and principal supporter of the stock, D. H. Blair, remains under investigation by the Securities and Exchange Commission. While the existence of such a probe by itself isn't news, the prospectus makes the inquiry sound more serious than Blair previously let on.

The SEC probe is "broad in scope," and involves "nearly all aspects" of Blair's compliance with federal securities laws, the prospectus says. In other words, this could be a bigger deal than when Blair settled an unfair-pricing case with the National Association of Securities Dealers in 1989, paying a $25,000 fine.

D. H. Blair's president, Kenton E. Wood, says the SEC investigation "has been going on now for close to four years, so that's not a new event." His firm blames the SEC probe on competitors and disgruntled ex-employees. "We know of nothing we've been doing wrong," he says.

An SEC spokesman yesterday declined to comment about the investigation.

Even considering the red-hot IPO market and Blair's salesmanship, some traders say it's astounding that investors hopped aboard this ride.

As described in a front-page article in *The Wall Street Journal* in 1991, Blair has underwritten stocks of more than 200 small companies since 1980. Often the issues rise in price for months or years—which benefits Blair's owner, J. Morton Davis, who often takes a stake in the

offerings. But the SEC is investigating whether Blair blocks small investors from selling shares when they want to, allowing Mr. Davis and others to sell out at a profit before the new issues decline.

"An unfavorable resolution" of the SEC's investigation of Blair "could have the effect of limiting" Blair's ability to make a market in Advanced Mammography shares, says the prospectus. The same warning could apply to Blair's handful of other recent offerings, including Laser Video Network, Life Medical Sciences, Las Vegas Entertainment and Health Image Media.

So why would any investor buy the Advanced Mammography deal? "They like the risk/reward opportunity," says D. H. Blair's president, Mr. Wood.

IPO watchers say they're seeing more new-issue gambits like Advanced Mammography during the current bull market for IPOs. Several companies lately "have been trying to go public without having any revenues, or without having any strong prospects," says Keith Goggin, managing editor of IPO Reporter, a newsletter. "I really don't know who they sell this stuff to."

Mr. Goggin has a theory about why risky new issues succeed: the SEC requires so much disclosure about risk in prospectuses that even offerings as risky as Advanced Mammography don't look too bad by comparison. "It's almost like crying wolf," he says. Investors read so much about risks that they start to ignore them.

Certainly there's no reason to ignore the risks in the Advanced Mammography deal. The company says it paid $1.7 million for a license from its corporate parent so that it can develop a new and safer breast-scanning device using magnetic resonance imaging.

The parent is Blair-underwritten Advanced NMR Systems—itself a development-stage company with an accumulated deficit of $17.6 million as of September—with which Advanced Mammography shares officers and offices in Wilmington, Mass. (Blair's Mr. Davis owns 10.5 percent of Advanced NMR and his brother owns 11.9 percent, the prospectus says.)

Advanced Mammography's auditor is Richard A. Eisner & Co. of Cambridge, Mass. It's highly unusual to find a "going-concern" qualification in an auditor's report for a company going public; such statements are the stock-market equivalent of a flashing red light. But this auditor's

(continued)

(continued)

opinion contains just such a warning and boldly states: "Management anticipates incurring substantial additional losses as it pursues research and development efforts."

Say this about Blair: It isn't shy. Despite the continuing SEC investigation, the company has been beating its breast with newpaper advertisements—featuring a photograph of Abraham Lincoln—that claim it is the No. 1 underwriter of IPOs on Wall Street, with postoffering prices of the Blair-underwritten stocks rising an average 93.4 percent.

Blair makes the astounding claim by using 1991 deals—nine of them—and including the value of "unit" offerings. Many Blair offerings are unit deals, which consist of both stock and warrants giving holders the right to buy shares later at a higher price. This structure can work

out fine for investors in a bull market. But most independent performance-ranking services prefer to look at stock prices alone rather than units, because the warrant portion may prove worthless down the road.

Blair's Mr. Wood prefers to count the value of his firm's unit deals. Doing otherwise, he says, is "ridiculous." Doing it Blair's way, its eight 1992 deals rose an average 57.4 percent, the fourth-best performance on Wall Street. But Securities Data Co., an independent data service, calculates the rise as just 17 percent if only the stock portions of the deals are tracked.

Source: William Power, "D. H. Blair & Co.'s Most Recent Offering Shows How Speculative IPOs Are Getting," *The Wall Street Journal*, February 3, 1993, p. C1. Reprinted by permission of The Wall Street Journal, © 1993 Dow Jones & Company, Inc. All Rights Reserved Worldwide.

Japanese stock prices soared between 1985 and 1989. From its low in 1985 (which occurred on January 4) to its high in 1989 (which occurred on December 18), the TOPIX more than tripled, increasing from a little more than 900 to almost 2,900.[29] By contrast, the S&P 500 rose slightly more than 111 percent during the period. At the same time, the average price/earnings ratio of stocks listed on the Tokyo Stock Exchange rose from 35 to 71. Trading volume also exploded. In 1986, average daily trading volume was about 428 million shares; by 1988 it was over 1 *billion* shares. The 1987 market break had only a very temporary effect on the frenzy. While the Tokyo market lost about 14 percent on October 20, 1987, it gained back almost 9.5 percent the next day. For all of 1987, the TOPIX increased by almost 11 percent. During the next two years, 1988 and 1989, the Japanese market rose another 50 percent.

Finally, Japanese stocks reached a point where more and more investors began to realize that stocks' prices were far out of line with their intrinsic values and started selling. Fears of slower growth in the Japanese economy, coupled with higher interest rates, also helped to break the bubble in Japanese stocks in 1990. Between the beginning of 1990 and October of that year, the Tokyo market lost almost 50 percent of its value, as the TOPIX declined from 2,900 to 1,500.

1993 Danger Zone? Some in the financial press are warning of a new bubble—this one in small stocks.[30] While we'll have to wait and see if, and when, this bubble breaks, the situation will bear an eerie resemblance to past stock market fads and frenzies.

An example of the speculative frenzy in new issues is Advanced Mammography Systems, subject of the article from *The Wall Street Journal* in the Investment Insights feature. Advanced Mammography went public in late January 1993 at $6 per share, jumped 29 percent, to $7\frac{3}{4}$, in one week, and is currently trading around $8\frac{1}{2}$. This increase has occurred in spite of the fact that the company has no products to sell, and won't for several years, if at all. The firm expects to lose money for the "foreseeable future," and its audi-

---

[29]As we discussed in Chapter 4, the TOPIX is a composite index made up of all first-section TSE shares, approximately 1,300 stocks.

[30]See, for example, "Danger Zone," *Forbes*, January 18, 1993, pp. 66–69.

tors have expressed "substantial doubt about the company's ability to continue as a going concern." Apparently when it's bubble time in the stock market, none of this matters.

Some Questions about Speculative Bubbles

After reading about past bubbles, you probably have lots of questions. You may wonder why seemingly rational people can't seem to learn from past mistakes and fall into the bubble trap over and over again. You may also be asking yourself whether bubbles can be predicted, and whether anything (such as regulatory changes) should be done to help prevent bubbles. In this section, we'll try to answer several questions about speculative bubbles.

Why Do Bubbles Occur?

This is perhaps the single most important question about speculative bubbles. Bubbles occur basically because investing involves people. Even in this age of technology, people still ultimately make investment decisions. Although they may rely on mathematical models and highly mechanical trading rules, investment decisions are still subject to the entire range of human emotions. This is one of the major lessons of bubbles; they reveal the powerful psychological and emotional influences on investment decision making and valuation.

Bubbles normally begin with significant economic or political events. The tulip bubble was a direct result of a period of sustained economic prosperity and political stability in 16th-century Holland. The biotech bubble began with the emergence of a new technology, genetic engineering, that held huge potential. The frenzy begins once people stop buying an investment for income, or to participate in its natural price appreciation through intrinsic value increases; instead they buy merely on the belief that the price will go higher because someone else will always be willing to pay more.[31] As long as buyers outnumber sellers, prices continue to rise and the bubble becomes, for a while, a self-fulfilling prophecy. Of course, once enough of those buyers become sellers, the balance changes and prices no longer rise. Usually another event (such as the critical *Forbes* article about Home Shopping Network) helps to break the bubble. Once the bubble breaks, prices tumble and the mad rush to get in turns quickly into a stampede toward the exit.

Why does this happen? Psychologists have long believed that, when confronted with uncertainty and incomplete information, people often imitate each other's behavior. Investing involves a lot of uncertainty. Some resolve the questions by assuming that, if other people think something is a good investment, then it must be. The frenzy surrounding a bubble usually becomes highly contagious as investors start to behave like an unthinking herd. If you think everyone around you is getting rich by investing in something, you may feel like a fool if you don't invest. As irrational as speculative bubbles are in retrospect, the pressure of the moment makes getting involved seem like the only rational thing to do. These powerful emotions are very difficult to control.

Several economists have set up experimental markets in order to gain more insight into the forces that cause bubbles. The article from *The Wall*

---

[31]Some cynically refer to this as the *greater fool theory*. Although I may be a fool to pay $100 per share for the stock, there is a greater fool out there who will be willing to pay more.

Stock Market Experiment Suggests Inevitability of Booms and Busts

Vernon L. Smith knows why the stock market crashed. He ought to. He's seen dozens of "bubbles"—booms followed by sudden crashes—in the past three years.

Almost every time, Mr. Smith says, the bubble occurred because inexperienced traders dominated the market. In fact, traders had to go through at least two booms and crashes before they collectively learned to avoid these bubbles.

Mr. Smith is one of a new breed of economists who test economic theories by setting up laboratory experiments. For the past few years he and his associate at the University of Arizona in Tucson, Gerry L. Suchanek, and Arlington W. Williams at Indiana University in Bloomington have been running experimental stock markets in their labs.

Heading for Another Crash?

If these experiments have any relevance to real markets, and the economists say they do, Wall Street is headed for another bubble of boom and crash. Moreover, many of the changes in trading practices being proposed, such as daily limits on price changes or restrictions on computer-assisted trading, will be of little help.

Trading Price

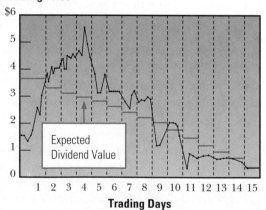

"It's not necessary to search for a cause (of the crash) hidden in the mechanics of trading, in the capital requirements of specialists and brokers, in the existence of futures-index markets, in program trading or in increased electronic assistance in trading," Mr. Smith asserts. "These are scapegoats, not fundamental causes."

In these experimental markets a dozen or so volunteers, usually economics students, are given a set number of "shares" of stock, along with some working capital. All the volunteers are connected by terminals to a computer, which is set up to duplicate trading on the stock-market floor. A trading "day" lasts about four minutes during which the traders may have entered two or three dozen bids and offers resulting in anywhere from five to a dozen trades. A typical experiment during an afternoon or evening runs 15 days.

The booms and crashes occurred in a recent series of 60 experiments aimed at testing an aspect of one of the most basic of all stock-market theories—rational expectations. This theory says a stock's price is determined by investors' expectations of what dividend the share will pay. If investors are rational in their expectations, they all place the same value on the stock and it will trade at a price reflecting its true dividend value. The price will change only when new information comes along that changes the dividend expectations.

Mr. Smith and his colleagues assumed, however, that even if investors had the same information, their dividend expectations would differ and they would value the stock differently. Price speculation would then be possible. But, they hypothesized, investors would soon realize that speculative profits are uncertain and unsustainable and they would begin changing their dividend expectations until, at some point, they all came to a common and rational expectation. The stock would then trade at its dividend value.

To find out how long this learning process would take, they set up a laboratory market in which all traders began with the same information about dividend prospects. Traders were told a payout would be declared after each trading day. The amount would be determined randomly from four possibilities—zero, eight, 28, or 60

Street Journal in the Investment Insights feature reports on one such study.[32] Each of the dozen or so volunteers in the study received a certain number of shares of stock, as well as some working capital. Volunteers were allowed to trade with one another using a computer network designed to duplicate a trading floor. The volunteers were told ahead of time that each session, which lasted only a few minutes, would end with the stock paying a dividend, randomly determined with an expected value of 24 cents. Over 15 sessions,

---

[32]The study cited in *The Wall Street Journal* article was published later in an academic journal. See Vernon Smith et al., "Bubbles, Crashes, and Endogenous Expectations in Experimental Spot Asset Markets," *Econometrica*, September 1988, pp. 1,119–1,151.

cents. The average daily payout would be 24 cents. Thus, a share's dividend value on the first trading day in a 15-day experiment was $3.60 (24 cents times 15 days). As the days passed and dividends were paid, the dividend value would drop.

One typical experiment involved nine students. On the first four-minute "day," trading opened when a student's offer to sell a share for $1.50 was quickly accepted. A moment later a bid to buy a share for $1.30 was snapped up. Such bargain prices triggered a flurry of rising bids, and a boom quickly developed. By the middle of the fourth trading day the price topped $5.50 even though the stock's dividend value had dropped to $3.

But at such high prices offers to sell began to outnumber bids to buy. A crash began and by day 11 prices were below the stock's $1 dividend value. Only on the last two trading days [did] prices settle at or near the dividend value.

Some of the more astute traders were able to post gains of as much as $50 in dividends and trading profits while others ended up with as little as $5, Mr. Smith says. If the stock had consistently traded at or near its dividend value, all nine students could have had a profit of $16.

Such market bubbles occurred repeatedly. "We find that inexperienced traders never trade consistently near fundamental value, and most commonly generate a boom followed by a crash in stock prices," Mr. Smith says. Moreover, traders who have experienced one crash "continue to bubble and crash, but at reduced volume," he says. But, he adds, "Groups brought back for a third trading session tend to trade near fundamental dividend value."

To counter any criticism that the boom and crash reflected students' naivete, the researchers used Tucson businessmen who had "real world" experience. They generated the biggest bubble of all and, like the students, had to go through two booms and crashes before settling down to trade at a mutually profitable dividend value.

The experiments show, the economists say, that market crashes are caused by nothing more than the traders themselves speculating on prices rather than paying attention to stocks' basic value.

The Real World

"People panic," Mr. Smith says. "They do it in our laboratory markets until they learn that trading away from fundamentals doesn't yield sustainable, continuing profits." In the real world, he says, "these bubbles and crashes would be a lot less likely if the same traders were in the market all the time." But, he notes, novices are always entering the market.

The experiments also suggest there are few regulatory steps that can be taken to prevent crashes. During the experiment with the businessmen, for example, traders had to stop for 20 minutes to service the computer, an action not unlike the trading halt in the Hong Kong exchange during the recent crash. The laboratory market was booming at the time. When trading resumed there was an initial selloff but then the boom resumed with more steam than before the shutdown. In fact, the shutdown seemed to fuel the boom instead of damping it, Mr. Smith notes.

Price curbs also have been tried in the lab, such as not allowing prices to change more than 15 cents a share in any trading day. "It doesn't work; it just makes things worse," Mr. Smith says. "The boom lasts longer because everyone knows prices can't fall more than 15 cents." The crash doesn't begin until later but when it does start it's worse than without price limits. "In a crash, no one is willing to buy even at a 15-cent lower price," he explains.

So, how did Mr. Smith himself fare in the recent crash? "I started getting off margin last January and February," he says of his investments. When the crash hit "I was about 50 percent out of the market. If I had been sure a crash was going to happen I would have been all the way out."

Source: Jerry E. Bishop, "Stock Market Experiment Suggests Inevitability of Booms and Busts," *The Wall Street Journal,* November 11, 1987, p. 33. Reprinted by permission of The Wall Street Journal, © 1987 Dow Jones & Company, Inc. All Rights Reserved Worldwide.

then, each share has an intrinsic value of $3.60 (15 × $0.24). The researchers repeated the experiment about 50 times, using different groups of volunteers.

In a typical experiment, several shares traded almost immediately during the first trading session at prices well below their intrinsic values. Those bargain prices soon attracted a frenzy of bids, driving prices up quickly. By the fourth session, share prices were double their intrinsic values. As happens with all bubbles, rising prices suddenly stimulate more offers to sell than to buy. Prices in the experimental market dropped quickly, and by the 11th session shares were actually trading *below* their intrinsic values. In only the last two or three sessions did shares trade for their intrinsic values. The researchers concluded that inexperienced traders never trade consistently near fundamental value, and thus the markets are prone to booms and busts. However, the tendency toward bubbles appears to decrease with trader experience.

Are Bubbles Inevitable?

Given the causes of bubbles, the answer to this question, alas, is probably yes. Events occur almost daily that could be catalysts for new bubbles. But why don't investors learn from past follies? After all, the results of the experimental study discussed above suggest that investors do have a learning curve. The trouble is, as the researchers pointed out, a continual influx of new, inexperienced traders enter the markets at the beginning of their learning curves.

While we certainly don't dispute the notion of a learning curve, at least for specific investors, reviewing past bubbles suggests that professional investors, supposedly some of the most experienced, are just as prone to bubbles as naive, individual investors. The nifty fifty episode is a good example. Many investors, whether institutions or individuals, seem to delude themselves into thinking that the current fad isn't a speculative bubble; *this* one, they say, will last. However, as John Templeton, a long-time respected investor and mutual fund manager, is quoted as saying, "The most dangerous words in the investment business are *this time it's different.*" It rarely is.

Can Bubbles Be Predicted?

Obviously if you could predict when bubbles were about to start and, perhaps more important, when they were about to break, you could make a great deal of money. Imagine having bought GE at 35 in 1921, sold it in 1929 when it peaked at $396\frac{1}{4}$, and then bought it back in 1932 after it had fallen to $8\frac{1}{2}$, and having held it until today.[33] Think about having invested in silver at $6.50 per ounce in 1979 and then cashing out when it reached $50 per ounce in early 1980.

Some pundits claim that they can predict bubbles, many using so-called *technical analysis* techniques which we'll discuss in the next chapter, and some of them have made correct calls over the years. However, we know of no one who has invented anything close to a foolproof system for predicting the beginning and end of a bubble in such a way that one could consistently profit. Our advice is always to be skeptical of anyone who claims to have such a system.

Why are bubbles so difficult to predict? For one thing, you can say that an episode was definitely a speculative bubble only in retrospect, that is after it has already burst. Another factor that makes bubbles difficult to predict is that no two are alike. Think about those we've examined in this chapter. They've involved a variety of assets ranging from land to silver, and involved both entire markets and specific types of stocks. In addition, some bubbles have lasted for years, while others have risen and burst within only a few months. While we can say that bubbles are likely to occur in the future, we really can't say when or where.

How Can an Investor Avoid Bubbles?

Given the difficulty of accurately predicting bubbles, even the most astute and careful investor may occasionally fall into the bubble trap. It is normal

---

[33]By the way, today that $850 investment in GE made in 1932 would be worth around $893,000, *excluding* dividends!

to hope that one or two clever investments will provide quick wealth. Investors must remind themselves constantly that, in Bernard Baruch's words, "two and two make four." The belief that one can get something for nothing is a very dangerous illusion that has led countless investors down the bubble path.[34]

More specifically, we offer three well-worn rules of investing. First, be wary of anyone who tries hard to get you to invest, says he or she wants to share the wealth with you, promises exceptional rates of return, and so forth. Second, if you don't understand it, don't buy it. Third, just because so-called *experts* like something, doesn't mean that you should invest in it.

Should New Issues Be Avoided?

Many of the bubbles we've discussed in this chapter have involved new issues—shares of companies that have recently gone public for the first time. (Think of Advanced Mammography Systems or Genentech.) Should investors, as a general rule, stay clear of new issues?

That's a difficult question to answer. The temptation to buy new issues can be very strong. After all, those who bought Home Depot when it went public did very well. The first shares were sold on September 30, 1981 at $0.21 per share (adjusted for subsequent splits). Recently, Home Depot was trading around $46, an astounding gain of almost *22,000* percent!

Investors must realize, however, that for every Home Depot, many new issues turn into disasters for investors. In fact, a recent study by *Forbes* of 2,223 companies that went public between January 1981 and April 1991 found that new issues, on average, substantially underperformed the overall stock market.[34] Further, 161 stocks on the *Forbes* list lost virtually all of their value between when they went public and April 1991.

Of course, we tend to remember the successes rather than the failures, so new issues remain tempting. Our advice is to be extraordinarily careful with new issues, strictly applying the three general rules we discussed above.[35]

Can, and Should, Regulators Do Anything to Prevent Bubbles?

Well-functioning securities markets are very important to modern economies. As we've seen, bubbles can damage securities markets by, among other things, destroying investor confidence. Also, many bubbles were caused by fraud and/or improper trading practices. Thus a case can be made for regulatory actions designed to prevent or minimize bubbles. On the other hand, the wrong type of regulation can actually hurt the markets. It is a difficult balancing act.

Our view is that the philosophy behind current U.S. securities regulation comes pretty close to the proper balance. Federal laws began to outlaw fraudulent trading and many of the most abusive practices in 1933. However, federal regulation is also based on the underlying notion of full and fair disclosure. It seeks to make sure that investors are given all relevant information, but to let them make their own decisions. This doesn't prevent bubbles, but it does recognize that investors should ultimately be responsible for their own actions, so long as everything has been disclosed and no frauds have been committed.

---

[34]Mark Hulbert, "Getting Taken," *Forbes,* June 24, 1991, pp. 216–220.

[35]Hulbert advises investors to completely avoid new issues unless they can get them at their inside prices (the actual offering prices), they buy them during a bear market, and they can sell the issues quickly.

Chapter Summary

1. **Provide some historical background for investing and investments.**

   Investing as an organized, legitimate human activity doesn't have a very long history. Three centuries ago there were no stock exchanges and only a handful of banks. As recently as the middle of the last century, the London Stock Exchange was a struggling weakling. Less than a century ago, few people in the United States owned any securities, much less any common stocks, which were considered to be wildly speculative investments. Stock price manipulation and insider trading were common practices in the 1920s. After the end of World War II, stock ownership, and investing in general, increased among Americans. However, as recently as 1970, over 80 percent of household financial assets consisted of savings accounts held at financial institutions. It wasn't until the late 1970s and 1980s that millions of Americans finally made the transformation from savers to investors.

2. **Examine some of Europe's most infamous speculative bubbles.**

   A speculative bubble is a situation where the price of some asset rises very sharply and quickly for no apparent reason other than the belief that the price will go still higher. Bubbles have taught two major lessons. First, while the long-run price of an investment will reflect its intrinsic value, in the short run a substantial difference can separate price and value. Second, bubbles illustrate that investors' emotions have affected the markets' performance in the past, and they will likely continue to affect performance in the future. Three infamous bubbles occurred in Europe in the 17th and 18th centuries. The Dutch went wild over, of all things, tulip bulbs in the 1630s. At the peak of the frenzy, a single, prized bulb could cost more than a new carriage complete with two horses. France was in a frenzy over the Mississippi Company (a company with a royal monopoly on trade with Louisiana and Canada) around 1720. Shares of the company often rose 10 or 20 percent per hour. A similar drama played out in England at the same time. Shares of the South Sea Company rose almost tenfold in less than six months in 1720. Hundreds of wildly speculative companies, some of them simple frauds, were formed to sell shares to the English public. These three bubbles eventually collapsed, causing all three countries serious economic consequences. For example, the English Parliament passed the Bubble Act in 1720 (and then repealed it in 1825) which made it difficult to raise capital in England for English ventures. As a result, English capital flowed overseas throughout the 18th and 19th centuries.

3. **Review some of the speculative bubbles that occurred in the United States early in this century.**

   Americans were no more immune from bubbles than their European ancestors' early bubbles. These were mere appetizers for the main course, the Great 1929 Stock Market Crash. A strong bull market turned into a bubble as stocks doubled and tripled in value over a period of months, helped along by low margin requirements and investment trusts. Stocks peaked on September 3, 1929 and the bubble broke on October 28 and 29, 1929. The Great Crash was only the beginning of a prolonged slide in stock prices. By 1932, the Dow Jones Industrial Average had lost about 90 percent of its peak value. Most investors shunned stocks throughout the 1930s and 1940s. It took a quarter of a century for the stock market to fully recover from the Great Crash.

4. **Examine several postwar speculative bubbles from the United States Market.**

   The postwar investment environment offered two notable changes: the increase in the importance of institutional investors and the substantial reduction in fraud and abusive trading practices. Neither change prevented bubbles. New issues and the so-called *'tronics boom,* were hot in the late 1950s and early 1960s, followed by the conglomerate boom of the late 1960s. In both periods, prices rose sharply to levels well above intrinsic values only to come crashing back to earth a few months later. The early 1970s saw a bubble in growth stocks, called the nifty fifty. Companies like McDonald's and Disney were selling, for a while, at 75 to 100 times earnings. The 1974 to 1975 bear market took care of the nifty fifty. The great bull market of the 1980s and early 1990s has seen its share of bubbles, many involving new issues such as biotechs, home shopping cable channels, and restaurants. The Tokyo stock market experienced a bubble similar to the American debacle of the 1920s. The great bull market also saw the largest one-day drop in history—Meltdown Monday—in 1987. Stock prices, however, soon recovered.

5. **Answer several important questions about speculative bubbles.**
Bubbles occur because people still make investment decisions in the heat of a wide range of human emotions. In the face of incomplete information and uncertainty, people tend to imitate each other. This makes bubbles both likely to reoccur and difficult to predict. Some commonsense rules could help investors avoid the bubble trap. New issues should be examined especially carefully. Despite many spectacular exceptions, most new issues underperform the market. Finally, no amount of regulation can prevent bubbles. Investors should ultimately be responsible for their own actions, so long as they are fully and fairly informed.

Key Terms

Speculative bubble	Babson Break
Discount a bill	'tronics boom
Stock exchange or bourse	New issue
Joint-stock association	Conglomerate
Tulipomania	Synergy
Mississippi Company	Bootstrap game
South Sea Company	Nifty fifty
Bubble Act	Meltdown Monday
Great 1929 Stock Market Crash	Biotech

Discussion Questions and Problems

1. As an organized, legitimate activity, how long of a history does investing have? When did investing enter mainstream American society?
2. List several characteristics of the U.S. investing environment prior to the Great Crash of 1929. How did these characteristics change following the end of World War II?
3. Compare and contrast tulipomania, the Mississippi scheme, and the South Sea bubble. What was the most serious consequence of each episode?
4. Explain how a speculative bubble differs from a standard bull market. Give an example of a bull market that turned into a speculative bubble.
5. Why do some professionals advise against investing in new issues? Give several examples of new issues that were successful and several that bombed.
6. What was the nifty fifty? How did it differ from other stock market bubbles?
7. Compare and contrast the Great Crash of 1929 and the 1987 market break. Was the 1987 market break the end of a speculative bubble?

8. Why do bubbles occur? Are bubbles likely to occur again?
9. Why are bubbles so difficult to predict? How can investors avoid falling into the bubble trap?
10. What are the two general lessons that speculative bubbles should teach investors? Should the government attempt to prevent bubbles?

Critical Thinking Exercises

1. This exercise requires library research. Identify the five top-performing industries during 1993 in terms of total stock returns. Most major financial publications (such as *Barron's* and *Business Week*) report industry performance, though different publications may define industries slightly differently.

   a. How well did each industry do relative to the overall market (e.g., the S&P 500)?

   b. Think about the characteristics of past speculative bubbles. Do you see bubbles developing in any of the five industry groups you identified? Why or why not?

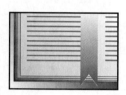

2. This exercise requires library research. Five of the possible bubble stocks of 1993 were Checker's Drive-In, Electronic Arts, EZ Corp, Lonestar Steakhouse, and President Riverboat.

   a. Find the highest and lowest price each sold for during the 1992–1993 period.

   b. Find the price of each at the end of 1993.

   c. Find their most recent prices.

   d. Are these bubble stocks? Why or why not?

Chapter 6

Technical and Fundamental Analysis: How the Pros Make Investment Decisions

Chapter Objectives

1. Define *technical analysis* and discuss its assumptions.
2. Identify the general categories of technical indicators and give examples.
3. Understand why technical analysis might work, and why it might not work.
4. Critically examine the track records of several technical indicators and technical analysts.
5. Define *fundamental analysis* and identify how it differs from technical analysis.
6. Examine part of the track records of fundamental analysts.

A recent study found that professionally managed pension funds, which invest primarily in common stocks, had a median yearly return (assuming reinvestment of all dividends) of 10.8 percent between 1974 and 1989.[1] While that might sound like a reasonable return, it is actually less than the average annual return for the S&P 500 stock index over the same 15-year period (12.1 percent). Further, the study found that the S&P 500 outperformed over 70 percent of the pension funds between 1974 and 1989. These performance figures don't even factor in the management fees the pension funds paid to their money managers. Depending on size, pension fund managers typically earn between 0.5 percent and 1.5 percent of the fund's assets as an annual management fee. It appears that a majority of pension funds would have enjoyed better performance, and saved costs as well, if they had simply bought and held the stocks that make up the S&P 500 index.

This is not an isolated example. Very few professional investors (money managers, advisors, securities analysts, market gurus, and so forth) seem to be able to consistently predict future market prices. In the late summer of

---

[1]See Josef Lakonishok et al., "The Structure and Performance of the Money Management Industry," *Brookings Papers on Economic Activity*, 1992, pp. 339–391.

1991, one well-known market guru told subscribers to his newsletter that his reading of various market indicators suggested that they should avoid common stocks.[2] Any investor who took the advice missed a year-end rally in stock prices that saw the S&P 500 increase by about 15 percent. Also in 1991, a securities analyst who had been praising America West Airlines for months failed to put out a sell recommendation until a couple of days before the airline filed for Chapter 11 bankruptcy protection; the stock had plunged prior to the analyst's change of heart.[3] Since advice from these managers, advisors, analysts, and gurus is rarely free, the natural question arises: Is professional investment advice worth the cost?

We are not prepared to answer the question unambiguously in this chapter. Rather, we will present a critical examination of the two techniques by which most professional investors make their investment decisions. Most professional investors rely on either fundamental or technical analysis, or some combination of the two, to make their investment decisions.

We begin Chapter 6 with a definition of *technical analysis* and an exploration of the assumptions on which it is based. Next, we identify the general categories of technical indicators and describe some of the best-known indicators. Then we discuss why technical analysis might work, and why it might not. We examine whether a technical indicator has provided correct buy and sell signals and review the past track records of three well-known technical analysts.

We focus next on fundamental analysis, beginning with a definition of the term and a discussion of how it differs from technical analysis. Next, we consider why fundamental analysis might work, as well as why it might not work. Finally, we examine some of the recent successes of fundamental analysts, and some of their recent failures. Our discussion of fundamental analysis is rather general in this chapter. The process of fundamental analysis will be covered in detail in Part III (Chapters 8 to 11).

What Is Technical Analysis?

Technical analysis refers to a broad group of indicators, all of them based on the belief that past patterns in security prices can reliably predict future price patterns.[4] Technical analysts believe that these patterns reflect the changing attitudes of investors to a variety of economic, political, and psychological factors. Technical analysis has been applied to stock indexes, individual stocks, bonds, foreign currencies, and many other investments. Those who believe in, or at least pay attention to, technical analysis are much more interested in a stock's past price record than how much the company is really worth.

Fundamental analysis, on the other hand, is based on the notion that every security has an intrinsic value. For common stocks, that value is based on the company's expected future earnings and dividend payments, the

---

[2]See "This Wall Street Seer Expects Stocks to Fall—and Soon," *Money,* August 1991, pp. 151–152. The seer, technical analyst Ned Davis, predicted that stocks would peak in August and then sharply decline.

[3]See "America West's Nose-Dive Puts Spotlight on Shearson 'Buy' Call," *The Wall Street Journal,* July 2, 1991, p. C1. The security analyst, Helane Becker of Shearson Lehman, strongly urged investors to buy America West Airlines in August 1989 when the stock was selling for about $12\frac{1}{2}$. The stock never traded above 10 during all of 1990. When Becker finally put out her sell recommendation the stock had dropped to $3\frac{7}{8}$.

[4]Several comprehensive, readable books have been written explaining technical analysis in detail. Two examples are Martin Pring, *Technical Analysis Explained* (New York: McGraw-Hill, 1980), and Martin Zweig, *Understanding Technical Forecasting* (New York: Dow Jones-Irwin, 1987).

expected growth rate of those earnings and dividends, and the degree of uncertainty surrounding these forecasts. Fundamental analysts, or fundamentalists, believe that the **intrinsic value** of a security can be estimated and that it must eventually sell for this intrinsic value. Fundamentalists search for **undervalued** or **overvalued securities,** securities whose prices are out of line with their intrinsic values, hoping to profit from the price correction.

Both technical and fundamental analysts believe that security prices depend on the interaction of **supply and demand.** They simply look at different factors to evaluate supply and demand. Fundamentalists believe that supply and demand are determined, at least in the long run, by such factors as the growth rate in earnings, dividends, and so forth. While technicians agree that intrinsic value plays a role in determining supply and demand, they argue that a wide range of other rational and irrational factors (such as investor emotions) govern these relationships. As a result, a technician would not hesitate to recommend a stock with indications of good technical strength, even if the stock appeared to be selling for more than its intrinsic value. In the technician's view, a favorable market supply and demand relationship is all that matters. Likewise, if the technician thought that a stock had poor supply and demand characteristics, he or she would probably not recommend the stock regardless of the relationship of its current price to its intrinsic value.

Analysts have developed literally dozens of different technical indicators. It may seem at times that there are more indicators than technicians! We will review just a few of the better-known indicators, divided into the following, somewhat rough and arbitrary, categories: indicators based on charting, indicators based on investor sentiment, and indicators based on market momentum.

Charting

Perhaps the best-known, and oldest, form of technical analysis is **charting.** This involves simply plotting the past price history of a security or index and then examining the chart for patterns that suggest shifts in the underlying supply and demand relationship, indicating shifts in investor attitudes. Anyone can draw a chart like that in Figure 6.1. The figure shows a chart of the daily high, low, and closing index values of the Dow Jones Industrial Average for November 1992. There is no hard and fast rule to determine how long a time period a chart should cover.

It isn't difficult to draw a chart, but interpreting it may be another matter. Since a technician who uses charts believes that price patterns accurately predict the future, the key is recognizing these patterns and understanding what they mean. One of the oldest and best-known forms of charting is the **Dow Theory,** which originated in a series of writings by Charles Dow in the early 1900s.[5]

Dow Theory. The Dow Theory is remarkably simple. It is based on the assumption that a demonstrated trend in stock prices will continue until a reversal in investor attitudes occurs. The theory identifies three types of moves in stock prices: primary, secondary, and minor moves. The **primary movement** is the major, or overall, trend in prices. The primary movement can be toward either rising prices **(bull market)** or falling prices **(bear market).** Within each primary movement, prices show secondary and minor movements. **Secondary movements** are defined as large changes (33 to 67

---

[5]Dow was a founder of Dow Jones & Company, which publishes the Dow Jones stock averages and *The Wall Street Journal.*

Figure 6.1

Example of a Price Chart: Dow Jones Industrial Average, November 1992

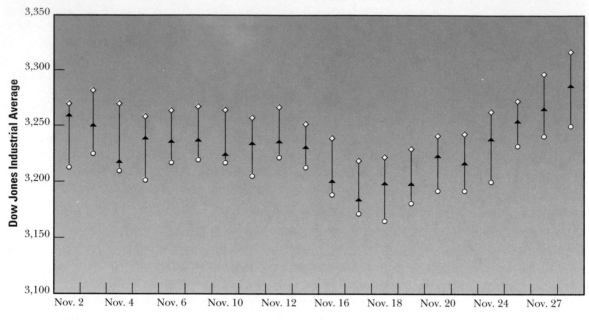

Source: *Barron's.*

percent of the primary change) in the opposite direction from the primary movement; secondary movements bring declines in a bull market or advances in a bear market. **Minor movements** are small advances or declines that last only a few days and, Dow Theory adherents believe, can usually be ignored. The objective is to determine changes in the primary movement of stock prices. In other words, the theory attempts to ascertain when a secondary move is about to become a change in the primary direction of prices. It does this by establishing what are known as **support levels,** below which prices tend not to fall, and **resistance levels,** above which prices tend not to rise.

Figure 6.2 shows a price chart of the weekly closing values of the Dow Jones Industrial Average between January 1993 and August 1993. Notice that the primary move throughout the period was positive, but a number of secondary moves carried prices lower. These secondary moves established support levels that the market never broke through during this period. In fact, each successive support level was higher than the prior support level. The market established a support level around 3,300 in February. Another support level was established in April at about 3,380, and still another was established in early June at around 3,460. Figure 6.2 also shows that once the secondary downward moves reversed themselves, the market broke through the established resistance level. Overall, this is a very bullish pattern.

Different technicians believe in support and resistance levels for different specific reasons, but they generally agree on the following explanation. As prices approach a support level, investors who failed to buy at the prior low start buying, pushing prices back upward. Similarly, when prices start to approach a resistance level, investors who failed to sell at the prior high start doing so, forcing prices back downward. If prices break through either a support or resistance level, this suggests a substantial change in investor attitude. Remember, no fundamental force has to propel this change in the market's supply and demand relationship.

Figure 6.2

Support and Resistance Levels: Dow Jones Industrial Average, January through August 1993

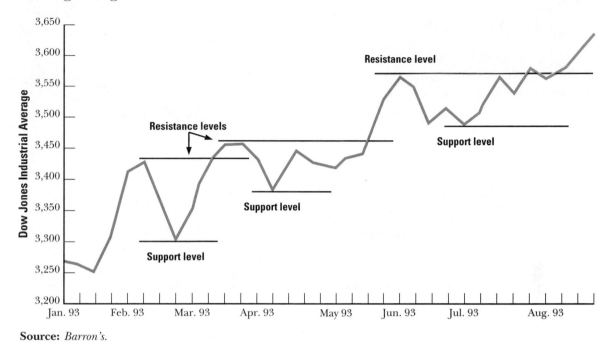

Source: *Barron's.*

Figure 6.3

Trading Range: Dow Jones Industrial Average, March through July 1991

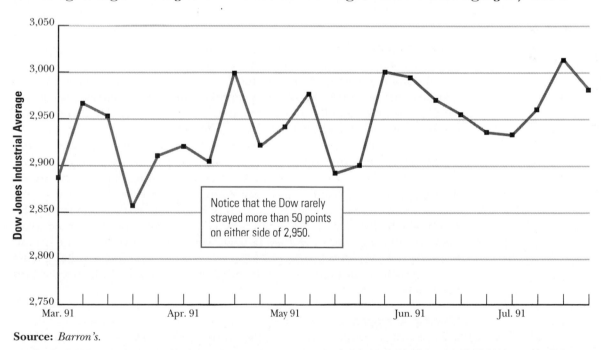

Source: *Barron's.*

Trading Range. Figure 6.3 presents another chart of weekly Dow Jones Industrial Average values from March through July 1991. This chart shows what technicians refer to as a **trading range.** Notice that no primary trend is evident; index values ranged between about 2,850 (the support level) and

Figure 6.4

Trendlines: Dow Jones Industrial Average, January through August 1993

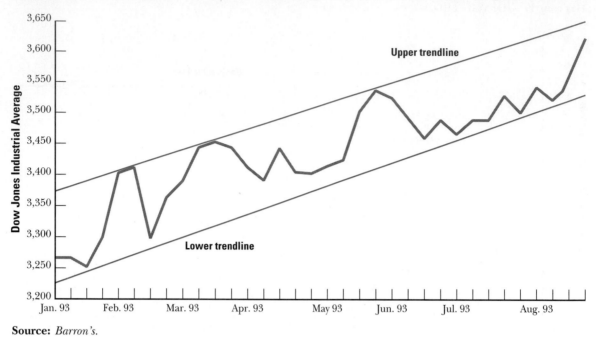

Source: *Barron's.*

3,010 (the resistance level) throughout the period, rarely straying more than 50 points on either side of 2,950. Some technicians see a trading range as a bullish indicator while others see it as a bearish indicator. We'll look at this issue again a little later.

More Complex Price Patterns. Beyond the Dow Theory, technicians may look for a variety of specific price patterns in their charts, including head-and-shoulders formations, double tops or bottoms, various broadening formations, and so forth. All of these complex price patterns are, we argue, simply variations, modifications, or extensions of the basic Dow Theory. All use the notions of support and resistance levels.

Figure 6.4 shows an example of a more complicated price pattern in the weekly Dow Jones Industrial Average between January and August 1993, plotting **trendlines.** The overall trend is clearly positive, but do the trendlines suggest that the bull market is running out of steam? Most technicians would answer no because the upper trendline (the line that connects all the secondary highs) and the lower trendline (that connects all the secondary lows) are moving closer together (a narrowing formation). Since the overall trend is positive, this formation suggests to some technicians that plenty of buyers still await even a small drop in prices to bring them surging into the market.

Moving Averages. Another type of charting uses **moving averages**—averages of prices over specified numbers of days (or weeks, or months) which move over time. Each day (or week, or month) the technician adds the most recent price and deletes the most distant price from the average. An example of a moving average is shown in Figure 6.5, which plots weekly values for the Dow Jones Industrial Average (again between January and August 1993), along with the index's 13-week moving average.

Figure 6.5

Dow Jones Industrial Average and Its 13-Week Moving Average

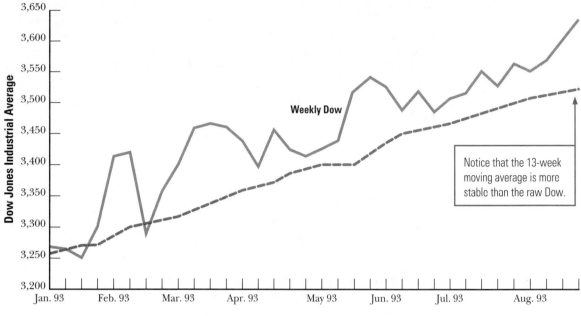

Source: *Barron's.*

Since a moving average smooths the variations in any series, technicians argue that a moving average can represent support and resistance levels. To see how this would work, go back to Figure 6.5. The 13-week moving average establishes a support level. With the exception of mid-January, the Dow remained above its 13-week moving average, giving a bullish signal consistent with the indications of the charts in Figures 6.2 and 6.4. Note that a couple of times a secondary decline dropped the index close to the 13-week moving average. Had the index broken through its 13-week moving average, most technicians would have taken the change as a signal that the bull market was over and a bear market was about to begin.

Investor Sentiment Indicators

Many technicians have moved beyond studying charts to looking at indicators that, they argue, measure **investor sentiment.** They seek to gauge whether investors are optimistic (bullish) or pessimistic (bearish). Some of these investor sentiment indicators are based on contrary opinion, while others are based on following the so-called smart money.

Contrary Opinion Theory. The notion behind **contrary opinion theory** is quite simple. As the market approaches a peak (i.e., the primary upward move in prices is about over), the consensus among investors tends to be bullish. Likewise, as the market approaches a trough, the consensus among investors tends to be bearish. Two indicators that technicians believe measure contrary opinion are the odd-lot sales ratio and the cash positions of mutual funds.

The odd-lot sales ratio is defined as odd-lot sales volume divided by odd-lot buying volume, where volume is usually measured in number of shares. (An odd-lot is a trade involving less than a round lot, or 100 shares.) The rationale behind this indicator is simply that small investors, who are much more likely to trade in odd-lots, are generally less sophisticated and more conservative. As a result, technicians argue, small investors tend to sell toward the end of a bear market (i.e., just before the primary downward move stops) and they tend to buy toward the end of a bull market (i.e., just before the market peaks). Thus, a declining odd-lot sales ratio, indicating increasing margins of odd-lot purchases over sales, tells technicians that the bull market has about run its course, so they consider selling.

The cash positions of mutual funds are another contrary opinion indicator. Every mutual fund holds a percentage of its assets in cash or cash equivalent securities (such as T-bills). Mutual funds can affect stock prices significantly by moving cash in and out of stocks. Some technicians see a sign of an impending market top if the cash positions of mutual funds are shrinking, or are near historic lows (say, less than 5 percent of total assets). In other words, they fear that demand for stocks is about to drop. On the other hand, if mutual funds have as much as 15 percent or so of their assets in cash, technicians may conclude that stocks are likely to enter, or continue, a primary bull market since the demand for stocks is likely to increase.

Smart Money Indicators. Other indicators of investor sentiment are based on the notion that investors should follow the **smart money,** investors who are more astute than average and, the argument goes, should lead bull and bear markets. Two examples of smart money indicators are short sales by specialists and the level of debit balances in brokerage accounts.

Specialists on the New York Stock Exchange, as part of their market-making function, often engage in short selling. Specialists are also allowed, with certain restrictions, to sell stocks short for their own accounts. Technicians believe that specialists may have access to better, more timely information, giving them a better feel for the future direction of prices compared to average investors. Therefore, if technicians see specialists engaged in heavy short selling, they take this as a bearish signal. Likewise, if short selling by specialists is relatively light, technicians take this as a sign of an impending bull market. To make this determination, technicians usually look at the ratio of specialist short sales to total short sales. This ratio is typically around 40 percent. If it rises above, say, 50 percent, technicians may conclude that specialists are selling short more heavily, and the market is about to fall.

Finally, technicians often look at the debit balances in brokerage accounts (that is, total margin debt). This indicator is based on the notion that only more sophisticated investors use margin debt. Thus, if the amount of margin debt in brokerage accounts is rising, these investors are buying. In fact, these supposedly more astute investors are borrowing to buy stocks. Technicians take this as a very bullish indicator.

Market Momentum Indicators

The final group of technical indicators we're going to review are based on a concept known as **market momentum.** Those who believe in market momentum equate the market for stocks (or any security) to a freight train: it takes a long time to get going (either upward or downward) and it takes a long time to stop (or change directions) once it gets going. Trendlines, which we discussed a little earlier, can be considered a measure of momentum.

Technicians use many other indicators to measure market momentum, the most obvious of which is simply trading volume. A technician sees a rising market on low, or perhaps even falling, volume as a sign of an impending peak since it indicates weak upward momentum. On the other hand, a rising market on increasing volume is a sign that the market has strong momentum and, therefore, prices are likely to go higher before peaking.

Advance–Decline Ratio. Another simple indicator of market momentum is the relationship between advancing and declining stocks, called the **diffusion index.** The diffusion index is often calculated as the number of advancing stocks plus one-half the number of unchanged stocks divided by the total number of stocks trading. A rising diffusion index is usually interpreted as a bullish signal, a signal that a primary upward move in the market has substantial momentum behind it. In contrast, if the diffusion index is falling as the market rises, technicians see a sign that the bull market is losing its momentum and approaching a peak.

A variation of an advance–decline ratio is to determine the number of stocks that are selling above or below their respective moving averages. For example, assume that 90 percent of the stocks that make up the S&P 500 are selling at prices above their 13-week moving averages. Many technicians would argue that this strongly suggests that a trend has enough momentum to carry the overall market higher in the coming months.

Relative Strength Indicators. Another example of technical indicators that purport to measure market momentum are **relative strength indicators.** A simple measure of relative strength divides the price of stock (or group of stocks) by a broad market average and examines the trend over time. Relative strength indicators can track individual stocks or groups of stocks, and evaluate the strength of a specific stock relative to the overall market. If a stock shows rising relative strength, that means it is rising in price by more than the overall market. This indicates that the stock has established a great deal of forward momentum and is considered to be a bullish indicator.

Assessment of Technical Analysis

We have described technical analysis and some of the better-known technical indicators. Many of these indicators are simple to calculate and their interpretations seem straightforward and full of common sense. For investors, however, the most important question is, how well does technical analysis work? This question evokes a great deal of controversy. A large number of investors believe, or at least follow, technicians. This group believes that charting, for example, really does work. While technical analysis has attracted a number of individuals who can best be described as crackpots, even charlatans, the field also includes a number of very serious, almost scholarly professionals who carefully examine their technical indicators. Some of these individuals have built impressive track records.

On the other hand, many critics, especially members of the academic community, argue that technical analysis does not, indeed cannot, work. These individuals view technicians the same way astronomers view astrologers. Burton Malkiel, one of the more articulate critics of technical analysis, flatly states: "I, personally, have never known a successful technician, but I have seen the wrecks of several unsuccessful ones."[6] This group asserts that

---

[6]Burton Malkiel, *A Random Walk Down Wall Street*, 5th ed. (New York: W. W. Norton, 1990), p. 131. Malkiel is a professor of economics at Princeton University and has extensive Wall Street experience. He currently sits on the boards of several investment companies and is a governor of the American Stock Exchange.

technical analysis cannot work because, if for no other reason, it is inconsistent with the efficient markets hypothesis (EMH). We will review the EMH, evidence that both confirms and contradicts it, and its implications for technical analysis in Chapter 7.

While we cannot hope to resolve the controversy over technical analysis, we would like to provide some basic insight into the question of how well it works. We begin with a discussion of some of the reasons why technical analysis might work, and why it might not work in actual investing situations.

Why Technical Analysis Might Work

In describing technical indicators, we explained some of the basic rationales behind them, in other words, why they might work. For example, recall that the basic rationale for the Dow Theory is that investors who held back from buying a stock at its prior low (or support level) will be anxious to buy as the stock approaches that price level again. There are other reasons why technical analysis might work, or at least appear to work. Many of these deal with the inadequacies of fundamental information.

It is quite possible that not all investors have equal access to fundamental information. Also, some investors might have access to relevant information before other investors. This suggests that a lag might separate the initial dissemination of information from the stock market reaction. Therefore, some investors may miss out on major moves if they wait for the fundamental information to reach them. Perhaps following the smart money (investors who presumably have better and/or more timely access to information) could produce higher returns than the general market over the long run.

Technical analysis might also work if fundamental information is incomplete or misleading. As we will see in Chapter 11, accounting information can be manipulated to represent a situation as something other than what it really is. In addition, fundamental information reveals very little about nonquantitative factors such as employee morale. Past stock price patterns might provide better insight into these nonquantitative factors, technicians argue.

Beyond the inadequacies of fundamental information, technical analysis might work because investor emotions can have a major impact on stock prices. We saw that impact time and time again in Chapter 5 when we discussed speculative bubbles. Sometimes investor fear and greed really do seem to drive prices. It is hard to explain the changes in Home Shopping Network shares any other way. Technicians argue that their indicators can spot a speculative bubble that is just beginning to rise and, perhaps more important, one that is about to burst.

Aside from these reasons, technical analysis might appear to work through the effects of a self-fulfilling prophecy. For example, assume that lots of investors believe in and follow moving averages. These investors abandon the market if a stock market index breaks below its moving average. Assume that the S&P 500's 13-week moving average is 450, and the index closes at 445. These investors are likely to sell. As a result, stock prices are likely to drop further, at least in the short run. Does this mean that the indicator works? One could argue that the answer is both yes and no.

For all the arguments for reasons that technical analysis might work, a number of strong arguments also give reasons that it might *not* work. For one thing, many technical indicators might give their signals only after it was too late. Since sharp reversals in prices can occur quickly and with little warning, by the time many charts give their signals, the market may have already turned. Furthermore, many traders may actually try to anticipate technicians' buy or sell signals. In other words, as the price of a stock approaches a resistance level, traders may assume that it will break through this time and buy before, not after, it crosses the resistance level.

Another reason that technical analysis might fail to work comes from the fact that the financial markets appear to function pretty well and prices appear to adjust very quickly to new information. A clear buy or sell signal from a technical indicator that has an established track record of success is likely to cause prices to adjust so quickly that most investors couldn't profit. This leads traders to try to anticipate the signal earlier and earlier, raising the possibility of mixed forecasts. The earlier one tries to forecast anything, the more uncertainty the forecast includes.

How Well Do Technical Indicators Work?

We have examined some reasons why technical analysis might work, and some reasons why it might fail. To resolve some of the controversy, we will evaluate the track records of some technical indicators and some well-known technicians. Again, our discussion will not attempt to be comprehensive.

Before we get to that question, however, we need to define how to determine whether technical analysis does or doesn't work. It is not enough to say that technical analysis works if it correctly predicts an event, say, a bull market. One can say that technical analysis works only if it consistently produces above-average returns for investors who follow its signals. Above-average returns must exceed the returns that the investor would have earned by simply buying and holding a similar investment over the same period of time. Since following technical advice usually implies more transactions compared to a buy-and-hold strategy, differences in transaction costs must also be taken into account.

Before we go further we should note a problem with testing how well technical analysis works: the interpretation of many technical indicators is often very ambiguous. In addition, most technicians examine several indicators when making their forecasts. This can make it quite difficult to scientifically evaluate the forecasts. Most technicians admit that interpreting technical indicators is very subjective, more an art than a science. Some technicians commonly believe that a certain indicator gives a bullish signal, while others see a bearish signal in the same data.

An example of this is shown by *The Wall Street Journal* article in the Investment Insights feature. The article points out that the Dow Jones Industrial Average's trading range between mid-February and mid-July 1991 gave a bullish indicator to some technicians, and a bearish indicator to others. (We looked at a portion of this trading range in Figure 6.3.) The bulls argued that "the long sideways move is a sturdy 'base' for further advances." The bears said that the "flatness of stock prices since February is a 'top' marking the end of the rally that started in October [1990]—perhaps even the end of the long-term bull market born in 1982." One of these forecasts was, of course, proved correct. The market broke out on the top side of the trading range in December 1991 as the Dow advanced from 2,950 to about 3,200, an increase of about 15 percent.

With that caveat in mind, we can say generally that the scientific evidence does not support technical analysis. Study after study has shown that simple buy-and-hold investing almost always outperforms an active strategy based on some technical indicator, after adjusting for transaction costs. Since this literature is reviewed in detail elsewhere, we thought it might be more interesting to construct one of our own tests.[7] Unlike the studies cited in the

---

[7]Most tests of technical analysis also test the efficient market hypothesis. Many sources provide a detailed bibliography of these studies. See, for example, Edwin Elton and Martin Gruber, *Modern Portfolio Theory and Investment Analysis,* 3rd ed. (New York: Wiley, 1987), pp. 361–405; see also Thomas Copeland and J. Fred Weston, *Financial Theory and Corporate Policy,* 3rd ed. (Reading, Mass.: Addison-Wesley, 1988), pp. 361–400.

Dow's Narrow "Trading Range" Fuels Bulls' Hopes, Bears' Fears

It's almost spooky. No matter how sharply the stock market zig-zags in a given day, it really isn't going anywhere.

For five long months now, the Dow Jones Industrial Average has hovered within 3.2 percent of 2,950. Known to Wall Street as a "trading range," this aimless flickering by itself holds no clues as to which way stock prices will head when they finally "break out." But analysts are saying that after months of confinement, any breakout could be powerful—for better or for worse.

"Trading ranges tend to end because of an extraneous, unexpected event," says Bob Nurock, editor of Bob Nurock's Advisory, a Paoli, Pa., market letter.

The current trading range is unusual in several ways. It's long—102 trading days so far. It's narrow—"the tightest one that I can recall," says Jack Solomon, technical analyst for Bear Stearns. And it's been peppered with sharp one-day moves, both up and down.

"The market has become a toy for huge [institutions] that can extract short-term profits out of it," says Henry Lowenthal, head of Equitron, a money-management and consulting firm in Highland Park, Ill.

In his view, the single-day surges reflect the big boys playing with options, futures, and other new types of securities. And he believes short-term trading overall is way up, compared with past years.

Both bulls and bears can find fuel for their arguments in the current trading range. Here's what the two camps are saying now, starting with the optimists, though they don't necessarily outnumber the pessimists.

In the optimists' view, the long sideways move is a sturdy "base" for further advances.

"The more time that passes in this narrow range, the better the chance that we'll get out of it on the upside," says James H. Morgan, president of Interstate/Johnson Lane, a brokerage firm based in Charlotte, N.C. "The market was definitely ahead of itself early in the year, but now it's had a chance to digest its January and February gains," he says.

Moreover, Mr. Morgan believes the Federal Reserve System will stay "accommodative" all year, meaning it won't clamp down on access to credit. He predicts the Fed governors "will not be tightening; they would even ease if they saw upward pressure on [interest] rates to the point" that the economy could suffer.

Edward Kerschner, strategist for Paine-Webber, thinks slightly higher corporate profits and slightly lower interest rates will combine to levitate the Dow industrials out of the trading range. He looks for a rise to 3,150 by year end and 3,300 early next year. His view: Inflation will level out at about 3.5 percent. Long-term interest rates will drift down below 8 percent, compared with the recent 8.5 percent on 30-year Treasury bonds.

Another bull is Mr. Nurock, who says: "I think the surprise may be that the Fed is going to ease again" this summer, after Alan Greenspan is reappointed chairman or another chairman is named.

To pessimists, the flatness of stock prices since February is a "top" marking the end of the rally that started in October—perhaps even the end of the long-term bull market born in 1982.

The arguments for a top are familiar by now. Stocks are high in relation to current corporate earnings, dividends, and other yardsticks. People, corporations, and government bodies

references, our test is more anecdotal than scientific. We will look at the track record over the past few years of the **Barron's Confidence Index.**

The Barron's Confidence Index. The Barron's Confidence Index, compiled and published by the weekly investment magazine *Barron's,* can be classified as a measure of investor sentiment. The Confidence Index is the ratio of the average yield on a small sample of high-quality corporate bonds (those with AAA or AA ratings) divided by the average yield on a small sample of medium-quality corporate bonds (those with A or BBB ratings). Since high-quality bonds always yield less than lower-quality bonds, the index is always less than 1. An index of 0.9, for example, means that high-quality corporate bonds are yielding about 90 percent of what medium-quality corporate bonds yield. As the index approaches 1, that is, as the yield spread between high-quality and medium-quality corporates decreases, investor sentiment is said to be more optimistic about the future. This is usually considered to be a bullish signal for stocks. Investors are considered to be more optimistic

remain heavily indebted. State and local tax increases may hamper the recovery. A banquet of new stock offerings has left many investors satiated.

What's new are some technical arguments, based on the market's internal indicators. Greg Kuhn, an Easton, Pa., money manager who relies on technical analysis, is unnerved by several signposts that have turned negative in the past month. Kuhn Asset Management has sold most of its stocks and is 75 percent in cash.

"The number of stocks making new highs is drying up, and the number of stocks making new lows is increasing," Mr. Kuhn says. Specifically, he likes to compare the number of new highs with the total of new highs and lows. "When that indicator goes above 90 percent, you're dealing with a very strong market," he says; "in February, it got as high as 98 percent."

Investors "can stay in stocks until that indicator drops below 70 percent," which happened at the end of June, Mr. Kuhn suggests. "Right now, we are below that, at 52 percent, and it is weakening. Now we're dealing with a strong sell signal."

Also disturbing Mr. Kuhn: "Horrid action" prevails in foreign stock markets, especially Tokyo. The percentage of stocks above their 30-week moving averages is falling. The public isn't short-selling, or betting on lower stock prices, but knowledgeable specialists on the New York Stock Exchange are. In addition, gold stocks are moving up, often a bad sign for the overall market.

During "five months of congestion," close to 20 billion shares have been traded, says Richard Arms, technical analyst with Principal Eppler Guerin & Turner. His work suggests that a similar amount of volume will propel the next big move. He thinks that move will be negative, carrying the Dow industrials all the way down to about

2,550 by September. He selected that number by extending a line through the market's low points in 1982, 1987, and 1990.

INVESTMENT INSIGHTS

History doesn't give much ammunition to the bulls—or to the bears. Laszlo Birinyi, head of Birinyi Associates, a New York market consulting firm, has studied 13 trading-range markets since 1973 that lasted at least 50 trading days and had tight ranges (roughly 3 percent above and below the midpoint). Three months after the breakout from the range, stocks were higher in seven cases, lower in six.

But Mr. Birinyi says the bulls' odds are better if a bull market prevailed when the trading range began. In such cases, he says, the most common results is a "continuation of the rally."

Mr. Nurock ruefully recalls the long trading range of 1976, when the industrial average was locked between 950 and 1,000. Stocks broke to the downside, recovered, then fell into an ugly bear market in 1977, dragging the average down to about 800.

But Mr. Birinyi thinks a better parallel may be 1985. The industrial average spent most of the year locked in a trading range around 1,300. In September, it broke to the upside, launching a big rally that went all the way to 1,900. He concludes that a flat market isn't a terrible thing: "Not going up doesn't mean going down."

Source: John R. Dorfman, "Dow's Narrow 'Trading Range' Fuels Bulls' Hopes, Bears' Fears," *The Wall Street Journal*, July 10, 1991, p. C1. Reprinted by permission of The Wall Street Journal, © 1991 Dow Jones & Company, Inc. All rights reserved worldwide.

because they appear more willing to buy lower-quality bonds. On the other hand, if the index is getting smaller, the indicator is said to be bearish because more pessimistic investors are avoiding lower-quality bonds. Therefore, a rising Confidence Index signals a coming rise in stock prices while a falling Confidence Index signals a coming fall.

How accurately did the Confidence Index predict market moves between the beginning of 1990 and August 1993? In order to make this assessment, we need to establish some criteria to state when the index gives buy and sell signals. Noting that any criteria are somewhat arbitrary (a difficulty that complicates proper tests of any technical analysis method), we take a Confidence Index above its 26-week moving average as a buy signal. A Confidence Index below its 26-week moving average gives a sell signal.

Figure 6.6 plots the Confidence Index against its 26-week moving average between January 1990 and August 1993. This suggests that the Confidence Index, using our criteria, gave nine fairly clear buy or sell signals between January 1990 and August 1993. Table 6.1 lists the date of each signal, the

Figure 6.6

Barron's Confidence Index versus Its 26-Week Moving Average: January 1990 through August 1993

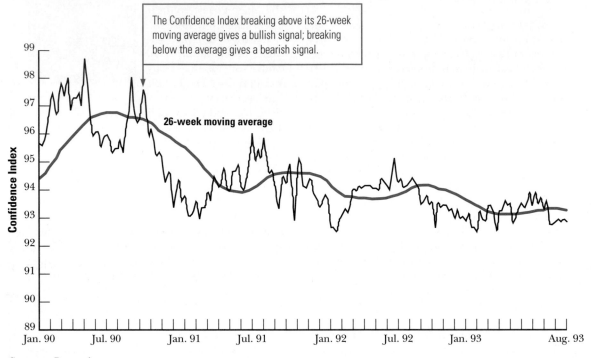

The Confidence Index breaking above its 26-week moving average gives a bullish signal; breaking below the average gives a bearish signal.

Source: *Barron's.*

nature of the signal (buy or sell), and the Dow Jones Industrial Average on the date of the signal. In addition, the table gives the percentage change in the Dow between that signal and the prior signal. The data suggest, at best, a mixed track record for the Confidence Index.

The Confidence Index gave a clear sell signal on May 18, 1990. This turned out to be the correct signal since the Dow proceeded to drop about 350 points (12.3 percent) between May and August 31, 1990, when the Confidence Index gave a buy signal. Between August 31, 1990 and October 5, 1990 (another sell signal), the Dow managed a small gain of less than 1.5 percent. The Confidence Index then missed the run-up in stock prices during late January and February 1991 (called *the war rally*). The Dow rose over 17 percent between the Confidence Index's October 5, 1990 sell signal and its tardy March 16, 1991 buy signal.

The Confidence Index also missed the big year-end rally in 1991. In December 1991, the Dow added close to 300 points, yet the Confidence Index, having given a sell signal in August 1991, didn't give another buy signal until late February 1992. The Confidence Index did slightly better during the rest of 1992. Between February's buy signal and August's sell signal, the Dow rose slightly (up 1.34 percent), and between August and the following January's buy signal, the index fell slightly (down 0.21 percent). The Confidence Index gave a buy signal on January 23, 1993, and the Dow advanced more than 6 percent until a sell signal in July 1993. Between July and the end of August 1993, however, the Dow added almost another 150 points.

In summary, then, six of the nine signals given by the Confidence Index between January 1990 and August 1993 correctly predicted market behavior, though some of the gains or losses were minimal. However, the Confidence

Table 6.1

Buy and Sell Signals from the Barron's
Confidence Index: January 1990 through
August 1993

Buy Signals			Sell Signals		
Date	Dow	Percentage Change	Date	Dow	Percentage Change
			5/18/90	2,831.7	−12.3%
8/31/90	2,483.4	+1.3%	10/5/90	2,516.8	+17.3
3/16/91	2,952.2	+1.6	8/16/91	2,998.4	+9.1
2/28/92	3,269.5	+1.3	8/14/92	3,313.3	−0.2
1/23/93	3,306.3	+6.2	7/2/93	3,510.5	+3.9[a]

[a]Through August 27, 1993 (not a buy signal), when the Dow
closed at 3,648.2.

Index missed the two largest-percentage increases in the Dow during this period. As a result, it is doubtful that an investor who used the Confidence Index to time market moves between 1990 and mid-1993 would have done any better than an investor who simply bought and held the Dow stocks throughout the period. Factoring in transaction costs, the active investor who followed the Confidence Index may have actually done worse than the passive investor who bought and held.

Track Records of Some Technical Analysts

Another way of assessing technical analysis is to critically examine the track records of well-known technicians. We will look at the track records of three: Robert Prechter, Elaine Garzarelli, and Martin Zweig.

Robert Prechter. Robert Prechter is best known for advocating the **Elliot wave**. The Elliot wave principle, first developed and published by R. N. Elliot in 1939, posits that stock prices exhibit basic wave characteristics common to all natural forces. These waves move with certain rhythmic regularity based on a numerical series discovered by a 13th-century mathematician. Elliot believed that one could predict major turning points in the stock market by examining its waves.

Prechter, the story goes, rediscovered the Elliot wave principle while working as a technical analyst for Merrill Lynch in the 1970s. He soon left Merrill Lynch and began writing his own investment newsletter. His first major forecast using the Elliot wave technique turned out to be pretty accurate. Prechter was one of the first market gurus to turn bullish in the early 1980s when the Dow was still under 1,000. His prediction of a 2,700-point Dow by the mid-1980s turned out to be pretty close to the mark. (The Dow hit 2,722 in August 1987.)

Unfortunately for his subscribers, some of Prechter's later forecasts were way off the mark. During late summer and early fall 1987, when the market had started to show signs of weakness, Prechter remained very bullish. Even in early October 1987, he urged clients to aggressively buy stocks and boldly predicted a 3,600 point Dow by the end of 1988. Those who took his advice probably wished they hadn't when the Dow dropped over 500 points on October 19, 1987.

After the 1987 market break, Prechter dramatically reversed direction, becoming very bearish. "The message of October 1987," he said, "is that the great bull market is over.'' He predicted that the Dow would fall below 400, losing about 85 percent of its value, by the early 1990s. Needless to say, Prechter missed the major rebound in stock prices that occurred in 1988 and 1989. The Dow finished 1989 at 2,753.20, an increase of over 57 percent from its 1987 low. As stocks continued to rise during both years, Prechter was recommending T-bills over stocks. In a February 1991 interview, Prechter stated that stocks would soon drop to a major bear market bottom within the next several years.[8]

Apparently, many investors have wiped out trying to ride the Elliot wave to success. When *Barron's* published the February 1991 article referring to Prechter as a top market timer, it received several letters attacking Prechter's track record, calling his forecasts "crummy," and labeling the Elliot wave theory as nonsense.[9]

Elaine Garzarelli. Another well-known market guru is Elaine Garzarelli, a senior vice president with Lehman Brothers. Unlike Robert Prechter's single-indicator forecast, Garzarelli claims to base her forecasts on at least a dozen indicators measuring such variables as monetary policy and investor psychology. The actual contents and form of her model are closely guarded secrets.

Garzarelli became famous as one of the few on Wall Street to predict the 1987 market break. She began to turn bearish in August, and by September 1, she had switched her model portfolio to 100 percent cash. By October 11, she became convinced that a major break was coming based on a steep drop in Japanese bond prices and hints from the Federal Reserve of higher interest rates to reduce inflationary pressures. In an interview on October 13, with the Dow at 2,508, Garzarelli told *USA Today* that she was convinced that a major market crash (possibly 500 points or more) would occur within a few days. Of course on October 19, the Dow dropped over 500 points; not a bad prediction as it turned out!

An analyst has to be right only once for people to listen, at least for a while, and Garzarelli became an almost overnight sensation. Unfortunately, her forecasts right after the market break were not quite as accurate. Garzarelli told investors that she wouldn't touch stocks for a while, expecting the Dow to drop another 200 to 400 points.[10] In fact, the Dow's low for 1987 was set on October 19. The index ended 1987 at 1,938.83, actually up slightly for the year and up about 12 percent from the October low. Garzarelli remained bearish or neutral throughout 1988 and much of 1989 as the market continued to rise.

Garzarelli's mixed track record since her famous 1987 prediction is illustrated in the article in the Investment Insights feature. As the article points out, the mutual fund she manages, the Shearson Sector Analysis Fund, has performed poorly since 1988 compared to both the S&P 500 and the average equity mutual fund. For example, $1,000 invested in the Shearson Sector Analysis Fund at the beginning of 1988 would have been worth about $1,400 at the end of 1992 (an average annual compound return of slightly less than 7 percent). By contrast, an investment of $1,000 in the S&P 500 would have been worth more than $2,000 at the end of 1992 (an average annual compound return of almost 16 percent).

---

[8]See *Barron's*, February 18, 1991, p. 8.

[9]See "Letters to the Editor," *Barron's*, March 4, 1991, p. 20.

[10]This prediction upset many on Wall Street, including colleagues in her own firm, because they felt it increased the instability in the stock market. Some even believe that her prediction contributed to a 157-point decline in the Dow on October 26, 1987.

But What Have You Done for Us Lately?

Elaine M. Garzarelli had already amassed a huge following on Wall Street when she made the call of the century. Weeks before the October 1987 stock market crash, the Shearson Lehman Bros. strategist urged her followers to dump their stocks, and days before, she warned that a drop in the Dow Jones Industrial Average of at least 500 points was imminent. Anyone who heeded her admonition will probably be forever grateful.

But those who've put their money in her hands since then have been sadly disappointed. True, the Shearson Lehman Bros. Sector Analysis Fund, the mutual fund the brokerage firm launched in the summer of 1987 to capitalize on her fame and talent, had a terrific start. Her months-old fund dodged the crash and even made a little from it.

Since then, however, the fund has been a sorry also-ran. Every year, it has underperformed the average U.S. diversified equity fund, and in four of the years, it underperformed the Standard & Poor's 500 to boot (table). In the first half of 1993, the fund was barely in the black, while the S&P 500 returned 4.9 percent. In all, $1,000 invested at the start of 1988 would have been worth $1,405 at the end of June 1993 compared to $2,122 for the average U.S. fund and $2,190 for the S&P. Not surprisingly, investors have left in droves. From over $700 million in 1988, the fund had dwindled to less than $200 million.

Garzarelli's experience shows that it's a far cry from giving advice to making real-world investment decisions. In February 1988 the same indicators that screamed "sell" in 1987 turned bullish. But she ignored her computer model and remained in cash. She later traded stocks furiously in a failed effort to catch up. So, while the S&P delivered a 16.6 percent return in 1988, Garzarelli's fund was a disaster—losing more than 13 percent. "Trading is not what I do well," she says.

Nor does she pretend to be a stock-picker. Garzarelli's models identify industry groups, or sectors, such as regional banks and newspaper stocks, her two most recent industry picks, which are expected to outperform the market. Her

models, however, do not select stocks. She says 80 percent of her sector picks are profitable. A review of her "Attractive Industry Group" list by Coopers & Lybrand indicates that her industry picks beat the S&P 500 by an average of

INVESTMENT INSIGHTS

five percentage points a year. To buy individual stocks for the fund, Garzarelli chooses companies rated No. 1 and No. 2 by Shearson analysts. Obviously, many of those picks underperformed their groups.

Garzarelli had a chance to redeem herself during the bear market of 1990. Her indicators turned bearish on July 7, when the Dow was just shy of 3,000, but her superiors had forbidden her to sell out the fund without their permission. After days of trying to get an O.K., she says: "I was told I could do a little selling but I couldn't go entirely to cash." The fund sank as the Dow slid below 2,400 into the fall. That was when her indicators turned bullish again, but her shareholders ended up in the red for 1990 anyway.

"Exorbitant" Pay. Since then, she has remained steadfastly bullish. She thinks the Dow could reach 4,000 by the spring of 1994 and does not foresee a significant market pullback until then.

Fortunately for Garzarelli, the fund is not her main source of income. That comes from commissions paid by institutional investors such as Fidelity Investments, T. Rowe Price, and the College Retirement Equity Fund. She writes voluminous reports and holds conference calls and face-to-face meetings with hundreds of clients every year. She also spends half her time on the road. For this, she says, "the company pays me an exorbitant amount of money"—believed to be in excess of $2 million.

With much of her own money invested in the fund, it's more than a matter of pride to turn it around. Garzarelli, who will remain with Lehman Bros. when Shearson merges with Smith Barney at the end of July, is negotiating with Lehman to set up her own investment management company. That would allow her to buy the fund from Shearson. She would then slash its fees, which drag down performance by eating up more than 2 percent a year, nearly twice the mutual-fund average. She's also considering cutting costs

(continued)

The article also illustrates just how difficult it can be to translate a general market prediction, like those Garzarelli makes, into actual, coherent investment strategies. As the article points out, Garzarelli's model points to the direction of the overall market and promising industries. It doesn't identify

(continued)

further by forgoing stock-picking and applying her market timing to an S&P index portfolio.

A Garzarelli management unit wouldn't just run one fund. She'd like to manage institutional and retail accounts as well and wants to pursue global investing. "I'm already building computer models for Japan, France, and Germany," she says. Still, the success of those ventures in enlist-

ing new investors will depend on whether she can ride her also-ran fund into the winner's circle.

Source: Jeffrey M. Laderman, "But What Have You Done for Us Lately?" *Business Week,* July 26, 1993, p. 71. Reprinted from July 26, 1993 issue of *Business Week* by special permission, © 1993 by McGraw-Hill, Inc.

A Sorry Fund Performance

Total Returns	1988	1989	1990	1991	1992	First Half 1993
Garzarelli[a]	−13.1%	22.5%	−7.2%	31.5%	7.7%	0.5%
Avg. Fund[b]	15.7	25.1	−6.1	36.7	9.1	4.8
S&P 500	16.6	31.7	−3.1	30.5	7.6	4.9

[a]Shearson Lehman Brothers Sector Analysis Fund
[b]Diversified U.S. Equity Fund
Source: Data Morningstar Inc.

specific stocks. For specific stock recommendations, Garzarelli relies on Shearson's analysts. Perhaps it's not her model that's the problem, but the quality of Shearson's securities analysts!

Martin Zweig. Martin Zweig, a former professor of finance, is the author of *The Zweig Forecast* and manages about $5 billion in mutual funds, pension funds, and partnerships using multiple indicator models. Like Elaine Garzarelli, Zweig is not strictly a technician; his models include many fundamental and technical variables. Unlike many gurus, however, Zweig is fairly open about the contents and workings of his model in various books and public appearances.[11] Consequently, we can get a pretty good idea of what criteria a well-known technician actually uses to make his investment decisions.

Zweig's market timing model is heavily weighted toward monetary indicators (his slogan is "Don't fight the Fed") and measures of market momentum (following another slogan, "The trend is your friend"). Specifically, Zweig's model uses the interest rates (both levels and changes), changes in Federal Reserve policy (such as discount rate policy), and changes in installment debt. The Zweig model also includes the advance/decline ratio, the ratio of up volume to down volume, and the weekly change in a broad market index. (A weekly increase in a broad market index of 4 percent or more is a bullish signal, according to Zweig.) Aside from monetary and momentum indicators, Zweig's model also considers market sentiment (such as insider trading data) and seasonal factors (such as always buying before holidays if you're going to buy anyway).

Aside from his market model, which tells him whether or not it is a good time to own stocks, Zweig also has a model for picking individual stocks. This model considers company fundamentals (such as the growth rate in revenues and earnings and the debt burden) and technical factors (such as the stock's relative strength).

---

[11]Zweig describes his model in detail in his *Martin Zweig's Winning on Wall Street* (New York: Warner Books, 1990). Zweig is also a regular guest on such television programs as PBS' *Wall Street Week with Louis Rukeyser.*

Table 6.2

Performance of the Zweig Model: 1981–1988

Buy Signals			Sell Signals		
Date	S&P 500	Percentage Change	Date	S&P 500	Percentage Change
9/21/81	117.24	+41.5%	10/21/83	165.95	−0.1%
10/15/84	165.77	+89.9	9/18/87	314.86	−20.9
12/18/87	249.16	+ 5.0	5/20/88	253.02	+ 9.4[a]

[a]Through December 27, 1988 (not a buy signal), the S&P 500 was at 276.83.

Source: *Martin Zweig's Winning on Wall Street* (New York: Warner Books, 1990), p. 114. Reprinted by permission of Warner Books/ New York from *Winning on Wall Street.* Copyright © 1990 by Martin Zweig.

It is difficult not to be impressed with aspects of Zweig's performance record; his performance has been both good and fairly consistent over the past ten years. For example, according to the *Hulbert Financial Digest,* which tracks the performance records of investment newsletters, Zweig's newsletters rank first out of 25 between 1982 and mid-1991.[12] His investment recommendations produced an average annual return of 17.2 percent per year, compared to 13.9 percent for the S&P 500.

Table 6.2 provides some anecdotal evidence on the performance of Zweig's market timing model between 1981 and 1988. (Note that the data in Table 6.2 were obtained from Zweig's book, not an independent source.) As the data show, five of the six signals given by the Zweig model turned out to be correct (the market moved upward after a buy signal, or downward following a sell signal). One signal is especially notable. Zweig's market timing model gave a sell signal on September 18, 1987, one month before the 1987 market break. As early as April 1987, Zweig was warning subscribers to be cautious, believing that stocks were showing signs of being overvalued.

Alas, Zweig's past performance record is far from perfect. For one thing, some argue that his investment philosophy is better suited to bear markets than bull markets. Indeed, the *Hulbert Financial Digest* gives Zweig's newsletter an A+ rating in bear markets, but only a C (average) rating in bull markets. Furthermore, several of the closed-end mutual funds managed by Zweig have exhibited only mediocre performance in recent years. For example, between 1988 and 1992 the Zweig Fund produced an average annual total return of 14.3 percent compared to 15.9 percent for the S&P 500. His newsletter recommendations have outperformed his mutual funds by a healthy margin. It is also worth noting that Zweig's investment philosophy involves very frequent trading. Thus a follower would incur high transaction costs. Zweig's investment approach also requires the investor to closely monitor the market and his or her portfolio; this type of attention may be inappropriate or unrealistic for certain types of investors.

What Is Fundamental (Securities) Analysis?

In one sense, technicians focus exclusively on a stock's current and past price patterns. Intrinsic value, what the stock really *should* be worth, plays only a

---

[12]*The Wall Street Journal,* July 18, 1991.

supporting role. Fundamentalists, on the other hand, try to determine the true value of a stock under the belief that all stocks, in the long run, will sell for their fundamental values. Therefore, fundamentalists are not as interested in passing effects like investor sentiment as in, say, the company's five-year projected growth rate of earnings.

Benjamin Graham and David Dodd are considered to be the fathers of modern security analysis. The first edition of their seminal work, *Security Analysis,* argued that common stocks were not wildly speculative investments, but rather belonged in the portfolios of prudent, long-term investors.[13] Graham and Dodd presented a methodology (often referred to as the *Graham & Dodd approach*) to analyze and value common stocks. What's remarkable about *Security Analysis* is that it was initially published during the depths of the Great Depression when interest in common stocks was weak. Graham and Dodd showed a great deal of faith in the long-run future of the capital markets and the American economy.

Fundamental analysis is usually completed in a three-stage process beginning with economic and aggregate market analysis and proceeding to industry analysis and then company analysis. The most important determinant of the fundamental value of a stock is its future stream of earnings and dividends. One cannot forecast future earnings and dividends without some idea of the company's future sales, operating expenses, depreciation costs, capital investment requirements, and so forth. Of course, all of these company-specific variables depend somewhat on the overall prospects for the industry (or industries) in which the company operates. In turn, the industry's prospects depend somewhat on the overall prospects of the overall economy.

We devote four chapters to the detailed process of fundamental analysis (Chapters 8 through 11). Chapter 8 presents several stock valuation models, Chapter 9 describes economic and industry analysis, and Chapters 10 and 11 discuss company analysis. At this point, a general example will suffice to introduce fundamental analysis; let's look at Peter Lynch's 1988 analysis of Ford.

Until 1989, Peter Lynch ran Fidelity's Magellan Fund, making his investment decisions on the basis of fundamental analysis. Instead of looking at charts, he read companies' annual reports and listened for stories he liked. Lynch and his associates must have done something right; Magellan has one of the best performance records of any mutual fund since 1980. In his best-selling book, *One Up on Wall Street,* Lynch summarizes the process he used to evaluate Ford in early 1988.[14] Ford had been one of the better performers in the Magellan portfolio, rising from about $4 a share (adjusted for splits) in 1982, when Lynch took his first big position, to about $38 a share in early 1988. Many analysts were predicting a cyclical downturn in the U.S. auto industry, however, eroding their opinions of Ford. Was it time to sell?

Lynch first looked at Ford's 1987 annual report. He noticed that Ford had about $10.1 billion in cash and marketable securities, an increase in its cash balance since 1986, which Lynch liked. At the end of 1987, Ford had about $1.75 billion in long-term debt, down from the total for 1986, giving Lynch another positive sign. This gave Ford a "net cash position," using Lynch's terminology, of $8.35 billion (cash and marketable securities minus long-term debt).[15] This net cash position of $8.35 billion translated into about $16.30 per share, convincing Lynch that Ford was not about to go broke regardless of the economy.

---

[13]Benjamin Graham and David Dodd, *Security Analysis* (New York: McGraw-Hill, 1934).

[14]Peter Lynch, *One Up on Wall Street* (New York: Penguin Books, 1989), pp. 193–196.

[15]Note that Lynch ignored current liabilities. He assumed that a company's other current assets (accounts receivable and inventories) were enough to cover short-term debts.

In early 1988, Ford's common stock was selling for about $38.00 per share. Thus, in Lynch's mind, Ford's noncash assets were selling for only $21.70 per share ($38.00 minus $16.30). Since analysts were expecting Ford to earn about $7.00 per share in 1988, Lynch evaluated Ford's "real" price/earnings ratio at only 3.1 ($21.70/$7.00). The stock was starting to look cheap.

Next, Ford's annual report told Lynch that the company's various financial-services units (Ford Motor Credit, etc.) had earned $1.66 per share on their own in 1987. Financial-services firms sold for about 10 times earnings, on average, in early 1988, so Ford's financial-services units were worth about $16.60 per share. With the company's net cash position of $16.30 per share and financial-services units worth about $16.60 per share, Lynch figured that Ford's auto business was selling for only $5.10 per share ($38.00 minus $16.30 minus $16.60) with a P/E of less than 1.

Based on this analysis, Lynch concluded that, unless Ford threw away its cash on bad acquisitions, the stock was an absolute "steal" at $38 per share. He decided not to sell. The market confirmed Lynch's analysis, at least for the rest of 1988. Ford generally rose throughout the year, trading as high as 54. It closed 1988 at $50\frac{1}{2}$, up about 33 percent for the year.

Assessment of Fundamental Analysis

Like our assessment of technical analysis, our review of the effectiveness of fundamental analysis makes no attempt to be comprehensive. We concentrate on some of the reasons why fundamental analysis might fall short and look at some of the notable mistakes and correct calls made by fundamental analysts over the past few years.

Before we get to that discussion, we'd like to point out that investment opinions by fundamental analysts can have major, though perhaps only temporary, impacts on stock prices. As an example, consider the effects on shares of biotechnology companies after a well-known analyst told investors to take profits. Michael Sorell, an analyst for Morgan Stanley, recommended on September 23, 1991 that investors sell biotech stocks.[16] Sorell concluded that biotech stocks had climbed in price much too quickly, calling their rise "indiscriminate" and out of pace with their fundamentals. Shares of biotech companies fell sharply. One stock, Synergen, lost more than 10 percent of its value in one day. Obviously, investors listened to this fundamentalist's recommendation. Look at today's edition of *The Wall Street Journal*. You will probably find several examples of stocks that rose or fell sharply as a result of comments made by securities analysts.

Track Records of Fundamental Analysts: Some Examples

A great deal of evidence, both anecdotal and scientific, lays out the track records of fundamental analysts. This record appears quite mixed. Some critics of fundamental analysts claim that their track results are no better than those of many technicians, which is to say, pretty poor. However, unlike critics of technical analysis, even the most severe detractors of fundamentalists criticize not the process or technique, but rather its execution. Many critics still see a great deal of value for investors in fundamental analysts' commentaries on companies and industries. We'll have more to say about this in Part III. Let's look at some examples of the successes and failures of fundamental analysis.

---

[16]See *The Wall Street Journal*, September 24, 1991, p. C6.

Forecasting Earnings. One of the more important tasks of a securities analyst is to forecast earnings. Some evidence suggests that analysts have less than a stellar record in forecasting earnings. One study found, for example, that a naive assumption that next year's earnings will equal this year's earnings produced better forecasts of earnings than professional security analysts did.[17]

Consider the case of IBM's first-quarter 1991 earnings.[18] Some 50 or so professional analysts spend most of their work days following IBM and trying to forecast its quarterly earnings. For the first quarter of 1991, these analysts blew it. On March 19, 1991, IBM told analysts that its first-quarter earnings would be only about $0.90 a share, less than half the consensus forecast ($1.82) of the analysts who follow IBM. Even the most pessimistic forecasts were above $1.50 per share. Ironically, the consensus forecast of $1.82 in early March was a downward adjustment from the consensus forecast in February ($1.99). As late as March 13, one IBM analyst forecast first-quarter earnings at $1.85 per share. IBM's stock was mauled after the announcement, losing $12\frac{3}{4}$ points (over 10 percent of its value) on March 19.

Columbia Gas. Columbia Gas illustrates both the success and failure of fundamental analysis. On June 19, 1991, Columbia Gas announced that it had a $1 billion surplus of natural gas that it had signed contracts to purchase, but could not sell to customers. In addition, Columbia Gas was committed to purchase the gas at above-market prices. Warm weather and oversupply had caused natural gas prices to plunge. Columbia Gas announced that unless it was able to renegotiate contracts with producers, it might be forced into bankruptcy. It also suspended its quarterly dividend. Investors headed for the exits and the company's stock lost more than 40 percent of its market value, over $700 million, on June 19.

Columbia's announcement surprised most analysts, though most appeared to have picked up some of the tell-tale signs of trouble prior to the announcement.[19] In general, analysts were neutral on the stock; however, some were actually positive on the long-run prospects for the company.

One analyst wasn't taken by surprise. Jack Egan, who works for the small investment firm of Pforzheimer & Company, ran the numbers several weeks before Columbia's announcement. He saw that Columbia's surplus of natural gas wasn't a temporary, weather-related issue, but rather a life-threatening, fundamental problem. After he failed to receive satisfactory answers from the company, Egan put out a sell recommendation, saving his clients a great deal of money. His example shows the success of fundamental analysis.

All-Star Analysts 1993 Survey. Each year *The Wall Street Journal* asks Zachs Investment Research, Inc. to rate earnings forecasts and buy/sell recommendations made during the prior calendar year by over 1,200 analysts at about 100 different investment firms. The *Journal* uses these rankings to compile its list of All-Star Analysts for the prior year.[20] Many analysts repeat year after year; they have excellent track records. Let's look at a couple of examples from the 1992 All-Star list.

The top-ranked beverage-industry analyst, Allan Kaplan of Merrill Lynch, told clients at the beginning of 1992 to avoid Coca-Cola and buy Pepsi. The

[17]James Cragg and Burton Malkiel, *Expectations and the Structure of Share Prices* (Chicago: University of Chicago Press, 1982).

[18]See "Red-Faced over Big Blue: Why the Analysts Blew It," *Business Week*, April 8, 1991, pp. 77–78.

[19]See "Columbia Gas: How Analysts Blew the Call," *The Wall Street Journal*, July 8, 1991, p. C1.

[20]See "All-Star Analysts 1993 Survey," *The Wall Street Journal*, September 15, 1993, pp. R1–R12.

market proved him right. Coke was basically flat throughout the year while Pepsi rose by more than 20 percent. Phil Friedman of Morgan Stanley was the top-ranked analyst of the defense and aerospace industries for 1992. He saved his clients money when he recommended at the beginning of the year that investors "avoid" (a euphemism for "sell") such well-known companies as Boeing and McDonnell-Douglas. Both stocks performed poorly throughout the year. Finally, Eleanor Kerns, of Alex. Brown, contradicted some analysts by making very bullish recommendations at the beginning of 1992 on HMOs (health maintenance organizations). She posted major gains in Foundation Health, PacifiCare Health Systems, United HealthCare, and U.S. Healthcare.

Why Fundamental Analysis Might Fail to Work

What makes fundamental analysis so difficult? Why do fundamental analysts occasionally "blow" calls? Essentially, we see two primary reasons: the nature of the task and data, and the behavior of the fundamental analysts themselves.

Fundamentalists must attempt to forecast the future stream of earnings and dividends using data that are often incomplete and ambiguous. Analysts must also try to anticipate major changes to key macroeconomic variables and overall industry conditions. Sometimes forecasting earnings in an uncertain environment can be a daunting task, leading to widely divergent forecasts among analysts. Let's look at an example.

Delta Airlines' 1991 and 1992 Earnings. Airlines had a bad year in 1991. Delta alone lost over $300 million for the fiscal year ending June 30, 1991. The outlook for 1992 was very cloudy, as well. Would airline traffic pick up in 1992? Would price wars continue to plague the industry? Would oil prices, and thus fuel expenses, remain stable? Specifically for Delta, would its recent acquisition of Pan Am's international routes add to or detract from earnings? Not surprisingly, different analysts answered these questions quite differently. One analyst forecast Delta's 1992 earnings to be $2.96 per share while another forecast that the company would *lose* $2.46 per share.[21]

Random events can also cloud an analyst's crystal ball, as the earnings forecasts for Delta Airlines for the fiscal year that ended on June 30, 1991 illustrate. In July 1990, the airline analyst for Standard & Poor's forecast that Delta would earn about $7.00 per share in the 1991 fiscal year, a healthy increase from its 1990 earnings of $5.79 per share. The analyst cited several reasons for the rosy forecast: moderate overall growth in airline passenger traffic due to continued economic expansion, an increase in average fare yields due to fewer price wars, and stable or perhaps even falling fuel prices. Then Iraq invaded Kuwait on August 2, 1990.

Perhaps the most significant of the initial impacts of the Iraqi invasion, for the airline industry, was a sharp increase in oil, and thus jet fuel, prices. The price index for crude petroleum was at 46.3 in July 1990 (1982 = 100); it shot up to 118.0 by October 1990, an increase of about 155 percent. The average July price of jet fuel of 56 cents per gallon (excluding taxes) increased to 114.4 cents per gallon by October. This increase significantly cut into airline operating margins, and thus earnings.[22] By the end of September, Standard & Poor's had cut its estimate of Delta's 1991 earnings from $7.00 per share to $2.75 per share.

---

[21]According to *Business Week*, the consensus forecast for Delta's 1992 earning was $0.25 per share. Of all the companies examined by *Business Week*, analysts agreed least on Delta.

[22]The general rule of thumb holds that a 1 cent increase in jet fuel prices will cause annual operating expenses for the U.S. airline industry to increase by $100 million.

Markets Can't Live Up to Analysts' Rosy Outlooks

Never mind that international currencies are in turmoil. Forget that most stocks are quite expensive relative to their earnings. Disregard all your concerns about the slow domestic economy and the presidential election.

Wall Street analysts have advice for you: Buy! Buy! Buy!

Despite an abundance of risks for investors, brokerage analysts are stoutly optimistic:

Among 2,800 stocks followed by 54 brokerages, 70 percent had consensus ratings of buy or strong buy, says First Call, a Boston information service that ran a computer check Wednesday at the request of *USA TODAY*.

Only 52 of the 2,800 stocks—less than 2 percent—had consensus ratings of sell or strong sell.

Sound unrealistic? It is. Even the most bullish of stock markets could not live up to so rosy an outlook.

A buy recommendation means the analyst predicts the stock will outperform the market as a whole. But 70 percent of stocks cannot outperform the market any more than 70 percent of a group of schoolchildren can be in the top half of their class.

Call it the Lake Wobegon Effect. Like Garrison Keillor's mythical hometown, Wall Street is a place where "all the children are above average."

Analysts tend to be smart, studious people. They pore over proxy statements and dissect footnotes in annual reports. They have access to top managers of the USA's biggest companies and aren't afraid to ask tough questions.

So why are they putting out such ridiculously optimistic recommendations? Simple: conflict of interest. Most analysts work for brokerages, which make money from commissions on stock trades. Buy recommendations bring in more business than sell recommendations.

Other reasons analysts are disproportionately bullish:

Office politics. All the leading brokerages have large underwriting units that handle sales of stock offerings. Investment bankers at a brokerage often woo the same companies the brokerage's analysts are sizing up as stock picks.

Morgan Stanley was embarrassed recently when a memo became public in which an investment banker leaned on analysts to make "no negative comments about our clients."

Morgan Stanley says the author of the memo was referring only to analysts' comments to reporters, not to the substance of analysts' reports.

Pressure from companies. Executives burned by criticism can refuse to talk to an analyst or even demand retractions. After a Shearson Lehman analyst made mildly negative comments

The sharp increase in oil prices, and overall war fears, also helped push the U.S. economy into recession. Typically, passenger traffic slows during economic downturns, forcing airlines to reduce fares. This further depressed operating margins and earnings. Thus, by December 1990, even with slightly lower jet fuel prices (90.1 cents per gallon), Standard & Poor's projected that Delta would lose $5.10 per share for the 1991 fiscal year.

After the Gulf War began in January 1991, oil prices rose sharply again, but then they started to fall after it became apparent that the United States and its allies would defeat Iraq without disrupting oil supplies. The crude petroleum price index fell from 87.9 in January to 54.1 in March. Jet fuel prices fell, as well, from 82.2 cents per gallon in January to 62.2 cents per gallon in March. Unfortunately for the airlines, passenger traffic also fell, as economic recession and fears of terrorism kept many travelers home. In fact, U.S. passenger traffic fell 7.7 percent for the first three months of 1991, compared to the same period in 1990. Even heavy price discounting and the end of the war failed to help very much. The U.S. economy started to grow again toward the summer of 1991, but only very slowly, and passenger traffic continued to be sluggish. By May 1991, Standard & Poor's forecasted that Delta would lose about $6.00 per share for the 1991 fiscal year. As it turned out, even *that* forecast was somewhat optimistic; Delta ended up losing $7.73 per share for the 1991 fiscal year. Comparing the July 1990 forecast to the actual result, Standard & Poor's overestimated Delta's 1991 earnings by almost

about a subsidiary of American International Group, company President M. R. Greenberg pressured the brokerage into putting out a second report that detailed Greenberg's point of view.

Any discussion of the sensitive issue of executive salaries is strictly verboten at Morgan Stanley. "In no event should commentary or reports contain negative analytical conclusions about management based on . . . levels of compensation of management," a manual for analysts states.

Pressure from investors. Every stock a brokerage covers is owned by some clients of the firm. They do not appreciate analysts bad mouthing stocks in their portfolios.

Brokerages acknowledge such pressures but say they resist them. "We try to avoid those conflicts of interest," says Terry Dessent, director of

research at A. G. Edwards. Relative to the rest of the industry, his firm issues a high proportion of sell recommendations. Since 1983, A. G. Edwards has made 1,000 buy recommendations and 500 sell recommendations, he says.

INVESTMENT INSIGHTS

Wall Street does have contrarians who buck the trend of optimism. But they could suffer for their independence, says John Keefe, a former Drexel Burnham analyst who works as an independent securities adviser in New York. On Wall Street, he says, "it's better to fail conventionally than succeed unconventionally."

Stocks Feel Impact of Downgrading

Brokerage	Stock	Old Rating	New Rating	Result
Bear Stearns	Chesapeake	Buy	Hold	Fell $1\frac{3}{4}$ to $22\frac{1}{8}$
Dain Bosworth	Merit Medical	Buy	Hold	Fell $2\frac{3}{8}$ to $4\frac{5}{8}$
Merrill Lynch	U.S. Surgical	Buy	Above Avg.	Fell $4\frac{3}{8}$ to $65\frac{1}{2}$
Morgan Stanley	Grand Metropolitan	Buy	Hold	Fell $2\frac{1}{2}$ to $30
PaineWebber	Honeywell	Attractive	Neutral	Fell 3 to $65\frac{3}{8}$
Vector Securities	Medco Research	Buy	Neutral	Fell $2\frac{1}{4}$ to $12\frac{7}{8}$

Source: Eric D. Randall, "Markets Can't Live Up to Analysts' Rosy Outlooks," *USA TODAY*, Sept. 24, 1992, 5B. Copyright 1992, USA TODAY. Reprinted with permission.

$15.00 per share![23] As an airline analyst, how could you have predicted all that would happen about a year before it did?

The Behavior of Analysts. The other major reason we see for the periodic failure of fundamental analysis deals with the behavior of the analysts themselves. A fair amount of evidence suggests that securities analysts are overly optimistic, and that they tend occasionally to exhibit a herd mentality in the face of uncertainty.

A study by the Institutional Broker Estimate System (IBES) found that analysts, on average, overestimated the annual changes in earnings for the individual companies that make up the Standard & Poor's 500 in eight out of the ten years from 1981 through 1990. In July 1981, for example, analysts forecast a 30 percent increase in earnings for the S&P 500 stocks for 1982. Earnings actually fell by about 15 percent.[24]

Another example of the general optimism of securities analysts can be found in the article from *USA Today* in the Investment Insights feature. As

[23]We do not mean to pick on Standard & Poor's. Analysts at other investment firms had similar results, nor was Delta the only airline to suffer in 1991. The entire industry lost around $5 billion during 1991, the worst year on record.

[24]See "Analysts, Grabbing Rose-Colored Glasses, See Earnings Leap," *The Wall Street Journal*, July 19, 1991, p. C1.

the article points out, a survey found that of the 2,800 or so stocks followed by 54 investment firms, about 70 percent carried buy or strong buy recommendations. By contrast, only 2 percent of the stocks had sell or strong sell recommendations. The article also gives examples of what happens to stock prices when analysts downgrade their recommendations. As we pointed out earlier, analyst opinions can move stock prices.

Why do analysts tend to be overly optimistic? The article summarizes some of the major reasons. For one thing, most analysts are employed by brokerage firms, which make most of their money through commissions on sales of stocks to investors. It is much easier to sell stocks if brokers can tell clients that analysts are predicting a good year. If an analyst gives brokers a list of ten stocks to buy and ten stocks to sell, which list do you think will interest the brokers more?

Another reason analysts tend to be optimistic may be the subtle, and not-so-subtle, pressure to which they are subjected by the companies they follow. Obviously, the companies want the analysts to say positive things about them. In order to do their jobs, analysts must be able to talk directly with the managers of the companies they follow, not to obtain illegal, inside information, but rather to provide more detailed explanations of public announcements and annual reports (often referred to as *guidance*). In a case we discussed earlier, when Columbia Gas refused comment about its natural gas surplus problem to analyst Jack Egan, he took that as another sign of impending disaster for stockholders. As it turned out, of course, he was right. An analyst may fear that if he or she fails to say positive things about a stock, the company will refuse to talk in the future, putting him or her at a competitive disadvantage against the other analysts who follow the same stock.

Occasionally companies have exerted much more overt pressure. Kidder Peabody banking analyst Charles Peabody had long been critical of NCNB Corporation (now NationsBank).[25] In a July 1991 report, Peabody asserted that NCNB was offering much less for shares of C&S/Sovarn (another bank holding company) than it appeared, since NCNB stock was overvalued by the market. NCNB was offering to buy C&S/Sovarn in a stock acquisition. Not only did NCNB take the unusual step of publicly rebuking the analyst, but it also severed all its business ties with Kidder.[26] Under this kind of threat, analysts often go out of their way to praise a company, its products, its management, and so forth, even if they resist recommending the stock as an investment.

Another reason analysts occasionally blow calls has been described as the **herd instinct.** We saw a good example of this in the discussion of IBM's first-quarter 1991 earnings earlier. Recall that IBM stunned Wall Street when it announced on March 19, 1991 that its first-quarter earnings would be less than half of analysts' consensus forecast. Critics contend that this episode showed how, in the face of uncertainty, analysts herd together, issuing forecasts with little variation. It is as though analysts say to themselves, "if I'm wrong, at least I won't be alone."

Implications for Investors

We've seen very mixed track records for both technical analysis and fundamental analysis. Following the advice of technicians or fundamentalists some-

---

[25]See "Analyst's Barbs Spur Retaliation by NCNB," *The Wall Street Journal,* July 18, 1991, p. C1.

[26]To its credit, Kidder appears to have resisted the pressure exerted by NCNB and stood behind its analyst. NCNB did successfully acquire C&S/Sovarn later in 1991.

times produces very good returns, and sometimes produces very poor returns. Some go so far as to argue that market efficiency prevents either technical or fundamental analysis from producing consistently above-average returns. They argue that an investor who simply buys and holds a well-diversified portfolio of securities will do as well as, and perhaps even better than, someone who follows the investment advice of professionals over a long period of time. We'll consider the issue of market efficiency in detail in the next chapter.

Critics often deride technicians as sellers of some modern-day snake oil. They argue that their methods are patently false and don't work. We will look at some more of the evidence in the next chapter, but, while we do agree that some technicians are crackpots and perhaps even charlatans, we are not prepared to dismiss technical analysis entirely. Some technicians' track records are hard to discount as mere luck. Remember, also, that many technical indicators, such as the Barron's Confidence Index, are based on fundamental relationships. Investors may well gain something of value by listening to what the serious technicians have to say about both what they think the market is going to do and why.

Likewise, it is easy to pick on the failures of fundamental analysts, though critics fault the execution rather than the technique. Fundamentalists have blown calls, sometimes quite badly, but they still have much to contribute to the investment analysis and selection process. You may not want to bet your life savings on their earnings forecasts, but they often have insightful and valuable things to say about a company's products, management, etc.

In conclusion, we would argue that some, though certainly not all, of the investment advice given by professionals is worth attention. Is professional investment advice worth its cost? Every investor must answer that question individually. We would like to give one final caveat to investors, one we've repeated many times: be careful, ask questions, and be very skeptical of anyone who claims to have a system that beats the market consistently. Good luck!

Chapter Summary

1. **Define** *technical analysis* **and identify its assumptions.**
   Technical analysis refers to a broad range of economic, political, and psychological indicators, all of which are based on the notion that past patterns in security prices can be used to reliably predict future price patterns. Technicians believe that security prices are determined solely by the interaction of supply and demand. They use indicators that, they believe, show upcoming shifts in supply and demand relationships, and thus security prices.

2. **Identify the general categories of technical indicators and give examples.**
   We grouped technical indicators into three general categories: charting, indicators based on investor sentiment, and indicators based on market momentum. Most charting techniques attempt to find support and resistance levels. Breaking through a support (resistance) level is a bearish (bullish) signal. Investor sentiment indicators attempt to measure how certain types of investors feel about the market. Indicators based on the notion of contrary opinion, say, for example, that the majority of investors become bullish only late in a bull market. Indicators based on the notion of following the smart money look for cues in the behavior of certain types of investors (such as NYSE specialists) who tend to lead bull and bear markets. Finally, indicators based on market momentum compare the market to a freight train; it takes a long time to get going, and once it gets going, it takes a long time to stop. Examples of momentum indicators are trading volume and various measures of relative strength.

3. **Understand why technical analysis might work, and why it might not work.**

   There are several reasons why technical analysis might work, or at least appear to work. Fundamental information can be incomplete and misleading, and all investors may not have the same level of access to fundamental information. Technical analysis might appear to work simply because it could become a self-fulfilling prophecy. On the other hand, technical indicators might fail to work because they might give clear buy or sell signals too late. A great deal of evidence confirms that security prices react very quickly to new information.

4. **Critically examine the track records of several technical indicators and technical analysts.**

   It can be difficult to assess the past track records of technical indicators and analysts. For one problem, technical indicators are often ambiguous. Different technicians can draw different conclusions from the same indicator. The scientific evidence (which we will review in more detail in the next chapter) generally does not support technical analysis. The Barron's Confidence Index did a mediocre job of predicting stock prices between 1990 and 1993. The track records of three well-known technicians (Robert Prechter, Elaine Garzarelli, and Martin Zweig) show that all three have made some successful predictions (such as Garzarelli's prediction of the October 1987 market break), but all have had their share of failures, as well.

5. **Define *fundamental analysis* and identify how it differs from technical analysis.**

   Fundamental analysis is based on the notion that every security has an intrinsic value. The intrinsic value of a common stock is based on such factors as the expected growth rate of the company's earnings and dividends. Since all securities should eventually sell for their intrinsic values, fundamental analysts look for undervalued or overvalued securities, those whose prices are out of line with their intrinsic values. We then looked at an example of the process by which a fundamental analyst might evaluate an actual stock.

6. **Examine part of the track records of fundamental analysts.**

   Fundamental analysts have made some correct calls in recent years, but they have also made some mistakes. Analysts' forecasts of earnings, for example, are often error-prone. In several conspicuous cases, analysts have failed to detect some serious problems with companies before they were announced. We see two general reasons that analysts occasionally blow calls: the nature of their data, and their own behavior. Analysts must base forecasts on data that can be ambiguous and incomplete. Analysts also cannot anticipate the impact of random events. We looked at examples of both problems. As a group, analysts tend to be overly optimistic, and often lapse into a herd mentality. The failures of fundamental analysis are caused, not by the process itself, but rather by its execution.

Key Terms

Technical analysis	Charting
Fundamental analysis	Dow Theory
Intrinsic value	Primary movement
Undervalued security	Bull market
Overvalued security	Bear market
Supply and demand	Secondary movement
	Minor movement

Support level	Smart money
Resistance level	Market momentum
Trading range	Diffusion index
Trendline	Relative strength indicator
Moving average	Barron's Confidence Index
Investor sentiment	Elliot wave
Contrary opinion theory	Herd instinct

Discussion Questions and Problems

1. What major assumptions underlie technical analysis? What role does supply and demand play?
2. Define the terms *support level* and *resistance level*. What happens if a price series breaks through a support (resistance) level?
3. What is a trendline? If the upper and lower trendlines are getting closer together in a bull market, is this a bullish or bearish indicator?
4. The table below lists 20 daily stock prices. Find the five-day moving averages. Plot both the moving averages and raw stock prices. Why is the moving average considered to be a better indicator of a trend than the raw data?

Trading Day	Stock Price	Trading Day	Stock Price
1	35.875	11	41.625
2	36.625	12	41.500
3	38.000	13	40.750
4	39.000	14	40.375
5	40.125	15	40.875
6	39.250	16	40.750
7	38.000	17	40.375
8	39.250	18	40.000
9	40.500	19	40.375
10	42.500	20	40.500

5. Define what technicians mean by *investor sentiment*. Give an example of an indicator that supposedly measures investor sentiment.
6. Why is trading volume considered to be an indicator of market momentum? Give an example of another market momentum indicator.
7. List and explain some reasons why technical analysis might work. List and explain some reasons why it might fail to work.
8. Why is it so hard to determine whether or not technical analysis really works? What standard should be used to test the effectiveness of technical analysis?
9. How does fundamental analysis differ from technical analysis? Why is intrinsic value so important to a fundamental analyst?
10. Explain the three-step process of fundamental analysis. Which step is the most important?
11. Why might fundamental analysis fail to work? Why is the criticism of fundamental analysis different from the criticism of technical analysis?
12. Why are analysts, as a group, optimistic? What role does pressure from companies play?

Critical Thinking Exercises

1. This exercise requires computer work. Open the file PRICE1.XLS on the data disk. The file contains weekly values for the S&P 500 index from the end of 1990 through the end of 1993. Use the data to complete the following activities:

   a. Graph the original data with time as the *x* variable and the index value as the *y* variable.

   b. Compute 4-week and 13-week moving averages. Graph the moving averages and the original data against time.

   c. On the first graph, find the support and resistance levels. When did the S&P 500 index break through a support and/or resistance level? Did stock prices behave as expected after breaking through support/ resistance levels (e.g., continue to drop after breaking through a support level)?

   d. On the second graph, determine when the moving averages gave buy and sell signals. Did these signals coincide with the signals given by the first chart?

   e. Discuss what this exercise illustrates about technical analysis.

2. This exercise requires computer work. File PRICE2.XLS on the data disk contains weekly price data for four industries: automobiles, computers (excluding IBM), drugs, and railroads. Use these data, along with the weekly data for the S&P 500, to answer the following questions and perform the following calculations:

   a. Compute relative strength measures for each industry. The most basic relative strength measure divides the industry index by the S&P 500.

   b. Compute 13-week moving averages for the relative strength measures.

   c. What do the relative strength measures tell you about these industries? Do they indicate rising or falling momentum?

   d. Which of the industries appears the strongest? Explain your answer.

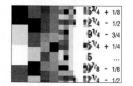

3. This assignment requires library research. *The Wall Street Journal* and other business newspapers publish quarterly earnings announcements. The *Journal* also identifies earnings surprises—situations where a firm's actual earnings were either higher or lower than analysts' expectations.

   a. Go back over a recent month's announcements and identify the five largest earnings surprises on both the upside and the downside. (Note: Quarterly earnings announcements are made almost continuously throughout the year. However, they are concentrated in February, April, July, and October. Firms make many more announcements during the second half of a month.)

   b. How much did the actual numbers differ from what analysts were expecting?

   c. Is there any correlation between the number of analysts following a stock and the size of the error?

   d. Pick one company from each list. Why were the analysts wrong? What did they miss?

Chapter 7

Market Efficiency: Concept and Reality

Chapter Objectives

1. Define the terms *random walk, market efficiency,* and *efficient markets hypothesis.*
2. Understand the important implications of market efficiency.
3. Outline the issues that arise with tests of the efficient markets hypothesis.
4. Examine evidence supporting the efficient markets hypothesis.
5. Review evidence that appears to contradict market efficiency.
6. Try to answer the question: Are the financial markets efficient?

One of the most controversial and far-reaching concepts to have emerged from investments theory over the last 40 years is the **efficient markets hypothesis** (sometimes referred to as the *random walk theory*). In a nutshell, the efficient markets hypothesis (EMH) states that securities' prices fluctuate randomly around their respective intrinsic values. Intrinsic values, in turn, rationally reflect all relevant publicly available information, and perhaps even privately available information, as well. Prices adjust very quickly to new information, which also enters the market in a random fashion.

The efficient markets hypothesis implies the logical conclusion that no person or system can accurately and consistently predict short-term movements in securities prices. As a result, the EMH questions the value of technical analysis and, to a lesser extent, fundamental analysis, as well. The efficient markets hypothesis also strongly suggests that investors may be better off simply buying and holding securities in passively managed portfolios. The EMH implies that higher transaction costs and management fees associated with active management are wasted, since active trading cannot consistently produce higher returns than passive management.

The efficient markets hypothesis has a number of strong proponents; most financial economists, and many Wall Street practitioners, believe in the EMH, at least up to a point. The proponents cite large amounts of evidence, both scientific and anecdotal, to support the concept of market efficiency. A great deal of evidence shows, for example, that past price patterns provide virtually no information about future price patterns.

Not surprisingly, many others dismiss ideas like efficient markets and security prices following random walks as academic nonsense. The detractors point to evidence, some anecdotal and some more scientific, and many common situations that seem to contradict the concept of market efficiency. As Peter Lynch, the famous mutual fund manager, wrote:

It's very hard to support the popular academic theory that the market is [unpredictable] when you know somebody who just made a twentyfold profit in Kentucky Fried Chicken, and furthermore, who explained in advance why the stock was going to rise.[1]

In this chapter, we examine both the concept and reality of market efficiency. We begin the chapter with a more formal definition of random walks and market efficiency, discussing the sources of efficiency and its traditional forms. Next, we review some of the important investment implications of market efficiency for such techniques as technical analysis, market timing, and professional management. Discussion of the evidence supporting market efficiency follows, focusing, among other things, on the usefulness of historical price information in predicting future price movements. We'll then review some of the evidence that appears to contradict the EMH, including well-known market anomalies (such as the January effect) as well as the apparent ability of some professional money managers to consistently outperform the market. Finally, we'll try to answer two big questions: just how efficient are the markets, and what does it all mean for investors?

Random Walks and Efficient Markets

In the early 1950s a statistician named Maurice Kendall was analyzing several economic time series using a new tool, the computer, when he discovered, to his surprise, that changes in stock prices appeared to be almost random in nature.[2] On any given day, a positive price change was as likely as a negative price change. Furthermore, Kendall concluded, past price patterns couldn't reliably predict future price patterns.

At first glance Kendall's findings, which a number of other researchers replicated, seemed to suggest that stock markets behaved almost irrationally. Perhaps prices were determined, not by rational valuation, but by the erratic behavior of investors. Some financial economists soon realized, however, that Kendall's findings might mean something quite different. Perhaps, random price changes weren't the results of irrational markets, but rather the results of well-functioning markets where prices rationally reflect all available information and adjust quickly to new information. The concept of market efficiency was born.

What Is a Random Walk?

Kendall's discovery about the time series behavior of stock prices is commonly referred to as a **random walk.** Mathematically, a random walk is a stochastic time series in which each successive change in a variable is drawn independently from a probability distribution with a constant mean and variance. What does it mean to say that stock prices follow a random walk?

To answer this question, assume the following time series best describes the behavior of stock prices:

$$P_t = P_{t-1} + a_t, \text{ where } a \sim N(0, \sigma^2). \tag{7.1}$$

---

[1] Peter Lynch, *One Up on Wall Street* (New York: Penguin Books, 1989), p. 35. Be careful not to take this type of anecdotal evidence as a strong contradiction of the efficient markets hypothesis.

[2] Maurice Kendall, "The Analysis of Economic Time Series, Part I: Prices," reprinted in *The Random Character of Stock Market Prices,* ed. by Paul Cootner (Cambridge, Mass.: MIT Press, 1967), pp. 86–99. Kendall had expected to find recurrent and predictable patterns in stock prices tied to the economic performance and prospects of companies.

Figure 7.1

Comparison of Two Series: Standard & Poor's 500 versus a Random Walk

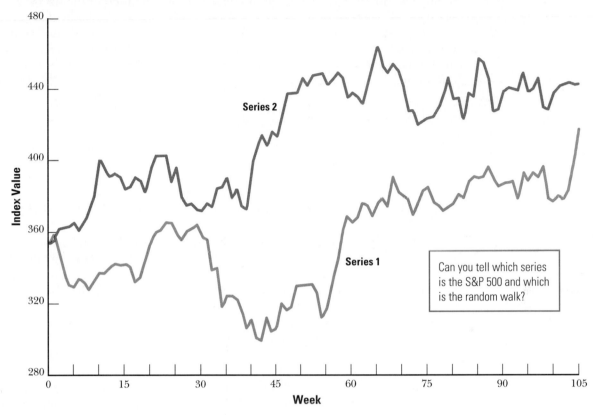

Can you tell which series is the S&P 500 and which is the random walk?

Source: *Standard & Poor's.*

Equation 7.1 identifies a random walk.[3] It says that today's price is equal to yesterday's price, plus a random variable, *a.* Each random variable is drawn from a normal distribution with a mean of 0 and a constant variance, σ^2. The change in price $(P_t - P_{t-1})$ equals the random variable, a_t.

Now, take a look at Figure 7.1. One of the two series is the weekly close for the S&P 500 from the beginning of 1990, at 353.4, through the end of 1991. The other series consists of a random walk, much like that defined by Equation 7.1. The random series also begins at 353.4, but each subsequent value equals the prior value plus a random variable. Each random variable is drawn from a normal distribution with a mean of zero and a standard deviation of 7.77 (the standard deviation of the weekly changes in the S&P 500 over this two-year period).

Which series is which? It's hard to tell; they look very similar. If you guessed that Series 1 is the S&P 500, you're correct. Series 2 is the random walk. This example demonstrates an important point: it's easy to see patterns in stock prices, even if none exist. Just like the S&P 500 series, the series produced by the random walk appears to have patterns, cycles, up trends, down trends, etc., but, by definition, there can't be any.

Random Walks and Forecasting. Suppose a time series of stock prices is best described by the random walk model in Equation 7.1 and someone wants to

---

[3]Equation 7.1 is only one realization of dozens of random walk models. The random variable, for example, need not be drawn from a normal distribution.

forecast its behavior. What will the forecast look like? Assume that, based on a history of price observations, $P_0, P_1, P_2, \ldots, P_T$, an analyst wants to forecast tomorrow's price, P_{T+1}. Using all the information contained in the historical price series, if the series follows a random walk, then it turns out that the best forecast of tomorrow's price is actually *today's* price, P_T.[4] We'll talk about this in more detail later, but as you can probably already see, if stock prices do follow a random walk, the value of technical analysis can be seriously questioned.

The Source of Market Efficiency

Why should anyone expect financial markets to be efficient markets in which prices reflect all available information? In a word, the answer to this question is *competition*. Financial markets in most parts of the world are very competitive. Literally millions of highly motivated participants (both individuals and institutions) hunt constantly for above-average profits (the "best" investments).[5]

After one participant discovers an investment with an above-average return, how long will it take before other participants also discover it? Probably not very long in a highly competitive market. As participants discover the investment, they bid up its price very quickly, eliminating the abnormal profit.

Further, many participants can devote substantial resources to search for the best investments. Say that a stock mutual fund with $5 billion in assets believes that buying the right stocks will boost its annual performance by 0.5 percent. One-half of 1 percent of $5 billion is $25 million. How much will this fund be willing to spend on research and analysis to uncover the best stocks? The fund probably would be willing to spend up to $25 million. Beating so many investors who have such deep pockets to the best investments isn't easy. Perhaps this elusive search for abnormal profits by so many investors is the single most important source of market efficiency.

Traditional Forms of Market Efficiency

Earlier we noted that market efficiency implies that security prices rationally reflect all available information. Using different assumptions about the meaning of the phrase *all available information,* financial economists traditionally distinguish between three levels, or forms, of market efficiency: the weak form, the semistrong form, and the strong form.[6] Let's briefly define each.

Weak-Form Market Efficiency. **Weak-form market efficiency** states that current security prices fully reflect all **historical information.** Further, it states that investors cannot earn abnormal returns using historical information.

---

[4]The practical definition of the "best" forecast is the one that produces the smallest, unbiased error. To show that the best forecast of tomorrow's price is today's price you must first note that P_{T+1} is a random variable. Why? Remember, $P_{T+1} = P_T + a_{T+1}$. Therefore, tomorrow's price is made up of a fixed number, P_T, plus a random variable, a_{T+1}. The expected value of P_{T+1} given all past prices equals:

$$E(P_{T+1}|P_0, P_1, \ldots, P_T) = E(P_T|P_0, \ldots, P_T) + E(a_{T+1}|P_0, \ldots, P_T)$$
$$= E(P_T) + E(a_{T+1})$$
$$= P_T$$

[5]We'll more formally define *above-average*, or *abnormal, profits* a little later in the chapter.

[6]Eugene Fama is credited by most with developing the first definitions of the three levels of market efficiency. See Eugene Fama, "The Behavior of Stock Market Prices," *Journal of Business,* January 1965, pp. 34–105.

Historical information includes not just price information, but information on trading volume, short interest, and so forth. Weak-form efficiency also implies that security prices do not follow recurrent and predictable patterns. Instead, it suggests that security prices follow a random walk.

An analyst may develop a trading model based on past prices over the prior 12 months, buying stock when the model gives one signal and selling when it gives another. Weak-form market efficiency doesn't imply that the model wouldn't generate a profit, just that the profit would match that of someone who simply bought and held the same stock over the same period.

Semistrong-Form Market Efficiency. **Semistrong-form market efficiency** states that security prices reflect all **public information** and react almost instantaneously to new public information. Public information includes all historical information, and adds all public information on a company's product lines, its financial policies, the quality of its management, and so forth. Therefore, semistrong-form efficient markets are also weak-form efficient, though weak-form efficiency does not necessarily imply semistrong-form efficiency.

As an example of semistrong-form efficiency, consider a company that announces quarterly earnings 10 percent higher than analysts were forecasting. This is good news, and the price of the company's stock should increase after the announcement. Semistrong-form efficiency says, however, that buying the stock after the public earnings announcement would fail to consistently produce abnormal returns. Why? The reason is simply because prices would adjust very quickly to the new information, so the price at the time of the purchase would fully reflect the new information.

Strong-Form Market Efficiency. **Strong-form market efficiency** makes the extreme statement that security prices reflect not only all public information, but all **private information,** as well. Again, price reactions to new information, whether public or private, occur rapidly. Thus, even insiders who have access to confidential information (e.g., corporate officers) cannot make abnormal returns consistently.[7]

Few would dispute that corporate insiders may have access to valuable information prior to the general investing public. Indeed, a principal focus of securities regulation is to prevent insiders from exploiting their potential information advantage. Laws that prohibit such practices as **insider trading** are examples of attempts to limit the information advantage of insiders. The NYSE and other major financial markets closely monitor records of trading activity, looking for abuses of inside information.

Implications of Market Efficiency

If the markets really are efficient (we'll look at the evidence in the next section), what implications would the theory have for such popular investment techniques as active portfolio management, fundamental analysis, or technical analysis? The efficient markets hypothesis has something to say about each.

---

[7]Corporate officers and directors are not the only ones who may have access to inside information. Mutual fund managers, securities analysts, and so forth, may also be privy to private information. Whether access to private information allows them to generate abnormal returns is a question we will examine later in the chapter.

Technical Analysis

Of all common investment tools, the efficient markets hypothesis has perhaps the most to say about technical analysis. Recall from the prior chapter that technical analysis is based on the notion that securities prices follow recurrent and predictable patterns. Technicians argue that investors can exploit these patterns. Even if the markets are only weak-form efficient, the EMH argues that technical analysis will not work since current securities prices already fully reflect all information contained in historical price data. In other words, charting, investor sentiment indicators, measures of market momentum, and so forth, cannot consistently produce abnormal profits. The EMH denies that technical analysis shows a path to investment wealth, except for brokers who earn commissions from trades and technicians who sell their advice.

Essentially the EMH attacks technical analysis on two points. First, it labels most of technicians' recurrent patterns in short-term securities prices as mere illusions. As an example, take another look at Figure 7.1; random walks can produce price series that appear to show trends and recurring patterns. It's easy to be fooled into seeing something where there is nothing.[8] Second, even if securities prices were to define recurrent and predictable patterns, many other investors would quickly recognize the patterns. Once that happened, any trading rules based on those patterns would rapidly self-destruct.

As an example of the second point, assume that a trading rule based on some historical price pattern indicates that a specific stock is about to rise from $50 to $55 per share. A technician who believed in the indicator would immediately buy the stock, as would other investors who recognized the price pattern. The price would jump almost instantaneously from $50 to $55 per share under the pressure of many buyers and no one willing to sell the stock at a price below 55. (Remember, every buyer has to find a seller.) In fact, some investors might have bought the stock even earlier, in anticipation of the pattern. In any event, the trading rule would no longer produce an abnormal profit.

That's the point of all this. Someone may be clever enough to uncover some profitable trading rule based on past patterns in security prices, but keeping this information a secret from other investors for very long to prevent it from self-destructing is quite another matter.

Fundamental Analysis

As the prior chapter explained, fundamental analysts study underlying economic data like interest rates, sales, and earnings to estimate the intrinsic values of securities. Fundamental analysis is based on the belief that every security eventually sells for its intrinsic value, and therefore analysts constantly hunt for undervalued or overvalued securities.

The efficient markets hypothesis also has something to say about the value of fundamental analysis. If analysts rely only on historical data and current, publicly available information, it states that their recommendations cannot consistently produce abnormal profits. Rather, an analyst must have superior forecasting ability to beat the market, gaining insight into the various fun

---

[8]Burton Malkiel likes to tell the following story about a price chart produced by a random process (flipping a coin):

> One of the charts showed a beautiful upward breakout from an inverted head and shoulders (a very bullish formation). I showed it to a chartist friend of mine who practically jumped out of his skin. "What is the company?" he exclaimed, "we've got to buy immediately." He did not respond kindly to me when I told him the chart had been produced by flipping a coin. [A Random Walk Down Wall Street (New York: Norton, 1991), p. 136.]

Figure 7.2

Closing Prices of Apple Computer: May 27–June 11, 1993

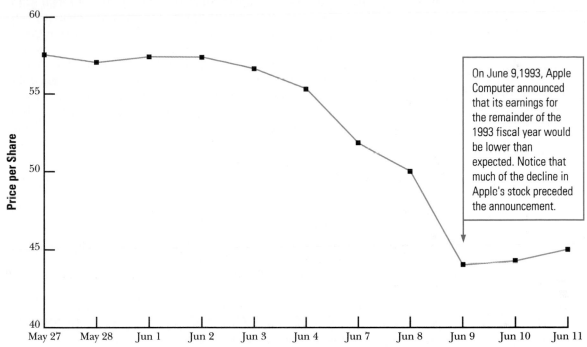

On June 9,1993, Apple Computer announced that its earnings for the remainder of the 1993 fiscal year would be lower than expected. Notice that much of the decline in Apple's stock preceded the announcement.

Source: *The Wall Street Journal,* various issues.

damental factors that drive stock prices before the market recognizes them. As we demonstrated briefly in Chapter 6, forecasting data like future earnings can be very difficult; it is as much an art as a science. It's not impossible, just very difficult, to be a consistently superior analyst, profiting from new, public information before others can react.

Consider the following example. On Wednesday, June 9, 1993, Apple Computer announced that fierce price competition in the personal computer market had reduced its profit margins. Most analysts who followed Apple Computer immediately slashed their 1993 and 1994 earnings estimates, cutting the consensus forecast for the firm's 1993 fiscal year earnings from $4.30 per share to $3.95 per share. Apple's stock dropped about $5 per share to $44\frac{1}{4}$ on volume of more than 10 million shares on June 9.

Could this new fundamental information have helped an Apple stockholder avoid this debacle? Probably not. For one thing, the stock fell so quickly after the announcement on June 9 that few could have sold their shares at prices much higher than $44\frac{1}{4}$. For another reason, Apple's stock had actually been falling for several days (see Figure 7.2). Between June 2 and June 8, the day before the earning announcement, Apple lost almost $8 per share (about 14 percent of its value). Therefore, an investor could have avoided the sclloff only by correctly *anticipating* the new information at least a week prior to the actual announcement, probably in late May.

Active versus Passive Portfolio Management

In Chapter 1 we briefly discussed the differences between active and passive portfolio management. Passive management employs a **buy-and-hold strategy;** the investor buys and holds a well-diversified portfolio of securities. By contrast, active management involves periodic changes to a portfolio in anticipation of price movements. For example, an actively managed stock portfolio might switch its holdings from growth stocks toward cyclical stocks (called *sector rotation*) in anticipation of an economic expansion. The managers of actively managed portfolios usually rely on technical analysis, fundamental analysis, or some combination to guide their portfolio changes.

Given the prior discussion of the implications of the EMH for technical and fundamental analysis, it probably shouldn't surprise anyone that market efficiency casts doubts on the possibility that an actively managed portfolio can produce consistently superior returns over a passively managed one (assuming that both have similar risk characteristics). Since EMH holds that securities prices reflect some level of all available information, consistently finding undervalued or overvalued securities is very difficult, especially since active management must profit enough to pay the higher transaction costs (e.g., brokerage commissions) associated with more frequent buying and selling of securities. You may recall from Chapter 6 that around 70 percent of actively managed equity pension funds failed to outperform the S&P 500 between 1974 and 1989.

Many investors have accepted this notion, at least implicitly. In recent years, their investments have caused **index funds** to grow rapidly. Index funds are mutual funds that match their portfolios to the compositions of market indexes. The assets of the Vanguard Index Trust—S&P 500 Portfolio, for example, grew more than 200 percent between 1989 and 1993. The Vanguard Index Trust is designed to replicate the performance of the S&P 500. Because index funds are more or less passively managed and make few changes to their portfolios, they have significantly lower annual operating expenses than actively managed funds.

Portfolio Management in an Efficient Market. It may seem that market efficiency implies that all investors should hold the same portfolio (say an index fund) and never make changes. Even in an efficient market, however, investors differ in their risk preferences, ages, income levels, and other characteristics.[9] As a result, the best portfolio for one investor might not suit another. Younger investors, for example, need less current income and are often more tolerant for risk than older investors. As a result, a younger investor might hold a diversified portfolio heavy in growth stocks while an older investor might hold a diversified portfolio skewed toward bonds and stocks with high dividend yields.

Testing Market Efficiency

As you're reviewing the evidence on market efficiency in the next two sections, you need to keep in mind a number of issues such as the type of tests, the benchmarks used, and other topics covered in the following discussion. These issues make interpreting the evidence somewhat subjective. In our opinion, the debate on market efficiency is likely to continue indefinitely and may never be settled one way or the other.

Types of Tests

There are several ways to test the efficient markets hypothesis. Analysts have devised direct and indirect tests of market efficiency. Direct tests assess the

---

[9]We'll explore this issue further in Chapter 13.

success of specific investment strategies or trading rules. An example of a direct test would be a test of the accuracy of predictions by some specific technical indicator. Indirect tests are statistical tests of prices or returns. For example, if prices follow a random walk, the *serial correlation* of returns should be close to zero.[10]

One can also test the efficient markets hypothesis by some scientific methodology, or simply by looking for anecdotal evidence. A scientific experiment develops a research design based upon a proven methodology. For example, we could scientifically examine market reactions to unexpected earnings announcements using a large sample over time. Results from the study would determine how rapidly the market responds to new public information. Anecdotal evidence involves looking for examples consistent, or inconsistent, with the efficient markets hypothesis. The earlier example of Apple Computer gave anecdotal evidence, in this case how rapidly investors responded to Apple's announcement on its 1993 fiscal year earnings.

The conundrum, of course, is that all types of tests can be criticized. Critics can argue that the test was applied improperly, was inadequate to measure its target, or both. For example, direct tests of technical trading rules can always be criticized because testing these trading rules requires applying them mechanically. These tests cannot hope to capture the subjective portion of technical analysis that, technicians argue, helps investors exploit historical price patterns. Even if a test provides evidence consistent with the efficient markets hypothesis, critics can always argue that the results were due to the test used, not necessarily the truth of the efficient markets hypothesis.

Establishing a Benchmark

Tests of the efficient markets hypothesis must usually establish some sort of a benchmark. For example, to say that some trading rule works, giving evidence inconsistent with the EMH, a test must find that a portfolio using the trading rule outperformed a similar portfolio that didn't use the trading rule, generating abnormal profits.[11] Like the type of test employed, critics can always question whether the benchmark chosen was appropriate.

The most common benchmark is the so-called *buy and hold portfolio.* As an example, a test may want to evaluate a trading rule that indicates when to switch between a stock index fund and a money market fund. How well does the trading rule perform? It would have to earn higher profits (or returns) than the profits from simply buying and holding the stock index fund over the same period of time. Of course, the test would have to account for differences in risk and transaction costs between the two investment strategies, as well. Active trading strategies usually involve higher transaction costs, and they often expose a portfolio to more risk, as well.

The Time Factor

As we noted in Chapter 6, on October 11, 1987, eight days prior to Meltdown Monday, Elaine Garzarelli, a well-known technical analyst, predicted the

---

[10]Serial correlation is essentially the correlation between the current value of a time series and past values of the same series. It is calculated as follows: Assume that you have a time series of equally spaced observations $(Z_1, Z_2, \ldots, Z_T)$. The serial correlation between Z_t and Z_{t-1} equals:

$$r_{-1} = \Sigma_{t=1}^{T} \left[(Z_t - M)(Z_{t-1} - M) \right] / \Sigma_{t=1}^{T} (Z_t - M)^2$$

where M is the mean of the time series. Serial correlation coefficients are interpreted in the same way as standard correlation coefficients and range from -1 to $+1$.

[11]This is analogous to the use of placebos in testing effectiveness of new drugs. The group of patients taking the drug have to show a significant change compared to the patient group taking the placebo in order to prove the drug effective.

upcoming market break. Was this prediction the result of her special insight into the market, application of her trading rules, and/or market inefficiency, or was this prediction merely luck? Of course, we'll never know. In retrospect, it's easy to find investment strategies that produced abnormal profits. Believers will call it skill, and skeptics will call it luck. The proper test evaluates how well the strategy works over different time periods.[12]

The time period(s) selected can, of course, always be criticized. A trading rule partisan may respond to a conclusion that the rule didn't work by saying "of course my trading rule didn't work over *that* period; everyone knows that period was an aberration in the market. The rule works fine during *normal* markets." There is no way to prove or disprove that assertion without testing it over every single possible time period, a rather daunting task.

Kiss and Tell

Suppose that someone discovered an investment strategy that really worked, and made a lot of money. Why would this person want to tell anyone? He or she could try to make money writing a book or an investment newsletter describing the strategy, but it would probably generate more money if kept secret. Suppose an analyst discovers that stocks beginning with the letter *K* rise on Wednesdays and fall on Fridays. Buying *K* stocks on Tuesdays and selling them on Thursdays makes the analyst lots of money. The dilemma, of course, is that once others know about the strategy, it will likely stop working. *K* stocks will probably start rising on Mondays and falling on Wednesdays as other investors try to anticipate the market. To avoid this, the analyst would probably keep the strategy a secret for as long as possible.[13]

Seriously, some argue that the inclination to keep successful strategies secret introduces a bias into tests of market efficiency and trading rules. (It's called *sample selection bias*.) Only those strategies that don't work are widely reported and, consequently, tested. Strategies that do work are not reported, so the results are biased in favor of the EMH, showing that trading rules don't produce abnormal profits by testing inferior trading rules. If the successful trading rules are kept secret, perhaps we can never fairly test the true ability of investors or the validity of the EMH.

Qualitative versus Quantitative Efficiency

We know that some investors pay more to trade than others. We also know that some investors can obtain information more cheaply than others. Perhaps we should replace the quantitative question "are the markets efficient?" with a more qualitative question "how efficient are the markets?" In other words, market efficiency may mean different things to different investors.

We'll use an actual example to illustrate this point. One familiar NYSE specialist firm has a small trading operation in addition to its normal specialist duties. The trading operation attempts to make money for the firm by buying and selling NYSE-listed stocks other than those for which the firm is the specialist.[14] The firm's traders employ a variety of technical indicators and trading rules, and the trading operation appears to make abnormal profits pretty consistently.

---

[12]This is true with any forecasting model. The true measure of the predictive power of a forecasting model is how well it performs over time periods other than the period used to develop the model.

[13]Cynics say that market gurus write their books, or start publishing their newsletters, only after their strategies begin to self-destruct!

[14]NYSE rules allow specialist firms to trade for their own accounts so long as they do not trade stocks assigned to them.

Does that mean that the NYSE isn't efficient? Not necessarily. For one thing, the specialist, being a member of the NYSE, pays virtually no transaction costs when it trades. For another, the firm rarely holds a position for more than a few minutes, and never overnight. Through electronic links with the NYSE's SuperDot System, the specialist firm's traders might buy 1,000 shares of Disney at 44 and then sell the shares a few minutes later for $44\frac{1}{4}$, making $250 (before transaction costs). The specialist tries to take advantage of what its traders believe are small, temporary mispricings of NYSE-listed stocks. The vast majority of investors could never profitably duplicate this firm's trading strategy. (Most investors' commissions on the Disney trade would probably exceed its $250 profit, and few have the timely access the strategy requires.) Perhaps this suggests that the markets are efficient for the vast majority of investors, though not necessarily for a few investors with special advantages. In fact, one could argue that these investors help to contribute to market efficiency by correcting mispricing.

Traditional Tests of the EMH

In this section we'll review some of the traditional tests of the three forms of the efficient markets hypothesis, most of which appear to support the concept of market efficiency, at least in its weak and semistrong forms. We examine tests based on historical prices, how rapidly the market reacts to new public information, and the value of private, or inside, information.

The vast majority of tests of the efficient markets hypothesis have examined the efficiency of *U.S.* stock markets. A few studies have attempted to test the efficiency of non-U.S. markets for stocks and other securities. The studies that have explored this question generally suggest that other security markets are at least as efficient as U.S. stock markets.[15]

Usefulness of Historical Prices

Tests of trading based on historical prices essentially evaluate the weak-form theory of market efficiency: that security prices fully reflect all historical information. These tests fall into two general categories: tests of the random nature of security prices and returns, and tests of specific trading rules.

Tests of the Random Nature of Security Prices and Returns. Tests of the randomness of securities prices over time have relied primarily on two statistical techniques: serial correlation and a so-called *runs test*. Both of these techniques have many other applications, as discussed in detail in most standard business statistics textbooks. Briefly, **serial correlation** measures the strength of the relationship between the current value of a time series (such as stock returns) and past share values. If stock prices follow something like the random walk described in Equation 7.1, serial correlation coefficients should be close to zero.

A **runs test** counts the number of times that price changes, each one designated positive or negative, change sign over a specific time period.[16] For example, say ten days of price changes produce this series: +, +, +, −, −, −, +, −, +, +. This sequence has five runs (the first three positive changes, the next three negative changes, a positive change, a negative change, and

[15]These studies are listed in several sources. See, for example, Edwin Elton and Martin Gruber, *Modern Portfolio Theory and Investment Analysis*, 3rd ed. (New York: Wiley & Sons, 1987), pp. 368–374; and Thomas Copeland and J. Fred Weston, *Financial Theory and Corporate Policy*, 3rd ed. (Reading, Mass.: Addison-Wesley, 1988), pp. 361–400.

[16]The runs test has the advantage that it tends to be less influenced by extreme observations than serial correlation coefficients.

the final two positive changes). Now consider the following sequence of ten price changes: +, +, +, +, +, +, −, −, −, −. This sequence has just two runs (the first six positive changes, and the final four negative changes). Too many, or too few, runs suggests that a series is not random.[17]

The results of these statistical tests from most studies have strongly suggested that stock prices and returns are essentially random, thus providing evidence in support of weak-form market efficiency.[18] For example, a test of price changes for each of the Dow Jones Industrial Average's 30 stocks over several years found that the average serial correlation coefficient was virtually equal to zero.[19] This study also conducted runs tests on price changes for each of the 30 Dow stocks (also over a period of several years) and found evidence supporting the contention that the price series were essentially random.[20]

Let's conduct our own test of the randomness of security prices, using the two series shown in Figure 7.1 generated by a random walk and the weekly averages for the S&P 500 during 1990 and 1991. We'll compute several serial correlation coefficients and conduct a runs test on the weekly changes for each series. We expect changes in the random walk should probably be random, but what about price changes for the S&P 500? The results are shown in Table 7.1.

The serial correlation coefficients are essentially equal to zero, with two exceptions. These results confirm that last week's price change provides virtually no information about next week's price change. Even though the series has statistically significant serial correlation coefficients, they are too small to support a profitable trading rule. The results of the runs tests reinforce the random nature of price changes for both series. The actual numbers of

Table 7.1

Tests of the Random Nature of Price Changes: The S&P 500 versus a Random Walk

A. Serial Correlation Coefficients

Lag	S&P 500	Random Walk
1	0.0027	−0.0693
2	0.0716	0.0243
3	0.0971	−0.1343
4	−0.0873	−0.0325
5	−0.1901	−0.0890

B. Runs Tests

Series	Total Changes	Positive Changes	Negative Changes	Actual Runs	Expected Runs
S&P 500	105	58	47	52	53
Random walk	105	62	43	56	52

[17]Assume that ten consecutive price changes produce the following run: +, +, +, +, +, +, +, +, +, +. The series has one run and doesn't appear to be random. On the other hand, assume the ten price changes produce the following series: +, −, +, −, +, −, +, −, +, −. The series has ten runs, but it still doesn't appear to be random.

[18]These studies are far too numerous to list here. As a reference, see Elton and Gruber, *Modern Portfolio Theory*, and Copeland and Weston, *Financial Theory*.

[19]See Fama, "Behavior of Prices." Fama found an average serial correlation coefficient of 0.026 (not significantly different from zero).

[20]Fama, "Behavior of Prices."

runs in both series are not significantly different from the number of runs expected for a random series.

Tests of Trading Rules. In addition to tests of the randomness of security prices and returns, a number of studies have examined trading rules based on historical prices to see if they produce abnormal profits. Weak-form efficiency, of course, states that such trading rules cannot produce abnormal profits. Again, the extensive evidence generally supports weak-form efficiency.[21] Let's look at one example of a trading rule, **filter rules.**

Filter rules are closely analogous to the support and resistance levels that we discussed in conjunction with the Dow Theory and technicians' charts in Chapter 6. Essentially a filter rule states that if a stock rises X percent from its most recent low (its support level), buy it because it has defined an up trend. Similarly, if a stock declines by Y percent from its most recent high (its resistance level), then sell the stock and hold cash (or sell the stock short if you don't own it) since the stock has defined a down trend.

How well do filter rules perform? Not very well, suggests the current evidence. One study compared buy-sell filters between 0.5 percent and 5 percent on each of the Dow Jones Industrial Average's 30 stocks against a simple buy-and-hold portfolio of those stocks. Only the smallest filter, 0.5 percent, outperformed the buy-and-hold portfolio, on average. The difference in performance, however, disappeared once the authors considered the higher transaction costs associated with the actively managed portfolio. Portfolios based on the larger filters all underperformed the buy-and-hold portfolio, even before accounting for higher transaction costs.

We will repeat a caveat about tests of trading rules: to allow testing, mechanical buy-and-sell criteria have to be established. As we discussed in Chapter 6, and earlier in this chapter, forecasts based on technical analysis are more subjective than objective by nature, and they're difficult to replicate. No test can really evaluate the subjective portion.

Market Reaction to New Public Information

A huge amount of widely varying new public information enters the financial markets each day. Semistrong-form market efficiency states that security prices reflect all of this information and react quickly to it. The reaction is so fast, in fact, that no one can consistently earn abnormal profits simply by buying or selling in response to new public information. Studies have examined market reactions to almost every conceivable type of new public information. Results of these studies generally support semistrong-form market efficiency. Let's look at some anecdotal evidence first.

Returning to the announcement by Apple Computer on June 9, 1993, we can see just how rapidly investors can react. Apple announced that its earnings for the rest of the 1993 fiscal year would be less than Wall Street was expecting and, in a matter of minutes, its stock fell sharply on the news. Yet the selloff actually started several days prior to Apple's announcement. (Take another look at Figure 7.2.) Between May 27 and June 9, Apple lost $13.625 per share (about 23.5 percent). However, more than half of the price decline ($7.875 per share) actually *preceded* the announcement (between May 27 and June 8).

This type of anecdotal evidence of semistrong-form market efficiency can be seen almost every day. Companies regularly make significant announcements with both negative and positive implications and their stocks react very quickly to the new information. In many cases, much of the reaction takes place before the announcement is made. Pick up today's edition of *The Wall*

---

[21]See Elton and Gruber, *Modern Portfolio Theory,* pp. 374–379; or Malkiel, *A Random Walk,* pp. 138–148.

Street Journal, and you'll probably find at least one or two examples similar to the Apple Computer situation.

Scientific Evidence. Of course anecdotal evidence doesn't prove that investors can't earn abnormal returns by acting on new public information. To find stronger evidence in support of semistrong-form market efficiency, we need to turn to the various scientific studies. These studies, often called **event studies,** typically examine market reactions to specific kinds of announcements. They analyze a large group of similar announcements using a statistical methodology that measures returns different from what would be expected, given no new information (called *abnormal returns* or *residuals*). Semistrong-form market efficiency implies that no abnormal returns should consistently occur after the announcement date.

To illustrate this approach, and the evidence presented by the vast majority of these studies, let's look at a study that examined market reactions to merger/takeover announcements.[22] As you know, shareholders of public companies that are taken over (often referred to as *target shareholders*) receive premium prices for their shares (prices higher than the existing market price). As a result, we would logically expect stock prices to jump in response to a takeover announcement. If the market is semistrong-form efficient, then this jump should occur prior to, and/or on, the announcement date, not afterward.

Figure 7.3 summarizes the researchers' results. It plots the **cumulative average abnormal return (CAAR)** against time relative to day of the announcement (Day 0).[23] The CAAR starts to rise, slowly at first, starting around 30 days prior to the announcement (Day -30) and the trend continues right up to the announcement date (Day 0). The two largest increases occur on the day prior to the announcement date (Day -1) and the announcement date itself. The CAAR then exhibits random drift following the announcement date (Day $+1$ through Day $+10$). These findings suggest that any significant price reaction of a target company stock due to a takeover announcement occurs prior to the announcement date. No one can earn an abnormal profit by acting on this new public information after it enters the market. This study's results are, therefore, consistent with semistrong-form market efficiency.

One has to be careful not to overinterpret the results of this, and other, event studies. Assume that Company A offers to buy Company B for $50 cash per share. The price of Company B's stock will jump on the announcement. If it doesn't jump to $50 per share, does that mean that the market isn't semistrong-form efficient? Not necessarily; think of all the things that can happen once a takeover offer becomes public. For one, Company A's bid may fail. Even if A does buy B, who knows, when the announcement is first made, just how long it will take to complete the deal. For another alternative, Company A may be forced to raise its offer price. The point is that takeovers, and other transactions, are complex and uncertain. As this uncertainty is resolved following the announcement, significant price reactions are likely to occur. The resolution of uncertainty can be thought of as new public information.

Value of Private Information

Tests of the value of inside, or private, information seek to evaluate strong-form market efficiency. These tests are perhaps the most difficult to conduct

---

[22]Arthur Keown and John Pinkerton, "Merger Announcements and Insider Trading Activity," *The Journal of Finance,* September 1981, pp. 855–870.

[23]The CAAR is the sum of the average abnormal returns up to day t, or $\text{CAAR}(t) = \text{CAAR}(t-1) + \text{AAR}(t)$. In the absence of new information, the expected value of $\text{AAR}(t)$ is zero. Therefore, in the absence of new information, the CAAR should exhibit random drift around zero. If the CAAR rises (or falls), then investors have reacted to new positive (or negative) information.

Figure 7.3

Example of the Market Reaction to New Public Information: Takeovers

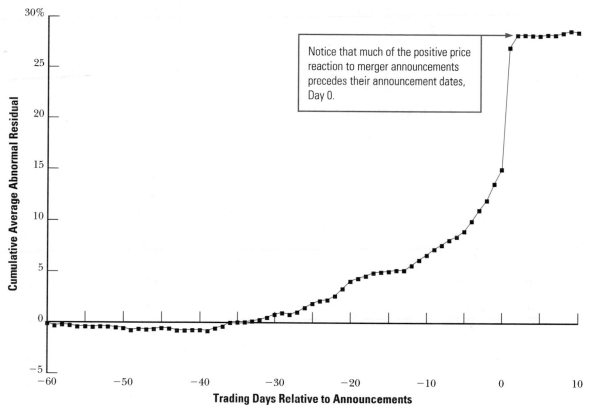

Notice that much of the positive price reaction to merger announcements precedes their announcement dates, Day 0.

Trading Days Relative to Announcements

Source: Arthur Keown and John Pinkerton, "Merger Announcements and Insider Trading Activity," *The Journal of Finance,* September 1981, pp. 855–870.

because there is no way to pinpoint exactly when new, private information, or inside information, enters the market. Further, the definition of *inside information* is ambiguous. Not surprisingly, the results from these studies are quite mixed.

One group of studies began with the assumption that mutual fund managers and securities analysts may have access to information before the general investing public. Securities analysts, for example, constantly talk to the companies they follow and may be able to learn some new information before it is made public.[24] These studies then examined the performance of mutual funds or securities analysts' recommendations, compared to some benchmark.

Results from these studies generally show that neither mutual fund managers nor securities analysts appear capable of consistently outperforming some market indicator like the S&P 500, after adjusting for differences in risk and transaction costs. Some additional, nonscientific evidence appears in Figure 7.4, which shows the total return from the average growth equity fund, the average growth and income equity fund, and the S&P 500 between 1984 and 1993. The average mutual fund did not post impressive results for this period. During the ten-year period, the S&P 500 produced an average

---

[24]This can be a very gray area. It is a violation of federal securities law for a securities analyst, or anyone else, to profit from the illegal use of inside information. The trouble is, as we've discussed, the definition of illegal use of inside information is very ambiguous. Most investment firms, however, have strict policies governing the public disclosure of material information that may be obtained by their analysts.

Figure 7.4

Performance of Equity Mutual Funds: 1984–1993

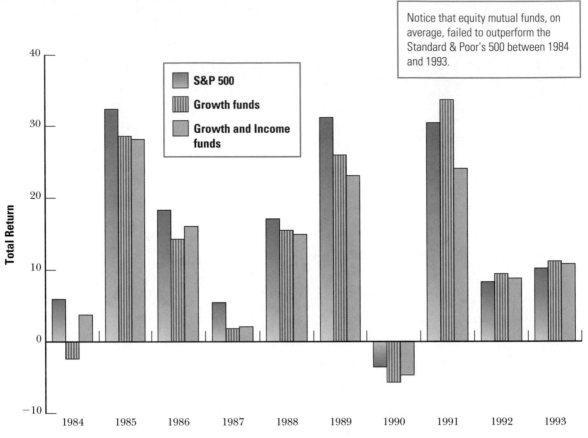

> Notice that equity mutual funds, on average, failed to outperform the Standard & Poor's 500 between 1984 and 1993.

Source: CDA/Weisenberger.

annual total return of 16.4 percent. By contrast, growth funds produced an average annual total return of only 13.6 percent, while growth and income funds produced an average annual total return of 13.7 percent. Further, the two most common types of stock mutual funds underperformed the S&P 500 in eight of the ten years.

Does all this evidence support strong-form market efficiency, or does it cast doubt on the assumption that mutual fund managers have access to private information? Obviously, there is no way to answer this question.

Event Studies. Event studies have provided more evidence about strong-form efficiency. Notice that Figure 7.3 showed evidence of positive price movements in takeover stocks well *before* the public announcements. Does this suggest that insiders were using private information about upcoming takeovers to make abnormal profits? The authors of the study thought so. They wrote: "Impending merger announcements are poorly held secrets, and trading on this nonpublic information abounds."[25]

Many event studies show the same pattern as Figure 7.3. Prices rise, or fall, before public announcements. Further, the rise or fall in prices is gradual, not immediate, suggesting that one can earn abnormal returns by possessing inside information. Perhaps the markets are not very strong-form efficient.

---

[25]Keown and Pinkerton, "Merger Announcements," p. 855.

On the other hand, since no one knows when private information becomes available, or even what really constitutes private information, perhaps these findings show only that some investors are good at anticipating significant new, public information. There's no way to say one way or the other.

Evidence Contradicting Market Efficiency

A number of well-documented instances and situations in the financial markets, often referred to as **anomalies,** appear to violate the concept of market efficiency. In this section, we'll review some of the evidence that appears to raise doubts about the efficient markets hypothesis.[26]

Financial Market Overreaction

One of the most intriguing issues to emerge in the last few years is the notion of **market overreaction** to new information (both positive and negative). Many practitioners have insisted for years that markets do overreact. Recent statistical evidence for both the market as a whole and individual securities has shown errors in security prices that are systematic and therefore predictable. Overreactions are sometimes called **reversals.** Stocks that perform poorly in one period suddenly reverse direction and start performing well in a subsequent period, and vice versa. Automobile manufacturers had one of the worst performance records of any industry group in 1991 based on total stock returns. The group reversed direction to become one of the top performers in 1992. Reversals suggest a number of possible trading strategies to earn abnormal profits, and they may also explain several other well-known anomalies. Let's look first at some evidence of market overreaction.

The markets seem to offer anecdotal evidence of reversals almost daily. Consider two recent examples: Disney and Warnaco. On June 5, 1992, SCA, the French owner of EuroDisney of which Disney owns 49 percent, announced that it was highly unlikely that the theme park would earn a profit during its first year of operation. In New York trading later that day, Disney's common stock was mauled, quickly losing almost 10 percent of its value.[27] The drop puzzled many analysts, who quickly reminded investors that any contribution of EuroDisney profits to Disney's overall net income would be quite small. Further, they pointed out, Disney makes money through various royalty and licensing arrangements with EuroDisney, regardless of whether or not the theme park turns a profit. Investors listened and Disney's shares recovered from the June 5 selloff within a few days.

The apparel maker Warnaco announced on February 11, 1993, that earnings for the 1992 fiscal year were $2.01 per share, about a penny higher than Wall Street estimates. Between February 11 and February 18, however, the stock dropped by almost 20 percent (from $33\frac{3}{4}$ to 27) because, on February 17, a Morgan Stanley analyst cut her 1993 earnings forecast from $2.75 to $2.35 (though she *reiterated* a buy recommendation on the stock).[28] Still, the falling earnings forecast was enough for the bears, who immediately beat the stock down. Analysts at other investment firms quickly issued their own buy

---

[26] The evidence is discussed in greater detail elsewhere. See, for example, Peter Fortune, "Stock Market Efficiency: An Autopsy?" *New England Economic Review,* March/April 1991, pp. 18–40.

[27] There were so many sell orders waiting to be executed that trading in Disney's common stock on the NYSE was delayed for about an hour.

[28] See *Business Week,* March 22, 1993, p. 79.

Figure 7.5

Evidence of Stock Market Overreaction

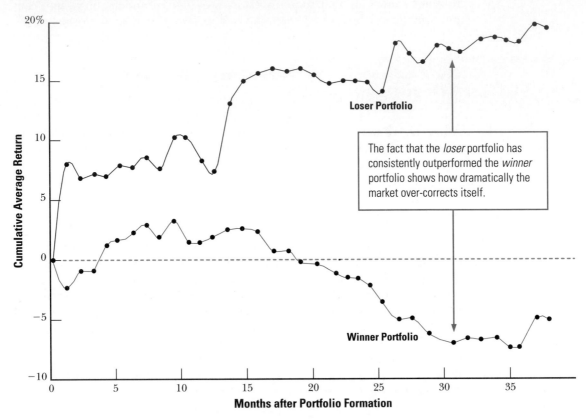

Note: Average of 16 Three-Year Test Periods Between January 1933 and December 1980; length of formation period: three years.

Source: Werner DeBondt and Richard Thaler, "Does the Stock Market Overreact?" *Journal of Finance,* July 1985, p. 800. Reprinted with permission of the Journal of Finance.

recommendations on Warnaco after the price drop, arguing that investors may have overreacted to a "slight revenue disappointment in a difficult environment for apparel makers," according to a report issued by analysts for Smith Barney on February 23. Warnaco drifted between 27 and 30 during the rest of February and March, and then started to recover. By the end of May the stock was trading in the upper 30s.

Scientific Evidence of Market Overreaction. In addition to this kind of anecdotal evidence, researchers have compiled a considerable amount of scientific evidence of reversals. Several studies have found that stock returns over longer time horizons (in excess of one year) display significant *negative* serial correlation. This means that high returns in one time period tend to be followed by low returns in the next period, and vice versa.

Other studies have tested for market overreaction by forming portfolios of winners and losers based on performance over a specific time period, and then measuring these portfolios' performance records over subsequent periods of time. These studies found that losers generally outperformed winners. An example of the results found by these studies is shown in Figure 7.5. This study found that the portfolios of losers outperformed portfolios of winners consistently over subsequent 36-month time periods.

Reversals and Other Anomalies. Market overreaction may offer the best explanation for several other well-documented anomalies. Some evidence suggests, for example, that stocks with low price/earnings ratios outperform stocks with high P/E ratios after adjusting for differences in risk. Low P/E stocks may be analogous to the losers we described above, or they may be stocks that are out of favor with investors. On the other hand, high P/E stocks may be the current investor favorites, or winners. As the market demonstrates almost daily, today's favorite stocks can fall from grace and reverse direction very quickly.[29]

Reversals may also explain the relationship between market-to-book ratios and subsequent performance. Two studies have shown that a good predictor of future returns is a stock's current market-to-book value ratio.[30] Both studies found that a lower ratio (in other words, a smaller difference between a stock's market value and its book value) corresponds to higher future returns. Like stocks with low P/E ratios, stocks with low market-to-book value ratios may be out of favor with investors.

Can Investors Profit from Reversals?

Market overreactions or reversals suggest a number of possible investment strategies to produce abnormal profits. Some possibilities include buying last year's worst performing stocks, avoiding stocks with high P/E ratios, or buying on bad news. At the risk of oversimplifying, any investment strategy based on market overreaction represents a **contrarian** approach to investing, buying what appears to be out of favor with most investors.

Contrarian investing has a number of strong proponents in the investment community. Respected investors such as Warren Buffet, Mario Gabelli, the late Benjamin Graham, Peter Lynch, and John Templeton all embrace aspects of contrarian investing. The success of several of John Templeton's mutual funds can be attributed, for example, to his willingness to invest in Japanese stocks in the 1970s, when most investors were ignoring Japan. When Japanese stocks got hot during the 1980s, Templeton moved money out of Japan and into other, less well-traveled markets, such as Mexico and Hong Kong.

The Investment Insights feature describes another investment strategy based on a contrarian approach. David Schafer buys only stocks with P/E ratios below the average P/E for the market. He also looks for reasonable expected growth rates in revenues and earnings. It's interesting to note that early in his career, Schafer was captivated by the nifty fifty. You may remember the nifty fifty from Chapter 5, which discussed their speculative bubble in the early 1970s.

Michael O'Higgins, a well-known money manager, has developed a system he claims will consistently outperform the overall market (which, for a number of reasons, he limits to the 30 Dow Jones Industrial Average stocks).[31] His system, a good example of contrarian investing, is explained in more detail in Figure 7.6. Essentially, the system involves buying the cheapest five Dow stocks (based on price and dividend yield), holding the stocks for a year, and then repeating the selection process.

[29]Amgen, the biotech company, is a good example of this. As we discussed in Chapter 5, biotechs were clearly investor favorites in 1991, only to reverse direction dramatically in 1992. At its peak in 1991, Amgen was selling for over 100 times earnings. In June 1993, its P/E ratio was down to 14, lower than the average P/E ratio for industrial companies such as automakers.

[30]See Eugene Fama and Kenneth French, "The Cross Section of Expected Stock Returns," *Journal of Finance,* June 1992, pp. 427–465; and Marc Reinganum, "The Anatomy of a Stock Market Winner," *Financial Analysts Journal,* March–April 1988, pp. 272–284. As you may remember, the book value of a stock equals common shareholders' equity (as given on the company's balance sheet, less the stated value of preferred stock, if any) divided by the number of outstanding shares.

[31]See Michael O'Higgins with John Downes, *Beating the Dow* (New York: Harper-Collins, 1992).

Reformed Sinner

There's no more zealous believer than a convert. That's why David Schafer is a believer in low-P/E investing. Long ago he favored stocks trading at giant multiples of their earnings. Now he's a fanatic for low earnings multiples.

Aged 52, Schafer has been around Wall Street since 1966. In late 1972 he left his job as an analyst to oversee International Nickel's pension fund. In the mass hypnosis then gripping Wall Street, the average multiple on the nifty fifty list of glamour stocks (Avon, Polaroid, 3M, and the like) topped 55. Schafer had the itch in the worst way. He recalls with a smile that his favorite was Avon Products—then priced around 140, or 65 times earnings. Its stock price would soon drop below 20.

Unlike a lot of other nifty fifty types, however, Schafer didn't get washed away in the debacle. His first job at Inco was to prepare an exhaustive report justifying why management of part of the pension fund should be moved in-house. It took Schafer over a year, during which he did no buying or selling. By late 1974, when Inco finally turned its pension fund over to Schafer to manage, the bear market was over. Says he: "After that, I didn't know how I was going to manage money, but I knew how I wasn't going to."

Schafer began by buying only stocks selling at lower multiples of earnings than the S&P 500. To that value angle he added a vestige of growth: He would buy only stocks that he thought could increase their earnings faster than the overall market over the next few years.

With 1973–74 burned in his memory, Schafer has never since bought a stock with a P/E bigger than a shoe size. And he has left big footprints: At Inco, he stomped out an average annual return of 20 percent from 1975 to 1981, outracing the S&P by 4 points. He left Inco in 1981 to start his own investment firm. His closed-end Schafer Value Trust was beating the market smartly when arbitragers, lured by the fund's discount to net asset value, forced Schafer to liquidate it in 1990. And his open-end, no-load Schafer Value Fund returned 19 percent last year—better than double the market's return. The fund, with only $14 million in assets, is just a showcase for Schafer's two investment firms, which handle $725 million in pension and private accounts.

Value stocks, Schafer's present religion, are usually defined as those fetching lower price/ earnings and price/book multiples than the market as a whole. Value seems to be back in style

these days: After several years of losing out to growth, value stocks outperformed the higher-multiple growth stocks by a wide margin last year, according to indexes kept by Frank Russell Co.

But, as Schafer well knows, the market tends to have alternating flings with growth and value. So his harmony of value and growth could be a nice hedge. He paid less than ten times earnings on average for the stocks in his fund, but he expects their earnings to grow at least 15 percent over the next three to five years. Other rules of his: He commits no more than 3 percent of the portfolio to any single stock, no more than 20 percent to a single industry, and rarely more than 3 percent to cash. When a stock's P/E rises as high as the market's (recently 16.5, the way Schafer calculates it), he dumps the stock. Thus he sold oil giant Atlantic Richfield and UJB Financial, the New Jersey bank, last year when their P/Es edged up.

Lately Schafer's biggest sector has been defense and aerospace, led by Northrop Corp., the defense contractor. "The smart operators in this business will come out okay," asserts Schafer.

Schafer tanked up on Progressive Corp., the Cleveland-based auto insurer, and Old Republic International, the liability and workers' compensation outfit, in 1989 and 1990. They were cheap because junk-bond jitters and California's Proposition 103 to restrict premiums were pummeling insurance stocks. He bought Old Republic at about five times earnings; he had to pay about eight times for Progressive. Progressive is now selling for 21 times trailing earnings; that has left Schafer with an impressive 190 percent gain in the stock.

Lately he's been buying Fleet Mortgage, the loan servicing outfit spun out of New England banking giant Fleet Financial. Another recent favorite: Ultramar Corp., the Tarrytown, N.Y.– based oil refiner, which Schafer started buying in December at seven to eight times earnings. When one of Ultramar's tankers ran aground off the Scottish coast in early January, the stock dropped nearly two points, to about 17. Schafer promptly bought more.

Schafer owns GM: "Car people, not financial people, are in charge again, and I like the new products." But IBM makes him shudder: "I think it has a lot further to go in resurrecting itself."

Source: "Reformed Sinner," *Forbes,* February 1, 1993, p. 111.

Figure 7.6

Example of a Contrarian Investment Strategy

The basic contrarian investment strategy advocated by money manager Michael O'Higgins consists of five simple steps:

1. List the current prices of the Dow Jones Industrial Average's 30 stocks. Next to each price list the stock's current dividend yield (current annual dividend divided by current price).
2. Circle the 10 highest-yielding Dow stocks.
3. Of these, identify the five with the lowest prices.
4. Buy equal dollar amounts of these five low-price/high-yield stocks.
5. Repeat the procedure around 12 months later.

Based on price and dividend information at the end of 1993, this strategy recommended equal dollar investments in the following five Dow stocks:

DuPont	Union Carbide
Eastman-Kodak	Woolworth
Merck	

Source: Michael O'Higgins with John Downes, *Beating the Dow* (New York: Harper-Collins, 1992).

Does it work? O'Higgins claims it does, though his evidence is not scientific. Between the beginning of 1973 and the middle of 1991, he claims that the five-stock portfolio selected using his method produced a cumulative total return of 2,819.4 percent versus only 559.3 percent for the entire Dow.[32] Further, the year-to-year variations in returns produced by the five-stock portfolio are less than the year-to-year variation in returns produced by the Dow.

Some Caveats about Contrarian Investing. While contrarian investing makes some sense, it requires a number of caveats. First, stocks with low P/E ratios are not necessarily cheap, nor are stocks with high P/E ratios necessarily expensive. The inverse relationship between value and P/E (or market-to-book value) ratios is far from perfect. Some stocks may have low (or high) P/E ratios for very good reasons. Further, value is definitely in the eye of the beholder; one person's bargain is another person's overvalued pariah.

For another caveat, remember that very good economic reasons may drive some reversals. Reversing prices may be responding to new information, and correcting an overreaction. Also, a poor performer may continue to perform poorly as the company continues to slide downhill. The fact that a company had a lousy year in 1992 doesn't mean it will have a good year in 1993. Further, the timing of a reversal can be very difficult to predict. Investors have shunned some individual stocks and groups of stocks for long periods of time, while other stocks have reversed direction quickly.

Finally, think about what would happen if every investor suddenly became a contrarian. If contrarian investing really does offer abnormal profit opportunities, we would expect the wise investors to exploit opportunities aggressively. Soon, competition would eliminate these opportunities. Remember, the past success of a system like the one O'Higgins proposes is no guarantee of future profits.

---

[32]We should note that these returns ignore commissions and taxes, both of which will be higher for O'Higgins' system than for a buy-and-hold strategy.

Bubbles and Fads

Recall from Chapter 5 that a speculative bubble is a situation where the price of some asset rises sharply for no apparent reason other than the belief that the price will go still higher. Bubbles can also be thought of as self-fulfilling, systematic deviations of market prices from fundamental values. These deviations continue until the conditions of self-fulfillment disappear. If a bubble was merely a random deviation of market price from fundamental value, the deviations would wash out over time. The bubble would not have to collapse.

Some argue that speculative bubbles and fads provide evidence that contradicts market efficiency. In one sense, bubbles and fads can be thought of as extreme market overreactions. Investors bid the price of something higher and higher, until, for some reason, the bubble breaks and prices reverse direction dramatically. While the bubble is building, prices tend to get onto one-way streets that lead only upward, so returns cannot follow a random walk.[33]

After reading Chapter 5, you should have little doubt that speculative bubbles are an unfortunate part of the investment landscape. Given the human factor in investments, bubbles are likely to occur over and over again. If one could predict bubbles, however, buying before they began and selling before they broke, one could make a great deal of money. Bubbles are very hard to predict, though, and can be identified only in retrospect. Identifying a fad while it is occurring is hardly an objective process.

Perhaps bubbles and fads seem inconsistent with the efficient markets hypothesis, then. Still investors cannot necessarily earn abnormal profits by avoiding the fad or predicting the bubble. Remember one other important thing about speculative bubbles: they may be systematic deviations of prices from fundamental values, but the market does correct itself—all bubbles eventually break.

January and Weekend Effects

A number of studies have identified persistent day-of-the-week and seasonal patterns in security returns, especially stock returns. These types of patterns are, of course, inconsistent with the EMH and, like all anomalies, may suggest some trading strategies. Let's look at some of the evidence first, and then discuss possible implications for investors.

Studies of daily returns began with the goal of testing whether the markets operate on calendar time or trading time. In other words, are returns for Mondays (that is, returns over Friday-to-Monday periods) different from the other day-of-the-week returns? The answer to the question turned out to be yes; the trend was called the **weekend effect.** Monday returns were substantially lower than other daily returns. Results from one study of daily returns from the S&P 500 between 1953 and 1977 are shown in Figure 7.7. On an annual basis (assuming 250 trading days per year), Mondays produced a mean return of almost −35 percent. By contrast, the mean annualized return on Wednesdays was more than +25 percent.

The January Effect. Stock returns appear to exhibit seasonal return patterns as well. In other words, returns are systematically higher in some months than in others. Initial studies found that returns were higher in January for

---

[33]As a bubble is building we would expect to find a positive serial correlation among returns or price changes. In other words, positive price changes tend to be followed by positive price changes.

Figure 7.7

Differences in Daily Returns from the Standard & Poor's 500: 1953–1977

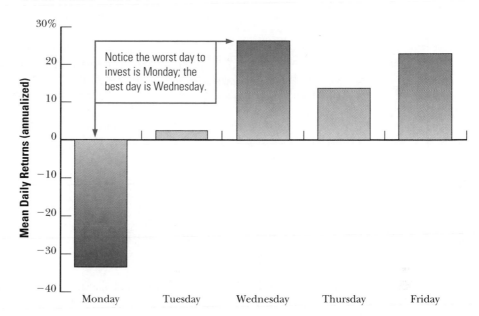

Source: Kenneth French, "Stock Returns and the Weekend Effect," *Journal of Financial Economics,* March 1980, p. 58. Reprinted with permission of Elsevier Science.

all stocks (thus this anomaly was dubbed the **January effect**). Later studies found a January effect only for small stocks.[34] The January effect has been shown in foreign stock markets, as well.[35]

As evidence of seasonal patterns in stock returns, look at Figure 7.8. Based on the Ibbotson Associates database, the figure illustrates average monthly total returns between 1926 and 1993 for both large and small stocks. While average January returns from large stocks are impressive (about 21 percent on an annual basis), two other months (July and August) have provided higher average total returns. On the other hand, January returns from small stocks are four times higher than average total returns from any other month. (Average January returns are a stratospheric 119 percent on an annual basis.)

One widely accepted explanation for the January effect is tax-loss selling by investors at the end of December. Since this selling pressure depresses prices at the end of the year, it would be reasonable to expect a bounce-back in prices during January.[36] Small stocks, the argument goes, are more susceptible to the January effect because their prices are more volatile and institutional investors (many of whom are tax-exempt) are less likely to invest in shares of small companies.

---

[34]For specific references to studies on the January effect, see Elton and Gruber, *Modern Portfolio Theory;* and Copeland and Weston, *Financial Theory.*

[35]See, for example, Philip Brown et al., "Stock Return Seasonalities and the Tax Loss Selling Hypothesis: Analysis of the Arguments and Australian Evidence," *Journal of Financial Economics,* March 1983, pp. 33–56.

[36]Several studies have found that virtually all of the January effect has occurred during the first few days of trading in January. See, for example, Donald Keim, "Size Related Anomalies and Stock Return Seasonality: Further Evidence," *Journal of Financial Economics,* June 1983, pp. 13–32.

Figure 7.8

Stock Market Seasonality: 1926–1993

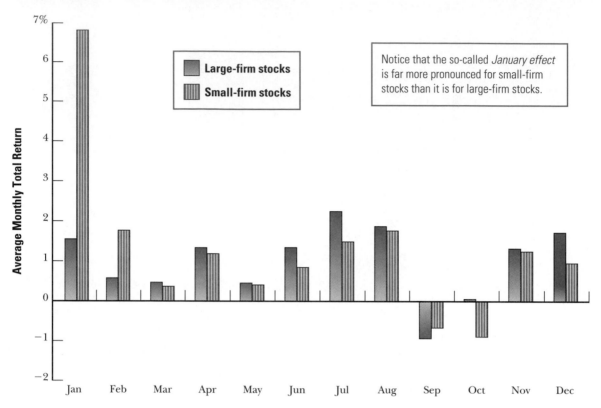

Source: *SBBI 1994 Yearbook* (Chicago: Ibbotson Associates, 1994), p. 114.

Seasonal Trading Strategies

Both seasonal and day-of-the-week effects are inconsistent with market efficiency since both suggests that historical information can generate abnormal profits. As with all anomalies, however, a more important issue is whether seasonal and/or day-of-the-week effects can create profit opportunities for investors. Should you, for example, always buy stocks at the close of trading on Mondays and sell them at the close of trading on Wednesdays? Technician Martin Zweig (you should remember him from Chapter 6) suggests that if you're going to buy stocks anyway, you should consider buying them prior to a holiday.[37]

However, it appears that trading rules based on either seasonal or day-of-the-week effects are unlikely to produce consistently abnormal profits, at least for investors who pay taxes and average transaction costs. Even Martin Zweig argues that seasonal and day-of-the-week effects are not large enough to offset other factors that he believes drive stock prices.

While differences in daily returns appear impressive, they are probably much too small to offset transaction costs. The daily mean return on Wednesdays, for example, is only 0.097 percent. A purchase at the end of trading on Tuesday followed by a sale at the end of trading on Wednesday, based on the mean Wednesday return, would pay only $9.70 on a $10,000 investment, before commissions. Most discount brokerage firms charge *minimum* commissions per trade of $25.

---

[37]See Martin Zweig, *Martin Zweig's Winning on Wall Street* (New York: Warner Books, 1990), pp. 155–174.

Figure 7.9

Seasonality in Small-Firm Stock Returns: 1971–1980 versus 1981–1990

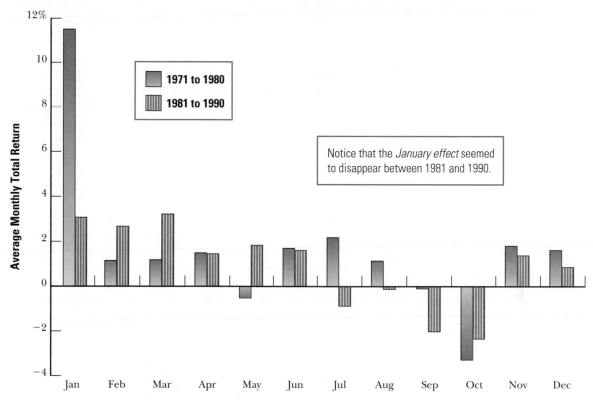

Source: *SBBI 1994 Yearbook* (Chicago: Ibbotson Associates, 1994).

The January effect appears to have far more profit potential. For example, the average January return suggests that buying a portfolio of small stocks at the end of December and selling them at the end of January could produce a profit of about $679 on a $10,000 investment, probably more than enough to offset transaction costs.[38]

If this sounds too good to be true, that's because it probably is. The average January return from small stocks of 6.79 percent is just that, a historical average. It hides substantial year-to-year variation in January returns between 1926 and 1992. In January 1990, for example, small stocks produced a total return of −7.64 percent. Remember, the past is no guarantee of the future.

Another reason we're skeptical that an investor can exploit the January effect to produce abnormal profits goes back to a point we've made over and over again in this chapter: once profitable investment strategies are recognized, it is reasonable to expect other investors to aggressively exploit them, eventually eliminating the profit potential. This may be happening to the January effect. Entire books have been published about this widely recognized anomaly, and it may be disappearing. Figure 7.9 shows average monthly total returns for the period 1971 to 1980 and 1981 to 1990. Notice that the difference between January returns differed from other months' returns far

---

[38]One thing worth remembering, however, is that transaction costs associated with buying and selling shares of small companies are higher than the cost of buying and selling shares of large companies. For one thing, the bid–ask spread on a small stock is much larger, on average, than the spread on a large stock. See "As Small Stocks Soar, So Do the Costs of Trading Them," *The Wall Street Journal*, October 27, 1991, p. C1.

less over the more recent decade. Between 1971 and 1980, the average January return was 11.5 percent, six times that of any other month. By contrast, the average January return was only 2.9 percent between 1981 and 1990, about the same as average monthly returns from February and March.

Small-Firm Effect

We saw in Chapter 2 that stocks of small companies substantially outperformed stocks of large companies between 1926 and 1993. An initial investment of $1,000 in large-firm stocks, made at the beginning of 1926, would have been worth slightly more than $800,000 at the end of 1993 (an average annual return of approximately 11 percent). By contrast, $1,000 invested in small-firm stocks at the same time would have been worth in excess of $2.7 million at the end of 1993 (an average annual return in excess of 17 percent). Of course, history has also shown that small stocks have exhibited more year-to-year variation than large stocks. However, even after correcting for differences in risk, some studies suggest that investors can earn abnormal profits by investing in shares of small companies, exploiting the **small-firm effect.**[39]

Two explanations for the small-firm effect seem plausible to us. The first is that analysts have applied the wrong risk measures to evaluate returns from small stocks. Small stocks may well be riskier than these traditional risk measures indicate. If proper risk measures were used, the argument goes, the small-firm effect might disappear. Small-firm stocks may not generate larger risk-adjusted returns than large stocks. While the risk of small stocks may not be adequately captured by standard risk measures, it's hard to believe that better measures of risk would eliminate the entire small-firm effect.

Another explanation for the small-firm effect is the fact that large institutional investors (such as pension funds) often overlook small-firm stocks. Consequently, less information is available on small companies. (They are also followed by fewer analysts.) One could argue that this information deficiency makes small-firm stocks riskier investments, but one could also argue that discovery of a neglected small-firm stock by the institutions could send its price rising as the institutions start buying it. The small-firm effect may arise from the continuous process of discovery of neglected small-firm stocks leading to purchases by institutional investors.

Whatever the explanation, small-firm stocks, though riskier than large-firm stocks, have historically provided substantial returns to investors, far higher than those produced by large-firm stocks. Of course, we can only speculate about whether this relationship will continue in the future.

Performance of Investments Professionals

As we've seen, investments professionals like pension fund managers or mutual fund managers seem to have a difficult time beating the overall market. Recall that Figure 7.4, for example, showed that average annual total returns from growth and growth and income equity mutual funds were less than total annual returns from S&P 500 in eight out of the ten years between 1983 and 1992. A study of pension fund performance found that all-equity pension funds underperformed the S&P 500 by an average of 1.3 percent per year between 1983 and 1989.[40]

---

[39]As we pointed out earlier, the January effect is observed only in small-firm stocks. The small-firm and January effects may be closely intertwined; one study found virtually all of the small-firm effect occurred in January. See Keim, "Size Related Anomalies."

[40]Josef Lakonishok et al., "The Structure and Performance of the Money Management Industry," *Brookings Papers on Economic Activity* (Washington, D.C.: Brookings Institution, 1992), pp. 339–379.

Of course these are average figures. In a particular year, some professionals will beat the market, while others will not. The key question is whether some professionals can *consistently* outperform the market. Some evidence suggests that the answer to this question may be *yes*.

A number of mutual funds appear to outperform the market on a regular basis, regardless of whether the market is rising or falling. For example, the Fidelity Contrafund (a stock fund) beat the S&P 500 each year between 1988 and 1992 by an average of 11.2 percent per year.[41] In 1990, the Contrafund had a total return of +3.9 percent versus −3.2 percent for the S&P 500. During 1991 the Contrafund had a total return of almost 55 percent, beating the S&P 500 by about 24.5 percent.

The Value Line Enigma. The performance of investment advisory services has been examined as well. In Chapter 4, we discussed the ranking system for stocks used by the investment advisory service Value Line. As you may recall, Value Line gives each of the 1,700 or so stocks it follows a timeliness rating of between 1 and 5 (1 being the highest).

Several studies have examined the predictive value of the Value Line ranking system.[42] These studies have found that an investor who bought stocks with Value Line rankings of 1, while avoiding or selling stocks with rankings of 5, would have earned abnormal risk-adjusted profits. We caution you, however, that studies of this **Value Line enigma** are over ten years old. The predictive value of the Value Line ranking system has not been tested with more recent data.

Playing Hot Hands. The same study that showed that the S&P 500 outperformed the average pension fund between 1983 and 1989 also found that the best-performing pension funds are likely to continue to perform well in future periods. The researchers ranked the three-year performance of 769 all-equity pension funds and divided the rankings into quartiles. Quartile 1 includes the 192 best-performing funds, Quartile 2 includes the next 192 funds, and so forth. The performance of each fund was then measured over the next three-year period. Some of the study's findings are shown in Table 7.2.

Table 7.2

Is Past Performance a Good Predictor of Future Performance?

	Future Performance[a]					Average Three-Year Return	
	Quartile 1	Quartile 2	Quartile 3	Quartile 4	Total	Past Three-Year Period	Future Three-Year Period
Past Performance							
Quartile 1	37%	29%	20%	13%	100%	24.3%	15.9%
Quartile 2	20	26	29	25	100	19.3	14.6
Quartile 3	19	24	30	26	100	16.1	14.5
Quartile 4	23	21	20	35	100	10.3	13.8

[a]Data in these columns show probabilities for movement from a past three-year performance quartile into various future three-year performance quartiles.

Source: Josef Lakonishok et al., "The Structure and Performance of the Money Management Industry," *Brookings Papers on Economic Activity* (Washington, D.C.: Brookings Institution, 1992), p. 361.

---

[41]This is not an endorsement of the Contrafund. We're using it only as an example and don't recommend you invest next year's tuition in the fund.

[42]See, for example, Thomas Copeland and David Myers, "The Value Line Enigma: A Case Study of Performance Evaluation Issues," *Journal of Financial Economics,* November 1982, pp. 289–321.

As you can see, the average total return over the previous three years for the top quartile was 24.3 percent compared to 10.3 percent for the bottom quartile. Returns over future three-year periods averaged 15.9 percent for the top group versus 13.8 percent for the bottom group. Further, 37 percent of the top-performing funds stayed in the top quartile over the next three years (66 percent stayed in the top half). By contrast, 35 percent of the worst-performing funds stayed in the bottom group over the next three years (55 percent stayed in the bottom half).

Contrary to the efficient markets hypothesis, is past perfromance a good guide to future performance? We would answer this question with a qualified *maybe*. It appears that investors can improve their probability of future success by betting on fund managers that have consistently beaten the market. Alas, however, like most things in life, there are no guarantees. For one thing, the winning fund manager may leave. Consider Fidelity's well-known Magellan mutual fund. Magellan had one of the best performance records of any stock mutual fund during the 1980s, beating the S&P 500 in eight of ten years. However, since Peter Lynch retired in 1990, the fund's performance has been somewhat more erratic.

Take another look at Table 7.2. Notice that there isn't a great deal of difference in the subsequent three-year performance figures between the top and bottom quartiles (about 2.1 percent per year). Further, while two-thirds of the top-performing funds stayed in the top half in the future, one-third, not an insignificant number, slipped into the bottom half. The moral is that, while there may be a few investment geniuses around, even the best pro occasionally lays an egg.

So, Are the Markets Efficient?

In an article entitled "Stock Market Efficiency: An Autopsy," financial economist Peter Fortune writes, "Our fundamental conclusion is that the efficient markets hypothesis is having a near-death experience and is very likely to succumb unless new technology, as yet unknown, can revive it."[43] We're not quite yet ready to bury the efficient markets hypothesis, but a considerable amount of evidence does contradict it, and more evidence seems to emerge daily. However, a considerable amount of evidence also supports the concept of market efficiency. Even if the markets aren't efficient in an academic sense, they may be efficient in a more practical sense. In most parts of the world, the financial markets are well-functioning, competitive institutions where consistent, abnormal profits based on public or historical information are rare. Arguments on both sides of the efficient markets debate are discussed in the Investment Insights box (reprinted from *The Wall Street Journal*).

There is an often-repeated joke about a Wall Street trader and a finance professor walking down the street. The trader notices a $100 bill lying on the street and stops to pick it up. "Why bother," the finance professor says, "If it had really been a $100 bill, someone would already have grabbed it."

In one sense, this joke sums up the debate over market efficiency. An unquestioning acceptance of the efficient markets hypothesis, and subsequent rejection of all investment analysis and research as worthless, can leave a lot of money lying on the street for someone else. Real-world situations defy a strict view of market efficiency often enough to justify the careful search

---

[43]Fortune, "Stock Market Efficiency."

Luck or Logic? Debate Rages on over "Efficient-Market" Theory

For just over five years now, the Investment Dartboard column has pitted investment pros against the forces of chance, in the form of darts heaved at the stock listings. One aim has been to provide a lighthearted test of the "efficient-market theory."

The theory, hated on Wall Street but accepted by many academics, states that stock-picking success is basically a "random walk," or a matter of luck. The notion is that, since all publicly known information is instantaneously factored into stock prices, an uninformed person—or a chimp throwing darts—can do as well as a knowledgeable professional.

Theorists allow for a couple of exceptions. People who possess nonpublic "inside information" can beat the market, they say. Since efficient market theorists also say people who pick riskier, more volatile stocks can beat the market. Such stocks exaggerate the overall market's up and down moves. In the average year, most stocks have more ups than downs, so the odds are with the risk-taker. Another way of looking at it is that investors demand to be compensated for the extra risk of holding a volatile stock.

Five years of Investment Dartboard columns have simply thrown gasoline on the flames of the debate. There's fuel for both sides of the argument.

On the surface, the results clearly favor the professionals and go against the theory. Since the contest adopted its current rules in 1990, the pros have won 24 times, the darts 17 times. The average six-month gain for the pros, 8.4 percent, has been much better than the 3.3 percent gain achieved by the darts. (Those figures are price changes only, without dividends.)

But Burton Malkiel, an economics professor at Princeton University and a leading exponent of the efficient-market theory, says there's less than meets the eye in the pros' apparent success in the contest.

According to Prof. Malkiel, the pros' favorable showing can be explained by two factors. First, they are picking riskier, more volatile, stocks than the darts are. Second, they benefit from a favorable publicity effect on the day the article is published.

INVESTMENT INSIGHTS

With Prof. Malkiel, Gilbert E. Metcalf, an assistant professor of economics at Princeton, recently wrote a paper analyzing the Dartboard contests from 1990 through 1992. The professors found that the pros' picks were about 40 percent more volatile—and therefore riskier—than the overall market. The dart stocks were only about 6 percent more volatile than the market.

In other words, the pros' selections tend to move up or down 14 percent for every 10 percent the overall market moves. Once you adjust for risk, the researchers say, the pros' margin shrinks to 0.4 percent, which is not statistically significant.

But that's not all. The researchers say the pros are riding the coattails of a strong "announcement effect" that causes the pros' picks to surge on the day they appear in this newspaper. Take away the announcement effect, they say, and the pros' superiority vanishes altogether.

In the contest, the starting price is the price at 4 P.M. Eastern time the day before the article appears. But Messrs. Metcalf and Malkiel found that if results were measured from 4 P.M. on the day the article appears, the pros' average gain in 1990–1992 would have been nearly a percentage point behind that of the darts.

Partisans of the pros would reply that starting the clock at 4 P.M. on publication day would unfairly penalize the pros. Their buy recommendations would have an artificially high starting point, having already been pushed up by several hours of column-inspired trading. Also, the six-month contest period allows plenty of time for the pros' picks to come back to earth.

So the great debate remains unsettled. Which, of course, allows the fun to continue.

for undervalued (and overvalued) securities. On the other hand, one should always be very skeptical of someone who claims to have a clever system or special insight to consistently beat the market. There aren't too many $100 bills lying on the sidewalk, waiting to be picked up.

Chapter Summary

1. **Define the terms** *random walk,* *market efficiency,* **and** *efficient markets hypothesis.*

   The concept of market efficiency evolved from research showing that stock price changes appeared to be independent over time, describing a random walk. A random walk is a stochastic time series where each successive change in a variable is drawn independently from a probability distribution with a constant mean and variance. If stock prices follow a random walk, tomorrow's price is simply today's price plus a random variable, so the best forecast of tomorrow's price is today's price. The competitive hunt for abnormal profits is probably a major reason to expect the markets to be efficient, as millions of highly motivated investors, many with substantial resources, search constantly for undervalued securities. Their actions probably mean that the easy pickings have already been picked over and profitable trading strategies will quickly self-destruct. Weak-form efficiency states that security prices reflect all information contained in historical prices. Semistrong-form efficiency states that, in addition to all historical information, current prices reflect all publicly available information and adjust quickly to new public information. Strong-form efficiency states that security prices reflect all private, as well as public, information.

2. **Understand the important implications of market efficiency.**

   The efficient markets hypothesis argues that technical analysis is essentially worthless because current prices already reflect all the information in historical prices. The recurrent and predictable patterns that technicians claim to see in securities prices are either illusions or they are recognized so quickly by investors that no one can expect to exploit them consistently to produce abnormal profits. Market efficiency also has a number of implications for fundamental analysis. For analyst recommendations to consistently produce abnormal profits, analysts must possess superior forecasting ability and be able to gain insight into the various fundamental factors that drive stock prices, before the market recognizes these factors. Finally, the efficient markets hypothesis argues that active portfolio management is unlikely to produce consistently higher returns than passive portfolio management, after adjusting for differences in transaction costs and risk. Market efficiency, does not, however imply that all investors should hold the same portfolio. Investors differ in terms of age, income, and risk preferences. These factors should influence portfolio selection, even in an efficient market.

3. **Outline the issues that arise with tests of the efficient markets hypothesis.**

   A number of issues make interpreting the evidence for and against the EMH somewhat subjective, so the debate over market efficiency will likely never be settled. Researchers have tested the EMH using direct tests of trading strategies and indirect tests such as serial correlation. All types of tests can be criticized, however, and one never can say whether the findings are due to market efficiency (or inefficiency) or the test. Establishing a benchmark and the timing of tests further complicate the question. Selection bias may plague such tests if successful trading strategies are kept secret. Finally, qualitative versus quantitative perspectives make *market efficiency* mean different things for different investors.

4. **Examine evidence supporting the efficient markets hypothesis.**

   Traditional tests of market efficiency have examined the usefulness of historical prices, the speed with which prices adjust to new public information, and the value of private information. Tests of the usefulness of his torical prices have generally found that price changes are essentially random and that common trading rules (such as filter tests) fail to outperform simple buy-and-hold strategies. Anecdotal and scientific evidence shows that securities prices adjust very quickly to new information, and trading on the basis of new public information is unlikely to produce abnormal profits. Tests of the value of private information are more ambiguous. It is difficult to measure exactly when new private information enters the market, or even to define what constitutes private information. Event studies suggest that many public announcements may be known by insiders prior to their announcement dates, and these insiders could be earning abnormal profits, even though use of inside information is a violation of federal securities laws.

5. **Review evidence that appears to contradict market efficiency.**

    Some research has produced evidence that appears inconsistent with the EMH, including market overreactions (reversals) along with related anomalies involving stocks with low price/earnings and market-to-book value ratios. This evidence suggests that a contrarian investment strategy might earn abnormal profits. In addition, the existence of bubbles and fads can be considered inconsistent with market efficiency. Seasonal, day-of-the-week, and small-firm anomalies cast further doubt on the EMH. Stock returns, especially for shares of small companies, are higher in January than in other months. Finally, some professional investors seem able to consistently outperform the market. The key point with all anomalies is not just that they are present, but whether investors can expect to continually profit from them. Some anomalies, such as the weekend effect, are quite small, while others, such as profits from contrarian investing, can be quite subjective. The moral to remember is that the past is no guarantee of the future.

6. **Try to answer the question: Are the financial markets efficient?**

    The answer to this question is an ambiguous *maybe*. In spite of the evidence that contradicts the EMH, we're not quite ready to bury it. Too much evidence still suggests that abnormal profits are very difficult to obtain in today's highly competitive financial markets. On the other hand, the potential value of creative and intelligent investment analysis and research should not be dismissed. The market always offers undervalued (or overvalued) securities, but it is never easy to find these securities before others do.

Key Terms

Efficient markets hypothesis	Runs test
Random walk	Filter rule
Weak-form market efficiency	Event study
Historical information	Cumulative average abnormal
Semistrong-form market	return (CAAR)
efficiency	Anomaly
Public information	Market overreaction
Strong-form market efficiency	Reversal
Private information	Contrarian
Insider trading	Weekend effect
Buy-and-hold strategy	January effect
Index fund	Small-firm effect
Serial correlation	Value Line enigma

Discussion Questions and Problems

1. Define the term *random walk*. Does a random walk imply that daily stock prices will be independent of each other?
2. If a series follows a random walk, what is the best forecast of tomorrow's price? Why?
3. How does competition produce market efficiency? What does competition imply about the future success of trading rules?
4. Distinguish between the weak, semistrong, and strong forms of market efficiency. What is meant by *all available information?*
5. What are the implications of the efficient markets hypothesis for technical analysis? On what points does the EMH attack technical analysis?
6. Is fundamental analysis inconsistent with market efficiency? Why or why not?
7. Distinguish between active and passive portfolio management. Why does the EMH tend to favor passive portfolio management?
8. Distinguish between direct and indirect tests of market efficiency. What major issues affect the selection of methods to test the EMH?
9. What is meant by *sample selection bias?* How does sample selection bias apply to tests of market efficiency?
10. Define the term *serial correlation*. If security returns follow a random walk, what results should you obtain from a serial correlation test?
11. Compute the number of runs in the following series of 20 daily stock prices. Do the price changes appear to be random?

Day	Price	Day	Price
1	30.25	11	33.00
2	30.50	12	33.25
3	30.75	13	33.00
4	32.25	14	33.50
5	31.75	15	33.75
6	31.25	16	33.50
7	32.00	17	34.00
8	32.25	18	34.25
9	32.00	19	34.75
10	32.75	20	35.00

12. What is a filter rule? Describe how you would go about testing it.
13. How would you go about testing how rapidly security prices respond to new public information? What would you look for?
14. Define the term *private* (or *inside*) *information*. Why is it so difficult to test for the value of private information?
15. What is meant by the term *reversal?* Explain how an investor might profit from reversals.
16. Discuss an investment strategy that you would classify as contrarian. What would happen if every investor decided to become a contrarian?
17. What is the January effect? How are the January and small-firm effects related?
18. Discuss the small-firm effect. List two explanations for the effect.
19. Is past performance a relatively good guide to future performance? What are some caveats about using past performance to assess likely future performance?

20. (CFA, Level I Question, 1991).
    a. List and briefly define the three forms of the efficient markets hypothesis.
    b. Discuss the role of a portfolio manager in a perfectly efficient market.

Critical Thinking Exercises

1. This exercise requires computer work. Open file Price 3.XLS on the data disk. It gives weekly values for the S&P 500 between the end of 1990 and the end of 1993. Use the data to perform the following exercises and answer the following questions:
   a. Compute the weekly percentage change. Plot both the index and percentage change against time.
   b. Design a filter rule. (Set your filter no lower than 0.5 percent, and no higher than 2.5 percent.)
   c. When do your filters tell you to buy and sell?
   d. Evaluate how well your filters worked. In other words, did your filters give you correct buy-and-sell signals compared to the performance chart?
   e. If you had simply bought the S&P 500 at the beginning of 1991 and held it until the end of 1993, how well would you have done? Is the performance of the buy-and-hold approach better or worse than the performance of the filter rules? Ignore dividends.

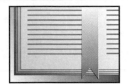

2. This exercise involves library research. Reviewing recent financial news, find an announcement that appears to be significant, new information. Collect stock price data for that company for several days around the announcement date, including the announcement date itself. Using your data, answer the following questions:
   a. How did the company's stock react to the announcement?
   b. How rapidly did the stock price react to the announcement?
   c. Can you detect any leakage of new information prior to the announcement date?
   d. Would you classify the stock price reaction as an overreaction? Why or why not?

   Hint: The best announcements to look for are those involving earnings. Look especially for earnings announcements that are higher or lower than analyst expectations. The best months for earnings announcements are February, April, July, and October, especially the last half of the month.

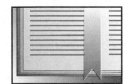

3. This exercise requires library research. Go back and look at the five stocks listed in Figure 7.6. They are the five highest-ranked Dow stocks using the O'Higgins system. According to the O'Higgins system, the five lowest-ranking stocks at the end of 1993 were Alcoa, Caterpillar, IBM, McDonald's, and Procter & Gamble.
   a. Since you now have the benefit of hindsight, how have each of the five highest-ranking stocks and the five lowest-ranking stocks performed since the list was prepared in December 1993?
   b. What do your results suggest about the O'Higgins system?

Part III

Principles of Security Analysis

The process of fundamental analysis was generally described in Chapter 6 in the prior section. Part III is devoted to a detailed discussion of the fundamental analysis and valuation of common stocks commonly referred to as *security analysis*. The goal of security analysis is to determine whether the price of a common stock reflects its intrinsic value. We begin with an overview of various common stock valuation models that attempt to evaluate the variables that determine the values of common stocks, such as earnings and dividends. We then turn to a detailed review of the process of security analysis. This process proceeds in a sort of inverted triangle, from the general to the specific, from economic analysis to industry analysis to company analysis. The overall purpose of our review of the process of security analysis is to show how analysts arrive at estimates of the variables that appear to determine the values of common stocks. We will see that the analyst has to consider both quantifiable and nonquantifiable factors and issues, making both subjective and objective judgments concerning the relationship between a stock's price and its intrinsic value.

Chapter 8

Fundamentals of Common Stock Valuation

Chapter Objectives

1. Understand the concept of intrinsic value.
2. Examine the Dividend Discount Model (DDM).
3. Develop the Earnings Model (EM).
4. Conduct a fundamental analysis.
5. Analyze a stock with nonconstant growth.
6. Develop an understanding of the market-to-book ratio.
7. Examine the price/earnings multiple (P/E ratio).

In 1987, IBM's net income declined 9.8 percent in the second quarter as compared to a year earlier; the firm reported net income of $1.18 billion or $1.95 per share. Analysts and investors alike were disappointed and the stock fell to $167.50.[1] At this time, IBM was still considered a premium growth stock and a market bellwether, as it had been for years. Four years later, in December 1991, many money managers were buying IBM stock because it looked cheap at around $85 per share.[2]

To rub salt in the wound, a September 1992 article in *The Wall Street Journal* reported that Microsoft's market value ($27.28 billion) had risen very close to IBM's at $27.83 billion and could soon exceed it.[3] By October 1993, IBM's stock was trading around $45.

This raises disturbing questions about the true value of IBM. Everyone following the news in 1991 seemed to agree that its true value had fallen below the $100 per share range. Some money managers, however, thought IBM was a good buy at around $85 per share. Does this place its true value above $85, but short of $100?

The true value of a stock is called its intrinsic value. Intrinsic value is important because the investor can base a relatively simple strategy on it. The investor would buy the stock if its market price were below the intrinsic value and sell it, or sell it short, if its market price were above the intrinsic value. In an efficient market, the market price should eventually match the intrinsic value, so an investor can profit by buying stocks selling below their intrinsic

---

[1] *The Wall Street Journal*, July 15, 1987, C3.

[2] *The Wall Street Journal*, December 20, 1991, C1.

[3] *The Wall Street Journal*, September 30, 1992, C1.

values, as their market prices should rise to match their intrinsic values. Conversely, selling short stocks whose market prices exceed their intrinsic values should generate profits as the market prices fall to the intrinsic values. This basic strategy focuses on finding securities whose prices are out of line with their intrinsic values.

We start this chapter with an intuitive discussion of intrinsic value, then we discuss quantitative models by which the analyst can determine intrinsic values. We begin with the basic Dividend Discount Model (DDM), which implies that a stock's value is simply the present value of its expected future dividends. Next, we turn to the Earnings Model (EM), which posits that stock prices are a function, not only of expected future dividends, but also of the growth of earnings due to companies' investment opportunities. The EM allows us to closely examine the real meanings of the widely used terms *growth company* and *growth stock*. Some stocks may be incorrectly labeled growth stocks. Finally, we will review two common measures of stocks' values, the market-to-book ratio (MV/BV) and the price/earnings (P/E) ratio. This discussion will highlight possible pitfalls of buying only stocks that appear to be cheap.

Intrinsic Value

Back in Chapter 6, we described the major differences between technical and fundamental analysis. Briefly, technical analysis is based on the belief that past patterns in security prices can be used to reliably predict future price patterns. Technicians believe that these patterns reflect the changing attitudes of investors toward a variety of rational and irrational factors. Technical analysts believe that security prices are determined solely by the interaction of supply and demand.

By contrast, fundamental analysis is based on the notion that every security has an intrinsic value. While some investors may not use the term *intrinsic value,* many accept this concept (money managers included) when they talk about a particular stock being cheap or expensive. In some manner, they assess an intrinsic value of the stock and decide, based on the relationship of that value to the market price, whether or not it is a good buy.

Our earlier characterization of an intrinsic value as the true value of a security gives little insight or assistance in estimating it. The **intrinsic value** of a stock is defined as the fundamental economic value of the issuing company's equity.[4] A simple, intuitive generalization of what creates value of a stock can clarify this.

A company produces goods and services, which it sells. We refer to these products as *projects* or *investment opportunities* of the company. For example, Ford's projects produce goods such as cars and trucks, and Walt Disney's projects provide services such as entertainment and relaxation. Both firms undertake their projects to generate sales. After paying taxes and other expenses from sales revenues, the remaining amount is the company's net profits or earnings. These earnings are the cash returns to the stockholders for investing in the equity of the company. Conceptually, then, the fundamental economic value of a stock is the economic value of these projects, or the present value of the cash returns to stockholders who invest in the company's equity.

---

[4]Economic value is calculated as the present value of a series of cash flows. Shortly, we will review the sources of the cash flows.

Though we admit this definition ignores other aspects of company operations, a fundamental, quantifiable economic value (or intrinsic value) is in essence the present value of the expected future earnings that its investment opportunities will generate. Based on some assumptions we'll discuss later, the intrinsic value of a common stock also equals the present value of the company's future dividends.

In this chapter, we present four models by which to estimate the intrinsic value of a common stock. At the outset we should point out that these models are simplified generalizations and may be difficult to apply to all common stocks. However, while the model might yield only a rough estimate in some cases, the process still builds important insights into the factors that determine stock prices in the real world.

The next section discusses the Dividend Discount Model (DDM). This model states that the intrinsic value of a stock is the present value of its expected future dividends.

Dividend Discount Model (DDM)

If any generalization is safe, we can surely say that most investors purchase common stocks with expectations of making profits from their investments. More specifically, though, profits come in two forms: periodic cash dividend payments and capital appreciation from selling the stock at a price higher than the purchase price. How can an investor evaluate the expected profit from an investment? Even when investors don't bother to formally determine values systematically, most make at least an informal assessment of intrinsic value.

Suppose for a moment that someone can travel forward 20 years (to Year 20) and find that a common stock will sell for $18.00 per share and pay an annual dividend of $1 per share. If that person expects a 16 percent return on the stock (that is, if the required rate of return on stock, ER_s, is 0.16), in Year 19, that investor would be willing to pay:

$$V_{s19} = \frac{\$1.00 + \$18.00}{(1 + 0.16)} = \$16.38$$

In symbols, this looks like:

$$V_{s19} = \frac{DIV_{20} + P_{s20}}{(1 + ER_s)} \tag{8.1}$$

In Year 19, the intrinsic price of the stock just equals the present value of its Year 20 cash flow, $16.38 at a 16 percent required return. Stated differently, if someone pays $16.38 for the stock in Year 19 expecting cash flows over the next year of $19.00, then the investment will earn an expected return, ER_s, of 16 percent (0.16).

Suppose that this time traveler decides to invest in Year 18, instead, to earn cash flows equal to the sum of Year 19 and Year 20 dividends (DIV_{19} and DIV_{20}) plus the selling price of the stock in Year 20 (V_{s20}). This investor would be willing to pay:

$$V_{s18} = \frac{DIV_{19}}{(1 + ER_s)} + \frac{DIV_{20} + V_{s20}}{(1 + ER_s)^2} \tag{8.2}$$

Assuming dividends in Years 19 and 20 equal to $1.00 and an expected Year 20 price of $18.00:

$$V_{s18} = \frac{\$1.00}{(1 + 0.16)} + \frac{\$1.00 + \$18.00}{(1 + 0.16)^2} = \$14.98$$

The stock's present value in Year 18 is less than its value in Year 19. Though it pays an extra dollar in dividends in Year 19, the cash flow from the dividend and expected selling price ($19.00) occurs a year later, in Year 20, and the present value of $19.00 is less two years earlier, in Year 18, than one year earlier, in Year 19.

This pattern continues as the traveler returns back from Year 17 through Year 1, and finally, to Year 0, today. To invest at Year 0, using the same logic, the investor would be willing to pay:

$$V_{s0} = \frac{DIV_1}{(1 + ER_s)} + \frac{DIV_2}{(1 + ER_s)^2} + \cdots + \frac{DIV_{19}}{(1 + ER_s)^{19}} + \frac{DIV_{20} + P_{s20}}{(1 + ER_s)^{20}} \quad (8.3)$$

Inserting values for expected dividends of $1 per year from Year 1 to Year 20, a Year 20 selling price of $18.00, and a required return of 16 percent, the value of the stock today equals:

$$V_{s0} = \frac{\$1.00}{(1 + 0.16)} + \frac{\$1.00}{(1 + 0.16)^2} + \cdots + \frac{\$1.00}{(1 + 0.16)^{19}}$$
$$+ \frac{\$1.00 + \$18.00}{(1 + 0.16)^{20}} = \$6.85$$

Would the Year 18 valuation of $V_{s18} = \$14.98$ give the same value, V_{s0}, today?

$$V_{s0} = \frac{\$1.00}{(1 + 0.16)} + \frac{\$1.00}{(1 + 0.16)^2} + \cdots + \frac{\$1.00}{(1 + 0.16)^{17}}$$
$$+ \frac{\$1.00 + \$14.98}{(1 + 0.16)^{18}} = \$6.85$$

Three Implications

Three major implications stem from these numerical examples.

Implication 1. The Year 18 price, V_{s18}, in the above example is just a present value of the Year 20 future dividends and future price, V_{s20}.

Implication 2. The present value of a selling price far in the future, such as Year 20 ($V_{s20} = \$18.00$), is very small; in fact, it is negligible. (The present value of $18.00 in Year 20 equals only 0.925.)

Implication 3. The third implication stems from the first one. It states that the holding period does not matter. With either 18-year or 20-year holding periods, the DDM gives an intrinsic value estimate of $6.85.

General Dividend Discount Model

Now, suppose the investor travels past Year 20 to an indefinite point in the future, Year N. The general **Dividend Discount Model** formula equals:

$$V_{s0} = \sum_{t=1}^{N} \frac{DIV_t}{(1 + ER_s)^t} + \frac{V_{sN}}{(1 + ER_s)^N} \qquad (8.4)$$

Remember from Implication 2 that the present value of the price in Year N, V_{sN}, can be ignored since it is virtually equal to zero. This allows the model to approximate the above equation by:

$$V_{s0} \approx \sum_{t=1}^{N} \frac{DIV_t}{(1 + ER_s)^t} \qquad (8.5)$$

If the dividends remain at $1 per year, the present value calculation is simple using Table A2 (a table of the present value of an annuity). However, if the expected dividends differ for each year, it can be a horrendous task (unless you are fortunate to have a financial calculator). Fortunately, a simpler formula can accommodate dividends that are expected to grow at a constant rate, g.

Let's define the future dividend stream relative to the current dividend as follows:

$$DIV_1 = DIV_0(1 + g)$$

$$DIV_2 = DIV_0(1 + g)^2$$

$$\bullet$$
$$\bullet$$
$$\bullet$$

$$DIV_N = DIV_0(1 + g)^N$$

The general formula of Equation 8.5 can be rewritten to allow for growth in the dividends at a constant rate, g:

$$V_{s0} = \frac{DIV_0(1 + g)}{(1 + ER_s)} + \frac{DIV_0(1 + g)^2}{(1 + ER_s)^2} + \ldots + \frac{DIV_0(1 + g)^N}{(1 + ER_s)^N} \qquad (8.6)$$

A constant-growth sequence like Equation 8.6 converges to:

$$V_{s0} = \frac{DIV_0(1 + g)}{(ER_s - g)} \qquad \text{or} \qquad \frac{DIV_1}{(ER_s - g)} \qquad (8.7)$$

This constant-growth Dividend Discount Model assumes, of course, that $ER_s > g$. For practical purposes, we will use Equation 8.7 exclusively since it is difficult, if not impossible, to accurately estimate future dividends for every year. We will almost always assume that firms' dividends will grow at a constant rate.

Let's go through an example for Sara Lee, the well-known frozen desserts company.[5] Suppose Sara Lee pays a current annual dividend of $0.56 per share, which should grow at a constant annual rate of 12 percent indefinitely. Also analysts estimate the company's expected rate of return, ER_s, at 15 percent. Using Equation 8.7, Sara Lee's intrinsic value is approximately $21:

$$V_{s0} = \frac{\$0.56(1 + 0.12)}{0.15 - 0.12} = \$20.90$$

---

[5]At this point we will just provide the numbers and go through the calculations; a later section will explain how to estimate each variable.

Figure 8.1

General Rule for Fundamental Analysis

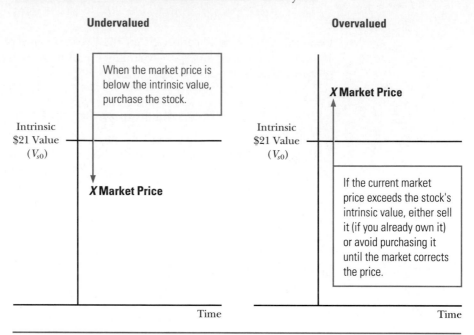

How does a fundamental analyst use this information? To compare the intrinsic value, V_{s0}, with the stock's market price, suppose Sara Lee is currently trading around $24.50 per share.[6] Comparing the V_{s0} of $21 to the market price of $24.50, Sara Lee appears to be **overvalued.** It's too expensive to buy, and a current stockholder may want to sell because the market price of $24.50 seems likely to fall to the fundamental economic value of $21.

The general rules for fundamental analysis prescribe trading strategies when a stock's market price differs from its intrinsic value. The two diagrams in Figure 8.1 depict the two possibilities. The horizontal line represents the intrinsic value ($21.00) and the Xs indicate market prices above or below the intrinsic value. A market price below the intrinsic value (V_{s0}) indicates an **undervalued** security. A market price above V_{s0} indicates an overvalued security.

General Rule for Fundamental Analysis

If the market price is below the estimated intrinsic value ($MP < V_{s0}$), then the stock is undervalued; purchase the stock, or hold it.

If the market price is above the estimated intrinsic value ($MP > V_{s0}$), then the stock is overvalued; sell the stock, or sell it short.

The development of the DDM implies that stock prices are valued by the dividends of the company alone. This seems implicit in Implication 1 above. But how can an analyst value stocks that pay no dividends? The next section discusses a technique to do this, the Earnings Model, and examines the major factors that add value to a stock.

---

[6]Its closing price on January 4, 1994.

Earnings Model (EM)

The **Earnings Model** is another way to estimate the intrinsic value of a common stock. It derives the intrinsic value by dividing the earnings generated by the firm's future investment opportunities into two parts: (1) earnings that the firm pays out as cash dividends and (2) earnings that it reinvests to fund future investment opportunities.

In fact, we could argue that future dividends are part of future earnings. Generally speaking, investors value expected dividend streams because those payments represent the return on their investments, but future dividend streams stem from future earnings, or profits, of the company. The Earnings Model takes this notion further, demonstrating that future earnings exist only because of investment opportunities, and increases in future earnings will exist if future investment opportunities exist. Also the Earnings Model adds another dimension to the analysis by clarifying the concept of growth companies; it provides five implications about growth companies and then contrasts a growth company and a growth stock. Through the Earnings Model, we hope to shed some light on these elusive terms.

Earnings Model Formula

The general formula for the Earnings Model is:

$$V_{s0} = \frac{EPS_1}{ER_s} + \frac{EPS_1}{ER_s} \left[\frac{g - ER_s(b)}{ER_s - g} \right] \tag{8.8}$$

where EPS_1 is the expected earnings per share, ER_s is the required rate of return or the expected return, g is the expected constant annual growth rate, and b is the retention rate or $(1 - $ dividend payout ratio$)$.

The equation can be viewed as having two parts: the no-growth term defined by EPS_1/ER_s and the growth term, which represents the present values of the firm's investment opportunities. These opportunities are expected to grow at a constant rate, g:

$$\frac{EPS_1}{ER_s} \left[\frac{g - ER_s(b)}{ER_s - g} \right]$$

Perhaps it's easiest to get an intuitive feel for the model by going through an example and then tying it to the formula. We will use data from Sara Lee to show how the model works.

Sara Lee: An Earnings Model Example

No-Growth Example. Suppose that Sara Lee is expecting earnings per share (EPS_1) to be \$1.55 next year, and that it anticipates no growth as it continues to produce only desserts, promising shareholders all the profits. The last condition sets the company's dividends per share equal to its earnings per share $(DIV_1 = EPS_1 = \$1.55$ per share$)$. If Sara Lee's profits remain at \$1.55 per share forever and the shareholders expect a return of 15 percent (ER_s), then the present value of the stock equals \$1.55 times the present value of an annuity factor for 15 percent in perpetuity.[7] This gives the present value of

---

[7]The PV of annuity factor at interest rate i for perpetuity equals $1/i$; for this example it is $1/0.15$ = 0.66667.

the stock as $10.33 per share. It is the amount that investors should pay for Sara Lee's stock if its future growth rate equals zero.

This value can also be calculated by the no-growth term of the Earnings Model:

$$\text{PV—no-growth term} = \frac{EPS_1}{ER_s} = \frac{\$1.55}{0.15} = \$10.33$$

Now suppose that the company begins innovative new projects that it expects to fuel growth at a constant rate. Let's explore how to determine the value of the constant-growth term.

Constant-Growth Example. Now suppose that Sara Lee decides to branch out from its desserts business and begin producing undergarments.[8] If investors expect these investments to return 20 percent to stockholders (ROE_1), how should Sara Lee finance the personal products business? Of the several methods, assume that Sara Lee chooses to invest some of the company's current earnings. Sara Lee expects to pay $0.65 per share (DIV_1) as dividends and to retain $0.90 per share (RE_1). The company will pay 42 percent of its earnings as dividends (0.65/1.55); that is its **dividend payout ratio.** Conversely, Sara Lee's **retention rate,** b, is 58 percent (0.90/1.55). This drop in dividends may seem disturbing, but actually Sara Lee is reinvesting 58 percent of its current earnings in investments that will benefit stockholders.

We can use this idea to define the growth rate, g:

$$g = ROE_1 \times b \tag{8.9}$$

where ROE_1 is the *expected* **return on equity** and b is the retention rate. This gives the company's growth rate because the additional earnings plowed back into the company are expected to generate a return on the stockholders' investment equal to ROE_1. (Remember that the ROE_1 should be the firm's *expected* return on equity in the future, not a historical value based on past projects.)[9] If additional investments in the company earn the rate ROE_1, then the shareholders' marginal return on earnings should also increase. This marginal increase or growth would be 58 percent of ROE_1, or:

$$58\% \times 20\% = 12\%$$

The general formula is $(ROE_1 \times b)$.

Now let's return to Sara Lee's new personal products venture. Sara Lee retains $0.90 per share and invests it in the undergarments business. Assuming that its sales generate an expected return of 20 percent (ROE_1), the venture's earnings per share come to $0.18 (20% × $0.90). At the company's expected return of 15 percent, the net present value of this venture to stockholders is $0.30 per share.[10] This says that the undergarment investment should add $0.30 to the stock price in Year 1. We must discount this Year 1 value to find its Year 0 or current value:

$$NPV_1/(1 + ER_s) = \$0.30/(1 + 0.15) = \$0.261$$

---

[8]Recently, the Personal Products division has been the fastest growing segment of Sara Lee. In 1993, it constituted 46 percent of the company's profits. Its better-known brand names are Hanes, Playtex, L'eggs, and Isotoner.

[9]Other caveats will be discussed later in the discussion of fundamental analysis.

[10]$NPV_1 = -\$0.90 + [\$0.18/0.15] = \$0.30$.

This return from the undergarment business investment is also reflected in Sara Lee's earnings per share in Year 2. Sara Lee's Year 1 earnings will increase to $1.73 per share ($1.55 from the dessert business and $0.18 from the undergarments business).

Now suppose this growth orientation continues in Year 2. Instead of being satisfied with the domestic market, suppose Sara Lee ventures into the European market. Again, it will retain 58 percent of Year 2 earnings (0.58 × $1.73, or $1.003 per share) and invests these funds in expanding its undergarments venture for the European market. At the same 20 percent return on this investment, it increases the value of the stock by $0.337 per share in Year 2; this is the NPV for the European investment in Year 2.[11] Again, to determine the Year 0 value, we must discount the Year 2 value:

$$\text{NPV}_2/(1 + ER_s)^2 = \$0.337/(1 + 0.15)^2 = \$0.255$$

The second term in Equation 8.8 summarizes the present values of all the firm's future growth opportunities (abbreviated as *PVGO*). From the discussion above, *PVGO* equals the sum of each investment opportunity over the years, or:

$$PVGO = \frac{\text{NPV}_1}{(1 + ER_s)} + \frac{NPV_2}{(1 + ER_s)^2} + \frac{NPV_3}{(1 + ER_s)^3} + \cdots$$

where:

$$NPV_1 = -b(EPS_1) + \left[\frac{b(EPS_1)(ROE)}{ER_s}\right]$$

NPV_2, NPV_3, and all subsequent *NPVs* represent investments that are expected to grow at a constant rate, *g*, so NPV_2 is 12 percent greater than NPV_1 and so on. To state the same thing in another way:

$$NPV_2 = NPV_1(1 + g)$$
$$NPV_3 = NPV_1(1 + g)^2$$

and so forth.

NPV_1 is the net present value at Year 1 a year after the investment is made. To find the present value at Year 0, we must divide by $(1 + ER_s)$. Similarly, we must divide NPV_2 by $(1 + ER_s)^2$ and so on.

This means that we can express *PVGO* as:

$$PVGO = \frac{NPV_1}{(1 + ER_s)} + \frac{NPV_1(1 + g)}{(1 + ER_s)^2} + \frac{NPV_1(1 + g)^2}{(1 + ER_s)^3} + \cdots$$

A constant growth sequence like this converges to:

$$PVGO = \frac{NPV_1}{(ER_s - g)}$$

[11]Retained earnings from Year 2 equal $1.003 and the investment is expected to provide a 20 percent return, so the cash flow per year equals (0.20 × $1.003) = $0.201. Assuming the investment will continue to perpetuity, the PV of annuity factor is 1/0.15 and $NPV_2 = -\$1.003 + (0.201/0.15) = \$0.337$.

Plugging in the terms given on the previous page for NPV_1:

$$PVGO = \frac{-b(EPS_1) + \left[\dfrac{b(EPS_1)(ROE)}{ER_s}\right]}{(ER_s - g)}$$

To simplify this horrendous equation, separate terms:

$$PVGO = \frac{-b(EPS_1)}{(ER_s - g)} + \frac{\left[b(EPS_1)(ROE)\right]}{ER_s(ER_s - g)}$$

Multiplying the first term by ER_s/ER_s and putting it under a common denominator, the equation equals:

$$PVGO = \frac{-b(EPS_1)(ER_s) + \left[b(EPS_1)(ROE)\right]}{ER_s(ER_s - g)}$$

Recall that $g = (b)(ROE)$. Gathering similar terms, $PVGO$ equals:

$$PVGO = \frac{EPS_1\left[g - b(ER_s)\right]}{ER_s(ER_s - g)}$$

This can be rewritten to resemble the growth term in Equation 8.8:

$$PVGO = \frac{EPS_1}{ER_s}\left[\frac{g - ER_s(b)}{ER_s - g}\right]$$

Now combining the present value of the firm's continuing growth opportunities, $PVGO$, with its no-growth present value, we have Equation 8.8:

$$V_{s0} = \frac{EPS_1}{ER_s} + \frac{EPS_1}{ER_s}\left[\frac{g - ER_s(b)}{ER_s - g}\right]$$

Equation 8.8 can be further simplified to:

$$V_{s0} = \frac{EPS_1}{ER_s}\left[1 + \frac{g - ER_s(b)}{ER_s - g}\right] \tag{8.10}$$

Using Equation 8.10, Sara Lee's intrinsic value equals:

$$V_{s0} = \frac{\$1.55}{0.15}\left[1 + \frac{0.12 - 0.15(0.58)}{(0.15 - 0.12)}\right] = \$21.70$$

Table 8.1 summarizes the results. It also shows that if Sara Lee can continue indefinitely to find other investment opportunities that earn 20 percent, the value of its stock should equal $21.70. This constant growth rate seems sustainable because the international undergarment market is fragmented and customers exhibit no brand loyalty. Sara Lee expects to capture new markets in Mexico, Asia, and central Europe.

Figure 8.2 depicts the cash Sara Lee generates and the marginal value of its stock as it accepts positive-NPV investments. The figure begins with the no-growth case which features constant earnings of $1.55 and an NPV of $10.33. Notice that each subsequent investment opportunity adds value to

Table 8.1

Summary of the Sara Lee Example

EPS_1 = \$1.55
DIV_1 = \$0.65   Dividend payout ratio = \$0.65/\$1.55 = 24 percent
RE_1 = \$0.90   Retention rate b = \$0.90/\$1.55 = 58 percent
ER_s = 0.15

No-Growth Company Value:

Value of Sara Lee if growth equals zero and all earnings are paid out as dividends:

PV = \$1.55/0.15 = \$10.333

Present Value of Growth Opportunities:

ROE_1 = 0.20

Growth rate, $g = ROE_1 \times b = 0.20 \times 58\% = 11.6$ percent ≈ 12 percent

$NPV_1 = -\$0.90 + [\$0.180/0.15] = \$0.30$

$\qquad PV[NPV_1] = \$0.30/(1+0.15) = \$0.26$

$NPV_2 = -\$1.003 + [\$0.201/0.15] = \$0.337$

$\qquad PV[NPV_2] = \$0.337/(1+0.15)^2 = \$0.255$

Intrinsic Value:

$$V_{so} = \frac{\$1.55}{0.15}\left[1 + \frac{0.12 - 0.15(0.58)}{(0.15 - 0.12)}\right] = \$21.70$$

the company's common stock. For example, the domestic undergarments investment opportunity adds \$0.26 per share to the stock price today and the European investment adds another \$0.26 per share to the current stock value. Additionally, each investment adds to the firm's earnings per share, which increases at a constant growth rate of 12 percent, or \$1.55 to \$1.73 to \$1.93, and so forth. One vertical axis indicates the marginal value to Sara Lee's stock price of each investment. Each horizontal step indicates another marginal investment, and the steps climb indefinitely into the future at a *constant* growth rate, *g*, of 12 percent. Each year, new projects increase the stock's value by 12 percent from \$0.300 (NPV_1) to \$0.337 (NPV_2) and so forth, indefinitely.[12] Notice that both the EPS and the marginal value of the stock increase at this constant rate. These growth opportunities plus $\left[\dfrac{EPS_1}{ER_s}\right]$ equals \$21.70 for Sara Lee.

Now we can conduct our fundamental analysis, as we did with the Dividend Discount Model. The rule is the same: if V_{s0} exceeds the market price, the stock is undervalued; if V_{s0} falls below the market price, it is overvalued. Given Sara Lee's V_{s0} equals \$21.70 and a market price of \$24.50, the stock is overvalued and we would not invest, or perhaps we would sell short.

The Earnings Model can serve two purposes other than intrinsic value estimation: (1) It can identify the underlying factors for a growth company's success. (2) It can contrast a growth company with a growth stock.

Implications for Growth Companies

The EM example showed that generally company growth leads to an increasing intrinsic value. Since undervalued stocks can produce abnormal profits, let's spend some time discussing how a **growth company** earns a higher intrinsic value.

---

[12] The numbers may differ slightly from equation results due to rounding.

Figure 8.2

Graphical Summary of the Sara Lee Example

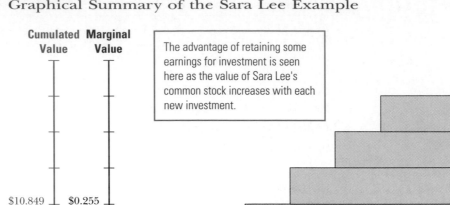

Cumulated Marginal
Value   Value

The advantage of retaining some earnings for investment is seen here as the value of Sara Lee's common stock increases with each new investment.

$10.849 $0.255

$10.594 $0.261

$NPY_2 = -\$1.003 + (0.201/0.15) = \$0.337$

$10.333 $10.333

$NPY_1 = -\$0.90 + (0.18/0.15) = \$0.300$

No-growth value $= \dfrac{\$1.55}{0.15} = \$10.333$

| | 0 | 1 | 2 | 3 | 4 | 5 | 6 | Time |

Earnings per Share	$1.550	$1.550	$1.550
		0.180	0.180
			0.201	0.201
	$1.550	$1.730	$1.931

EPS continues to increase at a constant growth rate of 12 percent.

Focus on the second term, or the growth term, of Equation 8.8. Since EPS_1 and ER_s are expected to be positive, notice that the growth term is positive only if $[g - ER_s(b)]$ is positive.[13] This means that g must be greater than $ER_s b$. Since g equals ROE_1 times b, $ROE_1(b)$ exceeds $ER_s(b)$ only if ROE_1 exceeds ER_s. This says that a growth company must have a return on equity greater than the return required by stockholders.[14] Five implications of this relationship can help investors identify the characteristics of a growth company.

Implication 1. Not every expanding company is a growth company. Suppose that a stockbroker informs you that GM is expanding extensively, building new warehouses and factories. Is GM a growth company? Its accounting data show growth in the form of increasing fixed assets. However, an astute investor should ask, "What is the company's return on these investments?" Expanding assets do not necessarily constitute growth; the return generated by the increased asset investment is critical.

Implication 2. If the company's investments earn an overall rate of return equal to the return required by stockholders, ER_s, then it is not a growth company, even if its investments earn positive returns.

---

[13]The growth term can be negative $(g < ER_s b)$. See Implication 3 below.

[14]Actually, an economically more meaningful term for ROE_1 is the internal rate of return, IRR, or the rate of return on investment. If we substitute IRR for ROE_1, we have $IRR > ER_s$. This is just the IRR decision rule for evaluating capital budgeting projects in corporate finance.

Implication 3. If the company's investments earn a positive overall rate of return below ER_s, then it is not a positive growth company, but a *negative* growth company. In fact, if g is less than $ER_s b$, then the stock has a negative growth rate. The stock's *PVGO* will be negative, indicating that company projects decrease the stock's value instead of adding value.

Implication 4. Retaining profits $(b > 0)$ by itself does not constitute growth. Again the return generated by the invested funds determines whether or not a firm is a growth company.

Implication 5. If a company cannot find any investments with returns (ROE_1) greater than the return that stockholders expect (ER_s), then it can maximize stockholder value by increasing cash dividends instead of retaining earnings to finance expansion.

Now that we understand what constitutes a growth company, let's determine the difference between a growth company and a growth stock. Though these terms seem synonymous, they're not.

Contrasting a Growth Company with a Growth Stock

Many investors may use these terms synonymously, but some subtle differences are worth mentioning. As defined above, a growth company is a company that undertakes positive NPV projects that increase its stock value. Generally, a growth company's stock tends to appreciate as shown by the EM example. However, there are some exceptions. For example, if investors overestimate growth opportunities for a company and bid up its stock's market price based on these rosy expectations, even a growth company may become overvalued. Technical analysts may also bid up market prices based on some perceived buy signal. As investors realize that they may have overestimated the company's opportunities, its excessive market price will decline. That's not to say that the market was wrong; the investors are simply adjusting to the economic value of the company as new information emerges.

Initial public offerings (IPOs) tend to follow this pattern. Snapple, the producer of natural fruit juices and iced tea, is an example of a growth company for which investors overestimated growth. After it went public in December 1992 at $20 per share, its stock price soared. On June 16, 1993, an article in *The Wall Street Journal* mentioned Snapple in a discussion of the most overpriced stocks in the market. At that time, Snapple's P/E ratio was 256 times (a huge multiple, as we will discuss later) at a market price of $62\frac{1}{4}$. The *Journal* article reported money managers' opinion that Snapple's intrinsic value based on its growth opportunities could not justify its $62\frac{1}{4}$ price. After all, the article reasoned, PepsiCo and Coca-Cola Company could easily enter the bottled iced tea market and burst Snapple's bubble. The article must have led the market to realize that expectations were too rosy because Snapple's stock price fell to $37\frac{3}{4}$ by June 30, 1993. Even six months later, it was trading in the 30s.

A **growth stock** is a stock that is currently undervalued enough to drive its return above those of other stocks at the same risk level. Shares in a growth company do not necessarily constitute a growth stock. For example, Sara Lee, based on our analysis, is a growth company (because $PVGO > 0$), but not a growth stock (because it is overvalued).

Alternatively, a stock can be a growth stock though the issuing company is not a growth company. Investors may ignore a stable, unglamorous company, undervaluing its stock to the point that it offers superior returns relative to other stocks at the same risk level, assuming that the efficient market eventually recognizes its intrinsic value.

Slower Earnings Growth May Spell Trouble for Stocks

Corporate America produced healthy profits in the third quarter. But even though some profits were stellar and most exceeded expectations, analysts now worry that companies may have trouble sustaining the recent strong pace of growth.

With interest rates already near rock-bottom levels, analysts say investors are relying ever more heavily on earnings to push prices higher. So slower earnings growth could hinder the stock market's performance.

Benjamin Zacks, executive vice president of Zacks Investment Research, says a survey of the nearly 700 companies in the Dow Jones Industry Groups shows that so far 62 percent have reported earnings as expected or better than analysts' estimates. Third-quarter earnings from continuing operations—before special charges and gains—grew 25.7 percent from the year before; that figure surpasses the 17.5 percent growth in the second quarter. (A separate *Wall Street Journal* survey of 597 companies showed that corporate after-tax earnings from continuing operations, but including special charges or gains, rose 24 percent, compared with an 11 percent gain for the second quarter.)

Indeed, stellar earnings reports from companies such as Ford, Xerox, and Caterpillar have buoyed the spirits of many investors about future earnings growth. But if the numbers look rosy, Mr. Zacks cautions investors to consider that analysts had drastically reduced their earnings estimates ahead of the reporting season.

Mr. Zacks says that though 25 percent earnings growth is quite healthy, he points out that the figure is partly the result of a very low year-earlier comparison. In addition, fourth-quarter earnings are expected only to match the third

quarter, indicating a slowdown in growth momentum. For the full year, Mr. Zacks estimates earnings for the Dow Jones universe will grow 22.76 percent from a year earlier; in 1994, earnings growth is projected to slow to 18.79 percent.

"One of the bigger negatives is that so much of the better earnings is from cost-cutting as opposed to revenue growth," Mr. Zacks says. "But cost-cutting soon reaches a point of diminishing returns."

That point may already be at hand, says Sung Won Sohn, chief economist at Norwest Corp. in Minneapolis. "What we're seeing is that cost control and productivity gains are beginning to peter out," Mr. Sohn argues. "We have a situation where we've squeezed this orange and gotten some good juice out of it, but the juice is running out."

A continuation of strong earnings requires a pickup in broad-based demand, Mr. Sohn says, but the signs of that pickup haven't emerged yet. Even without the power of strong earnings growth, Mr. Sohn believes the stock market isn't dead. He looks to subdued inflation and low interest rates to help keep stock prices climbing, albeit slowly. In today's low-interest-rate environment, Mr. Sohn expects investors to continue to seek higher yields in stocks.

"You have to look at liquidity," he says. "How much cash is around for investors to use, and right now there's a lot of it."

Despite their current lofty levels, Mr. Sohn is excited about the long-term potential for technology and communications stocks. "The next wave of innovation will come from companies like Microsoft and Intel," he says. "These will be like International Business Machines and Xerox were in the 1960s."

Faced with more modest earnings growth in coming quarters, analysts need to lower their profit estimates, says Hugh Johnson, chief investment officer at First Albany Corp. At current esti-

Now let's go back to a growth company whose shares do not constitute a growth stock. Sara Lee is a good example of a growth company that is not a growth stock because, despite its positive *PVGO*, the stock is currently overvalued. This says that stock in a growth company may not always be a good investment; the value of the investment still depends on how much it costs and returns! Someone who buys Sara Lee at $24.50 will earn a lower return than other stocks with the same risk because its market price should decline to its economic value of $21.70.

The moral of all this may be that the difference between real and false growth stocks often isn't obvious. Even if growth companies may be growth stocks, never assume it! Instead of assuming that a company with a positive *PVGO* (a growth company) is a good investment, always take that last step and compare the stock's V_{s0} with its market price to make sure it's under-

mates, he says, the stock market is expected to climb 10 percent to 15 percent next year. Mr. Johnson argues that based on the outlook for earnings those figures should have shaved to about 3 percent to 6 percent.

"It doesn't mean you should suddenly get bearish," he says. "What it means is the upside potential for stocks isn't what you thought it was."

Mr. Johnson attributes the slower earnings momentum to the anemic economic recovery, the weakest rebound in the postwar period. The sluggish recovery suggests that investors should focus on companies that aren't dependent on the economic cycle for profit gains, he says.

"Smart investors have moved back to the old growth stocks," Mr. Johnson says. "Find me a beaten down drug stock that the world hates, or a beaten-up tobacco, household products, or food stock. I think you'll find some value there, particularly in this environment."

But to other observers, the earnings landscape doesn't look nearly so bleak. Richard Pucci, senior vice president of I/B/E/S, a service that monitors analysts' earnings estimates, predicts that earnings will continue improving. He says analysts are now expecting earnings to climb 18 percent in 1994 compared with an estimated 13 percent to 14 percent growth this year. In 1992, earnings grew 12 percent from the year earlier.

"There are a lot of people out there looking for a negative story on earnings. But earnings keep beating the estimates," Mr. Pucci says. "I think the overall trend is up for the foreseeable future."

He believes some pickup in overseas economies will help lift earnings for large U.S. multinationals that benefit from rising exports. If a stock market correction comes, Mr. Pucci adds, it will most likely be caused by a modest rise in interest rates due to a stronger economy.

INVESTMENT INSIGHTS

"It's not going to be because earnings slow down," he contends. "A small uptick in inflation and interest rates may scare people a little."

Steven Resnick, senior investment strategist at Cowen & Co., is encouraged to see a preponderance of positive earnings surprises in such a sluggish economic environment. Even in a low-inflation climate that limits price increases, companies are still beating analysts' estimates because of continued restructuring, Mr. Resnick says.

"That tells me earnings momentum can still be better than the underlying economy," he adds.

Mr. Resnick tracks stock price movements on the day earnings reports are released to gauge the outlook for the stock. He notes that two-thirds of the financial stocks and other interest-rate-sensitive stocks in his database fell on reports of positive earnings surprises.

"This tells me that investors think financial stocks have had their run and that interest rates have reached bottom," Mr. Resnick says.

Stocks of consumer brand companies, including some of the giant drug firms, rose despite mixed earnings reports, Mr. Resnick says. "That tells you that market psychology felt that the group has been oversold," he says.

Mr. Resnick also is encouraged that the largest grouping of stocks in his database were those that rose on positive earnings surprises. "That's where bull market drive comes from," he says. "It's a positive indication for the stock market."

Source: Steven E. Levingston, "Slower Earnings Growth May Spell Trouble for Stocks," *The Wall Street Journal*, Nov. 1, 1993, C1.

---

valued before chasing those abnormal profits! (We'll discuss this further in Chapter 11 when we discuss company analysis.)

The two stock valuation models, the DDM and the EM, are just more formal ways of evaluating common stocks relative to their trading prices. An investor may suggest that Sara Lee isn't a good investment despite ample growth opportunities in the worldwide market for personal products, because the stock is currently priced too high. This investor is informally assessing the economic value relative to its traded price. Notice that the market confirms this opinion; Sara Lee's price listed by Value Line in November 1993 was $27, but by January 4, 1994, it had declined to $24.50.

The Investment Insights feature reprints a recent article in *The Wall Street Journal* entitled "Slower Earnings Growth May Spell Trouble for Stocks." This discusses some good news and bad news for companies with "stellar profits." The good news is that those profits have exceeded expectations in recent years, but the bad news is that it's next to impossible to sustain such earnings growth rates. The article reports that companies' third-quarter earnings from continuing operations grew 25.7 percent from the year before, but an analyst expected earnings growth for the Dow stocks to slow down to about 18.79 percent. The consensus seemed to be that analysts would have to reduce their earnings estimates as growth slowed. Another analyst had expected the stock market to climb by about 10 percent to 15 percent in 1994, but he said that he would revise his estimate to about 3 percent to 6 percent based on slower earnings growth. He attributed the slower earnings "momentum to the anemic economic recovery, the weakest rebound since the postwar" period. This analyst may have added that if someone had bought stocks assuming that these stellar profits would continue, that person may have overpaid. The article reinforces the importance of earnings growth in evaluating stock market performance.

Recap

Most investors believe that a stock has an intrinsic value and that, in an efficient market, the stock price will converge to that value. We have described two models, the DDM and the EM, by which to determine a stock's intrinsic value. A sound investment decision should be based on a careful study of a company's investment growth opportunities and an estimate of its intrinsic value. Finally, compare the stock's intrinsic value with its market price to identify any undervalued (or growth) stocks. This step is important because 2no one should ever assume that stock in a growth company is always a growth stock.

Fundamental Analysis in Practice

Value Line is one of many sources of information on which to base an estimate of an intrinsic value for Sara Lee. We used many numbers to explain the two valuation models; we will now go back to illustrate the calculation of those numbers.

Figure 8.3 reprints the one-page *Value Line* summary on Sara Lee. Given these data, we will assume that today is June 30, 1993, and that Sara Lee's earnings, and therefore its future dividend streams, can be estimated by a constant growth rate, *g*. Recall the DDM formula:

$$V_{s0} = \frac{DIV_0(1 + g)}{ER_s - g} \tag{8.7}$$

There are three basic steps in the process to estimate the intrinsic value of a common stock.

Step 1: Estimate Growth, *g*

Three ways to estimate a firm's growth rate are described next. Since the growth rate is such an important component of the estimate of intrinsic value, we'll use all three methods to gather as much information as possible. At the end, however, we must settle on one growth estimate.

A. Estimate a Historical Growth Trend for Dividends per Share. Using some historical time period that best illustrates the stock's expected growth

Figure 8.3

Value Line Report for Sara Lee

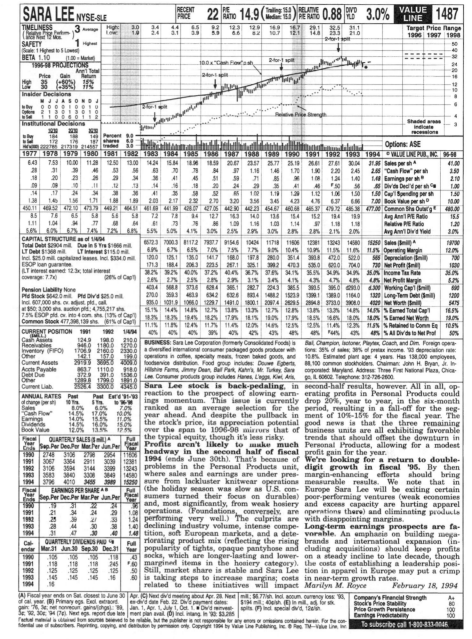

Source: *Value Line* report no. 1487, © 1993.

in dividends, estimate an average growth rate. The analyst must, of course, decide which period best represents *future* earnings for Sara Lee—not an easy task. There's no magical formula, but once a historical trend is designated as the best representation of future earnings, the analysis proceeds to estimate Sara Lee's geometric average growth rate, *g*.

Suppose that the time period from June of 1983 to June of 1993 best represents the company's expected future dividend growth. Dividends declared per share (*Value Line* abbreviates this as "Div'ds Dec'd per sh") were $0.14 in 1983 and $0.56 in 1993. Find the growth rate, *g*, using a compounded future value formula that would make $0.14 compound over ten years to equal $0.56:

$$0.14(1 + g)^{10} = 0.56$$

$$(1 + g)^{10} = 4.00$$

$$g = 14.9 \text{ percent}$$

Extrapolating from the historical dividend growth trend, the future growth rate should equal 14.9 percent.

B. Estimate a Historical Growth Trend for Earnings per Share. Using the same method over the same period, the earnings per share grew from $0.36 in 1983 to $1.40 in 1993. Thus g equals:

$$0.36(1 + g)^{10} = 1.40$$

$$(1 + g)^{10} = 3.889$$

$$g = 14.5 \text{ percent}$$

Extrapolating from Sara Lee's historical earnings trend, its estimated growth rate equals 14.5 percent.

C. Earnings Model Growth Definition. Finally, the growth definition in the Earnings Model (Equation 8.9) can give an estimate of Sara Lee's growth rate. Notice that Sara Lee has preferred stock outstanding; this analysis should focus on ROE for common equity only. Calculate ROE by subtracting preferred dividends from net profits after taxes, and by subtracting preferred stocks outstanding from net worth. Also to find *expected* ROE, ROE_1, use 1994 estimates.[15] Sara Lee's net profits equal $785 million and its net worth equals $4,395 million, while preferred dividends equal $28 million and preferred stock outstanding equals $675 million.[16] ROE_1 can be calculated as follows:

$$ROE_1 = \frac{\$785 - \$28}{\$4,395 - \$675} = 20.3 \text{ percent} \approx 20 \text{ percent}$$

The common stock dividend payout ratio has already been calculated as:

$$\text{Dividend payout ratio} = \frac{DIV_1}{EPS_1} = \frac{\$0.65}{\$1.55} = 42 \text{ percent}$$

Now, Sara Lee's growth, using Equation 8.9, is:

$$\begin{aligned} g &= ROE_1 \times b \\ &= ROE_1 \times (1 - \text{Dividend payout ratio}) \\ &= 0.20\% \times (1 - 0.42) \\ &= 11.6 \text{ percent} \approx 12 \text{ percent} \end{aligned}$$

This definition of growth gives an estimate of the expected growth rate equal to 12 percent.

Step 2: Estimate ER_s

Using the Capital Asset Pricing Model (CAPM), we can estimate the expected return on Sara Lee stock.[17] The CAPM states:

---

[15]Remember that today is the last day in 1993, so 1994 data will provide expected ROE (ROE_1) one year from today.

[16]We assume Sara Lee's preferred stock outstanding and dividends remain constant between 1993 and 1994.

[17]The CAPM will be discussed in detail in Chapter 13. The equation attempts to measure an investor's required rate of return for a given beta risk in relation to the risk of the overall market.

$$ER_s = RF + \beta(ER_M - RF) \tag{8.11}$$

The risk-free rate, *RF*, is found in *The Wall Street Journal* quotes for Treasury bond yields to be 6 percent annually. The yield spread for the market return [the $(ER_M - RF)$ term] is estimated to be approximately 8.6 percent using the results of historical spreads documented by Ibbotson Associates.[18] Beta, a relative risk measure, can be found in *Value Line* and equals 1.10 for Sara Lee.

Based on these numbers, Sara Lee's expected return equals:

$$ER_s = RF + \beta\left[ER_M - RF\right]$$
$$ER_s = 0.06 + 1.10\left[0.086\right]$$
$$= 0.15 = 15 \text{ percent}$$

Step 3: Estimate DIV_1 or $DIV_0(1 + g)$

Multiply Sara Lee's dividends per share declared for the current year-end by $(1 + g)$ to obtain DIV_1. An alternative method is to multiply EPS_1 by the dividend payout ratio.

To find DIV_1 in this way, we need to set a growth rate that is appropriate for Sara Lee. Since Equation 8.9 attempts to capture expected growth (instead of historical growth), it probably gives the best estimate. This means that DIV_1 equals:

$$DIV_1 = \$0.56(1 + 0.12)$$

Given the estimates from the three steps, the stock's intrinsic value is:

$$V_{s0} = \frac{0.56(1 + 0.12)}{(0.15 - 0.12)} = \$20.90 \approx \$21$$

Alternatively, using the EM to estimate Sara Lee's intrinsic value, we have:

$$V_{s0} = \frac{\$1.55}{0.15}\left[1 + \frac{0.12 - 0.15(0.58)}{0.15 - 0.12}\right]$$
$$= \$10.33\left[1 + 1.1\right]$$
$$= \$21.70$$

These estimates indicate that Sara Lee's intrinsic value is approximately $21 per share.[19] Compared to the recent price of $24.50, the fundamental analyst would say that the stock is overvalued and recommend against purchasing it, or suggest selling any currently owned shares.

Given reasonably efficient markets, and assuming that other market participants agree with our assessment and assumptions, Sara Lee should decline to $21. Before you call your broker, however, there are some caveats to consider.

Caveats for the Dividend Discount Model

"Assuming that other market participants agree with our assessment" expresses an important assumption called **homogeneous expectations.**

---

[18]See a summary of Ibbotson Associates' study in Appendix 8B.

[19]The difference in the intrinsic value estimates from the DDM and the EM stems from the different formulas to estimate DIV_1. The DDM uses the $DIV_0(1+g)$ formula and estimates the intrinsic value to be $21.00. If it used EPS_1 (Dividend payout ratio) instead, the two models would result in exactly the same intrinsic value, $21.70.

Without this condition, we cannot guarantee that the stock price will converge to the intrinsic value. If other investors have different expectations about Sara Lee, then they should arrive at different intrinsic values and different investment decisions, even if they use the same DDM formula.

Further, the DDM is very sensitive to the estimates of g and ER_s. For example, increasing the estimate of Sara Lee's growth rate by 1 percent to 13 percent would boost the stock's intrinsic value to $31.64 instead of $21.00. That's a $10.64 difference for a one percentage point difference in the growth estimate. This change would make Sara Lee appear undervalued, not overvalued.

Another variable is equally difficult to estimate: the yield spread between the market portfolio and the risk-free rate, or $[ER_M - RF]$. Ibbotson Associates estimates the yield spread for common stocks between 1926 to 1993 at 8.6 percent, but a yield spread estimate over a shorter period would fall to between 5 and 6 percent. Using a 6 percent yield spread and a 12 percent growth rate results in an intrinsic value estimate for Sara Lee of $104.53. This leads to our third caveat: Be wary of unreasonable numbers. It's highly improbable that Sara Lee has an economic value of $104.53 per share when the market price is only around $27. This means that the growth estimate or yield spread or both are suspicious and must be reconsidered.

This warning ties in with the earlier problem with the growth variable. Besides being very sensitive to the growth estimate, the DDM uses an ROE_1 value in the growth estimate that comes from accounting relationships, not a market value or an economic value. This value may not accurately reflect the stock's true expected return on investment. A more meaningful number may be the internal rate of return (IRR) on the firm's investment projects, but that number isn't publicly available. (Review footnote 13.) Use ROE_1 only with great caution. Again, if the final intrinsic value estimate is unreasonable, be suspicious of ROE_1 or g.

These caveats also apply to the Earnings Model, and the moral is the same. An investor needs to carefully study a company's investment opportunities before attempting to estimate its intrinsic value to determine whether the stock might be overvalued or undervalued.

Recap

We analyzed Sara Lee's intrinsic value using the DDM and the EM. Once we determined an intrinsic value (V_{s0}), we compared it to the stock's market price (MP). If MP is less than V_{s0}, the stock is considered to be undervalued. If MP is greater than V_{s0}, the stock is overvalued. In this way, fundamental analysis provides a decision rule to buy or sell.

Fundamental analysis clarifies the old adage, "Buy low, sell high." The analysis answers the equally old question, how low is low? When MP is less than V_{s0}, it's low enough and time to buy. How high is high? When MP is above V_{s0}, it's high enough to sell. The decision rule is an old one, but the process to find V_{s0} in a rational, logical way adds credibility to fundamental analysis.

This process has worked when dividends or earnings grow at nearly a constant rate, g. Suppose, however, that dividends and earnings do not follow a constant growth rate. Even worse, what if g is greater than ER_s? Notice in Equation 8.7 that V_{s0} is negative if g is greater than ER_s, but in a rational world, stocks rarely have negative values.[20] The next section discusses a nonconstant growth model that allows for variation in the growth rate, even to exceed ER_s in some years.

---

[20]A negative value says that you would pay me to take the stock from you. Rarely does someone pay to give up something. One example is garbage.

Nonconstant Growth Model

This section shows how to modify the DDM to apply it to stocks with different growth rates over various years, including growth rates that exceed expected returns. First, let's discuss whether a stock's growth rate *can* be greater than its required rate of return. Suppose a stock's expected growth rate is 20 percent and the return required by stockholders, ER_s, equals 15 percent. Corporate finance often defines the required rate of return as:

$$ER_s = \text{Dividend yield} + \text{Growth rate}$$

assuming a *constant* growth rate. Based on the formula, a stock cannot grow at a constant rate higher than ER_s for an indefinite period because growth is a component of the expected, or required, rate of return, ER_s. Constant higher growth would, therefore, drive the expected return higher, as well. Eventually, then, the growth rate must be less than ER_s. Stated differently, g cannot exceed ER_s forever (that is, the growth rate must be nonconstant). This implies that two growth phases must exist: (1) a phase with a nonconstant growth rate, g, higher than ER_s, and (2) a phase with a constant growth rate, g, less than ER_s. Let's see how we can apply a model with a two-phase growth rate.

Step 1: Determine the Value for the Nonconstant Growth Phase

Suppose that a company is expected to grow at a nonconstant rate of 20 percent for four years, and then to grow at a lower rate of 10 percent indefinitely. If the current dividend per share is $2.00, then we can determine the future dividend stream up to Year 4 in the following way:

Year	Dividend per Share	
1	$2.00(1+0.20)$	= $2.40
2	$2.00(1+0.20)^2$	= 2.88
3	$2.00(1+0.20)^3$	= 3.46
4	$2.00(1+0.20)^4$	= 4.15

Since the stock's intrinsic value is just the present value of its future dividend stream, we can find the present value of each dividend for the nonconstant growth period. If stockholders' required rate of return equals 15 percent, then each of these future dividends has a present value of:

Year	Dividend per Share	Present Value Factor at 15 Percent	Present Value
1	$2.40	0.8696	$2.087
2	2.88	0.7561	2.178
3	3.46	0.6575	2.275
4	4.15	0.5718	2.373
Total present value of nonconstant growth dividend stream			$8.913

A timeline illustrates the cash flows from the nonconstant growth phase, each cash flow's present value, and the sum of those present values.[21]

---

[21]Timelines are often used in corporate finance to display present value problems. See, for example, Eugene Brigham, *Fundamentals of Financial Management*, 7th ed., Ft. Worth, TX, The Dryden Press, 1995.

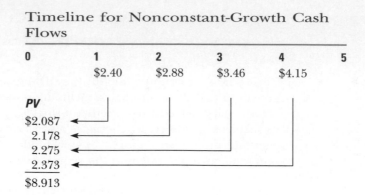

Timeline for Nonconstant-Growth Cash Flows

Therefore the present value of the stock in its nonconstant growth phase equals $8.913.

Step 2: Determine the Value for the Constant Growth Phase

Now let's examine the second phase when the stock's growth falls back to a constant rate. For a moment, suppose we jump forward to Year 4, after which the stock is expected to grow at 10 percent annually with a required rate of return of 15 percent; using the DDM, we can estimate a value for the stock during this period. Treating Year 4 as Year 0, DIV_4 ($4.15) replaces DIV_0 and the value of the stock equals:

$$V_{s4} = \frac{DIV_4(1 + g)}{(ER_s - g)} = \frac{\$4.15(1 + 0.10)}{(0.15 - 0.10)} = \$91.30$$

Recall that this is a Year 4 value. To really find the present value of this future value at Year 0, we need to multiply the future value by the present value factor for 15 percent:

$$\$91.30/(1 + 0.15)^4 = \$91.30(0.5718) = \$52.205$$

The timeline below illustrates how the present value of each constant growth cash flow at Year 4 becomes one cash flow, V_{s4}, for which we find the present value at Year 0:

Timeline of Constant Growth Cash Flows

0	1	2	3	4	5	6
				$4.15	$4.15(1 + g)	$4.15(1 + g)^2

	0	1	2

$$V_{s4} = \frac{DIV_0(1 + g)}{ER_s - g}$$

$$V_{s4} = \frac{\$4.15(1 + 0.10)}{0.15 - 0.10}$$

PV of constant growth phase

$$= \frac{V_{s4}}{(1 + ER_s)^4}$$

$$V_{s4} = \$91.30$$

$$= \frac{\$91.30}{(1 + 0.15)^4} = \$52.205$$

Therefore the value of the stock in its constant growth rate phase equals $52.205.

Step 3: Calculate the Intrinsic Value of the Two-Phase, Nonconstant Growth Stock

Finally, combine the present value of future dividends from the nonconstant growth phase with the present value of future dividends from the constant growth phase:

$$
\begin{aligned}
V_{s0} &= [\text{PV of nonconstant growth phase}] + [\text{PV of constant growth phase}] \\
&= \qquad\qquad \$8.913 \qquad\qquad + \qquad\qquad \$52.205 \\
&= \qquad\qquad \$61.12
\end{aligned}
$$

General Formula for the Nonconstant Growth Model

The general formula for the two-phase growth model assumes that the constant phase growth rate remains the same indefinitely, and that it is less than the required rate of return, ER_s:

$$
V_{s0} = \sum_{t=1}^{T} \frac{DIV_0(1 + g_n)^t}{(1 + ER_s)^t} + \frac{DIV_0(1 + g_n)^T(1 + g_c)}{ER_s - g_c}\left[\frac{1}{(1 + ER_s)^T}\right] \quad (8.12)
$$

where DIV_0 is the current dividend per share, g_n is the nonconstant growth rate, g_c is the constant growth rate when g_c is less than ER_s, ER_s is the required rate of return, and T is the number of years that the stock grows at the nonconstant growth rate.

The model can be extended to three or more phases as long as the last phase is a constant growth phase. The example below shows how to extend it to three different growth rates.

Three-Phase, Nonconstant Growth Model

Suppose that a firm's current dividend of $2.00 is expected to grow at 20 percent for the first two years, then to decline to 10 percent for the next three years, and finally to settle at an 8 percent constant rate thereafter. The timeline below illustrates the process, which closely resembles the two-phase model:

Timeline for Three-Phase Cash Flows

0	1	2	3	4	5	6
	$2.40	$2.88	$3.17	$3.49	$3.83	$3.83(1 + 0.08)

PV
$$
\begin{aligned}
\$\ 2.087 &\longleftarrow \\
2.178 &\longleftarrow \\
2.084 &\longleftarrow \\
1.996 &\longleftarrow \\
1.904 &\longleftarrow \\
\hline
\$10.249 &
\end{aligned}
$$

	0	1
		$3.83(1 + 0.08)

$$
\text{PV of constant growth phase} = \frac{V_{s5}}{(1 + ER_s)^5} \qquad\qquad V_{s5} = \frac{DIV_0(1 + g)}{ER_s - g}
$$

$$
= \frac{\$59.138}{(1 + 0.15)^5} \qquad\qquad V_{s5} = \frac{\$3.833(1 + 0.08)}{0.15 - 0.08}
$$

$$
= \$29.402 \qquad\qquad V_{s5} = \$59.138
$$

First, the timeline shows the present value of the nonconstant growth phase including both the 20 percent growth phase and the 10 percent growth phase (Step 1); this equals $10.249. It then shows the present value of the constant growth phase (Step 2), or $29.402. Finally, it combines the two nonconstant growth phase values with the constant growth phase value to find the intrinsic value: $10.249 + $29.402 = $39.651.

Notice that it doesn't matter how many different nonconstant growth rates a stock has. This process finds the present value of each cash flow separately in Step 1.

Estimating the Nonconstant and Constant Growth Rates

Now let's briefly discuss how we can estimate these growth rates. The nonconstant growth rate for Year 1 can be estimated using Equation 8.9:

$$g = ROE_1 \times b$$

Value Line reports usually provide estimates of companies' *ROE*s and dividend payout ratios for the following year in bold type. Remember, the retention rate, *b*, equals 1 minus the dividend payout ratio.

Value Line can provide data for next year, but how do you estimate a constant growth rate for a stock several years from today? This is more difficult. One suggestion is to enter an industry average *ROE* into Equation 8.9 and assume that the stock will approximate the return of the average industry firm when it can no longer grow at a nonconstant rate. *Value Line* provides industry data as do other sources.[22]

Recap

We examined the valuation process for a nonconstant growth stock where ER_s is less than g. We applied a modified, two-phase DDM with two growth rates, a nonconstant growth rate, g_n, that was greater than ER_s and a constant growth rate, g_c, that was less than ER_s.

The two-phase model may more accurately value a high growth company than a constant growth DDM could. For example, Wal-Mart Stores is expected to grow at 19 percent based on its ROE_1 and its retention rate (21.5% × 0.88); however, *Value Line* expects the retail industry overall to grow at 9 percent. It would be quite difficult for Wal-Mart to sustain a 19 percent growth rate indefinitely while its industry were growing at only 9 percent. The two-phase model should give a better value for a high growth company such as Wal-Mart.

Now we turn to a third method that investors use to find undervalued stocks. It has become increasingly popular due to recommendations by some researchers.[23]

Market-to-Book Ratio

Another valuation method based on the **market-to-book ratio (MV/BV)** has become popular in recent years as a way to find undervalued stocks. The ratio is defined as:

---

[22]Other sources are the Standard & Poor's Industry Survey and the Standard & Poor's Statistical Service.

[23]Eugene Fama and Kenneth French, "The Cross-section of Expected Stock Returns," *Journal of Finance*, June 1992, 427–466.

$$MV/BV = \frac{\text{Total market value of stock}}{\text{Total assets} - \text{Total debt} - \text{Preferred stock}} \qquad (8.13)$$

where MV, the total market value of the stock, equals the stock's market price per share multiplied by the number of shares outstanding, and BV, the company's total assets minus total debt minus preferred stock, measures the book value of common equity or common stock.

If the company does absolutely nothing to generate sales, the market value of its stock should approximately equal its book value. Book value measures the equity value of the firm if it were to sell all of its assets and pay off all of its debts and preferred stock at the values on its balance sheet. Book value presumably gives the company's value assuming it were to stop operating and liquidate. When the company does nothing, MV equals BV and the ratio MV/BV equals 1.0.

This means that if MV/BV is less than 1.0, then someone could profit by buying enough shares of the stock to gain a controlling interest in the company and sell its assets for book value. For example, suppose that a company has a ratio of MV/BV equal to 0.8. This ratio says that the stock is selling for $0.80 per share for every $1.00 of its equity's book value. Someone might buy up all the shares at $0.80 then take control of the company, then liquidate it for $1.00 per share making $0.20 per share on the investment, a 20 percent return. During the mergermania of the 1980s, corporate raiders like T. Boone Pickens became well-known doing this type of thing.

An investor who has smaller financial means could still reason that the stock was undervalued because its shares should be worth at least its book value. In an efficient market, investors would force management to take action so that the ratio becomes closer to 1.0. The stockholders may even replace the old management with a more efficient group or create incentives for them to make better investment decisions (positive-NPV investments).

Based on this kind of scenario, the MV/BV ratio strategy directs investors to buy stocks of firms that have low MV/BV ratios. A company turnaround should hopefully raise the stock's market value at least to its book value.

What type of stock has an MV/BV ratio greater than 1.0, or MV greater than BV? These could be the growth companies discussed in the section on the Earnings Model. Investors may bid up MV above BV because the value generated by the firm's investment opportunities is greater than its liquidated value. The ratio above 1.0 suggests that the firm is actually earning positive returns on its investments (positive NPVs) raising its value above that of a similar company doing nothing (which would be worth its BV).

Remember from the discussion of the EM, however, that shares in growth companies do not necessarily represent growth stocks. To invest in growth stocks, one must find stocks that are undervalued (with market values less than their intrinsic values) in order to earn returns superior to those of other stocks with the same risk level.

Beware of *MV/BV*

Unfortunately, the MV/BV ratio cannot distinguish between the overvalued stocks with MV/BV greater than 1.0 and undervalued growth stocks with MV/BV greater than 1.0. Stated differently, since MV is the market price, not intrinsic value, MV/BV can be greater than 1.0 in two cases: (1) $MV/BV >$ 1.0, with $MV >$ intrinsic value (an overvalued stock) and (2) $MV/BV > 1.0$ with $MV <$ intrinsic value (undervalued growth stock). Investors want to find the second type, not the first.

Another danger with MV/BV is that the book value may differ from the company's true liquidation value. Even if MV is less than BV, liquidation may not generate cash equal to *BV.* Book value is just an accounting number and may not reflect all the market forces that determine the firm's liquidation value.

For example, Value Line reported Sara Lee's book value per share as $6.66 in 1993, when its stock was trading for approximately $24.50 on January 4, 1994. Sara Lee's *MV/BV* ratio indicated that it was a growth company *(MV > BV)*. It was not a growth stock, however, since we found that it was overvalued when we compared its market value to its intrinsic value.

Again, don't lose sight of the importance of examining the stock in order to determine the company's investment opportunities and the returns they may generate in the future, rather than blindly applying a ratio-based decision rule that has seemed to work in the past. After careful analysis, compare the stock's market price with its estimated intrinsic value in order to determine whether it's undervalued. The *MV/BV* ratio may be part of a good initial sorting process to find potential good investments, but don't stop there; do the fundamental analysis described above.

Besides the *MV/BV* ratio, another ratio is popular with investors who hunt for undervalued stocks. It's called the *price/earnings ratio* or, more commonly, the *P/E ratio.*

Price/Earnings (P/E) Ratio

The **price/earnings ratio,** more often referred to as the *P/E ratio,* is a commonly used measure to which investors refer when searching for potential investments. However, many pitfalls complicate fundamental valuation using the P/E ratio. This section starts with a discussion of how an investor may view the P/E ratio and then it delves into some of the underlying problems.

The P/E ratio is defined as:

$$\text{P/E ratio} = \frac{\text{Market price per share}}{\text{Earnings per share}} \tag{8.14}$$

Interpreting P/E Ratios

Given the definition above, how would an investor interpret P/E to make an investment decision? Suppose two firms, Apple and IBM, have P/E ratios of 10× and 15×. An investor might interpret the P/E of 10 as indicating that the stock is selling for ten times the company's earnings, that is, the stock price per share is ten times the company's earnings per share (usually written as 10×). They often view the ratios as a unit-pricing scale. Apple's P/E of 10× means that the market values the stock at $10 per $1 of company earnings, while it values IBM at $15 per $1 of earnings. This resembles grocery shopping, where ground chuck may sell for $2.50 per pound while sirloin steak sells for $3.75 per pound. Both IBM and sirloin steak appear to be more expensive.[24] An investor may reason that Apple can provide the same dollar of earnings more cheaply than IBM, hence the stock may appear more attractive. This investor believes that the low-P/E stock pays a greater return since it cost less for the same $1 of earnings.

---

[24]There is no intent to imply that Apple is analogous to ground chuck and IBM to sirloin steak.

Table 8.2

Average, Raw, Year-by-Year Returns on
Common Stocks Stratified by P/E Ratios

	Low P/E		High P/E	
	Quartile 1	Quartile 2	Quartile 3	Quartile 4
1970	7.5%[a]	5.7%	−2.1%	−10.9%
1971	−7.8	−5.5	3.6	9.7
1972	−2.4	−1.4	−2.0	5.8
1973	−1.9	1.7	−3.2	3.3
1974	7.7	3.0	−2.4	−8.0
1975	11.3	8.0	−5.0	−14.1
1976	12.8	5.5	−2.2	−16.1
1977	10.2	2.4	−1.7	−10.9
1978	3.6	−2.5	−1.4	0.3
1979	0.7	0.4	−5.8	4.6
1980	−5.7	−6.8	−0.7	13.1
1981	12.2	4.9	−5.1	−12.0

[a]These numbers represent average one-year holding period
returns. The low-P/E ratio group consists of firms in the lowest two quartiles in terms of P/E ratios; the high-P/E ratio
group consists of firms with P/E ratios in the highest two
quartiles.

Another investor may reason that the market values IBM's $1 in earnings
at $15 while it values Apple's $1 at only $10, therefore the market considers
IBM to be more valuable and more likely to rise in price. This investor may
purchase IBM stock. As Table 8.2 indicates, both types of investors are right.
Unfortunately, they are only right some of the time.

Table 8.2 shows that firms with low P/E ratios earned handsome returns
over 1975 to 1977 and then again in 1981. The average one-year holding
period returns for those periods were 11.3 percent, 12.8 percent, 10.2
percent, and 12.2 percent, respectively. High-P/E firms fared well in some
years as well, as data for 1971 and 1980 exhibit. High-P/E stocks earned relatively high average returns of 9.7 percent and 13.1 percent in those years,
respectively.

A table from an article in *The Wall Street Journal* that illustrates some of the
inherent dangers of buying stocks with high P/E ratios is shown on the next
page. The table shows three points in time, lists the ten stocks with the highest P/E ratios at those times, and measures their performance to July 1991.
Many of these stocks disappointed investors. Of the ten stocks with the highest P/E ratios in December 1972, only one, Automatic Data Processing, had
a total return that exceeded that of the S&P 500. The ten stocks with the
highest P/E ratios in July 1981 all underperformed the S&P 500. On the
other hand, six of the ten stocks with the highest P/Es in July 1986 outperformed the S&P 500 over the test period. Wal-Mart's total return between
July 1986 and July 1991 was more than three times that of the S&P 500.

The article suggests that buyers of high P/E stocks may be buying glamour
stocks that are in high demand. Unfortunately, glamour stocks of today may
be very unglamorous in the future. Further, buying at a stock's peak price
increases the danger of buying overvalued investments. The message from
this article is simply that investors should not choose stocks solely on the basis
of P/Es.

The P/E ratio may have other uses, though. Can we use P/E to conduct
fundamental analysis?

Where Are the Stars of Yesteryear?

Investing in the most popular stocks is a dangerous game—witness what happened to many past market favorites. Shown are the fates of the Big Board stocks that had the highest price–earnings ratios (and market values over $200 million) in 1972, 1981, and 1986.

December 1972	P/E Ratio[a]	$18\frac{1}{2}$-Year Return[b]	July 1981	P/E Ratio[a]	10-Year Return[b]
Polaroid	90	−36%	Paradyne	45	−64%[c]
MGIC Investment	84	−35[c]	Computervision	37	−64[c]
McDonald's	83	418	Scientific Atlanta	33	−46
Baxter International	82	226	M/A Com	28	−76
Intl. Flavors & Frag.	81	214	Flightsafety Int'l.	26	325
Automatic Data Proc.	80	644	Rolm	24	109[c]
Walt Disney	76	447	Mary Kay Cosmetics	24	−13[c]
Rite-Aid	72	415	Dow Jones	23	89
Dr. Pepper	69	32[c]	Prime Computer	23	−74[c]
Colonial Penn	68	0[c]	Datapoint	23	−93
S&P 500	—	625	S&P 500	—	345

July 1986	P/E Ratio[a]	5-Year Return[b]	Today's High-P/E Lineup	P/E Ratio[a]
Marion Merrell Dow	61	142%	U.S. Surgical	64
Consolidated Stores	46	−51	Home Depot	55
Rollins Commun.	43	5[c]	Wal-Mart Stores	41
Rollins Environmental	40	−18	CUC International	40
Wal-Mart Stores	38	319	Mid-American Waste	36
Limited	36	103	Brinker International[d]	34
Toys 'R' Us	35	124	Continental Med. Sys.	34
Gap	32	316	Total System Services	32
Pep Boys	31	−40	Safety Kleen	31
Safety Kleen	30	135	Healthsouth Rehab.	30
S&P 500	—	95		

[a]Price divided by past 12 months per-share earnings
[b]Total investment return through July 1991, or through date trading stopped
[c]No longer traded, generally because of acquisition or leveraged buyout
[d]Name recently changed from Chili's

Source: John R. Dorfman, "Why Falling for High P–E Can Be Costly," *The Wall Street Journal*, August 15, 1991, C1–C2.

Determining Value from P/E

A quick and crude way of determining a stock's value is to multiply its P/E ratio by its expected earnings per share, EPS_1:

$$V_{s0} = (\text{P/E ratio}) \times (EPS_1) \tag{8.15}$$

For Sara Lee, this calculation would equal:

$$V_{s0} = 18.1 \times \$1.55 = \$28.055$$

Does this quick estimate approximate Sara Lee's intrinsic value? It does not because the P/E ratio was calculated using market price per share, just like the *MV/BV* ratio. Therefore, a value based on a P/E ratio may ignore many factors that an intrinsic value estimate must incorporate.

Let's carefully examine some of the factors that P/E-based fundamental analysis may ignore. First, the DDM can give a theoretical definition of P/E:

$$V_{s0} = \frac{DIV_1}{ER_s - g}$$

Dividing both sides of the equation by EPS_1 gives:

$$\text{P/E ratio} = V_{s0}/EPS_1 = \frac{DIV_1/EPS_1}{ER_s - g} \qquad (8.16)$$

This equation is a theoretical definition of the P/E ratio, substituting intrinsic value for price. It implies that the P/E ratio consists of three components:

1. DIV_1/EPS_1, the dividend payout ratio for next year's dividends and earnings
2. ER_s, the required rate of return by investors
3. g, the expected growth rate

Now let's examine the effects of these components on the P/E ratio. Suppose that someone believes that a high P/E indicates a better investment selection, devising a strategy to buy common stocks with high P/E ratios.[25] What factors might this person look for to assure high P/Es?

1. Suppose the P/E is high because the company truly has exceptional growth opportunities; that is, a high expected g leads to a high P/E. If P/E is high due to strong growth opportunities, then the stock may be a reasonable investment. This is analogous to a growth company with a high intrinsic value based on high expected growth.

2. Suppose the P/E ratio is high because the analysis ignored the level of risk inherent in ER_s. The future stream of expected earnings per share of IBM is probably less risky than the future stream of expected earnings per share for Apple.[26] In this case, P/E would be high only because the novice (due to ignorance) calculated the value based on IBM's required rate of return, ER_s, rather than Apple's required rate of return, assuming that the two computer firms have similar required rates of return. Using the rate of return of a stable company as the expected return for a riskier company leads the calculated P/E ratio to overstate the true P/E.

3. Most analysts calculate a P/E ratio by dividing a stock's price per share by the firm's current earnings per share (EPS_0). As our formula shows, the calculation should instead reflect expected earnings per share (EPS_1). For a firm with rising earnings, a P/E based on EPS_0 will overstate the true P/E ratio.

---

[25]One way of determining whether or not a P/E is high is to measure relative to the S&P 500 P/E or the market P/E; so if the market P/E is $10\times$, then $15\times$ is considered high.

[26]In effect, we are saying that the beta risk in Equation 8.10 is higher for Apple than IBM.

4.   Finally, an EPS_1 close to zero can give a large calculated P/E ratio. In fact, in the limit as EPS_1 approaches zero, the P/E ratio approaches infinity. As an example, if a company has estimated EPS_1 of $0.01 and a price per share of only $1.00, then its P/E ratio equals 100×.

After examining each component separately, we can draw the following conclusion: If P/E is high because of exceptional growth potential, then it may be a good reason to invest. If P/E is high because the calculation included the wrong expected return for the company's risk level, then it cannot support a decision to invest. P/E can also deceive the investor if it fails to reflect expected earnings, or if it reflects small earnings per share.

What about Low-P/E Stocks?

Many of the problems we discussed for high-P/E stocks disrupt analysis of low-P/E stocks, too. However, proponents of the low-P/E investment strategy believe that such stocks are the best investments because they are cheap. For example, Graham and Dodd suggest that one should never buy a stock with a P/E higher than 12 for "value" investing.

This strategy resembles contrarian investing (discussed in Chapter 7) which advocates buying last year's worst-performing stocks. Contrarians look for P/Es that are low because other investors have shunned the stocks, believing that low P/Es indicate likely candidates for undervalued stocks. Recall that Chapter 7 discussed results from several studies that examined low-P/E stocks. Generally, these stocks have seemed to earn excess returns in the past, and the studies seem to support the view that they earn superior returns. However, researchers are still looking for answers as to why low P/Es seem to indicate consistently strong performance. The relationship has been linked to the small-firm effect, which implies strong growth in companies with low market values, and the January effect, since much of the performance advantage of small firms has occurred in January. Still, no final judgment has been passed. Like the MV/BV ratio, P/E analysis may be a good initial sorting method to identify candidates for more thorough fundamental analysis. A sound investment decision still requires detailed research about the company.

Verdict on P/E

The foremost problem with P/E analysis arises from basing fundamental analysis on Equation 8.14 because it uses the market value to calculate price. Instead, Equation 8.16 gives a more accurate representation of company value. The best use of P/E comes from comparing values calculated by Equations 8.14 and 8.16 rather than comparing P/Es of different companies. This point helps clarify three problems with P/E-based investing.

1.   It is dangerous to compare two companies' P/Es. Instead, one should compare a company's intrinsic value to its market value. Comparing P/Es of two firms could ignore critical differences between them.

2.   Some investors avoid high-P/E stocks because the statistic makes them look too expensive.[27] A high P/E doesn't always mean that a stock is too expensive. Again, compare a company's P/E calculated from its market price (Equation 8.14) to that calculated from its intrinsic value (Equation 8.16). This comparison may make a high-P/E stock look like a bargain!

3.   Similarly, some investors believe that all low-P/E stocks are cheap and likely to be undervalued. Wise investors don't rely on this likelihood; they make direct comparisons of market prices with intrinsic values. The proper comparison may reveal that a lower-P/E stock isn't so cheap.

---

[27]These are usually the same investors who invest only in low-P/E stocks. More on them later.

At the risk of sounding like a broken record, if a company's investment opportunities offer solid potential, it is a growth company and its shares may be a growth stock. Identify a growth stock by comparing Equation 8.14 to Equation 8.16. If the P/E ratio is used correctly, it leads to the same investment decisions as the EM or the DDM. Given the potential of P/Es to mislead, most investors should use the EM or the DDM to perform a fundamental analysis. It's the same analysis and gives much more straightforward results!

Alternative Way to Use P/E

Those who must use P/E ratio as a way to make investment decisions could try Charles Holt's approach. He has developed a formula that provides a different perspective on the use of P/E ratios.[28] Instead of calculating a P/E ratio and investing based on whether it's low or high, Holt's method analyzes the stock's current growth rate and its stated P/E ratio. His formula determines the number of years the stock must grow at its current growth rate in order to justify the stated P/E ratio.

For example, suppose that a stock's stated P/E is 25× and its current growth rate is 20 percent while the stock market's growth rate is 8 percent. If Equation 8.17 yields 21, it says that the stock must grow at 20 percent for 21 years in order to justify the 25× P/E. Could this stock really grow at 20 percent for 21 years when the general market is growing at 8 percent? An alternative interpretation suggests that someone who pays 25× the stock's earnings must hold it for 21 years in order to recover the investment. This method puts the company's P/E ratio in a different perspective.

The formula is:

$$t \text{ (in years)} = \frac{\ln\left[P/E_g \,/\, P/E_s\right]}{\ln\left[\dfrac{(1 + g_g + d_g)}{(1 + g_s + d_s)}\right]} \tag{8.17}$$

where P/E_g is the P/E ratio for a growth stock, P/E_s is the P/E ratio for a stock market index (e.g., the S&P 500), g_g is the growth rate of a growth stock, g_s is the growth rate of a stock market index, d_g is the dividend yield of a growth stock, and d_s is the dividend yield of a stock market index.

Plugging in the appropriate numbers provided in Table 8.3 for Sara Lee (g) and the S&P 500 Index (s) the number of years (t) equals:

$$t \text{ (in years)} = \frac{\ln\left[18.0/10.0\right]}{\ln\left[\dfrac{(1 + 0.12 + 0.02)}{(1 + 0.05 + 0.05)}\right]}$$

$$= \frac{\ln\left[1.8\right]}{\ln\left[\dfrac{(1.14)}{(1.10)}\right]}$$

$$= \frac{0.58778}{0.03572}$$

$$= 16.5 \text{ years}$$

---

[28]Charles Holt, "The Influence of Growth Duration on Share Prices," *Journal of Finance*, September 1962.

Table 8.3

Effect of P/E Ratios when Measured in *T* Years

Company	P/E Ratio (P/E$_i$)	Growth Rate (g_i)	Dividend Yield (d_i)
Sara Lee (*g*)	18×	12.0%	2.0%
S&P 500 (*s*)	10×	5.0	5.0

Source: *Value Line* report no. 1487, © 1993 for Sara Lee and Standard & Poor's Statistical Service 1993 for S&P 500.

Sara Lee must grow at the rate of 12 percent for 16.5 years in order to justify a P/E ratio of 18 times.[29] What are the chances that any company can maintain a growth rate of 12 percent per year for 16.5 years when the stock market is growing at 5 percent? If this seems unlikely, it raises questions about the reasonableness of the P/E ratio. Perhaps the P/E ratio is high due to inappropriate use of EPS_0 rather than EPS_1 to calculate the ratio; perhaps the calculation ignores risk. Perhaps the stock is simply overvalued.

Recap

"If the shoe fits, wear it!" All kinds of investors, novices and money managers alike, follow this advice and use the *MV/BV* and P/E ratios to make investment decisions simply because they seem to work. Research studies have shown stocks with low *MV/BV* and P/E ratios tend to earn superior returns, and practical investors say "if it works, use it."

The article in the Investment Insights feature does exactly that; it identifies stocks that are "bargains," or undervalued, based on their P/E ratios and *MV/BV* market-to-book ratios. As the Dow Jones Industrial Average hit 3,850.31 on January 11, 1994, many investors began to wonder whether any bargain stocks remained.

The article complied a list of stocks thought to be bargains based on criteria of P/Es less than 14 times, *MV/BV* ratios less than 1.5 times, and price/sales per share ratios less than 1.0.

Money managers seemed to favor issues such as Cyprus Amax Minerals, a company that mines copper and other minerals; American Building Maintenance, a janitorial company for office buildings; and Russ Berrie, a toy and gift marketer. Notice the comments made by different money managers about these companies. Mr. Black of Delphi said American Building Maintenance's "fundamentals are decent," but he used estimated 1994 earnings and calculated a P/E of 11.5, not 12 as listed in the article. Mr. Black reinforced our emphasis on projected rather than historical figures. Ms. Burleigh of ASB commented that, at $20, Kmart was "dirt cheap." Perhaps her estimate of Kmart's intrinsic value was in the high 20s.

These money managers used terms similar to ours. They used low P/E and *MV/BV* ratios as part of initial sorting processes to find stocks that were likely to be undervalued, but they didn't stop there. Most money managers continue to examine the fundamentals and the growth opportunities for these companies to see if the stocks still look undervalued based on those assessments. When they use terms like "dirt cheap" or "a little expensive" or "realistic target," they seem to have estimated intrinsic values for these stocks and compared them to market prices before investment decisions.

---

[29]In his book, *One Up on Wall Street,* Peter Lynch also interprets P/E as the number of years it takes to recover an investment. Holt calls this number the "growth duration of share prices" which matches Lynch's interpretation.

Even above 3,800, a Few Bargains May Be Left

Records, records everywhere. Are any stocks still cheap?

That's a question many investors are asking now that the Dow Jones Industrial Average has plowed through the 3,800 mark like a knife through butter.

There are still *some* stocks on the bargain counter, investment professionals say, albeit precious few. The accompanying table, prepared by MarketBase, a Needham, Mass., information firm, shows two dozen stocks that rate as cheap, at least compared with many others in today's cloud-level market.

Some of these stocks are in the doghouse for a very good reason: They are dogs. But over the years, many professional money managers have made a good living bargain-hunting among out-of-favor stocks, starting with lists like this.

Upon scanning the cheap-stock list, a few money managers said they spied at least one gem in the rough—Cyprus Amax Minerals, an Englewood, Colo., company that mines copper and other minerals. Several managers are keeping an eye on the janitorial company American Building Maintenance and the toy and gift marketer Russ Berrie, though they hope to pick them up a bit cheaper. The sharpest debate is over Kmart: Defenders laud the cheapness of the retailer's stock; opponents attack the lethargy, as they see it, of the management.

Stocks shown in the table met three criteria:

INVESTMENT INSIGHTS

They have been trading for at most 14 times the past four quarters' per share earnings; 1.5 times book value (assets minus liabilities per share); and 1.0 times sales per share. Stocks that pass this triple screen are unusually cheap in today's very highly valued stock market. In normal times, however, such values would look rather ordinary.

Here are comments money managers offered this week about some of the names that show up on the cheap-stock list.

Cyprus Amax Minerals. "A whiff of economic recovery and a whiff of inflation" should help this stock in 1994, says Chris Bertelsen, a manager with Eagle Asset Management in St. Petersburg, Fla. "It's copper and gold and a lot of different minerals — a commodity play . . . I'm fairly high on it." At today's prices, Mr. Bertelsen says, "it's certainly a very low-expectation stock."

Scott Black, president of Delphi Management, is a Cyprus fan to the tune of 262,000 shares. "Cyprus is fine," he says, but copper prices, recently depressed by recessions in Europe and Japan, are beyond its control. "If somebody wants to make the bet that world economies are coming back, this is a smart way to play it because they're an efficient, low-cost producer."

American Building Maintenance. This one provides a good example of how "value managers," or professional bargain hunters, think.

(continued)

What We've Learned about Fundamental Analysis

We've learned some ways to determine whether or not to invest in certain stocks. One way is to calculate an intrinsic value using either the Dividend Discount Model (DDM) or the Earnings Model (EM), and then to compare the intrinsic value with the stock's market price. If the intrinsic value is greater than the market price, the stock is undervalued and an attractive investment. If the intrinsic value is less than the market price, the stock is overvalued, suggesting a decision to sell any currently owned shares or perhaps to sell short.

Investors have found shortcut methods for fundamental analysis. Two popular ones are based on market-to-book *(MV/BV)* and P/E ratios. These two ratios have some conceptual shortcomings but have been proven to be effective analytical tools. These ratios can underlie a very effective initial sorting process to identify stocks that are likely to be undervalued. The ratio-based strategy calls for buying stocks with low *MV/BV* or P/E ratios because those tend to be undervalued, relatively cheap issues. The analysis should not stop with just finding low-P/E stocks or low-*MV/BV* stocks; based on the DDM or the EM, further analysis can compare a stock's intrinsic value to its market

(continued)

While other managers who deal in hot growth stocks often want to be quick on the trigger, value managers often take their time, run the numbers just once more, and wait for a stock to weaken a little further before it falls into their clutches.

Roland Whitridge, manager of Babson Value Fund, says he thinks American Building Maintenance is an "interesting" stock. "It seems very attractive on the numbers," he says. "I just haven't put the case together to go out and write a ticket on it." One reason he hesitates: "A lot of its operations are in the Los Angeles area, which is still quite depressed."

Mr. Black of Delphi isn't pulling the trigger yet either. American Building Maintenance specializes in maintaining high-rise office buildings, he says. That's one of the soggiest parts of the real-estate realm today. So revenue growth is "very slow."

Does that mean Mr. Black is turning up his nose at the stock? Not at all. "The fundamentals are decent," he says. "But it's a little expensive at 11.5 times [estimated 1994] earnings. If you're a 10-multiple man like me, you've got to wait" for the stock price to sag a bit more.

Russ Berrie. The Oakland, N.J., maker of toys, candy, and impulse items rode high last year on the strength of its Troll dolls. But as the latest Troll fad has faded, the stock has ebbed 30 percent to a closing price yesterday of $13\frac{7}{8}$, down $\frac{1}{8}$.

Russ Berrie is a stock "that you can make money on if you buy it right," says Mark Boyar of Boyar Asset Management in New York. "You

can buy it in the low teens. That opportunity comes along once every couple of years."

Mr. Boyar says he sold the stock in the mid-20s because it "hit our target" during the Troll mania. Now that the stock is down to 14, "it's once again interesting," he says, though he hasn't bought it yet. The company, he says, has a "wonderful distribution network" with some 800 salespeople who call on card shops, gift shops, and other retailers.

Russ Berrie is "too small" for inclusion in her institutional portfolios, say Lois Burleigh, director of equity investments at ASB Capital Management, an institutional money manager in Washington. But she says, "I am planning to take a look at it for my own portfolio."

Guilford Mills. David Katz, chief investment officer at Matrix Asset Advisors in New York, is keeping a close watch on Guilford Mills, the Greensboro, N.C., textile maker. The stock is down about five points from its high, partly because "there were no strong fashion trends this year," Mr. Katz says. "If it came down to 19, we would have an interest." Guilford shares closed yesterday at $23\frac{1}{2}$, up $\frac{1}{8}$.

Kmart. The Troy, Mich., retailer generated the most vigorous arguments of any stock on the list. "We just started buying it" this week, says Mr. Katz. "The analyst community has given up on the company. It is selling for less than 10 times normalized earnings. And you get paid a 4.8 percent [dividend] yield while you wait."

Ms. Burleigh of ASB calls Kmart shares "dirt cheap." ASB already owns some, and she says she may add to the position. The stock was at 20,

---

price to make sure it's undervalued. Analyzing and studying a company's future investment opportunities increase the odds of finding undervalued, or growth, stocks. This analysis of the company's fundamental economic value must evaluate *future* opportunities and separate true growth opportunities from fluff.

The Gap is a good example of a company that used to be a growth company and growth stock. The firm sells quality casual clothing, especially jeans, with growth opportunities nationwide. If you had invested in 100 shares when it went public in 1976 for $18 per share, those shares would have been worth $46,725 at the stock's peak in 1987. The firm's earnings grew from $0.08 per share in 1977 to $0.49 in 1987 (an average growth rate of 20 percent per year).

The Gap *was* a good investment in the 1980s, but will it continue to please investors in the 1990s? The Gap continues to expand, opening new stores and updating its assortment of clothing in the 1990s. With expansion, sales rose by 12 percent in 1992 while expenses increased by only 6.5 percent. The firm has moved toward riskier, more fashionable clothing, but the change appears to have succeeded. Shoppers definitely continue to buy Gap clothes and shoes. Indeed, it still seems to be a growth company. Is it a growth stock? As always, the bottom line is that a "good" investment's market price must be lower than its intrinsic value.

unchanged, yesterday. She thinks a realistic target would be the high 20s.

But others say they wouldn't touch the stock. "Nice people, great art collection in the corporate offices, but . . ." says one money manager.

"I hate Kmart," says Mr. Bertelsen of Eagle Asset Management. "They are getting beaten up at the high end by JC Penney, at the low end by Caldor, and in the middle by Sears," he says. "And they certainly can't match Wal-Mart" in the low-price store wars. "They have to get a grip on what they're trying to do."

Source: John R. Dorfman, "Even above 3,800, a Few Bargains May Be Left," *The Wall Street Journal*, January 12, 1994, C1.

A Shopping List for the Tight-Fisted

These New York Stock Exchange shares are cheap by three yardsticks: their prices aren't higher than 14 times trailing earnings, 1.5 times book value, and 1.0 times sales per share.

	P/E Ratio[a]	Price/ Book[b]		P/E Ratio[a]	Price/ Book[b]
Giant Industries	7	1.1	Hudson Foods	12	1.2
Fleming Cos.	8	0.8	Kmart	12	1.3
Shopko Stores	9	1.0	Amer. Blg. Maintenance	12	1.4
Club Med	10	1.0	Syms	13	1.0
Northrop	10	1.3	Tultex	13	1.3
Windmere	11	0.9	Longs Drug Stores	13	1.4
Waban	11	1.0	Guilford Mills	13	1.4
Universal Health Serv.	11	1.2	Wynns International	13	1.4
Wellman	11	1.2	Hi-Lo Automotive	14	1.0
Cyprus Amax Minerals	11	1.3	Tredegar Industries	14	1.0
Russ Berrie	11	1.3	Tech-Sym	14	1.1
Delta Woodside	12	0.9	Nashua	14	1.4

[a]Stock price divided by past four quarters' per-share earnings
[b]Stock price divided by book value (assets minus liabilities) per share
Note: Ratios as of Friday. Excluded are companies with earnings of less than 10 cents a share, or debt exceeding 50 percent of total capital.

The discussion of fundamental analysis will continue as we explore a bigger picture of conditions in the economy and a firm's industry. No company operates in a vacuum. It is affected by economic and industrial conditions, and the investor must evaluate these effects. For example, when President Clinton announced that the U.S. health care system would be revamped, health care firms' stocks were hammered the following day in heavy trading. The announcement created uncertainties and the stocks suffered.

In the late 1980s and early 1990s recession showed how economic factors can affect companies and their stocks. The retail industry suffered tremendously during this recessionary period, as firms' depressed earnings prove. Liz Claiborne generated earnings per share of $2.61 in 1992, but this fell to $1.95 in 1993 due to soft retail conditions. Earnings per share for Nordstrom, an upscale retail department store, also fell, from $1.72 in 1992 to $1.60 in 1993. Similarly, Neiman Marcus, another pricey department store chain, reported losses in 1991 and 1992.[30] Chapter 9 will further explore why economic and industry analyses are important and review important components of an industry analysis.

---

[30]Information for Liz Claiborne, Nordstrom, and Neiman Marcus came from *Value Line* reports, in November and December 1993.

Chapter Summary

1. **Understand the concept of intrinsic value.**

   The intrinsic value of a common stock is its fundamental economic value. We found that fundamental analysts try to determine the intrinsic value of a stock by evaluating the future dividend payments and growth opportunities of the company. This chapter discusses the methods by which an investor may estimate an intrinsic value for a company's common stock.

2. **Examine the Dividend Discount Model (DDM).**

   The DDM is one method by which to estimate an intrinsic value of a common stock. The model defines common stock value as the present value of the stock's future dividend stream and its future value. A constant dividend growth model can be used if company dividends are estimated to grow at an average constant rate, g.

3. **Develop the Earnings Model (EM).**

   The EM is another method by which to estimate an intrinsic value for a common stock. The model assumes that a company's earnings grow at a constant rate, g, and defines common stock value as the present value of the future earnings stream of the company. It also shows that the future earnings stream is generated by the firm's future growth opportunities. We discussed some implications stemming from the EM, and we differentiated a growth company from a growth stock.

4. **Conduct a fundamental analysis.**

   Once an intrinsic value is calculated via the models described above, the analyst can assess whether or not the stock is an attractive investment. Intrinsic value is a benchmark value to which the analyst compares the stock's market price. If the market price is below the intrinsic value, the stock is undervalued and an attractive investment. If the traded price is above the intrinsic value, the stock is overvalued and should be avoided.

5. **Analyze a stock with nonconstant growth.**

   When g is greater than ER_s, the DDM breaks down. Nonconstant growth stocks with g greater than ER_s require a modified, two-phase DDM. It combines an estimate of a nonconstant growth rate and a constant growth rate to calculate the present value of dividends using the appropriate growth rates for each period of time.

6. **Develop an understanding of the market-to-book ratio.**

   The market-to-book ratio, defined as the market value of the stock divided by its book value, is another way to determine whether a stock is undervalued or not. The market value of a stock should at least equal its book value because that is the value of the firm's assets after it satisfies its liabilities. If the MV/BV ratio equals 1.0, then market value equals book value. If the ratio is less than 1.0, then the stock's price is depressed below the book value, and it may be undervalued because, by liquidating the company (selling the assets and paying off the liabilities), an investor may make a positive return.

7. **Examine the price/earnings multiple (P/E ratio).**

   Using the DDM, four components make up the P/E ratio. Whatever the P/E, only if the firm has solid growth opportunities is the stock a good investment. The DDM or EM could provide the same conclusion, without the potential problems of P/E. The chapter offers an alternative use of P/E that may not be as misleading.

Key Terms

Intrinsic value	Overvalued
Dividend Discount Model (DDM)	Undervalued

Earnings Model (EM)
Dividend payout ratio
Retention rate
Return on equity (ROE)
Growth company

Growth stock
Homogeneous expectations
Market-to-book ratio (MV/BV)
Price/earnings ratio (P/E)

Mini Case **1**   OBJECTIVE

Practice applying fundamental analysis on a company. See the following *Value Line* data on PepsiCo, Inc. (PEP). Suppose this is the end of 1993 and you are estimating PepsiCo's intrinsic value using DDM.

1. Estimate PEP's expected long-run growth rate using the dividend trend, the earnings trend, and Equation 8.9.

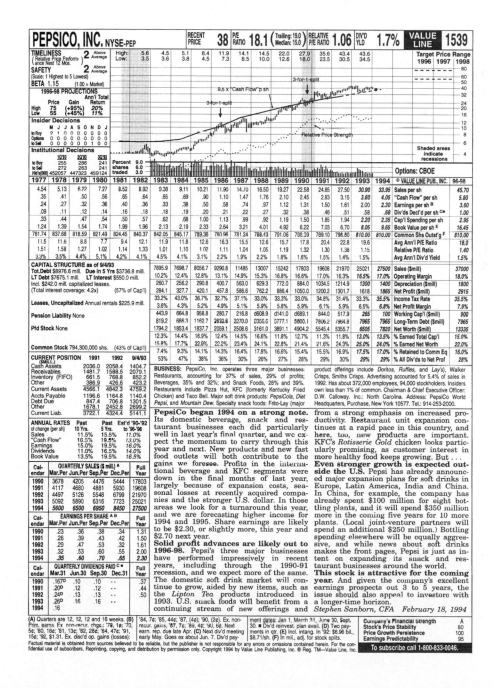

2. Estimate PEP's required rate of return using the CAPM, with the risk-free rate at 6 percent and Ibbotson & Associates' market risk premium of 8.6 percent.
3. Estimate DIV_1 using the equation $DIV_0(1 + g)$.
4. Estimate PEP's intrinsic value using the DDM.
5. Estimate PEP's intrinsic value using the EM.
6. Is PEP overvalued or undervalued? What investment decision would you make on PEP?

Mini Case **2**   OBJECTIVE

Apply the P/E ratio by using Equation 8.17 and learn to interpret it. Suppose it is currently 1992 and we have the following information about PepsiCo and the S&P 500 Index:

Name	P/E Ratio	Growth rate *(g)*	Dividend yield *(d)*
PepsiCo	23×	17.0%	1.5%
S&P 500 Index	21×	3.5	3.0

Apply Holt's model to determine the number of years that PEP must grow at 15 percent in order to justify its current P/E ratio. The S&P information was obtained from the S&P Statistical Service and PEP's data comes from *Value Line*.

Discussion Questions and Problems

1. What is a stock's intrinsic value and how do fundamental analysts use this figure?
2. Suppose that a stock's expected dividends are $1.50 per year for the next ten years and its expected price in Year 10 is $65.00. The required rate of return equals 0.12.
   a. What is the price of the stock in Year 5?
   b. What is the price of the stock today using the future value of $65.00?
   c. Determine the price of the stock today based on the stock price for Year 5.
   d. What can you conclude about your answers in Questions b and c? Explain.
3. Suppose that Stock A's current dividends per share are $1.55 and you expect it to grow at a 15 percent annual rate for the next five years. Also you speculate that it will sell for $95.00 five years from now. You would like to earn 18 percent on this investment.
   a. How much are you willing to pay for the stock today?
   b. Suppose it is selling for $42.50 today. Would you buy the stock or not? Explain.
4. Suppose that Stock W's expected dividends equal $1.65 and it is expected to grow annually at 9 percent for an indefinite period.
   a. If the required rate of return is 12 percent, what is the stock's intrinsic value?
   b. If Stock W's price today were $56.50, would you invest or not? Explain.
5. Stock X is currently trading at $29.50. Its current dividends per share equal $1.25, and this amount is expected to double in ten years.
   a. What is Stock X's growth rate?
   b. If you have a 12 percent required return on Stock X, what is its intrinsic value?
   c. Is it overvalued or undervalued? Explain.
6. Why is it incorrect to say that a stock's intrinsic value is equal to the present value of its earnings per share?

7. State the equation for an intrinsic value based on the Earnings Model. Based on the Earnings Model, how does one define the term *growth company*? (*Hint:* When is *PVGO* positive?)

8. Using the concept developed in the Earnings Model, comment on the following statement made by a tipster: "WXY Corp is purchasing a lot ($250 million) of machines and warehouses right now. They must be expanding and so they must be a growth stock. I would strongly recommend that you buy 200,000 shares today."

9. General Form has been investing in several projects this last month, but the stock price has not moved at all. A puzzled stock broker asks, "Is the market stupid?" Explain the possible reasons for the stable stock price by referring to the Earnings Model.

10. For what reasons can a company's P/E ratio be high? Why is this ratio not an accurate measure of a good investment?

11. Corie Kobb plans to invest in common stocks for a period of 12 years, after which she will sell out, buy a lifetime room-and-board membership in a retirement home, and retire. She feels that Odell Mines is currently, but temporarily, undervalued by the market. Kobb expects Odell Mines' current earnings per share and dividend to double in the next 12 years. Odell Mines' last dividend was $2.00 and its stock currently sells for $45 a share.
    a. In order to estimate Odell Mines' expected return, Kobb finds that the U.S. T-bill rate is at 4 percent while the S&P 500 Index has a 14 percent rate of return. Also, the stock's beta estimate is found to be 0.6. Estimate Odell Mines' discount rate.
    b. If Corie wants to earn a 10 percent return, would she buy the stock?
    c. If Corie purchases Odell Mines for $45 per share, what rate will she earn?

12. Stock ABC is considered to be a growth stock with a nonconstant growth rate of 25 percent for the next five years followed by 15 percent sustainable annual growth thereafter. ABC's current dividends per share are $1.10 and its required rate of return is 18 percent. Calculate its intrinsic value.

13. Explain how a low *MV/BV* ratio could contribute to a good investment strategy.

14. Suppose a stock's expected dividends are $1.50 per share and its expected earnings per share (EPS) are $5.00. The required rate of return, ER_s, for the stock equals 0.13 and the expected ROE is 0.12.
    a. Calculate the intrinsic value of the stock using the Earnings Model.
    b. Suppose *The Wall Street Journal* reports that the stock is trading at $35. Using the fundamental analysis, would you buy the stock? Why?
    c. Using the Earnings Model and the PVGO (Present Value of Growth Opportunities) term, determine if the stock is a growth company.
    d. Suppose your client comments that this stock has a growth rate that is greater than zero, so it should be a growth stock. Is he or she right or not? If so, how would you support his or her comment and, if not, how would you explain his or her error?

Critical Thinking Exercises

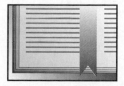

1. At the library, find information on McDonald's, the fast-food restaurant chain, and conduct a fundamental analysis. If necessary, use the nonconstant growth model instead of the DDM. Is McDonald's stock overvalued or undervalued? Carefully justify your answer with information to back your analysis.

2. Repeat the fundamental analysis conducted in the Mini Case 1 on Pepsico with more recent *Value Line* data. Do you concur with the analysis conducted in the Mini Case 1? Justify your answer.

3. Using *Value Line* or a similar source, find the ten stocks with the highest P/E ratios and the ten with the lowest P/E ratios as of December 31, 1989. Also find their stock prices at the end of 1989. Find today's stock prices for these 20 stocks. Calculate returns for the ten low-P/E stocks and the ten high-P/E stocks. (Remember to include dividends paid from 1987 to today.) Next, calculate an arithmetic mean return for each group of low P/Es and high P/Es. Does this return confirm or refute the contention that low-P/E stocks outperform high-P/E stocks?

4. Using *Value Line* again, find the ten stocks, as of December 31, 1989, with the highest and lowest MV/BV ratios. Find today's stock prices for these 20 stocks. Repeat the same process of calculating returns for each group, low-MV/BV and high-MV/BV ratios. Discuss your results. What is your conclusion?

5. Find a stock in a financial newspaper that has just announced its earnings (for either the quarter or the year). Determine the effect of any difference between forecasted earnings and actual earnings on the stock price. Discuss factors that may have affected the difference in forecasted and actual earnings.

Mini Case 1   SOLUTION

1. The long-run growth rate can be estimated using three methods: the dividend trend, the earnings trend, and Equation 8.9. Using Step 1 from the text, let's go through the dividend and earnings trend using a ten-year trend from 1982 to 1992. Using this time period assumes that PEP will repeat the last ten years' trend in the next several years.

   a. Dividend trend. $DIV_{1982} = \$0.18$; $DIV_{1992} = \$0.51$. This says that:

$$\$0.18(1 + g)^{10} = \$0.51$$
$$(1 + g)^{10} = \$0.51/\$0.18$$
$$(1 + g)^{10} = 2.833$$

   The tenth root of 2.833 equals 1.1097, or:

$$(1 + g) = 1.1097$$
$$g = 10.97 \text{ percent}$$

   b. Earnings trend. Repeating the same process for earnings per share, $EPS_{1982} = \$0.36$ and $EPS_{1992} = \$1.61$. This says that:

$$\$0.36(1 + g)^{10} = \$1.61$$
$$(1 + g)^{10} = \$1.61/\$0.36$$
$$(1 + g)^{10} = 4.472$$

   The tenth root of 4.472 equals 1.1616, or:

$$(1 + g) = 1.1616$$
$$g = 16.16 \text{ percent}$$

c. Equation 8.9 says:

$$g = ROE_1 \times b$$

where ROE_1 is the return on equity and b is the retention rate or (1 minus the dividend payout ratio). Remember that we are at the end of 1993, so ROE_1 is *ROE* for the end of 1994. Using the 1994 ROE and dividend payout ratio from *Value Line:*

$$g = (0.245) \times (1 - 0.28) = 0.1764$$

If we use the 1996 to 1998 estimates of ROE and the dividend payout ratio from *Value Line,* the growth rate estimate is:

$$g = (0.21) \times (1 - 0.28) = 0.1512$$

So the growth estimate for PEP ranges from approximately 11 percent to 18 percent using the three methods.

2. To estimate the required rate of return for PEP, apply Step 2 from the text. Using the CAPM or Equation 8.9:

$$ER_s = RF + \beta(ER_M - RF) \tag{8.11}$$

Using 6 percent for the risk-free rate, 1.20 for beta (obtained from *Value Line*), and 8.6 percent for the market risk premium, $(ER_M - RF)$, we can estimate ER_s.

$$ER_s = 0.06 + 1.20 \, (.086) = 0.1632 \approx 0.16$$

3. To estimate the expected dividends per share, DIV_1, apply Step 3 from the text. It says that DIV_1 equals $DIV_0(1 + g)$. This requires an estimated growth rate for PEP. We have a range from 11 percent to 18 percent. After carefully reading about PepsiCo's expected future opportunities, the long-run estimate for 1996 to 1998 using Equation 8.9 seems most appropriate (15 percent). *Value Line*'s analysts claim that "PepsiCo is clearly one of the world's premier consumer goods companies, with well-established operations in three diversified and growing businesses. Prospects for each look to be outstanding." With these endorsements, it seems that PepsiCo can sustain a 15 percent growth rate for the long-run. Using the 15 percent growth rate:

$$DIV_1 = DIV_0 \, (1 + g)$$

$$DIV_1 = \$0.58 \, (1 + 0.15) = \$0.667$$

4. Finally, estimate the intrinsic value for PEP. Using the DDM:

$$V_{s0} = \frac{DIV_1}{(ER_s - g)} = \frac{\$0.667}{(0.16 - 0.15)} = \$66.70$$

5. First, estimate EPS_1 using $EPS_0(1 + g)$:

$$\$2.05(1 + 0.15) = \$2.3575$$

Based on the EM, PEP's intrinsic value equals:

$$V_{s0} = \frac{\$2.3575}{0.16} \left[1 + \frac{0.15 - (0.16)(1.0 - 0.28)}{0.16 - 0.15} \right]$$

$$= \$14.7343 \left[1 + 3.48 \right] = \$66.01$$

6. So both models estimate PEP's intrinsic value to be around $66. Based on the stock's year-end price of $38, it is definitely undervalued. It may not be undervalued by as much as $28 ($66 minus $38), but we can comfortably say that it is undervalued. *Value Line*'s analysis seems to concur, so the decision is to buy shares of PepsiCo.

Mini Case **2** SOLUTION

In order to find the number of years a stock must grow to justify the P/E ratio, apply Equation 8.17:

$$t \text{ (in years)} = \frac{\ln \left[P/E_g \, / \, P/E_s \right]}{\ln \left[\dfrac{(1 + g_g + d_g)}{(1 + g_s + d_s)} \right]} \tag{8.17}$$

For PEP, this equals:

$$t \text{ (in years)} = \frac{\ln \left[23/21 \right]}{\ln \left[\dfrac{(1 + 0.17 + 0.015)}{(1 + 0.035 + 0.03)} \right]}$$

$$= \frac{\ln \left[1.0952 \right]}{\ln \left[1.112676 \right]}$$

$$= \frac{0.09097}{0.106768}$$

$$= 0.85 \text{ years}$$

The results tell us that PEP must grow at 17 percent for 0.85 years (about 10 months) in order to justify the 23× P/E ratio. Stated differently, if you invest in PEP at the current P/E ratio of 23×, it will take approximately 10 months to recover your investment. This certainly seems attractive and a good investment. These results are consistent with the fundamental analysis conducted in Mini Case 1.

Chapter 9

Economic and Industry Analysis

Chapter Objectives

1. Understand why economic and industry analyses are important.
2. Review the relationship between business cycles and investment decisions.
3. Examine economic forecasting techniques and issues.
4. Review industry definitions and classifications.
5. Outline the important components of an industry analysis.
6. Discuss the framework and techniques used in industry analysis.

In Chapter 6, we briefly discussed the basic steps for analyzing a common stock. Security analysis, or fundamental analysis, can be thought of as a three-step process describing an inverted triangle, with the analyst moving from the general to the specific. He or she begins with **economic analysis.** The analyst tries to determine where the domestic and international economies appear to be headed (expansion, recession, etc.), as well as the outlook for important economic variables such as inflation and interest rates. Among other things, the analyst will consider whether or not the overall economic outlook appears favorable or unfavorable for stocks.

After assessing the economic environment, the analyst completes an **industry analysis.** Is the company's industry in a growth phase or a mature phase? Is the industry subject to rapid technological change? Are demographic trends favorable or unfavorable for the industry? Are industry production costs rising more quickly or more slowly than the overall inflation rate? Is the industry subject to substantial government regulation? These are examples of questions an analyst might ask when examining a company's industry.

After assessing the economy and industry, the analyst examines the specific company in detail, looking at both its quantitative and qualitative characteristics. The analyst will examine the company's current financial statements in detail; the historical record of its sales, earnings, and dividends; the quality of its management; and so forth.

Building on the coverage of common stock valuation models in Chapter 8, we begin our detailed look at security analysis in this chapter with an examination of economic and industry analysis to assess the company's macroenvironment, which strongly influences common stock valuation. The chapter starts with a discussion of why economic and industry factors are important. Next, we review the relationship between business cycles and investment decisions, including the relationship of the business cycle with stock prices and interest rates. This is followed by an examination of economic forecasting, including a review of techniques, the accuracy of forecasts, and problems with economic statistics. We then turn our attention to industry analysis, beginning with a discussion of how industries are defined and classified. Next, we review the important components of an industry analysis. The chapter concludes with a discussion of the framework and techniques used in industry analysis.

Importance of Economic and Industry Analysis

We begin our look at the macroanalysis of securities by asking a simple question: Just how important are economic and industry factors in the valuation of individual common stocks? We believe that both are very important, though neither economic or industry analysis can substitute for a careful examination of a specific company.[1] History is replete with examples of poor stock performance despite favorable economic environments for stocks and good industry characteristics. The reverse situation (a good stock in poor economic and industry conditions) has occasionally occurred, as well. Economic and industry analysis should complement and enhance the analyst's examination of a specific company, not replace it.

Economic analysis is important, for one reason, simply because stock prices have a strong, positive relationship with overall economic performance. Since 1949, according to the National Bureau of Economic Research (NBER), the U.S. economy has passed through eight economic expansions and eight recessions. During the eight expansions, stock prices, as measured by the S&P 500, rose an average of 87.8 percent. By contrast, during the eight recessions, stock prices *fell* by an average of 18.2 percent. Not surprisingly, a stronger expansion (or contraction) in economic activity generally produces a larger increase (or decrease) in stock prices.[2] We'll have more to say about the relationship between stock prices and economic activity later in the chapter.

The same positive relationship between economic performance and stock prices exists in other countries, as well. For example, Britain experienced a recession between mid-1990 and late 1991; its real GDP (gross domestic product, stated in constant dollars, removing the effects of inflation) declined by approximately 2.6 percent. The associated decline in British stock prices (measured by the Financial Times 100 index) was slightly more than 16 percent.

It's important to note that, over the duration of a bull or bear market, performance levels among various industry groups often show substantial differences, as illustrated by the data in Table 9.1. It compares the cyclical price performance levels of the S&P 500 and several industry groups between October 1972 and December 1992. Notice that between March 1978 and November 1980 the S&P 500 increased by more than 52 percent, yet auto

---

[1]Many professional investment advisors argue that many individual investors are too concerned with short-term movements in the economy and overall stock market. Investors, they argue, should pay more attention to the specific characteristics of companies rather than trying to guess where the economy and overall stock market are headed. See, for example, Peter Lynch, *One Up on Wall Street* (New York: Penguin Books, 1989), 73–80.

[2]For example, during the 1973 to 1975 recession, real U.S. GDP declined by about 5 percent while stock prices fell by over 43 percent. By contrast, during the 1990 to 1991 recession, real GDP dropped by slightly more than 2 percent while stock prices fell by almost 15 percent. During the 1961 to 1969 expansion real GDP increased by over 47 percent, and the S&P 500 rose by more than 98 percent. In comparison, the 1970 to 1973 expansion saw an increase in real GDP of around 17 percent while stock prices rose about 56 percent.

Table 9.1

Comparison of the Cyclical Price Performance of the S&P 500 and Several S&P Industry Groups

Period	S&P 500	Industry Group					
		Airlines	Auto Makers	Computer Systems[a]	Drug Companies	Food Companies	Oil Companies
10/72 to 9/74	−42.0%	−65.0%	−53.3%	−46.5%	−33.8%	−45.5%	−30.8%
9/74 to 12/76	53.6	54.5	82.9	42.8	2.8	82.7	64.7
12/76 to 3/78	−15.1	−13.3	−18.5	−13.6	−12.1	−12.2	−10.7
3/78 to 11/80	52.7	9.2	−26.4	−5.5	40.6	−0.1	146.1
11/80 to 7/82	−19.4	11.1	−4.6	6.5	4.2	28.9	−42.9
7/82 to 10/83	53.3	49.5	98.0	93.3	34.7	44.7	37.5
10/83 to 7/84	−9.9	−10.4	−15.0	−18.5	−10.9	4.1	9.0
7/84 to 8/87	118.0	117.3	130.4	87.9	216.6	206.8	91.7
8/87 to 12/87	−26.8	−36.8	−33.5	−29.3	−32.4	−21.4	−23.2
12/87 to 6/90	49.5	89.2	31.7	−4.5	93.1	82.9	46.1
6/90 to 10/90	−14.8	−33.3	−28.8	−9.9	−3.6	−5.3	0.6
10/90 to 12/92	41.8	17.3	23.7	−40.2	36.9	53.0	1.5

[a]The computer systems group includes IBM, which explains the poor performance of the group between October 1990 and December 1992. Without IBM, this group actually *increased* by about 28 percent over the same time period.

Source: Standard & Poor's.

and computer stocks were down, and food stocks were virtually unchanged. By contrast, oil stocks gained over 146 percent. As another example, between November 1980 and July 1982, the S&P 500 lost about 19.4 percent of its value while airline, computer, drug, and food stocks all rose. The moral is simply that within general bull or bear market conditions, we can expect to see disparate performance among various industry groups; even if the economic outlook for stocks in general is favorable, the outlook for some industry groups may not be. Therefore, the analyst must examine the industry as well as the economy.

The security macroanalysis is important because it's naive to assume that the fortunes of individual companies, and thus the performance levels of their stocks, are not somehow tied to the prospects for the overall economy and the industries within which those companies operate. No company operates in a vacuum. One study, for example, found that over half of the variation in an individual stock's price could be explained by market and industry factors.[3]

The simple Dividend Discount Model from the last chapter gives the analyst one way to value a common stock. The model says that the intrinsic value of a common stock is a function of three variables: the current dividend, the expected growth rate in dividends, and the stock's required (or expected) rate of return. Without any economic or industry information, could you come up with reasonable estimates for any of these variables? The current dividend is known, but the other two variables are certainly influenced by economic and industry conditions.

The required rate of return, for example, reflects not only the risk of the individual stock but also the level of interest rates in the economy. The risk of an individual stock is likely influenced by industry, as well as company,

---

[3]See B. F. King, "Market and Industry Factors in Stock Price Behavior," *Journal of Business,* January 1966, pp. 139–190. One has to be careful not to overgeneralize King's findings, which were based on only 60 individual stocks and are almost 30 years old.

characteristics. The expected growth rate in dividends is likely tied to the firm's expected growth rate in earnings, but most companies' future earnings are heavily influenced by economic and industry conditions.[4]

Business Cycles and Investment Decisions

Having established the importance of an examination of economic and industry factors in the evaluation of individual stocks, we now turn to a discussion of the relationship between business cycles and investment decisions. First of all, what is a **business cycle?** Long-term economic growth in the United States (and in other developed, market-oriented countries) has exhibited nonperiodic, but recurrent, sequences of expansions and contractions (recessions) around the long-term, secular trend. Economists refer to these sequences as *business cycles.*

Since the end of World War II, the United States has experienced eight complete business cycles (measured from trough to trough). By comparison, Canada has experienced 12 complete business cycles since 1948, and Britain, France, Germany, and Japan have each experienced seven complete business cycles during the same period. The average business cycle in the United States since 1949 has lasted 62 months (slightly more than five years).

It is important to note, however, that no two business cycles have been exactly alike.[5] The longest postwar business cycle lasted 117 months (between February 1961 and November 1970) while the shortest lasted only 28 months (between July 1980 and November 1982). During the postwar era, U.S. expansions ranged from 12 to 106 months long, while contractions ranged between 6 and 16 months. During the average postwar expansion, real GDP increased by 5.1 percent per year, with a range between 4.0 percent and 7.3 percent. The average contraction saw real GDP decline by about 2.5 percent per year with a range between −0.1 percent and −4.4 percent per year.

Business Cycles and Stock Prices

As we discussed earlier, stock prices and economic activity are closely related; economic expansions are generally associated with rising stock prices and contractions are usually associated with falling stock prices. However, stock prices and economic activity are not *coincident;* they do not occur at the same time. Rather, stock prices tend to lead overall economic activity, typically by several months, in all developed, market-oriented economies. Stock prices could fall even when the economy was still expanding, and they could rise in a recession.

Table 9.2 illustrates the leading relationship between stock prices and economic activity in the United States. During expansions, stocks prices (measured by the S&P 500) have peaked almost six months before economic activity, on average. Stock prices, on average, have bottomed out roughly five months before the ends of recessions. Note, however, that the leading rela-

---

[4]We're not implying that the fortunes of all companies are tied equally tightly to economic and industry factors. The prospects of a company like Ford are probably much more closely tied to the overall economy than the future earnings of a company like Procter & Gamble.

[5]Since the mid-1800s, 34 complete business cycles have occurred in the United States according to the National Bureau of Economic Research. The NBER's data suggest that the "average" business cycle in the U.S. is getting somewhat longer (expansions are getting substantially longer while contractions are getting slightly shorter). Further, the data suggest that the average difference in economic activity between peaks and troughs of business cycles has gotten smaller over time.

Table 9.2

Turning Points in the Business Cycle and
U.S. Stock Prices: 1949–1991

S&P 500	GDP	Lead (months)
A. Peaks		
January 1953	July 1953	6
July 1956	August 1957	13
July 1959	April 1960	9
December 1968	December 1969	12
December 1972	November 1973	11
February 1980	January 1980	−1
April 1981	July 1981	3
June 1990	July 1990	1
Average		**5.8**
B. Troughs		
June 1949	October 1949	4
September 1953	May 1954	8
December 1957	April 1958	4
October 1960	February 1961	4
June 1970	November 1970	5
September 1974	March 1975	5
April 1980	July 1980	3
July 1982	December 1982	5
October 1990	March 1991	5
Average		**4.8**

Source: *Survey of Current Business,* various issues.

tionship between stock prices and economic activity has been far from consistent. Stock prices have peaked anywhere between 1 and 13 months prior
to peaks in economic activity. In 1980, stock prices didn't actually peak until
after the economic contraction had begun. The data in Table 9.2 also suggest
that the length of the lead time between the peak in stock prices and the
peak in economic activity is getting shorter.

To further complicate the relationship, many large declines in stock prices
have not led into recessions. The best, and most recent, example of this is
the 1987 market break. Between August and December of 1987, the S&P 500
dropped by more than 27 percent, yet no recession followed in either 1988
or 1989. In fact, real U.S. GDP grew by over 7 percent during both years. On
the other hand, in far fewer cases have large increases in stock prices failed
to presage economic expansions.

Why do stock prices tend to lead economic activity? One explanation is
that an increase or decrease in stock prices is a self-fulfilling prophecy.[6] Some
argue that stock price reversals affect consumer and business confidence,
and thus spending decisions. A sharp decline in stock prices, for example,
may lead to less consumer spending, depressing economic activity.

Another explanation is that the variables that drive stock prices (such
things as earnings, dividends, interest rates, and so forth) are based more on
expected business conditions than on current conditions. Stock investors may
be responding to what they think is going to happen, rather than what is
currently happening. Further, some of the fundamental factors that determine stock prices, such as companies' profit margins and earnings, also tend
to lead overall economic activity.

---

[6]This argument has been made about all so-called *leading economic indicators.*

Figure 9.1

Total Returns from Large-Firm Stocks versus Inflation: 1960–1993

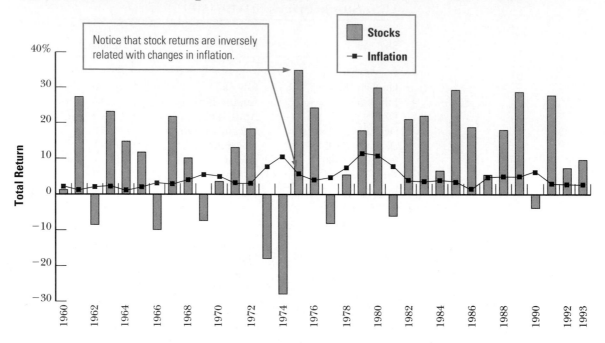

Source: *SBBI 1994 Yearbook* (Chicago: Ibbotson Associates, 1994).

Stock Prices and Inflation. Stock investors constantly watch for signs of a change in the rate of inflation. Any increase in inflation, actual or expected, is considered to be bad for the overall stock market. (The reverse is also true—lower inflation lifts stocks.) For one thing, rising inflation normally means rising interest rates. Rising interest rates, in turn, tend to depress stock prices, since the required rate of return on a stock moves up and down with general market interest rates.

Figure 9.1 shows the relationship between stock returns and inflation. The annual total return from large-firm stocks, as measured by Ibbotson Associates, is shown along with the annual inflation rate between 1964 and 1993. While the data indicate a generally inverse relationship between stock returns and inflation, it appears that changes in inflation, rather than a particular inflation rate, are more strongly associated with stock market performance.[7]

You have to be careful, of course, when interpreting the relationship between stock prices and inflation. Inflation tends to be at its highest around economic peaks, and at its lowest around economic troughs. Since stock prices generally lead economic activity, it is not surprising to see falling stock prices and rising inflation in anticipation of an economic peak and subsequent contraction.

The Overall Market and the Performance Levels of Industry Groups. If the overall stock market tends to lead economic activity, what relationship do specific industry groups have with the economy? The evidence suggests that certain industry groups tend do better during the early phases of bull mar-

[7]The correlation between stock returns and inflation between 1960 and 1992 equals −0.27, while the correlation between stock returns and the change in inflation (the inflation rate this year minus the inflation rate the prior year) equals −0.55. Remember, the closer a correlation coefficient is to −1.0 the stronger the inverse relationship between the two variables.

kets, while other groups often do better during the later stages. A study by Merrill Lynch found that cyclical stocks of credit and consumer goods firms (such as home-building companies and automobile manufacturers) generally outperform the overall market early in bull markets.[8] Energy stocks, defensive consumer goods stocks (such as food companies), and utilities exhibit the market's best relative performance late in bear markets. Growth stocks of consumer goods companies (such as cosmetics, soft drinks, and drug stocks) often outperform the market late in bull markets. Further, Merrill Lynch found that industries with high betas tend to do best early in bull markets, while stocks with low betas tend to do best later in bull markets.[9] Remember to interpret this, and all other studies of past performance, with caution: just because these relationships were true historically does not mean that they will be true in the future.

Business Cycles and Interest Rates

Even though no two business cycles are alike, there is little question that interest rates and business cycles are related. Generally, interest rates rise during economic expansions and fall during economic contractions. During the 1975 to 1980 economic expansion, for example, the yield on three-month T-bills rose 634 basis points.[10] In comparison, during the 1981 to 1982 recession, yields on three-month T-bills fell by 654 basis points.

One reason for the relationship between business cycles and interest rates, of course, is inflation. Actual and expected future rates of inflation tend to rise during economic expansions and fall during economic contractions. As actual inflation and inflationary expectations rise, so do interest rates.

In past business cycles, however, both inflation rates and interest rates have tended to rise (and fall) more sharply in the later stages of economic expansions (and contractions). For example, during the first two quarters of the 1975 to 1979 expansion (April through September 1975), the annual rate of inflation was about 7.3 percent. T-bill yields increased by about 80 basis points between April and October 1975. By contrast, during the last two quarters of the expansion (July through December 1979), the annual rate of inflation was more than 12.5 percent, and T-bill yields increased by over 300 basis points.

In addition, both inflation and interest rates have often continued to increase or decline for several additional quarters following turning points in economic activity. For example, the rate of inflation remained essentially constant during the first $2\frac{1}{2}$ years of the 1983 to 1990 expansion.

Aside from inflation, interest rate changes are related to economic activity in another way. The demand for loanable funds by businesses and households rises during expansions and falls during recessions. To illustrate this, Table 9.3 shows the change in a real rate of interest prior to, and during, postwar recessions.[11]

As expected, the real rate of interest rose, with one exception, during the four quarters preceding each peak in economic activity. During all postwar recessions, real interest rates have declined. Prior to the 1990 to 1991 recession, for example, the real rate of interest rose by 75 basis points. During the recession itself, real interest rates dropped by almost 300 basis points.

---

[8]This Merrill Lynch study is cited in Jerome Cohen et al., *Investment Analysis and Portfolio Management,* 5th ed. (Homewood, Ill.: Richard D. Irwin, 1987), 220–221.

[9]Beta is a standardized measure of the risk of a stock relative to that of the overall market. (The market's beta equals 1.0 by definition.) We'll discuss beta in more detail in Chapter 13.

[10]Remember, 100 basis points equals 1 percent.

[11]A real rate of interest is the stated (or nominal) rate of interest (or yield) on a security minus the rate of inflation.

Table 9.3

Changes in Real Rates of Interest before and during Recessions[a]

Recession	Prerecession Period[b]	During Recession
1953–1954	−0.55%	−0.99%
1957–1958	+1.05	−0.30
1960–1961	+1.90	−0.03
1969–1970	+1.82	−1.50
1973–1975	+0.64	−1.50
1980	+4.57	−5.68
1981–1982	+7.96	−3.69
1990–1991	+0.75	−2.99

[a]Figures are changes in real interest rates over the designed intervals. Real interest rates are defined as the rate on 90-day commercial paper minus a four-quarter average of current and past inflation as measured by the GDP deflator.
[b]The four quarters preceding the peak in economic activity.
Source: *Survey of Current Business,* various issues.

Business Cycles and Yield Spreads. A **yield spread** is the difference in yield between any two securities. Yield spreads are usually calculated for bonds that differ only in terms of credit (default) risk or maturity. (We'll use the term *bond* from now on to generically refer to all fixed-income securities.) Evidence from past business cycles suggests that yield spreads (based on both credit risk and maturity) often widen and narrow in response to changes in economic activity.

This is illustrated in Table 9.4, which shows the relationship between turning points in economic activity (both peaks and troughs) and the yield spreads between BBB-rated corporate bonds and Treasury bonds, and between Treasury bonds and Treasury bills.[12]

The data show that the yield spread between BBB-rated corporate bonds and T-bonds tends to be wider at the ends of contractions and narrower at the ends of expansions. This suggests that bond investors become more **quality conscious** during recessions. Investors may be worried that corporations are more likely to default on bonds during economic contractions.

The data presented in Table 9.4 show that the spread between T-bonds and T-bills is generally narrower at peaks in economic activity and wider at troughs. Notice that at some economic peaks, the yield on T-bills actually exceeded the yield on T-bonds. (This is referred to as an *inverted yield curve.*) One explanation for this pattern is that at economic peaks (or troughs), investors expect interest rates to fall (or rise).[13] Another explanation suggests that short-term rates are influenced by expected short-term inflation while long-term rates are influenced by expected long-term inflation. Inverted yield curves have normally coincided with high rates of both inflation and interest. Investors may believe, therefore, that the *average* rate of inflation may be higher in the short run than in the long run.

Investment Timing Implications

The relationships between business cycles, stocks prices, and interest rates discussed in the last few pages have a number of possible implications for

---

[12]The yield spread between long-term Treasury bonds and Treasury bills is sometimes referred to as the *yield curve.*
[13]We'll discuss several theories of the yield curve in more detail in Chapter 17.

Table 9.4

Turning Points in the U.S. Economy and Yield Spreads

Date	Turning Point	Yield Spreads			
		BBB, Absolute	T-Bonds, Relative	T-Bonds, Absolute	T-Bills, Relative
October 1949	Trough	120	0.55	114	1.09
July 1953	Peak	88	0.29	88	0.42
May 1954	Trough	101	0.40	173	2.21
August 1957	Peak	143	0.39	28	0.08
April 1958	Trough	203	0.73	166	1.48
April 1960	Peak	117	0.28	93	0.29
February 1961	Trough	144	0.38	137	0.57
December 1969	Peak	181	0.26	−86	−0.11
November 1970	Trough	287	0.44	122	0.23
November 1973	Peak	262	0.44	−195	−0.25
March 1975	Trough	144	0.18	236	0.41
January 1980	Peak	158	0.15	−151	−0.13
July 1980	Trough	190	0.19	208	0.26
July 1981	Peak	237	0.18	−119	−0.08
December 1982	Trough	276	0.26	251	0.31
July 1990	Peak	173	0.20	98	0.13
March 1991	Trough	164	0.19	257	0.43

Note: *BBB* refers to BBB rated corporate bonds: *T-Bond* refers to Treasury bonds with maturities in excess of 15 years; *T-Bill* refers to 90-day Treasury bills. Absolute yield spreads are stated in basis points. Relative yield spreads are equal to absolute yield spreads divided by the yields on T-bonds (or T-bills).

Source: *Survey of Current Business,* various issues.

investment timing. With our usual warning that the past is no guarantee of the future, Table 9.5 outlines some of these implications for both bond and stock investors. In anticipation of an economic upturn, for example, a stock investor should generally allocate a greater share of a portfolio to cyclical stocks, especially those with high betas. A bond investor should continue to lengthen the maturity of the bonds within the portfolio, and should shift some funds from high-quality bonds (such as Treasury bonds) to lower-quality bonds, anticipating a further decline in interest rates and a narrower yield spread between high-quality and lower-quality bonds.

On the other hand, in the middle of an economic expansion, a bull market is probably in its later stages. A stock investor should begin to take profits in cyclical stocks to build cash reserves, and start lowering the overall risk (beta) of the stock portfolio. Since interest rates have likely bottomed, a bond investor should begin to reduce the average maturity of his or her portfolio.

Economic Forecasting

The discussion in the prior section strongly suggests that an ability to forecast economic activity several months ahead improves the ability to forecast the general levels of stock prices and interest rates. Further, reasonable forecasts of future conditions in most industries depend on some idea of future economic activity.

Economic forecasting has two general objectives. The first is to foresee turning points in the business cycle (peaks and troughs), and the second is to provide estimates of specific economic variables such as the growth rate

Table 9.5

Business Cycles and Investment Timing

Stage of the Business Cycle	Stock Investors	Bond Investors
Late recession to trough	1. End of bear market, beginning of bull market 2. Begin to shift portfolio toward high-quality cyclical stocks.	1. Interest rates falling, yield spreads at their widest 2. Continue to lengthen the average maturity (or duration) of a bond portfolio; switch some funds into lower-quality bonds.
Early expansion	1. Early-to-middle bull market 2. Continue to move funds into cyclical growth stocks; buy other cyclical stocks and stock with high betas.	1. Yield spreads beginning to narrow, interest rates still falling 2. Continue to lengthen the average maturity of the portfolio and switch to lower-quality bonds.
Middle expansion	1. Middle-to-late bull market 2. Slowly lower the portfolio's beta and build cash reserves by taking profits.	1. Interest rates bottoming out and may begin rising, yield spreads continuing to narrow 2. Start to decrease the average maturity of the portfolio; continue the movement into lower-quality bonds.
Late expansion to peak	1. End of bull market, beginning of bear market 2. Take profits in cyclical stocks, build cash reserves, and reduce portfolio beta; slowly begin buying defensive stocks and utilities.	1. Interest rates rising, yield spreads at their narrowest 2. Start to move funds toward quality bonds; continue to reduce the average maturity of the portfolio.
Early recession	1. Early-to-middle bear market 2. Begin to shift cash into defensive stocks, utilities, and high-quality, noncyclical growth stocks.	1. Yield spreads widening, interest rates still rising 2. Hold short-term, high-quality bonds.
Middle recession	1. Middle-to-late bear market 2. Start to take profits in utilities and defensive stocks.	1. Interest rates peaking, and may begin falling, yield spreads continuing to widen 2. Begin to lengthen the average maturity of the portfolio.

in real GDP, inflation, unemployment, personal income, and so forth. Even if no recession is on the horizon, an investor still needs an idea about whether the economy is likely to grow slowly or rapidly.

Our goal in this section is not to turn you into an expert. (The best economic forecasters have spent their professional lives perfecting their trade.) Rather, we hope to give you an idea of how to generate an economic forecast, and how to interpret and use one. However, let's begin by examining accuracy and reliability of economic statistics.

Economic Statistics and Data

As we saw in Chapter 4, investors can refer to a massive amount of economic data with both domestic and international relevance. Much of the data are compiled and published by government agencies. Unfortunately, some of these data may not be as accurate or reliable as we'd like them to be. In fact, some economic statistics can be quite misleading. As a result, investors must interpret economic statistics and data with extreme care.

For one thing, one must understand what various economic statistics actually measure and how they are computed. As an example, consider how inflation, a critical economic variable, is measured. Inflation measures price changes. Probably the most widely disseminated measure of inflation, at least through the popular media, is the so-called **consumer price index (CPI).**[14] It is designed to measure the monthly change in the retail price to consumers of a selection, or *basket,* of goods and services.[15]

In 1993, the CPI rose by about 3.3 percent. Does that mean that everyone paid exactly 3.3 percent more for their particular goods and services in 1993 than they did in 1992? Of course not. The overall CPI hides substantial regional variation. In 1993, the CPI rose by almost 4 percent in New York City, but only by about 2 percent down the road in Philadelphia. Consumer prices rose by about 3.5 percent in Los Angeles, but by slightly more than 1 percent in Cleveland.

Interpretation of the CPI also depends on how the various goods and services that make up the index are weighted. Some argue that the contents of its basket of goods and services, and the weight of each item, don't change often enough to reflect changes in consumer buying patterns. One main concern is housing. Today, housing makes up about 45 percent of the CPI, and the index implicitly assumes that all consumers purchase new "shelter" (a combination of rents and housing costs) each month—obviously most don't. The problem, of course, is that sharp changes in housing prices can distort the CPI and give a misleading picture of the real rate of inflation faced by most consumers.[16] Therefore, a careful economist will look beyond the overall inflation rate to see what is happening to the prices of the goods and services he or she considers to be the most pertinent to a particular analytical problem.

Finally, one can argue that traditional inflation measures don't reflect changes in the quality of goods and services. For example, between 1988 and 1993, the prices of semiconductors (e.g., computer chips) actually fell by almost 10 percent. While that's impressive, it doesn't reflect the true economic change, since the chips produced in 1993 were, on average, far more advanced than the chips produced in 1988.

Seasonal Adjustments of Economic Statistics. More confusion can arise because many of the economic data reported by the government have been seasonally adjusted. The rationale for presenting **seasonally adjusted data** is fairly straightforward and can be illustrated with an example.

In the first quarter of 1993, retail sales in the United States were slightly more than $450 billion, a decrease of about 13 percent compared to the fourth quarter of 1992. Declining retail sales worry economists because consumer spending makes up approximately two-thirds of U.S. GDP. Did this drop in retail sales mean that the U.S. economy was headed for recession in

---

[14]Most economists do not use the CPI to measure inflation. Rather, they use something called the *GDP deflator,* a price index used to adjust the gross domestic product for changes in all the goods and services that make up the GDP. Economists believe that since the GDP deflator is broader than the CPI, it more accurately measures the true rate of inflation in an economy. Nevertheless, since the CPI gets more press, stock and bond prices tend to respond more to it than the GDP deflator.

[15]The U.S. Bureau of Labor Statistics, which publishes the CPI, also compiles and publishes the producer price index (PPI), designed to measure inflation at the wholesale level. Both the CPI and PPI are broken down into many sub-series that measure price changes of specific goods and services.

[16]This was a major issue in the late 1970s and early 1980s. For example, the CPI, including housing, increased by about 12.7 percent in 1980. Without housing, the CPI increased by less than 11 percent. The U.S. Bureau of Labor Statistics, the agency responsible for producing the CPI, has tried to make the housing cost component more realistic in recent years.

Figure 9.2

U.S. Retail Sales Adjusted and Unadjusted for Seasonal Variation: August 1991 through August 1993

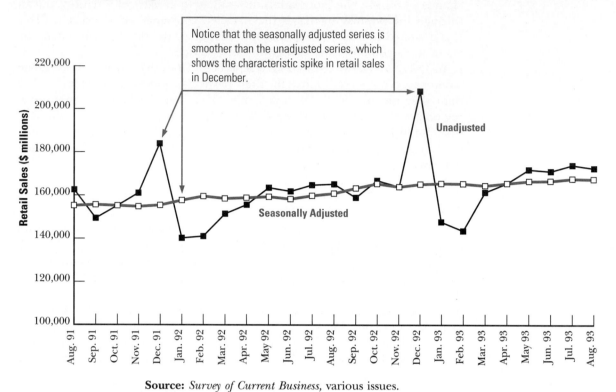

> Notice that the seasonally adjusted series is smoother than the unadjusted series, which shows the characteristic spike in retail sales in December.

Source: *Survey of Current Business,* various issues.

1993? No. Christmas buying always raises retail sales for the fourth quarter above the level for the first quarter of the following year. Without seasonally adjusting the data, comparing retail sales in the fourth quarter of one year to sales in the first quarter of the next year is pretty meaningless. Seasonally adjusted retail sales were actually slightly higher in the first quarter of 1993 than in the fourth quarter of 1992.

Economists argue that seasonally adjusted data present a better picture of the underlying trend of an economic series. This is shown in Figure 9.2, which compares seasonally adjusted retail sales to unadjusted retail sales between August 1991 and August 1993. Notice that the seasonally adjusted series is smoother than the unadjusted series and clearly exhibits a slow upward trend. This is considered to be a positive sign of future economic growth.

An economic analyst needs to know which series have been seasonally adjusted and which have not. This becomes more complicated since some economists and statisticians have criticized the techniques used to seasonally adjust data. Of course, no one should ever compare seasonally adjusted data to unadjusted data. Accurate analysis requires consistent data.

Accuracy of Economic Statistics. Critics have questioned the accuracy of much of the economic data compiled and published by the government with increasing frequency in recent years, as the article in the Investment Insights feature illustrates. The article suggests that the U.S. Commerce and Labor Departments, the main producers of U.S. economic statistics, cannot keep track of a rapidly changing, complex, global economy very well. This is especially true around peaks and troughs of business cycles. Thus, initially released statistics may give one signal, but revised data may give a completely different signal. Further, many traditional measures of such things as productivity are inadequate in a modern economy. (How do you measure productivity in a service industry like banking?)

One example cited by the article is the statistic for the U.S. trade deficit (imports minus exports), or balance of payments. The trade deficit should equal the amount of foreign capital coming into the country, since the United States must borrow from other countries in order to finance the deficit. Yet, in 1990 the official U.S. trade deficit was $73 billion more than the official figure for the amount of foreign capital coming into the country. Did the United States really have a problem with its balance of payments? What does this mean for investors? It means that they should be careful not to overreact to initially released economic statistics, especially those that are frequently revised.

Approaches to Economic Forecasting

Next, we'll review two common approaches for short-term forecasts of future economic activity. *Short-term* means forecasts that extend no longer than two years into the future. When short-term forecasts are matched chronologically, they can become a single long-term economic forecast that is constantly reviewed and revised.[17]

These perspectives can be roughly classified as **qualitative** and **quantitative forecasting.** In a qualitative forecast, the economist looks at a variety of economic data and then makes a subjective assessment about the economic outlook. A quantitative forecast is derived from econometric models. Of course, these two perspectives are not mutually exclusive. Many experienced economic forecasters emphasize one, while still using the other.

Qualitative Forecasts

As we just mentioned, a qualitative forecast results from subjective analysis of economic data. For example, an economist might observe an uptrend in the number of new household formations in the United States. He or she might conclude that this is a good sign for future economic growth, since it is likely to boost consumer spending on such things as new homes, appliances, and furniture.

In general, qualitative economists use two techniques to make their forecasts: leading indicators and anticipation surveys. Let's take a brief look at each.

Leading Indicators. A fairly simple approach to economic forecasting is to follow the behavior of specific variables which historically have been indicators, or barometers, of future economic activity. As an example of this approach, the U.S. Department of Commerce combines several specific variables, or indicators, of future economic activity into its **index of leading indicators,** published monthly.[18] Each month the index rises, falls, or remains unchanged. Analysts look for any clear reversal in the *direction* of the index. If the index reaches a certain level and then clearly declines, that is a signal

---

[17]This is similar to what investors should do. You may buy a stock as a long-term investment, but still review the stock periodically to make sure it continues to be appropriate for your changing investment objectives.

[18]In addition to the index of leading indicators, the Commerce Department also prepares coincident and lagging indexes of economic activity. These indexes are made up of components which tend to coincide with, or lag behind, general economic activity.

Washington's Misleading Maps of the Economy

Last autumn, Main Street was shivering in what seemed like the depths of recession. Yet, the government's official estimate of gross national product—its broadest measure of the nation's economic health—suggested things weren't so bad. The economy was contracting, according to the Commerce Dept., at a modest annual rate of 1.7 percent. So why did the economy feel so much worse?

One reason is that the official figures may be badly out of whack. A decade of budget cuts and benign neglect has left the government's main producers of statistics, the Labor and Commerce Depts., unable to track a rapidly shifting economy. Indeed, according to a new government measure of GNP, the economy was actually declining at a troubling 3.1 percent pace in the fourth quarter of 1989, nearly twice as fast as initially estimated. The cause for the dramatic shift: Commerce couldn't adjust its figures to reflect dramatic changes in the cost and quality of computers. That meant it was overestimating the true cost of the equipment and thus the real output of computer manufacturers. The new calculations should solve the problem, but they won't be officially published until next November.

The problems with the government's numbers go far beyond a single set of GNP figures, however. From retail sales to the trade gap, the statistics needed by policymakers and businesses are either misleading, late, or just not available. Observes Federal Reserve Board Chairman Alan Greenspan: "The economy has been changing faster than our ability to measure it."

Danger Signs. That's especially troubling when the economy is near a turning point. Looking back, it seems clear that the economy was showing early signs of distress by late 1989. Yet, after looking at relatively upbeat statistics, the Federal Open Market Committee decided not to lower short-term interest rates at a critical Mar. 27, 1990, meeting. Fed officials insist they received no "false signals" about the early signs of a downturn. And no one will ever know if the Fed would have cut rates in the spring of 1990 had it known how serious the slowdown was. But uncertainty over the reliability of data takes a toll. "It's not that the Fed went off 180 degrees," says William C. Melton, chief economist of IDS Financial Services Inc. "But it means policymakers tend to go real slow."

Capitol Hill, too, may have been misled. Congress hasn't moved to counter the recession, in part because lawmakers were convinced the downturn would be relatively mild. "The line has been that the recession would be short and shallow," says Joint Economic Committee Chairman Paul S. Sarbanes (D-Md.). "It would have been harder to sell that with more accurate figures."

Now that the U.S. economy may be heading upward, the lack of good data could once again be getting in the way of sound decisions. If, as many believe, consumer spending will lead the U.S. to recovery, the government's monthly measure of retail sales should be a major clue to how things are going. Yet, for the past two months, the initial report has seriously underestimated sales. For example, in April, Commerce reported that March sales declined by 0.8 percent. The report was widely interpreted to mean the recession was still in full swing. Then, on May 15, officials revised their estimates, reporting that March sales had actually increased by 0.4 percent. Government statisticians blame the problems on late reporting by businesses, and on a survey that hasn't kept pace with the rapid growth of new types of retailers, such as video rental outlets.

Drawing Blanks. The paucity of accurate and timely information has even more serious consequences for policy debates over such issues as international trade and competitiveness and health care reform. The oft-heated debates are riddled with assertions. But the hard evidence

of an impending peak in economic activity (and subsequent recession). On the other hand, if the index falls to a certain level and then starts to increase, that's a signal of an impending trough in economic activity (and subsequent expansion).

The index of leading indicators currently has 11 components, listed in Table 9.6 along with the expected direction (up or down) of each component preceding an economic peak or trough. Note that the S&P 500 is one of the components of the leading index. As we've seen, it should rise prior to an economic trough and fall prior to an economic peak. Since stock prices are a component of the index of leading indicators, any use of the index to forecast stock prices based on future economic activity can cause conflicts. Changes in stock prices may be driving changes in the overall index, so

policymakers need to steer them in the right direction just doesn't exist. "Increasingly, the government is run by people who think by the numbers," says Labor Statistics Commissioner Janet L. Norwood. "But the economy is so much more complex, you really need better data than we have ever had."

For example, it has become an article of faith that U.S. service-sector productivity is lagging. But government statisticians say they simply don't know how to count what many of these businesses produce. It's easy to measure the output of a steel mill. But what does a bank produce? "There's a general belief that we've had this long-term decline in productivity," says Patricia Ruggles, an economist at the Urban Institute in Washington. "It may perfectly well be true. But our output measures are so bad, there is no way to know."

That's especially true of health care. It's the fastest-growing sector of the economy, yet government statisticians have no handle on it at all. "We don't know how to define the output of the medical care industry," says Norwood, "and we don't know how to measure it." Not only do these problems distort productivity trends in services, but they also cast doubt on whether the overall growth of the U.S. economy is being accurately measured.

It's the same problem with international competitiveness. Almost everyone agrees research and development is critical, but no one knows how many researchers are working here or what they are doing. And no one knows how much money is going into key technologies, such as high-definition television or advanced ceramics. "We haven't a clue," says Jules J. Duga, senior research scientist at Battelle Memorial Institute.

The basic trade statistics are also flawed. In theory, the U.S. trade deficit should be roughly equal to the amount of foreign capital coming into the country, since the U.S. must borrow from abroad to finance the shortfall. But in 1990, the official current-account deficit was $73 bil-

lion more than the government's tally of the flow of money into the country. Says Rudolph G. Penner, a member of the National Association of Business Economists' statistical committee and former head of the Congres-

INVESTMENT INSIGHTS

sional Budget Office: "It's conceivable that if we did everything right, we'd find we don't have a competitiveness problem."

Out of Sync. The Bush Administration has taken some tentative steps to improve government data. Council of Economic Advisers Chairman Michael J. Boskin wants to spend $36 million to upgrade statistical programs—the first significant spending increase in more than a decade. But except for a handful of lawmakers, such as Sarbanes, there is very little interest on Capitol Hill in pumping up the budgets of statistical agencies.

For now, Labor and Commerce are trying to hold their tattered statistical operations together. The government's efforts to better measure the real output of computers are also a big step forward. Both agencies are upgrading their survey methods by refining both questions and targets to better reflect the changes in markets and the labor force. These improvements may help the government track cyclical changes. But the agencies have a long way to go before they can follow broader trends in productivity and international capital flows.

Indeed, without new resources, government statisticians will fall further behind a rapidly changing economy. The demand for instant, accurate information will only grow. But the ability of government agencies to deliver will continue to shrink.

Source: "Washington's Misleading Maps of the Economy," *Business Week*, June 3, 1991, 112–113. Reprinted from June 3, 1991, issue of *Business Week* by special permission, copyright © 1991 by McGraw-Hill, Inc.

you might be using changes in stock prices to forecast changes in stock prices!

Another component of the index of leading indicators is initial claims for unemployment insurance. As the pace of new layoffs slows, initial jobless claims tend to fall. This is normally interpreted as a sign that a recession may be about complete.

Figure 9.3 illustrates the relationship between the index of leading indicators and the business cycle since the mid-1950s. For comparison, the indexes of coincident and lagging indicators are also shown. While the index of leading indicators has generally given correct signals prior to turning points in economic activity, the timing of those signals has been far from consistent. For the last seven recessions, the leading indicator gave impending

Table 9.6

Components of the Index of Leading Indicators

Component	Direction Prior to Trough in Economic Activity	Direction Prior to Peak in Economic Activity
1. Average weekly hours, manufacturing	Up	Down
2. Average weekly initial claims for unemployment insurance	Down	Up
3. Manufacturers' new orders for consumer goods and materials	Up	Down
4. Vendor performance (slower deliveries index)	Down	Up
5. Contracts and orders for plant and equipment (constant dollars)	Up	Down
6. New, private housing units authorized by local building permits (index)	Up	Down
7. Change in manufacturers' unfilled orders (durable goods, constant dollars)	Up	Down
8. Change in sensitive materials prices	Up	Down
9. Stock prices (S&P 500 index)	Up	Down
10. Money supply (M2)	Up	Down
11. Consumer expectations (index)	Up	Down

recession signals anywhere between 2 and 20 months prior to actual peaks in economic activity, and it gave impending expansion signals anywhere between 1 and 10 months prior to actual troughs in economic activity.

Notice that the index of leading indicators has given some pretty ambiguous signals. Take a look at Figure 9.3, specifically the behavior of the index prior to the 1981 to 1982 recession. The index did peak in May 1981, prior to the peak in economic activity in July 1981, but you have to look pretty carefully to see it. In fact, the index rose less than 5 percent between April 1980 and May 1981. The index gave another ambiguous signal prior to the 1990 to 1991 recession. After about a 3 percent decline during the second half of 1987 (much of it attributable to the 1987 market break), the index of leading indicators stayed in a narrow range during all of 1988 and 1989. (The high was 146 and the low was 141.5.) The index rose in only 13 of the 24 months and didn't increase for any longer than three consecutive months, yet real GDP grew by about 4 percent in 1988 and 2.5 percent in 1989. The index of leading indicators peaked in May 1990 at 146.3, an increase of less than 1 percent from the end of 1989. Further, the index declined only about 2 percent before the peak in economic activity in July 1990.

The index of leading indicators has also given several false signals. For example, the index peaked in late 1983 and then declined by about 5 percent during the first half of 1984. (The index declined in five of six months.) No recession followed. Real GDP grew by 3.2 percent in 1985 and 2.9 percent in 1986.

Aside from the U.S. Commerce Department, other, nongovernment organizations compile and publish leading indicator indexes. For example, Stan-

Figure 9.3

Index of Leading Indicators

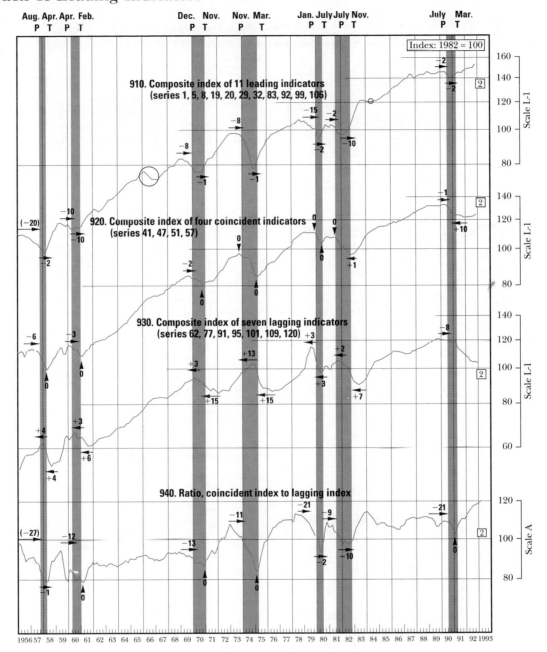

Note: The numbers and arrows indicate length of leads (-) and lags (+) in months from business cycle turning dates. Current data for these series are shown on page C-1.

Source: *Survey of Current Business,* March 1993.

dard & Poor's prepares a leading indicator index which is published in *Business Week.* (A sample is shown in Figure 9.4.) Several indexes are heavily weighted with monetary indicators such as the growth in the money supply and short-term interest rates, since some economists believe that future economic activity depends more on monetary conditions than anything else.

Anticipation Surveys. Another qualitative economic forecasting method examines surveys that attempt to measure the future economic behavior of

Figure 9.4

Alternative Leading Indicators

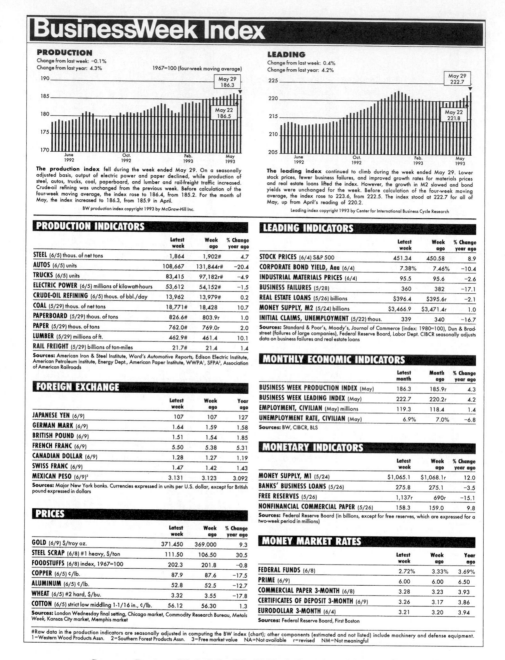

Source: *Business Week,* June 21, 1993, 6. Reprinted from June 21, 1993, issue of *Business Week* by special permission, copyright © 1993 by McGraw-Hill, Inc.

businesses, consumers, and government agencies. These are commonly referred to as **anticipation surveys.**

Because consumer spending is such a large component of U.S. GDP (comprising approximately 67 percent), many economists examine surveys that measure consumer confidence. For example, in Figure 9.5, the **consumer confidence index,** prepared by the Conference Board, a business group, is shown for the period between October 1992 and December 1993. The sharp rise in the index at the end of 1993 suggested strong economic growth for 1994. In other words, the more confident consumers are about their current

Figure 9.5

Conference Board's Consumer Confidence Index: October 1992 through December 1993

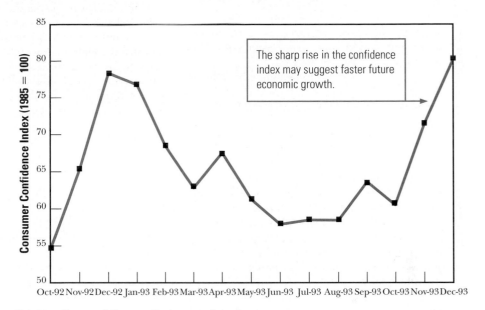

The sharp rise in the confidence index may suggest faster future economic growth.

Source: *Survey of Current Business*, various issues.

economic situation, the more money they'll spend, especially on big ticket items such as homes and automobiles.[19]

Anticipation surveys are obviously closely related to leading indicators. In fact, one measure of consumer attitudes, the **consumer expectations index,** prepared by the University of Michigan, is one of the components in the Commerce Department's index of leading indicators.

The major difference between leading indicators and anticipation surveys is that most leading indicators measure actual activity (jobless claims, building permits, and so forth) while anticipation surveys measure *planned* activity. Of course, a business's intention to add workers, for example, doesn't always result in new jobs.

Econometric Model Building

Econometric models apply mathematical and statistical techniques to economic forecasting. These models are the principal tools of the quantitative economist. While anticipation surveys and leading indicators provide fairly simple forecasts, econometric models provide perhaps the most complex. This most scientific approach to economic forecasting requires the user to specify the precise interrelationships between a variety of economic variables in order to come up with a model.

Econometric models predict not only the direction of future economic activity, but its duration and magnitude, as well. Instead of a general forecast (e.g., sluggish growth in real GDP), an econometric model yields a precise number (e.g., next year real GDP will grow by 2.5 percent). The accuracy of this precise forecast depends, of course, on the quality of the input data and validity of the assumptions made by the model builder.

---

[19]The consumer confidence index is referred to as a measure of consumer sentiment, how consumers feel about their current economic situation. That is, their situation within the next six months. There are also surveys, called expectation surveys, that are designed to measure how consumers feel about their longer-term economic situation, beyond the next six months.

How to Profit from Economists' Forecasts

We have two classes of forecasters: Those who don't know—and those who don't know they don't know.

John Kenneth Galbraith

Looking for an easy way to make money betting on interest rates?

Find out the consensus forecast among leading economists—and then bet against it.

That strategy would have paid off handsomely, according to two separate analyses of fearless forecasts from economists polled semiannually since 1981 by *The Wall Street Journal.*

"It's crazy," says Jack Miller, a New York investment specialist. "These guys get paid enormous sums to make these calls, but it turns out you would actually have been better off betting the other way."

That's certainly what Robert Beckwitt, a portfolio manager at Fidelity Investments in Boston, found when he studied data from the *Journal's* surveys. His conclusion: By betting against the consensus 30-year Treasury bond yield forecast every six months since December 1981, an investor would have earned a sparkling average annual return of 13.7 percent.

Betting against the consensus means rushing out and buying long-term Treasury bonds whenever the average forecast called for higher interest rates—and buying short-term Treasury bills whenever the experts predicted lower rates. By comparison, Mr. Beckwitt, portfolio manager of Fidelity Asset Manager Fund, found that a follow-the-herd approach would have netted an average

annual return of 8.8 percent, only slightly better than the 7.5 percent from investing in three-month T-bills.

"You really can't say enough bad things about how bad the consensus has been in forecasting interest rates," says Stephen K. McNees, an economist at the Federal Reserve Bank of Boston who also analyzed data from the *Journal's* surveys. "As an investor, you clearly would have done much better flipping a coin or assuming that rates would remain unchanged."

Some investment pros don't find that too surprising. "If you spend more than 14 minutes a year on economics, you've wasted 12," says Peter Lynch, the now semiretired investment wizard of Fidelity Investments.

Weather Forecasting

"If an economist at General Motors tells you steel prices are going up after being weak for four years, that's useful," Mr. Lynch says. "If an economist at Sears tells you about a new trend in the appliance business, that's useful. But if an economist tells you where interest rates and the economy will be 12 months from now, that's weather forecasting."

Economists have been particularly bad at predicting major turning points in the economy and interest rates—calls that are particularly important for investors and corporate budget planners because large amounts of money can be made or lost.

In mid-1990, for example, 35 of 40 economists in the *Journal* survey said the economy would growing for at least 12 more months. That was right before the 1990 to 1991 recession began. In early 1991, most forecasters predicted the recession would linger at least another six months; it

A variety of private and public organizations build econometric models and use them to produce econometric forecasts. Several of the better-known models have been developed by Chase Econometrics, DRI (Data Resources), G.E., the University of Michigan, and the University of Pennsylvania (Wharton School of Business). All of these models are extremely complex, containing many equations and dozens of variables. Their forecasts are widely reported in the financial press.

Accuracy and Applications of Economic Forecasts

It may come as no surprise that economic forecasters, as a group, are not revered for their accuracy. The article reprinted from *The Wall Street Journal* in the Investment Insights feature even suggests that investors should always expect the *opposite* of what economists predict (at least in their interest rate forecasts).

We need to consider three issues here. First, how accurate are economic

ended in March 1991—at least officially.

The consensus did come close to being correct for much of 1992. A year ago, economists were predicting a bleak winter followed by a mild recovery. Then in mid-1992, economists correctly predicted lower interest rates and lackluster growth. At that time, the consensus was aptly summarized by Robert Dederick, executive vice president of Northern Trust Co., who prophesied a "light-beer recovery—not very filling."

Accurate Inflation Predictions

Economists have proven fairly adept at forecasting inflation—or at least better than at many other things, according to data compiled by Mr. McNees and staffers at the Federal Reserve in Boston. He says every economist who appeared in 15 or more surveys produced better inflation forecasts for the next six months than a prediction of no change in the inflation rate from the previous six-month period.

But for some reason, good inflation forecasting doesn't always translate into accurate interest rate forecasting. Mr. McNees notes that Paul Boltz of T. Rowe Price Associates Inc. was among the best inflation forecasters but among the least effective in forecasting short-term Treasury bill rates.

Moreover, one year's hero often turns into the next year's goat. For example, Edward S. Hyman, president of ISI Group Inc., was tops in mid-1991 on the basis of his forecasts of interest rates in the second half of that year. He also ranked No. 1 as an economic guru among money managers surveyed by *The Wall Street Journal* early in 1992. But Mr. Hyman ranked dead last among 42 forecasters in the mid-1992 survey

INVESTMENT INSIGHTS

for his second-half interest-rate forecasts. The moral, he says, is: "Be persistent and be humble."

Noting Average Forecasts

Another moral, some analysts say, is to ignore all individual economic forecasts. "It may be more useful to look at the average forecasts in large surveys," instead of any one individual prediction, says Paul Volcker, former chairman of the Federal Reserve Board and now chairman of James D. Wolfensohn Inc. Economists who have studied this subject say the group average forecasts on the economy tend to be more accurate over time than any individual forecasters.

But group forecasts on interest rates are "much less reliable" than on the economy, says Robert J. Eggert, editor of Blue Chip Economic Indicators of Sedona, Ariz.

Why do so many high-paid forecasters, with high-powered computers and access to all the latest economic data, go so far astray?

Critics say the widespread failure to detect important economic shifts probably reflects a widespread tendency among forecasters to be "momentum-followers." That means assuming that whatever has happened over the past several months will continue over the next few months.

They also say too many economists, especially those at major financial institutions, are afraid to make forecasts that differ significantly from the conventional wisdom. Clinging close to the herd usually is a safer strategy, even if it means missing important changes.

(continued)

forecasts? Second, why is economic forecasting so difficult? Third, given the difficulty and accuracy of economic forecasting, how should investors use economic forecasts?

Several studies have examined the accuracy of economic forecasts. One recent study looked at the track records of 111 forecasters over 20 years (1970 to 1990) in predicting the following year's change in real GNP.[20] The group, on average, overestimated the change in real GNP in 8 of the 20 years by an average error of 0.5 percent. They underestimated the following year's growth rate in 9 of the 20 years by an average error of 1.2 percent. In three years, the group missed turning points by an average error of 2.8 percent. This group of forecasters was especially bad at predicting recessions.

Let's do our own, rather less scientific study of forecasting accuracy. At the

---

[20]See Victor Zarnowitz, *Business Cycles* (Chicago: University of Chicago Press, 1992). Zarnowitz is considered to be one of the deans of economic forecasting. Zarnowitz's findings suggest that forecasters are getting better at predicting future economic activity.

(continued)

"It makes you wonder if economists are more in touch with each other than they are with the realities of the marketplace," said Norman Robertson, who recently retired as chief economist at Mellon Bank in Pittsburgh.

Other statistics compiled by Fidelity's Mr. Beckwitt show:

—The consensus was right five times and wrong 17 times on which way long-term interest rates were heading over the next six months.

—Only five of the 34 economists who participated in 10 or more surveys managed to guess correctly which way long-term bond yields were going more than half the time. They were Carol Leisenring of CoreStates Financial Corp. (correct seven times out of 11, or 64 percent), Maury Harris of PaineWebber Inc. (eight out of 13, or 62 percent), David M. Jones of Aubrey G. Lanston & Co. (12 out of 22, or 55 percent), Lacy H. Hunt of Carroll McEntee & McGinley Inc. (seven out of 13, or 54 percent), and Irwin L. Kellner of Chemical Banking Corp. (11 out of 21, or 52 percent).

—But only two of those analysts (Ms. Leisenring and Mr. Harris) produced forecasts that would have beaten a strategy of being invested in intermediate-term bonds throughout the periods for which they were predicting. Buying and holding a basket of intermediate-term Treasury bonds would have produced an average annual return of 12.5 percent—or 3.7 percentage points more than betting on the consensus.

—The economist with by far the worst record on forecasting the economy and the unemployment rate is also the economist with by far the best record in picking when to buy long-term bonds: A. Gary Shilling, who heads an economic

consulting firm and manages money. During the 1980s, Mr. Shilling frequently made gloomy forecasts about the economy and thus saw sharply lower interest rates ahead. His forecasts often were a long way off the mark, but investors who bet on his rate forecasts by putting their money in long-term bonds did very well.

Despite the economists' unenviable record, Mr. Beckwitt is sympathetic. "I wouldn't want to have that job—and I'm glad I don't have it," he says.

Moreover, like many other investment managers, he says he still thinks it's important to keep up with consensus forecasts. "It helps me get a sense of literally what is priced in the market at the current time," he says.

Mr. Volcker once quipped that economists and arthritis specialists have several things in common. Both, he said, are better at diagnosis than at cures; and both are better at explaining what happened than at predicting.

"And despite our years of learning and our efforts at education, we still find our patients and clients longing for relief turning, with distressing frequency, to today's equivalent of snake oil and witchcraft," Mr. Volcker concluded.

As for John Kenneth Galbraith, the well-known professor, author and, yes, economist, he says the abysmal performance of so many high-paid forecasters "does not surprise me at all." He adds: "The association of intelligence with money is deeply suspect. This should be everyone's guiding rule."

Source: Tom Herman, "How to Profit from Economists' Forecasts," *The Wall Street Journal*, January 22, 1993, C1.

end of the third quarter of each year, *Business Week* asks 50 prominent economists to forecast economic activity for the upcoming year. How did the group do in 1992? Figure 9.6 shows their predicted and actual growth rates in real GDP for the forecast period. (The quarterly figures are seasonally adjusted at annual rates.)

As it turned out, the consensus forecast from the group was pretty much on the mark for 1992. The actual growth in real GDP turned out to be 2.1 percent compared to the consensus forecast of 2.2 percent. What the forecasters missed, however, was the erratic pattern of GDP growth during the year. The consensus forecast predicted slow growth during the first half of the year, followed by stronger growth during the second half. As it turned out, the economy grew much faster than the group expected during the first quarter of 1992 (2.8 percent versus 0.5 percent) and much slower than the group expected during the final quarter of the year (1.2 percent versus 3.2 percent). Even though the forecasters pretty accurately predicted growth for all of 1992, in only one quarter of the five shown did their forecast come

Figure 9.6

Actual versus Forecast Growth Rates in Real U.S. GDP: 1992

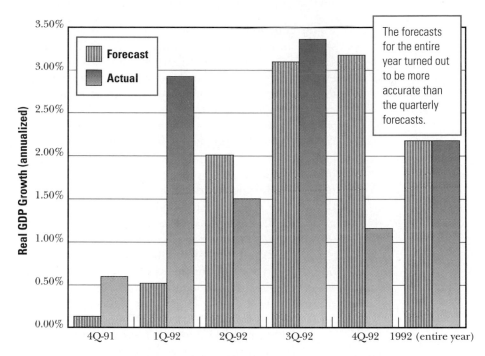

> The forecasts for the entire year turned out to be more accurate than the quarterly forecasts.

Source: *Business Week,* December 30, 1991, p. 63, and *Survey of Current Business,* March 1993.

close to the actual growth rate in real GDP. (That was the third quarter of 1992.)[21]

Why Is Economic Forecasting Difficult? If economists don't have a great record forecasting future economic activity, the next question is, why? In Chapter 6 we saw that security analysts don't have a great track record forecasting future earnings of companies, and we discussed some reasons for this. Many of the same explanations apply to economic forecasts. First, all forecasting is difficult, and forecasting economic activity is probably more difficult than forecasting earnings. Aside from data problems, the U.S. economy is an extremely complex system that has come to be interrelated with an even more complex system, the global economy. Second, the impact of random shocks on economic activity (like the flooding of the Mississippi River basin in the summer of 1993) can be both significant and unpredictable. Third, most economic forecasting models are derived from historic data, which give few clues about major structural or secular changes in the economy, such as corporate downsizings like those at Kodak, IBM, and Xerox, which have become so common today.

Critics argue that economic forecasters tend to respect momentum too much and believe that the next business cycle will look like the last business cycle, when in fact it may not due to major secular changes. Finally, human

---

[21]*Business Week* also asks the group to forecast inflation for the upcoming year, and the unemployment and prime interest rates at the end of the upcoming year. In 1991, the group forecasted a 1992 inflation rate (as measured by the CPI) of 3.3 percent, an end-of-year unemployment rate of 6.8 percent, and an end of year prime rate of 7.3 percent. The actual inflation rate turned out to be 2.9 percent, unemployment stood at 7.3 percent at the end of the year, and the prime rate was 6.0 percent.

psychology may play a role. Economic forecasters, like securities analysts, may be reluctant to forecast bad news. According to Victor Zarnowitz, "Few forecasters take the risk of signaling a recession prematurely, as the costs of such prediction to themselves and their customers can be quite high."[22]

Using Economic Forecasts. In light of their poor record of accuracy, how should investors use economic forecasts? The flip answer is that investors should take what economic forecasters have to say with a grain of salt. However, even if specific numbers aren't very accurate, the commentary behind the numbers may be valuable. How did economists come up with their forecasts? What variables did they consider? *Why* forecasters think the economy will grow slowly next year, for example, could be very useful to investors. Investors should ask why economists believe inflation and interest rates are likely to rise or fall, or why the dollar is likely to grow stronger against most other currencies. A good economic forecast will address these types of questions, and the answers deserve attention by investors. Like securities analysts, the general directions implied by economists' forecasts may provide much more insight than their forecasts of specific values like next year's GDP growth rate or inflation.

Say, for example, that an analyst wants to know about the airline industry, or possibly a specific airline stock. Trends in oil prices (and thus the price of jet fuel) have a major impact on airline profitability, and thus the attractiveness of airline stocks in general. If an economist forecasts falling oil prices for the next couple of years, and the reasons behind the forecast make sense, that's important and valuable information. Whether the economist's specific forecast of oil prices falling by $2.50 per barrel over the next 12 months turns out to be 15 cents too high or too low is much less important.

As another example, assume an analyst follows several retailing stocks, one of which is Nordstrom's, an upscale department store chain. Over half of Nordstrom's sales come from stores located in California. If an economist expects the California economy to grow far more slowly than the rest of the nation's economy, and the economist's reasoning makes sense, that's valuable information. It suggests that Nordstrom's prospects may be less favorable than those of other retailers who don't depend as much on California sales.

Industry Analysis

Having completed an economic analysis, an investor should turn to the next step in the securities analysis process: industry analysis. We begin with a discussion of how to define and classify industries.

Defining and Classifying Industries

In a broad sense, an industry might be considered a community that shares common interests that distinguish it from other communities. The dictionary defines an industry as, "a distinct group of productive or profit-making enterprises."[23] At first glance, this definition seems pretty clearcut. However, in practice, classifying industries can be difficult and the results somewhat ambiguous. Further, assigning specific companies to particular industries is sometimes no easy task.

There are several simple ways to classify industries. One obvious method is to classify industries by product or service (e.g., the chemical industry, the

---

[22]*Fortune,* January 27, 1992.

[23]*Webster's Ninth New Collegiate Dictionary* (Springfield, Mass.: Merriam-Webster, 1984), 617.

Table 9.7

Industry Classification Systems

		Dow Jones	Standard & Poor's
A.	**Major Groups**	1. Basic materials	1. Aerospace
		2. Conglomerates	2. Automotive
		3. Consumer cyclical	3. Banks
		4. Consumer noncyclical	4. Chemicals
		5. Energy	5. Conglomerates
		6. Financial services	6. Consumer products
		7. Industrial	7. Containers and packaging
		8. Technology	8. Discount and fashion retailers
		9. Utilities	9. Electrical and electronics
			10. Food
			11. Fuel
			12. Health care
			13. Housing and real estate
			14. Leisure-time industries
			15. Manufacturing
			16. Metals and mining
			17. Nonbank financial
			18. Office equipment and computers
			19. Paper and forest products
			20. Publishing and broadcasting
			21. Service industries
			22. Telecommunications
			23. Transportation
			24. Utilities and power

		Group 5 (Energy)	Group 11 (Fuel)
B.	**Subdivision**	a. Coal	a. Coal
		b. Oil (drilling)	b. Oil and gas
		c. Oil (integrated majors)	c. Petroleum services
		d. Oil (secondary)	
		e. Oilfield equipment	
		f. Pipelines[a]	

[a]In the S&P classification system, most pipeline companies are included in utilities and power (major group), oil and gas transmission (secondary group).

Sources: Dow Jones & Company; Standard & Poor's.

airline industry, the restaurant industry, and so forth). Another simple way of classifying industries is based on their reactions to the business cycle. A **cyclical industry** is one whose performance tends to be positively related to economic activity. Examples of cyclical industries include auto makers and home builders. A **defensive industry** is one whose performance tends to be relatively insensitive to economic activity, despite some cyclical ups and downs. Examples of defensive industries include electric and gas utilities and the drug industry. A **growth industry** is characterized by rapid growth in sales and earnings, often independent of the business cycle. Examples of growth industries during the 1990s include biotechnology and semiconductors.

A number of nongovernment organizations have industrial classification systems based on product (good or service) and business cycle characteristics. Two examples are Dow Jones and Standard & Poor's. Both divide companies initially into major industry groups, as Table 9.7 shows. They then subdivide each major industry group into secondary groups. As you can see,

Dow Jones divides companies into nine major groups, while S&P divides them initially into 24 major groups. Table 9.7 also breaks down the Dow Jones energy group and the S&P fuel group into their various subdivisions. The two systems differ substantially. Dow Jones, for example, includes pipeline companies as part of its energy industry, whereas S&P includes them as part of its utility industry. Investors should be aware of such differences in industry classifications.

These classification systems often define industries by grouping firms that are not very homogeneous. Take the airline industry as an example. Both Dow Jones and S&P put all airlines into one subgroup. Although each company in the industry provides the same service, flying people from Point A to Point B, grouping them masks difference among large domestic airlines (such as Delta), foreign airlines (such as British Airways), regional airlines (such as Southwest), and commuter airlines (such as Atlantic Southeast). Obviously all the companies in this industry are affected by some of the same general factors (e.g., the price of jet fuel), but this is still a diverse group. Today, many of the regional and commuter airlines are doing much better financially than the major domestic and international airlines.

Standard Industry Classification System. In an attempt to organize the massive amount of economic data it collects, the federal government developed the **Standard Industry Classification (SIC)** system.[24] The classification covers all organizations and is updated about every ten years to reflect the economy's changing industrial organization.

The SIC system goes from the general to the specific by initially dividing all organizations into 11 divisions identified by one-digit SIC codes. It subdivides each division into major groups, each with its two-digit SIC code. It further subdivides each major group into smaller groups with three-digit codes and, finally, into detailed groups with four-digit codes. Companies with the same four-digit SIC are considered to form a homogeneous industry group.

While it's very useful to the industry analyst, the SIC system is not perfect. Many divisions and subdivisions are arbitrary, and they can rapidly become outdated. Further, even though many four-digit industry groups are homogeneous, there are some notable exceptions. For example, all airlines, from majors to commuters, fall into a single four-digit industry group.

The point is, be careful when looking at any industry classification system. Otherwise, the quality of analysis may suffer. It isn't difficult, for example, to inadvertently compare a specific company's data to averages for the wrong industry.

Components of Industry Analysis

In a nutshell, industry analysis has two general objectives. The first is to determine the long-term, secular trend of the industry, while the second is to ascertain the industry's cyclical pattern around its long-term, secular trend. In order to meet these general objectives, a thorough industry analysis needs to consider a number of issues, both quantitative and qualitative. The following list includes brief discussions of eight of the most pertinent issues. The more qualitative issues are listed first.

1. Competitive Structure of the Industry. The analyst should start by listing all the companies that operate in the industry (both domestically and globally, if appropriate). It may also be useful to determine how many are publicly

---

[24]The United Nations has developed a similar system for international business and public organizations.

Figure 9.7

Projected Japanese Population Change by Age Group: 1991–2000

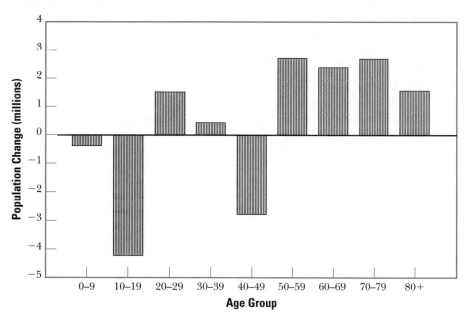

The projected trends in the age distribution of the Japanese population show a large increase in persons 50 and older and a decrease or only slight increase in persons 20 to 49. Most analysts view these demographic trends as unfavorable for the retailing industry.

Source: U.S. Census Bureau International Database.

traded, how many are privately owned or owned by other companies, and, perhaps, how many are government owned. The analyst should then consider some questions: Which companies have the largest market shares? Have their market shares been rising or falling (i.e., has the industry become more or less concentrated) during the last few years? Has the number of competitors been rising or falling in recent years?

2. Permanence. In this age of rapid changes in technology and major demographic trends, the permanence of an industry has become an important issue. Could technological changes, for example, make the industry obsolete in a short period of time? A single technological change, the electric refrigerator introduced in 1927 by GE, doomed the ice companies. Ice companies were among the most established and profitable companies in the United States at that time.

Demographic, economic, and lifestyle trends can also affect the permanence of an industry. Such trends in the United States have been very favorable over the last few years to home builders and related industries, such as appliances and furniture. In fact, furniture stocks were among the best performing industry groups in 1993.

Another example of the impact of demographic trends is shown in Figure 9.7. It shows projected changes in the population of Japan, by various age groups, between 1991 and 2000. The projections show an aging population, with an actual decline in the number of persons between 20 and 49. Since those 20 to 49 year olds are significant consumers, many experts contend that this demographic trend does not favor the retailing industry in Japan.

3. Vulnerability to External Shocks. How vulnerable is the profitability and performance of an industry to some dramatic economic, political, or natural event? As an example, consider what happened to the airline industry during the Persian Gulf crisis of 1990 to 1991. When Iraq invaded Kuwait on August 2, 1990, fear gripped the world oil market. The price of crude oil soared, and with it, the price of jet fuel. Between July and October 1990, the price of jet fuel more than doubled (from 55.3 cents to 115.8 cents per gallon). Since each penny increase in the price of jet fuel costs U.S. airlines something like $150 million per year, this increase devastated airlines' profitability. During the second quarter of 1990, U.S. airlines had an after-tax profit of $503 million; the industry lost $218 million in the third quarter, and $3,647 million in the fourth quarter. If airlines want to continue operating, they have little choice but to pay the going rate for jet fuel, over which they have little control.

4. Regulatory and Tax Conditions: Government Relations. The analyst should determine whether an industry is subject to any special or unusual government regulation at either the federal or state level. The electric utility industry, for example, is subject to much more government regulation than the typical industry. Some industries' foreign operations are subject to more regulation by other countries' governments than the U.S. government imposes.

Tax issues must be considered. The key question is whether the industry is subject to any special tax treatment with either positive or negative effects. The oil and gas industry, for example, has traditionally been subject to special tax treatment compared to most industries ranging from oil depletion allowances to windfall profits taxes.

The analyst should also keep an eye on emerging federal legislation that may have a special impact on an industry. The 1990 Clean Air Act Amendments, for example, require reduced emissions of air pollutants at around 800 coal-fired power plants. Standard & Poor's estimates that complying with the Clean Air Act will cost the affected electric utilities between $5 billion and $7 billion.

5. Labor Conditions. The key questions concerning labor conditions deal mostly with unions, including the percentage of the work force that is unionized and whether that percentage is rising or falling. The industry's overall relationship with the unions is important, as well. Further, even if the industry's work force is not heavily unionized, the analyst still needs to check for unusual labor conditions. For example, does the industry have a difficult time finding and retaining workers? Does it have an unusually high number of workers' compensation claims? The airline industry has been historically troubled by labor problems (both union and nonunion).

6. Historical Record of Revenue, Earnings, and Dividends. The analyst should compile a historical record of industry revenue, earnings, and dividends over at least two complete business cycles. This review should look for obvious patterns and trends. Have industry revenue and earnings been growing at above-average rates? Have industry earnings been growing more quickly or slowly than industry revenues? Do patterns in revenue and earnings suggest that the industry is cyclical? What percentage of industry earnings are paid in dividends? Has this percentage changed over time? The historical record can help answer these types of questions.

The analyst should also examine the industry's cost structure. Obviously, if earnings have risen faster than revenue, the industry's costs, as a percentage of revenue, are falling. However, the analyst needs to determine the relationship between fixed and variable costs (operating leverage), as well. High operating leverage means that a given increase in revenue can translate to a still larger increase in operating profits. The airline industry has a high fixed-cost component; it costs about the same for an airline to operate regardless of whether its load factor (the percentage of seats filled with paying passengers) is 50 percent or 80 percent.

Table 9.8

Balance Sheet of U.S. Airline Industry:
1991 and 1992

| | Year Ending 12/31/92 | | Year Ending 12/31/91 | |
	$ Millions	Percentage of Total	$ Millions	Percentage of Total
Current assets	$15,696	20.8%	$14,883	21.2%
Noncurrent assets	59,728	79.2	55,449	78.8
Total assets	$75,424	100.0%	$70,332	100.0%
Current liabilities	$24,017	31.8%	$24,023	34.1%
Noncurrent liabilities	33,690	44.7	25,569	36.4
Stockholders' equity	17,717	23.5	20,740	29.5
Total liabilities and equity	$75,424	100.0%	$70,332	100.0%

Source: U.S. Department of Transportation.

7. Financial and Financing Issues. What does the industry's balance sheet look like, and how has it changed over the last couple of years? The analyst should evaluate how much leverage is common in the industry, how asset-intensive its operations are (the ratio of revenues to assets), and so forth. If an industry needs to make substantial capital investments in the near future, how much of the needed funds will it have to raise externally?

Take a look at the airline industry balance sheet, shown in Table 9.8. (It's not a very pretty picture, is it?) Not surprisingly, about 80 percent of the industry's assets are noncurrent (most, of course, are aircraft). On the right side of the balance sheet, airlines are not awash in liquidity (current liabilities exceeded current assets at the end of 1992 by about $8.5 billion). Leverage is high in the industry. Long-term debt exceeded stockholder equity at the end of 1992 and the industry's debt ratio (total liabilities divided by total assets) was 76.5 percent, up from 70.5 percent at the end of 1991. The industry lost almost $2.4 billion in 1992. Given the state of the airline industry's balance sheet, substantial future capital investment will likely require external financing.

8. Industry Stock Price Valuation. Finally, the analyst needs to consider how investors have historically valued the industry's stocks, though, once again, the past is no guarantee of the future. For example, does the industry price/earnings ratio typically exceed that of the overall market? Has the industry's price/earnings ratio changed in recent years? How does the price/earnings ratio compare to the growth rate in industry earnings? As we discussed in Chapter 8, a stock's price/earnings multiple should generally have a positive relationship with its expected earnings growth rate.

Historically, some industries have sold for higher price/earnings multiples than other industries, which could be explained by differences in their expected earnings growth rates. At the end of 1992, for example, banking stocks and health care stocks had roughly the same expected growth rate in earnings for 1993 to 1995, about 15 percent per year. Banking had an average price/earnings ratio of 13, however, while health care stocks were selling for an average of 20 times earnings.

The analyst should also see how industry stocks have performed, measured by price appreciation as well as total returns, relative to an appropriate broad market average. As we saw in Table 9.1, both bull and bear markets have seen substantial variation in price performance among various industry groups.

Figure 9.8

Industry Life Cycle

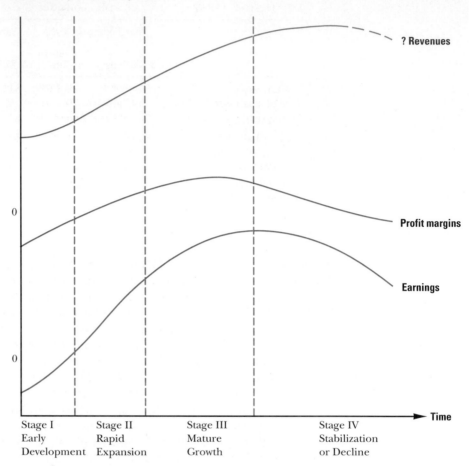

Source: Cohen et al., *Investment Analysis and Portfolio Management,* Fifth Edition, Irwin © 1987, page 376.

Industry Life Cycles

The **industry life cycle theory** provides a framework in which to understand many of the pertinent issues we just discussed. This theory argues that every industry goes through a life cycle consisting of four stages: birth, growth, mature growth, and stabilization/decline. These stages are illustrated in Figure 9.8. Gauging an industry's position in its life cycle may help the analyst gain some important insight into the industry's investment potential.

Before we briefly describe each phase of the industry life cycle, remember that the theory is very general and the life cycles of specific industries differ substantially. For one thing, the speed at which industries move from phase to phase varies. Some industries, for example, stay in a mature growth phase much longer than other industries. Industries even appear to have skipped entire phases. Further, the transition from phase to phase may be very subtle and gradual. Also, technological changes can sometimes cause a very mature industry to revert back to a growth industry. In the early 1900s, for example, the oil industry was considered to be a very mature, perhaps even declining, industry. Oil was used primarily to light lamps, and the development of electric lighting was eroding the demand for oil. The development of the automobile and the internal cumbustion engine suddenly launched the oil industry into a major new growth phase.

The oil industry example also illustrates that the industry life cycle is not always a one way progression. Industries can go backward as well as forward in their life cycles. For another example, consider the aluminum industry. In the 1930s, aluminum was considered to be a dying industry; production was falling rapidly, both in absolute terms and relative to overall industrial production. During the early 1940s, in order to supply the burgeoning aircraft industry during World War II, aluminum production rose much faster than overall industrial production. Between 1939 and 1945, U.S. industrial production rose 60 percent while aluminum production rose 110 percent. The growth in aircraft production slowed following the end of World War II, and aluminum production actually started to fall. The aluminum industry then entered another phase of rapid growth between 1950 and 1974. The index of aluminum production rose over 579 percent compared to a 170 percent increase in the index of overall industrial production. Since 1974, the aluminum industry has exhibited characteristics of a very mature industry and has grown at about the same rate as the overall economy. With these comments in mind, let's look at each phase in the industry life cycle.

Birth Phase. Industries are often born to exploit a major technical advancement or the invention of some new product. The development of the internal combustion engine, for example, helped give birth to the automobile industry. Infant industries often exhibit a number of important characteristics. Costs are high, product quality is uneven, sales growth is erratic, and profitability is low. (The industry may actually lose money for most, if not all, of the birth phase.) Birth-phase industries are often highly competitive and dynamic with many companies entering and exiting.[25]

The birth phase is perhaps the riskiest stage for stock investors, though the rewards can be substantial. A stock investor in an infant industry bets on two things: that the industry and its new good or service will survive infancy (some don't) and that a specific company will be among the survivors.

Growth Phase. An industry's growth phase is often characterized by a faster sales growth rate than the overall economy. Further, industry sales may be less vulnerable to a cyclical downturn in the overall economy compared to more mature industries. As the industry is growing, the quality of its product (either a good or a service) usually improves. Prices often fall, either in absolute or relative terms.[26] Costs tend to fall as production becomes more efficient and capital investment requirements decline. Industry profitability improves, as well. During the growth phase, more companies exit the industry than enter it. A few companies tend to grab the lion's share of the industry's growth.

Many analysts consider the growth phase to be the best time to invest in an industry. The product has proven itself and profits are growing rapidly. Stock investors should generally stick with industry leaders, since they're more likely to prosper; however, be careful of paying too much, as discussed in Chapter 8. Also, investors should not expect substantial cash dividends. Further, many industries have failed to make the transition from a short

---

[25]There have been some important exceptions to this. In the 1930s, the synthetic fibers industry was born when DuPont invented nylon. However, due to financial and technical factors, as well as patent protection, no companies emerged to compete with DuPont for many years.

[26]By a relative price decline, we mean that prices for the industry's product may not rise as quickly as prices in general. A relative price decline could also occur if the quality of the industry's products improves relative to price. Think about a car. This year's model is the same as last year's model, except it offers air bags and antilock brakes as standard equipment. If the price of this year's model was only $50 more than last year's model, wouldn't you say that the car's *relative price* had fallen?

period of very rapid growth to a longer period of slower, more sustainable growth to reach the next phase.[27]

Mature Growth Phase. During the mature growth phase, the sales growth rate starts to slow and industry performance may become more cyclical. Product demand starts to near its saturation point, and the industry may begin to face inroads from newer products competing for the same basic market. The competitive structure of the industry is generally quite stable; few companies either enter or exit the industry. In addition, large barriers to entry may have developed. As the industry matures, it becomes more difficult to increase demand by reducing prices or improving quality. Companies put more effort into gaining market share in mature industries. Capital investment requirements have fallen to relatively low levels and profits tend to be high. This is often the most profitable stage in the industry life cycle.

This phase imposes lower risk on investors than the rapid growth phase, especially if investors stick to the industry leaders. Even though growth is slowing, profits are high and dividend yields are likely to be above average. Investors shouldn't become complacent, however. If growth slows too much, for example, future profits could diminish as competitors start to aggressively cut prices to boost their market shares.

Stabilization or Decline Phase. A mature growth phase can last for a very long time, and an industry nearing the end of its mature growth phase may begin to grow more rapidly due to technological or demographic changes. Emerging global markets may help to pump more life into very mature industries. Barring those changes, however, a typical industry eventually reaches a stabilization or decline phase.

Conditions in this last phase are difficult to generalize. In the stabilization or decline phase, industry sales may continue to grow, but more slowly than the overall economy. Alternatively, sales may stabilize to meet replacement demand, which neither increases nor decreases. On the other hand, sales may actually start to fall in absolute terms and the industry may eventually disappear. Profitability generally follows the trend in sales.

This can be a difficult phase for investors. If the industry is stable, some companies may be good investments. These stocks may have less risk, and pay higher dividends, than the average stock. On the other hand, as a general rule, most investors should probably avoid declining industries. These companies often have falling profits and deteriorating balance sheets. Further, companies in declining industries face strong temptations to embark on ill-conceived, poorly planned diversification efforts to restore growth. These ventures often end up hurting shareholders even more. However, analysts should always carefully monitor declining industries for, as history has shown, their fortunes can rapidly improve due to external factors. (Remember what the automobile did for the oil industry, and what growth spurts in aircraft production did for the aluminum industry.)

Analyzing Industry Data

So far in our examination of industry analysis, we've discussed what the analyst ought to look for and what type of information he or she should obtain

---

[27]See "Emerging Growth Stocks: Why so Many Peak so Early," *Forbes,* January 28, 1985. According to the article, one common reason many government industries burn out is the industry's failure to develop followup products or services that build naturally on the initial success of the industry.

Figure 9.9

Worldwide Semiconductor Consumption by Type of
Product: 1992

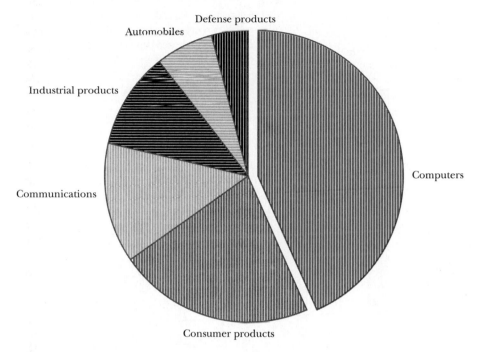

Source: Standard & Poor's, *Industry Survey (Electronics),* June 10, 1992, E17.

concerning the industry. At this point we turn our attention to ways investors
can analyze this information in order to further evaluate an industry.

End-Use Analysis. An important tool is **end-use,** or product-demand, **analysis,** in which the analyst attempts to identify the source of demand for the
industry's product and, in the process, to uncover relationships that help to
explain demand. Understanding these relationships will likely help the analyst make more accurate forecasts of future industry revenues and earnings.
One way to do this is to analyze who uses the industry's product and how
the demand for the product is likely to change for each user.

As an example, let's briefly look at the semiconductor industry. Who uses
semiconductors? Obviously the major user is the personal computer industry
(40 percent of semiconductors were computer chips in 1992), but the telecommunications, electronics, defense, and automotive industries use semiconductors, as well. Figure 9.9 shows in the distribution of worldwide semiconductor consumption in 1992.

What's the outlook for each user of semiconductors over the period from
1994 to 1998? According to Standard & Poor's, demand from the personal
computer industry should increase at an annual rate of about 10 percent,
the value of semiconductors in the typical new car should double by 1998,
and demand by the electronics and telecommunications industries should
also continue to show strong growth.[28] For example, sales of semiconductors
to the telecommunications industry for use in integrated services digital networks are expected to increase more than tenfold by 1998 to $400 million.
Among current users, only the defense industry's demand for semiconductors should remain flat. Defense, however, makes up only 3 percent of the

---

[28]Standard & Poor's, *Industry Survey (Electronics),* June 10, 1992.

Figure 9.10

Ratio of Auto Production to Overall Industrial Production: 1967–1993

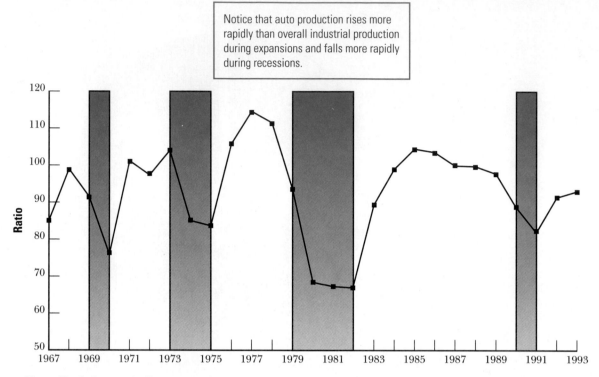

Notice that auto production rises more rapidly than overall industrial production during expansions and falls more rapidly during recessions.

Note: Shaded areas indicate recessions.

Source: *Survey of Current Business,* various issues.

market for semiconductors. Taken together, S&P forecasts worldwide semiconductor sales of $130 billion by 1998, up from approximately $69 billion in 1992.

Ratio Analysis. **Ratio analysis** with industries involves dividing industry data by aggregate economic data over a period of time. The movement, or lack of movement, in a ratio may suggest some important characteristics of the industry. Let's look at two examples.

Figure 9.10 illustrates the ratio of the auto production index to the overall industrial production index between 1967 and 1992. A ratio equal to 100 would mean that the two production indexes were the same. A rising ratio over time would suggest growth in the auto industry. On the other hand, a falling ratio over time would suggest decline. Figure 9.10 shows no obvious upward or downward trend, suggesting that the auto industry is a mature, cyclical industry. Notice, however, that the ratio between auto production and overall industrial production falls sharply prior to and during recessions (the shaded areas in Figure 9.10) and rises sharply early in economic expansions. This suggests that, while the auto industry is cyclical in nature, it is more volatile than the overall economy, especially around turning points in economic activity.

As we noted, one characteristic of growth industries is falling product prices. The semiconductor industry has been a growth industry throughout much of the 1980s and early 1990s, as reflected in its average prices. For example, between 1984 and 1993, the prices of all finished goods rose at an annual rate of slightly more than 2 percent. By contrast, the prices of semiconductors actually *fell* by an average of about 0.5 percent per year. The five-

Figure 9.11

Annual Auto Sales versus Gross Domestic Product: 1959–1992

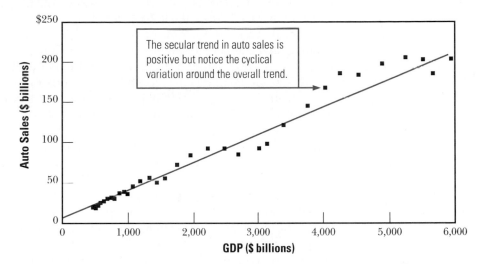

Source: *Survey of Current Business,* various issues.

year period between 1988 and 1993 showed an even more dramatic drop in the prices of semiconductors. The prices of all finished goods rose an average of 2.6 percent per year between 1988 and 1993; the prices of semiconductors fell by an average of 2.1 percent per year over the same period. As we discussed earlier, this price drop ignores the substantial improvement in the quality and performance of semiconductors in recent years.

Regression and Correlation Analysis. Statistics offers two useful and fairly simple techniques for analyzing demand and other industry data: **correlation analysis** and **regression analysis.**[29] For one thing, these techniques help to quantify many important relationships. As you may remember from statistics, bivariate regression (regression with two variables) is a mathematical process that fits a line to a series of points on an *XY* scatter diagram. *Y* is the dependent variable and *X* is the independent variable. The model states that *Y* is a function of *X* (for example, the level of industry sales is a function of GDP). Correlation analysis evaluates the strength of the relationship between *X* and *Y.*

Figure 9.11 shows an *XY* scatter diagram. The *X* axis measures GDP and the *Y* axis measures auto sales (both stated in nominal dollars). The regression line is also shown. In equation form, the regression line can be expressed as:

$$\text{Auto sales}_t = 1.7818 + 0.0367(\text{GDP}_t),\ R^2 = 0.97$$

where *t* refers to the year to be analyzed. The value of *Y* on the regression line is the predicted value of *Y,* for a given level of *X.*

The regression equation helps the analyst to forecast next year's auto sales, based on economic activity. Assume that a forecast states that the economy next year will grow, in real terms, at 2.5 percent with a 3 percent inflation

[29]A number of technical effects of regression and correlation analysis are beyond the scope of this textbook. Both techniques, for example, make a number of assumptions about the data being used. Violation of these assumptions can create problems in some situations. We suggest you consult a standard statistics or econometrics textbook.

rate. Nominal GDP, therefore, should increase by about 5.58 percent $(1.025 \times 1.030) - 1$. If this year's nominal GDP equals \$5,950.7 billion, next year's nominal GDP should equal \$6,282.8 billion (\$5,950.7 × 1.0558). For a nominal GDP of \$6,282.8 billion, the regression equation gives auto sales of \$232.36 billion $1.7818 + 0.0367(\$6,282.8)$.

Notice that most of the dots in Figure 9.11 fall close to the regression line, meaning that the actual and predicted values for annual auto sales match fairly closely. This suggests a strong relationship between GDP and auto sales. The R^2 statistic measures the strength of this relationship more precisely. It ranges from 0 to 1, and an R^2 closer to 1 indicates a stronger statistical relationship between the two variables.[30] A value of 0.97 for R^2 confirms the strong relationship between auto sales and GDP.

Does this strong historical relationship allow the analyst to rely on the forecast of \$232.36 billion for next year's auto sales? The answer to the question is both *yes* and *no*.

Figure 9.11 shows the secular trend in auto sales in relation to the trend in GDP. Both have increased at about the same rate as the overall economy. Notice that Figure 9.11 also shows the cyclical variation of auto sales around the secular trend. Remember from Figure 9.10, however, that the auto industry tends to be more volatile than the overall economy. Therefore, auto sales tend to be above the secular trend during periods of strong economic growth, especially when the economy is coming out of a recession. Auto sales tend to be below the secular trend during periods of slow economic growth, especially when the economy is entering a recession.

As a result, the forecast produced by the regression equation is a good starting point. The analyst might want to adjust the forecast upward or downward, depending on a number of factors. For example, if he or she feels that economic growth will be below normal next year, perhaps giving early signs of recession, the analyst should probably lower his or her forecast below the secular trend.

Regression and correlation analysis can help an industry analyst explore many other relationships. One important relationship is that between industry revenue and industry profits. Figure 9.12 shows another *XY* scatter diagram for the electric and gas utilities industry for the time period 1974 through 1993. The *X* axis measures operating revenue while the *Y* axis measures operating profits. Clearly, there is a strong, positive relationship between industry revenue and profits. The regression equation equals:

$$\text{Profits}_t = -1,476.56 + 0.18(\text{Revenues}_t), \ R^2 = 0.98$$

An increase in industry operating revenue of \$100 million produces an increase in industry operating profits of about \$18 million.

As before, the regression equation can help the analyst to forecast future industry profits. Assume that a forecast projects next year's industry revenue at \$200,000 million. At that level of revenue, the regression equation predicts operating profits of around \$34,523 million, $-1,476.56 + 0.18(200,000)$.

Finally, let's look at a relationship where regression and correlation have a different use. Figure 9.13 illustrates the relationship between airline industry revenue and profits between 1959 and 1993. The diagram appears to show no relationship between the two series. The estimated regression equation is:

$$\text{Profits}_t = 568.3 - 0.02(\text{Revenues}_t), \ R^2 = 0.28$$

A couple of comments are in order. First, notice that the estimated slope is

---

[30]For a bivariate regression, R^2 is the square of the correlation coefficient.

Figure 9.12

Operating Revenue versus Operating Income for U.S. Electric and Gas Utilities: 1974–1993

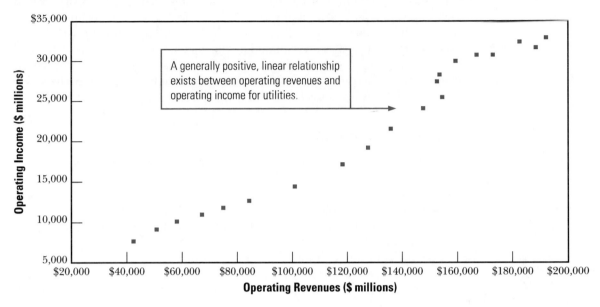

A generally positive, linear relationship exists between operating revenues and operating income for utilities.

Source: Edison Electric Institute.

Figure 9.13

Airline Industry Net Income versus Revenue: 1959–1993

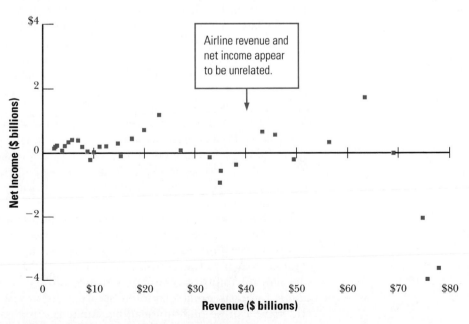

Airline revenue and net income appear to be unrelated.

Source: U.S. Department of Transportation.

negative, indicating an inverse relationship between airline revenue and profits. The more money airlines take in, the more they lose! Second, the R^2 is quite small, suggesting that the relationship is pretty weak. Obviously, this regression equation is not much of a forecasting tool. This means simply that airline revenue and profitability are not very closely related. Airlines cannot necessarily become more profitable merely by increasing their revenues.

Security macroanalysis must evaluate many economic and industry factors. While analyzing economic and industry factors can provide important insight, the process must continue with a thorough company analysis. We turn to company analysis starting in the next chapter.

Chapter Summary

1. **Understand why economic and industry analyses are important.**
   Economic and industry analysis are the macroanalytical components of securities analysis. While economic and industry analysis are important, neither can substitute for careful examinations of specific stocks and companies. Economic analysis is important simply because economic activity has historically shown a strong, positive relationship with stock prices. Industry analysis is important because during both up and down markets, performance has differed substantially between various industry groups. Finally, it is naive to assume that the fortunes of individual companies are entirely independent of the prospects for the overall economy and the industries in which those companies operate. The simple dividend growth model for valuing common stocks would be difficult to implement without some feel for future economic and industry conditions.

2. **Review the relationship between business cycles and investment decisions.**
   A typical business cycle runs through periodic phases of expansion and contraction, though no two have ever looked exactly the same. Historically, stock prices have led the overall business cycle, generally peaking about six months prior to economic peaks and bottoming out about five months prior to troughs. However, several large declines in stock prices have failed to foreshadow recessions. Stock prices are also related to inflation, though *rising* rates of inflation do appear to depress stock prices more than inflation itself. Historically, some industry groups have performed best, relative to the overall market, early in bull markets, while other industry groups have been the best performers later in bull markets. Interest rates tend to move up and down with the business cycle due to inflation and changes in the demand for loanable funds. Yield spreads (based on both maturity and quality) tend to widen and narrow at various points in the business cycle. Quality yield spreads, for example, tend to be the widest at the ends of recessions and the narrowest at the ends of expansions. Finally, with the usual warning that the past is no guarantee of the future, we examined some investment timing implications. In anticipation of an economic expansion, for example, stock investors should allocate greater shares of their portfolios to cyclical stocks, especially those with high betas.

3. **Examine economic forecasting techniques and issues.**
   Economic forecasting is important for investors, both to foresee turning points in the business cycle and to estimate important future economic variables (such as the growth rate in real GDP and inflation). The accuracy and reliability of economic statistics and data affect the value of economic forecasts. Some economic statistics are not as reliable as we'd like, and some can be quite misleading. Analysts often combine the two basic approaches to economic forecasting: qualitative and quantitative methods. Qualitative forecasting involves subjective analysis of economic data

and statistics in order to come up with general forecasts of future economic activity. Qualitative forecasters look at leading indicator series and anticipation surveys. Quantitative forecasters build econometric models to estimate both directions and magnitudes of future economic trends. Finally, we discussed the accuracy and applications of economic forecasts. Economists don't have a great track record in forecasting future economic activity, though they may be getting better. The reasons for their difficulty include the complexity of the economy, especially in a global context, and the impacts of random shocks. The commentary behind even very inaccurate numbers may be very useful to investors. If economists are forecasting a drop in inflation and interest rates, the reasons for their predictions may be more valuable than the actual numbers.

4. **Review industry definitions and classifications.**

   Industry analysis starts with the definition and classification of industries. Information sources have developed several classification systems, including the Standard Industry Classification (SIC) system. One problem with industry classifications is the lack of homogeneity within resulting groups. All airlines, for example, are classified into one industry group even though their financial performance levels and operating characteristics vary widely. Investors need to be careful when using any industry classification system.

5. **Outline the important components of an industry analysis.**

   A thorough industry analysis should consider at least eight quantitative and qualitative issues: the competitive structure of the industry (e.g., changes in the number of firms operating in the industry); the permanence of the industry (e.g., how changes in technology and demographics might affect the industry); the vulnerability of the industry to external shocks (e.g., the airline industry's vulnerability to rapid changes in oil prices); the industry's regulatory and tax environment (e.g., the industry's prospects for any unusual government regulation); labor conditions in the industry (e.g., a history of union problems); a historical record of revenue, earnings, and dividends (including an examination of the industry's cost structure); the industry's balance sheet (e.g., its need for external financing); and the industry's stock valuation (e.g., how the market values the industry's individual stocks).

6. **Discuss the framework and techniques used in industry analysis.**

   The industry life cycle theory provides a framework for understanding many of the industry's characteristics. This theory argues that industries go through a four-phase life cycle: birth, rapid growth, mature growth, and stabilization/decline. The rapid growth phase is usually considered the best time to invest in an industry, though each phase holds a different set of risks and rewards for investors. However, the speed with which industries move from phase to phase varies, and external changes can ignite a new growth phase even in a declining industry. Analysts use three techniques to analyze industry data. End-use analysis involves identifying the source of demand for an industry's product and, in the process, uncovers relationships that help to explain demand. Ratio analysis involves dividing industry data by aggregate economic data over a period of time and looking for trends. For example, a rising ratio of industry production to overall industrial production, even in a recession, suggests that the industry is in a rapid growth phase. Finally, regression analysis and correlation analysis can help to quantify relationships between such variables as GDP and industry revenue, or revenue and profits. If industry revenue has a strong, positive relationship to GDP, for example, then the industry is probably cyclical in nature. Regression analysis can be used as a forecasting tool, as well, in some instances.

Key Terms

Economic analysis	Consumer expectations index
Industry analysis	Econometric model
Business cycle	Cyclical industry
Yield spread	Defensive industry
Quality conscious	Growth industry
Consumer price index (CPI)	Standard Industry Classification (SIC)
Seasonally adjusted data	Industry life cycle theory
Qualitative forecasting	End-use analysis
Quantitative forecasting	Ratio analysis
Index of leading indicators	Correlation analysis
Anticipation survey	Regression analysis
Confidence index	

Mini Case   OBJECTIVE

The purpose of the Mini Case is to give you some practice interpreting some actual industry data.

Table 9.9 on the next page reports data on electric and gas utility industry revenue and operating income between 1974 and 1993, along with data on nominal GDP, overall industrial production, and utility production. Use these data to answer the following questions and perform the following exercises. (*Hint:* You'll save yourself some time and effort by entering the data in Table 9.9 into a computer spreadsheet file. You can use a spreadsheet program to perform the necessary calculations and draw the graphs.)

1. Compute the ratio of utility production to overall industrial production for each year and graph the result. Compare this graph with Figure 9.9. What conclusions concerning the utility industry can you draw from this exercise?
2. Graph the relationship between industry revenue and GDP. Regress industry revenue onto GDP. (Industry revenue is the *Y* variable and GDP is the *X* variable.) How strong is the relationship between GDP and industry revenue?
3. Assume you have a forecast that nominal GDP will grow by 5.5 percent in 1994. Using the regression you estimated in Question 2, forecast utility industry revenue. Based on your results, would you modify this forecast? If so, how would you modify it?
4. Assume you are satisfied with the forecast of industry revenue you obtained in Question 3. Can you now forecast industry operating income for 1994?

Discussion Questions and Problems

1. In general terms, why are economic and industry analyses important when evaluating specific common stocks? Discuss how economic and industry factors affect variable estimates in the constant growth model.
2. Define the term *business cycle*. Why does inflation typically increase toward the end of economic expansions and fall during the end of recessions?
3. Why do stock prices lead the business cycle? Cite an example of when a large decline in stock prices was not followed by a recession.
4. Why would we expect inflation to depress stock prices? Is there another explanation for the apparent relationship between rising (or falling) inflation and falling (or rising) stock prices?

Table 9.9

	Utility Industry ($ millions)		Nominal GDP ($ millions)	Production Indexes	
	Revenue	Income		Overall	Utility
1974	$ 42,174.6	$ 7,585.8	$1,458,600	72.7	83.5
1975	50,744.1	9,045.3	1,585,900	66.3	84.3
1976	57,970.3	10,060.0	1,768,400	72.4	87.6
1977	67,236.7	10,875.3	1,974,100	78.2	89.9
1978	74,688.2	11,734.0	2,232,700	82.6	92.7
1979	84,149.5	12,545.4	2,488,600	85.7	95.3
1980	100,811.8	14,379.4	2,708,000	84.1	95.9
1981	118,206.3	17,045.0	3,030,600	85.7	94.3
1982	127,745.1	19,086.4	3,149,600	81.9	91.8
1983	135,778.0	21,430.9	3,405,000	84.9	93.6
1984	147,893.7	23,954.9	3,777,200	92.8	97.0
1985	154,798.9	25,327.5	4,038,700	94.4	99.5
1986	152,831.7	27,226.1	4,268,600	95.3	96.3
1987	153,644.8	28,084.5	4,539,900	100.0	100.0
1988	159,488.3	29,757.9	4,900,400	105.4	104.4
1989	167,067.6	30,567.4	5,250,800	108.1	107.1
1990	173,000.0	30,528.6	5,522,200	109.2	108.0
1991	182,653.9	32,144.2	5,677,500	107.1	109.2
1992	188,535.4	31,466.0	6,038,500	106.6	111.9
1993	192,362.6	32,740.3	6,327,600	111.1	118.7

Source: *Survey of Current Business,* various issues.

5. What factors explain the relationship between interest rates and the business cycle? Historically, when during the business cycle have the sharpest declines in interest rates occurred?

6. Define the term *yield spread*. Why do yield spreads based on maturity and quality tend to rise and fall during the business cycles?

7. Why is economic forecasting important? What are the two objectives of economic forecasts?

8. What does the consumer price index measure? What are some of the issues to keep in mind when using the CPI?

9. What are the two general approaches to economic forecasting? How do the forecasts of future economic activity produced by the two approaches differ?

10. What is an anticipation survey designed to measure? Why is consumer confidence considered to be such an important leading indicator of future economic activity?

11. How effectively have economists forecasted future economic activity? Why is their track record so mixed?

12. Discuss various ways industries can be classified. What issues affect analysts' use of industry classifications?

13. List the major components of an industry analysis. What is meant by the term *permanence?*

14. What are the four stages (or phases) of the industry life cycle? Give several examples of industries that experienced renewed growth phases due to external changes.

15. What are some characteristics of the mature growth phase? Why is this phase generally the most profitable?

16. Define *end-use analysis* and *ratio analysis*. If the ratio of an industry's production index to the overall index of industrial production has remained constant over time, what kind of industry is it?

17. What is regression analysis? Discuss two industry relationships that can be examined using regression analysis.

Critical Thinking Exercises

1. This exercise requires library research. Consider the following industries: auto makers, electrical components, food, railroads, and semiconductors. Using Standard & Poor's *Industry Surveys,* find revenue and earnings growth over the most recent three-year period for each industry. In addition, find return on assets (earnings divided by assets), dividend payout, and capital expenditures for the most recent year for each industry. Using these data, answer the following questions:

   a. Classify each industry as being in a rapid growth phase, a mature growth phase, or a stabilization phase. (*Hint:* You should collect data on U.S. GDP growth during the most recent three-year period to help make these classifications. You should also consider how much revenue each industry generates from international sales.)

   b. What factors led you to make your classifications?

   c. The life cycle theory implies a negative relationship between return on assets and dividend payout. Why should such a relationship exist? Do the data you collected support this theory?

2. This exercise requires library research. Look through past issues of the *Survey of Current Business.* Each monthly issue publishes data on the 11 components that make up the index of leading indicators. Compile at least 36 consecutive monthly observations and answer the following questions:

   a. What was the overall trend in the index during your 36-month period? Did economic activity (measured by either GDP or industrial production) follow the index (e.g., move upward after the index moved upward)?

   b. Each month, how many of the 11 components moved in the same direction as the overall index? Did one or two components appear to account for all the change in the overall index during any particular month? What does this suggest to you about using the index of leading indicators to forecast future economic activity?

   c. How many of the components are seasonally adjusted? Why are these components seasonally adjusted? Pick one component which is seasonally adjusted. Compare the seasonally adjusted series to the seasonally unadjusted series. What kind of problems can seasonal adjustment present for users of economic data?

Mini Case   SOLUTION

1. The ratio equals the utility production index divided by overall industrial production. The resulting graph is shown in Figure 9.14. This graph provides an interesting contrast to Figure 9.9. That figure clearly shows that the auto industry has a strong cyclical component. Auto production rises more rapidly than overall industrial production during expansions and falls more rapidly than overall industrial production during recessions.

   The graph of utility production to industrial production doesn't show the same cyclical pattern. In fact, utility production appears to be almost unrelated to the business cycle. Utility production actually fell on a relative basis throughout much of the 1970s and early 1980s (perhaps due to rising energy efficiency). Utility production appeared to be rising slightly, relative to overall industrial production, during the early 1990s.

2. The relationship between utility industry revenue and GDP is shown in Figure 9.15. You could also graph the data on an *XY* scatter plot. (*X* would

Figure 9.14

Ratio of Utility Production to Overall Industrial Production

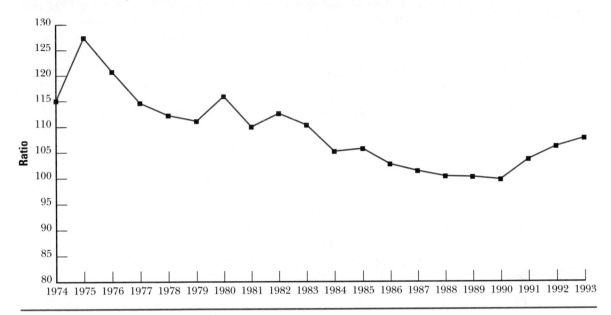

be GDP.) The graph shows that, with the exception of a period during the early 1980s, GDP and industry revenue rose at about the same rate. Indeed, over the entire 20-year period, industry revenue rose by an average of about 8.3 percent per year while nominal GDP rose by an average of approximately 8.1 percent per year. This relatively strong relationship between industry revenue and GDP is confirmed by the results of the regression:

$$\text{Industry revenue} = 14,023.54 + 0.03(\text{GDP}), \ R^2 = 0.94$$

3. Since utility industry revenue doesn't appear to exhibit the same type of

Figure 9.15

Utility Industry Revenue and Nominal GDP: 1974–1993

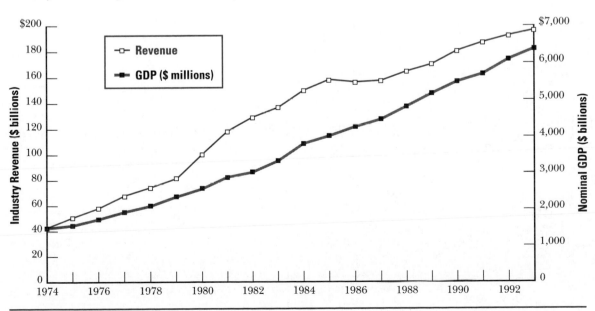

cyclical pattern as, for example, auto sales, and given the strong relationship between GDP and industry revenue, the regression equation estimated in Question 2 might give you a reasonable estimate of 1994 revenue. This assumes, of course, that the forecast of 5.5 percent growth in nominal GDP is fairly close to the mark. An increase of 5.5 percent gives us nominal GDP for 1994 of $6,675,618 million (or $6.676 trillion). Thus, the estimate of 1994 utility industry revenue, using the regression equation is:

$$14{,}023.54 + 0.03(6{,}675{,}618) = \$214{,}292 \text{ million}$$

The only modification you might want to make to this forecast is to increase it slightly because there is some evidence, from Figure 9.14, that utility production has been rising a little faster than overall industrial production in recent years.

4. Finding operating income, assuming our estimate of industry revenue is close, is not difficult. Recall from the chapter that we found a strong relationship between utility industry revenue and operating income ($R^2 = 0.98$). Using that regression equation, industry revenue of $214,292 million will produce operating income of around $37,000 million.

Chapter 10

Company Analysis: Qualitative Issues

Chapter Objectives
1. Provide an overview of company analysis.
2. Understand and analyze the competitive position of a company.
3. Describe the nature of management.
4. Review the criteria for evaluating the quality of management.
5. Discuss executive compensation and other such issues in corporate governance.

On March 16, 1992, after months of rumors and speculation, Chrysler Corporation finally announced a successor to chairman and CEO Lee Iacocca—Robert Eaton, a vice president at General Motors. Iacocca, who had been synonymous with Chrysler for over a decade, had indicated a desire to retire in 1990. Finding someone to take over had turned into one of the longest running soap opcras in U.S. corporate history. News reports named no fewer than five different individuals who had been groomed, at one time or another, to follow Iacocca.[1] For various reasons, all fell by the wayside. At the same time, some of Chrysler's directors began to worry that Iacocca was past his prime, but really didn't want to retire at the end of 1992, as he'd agreed. Finally, on March 12, 1992, the board named the outsider Eaton who took over on January 1, 1993; Iacocca remained on the board as chairman of the executive committee.

Turbulence in Chrysler's executive suite couldn't have come at a worse time for the company. Despite great strides in lowering costs and improving manufacturing efficiency, Chrysler was still considered the weakest financially of the big three auto makers. There was even talk that Ford was interested in acquiring Chrysler. In the spring of 1992, Chrysler was facing another enormous cash crunch after having lost over $795 million in 1991. The company was in the middle of bringing several promising new models to market, and, many analysts felt, Chrysler's survival depended on the success of these models.

The distraction over Iacocca's successor didn't help Chrysler's stock. From a high of 48 in 1987, Chrysler had fallen to as low as $9\frac{1}{2}$ in 1991. Investors, however, greeted the announcement of Iacocca's successor positively, and Chrysler's stock rose one-half of a point on March 17, 1992 on very heavy volume.

---

[1]See, for example, "Jockeying for Position," *Time*, March 30, 1992, 46–48.

The Chrysler story illustrates the importance of qualitative analysis of the investment potential of a company, especially the quality of the company's management. In this chapter we examine the qualitative factors and issues in company analysis. The more quantitative issues, such as those relating to financial statements and earnings forecasts, will be discussed in the next chapter. We begin Chapter 10 with an overview of company analysis, the type of information a typical company report contains, and the kinds of issues the analyst needs to consider. This is followed by a discussion of the competitive position of the company within its industry. Maintaining or expanding the company's competitive position should be one of the main objectives of management. Next, we discuss the nature of management, its objectives and functions, and the qualities managers must possess. This is followed by a discussion of criteria for evaluating the quality of a company's management. The chapter concludes with a review of some of the contemporary issues regarding executive compensation and corporate governance.

Overview of Company Analysis

Investors buy common stock hoping to earn satisfactory rates of return in relation to risk they assume in buying the stock. One key to determining whether a stock can produce the desired rate of return is its current price. A stock's attractiveness depends on the answer to the question, is it correctly priced today? As we discussed in Chapter 8, the correct price of a stock is essentially the present value of expected future cash flows (dividends and an expected future price). Since no one knows either the timing or the level of these future cash flows with certainty, investors must rely on estimates.

Future earnings are probably the most important determinant of a firm's future dividend stream and stock price. Since it pays dividends from earnings, higher future earnings often translate into higher future dividends. In addition, independent of the impact on future dividends, higher earnings usually drive a stock price higher. In a nutshell then, the major goal of company analysis is to forecast the **quality and quantity of future earnings.** All items that may materially affect future earnings must be considered in a company analysis report.

According to Graham and Dodd, the typical **company analysis report** contains the following four divisions:[2]

1. A description of the company's business and properties, including some historical data and details about senior management
2. Financial material including capitalization, a record of earnings and dividends for several complete business cycles, a flow of funds analysis, and recent balance sheets and income statements
3. Past stock price history and volume data
4. Prospects of the company in the form of projected future financial statements and analysis of the investment merits of the security

As an example of a company analysis, Investment Insights on page 312 reprints portions of a July 1993 report on Wal-Mart Stores, prepared by Donald Spindel of A. G. Edwards & Sons. (The rest of the report can be found on the data disk in the text file WMT.TXT.) The exhibit reprints the beginning of the report, which contains some basic fundamental information

---

[2]See Sidney Cottle et al., *Graham & Dodd's Security Analysis*, 5th ed. (New York: McGraw-Hill, 1988), 150.

(recent stock price, current earnings, etc.), and a summary of the analyst's appraisal of Wal-Mart's investment potential. The balance of the report consists of a review of some of the current issues and concerns facing Wal-Mart and its shareholders. These include pending health care reform, which may increase the company's labor costs, slowing momentum in its same-store sales, and its languishing stock price. Spindel then reviews some of Wal-Mart's numerous strengths (including its management) and some relevant financial data from both the balance sheet and income statement. He concludes the report by discussing the stock's current valuation (which he sees as fair, based on projections over the next 12 to 18 months) and its potential over the next three to five years ("shares should provide respectable price appreciation performance relative to the overall market. . . .").

In summary, the example analysis of Wal-Mart and guidance from Graham and Dodd suggest five general issues that a security analysis report should address: (1) the company's **competitive position** within its industry, (2) the **quality of its management,** (3) its current financial position (liquidity), (4) its long-term financial position (capital structure), and (5) its profitability and earnings. Of course, the analyst needs to both examine the historical record and make future projections about each issue. The first two issues will be considered in this chapter; the other three will be left to Chapter 11.

Competitive Position of the Company

As one task, the industry analyst must determine the competitive structure of the industry, as we saw in Chapter 9. For one thing, this will shed some light on the industry's position in its life cycle. Having evaluated the competitive structure of the industry, the company analyst must then assess the competitive position of the specific company within the industry. Initially, this requires answers to two questions.

First, why is the company's competitive position important? One factor that will clearly influence the future quality (or riskiness) and quantity of earnings of a firm is its competitive position in its industry. Simply put, a **leading** or **dominant company** in an industry should produce higher and more consistent future earnings than a company in a weak competitive position. This should be true for any stage of the industry life cycle. For example, if the industry is starting to show signs of stabilization, or even decline, the leading companies may be the only ones that survive for any length of time. Further, how well a company maintains its competitive position over time may reveal a great deal about the quality of its management.

The second question that drives analysis of competitive position asks, should one *always* restrict investment choices to industry leaders? This is a difficult question to answer. One theme we emphasize throughout this text, remember, is that investors can rely on few absolutes. An industry may seem attractive, but a company other than the industry leaders may have the most attractive valuation (e.g., price/earnings ratio). This fact, coupled with others, may confirm the decision to invest in the nonleading company.

Nevertheless, all other things being equal, leading companies offer lower-risk investment prospects than nonleading companies. Companies that have established dominant positions in their respective industries have proved that they can meet the competition. They have built high market shares for their products and services and demonstrated the ability to lead their industries. Further, these companies have demonstrated the ability to make money; they couldn't have achieved their dominant positions without operating profitably.

Growth Stock Perspective: Wal-Mart Stores, Inc.

May 26, 1993
DJIA   3540.11
S&P Indus.   523.67

Donald T. Spindel, CFA

Symbol/Exchange	WMT/NYSE
Recent Price	$27\frac{7}{8}$
1993 Price Range	$34\frac{1}{8}$—$25\frac{3}{4}$
Dividend	$0.13
Yield	0.5 percent

Fiscal Year Ends January 31[a]

	1991	1992	1993E
EPS	$0.70	$0.87	$1.05
P/E	—	—	26.5×
ROE	26.0%	25.3%	24.8%

[a] Of the following year.

Description The nation's largest retailer and still among the fastest-growing.

A.G. Edwards' Financial Strength Ranking   A−

CAGR—Compound Annual Growth Rate

Segment Contributions

	Sales		Est. Profits	
	FY92	FY93E	FY92	FY93
Discount Dept. Stores	73%	71%	87%	86%
Sam's	22	23	12	12
McLane (Distribution)	5	6	1	2

Fundamental Data

1987–1992 EPS CAGR	25%
Est. 1992–1995 EPS CAGR	20%
Trailing 12 Months' Sales (bil.)—4/93	$57.756
Total Debt & Cap. Leases to Total Cap.—4/93	45%
Current Ratio—4/93	1.47×
Cash Flow per Share—1/93	$1.15
Book Value per Share—1/93	$3.81
Price/Book Value	7.3×
Market Value (bil.)	$64.124
Market Value to Sales	1.1×
Relative P/E, FY 1993E, S&P Indus.	137%

Trading Data

Shares Outstanding (mil.)	2,300.4
Estimated Float (mil.)	1,365.0
Insider Holdings	40.6%
Institutional Holdings	30.5%
Average Daily Volume—April/May 1993	4,909,647
Listed Options	Chicago

The analyst owns a position in common or common equivalents.

Headquarters	Bentonville, AR 72716
Chairman	S. Robson Walton
President & CEO	David D. Glass

Rating: Hold*
Suitability: Aggressive

*For longer-term investors willing to look beyond 12 to 18 months and/or wishing to pursue a dollar cost averaging strategy, Wal-Mart shares provide attractive appreciation potential and are suitable for purchase.

This generalization requires another important caveat: *never* assume that a company will maintain its competitive position within its industry in the future. While many companies establish dominance and leadership and never lose them, history provides many examples of leading companies that have lost their dominant positions for a variety of reasons. An example is Lotus Development Company. Its best-known product is 1-2-3, the first commercially successful spreadsheet program. In the late 1980s, 1-2-3 had a commanding share of the spreadsheet market (something like 75 percent in 1987). Whether due to complacency, or some other factor, Lotus didn't respond quickly to major changes in computer technology, especially the move from DOS to Windows applications. As a result, Lotus's main competitors, Borland and Microsoft, got the jump and Lotus has been playing catch-up the last few years. Today, the company has less than 40 percent of the spreadsheet market.

Investment Appraisal and Summary

Our investment rating for Wal-Mart Stores, Inc.'s shares using our traditional 12- to 18-month time horizon is **hold** by aggressive investors. During this period, we believe there are other equity choices that trade at lower P/E multiples and possess similar or greater EPS growth potential and that are capable of significantly outperforming Wal-Mart's stock. However, over a more protracted period of time, we remain confident that Wal-Mart, with its very consistent, highly predictable and well above-average EPS growth prospects, should continue to provide its equity investors with superior returns versus the stock market in general. As such, we view WMT's stock as an attractive purchase by longer-term-oriented investors. In addition, the stock is an ideal dollar cost averaging vehicle.

Over the past six months the unthinkable has occurred. Wal-Mart, which for years has been extended a virtual untarnished image by the media and the investment community, has been the subject of a number of uncharacteristically unflattering articles and second guessing regarding the company's policies, practices and prospects. This negative publicity and related challenges, which are discussed in greater detail in this report, took their toll on Wal-Mart's stock price as the shares fell from their all-time high of approximately 34 in early March, to a low of $25\frac{3}{4}$ in mid-April and subsequently rebounded modestly. We contend that nothing is fundamentally wrong with WMT and it is just a matter of time before the stock should begin to regain its luster—although admittedly the company and its stock may never fully recapture the status of near invincibility they were once accorded.

In our view, one of the biggest problems impacting Wal-Mart has been bloated expectations among some analysts and portfolio managers. One could argue that Wal-Mart, which

INVESTMENT INSIGHTS

historically has "under-promised and overperformed," has spoiled Wall Street and, to a certain extent, has been victimized by its own exceptional success. Because the company has consistently exceeded expectations, Wall Street has, in effect, set the performance hurdles for Wal-Mart at extraordinarily high levels. In a retail environment such as the past several months (February through April), which was impacted by a variety of unusual conditions, it was virtually impossible for Wal-Mart to run true to the successful form that has typified the company.

In our opinion, Wal-Mart remains among the most tenacious and proficient retailers in the United States, if not the world. Investors, however, need to recognize that the company has reached the stage in its growth cycle where its sales and earnings gains, while still exceptional by nearly all standards, are likely to slowly recede from their current annual rates of more than 20 percent to the midteens (or possibly slightly lower) annually by the end of the decade. As a result, we believe investors should be prepared for 10 percent to 15 percent annual returns during the 1993–2000 time frame from their ownership of Wal-Mart. We would argue that if we are able to sustain the current relatively low inflation and interest rates, Wal-Mart's potential investment returns over the balance of the 1990s should still be quite respectable compared with the average performance of many other stocks.

Source: Courtesy of A.G. Edwards & Sons, Inc.

Evaluating a Company's Competitive Position

The discussion of the importance of the company's competitive position raises the question of how to ascertain whether or not a specific company enjoys a strong competitive position within its industry. In some cases, this could be a fairly straightforward, even easy, task; in others, it is more arduous.

Before we discuss criteria for a competitively strong company, we need to briefly revisit the issue, discussed in Chapter 9, of industry classification. Classifying industries can be difficult and may result in ambiguous classifications. Industries can be classified very broadly (e.g., computer software), or very specifically (e.g., spreadsheet programs). Further, assigning companies to specific industries can be equally difficult. There is no easy solution to these problems; the analyst must simply keep them in mind and allow for possible variation.

Many companies operate in several different industries. DuPont, for example, produces both chemicals and petroleum products. Johnson & Johnson makes hundreds of different products, from disposable contact lenses to baby shampoo. Should the analyst evaluate the competitive position of the company in *every* industry in which it operates? Probably, but experienced analysts concentrate their efforts on the industries that provide the largest shares of overall company revenue and earnings.

With respect for these complexities, let's now review the forces that determine the competitive position of a company. We'll discuss these forces generally, and then apply them to an examination of an actual company.

Revenues or Sales. In general, size is a good guide to competitive position. Higher annual sales or revenue often comes from success at meeting the competition, at least this has been true historically. Size alone doesn't guarantee continuing dominance in the future, however. A better indicator may be the *growth rate* in sales, relative to the industry. The leading company may not necessarily be the largest, but the one that is growing the fastest compared to its competitors.

Profitability. How profitable is the company, especially as compared to the industry? Analysts measure profitability not just in dollars, but also by such variables as profit margin and return on equity. This analysis should also determine whether the company is becoming relatively more or less profitable compared to the industry. As a general rule, a more profitable company, especially one that is becoming relatively more profitable compared to the industry, has a better competitive position.

Product Line. A longer and broader **product line,** compared to the industry, generally indicates a more competitive position. (The term *product* includes both goods and services.) Strong marketing and financial reasons drive a company to increase the length and breadth of its product line.[3] These include expanding growth opportunities, optimizing company resources, increasing the importance of the company in the market, and exploiting the product life cycle. Failure to increase the length and breadth of a company's product mix can have severe, negative consequences.

Lotus, for example, was considered by most in the software industry to be a one-product company for many years. When 1-2-3 sales started to soften in the late 1980s, the company didn't have much else to fall back on and its financial performance and stock price suffered. Lotus has since broadened its product line considerably.

A company's product line can also be too long, or too diverse, of course. The analyst must determine whether or not the length and breadth of a company's product line is optimal—seldom an easy task.

New Products and Product Innovation. Another sign of a competitively strong company is its ability to introduce new products (or improved versions of existing products) more rapidly than its competitors, to take advantage of changes in demand or technology. Chrysler, for example, now takes about half as long as most other auto manufacturers to bring a new car model to market (from initial design to manufacturing to actually selling vehicles to customers). This gives the company an edge over other auto manufacturers, both U.S. and foreign. While Chrysler will probably never become the world's largest auto maker, its success at innovation bodes well for its future in this highly competitive industry.

---

[3]These reasons are discussed in most basic marketing textbooks. See, for example, Louis Boone and David Kurtz, *Contemporary Marketing,* 7th ed. (Fort Worth, Tex.: Dryden Press, 1992), 329–331.

Operating Efficiency. Industry leaders, especially those that will be dominant in the future, usually produce goods and services more efficiently than their competitors. Companies that are **low-cost producers,** meaning that they can produce the same quality good or service more cheaply than competitors, are considered to be more efficient. These firms are more likely to build strong competitive positions within their respective industries.

Retail industry experts often cite the scrupulous attention to operating costs of Wal-Mart Stores. Wal-Mart simply spends less to operate than most other retailers. Lower costs, of course, allow it to offer lower prices to consumers, boosting sales. Many retailing experts believe that Wal-Mart's operating efficiency has helped the company become so dominant in its industry.

Pricing. Pricing is an important component of any marketing strategy. Dominant companies tend to follow certain pricing practices depending on the industry. For example, a **price leader** may hold the dominant competitive position, especially in a mature growth industry. A simple example will illustrate the meaning of price leadership. If Company A is the price leader in its industry, all of its competitors match its decision to raise (or lower) its prices. On the other hand, if a competitor raises (or lowers) its prices, competition will correct the price change unless A makes the same change. Pricing and operating efficiency are often related. A company that is a price leader is often a low-cost producer, as well.

Patents and Technology. Many companies have established dominant positions in various industries by exploiting patents and/or **proprietary technology.** Once the patent expires or the technology evolves, however, the company's dominant position in the industry becomes less secure.

Xerox, for example, dominated the photocopier industry for many years, protected from competitors by patents on the technology it invented for producing dry photocopies. As technology advanced and Xerox's patents started to expire, however, other companies, especially Japanese manufacturers, moved into the industry and began to take market share away from Xerox. These companies offered higher-quality, more technically advanced products at lower prices. While Xerox is still an important manufacturer of photocopiers, it no longer dominates the industry.

Competitive Position of Southwest Airlines

As an example of this analysis, let's examine the competitive position of Southwest Airlines. Our purpose is not to turn you into an expert on either Southwest or the airline industry, but rather to give you a taste of the kinds of things an analyst would examine to evaluate the competitive position of an actual company.

Southwest is the seventh largest air carrier in the United States, serving 37 cities. It has only a small share of the total market, however. In 1993 Southwest accounted for 2.9 percent of industry revenue passenger miles (RPM) and 2.2 percent of industry operating revenues.[4] In spite of its relatively small size, and recognizing that Southwest Airlines will never be the nation's largest airline, it is still a dominant carrier with a strong competitive position. Several statistics support this contention. (The Mini Case at the end of the chapter asks you to determine the competitive position of USAir, an interesting contrast to Southwest.)

Southwest's revenues (measured by both revenue passenger miles and dollars) are growing much faster than industry revenues, as Figures 10.1 and

---

[4]One revenue passenger mile equals one paying customer flying one mile.

Figure 10.1

Revenue Passenger Mile Index for Southwest and the Industry: 1988–1993

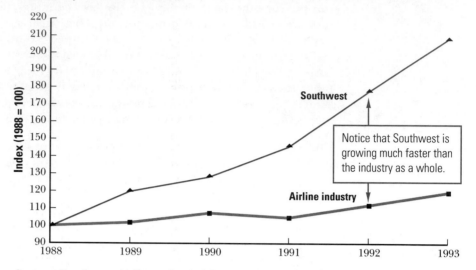

Source: Southwest Airlines, *Annual Report,* various issues; *Survey of Current Business,* various issues.

10.2 show. The figures show indexes of RPMs and dollar revenues, comparing Southwest to the industry, between the end of 1988 and the end of 1993.[5] During this five-year period, for example, Southwest's dollar revenues more than doubled, compared to an increase of about 40 percent for the industry.

Southwest has been far more profitable than the rest of the industry during the last few years. For example, between 1988 and 1993 the industry,

Figure 10.2

Revenue Index for Southwest and the Industry: 1988–1993

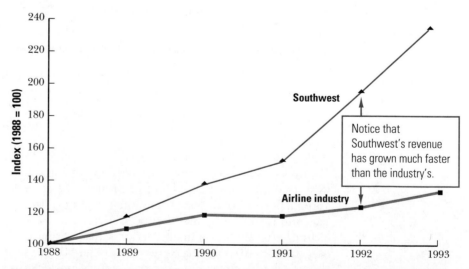

Source: Southwest Airlines, *Annual Report,* various issues; *Survey of Current Business,* various issues.

[5]The index value in year t (I_t) equals: $I_t = \left(\dfrac{X_t - X_{t-1}}{X_t}\right) I_{t-1}$, where X is either RPMs or dollar revenues. The index value in 1988 is set at 100.

excluding Southwest, had cumulative operating losses in excess of $1.3 billion. By contrast, Southwest had a cumulative operating *profit* of more than $500 million during the same five-year period. The company has consistently maintained this advantage: during the ten years from 1984 to 1993, Southwest has had an operating profit each year. On the other hand, the industry has had operating profits in only six of the ten years.

Although Southwest will likely never become the nation's largest air carrier, or even one of the largest, it dominates the markets (city-pairs) it serves. Further, Southwest usually grabs a large share of a market soon after starting service. A good example of this is the intrastate market in California. Southwest entered this market in the late 1980s and, by the end of 1993, it had approximately a 72.5 percent market share in every intrastate California city-pair it served. In fact, other airlines usually cut back their service once Southwest enters their markets because they find it very difficult to compete.

Most industry analysts consider Southwest to be the most efficient airline in the United States, if not the world. It has the highest aircraft utilization rate in the industry. (Its aircraft spend more time flying and less time sitting on the ground compared to the rest of the industry.) The airline turns an aircraft around, on average, in about 20 minutes; the industry average is about 45 minutes. Further, Southwest has the lowest operating costs in the industry. Figure 10.3 illustrates the cost per available seat mile (ASM) for Southwest and the industry between 1988 and 1993. Southwest's operating costs are clearly well below the industry standard (7.03 cents versus 10.54 cents per ASM in 1992, for example).

Finally, Southwest is clearly a price leader in the airline industry. By exploiting its comparative cost advantage over other airlines, the evidence strongly suggests that Southwest essentially sets fares on its routes, against any

Figure 10.3

Operating Expenses per Available Seat Mile (ASM) for Southwest and Industry: 1988–1993

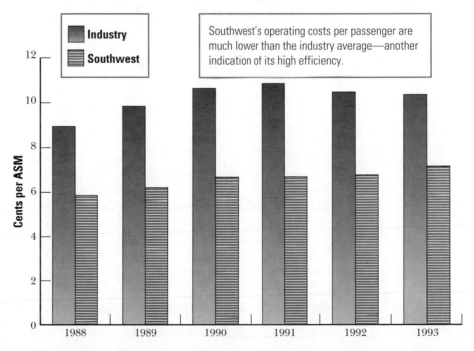

Source: Southwest Airlines, *Annual Report,* various issues; *Survey of Current Business,* various issues.

Figure 10.4

Management Process

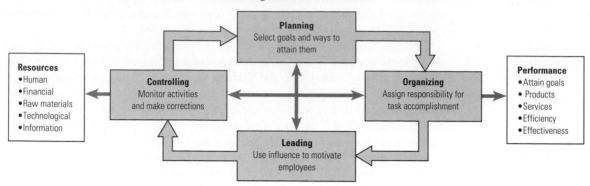

Source: Richard Daft, *Management,* 3rd ed. (Fort Worth, Tex.: Dryden Press, 1994), 8.

competition. Other airlines that can't, or won't, match Southwest's fares tend to quickly drop out of its markets, as happened in California in the early 1990s.

Nature of Management

Having established the competitive position of a company within its industry (or industries), qualitative company analysis turns next to an evaluation of the quality of a company's management. Some experts believe that the quality of a company's management may be the single most important influence on its future profitability and overall success. A company can have strong financial statements, for example, and yet be overly bureaucratic and incapable of responding quickly to changing business conditions.

In order to assess management quality, the analyst must understand what the work of management involves, starting with a definition. One leading expert defines *management* as follows:

> Management is the attainment of organizational goals in an effective and efficient manner through planning, organizing, leading, and controlling organizational resources.[6]

This general definition of management conveys two important ideas: First, managers are responsible for the attainment of various **organizational objectives** both effectively and efficiently. Second, management includes four basic functions: **planning, organizing, leading,** and **controlling.** The management process of deploying resources to achieve objectives (that is, promoting organizational performance), within the context of the four basic functions, is illustrated in Figure 10.4. Interpreting the figure requires some elaboration on organizational performance and the four management functions.

Organizational Performance

The first part of the definition of management deals with organizational performance. Managers are ultimately responsible for applying company

---

[6]Richard Daft, *Management,* 3rd ed. (Fort Worth, Tex.: Dryden Press, 1994), 8.

resources effectively and efficiently in order to accomplish the company's goals. *Effectiveness* is defined as the degree to which the company achieves its goals; *efficiency* is defined as the amount of resources required to produce a certain level of output. Performance depends on how effectively and efficiently the company attains its goals. This can be measured in a variety of ways.

For example, Southwest Airlines sets out to be the dominant carrier, measured in terms of market share, in each market (city-pair) it serves. In most markets, Southwest has achieved this goal, indicating strong effectiveness. In many markets, Southwest has become the dominant carrier very quickly, indicating high efficiency.[7] As we've seen, Southwest's operating costs are around 30 percent lower than those of any of its competitors. Also between 1989 and 1992, its revenue per employee increased by around 12 percent (from $132,000 to $148,000).

Chrysler provides another example of good organizational performance. By improving the organization and the operation of its manufacturing facilities, Chrysler has increased the number of vehicles it can build each day from around 4,500 in 1988 to about 8,000 in 1993. At the same time, it has reduced the number of worker-hours needed to build one vehicle from 175 to around 100. This boost in operating efficiency has reduced Chrysler's costs and, as we've discussed, probably has also improved the company's overall competitive position within the auto industry.

Management Functions

The second part of the general definition of management lists four functions: planning, organizing, leading, and controlling.[8] The *planning* function involves setting future goals for the organization and then identifying the tasks and resources necessary to obtain those goals. Figure 10.5 shows a popular planning tool, the nine-cell business screen used by senior management of General Electric to evaluate various business units based on industry attractiveness and business strength. A unit may rank high in industry attractiveness (for example, the industry may have a high growth rate and profit margin), while the unit ranks low in business strength (for example, the GE unit may have a small market share and no real price or quality advantages). The matrix suggests that GE should monitor the performance of the unit closely. Depending on its earnings, GE might choose to invest to develop the strength of the business unit or to divest the unit. As we'll see later, GE is considered to have executed the planning function very effectively in recent years.

The *organizing* function assigns tasks to various parts of the organization and allocates resources within the organization. Reorganization has helped Chrysler to reduce the amount of time it takes to bring a new model to market. Instead of a traditional linear process (from design to manufacturing to sales and marketing), Chrysler adopted a less rigid organizational structure that requires design, manufacturing, finance, and marketing to combine their efforts to produce a new vehicle.[9]

---

[7]Information on this question can be obtained from several sources, including airline industry analysts, trade publications (such as *Air Transport World*), and the U.S. Department of Transportation (Office of Airline Statistics).

[8]According to experts, the amounts of time individual managers spend at each function depend on their positions in the organizational hierarchy. See Daft, *Management*, 12–14.

[9]This approach has been adopted by other auto manufacturers, as well. Honda, for example, used this organizational approach to cut more than a year off of the time for the 1994 redesign of the Accord.

Figure 10.5

GE's Nine-Cell Business Screen

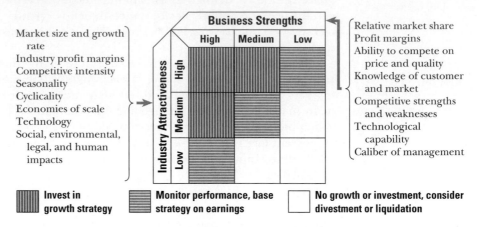

Market size and growth rate
Industry profit margins
Competitive intensity
Seasonality
Cyclicality
Economies of scale
Technology
Social, environmental, legal, and human impacts

Relative market share
Profit margins
Ability to compete on price and quality
Knowledge of customer and market
Competitive strengths and weaknesses
Technological capability
Caliber of management

| | Invest in growth strategy | | Monitor performance, base strategy on earnings | | No growth or investment, consider divestment or liquidation |

Source: Richard Daft, *Management,* 2nd ed. (Fort Worth, Tex.: Dryden Press, 1991), 163.

The *leading* function involves the motivation of employees to achieve the goals of the organization. One of the strengths of Southwest Airlines, noted by many observers, is the enthusiastic leadership of the company's CEO and chairman, Herb Kelleher.[10] By all accounts, Kelleher has done an outstanding job motivating and leading the airline's 13,000 employees. Relations with employees, for example, have never been antagonistic, as they are at many airlines. Further, Southwest is often ranked as one of the most employee-friendly companies in America.[11]

Finally, the *controlling* function is concerned with monitoring performance, keeping the organization moving toward its goals, and correcting deficiencies. The story of the decline of the E. F. Hutton brokerage firm illustrates what can happen in the absence of managerial control. For many years, Robert Fomon, Hutton's CEO, refused to set up any kind of control system because he wanted to supervise management personally. The company got too large for Fomon's personal supervision, and things soon got out of hand. For example, Hutton pleaded guilty in 1986 and 1987 to over 2,000 counts of mail and wire fraud in connection with a check-kiting scheme. Eventually, this lack of control led to the demise of both Fomon's tenure and E. F. Hutton as an independent firm. It was acquired in 1988 by Shearson Lehman Brothers.

Management Skills

What kinds of skills must managers exercise? Most experts identify three essential types of managerial skills: technical, conceptual, and human skills. Technical skills involve knowledge and mastery of such disciplines as engineering, manufacturing, basic science, finance, and so forth. Conceptual skills involve the ability to think and plan, to see the company as a whole as well as the relationships among all of its parts. Finally, human skills involve the ability to work with and through other people. Some human skills include leadership, motivation, communication, and conflict resolution.

---

[10]See, for example, "Hit 'Em Hardest with the Mostest," *Forbes,* September 16, 1991.

[11]Southwest ranked in the top ten in the R. Levering and M. Moskowitz, *The 100 Best Companies to Work for in America* (Reading, Mass.: Addison-Wesley, 1993).

Management experts argue that all managers need all three skills; however, the relative importance of each changes as a manager moves up the organizational hierarchy.[12] For example, technical skills may be very important for lower-level managers, but they are less important than conceptual and human skills for top managers.

Evaluating Management

The discussion of the nature of management leads to the critical question that investors must answer: How well-managed is the company? Determining the quality of management is neither easy nor totally objective. In a nutshell, the fundamental issue is how well the company's management performs the four basic functions. Of course, this analysis cannot stop with an assessment of how well management has performed in the past; it must extend to their likely future performance, as well.

In this section we'll review the techniques by which investors evaluate management. We'll start by listing some specific questions to ask, then we'll present two short case studies that illustrate good and bad management in actual companies. Many experienced analysts have trouble defining *good management*, but they often know it when they see it.

Some Questions to Ask

1. What Are the Age and Experience Characteristics of Management? Information on senior management appears in the company's annual report (to stockholders and its 10K report).[13] This usually includes ages, current titles, and brief biographic sketches of each individual.

Experts look for a senior management group that appears to have some depth of experience. At the same time, the group should exhibit some variation in terms of age, length of service with the company, and background. For example, some should have marketing backgrounds, while others have technical backgrounds. A group of senior managers that appear to be carbon copies of one another should raise concerns. As we'll discuss later in the chapter, this homogeneity may have been a source of some of GM's management problems during the 1980s.

Evaluating the senior management group includes considering likely successors to current leaders. This is especially important if the company bears the stamp of one individual (such as Lee Iacocca at Chrysler or Herb Kelleher at Southwest Airlines). The analyst should ask, could someone take over for the current CEO immediately? If the current CEO were to step down, would possible successors engage in a power struggle? Has the current CEO stayed too long?

As we saw in the chapter's opening story about Chrysler, the issue of CEO succession can be very distracting, diverting management's attention away from running the business. Contrast the succession story at Chrysler with that at Ford. In October 1993, Ford's CEO, Harold Poling, announced that he would retire at the end of the year. At the same news conference, Poling introduced his successor, Alexander Trotman. Trotman was the unanimous pick of Ford's directors and, by all accounts, the transfer of power was very smooth.

---

[12]Daft, *Management*, 15–17.

[13]Other sources of information about senior management include *Dun's Reference Book of Corporate Managements* and *Who's Who in Business*.

How J&J's Foresight Made Contact Lenses Pay

Bernard W. Walsh could see a lot of drawbacks when he was offered the chance to run J&J's Vistakon unit in 1987. Then serving the tiny corner of the contact-lens market for people with astigmatism, the operation garnered barely $20 million in annual sales. He would have to uproot his family from a cozy town on Philadelphia's Main Line and move to Jacksonville, Fla. Perhaps most worrying of all, Walsh would be building a brand-new company around a pricey, little-known product that Johnson & Johnson was investing millions to produce: disposable contact lenses. "There was a perception of high risk," he admits dryly.

If taking the job was a gamble, Walsh hit the jackpot. Now 49, he's in charge of one of the fastest-growing members of J&J's family of companies. Worldwide sales for Vistakon grew 50 percent last year, topping $225 million, mostly on the strength of its Acuvue disposable lens. Analysts say Vistakon has snared a quarter of the $650 million U.S. lens market alone, and it's No.

1 in the fast-growing disposable segment. Walsh, who came to Vistakon from a cardiovascular-equipment unit that J&J sold, is overseeing 1,800 employees, three times as many as he started with. He's in charge of fields as diverse as operations, marketing, advertising, and research and development. Walsh declines to comment on how his pay has changed, except to say he's "very happy" with it.

Vistakon is a typical J&J success story. Back in 1983, a J&J staffer in Europe got word of new Danish technology to produce disposable lenses cheaply. J&J bought the rights and began perfecting the packaging and manufacturing process. Within a few years, J&J had quietly assembled a management team and built a high-volume plant in Florida, where it started test-marketing the lens in the summer of 1987. Vistakon quickly set up distribution routes, developed consumer ads, and took the product national in June 1988, with trial lenses free to anyone who asked. The move was crucial, since Acuvue costs about $500 a year, including doctor's visits, compared with $350 to buy and care for conventional extended-wear lenses.

Small and Agile. The speed of the rollout and the novelty of big-budget ads left giants

---

2. How Effective Is the Company's Strategic Planning? Strategic planning (or *strategic management*) is defined as:

> The set of decisions and actions used to formulate and implement strategies that will provide a competitively superior fit between the organization and its environment so as to achieve organizational goals.[14]

Management experts suggest that strategic planning may be the single most important function of senior management because success or failure of this work determines much of the future prosperity of the company. Therefore, the effectiveness of the company's strategic planning efforts can reveal a great deal about the overall quality of a company's management. Some questions to ask about a company's strategic planning include whether the strategy is identifiable, consistent (both internally and externally), and feasible.

Management experts contend that effective strategic planning may be even more important for **multinational corporations (MNCs)**.[15] (The usual definition of a multinational company is one that generates more than 25 percent of its revenues outside its home country.) The strategic planning horizon for such a firm is much broader, of course, and planning must accommodate differences among multiple cultural, economic, and political environments. Some of the strategic decisions MNCs must make include whether to pursue global strategies (selling set product lines worldwide) or multidomestic strategies (designing products for individual markets). MNCs

---

[14]Daft, *Management,* 152.

[15]See Daft, *Management,* 617–620.

Bausch & Lomb Inc. and Ciba-Geigy Corp. seeing stars. J&J also had a manufacturing edge with its Florida factory, which could mass-produce thousands of lenses quickly and uniformly. Unable to take competing lenses coast-to-coast for six months or more, rivals conceded Vistakon an advantage that lingers.

J&J's structure made the guerrilla warfare possible. Walsh's unit was so small that he was able to make rapid-fire decisions on fronts as diverse as production and marketing, with little interference from a bureaucratic headquarters. He could hire ad agencies at will, for instance. Yet because Vistakon was backed by capital-rich J&J, it could count on the resources needed to attack a mature market with a little-tried and costly product. Kenneth S. Abramowitz, health care analyst at Sanford C. Bernstein & Co., estimates J&J has shelled out at least $75 million on Acuvue, including buying the rights, building the plant, and absorbing operating losses. He figures the business turned profitable in 1991.

Small though his company may be, Walsh's job just keeps getting bigger. To broaden its product line, Vistakon recently unveiled a longer-wear, pricier product called Surevue. Unlike Acuvue, users cannot sleep with Surevue

lenses in place. But they get twice the wear out of them, usually about two weeks, so Surevue is cheaper in the long run. As one of J&J's point men in the optical market, Walsh also must keep tabs on new technologies to make sure his products stay current.

One day, he would like to move into group management in J&J's New Jersey headquarters. That would give him oversight responsibility for a clutch of companies. But he clearly is torn about leaving the field for the home office. "A company presidency is probably the best job in the corporation," he says. "You're left alone to run your own business." That is, as long as you keep stomping the competition.

Source: Joseph Weber, "How J&J's Foresight Made Contact Lenses Pay," *Business Week*, May 4, 1992, 132. Reprinted from May 4, 1992 issue of *Business Week* by special permission, copyright © 1992 by McGraw-Hill, Inc.

must also decide between product-based and geographically based organization structures.

An example of the payoff from good strategic planning for a large company is illustrated in the Investment Insights feature. The article shows how Johnson & Johnson's organizational structure and strategic planning efforts have helped it to capture a large and growing share of the profitable market for contact lenses. In 1983 the company purchased the rights to a new technology developed in Denmark to produce disposable lenses cheaply. It then spent the next few years perfecting the manufacturing and packaging of the product. Johnson & Johnson rolled out the product nationwide in 1988, using its manufacturing and marketing strengths to blitz the competition. By the early 1990s, Johnson & Johnson had captured about 25 percent of the $650 million U.S. lens market and it had come to dominate the market for disposable contact lenses.

3. Has the Company Developed and Followed a Sound Marketing Strategy? An investor's analysis shouldn't discount the importance of a clear, well-planned **marketing strategy.** In order to prosper, every company must satisfy the demands of consumers. The basic components of a marketing strategy, shown in Figure 10.6 on page 324, illustrate two components of a marketing strategy: the target market and the marketing mix variables (distribution, price, product, and promotion). Environmental factors, the outer ring of Figure 10.6, form the framework for the marketing strategy.

An investor must evaluate how well the company has delineated its target market (or markets). Saab, the Swedish car maker, has done an excellent job of delineating its specific target market (professionals with annual incomes

Figure 10.6

Elements of a Marketing Strategy and Marketing's
Environmental Framework

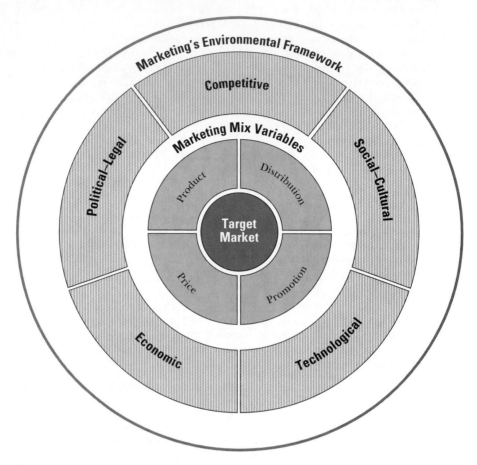

Source: Louis Boone and David Kurtz, *Contemporary Marketing*, 8th ed. (Fort Worth, Tex.: Dryden Press, 1995), 26.

between $50,000 and $100,000). Another important question deals with how well the company combines the four marketing mix variables (distribution, price, product, and promotion). While each variable should be examined individually, the analyst should also assess how well the company has blended the four variables together to satisfy chosen target markets.[16]

4. Does the Company Understand That It Is Part of a Global Environment? Even a company that is not classified as a multinational must operate in a global environment. How well a company has adapted to this fact may give some important insight into the quality of its management. Has the company recognized that it sells its products in a single, worldwide market and that competitors come from all over the world today? Does the company treat the entire world as a source of supply, as well as a market? Has it accepted the possibility that people in the United States do not necessarily know best in every situation? Companies such as AT&T, Coca-Cola, and Procter & Gamble are often cited as companies that have adapted well to the realities of the global business environment.

[16]Most basic marketing textbooks describe this process in general. See, for example, Boone and Kurtz, *Contemporary Marketing*, 22–26.

5. Has the Company Effectively and Nimbly Adapted to Changes in the External Business Environment?

The contemporary business environment is marked by rapid and sometimes unpredictable changes. How well a company anticipates and reacts to changes in its external business environment depends on the quality of its management. One thing to look at is the company's adoption of modern management techniques, especially those that have succeeded in other, similar companies. One example is the trend to adopt many of the Japanese production techniques and organizational structure characteristics (such as work teams) by U.S. auto makers. GM's Saturn plant has four levels of authority rather than the traditional six.[17] The bottom level consists of a "work unit" led by an elected counselor. The nearly self-sufficient team decides who does which jobs and maintains equipment, orders supplies, and so forth.

By contrast, members of the British sports car industry failed to adapt to changes in their business environment in the 1960s and 1970s.[18] Austin-Healy, MG, and Triumph actually stumbled into a lucrative U.S. franchise in the 1950s producing small, moderately priced sports cars. The cars proved very popular and profitable up until the late 1970s. The industry never recognized its real strengths, however (a virtual monopoly on low-priced, simple, fun cars). As those strengths diminished during the 1970s, the industry's organization structure proved so rigid that it couldn't meet the challenges of its changing business environment. By the early 1980s, the companies that created the sports car were all but gone, not only from the U.S. market, but from the roads of the entire world.

6. Has Management Maintained, or Improved, the Company's Overall Competitive Position?

We discussed this question at length earlier in the chapter. The company's competitive position is a prime responsibility of management. Well-run companies maintain or improve the competitive positions of all of their business units. If a specific business unit can't compete, a well-run company promptly reduces its investment in that unit, perhaps withdrawing from the business entirely. As we'll see later, one of GE's strengths is judgment of when to get into a business line, and also when to get out of one.

As another example, think about what happened to Xerox in the 1970s. The company that invented dry photocopying lost its dominant position as its patents started to expire. One explanation for this decline is the company's bureaucratic and insulated management. Its management structure simply couldn't respond quickly to the new competitive threats.[19]

7. Has the Company Grown in an Organized, Sustainable Manner?

History teaches that bigger is not always better. America West Airlines is one of many companies that have grown too quickly, outstripping their managerial and financial resources. Founded in the early 1980s, America West tried to reproduce the success of Southwest Airlines as a low-cost, regional airline. Its strategy had started to show signs of working by the mid-1980s. Unfortunately, America West embarked on an ambitious expansion program, including

---

[17]Daft, *Management*, 467.

[18]The decline of the British sports car industry is chronicled in, "Defeating the Triumph," *Audacity*, Fall 1993, 17–25.

[19]The fate of Xerox is chronicled in Douglas Smith and Robert Alexander, *Fumbling the Future* (New York: William Morrow, 1988). Failure to respond to competitive threats to its photocopier business wasn't the only failing of the company's management during the 1970s. It may surprise you to learn that Xerox *invented* the personal computer and the laser printer. Smith and Alexander suggest that management problems at Xerox contributed to the company's failure to bring either product to market.

initiating service to Hawaii and Japan. While its revenues more than doubled between 1987 and 1990, America West didn't have either the financial or managerial resources to compete effectively with the large airlines, such as Delta and United. Debt exploded and losses started to mount. (America West lost over $300 million in 1990 and 1991.) The airline finally ran out of cash and was forced to file for bankruptcy in 1991.

8. Has the Company Been Financed Adequately and Appropriately? We'll consider financial issues in detail in Chapter 11. However, for now note simply that a company's financial statements reflect on the quality of its management; as a general rule, better-run companies have better financials than poorly run companies. For example, prudent financial policy suggests that a company limit its **financial risk** (i.e., leverage) if it faces a high degree of **business risk.** The airline industry faces a high degree of business risk, yet it has an aggregate debt ratio in excess of 80 percent.[20] Many experts believe that this excess leverage is one of the industry's fundamental problems. By contrast, Southwest Airlines has a debt ratio around 55 percent. Its more conservative financial policies provide more evidence of the overall quality of the company's management.

9. Does the Company Have Good Relations with Its Unions and Employees? Managers have to lead and motivate employees; good and successful managers develop extremely effective human skills. Managers can't achieve the company's goals by themselves; they need employees working with them, not against them. As a general rule, well-run companies have better employee relationships than poorly run companies. As we mentioned earlier, one of the keys to Southwest Airlines' success has been its generally harmonious employee relations (something that's unusual in the airline industry). Even though Southwest's workforce is heavily unionized, about 83 percent, the company has been able to negotiate flexible work rules, such as job sharing, which reduce costs and improve operating efficiency.

10. What Is the Company's Public Image? Well-run companies know the importance of public image. Does a company's name convey a positive or negative image? Of course, well-run companies don't neglect their other responsibilities while cultivating positive public images.

One source of information concerning corporate reputations can be found in *Fortune* magazine. Each year the magazine presents a list of America's most admired corporations by polling several thousand senior executives, outside directors, institutional investors, and securities analysts. Each survey participant is asked to rate the top ten companies (or sometimes a shorter list) in his or her industry on each of eight attributes.[21] The ten most admired corporations according to the 1992 survey are listed in Table 10.1.

How closely are corporate reputation and total returns to stockholders related? You can form your own judgment, but consider this. The nine public companies listed in Table 10.1 had a median total annual return between 1983 and 1992 of 25.7 percent compared to 16.2 percent for the S&P 500. (Levi-Strauss is privately held.) Further, eight of the nine outperformed the S&P 500 during that period.

---

[20]The debt ratio is defined as total liabilities (both short-term and long-term) divided by total assets.

[21]The eight attributes are: quality of management, financial soundness, quality of products or services, ability to attract and keep talented people, use of corporate assets, value as long-term investments, innovativeness, and community and environmental responsibility.

Table 10.1

Fortune's 1992 Ten Most Admired List

Rank	Company	Fortune Score (maximum = 10)
1.	Merck	8.74
2.	Rubbermaid	8.58
3.	Wal-Mart Stores	8.42
4.	3M	8.41
5.	Coca-Cola	8.19
6.	Procter & Gamble	8.09
7.	Levi-Strauss	7.96
8.	Liz Claiborne	7.95
9.	J. P. Morgan	7.93
10.	Boeing	7.88

Source: *Fortune,* February 8, 1993, pp. 54–55.

Case Studies in Good and Bad Management

Having listed some questions to ask in evaluating management, we now turn to two brief case studies of good and poor management decisions by prominent companies.[22] Both cases provide some valuable lessons about management quality. On the good side we have picked General Electric, while on the poor side, we have selected General Motors. Obviously the distinction between good and poor is somewhat arbitrary and subjective. Of course, not every decision GE has made turned out well, and not every decision made by GM turned out badly. There is also evidence that GM has made progress in its attempt to change.[23]

General Electric. General Electric began the 1980s with around $25 billion in sales, earnings of $1.5 billion, 325 different business units, and over 300,000 employees. By the end of 1992, GE's annual revenues had more than doubled, to over $56 billion, while its earnings had almost quadrupled to around $4.5 billion. At the same time, however, GE's workforce had shrunk to around 268,000, distributed among only 12 different business units. The company's focus had shifted from core electrical manufacturing to high technology and services.

Stockholders benefited, as well. During the 1980s, no company increased its market value (price times number of outstanding shares) by more than GE. Between the end of 1980 and the end of 1992, GE stock had an average annual total return of around 19.5 percent, compared to 14.7 percent for the S&P 500. How did GE achieve this record of success? Much of the credit goes to GE's management, led by CEO Jack Welch.[24]

When Welch became CEO of the 110-year-old company in 1981, he saw storm clouds forming over American business. In order to compete in a global economy, replete with foreign competitors producing high-quality, inexpensive products, Welch believed that GE had to change. Further, Welch wanted to start the process of change *before* the business environment left no alternative.

---

[22]We could, of course, have selected hundreds of other good and poor examples. This group is certainly not any kind of a random sample.

[23]The company still has some distance to go. See, "GM: Not Fixed Yet," *Forbes,* November 8, 1993.

[24]Welch became CEO of GE in 1981. The transformation of GE during the 1980s is detailed in Robert Slater, *The New GE* (Homewood, Ill.: Business One-Irwin, 1993).

Welch took the helm of a huge company, albeit a profitable one, that he believed was too decentralized and too bureaucratic. (GE had 12 layers of management in the early 1980s.) Further, Welch believed that GE was trying to do too many things at the same time. Welch's overall strategic goal was to propel all of GE's businesses to positions of dominance in their respective markets. High-profit business units that offered little growth potential would have to be sold, for example.

In pursuit of his vision, Welch made substantial changes to GE. The firm sold its small-appliance business in 1984. GE had been producing electric irons for almost 100 years, but Welch saw no real future in the business for GE. The firm purchased RCA, which owned NBC, in 1986 for over $6 billion.[25] GE then sold its consumer electronics business in 1987 for $3.2 billion. At the same time, during the 1980s, GE greatly expanded in such areas as lighting, financial services, medical technology, and materials (both by internal growth and by acquisition). Much of this expansion was focused on non-U.S. markets.

GE's strategic planning is considered among the best in the corporate world. As an example, consider the company's sale of its consumer electronics division in 1987. GE had been producing consumer electronics, such as televisions, for years, yet profits were weak. In addition, GE had acquired another substantial consumer electronics business as part of RCA in 1986. The consumer electronics business was one of Welch's least favorite. At the same time, Welch wanted to expand GE's medical systems business, which made, among other things, X-ray and CAT scan equipment.

GE was strong in the United States and Japan, but weak in Europe. It approached Thomson, S.A., a French company, about acquiring its medical systems business. Thomson, in turn, suggested a swap: its medical systems business for GE's and RCA's consumer electronics business, plus some cash. Acquiring Thomson's medical systems business would boost GE's market share in Europe from 6 percent to 20 percent, the second largest share in Europe. Because GE's strategic objectives were so clear, and the company's management so nimble, it took Welch less than one hour to agree in principal to Thomson's offer. After only five days of negotiations, GE and Thomson had agreed on terms of the sale and signed a formal letter of intent.[26] The old, bureaucratic GE would have taken months to make a decision and complete such a deal.

GE's strategic planning efforts appear to have paid off. By the end of the 1980s most GE business units were leaders in their respective fields (measured by market share). GE led the U.S. and world markets for aircraft engines, electric motors, engineering plastics, power systems, and medical systems. It led the U.S. market for circuit breakers, and was tied with several other firms for world leadership. GE's railroad locomotives, lighting products, and major appliances have the largest shares of their respective markets in the United States, and the second largest in the world.[27]

Welch also made many changes to the human side of the corporation. Management layers diminished from 12 to 4, the size of the corporate staff was slashed, and line employees assumed far more responsibility and decision authority. As a result of these, and other changes, operating efficiency has increased substantially. For example, GE instituted a new program in 1990 to cut the amount of time necessary to bring a major appliance model (e.g.,

---

[25] We should note that the jury is still out concerning the long-term benefits of the RCA acquisition.

[26] Thomson retained the right to use the GE and RCA names on consumer electronic products. Slater, *New GE,* 195.

[27] Ibid., 235.

an electric range) to market.[28] At the time the new program was first instituted, the product cycle took about 18 weeks (6 weeks to forecast the number of appliances to build, 10 weeks to manufacture them, and 2 weeks to transport them to distributors). By the fall of 1991, the product cycle had been cut to around 5 weeks. By the end of the decade, productivity was rising by around 5 to 6 percent per year, compared to annual increases of around 1 to 2 percent at the beginning of the decade.

General Motors. The last few years have been difficult ones for General Motors, the world's largest automaker. During the three-year period 1990 through 1992, GM had cumulative losses of almost $10 billion; its U.S. car and truck business lost close to $5 billion in 1992 alone. GM has seen its share of the U.S. auto market fall from around 45 percent in 1980 to less than 30 percent in mid-1993. As losses mounted, GM's financial condition rapidly deteriorated. In 1983, GM's debt ratio was less than 50 percent, by 1990 it was close to 80 percent. GM has announced plans to close at least a dozen assembly plants, and reduce its workforce (both white collar and blue collar) by over 100,000 during the next few years. Shareholders have suffered, as well. Since 1987, GM's stock has lagged behind both the S&P 500 and shares of the other U.S. automakers.[29]

What happened to GM? In her book, *Rude Awakening,* respected auto analyst Maryann Keller provides some clues about why mighty GM was humbled.[30] Keller argues that GM knew that it had to change in the early 1980s, that its business environment had changed forever. However, the company found itself hopelessly entangled in a complex, myopic corporate culture that resisted change. Keller describes the following four elements of GM's corporate culture:

- **The Goliath Complex.** Bigger is better, the company believed. GM thought that its main strength was its ability to achieve monumental economies of scale. It had a difficult time understanding that in the contemporary fragmented and highly competitive auto market, it was becoming harder and harder to achieve scale economies. Further, as GM's market share fell, the company never attempted to downsize and, as a result, ended the 1980s with substantial excess production capacity and a bloated salaried workforce.
- **A Parochial World View.** GM saw no need to find out what customers really wanted because it had proven itself to be the industry leader.[31] GM merely assumed that people would buy whatever it produced. This parochial view of the world meant that GM never really understood foreign competition. Further, the company was unable to build the broad leadership base it probably needed. According to Keller, GM's senior executives tended to have similar backgrounds and, to a large extent, resembled one another remarkably.
- **Leadership by the Numbers.** GM's financial people determined every major investment and product initiative. This leadership by numbers was coupled with a resistance to hearing bad news about itself. Therefore, according to Keller, operating people learned how to make the numbers come out "just right" in order to get the financial people to sign off on a

---

[28]Ibid., 231–232.

[29]GM's average annual total return between the end of 1987 and the end of 1992 was around 7.0 percent, compared to 10.3 percent for Chrysler and Ford (combined) and 15.9 percent for the S&P 500.

[30]New York: William Morrow, 1989.

[31]As evidence of this, Keller notes that GM had no consumer market research division until 1985. Keller, *Rude Awakening,* 21.

project. Another example of financial tyranny appeared in frequent decisions to save comparably small amounts of money at the expense of product design, content, and quality.

- **Contemptuous Paternalism.** Apparently, firing an incompetent manager was a traumatic event at GM. (Only about 100 salaried employees were involuntarily let go in a typical year during the 1970s and 1980s.) Management compensation was based, not on performance or the company's bottom line, but on whatever new gains were negotiated with the United Auto Workers Union (UAW). Keller argues that this type of corporate paternalism is demoralizing to a workforce, since it gives no financial reward for high performance or concern for product quality and constant improvement.

This corporate culture, according to Keller's analysis, contributed to a number of disastrous decisions during the 1980s. Let's look at three examples. First, GM spent wildly on new technology. Roger Smith, GM's CEO during most of the 1980s, strongly believed that technology and automation could make a stronger competitor in the contemporary auto market. Smith was obsessed with robotics, for example. Therefore, GM committed its enormous financial resources to automation and technology during the 1980s. Keller estimates that GM spent over $40 billion on plant modernization alone (not including the $5 billion or so it invested in Saturn).[32] GM purchased equity in five machine-vision suppliers and a company working on artificial intelligence systems.

Unfortunately, however, GM lacked a continuous and consistent method for evaluating the effectiveness of its investments in technology. The company threw money at problems without any understanding of the real nature of the problems. Very few of these investments paid off. GM's operating efficiency improvements lagged well behind those made by Ford and Chrysler, and GM's production costs remained well above those of other domestic and foreign automakers. As a result, during the 1980s GM made less on each car it sold than either Chrysler or Ford.

A second example of the impact of GM's corporate culture is the 1986 introduction of the Cadillac Allante. Once GM's crown jewel, Cadillac's reputation had become tarnished by a series of well-publicized quality control problems and rapidly falling market share. Allante was supposed to restore Cadillac's image, attracting buyers of European luxury cars. By all accounts, Allante was a disaster. "[It] was under powered and plagued by mysterious rattles and squeaks. It was outrageously overpriced at $55,000—even if the car had worked perfectly."[33] Originally, GM projected sales of around 3,000 vehicles per year, assuming a price of $45,000. However, since at that price and volume, the car didn't meet GM's 15 percent return on investment standard, the price was increased, and the other numbers were manipulated to make the project appear to meet GM's ROI standard. Customer complaints began to roll in soon after the car went on sale for the first time. During the first two years, GM sold fewer than 3,000 Allantes, even with dealer rebates of $9,000. The model was finally discontinued.

According to Keller, the Allante fiasco illustrates the attitude GM had at the time toward its customers along with the company's lack of basic internal controls. She writes: "Everyone was scrambling to present the best picture [of the Allante project] to the top brass and no one was considering the customer."[34]

---

[32]Ibid., 205–206.

[33]Ibid., 215.

[34]Ibid., 217.

Finally, consider the acquisition of Hughes Electronics, a large defense contractor, in 1985. GM got into a bidding war for Hughes with Boeing and Ford (which already had a large aerospace and electronics business) and ended up buying Hughes for around $5.2 billion. Why did GM want to buy a defense electronics company? According to Keller, CEO Smith told the board: "Acquiring Hughes would allow top technical talent to be infused throughout GM and ultimately lead to its being a car company driven by advanced technology."[35] It was part of Smith's strategy to eliminate the Japanese cost advantage through technology. Yet, Hughes was considered to be the antithesis of the Japanese reputation of attention to minute, penny-pinching detail. Cost and quality control had never been a Hughes trademark, and it was far from a strong point with GM. Further, some questioned whether Hughes could offer any real synergy with GM's auto business. Ford saw *no* synergy with the auto business, according to Keller. Ross Perot, who was a member of GM's board at the time, strongly questioned why GM was spending all this money on something so peripheral to the car business as Hughes, when the firm really needed to figure out why its profit per car was about half what Chrysler or Ford made. None of this criticism mattered; Roger Smith, and the rest of GM's senior management, wanted to buy Hughes, and since the company had the money, it did.[36]

GE and GM are only two of hundreds of potential case studies of good and bad management we could have chosen. Both, however, clearly illustrate the kinds of things to look for, and types of issues to consider, when evaluating the quality of a company's management. Remember, you may not be able to clearly define "management quality," but it is an issue you can't ignore. There is often a strong relationship between the quality of a company's management and the returns to the shareholders.

Executive Compensation and Corporate Governance

One contemporary issue in corporation management that greatly affects investors is **executive compensation.** Many critics have questioned how much corporations pay senior executives and how well they earn their compensation. Many believe that executive compensation is part of a larger issue, **corporate governance.** This raises the question whether corporate managers run their companies in the best interests of stockholders. Evaluation of management's record in corporate governance may say a great deal about how well this work is done.

Understanding Executive Compensation

Executive compensation provokes strong controversy today. Many argue that senior managers receive excessive compensation. Further, critics argue there are poor links between compensation and performance. These critics also contend that excessive compensation hurts the global competitiveness of U.S. businesses, pointing to the fact that the average compensation of Japanese executives is far less than that of comparable U.S. executives.

---

[35]Ibid., 169–170.

[36]By most accounts, Hughes has been profitable for GM. Nevertheless, the question still remains whether GM should have spent over $5 billion on an acquisition that contributes only a small percentage of GM's total revenues (around 5 percent in 1992).

There is little question that compensation levels of senior managers of U.S. corporations have risen rapidly over the last 10 or 15 years. According to the annual survey conducted by *Business Week,* the average CEO of a U.S. corporation received more than $3.8 million in compensation in 1992, or more than five times what the average CEO received in 1980.[37] By contrast, median per capita U.S. income less than doubled during the same period. In comparison to U.S. CEOs' pay, Japanese CEOs received an average of around $870,000 in 1992.[38]

Types of Compensation. Executive compensation comes from four sources: salaries, bonuses, stock options (often called *long-term compensation*), and so-called *perks*. Because of new disclosure requirements, discussed in the next section, information on the first three sources is easy to obtain. Information concerning the value of many executive perks is next to impossible to obtain, however, without some cooperation from the executive involved. Perks include such things as company-paid insurance policies, golden parachute provisions, country club memberships, and use of company-owned apartments and cars.

Stock options are either restricted or unrestricted. Unrestricted options can be exercised (i.e., converted into common stock) at any time, while restricted options can be exercised only after a certain number of years. These options may, or may not, impose restrictions on the sale of stock obtained by exercising them. Options normally fix the exercise price (the price paid for each share of stock). These stock options typically have expiration dates between five and ten years after issue.

New Disclosure Rules. In 1992 the U.S. Securities and Exchange Commission (SEC) imposed new rules regarding the public disclosure of information about executive compensation. Normally, firms disclose executive compensation information in proxy statements that accompany notices of annual investors' meetings. As the Investment Insights feature on page 334 points out, it is now much more difficult to hide compensation of CEOs and other senior managers in the proxy statement. To paraphrase one pay consultant, the new disclosure requirement hits investors between the eyes; companies can no longer hide what they pay the boss.

As the article notes, the SEC now requires companies to provide a summary table showing how much they paid senior executives in each of the previous three years (broken down into salary, stock options, and other compensation). In particular, companies must provide details on stock options given to senior executives. This includes information on how many options each individual holds, their exercise prices, their current market values, and their potential market values. A table, or chart, must also compare the performance of the company's stock to two benchmarks (overall market and industry performance figures). It's interesting, as the article points out, that many companies have voluntarily disclosed more than the SEC requires.

Other countries are beginning to adopt similar disclosure requirements for executive pay. For example, in 1993, the Ontario Securities Commission, the most important securities regulatory body in Canada, adopted a set of disclosure rules on executive compensation. These rules are virtually identical to what the SEC now requires. All publicly traded companies in Ontario,

---

[37] *Business Week,* April 26, 1993, 56–57.

[38] We should point out that many argue that it is very difficult to fairly compare what Japanese and U.S. CEOs really make. For one thing, disclosure requirements are quite different. For another, Japanese CEOs typically receive more types of nonmonetary compensation than do their U.S. counterparts.

starting in 1994, will have to disclose how much they pay their CEOs and their four next-highest paid executives.

Analyzing Executive Compensation

Investors should ask two questions about executive compensation. First, is the amount paid to senior executives reasonable? Second, is executive compensation related to performance? The two questions are interrelated. For example, if two CEOs received the same compensation in 1992, but one CEO's pay was linked to performance while the other's appeared to defy the trend in company performance, an analyst might argue that the CEO whose compensation was linked to performance was earning a reasonable amount, while the other CEO was being paid excessively.

The line between reasonable and excessive compensation is, of course, very subjective. Obviously, a company must attract and keep top managerial talent, and that talent is not cheap. Further, if the company has delivered a good return for its investors consistently over a long period of time, they may consider almost any level of compensation reasonable. On the other hand, if the company has lost a pile of money, paying the CEO *anything* may seem excessive. Some people believe that *no* CEO should make more than a certain multiple of what the lowest-paid employee in the company earns, regardless of how well the company performs. For example, Ben & Jerry's Homemade, Inc., the maker of premium ice cream, pays its CEO no more than five times the salary of the lowest-paid employee. The company believes that equity in pay helps foster employee morale and loyalty, improving the performance of both employees and company.

Is excessive compensation really a major concern for investors? After all, the amount a company pays its CEO and other senior executives is a minute percentage of operating costs. Wal-Mart Stores, for example, paid its top five executives slightly over $3 million in 1992. The company probably spends more than $3 million each week on electricity.

Nevertheless, excessive compensation, however it's defined, can well be a problem. Many management experts believe that excessive executive compensation can be demoralizing to the rest of the company, especially if employees are being asked to tighten their belts. It can send the wrong signal, both internally and externally. For example, excessive compensation may be viewed as symptomatic of a larger inability to control costs. It might also suggest that management isn't running the company in the best interests of shareholders. Perhaps management is making suboptimal investment decisions and, thus, not maximizing intrinsic value.

In our view, the key is to reward senior executives for long-term performance. In other words, if the company prospers, senior management should benefit financially. This is impossible to evaluate based on a single year's data; longer time periods give more accurate pictures. For one thing, annual pay data can be skewed by the exercise of stock options. Also, the CEO should be rewarded more for long-term than short-term performance.

Compensation and Performance. Perhaps the best place to begin an examination of compensation and performance is with the company's guidelines for executive compensation. The new SEC rules require the company to publicly disclose these policies. Companies that closely link pay to performance usually set relatively modest salaries for top executives, and those amounts may be fixed for the lives of the employment contracts. A large percentage of the manager's total compensation, therefore, comes from bonuses and stock options, the amounts of which should be based on the performance of the company. Also, an analyst should assess how specific the guidelines are.

You Can't Bury CEO Treasure Chests Anymore

Only a year ago, Coca-Cola Co. awarded Chairman Roberto C. Goizueta an unprecedented grant of restricted stock worth more than $80 million. To uncover that generosity, however, shareholders had to search through dense prose in the proxy statement. Only then would they stumble upon a mention of the award—with the amount written out in words rather than numbers, making it even harder to find.

No more. The proxy, that archetype of obfus-

Fortunes Yet to Come

For all the big money being pulled down by the nation's top chief executives, there's plenty more to come. These CEOs are sitting on the 20 largest stock-option fortunes.

Executive	Company	Value of Nonexercised Stock Options (Thousands)[a]
D. Wayne Calloway	PepsiCo	$82,367
Leon C. Hirsch	U.S. Surgical	61,956
Roberto C. Goizueta	Coca-Cola	52,150
H. Wayne Huizenga	Blockbuster Entertainment	48,304
Paul Fireman	Reebok International	40,305
Lee Iacocca	Chrysler	35,553
Reuben Mark	Colgate-Palmolive	34,101
P. Roy Vagelos	Merck	28,803
Charles N. Mathewson	International Game Technology	26,464
William A. Schreyer	Merrill Lynch	25,499
Andrew S. Grove	Intel	21,231
Emerson Kampen	Great Lakes Chemical	20,382
Herbert M. Sandler	Golden West Financial	19,670
Harry A. Merlo	Louisiana-Pacific	18,620
Sanford I. Weill	Primerica	17,506
Walter J. Sanders III	Advanced Micro Devices	16,807
Stanley C. Gault	Goodyear	15,562
Daniel P. Amos	Aflac	15,054
William Farley	Fruit of the Loom	14,813
Maurice R. Greenberg	American International Group	14,529

[a]Based on stock price at end of company's fiscal year.

For example, if earnings fall, will the CEO automatically receive a smaller bonus? Finally, the analysis should try to determine who helps the board of directors set executive compensation. Many companies now rely on outside, independent pay consultants, who are often hired by the company's outside directors.[39]

Whatever the company's compensation guidelines say, an objective measure should try to relate compensation to performance. This implies choice of a measure of performance. The most obvious measure of performance is total returns to stockholders (dividends plus price appreciation) over a period of time.[40] As we noted, the SEC now requires that a company provide

---

[39]Outside directors are those other than the company's managers.

[40]Many investors and analysts will examine profitability measures, such as return on equity, as well as stock returns when measuring company performance.

cation, has been made more accessible to shareholders, thanks to new Securities and Exchange Commission rules. The huge grant to Goizueta, for example, is now disclosed in a summary table that provides a snapshot of three years of pay data. "It hits you between the eyeballs," says Paula H. Todd, of consultants Towers Perrin. "There's not much place to hide anymore."

True enough. Even a quick reading of Coca-Cola's latest proxy reveals Goizueta's treasure chest of more than $340 million in stock options, restricted stock, and so-called performance units. Previously, investors had to dig through years of proxy statements to make such a calculation.

Future Shock. Besides clearer statements of past pay, these newfangled proxies also provide some mind-boggling glimpses of future prospects. That's because they're now required to report on the value of nonexercised stock options based on the company's year-end stock price (table). D. Wayne Calloway, chairman of PepsiCo Inc., had a horde valued at $82.4 million. U.S. Surgical Corp. Chairman Leon C. Hirsch had options worth $62 million.

Another perennial winner of the pay sweepstakes, Reebok International Chairman Paul B. Fireman, boasted options worth more than $40 million. Even Lee Iacocca, who last year stepped down as chairman of Chrysler Corp., had $35.6 million more in profit on options yet to be exercised.

The new proxies also require a company to compare its stock's five-year performance with a broad market index and a peer group. But that still leaves room for a little spin control. Exxon Corp. added a 10-year performance chart to its proxy. The five-year one showed the company underperforming the Standard & Poor's 500-stock index. And Coca-Cola uses bright red ink to plot its stock, which outperformed both the S&P 500 and a peer group.

INVESTMENT INSIGHTS

Surprisingly, though, some companies are voluntarily disclosing information that makes them look bad. Citicorp charted its stock against an additional index of what it called "market-dominant global enterprises similar to Citicorp in size and complexity"—even though that made the bank's record appear worse. A $100 investment in that index, which includes such concerns as American Telephone & Telegraph Co. and General Electric Co., would have risen to $250 in five years, compared with an increase of only $155 for the bank—which also underperformed the two indexes required by the SEC.

Citicorp's candor may not be typical, but it's becoming less unusual amid today's hypersensitivity over executive pay. "Companies generally are tending to overreact to the new rules, giving more than is required," says Robert Salwen, a pay consultant at William M. Mercer Inc. "One of my clients has a record of paying its executives conservatively, yet their report on compensation goes into great depth justifying their modest pay packages." Sounds like just the thing the new proxy rules were designed to encourage.

Source: John A. Byrne, "You Can't Bury CEO Treasure Chests Anymore," *Busines Week,* April 26, 1993, 62. Reprinted from April 26, 1993, issue of *Business Week* by special permission, copyright © 1993 by McGraw-Hill, Inc.

investors with a chart that compares the total performance of the company's stock for at least five years with the total return produced by a broad market index, such as the S&P 500, and an index of industry stocks.

With a measure of performance settled, the analyst needs a methodology by which to compare compensation to performance, relative to other companies. As an example, *Business Week,* in its annual issue on executive compensation, evaluates pay in relation to performance: based on an index of total three-year stock return divided by the total amount paid to the CEO over the same three-year period (multiplied by 100). *Business Week* then divides the rankings into quintiles.[41] This simplifies ranking a specific company in relation to other companies in its industry.

---

[41]We must note that *Business Week* doesn't rank all publicly traded companies.

Yankee-Style Activists Strike Boardroom Terror Abroad

It came as no great surprise last spring when Andrew R. F. Buxton won the new slot of both chairman and chief executive at Barclays Bank PLC, effective Jan. 1, 1993. After all, Buxton, the scion of one of the bank's founding families, over 30 years had worked his way up the corporate ladder to No. 2. But by December, outside directors—goaded by big shareholders—had reconsidered, blaming Buxton for mounting bad debts and sagging earnings. Buxton was forced to cede the CEO job to another executive, probably by this spring.

The U.S. isn't the only place where shareholders are rising up to change the way companies are run. Britain, too, is being rocked by a campaign for better governance. Since 1990, angry shareholders have claimed the scalps of top executives at Burton Group, British Aerospace, and British Airways, among others.

More striking, the shareholder uprising is reaching across the globe. In Canada, Continental Europe, and Japan—where entrenched bank cliques, families, and governments hold sway over managers—shareholders are trying to change the balance of power. They often face stiff obstacles, such as the absence of the one share/one vote principle. Still, says Robert Sillcox, senior vice president for investments at Ontario's $13 billion Municipal Employment Retirement System: "The subject of corporate governance is on everyone's lips." Doubting corporate managers might well recall that as recently as two years ago, many U.S. and British executives dismissed out of hand the prospect of institutional uprisings.

The global economy will heighten pressure to give shareholders a bigger say. As national economies increasingly grow interlinked, more capital is flowing beyond national boundaries. Fund managers and institutions will open their wallets, but only in return for corporate openness, basic shareholder rights, and—possibly—more influence.

Countries and companies that don't respond have already turned off some foreign investors. Martin G. Wade, chief investment officer at $7.5 billion Rowe Price Fleming International, now steers clear of Italy, which gives minority shareholders short shrift. "Once you've been mugged enough times," snaps Wade, "you have to ask: Why hold the shares?"

At a minimum, big investors are demanding international standards of corporate behavior, accounting clarity, and disclosure. They're seeking an end to antitakeover poison pills. And they want to outlaw the outsized voting rights given certain classes of shareholders—for example, the 10 "priority shares" that hold all voting power at the Netherlands' Philips Electronics, which are in hands loyal to management. "We want to see the other European systems come into line with those of the U.S. and U.K.," says Anthony Bolton, senior investment officer for Fidelity Investments Services Ltd. in London and one of Europe's leading activists.

Investors also want better performance: Can-

Other Issues in Corporate Governance

Executive compensation isn't the only issue about which investors question companies. Traditionally even large institutional investors have tended to defer to senior management in almost all major decisions. They have dutifully elected management's chosen candidates to the board, approved management-sponsored proposals, and so forth. If investors didn't like what the company was doing, or how it was performing, they simply sold their shares—took a **Wall Street walk.** This is no longer true.

During the 1991 proxy season, for example, institutional investors (e.g., pension funds) and other organized investor groups sponsored 153 corporate governance proposals, a record. In addition to executive compensation, these proposals dealt with such things as antitakeover provisions, golden parachutes for executives, and guarantees that corporate boards would have majority blocs of outside directors. While only eight of these proposals were eventually approved, 20 were withdrawn after management made concessions to angry investors. Even in many cases where management prevailed, companies have become more receptive to investor demands and suggestions.

For example, investor groups helped force Time Warner to abandon an

ada's Sillcox, for one, pledges to begin working to influence strategy at laggard companies, though he prefers to work behind the scenes and avoid big public battles.

"Off Their Butts." In Britain, activism took off thanks to financial scandals at Maxwell Communications, Polly Peck International, and the Bank of Credit and Commerce International. Then, "with a lot of companies performing poorly," says Fidelity's Bolton, "institutions got off their butts."

They have found ammunition in the December publication of the Cadbury Report on corporate governance, the result of an 18-month study by leading regulators and industrialists. Endorsed by Britain's corporate elite, the Bank of England, and the London Stock Exchange, the report codifies "best" corporate practice. Among its key, but voluntary, recommendations: Split the posts of chairman and CEO, increase the say of independent directors on audit and compensation committees, and disclose executive pay more fully. British companies will have to report compliance to the stock exchange. And the report's influence may spread: fund managers in Canada and Australia are eyeing its impact.

Meanwhile, some British institutions are demanding representatives in the boardroom. Fidelity, for example, managed to install new outside directors at advertising giant WPP Group PLC and Teledanmark, the Danish phone company. Explains Alastair Ross Goobey, CEO of the $30 billion Possel Investment Management Ltd.: "We see ourselves playing a policeman's role."

INVESTMENT INSIGHTS

To maximize their clout, the British—particularly Fidelity—are increasingly joining in common cause with local fund managers in the Netherlands, Spain, and elsewhere. Increasingly, they're sharing data and tactics across borders.

American funds are helping to blaze the path. The $70 billion California Public Employees' Retirement System recently launched an international governance program, specifically targeting companies in Japan, France, and Britain. Last year, CalPERS voted unsuccessfully against a poison-pill takeover defense at French food giant BSN and tried unsuccessfully to push new directors onto the boards of Nomura Securities Co. and Daiwa Securities Co.

A Marker. In December, it joined forces with funds in Germany to try to undo an arrangement at electricity maker RWE that gave minority shareholders a majority of the voting rights. Nicolaus-Jürgen Weickart, a Frankfurt shareholder-rights lawyer, argues that even in defeat, CalPERS put down a marker. "It was impossible to win," says Weickart, "but it was the first time [Deutsche Bank and Dresdner Bank] abstained from voting their proxies." The CalPERS move and a series of recent hostile takeovers in Germany have emboldened others. A Mar. 11 shareholder proposal at Siemens, the electronics giant, to strip multiple voting rights from the descendants of

(continued)

unorthodox stock rights offering in 1991.[42] Investors complained that the rights offering, where stockholders could purchase shares at prices between $63 and $105 per share depending on how many investors participated, was simple coercion. If investors didn't want to risk seeing the value of their shares fall, they'd have to exercise the rights. Investor groups have claimed partial credit for the removal of CEOs at GM and IBM in 1992. They've also been partly responsible for forcing Eastman Kodak, Sears, and Westinghouse into major restructurings. As the Investment Insights feature shows, Yankee-style investor activism isn't limited to the United States. What's going on?

Part of this change in investor attitudes has been triggered, no doubt, by the poor performance of many prominent companies, many of them heavily owned by institutional investors. More fundamentally, however, many experts believe that increasing investor activism is due to the realization on the part of many large institutional investors that they must commit to their investments for the long term by default.[43] Given their sheer size, it is difficult for many institutional investors to sell shares in poorly performing companies without the stock price collapsing. For example, the California Public

---

[42]See "Time Warner Feels the Force of Shareholder Power," *Business Week,* July 29, 1991, 58–59.

[43]The SEC also helped by relaxing proxy regulations concerning private communication between shareholder groups.

(continued)

the founding von Siemens family is given a reasonable chance of succeeding.

A cadre of local gadflies, such as Weickart, also are sowing the seeds of wider shareholder activity. Former Nestlé manager André Baladi, now an independent investment adviser has been railing against the Swiss food giant's dividend policy for years and was in a camp of investors who succeeded in opening registered shares to foreign holders. And though the Dutch Shareholders Assn., a group of small investors and institutions, failed last year to block a merger of Nationale Nederlanden and NMB Postbank, it did manage to get the price raised. Meanwhile, Déminor, a Belgian company representing small holders in WagonsLits, a travel-services company, has won a court judgment against French hotelier Accor to get a higher price in a takeover. Accor is appealing.

Investor disenchantment is growing even in Japan, where crosslinks between corporate groups and banks is now seen as making managers too entrenched. Shareholders, growing restless with low dividends and paltry earnings, now have some heavy backing. A Japanese Justice Ministry committee just proposed changes to the commercial code to force companies to take on truly independent auditors and to ease the way for investors to sue company officials.

Proselytizing. Shareholders all over the world eagerly watch the U.S. CalPERS' CEO Dale M. Hanson is often sought out for advice by institutions in Canada and Japan. American activist Robert A. G. Monks, founder of Lens Inc., in February traveled to Australia, Singapore, the Netherlands, and Germany proselytizing to shareholders. The Dutch investment funds, with big international holdings, look particularly promising to him. Says Monks: "We'll probably help them devise a program [for Europe] through which they can become suitable active shareholders without creating undue problems."

None of this is being lost on heads-up managers. Britain's struggling Imperial Chemical Industries PLC, for example, has been moving fast to change course and to court institutions. On Feb. 25, its board approved the biggest corporate breakup in British history, splitting the manufacturing bulwark into separately quoted chemical and drug units. And in Germany, Boston Consulting Group Inc. is advising companies on enhancing shareholder value. "The trigger has been that international investors are exerting more pressure," says Thomas Lewis of BCG's Munich office.

From Tokyo to Toronto, Berlin to Birmingham, shareholders are demanding to be heard. And executives are beginning to learn that rebuffing them may well risk their jobs, access to capital, and eventually, the ability to compete in a global economy.

Source: Richard A. Melcher with Patrick Oster, "Yankee-Style Activists Strike Boardroom Terror Abroad," *Business Week,* March 15, 1993, 74. Reprinted from March 15, 1993, issue of *Business Week* by special permission, copyright © 1993 by McGraw-Hill, Inc.

Employees Retirement System (CalPERS) was unhappy with Sears management in the early 1990s, yet, because the pension fund owned 2.3 million shares, it felt it couldn't sell out without the market price plunging.

As a result, institutional investors have begun to follow a strategy called **relationship investing.**[44] Investors agree to take a long-term stake in the company, and in exchange the company agrees to talk with the investor group regularly, possibly giving the group a seat on the board. The company also allows investors to monitor performance more closely. The company gets more patient owners while investors get better management accountability.

Does Shareholder Activism Work? This new investor activism may seem to benefit shareholders, but does it work? Do companies perform better after listening, voluntarily or involuntarily, to investor groups? At this point no real scientific evidence can resolve the question one way or the other. Furthermore, the impact of investor activism should be felt more over the long term than the short term; this recent development has not had time to show results. Nevertheless, some anecdotal evidence may suggest that investor activism has had an effect.

Take a look at the four companies' performance illustrated in Figure 10.7.

---

[44]See, "Relationship Investing," *Business Week,* March 15, 1993, 68–75.

Figure 10.7

Four Examples of Potentially Successful Shareholder Activism

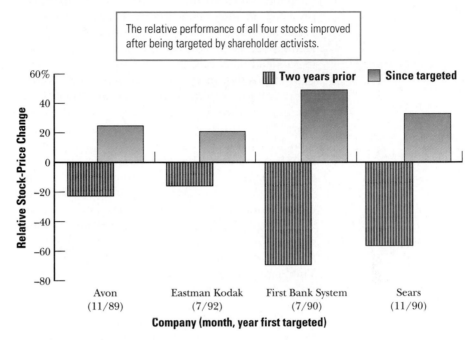

Source: *Business Week,* March 15, 1993, 70.

All four have been the target of investor activism in recent years, and all four have responded in various ways. Perhaps it is a coincidence, but the performance of all four companies improved markedly after they responded to investor activists. During the two years prior to being targeted by investor activists, all four stocks had lagged behind the S&P 500, some by substantial amounts. Since then, however, all four have outperformed the overall market.

For example, Eastman Kodak was first targeted by shareholder activists in July 1992. For the two years before that, Kodak's stock had a relative price change (its price change minus the change in the S&P 500 over the same period) of −15.3 percent. Between July 1992 and December 31, 1993, Kodak's stock had a relative price change of +20.6 percent.

Suppose a thorough qualitative analysis has identified a well-run company with a strong competitive position in its industry. Time to buy, right? Not yet. So far, we've considered only the first two aspects of company analysis; the other three, more quantitative, aspects will be examined in the next chapter. If the picture still looks good at the end of Chapter 11, it may be time to buy.

Chapter Summary

1. Provide an overview of company analysis.

The major goal of company analysis is to come up with forecasts of both the quality and quantity of future earnings that accommodates all material influences on earnings. A security analysis report should cover five general topics: the competitive position of the company within its industry, the quality of the company's management, its current financial position, its long-term financial position, and its profitability and earnings. It is important for the analyst to examine both the historical record of each topic and make future projections. We discussed the first two topics (competitive position and quality of management) in the balance of this chapter, leaving the other three topics for Chapter 11.

2. **Understand and analyze the competitive position of a company.**

Qualitative analysis must evaluate the competitive position of a company because, all else being equal, a stronger competitive position implies greater, and more consistent, future earnings. Further, investments in leading companies expose the stockholder to lower risk than investments in nonleading companies. The analyst can determine a company's competitive position in various ways. Size (measured in terms of revenues or sales) and growth rate in revenues are generally good indicators. A larger company, relative to its competitors, with more rapid growth is generally more dominant in its industry. Profitability is another good guide; dominant companies are generally more profitable. New products, product innovation, product line depth, and product diversification are other factors to consider. Leading companies generally have diverse product mixes, introduce new products more quickly, and are more innovative than their competitors. Leading companies are also, in general, more efficient making them pricing leaders. They may exploit proprietary technology. Southwest Airlines has a strong competitive position.

3. **Describe the nature of management.**

The general definition of management depends on two important ideas. First, managers are responsible for the attainment of various organizational objectives both effectively and efficiently. *Effectiveness* is defined as the degree to which the company achieves its goals; *efficiency* is defined as the resources used by the company to produce a certain level of output. The second part of the definition of management identifies four basic functions of management: planning, organizing, leading, and controlling. Planning involves setting goals for the company and deciding on the tasks and resources needed to obtain the goals. Organizing is concerned with the assignment of tasks to various parts of the organization. Leading involves the motivation of employees to achieve the organization's goals. Finally, the controlling function is concerned with monitoring performance, keeping the organization on track, and correcting deficiencies. Good managers demonstrate technical, conceptual, and human skills. The relative importance of each depends on the manager's position in the organizational hierarchy.

4. **Review the criteria for evaluating the quality of management.**

The qualitative analysis must answer some questions about the quality of management. These questions deal with such topics as the age and experience of management, the effectiveness of the company's strategic planning, the soundness of its marketing strategy, its effectiveness at adapting to changing business conditions, the company's finances, its competitive position, its growth, and its relations with employees and the general public. Two short case studies illustrate good management practices at General Electric and poor management practices at General Motors. One of GE's strengths, for example, is its strategic planning. Ge gets out of markets and products it can't dominate, and invests in products and markets that it can. Stockholders have been well rewarded; no company's market value increased more than GE's during the 1980s. On the other hand, GM has been characterized as having a Goliath complex in the 1980s, along with a parochial world view, tyranny by financial people, and an overall attitude of contemptuous paternalism. GM threw money at problems without first defining them, in the process losing a huge amount of money in recent years while remaining a high-cost manufacturer.

5. **Discuss executive compensation and other such issues in corporate governance.**

Executive compensation, what companies pay their CEOs and other top executives, is very controversial today, as compensation levels of U.S.

Table 10.2

USAir's Competitive Position

	RPMs (billions)		ASMs (billions)		Revenue ($ millions)		Operating Income ($ millions)	
	Industry	USAir	Industry	USAir	Industry	USAir	Industry	USAir
1988	423.3	31.3	677.3	52.1	$63,679	$5,707	$3,443	$434
1989	432.7	33.7	684.7	55.6	69,225	6,251	1,812	21
1990	457.9	35.6	733.8	59.5	75,967	6,559	(1,914)	(501)
1991	448.0	34.1	704.3	58.3	75,158	6,514	(1,785)	(174)
1992	478.1	35.1	763.7	59.7	78,119	6,686	(2,373)	(336)

Note: *RPMs* stands for *revenue passenger miles* and *ASMs* stands for *available seat miles.* Load factor is equal to RPMs divided by ASMs.

Sources: USAir Annual Report, *Business Statistics.*

senior executives have risen rapidly over the past 10 to 15 years. Executive compensation comes in four forms (salaries, bonuses, stock options, and so-called *perks*). The SEC now requires far more detailed public disclosure of executive compensation. Investors need to ask two basic questions concerning executive compensation: (1) Is the amount paid senior executives reasonable? (2) Is compensation linked to performance? Further, while the line between reasonable and excessive compensation is very ambiguous, excessive compensation can demoralize employees and indicate larger problems such as inability to control costs. The analyst can evaluate compensation based on performance by first reviewing the company's compensation policy—does it appear to be performance based? Then the analyst can compare compensation to company performance (such as stock returns over several years) using some sort of a standardized measure. An example is the pay-for-performance index published by *Business Week*. Finally, the debate over corporate governance has heated up as many investors, especially institutional investors, are becoming more proactive. These investors are challenging management decisions more frequently and, in a growing number of cases, getting results. Some anecdotal evidence indicates that shareholder activism can improve company performance.

Key Terms

Quality and quantity of future earnings	Organizing
Company analysis report	Leading
Competitive position	Controlling
Quality of management	Strategic planning
Dominant or leading company	Multinational corporation (MNC)
Product line	Marketing strategy
Low-cost producer	Financial risk
Price leader	Business risk
Proprietary technology	Executive compensation
Organizational objective	Corporate governance
Planning	Wall Street walk
	Relationship investing

Mini Case   OBJECTIVE

The purpose of this Mini Case is to analyze the competitive position of USAir Group in the airline industry. Data on the industry and USAir are presented in Table 10.2.

1. What is your overall assessment of USAir's competitive position? On what do you base your conclusion?

2. How does USAir's position compare with the competitive position of Southwest Airlines, as we discussed in the chapter?

3. What information other than that presented in the table, would you like to have to further assess USAir's competitive position?

Discussion Questions and Problems

1. What is the major goal of company analysis? What type of information does the typical company report contain?

2. Define what is meant by the competitive position of a company. Why is this important?

3. List some of the things you might examine when analyzing the competitive position of a company. When comparing a company to an industry, what do you have to be careful about?

4. The general definition of *management* contains two important ideas. What are they? What is the meaning of *organizational performance?*

5. What are the four functions of management? Give a brief example of each function.

6. What types of skills should good managers possess? How does the relative importance of each skill change as a manager moves up the organizational hierarchy?

7. List some of the most important questions to ask when evaluating management. Along with each question, list some possible sources of information.

8. Define the term *strategic management.* What kinds of questions should you ask concerning a company's strategic management?

9. What are the sources of executive compensation? Discuss the terms and conditions typically associated with executive stock options.

10. What new rules has the SEC adopted regarding public disclosure of executive compensation in the United States? Why is it harder for companies to hide what CEOs are really being paid?

11. When analyzing executive compensation, what two basic questions should investors ask? Should investors even care what the boss is being paid?

12. Explain one way of objectively comparing executive pay with performance. What are some other factors you may wish to consider?

13. What is shareholder activism? Why have institutional shareholders become more activist in recent years?

Critical Thinking Exercises

1. This exercise requires library research. Your library should have copies of the annual reports companies file with the Securities and Exchange Commission (Form 10K). These reports are also available on many computerized databases such as Compact Disclosure. Starting in 1992, companies were required to disclose executive compensation in more detail.

   Obtain the 10K and related proxy statements for The Gap for the most recent fiscal year you can find. Using this report, answer the following questions.

   a. What do the firm's compensation guidelines say? How specific are they?

   b. How much did The Gap pay its CEO that year?

   c. How much of his or her compensation was in the form of salary and how much was in the form of stock options?

d. How much are his or her stock options worth (at the time the report was prepared and today)?

e. Using the information provided in the 10K, compute a pay-for-performance measure for The Gap using the *Business Week* methodology.

f. Was the compensation paid The Gap's CEO during this year reasonable? Does CEO compensation appear to be linked to performance? Why or why not?

2. This exercise requires both computer work and library research. Open file WMT.TXT to access a company research report prepared by an analyst at A. G. Edwards & Sons on Wal-Mart Stores. According to Standard & Poor's (*Industry Surveys,* May 13, 1993), the following are some relevant questions an analyst should ask when assessing the corporate strategy of any retailer:

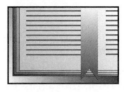

- Has the retailer stayed on top of major demographic and economic trends?
- What category of retailing is the company in? Does it appear to be diversified?
- Where are the company's key regional markets? Are those markets strong or weak economically?
- How strong is the competition relative to the company?
- How does the company position itself in terms of price, value, quality, and service? Where does it make tradeoffs between price, value, quality, and service?
- How effective is the company's merchandising and store presentation?
- How many more stores does the company plan to open? Has its past growth been orderly and well-managed?
- How effectively does the company keep its costs under control?

Considering these questions, and using the A. G. Edwards report, answer the following questions:

1. Why are these questions important to ask concerning a retailer?
2. How did the A. G. Edwards analyst answer each question about Wal-Mart?
3. Do you agree with his answers? Why or why not?
4. How do analysts at Value Line and Standard & Poor's answer these questions about Wal-Mart? If either had different answers than A. G. Edwards, why?

Mini Case   SOLUTION

1. Several calculations from the data given in Table 10.2 can contribute to an assessment of USAir's competitive position. Some of the most obvious are shown in Table 10.3. These data suggest that USAir's competitive position is not strong with respect to the rest of the industry.

   a. USAir has grown slightly more slowly than the rest of the industry since 1988 (measured by both dollar revenues and RPMs). Since 1988, industry dollar revenues have grown by about 23 percent while USAir's revenues have grown by about 17 percent.

   b. Dividing total revenues by ASMs (available seat miles) gives revenue (or yield) per ASM. While USAir's revenue per ASM has been consistently higher than that of the industry, the gap has narrowed. It was 1.55 cents in 1988 compared to 0.97 cents in 1992. This does not suggest that USAir is any kind of price leader in the markets it serves.

Table 10.3

	Revenue (index)		RPMs (index)		Yield/ASM		Cost/ASM		Yield/Cost	
	Industry	USAir	Industry	USAir	Industry	USAir	Industry	USAir	Industry	USAir
1988	100.0	100.0	100.0	100.0	9.40	10.95	8.89	10.12	105.7%	108.2%
1989	108.7	109.5	102.2	107.7	10.11	11.24	9.85	11.21	102.7	100.3
1990	119.3	114.9	108.2	113.7	10.35	11.02	10.61	11.87	97.5	92.9
1991	118.0	114.1	105.8	108.9	10.67	11.17	10.92	11.47	97.7	97.4
1992	122.7	117.2	112.9	112.1	10.23	11.20	10.54	11.76	97.1	95.2

Notes: Indexes are calculated as: $I_t = (X_t/X_t - 1) \times I_{t-1}$, where X is either revenue or RPMs. The index value for 1988 equals 100. Yield per ASM is equal to revenues divided by total ASMs. Cost per ASM is equal to operating costs (revenues minus operating income) divided by total ASMs. Yield and cost per ASM are in cents. Yield/cost equals the yield per ASM divided by cost per ASM.

    c. More telling are the data on cost per ASM. Operating costs equal operating revenues minus operating income. Dividing operating costs by total available seat miles gives cost per ASM. The data in Table 10.3 clearly show that USAir is a high-cost airline. This is also a measure of operating efficiency, suggesting that USAir is not as efficient as the industry average, not the sign of a leading company. You may have noticed, however, that industry costs have risen slightly faster than USAir's since 1988.

    d. Yield divided by cost compares yield per ASM with cost per ASM and confirms what we've discussed in relation to Questions b and c. While the industry's yield-to-cost ratio was hardly satisfactory in 1992, showing that the industry had an operating loss, it was higher than the yield-to-cost ratio for USAir.

2. The data on Southwest Airlines presented in the text show that Southwest is clearly a more dominant airline than USAir. Southwest is growing much faster and has far higher operating efficiency. In 1992, for example, USAir's cost per ASM was 4.73 cents higher than Southwest's. Further, Southwest's yield-to-cost ratio in 1992 was 112 percent compared to 95 percent for USAir.

3. In order to fully assess USAir's competitive position, it would be helpful to examine the airline's market share in each city-pair it serves, and whether its market share is rising or falling. Also, you might like to know how USAir responds to new competition in one of its major markets. Remember, Southwest tends to quickly dominate a market once it begins service.

Chapter 11

Company Analysis: Quantitative Issues

$\longrightarrow$

Chapter Objectives

1. Understand the importance of quantitative company analysis.
2. Examine the relationship between financial ratios and market value.
3. Review how to evaluate financial statements.
4. Conduct company analysis using financial ratios.
5. Understand business risk and operating leverage.
6. Estimate a sample company's earnings and expected return.

To many, unfortunately, quantitative analysis means simply plugging numbers into formulas; this exercise is meaningless by itself. A meaningful analysis requires careful interpretation of the input numbers and the implications of the resulting calculations.

For example, Chambers Development, Inc. was considered a dream growth stock back in the fall of 1991.[1] The company, which develops landfills, then announced on March 17, 1992 that it would start expensing indirect costs related to developing its sites. These costs, including public relations and legal fees to obtain permits, had been capitalized.[2] This change resulted in a $27 million charge against earnings, reducing Chambers's net income by half. The stock market reacted by reducing its market value by $1.4 billion.

We can learn three important lessons from this example. First, analysis of accounting numbers and financial data are critical to determining a company's earnings. Chapter 8 has already covered the importance of earnings to the estimate of the intrinsic value of a stock. In Chambers Development's case, a reduction in earnings led to a decline in market value. The second lesson teaches that we can't just apply these numbers blindly. Accounting has its gray areas that can create uncertainties. Analysis should carefully consider all assets, including unrecorded assets, of a company. An example is uncapitalized advertising that could have a major impact on sales and earnings for a company like Coca Cola. Finally, it's important to understand the implications of different accounting techniques, for example, expensing versus capitalizing costs.

A sound investment analysis procedure might take the following steps. First, understand the factors that affect a common stock's value (Chapter 8).

---

[1]"Fuzzy Accounting," *Forbes,* June 22, 1992.

[2]Capitalizing costs allowed the company to spread the cost (amortize it) over a number of years. Expensing forces the company to report all the costs against current sales.

Second, determine the conditions in the economy and industry that may affect the stock (Chapter 9). Finally, analyze the company itself, using qualitative and quantitative information, to see if it is a good investment. Chapter 10 outlined the competitive position of the company within its industry and the quality of its management. This chapter focuses on more quantitative issues, including the company's current financial position (liquidity), its long-term financial position (capital structure), and its profitability with the objective of determining the value of the company's stock. The final result of all this analysis is an answer to this question: Should one invest in this company's stock or not?

In this chapter, we will explore the importance of quantitative analysis of a company. We will critically examine financial data and use it to evaluate company performance, since strong financial performance implies higher earnings and a higher intrinsic value if risk remains constant. Further, as we already know from Chapter 8, a higher intrinsic value increases the likelihood of a good investment.

Importance of Quantitative Company Analysis

Why is quantitative company analysis important? Qualitative analysis develops an understanding of a company's financial status and risks. Strong financial condition can indicate that managers are doing a good job of increasing sales (by adding innovative products and/or increasing market shares) and cutting costs, thereby increasing earnings. As you already know, a well-run company has higher earnings and a higher intrinsic stock value.

Quantitative analysis also contributes to an understanding of a company's risk, including financial, operating, and business risks. This may not be as simple as it seems; certain types of risk may actually increase ROE and stock value! We will explore these areas as part of company analysis.

Finally, think of quantitative company analysis as a corporate checkup. Like a medical checkup, quantitative company analysis checks the vital signs of a company to determine whether it would be a healthy investment.

This chapter discusses two different approaches to quantitative company analysis and stock value assessment. One method examines past financial ratios, and then compares them to industry ratios, a competitor's ratios, or the company's historic ratios. Though the past is no guarantee for the future, examining the past can build some knowledge about the company's financial standing in the future.

Another method of quantitative analysis uses regression analysis techniques to forecast an expected future return, perhaps one year from today, for several companies. Comparing these expected returns can reveal the relative attractiveness of a number of companies.

Each method has some strengths and weaknesses. Ratio analysis conducts calculations on past data. Its strengths are the availability of data and the knowledge that the data must conform to accounting standard guidelines called GAAP (generally accepted accounting principles) making comparison easier.[3] Of course, the weakness is that past performance gives no guarantee for the future. Nevertheless, past data can give some feel about the company and its management.

---

[3]Despite these standards, we have already seen an example on the gray areas of accounting. Later in the chapter, we will discuss imperfections in information, even without gray areas.

Forecasting expected returns and earnings has its merits and downfalls, too. Its virtue is the resulting foresight of the return an investor can expect from a company relative to other companies. After the fact, however, the forecast can turn out to misrepresent reality, but no one can know until after investing money. The forecasting method trades off the correct orientation for a decision process (using expected rather than past returns) against accuracy of data.

Along with Graham and Dodd (as discussed in Chapter 10), we suggest evaluation of any investment by both methods. Also, before we start analyzing a company, remember what we said about growth companies with high intrinsic values fully valued by the market. Shares in a growth company may not necessarily be a growth stock. Recall that growth *companies* are firms with positive net present value investments, while growth *stocks* are undervalued stocks that can generate superior returns when compared to other stocks at the same risk level.[4] Company analysis can identify a growth company, but further analysis must compare its intrinsic value to its market value to determine whether it's a good investment or not. After all, no one wants to waste hard earned money for lack of a few minutes' research.

Our main objective in this chapter is to determine the quantitative factors that affect stock value. The next section examines some accounting ratios to determine their relationships to stock value.

Relationship between Financial Ratios and Market Value

In the previous section, we introduced the principle of ratio analysis to develop a financial profile of a company. In this section, we will show how a company's accounting ratios are related to the intrinsic value of its stock. The Dividend Discount Model (DDM), introduced in Chapter 8, will provide the linkage between intrinsic stock value and accounting ratios.

The DDM says that a stock's current intrinsic value equals:

$$V_{i0} = \frac{DIV_0(1 + g)}{Er_i - g} = \frac{DIV_1}{Er_i - g} \tag{8.7}$$

The growth rate, g, is defined by ROE times b, where ROE is the return on equity and b is the retention ratio or (1 minus the dividend payout ratio).[5]

Both ROE and b are obtained from the firm's financial statement. Both directly affect the intrinsic value of its stock. Further, recall that in an efficient market, a stock's market value should converge to its intrinsic value. Other ratios of accounting data can reinforce analysis of ROE and improve the analyst's understanding of how the financial status of a company can affect growth.

Analysis of *ROE*

Remember from your accounting classes that ROE equals:

$$\text{ROE} = \frac{\text{Net profits after taxes}}{\text{Common stockholders' equity}} = \frac{\text{Net profits}}{\text{Common equity}} \tag{11.1}$$

---

[4]See the section in Chapter 8 on the Earnings Model for a review of growth companies and growth stocks.

[5]Recall from Chapter 8 that the retention ratio, b, equals retained earnings divided by earnings per share, RE_1/EPS_1.

ROE attempts to measure the earnings generated by the company that belong to the stockholders; that is, stockholders' return, relative to what they have invested in the company (stockholders' equity). This number answers the question, what do the stockholders get back from their investment, based on book value or accounting data.

Decomposing ROE reveals what lies behind the basic formula showing how a company's operating and financial performance can affect ROE. ROE can be decomposed as:

$$\text{ROE} = \underbrace{\frac{\text{Net profits}}{\text{Equity}}}_{} = \underbrace{\frac{\text{Net profits}}{\text{Sales}}}_{\text{Ratio 1}} \times \underbrace{\frac{\text{Sales}}{\text{Total assets}}}_{\text{Ratio 2}} \times \underbrace{\frac{\text{Total assets}}{\text{Equity}}}_{\text{Ratio 3}} \quad (11.2)$$

Equation 11.2 shows that ROE can be decomposed into three ratios that measure the company's effectiveness. Briefly, Ratio 1 measures profitability, Ratio 2 measures company sales activity, and Ratio 3 measures leverage. Now let's discuss each one in detail and see how each affects ROE.

Ratio 1, the **profit margin,** measures how much of sales pass through to become net profits for the stockholders. A higher number indicates that a greater percentage of sales belongs to the stockholders in the form of earnings. This ratio attempts to answer the question, how profitable is the company? It's pretty easy to see how the profit margin affects ROE: it measures the amount of profits the firm generates out of sales, and these profits are the dollar returns generated for the stockholders. As this dollar return to stockholders increases, so does the stock value.

Ratio 2, **total asset turnover,** measures how effectively the company utilizes the assets. This is also referred to as the **asset utilization ratio.** A higher number indicates more efficient operation of the assets of the company. This ratio attempts to answer the question, how actively does the firm use its assets? How does this efficiency affect ROE? Think of equity as the funds invested by the stockholders to buy assets for the company (machines, warehouses, inventory, etc.). If the stockholders' assets are operated productively, then they will generate greater sales (and profits) than if some assets sit idle. In this way, a higher total asset turnover provides a greater return to stockholders.

Ratio 3, the **leverage ratio,** measures how much of a firm's total assets are financed by equity as opposed to debt (also called *leverage*). The leverage ratio essentially measures how much of the firm's assets it finances by debt and how much by equity. Since debt and equity appear on the right-hand side of the balance sheet and total assets appear on the left-hand side, debt and equity together must equal the total assets of the company.

Balance Sheet

	Debt
	Equity
Total assets	Debt and equity

Notice that a higher leverage ratio indicates less funding by equity (common stockholders) and a lower ratio indicates more funding by equity. As fewer assets are funded by equity and more by debt, the denominator becomes smaller and the leverage ratio increases beyond 1.00. This implies that 1.00 is the minimum value of the leverage ratio. For example, if total assets equal $100 and all funded by equity, then the leverage ratio equals 1.00. However, if equity funds $10 and debt $90, then the ratio equals $100/$10 or 10.00.

This ratio attempts to answer the question, how much debt (leverage) does the company have? Leverage affects ROE because as the firm uses more debt to finance its assets, ROE rises. If debtholders fund more and stockholders less, then the percentage return to stockholders is greater. This is a point we will discuss in greater detail later. In addition, after-tax profits are affected by leverage because interest expense on debt is tax deductible, and also because this expense is a fixed outflow.[6]

Next, we will review financial statements and some accounting practices to discuss how to use financial ratios and to evaluate the company's operating and financial effectiveness. Again, remember that more effective operations increase the company's earnings, and hence its stock's intrinsic value.

Review of Financial Statements

Firms create financial statements to provide interested parties with information on their available resources (funds), the sources of funding for those resources, and the uses of these funds. The three financial statements that provide this information are: (1) the balance sheet, (2) the income statement, and (3) the cash flow statement. Using Disney as an example, we will discuss each statement separately.[7]

Balance Sheet

The **balance sheet** is a snapshot of the company's asset holdings on the left-hand side and the sources of funding for those assets on the right-hand side. The two sides must balance, as all assets are financed by the sources on the right side. The left-hand side usually divides assets between two categories: (1) current assets, including cash, marketable securities, accounts receivable, and inventories, and (2) fixed assets, including plant and equipment and property such as warehouses.

The right-hand side of the balance sheet divides the firm's liabilities among the parties who have invested in the company. The two major classes of funders are debtholders and equityholders. Total debt is usually separated into short-term debt (or current liabilities) and long-term debt, while equity includes common stock and preferred stock issues. Common stock affects two balance sheet accounts: outstanding common stock and retained earnings. The balance sheet records outstanding common stock at par value and retained earnings equal the net profits that are reinvested in the company.

Table 11.1 presents Walt Disney's consolidated balance sheet for 1990, 1991, and 1992. Notice that it gives a snapshot of the firm on September 30 of each year. The balance of each account on that date is referred to as a **stock figure.** We will discuss Disney's balance sheet for 1992. (Accounts are reported in millions of dollars.)

Disney's current assets consist of cash and cash equivalents ($764.8); marketable securities, which include marketable equity securities and some interest rate swap agreements ($1,407.0); accounts receivable, which report sales for which payments are not yet received ($1,298.9); and merchandise inventories ($462.8).

---

[6]You may already be familiar with this *financial leverage* concept from a corporate finance class. If not, don't worry; we will discuss it in the next section.

[7]*Annual Report,* Walt Disney Company, 1992.

Table 11.1

Walt Disney Company
Balance Sheet
Fiscal Year-End September 30, 1990–1992
($ millions)

Assets

	1992	1991	1990
Current assets			
Cash and cash equivalents	$ 764.8	$ 886.1	$ 819.8
Marketable securities	1,407.0	782.4	588.1
Receivables	1,298.9	1,128.2	851.5
Merchandise inventories	462.8	311.6	269.2
Total current assets	$ 3,933.5	$3,108.3	$2,528.6
Fixed assets			
Film and television costs	$ 760.5	$ 596.9	$ 641.1
Theme parks, resorts, and property, net	4,798.7	4,571.6	3,910.5
Other assets	1,369.0	1,151.7	942.1
Total fixed assets	$ 6,928.2	$6,320.2	$5,493.7
Total assets	$10,861.7	$9,428.5	$8,022.3

Liabilities and Stockholders' Equity

	1992	1991	1990
Current liabilities			
Accounts payable and other accrued liabilities	$ 1,791.9	$1,433.8	$1,158.1
Income taxes payable	381.0	296.2	200.3
Total current liabilities	$ 2,172.9	$1,730.0	$1,358.4
Long-term debt			
Borrowings	$ 2,222.4	$2,213.8	$1,584.6
Unearned royalties and other advances	872.8	859.5	841.9
Deferred income taxes	889.0	753.9	748.8
Total long-term debt	$ 3,984.2	$3,827.2	$3,175.3
Stockholders' Equity			
Preferred stock ($0.10 par value, authorized—100.0 and 5.0 million shares, issued—none)	—	—	—
Common stock (0.025 par value, authorized—1,200 million shares, issued—552.2 million shares and 548.6 million shares)	$ 619.9	$ 549.7	$ 502.8
Retained earnings	4,661.9	3,950.5	3,401.1
Cumulative translation adjustments	86.9	35.2	67.7
Total	$ 5,368.7	$4,535.4	$3,971.6
Less treasury stock, at cost (27.8 million shares)	664.1	664.1	483.0
Total stockholders' equity	$ 4,704.6	$3,871.3	$3,488.6
Total liabilities and stockholders' equity	$10,861.7	$9,428.5	$8,022.3

Fixed assets include film and television costs ($760.5); theme parks, resorts, and property net of depreciation ($4,798.7); and other assets ($1,369.0). Interestingly, Disney reports film and television cost as assets, carried at cost much like a purchase of land. Other assets include "rights to the name, likeness and portrait of Walt Disney, goodwill, and other intangible assets which are being amortized over periods ranging from 2 to 40 years."[8]

The liabilities and stockholders' equity section begins with current liabilities, including accounts payable (unpaid bills) and other accrued liabilities ($1,791.9) and income taxes payable ($381.0). Short-term and long-term debt, referred to as *Borrowings* ($2,222.4), include subordinated notes at 6.2 percent, medium-term notes at 3.1 percent, securities sold under provisions to repurchase, and commercial paper. Two other liabilities are unearned royalties and other advances ($872.8) and deferred income taxes ($889.0).

The stockholders' equity consists of no preferred stock, just common stock. The common stock includes outstanding common stock and retained earnings, as well as cumulative translation adjustments, amounting to $5,368.7. Treasury stock is issued common stock that is repurchased in the market and recorded at cost (market value plus a premium) and subtracted from equity to obtain a final value of $4,704.6 for stockholders' equity.

Income Statement

The **income statement** provides information about the sales, cost, and profits of a company during some specified period of time (usually a quarter or a year). These accounts provide **flow figures** that represent accounts that receive additions over time as the information flows in. A good example is revenues or sales. As the firm sells products each day, it sums revenue over the year in order to represent total annual sales. Closely analyzing the income statement can reveal how effectively the company markets its products (sales), controls its costs (expenses) to generate the sales, and uses its debt. The final figure for income (profits after taxes) represents the earnings to the stockholders of the company. In this text we use the terms *net income* (or *income*), *net profits* (or *net profits after taxes*), and *earnings* interchangeably. Unfortunately, each company uses different terms. We follow the terms used by our sample company throughout the example.

Let's examine Walt Disney's income statement, given in Table 11.2. The Disney consolidated statement of income covers the years ending on September 30, 1990, 1991, and 1992. Because they are flow accounts, the figures represent information from October 1 of one year through September 30 of the next year (e.g., October 1, 1989 to September 30, 1990).

Disney generates its revenues or sales from theme parks and resorts, films, and sales of Disney character-related paraphernalia. Table 11.2 shows sales of $5,757.3 million in 1990. (That's $5.7573 billion.) This figure continued to increase in the following years. As expected, it's quite costly to run theme parks, produce films, and open Disney stores, and the firm's costs and expenses of $4,418.2 million in 1990 also increased. This produced operating income, revenues minus costs and expenses, of $1,339.1 million, $1,094.5 million, and $1,435.3 million, respectively, over the three years.

Notice that, despite higher revenues than 1990, operating income was lower in 1991 ($1,094.5 versus $1,339.1). This says that Disney's costs and expenses increased more than revenues in 1991 as compared to 1990; this trend could be a problem if it were to continue in 1992. Fortunately for Disney, it managed to control costs and expenses, increasing its operating income substantially from 1991 to 1992 (from $1,094.5 million to $1,435.3 million).

---

[8]Ibid.

Table 11.2

Walt Disney Company
Consolidated Income Statement
($ millions except per share data)

| | Year Ended September 30 | | |
	1992	1991	1990
Revenues			
Theme parks and resorts	$3,306.9	$2,794.3	$2,933.2
Filmed entertainment	3,115.2	2,593.7	2,250.3
Consumer products	1,081.9	724.0	573.8
Total revenues	$7,504.0	$6,112.0	$5,757.3
Costs and expenses			
Theme parks and resorts	$2,662.9	$2,247.7	$2,130.3
Filmed entertainment	2,606.9	2,275.6	1,937.3
Consumer products	798.9	494.2	350.6
Total costs and expenses	$6,068.7	$5,017.5	$4,418.2
Operating income			
Theme parks and resorts	$ 644.0	$ 546.6	$ 802.9
Filmed entertainment	508.3	318.1	313.0
Consumer products	283.0	229.8	223.2
Total operating income	$1,435.3	$1,094.5	$1,339.1
Corporate activities			
General administrative expenses	$ 148.2	$ 160.8	$ 138.5
Interest expense	126.8	105.0	43.1
Investment and interest income	(130.3)	(119.4)	(80.8)
Total corporate activities	$ 144.7	$ 146.4	$ 100.8
Income from investment in EuroDisney	$ 11.2	$ 63.8	$ 86.4
Income before income taxes	$1,301.8	$1,011.9	$1,324.7
Income taxes	485.1	375.3	500.7
Net income	$ 816.7	$ 636.6	$ 824.0
Earnings per share (EPS)	$ 1.52	$ 1.20	$ 1.50
Average number of common and common equivalent shares outstanding	536.8	532.7	549.0

Other expenses related to administrative costs and financial expenses (interest expenses on debt) appear under corporate activities on Disney's income statement. Also income from investment in EuroDisney is reported separately. Income before income taxes equals operating income minus corporate activities plus income from investment in EuroDisney. For 1990, this equals $1,324.7 million, $1,011.9 in 1991, and $1,301.8 in 1992. After income taxes, Disney had income of $824.0 million in 1990, $636.6 million in 1991, and $816.7 million in 1992.

Finally, Disney's **earnings per share (EPS)** is calculated as:

$$\text{Earnings per share} = \text{EPS} = \frac{\text{Profits after taxes}}{\text{Number of common shares outstanding}} \quad (11.3)$$

From the figures given in Table 11.2, we can calculate EPS as $1.50 in 1990, $1.20 in 1991, and $1.52 in 1992. Even though Disney's net income was lower in 1992 than 1990, its EPS was higher because of the lower number of shares outstanding. Remember that this figure, EPS, is used in the Earnings Model to calculate the intrinsic value of a company's common stock.

In general, Disney seems to have had a rough year in 1991, but the firm was able to recoup in 1992. What does this say about 1993? An up-and-down trend like this makes it even more difficult to predict results for future years, particularly if the economy is still relatively stagnant and competition is much keener in the entertainment industry.

Cash Flow Statement

The **cash flow statement** integrates the information provided in the balance sheet and income statement to report cash inflows and outflows. Since both the income statement and the balance sheet reflect inflows and outflows of funds, the cash flow statement integrates data from both. Its objective is relatively similar to the sources and uses statement, which provides information about the sources of funds and their uses.[9] Disney's consolidated statement of cash flows appears in Table 11.3.

As the table shows, Disney's foremost inflow of cash comes from income generated by operations, as it does for most firms. After taxes are paid, the amounts are $1,358.9, $1,496.7, and $1,838.1 in 1990 through 1992, respectively (all in millions of dollars).

As Table 11.3 indicates, the difference between income before income taxes in the income statement (Table 11.2) and the statement of cash flows is explained by the bottom half of the table. The differences are accounts that are charged as expenses in the income statement, but do not generate real cash outflows. Examples are depreciation and amortization of film and television costs. Additionally, some other charges that do not require cash outlays, are still sources and uses of funds. The changes in the balance sheet figures indicate whether they are sources or uses of funds.

Generally, increases in assets from one year to the next are uses of funds because the firm must pay cash to purchase assets. Alternatively, decreases in assets from one year to the next are sources of funds because decreases in assets must reflect sales of assets such as marketable securities, inventories, or fixes assets. For Disney, increases in receivables are uses of funds because the company is effectively lending money to its customers; merchandise inventories and prepaid expenses are also uses.

Generally, increases in liabilities or stockholders' equity from one year's balance sheet to the next are sources of funds because they reflect cash increases due to borrowing or selling equity shares. Of course, the reverse is also true; decreases in liabilities or stockholders' equity are uses of funds because they reflect the company spending cash to pay off debt or buy back shares. Accounts payable and other accrued liabilities are sources because they come from increased borrowing. Unearned royalties and other advances are sources because they represent IOUs the firm must repay. Together, income before income taxes and total charges equals cash provided by operations before income taxes, the first figure in Disney's cash flow statement.

From cash provided by operations before income taxes, the analyst subtracts income taxes paid and other outflows. For Disney, the outflows are investing activities and financing activities, which include reductions in borrowings, repurchases of common stock, and cash dividends paid. Additional inflows for Disney are added (borrowings and other financing cash flows). The result is an increase or decrease in the balance of the cash and cash equivalents account in the balance sheet from the beginning of the year. Adding this figure to the cash and cash equivalents account gives the new year-end balance, which equals the amount shown in Disney's balance sheet for cash and cash equivalents.

---

[9]Refer to an accounting textbook for a review of the sources and uses of funds statement.

Table 11.3

Walt Disney Company
Consolidated Statement of Cash Flows
($ millions)

| | Year Ended September 30 | | |
	1992	1991	1990
Cash provided by operations before income taxes	$2,132.0	$1,757.9	$1,780.3
Income taxes paid	(293.9)	(261.2)	(421.4)
Total cash from operations	$1,838.1	$1,496.7	$1,358.9
Investing activities			
Theme parks, resorts, and other property, net	$ 544.4	$ 924.6	$ 716.3
Film and television costs	606.0	486.8	533.0
EuroDisney investment and advances	68.3	50.6	(135.1)
Investments, net	624.5	194.3	(74.2)
Other investing cash flows	80.5	70.0	141.9
Total cash from investing	$1,923.7	$1,726.3	$1,181.9
Financing activities			
Borrowings	$ 182.8	$ 641.9	$ 965.0
Reduction of borrowings	(184.6)	(124.6)	(255.9)
Repurchases of common stock	0	(181.1)	(427.5)
Cash dividends	(105.3)	(87.2)	(74.1)
Other financing cash flows	71.4	46.9	54.5
Total cash from financing	(35.7)	295.9	262.0
Increase (decrease) in cash and cash equivalents	(121.3)	66.3	439.0
Cash and cash equivalents, beginning of year	886.1	819.8	380.8
Cash and cash equivalents, end of year	$ 764.8	$ 886.1	$ 819.8

The difference between income before income taxes as shown on the consolidated statement of income and cash provided by operations before income taxes is explained as follows:

Income before income taxes	$1,301.8	$1,011.9	$1,324.7
Charges to income not requiring cash outlays			
Depreciation	$ 317.3	$ 263.5	$ 203.1
Amortization of film and television costs	442.3	531.0	335.2
Other charges	155.4	29.7	(36.7)
Changes in receivables	(161.5)	(266.8)	(166.2)
Merchandise inventories	(151.2)	(42.4)	(44.9)
Prepaid expenses	(121.3)	(46.9)	(64.1)
Accounts payable and other accrued liabilities	335.9	280.1	300.0
Unearned royalties and other advances	13.3	(2.2)	(70.8)
Total charges	$ 830.2	$ 746.0	$ 455.6
Cash provided by operations before income taxes	$2,132.0	$1,757.9	$1,780.3
Supplemental cash flow information:			
Interest paid[a]	$ 89.8	$ 69.8	$ 67.3

[a]Interest paid is already deducted from Income Before Income Taxes and it is included in the Supplemental for information only.

The completed cash flow statement indicates the cash inflows and outflows during the fiscal year. Comparing these statements over the years can identify any excessive outflows or any significant declines in inflows. If any such problems arise, the analyst must determine the reasons. For example, receivables were a major use of Disney's funds in 1991, up from $166.2 in 1990 to $266.8 in 1991, and back down to $161.5 in 1992. This says that between 1990 and 1991, Disney significantly increased its lending to its customers by extending credit. Disney's management may have taken notice, too, because in 1992 this figure improved to fall in line with 1990s uses of funds. If 1992 data showed no improvement or a continued increase, an analyst should look more carefully at the receivables accounts. The analyst would want to see managers deciding to improve the company's competitive position as discussed in Chapter 10, by some change in the bill collecting policy. Are these data in line with those of competitors and the industry? Are Disney's credit terms more lenient than competitors'? Could Disney draw more sales because of this difference? These questions and further investigations, as suggested in Chapter 10, might be beneficial.

Finally, the analysis must extend beyond evaluating the potential weaknesses and strengths of a company's financial statements. It must evaluate the accuracy of the numbers that managers publish.

How Good Are Financial Statement Numbers?

Whenever a company publishes financial statements, the question arises, how reliable are these numbers? Do they represent a company's financial status in a realistic manner? Remember that corporate financial statements must be audited by qualified accounting firms to confirm the validity of the numbers; this does add quality control and accountability to the figures. However, the example at the beginning of the chapter pointed out that accounting rules aren't black and white. Further, a *Wall Street Journal* article, "Numbers Game, How Miniscribe Got Its Auditor's Blessing on Questionable Sales," confirms that investors cannot rely on others—they must always question and evaluate the numbers from the financial statements as part of their analysis.[10]

Briefly, the article describes how Miniscribe received a positive report from its auditors when in fact some records were fabricated, reserves were manipulated, questionable sales were included, and "growth figures were grossly exaggerated." Miniscribe subsequently filed for bankruptcy, but only after bondholders lost more than half their investment. Some of the bondholders sued Miniscribe's auditor, Coopers & Lybrand, alleging that it defrauded investors. This certainly casts doubt on the reliability of accounting figures, as well as responsibility for their accuracy.

Coopers is not the only accounting firm that has been sued for negligence in auditing; last year the Big Six spent $480 million to defend and settle lawsuits. The commentary in the following Investment Insights feature, entitled "They're Bean Counters, Not Gumshoes," argues some points on responsibility. Dean Foust says, "The public, in its never-ending quest for fail-safe investments, is coming to expect too much from accountants." Although accountants should be responsible for detecting blatant finagling and obvious inconsistencies or omissions, they cannot be "expected to check every slip of paper or trace the flow of funds to the penny." After all, they are hired by the company, so their audits usually try to avoid disrupting the firm's daily operations. The article basically says that, instead of blaming accountants, investors should focus on the real corporate culprits, the "managers who fall down on the job."

These articles reinforce the point that, although numbers are readily available, any analysis of a company must scrutinize them and judge their accuracy. Just plugging in numbers gives meaningless statistics. The analyst can add meaning only by carefully reviewing and assessing the reasons for the performance indicated by the numbers.

With that word of caution, let's return to the task at hand, that is, to perform a company analysis by applying our understanding of financial ratios to Disney's financial statements. First, we will briefly describe the use of each ratio, then calculate Disney's ratios for analysis.

---

[10]"Numbers Game, How Miniscribe Got Its Auditors' Blessing on Questionable Sales," *The Wall Street Journal*, May 14, 1992, A1.

They're Bean Counters, Not Gumshoes

Soon after Phar-Mor Inc. accused two of its executives in early August of embezzling at least $10 million from the drugstore chain, Chief Executive David S. Shapira made sure no one would mistake him for Harry Truman: He blamed the retailers' outside auditors, Coopers & Lybrand, for failing to detect phony financial ledgers and sued the firm. Never mind that Shapira himself caught on only after receiving a tip.

For the accounting profession, lawsuits such as Phar-Mor's are becoming increasingly common. As investors and taxpayers search for scapegoats in the wake of financial debacles, the Big Six accounting firms have come under siege. Last year, they spent nearly $480 million to defend and settle lawsuits charging them with shoddy accounting work—roughly 9 percent of their domestic audit revenues.

Some of those judgments may be defensible when auditors perform negligently. Yet unfortunately, the public, in its never-ending quest for fail-safe investment, is coming to expect too much from accountants. They aren't, shouldn't be, and really can't be prosecutors looking to root out all fraud and corruption. Their formal role is much more limited: They are hired by management to examine a company's books and records to determine whether management's financial statements abide by generally accepted accounting standards.

'Save Me.' By necessity, auditors rely mainly on information furnished by management. They typically visit company facilities, check samples of inventories, and assess a company's internal controls. They make sure depreciation schedules are appropriate and the arithmetic is correct. They see themselves as an ally of management, not its adversary. It's easy to see why: Management pays their fee.

If corporate executives are determined to cook the books to perpetrate some deceptive scheme that, say, shuttles inventory between warehouses, accountants say they can't always detect it. To avoid disrupting a company's operations, they usually schedule such functions as inventory checks in advance with management's cooperation.

Auditors can't be expected to check out every slip of paper and trace the flow of a company's every penny. That would be too time-consuming and expensive for executives to tolerate. "As an auditor, you don't make huge demands of management—that is, if you expect to be the auditor next year," says Howard Schilit, an accounting professor at the American University.

In the case of Phar-Mor, Coopers & Lybrand says it was intentionally misled by company exec-

Company Analysis Using Financial Ratios

Recall from your accounting classes that there are four major categories of company financial ratios: (1) liquidity ratios, (2) activity ratios, (3) leverage ratios, and (4) profitability ratios. We will discuss the general objective of each category of ratios and the definitions of some ratios under each category.

Liquidity Ratios

Liquidity ratios measure how much of its current liabilities a company could pay off with its current assets, if it were to liquidate at book value. Further, investors are also interested in how much liquid assets a company has to respond to unforeseen events. The question goes beyond whether a company can meet its current liability obligations in the event of liquidation, to ask, does it have enough cash (or liquid assets) to cover unforeseeables? How liquid is the company?

Liquidity is important to stock value for several reasons. A company has sufficient liquidity if its managers can pay its bills through recessionary periods and meet obligations without hindering operations. This should add to stock value. For example, if a liquidity ratio is weak, the company may be able to sell off an operation (or asset) to meet debt obligations, but in the long run this quick fix could damage the company. Suppose the sale is made at a relatively low price to finish the deal quickly; in the long run, this would

hurt the company (and its stockholders) because the valuable asset that was sold could have added earnings and increases to stock value by more than the sale price. Strong liquidity adds value to a company and its stock value by protecting against firesales of assets. More bluntly, no one wants to invest in a company that can't meet its obligations and is on its way to bankruptcy!

Investors rely on two common liquidity ratios: the current ratio and the quick ratio.

Current Ratio.   The **current ratio** measures how much current (liquid) assets a firm has available to repay its current liabilities. Current assets include cash and assets that can be easily converted to cash (such as marketable securities) or that are expected to be converted to cash soon (such as inventories or receivables). The ratio equals:

$$\text{Current ratio} = \frac{\text{Current assets}}{\text{Current liabilities}} \tag{11.3}$$

Disney's current ratios for 1990 to 1992 equal:

$$\text{Current ratio}_{1992} = \frac{\$3,933.5}{\$2,172.9} = 1.81$$

$$\text{Current ratio}_{1991} = \frac{\$3,108.3}{\$1,730.0} = 1.80$$

$$\text{Current ratio}_{1990} = \frac{\$2,528.6}{\$1,358.4} = 1.86$$

A ratio of 1.86 indicates that Disney has $1.86 of current assets for every dollar of current liabilities. If Disney had liquidated in 1990, it would have had $1.86 to repay every $1.00 of current liabilities. In 1991 and 1992, Disney's current ratio fell to 1.80 and 1.81, respectively. Does this indicate a problem? This and all ratios are meaningless without some comparison or reference point. Earlier in the chapter, we suggested comparing calculated ratios to the industry's, a competitor's, or the company's previous ratios. However, it is difficult to assign Disney to an industry category as it participates in several industries, and a similar competitor in all of these industries is difficult to find. Instead, we will examine changes in Disney's ratios over time.

Quick Ratio. For some companies and industries, current assets such as inventories aren't easily converted to cash. The **quick ratio** was designed to eliminate relatively nonliquid current assets so as to provide a more conservative liquidity ratio. A company with inventories that could fit only its machines, or that could easily become obsolete, has nonliquid inventories.

The quick ratio (also referred to as the *acid test ratio*) equals:

$$\text{Quick ratio} = \frac{\text{Cash} + \text{Receivables} + \text{Marketable securities}}{\text{Current liabilities}} \quad (11.4)$$

Disney's marketable securities represent interest rate swap agreements under which the company received interest at an average fixed rate of 8.0 percent. The quick ratios for Disney equal:

$$\text{Quick ratio}_{1992} = \frac{\$764.8 + \$1,407.0 + \$1,298.9}{\$2,172.9} = \frac{\$3,470.7}{\$2,172.9} = 1.60$$

$$\text{Quick ratio}_{1991} = \frac{\$886.1 + \$782.4 + \$1,128.2}{\$1,730.0} = \frac{\$2,796.7}{\$1,730.0} = 1.62$$

$$\text{Quick ratio}_{1990} = \frac{\$819.8 + \$588.1 + \$851.5}{\$1,358.4} = \frac{\$2,259.4}{\$1,358.4} = 1.66$$

These quick ratios can be interpreted the same way as the current ratios. Disney had $1.66 in liquid assets to pay off every dollar of current liabilities in 1990. The quick ratio decreased slightly from 1990 to 1991 and 1992, but again, the importance of this change depends on a comparison with the industry quick ratio. Since Disney doesn't fit any general industry category, it is not possible to make an industry comparison; however, overall industry quick ratios around 1.00 are considered safe. Based on this standard, Disney's liquidity appears very strong.

Activity Ratios

Activity ratios measure how effectively the company uses its assets to generate sales. By determining how efficiently the company runs, activity ratios help determine the stock value. Further, some activity ratios could function as indicators of future sales. For example, suppose The Gap starts stockpiling clothing because its fashion-sensitive inventory isn't selling. This would stimulate worries because company sales may be falling as unsold clothing lies in inventory. Activity ratios attempt to answer the question, how efficiently is the company using its assets to generate sales?

We will discuss four activity ratios: average collection period, inventory turnover, total asset turnover, and fixed asset turnover.

Average Collection Period. The **average collection period** measures the average number of days it takes to collect on receivables. Remember that receivables represent goods sold or services rendered, for which proceeds have not yet been collected. The average collection period equals:

$$\text{Average collection period} = \frac{\text{Average receivables}}{\text{Sales}/365} \qquad (11.5)$$

The average balances out any unusually low or high balances for a fiscal year-end.[11] To calculate average receivables, add the beginning receivables for 1992 (year-end 1991) and the year-end receivable balance for 1992, then divide by 2:

$$\text{Average receivables} = \frac{\$1,128.2 + \$1,298.9}{2} = \$1,213.55$$

For 1991, this equals:

$$\text{Average receivables} = \frac{\$851.5 + \$1,128.2}{2} = \$989.85$$

Next, calculate average sales per day by dividing annual sales by 365. For Disney, this equals:

$$\text{Daily sales}_{1992} = \$7,504.0/365 = \$20.559$$

$$\text{Daily sales}_{1991} = \$6,112.0/365 = \$16.745$$

The sales figure for this calculation should be limited to credit sales since receivables don't include cash sales. Disney's financial statements don't break down sales into credit and cash sales, so the ratio is less meaningful. However, since the credit sales figure is less than the combined sales figure (as reported in Disney's income statement), average collection period using both credit and cash sales should be *lower* than the average collection period calculated from just credit sales. Therefore, the average collection period calculated with Disney's sales should be a conservative estimate of the actual average collection period.

Disney's average collection period equals:

$$\text{Average collection period}_{1992} = \frac{\$1,213.55}{\$20.559} = 59 \text{ days}$$

$$\text{Average collection period}_{1991} = \frac{\$989.85}{\$16.745} = 59 \text{ days}$$

To interpret this value, it's important to determine what businesses Disney operates. Its theme parks and resorts include Disneyland, Disney World, EPCOT, and their associated hotels. Disney also operates other hotels and villas, shopping villages, conference centers, campgrounds, golf courses, and other recreational facilities. Royalties on revenues generated by Tokyo Disneyland and a 500-unit Disney Vacation Club at Lake Buena Vista, Florida are also considered revenues (or sales).

The average collection period says that Disney takes, on average, 59 days to collect its bills for these revenues. Again, only a comparison of this value to the industry's results can determine whether it is too long or too short. Too long a period means basically that Disney is lending too much money

---

[11]It's even better to use quarterly balance sheet figures to even out seasonal highs and lows. Most of the other balance sheet accounts used in ratios are averaged for the same reason.

to its customers and losing investment opportunities that these funds could have financed. Too short a period may mean that tight credit is driving customers to Disney's competitors.

An industry comparison is difficult because Disney is in so many different industries including theme parks, hotels, resorts, movies, shopping villages, golf courses, and others. Though it competes with other companies in these areas, not one operates in all of the same areas, so a well-matched comparison is almost impossible.

Further, interpreting the average collection period requires some knowledge of the company's credit policy. If, for example, Disney's policy is to collect within 60 days, its collection period of 59 days is not a concern. Additionally, different operations may have different policies; for example, it may collect in 30 days on theme park and resort receivables, but in 90 days for conference center receivables. So 59 days may be an acceptable collection period for the conference centers, but not for the hotels. In addition, 59 days seems an odd period for royalties collection, which probably occurs annually or at most quarterly. In summary, these calculated numbers must be used cautiously.

Inventory Turnover. Another activity ratio, the **inventory turnover,** measures how efficiently the company uses its inventory to generate sales. Too low a turnover means that the company is carrying too much inventory relative to sales, or perhaps carrying obsolete inventory. Too high a turnover means that the company isn't carrying enough to meet demand, and may be risking stockouts.

The inventory turnover equals:

$$\text{Inventory turnover} = \frac{\text{Sales}}{\text{Average inventory}} \text{ or } \frac{\text{Cost of goods sold}}{\text{Average inventory}} \quad (11.6)$$

Although some analysts use sales for the numerator, many prefer cost of goods sold because it represents the actual dollars spent by the company to turn inventory into finished goods (or services), while sales include accounting profits, as well as direct costs.

For Disney, let's first calculate average inventory figures for 1992 and 1991:

$$\text{Average inventory} = \frac{\text{Beginning inventory} + \text{Ending inventory}}{2}$$

$$\text{Average inventory}_{1992} = \frac{\$311.6 + \$462.8}{2} = \$387.2$$

$$\text{Average inventory}_{1991} = \frac{\$269.2 + \$311.6}{2} = \$290.4$$

Plugging in \$387.2 for 1992 average inventory, Disney's inventory turnover for that year equaled:

$$\text{Inventory turnover}_{1992} = \frac{\text{Sales}}{\text{Average inventory}} = \frac{\$7,504.0}{\$387.2} = 19.38\times$$

For 1991, it equaled:

$$\text{Inventory turnover}_{1991} = \frac{\$6,112.0}{\$290.4} = 21.05\times$$

This number means that Disney ordered inventory 19.38 times in 1992 (as measured by average inventory). Put differently, Disney ordered inventory approximately every 19 days (365 days/19.38, or 18.8 days). The firm's efficiency in its inventory use declined slightly from 1991 (21.05×).

Using cost of goods sold, Disney's 1992 inventory equaled:

$$\text{Inventory turnover}_{1992} = \frac{\text{Cost of goods sold}}{\text{Average inventory}} = \frac{\$6,068.7}{\$387.2} = 15.67\times$$

For 1991, it equaled:

$$\text{Inventory turnover}_{1991} = \frac{\$5,017.5}{\$290.4} = 17.28\times$$

The interpretations of these values are the same. They just present a more conservative picture than a ratio with sales in the numerator. The 1992 value says that Disney ordered inventory 15.67 times a year to produce its goods and services, while it ordered inventory slightly more often in 1991 (17.28 times). This slight decrease in Disney's inventory turnover could become a problem if the downward trend were to continue; however, it isn't an alarming trend yet.

Though these numbers seem high, the relationship between sales and inventory for Disney and other entertainment industries is not as direct as for manufacturing industries. Therefore, the ratios should be used more cautiously. For example, PepsiCo stores sugar and other ingredients to produce its soft drink syrup. These inventories are directly tied to sales of the soft drinks. Wal-Mart, a discount retailer, is another example of a company whose inventories are closely tied to sales. Additionally, Disney is in several industries, so its cost of goods sold and inventory figures should be separated by industry in order to obtain a clearer picture.

Total Asset Turnover and Fixed Asset Turnover. A more general activity ratio based on all firm assets is the total asset turnover, as discussed early in the chapter. This ratio measures how efficiently managers utilize all of the firm's assets. Inefficient use of total assets relative to sales will result in a relatively low turnover, while efficient use of assets will result in a relatively high turnover.

Remember though that either too high or too low a number could imply poor management decisions. Too low a turnover could imply that the company has obsolete equipment or too much equipment for the sales it generates, while too high a turnover could imply that the company is straining its present equipment and inventory to meet relatively high sales demand, resulting in a potential for equipment breakdowns and stockouts in inventory.

Since the total asset turnover can range from less than 1.0× for large capital companies such as steel producers to 10.0× for retailers, it is important to find the correct comparison. Also, if a firm's inventory turnover is within industry standards, but its total asset turnover isn't, it indicates a need to examine the utilization of fixed assets more closely. This illustrates the importance of combining the results of several ratios in order to diagnose an underlying problem.

Finally, the age of a firm's assets can affect total asset turnover. A company with relatively new fixed assets will tend to show a higher balance for both total assets and fixed assets, since both tend to increase in cost over time. This can reduce total asset turnover and fixed asset turnover as compared to a similar company with older facilities. Again, the reality must guide interpretation of the numbers.

The **total asset turnover** is defined as:

$$\text{Total asset turnover} = \frac{\text{Sales}}{\text{Average total assets}} \tag{11.7}$$

The **fixed asset turnover** is defined as:

$$\text{Fixed asset turnover} = \frac{\text{Sales}}{\text{Average net fixed assets}} \tag{11.8}$$

First, calculate Disney's average total assets, based on figures from the beginning of 1992 and the end of 1992:

$$\text{Average total assets} = \frac{\$9,428.5 + \$10,861.7}{2} = \$10,145.1$$

Average fixed assets for Disney in 1992 were:

$$\text{Average net fixed assets} = \frac{\$6,320.2 + \$6,928.2}{2} = \$6,624.2$$

Given the averages calculated above, the two ratios for Disney for 1992 are:

$$\text{Total asset turnover}_{1992} = \frac{\$7,504.0}{10,145.1} = 0.74\times$$

$$\text{Fixed asset turnover}_{1992} = \frac{\$7,504.0}{\$6,624.2} = 1.13\times$$

For 1991, Disney's asset turnover ratios were:

$$\text{Total asset turnover}_{1991} = \frac{\$6,112.0}{\$8,725.4} = 0.70\times$$

where average total assets were $8,725.4, and:

$$\text{Fixed asset turnover}_{1991} = \frac{\$6,112.0}{\$5,906.95} = 1.03\times$$

where average fixed assets were $5,906.95.

These results indicate that both total asset turnover and fixed asset turnover declined from 1991 to 1992 (from 0.74× to 0.70× for total asset turnover and 1.13× to 1.03× for fixed asset turnover). The decline in the total asset turnover can be attributed to less efficient use of both inventory and fixed assets in 1992 than in 1991.

Leverage Ratios

Leverage ratios measure a company's level of debt. This is an important factor to consider because debt has two major effects on ROE and hence market value, as discussed early in the chapter. First, debt interest expense is a fixed cost to the company, increasing the risk of financial trouble in difficult times. Also, an increased level of debt makes earnings per share and ROE more volatile. This concept of **financial leverage** says that a company with more debt will find that any changes in its operating earnings will result in a greater change in the firm's EPS. This enhances the return to stockholders nicely if operating income increases, but it can have an equally negative effect if operating income declines.

This increase in the volatility in earnings is called *financial risk,* as discussed in Chapter 10. It is the additional uncertainty of returns to stockholders (ROE) because the company uses securities with a fixed cost. Also, since debt is tax deductible, and debt increases earnings to the company, assuming everything else is constant. This, in turn, increases ROE, which may increase the stock's intrinsic value, as shown in Equation 11.1.

All of this implies that more debt is desirable. Notice, however, that the two effects can conflict with one another. In general, judicious use of debt is desirable, but too much debt will increase the firm's financial risk and too much may have dire consequences (such as bankruptcy).

Having established that leverage is an important component of ROE, we examine four leverage ratios, each of which gives a slightly different perspective about the company's financial risk. The first two leverage ratios measure the level of debt relative to equity or total assets. The last two are coverage ratios that determine the number of times a firm can pay interest charges from currently generated income.

Debt ratios use stock figures from the balance sheet to determine the amount of debt a firm uses relative to equity (the debt–equity ratio) or the amount of debt it uses to finance total assets (total debt–total assets ratio). The company's financial risk is reduced if both ratios are lower; however, there is an optimal combination of debt and equity for each company, depending on its industry and business risk.[12]

Debt–Equity Ratio. The **debt–equity ratio** equals:

$$\text{Debt–equity ratio} = \frac{\text{Total long-term debt}}{\text{Total equity}} \qquad (11.9)$$

It measures the total amount of long-term debt relative to the equity funding of the company.[13] Recall that higher levels of debt relative to equity would imply a financially riskier company.

Firms must also address the moral hazard problem. If a company is financed mostly by debt, then the managers (who report to the board and stockholders) may make riskier investment decisions than they might if the firm were funded primarily by stockholders. If the risky investments pay off, then the stockholders reap the benefits, while the debtholders receive their fixed payments. If the gamble fails, then stockholders are protected by their limited liability and the debtholders obtain rights to a worthless company, or end up in a long battle in bankruptcy court.

This provides an additional reason to carefully examine a firm's debt–equity ratio in order to verify that debt funding is not too high. Note that if the debt–equity ratio equals 1.0 (100 percent), then the company is financed equally by long-term debt and equity. If the ratio is less (or greater) than 100 percent, then the firm is financed more by equity (or debt).

Disney's debt–equity ratios for 1990 to 1992 equaled:

$$\text{Debt–equity ratio}_{1992} = \frac{\$3,984.2}{\$4,704.6} = 84.69 \text{ percent}$$

$$\text{Debt–equity ratio}_{1991} = \frac{\$3,827.2}{\$3,871.3} = 98.86 \text{ percent}$$

$$\text{Debt–equity ratio}_{1990} = \frac{\$3,175.3}{\$3,488.6} = 91.02 \text{ percent}$$

---

[12]Business risk is discussed later in the chapter.

[13]Only long-term debt is often used in debt ratios because current liabilities such as accounts payable and bank notes tend to be negotiable.

Disney's debt–equity ratio of 91.02 percent in 1990 increased to 98.86 percent in 1991, indicating that by 1991 the company was financed almost equally by debt and equity. In 1992, the company's debt level increased, but its equity level increased more, and so its debt–equity ratio fell to 84.69 percent. These numbers really indicate no substantial change, but at a debt–equity level of 98.86 percent, it's definitely better for it to decline than to increase.

Total Debt–Total Assets Ratio. The **total debt–total assets ratio** measures how much of the company's assets are financed by total debt. Total debt includes current liabilities and long-term debt, and total assets include current assets and net fixed assets. This ratio addresses similar issues to the debt–equity ratio, but total debt–total assets ratio can provide additional information.

The total debt–total assets ratio is defined as:

$$\text{Total debt–total assets ratio} = \frac{\text{Current liabilities} + \text{Long-term debt}}{\text{Total assets}}$$

(11.10)

Since total debt and stockholders' equity make up all of the right-hand side of the balance sheet, together, they must equal Total Assets, the left-hand side of the balance sheet. Therefore, if the long-term debt–equity ratio equals 100 percent, then the total debt–total assets ratio would equal approximately 50 percent, unless the company financed a large part of its assets by current liabilities (usually accounts payable or bank notes). An example may be helpful.

Suppose Company A has the following balance sheet:

**Company A
Balance Sheet
December 31, 1992**

Current assets	$1,000	Current liabilities	$2,000
		Long-term debt	500
Net fixed assets	$2,000	Stockholders' equity	500
Total assets	$3,000	Total debt and equity	$3,000

Company A has the following ratios:

$$\text{Debt–equity ratio} = \frac{\$500}{\$500} = 100 \text{ percent}$$

$$\text{Total debt–total assets ratio} = \frac{\$2,500}{\$3,000} = 83 \text{ percent}$$

Any relative differences between the debt–equity ratio and the total debt–total assets ratio probably indicates extensive, and potentially expensive, use of current liabilities to finance company assets. This practice of using current liabilities in place of long-term debt may be particularly prevalent among small- and medium-sized companies and start-up firms with limited access to the capital markets.

Disney's total debt–total assets ratios for 1990 through 1992 equal:

$$\text{Total debt–total assets ratio}_{1992} = \frac{\$2,172.9 + \$3,984.2}{\$10,861.7} = 56.69 \text{ percent}$$

$$\text{Total debt--total assets ratio}_{1991} = \frac{\$1,730.0 + \$3,827.2}{\$9,428.2} = 58.94 \text{ percent}$$

$$\text{Total debt--total assets ratio}_{1990} = \frac{\$1,358.4 + \$3,175.3}{\$8,022.3} = 56.51 \text{ percent}$$

The trend in this ratio is generally consistent with Disney's debt–equity ratio; however, the total debt–total assets ratio is greater than 50 percent even when the debt–equity ratio is less than 100 percent. This indicates *more* use of debt than equity (including all sources of total debt) and not less, as suggested by the debt–equity ratio.

The leverage ratios (debt–equity and total debt–total assets) provide information about the firm's stock of debt at each fiscal year-end. To supplement this information, it is also important to evaluate the flow of funds, or the firm's ability to repay fixed obligations with currently generated income. We discuss two ratios that provide this information, called **coverage ratios:** the interest coverage ratio and the fixed charge coverage ratio. Both measure the number of times the firm can repay fixed charges with generated income. Generally, higher coverage ratios indicate lower financial risk.

Interest Coverage Ratio, or Times Interest Earned. This ratio indicates the number of times the firm can pay its interest expenses with currently generated earnings. The **interest coverage ratio** equals:

$$\text{Interest coverage ratio} = \frac{\text{Income before interest and taxes}}{\text{Debt interest charges}} \quad (11.11)$$

Disney's income before interest and taxes equals operating income minus general administrative expenses plus investment and interest income plus income from EuroDisney. This gives interest coverage ratios of:

$$\text{Interest coverage ratio}_{1992} = \frac{\$1,435.3 - \$148.2 + (\$130.3) + \$11.2}{\$126.8}$$
$$= 9.21\times$$

$$\text{Interest coverage ratio}_{1991} = \frac{\$1,094.5 - \$160.8 + (\$119.4) + \$63.8}{\$105.0}$$
$$= 8.36\times$$

$$\text{Interest coverage ratio}_{1990} = \frac{\$1,339.1 - \$138.5 + (\$80.8) + \$86.4}{\$43.1}$$
$$= 27.99\times$$

Disney's tremendous interest coverage ratio for 1990 dropped drastically in 1991 and 1992, mostly due to increased interest charges. Though the coverage ratio dropped precipitously, it still seems more than adequate to cover the fixed charges. Since Disney doesn't fit in an industry category, an industry comparison is difficult.

Fixed Charge Coverage Ratio. This ratio measures the number of times the firm can cover its fixed obligations, including debt charges, lease payments, and pretax preferred dividend payments. The **fixed charge coverage ratio** equals:

Fixed charge coverage ratio

$$= \frac{\text{Income before interest and taxes}}{\begin{array}{c}\text{Debt} \\ \text{interest} \\ \text{charges}\end{array} + \begin{array}{c}\text{Lease} \\ \text{payments}\end{array} + \dfrac{\text{Sink fund}}{(1 - \text{Tax rate})} + \dfrac{\text{Pref Div}}{(1 - \text{Tax rate})}} \quad (11.12)$$

Why are the nontax-deductible, costs such as sinking fund payments and preferred dividends divided by (1 − Tax rate)? An example based on a sinking fund payment will show why. The same logic applies to preferred dividends. Suppose Firm A has the abbreviated income statement below, starting from income before taxes. Its tax rate equals 30 percent. Further, suppose that it makes sinking fund payments from generated income.

Firm A's
Sinking Fund Payments

Income before taxes	$100
Taxes	30
Net income	$ 70
Sinking fund payment	20
Funds left after sinking fund payment	$ 50

Notice that the firm subtracts its sinking fund payment after taxes, implying that its payment is not tax deductible. This example leaves ample income before taxes to pay off the sinking fund, but how much must Firm A have in income before taxes to give an amount that is just enough to pay taxes and the sinking fund payment?

A quick answer of $20 would be incorrect. The reason is that the sinking fund payment is not tax deductible, so Firm A must generate enough income before taxes to pay taxes first, then have enough left to pay the sinking fund. If *SF* denotes the sinking fund payment and *IBT* denotes income before taxes:

$$(1 - \text{Tax rate}) \times IBT = SF$$

The equation says that if (1 − Tax rate) times *IBT* equals *SF*, then the firm has allocated just enough after-tax income to cover the sinking fund payment. Solve the equation for the *IBT* that is necessary to pay off the sinking fund:

$$IBT = \frac{SF}{(1 - \text{Tax rate})}$$

In the example, Firm A must have:

$$IBT = \frac{\$20}{(1 - 0.30)} = \$28.57$$

This number says that the firm must have $28.57 in income before taxes in order to pay taxes on that amount and have enough left to cover the sinking fund payment. The abbreviated income statement looks like this:

Firm A's
Sinking Fund Payments

Income before taxes	$28.57
Taxes	8.57
Net income	$20.00
Sinking fund payment	20.00
Funds left after sinking fund payment	$ 0.00

The table verifies that the income before taxes of $28.57 is just enough to pay taxes on that amount and cover the sinking fund. Therefore, the fixed charge coverage ratio divides each nontax-deductible payment by $(1 - \text{Tax rate})$.

Disney's interest coverage ratio equals its fixed charge coverage ratio because the firm has no leases or preferred stock outstanding.[14]

Profitability Ratios

Remember that quantitative company analysis seeks to evaluate the intrinsic stock value, which depends directly on the company's ability to generate earnings. The ultimate ratios to consider are the company's earnings and associated profitability ratios.

Profitability ratios represent gross profits, operating profits, and net profits as percentages of sales revenues. Two additional profitability ratios measure the percentage return on a firm's total capital, and the return on its equity capital (ROE).

Gross Profit Margin. The **gross profit margin** measures gross profits, or sales minus cost of goods sold, relative to sales. The formula is:

$$\text{Gross profit margin} = \frac{\text{Gross profits}}{\text{Sales}} \tag{11.13}$$

The gross profit margin is more relevant for manufacturing firms than service-oriented companies such as Disney. A manufacturer's sales revenue must cover the direct costs of manufacturing its goods. Those costs are referred to as *cost of goods sold (CoGS)*. The gross profit margin indicates the percentage of sales that result in profits after deducting costs of production. For example, The Gap produces and sells casual apparel, with 1,385 stores as of 1993. The firm reported sales of $3,300.0 million and cost of goods sold of $1,270.5 million in 1993. The Gap's gross profits equal $3,300.0 minus $1,270.5, or $2,029.5 million, and its gross profit margin equals:

$$\text{Gross profit margin} = \frac{\$2,029.5}{\$3,300.0} = 38.5 \text{ percent}$$

Operating Profit Margin. Though Disney's gross profit margin isn't very relevant, its **operating profit margin** is. Notice that Disney's income statement details costs and expenses together, combining CoGS with operating expenses. Disney doesn't even report gross profits, but its operating profits are definitely more relevant. The operating profit margin measures operating profits relative to sales, where operating profits equal:

$$\text{Operating profits} = \text{Sales} - \text{CoGS} - \text{Operating expenses}$$

Operating expenses generally include general and administrative expenses, and it could include research and development costs. The operating profit margin formula is:

$$\text{Operating profit margin} = \frac{\text{Operating profits}}{\text{Sales}} \tag{11.14}$$

---

[14]Though Disney lists some lease payments in its annual report, no breakdown appears in the balance sheet or income statement.

Disney's operating profit margins for 1990 to 1992 equal:

$$\text{Operating profit margin}_{1992} = \frac{\$7,504.0 - \$6,068.7 - \$148.2}{\$7,504.0}$$
$$= 17.15 \text{ percent}$$

$$\text{Operating profit margin}_{1991} = \frac{\$6,112.0 - \$5,017.5 - \$160.8}{\$6,112.0}$$
$$= 15.28 \text{ percent}$$

$$\text{Operating profit margin}_{1990} = \frac{\$5,757.3 - \$4,418.2 - \$138.5}{\$5,757.3}$$
$$= 20.85 \text{ percent}$$

Disney's operating profit margin declined significantly from 1990 to 1991 (20.85 percent to 15.28 percent) and then increased slightly from 1991 to 1992 (15.28 percent to 17.15 percent). Disney definitely needs to keep this trend from declining further by controlling costs and expenses.

Since the aggregate economy can have a powerful influence on an individual company, let's see how the economy may have affected Disney's profits. According to *Value Line's Economic Series,* the real U.S. gross domestic product (GDP) fell between 1990 and 1991 from $4,877 billion to $4,821 billion, and it increased in 1992 to $4,923 billion.[15] In fact the real GDP has declined only twice since 1980, once in 1982, then in 1991. Many people had a very tough year in 1991! Also the national unemployment rate increased from 5.5 percent in 1990 to 6.8 percent in 1991 and to 7.4 percent in 1992. We expect increases in joblessness to affect the recreation industry much more than less cyclical industries, such as the food industry. Given the tough economy, then, Disney maintained a good operating profit margin, and even increased it from 15.28 percent in 1991 to 17.15 percent in 1992.

Net Profit Margin. The **net profit margin** measures net profits after taxes relative to sales to indicate how much of the firm's profits pass through to stockholders after all costs have been considered, as a percentage of sales. It equals:

$$\text{Net profit margin} = \frac{\text{Net profits after taxes}}{\text{Sales}} \tag{11.15}$$

Disney's net profit margin ratios are:

$$\text{Net profit margin}_{1992} = \frac{\$816.7}{\$7,504.0} = 10.88 \text{ percent}$$

$$\text{Net profit margin}_{1991} = \frac{\$636.6}{\$6,112.0} = 10.42 \text{ percent}$$

$$\text{Net profit margin}_{1990} = \frac{\$824.0}{\$5,757.3} = 14.31 \text{ percent}$$

These results confirm the analysis based on the operating profit margin. Net profit margin declined from 1990 to 1991 (from 14.31 percent to 10.42 percent) and remained relatively constant in 1992 (10.88 percent). Given the lack of improvement in the economy from 1990 to 1992 and increases in

---

[15] *Value Line Economic Series,* July 30, 1993.

unemployment during that period, it's not surprising to see Disney suffer along with the entire recreation industry.

This is a good example of the need to analyze ratios in the context of the overall economy to evaluate a firm's relative performance. It's important to recognize that Disney's decline in net profit margin is due in part to economic conditions, and to the cyclical nature of the industry and company.

Return on Total Capital. The **return on total capital** measures the rate of return on all long-term capital invested in the company, that is, all funds from long-term investors that appear on the right-hand side of the balance sheet (long-term debt, preferred stock, and common stock). The return on total capital is calculated as the cash flows to these investors, relative to their investments, or:

$$\text{Return on total capital} = \frac{\text{Net income} + \text{Interest expense}}{\text{Total long-term capital}} \quad (11.16)$$

Net income is calculated before dividend payments.

Disney's return on total capital ratios are:

$$\text{Return on total capital}_{1992} = \frac{\$816.7 + \$126.8}{\$3,984.2 + \$4,704.6} = \frac{\$943.5}{\$8,688.8}$$
$$= 10.86 \text{ percent}$$

$$\text{Return on total capital}_{1991} = \frac{\$636.6 + \$105.0}{\$3,827.2 + \$3,871.3} = \frac{\$741.6}{\$7,698.5}$$
$$= 9.63 \text{ percent}$$

$$\text{Return on total capital}_{1990} = \frac{\$824.0 + \$43.1}{\$3,175.3 + \$3,488.6} = \frac{\$867.1}{\$6,663.9}$$
$$= 13.01 \text{ percent}$$

Disney's return on total capital decreased from 1990 to 1991 (13.01 percent to 9.63 percent), but, much to Disney's credit, it increased from 1991 to 1992 (up to 10.86 percent). These results imply that, in spite of a tough economy, Disney's return to its investors increased.

Return on Stockholders' Equity (ROE). The **return on stockholders' equity (ROE)** encompasses much of the firm's operating and financing activities. Thus, ROE serves three functions: (1) it measures overall company performance, (2) it evaluates the return to the money that stockholders (the owners) have invested, and (3) it is a factor in determining the stock's intrinsic value. The formula for ROE was stated earlier in equation 11.1:

$$\text{ROE} = \frac{\text{Net profits after taxes}}{\text{Common stockholders' equity}} = \frac{\text{Net profits}}{\text{Common equity}}$$

Disney's ROEs for 1990 to 1992 are:

$$\text{ROE}_{1992} = \frac{\$816.7}{\$4,704.6} = 17.36 \text{ percent}$$

$$\text{ROE}_{1991} = \frac{\$636.6}{\$3,871.3} = 16.44 \text{ percent}$$

$$\text{ROE}_{1990} = \frac{\$824.0}{\$3,488.6} = 23.62 \text{ percent}$$

These results confirm those for the return on total capital. ROE decreased between 1990 and 1991, and then increased slightly from 1991 to 1992. As expected, these results correspond very closely to changes in GDP or aggregate economy.

A Brief Recap

These ratios do not exist in isolation. To show how they are related, let's reexamine the relationship between ROE and the company's profitability, activity, and leverage ratios. Equation 11.2 presented this relationship as:

$$\text{ROE} = \frac{\text{Net profits}}{\text{Sales}} \times \frac{\text{Sales}}{\text{Total assets}} \times \frac{\text{Total assets}}{\text{Equity}}$$

The first term is the net profit margin (Equation 11.15). The second is the total asset turnover (Equation 11.7). The third is the leverage ratio, a reciprocal of the total debt–total assets ratio (Equation 11.10). Equation 11.2 shows that ROE is positively related to the net profit margin, the total assets turnover, and the leverage ratio.

The leverage ratio may need some more explanation. Recall that the total debt–total assets ratio (Equation 11.10) equals:

$$\text{Total debt–total assets ratio} = \frac{\text{Current liabilities + Long-term debt}}{\text{Total assets}}$$

Notice that this differs from the leverage ratio (Total asset/Equity) which gives assets in relation to equity instead of total debt. However, total debt is the complement of equity from the right-hand side of the balance sheet. As debt increases, equity declines by the same amount. Also the leverage ratio places total assets in the numerator, but the total debt–total assets ratio (Equation 11.10) places assets in the denominator. This inversion gives debt the same effect on Equation 11.10 as it has on the leverage ratio. An increase in debt increases both ratios, assuming that total assets remain constant. Debt increases cause equity decreases in the leverage ratio, increasing this ratio of total assets to equity. The effect on Equation 11.10 is direct; as debt increases, the total debt–total assets ratio increases.

As the firm's net profit margin, total asset turnover, and leverage ratios increase, so does ROE. This raises the intrinsic value of a stock, as calculated by the Dividend Discount Model. Table 11.4 summarizes all the ratios discussed in this section.

The next section presents the DuPont Chart, an alternative method by which to show how these three ratios are related to ROE. The section also displays all the financial statement accounts that affect the three ratios.

DuPont Chart

A **DuPont Chart** summarizes the effects of the operating and financial activities of a company. It is a flow chart that serves two purposes: (1) it visually displays ratios and accounts that affect ROE, and (2) it shows the relationship of financial ratios and income statement and balance sheet accounts to the analyst's final ROE. Displaying this information in a chart that connects the accounts and ratios allows the analyst to trace an identified weakness back to its source through the series of accounts that determine ROE. Figure 11.1 provides an example of Disney's 1992 financials in a DuPont Chart.

Table 11.4

Summary of Ratios

I. Liquidity Ratios

A.
$$\text{Current ratio} = \frac{\text{Current assets}}{\text{Current liabilities}}$$

B.
$$\text{Quick ratio} = \frac{\text{Cash} + \text{Receivables} + \text{Marketable securities}}{\text{Current liabilities}}$$

II. Activity Ratios

A.
$$\text{Average collection period} = \frac{\text{Average receivables}}{\text{Sales}/365}$$

B.
$$\text{Inventory turnover} = \frac{\text{Sales}}{\text{Average inventory}} \text{ or } \frac{\text{Cost of goods sold}}{\text{Average inventory}}$$

C.
$$\text{Total asset turnover} = \frac{\text{Sales}}{\text{Average total assets}}$$

D.
$$\text{Fixed asset turnover} = \frac{\text{Sales}}{\text{Average net fixed assets}}$$

III. Leverage Ratios

A.
$$\text{Debt-equity ratio} = \frac{\text{Total long-term debt}}{\text{Total equity}}$$

B.
$$\text{Total debt-total assets ratio} = \frac{\text{Current liabilities} + \text{Long-term debt}}{\text{Total assets}}$$

C.
$$\text{Interest coverage ratio} = \frac{\text{Income before interest and taxes}}{\text{Interest charges}}$$

D. Fixed charge coverage ratio
$$= \frac{\text{Income before interest and taxes}}{\text{Debt charges} + \text{Lease payments} + \dfrac{\text{Sinking fund payments}}{(1 - \text{Tax rate})} + \dfrac{\text{Preferred Dividends}}{(1 - \text{Tax rate})}}$$

IV. Profitability Ratios

A.
$$\text{Gross profit margin} = \frac{\text{Gross Profits}}{\text{Sales}}$$

B.
$$\text{Operating profit margin} = \frac{\text{Operating profits}}{\text{Sales}}$$

C.
$$\text{Net profit margin} = \frac{\text{Net profits after taxes}}{\text{Sales}}$$

D.
$$\text{Return on total capital} = \frac{\text{Net income} + \text{Interest expense}}{\text{Total long-term capital}}$$

E.
$$\text{ROE} = \frac{\text{Net profits after taxes}}{\text{Stockholders' equity}} = \frac{\text{Net profits}}{\text{Equity}}$$

The left side of the chart displays the income statement accounts and the profitability ratios that result from the company's sales and net profits. If net profit margin seems lower than values in other years, the flow chart provides the cost and sales data to determine the cause. Perhaps management needs to cut costs or the marketing department needs to promote sales. Changes in data items can indicate which.

One way to determine the strength or weakness of each account is to examine it as a percentage of sales. This adjusts for size differences, which could complicate the analysis since changes in raw data cold be due simply

Figure 11.1

DuPont Chart for Disney

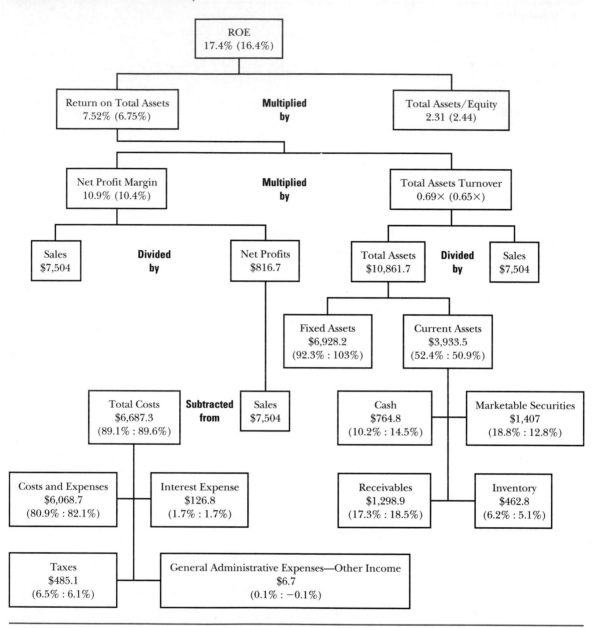

to a rise or fall in sales. For example, stating Disney's 1992 and 1991 accounts (in dollars) as percentages of sales allows comparisons between those accounts. Even though sales amounts differ ($7,504 in 1992 and $6,112 in 1991), the relationship of each amount to sales remains a valid basis for comparison.

The DuPont Chart in Figure 11.1 displays Disney's 1992 and 1991 accounts as percentages of sales. A colon separates each pair of percentages in parentheses (1992:1991). Of course, industry ratios or competitors' accounts could replace Disney's 1991 data as a benchmark for comparison.

On the right side of the chart, the balance sheet accounts sum to the firm's total assets. Sales divided by total assets gives the total asset turnover, which represents the company's activity ratio. Again, the flow chart shows the balance sheet accounts that affect the asset turnover ratio. If the ratio is lower than those in other years, the chart can show whether the firm had too much invested in assets, and which asset accounts it should decrease. Again, relative changes can be detected through percentage-of-sales comparisons.

Multiplying the net profit margin by the total asset turnover gives Disney's return on total assets: 7.52 percent. Next, multiplying return on total assets by the leverage ratio (Total assets/Equity) gives Disney's ROE of 17.4 percent, as compared to the previous year's value of 16.4 percent. However, notice that the leverage *ratio* (2.31) is lower than the previous year's (2.44) though the return on total assets is slightly higher (7.52 percent versus 6.75 percent). Further inspections of the net profit margin (10.9 percent versus 10.4 percent) and total asset turnover (0.69× versus 0.65×) show only slight differences between the two years' performance figures. The percentage-of-sales figures in parentheses reveal any differences. For instance, total costs rose slightly (89.1 percent versus 89.6 percent). Costs and expenses accounted for all of this rise (from 80.9 percent to 82.1 percent), as taxes fell and General administrative costs minus Other income remained stable.

Recall from the general discussion of ratio analysis that higher total asset turnover means greater efficiency. Disney's more efficient use of total assets came from lower fixed assets (92.3 percent versus 103 percent of sales), a lower cash balance (10.2 percent versus 14.5 percent), and lower receivables (17.3 percent versus 18.5 percent). Remember that a lower dollar investment in total assets for every dollar generated in sales means more efficient use of assets.

Conclusion. Disney's data show no significant changes in performance from 1991 to 1992. Owners of Disney stock see that as a good sign. If good results from a fundamental analysis conducted in 1991 led someone to invest, these results confirm that the company's financials remain very sound in 1992 and Disney remains a good investment.

For a company with significant changes, the DuPont Chart would break down the data to show how performance in all aspects of the company would affect its overall performance measure (ROE). The DuPont Chart shows how all balance sheet and income statement accounts contribute to the activity and profitability ratios, and finally to ROE. If this analysis were to identify changes for the worse, the investor may decide to sell the stock. However, the final decision should be based on a thorough fundamental analysis of expected ROE estimates.

So far we've examined financial ratios as static figures; we've used them as if the numbers would never change. However, profits (or earnings), for example, are dynamic flow figures that change annually, monthly, and even daily. Any profitability ratio calculation should raise the question: How reliable is this number? Company A's profits may vary over time more than Company B's profits. This makes any profit measure for A less certain than one for B. The profits of Company A are, therefore, riskier than those of B.

For example, profits of **cyclical companies** are more volatile than those of the average company over the economic phases. When the economy is in an expansionary phase, the cyclical company's earnings will increase by more than the economy's aggregate earnings, and the company's earnings will fall more during a recessionary phase. However, cyclical companies aren't necessarily bad investments. Companies known to be cyclical may not seem to do so poorly in relation to the economy. In contrast, if a noncyclical company exhibits volatile earnings, doubts may build about its prospects. Understanding a company and its stock value requires examining the risks associated with operating a business, or business risk. The next section discusses two types of business risk, sales risk and operating leverage.

Business Risk: Sales Risk and Operating Leverage

Business risk is the variability of a company's operating profits over time (usually measured over ten years). Because operating profits equal sales minus CoGS, the variability can be due to variability in sales and/or variability in production costs over time. For example, General Motors would have more business risk than Safeway or Winn-Dixie Stores because its sales vary more, and also because GM has higher fixed production costs than the retail grocery stores.[16]

Sales variability is a function of how a company reacts to the changing economy. Companies like Disney, Marriott, Toys "Я" Us, and United Airlines might be affected more by business cycles and aggregate economic conditions than companies like public utilities and retail grocery stores. Companies that are most affected by business cycles tend to have greater variability in sales.

Fixed production costs also increase operating profit variability. If fixed costs were to equal zero and all production costs were variable, then sales variability would equal operating profit variability (or business risk). However, any increase in fixed production costs above zero increases the variability of operating profits. To the extent that a company must pay fixed costs, its operating profit variability will be greater than its sales variability. This effect of fixed costs increasing variability in operating profits is referred to as **operating leverage.** Quantitative analysts measure business risk as the **coefficient of variation** (CV) of operating profits (OP) over time where CV(OP) is defined as:

$$CV(OP) = \frac{\text{Standard deviation of operating profits}}{\text{Arithmetic Mean of operating profits}} = \frac{SD(OP)}{M(OP)} \quad (11.17)$$

A statistical measure called **standard deviation** is a common measure of risk that quantifies the average variability of a series from its arithmetic mean. This value is used as a measure of risk because it measures how far an actual number may be dispersed around the arithmetic mean. SD(OP) is the average variability of operating profits over time. The arithmetic mean is calculated by adding operating profits over T years (usually ten years), divided by T. M(OP) is the arithmetic mean of operating profits over time. The mathematical formula for business risk equals:

$$\text{Business risk} = \frac{SD(OP)}{M(OP)} = \frac{\sqrt{\sum_{t=1}^{T} (OP_t - M(OP)^2/(T-1)}}{\sum_{t=1}^{T} (OP_t)/T}$$

where T is the number of observations (years) in the sample. Dividing the standard deviation by the mean allows the analyst to compare two companies' business risks regardless of their size because it normalizes each company's data. Let's examine some companies' business risks by calculating their SD(OP) and M(OP) values. Based on these values, Table 11.5 lists the coefficients of variation (CVs) as measures of business risk for ten companies from 1983 to 1992.

---

[16]Safeway is a retail grocery chain in the Northwest and West while Winn-Dixie is a retail grocery chain in the South and Southwest.

Table 11.5

Sample Companies' Business Risks

Company	M(OP)[a]	SD(OP)[a]	CV(OP)	CV (Sales)
American Home Products	$1,424.99	$ 244.50	0.172	0.181
Disney	917.24	482.95	0.527	0.563
Hewlett-Packard	1,456.21	377.94	0.260	0.405
Marriott	549.03	119.27	0.217	0.331
Paramount	311.24	98.50	0.316	0.265
Tootsie Roll	31.35	13.33	0.425	0.386
Toys "Я" Us	1,185.29	599.82	0.506	0.530
UAL	710.19	398.46	0.561	0.251
Wal-Mart	5,185.90	3,558.16	0.686	0.751
Winn-Dixie	1,938.25	268.52	0.139	0.131

[a]In millions of dollars.

For which companies would you expect relatively high sales variability, or sales risk? Sales variability, measured by the coefficient of variation of sales, equals $SD(\text{Sales})/M(\text{Sales})$ over time, as reported in Table 11.5. Cyclical companies are more likely to be affected by economic conditions, so they tend to have greater sales variability. In the table, look at Disney (0.563), Hewlett-Packard (0.405), Marriott (0.331), Toys "Я" Us (0.530), and Wal-Mart (0.751). These companies tend to prosper and falter with the economy's cycles. Disney and Marriott are cyclical because they provide recreation services, Hewlett-Packard because it sells computers and computer peripherals, and Toys "Я" Us and Wal-Mart because they rely on discretionary retail sales. All of these kinds of economic activity vary widely over a business cycle.

Which companies have high business risk? Table 11.5 lists Disney (0.527), Tootsie Roll (0.425), Toys "Я" Us (0.506), UAL (0.561), and Wal-Mart (0.686) with relatively high business risk. Notice that the business risk matches sales risk closely for both Disney (0.527 versus 0.563) and Winn-Dixie (0.139 versus 0.131). This implies that these companies have very little operating leverage; almost all of their business risk comes from sales risk. This is not surprising because Disney is in the service industry and Winn-Dixie is a retail grocery chain.

Since business risk is composed of sales variability and operating leverage, some companies may have low sales risk, but high business risk due to high operating leverage. UAL has very high business risk (0.561) and relatively low sales risk (0.251). Though the measures of sales risk and operating leverage aren't additive, the contrast is striking. This implies that UAL has more operating leverage than sales variability. The deep discounts that airlines offer to stimulate air travel allow UAL to control the variability of its sales somewhat, but the high fixed costs of running and owning airplanes still keeps UAL's business risk high.

Company Earnings and Estimating Expected Return

To conclude the chapter, let's analyze a company by estimating its expected return and earnings, then decide whether it's a good investment in two ways. One way is to actually conduct a complete fundamental analysis, comparing its expected return, $E(r_i)$, with the expected return estimated via the CAPM, ER_i. If $E(r_i)$ is above ER_i, then the stock is undervalued and a good investment; it's earning a greater return than required based on its risk level. If $E(r_i)$ is below ER_i, it's overvalued, earning a lower return than required based on its risk level. We'll discuss this point in much greater detail in Chapter 13.

The second way of evaluating a company's investment prospects is to rank a sample of stocks' expected returns in descending order. The better stocks appear higher on the list. Let's discuss these methods and apply them to Disney to determine whether it is a good investment or not.

Estimating Disney's 1994 Earnings and Expected Return

In addition to a careful examination of a company's past financial performance, perhaps based on financial ratios, the analyst also has the task of estimating future earnings and the return an investor could expect from buying the stock today. After all, even though a company under study may have an excellent financial history, it may fail to provide a satisfactory return at the current price. Let's outline the process and then go through a numerical example to forecast 1994 earnings and expected return for Disney.

Outline of the Process

The major objective is to forecast the expected return, $E(r_i)$, assuming that one would purchase the stock today and hold it for a period of time. (We'll assume a one-year holding period throughout this section.) Begin with the formula for finding the expected return:

$$E(r_i) = (P_{t+1} - P_t + DIV_{t+1})/P_t \qquad (11.19)$$

where P is price and DIV is dividend. Notice that only the current price, P_t, is known; variables with $t + 1$ subscripts must be estimated.

The basic steps of the process for estimating the expected return are shown in Table 11.6. Start by estimating earnings for next year. Based on an estimate of next year's earnings, one can estimate next year's dividends. Using the Dividend Discount Model (DDM) discussed in Chapter 8, or other techniques, the analyst can estimate next year's price-to-earnings ratio. Estimates for both earnings and the price-to-earnings ratio can combine to give an estimate of next year's stock price. With all the estimates completed, plug them into Equation 11.19 and find the expected return. Finally, compare the expected return to some required return. If the expected return is greater than the required return, the stock may seem like a good buy; if not, it may seem like a poor investment.

Forecasting Earnings and Dividends per Share

Forecasting earnings is the most important component of the process for finding a stock's expected return; analysts spend a great deal of their time on this task. A poor forecast of next year's earnings will likely skew other variables' estimates, as well. There are many ways of estimating earnings.

Table 11.6

One Approach for Estimating a Company's Earnings and Expected Return

Step 1   Estimate next year's earnings and dividends:
   A.   Estimate next year's revenue by extrapolating a historical trend.
   B.   Estimate next year's net profit margin.
   C.   Earnings = Revenue × Net profit margin
   D.   Dividends = Earnings × Dividend payout ratio

Step 2   Estimate next year's price/earnings ratio and stock price:
   A.   Estimate the dividend payout ratio two years from now.
   B.   Estimate the growth rate (g = Return on equity × Retention rate).
   C.   Estimate the required rate of return.
   D.   P/E = Dividend payout/(Required return − Growth rate)
   E.   Next year's stock price = Next year's earnings per share × P/E

Step 3   Find the expected return, E(r):

   E(r) = (Price in one year − Price today + Next year's dividend)/Price today

Step 4   Compare the expected return to the required return. If the expected return exceeds the required return, the stock may be attractive.

Some are more quantitative, others more qualitative. Some approaches work well for certain types of companies, but not for others.[17]

Assume that it's now mid-September 1993. At that time, Disney was selling for around $39 a share and most analysts expected it to report earnings for its 1993 fiscal year, which would end on September 30, 1993, of $1.64 per share. That would give Disney a P/E ratio of about 24 (39.00 divided by 1.64). Now forecast Disney's 1994 fiscal-year earnings. Using a relatively simple approach, forecast earnings by first estimating 1994 revenue and then estimating Disney's 1994 net profit margin. Multiplying revenue by net profit margin will give a forecast of 1994 earnings.

Estimate of 1994 Revenue. Estimate Disney's 1994 revenue by extrapolating the historical relationship between personal income and Disney's revenue. Since Disney is primarily a leisure-time service company (generating income from theme parks, movies, and so forth), a fairly strong relationship may hold between personal income and company revenues. Faster personal income growth should drive faster growth in Disney's revenues.

Figure 11.2 illustrates the relationship between personal income and Disney's revenue per share for the period 1984 to 1993. In addition to the actual relationship, the figure shows the results of a linear regression, where personal income is the independent variable and Disney's revenue is the dependent variable. In equation form, the regression model states:

$$RPS_t = -15.3673 + 0.0057(PI_t) \qquad (11.20)$$

where *RPS* is revenue per share and *PI* is personal income.

Assume that economists expect personal income to increase by about 6 percent between September 1993 and September 1994, to $5,737.5 billion. Plugging this figure into Equation 11.20 gives an estimate of Disney's 1994 revenue:

$$RPS_{1994} = -15.3673 + 0.0057(5,737.5) = \$17.08$$

---

[17]Techniques to forecast earnings and the issues associated with their use are discussed in depth by Graham and Dodd. See S. Cottle et al., *Graham and Dodd's Security Analysis*, 5th ed. (New York: McGraw-Hill, 1988), 511–555.

Figure 11.2

Relationship between Personal Income and Revenue for the Walt Disney Company: 1984–1994

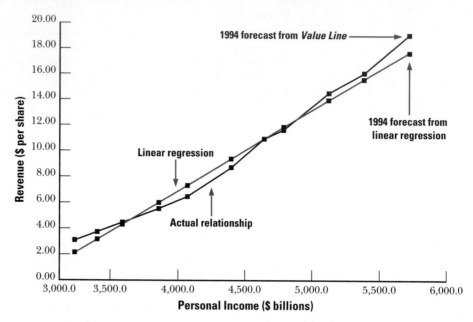

Source: *Value Line*, September 3, 1993, p. 1758; *Federal Reserve Bulletin* (various issues).

This figure represents an increase of about 7.2 percent from the company's 1993 revenue per share of $15.93, well below a *Value Line* forecast from early September 1993 of $18.45.[18]

Notice that, at first glance, the regression line appears to fit the actual relationship between revenue and personal income pretty closely. In recent years, however, Disney's actual revenues per share have been well-above the values predicted by the regression equation. In 1993, for example, actual revenue was $15.93 per share compared to a predicted value, from Equation 11.20, of $15.24. In fact, the increase between the 1993 predicted value and the 1994 predicted value is about 12 percent, more in line with *Value Line*'s forecast. A 1994 revenue increase of 12 percent would give a revenue estimate of $17.85. Let's use this figure.

Estimating Disney's Net Profit Margin. The next step is to estimate the firm's net profit margin. In recent years, Disney's net profit margin has declined from over 15 percent in 1989 to around 11 percent in 1993. Two factors often cited for the drop are higher corporate tax rates and lower operating margins for Disney's theme parks. For 1994, *Value Line* is forecasting a net profit margin of around 11.3 percent. Let's assume that the net profit margin in 1994 will remain around 11 percent. Multiplying 11 percent by our estimate of revenue per share gives an earnings forecast of $1.96.

Comparing Earnings Forecasts. We're forecasting fiscal 1994 earnings for Disney of $1.96 per share (an increase of 20 percent from 1993). By contrast, in September 1993 *Value Line* forecasted 1994 earnings of $2.05 per share (an increase of 25 percent). The consensus forecast of the 30 analysts who follow Disney was around $2.10 per share (an increase of 28 percent).[19] In

[18]*Value Line*, September 3, 1993, 1,758; *Federal Reserve Bulletin*, various issues.
[19]*Walt Disney Company*, Standard & Poor's Stock Report, October 1, 1993, 3.

fact, the lowest estimate from this group was $2.00 per share. Perhaps we've underestimated Disney's revenues and/or its net profit margin. Keep this difference in mind as you read further.

Forecasting 1994 Dividends. Forecasting next year's dividends is usually a lot easier than forecasting earnings. Historically, dividends are far more stable than earnings and most companies follow well-defined, predictable dividend policies. Disney doesn't pay a very high percentage of its earnings in dividends, and tends to raise dividends in small amounts, one or two cents per year. The 1993 dividend was 24 cents a share. The Disney analysts' consensus forecast for 1994 dividends, confirmed by *Value Line,* was about 29 cents per share. This figure seems pretty reasonable.

Forecasting the P/E Ratio and Stock Price

The next major step is to forecast Disney's 1994 price/earning ratio. This is not an easy task, but the analyst can find some clues. Historically, Disney's P/E has been larger than the P/E for the overall market. In September 1993, for example, Disney had a ratio of 22 compared to about 16.5 for the S&P 500, giving Disney a relative P/E of 1.33. Between 1977 and 1993, Disney's relative P/E has averaged 1.45. Many analysts predicted a market P/E in 1994 of 15, so one might estimate Disney's P/E at 21.75 (1.45 × 15). In September 1993, *Value Line* predicted a 1994 ratio for Disney of 22; the consensus forecast was also 22.

To get a somewhat more precise estimate of Disney's P/E, apply the Dividend Discount Model introduced in Chapter 8. One can rewrite the Dividend Discount Model as:

$$P/E_{t+1} = DPR_{t+2}/(ER_i - g) \qquad (11.21)$$

where DPR_{t+2} is the dividend payout ratio in Year $t+2$ (1995 in the example), ER_i is the required rate of return, and g is the firm's growth rate.

Value Line expected Disney's dividend payout ratio in 1995 to be around 15 percent. The firm's growth rate is equal to its return on equity (ROE) multiplied by its retention rate (1 minus the dividend payout ratio). *Value Line* predicted an ROE for Disney for 1994 of 17.5 percent. While that is lower than the firm's ROE in the middle-to-late 1980s, let's assume we're comfortable with it. If Disney retains 85 percent of its earnings, it has a projected growth rate of 14.9 percent (17.5 percent × 85 percent).

Now, what about the required rate of return? Back in Chapter 1, we suggested that the expected return on a risky asset like Disney stock can be considered as equal to the return on a risk-free asset plus a risk premium. A more risky asset must have a higher risk premium. In Chapter 13 we'll develop the Capital Asset Pricing Model, which attempts to formalize the relationship between risk and return for common stocks. Let's assume at this point that Disney, given its risk, should earn 15.5 percent.

Combining these figures and plugging them into Equation 11.21 gives an estimate for Disney's 1994 P/E ratio of 24 [15%/(15.5% − 14.9%)], somewhat higher than other estimates. Multiplying the projected P/E of 24 by the 1994 earnings forecast, $1.96, would give a stock price of $47.12. *Value Line's* numbers would give a projected stock price of $45.10 (22 × $2.05).

Calculating the 1994 Expected Return

We now have all the estimates we need in order to calculate an expected return for Disney. Assuming someone buys the stock at $39.00, holds it for one year, sells it for $47.12, after collecting cash dividends of $0.29. Using Equation 11.19, these figures give an expected return of:

$$(\$47.12 - \$39.00 + \$0.29)/\$39.00 = 21.6 \text{ percent}$$

Value Line's numbers give an expected return of around 16.4 percent.

Both expected returns are higher than the required rate of return, 15.5 percent, so Disney may seem like a good buy at $39.00 a share. In other words, if things were to work out as forecast, a Disney investor would earn a return higher than expected, given Disney's risk.

Some Caveats

Obviously we've oversimplified, but this section has reviewed the basic process by which analysts evaluate stocks. Instead of simply extrapolating a historical relationship to forecast revenues, for example, an analyst should examine each of Disney's three major business areas (theme parks, film entertainment, and consumer products) and then project revenue growth based on expected economic and industry conditions, in addition to historical trends. Perhaps Disney seems likely to have a lot of hit films in 1994. For example, "Lion King," due out in June 1994, is expected to be a blockbuster film. While the historical numbers support a 1994 revenue growth projection of 12 percent, this broader analysis may suggest a growth rate more like 15 percent.

Likewise, an analyst should develop a forecast of net profit margin by a more thorough analysis of Disney's income statement. Which costs are likely to rise, which are likely to fall, and why are these costs likely to change? Also, just because Disney's P/E has been higher than the overall market's for the last 15 years, it may not necessarily be higher next year.

Even the simplified forecast of Disney's 1994 earnings and expected return required estimates of six variables (1994 revenue per share, 1994 net profit margin, 1994 dividends, 1995 dividend payout ratio, 1994 return on equity, and required return). Obviously any or all of these estimates could be wrong. To evaluate this possibility, it is not a bad idea to ask a series of "what if" questions. What if revenue grows by 15 percent rather than 12 percent? How much higher will 1994 earnings be?

For example, if Disney's net profit margin were to turn out to be 12 percent (holding the other variables constant), rather than the 11 percent originally forecast, its 1994 earnings would be projected at $2.14 per share and its expected return would rise to 32.6 percent. By doing this analysis systematically, one can identify the variables to which the overall forecast is most sensitive. With this knowledge, then, one can direct any needed additional research to refining estimates of those critical variables.

Aside from illustrating the basic process of estimating earnings and returns, our discussion in this section teaches an important lesson: It is not easy to forecast earnings and expected returns. As we discussed in Chapter 6, even professional security analysts have only so-so records of forecasting earnings. Consequently, no analyst should simply rely on mechanically produced forecasts; specialized knowledge and skill can supply the best solutions to the problem. The good analyst is always alert to elements in the historical record of a company that may not continue in the future. Changes in the product line, significant demographic or technological changes, or drastic changes in management, just to name a few sources of disruption, could lead the analyst to reject the past record as a guide to the future.

In summary, a company analysis involves a process of research, research, and more research to determine what makes a company work. This process of qualitative and quantitative analysis, combined with some intuition (and guts), leads to a final decision to invest or not to invest.

Chapter Summary

1. **Understand the importance of quantitative company analysis.**

   Chapter 10 discussed the importance of qualitative company analysis, and now we discuss the importance of the quantitative analysis of a company. Quantitative information is important because it allows the analyst to summarize a company's past performance and to project trends for its future performance. Ranking companies by quantitative factors identifies those with better than market (or industry) performance and below market (or industry) performance. Given the vast pool of financial information available about a company, how can analysis summarize and identify relevant data? There are two methods: (1) ratio analysis and (2) forecasting expected return. Ratio analysis summarizes past financial information to identify a company's weaknesses and strengths with an expectation that if strengths outweigh weaknesses, it's a good investment. Another method is to forecast a rate of return from investing today and holding the stock for a specified period (usually a year). This expected return analysis combines forecasts of sales, EPS, and P/E in order to determine a stock's expected return, $E(r_i)$. Though quantitative analysis focuses on numerical data, qualitative issues are still very important. Both qualitative and quantitative criteria should guide final estimates of sales, EPS, P/E, and expected return.

2. **Examine the relationship between financial ratios and market value.**

   Ratio analysis is important because ratios are linked to the intrinsic value of a stock. Recall from Chapter 8 that the Dividend Discount Model (DDM) estimates a stock's intrinsic value based on a growth rate, g, where $g = ROE \times$ Retention ratio. We find that the profitability, activity, and leverage ratios all affect ROE, and in turn g, and thus the intrinsic value of a stock. This relationship between ratios and value makes ratios important tools to determine the true value of a stock. The relationship says that generally, higher profitability, higher activity, and higher leverage lead to higher ROE and growth.

3. **Review how to evaluate financial statements.**

   Firms provide financial statements to interested parties to distribute information on the resources (funds) available, the sources of funds for these resources, and the firm's use of these resources. Three financial statements typically appear in a company's annual report: the balance sheet, the income statement, and the statement of cash flows. The balance sheet provides information about sources of funds for company assets on the right-hand side and the assets on the left-hand side. The income statement provides information about the company's sales, costs and expenses, taxes, and net profits. The statement of cash flows provides information about the firm's cash inflows and outflows during a period (usually a year).

4. **Conduct company analysis using financial ratios.**

   Four categories of ratios drive analysis of the past performance and future prospects of a company. The four categories are: (1) liquidity ratios, (2) activity ratios, (3) leverage ratios, and (4) profitability ratios. Remember that ratios alone are meaningless; to add meaning they must be compared to aggregate economic indicators, industry ratios, a competitor's ratios, or the company's own past ratios.

5. **Understand business risk and operating leverage.**

   Business risk is the variability of the company's operating profits. Since the company's operating profits can be separated into two components, sales and costs, business risk decomposes further as: (1) variability in sales (sales risk) and (2) variability in operating profits due to fixed production costs (operating leverage). Business risk may be high for some companies because of high sales risk, high fixed costs, or both.

6. **Estimate a sample company's earnings and expected return.**

    Another way to analyze a company is to forecast its expected return, rather than conducting a past performance analysis (as in ratio analysis). This method forces the analyst to evaluate, not what the company has done, but what it will do in sales, EPS, P/E, and finally expected return. To forecast expected return: (1) forecast sales and EPS, and (2) apply the P/E model derived from the DDM. (See the process outlined in Table 11.6.) The expected return says that an investment today that holds the stock for a specified period (usually a year) will generate a particular expected return. Ranking expected returns for several companies reveals which ones are expected to be better investment. The strength of this method is that it bases investment decisions on forecasts, not past performance, and by using the DDM, it accounts for risk. Of course, its weakness is the accuracy of its forecasts, which can be off, sometimes way off.

Key Terms

Profit margin	Financial leverage
Total asset turnover	Debt–equity ratio
Asset utilization ratio	Total debt–total assets ratio
Leverage ratio	Coverage ratios
Balance sheet	Interest coverage ratio
Stock figure	Fixed charge coverage ratio
Income statement	Profitability ratio
Flow figure	Gross profit margin
Earnings per share	Operating profit margin
Cash flow statement	Net profit margin
Liquidity ratios	Return on total capital
Current ratio	Return on stockholders' equity (ROE)
Quick ratio	DuPont Chart
Activity ratios	Cyclical company
Average collection period	Operating leverage
Inventory turnover	Coefficient of variation
Fixed asset turnover	Standard deviation

Mini Case **1** OBJECTIVE

To determine business risk and sales risk for three companies: Intel, Osh-Kosh B'Gosh, and Procter & Gamble.

Open the file FINA1.XLS on the data disk. The file contains sales and operating profits data from 1983 to 1992 for each of the three companies. Use the data and a spreadsheet program or calculator to answer the following questions:

1. Calculate the arithmetic mean and standard deviation of sales for each company. Use a financial calculator or a spreadsheet program with statistical functions.
2. Discuss what each company sells and the expected level of sales variability or risk based on the major line of business for each. Compare the three companies and attempt to rank them from the most to the least risky. From what sources can you gather this information? (*Hint:* Go back to Chapter 4 to review the sources of information.)
3. Calculate the coefficient of variation (CV) for sales, or sales risk, for each of the three companies. Verify the sales variability rankings produced in Question 2.

4. Calculate the coefficient of variation (CV) for operating profits. Determine why the riskiest firm has so much variation and why the least risky firm is so stable.

Mini Case **2**   OBJECTIVE

To forecast a company's earnings for 1994 (1995 fiscal year). Also to see how difficult it is at times to finesse the forecasts.

Open the following file: FINA2.XLS on the data disk. The file contains Wal-Mart's sales per share and consumer spending data from 1984 to 1993. Use the data and information from Value Line to answer the following questions.

1. Estimate sales per share for 1994 using a simple linear regression with consumer spending as the independent variable. Discuss the explanatory power of the regression. The estimate for consumer spending in 1994 is given in the file.
2. Estimate EPS for 1994 (1995 fiscal year which ends on January 31, 1995).

Discussion Questions and Problems

1. Explain why the total debt–total assets ratio and the total assets–equity ratio are both called the *leverage ratio*. How are they related?
2. What is the relationship between *ROE* and the profitability, activity, and the leverage ratios?
3. What is a cyclical company? Give an example of a cyclical company.
4. What is financial leverage? Discuss what factors cause financial risk.
5. What is sales risk?
   a. Discuss the types of companies that may have low sales risk.
   b. Discuss the types of companies that may have high sales risk.
6. What is business risk? What are the components of business risk?
   a. Discuss the types of companies with low sales risk, but high business risk.
   b. Discuss the types of companies with high sales risk, but low business risk.

7. 1988 CFA Examination, Level I.
   Which of the following *best* explains a ratio of net sales to average net fixed assets that exceeds the industry average?
   a. The firm expanded its plant and equipment in the past few years.
   b. The firm makes less efficient use of its assets than other firms.
   c. The firm has a lot of old plant and equipment.
   d. The firm uses straight line depreciation.
   Explain your answer.
8. 1988 CFA Examination, Level I.
   The rate of return on assets is equivalent to:
   a. Profit margin × Total asset turnover.
   b. Profit margin × Total asset turnover × Leverage ratio/Interest expense.
   c. Net income + Interest expense net of income tax + Minority interest in earnings/Average total assets
   d. Minority interest in earnings/Average total assets
   Explain your answer.
9. 1987 CFA Examination, Level I.
   Use the financial statements for Seattle Manufacturing Corporation to compute the following ratios for 1986 (Tables 11.7 and 11.8).
   a. Return on total assets

Table 11.7

Seattle Manufacturing Corp. Consolidated Balance Sheet, as of December 31 ($ millions)

	1985	1986
Assets		
Current assets		
Cash	$ 6.2	$ 6.6
Short-term investment in commercial paper	20.8	15.0
Accounts receivable	77.0	93.2
Inventory	251.2	286.0
Prepaid manufacturing expense	1.4	1.8
Total current assets	$356.6	$402.6
Leased property under capital leases, net of accumulated amortization	181.4	215.6
Other assets	6.2	9.8
Total assets	$544.2	$628.0
Liabilities and Stockholders' Equity		
Current liabilities		
Accounts payable	$143.2	$161.0
Dividends payable	13.0	14.4
Current portion of long-term debt	12.0	16.6
Current portion of obligations under capital leases	18.8	22.6
Estimated taxes on income	10.8	9.8
Total current liabilities	$197.8	$224.4
Long-term debt	86.4	107.0
Obligations under capital leases	140.8	165.8
Total liabilities	$425.0	$497.2
Shareholders' Equity		
Common stock, $10 par value, 4,000,000 shares authorized, 3,000,000 and 2,680,000 outstanding, respectively	$ 26.8	$ 30.0
Cumulative preferred stock. Series A 8 percent; $25 par value; 1,000,000 authorized; 600,000 outstanding	15.0	15.0
Additional paid-in capital	26.4	27.0
Retained earnings	51.0	58.8
Total shareholders' equity	$119.2	$130.8
Total liabilities and shareholders' equity	$544.2	$628.0

    b. Earnings per share of common stock

    c. Quick ratio

    d. Interest coverage ratio

    e. Average collection period

    f. Leverage ratio − debt–equity ratio

10. Compute the ratios in Question 9 for Seattle Manufacturing Corporation for 1985. Compare each ratio between 1986 and 1985 and determine whether or not the data show improvement. Provide possible reasons for any significant changes.

11. Display the results of ratio analysis for Seattle Manufacturing in a DuPont Chart. It may be necessary to calculate additional ratios. State each account as a percentage of sales for 1986 and 1985. Discuss any significant changes that led to the differences in ROE.

12. Display ratios for Seattle Manufacturing in the ROE equation (Equation 11.2). Again, confirm your discussions in Question 11.

Table 11.8

Seattle Manufacturing Corp. Income Statement, Years
Ending December 31 ($ millions)

	1985	1986
Sales	$1,166.6	$1,207.6
Other income, net	12.8	15.6
Total revenues	$1,179.4	$1,223.2
Cost of sales	$ 912.0	$ 961.2
Amortization of leased property	43.6	48.6
Selling and administrative expense	118.4	128.8
Interest expense	16.2	19.8
Total costs and expenses	$1,090.2	$1,158.4
Income before income tax	$ 89.2	$ 64.8
Income tax	19.2	10.4
Net income	$ 70.0	$ 54.4

Critical Thinking Exercises

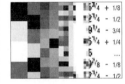

1. This exercise requires computer work. Balance sheets and income statements for Wal-Mart Stores for the years 1990–1994 are contained in file "Wal-Mart.XLS" on the data disk. Perform ratio analysis in each category listed below.

   a. Calculate Wal-Mart's liquidity ratios, including the current and quick ratios, for each of the three years. Discuss the trend.

   b. Calculate Wal-Mart's activity ratios, including the average collection period, inventory turnover, total asset turnover, and fixed asset turnover for the same periods. Discuss the trend over the years.

   c. Calculate Wal-Mart's leverage ratio, including the debt–equity, total debt–total assets, and interest coverage ratios over the three years. Discuss the firm's financial risk over the years.

   d. Calculate Wal-Mart's profitability ratios, including the gross profit margin, operating profit margin, and the net profit margin. Again discuss performance over time.

   e. Calculate Wal-Mart's return ratios, including the return on total capital and return on stockholders' equity (ROE) over the period. Discuss the trend for returns to investors. What is the possibility for future returns?

   f. Apply Equation 11.2's relationship between ROE and the three ratios, profitability, activity, and leverage over the three years. What can you conclude about Wal-Mart's performance and the impact of each of the three ratios?

   g. Create a DuPont Chart for Wal-Mart for 1992 and discover any possible strengths and weaknesses that may affect the firm's future.

2. This exercise requires computer work. Financial data for Kmart Corporation is contained in file K-Mart.XLS on the data disk. Use these data to answer the following questions.

   a. Calculate major liquidity, profitability, leverage, and activity ratios for Kmart Corporation.

   b. Apply Equation 11.2's relationship between ROE and the three ratios measuring activity, profitability, and leverage.

   c. Compare the results you found for Kmart in the prior three questions with the results you found for Wal-Mart in the prior exercise. Which company is more profitable? Which company is financially stronger?

3. This exercise requires computer work. Open file SWA.XLS on the data disk. Evaluate a 1994 earnings forecast for Southwest Airlines made by a major securities firm. The firm's airline analyst has come up with a 1994 earnings forecast of $1.58 per share. The analyst based her forecast on estimates of a number of variables.

   a. Based on the analyst's estimates for each variable, prepare a 1994 pro-forma income statement for Southwest Airlines which reconciles the analyst's forecast of 1994 earnings of $1.58 per share with the estimates given.

   b. Listed in the data file are original and revised estimates for several variables. Recompute 1994 earnings for each revision, holding other variables constant.

   c. Based on what you found in Question b, to which variables does the original 1994 earnings forecast of $1.58 per share appear to be most sensitive? Discuss your findings.

4. Open the following file: WMT.TXT on the data disk. It contains A. G. Edwards & Sons' report on Wal-Mart Stores prepared by Donald Spindel. Review his method of analysis and compare his forecasted EPS with the forecasted EPS in Mini Case 3. Critically analyze and contrast the results and the two methods. What are the strengths and weaknesses in each method?

Mini Case 1   SOLUTION

1. The arithmetic mean and standard deviation of sales are calculated for each of the three companies below:

Company	Arithmetic Mean[a]	Standard Deviation[a]
OshKosh	$ 241.70	$ 94.32
Intel	2783.40	1631.24
Procter & Gamble	21,057.30	6,453.84

[a]All results in millions.

2. Using Value Line, Moody's Industrial Record, or S&P Corporate, find information about each company's major line of business.

   OshKosh designs, manufactures, and markets clothing for kids up to age 7. (This market represents 96 percent of its 1992 sales.) The firm also manufactures men's and women's casual and work clothing, selling mainly to department stores and specialty stores. JC Penny accounts for 12.4 percent of 1992 sales and outlet stores for 13 percent of U.S. sales. Since the firm's children's clothes are known for moderate prices and durability, its sales variability may be moderate, as well. Though it is affected by the economy, it probably reacts less than the higher-priced clothing manufacturers.

   Intel is the leading manufacturer of integrated circuits. Intel serves markets in the personal computers (75 percent of sales), communications, industrial automation, military equipment, and other electronic equipment areas. The firm's main products are microprocessors, related peripherals, microcontrollers, and memory components. Intel may be greatly affected by business cycles as its customers are mainly computer manufacturers and communications companies. Relative to the other two firms (OshKosh and Procter & Gamble), Intel may have the greatest sales variability.

Procter & Gamble is a leading soap and detergent producer. It also produces toiletries, foods, paper, and industrial products. Well-known P&G brands include Tide, Cheer, Bold, Era, Crest, Ivory, Zest, Coast, Safeguard, Dawn, Joy, Cascade, Always, Downy, Bounce, Comet, Head & Shoulders, Prell, Scope, Secret, Pampers, Jif, Folgers, Cover Girl, and Hawaiian Punch. The firm would be the least affected of the three by business cycles as most households consider these products necessities for clean living. P&G may lose market share, but that would be a function of other companies in the industry developing better products, rather than changes in the overall economy.

Our guess is that Intel is the riskiest in terms of sales variability, while Procter & Gamble is the least risky.

3. The coefficient of variation of sales is calculated for each company:

Company	Coefficient of Variation
OshKosh	0.39
Intel	0.59
Procter & Gamble	0.31

The appearance; Question 2 seems to be correct based on these data. Intel is the most risky while Procter & Gamble is the least risky.

4. The coefficient of variation of operating profits for each firm is calculated below:

Company	Coefficient of Variation
OshKosh	0.37
Intel	0.88
Procter & Gamble	0.36

Intel has the highest business risk, while Procter & Gamble has the lowest. Intel's high sales risk gives it its business risk characteristics. The sales risk is associated with the sales variability of computer manufacturers purchasing Intel's products, while business risk comes from both sales risk and fixed costs of production. Intel is riskiest in both; it has both high sales variability and high fixed production costs. In contrast, Procter & Gamble has relatively low sales risk and low business risk. Compared to integrated circuit manufacturing, soap manufacturing has lower fixed costs as well as lower sales variability.

Mini Case **2**   SOLUTION

1. The coefficient estimates from regressing sales per share on consumer spending is given below. We will use a subscript of W for Wal-Mart.

$$\text{Sales per share }_{Wt} = -39.7446 + .0164CS_t + e_{wt}.$$

The R^2 for the regression equals .9445. This says that consumer spending does a good job in explaining the variability of sales per share. By plugging in the forecast for consumer spending provided in the file, we have:

$$\text{Sales per share}_{Wt} = -39.7446 + .0164(\$4750) = \$38.16$$

2. Multiplying the estimated sales per share by Value Line's estimate of 1994's net profit margin for Wal-Mart (1995 fiscal year), we estimate earnings per share$_{wt + 1}$. It equals:

$$\text{EPS}_{wt + 1} = (.035)(\$38.16) = \$1.34.$$

Part IV

Modern Portfolio Theory

The next four chapters will be devoted to a discussion of something called *modern portfolio theory* (MPT). We will discuss such topics as risk aversion, measuring risk and return (for both individual securities and portfolios), efficient frontiers, the capital asset pricing model, arbitrage pricing, and how to evaluate the performance of investment portfolios. The material in this section will probably seem more conceptual and theoretical than the material elsewhere in the text. However, we will show how modern portfolio theory can provide insight into many real-world investment situations. For example, the concept of diversification, the value of which is widely recognized by most investment professionals, really comes directly from MPT. Modern portfolio theory shows what diversification can do for investors (improve their risk and return tradeoffs), and MPT helps us understand why diversification works (securities' returns are not perfectly correlated over time). Keep this in mind as you're reading the next four chapters.

Chapter 12

Risk and Diversification

Chapter Objectives

1. Develop a definition of *risk aversion* and understand why investors, as a group, are risk averse.
2. Identify the general investment implications of risk aversion.
3. Understand why standard deviation is a good measure of risk, and learn how to compute standard deviations for both individual securities and portfolios.
4. Understand the impact of security correlations on portfolio risk.
5. Identify the benefits of diversification and how investors can achieve them.
6. Develop an understanding of efficient diversification and modern portfolio theory.

Two of the apparent truisms we discussed initially in Chapter 1, and have touched on many times since, were the positive relationship between historical returns and risk, and the beneficial effects of investment diversification. Investment instruments that have, at least over the last 65 years or so, exhibited higher rates of return, have also shown more variability around their average returns. You may recall from the historical data presented in Chapter 2 that common stocks have, on average, returned more than Treasury bills since 1926 (12.3 percent versus 3.7 percent, per year), but stock returns have also shown far more volatility. Therefore, if an investor wants to increase expected returns, she or he must be willing to accept higher levels of risk.

However, the historical evidence also suggests that owning a group of investment instruments can allow one to beat the risk/return tradeoff, at least up to a point. In other words, owning five stocks will generally produce a better risk/return profile over time than owning one stock. Both of these truisms form the basis of modern portfolio and investment theory, as we will discuss in more detail in this chapter. Many of the key ideas discussed in Chapter 12 have been touched on many times before. In this chapter, we try to tie many of these ideas together and more formally develop the concepts of risk and diversification.

Chapter 12 begins with a discussion of risk aversion, why most investors are risk averse, and what risk aversion implies about the long-term relationship between risk and return. The discussion establishes the importance of risk. Next, we turn to a discussion of how to actually measure risk, a subject we have attempted to avoid up to this point. This discussion will include the problem of measuring historical versus expected risk, measuring risk for an individual security, and measuring risk for a group of securities (a portfolio). After a discussion of risk measurement, we turn to a detailed discussion of diversification and two types of risk, market risk and firm-specific risk. We examine diversification across securities and the fallacy of time diversification. Naive versus efficient diversification will be scrutinized, as well. A discussion of efficient diversification naturally leads to a discussion of modern portfolio theory, which concludes the chapter.

What Is Risk Aversion?

Suppose your state were to begin a new lottery today. For five dollars, you would have an equal chance of losing or winning five dollars. If you play the game, you have a 50/50 chance of coming out five dollars richer, or five dollars poorer. The expected payoff is, of course, zero.[1] Would you play this new lottery game? You might answer *yes* as you're reading this, but if you were playing with real money, you would probably answer *no*. If you play this lottery, you can actually expect to be worse off. The lottery involves obvious **risk** (the chance you may come away poorer), with no compensation for that risk.

Now suppose your state offered another new game. For five dollars, you would have an equal chance of winning nothing, or winning ten dollars. Now the expected payoff is +$5; would you play the second game? Of course, not knowing you personally, we cannot answer the question definitively. We can say, however, that you are much more likely to play the second game than the first, because this second game offers some compensation for the risk involved with playing. Of course, in the real world neither game is likely to be offered since the purpose of state lotteries is to make money for states' treasuries. As a result, all state lottery games have negative expected payoffs for players. Why people voluntarily play these lottery games is a very interesting question that we will attempt to answer shortly.

As trivial as these lottery games sound, the two fundamental questions involved (would you play and why?) are really the same questions all investors must answer when making investment decisions. For example, assume you could buy a Treasury bill for $1,000, hold it for a year and receive $1,060 (a 6 percent return). As we've pointed out, Treasury bills are as close to a truly risk-free investment as you can get. Now also assume that you could invest your $1,000 in shares of a high-risk, junk bond fund. In a year, shares of the fund could be worth $1,500 (a 50 percent return), or only $500 (a *minus* 50 percent return); the expected return is 0 percent. Assuming each outcome has about a 50/50 chance of occurring, which investment would you choose? Most investors would likely choose to invest in Treasury bills simply because the junk bond fund doesn't offer any compensation for its added risk. In fact, the expected payoff from the fund is less than the almost certain payoff from the T-bill investment ($1,000 versus $1,060). It is hard to imagine any *rational* investor choosing the junk bond fund investment.

Make some changes to the example, however, and the decision becomes more interesting, and ambiguous. Assume that the T-bill still offers an almost certain 6 percent return and the junk bond fund has the same two possible outcomes ($1,500 or $500), but change the probabilities of those outcomes occurring. Now assume that there is a 75 percent chance that the fund will be worth $1,500 in one year, and only a 25 percent chance that it will be worth $500. The expected payoff becomes $1,250 (an expected return of 25

---

[1]Remember, the expected payoff is a weighted average of the possible outcomes. In this case, the expected payoff equals 0.5 (−$5) + 0.5($5).

percent). Which would you choose in this situation? It's hard to say. Some investors would choose to invest in the junk bond fund, while others would still choose to invest in T-bills.

While the above example is obviously simplified, it still serves to illustrate the important concept of **risk aversion.** Most investors appear willing to pay to avoid risky situations. Paying to avoid risk is exactly what we do when we purchase insurance. We pay premiums to shift some, or even all, of the risk of owning a home, driving a car, and so forth, to the insurance company. To put the notion of risk aversion another way, most of us will voluntarily take risks only if we receive proper compensation for that risk. Risk aversion is, in turn, related to the concept of utility and the utility of wealth.

Risk Aversion and the Utility of Wealth

Economists often rely on the concept of utility when explaining why individuals make certain economic decisions. The economic definition of utility is desiredness, or the capacity to satisfy a want, of whatever kind.[2] While utility cannot be measured directly, the concept of the **utility of wealth** is extremely useful in explaining investment behavior.

Not surprisingly, wealth provides utility to individuals. Since most of us prefer more wealth to less wealth, the utility of wealth increases as the level of wealth increases. This seems fairly obvious. The key question, however, is whether or not the amount of utility wealth provides increases at the *same rate* as the level of wealth. Perhaps the utility of wealth increases at a decreasing or increasing rate as the level of wealth rises.

While we cannot answer this question unambiguously, logic seems to suggest that the utility of wealth, for most of us at least, increases at a decreasing rate, as the level of wealth rises. For example, let's say your total wealth is $1,000. If you could increase your wealth level by $500, the increase in your utility of wealth would probably be substantial. By contrast, assume that Bill Gates (the founder of Microsoft, worth around $7 billion, give or take a billion) saw his wealth increase by the same $500.[3] His utility of wealth would increase, but probably not by very much. An important characteristic of the utility of wealth function is that for most people, as wealth increases, utility increases at a diminishing rate.

How does the concept of utility relate to risk aversion? The relationship, at least conceptually, is very straightforward. The key to understanding the relationship lies in the shape of the utility of wealth function. This function demonstrates how the utility of wealth changes as the level of wealth changes. It is best illustrated with a simple example. Assume a portion of your hypothetical utility of wealth function is as follows:

Wealth Level	Utility of Wealth (Utils)[4]	Percentage Change in Utils
1	0.00	—
10	2.30	—
20	3.00	30%
30	3.40	13
40	3.69	9
50	3.91	6

[2]The proper definition of utility has been debated throughout the history of economics. For example, see, *The New Palgrave Dictionary of Economics,* vol. 4 (London: Macmillan Press, 1987), 776–779.

[3]According to *Fortune* magazine's list of billionaires in the June 28, 1993 issue, Bill Gates ranked 12th after the Sam Walton family (founder of Wal-Mart Stores) and the Mars family (of M&M/ Mars candy).

[4]Economists often use the term *util* to represent utility. Even though utility cannot be measured in the scientific sense, we can say that 2 utils provide twice the utility of 1 util.

Figure 12.1

Utility of Wealth Function for a Risk-Averse Investor

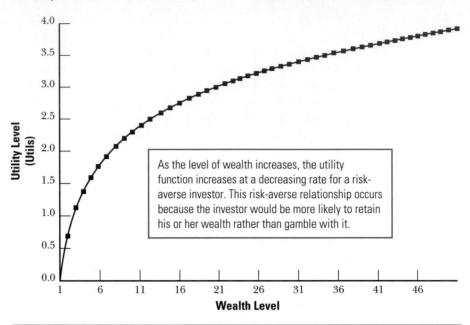

As the level of wealth increases, the utility function increases at a decreasing rate for a risk-averse investor. This risk-averse relationship occurs because the investor would be more likely to retain his or her wealth rather than gamble with it.

This utility of wealth function is graphed in Figure 12.1. Notice that over the range in which the function increases, the level of utility of wealth increases at a decreasing rate. The utility of wealth function in this example is a simple logarithmic relationship, where the utility of wealth equals the natural log of wealth $[U(W) = \ln(W)]$. This is one of many possible utility of wealth functions that could represent the risk aversion of investors, but it illustrates the characteristics we've described above: increasing wealth levels increase a person's utility at a decreasing rate. As the wealth level doubles from 10 to 20, the utility of wealth increases by 30 percent (from 2.30 utils to 3.00 utils), but the next increment of wealth from 20 to 30 increases utility by only 13 percent and utility continues to increase at a diminishing rate.

Let's go back to a simple, lottery-type game. Assume your current wealth level is 30, and your current utility of wealth is 3.40 utils. You could play a game that would either increase your wealth by 20 or decrease it by 20. Therefore, if you were to play the game, your wealth level would be either 10 or 50. As we discussed earlier, you most likely wouldn't play this game, assuming each outcome has a 50/50 chance of occurring, since you're not being compensated for the game's risk. The expected payoff from playing the game is zero. Knowing your utility of wealth function, we can easily show that you are actually worse off if you play the game. The function shows that your expected utility level is actually lower if you play the game. Remember your current utility is 3.400; if you were to play the game your expected utility would be only 3.105.[5] To put this another way, the wealth you might lose playing the game is worth more to you than the wealth you might make playing the game.

What could the promoter do to get you to play this game? At the very least, if you play the game your expected utility should be no less than your current utility. Using the same outcomes, if the probability of winning 20 were 0.68, while the probability of losing 20 were only 0.32, you might be

---

[5]The expected utility if you play the game is found by weighting the utility levels of each outcome by the probability of the outcome occurring. Thus, $E(U) = 0.5U(10) + 0.5U(50)$, which equals $0.5(2.30) + 0.5(3.91) = 3.105$.

Figure 12.2

Utility of Wealth Functions for Risk-Neutral Investors and
Risk Takers

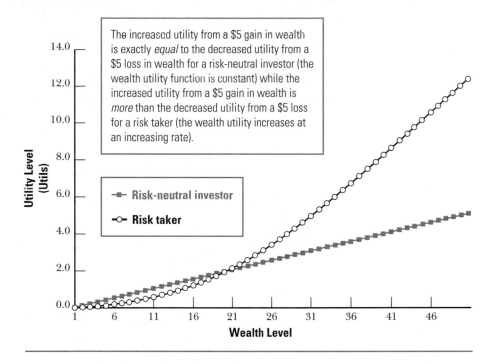

The increased utility from a $5 gain in wealth
is exactly *equal* to the decreased utility from a
$5 loss in wealth for a risk-neutral investor (the
wealth utility function is constant) while the
increased utility from a $5 gain in wealth is
more than the decreased utility from a $5 loss
for a risk taker (the wealth utility increases at
an increasing rate).

-■- **Risk-neutral investor**

-○- **Risk taker**

willing to play the game.[6] With these new odds, the game would set your
expected utility, *EU*, at 3.40, which is equal to your current utility.[7]

$$EU = 0.32U(10) + 0.68U(50) = 0.32(2.30) + 0.68(3.91) = 3.40$$

Notice that the expected payoff from the game is now positive and equals
$7.2 = [0.32(-20) + 0.68(20)]$.

This utility of wealth function is characteristic of a risk-averse investor, one
who voluntarily takes risk only in exchange for a sufficient reward. Risk aversion, in turn, is directly related to a utility of wealth function which increases
at a decreasing rate. Now consider the implications of two very different utility of wealth functions.

If the utility of wealth function graphed in Figure 12.1 represents that of
a risk-averse investor, then the utility of wealth functions graphed in Figure
12.2 represent those of a **risk-neutral investor** and a **risk taker.**[8] Notice that
the risk-neutral investor's utility function increases at a constant rate as
wealth increases, while the risk taker's function increases at an increasing
rate. How would both investors react to the same lottery game you just considered? Assuming each has a current wealth level of 30, and assuming the
odds of making 20 or losing 20 are 50/50, the risk-neutral investor would be
indifferent between playing or not playing. On the other hand, the risk taker
would actually pay to play the game. Both answers depend on the shape of
the investors' respective utility of wealth functions.

---

[6]If a utility of wealth function could be developed to precisely match your true preferences,
admittedly an almost impossible task, then you would be truly indifferent between playing and
not playing the game if the expected utility from playing the game were to equal your current
utility level.

[7]Now the expected utility of playing the game equals $0.32U(10) + 0.68U(50)$.

[8]The risk-neutral utility function is $U(W) = 0.1W$, while the risk taker's function is $U(W) =
0.005W^2$.

The risk-neutral investor has a current utility level of 3.00 utils, 0.1(30). The game would leave this utility at 3.00 utils, 0.5(1.00) + 0.5(5.00). The risk taker's current utility level is 4.50 utils. Playing the game actually increases this utility to 6.50 utils. The risk-neutral investor is neither better off nor worse off playing the game, while the risk taker is clearly better off. Therefore, the risk-neutral investor is indifferent to risk and the risk taker will actually pay to voluntarily take risk.

This example shows that investors exhibit very different responses to risky situations, such as the lottery-type game, depending on the shapes of their utility of wealth functions. We would expect major differences in investment behavior as well, depending on whether investors are risk-averse, risk-neutral, or risk takers.

Observation seems to suggest that investors, as a group, are risk-averse. It's hard to imagine anyone playing the lottery game described in the prior section, unless the expected payoff were greater than zero. Most investors, indeed most individuals, voluntarily purchase insurance to protect from adverse circumstances such as fire, theft, flood, earthquake, etc. This does not imply, however, that all investors are equally risk averse. Clearly various individual attributes (e.g., age and income) will make some investors more or less risk averse than others.

Risk Aversion and Expected Returns

Perhaps the most important implication of risk aversion is that an investment should show a positive relationship between expected returns and risk. As we've seen, risk-averse investors will take risk only in exchange for sufficient compensation, that is, returns. Therefore, higher-risk investments must offer risk-averse investors higher expected rates of return. If, at a certain price, a high-risk investment doesn't offer investors a sufficient expected rate of return, the price (or return) will have to fall (or rise). Now assume that investors are, as a group, risk-neutral. Risk-neutral investors would demand no relationship between risk and return. In fact, in a well-functioning market, all investments would have to have the *same* expected return, regardless of risk. Arbitrage would quickly eliminate any differences. As far-fetched as that sounds, consider the relationship between risk and return if investors are, as a group, risk takers. Since risk takers will pay to take risk, the relationship between expected returns and risk would have to be negative. In other words, high-risk investments would actually have to offer lower expected returns compared to safer investments!

If our logical argument doesn't convince you that investors are risk-averse, reviewing some of the historical evidence on risk and return might. Chapter 2 reviewed the long-term historical performance of the major investment instruments. We found that higher-risk investments have historically returned more, on average, than lower-risk investments. For example, between 1926 and 1993, the return on common stocks in the United States (represented by the Standard and Poor's 500) exceeded the return on U.S. Treasury bills by, on average, about 8.6 percent per year (12.3 percent versus 3.7 percent). By any conventional and reasonable measure, common stocks are more risky than Treasury bills. Figure 12.3 shows the distribution of yearly returns for both investments. Notice how the historical returns from T-bills are clustered together. For example, in 43 out of 68 years, T-bill returns ranged between 0 percent and 5 percent. By comparison, common stock returns have exhibited far more variability. Standard & Poor's 500 Index stocks earned more than 30 percent in seventeen different years, and lost more than 10 percent in 8 different years, between 1926 and 1993.

Figure 12.3

Distribution of Yearly Returns of Stocks and T-Bills:
1926–1993

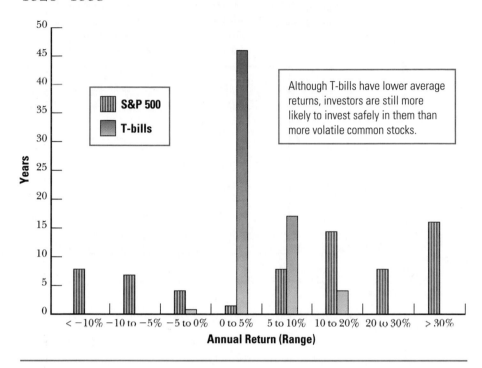

Although T-bills have lower average returns, investors are still more likely to invest safely in them than more volatile common stocks.

Relative Risk Aversion and Expected Returns

A little earlier we pointed out that some investors are probably more risk averse than others. In other words, Investor A may be relatively more risk averse than Investor B. What does this imply about the relationship between risk and expected returns? The answer is quite straightforward: relatively more risk aversion increases the expected return investors demand, for the same risk level. This is best illustrated with a simple example.

Let's say that Investor A is relatively more risk averse than Investor B. Figure 12.4 shows their hypothetical tradeoffs between risk and expected return.[9] Level *f* represents the expected return from a risk-free asset (e.g., a T-bill). As the level of risk increases (say to Level *a*), the expected return for both investors increases, consistent with the notion of risk aversion. Notice, however, that the expected return for Investor A (the more risk-averse investor) increases more (from Level *f* to Level *y*) than the expected return for Investor B (from Level *f* to Level *x*). In fact, the risk level would have to increase all the way to Level *b* before Investor B's expected return would reach Level *y*.

The notion of relative risk aversion helps to explain why certain investors hold only low-risk assets while others hold higher-risk assets. An investor who is relatively more risk averse may feel that the compensation for holding, say, stocks is not enough to justify their added risk. This investor would own mainly T-bills and CDs. On the other hand, another, relatively less risk-averse investor may feel the compensation for owning stocks is enough to justify the added risk, and thus this person would own mainly stocks.

---

[9]These are referred to as *indifference curves*. An investor is indifferent between each point on the curve. In other words, each point (investment) offers an identical risk/return tradeoff.

Figure 12.4

Risk Aversion and Expected Returns

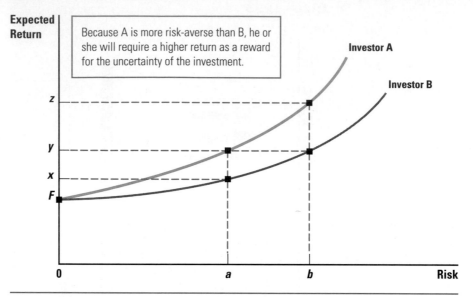

Because A is more risk-averse than B, he or she will require a higher return as a reward for the uncertainty of the investment.

Risk Aversion and Gambling

In spite of our logical argument, coupled with the historical evidence, perhaps you are still a bit skeptical about risk aversion. After all, how can we explain state lotteries, or any other form of gambling (legal or otherwise), if investors are really risk averse? After all, the expected payoff from games of chance is always negative. Also, what about the speculative bubbles we discussed in Chapter 5? Why would risk-averse investors fall into these traps, time and time again?

Economists and psychologists have debated answers to these questions for years, and have yet to answer them in any totally satisfactory manner. Clearly some investors periodically make irrational decisions, though this irrationality is often a conclusion drawn in retrospect. The psychology of the "madness of crowds" is well-documented. Some individuals view gambling as entertainment and derive utility from it, whether or not they win. These individuals probably voluntarily purchase insurance, which implies risk aversion, as well as gamble, which implies risk taking. In the extreme, sadly, some individuals actually become addicted to gambling, and there probably are a few true risk takers out there.

While we certainly can't answer all the questions associated with risk, a closer look at state lotteries might provide some insight. For a small wager, most state lotteries offer the chance, albeit a minuscule chance, of winning big. Given that states return in winnings, on average, only about one-third of what they take in, the expected return from these games is negative.[10] Why would risk-averse individuals play? Perhaps they are unable to properly compute or understand the odds of winning. Perhaps players want to help subsidize the state treasury!

A more rational explanation may be simply that, in spite of being risk averse, the utility of what they give up to play the lottery (a couple of dollars) is less than the potential utility of what they might win (millions), in spite of the odds. A couple of lottery tickets are a cheap dream for many.

---

[10]The odds of winning state lottery games are actually much worse that the odds of winning most Las Vegas–style casino games.

Brief Recap

We've tried to show in this section that most investors are probably risk averse, though probably to varying degrees. Examples showed that investors would not take a gamble (risk) unless its expected payoff (or return) were to exceed that of a sure thing. Clearly, risk and expected return must be closely related. As a result, we can assume that investors will prefer investments with higher expected returns and lower risk. Further, risk aversion is the basis upon which we can make statements about investment choices, as you'll see in Chapter 13. Given that risk and expected return are among the most striking features of the securities markets, and probably among the most important criteria in investment selection and analysis, the next question naturally becomes, How should (and can) risk and expected return be measured? We explore this issue in the next section.

Measuring Risk and Return: Individual Securities

In this section we will examine four topics: how to measure returns for individual securities, how to measure risk, how to calculate a standard deviation, and how investors can use risk and return measures to make security selections.

How to Measure Returns

Back in Chapter 3, we discussed how to measure a one-year (or one-period) return for a security. Recall that the holding period return for a Stock i can be calculated as follows:

$$HPR_{i,t} = \frac{P_{i,t} - P_{i,t-1} + DIV_{i,t}}{P_{i,t-1}} \quad \text{or} \quad \frac{P_{i,1} + DIV_{i,t}}{P_{i,t-1}} - 1 \quad (12.1a)$$

where $P_{i,t}$ is the price in period t (e.g., year t), $P_{i,t-1}$ is the price in period $t-1$, and $DIV_{i,t}$ is the dividend received in period t. For example, let's say that the closing stock price of Stock i one year ago was $15, the owner received $1.00 in dividend income during the year, and today's closing price is $17.00. The one-year return equals:

$$[(\$17.00 + \$1.00)/\$15.00] - 1 = 20 \text{ percent}$$

Next, consider a different type of problem. Someone is considering buying Stock i today at its current price of $20.00 per share. In one year, the investor *expects* the stock to sell for $25.00 per share and pay a $1.00 dividend. In this case, the expected return would be measured by:

$$ER_i = \frac{P_{i,t+1} - P_{i,t} + DIV_{i,t+1}}{P_{i,t}} \quad \text{or} \quad \frac{P_{i,t+1} + DIV_{i,t+1}}{P_{i,t}} - 1 \quad (12.1b)$$

where $P_{i,t}$ is today's price, $P_{i,t+1}$ is the expected price one period after t (usually one year), and $DIV_{i,t+1}$ is the expected dividend in period $t+1$.

Using Equation 12.1b, we can compute the one-year return:

$$[(\$25.00 + \$1.00)/\$20.00] - 1 = 30 \text{ percent}$$

Now even though Equations 12.1a and 12.1b are similar, there is a difference between them. The first computes an actual one-year return, while the second computes an expected one-year return. The expected return is based on a forecast (or guess) of future prices and dividends, while the holding period return is based on actual prices and dividends.

Now, let's consider the prior problem in a more sophisticated manner to account for several possible future prices. Assume that the investor is uncertain about the stock price one year from today; it may depend on the company's sales growth. (Assume the dividend will pretty certainly be $1.00.) The following table represents the possibilities:

Sales Growth Rate	Price One Year from Today	Return
Above average	$30.00	55%
Average	25.00	30
Below average	20.00	5

(Note that the returns were computed using Equation 12.1b.) Further assume a probability of each sales growth rate occurring next year. (These are sometimes referred to as *states of nature*.) The firm has a 30 percent chance of generating above-average growth, a 40 percent chance of average growth, and a 30 percent chance of below-average growth. We can now compute the expected return for Stock i a little differently:

$$ER_i = \sum_{s=1}^{S} R_{i,s}Pr(s) \qquad (12.2)$$

where R_{is} is the return for Stock i in State s (above-average, average, or below-average sales growth) and $Pr(s)$ is the probability of State s occurring. In our example:

$$ER_i = 0.55(30\%) + 0.30(40\%) + 0.05(30\%) = 30 \text{ percent}$$

Of course, it may be difficult, perhaps almost impossible, to forecast the future states of nature, the probability of each state occurring, and the rate of return from each state.

Then why, you may ask, should anyone bother? The answer is that in making an investment decision, an analyst strives to obtain a future return for the stock, and then to choose the stocks with the highest returns after adjusting for risk. Conceptually, it is very important to recognize that investment decisions must be based on the return one *expects* to earn. It does little good to know what one could have earned (or the historical return); the critical value is the return from investing today, so investors strive to estimate future returns, or **ex-ante returns.**

In most cases, it is easier and more convenient to calculate actual, historical, or **ex-post returns.** The historical equivalent of the expected return, computed using Equation 12.2, is the average (or mean) return over a specified period of time. In Chapter 1, we discussed how to compute an average return from an actual return series. It is worth repeating here. The general formula for calculating a mean return for Stock i is:

$$M_i = \frac{1}{T} \sum_{t=1}^{T} R_{i,t} \qquad (12.3)$$

Table 12.1

Walt Disney Company Stock Performance

t (month, year)	*Pₜ* End Price	*DIVₜ* Dividend	*HPRₜ* Return
Dec. 88	$ 65.75		
Jan. 89	75.00		14.07%
Feb. 89	74.00	$0.10	−1.20
Mar. 89	78.50		6.08
Apr. 89	85.13		8.44
May 89	93.00	0.12	9.39
Jun. 89	94.63		1.75
Jul. 89	107.50		13.61
Aug. 89	117.50	0.12	9.41
Sep. 89	120.88		2.87
Oct. 89	123.88		2.48
Nov. 89	129.00	0.12	4.23
Dec. 89	112.00		−13.18
Jan. 90	104.13		−7.03
Feb. 90	109.50	0.12	5.28
Mar. 90	111.13		1.48
Apr. 90	110.50		−0.56
May 90	129.00	0.15	16.88
Jun. 90	128.25		−0.58
Jul. 90	117.63		−8.28
Aug. 90	102.38	0.15	−12.84
Sep. 90	90.63		−11.47
Oct. 90	91.00		0.41
Nov. 90	99.63	0.15	9.64
Dec. 90	100.50		0.88
Sum			51.8%
Mean			2.16%

Note: HPR_t Return $= (P_t + DIV_t)/P_{t-1} - 1$. These prices were not adjusted for the 4-for-1 split that occurred in June of 1992.

where T is the number of time periods included in the sample and $R_{i,t}$ is the Stock i return for period t (calculated using Equation 12.1a).[11] A time period could be a day, a month, or a year. An example of how to calculate a mean return is presented in Table 12.1. The ending stock price for Walt Disney is given, along with the dividend (if any), on a monthly basis from the beginning of 1989 through the end of 1990. The monthly return is computed using Equation 12.1a. Summing the monthly returns and dividing by n (24 in this example) completes the calculation. Thus, over the two-year period, Disney had an average monthly return of 2.16 percent.[12]

How to Measure Risk

Up to this point, we've tried to discuss risk in a rather intuitive way. We've relied on basic observations and conventional wisdom in order to distinguish

[11]When we use historical returns, we assume each return has a $1/n$ probability of occurring. This is analogous to multiplying each return in Equation 12.2 by the probability of that return occurring.

[12]In Chapter 1 we saw how to annualize a monthly return. For Disney, if the average monthly return equals 2.16 percent, the annualized return equals:

$$[(1+\text{Monthly return})^{12} - 1] = (1.0216)^{12} - 1 = 29.23 \text{ percent}$$

Table 12.2

Alternative Risk Measures

| | Yearly Return | Risk Measures Based on Monthly Returns | | |
		Range	Number of Negative Returns	Standard Deviation
1980	32.42%	20.82%	2	18.31%
1981	−4.91	10.82	6	12.89
1982	21.41	17.79	6	19.14
1983	22.51	10.71	4	9.92
1984	6.27	16.59	5	10.01
1985	32.16	10.89	4	12.17
1986	18.47	15.70	4	17.94
1987	5.23	34.95	4	30.50
1988	16.81	8.01	4	10.07
1989	31.49	11.47	4	12.35
1990	−3.17	18.78	7	18.39
1991	30.55	20.49	3	16.00
1992	7.67	7.91	4	6.05
1993	9.99	6.69	4	6.26

Notes: Standard deviation has been annualized, range is the highest monthly return that year minus the smallest monthly return, and number of negative returns is the number of months during the year with monthly returns less than zero.

Source: *SBBI 1994 Yearbook* (Chicago: Ibbotson Associates, 1994).

between the riskiness of various securities. For example, in Chapter 2, we observed that the historical returns on common stocks have exhibited far more variation over time than returns on long-term, high-quality corporate bonds. We've argued that a stock, such as an electric utility stock, that pays a high dividend and grows at a slow, predictable rate, is probably a less risky investment over time than a cyclical stock (such as shares of an automobile manufacturer). In other words, the electric utility stock will show less variation in price and returns over most time periods. While we have yet to precisely define investment risk and discuss how it can (and should) be measured, the term we keep coming back to is *variation,* or *dispersion, around an average,* or *expected value.* Now we need to develop a risk measure that incorporates these intuitive observations into something more precise, allowing us to make risk comparisons between securities and portfolios.

Table 12.2 presents some data on returns for Standard & Poor's 500 stock index (including both dividends and capital gains) between 1980 and 1993. For each year the table gives a yearly return, along with three common measures of variation (or dispersion) around that average value. The risk measures are based on monthly returns. Each could be thought of, and used, as a risk measure. Let's briefly examine each.

Range. The range is simply the highest value minus the lowest value. In general, a larger range indicates greater risk. For example, during 1988, the monthly return for the S&P 500 index ranged between 4.70 percent and −3.31 percent (for a total of 8.01 percent). By contrast, during 1987, monthly returns ranged between 13.43 percent and −21.52 percent (for a total of 34.95 percent). Stock returns appear to have varied more during 1987 than during 1988.

Number of Negative Outcomes. In Table 12.2, this is the number of months during a year when the monthly return was less than zero.[13] For example, in seven months during 1990 the index generated negative monthly returns. By contrast, it had monthly returns less than zero in only two months during 1980.

Standard Deviation (or Variance). **Standard deviation** is a statistical measure of dispersion around the mean (average) of a distribution.[14] A higher standard deviation indicates a greater dispersion, or variation, around the mean. From Table 12.2, the year with the highest standard deviation of monthly returns was 1987 (30.50 percent); 1992 had the lowest standard deviation of monthly returns (6.69 percent).

From the table, it would not be unreasonable to conclude that all risk measures are equally good. After all, it does seem to show a close relationship between all three measures. Years that show greater variation by one measure tend to show greater variation by the others, and the measures agree on less-variable years, as well. In spite of this, we will argue that standard deviation is the superior measure of dispersion, and thus security risk. While range indicates the spread between the highest and lowest values, it says nothing about the distribution of returns in between. For example, how many values are closer to the high than the low? The number of negative returns indicates nothing about the range of the distribution, nor does it say anything about the returns that are greater than zero.

In contrast, the standard deviation provides rather full information about the distribution. For example, if we assume that the stock returns follow a normal distribution (a bell-shaped curve), one standard deviation from the mean accounts for about 67 percent of the possible returns, and two standard deviations from the mean account for 95 percent of the possible returns.

Calculating Standard Deviation

Standard deviation is a statistical measure of the dispersion, or variation, around the expected value, or mean, of a distribution. To illustrate this further, let's go back to the earlier example where the probability of a firm's sales growth being above average, average, or below average determined the expected return of 30 percent. Although the expected return is 30 percent, actual returns show dispersion around it. We can calculate the standard deviation of this expected, future return (or ex-ante return):

$$SD_i = \left[\sum_{s=1}^{S} (R_{i,s} - ER_i)^2 Pr(s) \right]^{1/2} \tag{12.4}$$

where $R_{i,s}$ is Stock i's return for State s, $Pr(s)$ is the probability of State s occurring, and ER_i is the expected return from the probability distribution.

[13]Zero need not be the only benchmark. Another could be the number of periods the index earned less than the return, over the same time period, on a low-risk investment such as Treasury bills or bank CDs.

[14]The variance is the square of the standard deviation. Unlike standard deviation, however, variance does not have the same unit of measurement as the mean and thus is not as useful for comparisons. If returns are normally distributed, 67 percent of the distribution lies within one standard deviation of the mean (plus and minus); 95 percent of the distribution lies within two standard deviations of the mean.

The example data are provided below:

State of Sales Growth Rate	Probability of State	Return
Above average	30%	55%
Average	40	30
Below average	30	5

To use the formula, first subtract each return from the expected return, ER_i; next square the difference, then multiply by its probability; finally sum the products for each and take the square root:

$R_{i,s} - ER_i$	$(R_{i,s} - ER_i)^2$	$(R_{i,s} - ER_i)^2 Pr(R_{i,s})$
0.55 − 0.30	$0.25^2 = 0.0625$	$0.0625(.30) = .01875$
0.30 − 0.30	$0.0^2 = 0.0$	$0.0(.40) = .00000$
0.05 − 0.30	$-0.25^2 = 0.0625$	$0.0625(30) = .01875$

$$\text{SUM} = 0.0375$$
$$\text{Standard deviation} = \sqrt{0.0375} = .1936$$

As for return measures, ex-ante standard deviations not ex-post values, should guide investment decisions. The decision should depend on the risk expected from investing in the stock. A future, expected, or ex-ante risk is important to assess to decide how risky it *will be* to invest in this stock.

A historical standard deviation can also be calculated using known, ex-post returns. As we've said, this may seem attractive, since historical returns can be measured more precisely and data on historical returns are more easily accessible. For historical returns, standard deviation equals:

$$SD_i = \left[\frac{1}{(T-1)} \sum_{t=1}^{T} (R_{i,t} - M_i)^2 \right]^{1/2} \tag{12.5}$$

where T is the number of time periods (usually years or months) in a particular sample, $R_{i,t}$ is the return for period t, and M_i is the mean return over the entire sample period.[15] An example of the mechanics of this calculation is presented in Table 12.3. The monthly returns we computed earlier for Disney are given in the first column. The second column gives the difference between each monthly return and the mean (2.16 percent). The third column squares the second column. Then, the third column is summed, divided by (24−1) or 23, and the square root taken. The result is a monthly standard deviation of 8.32 percent.[16]

Security Selection

Investors can use the risk/return measures just developed (mean or expected return and standard deviation) to choose between securities. To see this, consider the following stocks:

Stock	Mean Return	Standard Deviation
A	12%	12%
B	12	10
C	14	12

---

[15]Statistical theory suggests that one should divide by n for a population and divide by $(n - 1)$ for a sample. Technically speaking, we should divide by $(n - 1)$ since the return observation set is usually not the population, but a sample of historical returns.

[16]The monthly standard deviation can be annualized as follows: multiply the monthly standard deviation, calculated using Equation 12.5, by the square root of 12. In the Disney example, the annualized standard deviation equals 28.09 percent.

Table 12.3

Walt Disney Company Stock Risk Calculation

t month, year	P_t End. Price	DIV_t Dividend	1 HPR_t Return	2 $(HPR_t - M)$	3 $(HPR_t - M)^2$
Dec. 1988	$ 65.75				
Jan. 1989	75.00		0.1407	0.1191	0.0142
Feb. 1989	74.00	$0.10	−0.0120	−0.0336	0.0011
Mar. 1989	78.50		0.0608	0.0392	0.0015
Apr. 1989	85.13		0.0845	0.0629	0.0040
May 1989	93.00	0.12	0.0939	0.0723	0.0052
Jun. 1989	94.63		0.0175	−0.0040	0.0000
Jul. 1989	107.50		0.1360	0.1144	0.0131
Aug. 1989	117.50	0.12	0.0941	0.0726	0.0053
Sept. 1989	120.88		0.0288	0.0072	0.0001
Oct. 1989	123.88		0.0248	0.0033	0.0000
Nov. 1989	129.00	0.12	0.0423	0.0207	0.0004
Dec. 1989	112.00		−0.1318	−0.1533	0.0235
Jan. 1990	104.13		−0.0703	−0.0918	0.0084
Feb. 1990	109.50	0.12	0.0527	0.0312	0.0010
Mar. 1990	111.13		0.0149	−0.0067	0.0000
Apr. 1990	110.50		−0.0057	−0.0272	0.0007
May 1990	129.00	0.15	0.1688	0.1472	0.0217
Jun. 1990	128.25		−0.0058	−0.0274	0.0007
July 1990	117.63		−0.0828	−0.1044	0.0109
Aug. 1990	102.38	0.15	−0.1284	−0.1499	0.0225
Sept. 1990	90.63		−0.1148	−0.1363	0.0186
Oct. 1990	91.00		0.0041	−0.0175	0.0003
Nov. 1990	99.63	0.15	0.0965	0.0749	0.0056
Dec. 1990	100.50		0.0087	−0.0128	0.0002
				SUM =	0.1591
		SUM =	0.5176	SUM/(N − 1) =	0.0069
		MEAN =	0.0216	ST. DEV. =	0.0832

Note: $HPR_t = \dfrac{(P_t + DIV_t)}{P_{t-1}} - 1$; M is the arithmetic mean of monthly returns.

Clearly, a risk-averse investor would find Stock B a superior investment to Stock A. B offers the same return (12 percent), but has less risk (a lower standard deviation) than A. Similarly, Stock C is a superior investment to Stock A. C has the same risk level (a standard deviation of 12 percent), but offers a higher return (14 percent versus 12 percent) than A. In general, we can say that if two securities have the same standard deviation but different expected returns, the security with the higher expected return is superior to the security with the lower expected return. A risk-averse investor will always choose the security with the higher expected return for securities with equal risk. Also, if two securities have identical expected returns but different risk levels, the security with the lower standard deviation is superior to the security with the higher standard deviation. When one investment is clearly superior to another using mean return and standard deviation, it exhibits **mean-variance dominance** or **mean-variance efficient.** In the above example, B is mean-variance dominant over A.[17]

---

[17]Variance equals the standard deviation squared $(SD)^2$ and is also used as a risk measure. The relative level of risk between securities remains the same for the two measures, even if their scales differ.

The selection decision so far has been pretty straightforward. Let's make it more complicated. Which would you prefer, Stock B or Stock C? B has the smaller standard deviation, but also the lower expected return. On the other hand, C has the higher expected return, but also the higher standard deviation. Now the selection decision is more ambiguous. You may prefer B to C (or C to B for that matter), but you really can't say that one is superior to the other.

Another statistic, related to standard deviation, may help to clarify some investment selection decisions. This statistic, the **coefficient of variation (CV),** can be used as a crude assessment of the risk/return tradeoff of a security. The coefficient of variation equals the standard deviation divided by the mean *(SD/M)*. Statisticians use CV as a method of scaling standard deviations to account for differences in means. It measures the percentage of risk for every percentage return. Stock F in the table below has 0.67 percent of risk for every 1 percent of return. A lower CV indicates a better risk/return tradeoff.

To see how the coefficient of variation works, let's look at another hypothetical example:

Stock	Mean	Standard Deviation	CV
D	10%	10%	1.00
E	20	20	1.00
F	18	12	0.67

Again, the table gives little basis on which to choose between D and E. They have the same coefficient of variation and, one could argue, offer the same risk/return tradeoff. What about a choice between F and E or F and D? We really can't say that F is superior to either E or D, but we can say that F offers a better risk/return tradeoff (it has a lower CV). Why? Well, F has a lower mean than E (18 percent versus 20 percent), but it has substantially less risk, as well (a standard deviation of 12 percent versus a standard deviation of 20 percent). Also, F does have a higher standard deviation than A (12 percent versus 10 percent), but offers a much higher mean return (18 percent versus 10 percent). We can display these results on a return/risk graph like Figure 12.5. Generally, the stock that is farthest toward the upper-left corner usually offers the best risk/return tradeoff. (See the shaded area in Figure 12.5.)

Portfolio Risk and Return

A portfolio is simply a group, or collection, of securities. When looking at a portfolio, the investor broadens the focus beyond the risk and return levels of the individual securities to evaluate the risk and return level of the group as a whole. How do we measure portfolio risk and return? Your initial answer might be that a simple combination of the risk and return levels of the individual securities would equal the portfolio risk and return. When it comes to calculating the mean, or expected, return from a portfolio, this answer is correct. The expected, ex-ante return for a portfolio is defined as:

$$ER_p = \sum_{i=1}^{N} X_i ER_i \qquad (12.6a)$$

Figure 12.5

Risk/Return Graph for Security Selection

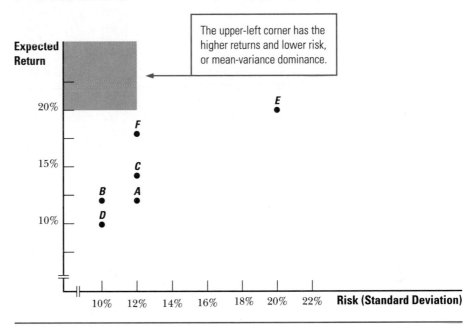

The mean historical, expost return from a portfolio is computed as:

$$M_p = \sum_{i=1}^{N} X_i M_i \qquad (12.6b)$$

where ER_i and M_i are the expected and mean returns from Security i and X_i is the percentage of the portfolio invested in Security i. An obvious condition of Equations 12.6a and 12.6b is that the sum of the Xs must equal 1.0.[18]

Calculating the standard deviation for a portfolio of securities can also be relatively simple. In fact, the formulas presented in the prior section can be used in most cases. For example, the standard deviation of monthly returns shown in Table 12.2 for the S&P 500 Index, which is of course a portfolio, were calculated using Equation 12.5. We simply calculated the portfolio return (i.e., the return for the S&P 500) for each time period, and then found the standard deviation of those returns. Calculating portfolio standard deviations becomes more challenging when one must understand the impact of the interrelationships between the returns of the individual securities in the portfolio. We will start with the simplest type of portfolio: one with two securities.

Standard Deviation of a Two-Security Portfolio

Let's begin by considering the following hypothetical example of the probability distributions for two individual stocks.

---

[18]Normally we would assume that all the Xs must be positive, as well, and thus all would have values between zero and one. This assumption is not necessary if the possibility of short sales is allowed. In other words, it is possible that some Xs could be negative while others gave a partial sum greater than 1.0.

| State of the Economy | Probability | Return | |
		Stock A	Stock B
Good	0.30	+30%	+ 5%
Normal	0.40	+15	+10
Poor	0.30	+ 0	+15
Expected return		**+15**	**+10**
Standard deviation		+11.7	+ 3.9
Coefficient of variation		0.78	0.39

The expected return for each stock was calculated using Equation 12.2 and the standard deviations were calculated using Equation 12.4. For example, Stock A's expected return equals:

$$0.30(30\%) + 0.40(15\%) + 0.30(0\%) = 15 \text{ percent}$$

as shown in bold type above.

Assume that Company A builds and sells automobiles. The auto maker does better when the economy does better. Assume that Company B makes antacids and aspirin, both of which may be in higher demand in a lousy economy. Further, suppose that the investor commits equal proportions of wealth to Stocks A and B: 50 percent is invested in A and 50 percent in B. The return distribution for the portfolio of Stocks A and B looks like this:

State of the Economy	Probability	Portfolio Return
Good	0.30	17.5%
Normal	0.40	12.5
Poor	0.30	7.5
Expected return		12.5
Standard deviation		3.9
Coefficient of variation		0.31

Notice that the expected return for the portfolio is simply a weighted average of the expected returns for the two stocks individually, and is consistent with the result of Equation 12.6b. For example, the portfolio return under the good state of economy equals:

$$0.50(30\%) + 0.50(5\%) = 17.5\%$$

The standard deviation, which was calculated using Equation 12.4, is not consistent with Equation 12.6b. In fact, the standard deviation of this portfolio, 3.9 percent, is exactly the same as the standard deviation of Stock B (the antacid and aspirin maker) and is considerably less than the standard deviation of Stock A (the automaker), even though half of the portfolio is made up of Stock A.[19] Note that the portfolio coefficient of variation is smaller than either Stock A's or Stock B's individual CV. How could this be?

The answer lies in the interrelationship between the return distributions for the two stocks. Notice that if the economy performs well, Stock A has a higher return than expected while Stock B has a lower return than expected. The situation is exactly reversed if the economy performs poorly. Statisticians refer to the interrelationship between probability distributions as **correlation**

---

[19]The portfolio standard deviation is calculated as:

$$SD_p = \sqrt{(0.175 - 0.125)^2 (0.30) + (0.125 - 0.125)^2 (0.40) + (0.075 - 0.125)^2 (0.30)}$$
$$= \sqrt{0.0015} = 0.039 \text{ or } 3.9 \text{ percent}$$

When calculating standard deviations, it is best to convert all the percentages to decimals.

or **covariance.** The two statistics, for ex-ante returns, are calculated as follows:

$$COV(A,B) = \sum_{s=1}^{S} [R_{A,s} - ER_A][R_{B,s} - ER_B]Pr(s) \qquad (12.7)$$

$$CORR\ (A,B) = COV(A,B)/SD_A SD_B \qquad (12.8)$$

where $R_{A,s}$ and $R_{B,s}$ are the returns for Stocks A and B for the various states of the economy, s; ER_A and ER_B are the expected returns for A and B; $Pr(s)$ is the probability of occurrence of state s; and SD_A and SD_B are the standard deviations for Stocks A and B.

In the above example, the returns for the two stocks have negative correlation or covariance.[20] In other words, as one stock's return gets larger, the other's return gets smaller, and vice versa. The actual covariance between the two stock returns is -0.0045 and the correlation coefficient is -1.0. The correlation is scaled so that its value, or **correlation coefficient,** can never be lower than -1.0 or higher than $+1.0$, or $-1.0 < CORR(A,B) < +1.0$. A positive sign implies that the two stocks generally move together, up or down, while the number between -1.0 to $+1.0$ conveniently provides the degree to which the two stocks covary together.[21]

The above example has obviously been concocted. Let's look at an example using some historical stock return data. If historical returns are used to calculate the correlation coefficient, the equation becomes:

$$COV(A,B) = \frac{1}{(T-1)} \sum_{t=1}^{T} [(R_{A,t} - M_A)(R_{B,t} - M_B)] \qquad (12.9)$$

where T is the number of time periods (usually annual, quarterly, or monthly returns), $R_{A,t}$ and $R_{B,t}$ are returns over period t for Stocks A and B, and M_A and M_B are mean returns for A and B.

The equation for the correlation coefficient equals:

$$CORR(A,B) = COV(A,B)/SD_A SD_B \qquad (12.10)$$

Table 12.4 presents monthly return data for American Home Products (AHP) and the Walt Disney Company (DIS), from the beginning of 1989 through the end of 1990. At the bottom of each column, the table gives mean monthly returns, standard deviations of returns, and coefficients of variation for both stocks. (All means and standard deviations were calculated using Equations 12.3 and 12.5.) AHP had an average monthly return of 1.46 percent with a standard deviation of 4.62 percent and a coefficient of variation of 3.16. DIS had an average monthly return of 2.16 percent with a standard deviation of 8.32 percent and a CV of 3.86.

Column 8 gives the portfolio return, assuming half of the portfolio is invested in AHP and half in DIS, for each time period. At the bottom, the table lists the mean, standard deviation, and coefficient of variation for the portfolio. Notice that the portfolio's average return, 1.81 percent, is exactly a weighted average of the mean returns for AHP and DIS, but the standard

---

[20]The correlation coefficient (CORR) always has a value of between -1.0 and $+1.0$. In this example, the two stocks' returns exhibit perfect negative correlation.

[21]In our example, covariance is calculated as:

$$(0.30 - .15)(0.05 - .10)0.3 + (0.15 - 0.15)(0.10 - 0.10)0.4 + (0.00 - 0.15)(0.15 - 0.10)0.3 = -0.0045$$

The correlation coefficient equals:

$$0.0045/(0.116)(0.039) = -1.0.$$

Table 12.4

Portfolio Return Calculation

1 t month, year	2 AHP End Price	3 AHP Dividend	4 AHP Return	5 Disney End Price	6 Disney Dividend	7 Disney Return	8 Portfolio Return
Dec. 1988	$41.63			$65.75			
Jan. 1989	43.00		0.0329	75.00		0.1407	0.0868
Feb. 1989	42.88		−0.0028	74.00	$0.10	−0.0120	−0.0074
Mar. 1989	43.00	$0.49	0.0142	78.50		0.0608	0.0375
Apr. 1989	45.75		0.0640	85.13		0.0845	0.0742
May 1989	46.38		0.0138	93.00	0.12	0.0939	0.0538
Jun. 1989	47.13	0.49	0.0267	94.63		0.0175	0.0221
Jul. 1989	51.50		0.0927	107.50		0.1360	0.1144
Aug. 1989	49.50		−0.0388	117.50	0.12	0.0941	0.0277
Sept. 1989	50.25	0.49	0.0251	120.88		0.0288	0.0269
Oct. 1989	52.13		0.0374	123.88		0.0248	0.0311
Nov. 1989	53.00		0.0167	129.00	0.12	0.0423	0.0295
Dec. 1989	53.75	0.49	0.0234	112.00		−0.1318	−0.0542
Jan. 1990	52.94		−0.0151	104.13		−0.0703	−0.0427
Feb. 1990	49.94		−0.0567	109.50	0.12	0.0527	−0.0020
Mar. 1990	50.44	0.54	0.0208	111.13		0.0149	0.0179
Apr. 1990	47.81		−0.0521	110.50		−0.0057	−0.0289
May 1990	52.88		0.1060	129.00	0.15	0.1688	0.1374
Jun. 1990	52.50	0.54	0.0030	128.25		−0.0058	−0.0014
July 1990	50.75		−0.0333	117.63		−0.0828	−0.0581
Aug. 1990	46.00		−0.0936	102.38	0.15	−0.1284	−0.1110
Sept. 1990	47.00	0.54	0.0335	90.63		−0.1148	−0.0406
Oct. 1990	49.13		0.0453	91.00		0.0041	0.0247
Nov. 1990	51.75		0.0533	99.63	0.15	0.0965	0.0749
Dec. 1990	53.00	0.54	0.0346	100.50		0.0087	0.0217
Mean			0.0146			0.0216	0.0181
St. Dev.			0.0462			0.0832	0.0572
Coefficient of Variation (CV)			3.1570			3.8564	3.1612

Note: The portfolio is weighted with one-half in AHP and one-half in Disney.

deviation, 5.72 percent, is not. It is closer to AHP's than to Disney's. As in the prior example, the explanation for this lies in the interrelationship between AHP's and Disney's returns, covariance, and correlation.

We next compute the covariance and correlation between the two sets of returns based on the historical, ex-post return formulas for covariance and correlation (Equations 12.9 and 12.10). The calculation is detailed in Table 12.5. The first two columns list the monthly returns for American Home Products and Disney. The third and fourth columns list the differences between each return and its respective mean. The fifth column is the product of Columns 3 and 4. If the products are generally positive (as in the example), they suggest that the two series move in the same direction (e.g., if one series is above its mean, the other tends to be above its mean). Column 5 is then summed and divided by (24 − 1) or 23, giving the covariance (0.00202). Dividing the covariance by the product of the two standard deviations gives the correlation coefficient, 0.53. Thus, it appears that the two series of returns generally moved in the same direction during 1989 and 1990, though not always together.

With these two examples serving as an introduction, let's look at the formula for finding the standard deviation of a two-security portfolio:

$$SD_p = [X_A^2 SD_A^2 + (1 - X_A)^2 SD_B^2 + 2X_A(1 - X_A)COV(A,B)]^{1/2} \quad (12.11a)$$

Table 12.5

Covariance and Correlation Calculations

1 t month, year	2 AHP Return	3 Disney Return	4 AHP Return-Mean	5 Disney Return-Mean	6 3 × 4
Jan. 1989	0.0330	0.1407	0.0184	0.1191	0.0022
Feb. 1989	−0.0029	−0.012	−0.0175	−0.0336	0.0006
Mar. 1989	0.0143	0.0608	−0.0003	0.0392	0.0000
Apr. 1989	0.0640	0.0844	0.0494	0.0628	0.0031
May 1989	0.0137	0.0939	−0.0009	0.0723	−0.0001
Jun. 1989	0.0267	0.0175	0.0121	−0.0041	0.0000
Jul. 1989	0.0928	0.1361	0.0782	0.1145	0.0090
Aug. 1989	−0.0388	0.0941	−0.0534	0.0725	−0.0039
Sept. 1989	0.0251	0.0287	0.0105	0.0071	0.0001
Oct. 1989	0.0373	0.0248	0.0227	0.0032	0.0001
Nov. 1989	0.0168	0.0423	0.0022	0.0207	0.0000
Dec. 1989	0.0234	−0.1318	0.0088	−0.1534	−0.0013
Jan. 1990	−0.0151	−0.0703	−0.0297	−0.0919	0.0027
Feb. 1990	−0.0567	0.0528	−0.0713	0.0312	−0.0022
Mar. 1990	0.0208	0.0148	0.0062	−0.0068	0.0000
Apr. 1990	−0.0521	−0.0056	−0.0667	−0.0272	0.0018
May 1990	0.1060	0.1688	0.0914	0.1472	0.0135
Jun. 1990	0.0030	−0.0058	−0.0116	−0.0274	0.0003
July 1990	−0.0333	−0.0828	−0.0479	−0.1044	0.0050
Aug. 1990	−0.0936	−0.1284	−0.1082	−0.15	0.0162
Sept. 1990	0.0335	−0.1147	0.0189	−0.1363	−0.0026
Oct. 1990	0.0452	0.0041	0.0306	−0.0175	−0.0005
Nov. 1990	0.0534	0.0964	0.0388	0.0748	0.0029
Dec. 1990	0.0346	0.0088	0.02	−0.0128	−0.0003
	0.0146	0.0216		Sum =	0.0465
				Covariance −	0.00202
				Correlation =	0.53

Remember from Equation 12.10 that

$$CORR(A,B) = COV(A,B)/SD_A SD_B$$

Rearranging terms gives:

$$COV(A,B) = SD_A SD_B CORR(A,B)$$

This gives an alternative formula for the standard deviation of a two-security portfolio:

$$SD_p = [X_A{}^2 SD_A{}^2 + (1 - X_A)^2 SD_B{}^2$$
$$+ 2X_A(1 - X_A)(SD_A)(SD_B)CORR(A,B)]^{1/2} \qquad (12.11b)$$

where X_A is the percentage of the portfolio invested in Stock A, and $(1 - X_A)$ is the percentage of the portfolio invested in Stock B. From Equation 12.11a you should see that the standard deviation of a two-security portfolio is really made up of three things: the standard deviation of Stock A, the standard deviation of Stock B, and the covariance between A and B.

Applying Equation 12.11b to the American Home Products/Disney example, the standard deviation of the portfolio (weighted one-half in AHP and one-half in DIS) equals:

$$SD_p = [0.25(0.0462)^2 + 0.25(0.0832)^2 + 2(0.5)(0.5)(0.00202)]^{1/2}$$
$$= 0.0572 \text{ or } 5.72 \text{ percent}$$

This is exactly the number reported in Table 12.4 based on Equation 12.5! Since there are easier ways to compute the standard deviation of a two-security portfolio, how useful is Equation 12.11b? As a simple calculation tool, perhaps not that useful. However, the most important feature of Equation 12.11b is that it explicitly shows that the standard deviation of a two-security portfolio is not simply the weighted average of the two individual standard deviations. The two securities' variations with each other must also be taken into account. You can see from Equation 12.11b that, if the two securities move in opposite directions, and thus have negative covariance and correlation, the standard deviation of the portfolio could be less than the standard deviation of either security individually. The portfolio could easily offer a better risk/return tradeoff than the individual securities. It all depends on the correlation between the two sets of returns. We explore this issue in detail next.

Correlation and Portfolio Standard Deviation

The prior discussion has shown, albeit indirectly, that the correlation between two sets of security returns can have a major impact on the risk of the resulting two-security portfolio. Let's look at the relationship in more depth. The relationship between correlation and portfolio standard deviation is best illustrated with an example.

Consider two securities, labeled A and B. Security A has an expected return of 12 percent and a standard deviation of 6 percent, while Security B has an expected return of 20 percent and a standard deviation of 10 percent. Is one a better investment than the other? Not really. Both securities, for example, have the same coefficient of variation (CV = 0.50). An individual may prefer one to the other, but no one can really say that one is better than the other.

Now, combine A and B into a portfolio. The expected portfolio return will be a simple weighted average of the two individual expected returns, or 16 percent, if one-half of the portfolio is invested in A and one-half is invested in B. We also know that the portfolio standard deviation will depend on the covariance, or correlation, between A and B. Let's look at three possible scenarios, summarized in Figure 12.6.

Figure 12.6a assumes that the returns for A and B move together perfectly, and in the same direction [CORR(A,B) = +1.0]. In other words, the correlation coefficient between A and B equals +1.0. The **investment opportunity set** provides all the possible combinations of A and B and is graphed in Figure 12.6a. Moving along the line from Point A to Point B, the percentage of the portfolio invested in A decreases while the percentage invested in B increases. Portfolio P1 consists of one-half A and one-half B. Notice that Portfolio P1 has a standard deviation that is a weighted average of those of A and B, 8 percent. Since P1 has an expected return of 16 percent, it has the same coefficient of variation as A and B. Does P1 offer a better risk/return tradeoff than either A or B? No. In fact, none of the possible combinations of A and B, in this scenario, offer a better risk/return tradeoff than the two individual stocks. If the correlation between any two stocks equals +1.0, then a better risk/return tradeoff cannot be found; an investor can increase expected return only by increasing risk.

Now pick a different stock, C, to pair with A, and assume for simplicity that C's return and risk are the same as B's, but its correlation with A equals zero. Suppose returns from A and C move completely independently of each

Figure 12.6

Two-Security Portfolio Combinations with Various Correlations

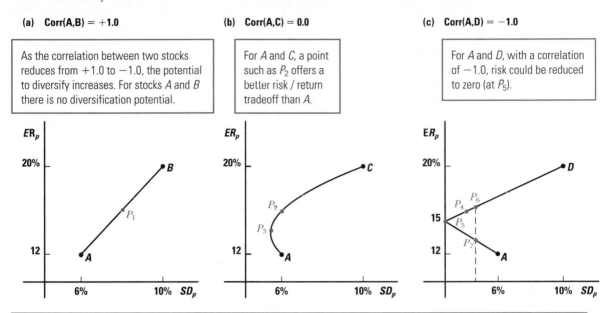

(a)   Corr(A,B) = +1.0

As the correlation between two stocks reduces from +1.0 to −1.0, the potential to diversify increases. For stocks *A* and *B* there is no diversification potential.

(b)   Corr(A,C) = 0.0

For *A* and *C*, a point such as P_2 offers a better risk / return tradeoff than *A*.

(c)   Corr(A,D) = −1.0

For *A* and *D*, with a correlation of −1.0, risk could be reduced to zero (at P_5).

other or CORR(A,C) = 0.0. All the possible combinations of A and C are graphed in Figure 12.6b. For example, Portfolio P2 consists of one-half A and one-half C. Portfolio P2 also has an expected return of 16 percent, but a standard deviation of only 5.8 percent and its coefficient of variation (CV) equals 0.36. One could argue that P2 offers a better risk/return tradeoff because its CV is lower than those of A or C. P2, for example, has only slightly less risk than A (5.8 percent compared to 6.0 percent), and a much higher expected return (16 percent versus 12 percent).

This potential to obtain a better risk/return tradeoff by combining imperfectly correlated securities is called **diversification.** This case shows that any correlation between two stocks less than +1.0 indicates a potential to diversify. Graphically, the range of combinations between two stocks gives a nonlinear (bow-shaped) curve that allows diversification to occur. As Figure 12.6b shows, several possible combinations of A and C offer better risk/ return tradeoffs than either stock alone. A point such as P3 has the minimum risk for a portfolio combination of A and C. Its expected return equals 14.1 percent (A's is 12.0 percent) and its risk equals 5.1 percent (A's is 6.0 percent). In fact, any combinations of A and C from P3 to C offer better risk/ return tradeoffs than combinations between A and P3. Of course, the choice of the actual portfolio between P3 to C depends on the amount of risk the investor is willing to take.

As a final scenario, let's assume that the two return series move together perfectly, though in opposite directions. Thus, A and D have perfect negative correlation [CORR(A,D) = −1.0]. Again, let us assume that D has the same return and risk as Stock B.[22] The investment opportunity set for A and D is shown in Figure 12.6c. Portfolio P4 consists of one-half A and one-half B. Like P1 and P2, P4 has an expected return of 16 percent, but its standard deviation is only 2.0 percent. Portfolio P4 not only offers a better risk/return

---

[22]In reality, perfect negative correlation is not possible, though negative correlation can be achieved using derivative securities in hedging (more on that in Chapter 18). Generally, securities are positively correlated to each other; negative correlation is very rare.

tradeoff than A, but a risk-averse investor would actually prefer it—P4 has a higher expected return and less risk than does Stock A. In fact, a risk-averse investor would not choose any combination of A and D between Point A and Point P5 because other combinations offer higher expected returns, for the same level of risk, such as P6 compared to P7. Furthermore, Portfolio P5 is a combination of A and D (62.5 percent in A and 37.5 percent in D) that reduces the portfolio risk to zero with an expected return of 15.0 percent.

In summary, as the correlation coefficient decreases from +1.0 to −1.0, potential diversification benefits grow. Also notice that diversification improves the risk/return tradeoff only if the correlation is less than +1.0. Stated differently, as long as the correlation is less than +1.0, combinations of securities offer diversification potential.

Another way to see the effect of the correlation coefficient on the portfolio standard deviation (and diversification potential) is to examine Equation 12.11b again. Recall the formula:

$$SD_p = [X_A^2 SD_A^2 + (1 - X_A)^2 SD_B^2 \qquad (12.11b)$$
$$+ 2X_A(1 - X_A)(SD_A)(SD_B)CORR(A,B)]^{1/2}$$

Let's examine the three terms in the formula. The first term, $X_A^2 SD_A^2$, is always positive because both terms are squared, so it will only add to the portfolio risk. Similarly with the second term, $(1 - X_A)^2 SD_B^2$. The third term, $2(X_A)(1 - X_A)(SD_A)(SD_B)CORR(A,B)$, however, can be positive or negative because every term is positive except for the correlation coefficient, $CORR(A,B)$. The correlation coefficient can be negative, which would reduce portfolio risk. In fact, that's what we found in the earlier examples; if the correlation between pairs of stocks was low or negative, it provides the greatest diversification benefit or reduction in portfolio risk.

Investment Opportunity Set for a Two-Security Portfolio

An investment opportunity set which identifies the portfolio combinations is not very difficult to define for a two-security portfolio. Apply Equation 12.6b to find M_p and Equation 12.11b to find SD_p, varying the proportions invested in each security (X), as shown in the example below.

Suppose that you have already calculated the mean, M_j, and standard deviation, SD_j, of each security, A and E, and their correlation coefficient, $CORR(A,E) = -0.20$.

	M_j	SD_j
Security A	12%	6%
Security E	20	10

Now the investment combinations can be determined by varying the amount invested in A and E in Equations 12.6b and 12.11b (where X_A is the percentage invested in A and X_E is the percentage invested in E). Since the percentages invested must add up to 100 percent, X_E can be written as $(1 - X_A)$, and Equations 12.6b and 12.11b can be written as:

$$M_p = X_A(M_A) + (1 - X_A)(M_E)$$
$$SD_p = [(X_A)^2(SD_A)^2 + (1 - X_A)^2(SD_E)^2$$
$$+ 2X_A(1 - X_A)(SD_A)(SD_E)CORR(A,E)]^{1/2}$$

Table 12.6

Various Combinations of Securities A and E

X_A	$(1 - X_A)$	M_p	SD_p
0%	100%	20.0%	10.0%
10	90	19.2	8.9
20	80	18.4	7.8
30	70	17.6	6.9
40	60	16.8	6.0
50	50	16.0	5.3
60	40	15.2	4.8
70	30	14.4	4.6
80	20	13.6	4.8
90	10	12.8	5.3
100	0	12.0	6.0

Note: M_p is the portfolio's mean return and SD_p is the portfolio's standard deviation.

For example, if $X_A = 0.10$ percent then $1 - X_A = 0.90$. Plugging in these percentages:

$$M_p = 0.10(12\%) + (0.90)(20\%) = 19.2 \text{ percent}$$

$$SD_p = [(0.10)^2(0.06)^2 + (0.90)^2(0.10)^2$$
$$+ 2(0.10)(0.90)(0.06)(0.10)(-0.20)]^{1/2} = 8.9 \text{ percent}$$

This calculation represents one point on the $M(P) - SD(P)$ graph. In order to find several more combinations of Securities A and E, just change the percentages X_A and $(1 - X_A)$. Table 12.6 displays several combinations. Graphing the results in the table gives Figure 12.7, which resembles the curves in Figure 12.6.

One use of an investment opportunity set might be to find the **minimum risk portfolio.** Using calculus, solve for X_A and E's proportion $(1 - X_A)$. An investment of X_A in Stock A [and $(1 - X_A)$ in Stock E] provides the lowest portfolio risk:

$$X_A = \frac{SD_E^2 - SD_A SD_E \text{CORR}(A,E)}{SD_A^2 + SD_E^2 - 2(SD_A)(SD_E)\text{CORR}(A,E)} \quad (12.12)$$

For our example, above, it equals:

$$X_A = \frac{(0.10)^2 - (0.06)(0.10)(-0.20)}{(0.06)^2 + (0.10)^2 - 2(0.06)(0.10)(-0.20)} = 0.70$$

The proportion invested in E must equal $(1 - X_A)$ because the two securities must add to 100 percent:

$$X_E = (1 - X_A) = (1 - .70) = 30 \text{ percent}$$

We can also find the portfolio expected return M_p and risk SD_p for the percentage that provides the minimum risk portfolio. Again, using Equations 12.6b and 12.11b:

$$SD_p = [(0.70)^2(0.06)^2 + (0.30)^2(0.10)^2$$
$$+ 2(0.70)(0.30)(0.06)(0.10)(-0.20)]^{1/2} = 4.6 \text{ percent}$$

Figure 12.7

Two-Security Portfolio Combinations of Securities
A and E

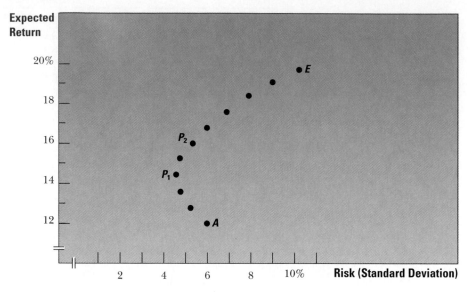

Note: $P1$ is 70 percent in Security A and 30 percent in E. It is the minimum-variance portfolio. $P2$ is 50 percent in Security A and 50 percent in E.

Actually, the results in Table 12.6 already showed that the SD_p is lowest with 70 percent in Security A and 30 percent in Security E. Also, Figure 12.7 shows that these percentages are indeed the lowest-risk portfolio combination. By examining the SD_p Equation 12.11b, and Figure 12.7, it is clear that the risk can be reduced because SD_p is a nonlinear equation. It is also evident that correlation plays a major role in diversification. It is the only term in Equation 12.11b that contributes to reducing risk.

Standard Deviation of an *N*-Security Portfolio

Finding the standard deviation of a portfolio that contains more than two securities is a logical extension of what we've discussed so far. Extending Equation 12.11b to *N* assets creates:

$$SD_p = \left[\sum_{i=1}^{N} X_i^2 SD_i^2 + \sum_{i=1}^{N} \sum_{\substack{j=1 \\ i \neq j}}^{N} X_i X_j COV(i,j) \right]^{1/2} \qquad (12.13)$$

where X_i is the percentage of the portfolio invested in Security i (as before, the X values must sum to 1.0), SD_i is the standard deviation of Security i, and $COV(i, j)$ is the covariance between Security i and Security j.

Now, Equation 12.13 may look horrible at first glance, but it isn't as complicated as it seems. Like Equation 12.11b, it states that the standard deviation of a portfolio is a function of two elements. The first element is the variances (the squares of the standard deviations) of the individual securities and the second element is the covariances between each possible pair of securities. The double summation operator ($\Sigma\Sigma$) in the covariance element means that each covariance term appears twice. (Look at the covariance term in Equation 12.11b.)

Table 12.7

Three Stock Portfolio Risk

1 month, year	2 AHP Return	3 Disney Return	4 Duke Return	5 Portfolio Return
Jan. 1989	0.0330	0.1407	−0.0028	0.0570
Feb. 1989	−0.0029	−0.0120	−0.0650	−0.0266
Mar. 1989	0.0143	0.0608	0.0492	0.0414
Apr. 1989	0.0640	0.0844	0.0281	0.0588
May 1989	0.0137	0.0939	0.0492	0.0523
Jun. 1989	0.0267	0.0175	0.0442	0.0295
Jul. 1989	0.0928	0.1361	0.0656	0.0982
Aug. 1989	−0.0388	0.0941	−0.0331	0.0074
Sept. 1989	0.0251	0.0287	0.0252	0.0263
Oct. 1989	0.0373	0.0248	0.0269	0.0297
Nov. 1989	0.0168	0.0423	0.0095	0.0229
Dec. 1989	0.0234	−0.1318	0.0683	−0.0134
Jan. 1990	−0.0151	−0.0703	−0.0422	−0.0425
Feb. 1990	−0.0567	0.0528	0.0186	0.0049
Mar. 1990	0.0208	0.0148	0.0188	0.0181
Apr. 1990	−0.0521	−0.0056	−0.0385	−0.0321
May 1990	0.1060	0.1688	0.0424	0.1057
Jun. 1990	0.0030	−0.0058	0.0279	0.0084
July 1990	−0.0333	−0.0828	0.0379	−0.0261
Aug. 1990	−0.0936	−0.1284	−0.0431	−0.0884
Sept. 1990	0.0335	−0.1147	0.0169	−0.0214
Oct. 1990	0.0452	0.0041	0.1462	0.0652
Nov. 1990	0.0534	0.0964	−0.0314	0.0395
Dec. 1990	0.0346	0.0088	0.0052	0.0162
Mean	0.0146	0.0216	0.0177	0.0180
St. Dev.	0.0462	0.0832	0.0458	0.0449
CV	3.16	3.86	2.60	2.50

Note: The portfolio is made up of one-third AHP, one-third Disney, and one-third Duke.

Let's use Equation 12.13 to calculate the standard deviation of a sample multi-stock portfolio. First, if the portfolio contains three securities (A, B, and C), Equation 12.13 becomes:

$$SD_p = [X_A^2 SD_A^2 + X_B^2 SD_B^2 + X_C^2 SD_C^2 + 2X_A X_B \text{COV(A,B)} \quad (12.14)$$
$$+ 2X_A X_C \text{COV(A,C)} + 2X_B X_C \text{COV(B,C)}]^{1/2}$$

Notice that there are three covariance terms because there are three possible pairs of securities (A and B, A and C, B and C).[23]

Turning to some real data, Table 12.7 adds another stock, Duke Power, to American Home Products (AHP) and Disney. Again, measure the monthly return for each stock from the beginning of 1989 through the end of 1990. The portfolio consists of one-third AHP, one-third Disney, and one-third Duke Power; its returns are presented in the last column. The portfolio's standard deviation, calculated from that column using Equation 12.5, equals

---

[23]The number of possible pairs of securities equals: $n!/2!(N - 2)!$, where n is the number of securities. The ! means factorial, which mathematically is equal to $(1)(2)(3) \ldots (n)$. For example, $4! = (1)(2)(3)(4) = 24$. So, a four-security portfolio would have: $24/4 = 6$ covariance terms (each appearing twice); there are six possible pairs of securities. A ten-security portfolio would have 45 covariance terms!

4.49 percent. The portfolio's mean return, 1.80 percent, is, of course, simply a weighted average of the three stocks' mean returns.

We can also find the portfolio's standard deviation using Equation 12.14. Recall that the covariance between AHP and Disney equals 0.00202. (We went through the calculation in Table 12.5.) Using the same procedure, the covariance between AHP and Duke Power equals 0.00044 and the covariance between Disney and Duke Power equals 0.00104. The respective correlation coefficients equal 0.21 and 0.27, indicating that the returns move together, generally, but not perfectly. Each stock makes up one-third of the portfolio and the respective standard deviations are: 4.62 percent (AHP), 8.31 percent (Disney), and 4.58 percent (Duke). Using Equation 12.14, the portfolio's standard deviation equals, not surprisingly, 4.49 percent.

Again, you may question the value of using Equation 12.13 to find the standard deviation of an N-asset portfolio. We agree that as a computational device only, it's not that critical to remember. However, as we've said before, Equation 12.13 illustrates explicitly the impact of security correlation and covariance on portfolio risk. The standard deviation of a portfolio is not simply the weighted average of the standard deviations of the individual securities. The procedure for calculating the standard deviation of a portfolio also provides a good illustration of the concept of diversification.

Diversification

When we discussed how to calculate the standard deviation of a portfolio in the prior section, we illustrated, albeit indirectly, two important points about diversification. They can be summarized as follows:

1. Diversification can improve the risk/return tradeoff if the correlation between individual security returns in the portfolio is less than 1.0 (i.e., returns are not perfectly correlated).
2. The benefits of diversification increase as the correlation coefficient gets smaller (i.e., approaches −1.0).

The benefits of diversification appear to be obvious; the prior examples have shown this. Further, the benefits of diversification may not be very difficult to obtain. Let's now consider how to obtain the benefits of diversification in some realistic investment settings.

Diversification across Securities

Perhaps the most straightforward way for investors to diversify is by spreading their investment funds across several different securities. We've seen this already, both with manufactured and real return data. For example, we saw that owning two stocks instead of just one can produce a risk/return tradeoff that would be preferred by most risk-averse investors.

The benefits of diversification across securities are clearly shown in Figure 12.8. The data used to generate this graph were taken from the CRSP database. (We discussed the CRSP database briefly in Chapter 4.) One stock was randomly selected from the CRSP database, another stock was randomly selected, creating a portfolio of two stocks, then another stock was randomly added to the portfolio, and so forth. (All portfolios are equally weighted combinations of the stocks.) Daily returns for each portfolio were then calculated for 1989. Notice how the portfolio standard deviation generally falls as the number of securities increase. The one-stock portfolio has an annu-

Figure 12.8

Example of Diversification across Securities

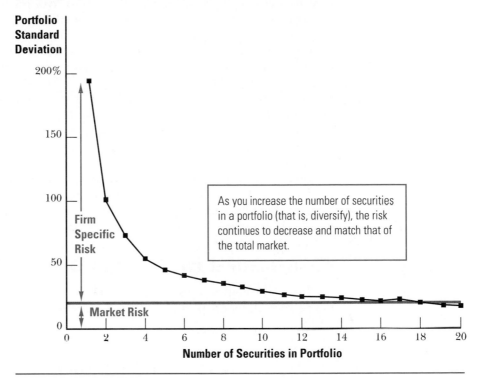

As you increase the number of securities in a portfolio (that is, diversify), the risk continues to decrease and match that of the total market.

alized standard deviation of 193.6 percent, the two-stock portfolio has an annualized standard deviation of 100.7 percent, and so forth.[24] By contrast, the 20-stock portfolio has a standard deviation of only 15.3 percent.

This occurs simply because returns between pairs of securities are not perfectly correlated. For example, the correlation coefficients between the first stock and the other 19 range from −0.10 to 0.09. Recall that some diversification potential exists so long as the correlation coefficient between two pairs of returns is less than 1.0.

Two Types of Portfolio Risk

The need to diversify leads to a distinction of two types of risk: **market risk** and **firm-specific risk.** Let's discuss this further.

Suppose you own just shares in Disney stock in your investment portfolio. The return on the stock is affected by economic factors such as business cycles, the inflation rate, interest rates, and others (as discussed in Chapter 9), as well as factors that are firm specific such as labor contracts, managerial policies, new product development, and more (as discussed in Chapters 10 and 11). Every stock return is affected by both kinds of factors in varying degrees.

Now suppose you own two stocks, Disney and Duke Power. Though these stocks are both affected by market-related factors (perhaps not to the same degree), their firm-specific factors may differ. For example, if the weather becomes extremely cold and rainy, sales receipts at Disney's theme parks may suffer, but utility bills may rise. The firm-specific factors can lead to offsetting

---

[24]Since there were 252 trading days in 1989, the annualized standard deviation equals the standard deviation of daily returns multiplied by the square root of 252.

returns between two stocks. Of course, this is the crux of the power of diversification; as the number of stocks in a portfolio increases, the firm-specific risk becomes negligible. However, the market risk related to economic factors affects all stocks, so it cannot be eliminated through diversification. This can also be seen in Figure 12.8. As diversification across securities increases, firm-specific risk decreases until the only risk left is the market risk.

The market risk that exists even with diversification is also called **systematic risk** or **nondiversifiable risk.** The firm-specific risk that can be eliminated by diversifying is also called **diversifiable risk** or **nonsystematic risk.** Two important points stem from this discussion: (1) a portfolio of stocks can virtually eliminate firm-specific risk, and (2) the only relevant risk is the market risk when portfolios are held because the firm-specific risk decreases to virtually zero.

A mathematical example can illustrate the power of diversification. The next section shows that as the number of securities increases, the effect of each company's standard deviation, *SD*, is virtually zero and the portfolio risk is measured entirely by the covariance, COV, between the securities.

Mathematical Effects of Diversification

We can mathematically show that the standard deviations of securities have minuscule effects on portfolio standard deviation risk, SD_p, using Equation 12.13:

$$SD_p = \left[\sum_{i=1}^{N} X_i^2 SD_i^2 + \sum_{i=1}^{N}\sum_{\substack{j=1 \\ i \neq j}}^{N} X_i X_j \mathrm{COV}(i,j) \right]^{1/2} \tag{12.13}$$

Square the standard deviation to avoid the square root sign:

$$SD_p^{\,2} = \sum_{i=1}^{N} X_i^2 SD_i^2 + \sum_{i=1}^{N}\sum_{\substack{j=1 \\ i \neq j}}^{N} X_i X_j SD_i SD_j \mathrm{CORR}(i,j)$$

Suppose we create a naive portfolio where stocks are randomly chosen and invested in equal proportions. If there are *N* stocks, each *X* equals (1/*N*). The equation becomes:

$$SD_p^{\,2} = \frac{1}{N} \sum_{i=1}^{N} \frac{1}{N} SD_i^2 + \sum_{i=1}^{N}\sum_{\substack{j=1 \\ i \neq j}}^{N} \frac{1}{N^2} \mathrm{COV}(i,j)$$

It's difficult to figure out from the formula, but there are *N* variances (SD_i^2) and $N(N-1)$ covariances. Now just for simplicity (and also to make our point) suppose that each SD_i^2 is the same for each stock. This reduces the term to SD^2 (no subscript since they're all the same). Similarly for the covariances, suppose they all equal COV, then $SD_p^{\,2}$ equals:

$$SD_p^{\,2} = \frac{1}{N} SD^2 + \frac{(N-1)}{N} \mathrm{COV}$$

Now we can really see the power of diversification. As the number of stocks *(N)* increases, (1/*N*) decreases. When *N* becomes very large, (1/*N*) becomes virtually equal to zero. This makes the standard deviation of each stock almost irrelevant! Similarly, the covariance term becomes more important as *N* increases because $(N-1)/N$ approaches 1.0 as *N* becomes large. Why?

Table 12.8

Returns for Stocks and Treasury Bonds over Various Holding Periods: 1926–1993

Holding Period	Stocks			T-bonds		
	Mean	Standard Deviation	Coefficient of Variation	Mean	Standard Deviation	Coefficient of Variation
1 year	12.32%	20.30%	1.65	5.36%	8.72	1.63
2 years	11.37	14.58	1.28	5.10	6.38	1.25
5 years	10.25	8.26	0.81	4.81	4.65	0.97
10 years	10.56	5.43	0.51	4.50	3.65	0.81
25 years	10.78	2.22	0.21	3.51	1.93	0.55

Note: All returns are annualized.

Source: *SBBI 1994 Yearbook* (Chicago: Ibbotson Associates, 1994).

Because $(N - 1)/N = 1 - (1/N) = 1$ as N becomes very large. This exercise shows that the standard deviation of stocks has almost no effect on the portfolio risk SD_p^2; this leaves the covariance between stocks as the only important term.

Diversification Across Time

Table 12.8 presents mean annualized total returns from Standard & Poor's 500 Index and an index of long-term U.S. Treasury bonds, between the end of 1925 and the end of 1993, for different assumed holding periods. For one-year holding periods, buying at the beginning of the year and selling at the end of the same year, the S&P 500 produced a mean annualized return of 12.32 percent. However, the data show considerable variation around this mean (SD = 20.30 percent and CV = 1.65). On the other hand, for 25-year holding periods (i.e., buying at the beginning of Year 1 and selling at the end of Year 25, reinvesting all dividends along the way) the mean annualized return from the S&P 500 was about 2 percent per year less, 10.78 percent, but this return also showed far less variation around the mean (SD = 2.22 percent and CV = 0.21). In fact, the standard deviation and coefficient of variation both fall consistently as the length of the holding period increases.

The same pattern is evident, though not as dramatic, for Treasury bond returns. For one-year holding periods, long-term U.S. Treasury bonds produced a mean annual return of 5.36 percent, again with a fair amount of variation around the mean (SD = 8.72 percent and CV = 1.63). Increasing the holding period to 25 years, however, improves the risk/return profile. The mean annualized rate of return does fall to 3.51 percent, but the standard deviation, and thus the coefficient of variation, fall even more (SD = 1.93 percent and CV = 0.55). As with stock returns, the standard deviation and coefficient of variation fall consistently as the length of the holding period increases. This phenomenon where the annualized standard deviation declines as the time horizon increases is called **time diversification.**

Many articles in the financial press attest to the benefits of time diversification. A *Wall Street Journal* article illustrates that longer holding periods have historically lowered the risks associated with stock investing, as Table 12.8 also illustrates.[25] The article shows that if the S&P 500 Index was held for only a one-year period, the stock index return would have trailed a T-bill

---

[25]Karen Slater, "Long Haul Investing: Riding Out the Risk in Stocks," *The Wall Street Journal,* December 16, 1991, C1.

Averaging Can Take the Worry Out of Market Moves

With the stock market hovering near historical highs, many investors are torn.

They don't want to miss out on any further gains, but they're afraid of buying just before prices start to slide.

What to do? One answer for skittish investors is dollar cost averaging—buying equal dollar amounts of a mutual fund at regular intervals, usually monthly or quarterly. That way, investors avoid the risk of buying only at market peaks.

But while dollar cost averaging can be a useful strategy, it's no panacea. The strategy doesn't protect investors from a loss, nor does it work equally well in all markets. Further, people who don't invest for the long term can face tax-time headaches.

"If you shouldn't be buying the stock fund in the first place, dollar-cost averaging won't help," says Michael Price, president of Mutual Series Fund Inc., a mutual fund company in Short Hills, N.J. "But once you know it's the fund you want to own, you get more bang for the buck—more shares for better prices."

With dollar cost averaging, investors automatically buy more shares when prices are lower, and fewer shares when prices are high. As a result, the average cost of the shares they buy is usually lower than the average price during the period.

Say you invest $200 a month in a mutual fund. If the price of each individual share is $25 in June, the money buys eight shares. If the share price rises to $30 in July, the $200 will buy 6.66 shares; if the price falls back to $20 in August, you get 10 shares. The average price of the shares during this period was $25. But because your $600 investment bought 24.66 shares, your average cost was only $24.33.

Many people already dollar cost average without realizing it. If they participate in a 401(k) or profit-sharing retirement plan at work, they are investing a set percentage of their salary on a regular basis. Many employees also have set amounts withheld from their paychecks to buy U.S. savings bonds.

"It's really an anti-timing technique," says John Markese, research director at the American Association of Individual Investors. People using this auto-pilot approach long term can generally cruise along and ignore the occasional war, interest-rate spike, or industry meltdown.

"The real value is that it gets you used to investing in all environments and gives you discipline," says Mr. Markese.

Still, dollar cost "doesn't guarantee a gain or protect you from a loss," says Brian Mattes, a vice president at Vanguard Group, a mutual-fund company in Valley Forge, Pa. That's something investors don't always understand, he says.

If the price of the shares falls consistently, investors will lose money, although not as much as if they had made an ill-timed lump-sum investment just before the price started to skid.

The Downside

For instance, if the share price in the previous example fell from $25 to $20 to $15, the investor's $200 a month would have bought 34 shares. At $15 each, the value of those shares would be $510—a $90 loss on the investor's $600 investment. But if the entire $600 had been put into the fund when shares were $25, the investor would have bought 24 shares. At $15 each, those shares would now be worth $360—a loss of $240.

On the downside, however, dollar cost averaging limits an investor's gain when prices are rising. "If the market were to keep going up, you'd be better putting all your money in up front" rather than dollar cost averaging, says Mr. Mattes.

For example, if an investor put $6,000 into a fund mirroring Standard & Poor's 500 stock index on May 1, 1986, the value of the investment would have grown to $11,327 in the five years through April, says Mr. Mattes. But if the investor had dollar cost averaged into the index fund at a rate of $100 a month, the value of the $6,000 total investment would have grown to only $8,479 (although the investor would have earned something on the money that was sidelined until it was invested in the stock-index fund).

"Depending on what time period you pick, dollar cost averaging can work for you or against you," says Mr. Mattes.

Of course, no one invests only in pure market rises or declines. Typically, markets fluctuate, and investors never know which way the wind is blowing. For the strategy to work, "You can't alter your course in the middle or you'll be buying at highs and selling at lows," says Michael Hirsch, president of Fund Trust Management, an investment advisory firm in New York. "You have to have iron will and discipline and stick to your game plan."

Another reason that dollar cost averaging is better for long-term investments is that otherwise tax reporting can get onerous. Every time an investor sells shares or switches money among mutual funds, it triggers a loss or a gain. An investor who dollar cost averages will have to add up each monthly purchase to calculate the average price of the shares.

While this isn't difficult, it can get cumbersome and isn't the sort of thing most people like to do too often. For this reason, investing experts recommend dollar cost averaging only if a person plans to leave the money intact for a long period, such as in an individual retirement account.

A simple way to start dollar cost averaging is to set up an automatic savings program with a mutual fund company. Most can arrange automatic transfers from checking or savings accounts.

INVESTMENT INSIGHTS

Source: Ellen E. Schultz, "Averaging Can Take the Worry Out of Market Moves," *The Wall Street Journal,* June 17, 1991, C1.

Dollar Cost Averaging Can Help—or Hurt

Investing a fixed dollar amount at regular intervals can lower the average cost for shares. But while it can cushion a loss if the share price declines, it will retard a gain if prices rise.

If Share Prices Fall

Avg. transaction price:	$25 a share	Monthly Investment	Share Price	Shares Bought	Value
Avg. total cost: ($600 ÷ 24.66)	$24.33 a share	$200	$30	6.66	
		200	25	8.00	
		200	20	10.00	
		Total $600		24.66	$493

Value if lump sum of $600 were made at beginning: $400
($600 ÷ $30 share = 20 shares; 20 × current share price of $20)

If Share Prices Rise

Avg. transaction price:	$30 a share	Monthly Investment	Share Price	Shares Bought	Value
Avg. total cost: ($600 ÷ 20.37)	$29.45 a share	$200	$25	8.00	
		200	30	6.66	
		200	35	5.71	
		Total $600		20.37	$713

Value if lump sum of $600 were made at beginning: $840
($600 ÷ $25 share = 24 shares; 24 × current share price of $35)

	Value
If you had dollar cost averaged the entire 6-month period: (Total shares bought [45.03] × current share price [$35])	$1,576
If you had invested $1,200 at beginning [40 shares]:	$1,400

investment 40 percent of the time. If the stock index was held for a five-year period, it would have trailed T-bills 31 percent; however, over a 20-year holding period, the stock index earns a higher return than T-bills 100 percent of the time.

An Investment Insights features another article from *The Wall Street Journal* which argues that buying equal dollar amounts of a mutual fund at regular intervals (weekly, monthly, etc.) will help investors "even out" temporary market highs and lows. This strategy, often referred to as **Dollar Cost Averaging,** may well produce less variable returns over the long run, as the example in the article shows.

If this is true, an investor can reduce risk simply by increasing the investment period, a perfect tactic for retirement funds! Unfortunately, time diversification is a fallacy. It is true that the annualized standard deviation falls as the investment time horizon increases based on rates of return. It is also true, however, that the uncertainty compounds over a greater number of years. This implies that the total dollar return becomes more uncertain as the investment horizon becomes longer. Stated differently, the annualized standard deviation does not say anything about the total dollar return; as the holding period becomes longer, the risk of the total dollar return becomes greater. Most investors worry about the total dollar return on a retirement fund rather than the decreasing annualized standard deviation, so it is important to note that to feel safer with time diversification is only illusionary.

Ibbotson Associates provides evidence with real and simulated data that, although the confidence interval around the expected return narrows as investment period increases over time (that is, the standard deviation around the mean decreases over longer investment periods), the confidence interval of the dollar return widens as investment periods increase (that is, risk increases as the investment period lengthens).[26] Figure 12.9 illustrates how the confidence intervals around the expected return become narrower as the investment horizon increases; Figure 12.10 displays how the confidence intervals around the dollar return widen as the investment horizon increases.

What does all this mean? It means that investors must be careful when using these measures and not lose sight of the objective. To maximize long-term dollar return (perhaps for a retirement fund), one must be aware that risk increases for investments over longer periods, even if the standard deviation of the rate of return decreases. Perhaps a good (though sad) example is IBM. Many investors considered IBM stock to be a good retirement investment since it had been a market bellwether, earning the nickname "Big Blue" for its stature as a leader among blue-chip stocks. If you purchased 100 shares of IBM in 1964 for $492 (total investment of $49,200) as a retirement fund and sold at its peak in 1987, adjusted for stock splits, it would be worth $329,766! It would have been a great retirement investment; your dollar return would have been huge. Suppose, however, that you didn't (or couldn't) retire until 1993 when IBM was selling in the high $40s and low $50s. Your retirement nest egg would only be worth around $76,172, a real drop in dollar return as compared to 1987. Despite the longer investment horizon, IBM was certainly a riskier investment based on dollar returns. Louis Gerstner, new CEO for IBM, had the sad duty of speaking to livid stockholders reaching retirement age and trying to appease them by vowing to turn IBM around.[27]

---

[26]*SBBI 1994 Yearbook* (Chicago: Ibbotson Associates, 1994, pp. 157–161)

[27]*The Wall Street Journal*, April 27, 1993, A3.

Figure 12.9

Compound Annual Return Rates

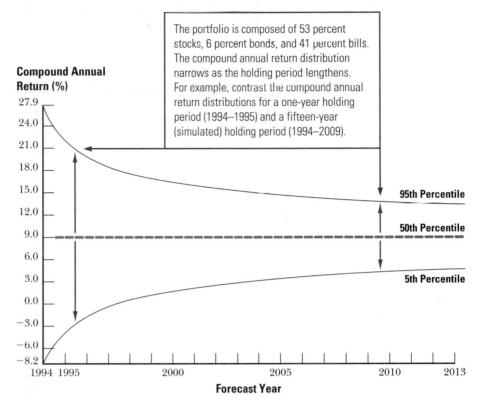

Note: The portfolio is composed of 53 percent Stocks, 6 percent Bonds, and 41 percent Bills. The compound annual return distribution narrows as the holding period lengthens. For example, contrast a one-year holding period (1994–1995) and a fifteen-year (simulated) holding period (1994–2009) compound annual return distributions.

Source: *SBBI 1994 Yearbook* (Chicago: Ibbotson Associates, 1994). © *Stocks, Bonds, Bills, and Inflation 1994 Yearbook.*[TM] Ibbotson Associates. Chicago (annually updates work by Roger G. Ibbotson and Rex A. Sinquefield). Used with permission. All rights reserved.

Efficient Diversification

Most of the examples of diversification we've discussed up to this point are examples of **naive diversification.** The stock selection technique we used to produce Figure 12.8 is a classic example of naive diversification: the stocks were added to the portfolio randomly. While adding additional securities to a portfolio will generally improve its risk/return profile, there is no guarantee that it will produce the *best* risk/return profile. In other words, naive diversification will not necessarily maximize return for a given level of risk, nor will it necessarily minimize risk for a given level of return.

By contrast, **efficient diversification** involves finding the portfolio combinations that produce the best risk/return profiles. It involves the use of mathematical techniques to search through all possible combinations of securities

Figure 12.10

Wealth Distribution Forecast

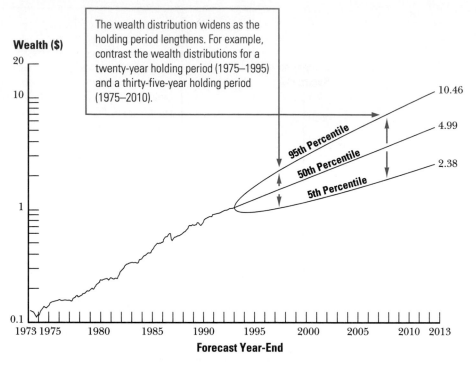

Note: The wealth distribution widens as the holding period lengthens. For example, contrast a twenty-year holding period (1975–1995) and a thirty-five-year holding period (1975–2010) wealth distributions. © *Stocks, Bonds, Bills, and Inflation 1994 Yearbook.*[TM] Ibbotson Associates. Chicago (annually updates work by Roger G. Ibbotson and Rex A. Sinquefield). Used with permission. All rights reserved.

to determine which provide maximum expected returns for given risk levels or which subject the investor to the minimum amount of risk for given levels of return. In the process, all diversifiable risk is eliminated. These mathematical techniques are derived from a body of theory usually referred to as **modern portfolio theory (MPT).**

The origins of modern portfolio theory can be traced by an article published in 1952 by Harry Markowitz.[28] Markowitz argued that an investor could produce an optimal allocation of securities within a portfolio that would achieve the best possible risk/return tradeoff. In other words, one can build a portfolio that minimizes risk for a given level of return or, alternatively, that maximizes expected return for a given level of risk. The basic technique employed by Markowitz finds, for a given set of securities, what's called the *efficient frontier.* Portfolios that lie along the efficient frontier offer investors the optimal risk/return combinations; these portfolios are called **mean-variance efficient portfolios.**[29]

---

[28]See "Portfolio Selection," *The Journal of Finance* (March 1952), 77–91. In 1990, Markowitz, Merton Miller, and William Sharpe were awarded the Nobel Prize in Economics for their work developing modern portfolio theory.

[29]In this text, we measure risk by portfolio standard deviation, *SD(P)*, rather than variance, which equals $SD(P)^2$. There is really no major difference between the two measures; the numerical value differs, but the relative risk level remains the same between securities or portfolios. To label a portfolio *mean-variance efficient* is the same as labeling it *mean-standard-deviation efficient.* We will stick to the conventional phrase here and use *mean-variance efficient.*

Figure 12.11

Efficient Frontier

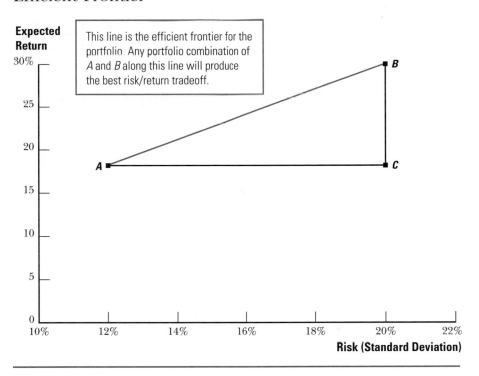

Let's illustrate an efficient frontier by considering a very simple example with just three assets (A, B, and C), presented in Figure 12.11. Each asset is plotted based on its standard deviation and expected return. Notice that A and C have identical expected returns while B and C have identical standard deviations. Clearly A is superior to C since it has less risk (i.e., a lower standard deviation) for the same expected return. By the same token, B clearly offers a superior risk/return tradeoff compared to C since it has a higher expected return for the same level of risk.

How can one choose between A and B? While someone may prefer A to B, or vice versa, remember that no one can really say one is better than the other. In this simple example, A and B form endpoints along the efficient frontier.

Assume that a straight line connects A and B. By definition, all the portfolios along that line would be combinations of A and B, and all, including A and B, would maximize expected return for a given risk level and minimize risk for a given expected return. All portfolios that lie along the efficient frontier produce the optimal risk/return tradeoffs of all feasible combinations of the securities; at the same time, these efficient portfolios minimize nondiversifiable risk. Thus the Markowitz model allows an investor to reduce the number of feasible combinations under consideration to only those that lie along the efficient frontier, even though hundreds or even thousands of portfolios may remain.

How to Find an Efficient Frontier

The data necessary to find the efficient frontier for a set of securities, using the Markowitz model, consist of three items: the standard deviation of returns for each security, the mean (or expected) return for each security,

Table 12.9

Inputs Needed to Find an Efficient
Frontier

Stock	Mean Return	Standard Deviation	Coefficient of Variance
AHP	17.46%	15.59%	0.89
Boeing	32.16	21.76	0.68
Disney	23.99	28.09	1.17
Duke Power	21.76	15.17	0.70
Texaco	22.53	14.59	0.65

Stock	Correlation Matrix				
	AHP	Boeing	Disney	Duke	Texaco
AHP	1.00				
Boeing	0.49	1.00			
Disney	0.52	0.69	1.00		
Duke	0.50	0.38	0.12	1.00	
Texaco	0.25	−0.04	−0.18	0.28	1.00

and the correlation coefficient between returns for each possible pair. The
Markowitz model can be used with either ex-ante (expected future) data or
ex-post (historical) data.

The Markowitz model involves solving a set of mathematical equations to
minimize portfolio standard deviation, subject to a minimum stated expected
return. It does this by varying the percentages of the total portfolio invested
in the individual securities. Computer software has simplified the work; so
finding an efficient frontier is not difficult. (The *Investment Wizard Software*
included with your textbook has a routine which finds an efficient frontier
based on input data.) Let's look at an example. Table 12.9 lists the data necessary to find an efficient frontier for five stocks: American Home Products,
Boeing, Disney, Duke Power, and Texaco. For each stock, historical monthly
returns were calculated starting in January 1989 and ending in December
1990 (24 observations). Table 12.9 gives the mean annualized monthly
return and annualized standard deviation for each stock, along with the correlation coefficient for each pair of stocks.

Investment Wizard identifies the efficient frontier shown in Figure 12.12.
Ten portfolios create different combinations of the five stocks that lie along
the efficient frontier; they are plotted along with an equally weighted portfolio of the five stocks. The relevant characteristics of the portfolios (mean
returns, standard deviations, and percentages invested in each security) are
presented in Table 12.10. Notice that the equally weighted portfolio does not
lie along the efficient frontier.

The ten that do lie along the efficient frontier vary widely in their make-
ups. Portfolio 1 is the only one of the ten that contains American Home
Products (albeit only 7.29 percent). None of the ten efficient portfolios contain all five stocks. In fact, Portfolios 5 through 9 are made up of only two
stocks (Boeing and Texaco). Portfolio 10 is even 100 percent Boeing! Of
course, the Markowitz method does not guarantee that all stocks will be
included in all, or even any, efficient portfolios. The makeup of an efficient
portfolio depends upon the risk/return characteristics of the individual securities as well as the correlations between them.

By definition, remember, any portfolio that lies along the efficient frontier
maximizes return for a given risk level, and minimizes risk for a given return.
To check this, let's compare the equally weighted portfolio to portfolios that

Table 12.10

Characteristics of the Efficient Frontier

| Portfolio | Portfolio | | Percentage of the Portfolio Invested In | | | | |
	Mean Return	Standard Deviation	AHP	Boeing	Disney	Duke Power	Texaco
1	22.13%	10.68%	7.29%	0.00%	14.95%	29.49%	48.27%
2	23.29	10.95	0.00	7.38	13.89	26.25	52.48
3	24.31	11.68	0.00	19.20	15.97	18.20	54.86
4	25.49	12.73	0.00	31.02	1.60	10.15	57.23
5	26.53	14.13	0.00	41.93	0.00	0.00	58.07
6	27.57	16.10	0.00	53.54	0.00	0.00	46.46
7	28.78	18.63	0.00	65.16	0.00	0.00	34.84
8	29.84	21.46	0.00	76.77	0.00	0.00	23.23
9	31.07	24.55	0.00	88.39	0.00	0.00	11.61
10	32.16	27.77	0.00	100.00	0.00	0.00	0.00
Equally weighted	23.43	14.03	20.00	20.00	20.00	20.00	20.00

lie along the efficient frontier. The equally weighted portfolio has about the same return as Portfolio 2 (23.43 percent versus 23.29 percent), but a higher standard deviation (14.03 percent versus 10.95 percent). Similarly, the equally weighted portfolio has about the same standard deviation as Portfolio 5 (14.03 percent versus 14.13 percent), but a lower mean return (23.43 percent versus 26.53 percent). Thus, most risk-averse investors would choose Portfolio 2 or Portfolio 5, over the equally weighted portfolio, since the efficient portfolios offer superior risk/return tradeoffs. We cannot say, however, that risk-averse investors would choose Portfolio 2 over Portfolio 5 (or vice versa).

Figure 12.12

Efficient Frontier

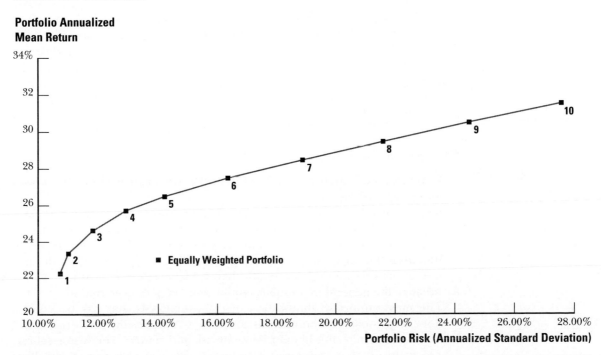

Portfolio Annualized Mean Return

■ Equally Weighted Portfolio

Portfolio Risk (Annualized Standard Deviation)

Figure 12.13

Full-Market Efficient Frontier

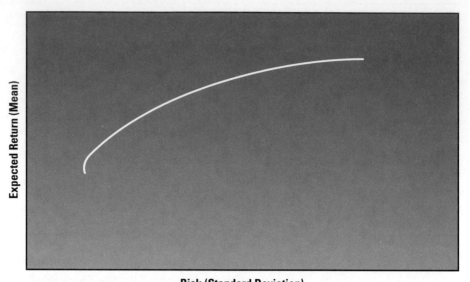

This example has considered only five stocks. Could an efficient frontier be computed for all publicly traded stocks? If so, what would its shape look like? The answer to the first question is *yes;* even though the amount of data required would be enormous, the mathematical process would be the same. As for the shape, most agree that the full-market efficient frontier would look something like Figure 12.13. It starts at the minimum risk portfolio and extends upward and to the right.

The notion that risk-averse investors will invest in portfolios with optimal risk/return tradeoffs is used in the next chapter to develop a risk/return relationship for securities. Chapter 13 provides a way to quantify security risk and develops a model called the capital asset pricing model (CAPM) to relate risk to return. You may ask, Why is this important to security analysis? Only by quantifying a stock's risk can one determine a reasonable expected return (via CAPM) for the stock and then compare our predicted return with the CAPM required return to decide whether it's a good investment or not. Chapter 13 will also cover security analysis, and show that it is very similar to the fundamental analysis discussed in Chapter 8.

Chapter Summary

1. **Develop a definition of *risk aversion* and understand why investors, as a group, are risk averse.**
   Some simple lottery type games suggest that most individuals are unlikely to play a risky game unless they receive some compensation for that risk. The reason for this is that most individuals probably have utility of wealth functions that increase at decreasing rates. Thus, a typical individual cares less about a $1 increase in wealth than a $1 decrease in wealth.
2. **Identify the general investment implications of risk aversion.**
   The most important implication of risk aversion is that risk becomes a dominant consideration in security selection. As a result, over time, a positive relationship should exist between risk and return. The historical record confirms that higher-risk investments, such as common stocks, have

returned more, on average, than lower-risk investments such as U.S. Treasury bills.

3. **Understand why standard deviation is a good measure of risk, and learn how to compute standard deviations for both individual securities and portfolios.**

   Among several alternative measures of risk, standard deviation is a good measure because it uses the entire return distribution, and because it expresses, in a single statistic, the degree to which two securities have similar return distributions. We saw how to measure standard deviation for both individual securities and groups of securities (portfolios) using either historical return data (ex-post returns) or expected future returns (ex-ante returns). We looked at how to compare securities and portfolios based on their risk/return tradeoffs.

4. **Understand the impact of security correlations on portfolio risk.**

   Several examples (with both real and concocted data) suggest that, while the expected (or mean) return for a portfolio is simply the weighted average of expected returns of the individual securities, the standard deviation of a portfolio is not a simple function of individual security's standard deviations. The reason for this lies in the interrelationships (or correlations) between the return distributions of the securities.

5. **Identify the benefits of diversification and how investors can achieve them.**

   Diversification can help investors achieve better risk/return tradeoffs, reducing risk without significantly reducing expected returns. Diversification is possible so long as security returns are not perfectly correlated (their correlation coefficient is less than 1.0). Also, some actual historical data confirm that diversification is not a difficult goal for investors to achieve. Investors can easily diversify by spreading investment funds across several different investments. In doing so, they can eliminate firm-specific or diversifiable risk, leaving only market or systematic risk.

6. **Develop an understanding of efficient diversification and modern portfolio theory.**

   We ended the chapter with a discussion of efficient diversification and the basics of modern portfolio theory. Modern portfolio theory seeks the combinations of securities that offer optimal risk/return tradeoffs, the so-called *efficient frontier*. An efficient frontier based on a set of five actual stocks verified that all portfolios that lie along the efficient frontier do indeed minimize risk for a given level of return, and maximize return for a given level of risk.

Key Terms

Risk	Correlation coefficient
Risk aversion	Investment opportunity set
Utility of wealth	Minimum risk portfolio
Risk neutral investor	Diversification
Risk taker	Efficient frontier
Ex-ante return	Market risk
Ex-post return	Firm-specific risk
Standard deviation	Systematic risk
Mean-variance dominance	Nondiversifiable risk
Mean-variance efficient	Diversifiable risk
Coefficient of variation (CV)	Nonsystematic risk
Correlation	Time diversification
Covariance	

Dollar Cost Averaging
Naive diversification
Efficient diversification

Modern portfolio theory (MPT)
Mean-variance efficient portfolios

Mini Case **1**   OBJECTIVE

To practice calculating the mean, standard deviation, and coefficient of variation, and to select stocks for a risk-averse investor.

Open the file FINA3.XLS on the data disk. The file contains monthly returns for ten stocks from January 1987 to December 1991. Use the data and a spreadsheet or calculator to answer the following questions:

1. What is the mean return for the first five stocks over the entire five-year period?
2. What is the standard deviation for each stock?
3. What is the coefficient of variation (CV) for each stock? Which stock offers the best risk/return tradeoff?
4. Graph the results of the five stocks on a risk/return graph (with ER–SD risk). Which one lies the farthest toward the northwest (upper-left) corner? What does that imply?

Mini Case **2**   OBJECTIVE

To create a two-security efficient frontier.

Open the file FINA3.XLS on the data disk. The file contains monthly returns for ten stocks from January 1987 to December 1991. Use the data on Pepsi and Abbott Labs to answer the following questions:

1. What are the mean returns and standard deviations for both stocks?
2. What is the correlation coefficient for the pair?
3. Create a table like Table 12.6 and determine the portfolio return and standard deviation for various percentage holdings in Pepsi and Abbott Labs. Start with 0 percent as X percent for Pepsi and change it by 10 percent increments.
4. Graph the results on an expected return/standard deviation graph.
5. Using the table and graph, find the proportional investment in Pepsi and Abbott Labs that has the minimum variance.
6. What are the exact proportions for the minimum variance portfolio?
7. What proportions would you invest in Pepsi and Abbott Labs? Discuss.

Discussion Questions and Problems

1. How would you describe a risk-neutral investor versus a risk-averse investor?
2. What does risk aversion imply about the long-term relationship between risk and return?
3. Suppose you have an option of investing $10,000 in Treasury bills to earn a guaranteed 4 percent annual return, or investing in Snapple, which went public in October 1992. Suppose the stock has a 40 percent chance of earning 100 percent in a year and a 60 percent chance of going bankrupt (because Pepsi and Coke will market similar products) within a year. Which investment would a risk-averse investor choose?
4. Suppose someone has the utility of wealth function given by the table on next page:

Wealth Level	Utility of Wealth (Utils)
1	0.00
10	2.50
20	3.20
30	3.60
40	3.89
50	4.11

   a. Graph the utility function. What type of investor is this (risk-neutral, risk-averse, or risk taking)?
   b. Suppose this investor has a current wealth level of 30. What are the current utils?
   c. Suppose this person has a 50/50 chance of increasing wealth level by 10 or decreasing them by 10 from 30. What is the expected utility from taking the chance?
   d. Will this person take the chance or not? Explain.
5. Suppose you had invested in three stocks during 1993. Calculate the stocks' holding period returns:

Stock	Year-End 1992 Price	1993 Annual Dividend	Year-End 1993 Price
Toys "Я" Us	$37.000	$0.00	$42.000
Tootsie Roll	71.000	4.20	78.000
Hewlett-Packard	72.500	2.60	80.625

6. What is the difference between an actual holding period return and an expected return?
7. Suppose today is year *t*, last year was *t* − 1, and next year will be *t* + 1. The prices and disbursed cash dividends for a stock for these years are listed below:

Year	Price	Dividend
t − 1	$58	$1.00
t	65	1.50
t + 1	72	2.00

   a. Calculate the actual holding period return.
   b. Calculate the expected return.
8. Suppose the following probabilities are given for each state of the economy and the respective stock returns:

		Returns	
State of Economy	Probability	Anheuser Busch	Toys "Я" Us
Good	50%	+10%	+30%
Normal	30	+15	+20
Poor	20	+25	+ 5

   a. What is the expected return for each state of the economy for each stock?
   b. What is the standard deviation for each stock?
   c. What is the portfolio expected return from investing 50 percent in each stock?
   d. Calculate the correlation coefficient.
   e. What is the portfolio standard deviation for an equally weighted portfolio of Anheuser Busch and Toys "Я" Us?

9. Five years of returns are given for Pepsi and Hewlett-Packard:

	Pepsi	Hewlett-Packard
1987	30.79%	39.65%
1988	20.88	−8.08
1989	64.89	−10.59
1990	23.84	−30.20
1991	32.22	80.56

   a. Calculate the actual mean return for each stock.

   b. Suppose someone invests 50 percent in each stock. Calculate the mean return for the portfolio using Equation 12.3, and again using Equation 12.6b.

   c. Calculate the correlation coefficient between Pepsi and Hewlett-Packard.

   d. If someone invests 50 percent in each stock, calculate the portfolio standard deviation using Equation 12.5, and again using Equation 12.11b.

10. Two stocks, A and B, have the expected returns of 10 percent and 25 percent with standard deviations of 15 percent and 20 percent, respectively. The correlation coefficient is +0.30. If one invests 40 percent in stock A and 60 percent in B, what are the portfolio expected return and standard deviation?

11. Determine the proportional investment in Stocks A and B from Question 10 that provides the minimum-variance portfolio.

   a. What is the expected return of the minimum-variance portfolio?

   b. What is the standard deviation of the minimum-variance portfolio?

12. Compare the two Portfolios in Questions 10 and 11. Is one preferred over another? Explain.

13. Suppose the two stocks, A and E, in Chapter 12 have a correlation coefficient equal to −1.0. Determine the proportional holdings in A and E that would give the minimum-variance portfolio.

   a. What is the portfolio's expected return?

   b. What is the portfolio's standard deviation?

14. Suppose that two stocks, X and Y, have the following mean returns and standard deviations. The correlation between the two stocks is −0.50.

Stock	Mean Return	Standard Deviation
X	15%	8%
Y	25	14

   Graph an investment opportunity set for these two stocks.

   a. Estimate the proportions of X and Y that make up the minimum-variance portfolio from the graph.

   b. Calculate the proportions of X and Y that make up the minimum-variance portfolio. How close was your estimate?

15. Explain why the correlation coefficients between securities are the key determinants of a portfolio's degree of diversification.

16. Suppose four stocks have the following risk and return characteristics:

Stock	Expected Return	Standard Deviation
A	0.10	0.05
B	0.20	0.10
C	0.20	0.10
D	0.20	0.10

The correlations between A and each of the other stocks are:

$$CORR(A,B) = +1.0$$
$$CORR(A,C) = +0.50$$
$$CORR(A,D) = -0.90$$

Graph an investment opportunity set for A and B, A and C, and A and D by the process described in Chapter 12. Which combination offers the greatest diversification benefits? Explain.

17. What is the difference between market risk and firm-specific risk? Name two other terms for market risk. Name two other terms for firm-specific risk.

18. Suppose a manager of a fund must decide which of two stocks, B or C, to combine with Stock A. The portfolio will hold 50 percent in A and 50 percent in B *or* C. The stocks' expected returns and risk characteristics are given below:

Stock	Expected Return	Standard Deviation	Coefficient of Variation
A	15%	15%	1.00
B	20	10	0.50
C	20	15	0.75

The correlation coefficient CORR(A,B) is +0.90 and CORR(A,C) equals −0.80. The manager concludes that B has a lower risk (and CV) so it is the obvious choice. Do you agree or disagree? Explain why!

Critical Thinking Exercise

Open the file STKRET1.XLS on the data disk. The file contains quarterly returns for ten stocks. Use the data in the file to answer the following questions:

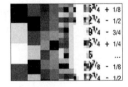

1. What are the mean returns, standard deviations, and pairwise correlation coefficients for the stocks?
2. Display the ten stocks' mean returns and standard deviation (SD) risk on a return–SD risk graph.
3. Choose three stocks for a portfolio and discuss your reasons for your choices.
4. Create at least 10 portfolios with your three stocks by varying the percentages invested in the three stocks. Remember, the percentages must sum to 100%.
5. Which of your 10 portfolios appear to be the most "efficient" compared to the others? Justify your answer.

Mini Case 1 SOLUTION

1. The first five stocks are Abbott Labs, American Home Products, Hewlett-Packard, Johnson & Johnson, and Kmart. The arithmetic average or mean is calculated using Equation 12.3:

$$M_i = \frac{1}{T} \sum_{t=1}^{T} R_{i,t}$$

2. The standard deviation for each stock can be calculated using Equation 12.5:

$$SD_i = \sqrt{\frac{1}{(N-1)} \sum_{t=1}^{T} (R_{i,t} - M_i)^2}$$

The mean and standard deviation for each stock is given below:

Stock	Mean Return	Standard Deviation
Abbott Labs (Ab)	2.24%	6.49%
AHP (AHP)	1.82%	5.45%
Hewlett-Packard (HP)	1.11%	10.32%
Johnson & Johnson (JJ)	2.49%	6.64%
Kmart (KM)	1.62%	9.55%

3. The table below gives the coefficients of variation (CVs), equal to *SD/M:*

Stock	CV
Abbott Labs	0.06491/0.02240 = 2.8981
AHP	0.05448/0.01823 = 2.9890
Hewlett-Packard	0.10324/0.01110 = 9.3399
Johnson & Johnson	0.06641/0.02492 = 2.6649
Kmart	0.0955/0.01615 = 5.9105

Johnson & Johnson offers the best risk/return tradeoff, followed very closely by Abbott Labs and AHP. It has a 2.6649 percent risk per 1 percent of return, while Hewlett-Packard has 9.3399 percent risk per 1 percent of return. It's easy to see that HP had the highest risk level and a relatively low mean return over this past period.

Figure 12.14

ER–SD Risk Graph

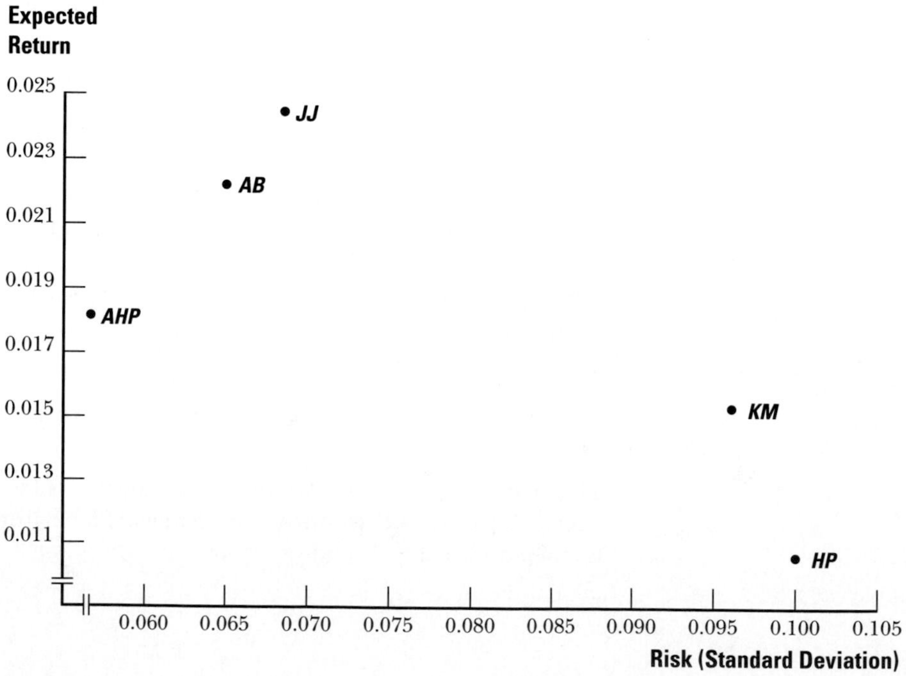

It's pretty clear that Johnson & Johnson, Abbott Labs, and AHP lie farthest toward the northwest corner, indicating that these three have the most attractive risk/return tradeoff, consistent with the results of Part 3.

Mini Case **2**   SOLUTION

1. The mean return is calculated using Equation 12.3 and the standard deviation is calculated using Equation 12.5. (See the Mini Case 1 solution for the equations.) For Pepsi, the mean return equals 2.694 percent and its standard deviation is 0.07154, while Abbott Labs' mean return is 2.240 percent and its standard deviation is .06491.

2. The correlation coefficient is calculated by using Equations 12.9 and 12.10:

$$\text{COV(A,B)} = \frac{1}{(N-1)} \sum_{t=1}^{T} [(R_{At} - M_A)(R_{Bt} - M_B)] \qquad (12.9)$$

$$\text{CORR(A,B)} = \text{COV(A,B)} / SD_A SD_B \qquad (12.10)$$

The easiest way is to set up a table like Table 12.5 and take it step by step or use a spreadsheet. The correlation coefficient for Pepsi and Abbott Labs is 0.685. Recall that the correlation coefficient ranges from -1.0 to $+1.0$, so the two stocks seem to move pretty closely together.

3. As shown in Chapter 12, a table can list various combinations of investments in Pepsi (PEP) and Abbott Labs (AB):

X%PEP	1 − X%PEP	M_p	SD_p
0%	100%	0.02240	0.06491
10	90	0.02285	0.06346
20	80	0.02331	0.06247
30	70	0.02376	0.06196
40	60	0.02422	0.06195
50	50	0.02467	0.06245
60	40	0.02512	0.06339
70	30	0.02558	0.06481
80	20	0.02603	0.06667
90	10	0.02649	0.06892
100	0	0.02694	0.07154

4. The ER–SD risk graph is shown on the following page. The graph starts at 0 percent in Pepsi (or 100 percent in Abbott Labs), and then invests progressively larger amounts in Pepsi.

5. Based on the table and graph, investing 30 percent in Pepsi and 70 percent in Abbott Labs provides the lowest-risk level, or the minimum-variance portfolio.

6. To find the exact proportion, Equation 12.13 gives the proportional investment with the minimum variance:

$$X_A = \frac{SD_E^2 - SD_A SD_E \text{CORR(A,E)}}{SD_A^2 + SD_E^2 - 2(SD_A)(SD_E)\text{CORR(A,E)}}$$

In this case, Stock A is Pepsi and Stock E is Abbott Labs. Plugging in the values gives:

Figure 12.15

ER–SD Risk Graph

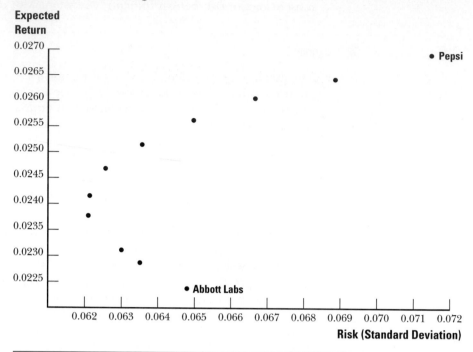

$$X_{PEP} = \frac{0.06491^2 - (0.07154)(0.06491)(0.685)}{0.07154^2 + 0.06491^2 - 2(0.07154)(0.06491)(0.685)}$$

$$X_{PEP} = \frac{0.0042133 - 0.0031809}{0.005118 + 0.0042133 - 0.0063618}$$

$$= \frac{0.0010324}{0.0029695} = 0.347668$$

7. The proportional investment in Pepsi and Abbott Labs should be the minimum-variance portfolio or more investment in Pepsi. The reason is that any point below the minimum-variance portfolio can be replicated by using some combination of Pepsi and Abbott Labs that lies above it (with the same risk but a higher return). What about a point beyond the minimum-variance portfolio? It would depend on the investor's level of risk aversion or utility function. A really risk-averse investor would probably be at the minimum-variance portfolio, approximately 35 percent in Pepsi and 65 percent in Abbott Labs. A less risk-averse investor might land anywhere above it. Now it's easy to see the significance of the minimum-variance portfolio; it determines the viable portfolios between itself and the others above it.

Chapter 13

Capital Asset Pricing Theory

Chapter Objectives

1. Understand the capital market line (CML).
2. Develop the Capital Asset Pricing Model (CAPM).
3. Contrast the standard deviation and beta risk measures.
4. Apply the CAPM to security analysis.
5. Learn to estimate beta.
6. Review the good news and bad news about beta.

In Chapter 12, we examined how a portfolio of securities can provide diversification, which offers the potential to reduce risk and increase return. In fact, we established that any rational investor would hold a diversified portfolio instead of one or two securities. This raises the question: How can individual securities be priced when everyone holds combinations of securities? More specifically, you may be wondering how this is going to help with security selection, as discussed in Chapter 8.

Chapter 12 discussed securities only in the context of a portfolio. However, Chapter 12 developed two important ideas that will link portfolio theory to a security risk/return relationship. It showed that risk-averse investors require higher returns to compensate them for risk. Further, investors who hold well-diversified portfolios eliminate firm-specific risk, so their only relevant risks are market risks (also referred to as *systematic risk*).

This chapter will develop techniques to measure market risk and security risk. By quantifying a security risk measure, we can determine a risk/return relationship for individual securities. The risk/return relationship is specified by the **Capital Asset Pricing Model (CAPM).** It provides an objective way of determining the risk and return for each security in the context of portfolio diversification. The general notion presented in CAPM, that investors will accept higher risk only if compensated with higher returns, is also central to modern portfolio theory, as Chapter 12 showed.

Before we embark on a development of the theory, let's discuss the assumptions. These assumptions are necessary to develop a model that provides a linear representation of the risk/return relationship; some assumptions are necessary to make decisions while others just simplify things. We admit that these assumptions may be unrealistic, but they help to simplify the model so we can gain some insights on how security risk and return are related. Also, it's important to recognize that the value of the model resides in the insights it provides with respect to the real world and not in the realism of its assumptions. Later in Chapter 14, we will discuss other developments of the model that relax some of the assumptions listed here; for now, however, we start by including all the assumptions in order to develop the original capital asset pricing model.

Assumptions of the Capital Asset Pricing Model

Several assumptions are necessary in developing the capital asset pricing theory. These assumptions are:

1. Investors have homogeneous expectations. This means that everyone has equal information and the same perceptions about the securities and the market. This assumption is necessary so that everyone will perceive the same efficient frontier. Otherwise, market equilibrium would be elusive.
2. Frictionless capital markets. This means that no impediments prevent investors from creating their optimal portfolios. This assumption prevents additional costs or constraints (which may vary among investors) from affecting investment decisions to create frictionless markets. These listed restrictions include:
   a. No transaction costs, brokerage fees, or bid–ask spread fees exist.
   b. No taxes are payable.
   c. Securities can be divided in any proportions investors want to optimize their portfolios.
   d. One person's trading activity will not affect prices.
3. Investors are rational and seek to maximize their expected utility functions. This assumption allows us to determine investment choices for a standard group of risk-averse investors.
4. Investment is for one period only. This assumption is important to prevent future investment strategies from affecting today's prices. For example, if investment horizons vary from 2 years to 20 years, it may affect investment choices (and prices) today.
5. All investors can borrow or lend at the risk-free rate. This assumption simplifies the risk/return relationship. Without it, the risk/return relationship may be nonlinear.[1]

Efficient Frontier and the Optimal Risky Portfolio

In Chapter 12, we learned that the efficient frontier represents a series of portfolios that provide the highest return for a given risk or the lowest risk for a given expected return. See Figure 13.1.

As expected, a security's expected return and standard deviation will be inferior to those at any point on the efficient frontier, and hence any security will lie below the efficient frontier. Although an individual security may lie below the efficient frontier, it may be part of one (or several) of the portfolios on the efficient frontier. It may represent 5 percent of the value of a portfolio and 8 percent of another portfolio that lie on the efficient frontier.

[1] Economists and finance academics have a biased expectation that the risk/return relationship should be linear. Also only with a linear relationship can we separate the personal (utility function) decisions from objective investment decisions. This point will be clearer after we discuss the portfolio separation theorem. Until then, don't worry about it too much.

Figure 13.1

Efficient Frontier

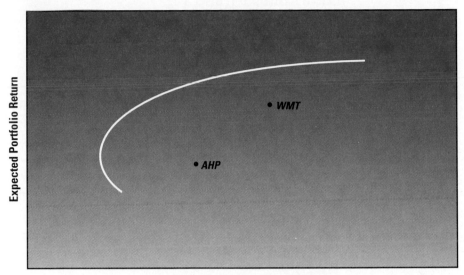

Portfolio Risk (Standard Deviation)

A rational investor will always choose a portfolio that lies on the efficient frontier, but which one? Remember a portfolio on the efficient frontier has the maximum return for a given risk level, so the answer depends on an individual's preference for risk and return. Earlier in Chapter 12, we discussed the investor's utility function (or curve). Two investors with different utility functions will choose different risky portfolios. Figure 13.2 combines the efficient frontier with two investors' utility curves.[2]

Figure 13.2

Efficient Frontier and Utility Curves for Investors A and B

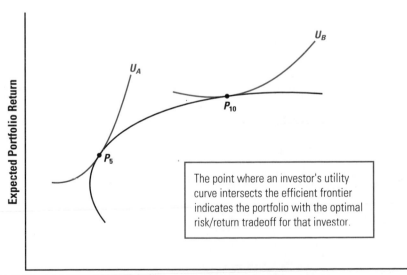

Portfolio Risk (Standard Deviation)

> The point where an investor's utility curve intersects the efficient frontier indicates the portfolio with the optimal risk/return tradeoff for that investor.

---

[2]Assumption 3, that investors are rational and maximize their utility functions, allows us to make portfolio choices for investors with different utility functions. Given this assumption, an investor will choose a risky portfolio that maximizes his or her utility function.

Figure 13.3

Combination of the Risk-Free Asset, RF, and Risky
Portfolios P1 and P2

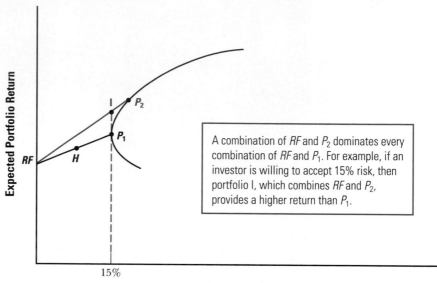

A combination of *RF* and P_2 dominates every combination of *RF* and P_1. For example, if an investor is willing to accept 15% risk, then portfolio I, which combines *RF* and P_2, provides a higher return than P_1.

Portfolio Risk (Standard Deviation)

Investor A, who is very risk averse, chooses P5 which exposes the portfolio to relatively low risk. Investor B, who is less risk averse, chooses P10 which is riskier, but also provides a higher return.[3] This is helpful, but practically speaking, utility curves are difficult to assess. More importantly, it does not provide an objective portfolio choice. The portfolio chosen (and the percentage invested in each security) will differ depending on the individual's utility curve. For example, Investor A's choice of P5 may consist of 2 percent in AHP while Investor B's choice of P10 may have 35 percent invested in AHP. Besides, how often have you been asked by your stockbroker to describe your utility function?

Developing the Capital Market Line (CML)

To solve this problem, we introduce a risk-free asset, RF. The closest asset to a truly risk-free investment is a short-term U.S. Treasury bill. With a zero standard deviation, or risk, it lies on the *y*-axis. Now combine RF with a **risky portfolio** such as P1. Figure 13.3 shows the combination between RF and P1.

The combination of RF and P1 is also a portfolio and its expected return ER_p, using Equation 12.6a, equals:

$$ER_p = (X)ER_{p1} + (1 - X)RF \qquad (13.1)$$

where X is the proportion of wealth invested in the risky portfolio P1 and $(1-X)$ is the proportion invested in the risk-free asset, RF. The standard deviation risk of the RF–P1 combination can be calculated using Equation 12.11b:

$$SD_p = \left[X^2 SD^2_{p1} + (1 - X)^2 SD^2_{RF} \right.$$
$$\left. + 2X(1 - X)SD_{p1}SD_{RF} \text{CORR}(\text{P1,RF}) \right]^{1/2}$$

---

[3]Investor A may be a retired, middle-income individual while Investor B may be someone like Ross Perot or Donald Trump.

Figure 13.4

Combination of the Risk-Free Asset, RF, and the Risky Portfolio, M

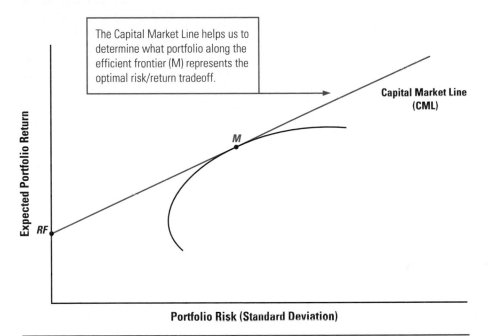

The Capital Market Line helps us to determine what portfolio along the efficient frontier (M) represents the optimal risk/return tradeoff.

Capital Market Line (CML)

Expected Portfolio Return

RF

M

Portfolio Risk (Standard Deviation)

The last two terms equal zero because SD_{RF} equals zero. This leaves:

$$SD_p = \sqrt{(X)^2 SD^2_{p1}}$$
$$= (X)SD_{p1}$$

(13.2)

The standard deviation of the portfolio combination RF–P1 is linear because the risk-free rate has a zero standard deviation.

The line between *RF* and *P1* can be interpreted in the same way as that between two security combinations in Chapter 12. Point *RF* represents a 100 percent investment in the risk-free asset while Point *P1* represents a 100 percent investment in the risky portfolio P1. The halfway point, *H*, represents a 50 percent investment in each. Remember, investors want to maximize their expected returns for a given risk.

As shown in Figure 13.3, a combination of RF and P2 dominates any point on the line created between RF and P1. For example, suppose an investor is interested in maintaining a 15 percent risk level. He or she could invest 100 percent in P1, or better yet invest 90 percent in P2 and 10 percent in RF to reach Point *I*. The P2 and RF combination has the same 15 percent risk, but a higher expected return, ER_p. Being rational, an investor would choose P2 over P1.

Of course, why stop there! Other combinations with RF, such as P3, P4, etc., will dominate those before. As shown in Figure 13.4, Portfolio M, where a tangent line from RF touches the efficient frontier, is the line that dominates any other line that can be drawn from RF to any point on the efficient frontier, even P10. This line from RF to M is called the **capital market line (CML).** The CML identifies all efficient portfolios and surpasses the old (curved) efficient frontier, except at Point M. Recall that *efficient* means that it has the highest expected return for a given risk, or the lowest risk for a given expected return. The CML will be discussed in more detail later.

Like the earlier examples, the line represents percentage investment in RF and the risky portfolio, M. For example, a point halfway between RF and M represents a 50 percent investment in RF and M each. Once an investor

Figure 13.5

CML and Individual Utility Curves

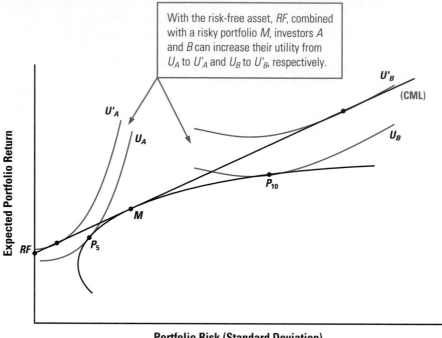

With the risk-free asset, *RF*, combined with a risky portfolio *M*, investors *A* and *B* can increase their utility from U_A to U'_A and U_B to U'_B, respectively.

has decided on a personally desirable combination of RF and M, he or she can calculate the expected portfolio return and its expected standard deviation risk using Equations 13.1 and 13.2. For 50 percent investments in each, the ER_p and SD_p equal:

$$ER_p = (0.50)ER_M + (1 - 0.50)RF \qquad (13.3)$$
$$SD_p = (0.50)SD_{p1} \qquad (13.4)$$

If RF equals 6 percent and ER_M equals 16 percent with an 8 percent SD_M, the portfolio expected return, ER_p, is 11 percent and SD_p is 4 percent.[4]

$$ER_p = (0.50)(0.16) + (1 - 0.50)(0.06) = 0.11 \text{ or } 11 \text{ percent}$$
$$SD_p = (0.50)(0.08) = 0.04 \text{ or } 4 \text{ percent}$$

At Point M, 100 percent is invested in the risky portfolio, M. What about beyond point M? We will defer this discussion until later to deal with the significance of the CML to investors who are choosing their optimal risky portfolios.

Remember the utility curves and how we determined which portfolio Investors A and B would choose? A chose P1 and B chose P10. Now recall from earlier discussions in Chapter 12 that investors gain utility as their utility curves move upward and to the left (toward the northwest). As shown in Figure 13.5, Investor A's utility increases as the curve moves out from U_A to U_A'. U_A' is tangent to the CML and represents perhaps a 90 percent investment in RF and only 10 percent in the risky portfolio M. As we observed earlier, Investor A is very risk averse, choosing between RF and M consistently with his or her conservative utility function. What about Investor B?

---

[4]When using Equations 13.1 and 13.2, it's easiest to convert all percentages into decimals, then later convert back to percentages.

Figure 13.6

CML: The Borrowing–Lending Line

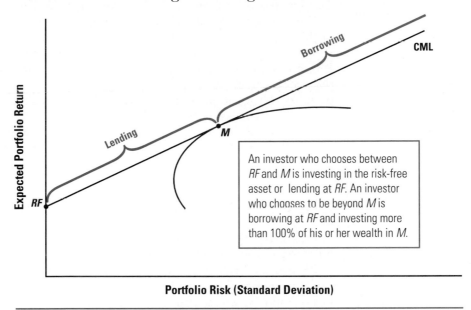

An investor who chooses between *RF* and *M* is investing in the risk-free asset or lending at *RF*. An investor who chooses to be beyond *M* is borrowing at *RF* and investing more than 100% of his or her wealth in *M*.

B also increases his or her utility by moving from U_B to U_B'. B chooses to invest −100 percent in RF and 200 percent in the risky portfolio, M. What does it mean to invest a negative percentage in RF? To be beyond *M*, it means that an investor has borrowed at the risk-free rate, RF, and invested over 100 percent in Portfolio M. (A negative percentage allocation means borrowing.) In reality, it just means that a person bought on margin or borrowed money to invest more wealth than he or she has. Investor B is borrowing 100 percent at the risk-free rate and investing twice his or her wealth (200 percent) in Portfolio M. If $100 represents his or her invested wealth, B borrows an additional $100 and invests $200 in M. This example implies a 50 percent margin, borrowing half of what is invested. Investor B is definitely not as risk averse as A, and is willing to take more risk for a higher return.

Using the examples of Investors A and B and their choices, we can segment the CML between lenders and borrowers. For that reason, the CML is sometimes called the **borrowing–lending line.**[5] The section between RF and M is called the *lending line* and beyond M, it is called the *borrowing line.* Why? Let's go back to Investor A who invested 90 percent in RF and 10 percent in M. If A invests in RF, he or she is basically lending money at the risk-free rate. Therefore by investing 90 percent of his or her wealth in RF, A is lending 90 percent of his or her wealth. Investor B, by investing −100 percent of his or her wealth in RF, is borrowing 100 percent of his or her wealth at the risk-free rate. Figure 13.6 shows how the CML is segmented between lenders and borrowers.

At this point we have made an important discovery. Both Investors A and B will now choose to invest in the risky portfolio M along with the risk-free asset, RF. Though they are diametrically different in their risk preferences, both investors will now choose M instead of P1 or P10. Notice that Assumption 1 (homogeneous expectations) is critical here. If investors did not have homogeneous expectations, then even with the risk-free asset, Investors A and B may perceive different efficient frontiers and choose different risky portfolios instead of M. Also Assumption 2 (frictionless markets) is necessary because impediments might lead investors to perceive different efficient frontiers based on their tax brackets or transaction fees.

Now going back to the choice of Portfolio M, we have resolved the earlier problem of dealing with utility curves and different risk preferences. It now seems that all investors will choose the risky Portfolio M; not P1, P2, P5, or P10, but M! This is a very profound discovery because we can now separate the risky portfolio choice from the subjective individual utility functions. This premise, called the **portfolio separation theorem,** states:

> Individuals choose the risky portfolio independently of their utility functions. All risk-averse investors choose the same risky portfolio regardless of utility functions, then they decide on the combination of RF and the risky portfolio, based on their utility functions.

For example, Investors A and B chose portfolio M as their risky portfolio despite their differences in risk aversion because M combined with RF is efficient. (It has the highest expected return for a given risk or the lowest risk for a given expected return.) Once M is chosen, the proportion (X) invested in RF, and the balance invested in M, depend on risk preference; how much risk is someone willing to take for a higher return? A invested only 10 percent in Portfolio M, while B invested a whopping 200 percent in M. Note that their portfolio combinations of RF and M will have different ER_p and SD_p values, which can be calculated using Equations 13.1 and 13.2.

The portfolio separation theorem emphasizes the importance of M as the *only* risky portfolio chosen by *all* investors. Since M is the only risky portfolio, it must include all traded assets from art, stamps, and coins to financial securities. If so, it is appropriate to call it the **market portfolio.** Also, if it contains all traded assets, it must be well-diversified.

Furthermore, theoretically, the securities in the market portfolio are value-weights of each security's proportion in the market portfolio. It is calculated as the security's total market value (price per share × number of shares outstanding) divided by the total market value of all the securities in M. In practice, however, a proxy such as the S&P 500 index, which is considered to be well-diversified, substitutes for the market portfolio.

Finally, the capital market line (CML) that combines RF and M holds an important position, too. It defines all efficient portfolios, which are just combinations of RF and M. It can also be interpreted as a unique linear relationship between standard deviation risk, SD_p, and its expected return, ER_p, for all the $RF–M$ choices for individuals. The equation of the CML equals:

$$ER_p = RF + \left(\frac{ER_M - RF}{SD_M} \right) SD_p \qquad (13.5)$$

where the y-intercept (where the CML crosses the y-axis) is RF and the slope equals $(ER_M - RF)/SD_M$. Keep this in mind; it will be an important factor in developing the CAPM!

Now we've almost reached our goal, to find a model that shows how securities are priced. Recall that it is called the Capital Asset Pricing Model (CAPM).

Brief Recapitulation

The CML defines efficient combinations of RF and Portfolio M. It defines only one optimal risky portfolio, M; all investors prefer to combine M with the risk-free asset, RF. If M is preferred by all rational, risk-averse investors, then it must be the market portfolio.

Figure 13.7

CML and Individual Securities

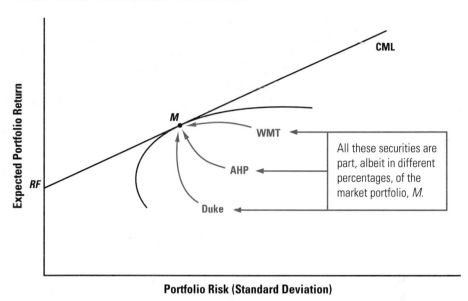

So far we have only developed the Portfolio M and justified why everyone will invest in M. If all rational, risk-averse investors prefer only one risky portfolio, M (which is the market portfolio), then the risk that each security contributes to M is the only relevant risk for a security. The relevant risk of securities such as AHP, WMT, and DUKE is just what they contribute to M's risk. Figure 13.7 shows how all those securities are parts of the market portfolio, M; and the next section will discuss how to measure their risk, defined as each security's risk contribution to the market portfolio's risk.

Capital Asset Pricing Model (CAPM)

M must contain all tradable securities, as everyone invests only in M, and it must be well-diversified. We also know from Chapter 12 that if everyone invests in a well-diversified portfolio, then only market risk is relevant. Any firm-specific risk is eliminated purely through portfolio diversification. Since everyone invests in a well-diversified portfolio, M, by determining Portfolio M's market risk, investors will know the risk level of their investment. Portfolio M's risk can be written as:

$$\text{Portfolio M's risk} = \text{Market risk}$$

Further, since M is the only risky portfolio to consider, the relevant risk for each security is the amount of risk it contributes to M, or the security's market risk, ignoring firm-specific risk. If each security risk is stated as:

$$\begin{aligned} \text{Security risk} &= \text{Total risk} \\ &= \text{Market risk} + \text{Firm-specific risk} \end{aligned}$$

then we could restate Portfolio M's market risk as:

$$\text{Portfolio M's risk} = (\text{Security 1's market risk} + \text{Security 2's market risk} + \ldots + \text{Security } N\text{'s market risk})$$

We are no longer interested in total risk (or standard deviation) of a security, but its risk contribution to the larger market portfolio.

Also recall from Chapter 12 that, as the number of securities (N) increases, the security risk, SD, falls virtually to zero; the only relevant risk is the security's covariance with the other securities in a well-diversified portfolio (in this case, the market portfolio, M). We need to develop a measure of the security's risk contribution to the market portfolio, which we'll call the security's *relative risk measure*.

Developing a Relative Risk Measure

Recall that Equation 12.13 defined the total risk of any portfolio, p, as:

$$SD_p = \left[\sum_{i=1}^{N} X_i^2 SD_i^2 + \sum_{i=1}^{N} \sum_{\substack{j=1 \\ i \neq j}}^{N} X_i X_j \text{COV}(i,j) \right]^{1/2}$$

Instead of any portfolio, p, we will use Equation 12.13 to define the market portfolio and the risk contribution of Security i to M. First, take the square of Equation 12.13 to ignore the square root sign. Rewrite it as:

$$SD_M{}^2 = \sum_{i=1}^{N} X_i^2 SD_i^2 + \sum_{i=1}^{N} \sum_{\substack{j=1 \\ i \neq j}}^{N} X_i X_j SD_i SD_j \text{CORR}(i,j) \tag{13.6}$$

We'll further rewrite Equation 13.6 by separating the summation over i from the summation over j, which adds up all the securities to make portfolio M. Now we can identify Security i's contribution to the market portfolio, M, as:

$$SD_M{}^2 = \sum_{i=1}^{N} X_i [X_i SD_i^2 + \sum_{j=1}^{N} X_j SD_i SD_j \text{CORR}(i,j)] \tag{13.7}$$

Let's examine the term in brackets, which equals the total risk contribution of Security i to the market portfolio:

$$\begin{array}{l}\text{Total risk} \\ \text{contribution} \\ \text{of Security } i \end{array} = [X_i SD_i^2 + \sum_{j=1}^{N} X_j SD_i SD_j \text{CORR}(i,j)] \tag{13.8}$$

Equation 13.8 represents the total risk contribution of Security i to the market portfolio M, where the first term is $X_i SD_i^2$ and the second term, $X_j SD_i SD_j \text{CORR}(i,j)$, equals $X_j \text{COV}(i,j)$.[6] The first term measures the contribution of Security i's total risk, multiplied by the proportion of Security i in M; the second term measures the amount of risk Security i contributes to Security j and Security j's proportion in portfolio M. By summing the COV(i,j) over j [$\sum_{j=1}^{N} X_j \text{COV}(i,j)$], we are capturing how Security i contributes to the risk of each of the other securities that make up the market portfolio, M. The two terms together capture the total risk of Security i in the market portfolio.

---

[6]Remember that CORR(i,j) is defined as $\text{CORR}(i,j) = [\text{COV}(i,j)/(SD_i(SD_j)]$ so we can rearrange terms and have $\text{COV}(i,j) = (SD_i)(SD_j)\text{CORR}(i,j)$

Now suppose that we want to measure the total risk of Security i relative to the market portfolio risk, SD_M^2. Equation 13.8 can be rewritten as:

$$\text{Relative risk contribution of Security } i = \frac{\text{Total risk contribution of Security } i}{\text{Total risk of market portfolio, M}} \quad (13.9)$$

$$= \frac{X_i SD_i^2}{SD_M^2} + \frac{\sum_{j=1}^{N} X_j SD_i SD_j \, \text{CORR}(i,j)}{SD_M^2}$$

Similar to the portfolio risk equation (Equation 12.12), this equation states that the relative security risk is composed of two types of risk: total risk of Security i (SD_i^2) and its correlation (or covariance) with other securities. Since the market portfolio, M, consists of several thousand securities, each security's contribution, denoted by X_i, is very small. This makes $X_i SD_i^2 / SD_M^2$ virtually equal to zero. (Remember this is the power of diversification discussed in Chapter 12.)

This makes the relative risk contribution of Security i equal to:

$$\text{Relative risk contribution of Security } i \approx 0 + \frac{\sum_{j=1}^{N} X_j SD_i SD_j \, \text{CORR}(i,j)}{SD_M^2} \quad (13.10)$$

If the summation is taken over all Securities j, it equals the risk of the market portfolio, and Equation 13.10 becomes:

$$\text{Relative risk contribution of Security } i \approx 0 + \frac{SD_i [SD_M \text{CORR}(i,M)]}{SD_M^2} \quad (13.11)$$

$$\approx \frac{SD_i}{SD_M} \text{CORR}(i,M)$$

Equation 13.11 says that the relative risk of Security i equals Security i's total risk relative to the market portfolio risk (SD_i / SD_M) multiplied by Security i's risk contribution to the larger portfolio, M, measured by CORR(i,M).

Since $\text{CORR}(i,M) = \text{COV}(i,M)/SD_i SD_M$, we can rewrite Equation 13.11 as:

$$\text{Relative risk contribution of Security } i \approx \frac{\text{COV}(i,M)}{SD_M^2} = \beta_i \quad (13.12)$$

This relative risk is better known as **beta,** β_i, for Security i. The relative risk contribution of Security i equals β_i.

Now let's determine the beta for the market portfolio, M. Using Equation 13.11:

$$\beta_M = \frac{SD_M}{SD_M} \text{CORR}(M,M)$$

Any variable must be perfectly correlated with itself, or CORR(M,M) = +1.0, so the market portfolio beta, β_M, equals 1.0. Because the market portfolio is a value-weighted average of all the traded securities, it says that an average security risk contribution is equal to 1.0. If Security i's beta, β_i, is greater than 1.0, then Security i's risk contribution is higher than the average security or the market portfolio risk. If β_i is less than 1.0, then its risk contribution is less than the average security or the market portfolio risk. The market portfolio's beta can be used as a reference point for security risk. Let's continue our discussion on beta to obtain an intuitive feel about it and determine how to interpret it.

Understanding Beta

This section discusses the meaning and interpretation of beta. We will start with a list of four ways to view beta and then discuss the difference between beta and the standard deviation risk (or total risk) of a stock.

1. All security betas are measured relative to the market portfolio beta which equals 1.0. If a security beta is greater than 1.0, its risk is greater than the market portfolio's risk; if it is less than 1.0, its risk is less than the market portfolio's. The market beta of 1.0 serves as a reference point for security betas.
2. Alternatively, we can interpret a beta greater than 1.0 to mean that the security contributes more than average risk to the well-diversified market portfolio.
3. Also, the numerical value of beta, such as AHP's beta of 0.66, implies something about returns. If the return on the market portfolio changes by 1 percent, then AHP's return will move up or down by 0.66 percent. Therefore, high-beta securities returns move more aggressively than the market portfolio while low-beta securities are more conservative. Money managers have created strategies to invest heavily in high-beta stocks in bull markets. Using the same analogy, many will invest in money markets (risk-free assets) or low-beta stocks when they expect bear markets or unpredictable conditions.
4. Finally because beta is a relative measure, the index used as a proxy for the market portfolio can make a big difference in the beta estimate. For example, if IBM were measured relative to the Dow Jones Industrial Average (DJIA), it would be very closely correlated as the Dow is a price index made up of only 30 stocks. When the DJIA fell 9.46 points to 3266.80 on September 29, 1992, its decline was blamed in part on IBM cutting 40,000 jobs and charging $2.1 billion against 1992 earnings.[7] On the other hand, if IBM's beta is measured relative to the Wilshire 5,000 index, IBM's beta may show less correlation, and so the beta estimate will be less than one measured relative to the Dow. This just says that it's very important to know what market index serves as a proxy for the market to measure each security beta.

Two Types of Risk Revisited. Next, let's examine intuitively how to use the beta instead of standard deviation risk. In Chapter 12, we discussed two types of risk: market risk and firm-specific risk. Also remember that a security's total risk is composed of market risk plus firm-specific risk. Now we can define the relative market risk for a security as its beta, so the total risk of a security return can be divided into beta and firm-specific risk. Beta is also referred to as the systematic or nondiversifiable risk; it is the component of a security's risk that is associated with the market portfolio, M. Alternatively, it is the part of the security's risk that is inherent in the market, and the extent to which it moves with the system; hence, this systematic risk cannot

---

[7]*The Wall Street Journal,* September 30, 1992, C2.

be diversified away. In contrast, the firm-specific risk, or risk that is unique to the firm, can be eliminated simply by holding a well-diversified portfolio like M; this is diversifiable risk. Often cited sources of firm-specific risk are labor disputes or negotiations, product tampering (as in the Tylenol and Pepsi episodes), resignations of CEOs, and awards of government contracts.

Now let's contrast investment decisions made by total risk versus beta. Suppose AHP's total risk, SD_{AHP}, is 10 percent, and Wal-Mart's, SD_{WMT}, equals 15 percent. Assume, for simplicity, that the expected return equals 20 percent for both securities. Based on what we said in Chapter 12, a risk-averse, rational single-security investor would prefer AHP with 10 percent total risk. However, now that the investor can hold a well-diversified portfolio such as M, the total risk is no longer relevant. Only the systematic risk (beta) or the risk that the security contributes to the large portfolio M, is relevant.[8]

Suppose that total risk can be decomposed as follows for AHP and Wal-Mart:

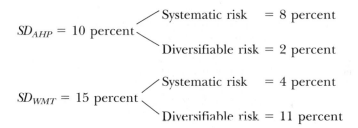

$$SD_{AHP} = 10 \text{ percent} \begin{cases} \text{Systematic risk} & = 8 \text{ percent} \\ \text{Diversifiable risk} & = 2 \text{ percent} \end{cases}$$

$$SD_{WMT} = 15 \text{ percent} \begin{cases} \text{Systematic risk} & = 4 \text{ percent} \\ \text{Diversifiable risk} & = 11 \text{ percent} \end{cases}$$

Given that the two securities have the same expected return, an investor naively using the total risk measure would incorrectly choose AHP (which has a lower SD of 10 percent) when in fact, Wal-Mart has a lower systematic risk of 4 percent as compared to AHP's 8 percent.

CAPM Derivation

A risk/return measure for securities can be developed now that we have an intuitive feel for the security's relative risk contribution, β_i. To take that final step to derive the CAPM, let's go back to the investment choice and reiterate some points. Remember, all risk-averse investors will invest in one risky portfolio, M. If so, Portfolio M must be the market portfolio consisting of all traded securities. Recall that M is optimal because it lies on the CML and is preferred over all other risky portfolios. Now what does it take for M to be on the CML? To lie on the CML, it must have the same slope as the CML. From Equation 13.5:

$$\text{Slope of CML} = \frac{(ER_M - RF)}{SD_M}$$

This is interpreted as the market portfolio's ratio of reward $(ER_M - RF)$ to risk (SD_M).

What is the reward-to-risk ratio for a security? Let's first discuss how to measure reward for securities, and then cover risk.

---

[8]We use systematic risk, defined as $\beta_i SD_M$ instead of beta because it provides a percentage risk measure comparable to total risk (which is also in percentage terms). Beta is a risk measured relative to the market portfolio, so it is an absolute number and cannot be compared to total risk given as a percentage.

Reward for Investing in a Security. In Chapter 12, we found that risk-averse investors are enticed to invest in risky securities only if they are compensated for risk. Chapter 1 defined this risk/return relationship as:

$$ER_i = RF + \text{Risk premium}$$

The compensation for accepting risk equals:

$$(ER_i - RF) = \text{Risk premium}$$

The left side of the equation $(ER_i - RF)$, is the reward for accepting risk. Now how do we measure security risk?

Security Risk. Recall that Security i's risk is only relevant to the extent that it contributes to the market portfolio, M. That risk contribution is beta, β_i, also known as *systematic risk,* which can be defined as $\beta_i SD_M$. The term $\beta_i SD_M$ redefines Security i's risk contribution to the market portfolio as a percentage rather than an absolute number, like beta. For example, if β_i equals 1.2 and SD_M equals 20 percent, then Security i's percentage risk contribution equals $\beta_i SD_M$ or $(1.2)(0.20) = 0.24$ or 24 percent. Now we can define reward-to-risk ratios for a security.

Security's Reward-to-Risk Ratio. Using this definition of the risk contribution of Security i, its reward-to-risk ratio can be defined as:

$$\text{Security } i\text{'s reward-to-risk ratio} = \frac{(ER_i - RF)}{\beta_i SD_M}$$

Because Security i is part of the larger market portfolio, M, its reward-to-risk ratio must equal M's reward-to-risk ratio from the CML:

$$\frac{(ER_i - RF)}{\beta_i SD_M} = \frac{(ER_M - RF)}{SD_M} \tag{13.13}$$

Why? Remember, that $\beta_i SD_M$ is Security i's risk contribution to M. As this contribution increases, its reward must increase proportionately; otherwise M's reward-to-risk ratio would change and may no longer be optimal (that is, may no longer lie on the CML).[9] To be in market equilibrium and for M to maintain its optimal position, the reward-to-risk ratio for each security must maintain its proportion of the market portfolio's reward-to-risk ratio.

Risk/Return Relationship. Now that we have determined the relationship between reward-to-risk ratios necessary to maintain an optimal portfolio, M, we can use it to find a security's risk/return relationship. Solve Equation 13.13 for ER_i:

$$ER_i = RF + \beta_i(ER_M - RF) \tag{13.14}$$

Finally, we have developed a risk/return measure for securities such as AHP. It is called the *Capital Asset Pricing Model* (CAPM). The security risk pre-

---

[9]We need to use calculus to prove this. If you are interested in a mathematical proof, go to the following references. William Sharpe, "Capital Asset Prices: A Theory of Market Equilibrium," *Journal of Finance,* September 1964; John Lintner, "The Valuation of Risk Assets and the Selection of Risky Investments in Stock Portfolios and Capital Budgets," *Review of Economics and Statistics,* February 1965; and Jan Mossin, "Equilibrium in a Capital Market," *Econometrica,* October 1966.

Figure 13.8

Security Market Line (SML)

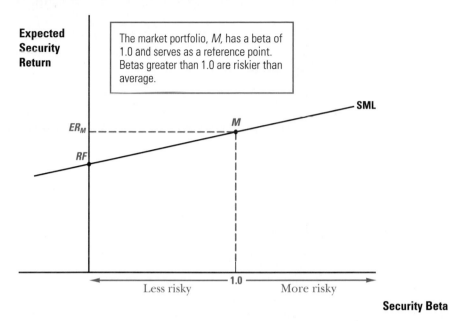

mium, $\beta_i(ER_M - RF)$, equals the risk contribution to the market portfolio multiplied by the market portfolio's risk premium. This makes sense because we presume that all risk-averse investors will purchase the market portfolio, so all security risk must be measured relative to the market portfolio risk. The CAPM is important because it allows us to quantify the *security's* risk premium and define a linear representation of risk/return relationship for all securities and portfolios. This relationship comes from modern portfolio theory (MPT) because it relies on the idea that risk-averse investors will diversify away as much risk as they can; beyond that, expected return increases only with added risk.

The CAPM (Equation 13.14) can also be displayed graphically. This gives the **security market line (SML),** as displayed in Figure 13.8.

Notice that this graph uses beta, as opposed to standard deviation, as a measure of risk. The expected return equals the risk-free rate, RF, at zero beta; it increases as beta increases. The expected return when beta equals 1.0 is just the expected return on the market portfolio, ER_M. Since we have two points, RF at zero beta and ER_M at beta 1.0, we can draw a line to obtain the SML. Remember that Equation 13.14, the CAPM formula, creates the SML. To verify this, let's find the equation of the line for the SML.

Recall that the equation of a line equals:

$$Y = a + bX$$

where a is the y-intercept of the line, b is its slope, X is the independent variable, and Y is the dependent variable. For the SML, β_i is the independent variable and ER_i is the dependent variable. What are the y-intercept and the slope?

The y-intercept is just the point at which the line crosses the y-axis, RF in Figure 13.8. Recall that the slope is defined as:

$$\frac{\text{Rise}}{\text{Run}} = \frac{\Delta Y}{\Delta X} = \frac{(ER_M - RF)}{1.0 - 0.0} = (ER_M - RF)$$

For the SML, the slope equals $(ER_M - RF)$ so the equation of the SML is:

$$ER_j = RF + (ER_M - RF)\beta_j$$

This equation for the SML equals Equation 13.14, the CAPM equation. The CML and SML sound similar at first. The next section contrasts the two lines to clear up this confusion.

Differences between the CML and SML

At this point, we have introduced terms with two similar names, the capital market line (CML) and the security market line (SML). The latter graphs the CAPM equation. Let's contrast the two to avoid any confusion.

The lines differ in two ways. The most obvious is the risk measure; the CML measures risk by standard deviation, or total risk, while the SML measures risk by beta to find the security's risk contribution to Portfolio M. The second difference is more subtle. The CML graph defines only efficient portfolios, while the SML graph defines both efficient and nonefficient portfolios and securities. Let's embellish on these points.

Firm-specific risk or diversifiable risk for portfolios on the CML is virtually zero because the CML contains only well-diversified, efficient portfolios. Even though it measures total risk (by standard deviation), it contains only market risk and almost no firm-specific risk. Also remember that when the risk-free asset was introduced, all risk-averse investors preferred only one risky portfolio, the market portfolio, M. All portfolios on the CML are just combinations of the risk-free asset and the market portfolio, M.

The SML includes all portfolios and securities that lie on and below the CML. Since everyone invests in M, each security (or portfolio) risk is determined as its risk contribution to M. This risk contribution is defined as beta. Every security (or portfolio) on the SML exists only as part of M, and the relevant risk is the security's contribution to M's risk. Again, firm-specific risk is irrelevant to the SML, but for a different reason than the reason it is irrelevant to the CML.

Brief Recapitulation. The CAPM (or its graph, the SML) provides a risk/return relationship for every security and portfolio. It measures risk as beta, a relative risk contribution to the market portfolio, M, because all investors are assumed to hold only M as their risky portfolio choice. The total risk (or standard deviation) of a security is no longer relevant, because the firm-specific part of risk can be diversified away leaving only beta. The CAPM quantifies the risk premium for securities as $\beta_i(ER_M - RF)$ or the security risk contribution, β_i, multiplied by the market risk premium. The market beta equals 1.0 and serves as a reference point for other security betas. If a security's beta is greater than 1.0, then it is riskier than the average security, or the market portfolio; if its beta is less than 1.0, then it is less risky than the market.

Now that you have some insights on the development of the CAPM, let's apply this model to security analysis; this will also promote a better understanding of the SML. The analysis really repeats the fundamental analysis conducted in Chapter 8. The only difference is that the CAPM replaces intrinsic values measured in dollars with expected returns measured in percentages. (We'll compare the two approaches later.) The next section will illustrate how to conduct a security analysis using the CAPM.

CAPM and Security Analysis

Suppose that U.S. Treasury bills are currently yielding 7 percent and the current traded prices for AHP, Washington Water Power, Wal-Mart, and Mainstay Gold & Precious Metals Fund, as of 1992, are $66.00, $34.00, $62.00, and $22.00, respectively. The analysis begins with a description of each of the four securities. (The fourth is actually a mutual fund that holds securities of firms that produce gold and other precious metals.)

Security Descriptions

American Home Products (AHP). American Home Products is a leading manufacturer of prescription and ethical drugs, specialty foods and candies, and proprietary drugs (infant formulas, cold remedies, etc). AHP's major products include Advil, Anacin, Dimetapp, Norplant, and Robitussin. The company is attempting to create niches that are protected from competition with other, larger drug companies. In a joint venture, it produces fetal heart monitoring equipment. Other areas include central nervous system and cell-trafficking drugs and drug delivery systems. Management's target growth rate is 15 percent.

Washington Water Power (WWP). Washington Water's revenues are distributed as 73 percent in electricity, 13 percent in gas, and 14 percent in various nonutility businesses. Earnings for the third quarter were well ahead of last year's, but Value Line expects the year-end total to about match that of 1992. WWP is expecting to increase earnings by acquisition of electric or gas operations. The firm also proposes to diversify into nonutility firms such as a natural gas marketing company and, perhaps, low-technology manufacturing operations.

The firm's dividend payout ratio is currently 96 percent. Earnings are expected to remain somewhat constant.

Wal-Mart Stores (WMT). Wal-Mart Stores is the largest U.S. retailing operation with its chain of modern discount retail stores in cities and towns in 43 states. It also operates a growing chain of Sam's Wholesale Clubs and Supercenters in metropolitan areas. The firm's main theme is to give customers "a good value." For the first nine months of the 1992 fiscal year, which ended January 31, store sales rose 12 percent despite a weak economy. Wal-Mart will probably remain strong as profits rose 25 percent in 1991 to 1992 and were expected to increase for 1992 to 1993 by 20 to 25 percent due to new openings. The new supercenter concept, which combines a full-line supermarket with a traditional Wal-Mart store, may provide more growth potential in the future.

Wal-Mart's recent P/E ratio of 34.1 is considered to be high by many investment advisors. The firm's recent stock price around $62 (before the stock split) may leave some growth potential.

Mainstay Gold & Precious Metals Fund (MN). Mainstay Gold & Precious Metals Fund is a mutual fund that specializes in securities of firms that produce gold and precious metals. The fund's holdings distribution between gold and various other precious metals varies from year to year.

Security Analysis Methods

Value Line gives recent beta estimates for the four stocks of 1.00, 0.55, 1.25, and −.20.[10] Also, data from Ibbotson Associates gives an average yield spread between the S&P 500 Index and the U.S. T-bill rate of 0.086.

Given these data and Equation 13.14, we can estimate the expected return for each of the four securities.

$$ER_i = RF + \beta_i(ER_M - RF) \tag{13.14}$$

For AHP, it equals:

$$ER_{AHP} = 0.07 + 1.0(0.086) = 0.156$$

For Washington Water Power it equals:

$$ER_{WWP} = 0.07 + 0.55(0.086) = 0.1173$$

For Wal-Mart it equals:

$$ER_{WMT} = 0.07 + 1.25(0.086) = 0.1775$$

For Mainstay Gold & Precious Metals Fund (MN) it equals:

$$ER_{MN} = 0.07 + -0.20(0.086) = 0.0528$$

Let's find these expected returns on an SML graph, Figure 13.9. Since the SML is the graph for Equation 13.14 (the CAPM), they must all lie on the SML.[11]

The first three securities, those with positive betas, lie on the SML, and their corresponding expected returns are greater than the risk-free rate, RF. What about Mainstay Gold & Precious Metals Fund with its negative beta? What does it mean to have a negative beta and a corresponding ERs less than RF? Though quite unusual, this is certainly possible. A negative beta means that the fund is negatively correlated with the market portfolio. This negative correlation can help to improve diversification benefits for the market portfolio. Remember the ultimate diversification benefit is derived from two assets that are perfectly negatively correlated (CORR = −1.0); this can reduce the combined portfolio risk to zero. To achieve this risk reduction, investors are willing to purchase the security even if it earns less than the risk-free rate, RF.[12]

Next, we calculate the predicted return for each security based on today's price, $P_{i,t}$, a predicted price a year from today, $P_{i,t+1}$, and expected dividends

[10]Interestingly, from 1987 to 1992 many small company growth funds had negative betas. Examples are Flag Investors Emerging Growth Fund (−0.18), Quest for Value Small Capitalization Fund (−0.25), Shearson Small Capital Fund (−0.31), and Warbug Pincus Emerging Growth Fund (−0.34).

[11]If an expected return doesn't lie on the line, you need to redo the calculations for Equation 13.14 or straighten your line.

[12]Why might gold and other precious metals tend to be negatively correlated with the market portfolio? Typically when a financial market is in a severe downturn (e.g., a war or a depression), financial assets are riskier, sometimes even worthless, and a greater demand for tradeable precious goods such as gold results. In Chapter 2 we reviewed evidence which showed that gold did well in the 1970s, while stocks did poorly. During the 1980s and early 1990s, stocks have outperformed gold, on average.

Figure 13.9

Security Market Line Analysis

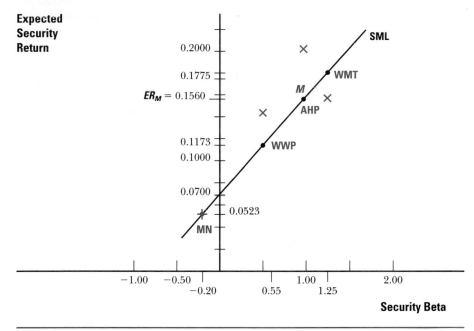

during the coming year, $DIV_{i,t+1}$. Table 13.1 provides the data for the four securities.

Predicted prices and dividends can be estimated by the procedure described in Chapter 11 on company analysis, which presented a procedure to estimate $P_{i,t+1}$ and $DIV_{i,t+1}$ in order to calculate $E(r_i)$. Of course, you may wonder whether every investor will make the same predictions. This is where Assumption 1, that all investors have homogeneous expectations, is important. Recall that this means that everyone has the same perceptions about securities and the market.

Now, this information will allow us to calculate an annual predicted holding period return, $E(r_i)$, for Security i. An expected return is calculated by Equation 11.19:

$$E(r_i) = (P_{i,t+1} - P_{i,t} + DIV_{i,t+1}) / P_{i,t} \tag{11.19}$$

Table 13.1

Price, Dividend, and Predicted Holding Period Return

Security Name	Today's Price, $P_{i,t}$	One-Year Predicted Price, $P_{i,t+1}$	Expected Dividends, $DIV_{i,t+1}$	Predicted Holding Period Return, $E(r_i)$
AHP	$66.00	$77.25	$2.60	0.2098
WWP	34.00	36.63	2.48	0.1406
WMT	62.00	71.75	0.21	0.1608
MN	22.00	23.16	0.00	0.0528

Note: Wal-Mart price reported here is not adjusted for its 2-for-1 stock split in 1992. $P_{i,t}$ are 1992 prices.

Table 13.2

Decision Rules for Fundamental Analysis and CAPM Analysis

Fundamental Analysis

$V_{i,0}$ is the intrinsic value of Security i.

$P_{i,0}$ is the current market price for Security i.

CAPM Security Analysis

ER_i is the expected return according to the CAPM.

$E(r_i)$ is the predicted return using the predicted market price, $P_{i,t+1}$, expected dividends, $DIV_{i,t+1}$, and the current price, $P_{i,t}$.

Decision Rules

$P_{i,0} < V_{i,0}$ implies $E(r_i) > ER_i$; Security i is undervalued.

$P_{i,0} > V_{i,0}$ implies $E(r_i) < ER_i$; Security i is overvalued.

Predicted holding period returns are calculated for each of the four securities.

$$E(r_{AHP}) = (77.25 - 66.00 + 2.60) / 66.00 = 0.2098$$
$$E(r_{WWP}) = (36.63 - 34.00 + 2.48) / 34.00 = 0.1503$$
$$E(r_{WMT}) = (71.75 - 62.00 + 0.22) / 62.00 = 0.1608$$
$$E(r_{MN}) = (23.16 - 22.00 + 0.00) / 22.00 = 0.0527$$

These predicted holding period returns are graphed onto Figure 13.9 with an X at the specified beta for each security. If the X lies above the SML [or $E(r_i) > ER_i$], the security is undervalued; if the X lies below the SML [or $E(r_i) < ER_i$), the security is overvalued. See Figure 13.9 again: AHP and WWP are undervalued and Wal-Mart is overvalued. Mainstay is priced as expected by the CAPM.

Since the CAPM is an ex-ante (or expectation) model, it provides estimates of an appropriate future return, for a given risk, from investing today. Comparing this value to an expected return based on current and future market data, $E(r_i)$ suggests a decision rule. If a security seems likely to have a higher return than its risk level justifies [$E(r_i) > ER_i$], then it is undervalued and a good investment. However, a lower return than its risk would justify [$E(r_i) < ER_i$], suggests that a security is overvalued, and not a good investment.

This analysis should sound familiar. It is just like the intrinsic value method of fundamental analysis. Recall from Chapter 8 that we estimated an intrinsic value of a security and then compared it with the traded price. A traded price higher than the intrinsic value characterized an overvalued security; a price lower than the intrinsic value characterized an undervalued security. SML analysis is just another form of fundamental analysis using percent returns instead of dollar values. However, since SML analysis measures predicted returns, it reverses the decision rule. Be careful not to confuse the two rules for SML and intrinsic value analyses! The two analyses and their decision rules are summarized in Table 13.2.

Why do SML and intrinsic value analysis reverse their decision rules? The reason is that we assume that all investors predict the same price a year from now, $P_{i,t+1}$. Given this predicted price, SML analysis calculates a predicted holding period return, $E(r_i)$. If the return is higher than the required return according to the CAPM, it plots above the line, indicating that an investor can earn more than expected. This also means that the investor paid less than expected, making the security undervalued and a bargain.

If all investors agree that AHP is undervalued, demand for AHP will rise, driving the current price upward. How high will it rise? It will go up to $69.074, a price that will allow investors to earn just 15.6 percent, the required return for the stock's market risk as calculated by the CAPM. Since current price (on which intrinsic value is based) and expected return (on which SML analysis is based) are inversely related, the decision rules are reversed.

The analysis might proceed to find the equilibrium price at which the investor would earn a just return. Solve Equation 11.19 for $P_{i,t}$.

$$E(r_i) = (P_{i,t+1} - P_{i,t} + DIV_{i,t+1})/P_{i,t} \qquad (11.19)$$

$$P_{i,t} = P_{i,t+1} + DIV_{i,t} / [1 + E(r_i)] \qquad (13.15)$$

To set $E(r_i)$ equal to the CAPM expected return, substitute ER_i for $E(r_i)$:

$$P_{i,t} = P_{i,t+1} + DIV_{i,t} / (1 + ER_i) \qquad (13.16)$$

It does make sense that the current price should just equal the present value of future cash flows, $P_{i,t+1}$ and $DIV_{i,t+1}$. For AHP this equals:

$$P_{AHP,t} = \$77.25 + \$2.60 / (1 + 0.156) = \$69.074$$

All of this relies on an accurate beta value. In the next section, we discuss how to estimate beta and introduce two new terms, the *security characteristic line* and the *market model*.

Estimating Beta

A beta estimate measures the changes of a security's return relative to the market return. A **security characteristic line** shows this graphically as the relationship between the return on the market portfolio, M, and a security return, $R_{i,t}$. The relationship can be estimated mathematically by a simple linear regression model called the **market model:**

$$R_{i,t} = a_i + b_i R_{M,t} + e_{i,t} \qquad (13.17)$$

where a_i is the y-intercept estimate of the regression, b_i is the slope estimate for the regression line (also referred to as *beta)*, $R_{M,t}$ is the return on the market portfolio in time t (usually measured in months or years), $R_{i,t}$ is the return on Security i in time t, and $e_{i,t}$ is a random error term for the variation of Security i's return around the regression line in time t.

Figure 13.10 graphs AHP monthly returns based on data from Table 13.3. The parameter estimates, using ordinary least squares regression, give this market model equation:

$$R_{i,t} = 0.012 + 0.66 R_{M,t} + e_{i,t}$$

A statistical package estimates a_i and b_i as 0.012 and 0.66. The slope coefficient, b_i, is the estimate of systematic risk or beta. This confirms beta's role as the measure of volatility relative to the market return. If the market return changes by 1 percent, AHP's return will change by 0.66 percent; this is just the definition of a slope. Alpha, a_i, also has a special interpretation; however, we reserve its detailed discussion until Chapter 15.

Figure 13.10

Regression Analysis to Estimate Beta

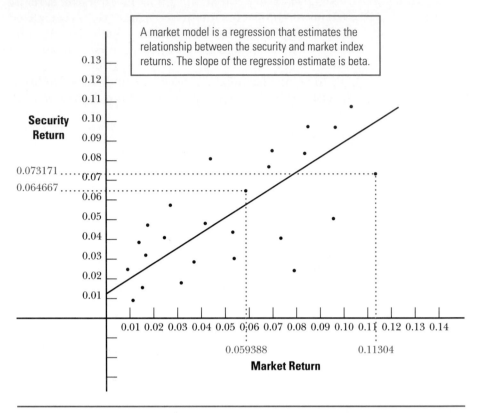

Information Service Beta Estimates

Many financial advisory firms such as Merrill Lynch, Value Line, and others provide estimates of beta. Table 13.4 displays a sample of securities and their betas, estimated by an ordinary least squares regression model. Notice that the utility stocks generally tend to have betas less than 1.0, the beta of the market portfolio. Since most consumption of gas and electricity is unrelated to market moves, these firms are typically not highly correlated to the market. Duke Power has a 0.11 beta while Washington Water Power has a 0.41 beta. Other betas are around 1.0 and some are much greater than 1.0; Charles Schwab's beta is more than twice the market level at 2.11. It makes sense for Schwab to be more volatile than the market as its business is pretty closely tied to trading volume, which tends to be high when the market is doing well. Betas tend to range from −0.9 to almost 4.0. Many high-technology firms have high betas, reflecting their participation in a risky, competitive industry. Advanced Micro Devices (2.04) and Hewlett-Packard (1.43) fall in this category. Securities with betas close to 1.0 are Lockheed (0.93), Philip Morris (0.89), Tootsie Roll (0.96), and Wal-Mart (1.07).

Calculating Beta: Separating Systematic Risk from Diversifiable Risk

Using the market model, one can calculate systematic risk and diversifiable risk. Recall the market model:

$$R_{i,t} = a_i + b_i R_{M,t} + e_{i,t}$$

Table 13.3

Monthly Returns for AHP and a Market Portfolio: 1987–1991

Date Mo-Date-Yr	AHP Return	Equally Weighted Market Portfolio	Date Mo-Date-Yr	AHP Return	Equally Weighted Market Portfolio
01-30-87	0.073171	0.113040	07-31-89	0.092838	0.050313
02-27-87	0.064667	0.059388	08-31-89	−0.029369	0.020558
03-31-87	−0.002874	0.025149	09-29-89	0.015152	−0.006380
04-30-87	−0.031700	−0.025751	10-31-89	0.037313	−0.057945
05-29-87	−0.006429	0.007515	11-30-89	0.026139	0.008758
06-30-87	0.030257	0.038271	12-29-89	0.014151	0.002764
07-31-87	0.058737	0.048282	01-31-90	−0.015116	−0.052310
08-31-87	0.049487	0.023300	02-28-90	−0.046517	0.010419
09-30-87	−0.086667	−0.017401	03-30-90	0.010013	0.020365
10-30-87	−0.170803	−0.256100	04-30-90	−0.052045	−0.043001
11-30-87	−0.058662	−0.051834	05-31-90	0.117124	0.059519
12-31-87	0.102273	0.061361	06-29-90	−0.007092	−0.001755
01-29-88	0.097938	0.067241	07-31-90	−0.033333	−0.018971
02-29-88	−0.007512	0.072515	08-31-90	−0.083005	−0.104746
03-31-88	−0.020734	0.013677	09-28-90	0.021739	−0.079007
04-29-88	0.013029	0.008756	10-31-90	0.045213	−0.044239
05-31-88	−0.051125	−0.009440	11-30-90	0.064377	0.061834
06-30-88	0.013722	0.061050	12-31-90	0.016908	0.014858
07-29-88	0.015228	−0.007524	01-31-91	−0.040380	0.091523
08-31-88	0.048667	−0.025668	02-28-91	0.140099	0.121503
09-30-88	0.027331	0.026990	03-28-91	0.026316	0.047543
10-31-88	0.037559	0.002575	04-30-91	0.010684	0.004984
11-30-88	−0.019306	−0.027984	05-31-91	0.009725	0.036212
12-30-88	0.035770	0.026101	06-28-91	0.008457	−0.041854
01-31-89	0.033033	0.060382	07-31-91	0.054507	0.030650
02-28-89	0.008430	−0.001611	08-30-91	0.038966	0.024877
03-31-89	0.002915	0.016004	09-30-91	0.052124	−0.005748
04-28-89	0.063954	0.037032	10-31-91	0.078899	0.010022
05-31-89	0.024317	0.034190	11-29-91	0.019048	−0.037694
06-30-89	0.016173	−0.002558	12-31-91	0.139731	0.063360

The variance of this relationship, SD_i^2, would equal:

$$SD_i^2 = \beta_i^2 SD_M^2 + SD_e^2$$

The previous equation has two terms. The first can be interpreted as a security's correlation with the market portfolio, or its systematic risk; the second term is interpreted as the portion of risk not explained by the independent variable, $R_{M,t}$. This is the firm-specific or diversifiable risk. To simplify the equation, substitute in the definition for beta (Equation 13.11):

$$\beta_i = (SD_i/SD_M)\text{CORR}(i,M)$$

This makes β_i^2 equal to:

$$\beta_i^2 = (SD_i^2/SD_M^2)(R^2)$$

where $\text{CORR}(i,M)^2$ is shortened to R^2. This means that the diversifiable risk, SD_e^2 must equal:

$$SD_e^2 = (1 - R^2)SD_i^2$$

This allows one to rewrite the total risk, SD_i^2, as:

$$SD_i^2 = R^2(SD_i^2) + (1 - R^2)(SD_i^2) \tag{13.18}$$

Table 13.4

Beta Estimates for Select Firms

Security	Beta	R-square	Residual Standard Deviation
Abbott Labs	0.71	0.37	0.0520
Advanced Micro Devices	2.04	0.42	0.1346
American Home Products	0.66	0.46	0.1094
Bank of America	1.18	0.29	0.1038
Barnett Banks	1.29	0.43	0.0848
Charles Schwab	2.11	0.44	0.1277
Chrysler	1.45	0.45	0.0908
Duke Power	0.11	0.01	0.0496
Hewlett-Packard	1.43	0.61	0.0652
Johnson & Johnson	0.86	0.52	0.0462
Kmart	1.41	0.69	0.0540
Lockheed	0.93	0.41	0.0637
Occidental Petroleum	0.82	0.42	0.0545
Orion Pictures	1.46	0.15	0.2000
Pennzoil	0.51	0.11	0.0831
Philip Morris	0.89	0.45	0.0561
Ralston Purina	0.58	0.31	0.0495
Tootsie Roll	0.96	0.39	0.0684
Toys-R-Us	1.19	0.54	0.0630
United Airlines	1.35	0.28	0.1238
Wal-Mart	1.07	0.61	0.0499
Washington Water Power	0.41	0.27	0.0380

R^2 is equal to $CORR(i,M)^2$ for a simple regression (one with just one independent variable). It ranges from 0.0 to +1.0. As R^2 approaches 1.0, the explanatory power of the independent variable for the dependent variable increases. This indicates how closely the security return correlates to the market return. A higher R^2 indicates a higher predictive power of the market return for the security return; this gauges the reliability of the beta estimate from the regression, helping the analyst to interpret Table 13.4.

Using the beta and R^2 data presented in Table 13.4 and Equation 13.18, one can separate total risk into its systematic and diversifiable components for AHP:

$$SD_i^2 = 0.46(0.054) + (1 - 0.46)(0.054)$$

This can be interpreted to mean that 46 percent of *AHP*'s total risk is systematic risk and 54 percent of total risk is firm-specific or diversifiable risk. The formula gives a convenient way to find how much of total risk can be eliminated in a well-diversified portfolio. Furthermore, in regression analysis, R^2 measures the explanatory power of the independent variable ($R_{M,t}$) for the dependent variable ($R_{i,t}$); this indicates how much of the variation of $R_{i,t}$ (denoted by $SD_{i,t}^2$) is explained by variation in $R_{M,t}$.

Having explained how to estimate beta, we can now show how to interpret its graphic representation, the security characteristic line. This will reduce the confusion between the SML and the security characteristic line. They appear very similar, but they perform different roles.

Differences between the SML and the Security Characteristic Line

The most obvious difference is the variables graphed by the x-axis and the y-axis. The SML displays expected return, ER_i, values for a cross-section of securities on the vertical axis and betas on the horizontal axis. It shows the relationship of *two variables* for many securities. In contrast, the security characteristic line measures a security's returns on the vertical axis and the market portfolio's returns (usually S&P 500 returns) on the horizontal axis, using time series data, which shows the relationship between the security's return and that of the market over time. The slope of the SML equals $(ER_M - RF)$ while the slope of the security characteristic line equals β_i. The y-intercept of the SML is the risk-free rate, RF, and the y-intercept of the security characteristic line equals a_i. Because the relationships are different, the uses of the lines differ, too.

The security characteristic line is primarily used to determine how a security return correlates to a market index return. The R^2 that results from regressing the security return on the market index return indicates how well the market index return can explain the security return. A higher R^2 indicates greater explanatory power. Its other use is to estimate beta, which is the slope of the security characteristic line.

The SML, in contrast, is used for estimating the required return for a security relative to its risk measured by beta, β_i. The β_i value for the SML comes from the slope estimate of the security characteristic line. The security characteristic line estimates beta, and the SML graphs it.

In Chapter 15, we will explain how to interpret the slope of the SML as a reward-per-risk measure called the *Treynor measure*. That chapter will show that the y-intercept of the characteristic line can be interpreted as a reward measure, too.

We conclude this chapter by reviewing some research studies and opinions about beta. What is the practical value of beta and what are some problems with beta?

Good News and Bad News about Beta

Of course, researchers and practitioners have estimated beta since its discovery and found some good news and some bad news. They have focused on two real issues. One is how well one can estimate beta; this is a purely statistical question. The other is how well one can predict future betas using past beta estimates. After all, the goal of security analysis is to measure its future systematic (beta) risk to determine what returns to expect.

Researchers and practitioners have found that a single measure of the actual relationship between a security return and the market portfolio return is dubious at best. They have found very little correlation between security returns and market portfolio returns, which beta attempts to measure. Table 13.4 listed low R^2 values, which evaluated the explanatory power of the market portfolio's return for a security return. Duke Power, for example, has an R^2 of 0.01 and most are below 0.50. (The maximum is 1.0.) Studies have found that portfolio betas have a much higher correlation with the market portfolio, so portfolio beta estimates may be more reliable than security beta estimates.[13]

The issue of measuring future betas can be addressed by summarizing Marshall Blume's study, "On the Assessment of Risk."[14] He shows that historical betas can be better predictors of future betas for large portfolios, even

---

[13]For a more complete discussion, see Fischer Black, Michael C. Jensen, and Myron Scholes, "The Capital Asset Pricing Model: Some Empirical Tests," in Michael C. Jensen, ed. *Studies in the Theory of Capital Markets* (New York: Praeger Publishers, 1972).

[14]Marshall Blume, "On the Assessment of Risk," *Journal of Finance* (March 1971), 1–10.

Beta Is Dead

Capital Ideas (Free Press, $24.95), by Peter Bernstein, the founder and first editor of the *Journal of Portfolio Management,* is a fine book and should be read by anyone wanting to understand modern Wall Street. Unfortunately for the book, almost as soon as it came out, the investment theory it highlights became discredited.

The book tells how the capital assets pricing model got its modest beginnings among a few upstart professors, took the rest of academia by storm, won Nobel Prizes for several economists, and in the process became standard operating procedure for institutional investors.

Bernstein's book was in bookstores only a few weeks when a revolutionary study was published by one of the heroes of Bernstein's story, University of Chicago Professor Eugene Fama. Fama and coauthor Professor Kenneth French discovered that beta, a central analytical tool of the capital assets pricing model, is worthless as an explanation of stocks' relative performance over time.

Beta is a scoring system that rates individual stocks according to their volatility. The theory holds that the only way you can beat the market is by buying high-beta stocks—which also means you take a lot of risk. Despite several decades of confident academic assertions to the contrary, Professors Fama and French found that high-beta stocks don't do any better than low-beta stocks.

So far, other than an article by fellow columnist David Dreman (FORBES, Mar. 30), the reaction to Fama and French's study has been remarkably muted, but it means that the foundation of much of Wall Street's research has been yanked away. It leaves finance departments and business schools with the unsavory prospect of teaching theories to their students and then having to concede that those theories are wrong.

All this is reassuring for the individual investor, however. Despite the theoretical anarchy in academia and the cries of anguish from computer jocks whose programs are now pointless, beta's death gives the investor new hope. No longer can market-beating strategies be dismissed on the grounds that they must have incurred above-market risks. No longer can promising approaches be ignored because they don't conform to theoretical orthodoxy.

One of the best illustrations of this need for theoretical humility is the diversity of approaches pursued by the four investment letters that have beaten the market since 1980, when the *Hulbert Financial Digest* began tracking the industry's performance. Not only are their approaches theoretically distinct, some actually contradict each other. But in a world that recognizes more than one road to riches, this need not pose a problem.

---

if they are unreliable for individual securities. His study correlated beta estimates for individual securities from July 1954 to June 1961 with estimates from July 1961 to June 1968. He found correlations for single security beta estimates for the two periods of only 0.60 with an R^2 value of 0.36; if the number of securities in a portfolio increased from one to two, however, the correlation also increased to 0.73 with an R^2 of 0.53. When Blume included 50 securities in a portfolio and estimated its beta over the same two time periods, he found that the correlation increased to 0.98.

Table 13.5 suggests that, as the number of securities in a portfolio increases, beta estimates become better predictors of subsequent-period beta estimates. Blume's study may suggest that historical betas are better predictors of future betas for mutual funds. However, other evidence suggests that mutual fund betas change because fund managers deliberately change the risk compositions of their funds. Remember, though, the risk level must still comply with the portfolio objective, so it should change only within limits.

To summarize, the good news may be that portfolio (and mutual fund) betas are relatively stable. Analysts can use them with some degree of confidence. Be wary of security beta estimates, however.

Academics and practitioners alike seem doubtful as to the value of beta as a risk measure. In a shocking confession, an article by Eugene Fama and Kenneth French states that beta is nearly worthless as an explanation of a stock's relative performance over time. They suggest that strategies based on investing in stocks with low price-to-book ratios and small-capitalization firms

For example, in first place since 1980 is Dan Sullivan's *The Chartist,* which utilizes only technical analysis. In second place is the *Value Line Investment Survey,* whose famed ranking system focuses on several different factors, such as price and earnings momentum. In third place is Martin Zweig's *The Zweig Forecast,* which uses a wide variety of technical, fundamental, and monetary indicators. And in fourth place is another Value Line service—*OTC Special Situations Survey,* which utilizes strictly fundamental valuation criteria.

That's pretty interesting, isn't it? Each of the four leading services uses an approach significantly different from the other three.

Or consider the outstanding performance of a newer letter. Editor Louis Navellier was trained in the intricacies of modern portfolio theory, and reportedly stopped short of completing his Ph.D. thesis only because he was impatient to begin applying his academic research to the investment world.

Navellier's success suggests that, even if beta is dead, the trip from gown to town is still worth making. Focusing on over-the-counter stocks, he has achieved a 37 percent compound annual return since the beginning of 1985 (when *HFD* began monitoring his performance), more than doubling the market's annualized total return over the same period. Navellier isn't surprised by Fama's findings. He tells me that his own

research found no more than about a 30 percent correlation between a stock's performance and its beta.

How can we make sense of all this? One finance professor remarks that, in the wake of the Fama/French study, his profession today is where Newtonian physics was prior to Einstein: waiting and searching for a theory that makes sense of the markets, recognizing that previous explanations are woefully inadequate.

As a monitor of investment letter performance, perhaps I'm biased, but I believe advisory letters have a valuable role to play. Innovation comes more easily to letter editors than to institutions. And the lesson of Bernstein's book and Fama's research is the need for innovation and keeping an open mind.

Most of the myriad letters out there won't beat the market. That's why it is so crucial to monitor their performance rigorously and objectively, so that we can discover those methods that genuinely have promise. But we're all better off because so many of them are willing to try.

Source: Mark Hulbert, "Beta Is Dead," *Forbes,* June 22, 1992, 239.

produce better long-term performance than strategies based on beta.[15] The favored strategies basically look for firms selling cheaply compared to the book values of their assets, while avoiding those that sell way above their asset values. Also, firms with smaller market values appear to outperform firms with larger market values. These findings reduce the analytical value of beta to the point that some favor ignoring it, as discussed in the Investment Insights feature.

Mark Hulbert, who follows investments newsletters, almost gleefully announces that "Beta Is Dead." He points out that beta is no longer regarded as sacred, allowing securities analysts to consider other strategies. Hulbert's work is to rank investment strategies; he feels this task is more important with the loss of beta.

Though there is merit to ranking performance, Hulbert needs to be careful not to mislead investors. To say that beta is dead, making his task all the more important, may seem to be biased. In fact, we must be careful with analysts who dismiss betas too quickly. It still serves a purpose of quantifying risk. Moreover, it's important to remember that ranking past performance provides some information, but what worked during the 1980s may not work in the 1990s. In Chapter 15, we will discuss whether a money manager's past performance can predict future performance.

[15]Eugene Fama and Kenneth French, "The Cross-Section of Expected Stock Returns," *Journal of Finance* (June 1992), 427–446.

Table 13.5

Correlation of Beta Estimates from One
Time Period to a Subsequent Period

Number of Securities in Portfolio	Correlation Coefficient[a]	R[2b]
1	0.60	0.36
2	0.73	0.53
4	0.84	0.71
7	0.88	0.77
10	0.92	0.85
20	0.97	0.95
35	0.97	0.95
50	0.98	0.96

[a]The correlation coefficient (CORR) ranges from -1.0 to $+1.0$ where $+1.0$ is a perfect correlation in which one variable (past beta) can perfectly predict the other (future beta).
[b]R^2 is the correlation coefficient squared. It has the same interpretation as the correlation but is limited to a range from 0.0 to $+1.0$.
Source: Marshall Blume, "On the Assessment of Risk," *Journal of Finance* (March 1971), 1–10.

In response to Hulbert, another practitioner, Peter Bernstein, wrote an article, which appears in a second Investment Insights feature. Bernstein cautions readers against totally dismissing beta. He summarizes the implications of Fama and French's study and writes that even if beta may be pronounced dead, it does not invalidate the importance of the risk/return relationship. As we have also emphasized, investors are smart enough to accept riskier investments only in exchange for compensation in the form of higher returns. (We have called it a *risk premium.*) Based on this premise, Bernstein notes that small-capitalization stocks are riskier, so their stock returns must be higher. Also, stocks of firms with low price-to-book ratios would not sell cheaply if these companies were "prospering and growing"; this suggests that these firms, too, are unusually risky investments.[16] Since risk is a very important factor in making investment decisions, even without a perfect measure of risk, one must incorporate some kind of risk measure to allow for these risk/return differences.

As Bernstein says, no one should despair just because beta was found to be less than perfect. It is still helpful in objectively quantifying risk and in recognizing a positive relationship between risk and return. Beta is still used by practitioners and academics alike. Recent developments have pointed out weaknesses, but they haven't invalidated the concept that higher risk implies a higher expected return. Finally, understanding how risk measures are developed is helpful in discovering an underlying meaning of risk.

The next chapter expands on the CAPM and relaxes some of its assumptions to determine a more general risk/return relationship. Chapter 14 also examines some empirical studies of the CAPM and shortfalls of the studies, and it develops another measure of the risk/return relationship using arbitrage as its driving force.

---

[16]We discussed this point back in Chapter 8 when we explained the role of the price-to-book ratio in security analysis.

If Beta Is Dead, Where Is the Corpse?

After Mark Hulbert's high compliment to my book, *Capital Ideas,* I hope I do not appear ungrateful if I take issue with his conclusions. He invokes the study by Professors Fama and French to assert that "beta's death gives the investor new hope. . . . No longer can market-beating strategies be dismissed on the grounds that they must have incurred above-market risks."

With all due respect, I think Mr. Hulbert may be reading more into the Fama–French study than is there.

The essential message of Fama–French is that long-term average returns are inversely correlated with price/book ratios and the size of a stock's market capitalization. In other words, small stocks do better than big ones, and stocks that sell cheaply relative to book value do better than those that sell at large premiums to book. As these two factors appear to dominate long-run performance, a stock's volatility relative to the market—its beta—loses its significance as a predictor of returns. As beta is often considered the most useful gauge of a stock's riskiness, the traditional linkage between risk and expected return appears to have crumbled. Hence, Mark Hulbert's good cheer.

Yet Fama–French cannot have sundered the relationship between risk and return unless we make the dangerous assumption that all investors are off their trolleys. Investors are not likely to take risks unless they expect returns above what they could expect on riskless investments. You do not drill for oil if all you can hope for is what a Treasury bill would provide. This requirement for higher returns from riskier investments pervades all investment decisions.

Consequently, investors tend to price riskier assets so that those assets will provide the higher returns demanded. In the long run and on the average, wildcat oil drillers earn more than investors in Treasury bills. When they do not, drilling dries up.

From this follows a second consequence. Predicting return is tough. But if return is related to risk, and if we can somehow measure risk, then risk will give us a guide to the probable rate of return! That upside-down use of the risk–return tradeoff is what lent beta its attraction. Fama–French's demonstration that beta is a poor predictor of return is the source of Mr. Hulbert's cry of joy.

INVESTMENT INSIGHTS

Yet beta has been moribund for some time as a predictor of returns, as many types of multifactor models have supplemented the single influence of the market on asset valuation. In addition, the current popularity of small-cap investing and of "value" strategies indicates that the professors were by no means the first to find an interesting road to the mother lode.

Thus, Mr. Hulbert neglects two elements of the Fama–French study. First, there is nothing in the Fama–French story to suggest that risk and return are unrelated. Fama and French focus on expected returns. The issue of whether small-cap and value stocks have outperformed because they are *riskier* than large companies and growth companies remains unresolved. This anomaly has haunted the Capital Asset Pricing Model, which is based on beta, for many years. But we do know that small companies are riskier than large companies. We also know that stocks do not sell at low prices relative to their assets if a company is prospering and growing. Although quantifying these risks is an elusive task, the Fama–French findings merely suggest that we do not yet have a good handle on calibrating risk.

Second, the implication that small-cap stocks and value stocks will *systemically* outperform after adjustment for risk flies in the face of common sense. The opposite conviction, that large-cap growth stocks would always outperform the market, led many prominent investment managers into Disasterville in the crash of 1974. These notions violate the one overriding lesson of investment theory: Do not put all your eggs in one basket. Tilting in one direction may be acceptable; abandoning diversification is perilous.

Investment is still a process of reaching decisions under conditions of uncertainty. Risk is still the dominant consideration for investors. The stock market is still a volatile arena that does not feature free lunches. You makes your choice, but never forget that you pays your money for doing so. There is nothing in Fama and French to contradict any of these truths or to overcome the nastiest truth of them all—that past performance, no matter how impressive, is no guarantee of future returns.

Source: Peter L. Bernstein, "If Beta Is Dead, Where Is the Corpse," *Forbes,* July 20, 1992, 343.

Chapter Summary

1. **Understand the capital market line (CML).**

   By making a few assumptions about rational investors and capital markets, and adding the risk-free asset, we can determine that all investors will choose M as their risky portfolio. The line that starts at the risk-free rate, RF, and extends to M is called the *capital market line* (CML). It is also called the *lending–borrowing line* because it distinguishes investors that lend and borrow at the risk-free rate, RF.

2. **Develop the Capital Asset Pricing Model (CAPM).**

   Since all investors will invest in the same risky portfolio, M, we can show that each security risk should be measured by its contribution to the risk of the well-diversified portfolio, M. The relative risk contribution of Security i to Portfolio M is defined by beta, β_i. This allows us to develop a model in which a security's expected return, ER_i, equals $RF + \beta_i(ER_M - RF)$.

3. **Contrast the standard deviation and beta risk measures.**

   We can now decompose the standard deviation, or total security risk, into two components: (1) systematic or beta risk, and (2) firm-specific or diversifiable risk. Since we assume that all investors hold well-diversified portfolios based on M, we can assume that they eliminate all diversifiable risk. Therefore, the only risk to consider for investment purposes should be the systematic risk.

4. **Apply the CAPM to security analysis.**

   First, calculate a security's expected return via the CAPM. This is the return that a security should earn, given its beta. Next, calculate the predicted holding period return, $E(r_i)$ and compare it to the expected return estimated from the CAPM, ER_i. If $E(r_i) > ER_i$, then the security is undervalued; if $E(r_i) < ER_i$, then the security is overvalued.

5. **Learn to estimate beta.**

   Beta is estimated by a regression estimation process called the ordinary least squares method. The independent variable is the return on a proxy for the market portfolio (usually the S&P 500 index): the dependent variable is the security's return. The slope of the resulting regression line equals beta.

6. **Review the good news and bad news about beta.**

   Research has found two items of bad news about beta. Security beta estimates have very low explanatory power, and the predictability of a future beta isn't very good. In fact, some academics and practitioners believe that beta has all but lost its usefulness. The good news is that portfolio beta estimates are relatively reliable predictors of future portfolio betas; for a portfolio of approximately 20 stocks, beta's predictability is approximately 90 percent or better. These news flashes imply that, even if beta's power over the investment community has waned, some risk measure is still necessary to make good investment decisions.

Key Terms

Capital Asset Pricing Model (CAPM)	Market portfolio
Risky portfolio	Beta
Capital market line (CML)	Security market line (SML)
Borrowing–lending line	Security characteristic line
Portfolio separation theorem	Market model

Mini Case **1**   OBJECTIVE

To conduct a security analysis using the SML.

An assistant has compiled the following data from various sources:

Security Name	Today's Price, $P_{i,t}$	Predicted Price After One Year, $P_{i,t+1}$	Expected Dividends, $DIV_{i,t+1}$	Beta, β_i
Hewlett-Packard (HP)	$78\frac{3}{8}$	$92	$1.00	1.43
Tootsie Roll (TOOT)	$70\frac{5}{8}$	77	3.55	0.96
Toys "Я" Us (TOY)	35	38	0.00	1.19

The market risk premium, taken from Ibbotson Associates data, equals 0.086 and the risk-free rate (T-bill rate) is 0.05.

1. What expected return does the CAPM give for each security?
2. Graph the SML and place each of the three securities along it.
3. Find the predicted holding period return, $E(r_i)$, for each security.
4. Which stocks are overvalued or undervalued? Display the results on the graph from question 2.
5. What will happen to Tootsie Roll's price? At what price will it be in equilibrium?
6. What will happen to the price of Toys "Я" Us? What is its equilibrium price?

Mini Case **2**   OBJECTIVE

To estimate betas and to interpret the market model regression.

The 60-monthly returns for three stocks are available on the data disk. Open file FINA3.XLS and, using software such as Lotus or Excel, run a market model regression. Answer the following questions.

1. The market model is:

$$R_{i,t} = a_i + b_i R_{M,t} + e_{i,t}$$

What are the beta estimates for Hewlett-Packard (HP), Tootsie Roll (TOOT), and Toys-R-Us (TOY)?
2. Interpret the R^2 values. How are they related to the correlation coefficient, CORR(i,M)?
3. What is the total risk for each security?
4. What can we say about each security's systematic and diversifiable risks?

Discussion Questions and Problems

1. How do Assumptions 1 through 5 help to develop the CAPM? Which ones are necessary and which just simplify the model?
2. You choose a risky portfolio, P3, with an expected return of 0.12 and a standard deviation of 0.15. The risk-free rate, RF, equals 0.05. You want to invest 20 percent in RF and 80 percent in P3.
   a. What is the RF–P3 portfolio's expected return?
   b. What is the portfolio's standard deviation?
   c. Draw the CML for Portfolio P3.
3. What is the significance of introducing the risk-free asset to the investment opportunity set?
   a. What theorem results from introducing the risk-free asset and what is the significance of the theorem?

b. What line results from the introduction of the risk-free asset?

c. What is the significance of Portfolio M in the line defined in Part b?

4. What two types of risk make up the standard deviation of a security return?

a. Discuss the two types of risk.

b. Why is only one relevant in the CAPM?

5. You expect UAL (United Airlines) to hit $170 per share with expected dividends of $2.00 per share in one year. Its current price is $148 and your research sets UAL's beta at 1.25. The market risk premium is 0.086 with T-bills yielding 0.06. Is UAL a good investment? Conduct a security analysis using the CAPM and explain your answer.

6. The correlation coefficient of GM with the market portfolio is +0.80, SD_{GM} is 45 percent, and SD_M is 40 percent. The correlation between Pepsi and the market portfolio is +0.50 and SD_{PEP} is 72 percent.

a. Calculate separate betas for GM and Pepsi.

b. Compare the two and explain the results.

c. What factors affect betas and what can we conclude about how they affect GM and Pepsi's betas?

7. You are given the following information about two mutual funds, A and B:

	Current Price	Expected Price	Expected Dividend	Estimated Beta
A	$53.50	$60.00	$2.00	1.10
B	76.75	82.00	1.00	0.80

$$(ER_M - RF) = 0.086 \qquad RF = 0.02$$

a. Estimate the expected returns using the CAPM.

b. Graphically, show the CAPM's expected returns for the market portfolio, the risk-free asset, and the two funds.

c. Represent the predicted returns on the graph with Xs. Is either fund overvalued or undervalued?

d. At what current price would the two funds be at equilibrium?

8. You expect stock of Firm C to sell for $100 a year from now and to pay a $5.00 dividend during the year. If the stock's correlation coefficient with portfolio M is +0.40, $SD_C = 50$ percent, $SD_M = 30$ percent, $RF = 6$ percent, and $ER_M = 15$ percent, at what price should the stock sell today? Explain your results.

9. You are interested in estimating IBM's beta. IBM's correlation with the Dow Jones Industrial Average is +0.85 and SD_{IBM} equals 40 percent while SD_{DJ} is 20 percent. You also decide to look into the Wilshire 5,000 stock index as a proxy for the market portfolio. SD_W is 25 percent and its correlation with IBM is +0.20.

a. Calculate IBM's beta with the Dow.

b. Calculate IBM's beta with the Wilshire 5,000.

c. Under what conditions would you use the Dow versus the Wilshire index?

10. The Dow's expected return is 30 percent and T-bills are yielding 10 percent. Suppose the expected return of the Wilshire 5,000 is 40 percent. Using the data given here and in Discussion Question 9, answer the following questions:

a. Draw an SML with the Dow as the market portfolio.

b. Draw an SML with the Wilshire 5,000 as the market portfolio on the same graph.

c. What is the drawback of using the wrong market index?

11. A security's standard deviation equals 20 percent and its market model results are summarized below:

$$R_{i,t} = 0.03 + 1.32R_{M,t} + \epsilon_{j,t}$$
$$R^2 = 0.35$$

  a. What is the correlation coefficient between Security i and the market portfolio?
  b. What is the security's beta?
  c. What are its systematic and diversifiable risks?

12. Firm XYZ, which invests in precious metals, has a beta of -0.54. What does it mean to have a negative beta? What are its benefits?

13. The following data for McDonald's (MAC), Waste Management (WM), and Abbott Labs (ABT) were compiled for your information:

	ER_i	Standard Deviation	Systematic Risk	Diversifiable Risk
MAC	0.10	0.122	0.068	0.054
WM	0.20	0.200	-0.005	0.205
ABT	0.05	0.080	0.075	0.005

Correlation coefficients: CORR(MAC, WM) = -0.60
CORR(MAC, ABT) = 0.25
CORR(WM, ABT) = 0.05

  a. If a client wants to invest equal proportions in only two securities, which two would you recommend? Answer the question without performing any calculations, based simply on your knowledge about portfolio theory. Explain in words.
  b. Suppose your client already holds a well-diversified portfolio such as the S&P 500 index. Which stock would you recommend? Why?
  c. Your client says that WM is far too risky with a standard deviation of 0.20, especially compared to the other two firms' standard deviations of 0.12 and 0.08. How would you address his concern? Carefully explain, assuming that your client holds a well-diversified portfolio.

14. What are the differences between the CML and the SML?

15. What are the differences between SML and the security characteristic line?

Critical Thinking Exercise

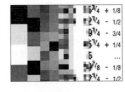

Open the file STKRET2.XLS on the data disk. The file contains quarterly returns for ten stocks along with a market index. It also contains *Value Line* estimates of the current prices, P_t, for the stock, expected earnings per share, EPS_{t+1}, expected dividends per share, DIV_{t+1}, and expected P/E ratios a year from today. Use the data and a spreadsheet program to answer the following questions:

1. Using the market model, estimate betas for the ten stocks.
2. If T-bills are yielding 0.04 and the market risk premium equals 0.086, estimate the expected return for each stock using the CAPM.
3. Using the *Value Line* information, each stock's predicted price, P_{t+1}, can be calculated by:

$$P_{t+1} = EPS_{t+1} \times P/E_{t+1}$$

Calculate each stock's predicted holding period return for the coming year.

4. Determine which stocks seem overvalued or undervalued. Explain.
5. Using the data provided and the expected return calculated in question 2, estimate each stock's price today.
6. Determine which stocks are currently overvalued or undervalued. Explain.
7. Show that the results of Parts 4 and 6 are consistent and really the same analysis.

Mini Case 1   SOLUTION

The case requires security analysis using the CAPM.

1. To find the expected return via CAPM, use Equation 13.13:

$$ER_i = RF + \beta_i(ER_M - RF)$$
$$ER_{HP} = 0.05 + 1.43(0.086) = 0.1730 \qquad (13.13)$$
$$ER_{TOOT} = 0.05 + 0.96(0.086) = 0.133$$
$$ER_{TOY} = 0.05 + 1.19(0.086) = 0.152$$

2. Graph the RF, the market portfolio, and the three securities on the SML. First, graph RF (0.05) with a zero beta and ER_M (ER_M = Market risk premium + RF = 0.086 + 0.05 = 0.136) with beta of 1.0.

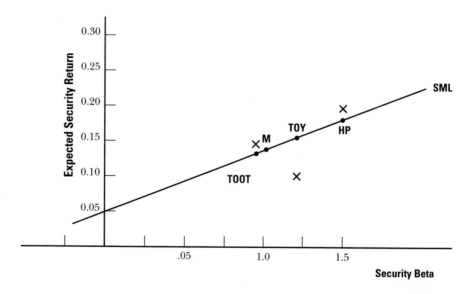

3. The holding period predicted return equals:

$$E(r_i) = (P_{i,t+1} - P_{i,t} + DIV_{i,t+1})/P_{i,t}$$

For each of the securities, it is:

$$E(r_{HP}) = (92.000 - 78.375 + 1.00)/78.375 = .187$$
$$E(r_{TOOT}) = (77.000 - 70.625 + 3.55)/70.625 = .141$$
$$E(r_{TOY}) = (39.000 - 35.000 + 0.00)/35.000 = 0.114$$

4. Stocks are undervalued if $E(r_i)$ lies above the SML, or $E(r_i) > ER_i$. They are overvalued, however, if they lie below the SML, or $E(r_i) < ER_i$. The sample stocks' ratings are summarized in the following table:

Stock	$E(r_i)$		ER_i	Valuation
HP	0.187	>	0.173	Undervalued
TOOT	0.141	>	0.133	Undervalued
TOY	0.114	<	0.152	Overvalued

Also note the X marks on the SML graph for the $E(r_i)$ values, as compared to the dots on the SML for the ER_i values.

5. Since the CAPM sets Tootsie Roll's appropriate expected return at 13.3 percent while its predicted return will be 18.3 percent, the demand for Tootsie Roll will rise and so will its price. Its equilibrium price is:

$$P_{i,t} = \frac{P_{i,t+1} + DIV_{i,t+1}}{(1 + ER_i)} = \frac{\$77 + \$3.55}{(1 + 0.133)} = \$71.094$$

The price will rise from \$70.625 to \$71.094, which will provide the appropriate 13.3 percent expected return.

6. Since Toys "Я" Us is overvalued at \$34.875, investors will sell the stock; as demand declines, so will the price until the expected return rises from 11.4 percent to 15.2 percent. Its equilibrium price is:

$$P_{i,t} = \frac{P_{i,t+1} + DIV_{i,t+1}}{(1 + ER_i)} = \frac{\$39.00 + \$0.00}{(1 + 0.152)} = \$33.854$$

The price will fall from \$35.000 to \$33.854 in order to earn the expected 15.2 percent return.

Mini Case **2**   SOLUTION

The problem requires a regression package to run the market model and to interpret the results.

1. The data on the diskette report 60 monthly returns for three securities and a proxy for the market portfolio. The regression results for the market model are:

	$R_{i,t} = a_i + b_i R_{M,t} + e_{i,t}$	R^2	$SD(e_{i,t})$	$SD(R_{i,t})$
HP	$R_{HP,t} = -0.0024 + 1.43R_{M,t} + e_{HP,t}$	0.61	0.0652	0.1032
TOOT	$R_{TOOT,t} = 0.0151 + 0.96R_{M,t} + e_{TOOT,t}$	0.39	0.0684	0.0867
TOY	$R_{TOY,t} = 0.0087 + 1.19R_{M,t} + e_{TOY,t}$	0.54	0.0630	0.0917

The beta estimates are just slope estimates of the market model regressions.

	Beta Estimate
HP	1.43
TOOT	0.96
TOY	1.19

2. R^2 measures the explanatory (or predictive) power of $R_{i,t}$ by the independent variable, $R_{M,t}$. It explains perfectly when R^2 equals 1.00. The market has the highest explanatory power for HP at 61 percent and the lowest for TOOT at 39 percent. The $\sqrt{R^2}$ equals R, the correlation coefficient, which measures the degree of diversification benefits. (Remember, a lower correlation implies a greater benefit of holding the well-diversified portfolio, M.) The correlations are 78 percent ($\sqrt{0.61}$) for HP, 62 percent

($\sqrt{0.39}$) for TOOT, and 73 percent ($\sqrt{0.54}$) for TOY. This says that TOOT has the greatest diversification benefit, through differences between the three stocks aren't significant.

3. The total risk of a security is just the standard deviation of the security's return, $SD(R_{i,t})$. As shown in the table above, the total risk values are: 0.1032 for HP, 0.0867 for TOOT, and 0.0917 for TOY.

4. As shown in the chapter, total risk includes systematic risk and diversifiable risk components, in the formula:

$$
\begin{aligned}
SD_i^2 \quad & = \text{Systematic risk} + \text{Diversifiable risk} \\
& = R^2 SD_i^2 + (1 - R^2) SD_i^2 \\
SD_{HP}^2 \quad & = (0.61)(0.0107) + (1 - .61)(0.0107) \\
& = 0.0065 + 0.0042 \\
SD_{TOOT}^2 & = (0.39)(0.0075) + (1 - 0.39)(0.0075) \\
& = 0.0029 + 0.0046 \\
\\
& = (0.54)(0.0084) + (1 - 0.54)(0.0084) \\
& = 0.0045 + 0.0039
\end{aligned}
$$

Therefore, the systematic risk values are 0.0065 for HP, 0.0029 for TOOT, and 0.0045 for TOY while the diversifiable risk values are 0.0042 for HP, 0.0046 for TOOT, and 0.0039 for TOY. As expected, HP has the highest systematic risk (0.0065) as its correlation is highest with M (78 percent), while TOOT has the highest diversifiable risk (0.0046) because its correlation is the lowest (62 percent).

Chapter 14

Extensions of Capital Asset Pricing Theory[1]

───▶

Chapter Objectives

1. Develop an understanding of the zero-beta portfolio model.
2. Overview some empirical tests of the CAPM.
3. Review Roll's critique of the CAPM.
4. Understand Arbitrage Pricing Theory (APT).

We spent quite a bit of time and energy developing the Capital Asset Pricing Model (CAPM) in Chapter 13. The final results can be summarized as follows:

1. Securities are priced in relation to their beta risk levels because all rational investors hold well-diversified portfolios equivalent to the market portfolio.
2. A security's total risk (standard deviation) is composed of two types of risk, beta risk and diversifiable risk.
3. Beta is estimated by a market regression model.
4. Beta estimates can accurately predict future portfolio betas but not individual securities' betas.

In this chapter we turn to several other issues which can be viewed as extensions, or empirical tests, of the Capital Asset Pricing Model. Three issues are discussed, grouped under three topics: modifications of the CAPM, empirical tests and critiques of the CAPM, and Arbitrage Pricing Theory (APT).

The first section deals with practical modifications to the CAPM. Recall that Chapter 13 required several restrictive assumptions to derive the CAPM. We discuss the Black's zero-beta model, which drops one particular assumption: that investors can borrow and lend at the risk-free rate.[2] This less restrictive model seems to produce results that conform more closely than those of the CAPM to empirical market performance.

This leads to a discussion of empirical tests of the CAPM and the more robust zero-beta model, followed by a critique of the CAPM. This section

───────────────────────────

[1]This chapter covers advanced material and can be omitted without loss of continuity.

[2]Fischer Black, "Capital Market Equilibrium with Restricted Borrowing," *Journal of Business,* July 1972, 444–455.

outlines the steps required to conduct the empirical tests to develop a clear idea of the procedures adopted by researchers and some appreciation of their tremendous efforts.

Although we've already discussed some of the problems with the CAPM in Chapter 13, the second section also deals with Roll's critique of the CAPM and its empirical tests.[3] Roll mathematically proves that the CAPM cannot be empirically tested (in spite of all the tests that researchers have conducted). His critique provides some insights on what researchers can test and what they have actually tested.

Finally, given the state of CAPM, the third section reviews Ross's alternative security pricing model called *Arbitrage Pricing Theory (APT)*.[4] Ross uses the principle of arbitrage to develop a model with several factors and corresponding betas to price securities. The model's premise states that identical assets (assets of similar risk) must sell at identical prices. Stated differently, it says that each security return can give a price based on a linear combination of factors (or portfolios) that mimic that security's return. If the risk for the security and the linear combination of portfolios are equal, but the returns aren't, then the market will arbitrage the profits away to set identical prices for all identical assets. The last section of the chapter will elaborate on the concept of APT.

Now let's start with the zero-beta model, which is a modification of the CAPM.

Modifications of the CAPM

As you may have noted, some of the assumptions required for the CAPM seem very restrictive (see p. 440 of Chapter 13). One particularly unlikely assumption states that all investors can borrow or lend at the risk-free rate, *RF.* If investors cannot all borrow at the same risk-free rate, some may choose risky portfolios based on their risk–return preferences (utility curves). This returns asset pricing theory to square one; recall that introducing the risk-free rate separated the objective choice of all investors to invest in Portfolio M from the subjective choices of percentages to invest in the risk-free asset and Portfolio M.[5] A common rate at which investors can borrow or lend allows them to adjust these percentages to achieve their own preferred combinations of risk and return. Without the common rate, they must choose different risky portfolios to meet their individual needs.

To address this problem, Black suggests that each investor creates a personal combination of the chosen risky portfolio, *P*, and a portfolio of stocks that is uncorrelated to Portfolio P, as shown in Figure 14.1. The portfolio that is uncorrelated to P is called the **zero-beta portfolio.** The zero-beta portfolio consists of a combination of securities that has a beta equal to zero, or that has a zero correlation to the chosen risky portfolio, P. The expected return of the zero-beta portfolio $ER[Z(P)]$, is calculated as the weighted average return of all the securities in the portfolio. Notice that each risky portfolio has a different zero-beta portfolio associated with it. For example, consider P_1 and P_2 in Figure 14.1. An investor who chooses risky portfolio P_1 will choose $Z(P_1)$ as the uncorrelated, zero-beta portfolio with expected return

[3]Richard Roll, "A Critique of the Asset Pricing Theory's Tests," *Journal of Financial Economics,* June 1977, 129–176.

[4]Steven Ross, "Return, Risk, and Arbitrage," ed. by I. Friend and J. Bicksler, in *Risk and Return in Finance,* vol. 1 (New York: Ballinger Publishing, 1976).

[5]Go back to reread pp. 442–446 for a quick refresher, if you need to.

Figure 14.1

Zero-Beta Portfolio Model

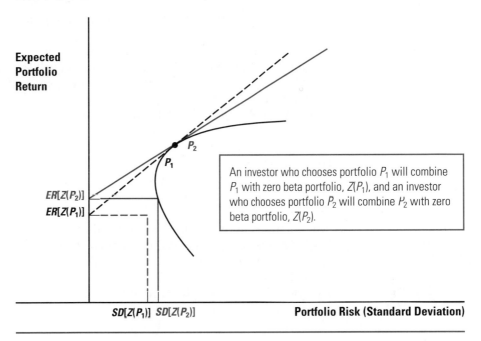

An investor who chooses portfolio P_1 will combine P_1 with zero beta portfolio, $Z(P_1)$, and an investor who chooses portfolio P_2 will combine P_2 with zero beta portfolio, $Z(P_2)$.

$ER[Z(P_1)]$ and risk $SD[Z(P_1)]$. Notice that $Z(P_1)$ may differ from the risk-free rate. This is a result of dropping the assumption that investors can borrow and lend at the risk-free rate, RF.

Black's model has three major implications:

1. Any combination of the portfolios on the efficient frontier will also be on the efficient frontier.
2. Any efficient portfolio, like P_1 or P_2 in Figure 14.1, will have associated with it a zero-beta portfolio. The expected return of this zero-beta portfolio is found by the intersection of tangent line from P_1 or P_2 with the y-axis; its standard deviation is found by drawing a horizontal line from the intersection to the efficient frontier.
3. The expected return of any security, i, can be expressed as a linear relationship of any two efficient portfolios, such as P_2 and P_1. The relationship is:

$$ER_i = ER_{P1}$$
$$+ [ER_{P2} - ER_{P1}] \left[\frac{COV(i,P_2) - COV(P_1,P_2)}{SD^2(P_2) - COV(P_1,P_2)} \right] \quad (14.1)$$

These implications are sufficient to derive the zero-beta model. To find a market equilibrium risk–return relationship, aggregate the efficient risky portfolio choices of all investors; this becomes the market portfolio. Since any combination of efficient portfolios is itself efficient, the market portfolio identified in this way must be efficient. Into Equation 14.1, substitute the market portfolio, M, for the risky portfolio, P_2, and the market portfolio's zero-beta portfolio, $Z(M)$, for P_1. Note also that $COV[M,Z(M)]$ equals 0.0 by definition. By rearranging terms, Equation 14.1 simplifies to:

$$ER_i = ER[Z(M)] + \{ER_M - ER[Z(M)]\} \left[\frac{COV(i,M)}{SD_M^2} \right] \quad (14.2)$$

Recognize that $COV(i,M)/SD_M^2$ is beta, β_i. This gives a revised expression of the risk–return relationship as:

$$ER_i = ER[Z(M)] + \beta_i\{ER_M - ER[Z(M)]\} \qquad (14.3)$$

Figure 14.2 provides a graphic example of the *Zero-Beta Model* described by Equation 14.3. Notice that the beta still equals 1.0 for the market portfolio; however, the *y*-intercept is equal to the expected return for the zero-beta portfolio, $ER[Z(M)]$, and the slope equals $ER_M - ER[Z(M)]$.

This is similar to the CAPM expressed in Equation 13.14. In fact, Equation 14.3 is simply a more general expression of the risk–return relationship.[6] If the CAPM truly defines the relationship between risk and return, then, empirically, the return on the zero-beta portfolio should equal RF. To determine whether $ER[Z(M)]$ equals *RF*, first define the market portfolio, *M*, then mathematically solve for the associated zero-beta portfolio. For practitioners, this implies the possibility of a linear risk-return relationship, even if the *y*-intercept of the equation doesn't equal the risk-free rate. Simply identify a market index portfolio, and then mathematically solve for the return on the zero-beta portfolio, which need not equal *RF*.

In the next section, we will outline the procedures by which researchers have empirically tested the CAPM. In that process, they have also tested the Zero-Beta Model simply by determining whether or not $ER[Z(M)]$ equals *RF*. If not, a test would support the Zero-Beta Model, but not the CAPM.

Empirical Tests and Critique of the CAPM

Empirical Tests

Once a theory is developed, researchers need to test the model to determine how valid it is. To put it more scientifically, tests must evaluate whether the hypothesis implied by the model can be refuted empirically. Before we discuss the procedure for testing the CAPM, let's talk about the implications being tested; that is, what is testable about the CAPM?

Unfortunately, along with its apparently unrealistic assumptions, any test of the CAPM must evaluate two implications jointly. That is, if the data contradict the theory, the problem could arise from either implication or both. The two implications of the CAPM are that:

1. The risk–return relationship is consistent with the data.
2. The market is efficient.

The first implication is straightforward; what about the second? Remember, one of the major requirements of CAPM is that the efficient market prices securities based on all information and market equilibrium prevails. The second implication of the CAPM is important because empirical testing assumes that securities are at equilibrium; an empirical test cannot tell failure due to a deficient model from failure due to market disequilibrium. If empirical tests find evidence rejecting the CAPM, they could have three consequences: (1) reject the CAPM, (2) label the market inefficient, or (3) both.

Given the evidence provided in Chapter 7 on market efficiency, it may be safe to assume that the market is relatively efficient and proceed with empir-

---

[6]This is generally the case. Relaxing assumptions makes a model more general, with the more restrictive model as a subset. Remember, this version of the asset pricing model no longer assumes that all investors can borrow or lend at the risk-free rate, *RF*.

Figure 14.2

Zero-Beta Portfolio Model

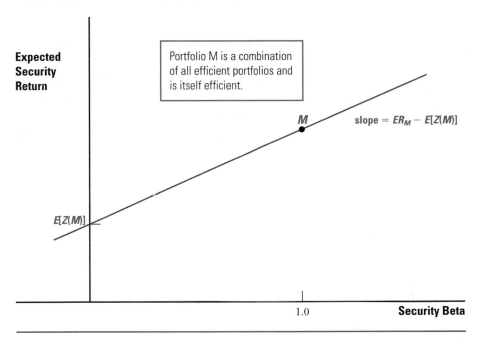

ical testing. This jump past market efficiency is possible because the testing will consider several hundred *randomly* selected securities, which should eliminate any systematic inefficiencies such as small-firm effects or low-P/E effects.[7]

Several researchers have conducted empirical tests of the CAPM.[8] The empirical studies have followed a similar series of basic steps. First, a typical test uses the market model in a regression of excess returns for a Security i on the excess return for the market portfolio, $(R_{M,t} - RF_t)$, over a 60-month period. (**Excess return** is defined as the difference between the risk-free rate and the return on Security i or $R_{i,t} - RF_t$.) This is often called the **first pass regression** because it is the first of two regressions in the CAPM empirical testing procedure. It estimates the beta for each Security i. The test must run this regression individually for several hundred securities, with each **time series regression** equal to:

$$(R_{i,t} - RF_t) = a_i + b_i(R_{M,t} - RF_t) + e_{i,t} \qquad (14.4)$$

Recall from the discussion of the market model that a time series regression compares time-based data (e.g., returns over 60 months) for a single variable (e.g., $R_{i,t}$).

In the second step of a test of the CAPM, the estimated beta values, b_j, serve as independent variables for **cross-sectional regressions** which regress securities' mean excess returns $M(R_{j,t} - RF_t)$ on their b_j values. This is called the **second pass regression** because it is the second set of regressions run to test the CAPM.

[7]Remember that the small-firm or low-P/E effects can skew results only if securities are sorted by size or P/E.

[8]Two of the first empirical studies are: J. Lintner, "Security Prices, Risk, and Maximal Gains from Diversification," *Journal of Finance,* December 1965, 587–615; and M. H. Miller and M. Scholes, "Rate of Return in Relation to Risk: A Reexamination of Some Recent Findings," in *Studies in the Theory of Capital Markets,* ed. M. C. Jensen (New York: Praeger Publishers, 1972).

The cross-sectional regression equals:

$$M(R_{i,t} - RF_t) = \gamma_0 + \gamma_1 b_i \qquad i = 1,2,3, \ldots, N \qquad (14.5)$$

where N equals the number of securities in the sample, $M(R_{i,t} - RF_t)$ is the mean of the security return minus the risk-free rate (T-bill rate) over the entire testing period; b_i is the estimated beta from the first pass regression; γ_0 is the y-intercept of the second pass regression; and γ_1 is the slope of b_i. This is a cross-sectional regression because the regression data consist of several hundred securities' returns regressed on their corresponding beta values, b_i.

A second independent variable, SD_e^2, which represents diversifiable or firm-specific risk, is added to determine whether this factor affects security returns. This gives the following regression:

$$M(R_{i,t} - RF_t) = \gamma_0 + \gamma_1 b_i + \gamma_2 SD_e^2 \qquad (14.6)$$

The theoretical CAPM model in Chapter 13 is stated as:

$$ER_i = RF + \beta_i(ER_M - RF) \qquad (13.14)$$

This can be rewritten as:

$$ER_i - RF = \beta_i(ER_M - RF)$$

If the mean excess return for the security estimates the ex-ante expected excess return for the security, then Equation 14.6 equals Equation 13.14. Therefore, if the CAPM correctly describes the risk–return relationship for securities, then:

$$\gamma_0 = 0 \qquad \gamma_1 = (ER_M - RF) \qquad \gamma_2 = 0$$

Unfortunately, the empirical results are far from satisfying. Lintner and Miller and Scholes both found that:

1. γ_0 was statistically significantly different from zero.
2. γ_1 was statistically significantly less than the mean market portfolio excess return, or $M(R_{M,t} - RF)$.
3. γ_2 was statistically significantly different from zero.

This should not provoke despair, however. Black, Jensen, and Scholes suggested that the poor results could have been due to measurement errors for b_i values, which served as independent variables in the second pass regressions.[9] These authors reasoned that measurement errors in the b_i estimates caused biases in the second pass regression, and hence reduced the power of the tests. They improved the empirical technique by evaluating security portfolios instead of individual securities in the second pass regressions. The researchers created a three-step procedure to reduce estimation errors and applied the new technique to data from 1931 to 1965.

Step 1. Based on 60 months of return data (e.g., from 1931 to 1935) for each security, estimate a security beta. If the sample includes 600 securities, rank the estimated 600 security betas in descending order. Divide these betas into 10 portfolios and identify the firms that belong in each portfolio.

---

[9]F. Black, M. C. Jensen, and M. Scholes, "The Capital Asset Pricing Model: Some Empirical Tests," *Studies in the Theory of Capital Markets,* ed. M. C. Jensen (New York: Praeger Publishers, 1972).

Figure 14.3

Empirical Findings for the CAPM

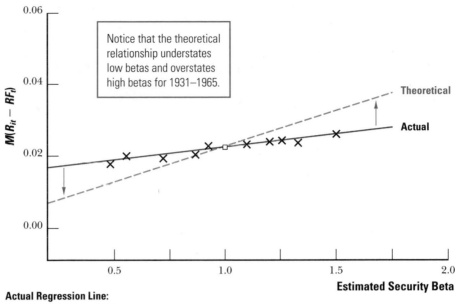

Notice that the theoretical relationship understates low betas and overstates high betas for 1931–1965.

Actual Regression Line:
$$M(R_{it} - RF_t) = 0.00359 + 0.01080\ b_i + e_i$$

Source: F. Black, M. C. Jensen, and M. Scholes, "The Capital Asset Pricing Model: Some Empirical Tests," *Studies in the Theory of Capital Markets,* ed. M. C. Jensen (New York: Praeger Publishers, 1972).

Step 2. Estimate betas for the 10 portfolios created in Step 1. Conduct the regression on results for a different time period (e.g., 1936 to 1940) so that the measurement errors for security betas are independent of any measurement errors in portfolio betas. This is the first pass regression described earlier. Estimating betas for portfolios reduces the variance of the error term or SD_e^2. Stated differently, portfolios are more highly correlated with the market portfolio than with individual securities.

Step 3. Run the second pass regression on the 10 portfolios' excess returns, averaged over another time period (e.g., 1941).

Figure 14.3 summarizes the results. Black, Jensen, and Scholes found that the theoretical CAPM relationship understated low betas and overstated high betas over the period from 1931 to 1965. The Zero-Beta Model seemed to fit the data better than the CAPM, though it did not give totally consistent results. The researchers also found that the average zero-beta portfolio return is much greater than the risk-free rate. Undaunted by the poor findings, these authors continue to pursue the modified version of the CAPM, or the Zero-Beta Model.

The major difficulty with this test of the CAPM is the use of ex-post data to evaluate ex-ante returns. Even if the test results are less than perfect, therefore, one could attribute the difference to the fact that historical data do not determine ex-ante results. For example, Black, Jensen, and Scholes split their second pass regression over several subperiods. They found that from April 1957 to December 1965, ex-post data gave a regression line with a slightly negative slope, as displayed in Figure 14.4. In reality, of course, a negative risk–return relationship is impossible. Would you invest in a security for which you expected a lower return for greater risk? In an efficient market, investors would sell those securities, forcing their prices to decline until the

Figure 14.4

Empirical Findings for the CAPM: April 1957 to
December 1965

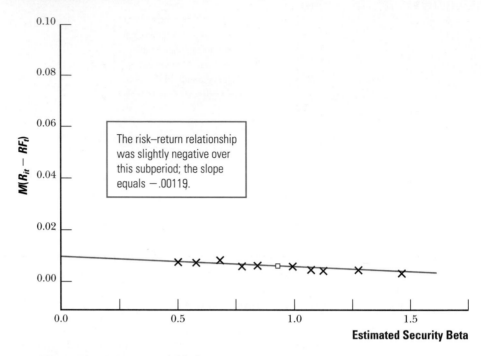

> The risk–return relationship
> was slightly negative over
> this subperiod; the slope
> equals −.00119.

$$M(R_{it} - RF_t) = 0.01020 + -0.00119\, b_i + e_i$$

Source: F. Black, M. C. Jensen, and M. Scholes, "The Capital Asset Pricing Model:
Some Empirical Tests," *Studies in the Theory of Capital Markets,* ed. M. C. Jensen (New
York: Praeger Publishers, 1972).

securities earned returns commensurate with their risk levels. This result just
emphasizes the fact that expectations (like the weather forecasts) may not
match actual results.

We have reviewed some obvious problems revealed by empirical tests of
the CAPM. The next section will outline even more damaging evidence from
these kinds of empirical tests.

Critique of the CAPM

To add to the chorus of detractors, Richard Roll provides a critique of the
CAPM and creates doubt about the value of empirical testing and results of
CAPM.[10] His critique can be summarized in six premises.

1. Limits on Tests. The only testable implication from the CAPM is whether
the market portfolio is mean-variance efficient, that is, whether it lies on the
efficient frontier.

2. Linear Risk–Return Relationship. If the market portfolio is mean-variance efficient, then mathematical relationships require that the beta
risk–return relationship (graphed by the SML) is exactly linear. Once the
market portfolio is established as efficient, then the second pass regression

---

[10]Richard Roll, "A Critique of the Asset Pricing Theory's Tests," *Journal of Financial Economics,*
June 1977, 129–176.

Figure 14.5

Different Well-Diversified Portfolios and Their Corresponding SMLs

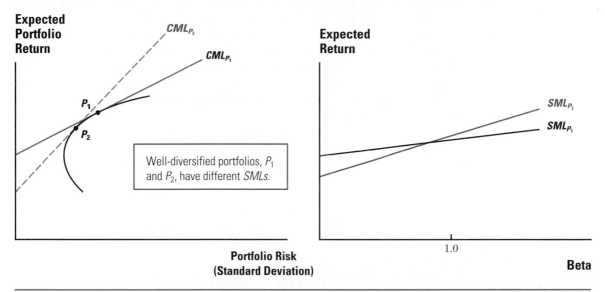

adds nothing; the relationship must be linear. However, this creates further problems, outlined in the next three premises.

3. Market Portfolio Composition. The true composition of the market portfolio is unobservable, so it's not possible to test the first two premises accurately. Conceptually, the true market portfolio should consist of all traded assets, which includes common stocks, bonds, preferred stocks, real estate, art, and all other traded assets. Could professional baseball, basketball, and football players fall under the category of traded assets?

4. Range of SMLs. The vast market proxies offer an infinite number of ex-post mean-variance efficient portfolios, each with an SML that tracks an exact linear beta risk–return relationship. Essentially, every efficient portfolio has a different SML. Therefore, each Security i has a different beta estimate, based on the efficient portfolio with which it is correlated. Using different sample portfolios as market proxies, even if they are mean-variance efficient, will produce different beta esitmates for each security; these differences can be significant. Figure 14.5 displays individual SMLs for two different efficient portfolios, P1 and P2 (SML_{P1} and SML_{P2}).

5. Market Efficiency Effects. In a nutshell, Roll states that using a substitute, such as the S&P 500 index, for the market portfolio creates two problems:

1. Even if the proxy is mean-variance efficient, it doesn't accurately represent the true market portfolio.
2. Even if the proxy is not efficient, the true market portfolio may still be efficient.

6. Conflicts between Proxies. Finally, more confusion may arise when different substitutes for the true market portfolio may be very closely correlated, even though some may be efficient while others are not. This difference leads to different conclusions with regard to the beta risk–return relationship. Remember, efficient portfolios give perfectly linear beta risk–return relationships, while inefficient portfolios give linear estimates that aren't perfect fits.

What can we conclude about the empirical test results presented earlier? The empirical tests confirmed only that their substitutes for the market portfolio were not mean-variance efficient. The researchers certainly did a lot of work, but they didn't test the CAPM!

Roll convincingly showed that the CAPM is untestable, but this does not make it valueless. The general agreement is that the CAPM has its merits and should be used carefully. Though some controversy remains about its merits, it is still regarded as a useful tool by many. It does provide a theoretical justification for the risk–return relationship and it does describe a quantifiable measure of risk. Though the CAPM's beta must be used very cautiously, some will argue that having an inexact quantifiable risk measure is better than having none at all. Peter Bernstein's comments in the Chapter 13 Investment Insights feature summarize the consensus; the CAPM is a useful framework in which to see how riskier investments provide higher returns.[11]

While Roll was adding to the demise of the CAPM, Stephen Ross was developing an alternative way to look at asset pricing. His work culminated in the Arbitrate Pricing Theory (APT), discussed in the next section.

Arbitrage Pricing Theory (APT)

Given the theoretical and empirical problems with the CAPM, some researchers have turned to alternative theories to explain asset pricing. Ross has used the old idea of arbitrage to develop another way to view asset returns. The resulting Arbitrage Pricing Theory (APT) is another way to price securities. While its final equation seems to be an extension of the CAPM, its logical development is different. The CAPM stems from utility theory concepts of investor preference for risk and return, while APT is built on the principle of arbitrage.

Concept of Arbitrage

The general **arbitrage principle** states that two identical securities (or goods) will sell at identical prices. Another way of stating the same thing is to say that if one invests nothing, one should get nothing in return.[12]

Although this sounds pretty straightforward, an example can help illustrate its application to securities. Remember the concept of selling short? Suppose one could borrow a stock with no margin requirements or transaction costs and sell it for $69. The proceeds of the sale could finance a purchase of the stock for $69. This would constitute a zero investment, and it would generate zero profits; for every dollar gained (or lost) in the long position, the investor would lose (or gain) the same amount in the short position. For instance, if the example stock were to rise to $70, the long position would make $1, but the short position would lose $1. This eliminates any possibility of profits from arbitrage. Investing nothing gains nothing.

Now look at an example that offers arbitrage opportunities, but still requires no investment. The theory holds that this situation will disappear quickly as arbitragers' trades drive prices toward equilibrium. Suppose that two stocks, A and B, have identical risk levels. If Stock A is expected to earn 12 percent and Stock B 10 percent, careful trading can create arbitrage prof-

---

[11]Peter Bernstein's article, "If Beta Is Dead, Where Is the Corpse?" is reprinted in Chapter 13.

[12]This sounds similar to the old adage, "nothing lost, nothing gained," or the slogan from aerobics classes: "no pain, no gain."

its. Since all investors perceive Stocks A and B to have identical risk, an arbitrager can sell short \$100 of B and invest long \$100 in A and receive a \$2 in arbitrage profits:

	Today	One Year Later
Short position in B	\$100	\$100(1 + 0.10 = (\$110)
Long position in A	(100)	\$100(1 + 0.12) = 112
Investment	0	Net profits \$2

Of course, if this is a sure thing, why stop with \$100? Arbitragers will sell B and buy A to make unlimited profits while investing no money until the prices of Stocks A and B reach equality.[13] This is a simple example of arbitrage; now we will discuss how the principle can suggest a model for security prices in the context of developing a single-factor APT.

Single-Factor APT

Let's formulate a **single-factor APT model** to describe how arbitrage operates. Suppose that ex-post returns, $R_{i,t}$, are generated according to some stochastic relationship described as

$$\tilde{R}_{i,t} = E_{0,t} + \beta_{i,1}\tilde{F}_{1,t} + \tilde{e}_{i,t} \quad \text{for } i = 1, 2, \ldots, N \quad (14.7)$$

where $E_{0,t}$ is the security's expected return if $\beta_{i,1}\tilde{F}_{1,t}$ equals zero; $\tilde{F}_{1,t}$ is a factor (which we'll call *F1*) that affects Stock i's ex-post return for year t; $\beta_{i,1}$ is the sensitivity (systematic risk or beta) of Stock i to factor *F1*; $\tilde{e}_{i,t}$ is the firm's stock price movement that is uncorrelated to *F1*. (This is essentially the firm-specific risk for year t.) $E(\tilde{e}_{i,t})$ is assumed to equal zero.

The *F1* factor can be decomposed into two types of factors: (1) one that is expected by investors ($EF_{1,t}$) and (2) another that is unexpected ($\tilde{f}_{1,t}$). Rewrite Equation 14.7 more explicitly:

$$\tilde{R}_{i,t} = E_{0,t} + \beta_{i,1}(EF_{1,t} + \tilde{f}_{1,t}) + \tilde{e}_{i,t} \quad \text{for } i = 1, 2, \ldots N \quad (14.8)$$

where $EF_{1,t}$ is *F1*'s expected effect on Stock i's ex-post return for year t and $\tilde{f}_{1,t}$ is the effect of the unanticipated change in Stock i's ex-post return, which is also uncorrelated to $e_{i,t}$.

Finally, rewrite Equation 14.8 as:

$$\tilde{R}_{i,t} = ER_{i,t} + \beta_{i,1}\tilde{f}_{1,t} + \tilde{e}_{i,t} \quad (14.9)$$

where $ER_{i,t}$ equals stock i's expected return, or $(E_{0,t} + \beta_{i,1}EF_{1,t})$.

An example may help to clarify this relationship between $EF_{1,t}$ and $\tilde{f}_{1,t}$. Suppose that Stock i is AHP and factor *F1* represents the change in the rate of inflation. If the change in inflation rate is zero, then AHP's return is 10 percent ($E_{0,t} = 10$ percent).

Suppose, however, that everyone believes that inflation will increase by 3 percent. ($EF_{1,t}$ is 3 percent.) Since stocks tend to suffer during periods of high inflation, AHP should decline. If AHP's beta relative to the *F1* factor

---

[13]Other investors catch onto a scheme like this pretty quickly and their demand for the stock with the lower price drives prices toward equality. (Academics refer to this as *market equilibrium*.)

equals -1.5, its return is expected to fall by 4.5 percent (-1.5×3 percent) and its expected return, ER_{AHP}, equals 5.5 percent:

$$ER_{AHP} = 10\% + [-1.5(3\%)] = 5.5 \text{ percent}$$

Remember, however, that 3 percent is just a predicted change in $F1$. If the actual change in the rate of inflation is equal to $+4$ percent, so $\tilde{f}_{1,t}$ is $+1$ percent, then the effect on AHP's actual, realized return is:

$$R_{AHP,t} = ER_{AHP} + [-1.5(1\%)] = 5.5\% - 1.5\% = 4.0 \text{ percent}$$

The difference between actual and expected inflation causes the actual, realized return ($R_{AHP,t}$) to be 1.5 percent lower than the expected return, ER_{AHP}; the stockholder expects 5.5 percent, but actually realizes 4.0 percent.

Now what is $e_{i,t}$, the firm-specific effect on the stock's actual return? The variable $e_{i,t}$ might measure the effects of a product tampering episode (remember the Tylenol case?) or litigation on a product that causes side-effects. This effect would cause the actual return to differ from ER_{AHP}. This may create some confusion between $e_{i,t}$ and $\tilde{f}_{1,t}$. The latter captures the effect of $F1$ that is not predicted correctly (unexpected inflation) while $e_{i,t}$ captures the firm-specific effect, which is not captured by $\tilde{f}_{1,t}$ and uncorrelated to $\tilde{f}_{1,t}$.

Single-Factor APT for a Well-Diversified Portfolio. Next let's discuss the risk–return relationship for a well-diversified portfolio. Start with the same ex-post relationship (Equation 14.9), but modify it for a portfolio:

$$\tilde{R}_{p,t} = ER_{p,t} + \beta_p \tilde{f}_{1,t} + \tilde{e}_{p,t} \qquad (14.10)$$

One benefit of diversification is elimination of virtually all firm-specific risk, as described in Chapter 12. Recall from that chapter that the effect of a security's standard deviation, SD_i, on a well-diversified portfolio's standard deviation, SD_p, is virtually zero; the only relevant risk is the covariance of each security with the portfolio. Another way of saying this is that the standard deviation of unexpected, ($\tilde{e}_{p,t}$) or firm-specific, risk equals zero. Since the expected value of firm-specific risk [$E(\tilde{e}_{p,t})$] equals zero and its standard deviation [$SD(\tilde{e}_{p,t})$] is zero, then the actual effect on the portfolio return of $\tilde{e}_{p,t}$ must equal zero for a well-diversified portfolio. The ex-post return relationship for a well-diversified portfolio becomes:[14]

$$\tilde{R}_{p,t} = ER_{p,t} + \beta_p \tilde{f}_{1,t} \qquad (14.11)$$

Well-diversified portfolio risk equals:[15]

$$SD_p^2 = \beta_p^2 SD_{f,1}^2 \qquad \text{or} \qquad SD_p = \beta_p SD_{f,1}$$

---

[14]This involves constructing portfolios so that $E(\tilde{e}_{pt})$ equals zero. Also, remember from statistics that if an expected value is zero and actual values show no deviation from it (standard deviation is zero), then all the values that make up e_{pt} must be zero.

[15]Portfolio risk can be shown mathematically to equal:

$$SD(P) \ \beta_p SD_{F,1}$$

Recall that:

$$SD^2(P) = \beta_p^2 SD_{F,1}^2 + SD_{ep}^2$$

Having established that SD_{ep}^2 is virtually zero for a well-diversified portfolio, then:

$$SD^2(P) = \beta_p^2 SD_{F,1}^2$$

Taking the square root gives:

$$SD(P) = \beta_p SD_{F,1}$$

The APT imposes three conditions:

1. No wealth is invested.
2. A portfolio can eliminate firm-specific risk, $\tilde{e}_{p,t}$. (Of course, this is possible by holding a well-diversified portfolio.)
3. If arbitrage opportunities exist, the market can risklessly and costlessly arbitrage the profits to eliminate any discrepancies between any combinations of portfolios or securities at the same risk level.

If these conditions hold, it follows mathematically that portfolio expected return, $ER_{p,t}$, has a linear relationship with beta, β_p:

$$ER_{p,t} = E_{0,t} + \beta_p EF_{1,t} \tag{14.12}$$

An example may be helpful here. Besides the rationale for security return, the following example also shows how the arbitrage process is truly riskless; the dollar payoff is the same, regardless of any unanticipated changes in the portfolio return. Based on that premise, the example shows that Equation 14.12 follows from the assumptions of the single-factor APT.

Suppose that a single-factor model defines expected and realized returns as:

$$\text{Realized return:} \qquad \tilde{R}_{p,t} - ER_{p,t} + \beta_{p,1}\tilde{f}_{1,t}$$

$$\text{Expected return:} \qquad ER_{p,t} = E_{0,t} + \beta_{p,1}EF_{1,t}$$

Suppose, also, that three portfolios C, D, and K have expected returns of 14 percent, 16 percent, and 17 percent with $\beta_{p,1}$ (systematic risk) measures of 0.7, 1.7, and 1.2, respectively. So Portfolio K has a systematic risk of 1.2 and an expected return of 17 percent. Investing 50 percent of one's wealth in C and 50 percent in D gives a systematic risk of combined Portfolio CD as:

$$\beta_{CD} = X_C \beta_{C,1} + (1 - X_C)\beta_{D,1} \tag{14.13}$$

where X_C is the proportion invested in Portfolio C. For the example:

$$\beta_{CD} = 0.50\ (0.7) + (1 - 0.50)(1.7) = 1.2$$

Portfolio CD has the same systematic risk as Portfolio K; however, its expected return equals 15 percent. Using Equation 12.6a, the portfolio expected return is:

$$ER_{CD} = X_C(ER_C) + (1 - X_C)(ER_D)$$
$$= 0.50(0.14) + (1 - 0.50)(0.16) = 0.15 \text{ or } 15 \text{ percent}$$

This example presents an arbitrage opportunity because Portfolios K and CD have the same systematic risk ($\beta = 1.2$), but K's expected return is 17 percent while CD's is 15 percent. Arbitrage with no risk and no investment can be constructed by selling short \$100 of Portfolio CD and using the proceeds to buy \$100 of Portfolio K. This results in zero investment and zero risk, as displayed in the first part of Table 14.1.

Now let's see what happens a year from today if the unanticipated change ($\tilde{f}_{1,t}$) equals -3 percent, 0 percent, or +5 percent. Table 14.1 displays the results of the realized dollar payoffs, calculated as:

$$\text{Dollar payoff} = INV + INV(ER_{p,t} + b_{p,1}\tilde{f}_{1,t}) \tag{14.14}$$

Table 14.1

Arbitraging Portfolio *K* with Portfolio *CD*

A. Investment Today

	Dollar Investment	Systematic Risk
Sell Portfolio *CD* short:		
Short Portfolio *C*	$ +50	−0.35
Short Portfolio *D*	+50	−0.85
Buy Portfolio *K:*	−100	+1.20
Net investment	$ 0 Net risk	0.00

B.   One Year Later

Unanticipated Changes	Realized Dollar Payoffs
$f_{1,t}$	$= INV + INV(ER_{p,t} + b_{p,1}\tilde{f}_{1,t})$

Low $f_{1,t}$

C:	Dollar payoff $= -\{\$50 + \$50[0.14 + 0.7(-0.03)]\}$	$−55.95
D:	Dollar payoff $= -\{\$50 + \$50[0.11 + 1.7(-0.03)]\}$	−55.45
K:	Dollar payoff $= \$100 + \$100[0.17 + 1.2(-0.03)]$	113.40
Net profits		$+ 2.00

Expected $f_{1,t}$

C:	Dollar payoff $= -\{\$50 + \$50[0.14 + 0.7(0)]\}$	$−57.00
D:	Dollar payoff $= -\{\$50 + \$50[0.16 + 1.7(0)]$	−58.00
K:	Dollar payoff $= \$100 + \$100[0.17 + 1.2(0)]$	117.00
Net profits		$+ 2.00

High $f_{1,t}$

C:	Dollar payoff $= -\{\$50 + \$50[0.14 + 0.7(+0.05)]\}$	$−58.75
D:	Dollar payoff $= -\{\$50 + \$50[0.16 + 1.7(+0.05)]\}$	−62.25
K:	Dollar payoff $= \$100 + \$100[0.17 + 1.2(+0.05)]$	123.00
Net profits		$+ 2.00

where *INV* is the dollar amount invested ($100 in the example) and ($ER_{p,t}$ $+ b_{p,1}\tilde{f}_{1,t}$) is the actual realized return, from Equation 14.11. These results show that the dollar payoffs are exactly the same regardless of the unanticipated changes; whether the model's single factor changes by −3 percent, 0 percent, or +5 percent, the net profits equal $2.00. This is the meaning of riskless arbitrage; the technique guarantees a known dollar payoff a year from today, regardless of the unanticipated changes. This allows arbitragers to exploit mispricing between portfolios of equal systematic risk until the profits become zero (that is, the portfolios' returns become equal).

This says that the risk caused by the unanticipated changes, $\tilde{f}_{1,t}$ can be eliminated by constructing two portfolios (*CD* and *K*) that have offsetting effects; therefore, $\tilde{f}_{1,t}$ is not relevant in pricing security if it can be eliminated with offsetting arbitrage portfolios. This suggests removing $\tilde{f}_{1,t}$ from Equation 14.11:

$$\tilde{R}_{p,t} = ER_{p,t} + \beta_{p,1}\tilde{f}_{1,t}$$

If so, the realized return, $R_{p,t}$, can be best described by the expected return, $ER_{p,t}$. Recall, however, that $ER_{p,t}$ is defined by Equation 14.12 as:

$$ER_{p,t} = E_{0,t} + \beta_{p,1}EF_{1,t}$$

This shows intuitively that if one portfolio (K) can be replicated by combinations of other portfolios, then its expected return can be described by Equation 14.12.

Let's rework the example of Portfolios C, D, and K to develop another intuitive technique to evaluate returns describing the arbitrage process. Suppose the realized returns for Portfolio K and Portfolio CD are defined by Equation 14.11 as:

$$\tilde{R}_{K,t} = ER_{K,t} + \beta_{K1,t}\tilde{f}_{1,t} \quad \text{and} \quad \tilde{R}_{CD,t} = ER_{CD,t} + \beta_{CD,1}\tilde{f}_{1,t}$$

Since $ER_{K,t}$ equals 0.17 and $\beta_{K,1}$ equals 1.2, rewrite Portfolio K's realized return as:

$$\tilde{R}_{K,t} = 0.17 + 1.2\,\tilde{f}_{1,t}$$

Portfolio CD's $ER_{CD,t}$ equals 0.15 and its $\beta_{CD,1}$ equals 1.2, so its realized return equals:

$$\tilde{R}_{CD,t} = 0.15 + 1.2\,\tilde{f}_{1,t}$$

Since the portfolio combination in CD has the same systematic risk of 1.2, but earns only 15 percent, an arbitrager will sell CD short and buy Portfolio K with the proceeds of the short sale giving a net investment of zero. The results can be displayed as:

Buy Portfolio K	$\tilde{R}_{K,t}$	$= (0.17 + 1.2\,\tilde{f}_{1,t})$
Sell short Portfolio CD	$-\tilde{R}_{CD,t}$	$= -(0.15 + 1.2\,\tilde{f}_{1,t})$
Arbitrage profits	$(\tilde{R}_{K,t} - \tilde{R}_{CD,t})$	$= +0.02$

The arbitrage generates a 2 percent profit. Notice, also, that the effects of any unanticipated changes, $\tilde{f}_{1,t}$, are offset so it doesn't matter what that number is: -3 percent, 0 percent, or $+5$ percent. This says that the arbitrage investment risk is zero. Since all arbitragers are guaranteed to realize this profit, they will continue to make these trades until Portfolio K's price rises enough to reduce its return to 15 percent.

Generally, if a portfolio (such as K) with a higher return can be replicated as a combination of other portfolios (such as C and D), then arbitrage profits exist. However, arbitragers quickly eliminate this mispricing between portfolios. For that reason, all portfolios with the same systematic risk must lie on the same line, defined by Equation 14.12. Stated differently, portfolios with the same systematic risk must have the same expected return.

The linear relationship for Portfolios CD and K may be:

$$ER_{p,t} = 0.03 + 1.2\,(0.10) = 0.15 \text{ or } 15 \text{ percent}$$

This relationship is displayed in Figure 14.6.

The risk–return relationship defined by Equation 14.12 needs one last modification. The systematic risk factor in Equation 14.12 can be normalized so that the average $\beta_{p,1}$ equals 1.0. This gives a general normalized risk–return relationship of:

$$ER_{p,t} = E_{0,t} + \beta_{p,1}(EF_{1,t} - E_{0,t}) \tag{14.15}$$

where $E_{0,t}$ is the expected return for the portfolio if the systematic risk for

Figure 14.6

Arbitraging Portfolio *K* Using Portfolio *CD*

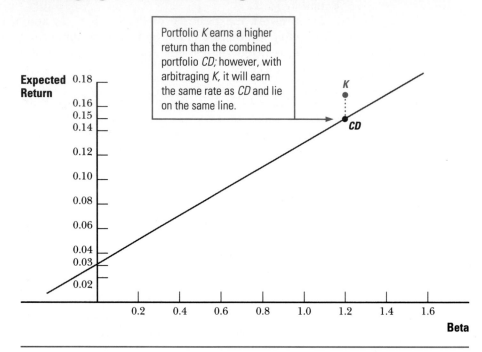

> Portfolio *K* earns a higher return than the combined portfolio *CD*; however, with arbitraging *K*, it will earn the same rate as *CD* and lie on the same line.

the portfolio is zero; $\beta_{p,1}$ is the systematic risk for a portfolio (equal to 1.0 for the average systematic risk for *F1*); and $(EF_{1,t} - E_{0,t})$ is *F1*'s risk premium.

This normalization allows us to interpret APT's measure of systematic risk like the CAPM's beta. If systematic risk is greater than 1.0, then the portfolio's systematic risk is higher than the average of all portfolios; if it is less than 1.0, the portfolio is less risky than average. Again, this provides a reference point for factor F_1's systematic risk.

Having developed an intuitive feel for arbitrage, we make a leap by induction to apply the principle to valuation of securities. If a well-diversified portfolio can be valued by Equation 14.12, what about individual securities? Each security must also follow Equation 14.12 as long as arbitragers can create well-diversified portfolios to mimic a security's extraordinary return. Put differently, if AHP were compensating investors for firm-specific risk such as product tampering, that is, if $SD(e_i) \neq 0$, then shrewd investors could create combinations of other stocks in a portfolio that would have the same systematic risk level as AHP. They would sell the portfolio short and buy more AHP, driving AHP's price upward until its return came to equal the portfolio's, or until AHP's $SD(e_i)$ would no longer affect its security return.

Therefore, if a security return could be re-created by a combination of other securities' returns (in a portfolio), then no arbitrage profits would remain and all securities would be priced to reflect only the systematic risk associated with the factor. This says that Equation 14.15, which we have applied only to well-diversified portfolios, can be extended to Security *i*'s return:

$$ER_{i,t} = E_{0,t} + \beta_{i,1}(EF_{1,t} - E_{0,t}) \qquad \text{for } i = 1, 2, \ldots, N \qquad (14.16)$$

This equation should look vaguely familiar. It resembles the CAPM formula, if some assumptions are made. We will see in the next section that the single-factor APT model and the CAPM take on exactly the same form. However, the next section will examine differences between the two processes.

Single-Factor APT and the CAPM. Since $\beta_{i,1}$ is defined as a security's sensitivity to factor *F1,* this APT variable has the same definition as beta in the CAPM. Given a single-factor APT model, and defining *F1* as the market portfolio, M, the term $EF_{1,t} - E_{0,t}$ in Equation 14.16 becomes $ER_{M,t} - RF$. Also, if $E_{0,t}$ equals *RF,* it makes Equation 14.16 equal to:

$$ER_i = RF + \beta_{i,M}(ER_M - RF)$$

The term $ER_M - RF$ is the market risk premium and $\beta_{i,M}$ is Security *i*'s systematic risk relative to the market portfolio, *M.*

The result is the same formula as the CAPM. However, the process of arriving at the final formula is quite different; the APT model uses the arbitrage principle while the CAPM uses utility theory. Let's discuss how the APT develops the single-factor model.

Development of the Single-Factor APT. In Chapter 12, we found that risk-averse investors are enticed to invest in risky securities only if they are compensated for risk. Even in Chapter 1, we defined a risk–return relationship as:

$$ER_i = RF + \text{Risk premium}$$

The compensation for accepting risk equals:

$$ER_i - RF = \text{Risk premium}$$

The left side of the equation, $ER_i - RF$, is the reward for accepting risk. How can one measure security risk?

Recall from the previous section that systematic risk is the only relevant risk for a well-diversified portfolio because a portfolio diversifies away any firm-specific risk. Therefore, a reward-to-risk ratio for a well-diversified portfolio can be defined as:

$$\text{Reward-to-risk ratio} = \frac{(ER_p - RF)}{\beta_p}$$

In market equilibrium, the reward-to-risk ratios for all well-diversified portfolios must equal; otherwise market forces would arbitrage any profits until they reached equality. In essence, the reward-to-risk ratio must increase proportionately or else arbitrage opportunities, as described earlier, are possible. If so, arbitragers will eliminate any discrepancies in portfolios with arbitrage profits. For two well-diversified portfolios, *P* and *Q,* then:

$$\frac{(ER_P - RF)}{\beta_P} = \frac{(ER_Q - RF)}{\beta_Q}$$

Now what about securities? If securities' returns can be duplicated by combinations of other portfolios, then in market equilibrium, they too must have reward-to-risk ratios that are equal to those of the portfolios. For example, suppose a well-diversified portfolio, *M,* can combine other securities so that its systematic risk is the same as Security *i.* Their reward-to-risk ratios must equal:

$$\frac{(ER_i - RF)}{\beta_i} = \frac{(ER_M - RF)}{\beta_M}$$

If not, arbitrage would drive them into equality. Suppose that Security i's reward-to-risk ratio equals 0.8 while the ratio of the combination portfolio, M, equals 0.6.

$$\frac{(ER_M - RF)}{\beta_M} = \frac{(0.12 - 0.06)}{1.0} = 0.6$$

$$\frac{(ER_i - RF)}{\beta_i} = \frac{(0.30 - 0.06)}{0.3} = 0.8$$

Investors who notice that Security i has a greater reward-to-risk ratio than Portfolio M will purchase Security i and sell Portfolio M short until the two reward-to-risk ratios become equal. This says simply that as risk increases, reward must increase in the same proportion for every security in the market; otherwise mispricing occurs. However, arbitrage quickly corrects any mispricing to prevent a security from earning a reward out of proportion to its risk.

If securities can be combined into a portfolio that duplicates the return of Security i, but with a different reward-to-risk ratio, then arbirage will occur. In the end, most securities and portfolios have a single reward-to-risk ratio:

$$\frac{(ER_j - RF)}{\beta_j} = \frac{(ER_i - RF)}{\beta_i} = \frac{(ER_M - RF)}{\beta_M}$$

In equilibrium, all securities, including portfolios, must have the same reward-to-risk ratio or:

$$\frac{(ER_i - RF)}{\beta_i} = \frac{(ER_M - RF)}{\beta_M}$$

Remember that if beta is normalized, the average beta equals 1.0, where the average portfolio is represented by a well-diversified portfolio, M. Therefore, the reward-to-risk ratio equals:

$$\frac{(ER_i - RF)}{\beta_i} = \frac{(ER_M - RF)}{1.0}$$

Solve for ER_i to determine the risk–return relationship for Security i:

$$ER_i = RF + \beta_i(ER_M - RF) \qquad (14.17)$$

If Portfolio M is defined as the market portfolio, then beta, β_i, is Security i's risk contribution to the market portfolio and $ER_M - RF$ is the market risk premium.

You probably recognize Equation 14.17 as the CAPM from Chapter 13; however, the process of developing the formula using APT is different from that in Chapter 13, which used utility theory and the CML. The next section outlines the differences between the single-factor APT and the CAPM.

Differences between the Single-Factor APT and the CAPM. Four major differences separate the single-factor APT and the CAPM:

1. The APT is appealing because it relies only on the premise that arbitrage will preclude any mispricing in a rational capital market, maintaining market equilibrium. The CAPM relies on utility theory and risk aversion in order to develop the risk–return relationship. This gives CAPM a less intuitive basis than the Arbitrage Pricing Theory.

2. The development of the single-factor APT assumes a well-diversified portfolio that affects returns on individual securities. The APT does not rely on any unobservable market portfolio, as the CAPM does.
3. However, the CAPM does have its strengths. Its development shows that all traded securities will lie on its risk–return line; the APT guarantees that diversified portfolios must lie on the line, but individual securities may diverge somewhat. It recognizes the possibility of small mispricing errors, though it is virtually impossible for most securities to systematically deviate from the APT's risk–return line.
4. Both models have drawbacks that become apparent when conducting empirical tests. The CAPM is not testable because no one can observe the true market portfolio, while the APT does not define its factors, nor does it rely on a set number of factors.

Both models have weaknesses and strengths, so it's impossible to say that one model is clearly better. However, both models help the analyst to quantify a risk premium and both define risk–return relationships that are still useful in evaluating securities for investment decisions.

The final step we'll take is to develop a multifactor APT, which assumes that many factors are significant in explaining security returns. We start with a two-factor APT, and then generalize to the N-factor APT. In either case, the underlying principle is still the same; the only difference is the initial premise that more than one factor can affect an ex-post security return.

APT with Multiple Factors

The concept of security pricing based on arbitrage can be extended to more than one factor. In fact, introduction of several factors just says that Security j's return depends on more than one force, so it can be re-created by holding a linear combination of different factors. Using the same arbitrage principle, we show that if a security's return can be mimicked by combining several stocks in a portfolio, then no arbitrage profits remain. We begin by extending the single-factor relationship to a two-factor relationship.

Two-Factor APT. A two-factor APT extends the single-factor APT by defining a security's realized returns and expected returns as:

$$\text{Realized return} \qquad \tilde{R}_i = ER_i + \beta_{i,1}\tilde{f}_{1,t} + \beta_{i,2}\tilde{f}_{2,t} + \tilde{e}_{i,t} \qquad (14.18)$$

$$\text{Expected return} \qquad ER_{i,t} = E_{0,t} + \beta_{i,1}EF_{1,t} + \beta_{i,2}EF_{2,t} \qquad (14.19)$$

where $E_{0,t}$ is Security i's expected return if it is uncorrelated to $F1$ and $F2$; $EF_{1,t}$ and $EF_{2,t}$ are the factors' expected effects, based on $F1$ and $F2$, respectively; $\tilde{f}_{1,t}$ and $\tilde{f}_{2,t}$ are the effects of unanticipated changes in Stock i's ex-post return, which are uncorrelated to $\tilde{e}_{i,t}$ ($\tilde{f}_{1,t}$ and $\tilde{f}_{2,t}$ are also uncorrelated); $\beta_{i,1}$ and $\beta_{i,2}$ are the systematic risk effects of $F1$ and $F2$, respectively; finally, $e_{i,t}$ is the firm-specific risk, which is uncorrelated to $F1$ and $F2$.

Well-diversified portfolios can eliminate firm-specific risk through diversification, so their realized returns equal:

$$\text{Realized return} \qquad \tilde{R}_{p,t} = ER_{p,t} + \beta_{p,1}\tilde{f}_{1,t} + \beta_p\tilde{f}_{2,t} \qquad (14.20)$$

Again, an example can illustrate that the effects of unanticipated changes $\tilde{f}_{1,t}$ and $\tilde{f}_{2,t}$) are offset in arbitrage, leaving the expected return, $ER_{p,t}$, in a linear relationship with systematic risk, or beta, as defined in Equation 14.19.

Suppose that two portfolios, P and Q, have the following systematic risks to $F1$ and $F2$ and expected returns, ER_P and ER_Q:

Portfolio	β_{p1}	β_p	ER_{pt}
P	0.1	0.2	0.05
Q	0.3	0.6	0.18

Investing 300 percent in Portfolio P would give the following risk levels and expect return:

$$\beta_{p1} = 3(0.1) = 0.3$$

$$\beta_p = 3(.02) = 0.6$$

$$ER_{p,t} = 3(0.05) = 0.15$$

Notice that Portfolio P's risk levels are now equal to those of Portfolio Q, but its return is lower (15 percent versus 18 percent). This suggests a strategy of selling short a dollar of Portfolio P for every dollar invested in Portfolio Q. This results in the following realized returns for Portfolios P and Q:

Realized return for investment in Portfolio Q	$\tilde{R}_{Q,t}$	$= 0.18 + 0.3\,\tilde{f}_{1,t} + 0.6\,\tilde{f}_{2,t}$
Realized return for short sale of Portfolio P	$-\tilde{R}_{P,t}$	$= -(0.15 + 0.3\,\tilde{f}_{1,t} + 0.6\,\tilde{f}_{2,t})$
Arbitrage Profits	$\tilde{R}_{Q,t} - \tilde{R}_{P,t}$	$= +0.03$

Again, the unanticipated effects, $\tilde{f}_{1,t}$ and $\tilde{f}_{2,t}$, offset each other for well-diversified portfolios, generating a 3 percent arbitrage profit. The arbitrage will continue until the expected returns from the portfolios are equal, so the two-factor APT for a well-diversified portfolio can be described by:

$$ER_{p,t} = E_{0,t} + \beta_{p,1}EF_{1,t} + \beta_{p,2}EF_{2,t}$$

Again this assumes that most securities' returns can be replicated as combinations of other securities or portfolios, so arbitrage profits will be virtually zero for securities, too. If so, then Security i's expected return can also be written as a linear relationship of the beta risks of the two factors:

$$ER_{i,t} = E_{0,t} + \beta_{i,1}EF_{1,t} + \beta_{i,2}EF_{2,t}$$

As in the single-factor APT, standardizing each beta can set the average beta equal to 1.0 for each factor's beta. The standardized two-factor APT equals:

$$ER_{p,t} = E_{0,t} + \beta_{p,1}(EF_{1,t} - E_{0,t}) + \beta_{p,2}(EF_{2,t} - E_{0,t}) \qquad (14.21)$$

where $E_{0,t}$ is the expected return value when all factors equal zero; $(EF_{1,t} - E_{0,t})$ and $(EF_{2,t} - E_{0,t})$ are risk premiums for factors $F1$ and $F2$, respectively; $\beta_{i,1}$ and $\beta_{i,2}$ are systematic risks for factors $F1$ and $F2$, respectively.

The two-factor APT is derived much like the single-factor APT. The only difference is that it includes more than one factor to describe the realized return.

N-Factor APT. Now suppose that N factors describe the realized return for a security. Security j's realized return equals:

$$\tilde{R}_{j,t} = E_{0,t} + \beta_{j,1}(EF_{1,t} + \tilde{f}_{1,t}) + \beta_{j,2}(EF_{2,t} + \tilde{f}_{2,t}) + \ldots$$
$$+ \beta_{j,N}(EF_{N,t} + \tilde{f}_{N,t}) + \tilde{e}_{j,t}$$

where the $EF_{k,t}$ terms are the expected values of the k factors in period t; the $\tilde{f}_{k,t}$ terms are the unexpected values of the k factors in period t; $\tilde{e}_{j,t}$ is the firm-specific risk that is uncorrelated to any of the unexpected $\tilde{f}_{k,t}$ values; $\beta_{j,k}$ are the sensitivities or systematic risks associated with each of the k factors; $E_{0,t}$ is the expected return value when each of the N factors equals zero.

First, separate and collect the expected values of all the k factors as one term and the unexpected values as the second term:

$$\tilde{R}_{j,t} = (E_{0,t} + \beta_{j,1}EF_{1,t} + \beta_{j,2}EF_{2,t} + \ldots + \beta_{j,N}EF_{N,t}) \qquad (14.22)$$
$$+ (\beta_{j,1}\tilde{f}_{1,t} + \beta_{j,2}\tilde{f}_{2,t} + \ldots + \beta_{j,N}\tilde{f}_{N,t}) + \tilde{e}_{j,t}$$

Since the first term in parentheses can be defined as the expected return for all the factors that are correlated with Security j, make the following substitution:

$$ER_{j,t} = (E_{0,t} + \beta_{j,1}EF_{1,t} + \beta_{j,2}EF_{2,t} + \ldots + \beta_{j,N}EF_{N,t})$$

Inserting this into Equation 14.22 gives:

$$\tilde{R}_{j,t} = ER_{j,t} + (\beta_{j,1}\tilde{f}_{1,t} + \beta_{j,2}\tilde{f}_{2,t} + \ldots + \beta_{j,N}\tilde{f}_{N,t}) + \tilde{e}_{j,t} \qquad (14.23)$$

This formula says that if an expected return on a security can be re-created by factors and their systematic risks are equal (or portfolios of other securities) then arbitragers will price the two the same, assuming they must pay no transaction costs. This means that the security's realized return must equal its expected return, which is explained by many factors, plus the unanticipated changes of those factors. Therefore, each $\beta_{j,k}$ is composed of two components: the part of security return that is sensitive to and explained by factor $F_{k,t}$ and the part that is sensitive, but not explained by $F_{k,t}$; the second part is captured by a random term, $\tilde{f}_{k,t}$. The unpredictable component can be unexpected factor outcomes ($\tilde{f}_{k,t}$) or unexpected firm-specific events ($\tilde{e}_{j,t}$). If a factor to explain a security return were an industry index, an unanticipated outcome might be a new drug breakthrough; a firm-specific outcome could be a product tampering episode. Again, if the three conditions outlined for the single-factor APT model hold, then virtually no arbitrage opportunities exist, implying the relationship:

$$ER_{j,t} = E_{0,t} + \beta_{j,1}(EF_{1,t} - E_{0,t}) + \beta_{j,2}(EF_{2,t} - E_{0,t}) + \ldots \qquad (14.24)$$
$$+ \beta_{j,N}(EF_{N,t} - E_{0,t})$$

where $EF_{k,t} - E_{0,t}$ is the risk premium for the kth factor; $E_{0,t}$ is the expected return value when all N factors equal zero (this value is uncorrelated to all the factors); $\beta_{j,k}$ equals the systematic risk or beta of Security j with the kth factor. Also, each factor must be uncorrelated with the other factors, that is, $CORR(F1,F2) = 0.0$. The same relationship must hold for other pairs of factors.

This formula says that each factor, F_k, captures an independently different effect and its sensitivity is measured by its corresponding beta, $\beta_{j,k}$. The only requirement is that the number of factors must be less than the number of securities being evaluated. Researchers have found that three to six factors can eliminate virtually all arbitrage opportunities.[16]

Final Synopsis of APT

The **multifactor APT model** is more robust than the CAPM because it allows for several factors that may affect security returns and it avoids the need to identify a true market portfolio. However, it has some empirical problems of its own. The factors aren't well-defined, so the analyst must empirically attempt to identify the factors that are significant in describing security returns. This creates two types of problems: (1) The factors may change, depending on the sample of securities used to ascertain them. (2) Factors may change over time.

Researchers have found that increasing the sample size also increases the number of factors that significantly affect security returns. The question, what are the factors, is difficult to resolve. Furthermore, the number of factors appears to vary, not only with the sample, but with time periods, as well.

An alternative strategy is to define factors that seem like plausible descriptions of security returns. For example, Chen, Roll, and Ross conducted a test of specified factors and found that a large part of a security's return can be explained by four factors: (1) differences between yields to maturity on long-term and short-term Treasury securities, (2) inflation rates, (3) differences between yields to maturity on BB-rated corporate bonds and T-bills, and (4) growth of industrial production (GNP).[17]

In conclusion, extensive research is still being conducted to determine the appropriate risk measures, but both academics and practitioners agree that risk level is an important component in making good investment decisions.

Chapter Summary

1. **Develop an understanding of the zero-beta portfolio model.**
   The zero-beta portfolio model relaxes the CAPM's assumption that all investors can borrow and lend at the risk-free rate, RF. It results in a similar linear, beta risk–return relationship; however, it replaces the risk-free asset with a zero-beta portfolio, or a stock portfolio that is uncorrelated to the market portfolio.

2. **Overview some empirical tests of the CAPM.**
   Empirical findings for the CAPM are less than satisfactory. Major findings indicate that: (1) actual beta risk–return relationships are flatter than theory suggests, (2) the y-intercept does not equal the risk-free rate, RF, and (3) the slope for the SML was slightly negative during some periods in 1957 to 1965.

3. **Review Roll's critique of the CAPM.**
   Roll mathematically proves that the CAPM cannot be empirically tested because any efficient portfolio will have an exactly linear beta risk–return relationship, as described by the CAPM. Unless the analyst can identify an ex-ante market portfolio (which is impossible), no one can test the CAPM. One can test only whether the proxy for the market portfolio is mean-variance efficient or not.

4. **Understand Arbitrage Pricing Theory (APT).**
   The APT is based on the theory that identical assets must be priced

---

[16]Richard Roll and Stephen Ross, "An Empirical Investigation of the Arbitrage Pricing Theory," *Journal of Finance*, December 1980, 1073–1103.

[17]Nai-Fu Chen, Richard Roll, and Stephen Ross, "Economic Forces and the Stock Market," *Journal of Business*, September 1986, 383–404.

exactly the same; otherwise, investors will arbitrage the profits to zero. Ross developed an alternative way of viewing asset pricing based on this principle. His model is more robust than the CAPM and incorporates a formula exactly like the CAPM. However, the process of arriving at the final formula is quite different. (CAPM uses utility theory and APT uses arbitrage theory.) Also, the APT can include multiple factors.

Key Terms

Zero-beta portfolio
Excess return
First pass regression
Time series regression
Cross-sectional regression

Second pass regression
Arbitrage principle
Single-factor APT model
Multifactor APT model

Discussion Questions and Problems

1. What assumption of the CAPM is relaxed to develop the zero-beta port-folio model?
2. What are the general results of the empirical tests for the CAPM and zero-beta portfolio model?
3. How would you explain the negative risk–return relationship that is doc-umented for the April 1957 to December 1965 period?
4. What are the premises of Roll's critique of the CAPM?
5. According to Roll, what are the implications of the empirical results pro-vided by Black, Jensen, and Scholes?

6. CFA Exam, Level III, 1981

   Richard Roll, in an article on using the Capital Asset Pricing Model (CAPM) to evaluate portfolio performance, indicated that it may not be possible to evaluate portfolio management ability if there is an error in the benchmark chosen for comparison.

   a. Describe the general procedure for evaluating portfolio performance, with emphasis on the benchmark employed.
   b. Explain what Roll meant by *benchmark error* and identify the specific problem with this benchmark.
   c. Draw a graph that shows how a portfolio that has been judged as supe-rior relative to a measured security market line (SML) can be inferior relative to the true SML.
   d. Assume that you are informed that a given portfolio manager has been evaluated as superior when compared to the Dow Jones Indus-trial Average, the S&P 500, and the NYSE Composite Index. Explain whether this consensus would make you feel more comfortable regarding the portfolio manager's true ability.
   e. While conceding the possible problem with benchmark errors as set forth by Roll, some contend this does not mean that the CAPM is incorrect, but only that there is a measurement problem when imple-menting the theory. Others contend that, because of benchmark errors, the whole technique should be scrapped. Take and defend one of these positions.
7. The chapter example on Portfolios CD and K shows the dollar payoffs if $\tilde{f}_{1,t}$ equals -3 percent, 0 percent, and $+5$ percent. What are the dollar payoffs if $\tilde{f}_{1,t}$ equals -5 percent and 2 percent?
8. What are the conceptual differences between the single-factor APT and the CAPM?
9. Suppose that two factors affect ex-post realized returns and expected returns. The systematic risks, $\beta_{p,1}$ and $\beta_{p,2}$, and expected returns for two well-diversified portfolios, R and S, are on the next page.

Portfolio	$\beta_{p,1}$	$\beta_{p,2}$	$ER_{p,t}$
R	0.5	0.3	0.12
S	1.0	0.6	0.09

a. Write the expected return and systematic risk relationship for Portfolios R and S.

b. Write the realized return and systematic risk relationship for Portfolios R and S.

c. Do these portfolios offer any arbitrage opportunities? If so, how would you construct the arbitrage?

10. **CFA Exam, Level I**

Research on the CAPM and beta has concluded that:

a. Short-term results may contradict the CAPM.

b. Estimated betas change over time.

c. Estimated betas depend on the choice of the market index.

d. All of the above.

Explain your answer.

11. **CFA Exam, Level I**

Compared to the CAPM, in the APT:

a. Beta is eliminated as a pricing factor.

b. Inflation is eliminated as a pricing factor.

c. The risk-free rate loses its significance.

d. Multiple factors affect the return generation process.

12. **CFA Exam, Level I**

The feature of APT that offers the greatest potential advantage over the CAPM is the:

a. Use of several factors instead of a single market index to explain the risk–return relationship.

b. Identification of anticipated changes in production, inflation, and term structure as key factors explaining the risk–return relationship.

c. Superior measurement of the risk-free rate of return over historical time periods.

d. Variability of coefficients of sensitivity to the APT factors for a given asset over time.

Critical Thinking Exercise

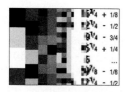

This exercise requires computer work. Find file MRETURN.XLS on the data disk. The file contains 1993 returns for 40 mutual funds, their respective betas, and the U.S. T-bill rates. The betas are estimated using the S&P 500 Index as the market proxy. Suppose these mutual funds represent portfolios identified in the first pass regression. Run the second pass regression described by Equation 14.5 and answer the questions below. Equation 14.5 is:

$$M(R_{i,t} - RF_t) = \gamma_0 + \gamma_1 b_i$$

1. What should γ_0 and γ_1 equal if the mutual fund returns follow the CAPM relationship?

2. What are the estimates for γ_0 and γ_1? Does it support the CAPM relationship? Explain.

3. Graph the actual regression line and the theoretical relationship. What conclusions can you draw from the difference?

4. According to Roll's critique of the CAPM, what do the results imply about the market proxy, S&P 500?

Chapter 15

Applications of Modern Portfolio Theory

Chapter Objectives

1. Develop and apply three measures of investment performance based on modern portfolio theory.
2. Reconsider whether past performance is a good predictor of future performance.
3. Understand how different groups of investors might apply MPT to investment decisions.
4. Examine the Treynor–Black portfolio combination model.

Together, Chapters 12, 13, and 14 have developed **modern portfolio theory (MPT).** Those discussions of risk aversion, diversification, efficient frontiers, beta, and arbitrage pricing have not directly addressed the question of the value of MPT to real-world investors.

Actually, as we have developed MPT in Chapters 12, 13, and 14, we've already discussed many important insights that MPT provides into real-world investment situations. Modern portfolio theory, for example, uses the concept of the tradeoff between risk and return, which implies that one cannot expect higher returns without accepting additional risk. MPT shows a way to measure risk and return, and how to compare different investments on the basis of risk and expected return. Modern portfolio theory uses the concept of diversification, which can improve a portfolio's risk/return tradeoff by combining security returns that are not perfectly correlated. The benefits of this technique are widely recognized by investment professionals. Even the capital asset pricing model (CAPM), in spite of its faults, can provide the basis for several techniques by which to evaluate the performance of investment portfolios.

In this chapter, we demonstrate more explicitly the usefulness of modern portfolio theory in practical investment situations. We begin by developing three measures of investment performance and applying them to some real data. These Treynor, Sharpe, and Jensen measures are named for the individuals who developed them. All three are natural outgrowths of MPT. Next, because all three measures use historical data, we revisit the question of whether past performance is a good predictor of future performance. We then turn our attention to how the forms of the efficient markets hypothesis lead different groups of investors to apply modern portfolio theory to investment decisions. Finally, we examine the Treynor–Black portfolio combination model, which applies MPT to practical investment selection decisions.

Three Performance Measures

In many financial publications, portfolio performance is examined; however, it's impossible to compare different portfolios' performance because their risk levels differ. Each of the three measures solves this by adjusting performance for a standard level of risk. First, reward or compensation for undertaking risk is defined, then risk is defined separately by each measure.

Recall from Chapter 1 that an expected return for any risky security must exceed the risk-free rate, *RF*, in order to compensate investors for risk. Generally this relationship can be stated:

$$ER_p = RF + \text{Risk premium} \tag{15.1}$$

The additional return or reward an investor expects for undertaking risk equals:

$$ER_p - RF = \text{Risk premium} \tag{15.2}$$

Equation 15.2 says that the reward for taking on risk is not equal to ER_p, but to ER_p minus *RF*. Both the Treynor and Sharpe measures focus on this measure of reward relative to risk. For example, if ER_p and *RF* equal 10 percent and 4 percent respectively, then only 6 percent is compensation for additional risk; the 4 percent is guaranteed from an investment in a risk-free asset. With this background, let's examine each of three portfolio performance measures separately.

Treynor Performance Measure

The equation for the **Treynor measure** for the performance of portfolio p, T_p, equals:[1]

$$T_p = [ER_p - RF]/\beta_p. \tag{15.3}$$

This measure is interpreted as stating the reward (return minus the risk-free rate) in relation to a portfolio's **beta risk.** The equation stems from the security market line (SML) discussed in Chapter 13. Recall that the SML for a portfolio p is defined by:

$$ER_p = RF + \beta_p[ER_M - RF] \tag{15.4}$$

From Equation 15.2, the reward for taking risk equals $[ER_p - RF]$. Solving for the reward in Equation 15.4 gives:

$$ER_p - RF = \beta_p[ER_M - RF] \tag{15.5}$$

Dividing by beta gives:

$$[ER_p - RF]/\beta_p = [ER_M - RF] \tag{15.6}$$

The left-hand side of Equation 15.6 is simply the Treynor measure for

---

[1] Jack Treynor, "How to Rate Management of Investment Funds," *Harvard Business Review,* January–February 1965, 119–138.

Figure 15.1

Security Market Line when $T_p = T_M$

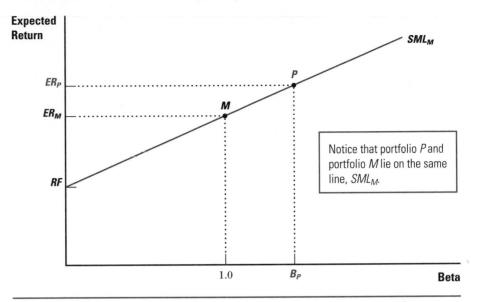

portfolio p, T_p. Note that Equation 15.6 originated from the SML, and $[ER_M - RF]$ is the slope of SML. Equation 15.6 implies that, if portfolio p lies on SML, then the portfolio's Treynor measure, T_p, must equal the slope of the market portfolio's SML, SML_M. In fact, dividing $[ER_M - RF]$ by β_M gives:

$$T_M = [ER_M - RF]/\beta_M \qquad (15.7)$$

Since the market portfolio's beta is 1.0 by definition, Equation 15.7 is equivalent to the right-hand side of Equation 15.6 or $[ER_M - RF]$. T_p is the slope of the portfolio's SML, SML_p. Therefore, the Treynor measure says that, if the slope of SML_p equals the slope of SML_M, that is, if T_p equals T_M, then the portfolio must lie on the market SML. Recall from the discussion in Chapter 13 of the SML that the performance of any portfolio or security that lies on the line matches the expectations of the CAPM. See Figure 15.1.

Suppose a different portfolio p_1 lies above the SML, as shown in Figure 15.2. Its slope, calculated by the Treynor measure, would be steeper than that of SML_M:

$$T_{p1} = [ER_{p1} - RF]/\beta p_1 > [ER_M - RF] = T_M \qquad (15.8)$$

As in the SML analysis, this implies that portfolio p_1 is undervalued; it is outperforming the expectations of SML_M (as defined by the CAPM). Since, the SML represents the market portfolio, most interpret this relationship to mean that p_1 is outperforming the market portfolio.

Another interpretation is that the Treynor measure normalizes the portfolio's reward by the market's beta of 1.0. Suppose that T_{p1} is 0.245 and T_M is 0.210. This means that at a beta of 1.0, the reward to p_1 equals 0.245 while the market portfolio's reward equals 0.210. Figure 15.2 shows this graphically. The Treynor measure compares the rewards of two portfolios, p_1 and M, adjusted to reflect the same risk level. If the reward for p_1 is greater than that for M at the same risk level, p_1 outperforms M, the market portfolio.

Figure 15.2

Security Market Lines when $T_P > T_M$

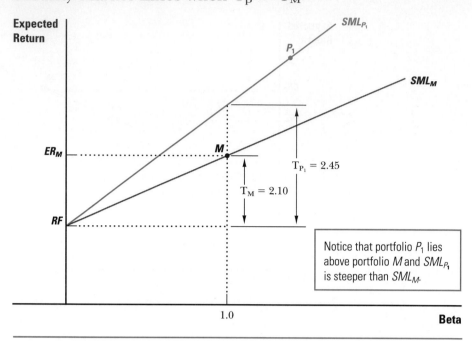

Notice that portfolio P_1 lies above portfolio M and SML_{P_1} is steeper than SML_M.

Finally, if a portfolio p_2 lies below the SML, as shown in Figure 15.3, then its slope will be flatter than the slope of the SML_M:

$$T_{p2} = [ER_{p2} - RF]/\beta_{p2} < = T_M [ER_M - RF] \qquad (15.9)$$

Portfolio p_2 is overvalued; it underperforms the expectations of the SML, or the market portfolio, since the slope of the market portfolio is the benchmark. Again, if the two portfolios, p_2 and M, are aligned by beta risk of 1.0, then a comparison shows that p_2 generates a smaller reward than M at the same level of beta risk. All three cases are summarized in Table 15.1.

Figure 15.3

Security Market Lines when $T_p < T_M$

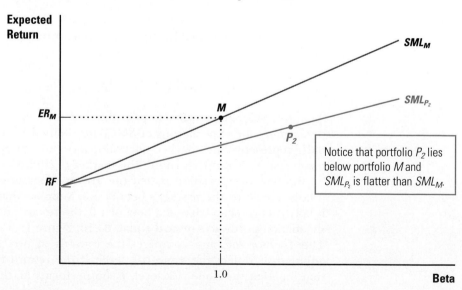

Notice that portfolio P_2 lies below portfolio M and SML_{P_2} is flatter than SML_M.

Table 15.1

Interpretation of the Treynor Measure

If $T_p > T_M$	Portfolio p outperforms the market.
If $T_p = T_M$	Portfolio p performs exactly as well as the market, adjusted for beta risk.
If $T_p < T_M$	Portfolio p underperforms the market.

Using data provided in Table 15.2, let's calculate ER_p and the Treynor measure for the Pax World Fund portfolio and the Standard & Poor's 500 Index (to represent the market portfolio).[2] First, calculate ER_p as the arithmetic average of returns over the years 1982 through 1991; this gives mean returns of 15.44 percent for Pax and 17.42 percent for the S&P 500.[3] The risk-free rate also appears in Table 15.2 as the return on T-bills; its mean equals 7.65 percent.[4] Now estimate beta by the market model, using the data above. (It can be obtained from IBC/Donoghue's *Mutual Fund Almanac,* Value Line's *Mutual Fund Forecaster,* and several other sources.) Pax World Fund's beta is estimated to be 0.44, so the Treynor measure for Pax World Fund can be calculated as:

$$T_p = [ER_p - RF]/\beta_p = [15.44\% - 7.65\%]/0.44 = 17.7$$

The Treynor measure for the Standard & Poor's 500 equals:

$$T_M = [ER_M - RF] = [17.42\% - 7.65\%] = 9.8.$$

Since T_p exceeds T_M (17.7 > 9.8), Pax World Fund appears to outperform the S&P 500, the proxy for the market. Figure 15.4 graphically illustrates the

Table 15.2

Data on a Sample Mutual Fund (Pax World), S&P 500, and T-Bills

	Pax World Fund[a]	S&P 500	30-Day T-Bills
1982	18.30%	21.41%	10.53%
1983	24.20	22.51	8.80
1984	7.40	6.27	9.78
1985	25.90	32.17	7.73
1986	8.40	18.62	6.07
1987	2.50	5.25	5.13
1988	11.70	16.62	6.58
1989	24.80	31.59	8.14
1990	10.50	−6.56	7.50
1991	20.70	26.31	6.25
Expected return	15.44%	17.42%	7.65%
Beta	0.44	1.0	0.0
Standard deviation	8.36%	12.42%	—

[a]**Source:** *IBC/Donoghue's Mutual Fund Almanac,* 24th ed. (Ashland, MA: IBC/Donoghue, Inc., 1993).

[2]The source for the data is IBC/Donoghue's *Mutual Funds Almanac,* 24th ed. (Ashland, MA: IBC/Donoghue Inc., 1993), 40–86.

[3]Note that theory assumes ex-ante returns; practitioners use ex-post returns. Nevertheless, we will continue to use the same notations.

[4]Ignore the standard deviation data for now. We will use them a little later for the Sharpe measure.

Figure 15.4

Graphic Example of the Treynor Measure for the Pax World Fund

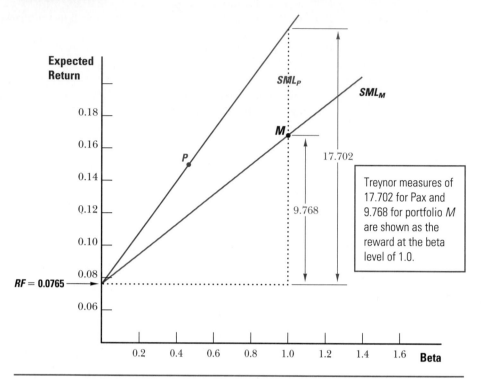

results of this example. It also indicates how the Treynor measure can be graphically interpreted.

The graph shows the SML_M based on a risk-free rate of 7.65 percent with a zero beta and a market portfolio return of 17.42 percent with a 1.0 beta. The graph shows the SML_p based on the same risk-free rate, but with Pax World Fund's portfolio beta of 0.44. SML_p is steeper than SML_M. Also, the Treynor measures of 9.768 for the S&P 500 and 17.702 for Pax World Fund measure the differences in their rewards at the 1.0 beta level. Pax provides a 7.934 percent higher reward (17.702 minus 9.768) at the 1.0 beta level.

Sharpe Performance Measure

The **Sharpe measure,** S_p, adjusts portfolio performance by **total risk** rather than beta risk.[5] The formula is:

$$S_p = [ER_p - RF]/SD_p \qquad (15.10)$$

Sharpe's logic for introducing total risk (measured by standard deviation, SD_p) instead of beta lies with the assumption behind the beta risk. Beta risk assumes that a portfolio is well-diversified with no remaining diversifiable risk. Sharpe argues, however, that a portfolio manager who does not hold a well-diversified portfolio should be penalized for exposing returns to diversifiable risk. Hence, the Sharpe measure adjusts portfolio returns for total risk, SD_p, which includes both systematic (beta) risk and diversifiable risk. Generally, if mutual funds or other portfolios are well-diversified, the Sharpe and Treynor measures will give them the same rankings. If the measures give different rankings, the portfolio ranked higher by Treynor, but lower by

[5]William Sharpe, "Mutual Fund Performance," *Journal of Business,* January 1966, 119–138.

Figure 15.5

Capital Market Line and the Sharpe Measure

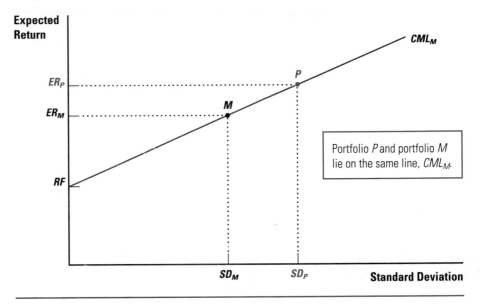

Sharpe may not be well-diversified. In this way, the Sharpe measure is considered to be more stringent than the Treynor measure.

While Treynor used the security market line, the Sharpe measure relies on the capital market line (CML) from Chapter 13. Recall that Equation 13.5 defined the CML as:

$$ER_p = RF + \{[ER_M - RF]/SD_M\}SD_p \tag{15.11}$$

Again, the reward for taking risk equals $[ER_p - RF]$, which comes from some manipulation of Equation 15.11:

$$[ER_p - RF] = \{[ER_M - RF]/SD_M\}\, SD_p \tag{15.12}$$

Dividing both sides by SD_p gives:

$$[ER_p - RF]/SD_p = [ER_M - RF]/SD_M \tag{15.13}$$

The left-hand side of Equation 15.13 is the Sharpe measure for portfolio p, S_p, and the right-hand side is the Sharpe measure for the market portfolio. More importantly, the right-hand side gives the slope of the CML_M. Again, the logic resembles that for the Treynor measure. If the slope (S_p) of a line, CML_p, equals the slope of the CML_M, then portfolio p must lie on the CML_M as Figure 15.5 illustrates.

If, however, a portfolio such as p_1 lies above the CML_M, the slope of CML_{p1} (S_{p1}) will be steeper than the slope of the CML_M. This suggests that p_1 outperforms the market. The Sharpe measure adjusts portfolio risk to the equivalent of the market's 1 percent standard deviation so the analyst can compare the rewards for p_1 and M. Suppose that S_{p1} equals 0.55 and S_M is 0.45; this relationship implies that the reward to p_1 is greater (by 0.10) than the market portfolio's return at the same level of SD_p risk. Figure 15.6 illustrates this situation.

Suppose another portfolio, p_2, lies below the CML_M; its slope (S_{p2}) must be flatter than the slope of the CML_M. This implies that p_2 underperforms

Figure 15.6

Capital Market Lines when $S_p > S_M$

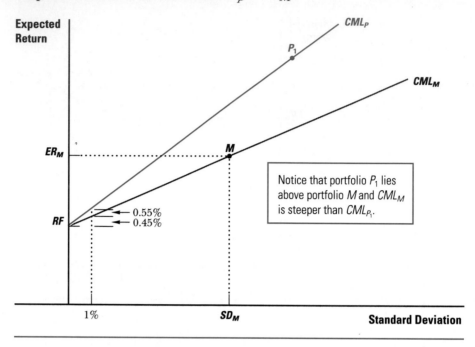

the market. Again, the Sharpe measure shows that the reward to p_2 is less than the market portfolio's reward at the same level of risk, as in Figure 15.7. Table 15.3 summarizes the three cases.

Let's apply the Sharpe measure to Pax World Fund and see if the relative performance picture changes. Table 15.2 reported ER_p for the portfolio (Pax), the S&P 500, and 30-day T-bills, so now we must calculate standard

Figure 15.7

Capital Market Lines when $S_p < S_M$

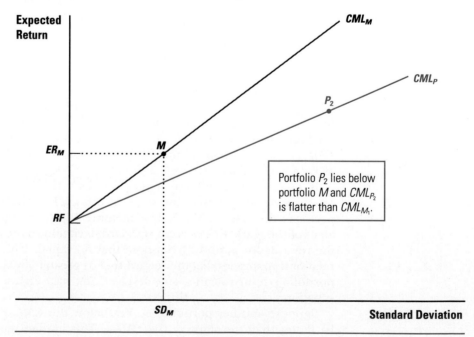

Table 15.3

Summary of the Sharpe Measure

If $S_p > S_M$	Portfolio p outperforms the market.
If $S_p = S_M$	Portfolio p performs exactly as well as the market portfolio, adjusted for total risk.
If $S_p < S_M$	Portfolio p underperforms the market.

deviations for Pax and the S&P 500. We calculated standard deviations in Chapter 12, but if you need a quick review, see Table 15.4. The standard deviation of returns on Pax equals 8.36 percent; for S&P 500, the standard deviation is 12.42 percent, as displayed in Table 15.2. Now let's calculate the Sharpe measure for Pax:

$$S_p = [ER_p - RF]/SD_p = (15.44\% - 7.65\%)/8.36\% = 0.93$$

The Sharpe measure for the S&P 500 equals:

$$S_M = [ER_M - RF]/SD_M = (17.42\% - 7.65\%)/12.42\% = 0.79$$

Since Pax's Sharpe measure is greater than that of the S&P 500, the mutual fund appears to outperform the market (S&P 500). CML_p has a

Table 15.4

How to Calculate a Standard Deviation

Using Pax World Fund as an example, this exhibit reviews how to calculate a standard deviation. It applies the procedure displayed in Table 12.3 to a portfolio of securities or a mutual fund.

Period (1)	Return (2)	Return − Mean (3)	$(R - M)^2$ (4)
1	18.20%	2.77%	7.6729%
2	24.20	8.77	76.9129
3	7.40	−8.03	64.4809
4	25.90	10.47	109.6209
5	8.40	−7.03	49.4209
6	3.50	−23.94	167.1849
7	11.70	−3.73	13.9129
8	24.80	9.37	87.7969
9	10.50	−4.93	24.3049
10	20.70	5.27	27.7729
Sum	154.30%		629.0810%

Step 1: Calculate the arithmetic average or mean, M, of Pax returns, R. The mean equals the sum of Column 2 divided by the number of returns, N:

$M = $ (Sum of Column 2)$/N = 154.3\%/10 = 15.43$ percent.

Step 2: Create Column 3 by subtracting the mean, M, from each return in Column 2.

Step 3: Create Column 4 by squaring each $(R - M)$ in Column 3.

Step 4: Sum Column 4 and divide by $(N - 1)$ to find the sample standard deviation, SD: 8.36 percent.

Most of the Larger Investment Advisers Appear to Be Beating the Stock Market

Most investment advisers apparently are beating the stock market.

A survey of filings with the Securities and Exchange Commission finds that the average adviser managed an 11.7 percent gain in the first quarter, compared with a 10 percent gain for the overall market, as measured by the Standard & Poor's index of 500 stocks. Dividend income is included.

The survey, covering 182 of the largest of the some 6,000 advisers registered with the SEC, found that three out of four were able to at least match the market's performance. Only the largest advisers are required to file reports with the agency.

And in the 12 months ended March 31, during which the market was declining in the first half and rising in the second half, 80 percent of the investment advisers were able to at least match the 44 percent rise in the S&P 500. The average gain for the period was 49.7 percent.

The statistics, compiled by Computer Directions Advisors Inc. of Silver Spring Md., cover stock performance only. Gains are computed on issues held in portfolios at the beginning of the period. Although trading activity during the period isn't reflected, Computer Directions says the discrepancy typically is insignificant.

The 182 money managers included in the survey reported stock portfolios at the beginning of the quarter totaling $161 billion.

INVESTMENT INSIGHTS

Some of the best first-quarter performances were turned in by advisers who were heavily invested in technology issues, which were strong during the quarter. Gregg, McKay, Knight & McKay Inc. of Boston, a two-year-old firm that began reporting its results this year, topped the quarterly rankings with a gain of 26 percent from 1982's fourth quarter.

Robert Knight, a partner, says the firm seeks stocks of companies whose per-share earnings are growing at an average of 30 percent a year or better. "When you look around for industries capable of this kind of growth, it puts you into telecommunications, microcomputers, telephone systems, and health care," he says. "These are the areas we've concentrated on."

Mr. Knight says the firm hasn't sold any stocks recently, and has been buying such issues as Emulex Corp., Micom Systems Inc., and Convergent Technologies. As for the fears of some market watchers that technology-stock prices are overinflated, Mr. Knight asserts that the outlook, assuming an economic recovery is under way, is bullish. "We're hoping for a correction in stock prices," he adds, "so we can go back to our clients for more money to buy at lower prices." The firm manages about $200 million of pension-fund money.

Those advisers unable to at least match the market's performance included some who bet early in lagging smokestack issues. Standish, Ayer & Wood, Inc., also Boston-based, managed a gain

steeper slope than CML_M. Finally, at a 1 percent level of total risk (SD_p), Pax's reward is .14 (0.93 minus 0.79) greater than that of the S&P 500. For a graphic display of the results, see Figure 15.8 on page 510.

The Investment Insight feature reprints a *Wall Street Journal* article from 1983 that ranks the top 20 investment advisory firms during the first quarter of that year and then measures their performance over the year from April 1982 to March 1983. The rankings reflect only holding period returns generated by these firms over the two periods, though. For example, Gregg, McKay, Knight, & McKay had an impressive 26.0 percent return over the first three months of 1983 followed by Torray, Clark & Co. with 25.4 percent, and so on. These advisors' annual returns were more impressive, as Provident Investment Counsel earned an 80.5 percent return over one year, followed by Quest Advisory Corp. with 80.4 percent, Torray, Clark & Co. with 77.5 percent, and so on. The S&P 500 didn't perform as well, but it had a 44.0 percent annual return.

Note, however, that these rankings do not account for risk, measured by beta, standard deviation, or otherwise. The Treynor measure for Provident Counsel's portfolio, assuming it had an average beta of 2.0 and 30-day T-bills were yielding approximately 10 percent, equaled:

of just 7 percent for the quarter, according to the survey. "We shifted gears during the quarter to highlight cyclical sectors of the market, especially basic industries," says Bart Clayson, chief investment officer.

"We were out of sync with the market," he adds, "but longer term we think it will pay off when the pickup in revenue and earnings come through."

The following tables list the top 20 investment advisers by percentage gains for the first quarter and for the 12 months ended March 31:

Top 20 Investment Advisers

First Quarter, 1983	Percentage Gain
Gregg, McKay, Knight & McKay	26.0
Torray, Clark & Co	25.4
BMI Capital Corp	25.4
Fidelity Intl Ltd	21.3
Hathaway & Associates	20.0
William D. Witter Inc	19.7
First Wilshire Securities Mgmt	19.6
Weingarton Mgmt Corp	18.8
Reams Asset Mgmt Co	18.8
Quest Advisory Corp	18.7
Manning & Napier Advisor	18.6
Investors Research Corp	18.5
Sterling Capital Mgmt	18.5
Frontier Capital Mgmt	18.4
Delafield Asset Mgmt	17.5
Montag & Caldwell	17.0
Strong/Cornegluson Cap	16.9
Harris Associates	16.2
Cashman, Farrell & Assoc	16.1
Templeton Investment Counsel	15.7
Standard & Poor's 500	10.0

12 months ended March 31	Percentage Gain
Provident Investment Counsel	80.5
Quest Advisory Corp	80.4
Torray Clark & Co	77.5
E.W. Axe & Co	75.8
Brokaw Capital Mgmt	75.3
Fidelity Intl Ltd	75.2
Fred Alger Mgmt	70.6
Rollert & Sullivan	70.2
Atlanta Capital Corp	68.6
Penmark Investments Inc	67.3
Investors Research Corp	65.2
Lynch & Mayer Inc	63.9
L. F. Rothschild, Unterberg	63.6
Lieber & Co	63.2
Arnold & S. Bleichroeder	62.6
Montag & Caldwell	62.4
Markston Intl	61.0
Essex Investment Mgmt	60.9
Management Asset Corp	60.3
Ruane Cunniff & Co	59.3
Standard & Poor's 500	44.0

Notes: The 1983 first-quarter gains are measured from the end of the 1982 fourth quarter. Gains for the 12 months are measured by linking the results of each quarter in the period.

Gains are for the equity portion of managed assets only. Total firm performance may vary depending on the mix of investments and other factors.

Source: R. Foster Winans, "Most of the Larger Investment Advisers Appear to Be Beating the Stock Market," *The Wall Street Journal*, April 12, 1983, 8. Reprinted by permission of The Wall Street Journal, © 1992 Dow Jones & Company, Inc. All Rights Reserved Worldwide

$$T_p = [ER_p - RF]/\beta = [80.5 - 10.0]/2.0 = 35.25$$

while the Treynor measure for the S&P 500 equaled:

$$T_M = [ER_M - RF] = [44.0 - 10.0] = 34.0$$

Remember, the market's beta equals 1.0. These results imply that Provident's portfolio outperformed the market portfolio, but not quite as impressively as the returns ignoring risk indicated. In fact, the other mutual funds further down the list may not have outperformed the market at all after adjusting for risk. This exercise shows how important it is to include risk when evaluating portfolio performance.

Alternatively, the Pax World Fund example shows that it is equally important not to assume that because a fund earns less than the S&P 500 Index, it underperforms the market. Pax had only a 15.44 percent return while the S&P 500 returned 17.42 percent; however, Pax's beta risk was only 0.44, less than half the market's, so its Treynor measure was higher than that of the S&P 500 ($T_p = 17.7$ and $T_M = 9.8$).

Now let's compare 10 mutual funds using the Treynor and Sharpe measures to determine whether they beat the market and how they rank against

Figure 15.8

Graphic Example of the Sharpe Measure for the Pax
World Fund

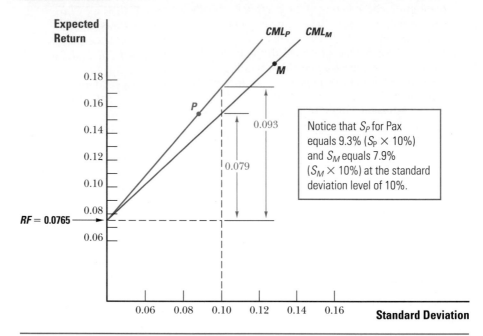

each other. Table 15.5 shows the Treynor and Sharpe measures for each fund
and for the market proxy (in this case the S&P 500). The table also includes
the Jensen measure, which will be discussed later.

The two performance measures produce very similar rankings.[6] The consistency of the rankings suggests that all ten funds are fairly well-diversified.
The top three funds according to both the Treynor and Sharpe measures are
Income Fund of America, Vista Growth & Income, and Putnam Fund for
Growth & Income. All three funds outperformed the market, based on both
measures. For example, Vista Growth & Income Fund has a Treynor measure
of 0.153 and a Sharpe measure of 1.006. The Treynor measure for the S&P
500 is 0.074 and the market has a Sharpe measure of 0.579. In fact, six of
the ten funds listed in Table 15.5 beat the market based on the Treynor measure; five of the ten funds beat the market based on the Sharpe measure.

The two measures also evaluate the bottom-ranked funds fairly con-
sistently. The worst-ranked funds, according to both measures, are SIT
New Beginning Growth & Income, State Street Investment, and TNE Value
Funds.

Jensen's Alpha

Another measure of risk-adjusted return, **Jensen's alpha,** utilizes the characteristic line estimated by the market model and again, the CAPM is its
benchmark.[7] Let's review the CAPM and then subtract RF from both sides
of the equation:

---

[6]In much larger samples, over longer time periods, the Treynor and Sharpe measures have been
shown to produce very similar rankings. See, for example, Hany Shanky, "An Update on Mutual
Funds: Better Grades," *Journal of Portfolio Management,* Winter 1982, 28–34; and Emery Trahan,
"Mutual Fund Performance: An Update for the 1980s," working paper, Northeastern University,
Boston, 1993.

[7]Michael Jensen, "Performance of Mutual Funds in the Period 1945–1964," *Journal of Finance,*
May 1968, 389–415.

Table 15.5

Ranking the Performance of Ten Mutual Funds Using the Treynor, Sharpe, and Jensen Measures

Mutual Fund	Treynor		Sharpe		Jensen's Alpha		
	Statistic	Rank	Statistic	Rank	Alpha	Rank	r-square
Income Fund of America	0.194	1	1.303	1	6.0	2	75%
Putnam Fund for Growth & Income	0.111	3	0.823	3	2.8	3	89
SAFECO Equity	0.084	5	0.566	6	1.4	5	73
Salomon Brothers Investors	0.073	7	0.552	7	0.0	7	95
SIT New Beginning Growth & Income	0.057	9	0.422	8	−1.2	8	89
State Street Investment	0.053	10	0.408	10	−1.9	10	96
TNE Value	0.058	8	0.420	9	−1.6	9	85
Vanguard Quantitative	0.082	6	0.634	5	1.0	6	98
Vista Growth & Income	0.153	2	1.006	2	8.9	1	71
Washington Mutual Investors	0.092	4	0.683	4	1.7	4	92
S&P 500 Stock Index (market proxy)	0.074	—	0.579	—			

Source: *Morningstar,* July 23, 1993 (based on returns through June 1993).

$$ER_p = RF + \beta_p[ER_M - RF], \tag{15.14}$$

$$ER_p - RF = \beta_p[ER_M - RF]. \tag{15.15}$$

Now let's review the market model, Equation 13.14, and then subtract RF from the independent and dependent variables $(R_{Mt}$ and $R_{jt})$: Recall that the market model estimates the α_p and β_p for a regression between R_{Mt} and R_{pt}.

$$R_{pt} = \alpha'_p + \beta_p R_{Mt} + \epsilon_{pt} \tag{15.16}$$

$$(R_{pt} - RF_t) = \alpha_p + \beta_p(R_{Mt} - RF_t) + \epsilon_{pt} \tag{15.17}$$

The difference between Equations 15.16 and 15.17, subtracting RF from both the independent and dependent variables, leaves the slope the same. The change causes a parallel shift in the market model to a new y-intercept, as Figure 15.9 shows.

The expected value of the regression equation in Equation 15.17 equals:

$$[ER_{pt} - ERF_t] = a_p + b_p [ER_{Mt} - ERF_t] + Ee_{pt} \tag{15.18}$$

where a and b are least-squares estimates of α and β. Recall from your statistics class that the ordinary least squares estimation procedure assumes that $Ee_{pt} = 0$ and that the expectations operator E is an arithmetic mean. This allows us to rewrite Equation 15.18 as:

$$ER_{pt} - ERF_t = a_p + b_p[ER_{Mt} - ERF_t] \tag{15.19}$$

Now let's compare Equation 15.19 with the CAPM, remembering that the ER_p, RF, and ER_M for the CAPM are calculated as arithmetic means using historical data over time. This implies they are equivalent in value to ER_{pt}, ERF_t, and ER_{Mt}.

$$ER_{pt} - ERF_t = a_p + b_p[ER_{Mt} - ERF_t]$$

$$ER_{pt} - RF = 0 + \beta_p[ER_M - RF]$$

The two equations are equivalent only if a_p equals zero. This value is called Jensen's alpha. It equals zero only if the ER_{pt} of portfolio p equals the CAPM

Figure 15.9

Market Model Less the Risk-Free Rate

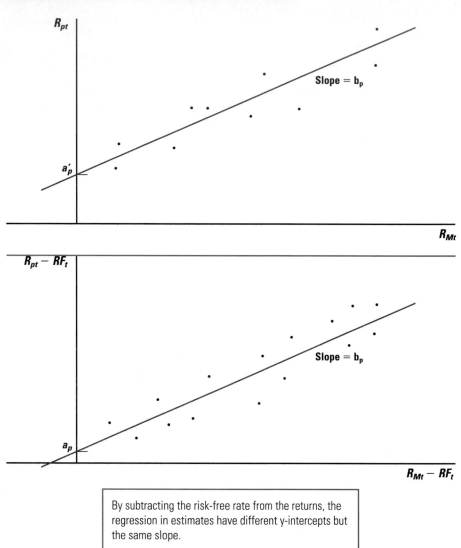

By subtracting the risk-free rate from the returns, the regression in estimates have different y-intercepts but the same slope.

equation. This means that p must lie on the SML. This essentially duplicates the SML analysis we conducted in Chapter 13. In fact, ER_{pt} can be interpreted as the predicted return, $E(r_i)$, in the SML analysis. If a_p equals zero when a portfolio lies on the SML, then a_p must be greater than zero $(a_p > 0)$ when a portfolio lies above the SML. Stated differently, $a_p > 0$ when the actual return from the regression exceeds the required CAPM return. Conversely, if $a_p < 0$, then a portfolio must lie below the SML or the actual return is less than the required CAPM return. The three decision rules for Jensen's alpha are summarized in Table 15.6. Figure 15.10 compares SML analysis and Jensen's alpha.

Since Jensen's alpha is estimated using regression, the analysis also provides the r-square statistic. In general, r-square indicates how well the independent variable "explains" the dependent variable. More specifically, when the regression equation is in the form of a market model, r-square states the percentage of a security's, or portfolio's, total risk that is systematic. (We discussed this back in Chapter 13.) Since one goal of a portfolio is to minimize, or even eliminate, unsystematic risk through diversification, the degree to

Table 15.6

Summary of Jensen's Alpha

If $a_p > 0$ Portfolio p outperforms the market.
If $a_p = 0$ Portfolio p performs as expected by the CAPM.
If $a_p < 0$ Portfolio p underperforms the market.

Figure 15.10

SML Analysis and Jensen's α

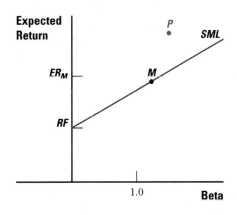
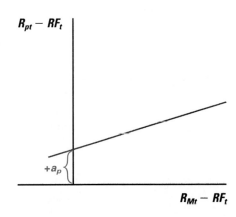

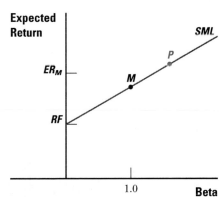
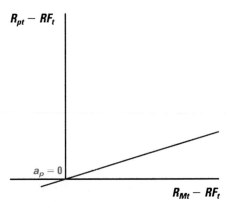

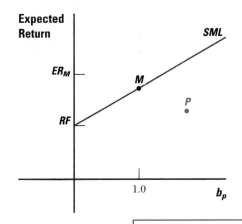
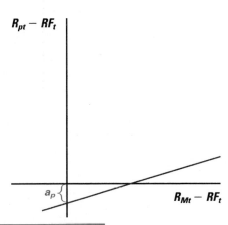

Notice the relationship between the SML and
Jensen's α. If P lies above SML, α is positve,
if P lies on SML, α equals zero, and if P lies
below SML, α is negative.

which *r*-square approaches 1.0 indicates how well-diversified the portfolio is.

Let's return to Table 15.4 to review the ranks of the ten mutual funds based on Jensen's alpha. Clearly, Jensen's alpha produced very similar rankings to those of the Treynor and Sharpe measures; the top three and bottom three funds are the same, although the individual rankings differ slightly. For example, the highest-ranked fund according to Jensen's alpha, Vista Growth & Income, ranks second according to the other two measures. Furthermore, the funds that appear to beat the market based on the Treynor and Sharpe measures all have positive alphas.

The three performance measures account for the reward relative to a risk measure and provide more appropriate portfolio performance measures. However, all three portfolio performance measures were applied to historical data, although the theoretical developments were based on ex-ante models. Obviously, historical performance is easier to evaluate than future performance even though we are really interested in future performance. The next section will focus on how well past performance predicts future performance and how we might use past data to, perhaps, find superior future investment portfolios.

How Well Does Past Performance Predict Future Performance?

At this point, we need to revisit the issue of whether or not past performance is a good predictor of future performance. All the performance measures we've just discussed use historical returns, so they evaluate *historical* performance. Of course, history may not repeat itself, at least during a particular investment horizon. Thus the results from using ex-post data even in a theoretically sound technique are dubious at best if the past is no guarantee of the future. Does the past predict the future? As we've seen before, and will see again, the answer is, alas, both *yes* and *no*.

The Wall Street Journal article reprinted in the Investment Insights feature points out that, although a "great track record may seem very alluring, it's just as likely to be dangerously misleading." The article admonishes investors to resist the temptation to rate money managers by short-term performance. Short-term results could easily be attributed to luck rather than skill. For example, managers look great if very risky investments pan out, but their success may depend on luck. Most pros track the long-term performance of money managers to assess their capabilities. The bar graph in the article shows that the best managers, those with approximately 32 percent cumulative return for four years from 1983 through 1986, had approximately an 8 percent cumulative return for a subsequent four-year period (1987 through 1990). Furthermore, the graph shows that from 1987 through 1990, the previously identified worst managers did about as well as the best (9 percent versus 8 percent). In fact, Ronald Peyton, president of Callan Associates, a pension consultant, says, "If you hire a manager for knockout returns over the last few years, you're in danger of signing on at the peak of the cycle, just before the [manager's style] declines." Columbia finance professor William Goetzman, adds "Investors appear to respond to raw returns."

However, evidence also suggests that investors shouldn't ignore past performance. (We looked at some of it in Chapter 7.) The article entitled "Playing Hot Hands" in the Investment Insights feature reports a conclusion from a recent study of pension fund managers that money managers with outstanding records are better bets for future gains than those with dismal past performance records.[8] The study measured the results of investing with managers whose performance records over the previous three years placed them in the top 25 percent of all pension funds. This strategy provided a 2.1 percent greater annual return than investing with managers whose performance records for the previous three years placed them in the bottom 25 percent. The Hulbert Financial Digest expanded on this study and found that performance records over periods longer than three years provided even more accurate predictions of money managers' future performance. Six-year performance data revealed that managers who beat the market between mid-1980 and mid-1986 made 5.1 percent per year more from mid-1986 to mid-1992 than those who did not beat the market.

Both articles argue that investors should evaluate returns over a fairly long period (three to six years) to measure the performance of money managers. Even long-term results give no guarantee that past performance can predict future performance, though. This uncertainty just reinforces the importance of risk in any investment decision. Returns alone cannot accurately measure performance; investors should always rely on some measure of reward in relation to risk.

Applying MPT to Investment Decisions

Different groups of investors apply MPT to investment decisions in different ways. Investors seem to accept MPT in varying degrees depending on how strongly they believe in market efficiency. (We discussed market efficiency in Chapter 7.)

Let's break investors into two groups on that basis. **Group 1 MPT investors** believe that the markets are so efficient that any well-diversified portfolio will provide a just return relative to its risk. These investors believe that all securities are correctly valued, or at least that they cannot discover undervalued securities before every one else does.[9] This is a **passive** or **naive strategy.** A strong belief in market efficiency implies that any portfolio will provide the appropriate return based on its risk level. As we discussed in Chapter 12, a randomly selected, equally weighted portfolio of about 20 stocks can eliminate virtually all unsystematic risk.[10] Group 1 MPT investors will base their portfolio decisions on this premise and invest in any well-diversified portfolio without worrying about individual securities. The only decision a Group 1 investor must make is what proportion of wealth to invest in the risky portfolio, p, and the risk-free asset, RF. In reality, such an investor would probably choose an index fund and a money market fund and determine the appropriate split between the two, depending on the individual investor's utility function for risk and return.

Group 2 MPT investors believe that the market is essentially efficient, but that some securities are always temporarily mispriced. They, too, accept the need to hold well-diversified portfolios; however, they see potential gains from selecting stocks that are undervalued, instead of naively choosing stocks randomly.[11] They also pursue optimal combinations of stocks in the portfolio,

---

[8]Josef Lakonishok et al., "The Structure and Performance of the Money Management Industry," *Brookings Papers on Economic Activity,* 1992, 339–391.

[9]Given Richard Roll's critique of the CAPM, which we discussed in Chapter 13, it's just as well to choose any efficient portfolio, especially since the "true" market portfolio is unobservable.

[10]Theoretically, portfolio weights should be based on market values.

[11]Security analysis could focus on such indicators as low P/E ratios, Value Line timeliness ratings, price-to-book ratios, small capital values, etc.

Past Is No Guarantee of Manager's Future

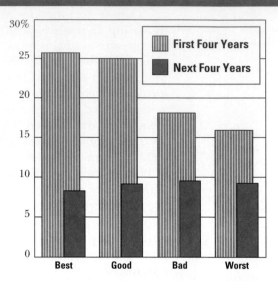

Everybody loves a winner, and investors are no exception.

A winning track record is the first—and sometimes the only—thing that most investors look for when entrusting their money to a professional manager. That's true of well-heeled folk with individually managed portfolios, as well as mutual-fund investors.

But while a great track record may seem very alluring, it's just as likely to be dangerously misleading.

To start with, impressive performance numbers tell nothing about how the portfolio stacks up today. Which of yesterday's winning managers are hedging their bets by diversifying into other investments? Which are riding the same investments that did so well in the past? Those are crucial questions because it's today's investment choices—not yesterday's—that determine how a manager will do in the future.

"The predicament that you get into looking at past performance is that portfolios are dynamic. Two managers who did equally well in the past may be making diametrically opposed bets today," says Dennis Trittin, director of stock research at Frank Russell Co., a pension-consulting firm. Looking at past performance wouldn't give investors any clue that such a transformation had taken place.

Impressive performance numbers also may gloss over other important questions—in particular, whether those gains were attributable to luck or skill.

Because the best short-term performers often come with highly volatile track records, short-term winners often aren't very capable managers. They may just be the ones who took big risks that happened to pan out.

Conversely, short-term losers aren't necessarily bad managers. They may just be the victims of bad luck. The shorter the track record under consideration, the harder it is to know for sure who's competent and who's not.

For that reason, most pros give little weight to recent performance numbers in trying to identify superior managers. They focus instead on the strength, consistency and discipline of a manager's investment process over the very long term.

"One of the biggest traps investors fall into is to put money into the absolute top performer," says Marshall Blume, a finance professor at the University of Pennsylvania's Wharton School who also advises investors in selecting managers.

Like roulette players, big winners "become top performers by having a very undiversified portfolio, with a big bet in one area that happens to work out," he says. As soon as they hit the jackpot, however, "the odds are very low that that will repeat itself in the future."

Unfortunately, unsophisticated investors do tend to rely heavily on short-term results in judging managers and mutual funds. As a result, they often end up making bad risk–return tradeoffs.

"Individual investors appear to use the preceding year's performance ranking as the basis for their investment decisions," says William Goetzman, a finance professor at Columbia University. That observation is supported by investor surveys, as well as Mr. Goetzman's own research on how mutual-fund performance correlates with inflows of new money from investors. Such behavior means "investors end up buying volatility not return," he adds.

rather than investing equally in the stocks. Group 2 MPT investors may conduct two-stage analyses: (1) securities analysis to determine which stocks to include in a well-diversified portfolio, and (2) an analysis to determine the optimal percentage of the well-diversified portfolio to devote to each stock.[12] Some professional money managers are paid to do essentially this work.

---

[12]The Sharpe performance measure can serve this purpose.

Extracting meaning from managers' track records becomes more confusing still, considering that even gifted managers with consistently good long-term records don't seem reliably to outperform over time.

For instance, a recent Frank Russell study tested whether an investor could predict future performance from the track records of 106 hand-picked managers monitored by the firm. It found that the winners' chances of repeating their success were "statistically indistinguishable from a proportion of 50 percent (the coin-flipping chance of success)."

In other words, investors have only a coin-flip chance of success that proficient managers with winning records will continue to outperform in the future. "There is no indication that there is any information on future prospects for return success contained in the manager's past performance," the study said.

There's less doubt, however, that investors should shun managers with consistently bad long-term records. When a broad mass of mutual-fund managers are held up to scrutiny, "the persistence of bad performance among losers is really striking," says Stephen Brown, a finance professor at New York University who coauthored a recent study on variations in funds' performance from 1976 to 1987.

"Really poor performance is kind of unambiguous," he says. "It's the good performance that's ambiguous."

Even good performers with well-defined, disciplined strategies can't always defend themselves against the market's vagaries. For one thing, investment styles rotate in and out of fashion at unpredictable intervals over time, and managers' strategies typically contain biases— whether overt or hidden—toward one style or another. In the very long run, style biases don't appear to vastly help or hinder the returns of one group of managers relative to the rest. But over periods of three, five, or even ten years, they can make significant differences to managers' relative performance.

For instance, managers who bought small-capitalization stocks enjoyed stunning performance in periods such as 1975 to 1983 and 1991, when small stocks trounced the rest of the market. But at other times, when small stocks were in eclipse, even top-performing small-stock managers showed relatively poor returns.

INVESTMENT INSIGHTS

In a similar vein, "growth" managers, who buy stocks with great earnings trends, may be the market's winners for years at a stretch, then abruptly hit dry spells when "value" strategies—or picking stocks that look cheap relative to earnings, dividends, and other fundamentals—become the rage. At that point, value managers will look like geniuses until that fad exhausts itself and these managers, in turn, get torpedoed by a rebound in growth investing.

Because many investors don't jump on any given style bandwagon until it's already in high gear—that is, once it's already reflected in managers' track records—they're constantly in danger of getting whipsawed by styles' changing fortunes.

"If you hire a manager for his knockout returns over the last few years, you're in danger of signing on at the peak of the cycle, just before [the manager's style] declines," says Ronald Peyton, president of Callan Associates, a pension consultant. "Over time, those who try to chase the market typically get killed."

Given this ebb and flow in the performance of different investment styles, investors should be careful to judge particular managers' records relative to managers with like styles and like levels of risk. Unfortunately, the evidence is that most individual investors don't compare apples to apples when gauging managers' performance.

"Investors appear to respond to raw returns—adjustment for risk makes little difference," says Columbia's Mr. Goetzman.

Source: Barbara Donnelly, "Past Is No Guarantee of Manager's Future," *The Wall Street Journal*, December 27, 1992, C1. Reprinted by permission of The Wall Street Journal, © 1992 Dow Jones & Company, Inc. All Rights Reserved Worldwide

Next, Group 2 MPT investors will follow Group 1 MPT investors and decide the right combination of the risky portfolio, p, and the risk-free asset, RF.

A third group of MPT investors falls somewhere between Group 1 and Group 2 investors. These investors believe that the market offers undervalued and overvalued securities, but that finding these securities, given the limited resources of an individual investor, is next to impossible. As a result, while they share some beliefs with Group 2 investors, these investors make

Playing Hot Hands

I recently had an unexpected telephone call from Professor Josef Lakonishok of the University of Illinois at Urbana-Champaign. He wanted to talk with me about his recent study on the performance of the money management business.

He was flabbergasted at reports on the study that appeared in the *Economist* and *The Wall Street Journal*. Not that he doesn't appreciate the publicity—anyone likes to see his views get wide exposure. But he was upset that these two widely read publications had misunderstood one of his quite remarkable conclusions—that there is such a thing as genuine advisory ability. Both publications had fastened on to the idea that the study showed that professional investment managers couldn't beat the market. But in so doing, they missed a far more noteworthy and helpful conclusion. The study found that—the efficient market hypothesis notwithstanding—money managers with outstanding records are better bets for future gains than those with dismal past performances.

Coming from a perennially skeptical academia, this is a truly newsworthy revelation. Lakonishok and his colleagues arrived at it by exhaustively studying the performance of 769 all-equity pension funds from 1983 through 1989.

They searched for any consistency in those funds' performances over time: Are the best performers more likely to continue outperforming others, and are the losers more likely to continue as losers?

Their answer: "Yes"—there are consistent winners, provided performance is measured over a sufficiently long period of time. One year is not enough. But performances over a three-year period provide "very clear consistency."

The study asked what would happen if one entrusted one's money to those managers whose performances over the previous three years placed them in the top 25 percent of all pension funds. Lakonishok and his colleagues calculate that such a strategy can expect to do 2.1 percent per year better than a strategy of betting on those managers who are in the bottom quartile for three-year past performance.

Lakonishok et al. don't claim that investing in the top 25 percent of three-year performers is the best way of using past data to pick a manager. A three-year period isn't very long, and segregating managers into quartiles still groups together advisers of widely varying abilities. Nevertheless, 2.1 percent per year isn't insignificant by any means: Over the 30 years that many invest in their companies' pension plans, for example, betting on the three-year winners rather than three-year losers would lead a pen-

investment decisions as if they belonged to Group 1. As a result, they try to combine well-diversified risky portfolios with risk-free assets.

Of course, some investors scorn MPT entirely. Many technicians may fall into this group. These investors, as a group, probably don't believe in market efficiency, either. Despite this skepticism, however, many of these investors do believe in the benefits of diversification and some of the other contributions of MPT. The well-known market technician Martin Zweig, for example, flatly states: "When you buy stocks, you *must* diversify."[13] Excluding the group of skeptics, who have their own investing decision techniques, let's see how the two groups of MPT investors might apply what we have learned so far in Chapters 12 through 15.

Group 1 MPT Investors

How would Group 1 MPT investors apply the theory? Since they believe strongly in market efficiency, their only decision is how to divide their funds between the well-diversified portfolio and the risk-free asset. Suppose an investor naively chooses a well-diversified portfolio, p_1, that has an annual ER_{p1} equal to 16 percent and $SD(P_1)$ equal to 12 percent. The risk-free rate

---

[13]Martin Zweig, *Winning on Wall Street* (New York: Warner Books, 1990), 275. A careful reading of Zweig's book leads one to believe that he accepts more of MPT than many of his fellow technicians.

sion fund to be worth nearly twice as much at retirement.

Lakonishok's findings are right in line with what my *Hulbert Financial Digest* has discovered from its research into the performance of investment advisory letters. In a just-completed summary of its findings over the last 12 years, the *HFD* found that letters beating the market over a three-year period make an average of 2.8 percent per year more over the subsequent three years than the market laggards—quite close to the 2.1 percent differential in the Lakonishok study.

But that's not all: The *HFD* found that performances over periods longer than three years have even more predictive power. Consider gains over a six-year period. Those letters that beat the market between mid-1980 and mid-1986, for example, made 5.1 percent per year more over the mid-1986 to mid-1992 period than did those that failed to beat the market in the earlier period.

How could *The Wall Street Journal* and the *Economist* miss these important findings contained in Lakonishok's study? By failing to look beyond the average performance of all pension funds. And when focusing on the average, it is easy to dismiss the entire industry: As the Lakonishok study reports, the typical all-equity pension fund underperforms the stock market by 1.3 percent per year.

INVESTMENT INSIGHTS

Which investment letters should you thus bet on? Out of the 67 that the *HFD* has tracked over the last six years, just under a quarter of them, or 15, are ahead of the market itself. These six-year market beaters include Louis Navellier's *MPT Review* (which gained 294 percent over these six years, in contrast to the average stock's 86 percent), Geraldine Weiss' *Investment Quality Trends* (128 percent), Dan Sullivan's *The Chartist* (116 percent), and Martin Zweig's *Zweig Forecast* (101 percent).

There is no guarantee that these and the other six-year market-beaters will continue to outperform the market into the future. But the *HFD*'s research, as does this new academic study, gives us confidence in betting that they will do significantly better than those who have failed to beat the market over the last six years.

But then why should this be surprising? In any field, whether sports, business, or the arts, past performance *is* a reasonable basis for predicting future performance.

Source: Mark Hulbert, "Playing Hot Hands," *Forbes,* August 17, 1992, 135.

---

equals 6 percent. Using the capital market line (CML) equation, the risk–return relationship can be stated as:

$$ER_p = RF + \left[\frac{ER_{p1} - RF}{SD_{p1}} \right] SD_p \qquad (15.20)$$

Plugging in the values for p_1 gives:

$$ER_p = 0.06 + [(0.16 - 0.06)/0.12] SD_p$$
$$= 0.06 + 0.833\ SD_p$$

Notice that the relationship in Equation 15.20 exists for every risky portfolio (efficient or not); however, we assume that all rational investors choose portfolios on the efficient frontier (that is, efficient portfolios).

Group 1 MPT investors don't care which efficient portfolio they hold; they simply adjust their risk levels by investing in varying proportions of p_1 and the risk-free asset, *RF*. A risk adverse investor might set a risk objective of a 10 percent standard deviation, which is less than portfolio $p1$'s risk of 12 percent. The following steps would meet this objective.

First, plug 10 percent into the equation above to determine the level of ER_p:

$$ER_p = 0.06 + 0.833\ (0.10) = 14.33\ percent$$

Next, determine what percentages of risky and risk-free assets would give the expected return of 14.33 percent. This requires using the equation from Chapter 12 for the expected return from a two-asset portfolio:

$$ER_p = X\% \times ER_{p1} + (1 - X\%) \times RF$$

where X equals the percentage investment in the risky portfolio, p_1. This equation can be rewritten as:

$$ER_p = [ER_{p1} - RF]X\% + RF$$

$$0.1433 \text{ percent} = [0.16 - 0.06]X + 0.06$$

$$0.1433 \text{ percent} = [0.10]X\% + 0.06$$

$$X = 0.833 \text{ or } 83.3 \text{ percent}$$

The percentage invested in RF, $(1 - X)$ equals $(1 - 0.833)$, or 16.7 percent. A Group 1 MPT investor will naively choose p_1 and then invest 83 percent of available funds in that portfolio. The remaining 17 percent would go into a money market fund to achieve the target risk level (10 percent).

Group 2 MPT Investors

Now what will a Group 2 MPT investor do? Remember, this investor also believes in market efficiency, but still sees some benefits in security analysis. This person hopes to identify undervalued stocks, and to define some optimal portfolio combination.

As stated earlier, a Group 2 MPT investor would conduct two analyses: (1) security analysis to identify undervalued stocks, and (2) an analysis based on the Sharpe performance measure (supplemented by lots of intuition) to determine the optimal combination of securities.

Recall that Chapter 13's SML analysis (along with intrinsic value analysis from Chapter 8) found that American Home Products (AHP) and Washington Water Power (WWP) were undervalued. This is the first step for a Group 2 MPT investor; to identify stocks in which to invest. Next, the investor determines what percentage (X) of available funds to invest in specific stocks. This person is not naive enough just to buy 50 percent of each security (called an equally weighted portfolio). To determine the optimal percentage holdings for just two stocks, AHP and WWP,[14] follow the steps outlined below.

In Chapter 12, Table 12.6 illustrated different percentage holdings of each of two securities. In order to determine their optimal percentages, first use the method discussed on page 415 to create various combined holdings of AHP and WWP, then use the Sharpe measure to determine the optimal combination.[15]

Table 15.7, like Table 12.6, displays various percentage investments in AHP and WWP, along with the expected returns, standard deviations, and Sharpe

---

[14]This method is also applicable for a capital allocation decision between categories of funds such as a stock fund and a bond fund.

[15]In reality, this analysis should consider several hundred stocks to gain maximum benefits of diversification. This work requires linear programming techniques or a computer program that creates an efficient frontier with a large number of stocks. The wizard program, which accompanies the text, can create efficient frontiers.

Table 15.7

Expected Returns, Standard Deviations, and Sharpe Measures for Various Combinations of AHP and WWP

Portfolio	X percent in AHP[a]	(1 − X percent) in WWP	E(R_p)	SD_p	Sharpe Measure[b]
p_1	100%	0%	21.876%	18.872%	0.8412
p_2	90	10	21.216	17.878	0.8511
p_3	80	20	20.556	16.984	0.8571
p_4	70	30	19.908	16.205	0.8583[c]
p_5	60	40	19.248	15.564	0.8512
p_6	50	50	18.588	15.072	0.8352
p_7	40	60	17.940	14.743	0.8099
p_8	30	70	17.292	14.594[d]	0.7737
p_9	20	80	16.620	14.629	0.7259
p_{10}	10	90	15.972	14.844	0.6718
p_{11}	0	100	15.240	15.235	0.6065

[a]We will calculate only an approximate optimal percentage because the ultimate decision should rest with the portfolio manager's intuition for the security and its expected performance. Therefore the X percent will be in increments of 10 percent.

[b]The Sharpe measure is calculated using a 0.06 annual return for the risk-free rate.

[c]Portfolio p_4 has the highest Sharpe measure and provides the percentage for an optimal investment in AHP and WWP.

[d]Portfolio p_8 has the minimum variance, or the lowest portfolio risk.

measures for those portfolios. The portfolio with the highest Sharpe measure is considered to have the optimal percentage investment in AHP and WWP. Table 15.6 indicates that 70 percent in AHP and (1 − 0.70), or 30 percent, in WWP (portfolio p_4) is the optimal combination of these stocks. A naive holding of 50 percent in each does not have the highest Sharpe measure. Figure 15.11 shows graphically that portfolio p_4 has the highest CML. Figure 15.11 also shows that the minimum-variance portfolio is just the reverse: 30 percent in AHP and 70 percent in WWP. This low-risk option is not necessarily the optimal portfolio.

The CML equation for the optimal portfolio, p_4, the one with the highest Sharpe measure, equals:

$$ER_p = RF + \{[ER_{p4} - RF]/SD_{p4}\}SD_p \qquad (15.21)$$

Since $[ER_{p4} - RF]/SD_{p4}$ is the Sharpe measure for portfolio $p4$, replace it with 0.8583 (assuming that the risk-free rate still equals 6 percent):

$$ER_p = 0.06 + 0.8583SD_p$$

This CML equation is helpful in determining the ER_p at a specific risk level (measured by standard deviation). At a set SD_p of 10.0 percent Equation 15.21 gives:

$$ER_p = 0.06 + 0.8583 (0.10) = 0.14583 \text{ or } 14.583 \text{ percent}$$

Knowing that ER_p equals 14.583 percent, we can find how much of the risk-free rate asset and the optimal portfolio p_4 should be held in the overall portfolio. Using Equation 15.20 for p_4 and RF, solve for X percent.

Figure 15.11

Various Combinations of Portfolio Investments in AHP and WWP

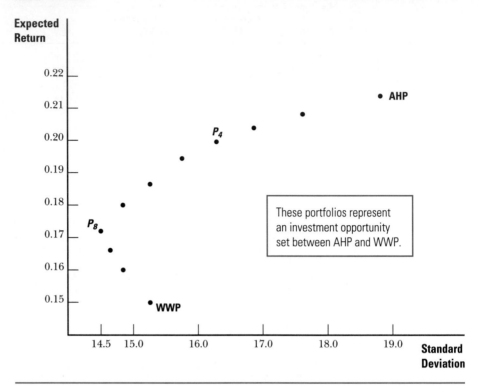

Remember that *RF* equals 0.06 (6 percent) and Table 15.7 gives ER_{p4} as 19.908 percent, so:

$$14.583 \text{ percent} = [0.19908 - 0.06] \, X + 0.06$$

$$X \text{ percent} = 0.617 \text{ or } 61.7 \text{ percent}$$

The portfolio manager would hold 61.7 percent of portfolio p_4 and $(1 - X)$ or 38.3 percent of *RF* (or a money market fund). Now, recall that p_4 consists of 70 percent AHP and 30 percent WWP, so the *entire* portfolio consists of 43.19 percent of AHP (.617 × 70 percent), 18.51 percent of WWP (.617 × 30 percent), and 38.3 percent of a money fund. The entire portfolio provides an expected return of 14.567 percent, with the specified risk level of 10 percent.

In reality, a Group 2 MPT investor or portfolio manager may not match these percentages exactly to the second decimal place. This is a systematic method by which a portfolio manager may wish to determine optimal holdings of several securities. In the end, however, the manager's intuition probably will (and should) outweigh the calculated percentages. These equations set some helpful, systematic guidelines for optimizing risk and return.

The key difference between MPT investors in Groups 1 and 2 is that the first group will accept any well-diversified portfolio, while the second group will attempt to find undervalued stocks and optimize the portfolio combinations of these stocks. The next section outlines a more mathematical process for finding optimal combinations in a passive, well-diversified portfolio that includes some select, undervalued or overvalued stocks.

Treynor–Black Portfolio Combination Model[16]

Jack Treynor and Fisher Black have developed a method by which portfolio managers can naively select well-diversified portfolios then enhance their performance by investing in more selected stocks found through securities analysis.[17] This is referred to as the **Treynor–Black portfolio combination model.** Group 2 MPT investors might embrace this type of procedure in order to systematically increase their expected returns by optimizing their selections and combinations of securities. The process also accommodates the tradeoff between the benefits of selecting undervalued securities and the cost of incurring diversifiable risk associated with choosing only a limited number of stocks. This method gives the individual a more realistic procedure that recognizes the impossibility of conducting security analysis on every stock; the best MPT alternative is to find a few undervalued stocks called portfolio U, and a naive, well-diversified stock portfolio fund (perhaps an index fund based on one of the broad market averages such as the S&P 500), then find an optimal combination of these two portfolios. Of course, the combination model can also find the optimal proportions of the stocks in just portfolio U, which essentially duplicates the above example.

Conceptually, the model determines a well-diversified portfolio on the efficient frontier, assuming that all securities are priced according to the CAPM. (See Figure 15.12 for a graphic representation.) Consistent with the earlier discussion, we'll call this the market portfolio, M. We will assume that it is efficient based on the premise that all stocks are priced fairly, as expected by the CAPM.

Now suppose that security analysis techniques help a portfolio manager to identify a group of undervalued stocks, portfolio U. (An investor could also sell short overvalued stocks where the proportional investments equal negative percentages.) Now the well-diversified portfolio could be improved by creating a new efficient frontier that encompasses the naive portfolio, plus U. The optimal proportion of this combined portfolio with the risk-free asset is designated as portfolio p^*, as in Figure 15.12.

With this background established, let's review the process in detail. First, naively choose a well-diversified portfolio, M. It could be any broad-based index fund, for example. Second, find a group of undervalued stocks. Jensen's alpha could help to identify undervalued (overvalued) stocks, which would have positive (negative) alphas, based on Equation 15.19.[18] The portfolio manager could add as many stocks as available research time reveals.

Suppose a combination of these undervalued stocks is represented by portfolio U. The expected return on portfolio U can be written as:

$$ER_{ut} - ERF_t = a_u + b_u[ER_{mt} - ERF_t].\tag{15.22}$$

Remember that a and b are least-squares estimates of α and β.

The third step is to determine the optimal combination of M, the market portfolio, and undervalued portfolio U. Call this optimal portfolio p^*. The

---

[16]This section is more rigorous than prior sections and can be skipped without any loss of continuity.

[17]Jack Treynor and Fisher Black, "How to Use Security Analysis to Improve Portfolio Selection," *Journal of Business,* January 1973, 66–86.

[18]Alternatively, the technique could identify overvalued stocks and expect to sell them short.

Figure 15.12

Treynor-Black Portfolio Combination Model

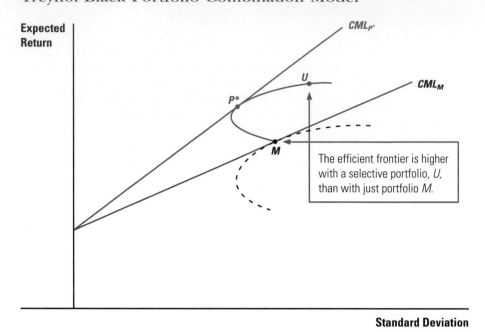

return to p^* should equal a proportion X^* of portfolio U and $(1 - X^*)$ of the market portfolio:

$$ER_p^* = X^*ER_u + (1 - X^*)ER_M$$

To identify the optimal combination by the Sharpe measure, as in the earlier example, the portfolio with the highest Sharpe measure provides the optimal combination of U and M. Using calculus, we could mathematically find the X^* proportion in portfolio p^* that would maximize the Sharpe measure. The proportion X^* equals:

$$X^* = \frac{X'}{1 + (1 - b_u)X'} \tag{15.23}$$

where:

$$X' = \frac{a_u / SD^2(e_u)}{[ER_M - RF] / SD_M^2}$$

What do the proportions tell us? Notice that if b_u equals 1.0 then, $X^* = X'$. Let's dissect X' now. The numerator, $a_u / SD^2(e_u)$, measures the degree of underpricing, or alpha, relative to the diversifiable risk, $SD^2(e_u)$, embedded in the select stock portfolio. This ratio expresses the tradeoff between excess profits from underpricing and the risk of not diversifying. Finally, it is divided by $[ER_M - RF] / SD_M^2$. This equals the Sharpe measure for the market portfolio, which provides the reward-to-risk ratio for a well-diversified portfolio.

Although the two ratios in Equation 15.23 seem horrendous, they can be intuitively interpreted. The whole expression says that the optimal combination of U and M depends on two things. (1) The optimal combination depends on the tradeoff between the excess return and its diversifiable risk, which is also the tradeoff between the excess return and a well-diversified portfolio M (as measured by Sharpe). (2) The optimal combination of U and

M also depends on how they are correlated (measured by β_u), providing the opportunity of diversifying further by holding U alone.

Now, take the squared value of the Sharpe measure for the optimal portfolio, p^*. (Remember, this is some combination of the market, or naive, portfolio, M, and the portfolio of undervalued stocks, U.)

$$S_p^{*2} = \left[\frac{ER_M - RF}{SD_M}\right]^2 + \left[\frac{a_u}{SD(e_u)}\right]^2, \text{ or}$$

$$S_p^{*2} = S_M^2 + \frac{a_u^2}{SD^2(e_u)}.$$

(15.24)

Note that this relationship holds only for the optimal portfolio, p^*. The first term in Equation 15.24 is the squared Sharpe measure for the market portfolio. The second term is the contribution to the optimal portfolio made by the undervalued securities. Three important facts guide selection of stocks based on Equation 15.24.

1. The Sharpe measure of p^* increases over the naive portfolio M by the second term in Equation 15.24, $a_u^2 / SD^2(e_u)$. To the extent that undervalued stocks can be found, it pays to be selective. An investor should choose stocks with the highest ratios of excess returns to diversifiable risk.

2. The second term in Equation 15.24 also suggests the appropriate proportion for each of the selected stocks. It says that the portfolio's Sharpe measure is maximized by investing the largest proportions in the stocks with the highest individual ratios of excess returns to diversifiable risk. Assume a pool of N undervalued stocks; the investor can find the proportion in which to invest in each, X_j, in order to maximize the second term, and thus the Sharpe measure for the optimal portfolio:

$$X_j = \frac{a_j SD^2(e_j)}{\sum\limits_{j=1}^{N} a_j / SD^2(e_u)}$$

(15.25)

The denominator in Equation 15.25 is, of course, the same as the second term in Equation 15.24.

To sort out all of these terms, a little numerical example may help. Assume an undervalued group of three stocks:

Stock	$a_j/SD^2(e_j)$	X_j
One	0.4	0.33
Two	0.6	0.50
Three	0.2	0.17
Sum	1.2	1.00

The last column is the proportion of each of the three stocks in the undervalued portfolio. It's found by dividing the number in the second column (the ratio of individual stocks' excess returns to their diversifiable risk) by the sum of the ratios for the three stocks (1.2 in this example). Since Stock 2 has the highest ratio of excess return to diversifiable risk of the three, the investor should invest the most, proportionally, in that stock or X_j is 50 percent. Stock 3 has the lowest ratio of excess return to diversifiable risk, so the investor commits the least amount to that stock, or X_j is 17 percent.

3. The ability of the portfolio manager to find undervalued stocks can be measured by how well the optimal portfolio performs, relative to the naive portfolio M. The second term in Equation 15.24, sometimes called the

appraisal ratio, defines this relationship. A higher appraisal ratio indicates better performance relative to the market (that is, how good the investor is at picking stocks). We can even calculate how much each stock contributes to the overall appraisal ratio: $a_j^2 / SD^2(e_j)$.

Let's review the numerical example with AHP and WWP as the undervalued stocks. This time, however, we will combine them with a well-diversified portfolio, the S&P 500. Suppose the S&P 500 index fund is expected to return 16 percent per year with a standard deviation of 18 percent. Assume that the risk-free rate is 6 percent. The procedure requires seven steps.

Step 1. Complete the market model regressions for AHP and WWP to produce the following results taken from Table 13.3:[19]

Stock	a	b	$SD(e_j)$	$SD^2(e_j)$
AHP	0.09	0.66	0.378	0.1429
WWP	0.01	0.41	0.132	0.0174

Step 2. Construct the individual stocks' appraisal ratios in order to determine their excess returns relative to their added diversifiable risk, $SD^2(e_j)$.

Stock	$a_j^2/SD^2(e_j)$	X_j
AHP	0.630	0.630/1.205 = 0.523
WWP	0.575	0.575/1.205 = 0.477
Sum	1.205	1.000

The last column in this table indicates the optimal combination of the selected stocks in portfolio *U;* approximately 52 percent in AHP and 48 percent in WWP.

Step 3. Using the appraisal ratio from each stock, calculate a, *b,* and *SD(e)* for portfolio *U.* Portfolio *U*'s a is equal to a weighted average of the alphas of the two stocks:

$$a_U = 0.523(0.09) + 0.477(0.01) = 0.05184$$

Similarly, the beta of Portfolio *U* is a weighted average of the betas of the two stocks:

$$b_U = 0.523(0.66) + 0.477(0.41) = 0.541$$

Finally, diversifiable risk, $SD(e_U)$, equals:

$$SD(e_U) = \sqrt{\sum_{j=1}^{N} X_j^2 SD^2(e_j)}$$

$$SD(e_U) = \sqrt{(0.523)^2(0.1429) + (0.477)^2(0.0174)}$$

$$SD(e_U) = 0.2075$$

This assumes that the error terms from the two market model regressions are independent of each other.

Step 4. Calculate the proportions of *U* and *M* in the optimal portfolio *p**. Remember that *p** is composed of *U* and *M* and the proportions are defined by *X'* and *X**. Equation 15.23, with the data developed in the first three steps, gives:

---

[19]Recall that *a* and *b* are estimates for α and β.

$$X' = \frac{0.05184/(0.2075)^2}{(0.16 - 0.06)/(0.18)^2} = 0.39$$

$$X^* = 0.39/[1 + (1 - 0.541)(0.39)] = 0.331$$

The optimal portfolio consists of about 33 percent of portfolio U and about 67 percent of the market portfolio.

Step 5. Now determine how much of the optimal portfolio will consist of the two stocks, AHP and WWP. Since Equation 15.24 gives X_s, the amount invested in AHP and WWP, combine it with X^* to find the final holdings:

Stock	Optimal Holding, X_j^*
AHP	$(0.331)(0.523) = 0.173$
WWP	$(0.331)(0.477) = 0.158$
Portfolio U total holdings	0.331

If 0.331 of portfolio p^* is invested in U, then $(1 - 0.331) = 0.669$ is invested in M. To summarize, the total investment between U and M consists of:

Stock/Portfolio	Final Holdings
AHP	0.173
WWP	0.158
Portfolio U	0.331
Portfolio M	0.669
Total invested in p^*	1.000 or 100%

Step 6. Find the expected return on p^*, ER_p^*. Using the standard formula for expected return from a two-asset portfolio:

$$ER_p^* = X^*ER_U + (1 - X^*)ER_M$$

Since U consists of 52.3 percent of AHP and 47.7 percent of WWP, so:

$$ER_U = 0.523ER_{AHP} + 0.477ER_{WWP}$$

Substituting these values for $E(R_U)$ gives:

$$ER_p^* = X^*[0.523ER_{AHP} + 0.477ER_{WWP}] + (1 - X^*)ER_M.$$

Using the values for ER_{AHP}, ER_{WWP}, and X^*, find the value for ER_p^*,

$$
\begin{aligned}
ER_p^* &= (0.331)[0.523(21.876\%) + 0.477(15.24\%)] + 0.669(16\%) \\
&= 6.19\% + 10.70\% \\
&= 16.9 \text{ percent}
\end{aligned}
$$

As expected, this return is higher than the return on the naive portfolio, M, but not by much! The naive portfolio is expected to return 16 percent compared to the optimal portfolio's 16.9 percent.

Step 7. Having identified portfolio, p^*, along with its expected return, let's examine the benefits from the process by finding the Sharpe measure for portfolio p^*, S_p^*.

$$S_p^{*2} = 0.3136 + 0.0624 = 0.376$$

$$S_p^* = 0.613$$

The optimal portfolio's Sharpe measure equals 0.613 compared to the naive/ market portfolio's Sharpe measure of 0.56. Stock selection has provided a small benefit, 0.053. The bottom line is that there is a tradeoff between stock selection and diversification. One should *never* ignore the benefits of diversifying, no matter how confident of one's stock picking ability.[20] It's definitely a wise decision to balance the two!

After identifying the optimal portfolio p^*, the individual investor must choose the percentage of p^* and the risk-free rate to hold, and this depends on an individual's utility function. This last step is the only part that requires a subjective decision about risk preference.

Modern portfolio theory is extremely valuable to real-world investors. MPT can provide insight into evaluating the performance of portfolios, how they rank against each other, and whether they beat the market over a period of time. Modern portfolio theory can also incorporate security analysis to help improve portfolio selection and performance.

Chapter Summary

1. **Develop and apply three measures of investment performance based on modern portfolio theory.**

   We developed, and applied to actual return data, three measures of portfolio performance: the Treynor measure, the Sharpe measure, and Jensen's alpha. All three come from modern portfolio theory. The Treynor measure, based on the security market line (SML), determines the reward (return minus the risk-free rate) per beta risk for a portfolio or an individual security. If an investment's Treynor measure exceeds that of the market, the investment has outperformed the market over a specified period of time; if its Treynor measure falls short of the market's, it has underperformed the market. The Sharpe measure, based on the capital market line (CML), determines the reward (again, return minus the risk-free rate) per total risk for a portfolio or an individual security. If an investment's Sharpe measure exceeds that of the overall market, the investment has outperformed the market over a specified period of time; if its Sharpe measure falls short of the market's, it has underperformed the market. Finally, Jensen's alpha comes from the market model. Alpha is the y-intercept of the regression model. The dependent variable is excess returns from a portfolio or individual security (return minus the risk-free rate), while the independent variable is the market's excess return over the same time period. If alpha does not equal zero, then the investment has outperformed or underperformed the overall market, depending on the sign of alpha. As we saw, all three measures generally rank investments and portfolios consistently, but not always.

2. **Reconsider whether past performance is a good predictor of future performance.**

   Because all three measures of investment performance are based on historical returns, we reconsidered whether or not past performance is a good predictor of future performance. As we've seen before, the evidence is quite mixed. Many investors appear to base decisions on raw, short-term returns. Evidence suggests that these returns, unadjusted for risk, are poor predictors of future returns. On the other hand, a recent study of pension fund managers found that managers who performed well over a three-year-period were more likely to do better than average over the subsequent three-year period. This reinforces familiar advice: consider past

---

[20]Even the legendary mutual fund manager Peter Lynch admitted that about one-third of his "hot" stock picks for Fidelity's Magellan Fund turned out to be duds.

performance as only one of several important factors when making investment decisions.

3. **Understand how different groups of investors might apply MPT to investment decisions.**

Two groups of investors may apply modern portfolio theory differently, depending on how strongly they believe in the efficient markets hypothesis. Group 1 MPT investors believe so strongly in market efficiency that they will accept *any* well-diversified portfolio. This group believes that no one can uncover undervalued securities before everyone else does. Investors in this group would allocate their investment funds between the market portfolio (say an index fund) and a risk-free security (say a money market fund) depending upon their individual risk preferences. Group 2 MPT investors believe the market is *generally* efficient, but that undervalued securities can be discovered through careful security analysis. Investors in this group would allocate investment funds between the market portfolio, a risk-free security, and the undervalued securities, again depending upon individual risk preferences.

4. **Examine the Treynor–Black portfolio combination model.**

The Treynor–Black portfolio combination model is a more formal, and mathematical, process for the analysis performed by Group 2 MPT investors. An investor initially identifies a portfolio of undervalued securities and then allocates funds based on the tradeoff each security offers between excess returns and diversifiable risk. A higher ratio leads the investor to allocate more funds to a particular security. The investor then goes through a process of combining the portfolio of undervalued securities with the market portfolio and a risk-free security. This produces a portfolio that should maximize expected return, given the individual investor's risk preference.

Key Terms

Modern portfolio theory (MPT)	Group 1 MPT investor
Treynor measure	Passive (naive) strategy
Beta risk	Group 2 MPT investor
Sharpe measure	Treynor–Black portfolio combination
Total risk	model
Jensen's alpha	Appraisal ratio

Mini Case **1**   OBJECTIVE

Calculate and interpret the Treynor, Sharpe, and Jensen performance measures based on the following ten-year annual mutual fund performance data:

	State Farm Balanced Fund (1)	Bull & Bear Capital Growth Fund (2)	Keystone Custodian Series/S-1 (3)	Lexington Growth & Income (4)
1982	22.8%	12.2%	24.6%	12.0%
1983	13.8	15.5	20.4	28.7
1984	4.1	−5.2	−2.2	−4.1
1985	36.2	27.7	24.2	26.4
1986	14.8	3.7	17.3	20.5
1987	7.8	−4.6	3.7	0.1
1988	11.4	13.9	8.5	9.5
1989	25.7	30.3	29.3	27.6
1990	10.0	−26.2	−5.2	−10.3
1991	39.2	21.3	28.8	24.9
Beta	0.74	1.38	1.03	0.94

1. Calculate the expected return and standard deviation for each mutual fund, designated by column number: State Farm is 1, Bull & Bear is 2, Keystone is 3, and Lexington is 4.
2. Suppose the U.S. T-bill rate equals 7.65 percent. Calculate the Treynor and Sharpe performance measures.
3. Suppose the S&P 500 Index had a 17.42 percent average annual return for this period with a standard deviation of 12.42 percent. Compare its Treynor and Sharpe measures with those of the mutual funds.
4. Rank the funds by the Treynor measure.
5. Rank the funds by the Sharpe measure.
6. Do the two measures give consistent rankings? If so, what does it imply? If not, what does it imply?
7. (Optional) Using the data in Table 15.2 and a spreadsheet package (e.g., Excel), run a market model regression of $(R_{it} - RF_t)$ on $(R_{Mt} - RF_t)$ and estimate Jensen's alpha. Discuss which funds are undervalued and overvalued as well as what will happen to their prices as they reach equilibrium.

Mini Case 2   OBJECTIVE

Determine how different groups of MPT investors might determine their investment holdings.

Two clients approach you and explain their beliefs about investments and the capital markets. Mr. Naive believes that the market is pretty much strong-form efficient and that the best one can do is to choose a well-diversified portfolio. He chooses portfolio p_1, which has an 18 percent annual return and a 20 percent total risk. The annual risk-free rate is 5 percent.

Ms. Combo believes that the market is semistrong-form efficient, but that some undervalued stocks await discovery. Based on her analysis, she thinks that Hewlett-Packard (HP) and Tootsie Roll (TOOT) are undervalued stocks. The expected returns (based on historical arithmetic means) are 27 percent for HP and 23 percent for TOOT and their standard deviations are 25 percent and 20 percent, respectively. The correlation between HP and TOOT [CORR(HP,TOOT)] is +0.32.

1. Mr. Naive would like to combine p_1 with the money fund *(RF)* in order to hold a 22 percent risk level. He has asked you to construct his portfolio and estimate his expected return for the combined portfolio.
2. Ms. Combo would like to combine the two securities with some money fund shares. She would like you to figure out what percentage of her holdings should be in HP, TOOT, and the money fund. Finally, she too is willing to accept a 22 percent risk level, and would like to know her expected return on the combination, as well as the proportional (percentage) holdings each of HP, TOOT, and the money fund.

Mini Case 3   OBJECTIVE

Apply the Treynor–Black portfolio combination model.

Suppose your client, Ms. Combo now realizes that two stocks aren't enough to gain diversification benefits, so she chooses a well-diversified portfolio M and wants you to combine M with portfolio U, which consists of HP and TOOT. M's expected annual return equals 18 percent and its standard deviation is 20 percent. The risk-free rate equals 5 percent per year. Suppose your assistant runs the market model regression and provides the following data:

Stock	a	b	$SD(e_j)$	$SD^2(e_j)$
HP	0.05	1.43	0.226	0.051
TOOT	0.04	0.96	0.237	0.056

1. Calculate the proportional holdings of portfolios U and M.
2. Calculate the proportional holdings of stocks, HP and TOOT, and the naive portfolio, M, in the optimal portfolio, p^*.
3. Calculate the benefits of selecting stocks over the naive portfolio.

Discussion Questions and Problems

1. What are the major contributions of modern portfolio theory to investment practice? Which is the most significant?
2. Define the Treynor performance measure. From what market measure does it stem?
3. What is the Sharpe performance measure? What is the logic behind using a security's (or portfolio's) total risk rather than its beta?
4. Using the following data, find the portfolio's Treynor and Sharpe performance measures. Why are the performance measures different?

   Portfolio return = 14 percent
   Portfolio beta = 0.95
   Portfolio standard deviation = 8 percent
   Market return = 14.5 percent
   Market standard deviation = 7 percent
   Risk-free rate = 3.5 percent

5. What is Jensen's alpha? If a portfolio's alpha is less than zero, what does that imply about its relative performance?
6. How well does past performance predict future performance? Why is this issue so important?
7. What are the differences between Group 1 and Group 2 MPT investors? What views does each hold of market efficiency?
8. Explain how a Group 1 MPT investor would select an investment portfolio. How would a Group 2 MPT investor go about the same task?
9. What is the Treynor–Black portfolio combination model? To which group of MPT investors would this model appeal?
10. Explain the seven steps in the Treynor–Black portfolio combination model. When does the investor need to make subjective decisions?

11. CFA Level III, 1991. A number of different management "styles" are utilized by investment managers. Performance evaluation, however, is not standardized either within or across management styles. One development aimed at mitigating this problem is the emergence of the "benchmark portfolio" concept.

    Against this background, **comment** on the role of benchmark portfolios in evaluating a manager's investment performance, and **contrast** the suitability of benchmark portfolios for this purpose with that of the "median manager" approach often employed. Include *four* elements of comparison in your discussion.

Critical Thinking Exercise

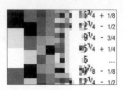

This exercise requires computer work. Open file RETURN2.XLS on the data disk. The file contains 44 holding period returns for 20 stocks, along with relevant market data. Using the data, perform the following calculations and answer the following questions:

a. Form four portfolios, each with five stocks. You may form the portfolios any way you wish, but use each stock only once.

b. Assume the portfolios are equally weighted (i.e., each stock makes up 20 percent of each portfolio). Compute the portfolio returns. You should have 44 holding period returns for each portfolio.

c. Find the mean return and standard deviation of returns for each portfolio.

d. Find the covariance between the returns for each portfolio and returns for the market. Find each portfolio's beta.

e. Calculate the Sharpe, Treynor, and Jensen performance measures for each portfolio.

f. Which ranked highest according to each measure? Can you explain any differences in the rankings?

g. Which of the five portfolios appears, based on these data, to contain the most undervalued stocks? Which portfolio appears to contain the most overvalued stocks?

h. How well-diversified does each portfolio appear to be?

Mini Case **1**   SOLUTION

This problem provides practice to calculate and interpret the chapter's performance measures.

1. To calculate the expected return, take an arithmetic average over the ten-year period for each fund. Funds 1, 2, 3, and 4 have expected returns of 18.58 percent, 8.86 percent, 14.94 percent, and 13.53 percent, respectively. The standard deviations can be calculated using the method shown in the chapter: 11.98 percent, 17.27 percent, 12.82 percent, and 14.33 percent for Funds 1, 2, 3, and 4, respectively.

2. The Treynor measure is defined as: $[ER_p - RF]/\beta_p$, so the measures for the funds are:

Fund 1:	14.77
Fund 2:	0.88
Fund 3:	7.07
Fund 4:	6.25
S&P 500:	9.77

The Sharpe measure is defined as $[ER_p - RF]/SD_p$, so the measures for the funds are:

Fund 1:	0.912
Fund 2:	0.070
Fund 3:	0.568
Fund 4:	0.410
S&P 500:	0.786

3. According to both the Treynor and Sharpe measures, Fund 1 (State Farm) is the only one that beats the market or the S&P 500 ($T_p = 14.787 > T_M = 9.77$ and $S_p = 0.912 > S_M = 0.786$). Both measures indicate that Funds 2, 3, and 4 are underperforming the market, adjusted for risk.

4. The Treynor measure ranks the four funds as follows:

Rank	Fund
1	Fund 1: State Farm
2	Fund 3: Keystone
3	Fund 4: Lexington
4	Fund 2: Bull & Bear

5. The Sharpe measure ranks the four funds as follows:

Rank	Fund
1	Fund 1: State Farm
2	Fund 3: Keystone
3	Fund 4: Lexington
4	Fund 2: Bull & Bear

6. The two measures rank the funds consistently, which indicates that all of the funds are well-diversified.

7. The market model regression of $(R_{it} - RF_t)$ on $(R_{Mt} - RF_t)$ gives the following estimates of Jensen's alpha:

Fund	α	$SE(\alpha)$	R^2
1	3.47	3.36	0.60
2	−12.13	1.525	0.96
3	−2.206	1.903	0.88
4	−4.887	2.134	0.89

Only Fund 1 (State Farm) has a positive alpha, indicating that it beat the market. The other funds' alphas are negative, indicating that they underperformed the market. State Farm would lie above the SML and is considered undervalued, while the others would lie under the SML and are overvalued. If markets are efficient and all investors agree on this assessment of the funds, then State Farm's price will rise until its return equals its CAPM required return:

$$ER_p = RF + [ER_M - RF]$$
$$= 0.0765 + 0.74[0.1742 - 0.0765] = 0.1488 \text{ or } 14.88 \text{ percent}$$

In contrast, Funds 2, 3, and 4 will decline in price until their returns equal those expected via the CAPM. For example, Fund 3's price should fall until its return equals:

$$ER_p = 0.0765 + 1.38[0.1742 - 0.0765] = 0.2113 \text{ or } 21.13 \text{ percent}$$

Even though Fund 1 ranks at the top based on all three performance measures, it also appears to be the least diversified of the four. Its R^2 is only 0.60.

Mini Case **2**   SOLUTION

The intent of this problem is to contrast Mr. Naive (a Group 1 MPT investor) with Ms. Combo (a Group 2 MPT investor).

1. To determine the investment proportions for Mr. Naive, first select a well-diversified portfolio, p_1 (which we'll assume is mean-variance efficient portfolio and lies on the efficient frontier). Suppose p_1 has an 18 percent expected return with a 20 percent standard deviation. Given a portfolio on the efficient frontier, define a CML equation for p_1.

$$ER_p = RF + \{[ER_{p1} - RF]/SD_{p1}\}SD_p$$
$$= 0.05 + SD_p$$
$$= 0.05 + (0.65)SD_p$$

Find ER_p for a 22 percent risk level by plugging in 0.22 for SD_p:

$$ER_p = 0.05 + (0.65)(0.22) = 0.193$$

The CML expects a 19.5 percent return for accepting a 22 percent risk level. Notice that the expected return is 19.3 percent, greater than p_1's 18 percent, so Naive must invest beyond 100 percent in p_1. This means borrowing at the risk-free rate, RF, in order to buy p_1 on margin. Now, determine the percentage investment in p_1 and RF. Using Equation 15.21, find the X in p_1 and $(1 - X)$ in RF.

$$ER_p = [ER_{p1} - RF]X\% + RF$$

$$0.193 = (0.19 - 0.05)X + 0.05$$

$$0.143 = (0.13)X$$

$$X = 1.10 \text{ or } 110 \text{ percent}$$

Naive must invest 110 percent in p_1 and -10 percent $(1.0 - 1.10)$ in RF, which means borrowing 10 percent at the risk-free rate and investing 110 percent in p_1. Using these percentages provides a 19.3 percent return with a 22 percent risk level, as specified by Mr. Naive.

2. What about Ms. Combo's investment? First, determine the optimal combination of undervalued stocks HP and TOOT. Create a table like Table 15.6 to determine the Sharpe measures at various levels of investment in HP and TOOT. The highest Sharpe measure indicates the optimal combination of HP and TOOT.

Portfolio	X in HP	(1 − X) in TOOT	ER_p	SD_p	Sharpe Measure, S_p
p_1	100%	0%	27.0%	25.0%	0.880
p_2	90	10	26.6	23.2	0.930
p_3	80	20	26.2	21.6	0.981
p_4	70	30	25.8	20.2	1.028
p_5	60	40	25.4	19.1	1.067
p_6	50	50	25.0	18.3	1.091
p_7	40	60	24.6	17.9	1.094
p_8	30	70	24.2	17.9	1.074
p_9	20	80	23.8	18.2	1.031
p_{10}	10	90	23.4	18.9	0.970
p_{11}	0	100	23.0	20.0	0.900

Portfolio p_7 with 40 percent in HP and 60 percent in TOOT is the optimal combination. Now find the combination of p_7 and the risk-free asset, RF, that provides a 22 percent risk level. The process is exactly like Mr. Naive's. Again, start with the CML equation using p_7 as the portfolio. (It should be a well-diversified portfolio, but two stocks reduce the amount of work necessary for a large portfolio. In reality, the computer can do this part of the work, so the calculations for a large portfolio can be performed relatively effortlessly.)

$$ER_p = RF + \{[ER_{p7} - RF]/SD_{p7}\}SD_p$$
$$= 0.05 + (1.094)SD_p$$

Now substitute 22 percent for SD_p to solve for ER_p:

$$ER_p = 0.05 + (1.094)(0.22)$$
$$= 0.2907 \text{ or } 29.07 \text{ percent}$$

Using Equation 15.21, find the proportional holdings in p_7 and RF:

$$ER_p = [ER_{p7} - RF]X + RF$$
$$0.2907 = (0.246 - 0.05)X + 5\%$$
$$0.2107 = (0.196)X$$
$$X = 1.23 \text{ or } 123 \text{ percent}$$

This says to invest 123 percent in p_7, borrowing 23 percent ($1.00 - 1.23 = -0.23$) at the risk-free rate to buy p_7 on margin. Finally, determine the percentage investment in HP, TOOT, and RF. This is easily accomplished using the standard equation:

$$ER_p = X\%ER_{p7} + (1 - X\%)RF$$
$$123 \text{ percent} = ER_{p7} + (-23\%)RF$$

Since p_7 is composed of 40 percent in HP and 60 percent in TOOT, make that substitution in the standard equation:

$$ER_p = 123\%[0.40E(R_{HP}) + 0.60E(R_{TOOT})] - (23\%)RF$$
$$= [49.2\%E(R_{HP}) + 73.8\%E(R_{TOOT})] - (23\%)RF$$

Invest 49.2 percent in HP, 73.8 percent in TOOT, and borrow 23 percent at the risk-free rate, RF.

Finally, verify that the expected return of this portfolio is 29.07 percent based on Ms. Combo's desired 22 percent risk level:[21]

$$ER_p = [49.2\%(0.27) + 73.8\%(0.23)] - 23\%(0.05)$$
$$= 29.10 \text{ percent}$$

Ms. Combo will achieve her desired risk level of 22 percent and expect a 29.10 percent (29.07 percent) return by investing 49.2 percent in HP and 73.8 percent in TOOT, and buying these stocks on margin by borrowing 23 percent of her investment at the 5 percent risk-free rate.

Mini Case **3**   SOLUTION

This problem is an exercise in applying the Treynor–Black portfolio combination model. The first step in the Treynor–Black model is to calculate a_j and $SD(e_j)$. Since your assistant has done this grunt work, start with Step 2.

1. Calculate the proportional holdings of HP, TOOT, and M, by Treynor–Black Steps 2 through 5. Step 2 determines the reward relative to diversifiable risk, $SD(e_j)$:

Stock	$a_j SD(c_j)$	X_j
HP	$0.05/0.051 = .980$	$0.980/1.694 = 0.579$
TOOT	$0.04/0.056 = 0.714$	$0.714/1.694 = 0.421$
	1.694	1.000

---

[21]The difference between the earlier calculation of 29.07 percent and 29.10 percent is due to rounding errors.

2. Given the individual stock's reward to diversifiable risk, invest 57.9 percent in HP and 42.1 percent in TOOT. Now construct portfolio U, which consists of 57.9 percent HP and 42.1 percent TOOT in Step 3.
   Step 3   Calculate α for portfolio U.

$$a_U = (0.579)(0.05) + (0.421)(0.04) = 0.04579$$

The portfolio beta equals:

$$b_U = (0.579)(1.43) + (0.421)(0.96) = 1.232$$

Next calculate portfolio U's diversifiable risk, $SD(e_U)$.

$$SD(e_U) = \sqrt{(0.579)^2(0.051) + (0.421)^2(0.056)}$$
$$= 0.1644$$

Next, in Step 4, calculate the proportional investment of U and M together in an optimal portfolio p^* using Equation 15.23:

$$X' = \frac{0.04579/(0.1644)^2}{(0.18 - 0.05)/(0.20)^2} = 0.521$$

$$X^* = \frac{0.521}{1 + (1 - 1.232)(0.521)} = 0.593$$

Notice, that the proportional holding in U increases since b_u is greater than 1.0 and the optimal portfolio p^* consists of 59.3 percent of portfolio U and 40.7 percent $(1 - 0.593)$ of the naive portfolio M.

Finally, determine the proportional holdings of HP and TOOT, using the following equation from Step 5:

$$X_s^* = X^*(X_s), \text{ where } s = \text{HP and TOOT}$$

Stock	Optimal Holding, X_s^*
HP	$(0.593)(0.579) = 0.343$
TOOT	$(0.593)(0.421) = 0.250$
Total, portfolio U	0.593

Additionally, portfolio p^* consists of 40.7 percent of portfolio M (the market portfolio).

3. To calculate the benefits of selecting stocks, calculate the Sharpe measure for the optimal portfolio, p^*, and compare it with the Sharpe measure for the naive portfolio, M. This requires us to complete Step 7.

$$S_{p^*}^2 = \left(\frac{ER_M - RF}{SD_M}\right)^2 + \left[\frac{\alpha_U}{SD(e_U)}\right]^2,$$
$$= (0.65)^2 + (0.2785)^2$$
$$= 0.5001$$

This says that the Sharpe measure, S_p^*, equals:

$$S_p^* = 0.707.$$

This is higher than the Sharpe measure for the naive portfolio, M ($S_M = 0.65$), but not by much; the benefit of stock selection is only 0.057 (0.707 − 0.65).

Part V

Beyond Common Stocks

Up to this point we've concentrated much of our attention on common stocks. While we believe that common stocks are among the most interesting, and in some ways the most complicated, investment alternatives, the world of investments doesn't end with common stocks. It's now time to look beyond common stocks, starting with fixed-income securities (generically referred to as *bonds*). There are good reasons to invest in bonds, and bonds make up large percentages of many investment portfolios. After bonds, we turn to so-called *derivative securities,* options and futures. Most investors never directly participate in either the options or futures markets, but both markets are linked to the stock and bond markets. It's important for every investor to understand the basics of options and futures. Finally, we consider investment companies, most notably mutual funds. These investment vehicles allow investors to purchase securities indirectly. Today, many investors invest all their funds through mutual funds and other investment companies.

Chapter 16

Fixed-Income Securities: Valuation and Risks

⟶

Chapter Objectives
1. Understand why bonds are viable investment alternatives.
2. Review the risks facing bond investors.
3. Examine how bonds are priced.
4. Review the basic bond pricing theorems.
5. Measure bond price volatility and interest rate risk.
6. Evaluate credit risks of bonds.
7. Review the relationship between bond risk and required return.

Back in Chapter 2, we mentioned many different types of fixed-income securities. The U.S. government issues bonds and notes through the Treasury Department and various federal agencies; state and local governments issue municipal bonds, and domestic corporations, foreign governments, foreign corporations all issue their own bonds. Mortgage pass-through securities and preferred stock issues are also considered to be fixed-income securities.[1]

The market offers literally thousands of different bonds. The U.S. Treasury, for example, currently has more than 200 different bond and note issues outstanding. Billions of dollars' worth of new bonds are issued each year by a variety of corporations and governments.

At first glance bonds may seem to be relatively simple securities, at least compared to common stocks. A bond represents a debtor/creditor relationship; the investor is the creditor and the issuer is the debtor. Most investors purchase bonds primarily for current income rather than capital appreciation. A bondholder collects interest payments, usually twice a year, and then the issuer returns the principal when the bond matures. In the process, the bondholder earns a fixed rate of return. Bonds seem like simple securities, right? Well, in the real world, bond investing can get quite complicated.

The next two chapters will take a much closer look at the investment characteristics and potential of bonds. In this chapter, we concentrate on two basic issues: bond valuation and the risks associated with investing in bonds. We begin with a seemingly very simple question: Why invest in bonds at all? Next, we introduce the risks associated with bond investing and discuss each briefly. This is followed by a discussion of bond pricing. We will develop the

---

[1]From now on, we'll use the term *bond* to refer to all fixed-income securities.

basic bond pricing equation and discuss some of the issues it raises. We will also review a number of important bond pricing theorems. The discussion of bond pricing leads to methods by which investors can measure price volatility and interest rate risk. The concept of duration will be explored in depth. Finally, we will examine the other risks facing the bond investor, especially the risk that the issuer will default. For example, we will see how to assess credit risk and the default premium built into bond prices and yields.

Why Bonds?

Even though bond trading makes up a substantial portion of total trading volume in the world's financial markets, bonds have a reputation as being rather dull, conservative investments. Images of people leisurely sitting by a pool clipping coupons might come to mind. Others argue that bonds offer poor risk/return tradeoffs when compared to stocks. Even legendary investment guru Peter Lynch has had less than kind things to say about investing in bonds: "In stocks you've got the company's growth on your side," he writes, "you're a partner in a prosperous and expanding business. When you lend money (buy bonds), the best you can hope for is to get it back, plus interest."[2] Lynch then recites a list of all the things that can go wrong if one buys bonds and concludes that bond prices fluctuate as wildly these days as stock prices.

While some of what Lynch, and others, have to say about bonds is probably true, we regret the attitude that bonds generally are dull and/or poor investments.[3] For many investors, both individuals and institutions, bonds are a viable and important investment option. What do bonds offer investors?

Income

Investors who want predictable, regular income have to consider buying bonds. While many common stocks do pay cash dividends, and these dividends often increase regularly, few common stocks have dividend yields that exceed the current yield on bonds. This is illustrated in Figure 16.1, which compares the S&P 500 dividend yield to the average yield on Treasury bonds between 1964 and 1993. Notice that the dividend yield on the S&P 500 has generally been about half the current yield on long term T-bonds.

In addition, the financial trauma associated with reducing cash dividends on common stocks is much less than the trauma associated with suspending interest payments on bonds (which, of course, constitutes default). A source of reliable, regular income can also improve the liquidity of any well-diversified portfolio.

Potential for Capital Gains

Looking over the data on historical returns presented in Chapter 2, it is difficult to argue that bonds have been dull investments in recent years. For example, during a three-year period from the beginning of 1991 through the end of 1993, bonds (both corporate and government) produced average annual compound returns that exceeded the average annual return on com-

---

[2]Peter Lynch, *One Up on Wall Street* (New York: Penguin Books, 1989), 57.

[3]We should point out that Lynch, and others, are not *totally* against buying bonds; they just aren't very enthusiastic, especially given today's interest rate environment.

Figure 16.1

Yield on Long-Term T-bonds versus Dividend Yield on the Standard & Poor's 500: 1964–1993

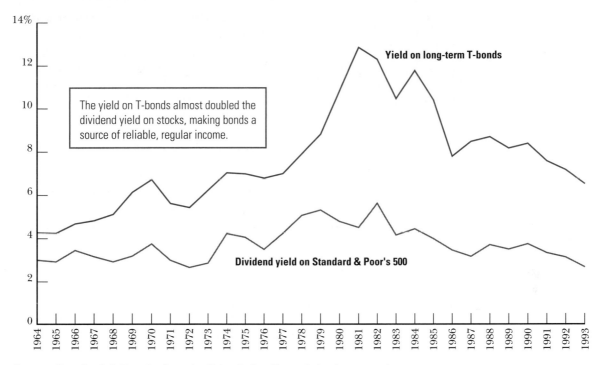

The yield on T-bonds almost doubled the dividend yield on stocks, making bonds a source of reliable, regular income.

Yield on long-term T-bonds

Dividend yield on Standard & Poor's 500

Source: Standard & Poor's, Security Price Index Record (various years).

mon stocks.[4] In 1982, long-term Treasury bonds produced an annual return in excess of 40 percent. In periods of falling interest rates, bonds can produce spectacular returns.

Paper versus Real Losses

Of course, rising interest rates can also clobber bond prices. Still, it is important to remember that rising interest rates produce only paper losses, not real losses, unless the investor sells the bond at the depressed price. Assume that someone buys a bond for its face value of $1,000 and rising interest rates drop the bond's price to $900. This is only a paper loss, unless the bondholder turns around and sells the bond. Furthermore, holding the bond to maturity guarantees return of the $1,000 (assuming that the issuer doesn't default). Now, if someone buys a stock at $50 per share and it declines to $40 per share, the investor suffers only a paper loss, not a real loss, of $10 per share. However, unlike a bond, there is no guarantee that the stock will *ever* get back to $50 per share, regardless of how long it is held.

Diversification

Bonds may expand the risk/return opportunities available to investors by further diversifying a portfolio of common stocks. Consider, for example, the correlation coefficients between stock and bond returns shown in Table 16.1. Recall that any correlation coefficient less than 1.0 between two sets of

---

[4]Stocks produced an average annual return of 10.8 percent compared to 11 percent from long-term T-bonds and 11.9 percent from investment grade corporate bonds.

Table 16.1

Correlations of Historical Annual Returns: 1926–1993

Series	Correlation with	
	Large-Firm Stocks	**Small-Firm Stocks**
Large-firm stocks	1.00	0.81
Small-firm stocks	0.81	1.00
Long-term corporate bonds	0.22	0.10
Long-term Treasury bonds	0.14	−0.01
Intermediate-term Treasury bonds	0.06	−0.06
Treasury bills	−0.05	−0.10

Source: *SBBI 1994 Yearbook* (Chicago: Ibbotson Associates, 1994), 105.

returns indicates some diversification potential. The data show that the correlation between stock and bond returns is generally close to zero, ranging between 0.20 and −0.10.

Tax Advantages

The Tax Reform Act of 1986 eliminated many popular tax shelters. One that remained was the tax treatment of municipal bond interest; interest received from municipal bonds remains exempt from individual federal income taxes. Municipal bonds are one of the few tax shelters still available to a wide range of individual investors.

Risks Associated with Investing in Bonds

While bonds have much to offer investors, buying bonds is not without risk. Further, some bonds expose investors to more risk than other bonds. U.S. government bonds, for example, don't have any default risk, but still expose investors to other risks.

Components of Bond Risk

Credit Risk. Whenever anyone lends money the biggest concern is probably getting it back. Essentially, **credit risk** involves the possibility that the bond's issuer will not make interest and principal payments when due. (The technical term is **default**.) As we discussed in Chapter 2, bonds' levels of credit risk vary widely. Some bonds, such as those issued by the U.S. Treasury, have no credit risk, while other bonds have much greater probabilities of default. Generally, we would expect to see a positive relationship between credit risk and expected returns. We'll have a lot more to say about credit risk later in this chapter.

Interest Rate Risk. As interest rates rise, bond prices fall, and vice versa. If an investor were forced to sell a bond when rates were high, he or she could suffer a capital loss. Even if the investor doesn't sell prior to maturity, rising interest rates also create an opportunity cost. For example, if someone buys a bond with a coupon rate of 8 percent and rates rise to, say, 10 percent, the bondholder loses the opportunity to get the higher rate; the bond is locked in at 8 percent. All bonds expose investors to interest rate risk, but, as we'll see, some bonds have more interest rate risk than others. We'll also discover, in the next chapter, that investors can manage, and perhaps almost eliminate, interest rate risk.

Reinvestment Risk. If a bond promises a return (referred to as *yield-to-maturity*) of 8 percent, when it matures, assuming that the issuer doesn't default, will its actual rate of return equal 8 percent? Not necessarily since, as we'll see, part of the actual return from owning a bond comes from reinvesting the intermediate cash flows (i.e., the coupon payments). Reinvesting the coupon payments at a rate higher than the bond's yield-to-maturity could raise the actual rate of return above the promised return when the bond was initially purchased.[5] Note that interest rate risk and reinvestment risk tend to offset each other to some extent. The immunization techniques discussed in the next chapter are based on this offsetting effect.

Purchasing Power Risk. **Purchasing power risk** deals with the impact of future rates of inflation on cash flows. If a bond has a coupon rate of 6 percent when inflation is raging at 8%, the purchasing power of the invested money actually declines. Purchasing power risk hurts a bond investor if actual inflation exceeds the rate the investor expected when he or she first purchased the bond. Second, purchasing power risk and interest rate risk are closely related. As we know, rising expected inflation leads to higher interest rates.

Call Risk. In Chapter 2 we pointed out that many bonds (especially corporate and municipal bonds) are **callable.** A call provision gives the issuer the option of buying the bond back from the investor at a specified price during a specified period of time, prior to maturity. Why should bond investors care about this **call risk?** An issuer is most likely to call a bond when interest rates are low, or have fallen substantially from when the bond was initially issued. To replace the called bond in such an environment, the investor would probably have to accept a lower coupon rate. A bond may offer investors a period of **call protection** during which the bond is not callable.

Liquidity Risk. As we discussed in Chapter 3, some bonds trade in poor secondary markets, so the spreads between their respective bid prices and ask prices (prices at which a dealer would buy or sell the bond, respectively, in response to a customer order) could be quite high. It may be difficult for investors to sell certain bonds prior to maturity for anything approaching their true values. **Liquidity risk** is a special problem for small municipal bond issues.

Foreign Exchange Risk. In recent years, many U.S. investors have been attracted to bonds issued by foreign governments and corporations; many foreign issuers' bonds have offered yields well above those offered by domestic bonds. Many foreign bonds are denominated in foreign currencies, however, so their returns depend on both interest rates and foreign exchange rates. For example, a bond denominated in British pounds (£) may have a par value of £1,000 and a coupon rate of 10 percent. (It pays annual interest of £100.) If the exchange rate between the dollar and the pound ($/£) when the bond is purchased is $1.50 per pound, the bond would cost $1,500 and pay $150 per year in interest. However, if the dollar were to gain strength relative to the pound and the $/£ exchange rate declines to $1.20 per

---

[5]This assumes, of course, that the bond is held to maturity and the issuer doesn't default.

pound, the bond's £100 in annual interest would translate into only $120.[6] Even if everything else remained the same, the bondholder loses $30 a year merely due to the U.S. dollar's increasing strength relative to the British pound. This is **foreign exchange risk.**

Bond Valuation

So far we've examined the reasons for buying bonds as well as the general risks investors take when they buy bonds. In this section, we turn to a detailed discussion of bond valuation. An understanding of bond valuation is critical to an understanding of the general risk/return profile of bonds, as well as how to select and evaluate individual bonds.

Basics of Bond Pricing

The price of a bond depends on the values of four variables: (1) **face value,** FV (also called *par value*), (2) **coupon rate,** CR, (3) **time to maturity,** T, and (4) **promised return.** For a noncallable, default-free bond, the first three variables are fixed at issue. These first three variables also determine the cash flows associated with a bond. The fourth variable, the promised return, is also the bond's required rate of return, the interest rate used to discount its cash flows to determine its present value. Given these four variables, we can calculate the present value of the bond's cash flows, which, added up, equals the bond's price, P(b).

For example, a five-year bond ($T = 5$) has an 8 percent coupon rate, CR, and a $1,000 face value, F. The promised, or required, return, r, equals 6 percent per annum. The bond's price can be calculated in two steps.

Step 1. Calculate cash flows. The coupon payment (or interest payment per year in dollars), C, equals:

$$C = CR \times F \tag{16.1}$$

In our example, 8 percent times $1,000 equals $80. The final cash flow at maturity equals $1,000, the face value, which is repaid in five years.

Step 2. Calculate the present value of these cash flows to find bond value, P(b).

$$
\begin{aligned}
P(b) &= \text{PV of coupon payments} + \text{PV of face value} \\
&= \$80(\text{P/A}; 6\%; 5) + \$1,000(\text{P/F}; 6\%; 5) \\
&= \$80(4.2124) + \$1,000(0.7473) \\
&= \$1,084.25 \text{ (rounded to the nearest penny)}[7]
\end{aligned}
\tag{16.2}
$$

---

[6]When we say that one currency gains strength (or gets stronger) relative to another currency, it takes fewer units of the first currency to buy one unit of the other currency. In our example, the exchange rate between dollars and pounds starts at 1.5, meaning it takes $1.50 to buy £1.00. If the exchange *falls* to 1.2, meaning that the dollar gains strength relative to the pound, it now takes only $1.20 to buy £1.00.

[7]From now on, the following notation will be used: (P/A, r percent, T) represents the present value of an annuity, received for T periods, and discounted at r percent. (P/F, r percent, T) represents the present value of a single sum, received in T periods, and discounted at r percent. Mathematically,

$$
(\text{P/A}; i; T) = \frac{1 - \dfrac{1}{(1 + r)^T}}{r} \quad \text{and} \quad (\text{P/F}; i; T) = \frac{1}{(1 + r)^T}.
$$

Semiannual Coupons. Equation 16.2 assumes that the bond pays coupon interest once a year, or annually. The vast majority of bonds actually make coupon payments every six months. To accommodate the **semiannual coupon,** the bond pricing equation (Equation 16.2) needs three modifications. The first is to divide the annual coupon by two. This represents the coupon payment per six-month period. The second change is to divide the required rate of return by two, and the third is to multiply the time to maturity by two. For the example above, Equation 16.2 becomes:

$$P(b) = \$40(\text{P/A}; 3\%; 10) + \$1,000(\text{P/F}; 3\%; 10)$$
$$= \$40(8.5302) + \$1,000(0.7441) \qquad (16.3)$$
$$= \$1,085.30 \text{ (rounded to the nearest penny)}$$

Notice that the price of the bond with semiannual coupon payments rises slightly above the price with annual coupon payments ($1,084.25 versus $1,085.30). To see why, consider an investment paying $80 over a one-year period; the investor may choose to receive $80 after one year, or $40 after six months and the other $40 after one year. Which would you choose? The answer is simple. A rational investor would prefer two $40 payments versus one $80 payment, because it's better to receive money earlier. The *present value* of the two $40 payments is higher than the present value of the $80 payment, discounted at the same rate of interest.[8] This principle gives a bond with semiannual coupons a higher price (assuming the same required rate of return) compared to an otherwise identical bond with annual coupons.

Some argue that technical accuracy demands more than simply dividing the annual required rate of return by two when a bond pays coupon interest semiannually. This simple adjustment actually discounts the bond's cash flows at a higher rate of interest than the stated annual required rate of return. Remember from the discussion of the time value of money that money in a savings account with a stated annual interest rate of 6 percent earns a higher rate of return if it is compounded semiannually than if it is compounded annually. The effective rate of interest is actually higher than 6 percent (6.09 percent to be more precise).[9]

In the bond example, if the annual required rate of return, 6 percent, is divided by two to discount the semiannual cash flows at 3 percent, the effective annual discount rate is actually 6.09 percent. Of course, a higher rate of interest gives a lower present value. If the required rate of return is really 6 percent per annum, then the six-month discount rate should be 2.96 percent.[10] Substituting 2.96 percent for 3 percent in Equation 16.3 changes the price of the bond to $1,089.23, admittedly not a huge difference. However, it's important to recognize and understand this issue.[11]

Accrued Interest. Someone who buys a bond between coupon payment dates must pay the seller, in addition to the bond's price, the **accrued interest** since the last coupon payment date. When the bond makes its next coupon

---

[8]Skeptical? At a 6 percent discount rate, the present value of $80 received in one year equals $80/(1.06), or $75.47. The present value of $40 received in six months plus $40 received in one year equals $40/(1.06)^{0.5} + $40/(1.06), or $76.59.

[9]The general formula to find the effective rate of interest is: $(1 + r/m)^m - 1$, where m is the number of compounding periods per year. In the example, $m = 2$ and the effective rate equals $(1.03)^2 - 1$, or 6.09 percent, rounded to two decimal places.

[10]To find this, modify the equation in the prior footnote; 2.96 percent $= (1.06)^{0.5} - 1$.

[11]This issue has been analyzed and debated in detail elsewhere. See, for example, Frank Fabozzi, *Bond Markets, Analysis and Strategies,* 2nd ed. (Englewood Cliffs, N.J.: Prentice-Hall, 1993), pp. 39–42; and, especially, James Lindley et al., "A Measurement of the Errors in Intra-period Compounding and Bond Valuation," *The Financial Review,* February 1987, 33–51.

payment, the new owner receives the entire amount. Virtually all bonds accrue interest daily and pay every six months.

Say, for example, a bond with an 8 percent coupon pays coupon interest on February 1 and August 1. Assuming a 360-day year and a face value of $1,000, this bond accrues about $0.22 per day in interest. Someone who buys this bond on May 1, 90 days after its last coupon payment, must pay the seller $20.00 in accrued interest ($0.22 times 90). When the bond makes its next coupon payment, on August 1, the new owner receives the entire six-month (180-day) coupon of $40.

Accrued interest may seem like a trivial issue, but it does affect the prices of bonds slightly. One reason goes back to a basic rule of present value. Continuing the above example, the new owner pays $20.00 today (May 1) and gets the $20.00 back in three months (on August 1, when the bond makes its next coupon payment). Since this money has a time value, the $20.00 received on August 1 is worth less than the $20.00 paid on the purchase date. Furthermore, buying the bond on May 1, instead of on its last coupon payment date (February 1), entitles the new owner to receive the first coupon payment in three months rather than six months.

Adding accrued interest, the basic bond valuation equation, assuming semiannual coupons, becomes:

$$P(b) = \frac{C}{2} \sum_{t=1}^{2T} \frac{1}{(1 + r^*)^v (1 + r^*)^{t-1}} + \frac{F}{(1 + r^*)^v (1 + r^*)^{2T-1}} \quad (16.4)$$

where, v is the days until the next coupon divided by the number of days in the six-month period, and r^* is the appropriate semiannual rate of interest. Accrued interest is then added to the bond's price. While Equation 16.4 looks confusing, it isn't as bad as it seems. Let's look at an example.

Maintaining the same example bond we've been using throughout this section (face value of $1,000, term of five years, 8 percent annual coupon, and 6 percent annual required rate of return—2.96 percent per six months). Assume someone buys the bond exactly three months after its last coupon payment and exactly three months before it makes its next coupon payment (so, $v = 0.5$). Now compare the prices of the bond with and without accrued interest. The relevant numbers are summarized below:

	Without Accrued Interest	With Accrued Interest
Maturity	Five years	Four years and nine months
Number of coupons	10 (first coupon payment received in six months)	10 (first coupon payment received in three months)
Price of bond	$1,089.23	$1,105.21

The new owner still receives 10 coupon payments of $40, but now the bond matures in four years and nine months. The bond's price now equals $1,105.21 (*plus* $20 in accrued interest). Why is the bond's price about $15 higher than it is without accrued interest? There are two reasons. First, the bond matures three months sooner, and second, the owner receives the first coupon payment in three months rather than six months.

Yield-to-Maturity. We can interpret the continuing bond example as follows: What rate of return would an investor earn by buying a bond today for $1,089.23, receiving $40 every six months for five years (a total of ten payments), and receiving the bond's face value, $1,000, at the end of five years? The answer is 6 percent per annum. The return on a bond, held to maturity, is referred to as the **yield to maturity.** This is a new name for the promised return, discussed earlier.

A bond's yield to maturity represents the market's current assessment of the rate the bond ought to pay given current market conditions. On the other hand, the coupon rate represents the market's assessment of the rate the bond should pay at the time of issue. As a result, yield to maturity can be higher or lower than the coupon rate, and will change over time as market conditions change.

From another perspective, the yield to maturity is the interest rate that equates the present value of a bond's cash flows to its current price. Technically, a bond's price determines its yield to maturity, not vice versa. Based on the price of a bond and its coupon rate, face value, and maturity, we can compute its yield to maturity. Let's consider a simple example. The market offers a bond today for $1,100. It has a coupon rate of 7.5 percent and a face value of $1,000, and it matures in 20 years. Assume semiannual coupons and that the bond made a coupon payment today (eliminating accrued interest). The bond pricing equation is:

$$\$1,100 = \$37.50(P/A, r^*\%, 40) + \$1,000(P/F, r^*\%, 40)$$

Find r^* (the semiannual discount rate) and r (the effective annual rate or yield to maturity). In the dark ages when the authors went to school, this used to be a fairly tedious task, using present value tables and trial and error. These days, financial calculators and PCs have taken over this work.[12] Still, you need to understand what the yield to maturity means, and why it's an important number.

Relationship between Coupon Rate and Yield to Maturity. The relationship between a bond's coupon rate (CR) and yield to maturity (YTM) can be stated as follows:

1. If $P(b) = F$, then $YTM = CR$.
2. If $P(b) < F$, then $YTM > CR$.
3. If $P(b) > F$, then $YTM < CR$.

Let's get an intuitive understanding of the relationship between CR and YTM. If the bond's price, $P(b)$, equals its face value, F, then YTM equals CR. Why? Since the bond price already equals its face value (a known cash flow at maturity, assuming a default-free bond) its only return comes in the form of coupon payments. Thus, the yield on this investment if held to maturity (YTM) must exactly equal the return generated from the coupon payments, which is, of course, the coupon rate (CR).

A bond selling below its face value ($1,000) is called a *discount bond*. The total return on a discount bond comes from two cash flows: the coupon payments and the certain payment of the bond's face value at maturity. Thus, YTM is greater than CR because the bond's price appreciation will add value, over and above the return generated by the coupon payments.

A bond selling for more than its face value is called a *premium bond*. For a premium bond, the relationship between YTM and CR is the exact opposite from that for a discount bond. In this case, the certain depreciation of the bond price to its face value reduces the YTM below the CR. Consider the bond with an 8 percent coupon and a five-year term to maturity. Since the bond's price exceeds its face value ($1,089.23 versus $1,000), its yield to maturity is less than its coupon rate, 6 percent.

Current Yield. Quotes of a bond price printed in the financial press (as discussed in Chapter 4) often state the **current yield** on the bond. The current

---

[12]The yield to maturity in this example works out to 6.59 percent (annualized).

yield is simply the coupon rate divided by the bond's price (stated as a percentage of face value). For example, the bond we've been using has a price of $1,089.23 (or 108.923 percent of par) and a coupon rate of 8 percent. Therefore, this bond has a current yield of 7.34 percent (8 percent divided by 1.08923). Notice that the current yield is more than the yield to maturity.[13]

Yield to Call. A call provision may lead a bond investor to calculate another measure of return, the **yield to call.** Basically, this analysis asks the following question: If a bond bought today is called by the issuer at some point in the future, prior to maturity, what return should the owner expect to earn? An answer to this question requires two modifications to the basic bond pricing equation. First, substitute the call price for the bond's face value, and second, substitute the call date for the maturity date. Assume a 20-year bond with a current price of $975, a coupon rate of 6.5 percent, and a face value of $1,000. Also assume the bond is callable in 15 years at a price of $1,065. Ignoring any accrued interest, the yield to call would be the discount rate that equates $975 to the present value of $65 per year (or $32.50 per six months) for 15 years, plus $1,065 received at the end of 15 years. Not surprisingly, the yield to call exceeds the yield to maturity, in this example (7.02 percent versus 6.73 percent).[14]

Actual Return versus Yield to Maturity

Suppose that someone buys the bond discussed in the prior section (8 percent coupon, five-year maturity, face value of $1,000, current price of $1,089.23, and annual yield to maturity of 6 percent). The owner holds the bond for the entire five-year period, and the issuer pays all interest and principal when due. This investment actually earns 6 percent per annum, right? Not always! Even if an investor holds a bond until maturity, and the issuer doesn't default, his or her **actual rate of return** may differ from the promised return (the yield to maturity) when the bond was first purchased. We referred to this variation earlier in the chapter as *reinvestment risk.* The yield to maturity, or promised rate of return, assumes reinvestment of the coupon payments at the yield to maturity. If the reinvested coupon payments earn a rate other than the yield to maturity, then the investor's actual return differs from the promised return.

Having bought the example bond for $1,089.23 (again, ignoring accrued interest), the owner holds it to maturity, spending the coupon payments when received. How much cash did the bond actually pay over its five-year life? The bondholder received $1,400 (ten coupon payments of $40 each plus the face value of $1,000). Since the coupon payments were not reinvested, the future value of all the cash received from the bond at maturity (after five years) also equals $1,400. Remember from the basic time value of money discussion, if we know the present and future values of an investment, and the length of time it is held, we can calculate the actual rate of return using the following formula:

$$ARR = [FV/PV]^{1/n} - 1 \qquad (16.5)$$

---

[13]This is true for all bonds selling for more than their face values. If a bond is selling for less than its face value (a discount bond), the current yield is less than the yield to maturity.

[14]The yield to call almost always exceeds the yield to maturity. You have to be careful, however, when considering the yield to call. Most corporate and municipal bonds remain callable for several years, so you never know exactly when, or even if, they will be called. Further, the call price typically declines over the period of time the bond is callable, usually approaching the face value as the bond approaches maturity. We know of no actual bonds where the call price is less than the face value.

where, *ARR* is the actual rate of return, *FV* is the future value of cash flows, *PV* is the present value (or price), and *n* is the length of time the investment is held. Using our example, *FV* = $1,400, *PV* = $1,089.23, and *n* = 10. Substituting these values into Equation 16.5 gives an actual rate return of 5.15 percent. (This is also called the *effective annual rate.*) That rate is less that the yield to maturity (an effective annual rate of 6 percent).

Now, change the example slightly. Assume that, instead of spending the coupon payments, the bondholder deposits them in a bank account that pays 3 percent per annum (a semiannual rate 1.49 percent). The new value of the bond investment at the end of five years equals $1,427.89; the extra $27.89 is interest earned on interest (the return from the reinvested coupons).[15] Equation 16.5 gives an actual rate of return of 5.56 percent (effective annual rate). That's still less than the yield to maturity, but higher than not reinvesting coupons at all (for an effective reinvestment rate of 0 percent).

Now, assume that the bondholder can reinvest the bond's coupons in an account that pays 9 percent per annum (a semiannual rate of 4.40 percent). Under this assumption, the future value of cash flows in five years equals $1,489.32 and the actual rate of return equals 6.46 percent (effective annual rate).

By now it should be clear: reinvesting a bond's coupon payments at a higher rate increases the bond's actual rate of return. If the coupons are reinvested at a rate lower (or higher) than the yield to maturity, the actual rate of return will be lower (or higher) than the yield to maturity, or promised rate of return. Of course, this still assumes that the bond is held to maturity and the issuer doesn't default. Figure 16.2. illustrates the relationship between the reinvestment rate and the actual rate of return for the example bond. Notice that the actual rate of return equals the promised rate of return only when the reinvestment rate equals the yield to maturity.

The relationship between reinvestment rates and actual rates of return illustrate that bond investors can be hurt by falling interest rates as well as rising interest rates. Interest rate risk, therefore, reflects the risks associated with interest rates changing (whether upward or downward) during the time an investor owns any bond. We'll have more to say about this later.

Five Bond Pricing Theorems

In this section we review five well-known bond pricing theorems that attempt to explain various mathematical relationships between bond prices and interest rates. These theorems are important for understanding bond investing. They also provide an important link between understanding bond valuation and interest rate risk.

Before we get to the bond pricing theorems, two things need to be made clear. First, if interest rates are generally rising (or falling), the yield to maturity on every existing bond will rise (or fall). Think about it this way, if the yield on a newly issued five-year Treasury note increased from 6 percent to 6.5 percent, what would happen to the yield on already issued Treasury securities that mature in five years? Obviously, market forces would push their yields upward, as well, probably to around 6.5 percent.

Second, yields on short-term and long-term bonds can move in different directions for short periods of time. For example, during the summer of

---

[15]Mathematically, $1,428.11 = $1,000 + $40(F/A; 1.49%; 10), where (F/A; 1.49%; 10) =

$$(F/A; 1.49\%; 10) = \frac{(1.0149)^{10} - 1}{.0149} = 10.6978$$

Figure 16.2

Reinvestment Rate and Actual Rate of Return for a Bond

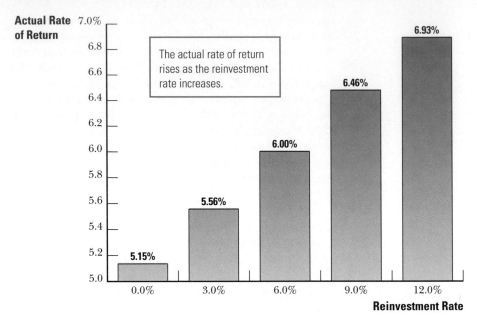

Note: The bond has a coupon rate of 8 percent, a maturity of exactly five years, a face value of $1,000, a yield to maturity of 6 percent (effective annual rate), and a current price of $1,089.23.

1993, the yield on T-bills (which are essentially short-term bonds) rose slightly, while the yield on long-term T-bonds fell substantially. With these preliminaries out of the way, let's look at the five bond pricing theorems.

1. Bond Prices Move Inversely to Changes in Interest Rates

This first theorem comes from basic valuation principles: as interest rates rise, bond prices fall (and vice versa). The reason, of course, is that bond investors discount fixed future cash flows at higher interest rates, and higher discount rates give lower present values. This is shown in Figure 16.3, which illustrates the various prices of a bond with a 30-year maturity and a 6 percent coupon, assuming a yield to maturity between 4 percent and 12 percent. For example, at a yield to maturity of 4 percent per annum, the bond has a price of $1,347.61. To increase the bond's yield to maturity to 7 percent, the market would drive its price down to $875.28.

2. Longer Maturity Makes a Bond Price More Sensitive to Interest Rates

The best way to illustrate this pricing relationship is with an example. Consider several bonds, each of which has a coupon rate of 8 percent, a current yield to maturity of 8 percent, and a face value of $1,000. One bond matures in 5 years, another in 10 years, still another in 15 years, and so forth. How much will the price of each bond change if the market yield to maturity falls from 8 percent to 6 percent? The answer indicates each bond's **price sensitivity.** We already know that the price of each bond will rise, but will they all rise by the same amount? The answer is *no*. Figure 16.4 shows the percentage

Figure 16.3

Bond Price versus Yield to Maturity

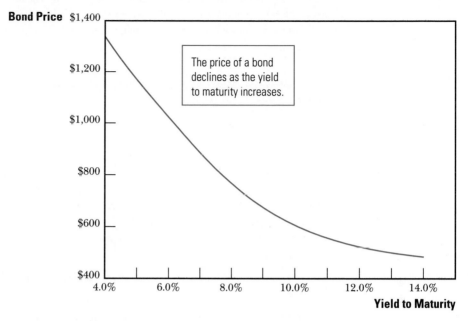

Note: The bond has a coupon rate of 6 percent, a maturity of 30 years, and a face value of $1,000.

Figure 16.4

Price Sensitivity and Maturity

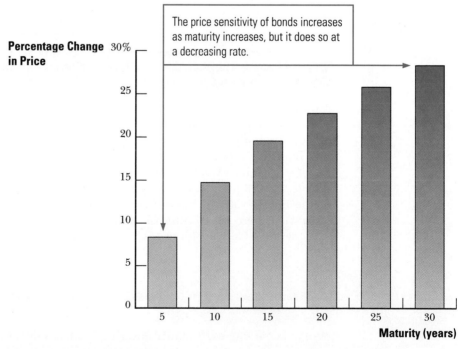

Note: All bonds have coupon rates of 8 percent and face values of $1,000; price changes assume a drop in the yield to maturity from 8 percent to 6 percent.

price changes for all the bonds. Clearly, longer maturities bring greater percentage price increases. (Remember, other than maturity, all the bonds are identical, with initial prices of $1,000.) For example, the 5-year bond increases in price from $1,000 to $1,085, or about 8.5 percent. By contrast, the 30-year bond increases in price from $1,000 to $1,277, or about 27.7 percent.

3.   Price Sensitivity Increases with Maturity at a Decreasing Rate

Take another look at Figure 16.4. When the yield to maturity on the bonds falls from 8 percent to 6 percent, the 5-year bond increases in price by about $85, the 10-year bond increases in price by about $149, and the 15-year bond increases in price by about $196. The 10-year bond is more price sensitive than the 5-year bond, and the 15-year bond is more price sensitive than the 10-year bond. However, the difference in sensitivity between the 15-year and 10-year bonds is *less* than the difference in price sensitivity between the 10-year and 5-year bonds ($47 versus $64).

4.   Lower Coupon Rates Increase Price Sensitivity

Again, this theorem is easiest to illustrate using an example. Assume a series of bonds each having a ten-year maturity, face values of $1,000, and current yields to maturity of 8 percent. The bonds differ only in their coupon rates. One bond has a coupon rate of 4 percent, another has a coupon rate of 6 percent, another has a coupon rate of 8 percent, and so forth. Let's assume the yield to maturity on all the bonds falls from 8 percent to 6 percent. Figure 16.5 shows that the prices of all of the bonds rise, with the low-coupon bonds rising the most. For example, the price of the 4 percent bond increases from $728 to $851 (16.9 percent) while the price of the 12 percent bond increases from $1,272 to $1,446 (13.7 percent).

5.   A Price Increase Caused by a Yield Decrease Exceeds a Price Decrease Caused by a Similar Yield Increase

Consider a bond with a coupon rate of 8 percent, a maturity of ten years, a face value of $1,000, and a current yield to maturity of 8 percent. Basic bond valuation confirms that, since the yield to maturity equals the coupon rate, the bond is currently selling for its face value. What would happen to the bond's price if its yield to maturity were to fall from 8 percent to 6 percent, or rise from 8 percent to 10 percent. The results are shown in Figure 16.6. If the bond's yield increases from 8 percent to 10 percent, its price falls by about 12.5 percent. By contrast, if the bond's yield decreases from 8 percent to 6 percent, its price increases by about 14.9 percent.

Assessing Interest Rate Risk

So far we've discussed bonds' investment characteristics, including the general risks investors take when they buy bonds and how bonds are valued. In this section, we'll take a more detailed look at how to evaluate the most important risk to a bondholder: interest rate risk. Much of this material flows directly from the bond valuation principles we examined in the prior section.

Figure 16.5

Price Sensitivity and Coupon Rate

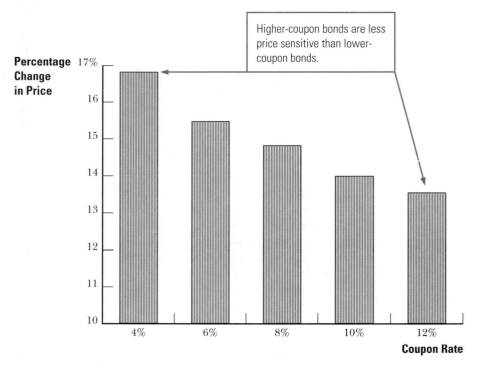

Note: All bonds have maturities of ten years, and face values of $1,000; price changes assume a drop in yield to maturity from 8 percent 6 percent.

Figure 16.6

Price Changes for Increase and Decrease in Yield

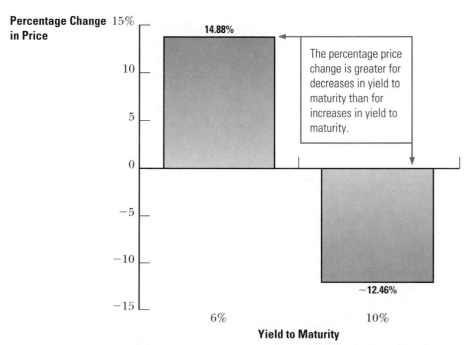

Note: Bond has a coupon rate of 8 percent, a maturity of ten years, and an original yield to maturity of 8 percent.

At this point it might be useful to summarize what we already know about interest rate risk. As interest rates move up and down, the prices of all bonds change, as well. Furthermore, some bonds are more price sensitive than others. Bonds with low coupon rates, for example, are more price sensitive than similar bonds with high coupon rates. Therefore, some bonds expose investors to more interest rate risk (i.e., are more price sensitive) than other bonds.

While the bond pricing theorems are important for understanding bond investing, each assumes that various factors remain constant while only the one under examination varies. When trying to compare various bonds' price sensitivity levels, these theorems may provide only limited insight. Consider the following two bonds:

Bond A: Coupon = 10%, maturity = 20 years
Bond B: Coupon = 6%, maturity = 10 years

Assume that both bonds have the same yield to maturity and face value. Which bond is more price sensitive? So far, we really can't say. Bond A has the longer maturity which, according to Theorem 2, makes it more price sensitive. However, Bond A also has a higher coupon which, according to Theorem 4, makes it less price sensitive. Some sort of a measure is needed to compare the price sensitivity of various bonds, regardless of individual coupons and maturities. This measure is called **duration.**

Duration

The concept of bond duration was formalized by Frederick Macaulay in 1938.[16] Duration provides a measure of price sensitivity, and thus interest rate risk, that takes into account three important factors: coupon rate, time to maturity, and yield to maturity. A longer duration characterizes a more price-sensitive bond.

Technically, duration summarizes the effective maturity of a bond, measuring when an investor receives the average promised cash flow from the bond. More intuitively, duration measures the number of periods it takes to *recover* the bond's price. As an example, consider a zero coupon bond with a maturity of five years.[17] Since it pays only one cash flow, at maturity in five years, the average cash flow is received in five years. Therefore, the bond has a duration of five years.

Finding the duration for a bond with a coupon rate not equal to zero is somewhat more complicated. For any bond, duration (D) is calculated as follows:

$$D = \frac{\sum_{t=1}^{T} t(CF_t)(1 + r)^{-t}}{P(b)} \tag{16.6}$$

where CF_t is the cash flow received in period t, T is the number of periods, and r is the appropriate yield to maturity (also adjusted for semiannual coupons, if needed). If the bond pays interest semiannually, Equation 16.6 will state D in half-year periods. In order to restate duration in years, divide D by 2. Let's look at an example.

---

[16]Frederick Macaulay, *Some Theoretical Problems Suggested by the Movements of Interest Rates, Bond Yields, and Stock Prices in the United States since 1856* (New York: Columbia University Press, 1938).

[17]We briefly discussed zero coupon bonds in Chapter 2. Since the coupon rate is zero, the price of a zero coupon bond is merely the present value of the face amount, discounted at the yield to maturity, or: $P(b) = FV/(1 + r)^T$.

Table 16.2

Example Duration Calculation

Basic information:

Coupon rate = 8 percent
Term = Five years
Yield to maturity = 6 percent (2.96 percent semiannually)
Price = $1,089.23

t (1)	Cash Flow (2)	Col. 1 × Col. 2 (3)	PV factor (4)	Col. 3 × Col. 4 (5)
1	$ 40	40	0.9713	38.8514
2	40	80	0.9434	75.4717
3	40	120	0.9163	109.9569
4	40	160	0.8900	142.3994
5	40	200	0.8644	172.8882
6	40	240	0.8396	201.5086
7	40	280	0.8155	228.3429
8	40	320	0.7921	253.4700
9	40	360	0.7693	276.9658
10	1,040	10,400	0.7473	7,771.4850

Sum of Column 5	9,271.3399
Duration in half-years (Sum/Price)	8.5118
Duration in years (Duration in half-years/2)	4.26

Note: PV factor = $1/(1.0296)^t$

Table 16.2 details the duration calculation for the familiar bond with a face value of $1,000, a coupon rate of 8 percent, a term of five years, a yield to maturity of 6 percent (2.96 percent per half-year), and a price of $1,089.23. The process to calculate duration consists of five steps:

1. List the cash flow received in each period (t). This is Column 2 in Table 16.2.
2. Multiply the cash flow (Column 2) by the period (the number in Column 1). The result, $t \times CF(t)$, is shown in Column 3.
3. Find the present value of the amount in Column 3. This involves multiplying Column 3 by the present value factors shown in Column 4. The result is shown in Column 5.
4. Sum Column 5. In Table 16.2, the sum of Column 5 is equal to 9,271.3399.
5. Divide the sum by the bond's current price. In the example 9,271.3399 divided by 1,089.23 gives 8.5118. This is the duration of the bond in half-years. Dividing 8.5118 by 2 gives the duration of the bond in years, 4.26.

An investor would receive the bond's average cash flow in about 4.26 years. It should come as no surprise that the duration is close to the bond's maturity, five years, since the single largest cash flow, the face value and the final six months' interest ($1,040) arrives when the bond matures.

Investors often look at the ratio $D/(1 + r)$. This measure is referred to as **modified duration (MD).** The above bond's modified duration is equal to 4.20 (4.26/1.06). Modified duration reflects the approximate percentage change in price for a given change in yield to maturity.

As mentioned earlier, duration takes into account three important bond pricing factors (maturity, coupon rate, and yield to maturity). The relationship of duration to all three is summed up in three general statements:

1. A longer maturity gives a longer duration, holding the other two factors constant.
2. A higher coupon rate gives a shorter duration, holding the other two factors constant.
3. A higher yield to maturity gives a shorter duration, holding the other two factors constant.

The first two statements are fairly intuitive. Bonds with longer maturities spread out their periodic cash flows over longer periods of time. In addition, they take longer to return their face values to investors. Bonds with higher coupon rates have larger intermediate cash flows (those prior to maturity) so it takes less time to get back the average dollar.

Figures 16.7 and 16.8 illustrate the relationships between duration, maturity, and coupon rates. Figure 16.7 shows the durations of four bonds, all with coupon rates of 8 percent and yields to maturity of 6 percent; the bonds have maturities of 5, 10, 20, and 30 years. The positive relationship between duration and maturity is shown clearly. For example, the 10-year bond has a duration of 7.29 years, whereas the 30-year bond has a duration of 13.56 years.

Figure 16.8 shows the negative relationship between coupon rate and duration. All five bonds have maturities of ten years and yields to maturity of 8 percent. Notice that the 4 percent coupon bond has a duration of almost 8 years while the 12 percent coupon bond has a duration of about 6.5 years.

The relationship between duration and yield to maturity is illustrated in Figure 16.9. All the bonds have equal coupon rates (8 percent) and maturities (ten years). Since their yields differ, so do their durations. The bond that has a yield to maturity of 4 percent, for example, has a duration of 7.5 years compared to about 6.6 years for the bond with a yield to maturity of 12 percent.

Figure 16.7

Relationship between Duration and Maturity

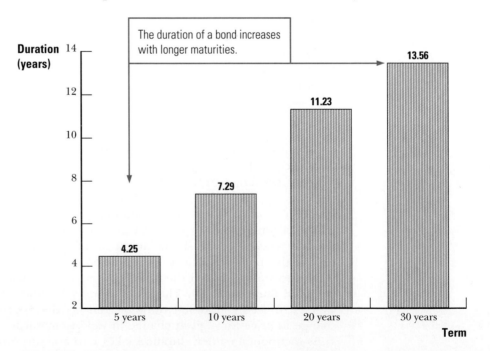

Note: All bonds have coupon rates of 8 percent and yields to maturity of 8 percent.

Figure 16.8

Relationship between Duration and Coupon Rate

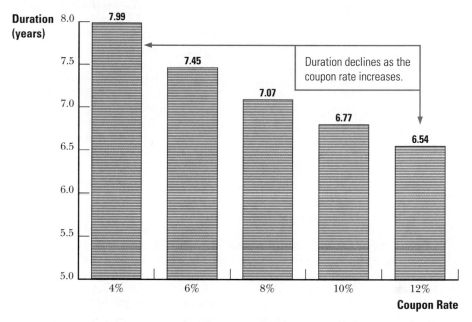

Note: All bonds have terms of ten years and yields to maturity of 6 percent.

The relationship between yield to maturity and duration is probably less intuitive than the relationships between coupon rates or maturity and duration. The inverse relationship between yield to maturity and duration results from the nonlinear relationship between the bond's interest rate and its present value. Take another look at Figure 16.3. Notice that the relationship

Figure 16.9

Relationship between Duration and Yield to Maturity

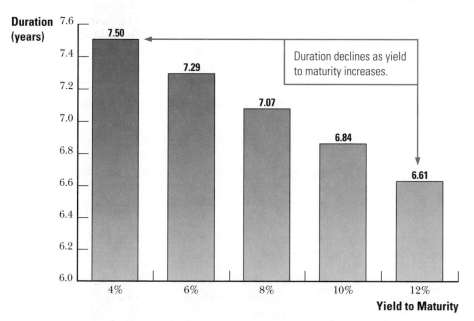

Note: All bonds have terms of ten years and coupon rates of 8 percent.

Bond's Duration Is Handy Guide on Rates

Suppose you buy a ten-year Treasury note today at a yield to maturity of 6 percent and interest rates shoot up to 8 percent. What happens to your investment?

    A. You lose money.

    B. You make money.

    C. Nothing happens.

    D. All of the above.

    The answer: D. All of the above.

How is that possible? The trick is how long you hold the investment.

In the short run, you lose money. Since interest rates and bond prices move inversely to one another, higher rates mean the value of your bond investment withers when rates go up. For a ten-year Treasury yielding 6 percent, a two percentage-point rise in rates would cause the value of your principal to sink by roughly 14 percent, according to Capital Management Sciences, a bond research company.

However, if you hold the note, rather than selling it, you'll get to reinvest the interest received from it at the new, higher 8 percent rate. Over time, this higher "interest on interest" adds up, allowing you not only to offset your initial loss of principal but also to profit more than if rates had never moved at all.

Over ten years, for instance, a Treasury note with an initial yield of 6 percent would produce a total return—price change plus interest—of 6.5 percent a year if you could reinvest the interest payments at 8 percent, according to Capital Management Sciences. That compares with an average return of 6 percent if rates remain unchanged. If rates dropped, so that the reinvestment rate declined to 4 percent, the ten-year return would average just 5.5 percent a year.

Perhaps the best way to judge a bond's interest-rate sensitivity is to get a handle on its "duration." Duration is one measure of a bond's life. It's that sweet spot, somewhere between the short term and the long term, where a bond's return remains practically unchanged, no matter what happens to interest rates.

Exactly where that point is does tend to slide round a bit as interest rates reach different levels. To be precise, it tends to come earlier as rates go up, and move later as rates shrink. The net result is often a plus for investors because the potential gains tend to be bigger than the potential losses, for a given rate move in either direction.

Bond's Duration

Unlike maturity, the more widely understood measure of a bond's life, duration adjusts for the "present value" of the money generated by the bond throughout its life, through interest and principal payments. Present value simply means that it's worth more to have a dollar in hand today than it is to receive it, say, ten years in the future. To account for this, earlier payments in a bond's life are given greater weight than later payments in figuring its duration. As a result, a bond's duration almost always ends up being shorter than its maturity.

For instance, the duration of a ten-year Treasury note yielding 6 percent in today's market is between seven and $7\frac{1}{2}$ years. By that time in that note's life, potential price changes as rates go down or up would be about equally offset by consequent changes in the amount of interest-on-interest that would be received.

As a result, the bond's total return [would] about equal its initial yield to maturity, even if rates change. Anyone who holds a ten-year Treasury note for $7\frac{1}{2}$ years, and diligently reinvests the interest payments, can expect a total return

between yield to maturity and price is more a convex curve than a straight line. How does this affect duration? Duration measures the slope of a straight line tangent to each point along that curve. As a bond moves up or down the curve, the slope of the line changes. Moving down the curve (i.e., as yield to maturity increases), the slope of the line decreases. The relationship between duration and yield is important to understanding the uses, and limitations, of duration as a precise measure of price sensitivity and, thus, interest rate risk.

Duration and Price Sensitivity. The prior section explained how to compute duration and the relationship between duration and the three factors that determine bond prices. These discussions lead to an obvious conclusion: a longer duration indicates greater price sensitivity, for a given change in yield. This suggests one use of duration: to compare the price sensitivity levels of

that's roughly in line with the initial 6 percent yield, no matter if rates rise or fall.

In the case of zero-coupon bonds, durations are equal to, not shorter than, maturities. Zero-coupon bonds don't make interest payments; instead, they are sold at a discount to the face value that is paid to investors at maturity. Over the years between original issue and maturity, the market value of zero-coupon bonds can fluctuate widely. Investors have to hold these bonds until maturity to be assured of locking in their initial yield.

Duration is a reassuring feature for investors who have expenses coming due in the future— for retirement or tuition payments, for instance—that they need to cover with the proceeds of their bond investments. By making sure the duration of their investments roughly matches the due date of their expenses, they can avoid being caught off guard by adverse rises in interest rates.

Gauge of Risk

But the best thing about duration may be that it provides an extremely handy gauge of interest-rate risk in a given bond or bond fund. To figure out how much prices will move in response to rate changes, simply multiply the percentage change in rates by the duration of the bond or bond fund and, voila, you have a pretty good estimate of what to expect.

Because duration shifts around somewhat as rates change, the numbers don't work out exactly. However, the results of this analysis still get you in the ballpark.

For instance, if rates go from 6 percent to 8 percent, a ten-year Treasury note with a duration of 7.4 will take a price hit of about 13.5 percent, or a bit less than two percentage points times the duration, according to Capital Management Sci-

INVESTMENT INSIGHTS

ences. If rates go from 6 percent to 4 percent, on the other hand, that same note can be expected to gain about 16 percent in price, or a bit more than two percentage points times the duration, the data show.

A 30-year Treasury, meanwhile, with a duration of about 12.5, would be much more volatile. It would lose about 21 percent if rates rose two percentage points, or a bit less than the rate change times the duration, and gain about 31 percent if rates fell by the same amount, or a bit more than the rate change times the duration. By contrast, a 30-year zero coupon bond, with a duration of 30, could be expected to react even more drastically to a given change in rates.

How much can duration shift? For Treasurys and other noncallable bonds, duration remains relatively stable within quite a wide band of interest-rate swings. For instance, the duration of ten-year Treasurys would remain between seven and eight years even at rates as low as 3 percent or as high as 9 percent.

However, for trickier types of bonds—including many mortgage-backed securities and callable bonds—durations can snap around quite sharply with interest-rate moves. As a result, current duration estimates for these kinds of bonds can be quite misleading. That's particularly true if these bonds are priced at premium to their face value, as most of the mortgage-backed bonds and callable bonds are these days.

two bonds regardless of their individual coupon rates and maturities.

As an example, reconsider the two bonds we tried to compare earlier:

Bond A: Coupon rate = 10 percent, maturity = 20 years,
              YTM = 8 percent
Bond B: Coupon rate = 6 percent, maturity = 10 years,
              YTM = 8 percent

Before the concept of duration was introduced, there was no way to say, unequivocally, that one was more price sensitive than the other. Duration more accurately measures this important relationship. The duration of Bond A is 9.87 years and the duration of Bond B is 7.45 years. Therefore, if yields rise by a given amount (say from 8 percent to 8.5 percent), the prices of both bonds will fall, but Bond A's price will fall by a greater amount. Therefore,

Bond A has more interest rate risk than Bond B. This feature, by itself, makes duration a useful tool for bond investors. As the article from *The Wall Street Journal* reprinted in the Investment Insights feature on pages 558–559 points out, duration is widely used by bond investors.

Duration and Price Changes. Can this comparison become any more specific, however? It can, to a point. It has been shown that the price change for a bond, given a change in yield to maturity, can be approximated by the following equation:

$$\Delta P = -D[\Delta(1 + r) / (1 + r)]P(b) \tag{16.7}$$

where ΔP is the change in price, D is the bond's duration, $\Delta(1 + r)$ is the change in the yield to maturity, and $P(b)$ is the current price of the bond.[18] Consider the two bonds above, A and B, and assume the yield to maturity on both increases from 8 percent to 8.5 percent. Their approximate price changes can be calculated as follows:

Bond A: $\Delta P \approx -9.87[0.005/(1.08)]119.79$
≈ -5.47 (per \$100 face value)

Bond B: $\Delta P \approx -7.45[0.005/(1.08)]86.41$
≈ -2.98 (per \$100 face value)

Why is this only an approximate price change? The reason goes back to our discussion in the prior section: as a bond's yield to maturity changes, so does its duration. Duration is a measure of price sensitivity, but only a *point* measure. A greater change in yield to maturity gives a less precise statement of price change calculated using duration.[19] This is sometimes referred to as *duration tracking error*.

Brief Recapitulation

Let's try to recap what we've learned about interest rate risk. First, interest rate risk can be described as the price sensitivity of a bond to a change in its yield to maturity. Second, we determined that all bonds expose investors to interest rate risk, though some have more than others. Third, the usefulness of a summary measure of price sensitivity (duration) was demonstrated. We haven't yet discussed how bond investors can minimize interest rate risk, if they wish to, nor how investors might take advantage of the price sensitivity of a particular bond. These issues form the basis of passive and active bond portfolio management strategies and will be explored in the next chapter.

Credit Risk

In this section we'll examine the other major risk to which bond investors are exposed, the risk of not receiving promised cash flows in a timely fash-

---

[18]If modified duration is substituted for duration, Equation 16.7 becomes: $\Delta P = -MD(\Delta r)P(b)$.

[19]The actual price change for Bond A is -5.48 (per \$100) and for Bond B it is -3.03 (per \$100) if the yield to maturity increases from 8 percent to 8.5 percent. Now, assume that the yield to maturity on both bonds increases from 8 percent to 9.5 percent; the actual price changes for both bonds are 15.35 (Bond A) and 8.69 (Bond B). Using Equation 16.7, the approximate price changes are 16.42 (Bond A) and 8.94 (Bond B).

ion—credit or default risk. While all bonds feature interest rate risk, some expose investors to zero credit risk. These are bonds issued by the U.S. Treasury. (Remember, since the Treasury owns the government's financial printing press, it can always print money to pay its bills.) Bonds issued by corporations and municipalities all have varying degrees of credit risk. Some of these bonds are almost as safe as Treasuries, while others are far more speculative. In this section we'll discuss how to evaluate credit risk. We'll also take a detailed look at an actual bond default to see how it affected issuers and investors. First, let's take a detailed look at **bond ratings**—perhaps the most common tool for assessing credit risk.

Bond Ratings

Most, though not all, publicly traded corporate and municipal bonds are rated by independent investment information services. The two best-known rating agencies are Moody's and Standard & Poor's (S&P). Table 16.3 presents a brief description of Moody's and S&P's bond ratings. In addition to those letter ratings, Moody's will occasionally assign a number to a bond rating to indicate where a bond ranks within its rating category. For example, a bond with a rating of A1 is considered to be of slightly higher quality than

Table 16.3

General Description of Bond Ratings

Description of Potential Credit Risk	Standard & Poor's Rating	Moody's Rating
Capacity to pay interest and repay principal is extremely strong	AAA	Aaa
Very strong capacity to pay interest and repay principal; only slightly less safe than debt rated triple A	AA	Aa
Strong capacity to pay interest and repay principal, though somewhat susceptible to adverse changes in financial and economic conditions	A	A
Adequate capacity to pay interest and repay principal, though more susceptible to adverse changes in economic and financial conditions	BBB	Baa
Speculative; faces ongoing uncertainties or exposure to adverse conditions which could lead to the inability to pay interest or repay principal	BB	Ba
Vulnerable to default, but currently has the capacity to meet interest and principal obligations	B	B
Currently identifiable vulnerability to default and is dependent on favorable conditions to meet obligations	CCC	Caa
More vulnerable to default and highly speculative	CC	Ca
Extremely speculative, poor prospects for attaining any real investment standing	C	C
Currently in default	DDD or below	—

a bond with a rating of A3. Standard & Poor's sometimes adds a plus (+) or minus (−) to a letter rating to show relative standing within a rating category.

Moody's and S&P rate bonds very similarly. Both rate bonds primarily on the issuers' ability to make required principal and interest payments in a timely fashion. Bonds that receive the highest rating (Aaa or AAA), for example, are considered to have virtually no credit risk, regardless of the economic environment. An issuer whose bond receives a middle rating (say Baa or BBB) is considered to have adequate capacity to make interest and principal payments, but that capacity may be adversely affected by deteriorating economic conditions. Both Moody's and S&P divide bonds into two general categories based on their ratings: **investment grade bonds** (Baa/BBB-rated issues, or above) and **speculative grade bonds** (Ba/BB-rated issues, or below).[20] Speculative grade bonds are commonly referred to as **junk bonds**.

Moody's and S&P rate newly issued bonds and update their ratings on existing bonds. Both companies publish lists of bonds whose ratings are under review. (The list published by Standard & Poor's is called *Credit Watch*.) As an example, let's look at the bond ratings produced by Moody's and S&P during just one month, October 1992. Data on bond rating activities conducted by Moody's appear in Table 16.4. During the month, Moody's initiated ratings on 663 bond issues (352 municipal issues and 311 corporate issues) and reviewed existing ratings on 657 issues (469 municipal issues and 188 corporate issues). It confirmed its ratings on the majority of bonds (468 out of 657); on 189 bond issues, Moody's either raised or lowered its rating (81 were lowered and 108 were raised).[21] A word of caution seems warranted: both Moody's and Standard & Poor's have been criticized for being somewhat tardy in keeping up with outstanding bond issues.

Table 16.5, reports S&P *Credit Watch* activity for corporate bonds. At the end of October 1992, 186 corporate issuers were on *Credit Watch*.[22] During October, 56 issuers were added and 47 issuers were deleted. Of the issuers deleted from *Credit Watch* during the month, 17 had their ratings reaffirmed, 23 had their ratings lowered, and 7 had their ratings raised.

Determinants of Bond Ratings. Why do some bonds receive higher ratings than other bonds? As we indicated, Moody's and S&P base a bond rating primarily on the ability of the issuer to make required principal and interest payments in a timely fashion. Not surprisingly, the financial characteristics of issuers that receive high ratings differ from those that receive lower ratings. For example, a corporate issuer that receives an Aaa/AAA rating should be stronger financially than a corporation that receives a Baa/BBB rating. This is illustrated in Table 16.6, which breaks down three-year median values of selected financial ratios by S&P rating category. (These data refer to corporate issuers only.) The data show that higher-rated corporations are, on average, less levered and more profitable, and they have greater capacity to cover fixed financial charges, when compared to lower-rated corporations.[23]

In addition to the issuer's financial characteristics, both Moody's and S&P examine other factors when determining bond ratings. These include the

---

[20]This distinction is important; some large institutional investors are prohibited from buying bonds that do not have investment grade ratings.

[21]These numbers may seem high to you, however, it's important to point out that Moody's rates each *individual* issue, not issuer. For example, a corporation might have five subordinated debenture issues outstanding. If Moody's downgrades the corporation (issuer), it would count as five rating changes in Table 16.6.

[22]Unlike Moody's S&P counts only issuers. For example, if a corporation has five subordinated debenture issues outstanding, and has its rating lowered, it counts as one rating downgrade.

[23]Note that these data are *medians* for each rating category and should not be considered *minimum* standards.

Table 16.4

Moody's Bond Rating Activity: October 1992

| | Number of Issues | | |
Activity	Municipal Issues	Corporate Issues	Total
New ratings	352	311	663
Ratings reviewed	469	188	657
Confirmed	403	65	468
Lowered	19	62	81
Raised	47	61	108

Source: *Moody's Bond Record,* November 1992.

Table 16.5

Standard & Poor's *Credit Watch* Activity: October 1992 (corporate issuers only)

Number of issuers (end of month)	186
Issuers added during the month	56
Issuers deleted during the month	47
Ratings confirmed	17
Ratings lowered	23
Ratings raised	7

Source: *Standard & Poor's Bond Guide,* November 1992.

Table 16.6

Median Financial Ratios by S&P Rating Category

Rating Category	Fixed-Charge Coverage Ratio	Cash Flow to Long-Term Debt	Long-Term Debt to Capital
AAA	7.48	3.09	8.85%
AA	4.43	1.18	18.88
A	2.93	0.75	24.46
BBB	2.30	0.46	31.54
BB	2.04	0.27	42.52

Source: *Debt Rating Criteria,* Standard & Poor's, 1986, 51.

nature of the bond, its specific provisions, and the protection it affords creditors in the event of bankruptcy. Standard & Poor's, for example, assigns a rating of BB to a corporation's subordinated debt if its senior debt has a BBB rating. As another example, a municipal bond that's insured will generally receive an Aaa/AAA rating regardless of other characteristics.

Bond Ratings and Default Rates. Bond ratings raise a number of important questions. Perhaps the most important is whether or not bond ratings predict default reasonably well. In other words, has the historical default rate been higher for bonds with lower ratings? Available evidence appears to answer this question *yes.* For example, Table 16.7 lists one-year and ten-year default rates for corporate bonds between 1970 and 1990, broken down by original bond ratings.

Table 16.7

Historical Default Rates for Corporate Bonds: 1970–1990

	Default Rates	
Original Rating	One Year from Issue	Ten Years from Issue
Aaa	0.00%	0.37%
Aa	0.04	0.65
A	0.01	0.99
Baa	0.17	3.78
Ba	1.80	11.29
B	8.08	24.17

Source: J. S. Fons and A. E. Kimball, "Corporate Bond Defaults and Default Rates," *Journal of Fixed Income,* June 1991, 36–47.

Less than one-half of 1 percent of bonds originally rated Aaa defaulted within ten years of issue. (None defaulted within one year of issue.) By contrast, slightly over 8 percent of bonds originally rated B defaulted within one year of issue, and almost one-quarter defaulted within ten years of issue. In addition, notice the dramatic difference in the historical default rates between investment grade bonds (Baa and above) and speculative grade, or junk, bonds (Ba and B). For example, the ten-year default rate for bonds rated Baa was less than 4 percent compared to a ten-year default rate of more than 11 percent for bonds rated Ba.[24]

Another way of assessing the effectiveness of bond ratings is to see whether (and how) they have changed prior to default. We would expect to see bond ratings falling well before issuers actually defaulted, as issuers' financial conditions deteriorate. This appears to be the case. Table 16.8 lists the distribution of original ratings on 556 corporate bond issues that eventually defaulted between 1970 and 1991, as well as the rating distributions one year and six months prior to actual default.

Only about one-quarter of the 556 corporate issues that actually defaulted between 1970 and 1991 were originally classified as investment grade. (Five bonds were even initially rated AAA.) The rest were originally classified as junk bonds. The most common original bond rating was B.[25] The data suggest that, as default approached, the average rating did indeed decline. One year prior to default, over half the bonds were rated B, CCC, or CC, while less than 10 percent were still classified as investment grade. Finally, six months prior to reaching default status, less than 8 percent of the bonds carried investment grade ratings while almost 90 percent were rated B, or below.

Graham and Dodd on Credit Risk and Bond Selection

While bond ratings are useful tools for assessing credit risk, they aren't perfect predictors. Further, many bonds aren't even rated. Investors often need to look beyond bond ratings, to evaluate the specific characteristics of issues

---

[24]A number of older studies found the same expected relationship between bond ratings and default rates. (Lower-rated bonds have higher default rates.) See, for example, W. B. Hickman, *Corporate Bond Quality and Investor Experience* (Princeton: Princeton University Press, 1985).

[25]Recall the rating criteria from Figure 16.1: "Vulnerable to default, but currently has the capacity to meet interest and principal obligations. Adverse business, financial, or economic conditions will likely impair capacity or willingness to pay interest or repay principal."

Table 16.8

S&P Rating Distributions of Defaulting Bond Issues

		Rating Prior to Reaching Default Status	
Rating Category	**Rating when Issued**	**One-Year Prior to Default**	**Six Months Prior to Default**
AAA	0.9%	0.0%	0.0%
AA	3.4	0.0	0.0
A	10.8	0.4	0.4
BBB	11.2	9.3	7.3
BB	10.6	9.8	5.9
B	47.8	49.4	40.4
CCC	14.6	28.4	40.2
CC	0.7	2.1	5.1
C	0.0	0.6	0.6

Note: The table shows the distribution of bond ratings at the time of issue, one year prior to default, and six months prior to default. For example, almost 48 percent of bonds that eventually defaulted were rated B when issued; almost half of bonds that eventually defaulted were rated B one year prior to reaching default status.

Source: E. I. Altman, "Revisiting the High-Yield Bond Market," *Financial Management,* Summer 1992, 85.

and issuers, when selecting bonds. In addition to being the fathers of modern stock analysis, Graham and Dodd also had a lot to say about bond investing.[26]

Graham and Dodd argued that bond investors should focus primarily on avoiding losses. Therefore, bond selection is "primarily a negative art. . . . [I]t is a process of exclusion and rejection, rather than [of] search and acceptance."[27] To meet this objective, Graham and Dodd established a set of qualitative and quantitative standards of safety. After reviewing these standards, it's probably reasonable to say that Graham and Dodd wouldn't be big fans of junk bonds!

Graham and Dodd's qualitative standards include stability, issuer size, and issue terms. They argue that more stable companies with better interest coverage ratios and profitability over several business cycles are better credit risks. For example, a company whose interest coverage ratio stays around 3.0× over several business cycles is a better credit risk than one whose interest coverage ranges from, say, 1.5× to 4.5× depending on the economic environment. Larger issuers, according to Graham and Dodd, are safer than smaller issuers. Indeed, the historical default rate is higher for smaller issuers (measured in terms of total assets) than the rate for larger issuers. Finally, the terms of the issue are also important. Shorter maturities, more secure types of securities (e.g., mortgage bonds), and protective provisions make for safer bonds. For example, Graham and Dodd believed that bonds with sinking funds are better, safer investments compared to bonds without sinking funds.[28]

---

[26]The updated version of Graham and Dodd's classic, *Security Analysis,* devotes four chapters to bond investing. See, S. Cottle et al., *Graham and Dodd's Security Analysis,* 5th ed. (New York: McGraw-Hill, 1988), 403–482.

[27]Ibid, 441.

[28]A sinking fund is a provision that requires the issuer to retire (i.e., call) a fixed percentage of bonds each year, over a specified period, prior to maturity. For example, a sinking fund might require the issuer of a 30-year bond to retire 10 percent of the outstanding bonds each year starting 21 years from the issue date. In essence, a sinking fund shortens the effective maturity of a bond issue and also stretches the repayment of principal over a number of years. The market tends to look on sinking funds favorably and, therefore, bonds with sinking funds usually have lower yields compared to similar bonds without sinking funds.

Table 16.9

Graham and Dodd's Standards for Safety: Investment Grade Bonds

1. Retained earnings equal to 40 percent of assets, except in capital intensive businesses where 25 percent may be adequate.
2. Positive trends in growth and profitability relative to trends in the economy and in the company's industry.
3. Reasonable stability of earning power, with no or infrequent loss years.
4. A minimum size of $50 million as measured by the five-year average market value of the borrower's net worth.
5. Reasonable protection against excessive dilution of the priority of claim on earning power.
6. Net current assets equal to 100 percent of total long-term debt.
7. A working capital ratio of at least 1.75:1.
8. A quick ratio of 1:1.
9. An equity cushion of 200 percent of total debt as measured by the five-year average of the market value of the borrower's net worth.
10. Interest charges earned an average of five times before taxes for industrials and three times for public utilities, with a poorest-year minimum of twice.
11. Total debt service coverage averaging twice and not below once in the poorest year.

Source: S. Cottle et al., *Graham and Dodd's Security Analysis,* 5th ed. (New York: McGraw-Hill, 1988), 465. Cottle et. al., *Graham and Dodd's Security Analysis,* Copyright 1988, McGraw-Hill. Reproduced with permission of McGraw-Hill.

In addition to these qualitative standards, Graham and Dodd also list 11 minimum quantitative standards for investment grade bonds. They believed, for example, that issuers of investment grade bonds should have net total current assets (current assets minus current liabilities) equal to at least 100 percent of outstanding long-term debt. We reprint this list in Table 16.9. Unfortunately there is no information on how Graham and Dodd came up with these standards. In addition, these standards are quite strict; many companies with investment grade bond ratings probably don't meet them.

Anatomy of a Default

On July 23, 1983, the Washington Public Power Supply System (WPPSS, often referred to in the financial press as *Whoops*) defaulted on approximately $2.25 billion worth of bonds.[29] The default, the largest municipal bond default in U.S. history, was caused by problems associated with two partially completed nuclear power plants in Washington state. Financial problems (e.g., cost overruns), regulatory factors, and market forces (such as slower growth in demand for electric power) led to project cancellations and bond default. What follows is a very brief chronology of the events following the WPPSS default.

The default had been expected for several months, though the exact timing took the financial markets somewhat by surprise.[30] The market price of WPPSS bonds collapsed; some of the defaulted bonds were trading for as little as 8.5 cents on the dollar. In response to the default, a series of class action federal and state lawsuits were filed on behalf of WPPSS bondholders.

---

[29]This represented approximately one-third of WPPSS's outstanding bond issues. The other WPPSS bonds were not directly affected by the default.

[30]It had been expected to occur no earlier than October 1983.

Does the Future Hold Another 'Whoops'?

Ten years ago this week, one of the more notorious names in Wall Street history, the Washington Public Power Supply System, defaulted on $2.25 billion of municipal bonds.

It was the largest default in the history of the municipal-bond market. And it thrust that market, previously the sleepy backwater of the securities business, into the limelight, changing forever the way it operated and the tax-exempt bond's image as a widow-and-orphan investment.

A decade later, the name "Whoops," as the issuer came to be dubbed derisively, still evokes unpleasant memories for many investors. Those who've held their bonds from the beginning have recouped only about 34 cents on the dollar.

Could it happen again?

The good news is that there is much more scrutiny, oversight and disclosure of financial information in the municipal bond market than there was a decade ago. That argues strongly that a default of such magnitude is unlikely.

But many bond attorneys, analysts, and investment bankers warn that if a municipal market disaster did happen again, investors would still have few advocates and scant protection.

The lesson of the Washington Public Power default is that the greatest risk in the bond market "is political risk," says C. Richard Lehmann, a WPPSS bondholder who is the publisher of the

"Defaulted Bonds" newsletter in Miami Lakes, Fla. If allowed to, he says, "the powers that be will find whatever means they can to abrogate their obligation."

INVESTMENT INSIGHTS

The Washington Public Power Supply System was one of the biggest borrowers in the municipal bond market in the mid-1970s and early 1980s. The agency sold $8 billion of municipal bonds to about 75,000 investors, using the proceeds to build five nuclear power plants in Hanford and Elma, Wash. It canceled the last two plants midway, Project Nos. 4 and 5, in January 1982, as costs soared, estimates of the region's power needs dropped, and local resistance to nuclear power mounted.

On June 15, 1983, in a decision that turned the genial-handshake business of selling local debt on its head, the Washington state Supreme Court ruled that the state's utilities never had the authority to pledge customer money to pay off bonds. The default didn't become final until two months later, but for investors it was all over but the shouting—most of which took place in court.

So far, investors, after a series of lawsuits including a huge class-action lawsuit with 27,000 plaintiffs, have ended up with $915 million in settlements, including interest, from such defendants as Washington Public Power, Wall Street

(continued)

(The state lawsuits were eventually dismissed.) In late 1988, over five years after WPPSS defaulted, the plaintiffs (the bondholders) and defendants (the State of Washington, over 100 utilities, securities firms, and plant contractors) reached a preliminary settlement of the federal lawsuits. The settlement called for the payment of approximately $750 million to the plaintiffs. The allocation of these funds to individual bondholders was approved by a federal court in October 1990 and final payment was made in September 1992. Bondholders received about 45 cents on the dollar after legal expenses were paid.

Investors can learn a number of important lessons from the WPPSS default. First, large, well-known bond issues can go into default. The WPPSS bonds were originally rated A by S&P and A1 by Moody's, both investment grade ratings. Even 18 months prior to default, the WPPSS bonds still carried an A rating. It wasn't until about eight months prior to default that S&P dropped the WPPSS bonds below investment grade. At the time of actual default, the bonds were rated B.

A second lesson to be learned is that default is very costly to bond investors. While they settled the lawsuit for a record amount, recovering far more than most investors do in defaults, investors received less than half the face value of their bonds. In addition, it took more than nine years to come to a

(continued)

securities firms, utilities, bond counsel, and Washington state, according to plaintiffs' attorney Melvin Weiss.

"Was that sufficient justice?" asks Howard Sitzer, senior vice president at Greenwich Partners and one of the first bond market Cassandras to warn, over a dozen years ago, of the coming collapse. "I don't believe so. The Northwest has since prospered, WPPSS has returned to the bond market, and citizens of Washington are paying substantially cheaper electric rates than in most other parts of the country." Wall Street underwriters made "tremendous profits" and WPPSS bondholders suffered "extraordinary angst."

Still, the $1.15 trillion municipal bond market is more policed than it used to be. The ranks of municipal analysts, a meager 80 or so a decade ago, have now swelled to near 1,000, with every major mutual-fund firm retaining a credit overseer on staff.

All told, less than 2 percent of all municipal bonds default, according to the Bond Investors Association. Nonetheless, municipal-bond insurance for cautious investors has burgeoned into a major business, with one firm that had insured a parcel of Washington Public Power bonds actually using the default as a selling point in its ads.

Most important, in the wake of a 1984–1988 investigation of the default by the Securities and Exchange Commission, state and local governments are held to a higher standard of financial disclosure and Wall Street has more responsibil-

ity for the accuracy of information in bond offerings it underwrites. A central computer database of financial information has been set up in Washington, D.C., by the Municipal Securities Rulemaking Board, an industry watchdog.

Yet while that database now has information on more than 30,000 bond issues, the information isn't updated in any way if an issuer's fortunes change.

As a group, the dozens of Wall Street securities firms who sold the bonds settled a class-action lawsuit by bondholders for $92 million. That was less than the Wall Street community earned from selling Washington Public Power debt in 1980–1983 alone, records from Securities Data Co. show. The securities firms successfully argued that, because the bonds were sold to underwriters in a competitive bidding process, the firms shouldn't be held to the same standards of due diligence as if they had structured the deals themselves. The SEC took issue with that argument, but pressed no charges.

That could be of importance to investors because competitive bond offerings are coming back into favor on Wall Street.

As for the investors in the defaulted bonds, more than half of the total settlement pot was disbursed in November, after the U.S. Supreme Court declined to hear the class-action lawsuit. A number of suits remain outstanding, and former and present bondholders could receive another distribution, although probably much smaller than the first.

settlement, and, of course, investors received nothing during the nine plus years between default and settlement.

These and other important lessons of the WPPSS default are discussed in the *Wall Street Journal* article reprinted in the Investment Insights feature. The bottom line of the WPPSS story is that bond investors ignore credit risk at their peril.

Risk and Required Returns for Bonds

Throughout this text we've discussed the notion that risk and return are related; riskier investments must promise higher returns. Therefore, we would expect to see bond investors demanding higher promised returns on higher-risk bonds. Given that bonds expose investors to several different types of risk, we can relate the promised (required or expected) return on a bond to a number of factors, as follows:

$$r = f(i, \Delta p, ir, rr, dr, cr, lr, fxr) \tag{16.8}$$

where, i is the **real rate of interest,** Δp is the expected rate of inflation over the bond's term, ir is interest rate risk, rr is reinvestment risk, dr is default (credit) risk, cr is call risk, lr is liquidity risk, and fxr is foreign exchange risk.

Still to be decided in court: whether WPPSS improperly allocated certain costs to the two terminated plants from the plants completed earlier. Also at issue are lawyers' fees: Attorneys continue to appeal a federal court's award of $32.7 million in legal fees; they request $103 million.

As for Washington Public Power, the agency has sold 10 bond issues since 1989, refinancing the bonds for Project Nos. 1, 2, and 3, "saving the region about $1.4 billion," according to a spokeswoman. But only one of the five nuclear power plants is up and running. And in a May report, the Nuclear Regulatory Commission faulted that plant for "instances of repeated equipment failures," "insufficient quality assurance," and "ineffective senior management oversight to aggressively assure the corrective action process is successful."

Washington Public Power says "in response to the NRC's report, the supply system developed a comprehensive plan for improvements that will improve the areas in which the supply system was found to be deficient."

Source: Alexandra Peers, "Does the Future Hold Another 'Whoops'?" *The Wall Street Journal*, August 18, 1993, C1. Reprinted by permission of The Wall Street Journal, © 1993 Dow Jones & Company, Inc. All Rights Reserved Worldwide

Learning the Lessons of WPPSS

Bond analysts and attorneys offer this advice for avoiding defaults:

AVOID "POLITICAL FOOTBALLS": any bonds for projects such as nuclear power plants which face local opposition or may be subject to a voter referendum. Hospital and nursing home bonds also have a slightly higher-than-average default rate, and may be affected by new regulations from the Clinton administration.

AVOID BONDS FOR HUGE, NEW PROJECTS that don't have established revenue streams paying off the bonds. Bonds that pay for the expansion or repair of existing facilities, such as electric power plants or bridges, are generally safer.

AVOID ANY PROJECT IN WHICH A NEW TAX, which could later be overturned or declared unconstitutional by the state, pays off the debt.

DON'T GO BY BOND RATINGS ALONE. Both Moody's and Standard & Poor's didn't downgrade WPPSS bonds to below investment-grade status until after the projects were canceled.

AT THE FIRST SIGN OF SERIOUS TROUBLE, SELL. Investors who held onto their WPPSS bonds did worse than those who bailed out when the bonds went into "technical default" in June 1983. Essentially, the federal court held that investors who kept their WPPSS bonds after the default were speculators, and some recovered a lower percentage of their losses.

As each risk factor rises (or falls), the promised return on a bond also rises (or falls).

The first two factors in Equation 16.8 (i and Δp) make up the required return on a risk-free bond. (The closest thing to a truly risk-free security is a short-term T-bill.) The other seven factors can be thought of as compensation (or risk premiums) for investing in bonds that expose investors to various types of risk. For some bonds, certain risk premiums may be zero (or very close to zero). For example, T-bonds have no credit risk, thus investors can demand no risk premium to the bonds' required returns to compensate investors for credit risk. However, T-bonds do expose investors to other types of risk (e.g., interest rate risk) and thus those risk premiums will be added to the bonds' promised returns.

Equation 16.8 represents only a very general model of the determinants of bond yields and is difficult to quantify. Nevertheless, the model can give some insight into the determinants of bond yields. Let's now take a more detailed look at the relationship between bond yields and two important factors: maturity and credit risk.

Bond Yields and Maturity

The relationship between bonds yields and maturity is often referred to as the **term structure of interest rates,** or **yield curve.** The yield curve shows the relationship between yield and maturity for a group of bonds that are

Figure 16.10

Yield Spread between Long-Term T-Bonds and T-bills: 1964–1993

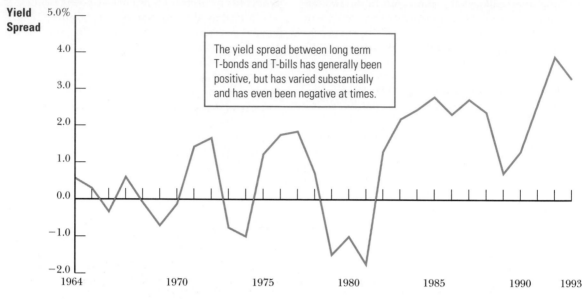

The yield spread between long term T-bonds and T-bills has generally been positive, but has varied substantially and has even been negative at times.

Source: *Federal Reserve Bulletin* (various issues).

similar in other respects. U.S. Treasury securities are often used to represent the yield curve since all are free of default risk and have excellent secondary markets.

While the yield curve raises a number of important and interesting questions, for our purposes in this chapter we need to examine only two. What is the expected shape of the yield curve? Does the shape of the yield curve change over time?

Based on our discussion in this chapter, one could argue that the normal shape of the yield curve should be upward sloping. In other words, as the term to maturity increases, so should the yield. There are several reasons for this. We've seen that a longer-maturity bond exposes the investor to greater interest rate risk (holding other factors constant). Also, as one holds a bond longer, the probability of unfavorable changes in interest rates rises. Thus, one could argue that longer-term bonds expose investors to greater amounts of reinvestment risk. Furthermore, longer-term bonds also expose investors to greater amounts of purchasing power risk. After all, it's easier to forecast inflation for next year than to forecast inflation for the next 30 years. Investors who bought bonds back in the 1950s never expected the inflation of the 1970s.[31]

Adding all of this up suggests that, all things being equal, investors would rather own short-term bonds than long-term bonds; investors require inducements (in the form of higher yields) to purchase longer-term bonds. Therefore, the normal shape of the yield curve should be positive. The evidence does indeed suggest that the yield curve is normally upward sloping. But is it always upward sloping? The answer is *no*.

Figure 16.10 shows the general shape of the Treasury yield curve between 1964 and 1993. To simplify the shape, the figure shows the **yield spread** between three-month T-bills and long-term T-bonds (with at least ten years to maturity). A yield spread is just the difference in yield between the

---

[31]Remember, Graham & Dodd argued that longer-term bonds have more credit risk than shorter-term bonds. This, of course, doesn't affect Treasury securities.

Figure 16.11

Quality Yield Spreads in the U.S. Capital Markets: 1964–1993

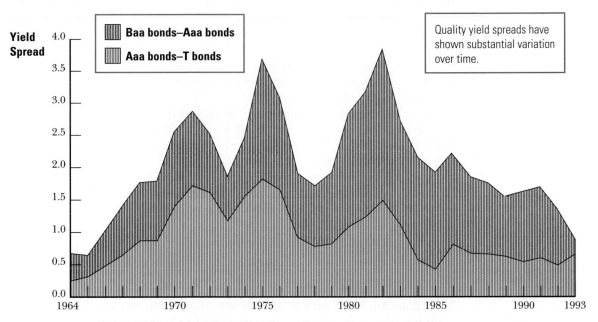

Source: *Federal Reserve Bulletin* (various issues).

two instruments. For example, if the yield on three-month T-bills is 4.30 percent and the yield on long-term T-bonds is 7.00 percent, then the yield spread (bonds minus bills) is 2.70 percent. If the yield spread is positive, then the yield curve is upward sloping. Notice that the shape of the yield curve has changed from time to time.

The yield spread between three-month bills and long-term bonds has generally been positive over this time period (indicating an upward-sloping yield curve). However, the slope has been much steeper in some years than other years. In 1992, for example, the spread was over 4.00 percent compared to 1990 when it was 1.24 percent. In some years, the yield spread has been virtually zero. In 1970, for example, the yield spread was about 0.10 percent. A yield spread close to zero defines a flat yield curve. Finally, in other years, yields on T-bills have actually exceeded yields on long-term T-bonds. In 1981, for example, T-bills were yielding almost 2.00 percent more than long-term bonds. A negative yield spread defines an inverted (i.e., downward-sloping) yield curve.

What do differently shaped yield curves mean? We'll discuss a number of interesting theories of the yield curve in the next chapter. Each theory has a number of implications for active and passive bond portfolio management strategies. We'll discuss these in Chapter 17, as well.

Bond Yields and Credit Risk

Just as interest rates have a term structure, one can also define a **risk structure of interest rates,** which takes into account differences in bond yields across bonds with different degrees of credit risk. In general, of course, bonds with higher credit risk always have higher yields. However, the yield spreads between bonds of varying credit risk do not remain constant over time. The risk structure of interest rates changes from time to time. As an example, look at Figure 16.11. It shows two yield spreads (Aaa corporates minus long-term T-bonds, and Baa corporates minus Aaa corporates) between 1964 and 1993.

Both yield spreads were positive throughout this 30-year period; the yield spread between Aaa corporates and T-bonds, as well as the spread between Baa corporates and Aaa corporates, averaged about 1.00 percent. However, both spreads show a good deal of variation around their averages. In 1992, for example, the spread between Aaa corporates and long-term T-bonds was less than one-half of 1 percent (0.48 percent). By contrast, in 1985 the spread was almost 2.00 percent. During this 30-year period, the yield spread between Baa and Aaa corporates has been as low as 0.38 percent (1968) and as high as 2.32 percent (1982).

Several theories try to explain the risk structure of interest rates. One popular theory suggests that yield spreads widen and narrow in response to economic expectations. If investors are pessimistic about the economy, yield spreads widen; if investors are optimistic, spreads narrow. Apparently, the argument goes, investors are more quality conscious in a poor economic environment than they are in a good environment. Investors are willing to hold lower-quality bonds in a poor economy, but require higher credit risk premiums.

Chapter Summary

1. **Understand why bonds are viable investment alternatives.**
   Bonds offer a number of things to investors that make them an important investment alternative. These include income (bonds are a better source of consistent income than stocks), potential for capital gains in the right kind of interest rate environment, eventual return of principal to investors (assuming no default), portfolio diversification, and one of the few remaining tax shelters (tax-exempt municipal bonds).

2. **Review the risks facing bond investors.**
   While bonds offer a number of advantages to investors, they also expose investors to a variety of risks. Perhaps the most basic is credit risk—the possibility of not receiving interest and principal payments as promised. Bonds also expose investors to interest rate risk, reinvestment risk, purchasing power risk, call risk, liquidity risk, and foreign exchange risk. Not all bonds expose investors to each type of risk. Treasury bonds, for instance, have no credit risk.

3. **Examine how bonds are priced.**
   The price of a bond is simply the present value of its expected future cash flows (coupon interest and principal) discounted at a promised rate of return called the *yield to maturity*. The impact on bond pricing of two complications was examined: semiannual interest and accrued interest (interest due the seller of a bond that changes hands between coupon payment dates). We found how to compute yield to maturity assuming the bond's price was known. In addition, computing yield to call was discussed. We also discussed how to find a bond's actual rate of return and discovered that the actual return will differ from the yield to maturity (promised return) unless coupon payments can be reinvested at the yield to maturity.

4. **Review the basic bond pricing theorems.**
   Five theorems deal with various mathematical relationships between bond prices and interest rates. First, bond prices move inversely to changes in interest rates. Second, a longer maturity makes a bond's price more sensitive to a change in interest rates, holding other factors constant. Third, the price sensitivity of bonds, with respect to maturity, increases at a decreasing rate. Fourth, bonds with lower coupon rates are more price sensitive than bonds with higher coupon rates, all other factors being the same. Fifth, for a given bond, the price increase caused by a yield decrease

exceeds the price decrease caused by a yield increase of the same magnitude.

5. **Measure bond price volatility and interest rate risk.**

   While the bond pricing theorems are important for understanding price volatility, and thus interest rate risk, some sort of measure is needed that allows a comparison of the price sensitivities of various bonds with different coupons and maturities. One such measure, duration, measures when the bondholder receives the bond's average promised cash flow. Bonds with longer durations are more price sensitive than bonds with shorter durations. We found that duration is related to coupon rate, maturity, and yield to maturity. Duration can be used to approximate the price change of a bond, given a change in its yield to maturity.

6. **Evaluate credit risks of bonds.**

   We started this section by reviewing bond ratings. The determinants of bond ratings were discussed. We also examined how accurately bond ratings predict default. Next, we discussed Graham and Dodd's belief in safety of principal as the investor's primary objective. They set forth a set of qualitative and quantitative standards of safety. Finally, we briefly reviewed an actual bond default by the Washington Public Power Supply System (or Whoops). The important lessons are that even large, well-known bonds can default, and default is very costly to bond investors.

7. **Review the relationship between bond risk and required return.**

   Finally, we developed a simple model which states the required (expected or promised) return on a bond as a function of several different factors. To some real rate of interest plus compensation for expected inflation, investors add risk premiums as compensation for the various risks to which the bond investor is exposed. A bond that exposes an investor to greater purchasing power risk, for example, will have to have a higher expected rate of return. We examined the relationships between bond yields and two factors: maturity and credit risk. We found that the yield curve is generally upward sloping, meaning that long-term bonds have higher yields than short-term bonds (holding other factors constant). However, at times the yield curve has been flat, or even downward sloping. Also, while lower-quality bonds always yield more than higher-quality bonds, the yield spreads between bonds of different quality levels have not been constant over time.

Key Terms

Credit risk	Yield to maturity
Default	Current yield
Interest rate risk	Yield to call
Reinvestment risk	Actual rate of return
Purchasing power risk	Price sensitivity
Callable bond	Duration (D)
Call risk	Modified duration (MD)
Call protection	Bond rating
Liquidity risk	Investment grade bond
Foreign exchange risk	Speculative grade bond
Face (par) value	Junk bond
Coupon rate	Real rate of interest
Time to maturity	Term structure of interest rates
Promised return	Yield curve
Semiannual coupons	Yield spread
Accrued interest	Risk structure of interest rates

Mini Case   OBJECTIVE

The purpose of this Mini Case is to give you practice with basic principles of bond valuation. Use the bond data below to answer the following questions:
  Coupon rate = 7 percent
  Yield to maturity = 6 percent
  Face value = $1,000
  Maturity = 5 years

a. Assuming annual coupon payments, and maturity in exactly five years, find the price of this bond.
b. Assuming semiannual coupon payments, maturity in exactly five years, and an effective annual yield to maturity of 6 percent, find the price of this bond.
c. Why are the prices you found in Parts a and b different?
d. Now, assume that the bond matures in exactly four years and three months. (Also assume semiannual coupons and an effective annual yield to maturity of 6 percent.) Find the bond's price. How much accrued interest could a buyer owe?
e. Go back to the assumptions in Part b. If someone were to buy the bond today and hold it until maturity, and the issuer didn't default, would the actual annual rate of return be equal to 6 percent? What would the actual rate of return be if the owner were simply to spend the coupon payments?

Discussion Questions and Problems

1. List some of the reasons investors should consider buying bonds. Elaborate on one of the reasons you listed.
2. What are the risks associated with investing in bonds? To which type(s) of risk are all bond investors exposed?
3. List the variables you need to know in order to find the price of a bond. What does *yield to maturity* mean?
4. If the effective annual yield to maturity on a bond is 7 percent, what is the appropriate semiannual rate of interest?
5. Define *accrued interest*. What impact does it have on the price of a bond?
6. Define *yield to call*. Will yield to call be more or less than yield to maturity?
7. Assume a bond has a current price of $1,100, a face value of $1,000, a coupon rate of 8 percent, and exactly ten years to maturity (assume annual coupon payments). Find the bond's yield to maturity. If this bond is callable in exactly eight years at $1,080, what is the yield to call?
8. If you were to buy a ten-year, 7 percent coupon bond today for its face value of $1,000, what would your actual rate of return be if you reinvested the coupon payments at 8 percent? Assume you would hold the bond to maturity and the bond would pay interest once a year.
9. Why is the actual rate of return always equal to the yield to maturity for a zero coupon bond (assuming it is held to maturity and the issuer doesn't default)?
10. List the five basic bond pricing theorems. How do these theorems relate to interest rate risk?
11. Define *duration*. How does duration relate to interest rate risk?
12. Assume a bond has a duration of 4.5 years, a current price of $1,000, and a yield to maturity of 7 percent. If the bond's yield to maturity declines from 7 percent to 6.5 percent, how much will the price of the bond increase? What will happen to the bond's duration?
13. What is duration tracking error? What causes it?

14. What are the major issues associated with the use of bond ratings? How well do bond ratings predict actual default rates?

15. According to Graham and Dodd, what should the investor's most important criterion be in selecting bonds? What types of things did they look at when assessing the risk of a bond?

16. Explain the relationship between risk and required return for a bond. Why do bonds generally have positive relationships between maturity and required return?

17. Define *risk structure of interest rates*. Has it remained constant over time? Why or why not?

18. CFA Level I Examination, 1992

The following table shows selected data on a German government bond (payable in D-marks) and a U.S. government bond. Identify the components of return and calculate the total return in U.S. dollars for both of these bonds for the year 1991. Show the calculations for each component. (Ignore interest on interest, in view of the short time period.)

		Market yield		Modified	FX rate (DM/$)	
	Coupon	1/1/91	1/1/92	Duration	1/1/91	1/1/92
German bond	8.5%	8.5%	8.00%	7.0	1.55	1.50
U.S. bond	8.0	8.0	6.75	6.5		

19. CFA Level I Examination, 1992

A bond analyst is looking at a 20-year, AA-rated corporate bond. The bond is noncallable and carries a coupon of 7.5 percent. The analyst computes both the standard yield to maturity and horizon return for the bond, which are as follows:

Yield to maturity: 8.00 percent
Horizon return: 8.96 percent

Assuming the bond is held to maturity, explain why these two measures of return differ.

Critical Thinking Exercise

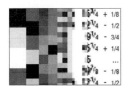

1. This exercise requires computer work. Open file BOND1.XLS on the data disk. It contains the data you will need to answer the following questions. You can do this problem by hand, but it is easier to set it up on a spreadsheet.

   a. Find the bond's duration.

   b. Assume that the bond's yield to maturity increases from 7.25 percent to 7.75 percent (effective annual rate). Find the estimated price change using duration.

   c. Assume that the bond's yield to maturity decreases from 7.25 percent to 6.5 percent. What will happen to the bond's duration? Why?

   d. If this bond had a coupon rate of 8.0 percent (not 6.5 percent), a maturity of ten years, a yield to maturity of 7.25 percent, and a face value of $1,000, what would its duration be, compared to what you found in Part a?

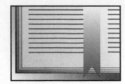

2. This exercise requires library research. Go back over the last few issues of Standard & Poor's *Bond Guide*, which is published monthly, and answer the following questions.

   a. How many corporate bond issuers were added and removed from *Credit Watch* each month? How many issues remained on the *Credit Watch* list at the end of each month?

   b. What happened to the issuers that were removed from *Credit Watch*?

   c. Identify one of the issuers that was removed from *Credit Watch*. Why was the issuer removed from the list? What happened to its stock price and, if you can find it, the prices of its bonds, when the company was removed from the *Credit Watch* list?

Mini Case   SOLUTION

a. Using Equation 16.2, the price of the bond equals $1,042.12.

b. If the effective annual yield to maturity equals 6 percent, then the appropriate semiannual rate equals: $(1.06)^{0.5} - 1 = 2.96$ percent. Using Equation 16.3, the price of the bond equals $1,046.48.

c. The difference between the prices found in Parts a and b can be explained by the fact that the investor receives coupon payments earlier from the bond that pays semiannual interest. The earlier a dollar is received, the higher its present value when discounted at the same rate.

d. The price of the bond, using Equation 16.4, will equal $1,061.84 plus accrued interest. Assuming a 360-day year, and 90 days since the last coupon payment, the amount of accrued interest equals: $(0.06 \times \$1,000)/360 \times 90 = \$16$.

e. Under these conditions, the investor's actual rate of return will equal 6 percent (effective annual rate) only if he or she can reinvest the coupons at 6 percent (effective annual rate). If the coupon payments are spent when received, then the investor receives a total of $1,350 from this bond ($350 in coupon payments, $1,000 face value, and no interest on interest). The actual rate of return equals:

$$(\$1,350.00/\$1,046.48)^{0.1} - 1 = 2.58 \text{ percent, semiannual rate}$$
$$(1.0258)^2 - 1 = 5.23 \text{ percent, effective annual rate}$$

Chapter 17

Managing Bond Portfolios

→

Chapter Objectives

1. Briefly discuss the history of bond price volatility.
2. Analyze the term structure of interest rates.
3. Discuss active bond portfolio management strategies.
4. Understand how to passively manage bond portfolios.
5. Outline the basics of interest rate swaps.

Bond investors had a wild ride during the first half of the 1980s.[1] In 1979, yields on long-term U.S. Treasury bonds broke the 10 percent psychological barrier for the first time in history. Even though rates had been rising almost steadily for several years, the bond market was not especially volatile. Day-to-day (or month-to-month) swings in bond prices and yields were not that extreme. During 1978, for example, the range between the highest and lowest yields on long-term T-bonds was less than 1 percent. That changed abruptly in late 1979.

Between September 1979 and March 1980, yields on T-bonds shot up from about 9 percent to over 12 percent. Bond yields then changed direction and proceeded to fall by more than 2 percent between March and June 1980. Just as quickly, bond yields reversed direction again and rose sharply, peaking at just over 15 percent in September 1981. Bond yields then fell sharply again, falling as low as 10 percent in 1982. T-bond yields then started up again, reaching almost 14 percent in June 1984, only to fall sharply again for about the next two years, dropping to as low as 7.3 percent in late 1986.

This volatility shattered, perhaps for many years, the image of bonds as staid, conservative securities that investors could safely buy and hold. The major lesson of the volatile bond market of the 1980s, we believe, is the importance of bond portfolio management. Careful management is essential. The investor wants to take advantage of anticipated changes in interest rates to boost returns, or to protect the value of the portfolio from adverse changes in interest rates.

In Chapter 16, we discussed bond valuation principles and the major risks facing bond investors, especially interest rate risk and credit risk. While investors must never disregard credit risk, always carefully evaluating the creditworthiness of individual bond issuers and issues, the major risk to which *all* bond investors are exposed is changing interest rates.

---

[1]As in Chapter 16, we use the term *bond* generically to refer to all long-term, fixed-income securities.

577

Figure 17.1

Range of Long-Term Treasury Bonds' Annual Yields: 1948–1993

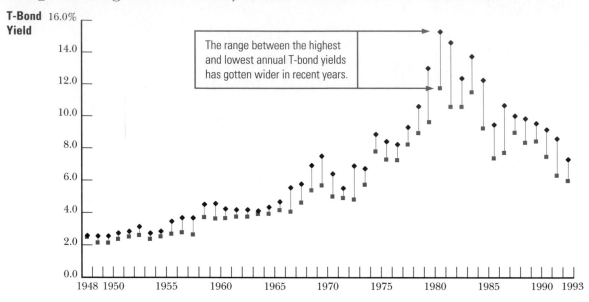

Source: Standard & Poor's Security Price Index Record (various issues).

This chapter explores bond portfolio management techniques, building on the material we discussed in Chapter 16. We begin Chapter 17 with a brief history of bond market volatility. We will see, for example, that bonds have occasionally been more volatile than common stocks in recent years. Next, we discuss and analyze the portfolio management implications of the term structure of interest rates (also called the *yield curve*). As we saw in the last chapter, the term structure shows the relationship between yield and maturity at a specific point in time. Understanding the information provided by the term structure can help to improve the bond portfolio manager's insight. After our discussion of the term structure, we discuss various active bond portfolio management strategies, such as intermarket spread swaps and pure-yield pick up swaps. We then examine more passive bond portfolio management strategies. These include strategies such as immunization and buying bond-index funds. Finally, we conclude Chapter 17 with a brief discussion of a fairly new tool in bond portfolio management, interest rate swaps.

Brief History of Bond Market Volatility

As we've noted several times, 25 years ago, bonds were considered to be dull, almost boring, securities. Investors bought bonds for regular income, usually with the intention of holding them to maturity. Investors worried about credit risk, of course, but the risk of not receiving interest and principal when due could be minimized by careful selection and analysis of individual issuers. This was an era when interest rates, and thus bond prices, changed little from month to month. In fact, interest rates often changed little from year to year.

Figure 17.1 illustrates this stability. It shows the annual range of yields on long-term U.S. Treasury bonds (those with maturities in excess of ten years) between 1948 and 1993. Notice that from 1948 to the early 1970s, the annual difference, or range, between the high and low yields on T-bonds was gen-

Figure 17.2

Monthly Returns on Long-Term Treasury Bonds:
1926–1993

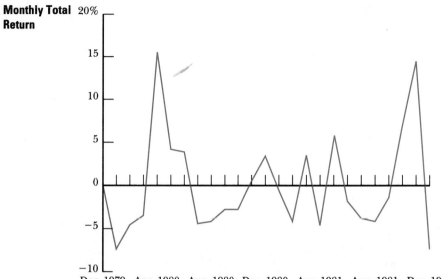

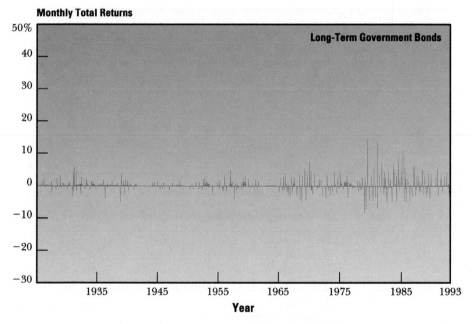

Source: *SBBI 1994 Yearbook* (Chicago: Ibbotson Associates, 1994).

erally quite small. Between 1948 and 1972, it averaged less than 0.6 percent and exceeded 1 percent in only 4 of the 25 years. During the last 20 years shown in Figure 17.1 (1974 through 1993), however, the range between the annual high and low yields on T-bonds averaged more than 1.8 percent. The range exceeded 1 percent in 15 of the 20 years, and in 7 of the 20 years, it exceeded 2 percent.

As interest rates have become more volatile, so too have bond returns. This seems reasonable since bond prices and interest rates are inversely related; as interest rates move up, bond prices fall, and vice versa. Bond holding period returns, therefore, are also inversely related to changes in interest rates.

Figure 17.3

Bond Market and Stock Market Volatility: 1926–1993

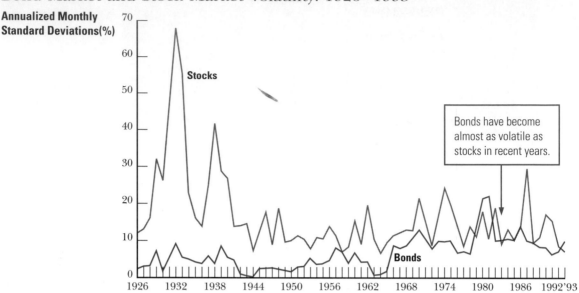

Source: *SBBI 1994 Yearbook* (Chicago: Ibbotson Associates, 1994), 102–103.

Figure 17.2 shows month-by-month total returns on long-term Treasury bonds between 1926 and 1993. The figure vividly illustrates the increasing volatility of bond returns over time. With the exception of a few years, month-to-month bond returns were relatively stable until the late 1960s. By the late 1970s and early 1980s, substantial swings in month-to-month bond returns became common. (The detailed insert in Figure 17.2 shows the month-to-month returns for 1980 and 1981.) For the last three months of 1981, for example, returns from long-term Treasury bonds were 8.3 percent, 14.1 percent, and −7.1 percent.

Comparing Stock Market and Bond Market Volatility

The increase in bond market volatility over the past 20 years raises the question of how bond market volatility compares to that of the stock market. Figure 17.3 shows the annualized standard deviations of monthly returns by year for large-firm stocks (e.g., the S&P 500) and long-term Treasury bonds between 1926 and 1993.

Stocks were clearly very volatile during the beginning of the period, especially prior to 1940. The stock market settled down somewhat during the 1940s and 1950s and, while volatility has increased somewhat since the mid-1970s, with the exception of a few years (most notably 1987) it has not approached the frantic variability of the 1920s and 1930s.

On the other hand, Figure 17.3 confirms prior evidence on increasing bond market volatility. Further, since the mid-1960s, the bond market has frequently changed almost as erratically as the stock market. In the early 1980s, bond market volatility briefly exceeded stock market volatility.

Impact of Bond Market Volatility on Investors

It is difficult to know exactly what caused the bond market to become more volatile during the last 20 years. Both inflation and institutional changes in the bond market probably contributed. Further, while some evidence suggests that the bond market may have regained some of its former stability during the last couple of years, questions still cloud any prediction of how volatile the bond market will be in the future. Whatever the causes of volatility swings, and whatever the outlook, bond market volatility affects both active and passive investors.

The most obvious impact of increased volatility in the bond market is the potential to profit from anticipated changes in interest rates by actively managing a bond portfolio. Volatility also increases the potential for losses, however. We'll assess the potential to increase risk-adjusted profits by actively managing a bond portfolio later in this chapter.

How does volatility affect passive investors? Remember from Chapter 16, that bonds have set par (or face) values. Barring default, a bond will eventually mature and return its par value, regardless of its price in the secondary market prior to maturity. Why should a passive (buy-and-hold) bond investor care about volatility, since the bond will return the investment at maturity? The short answer is that increased volatility increases the various risks associated with changes in interest rates, and these risks affect *all* bond investors. For example, increased volatility makes it more difficult to accurately predict an actual rate of return when purchasing a bond. Increased volatility in the bond market, therefore, increases the importance of strategies designed to minimize the risks associated with changes in interest rates. We'll discuss some of these strategies later in this chapter.

Analyzing the Yield Curve

To structure a sound bond portfolio, passive and active investors alike must understand the relationship between yield and maturity. This knowledge helps the portfolio manager determine the appropriate mix of bond durations in a portfolio. Understanding the relationship between yield and maturity can also indicate when to adjust the average duration of the portfolio. As we discussed in Chapter 16, adjusting the average duration of the bond portfolio will alter its sensitivity to changes in interest rates. Making the correct adjustments can dramatically improve the risk and return characteristics of any bond portfolio.

The term structure of interest rates, or yield curve, is an important tool by which to evaluate the relationship between yield and maturity; a great deal of important information about interest rates lies embedded in the yield curve. In order to better comprehend this information, the investor must understand the nature of the term structure of interest rates, and this understanding begins with a review of the various theories of the yield curve.

What Is the Yield Curve?

In Chapter 16 we briefly defined the yield curve when discussing the historical relationship between yield and maturity. Recall that the yield curve graphs the relationship between maturity and yield for a group of bonds that are similar in every respect other than maturity. Because Treasury securities all have similar default risk, call provisions, tax status, etc., they are usually used to construct the market term structure of interest rates. Further, yields on Treasury securities often serve as benchmarks for determining yields on non-Treasury bonds. Therefore, analysis of the Treasury yield curve can

Figure 17.4

U.S. Treasury Securities Yield Curve: November 1993

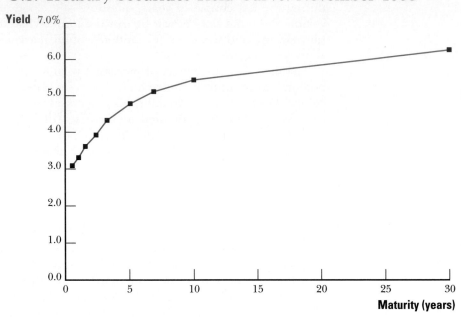

Source: *Federal Reserve Bulletin,* February 1994, A26.

provide insight into the relationship between yield and maturity of non-Treasury bonds, as well.

Figure 17.4 shows a Treasury bond yield curve based on yields as of November 1993. Notice the classic upward slope, which indicates that yields on short-term Treasuries are lower than yields on long-term Treasuries. As we discussed in Chapter 16, short-term yields are generally lower than long-term yields, but not always. Variations in this relationship have given yield curves a variety of shapes. Occasionally, as in early 1989, the yield curve has been flat, meaning that short-term and long-term yields were roughly the same. At other times, the yield curve has had a hump, as in late 1989 and early 1990; this means that, as maturities increased, yields rose and then fell. In a few cases (most notably 1981 and 1982), the yield curve has actually been inverted; long-term Treasuries yielded less than short-term Treasuries.

Changes in the yield curve's slope, and even its shape, over short periods of time give rise to a number of questions. What do the different shapes mean? Does the yield curve contain information about future interest rates? The various theories of the yield curve, which we'll discuss shortly, address these questions. To fully understand these theories, however, one must understand **forward rates** and how to calculate them.

Implied Forward Rates

A **spot rate** of interest is today's prevailing yield on a bond with a particular maturity; a forward rate is the expected rate on a bond with a particular maturity at some point in the future, that is, tomorrow's projected spot rate. For example, the current yield on a one-year bond is a spot rate; the expected rate on a one-year bond, one year from today is a forward rate. If forward rates are *implied* by current spot rates, then knowing current spot rates would allow the bond investor to calculate forward rates.

Suppose someone wants to make a two-year bond investment. This investor must choose between two alternatives:

- Alternative A: Buy a two-year Treasury security
- Alternative B: buy a one-year Treasury security today and another one-year security one year from today

Further, assume indifference between the two alternatives if they produce the same expected dollar return. The one that could produce a higher dollar return would, of course, be preferred. The spot rates are the current market yields on one-year and two-year Treasuries. Knowing these spot rates, can one find the forward rate on a one-year Treasury, one year from today, that is, the rate that would make one indifferent between Alternatives A and B?

The answer depends partially on the timing of interest payments. The example assumes that all of the example bonds are **pure discount bonds,** or zero coupon bonds. Coupon payments would not change the basic relationships we're about to discuss, but they would complicate the mathematics of the relationships between spot and forward rates.

Given the assumption that all bonds are pure discount bonds, we can express the relationship between the two alternatives mathematically. In order to be indifferent between Alternatives A and B, the following relationship must hold:

$$(1 + R_2)^2 = (1 + R_1)(1 + {}_1r_1) \qquad (17.1)$$

where R_2 is the spot rate on a two-year bond, R_1 is the spot rate on a one-year bond, and ${}_1r_1$ is the forward rate on a one-year bond, one year from today.[2] To solve for the forward rate implied by the spot rates, manipulate Equation 17.1 as follows:

$$_1r_1 = \frac{(1 + R_2)^2}{(1 + R_1)} - 1 \qquad (17.2)$$

For example, if the spot rate on a one-year bond is 3.50 percent and the spot rate on a two-year bond is 3.75 percent, then the implied forward rate on a one-year bond, one year from today is:

$$(1.0375)^2 / (1.0350) - 1 = 4.00 \text{ percent}$$

We can also write this relationship as:

$$(1.0375)^2 = (1.0350) \times (1.0400)$$

Thus, buying two consecutive one-year bonds with spot rates of 3.5 percent and 4 percent would produce the same total return as buying a single two-year bond at 3.75 percent.

Now let's extend the example to a three-year investment. Four alternative investment combinations are listed, along with their expected return formulas, in Table 17.1. In order to be indifferent between these four alternatives, all four would have to have the same expected return. Therefore we can find the forward rates implied by the spot rates calculated from Table 17.1.

---

[2] In general, R_n is the spot rate on an n-year bond, and ${}_tr_n$ is the forward rate on an n-year bond, t years from today.

Table 17.1

Alternative Three-Year Investments

Alternative	Expected Return Formula
One three-year bond	$(1 + R_3)^3$
Three one-year bonds	$(1 + R_1)(1 + {}_1r_1)(1 + {}_2r_1)$
One two-year bond and one one-year bond	$(1 + R_2)^2(1 + {}_2r_1)$
One one-year bond and one two-year bond	$(1 + R_1)^1(1 + {}_1r_2)^2$

Note: ${}_1r_1$ is the forward rate on a one-year bond, one year from today; ${}_2r1$ is the forward rate on a one-year bond, two years from today; ${}_1r_2$ is the forward rate on a two-year bond, one year from today.

To illustrate this, assume that the spot rate on a one-year bond is 3.50 percent, the spot rate on a two-year bond is 3.75 percent, and the spot rate on a three-year bond is 4.00 percent. As before, assume that all bonds are pure discount bonds. The formula for finding an implied forward rate (the general form of Equation 17.2) is:

$$ {}_tr_n = \left[\frac{(1 + R_{n+t})^{n+t}}{(1 + R_t)^t} \right]^{1/n} - 1 \qquad (17.3) $$

where t is the number of years from today and n is the bond's time to maturity.

Plugging the assumed spot rates into Equation 17.3 gives the implied forward rates shown below:

$$ {}_1r_1 = (1.0375)^2/(1.0350) - 1 = 4.00 \text{ percent} $$

$$ {}_2r_1 = (1.0400)^3/(1.0375)^2 - 1 = 4.51 \text{ percent} $$

$$ {}_1r_2 = [(1.0400)^3/(1.0350)]^{1/2} - 1 = 4.25 \text{ percent} $$

Locking in Future Returns. Computing forward rates from spot rates implies that investors can lock in future rates of return. To illustrate this, compute the market values of discount Treasury bonds with one-year and two-year maturities. Using the spot rates from the prior example, their prices would be:

$$ \text{One-year bond price (per \$100)} = \$100/(1.0350) = \$96.62 $$

$$ \text{Two-year bond price (per \$100)} = \$100/(1.0375)^2 = \$92.90 $$

To lock in the return on a one-year bond, one year from today, an investor would sell short the one-year bond today and purchase some multiple of the two-year bond today, to return the initial cash outlay to zero. Table 17.2 details the effects of this strategy. If these bonds are risk-free, this strategy locks in a 4 percent return on a one-year bond, one year from today.[3]

The potential to lock in future rates suggests a close interrelationship between spot rates and implied forward rates with a yield curve of any shape. One can, then, think of all market interest rates as consisting of explicitly

---

[3] We should note that borrowing the present value of $100 would be equivalent to a short sale if the loan's interest rate matched the yield on a one-year Treasury bond. How realistic is this strategy? For most small investors, selling a bond short is difficult, and they pay more than the government to borrow money. On the other hand, some large institutional investors and government bond dealers can sell bonds short. These investors can also borrow money at rates close to what the government pays.

Table 17.2

Locking in a Future Return

		Cash Flows		
		Year 0	**Year 1**	**Year 2**
1.	Short a single one-year bond	+$96.62	($100)	—
2.	Buy 1.04 two-year bonds	($96.62)	—	+$104
	Cash Flow	$0.00	($100)	+$104

One-year return, one year from today = ($104 − $100)/$100 = 4 percent

known spot rates, as well as implied forward rates.[4] The interrelationship between spot and forward rates suggests a potential to use implied forward rates to *forecast* future spot rates. Thus, the shape of the yield curve may indeed give clues about the future direction of interest rates. This is the basic issue addressed by the various theories of the yield curve, as discussed in the next section.

Theories of the Yield Curve

Three general theories seek to explain the shape of the yield curve: the pure expectations theory, the liquidity preference theory, and the market segmentation theory. Each theory draws different conclusions about the interrelationships between spot and forward rates, and, as a result, the amount of information contained in the yield curve. We'll describe each theory and then look at some empirical evidence.

Pure Expectations Theory. The **pure expectations theory** holds that forward rates are unbiased estimates of expected future spot rates.[5] It is based on the assumption that many, if not all, investors are indifferent between various combinations of maturities that add up to the same term. Investors choose the combination that offers the highest expected return, eliminating any differences in returns between combinations. Going back to the investments shown in Table 17.1, the pure expectations theory says that investors are indifferent between any of those three-year investment combinations. The theory states that all four combinations must offer the same expected rate of return.

If the pure expectations theory is correct, then the shape of the current yield curve reveals investors' expectations for the future direction of interest rates. An upward sloping curve indicates that investors expect rates to rise. In other words, they think that the spot rate on a one-year bond will be higher one year from today than it is today. On the other hand, a flat curve suggests that investors expect rates to remain about the same. An inverted curve indicates that investors expect rates to fall.

In addition to the shape of the yield curve, changes in its slope are also important indicators of the market's expectations concerning future spot rates, according to the pure expectations theory. For example, if the slope of the yield curve becomes less steep, the theory says that investors expect smaller magnitudes for future interest rate changes, whether upward or downward.

---

[4]We can think of a discount bond's yield to maturity as being equal to the geometric average of many shorter-term implied forward rates. For example, the spot rate, R_n equals:

$$R_n = [(1 + R_1)(1 + {}_1r_1)(1 + {}_2r_1) \ldots (1 + {}_{n-1}r_1)]^{1/n} - 1$$

[5]Pure expectations theory doesn't imply that forward rates always perfectly forecast future spot rates, only that they give unbiased forecasts. An unbiased forecast is one where the average forecast equals the true value of the variable being estimated.

Liquidity Preference Theory. The **liquidity preference theory** holds that forward rates are good predictors of future rates, but they do not provide unbiased projections because, all things being equal, investors prefer short-term bonds to long-term bonds. Investors will hold longer-term bonds only in exchange for a **liquidity premium.**

Going back to the alternative three-year investment combinations in Table 17.1, the liquidity preference theory states that investors would rather hold three one-year bonds than one three-year bond. Therefore, the expected return from three one-year bonds should be lower than the return from one three-year bond:

$$(1 + R_3)^3 > (1 + R_1)(1 + {}_1r_1)(1 + {}_2r_1)$$

If the liquidity preference theory is correct, the yield curve should generally slope upward. Further, according to the liquidity preference theory, forward rates should consistently overestimate future spot rates. That is, if the yield curve is upward sloping, the forward rate on a one-year bond, one year from today will be, on average, higher than the current spot rate on a one-year bond. However, depending on the size of the liquidity preference, the actual spot rate on a one-year bond, one year from today may be the same, or even lower, than the current spot rate on a one-year bond.

Market Segmentation Theory. The **market segmentation theory** argues that forward rates have essentially no relationship with future spot rates. The reason, according to the theory, is that bonds with different maturities are not substitutes for each other. Some issuers wish to borrow short-term and some wish to borrow long-term. Short-term borrowers will not borrow long-term, and vice versa. Similarly, some investors prefer short-term bonds, and some prefer long-term bonds. Long-term investors do not see short-term bonds as substitutes, and vice versa. Going back to Table 17.1, market segmentation theory denies that the four alternative three-year investment combinations are substitutes for each other, regardless of their expected returns. One group of investors will buy one-year bonds and a different group of investors will buy three-year bonds.

Therefore, the market segmentation theory argues, spot rates for different bonds are determined solely by interactions of supply and demand with maturity categories. If the market segmentation theory is correct, the shape and slope of the yield curve reveal nothing about the future direction of interest rates. This theory sees implied forward rates as poor forecasts of future spot rates. If, for example, the upward slope of the yield curve becomes steeper, the change means only that supply and demand conditions in either the short or long ends of the bond market have changed.

Empirical Evidence of Yield Curve Relationships

Some evidence, both anecdotal and scientific, supports all three theories of the yield curve.[6] Some evidence suggests, for example, that implied forward rates forecast future spot rates reasonably well, supporting the pure expectations theory. Supporters of the pure expectations theory note that inverted yield curves have generally occurred during recessions, when current interest rates are high, but declining future interest rates are likely. On the other

---

[6]Much of the scientific evidence, both pro and con, on the pure expectations theory is summarized in Kenneth Froot, "New Hope for the Expectations Hypothesis of the Term Structure of Interest Rates," *Journal of Finance,* June 1989, 283–305. Evidence on all three theories is briefly summarized in James Van Horne, *Financial Market Rates & Flows* (Englewood Cliffs, N.J.: Prentice-Hall, 1993), 108–116.

hand, a great deal of evidence finds that forward rates have little value as forecasts of future spot rates. Upward-sloping yield curves are common, but they do not necessarily give way to rising interest rates. For example, in June 1992 the yield curve sloped sharply upward, yet interest rates continued a general falling trend through the rest of 1992 and much of 1993.

Evidence also gives somewhat ambiguous signals about liquidity preference theory. The typical upward slope of the yield curve is often cited as evidence of a liquidity preference that leads investors, as a group, to prefer short-term bonds to long-term bonds. Average annual yields on Treasury bills, for example, have exceeded yields on long-term Treasury bonds only seven times since 1948. Yet other scientific evidence implies that if a liquidity premium exists, it isn't very large and is probably limited to short-term bonds.

Evidence of Market Segmentation. The market segmentation theory is difficult to believe in its purest form. Can the markets for long-term bonds and short-term bonds be *completely* separate from one another? Corporations and governments issue both long-term and short-term bonds. Further, many investors seem willing to own varying mixes of maturities, adjusting the average maturities of their bond portfolios as market conditions change. In addition, if the bond market were segmented enough to sever any relationship between current spot rates, forward rates, and future spot rates, the differences could create substantial arbitrage opportunities.

Nevertheless, some evidence supports the contention that shifts in supply and demand conditions can affect the shape and slope of the yield curve. For example, in the early 1980s the municipal yield curve was far steeper than the Treasury yield curve. One study attributed this difference, in large part, to a supply and demand imbalance in the municipal bond market.[7] In the early 1980s tax-exempt money market funds had grown very rapidly. As a result of this heavy demand, the study concluded, yields on tax-exempt money market instruments were "artificially" depressed.

Anecdotal evidence of market segmentation can also be seen in the slope of the Treasury yield curve during the early 1990s. From the middle of 1990 through the middle of 1992, the Federal Reserve began pushing short-term interest rates lower in an attempt to stimulate economic activity. The federal funds rate, for example, fell from 8.29 percent to 3.25 percent between June 1990 and June 1992. The effect of this change on the Treasury yield curve appears in Figure 17.5. It shows the spread between three-month T-bills and ten-year T-bonds at various points in time between June 1990 and November 1993.

In June 1990, this Treasury yield curve was essentially flat; the spread between ten-year bonds and three-month bills was only 0.06 percent. As the Fed pushed short-term rates downward, the yield on T-bills fell rapidly from over 8.2 percent in June 1990 to 5.6 percent in June 1991, and to 3.7 percent in June 1992. The yield on ten-year Treasuries also fell, but not nearly as far, from 8.28 percent in June 1991 to 7.26 percent in June 1992. The difference in changes between long-term and short-term rates made the yield curve steeper. The spread between short-term and long-term Treasuries reached record levels in 1991 to 1992. Only in 1993 did the yield on longer-term Treasuries come down and the slope of the yield curve start to become less steep. In November 1993, for example, the spread between ten-year Treasuries and T-bills was 2.50 percent, down from 3.56 percent in June 1992.

---

[7]See David Kidwell and Timothy Koch, "Market Segmentation and the Term Structure of Municipal Yields," *Journal of Money, Credit & Banking,* Spring 1983, 40–55.

Figure 17.5

Slope of the Treasury Yield Curve: June 1990–November 1993

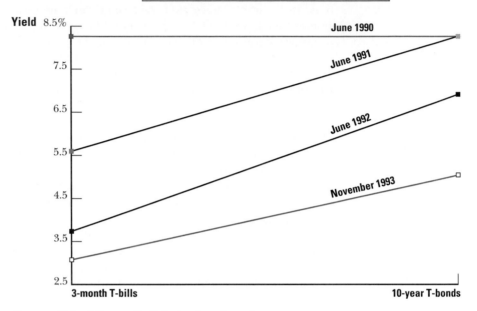

As the Fed reduced short-term interest rates, the yields on short-term T-bills declined, indicating that, perhaps, market segmentation does exist and that the maturity of the security may influence its yield.

Source: *Federal Reserve Bulletin* (various issues).

One explanation for this behavior is that investors kept long-term rates high due to worries about future inflation and therefore, higher interest rates. (Perhaps, they may have thought, the Fed was easing too much and risking overstimulating the economy.) Investors may also have been worried that the federal budget deficit (which set records throughout the early 1990s) would cause heavy demand for funds by the Treasury. This could alter supply and demand factors in the long-term portion of the bond market, influencing the slope of the Treasury yield curve in the early 1990s. Is this evidence of market segmentation? It's hard to say, but in any case, actions by the Federal Reserve to lower interest rates in the early 1990s took an unusually long time to affect the long-term portion of the bond market.

Brief Recapitulation

Up to this point, we've discussed the slope and shape of the yield curve, and important information it may contain for all types of bond investors. These effects are critical regardless of whether the pure expectations, liquidity preference, or market segmentation theory (or a combination of the three) best explains the yield curve. Changes in the slope and shape of the yield curve may forecast future spot interest rates, changes in the size of the liquidity premium, and changes in supply and demand conditions in various segments of the bond market. All bond investors should pay close attention to these implications of the yield curve.

Actively Managing Bond Portfolios

Investors can manage their portfolios actively or passively, or employ strategies that have both passive and active elements. All active strategies require the investor to specify expectations about variables that determine the performance of the assets in the portfolio. For a stock portfolio, important variables include such things as company earnings, dividends, and risk. For a bond portfolio, the investor must estimate interest rates, interest rate volatility, yield curves, and yield spreads. (An estimate of foreign exchange rates should guide any transaction in bonds denominated in a foreign currency.)

Most active bond strategies involve swaps in which the investor buys one set of bonds with certain characteristics while selling another set of bonds with different characteristics. Swaps are based on expectations regarding future interest rates, yield spreads, and so forth. Passive portfolio strategies, by contrast, require little attention to expectations. They make no real attempt to forecast the variables that determine the performance of a portfolio's assets. These strategies generally follow buy-and-hold decision rules. The investor buys a well-diversified portfolio and holds those securities, making few if any changes regardless of either current or expected market conditions. In one popular passive portfolio strategy, indexing, the investor tries simply to replicate the performance of a well-known, predetermined market index.

In this section we examine several active bond portfolio strategies. (More passive strategies will be discussed in the next section.) We also try to assess how well active bond management strategies actually work. Active strategies can be classified as:

1. Interest rate expectations strategies
2. Yield curve strategies
3. Yield spread strategies
4. Foreign exchange strategies
5. Individual bond selection strategies

Of course specific strategies can span these categories. For example, we observed in the last chapter that changes in interest rates and changes in yield spreads are often interrelated. Therefore, bond strategies based on expected changes in interest rates may also evaluate expected changes in yield spreads.

Interest Rate Expectations Strategies

We know that as interest rates rise (or fall), bond prices fall (or rise). We also know that certain bonds are more price sensitive than others, and that duration measures the relative price sensitivity of bonds. These premises suggest a fairly basic bond portfolio strategy: lengthen or shorten the average duration of the bond portfolio based on expectations for future interest rates. If rates are expected to fall (or rise), try to lengthen (or shorten) the average duration of the portfolio. One can increase the duration of a bond portfolio by swapping bonds with high coupon rates and short maturities for bonds with low coupon rates and longer maturities. Of course, the opposite swap would shorten the portfolio's duration.

As an example, assume that a bond portfolio has a current market value of $500,000, an average coupon rate of 7 percent, an average yield to maturity

Table 17.3

Impact of Adjusting Duration on Price Appreciation of a Bond Portfolio

Basic Data

Average coupon rate = 7 percent
Average maturity = 10 years
Current average yield to maturity = 7 percent
Current market value = $500,000
Current duration = 7.36 years
New yield to maturity = 6 percent

Duration	Approximate Price Change	Percentage Change
7.36	$34,393	6.88%
7.50	35,047	7.01
8.00	37,383	7.48
8.50	39,720	7.94
9.00	42,056	8.41

of 7 percent, and an average maturity of ten years. These characteristics give the bond portfolio an average duration of about 7.36 years. Suppose that interest rates are about to fall, dropping the average yield to maturity of the bonds in the portfolio from 7 percent to 6 percent. Table 17.3 shows that, without any adjustment to the portfolio's duration, its market value would increase by approximately $34,393 (or 6.88 percent). On the other hand, lengthening the duration of the portfolio would cause a larger increase in the portfolio's value. If the portfolio's duration could be increased from 7.36 years to, say, 8.00 years, the portfolio would increase in value by approximately $37,383 (or 7.48 percent). The change in duration caused about a $3,000 difference in return. If the duration could be increased to 9.00 years, the portfolio's value would increase by approximately $42,056 (or 8.41 percent). Of course, this strategy brings the risk of inaccurate expectations. If interest rates rise as the duration of the portfolio becomes longer, the price decline will be greater than if no change had been made.

Riding the Yield Curve (Horizon Analysis). Another strategy based on interest rate expectations is sometimes called **riding the yield curve.** If the yield curve is upward sloping, and expectations predict that neither the shape nor the slope of the yield curve will change over the investment horizon, then yields on specific bonds will fall as they ride the yield curve downward (i.e., as they approach maturity).

As an example, assume that the current yield on a one-year bond is 3.5 percent and the yield on a two-year bond is 4.0 percent. If both bonds are discount bonds, the price of a one-year bond is $96.62 and the price of a two-year bond is $92.46. An investor with a one-year investment horizon could buy the one-year bond and earn 3.5 percent. Expectations for stable rates in a year could lead the investor to ride the yield curve by buying the two-year bond and selling it after one year, when it would have one year left to maturity and be priced as a one-year bond. If rates remained unchanged, the two-year bond would sell for $96.62 generating a one-year return of 4.5 percent [($96.62 − $92.46)/$92.46].

Someone who rides the yield curve hopes, of course, that a rising yield curve doesn't portend rising interest rates, as predicted by the pure expectations theory. If the pure expectations theory is correct, the one-year return from the strategy we just described would be only 3.5 percent.[8] Riding the yield curve should not produce consistently higher returns, therefore, if the pure expectations theory is correct (i.e., forward rates are reasonably accurate predictors of future spot rates).

Yield Curve Strategies

As we observed earlier in this chapter, historically both the shape and slope of the yield curve have shifted over time. For example, the Treasury yield curve was essentially flat in mid-1990. It then became upward sloping and became progressively steeper until late 1992. Since the end of 1992, the yield curve has remained upward sloping but at a somewhat flatter slope. Changes in the shape and slope of the yield curve create several possible trading strategies.[9]

Before we review some yield curve strategies, let's describe the types of changes to the yield curve that have been observed historically. Figure 17.6 illustrates three types of changes:

1. *Parallel shifts.* Yields rise or fall over all maturities. The slope of the yield curve remains essentially unchanged as the entire curve moves.
2. *Changes in slope.* The slope of the yield curve gets either flatter or steeper. A flatter yield curve means that short-term yields rise more than intermediate-term yields, which in turn rise more than long-term yields. A steeper yield curve means the exact opposite; short-term yields decline by more than intermediate-term yields, which decline by more than long-term yields.
3. *Butterfly shifts.* This is a change in the "humpedness" of the yield curve. In a positive butterfly shift, long-term and short-term yields rise more than intermediate-term yields. In a negative butterfly shift, long-term and short-term yields fall more than intermediate-term yields.

Historically, parallel shifts and changes in slope are responsible for about 92 percent of observed changes to the yield curve.[10] Furthermore, history shows a high degree of correlation between parallel shifts and changes in slope. Rising yields are often associated with flatter slopes, and falling yields often accompany steeper slopes.

Optimal Yield Curve Strategies. An expected parallel shift in the yield curve, with no other changes, implies probable success for a simple strategy of adjusting the average duration of the portfolio in the opposite direction of the expected change in interest rates. On the other hand, a parallel shift combined with some sort of change in slope implies somewhat more complex bond portfolio strategies. Let's look at an example.

---

[8]If the spot rate on a one-year bond is 3.5 percent and the spot rate on a two-year bond is 4 percent, then the forward rate on a one-year bond after one year would be 4.5 percent. According to the pure expectations theory, this is the best forecast case of the spot rate on a one-year bond after one year. If the rate on a one-year bond after one year were to reach 4.5 percent, then the price of the original two-year bond would be $95.69 [$100/(1.045)] after one year. The one year return would then be [(95.69/92.46) − 1] = 3.5 percent.

[9]Yield curve strategies can get quite complicated. For a more detailed discussion of yield curve strategies, see Frank Fabozzi, *Bond Markets, Analysis & Strategies,* 2nd ed. (Englewood Cliffs, N.J.: Prentice-Hall, 1993), 490–495; or Frank Jones, "Yield Curve Strategies," *Journal of Fixed Income,* September 1991, 43–51.

[10]The three types of yield curve shifts are not independent of each other. For example, upward parallel shifts in the yield curve (rising yields) tend to be associated with flatter slopes. See, Jones, "Yield Curve Strategies," 49–51.

Figure 17.6
Types of Yield Curve Shifts

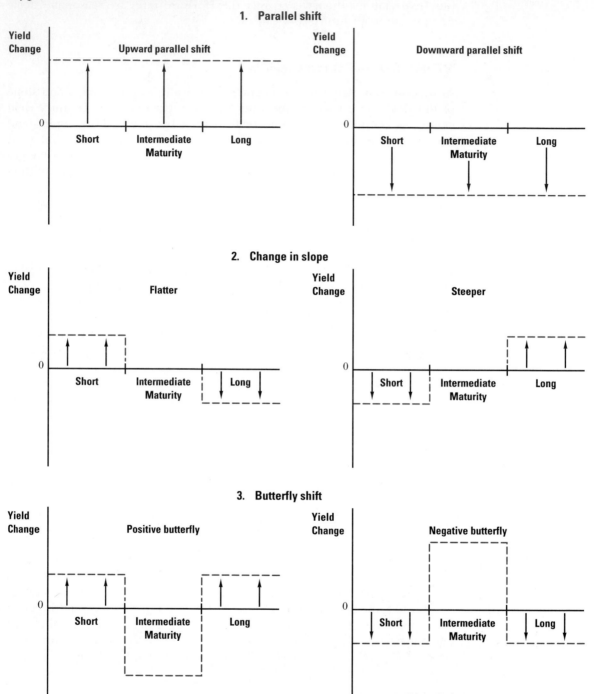

Source: Frank Fabozzi, *Bond Markets, Analysis & Strategies,* 2nd ed. (Englewood Cliffs, N.J.: Prentice-Hall, 1993), 496.

Table 17.4 lists yields and prices (as of November 1, 1993) on three Treasury securities (one short-term, one intermediate-term, and one long-term security). Based on these data, the table outlines optimal yield curve strategies for four scenarios of different parallel shifts and changes in slope. All

Table 17.4

Examples of Optimal Yield Curve Strategies

A. Price and Yield Data

Bond	Maturity (years)	Yield	Price
Short-term	2	3.95%	$92.54
Intermediate-term	7	5.30	69.66
Long-term	15	6.32	39.88

B. Optimal One-Year Returns, Given Expected Yield Curve Changes

Scenario	Expected Change in the Yield Curve — Parallel Shift	Change in Slope	Optimal Bond to Hold	Yield in One Year	Price in One Year	One-Year Return
1	Down	Steeper	Intermediate-term	4.80%	$75.48	8.35%
2	Up	Steeper	Short-term	3.94	96.21	3.95
3	Down	Flatter	Long-term	5.32	48.40	21.36
4	Up	Flatter	Long-term	6.32	42.40	6.32

Notes: Yields and prices are based on the Treasury yield curve that prevailed on November 1, 1993. All bonds are assumed to be zero coupon bonds. Both parallel shifts and slope changes are plus/minus 0.5 percent. The new short-term yield is 3.95 percent + Parallel shift − Slope change; the new intermediate-term yield is 5.30 percent + Parallel shift; the new long-term yield is 6.32 percent + Parallel shift + Slope change.

three bonds are assumed to be zero coupon bonds.[11] The table states one-year holding period returns, given each scenario's relative yield curve change. The optimal strategy is the one that produces the highest one-year holding period return.

In Scenario 1, the yield curve has a parallel, downward shift of 0.50 percent, but at the same time, the slope gets steeper by the same amount. The optimal bond to own is the intermediate-term bond, which produces the highest one-year holding period return, 8.35 percent. In Scenario 2, the yield curve shifts upward 0.5 percent while the slope gets steeper by the same amount. In this case, the short-term bond produces the highest one-year return of the three, 3.94 percent. If the yield curve shifts downward by 0.5 percent and the slope gets flatter by the same amount (Scenario 3), the long-term bond is optimal, producing a one-year holding period return of 21.36 percent. Finally, if the yield curve has an upward, parallel shift of 0.5 percent, while the slope gets flatter (Scenario 4), the long-term bond again produces the highest one-year holding period return of the three, 6.32 percent.

Depending on the relative change in the yield curve, the optimal strategy is sometimes to hold a short-term bond, sometimes to hold an intermediate-term bond, and sometimes to hold a long-term bond. The optimal yield curve strategies are summarized in Table 17.5.

Yield Spread Strategies

Yield spread strategies involve altering the contents of the bond portfolio to capitalize on existing yield spreads or expected changes in yield spreads. As we discussed in Chapter 16, a yield spread measures the difference in yields

[11] Pure discount bonds simplify the analysis, but they don't change essential relationships.

Table 17.5

Optimal Yield Curve Strategies for Parallel Shift and Change in Slope of the Yield Curve

| | | Parallel Shift in the Yield Curve | | |
		Decrease	**No Change**	**Increase**
	Steeper	Long-term or intermediate-term bonds (A less steep curve relative to the yield decrease favors long-term bonds.)	Intermediate-term bonds	Short-term bonds
Change in the Slope of the Yield Curve	**None**	Long-term bonds	Long-term bonds	Short-term bonds
	Flatter	Long-term bonds	Long-term bonds	Short-term or long-term bonds (A flatter curve relative to the yield increase favors long-term bonds.)

Source: Adapted from Exhibit 20–6 in Frank Fabozzi, *Bond Markets, Analysis & Strategies,* 2nd ed. (Englewood Cliffs, N.J.: Prentice-Hall, 1993), 499.

between bonds of different qualities. We also observed in the prior chapter that quality-based yield spreads become wider and more narrow at various points in time. Further, yield spreads are often related to interest rate levels. Yield spreads tend to increase (or decrease) when interest rates are rising (or falling) and tend to be at their maximums (or minimums) when interest rates are historically high (or low). As a result, expectations regarding yield spreads are closely related to expectations regarding interest rates.

However, rising interest rates may also foreshadow an improving economy. As the economy improves, investors may see less risk in lower-quality bonds and become more willing to buy them. Consequently, yield spreads may continue to narrow even as interest rates, in general, rise.

A simple yield spread strategy is often referred to as a **pure yield pick up swap.** In this strategy the bond investor swaps lower-yielding bonds for higher-yielding bonds with roughly similar maturities in order to earn a higher return. At the end of 1992, for example, AAA-rated corporate bonds were yielding almost 0.5 percent more than long-term Treasury bonds (8.28 percent versus 7.80 percent). Someone might swap Treasuries for AAA corporates in an attempt to earn the higher term premium associated with the higher-yielding bonds. This strategy implicitly assumes that neither interest rates nor yield spreads will change significantly over the expected holding period.

Other yield spread strategies are designed to capitalize on expected changes in yield spreads. As we observed in both Chapter 9 and Chapter 16, yield spreads between bonds with varying quality levels tend to be at their maximums when interest rates are at their maximums. This tends to occur right after a peak in economic activity. The usual explanation for this phenomenon is that the risk of default rises in a declining economy. Consequently, investors demand higher premiums to hold non-Treasury bonds. The reverse is true during an economic expansion. Therefore, as the economic outlook improves, the yield spread between Treasury and non-Treasury bonds should start to narrow. In such a situation, the optimal strategy is to swap high-quality bonds for lower-quality bonds if interest rates are expected to remain the same, or even decline, with narrowing yield spreads.

Table 17.6 details a hypothetical example. Assume the current yield on ten-year Treasuries is 10.0 percent and the yield on ten-year AAA corporates is 11.5 percent (giving us yield spread of 1.5 percent). As interest rates gen-

Table 17.6

Illustration of a Yield Spread Strategy

	Treasury Bond	AAA Corporate Bond
Initial term	10 years	10 years
Initial yield	10.00%	11.50%
Initial price (per $100)	$38.55	$33.67
Expected yield (one year hence)	8.00%	8.75%
Expected price (one year hence)	$50.02	$47.00
One-year holding period return	29.75%	39.60%

Note: Both bonds are assumed to be pure discount bonds.

erally decline over the next year, the yield spread between Treasuries and AAA corporates should decline to around 0.75 percent. Both bonds are expected to earn impressive one-year returns, but the AAA corporate bond is expected to earn a higher return (39.6 percent compared to 29.8 percent) due to the decline in the yield spread between Treasuries and AAA corporates.

Another scenario involves narrowing yield spreads during a general rise in interest rates. As we noted earlier, interest rates could rise due to an improving economy, even as yield spreads continue to narrow. In this scenario, an investor might consider making two changes to a bond portfolio: swapping Treasuries and other high-quality bonds for lower-quality bonds, and at the same time reducing the portfolio's average duration.

Tax Swaps. Market forces create yield spreads based on other characteristics besides quality level. One of these spreads compares the yield on taxable bonds to that on tax-exempt bonds.

Over the last 30 years, high quality (AAA-rated or AA-rated) municipal bonds have yielded about 86 percent of the yield on Treasury bonds with similar maturities on average. (The difference arises because the interest from municipal bonds is exempt from federal income taxes.) That ratio has varied substantially, though. For example, it was over 90 percent in 1986 and under 80 percent in the late 1970s. A taxable investor who feels that the ratio between municipal and Treasury yields is too high might switch from Treasuries to municipals, and vice versa. Further, if an investor's marginal federal tax rate goes up (or down), the attractiveness of municipal bonds relative to Treasury bonds goes up (or down).

For example, consider an investor in a 28 percent federal marginal tax bracket. (This person pays $0.28 in additional taxes on every additional dollar of income.) Also assume that AAA-rated corporate bonds are currently yielding 7.0 percent while AAA-rated municipal bonds with similar durations are yielding 4.8 percent. To compare these yields, one must adjust for the fact that interest from municipal bonds is not subject to federal income tax. The municipal bond's **taxable equivalent yield** of 6.67 percent [4.8%/(1 − 28%)] is less than the yield on corporate bonds. If all other factors are the same, the investor is better off holding corporate bonds, rather than municipal bonds.

Now, assume that interest rates in general decline; AAA corporates are now yielding 6.0 percent while AAA municipals are yielding 4.5 percent. The marginal tax rate remains at 28 percent, but the investor is now better off holding municipal bonds since they have a higher taxable equivalent yield than corporate bonds (6.25 percent versus 6.00 percent).

Foreign Exchange Strategies

As we discussed in Chapter 16, bonds denominated in foreign currencies expose investors to foreign exchange risk, since the coupon payments have to be translated back into dollars. Expected changes in foreign exchange rates create some possible bond trading strategies.

One simple strategy is based on the expectation of no significant changes in foreign exchange rates. Investors switch to bonds denominated in foreign currencies if they offer higher yields. In 1992, for example, German government bonds were yielding close to 10 percent compared to around 5 percent for U.S. Treasury bonds with comparable maturities. Even if rates were to fall in Germany, an investor would get the added benefit of rising bond prices.

Another, more complicated foreign exchange strategy is based on buying bonds denominated in currencies that should gain strength relative to the dollar over time. For example, assume a current exchange rate between the Canadian and U.S. dollars of 0.75 (C\$1 = US\$0.75). Also assume that a five-year Canadian government bond yielding 6 percent is priced at par (C\$5,000). At the current exchange rate, the bond would cost US\$3,750 and would provide US\$225 per year in coupon interest. If the Canadian dollar were to gain value relative to the U.S. dollar, then buying the Canadian bond would provide a higher rate of return. If the exchange rate were to rise to 0.80 while Canadian interest rates remained constant, the value of the bond would rise to US\$4,000 and the annual coupon interest would come to be worth US\$240.

Strategies based on foreign exchange rates can be tricky, however. They can also be very risky. The main reason is that interest rates are a major determinant of foreign exchange rates. If the U.S. dollar loses value relative to the Canadian dollar, it may be because interest rates in Canada have risen. If this is the case, the bond's increase in value from the change in exchange rate could be offset by the decline in the bond's price, stated in Canadian dollars.

For example, many investors who bought high-yielding German bonds and other foreign bonds in 1992 received a rude shock in early 1993. German interest rates fell sharply, with the yield on German government bonds dropping from around 9.0 percent to about 6.5 percent. At the same time, however, the German mark (DM or D-mark), lost about 15 percent of its value relative to the dollar. A hypothetical example can illustrate the impact of these changes on an American investor who owned German government bonds.

Assume that one year ago someone purchased a five-year, zero coupon German government bond with a face value of DM100. At the time, the bond had a yield to maturity of 9 percent and a price of DM64.99. If the exchange rate was \$0.75/DM, the bond's price, in dollars, was \$48.75. Now, assume that one year later the yield on the bond has fallen to 6.5 percent, bringing its price to DM77.73. However, also assume that the DM has lost 15 percent of its value relative to the dollar, giving an exchange rate of \$0.64/DM. In dollars, the bond's new price is \$49.75. Measured in D-marks, the one-year return would be an impressive 19.6 percent. Measured in dollars, on the other hand, the one-year return would be only around 2 percent. While the price of the bond appreciated in D-marks as rates in Germany fell, most of this gain was wiped out by the decline in the value of the D-mark relative to the dollar.

Individual Bond Selection Strategies

Individual bond selection strategies seek to uncover individual bonds that are undervalued for some reason. Once the market recognizes that these bonds are undervalued, their prices should rise (as their yields decline) providing a high rate of return. Individual bond selection techniques really look for one of two situations: (1) a bond with a higher yield than other, similar bonds (e.g., those with the same maturity or bond rating), and (2) a bond for which credit analysis suggests that its rating will improve. Let's look at an example.

In the early 1990s, Chrysler was struggling financially. Some observers even speculated about whether or not the company could survive. As its financial woes mounted, Chrysler's bond rating fell. In July 1990, Standard & Poor's and Moody's dropped Chrysler's bond rating below investment grade. Chrysler bonds fell sharply in price as a result of the downgrade, but some investors felt that the market overreacted. They may have been right. As Chrysler's fortunes improved, so did the prices of Chrysler bonds. Between August 1990 and December 1993, for example, the price of Chrysler's 10.95 percent, 2017 debentures rose from 86 percent of par value to over 120 percent of par value, an increase of over 41 percent.

Guilt by Association. We refer to a situation where an entire class of securities is affected by problems of a few individual securities in the class as guilt by association. A good example of this affected high-yield corporate bonds (junk bonds) from 1989 through 1991.

As you probably remember, junk bonds are bonds rated below investment grade (below BBB or Baa). These issues became popular during the 1980s to finance acquisitions, leveraged buyouts, and so forth. By the end of the 1980s, many junk bond issuers faced financial trouble. Several major defaults rocked the junk bond market (notably the 1990 defaults of Campeau Corporation and Southland Corporation). As a result, prices of all junk bonds were mauled. By April 1990, the average yield on B-rated corporate bonds was over 8.0 percent higher than the average yield on Treasury bonds, setting a record.

Some analysts felt that the market had punished all junk bonds too severely, especially those that carried only moderate credit risk. They started to recommend selected junk bonds.[12] Prices of higher-quality junk bonds soon started to recover. In fact, over the three-year period ending on December 31, 1993, mutual funds that invested in junk bonds had an average annual return of 24.2 percent, compared to 11.7 percent for all taxable bond funds.

Do Active Bond Management Strategies Work?

These technical discussions haven't answered an important question: Do active bond portfolio management strategies work? Before we can answer the question, we have to state criteria by which to make the judgment. As we've discussed in prior chapters, a successful active strategy must *consistently* produce higher returns than a simple buy-and-hold strategy. This comparison must adjust returns for higher transaction costs (since all active strategies involve more trading than a buy-and-hold strategy) and differences in risk (since many active strategies expose the portfolio to more risk than a buy-and-hold strategy).

So do active bond portfolio management strategies work? The evidence is far from conclusive. A handful of bond mutual funds, for example, appear to outperform their respective averages pretty consistently, year after year.

On the other hand, interest rates are notoriously difficult to forecast, and many active bond management strategies rely on correct interest rate forecasts. The article in the Investment Insights feature argues that it is next to impossible to outguess the bond market. The author claims that "not one of

---

[12]See, for example, "Why You Should Buy Junk Now," *Forbes*, April 30, 1990, 440–441.

A Fool's Game

Can you make money playing the swings in the bond market? Or should you think of bonds chiefly as a means of hedging the risks of holding stocks and of collecting interest?

Rarely does the research from my tracking of investment letters yield as strong a conclusion as it does in answering this question: Don't try to outguess the bond market. The odds of successfully timing the bond market are so poor that not one of the seven timing strategies the *Hulbert Financial Digest* has followed since 1986 has bettered what could have been achieved simply by buying bonds and holding them.

While successfully calling the ups and downs in any market is difficult, at least some of the timers I follow have succeeded in beating a buy-and-hold approach in both the stock and gold markets. But not so in bonds, at least over the longer term.

The best of the bond timers over the past $5\frac{1}{2}$ years was Gerald Appel, editor of *Systems & Forecasts*, with a compound annual return of 8.6 percent. The worst was the trading strategy of Robert Prechter's *Elliott Wave Theorist*, with a compound annual loss of 1.1 percent. Contrast these returns with that of Shearson's all-maturities Treasury bond index, which averaged 9.4 percent.

Of course, there have been shorter periods since 1986 in which some bond timers have

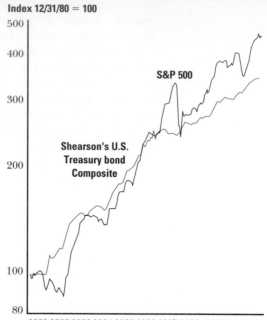

Index 12/31/80 = 100

beaten a buy-and-hold. But in every case, these timers eventually dropped below the return they could have obtained from buying and holding. In the bond market hot hands soon turn cold. Not one of the 20 bond timing strategies that I have followed over the past three years is ahead of the market.

Why would the bond market be more difficult to time than the gold or stock markets? The contrast with the gold market can be explained quite

the 20 bond timing strategies that I have followed over the past three years is ahead of the market [a buy-and-hold strategy]." The reason, he believes, is that "the bond market is so efficient that it leaves few anomalies for investors to exploit." In addition, a study by the investment advisory service SEI Funds Evaluation found that 75 percent of active bond investment advisors underperformed the broad bond indexes over varying periods, ending in 1989.[13]

A few bond investment geniuses may have consistently outperformed the market. Remember, however, as we've said many times before, that the past is never a guarantee of the future. Just because some system or strategy has produced higher risk-adjusted returns, that doesn't mean that it will produce those higher returns tomorrow.

Passively Managing Bond Portfolios

Active bond portfolio management strategies attempt to profit from anticipated changes in such variables as interest rates and yield spreads by buying and selling bonds. Passive strategies are more concerned with controlling the

---

[13]Fabozzi, *Bond Markets*, 515.

easily: Gold has been in a bear market for much of the last five years, and it's much easier for a timer to beat a bear than a bull market. Since the beginning of 1986, for example, a period in which gold bullion has averaged a 2 percent annual gain, 10 of the 14 different gold timing strategies I follow have beaten a buy-and-hold. Yet, even in the stock market, which has been more bullish than bonds over the last five years, and thus should have been more difficult to time, no fewer than 8 of the 32 stock market timers I follow have beaten a buy-and-hold since 1986. Why have no bond timers been able to beat the market?

The answer, I think, is simply this: The bond market is so efficient that it leaves few anomalies for investors to exploit. This is especially the case for the government bond market, which the nearly universal consensus among academia holds to be the most efficient market in the world. Unlike stocks, whose prices reflect everything from broad macroeconomic forces to factors unique to each company, government bond prices are determined by just one thing—interest rates. And there are so many tens of thousands of very smart people watching the key variables—and each other—that it is nearly impossible for one to get an edge over the others. Not so in stocks, especially small-company stocks, where there are far fewer watchers and far more variables to be watched.

Consistently beating the stock market by moving in and out is something accomplished by rel-

INVESTMENT INSIGHTS

atively few humans—yet it can be done. But timing the bond market is just about impossible. My advice is: Resist the temptation to try.

Instead, take the portion of your portfolio allocated to bonds and invest it in a bond index fund. One such fund is Portico's Bond Index fund (sales load, 0.25 percent), which tracks Shearson's corporate/government bond index. Vanguard's Bond Market fund (no load) tracks the Salomon investment-grade bond index. The Vanguard fund has a significantly lower expense ratio—0.21 percent of assets annually, to Portico's 0.5 percent.

An index fund is a pretty cheap way of investing in the bond market, but there's a cheaper way still: purchasing Treasury bonds directly from a Federal Reserve bank and holding to maturity. You don't pay any commissions doing this. This makes particular sense if you don't need to be diversified among many different bond maturities (as are both of these bond index funds). Treasury coupons are a bit lower than those on high-quality corporates, but have the added advantage of being exempt from state income tax.

Source: Mark Hulbert, "A Fool's Game," *Forbes*, August 5, 1991, 119.

---

risk of a bond portfolio. Passive bond management strategies fall into two broad categories. **Indexing strategies** are designed to replicate the performance of broad market indexes. The second type of strategies, commonly referred to as **immunization,** are designed to reduce the risks associated with fluctuations in interest rates.

Indexing Bond Portfolios

As we've discussed before, indexing is perhaps the ultimate in a passive investment strategy. Indexing has become a popular choice among bond investors in recent years.[14] The amount of pension money currently invested in bond index funds is close to $100 billion. The Vanguard Bond Fund, an indexed bond mutual fund, currently has over $3 billion in net assets.

Investors have two basic rationales for indexing bond portfolios. First, indexing tacitly recognizes the extreme difficulty of an active bond investor consistently outperforming the overall market. (We discussed this in the prior section.) Second, indexing reduces transaction costs and management expenses compared to actively managed portfolios. For example, a typical pension fund pays advisory fees between 0.15 percent and 0.50 percent per

---

[14]The issues associated with indexing bond portfolios are discussed in detail in Sharmin Mossavar-Rahmani, *Bond Index Funds* (Chicago: Probus Publishing, 1991).

year for active management of a bond portfolio compared to between 0.01 percent and 0.20 percent for an index fund.

This is not to say, however, that indexing has no drawbacks. For one thing, indexing restricts the investor to the sectors of the bond market that the index tracks, even though attractive opportunities may exist in other sectors. Further, indexing does not ensure that sufficient funds will be available at a specific point in time to meet a predetermined liability. This is a common problem for institutional investors such as life insurance companies and pension funds. Other passive bond management strategies are designed to ensure that future liabilities are fully funded.

Choosing an Index. One of the most important decisions to make when indexing a portfolio is choosing the appropriate index. The most popular index for stock index funds is the S&P 500, though some index funds track broader indexes such as the Wilshire 5,000. Bond index funds may try to replicate the domestic, taxable bond market by tracking one of three indexes: the Salomon BIG index, the Lehman Brothers Aggregate index, or the Merrill Lynch Domestic Master index. Each index contains over 4,500 different bond issues with a total market value in excess of $2.5 trillion. Investors who wish to replicate the performance of a specific sector of the bond market (e.g., Treasuries, municipals, or foreign bond markets) can choose among several indexes. Examples include the Moody's Bond Buyer index, a municipal bond index, and the Salomon World Government Bond index.

Three criteria should guide the choice of an index. First, the index should match the investor's risk tolerance. For example, an investor who wants to eliminate any exposure to credit risk should avoid indexes that include corporate bonds. The second criterion is the investor's set of objectives and goals. An investor who has a short-term investment horizon may find some indexes more appropriate than others. The final criterion is regulatory constraints. Some institutional investors are restricted to investment grade bonds. These investors would have to avoid any indexes that included below investment grade bonds.

Indexing Methodologies. Indexing methodologies are more difficult for bond portfolios than for stocks. For one thing, bond indexes contain thousands of individual bond issues. Purchasing each individual bond in proportion to its market value may be very difficult, especially since many bonds are thinly traded. In addition, **rebalancing** presents more of a problem with bond index funds than with stock index funds. Most indexes drop individual bonds once their times to maturity fall below six months or one year. Thus new bonds are constantly being added to the index and the index fund must be rebalanced each time. Also, the portfolio manager must decide what to do with all the interest income when it is received.

Several indexing methodologies can be employed. The most common, the stratified sampling or cell approach, stratifies the bond market into several subclasses based on criteria such as credit risk, maturity, and issuer.[15] The resulting cells are considered to consist of reasonably homogeneous groups, from which the index selects a sample.

Let's illustrate this approach using a simple example. To design a bond portfolio that is tied to a Treasury index consisting of all U.S. Treasury securities with times to maturity in excess of one year, first divide the Treasury market by maturity. Next, stratify each maturity class by type of security, bonds or notes. As you may recall from Chapter 2, the only difference between bonds and notes, other than maturity when issued, is the fact that some bonds are callable starting five years from their maturity dates. The resulting cells are shown in Table 17.7.

---

[15]Other indexing methodologies are discussed in Fabozzi, *Bond Markets*, 518–522.

Table 17.7

Stratification of Treasury Securities into
Cells

| | Type of Security | | |
Maturity	Notes	Bonds	Total Percentages
1 to 5 years	99%	1%	57%
5 to 10 years	94	6	19
10 to 20 years	0	100	5
More than 20 years	0	100	19
Total percentages	78	22	100

Note: Composition of the market as of June 30, 1993.
Excludes Treasury bills and other Treasury securities with
times to maturity of less than one year.

The bottom row shows the breakdown between notes and bonds. Since 78
percent of outstanding Treasuries with over one year remaining before maturity are notes, and 22 percent are bonds, 78 percent of the entire portfolio
should consist of notes and 22 percent should consist of bonds. The last column shows the general breakdown of the portfolio by maturity. For example,
19 percent of the portfolio should consist of Treasuries with maturities
between five and ten years. The other cells show the breakdown between
notes and bonds within each maturity group. The group of securities with
maturities between five and ten years should be broken down as 94 percent
notes and 6 percent bonds.

Tracking Error. **Tracking error** is one way of assessing how well an index fund
replicates the performance of its benchmark index. Tracking error simply
measures the difference between the total return of the portfolio and that
of the index. This measure is usually calculated monthly. A Salomon Brothers
study found that portfolios indexed to broad bond market indexes (such as
Salomon's BIG index) had the lowest tracking errors. Portfolios indexed to
specific sectors of the bond market (such as corporate bonds) had the highest tracking errors.[16] Further, indexing a larger portfolio generally leads to
smaller tracking error.

Immunization

In contrast to indexing, immunization is an attempt by a bond investor to
reduce a portfolio's exposure to the risks associated with changing interest
rates. As we discussed in Chapter 16, bond investors are exposed to both
interest rate and reinvestment risk. As interest rates rise, bond prices fall. At
the same time, however, bond investors can reinvest coupon payments at
higher rates, earning more interest on interest. When interest rates fall, bond
prices rise, but investors are forced to reinvest coupon payments at lower
rates. Therefore, both rising and falling interest rates can hurt bond
investors.

While it is probably impossible to totally eliminate these risks, careful
immunization can substantially reduce them. The specific immunization
strategy employed by an investor will depend on the risk from which the portfolio needs protection.[17] Let's examine three immunization strategies.

---

[16]Reported in Fabozzi, *Bond Markets*, 522–523. Average annual tracking errors ranged from 0.34
percent for broad bond market index funds to 1.56 percent for corporate bond index funds.

[17]In practice immunization strategies can get more complicated than what we're about to
describe. See, for example, Fabozzi, *Bond Markets*, 511–549. Furthermore, financial futures can
reduce interest rate exposure, as discussed in Chapter 19.

Table 17.8

Three Bonds for Funding a Future Liability

Bond	Term (years)	Coupon Rate	Yield to Maturity	Duration (years)	Price (per $100)
A	10	10%	6.8%	6.91	$122.95
B	17	8	6.8	9.99	111.99
C	25	5	6.8	13.15	78.50

Note: Bonds pay interest semiannually.

Target Date Immunization. Target date immunization seeks to ensure that an investor has sufficient funds available at a point in time to meet a single liability. It does this by setting the duration of the bond portfolio equal to the horizon date, that is, the point in time when the single liability will fall due. This protects the future value of the portfolio from fluctuations in interest rates between the current date and the horizon date. Let's illustrate target date immunization with a simple example.

A pension fund manager determines that the fund will need $10 million in ten years in order to meet obligations to retiring employees. The current yield to maturity on ten-year bonds is 6.8 percent. Therefore, in order to have $10 million in ten years, the pension fund needs to invest $5,123,765 (the present value of $10 million discounted at 6.8 percent for ten years). The pension fund manager decides to invest the money in bonds, leaving the three choices listed in Table 17.8. For simplicity, assume that all three bonds have the same yield to maturity and are free of credit and call risk.

Does it matter which bond the pension fund buys? Absolutely! Table 17.9 shows the future values of the cash flows after ten years for the bonds under three different interest rate scenarios. The future value of each cash flow is made up of the price of the bond after ten years (in the case of Bonds B and C) or the face value (in the case of Bond A), the coupon payments, and interest on the coupon payments.

Table 17.9

Target Date Immunization

Rate of Interest	Future Value of Cash Flows in Ten Years (per bond)			Value of Bonds in Ten Years ($ millions)		
	Bond A	Bond B	Bond C	Bond A	Bond B	Bond C
5.8%	$232.99	$218.91	$158.55	$ 9.71	$10.01	$10.35
6.8	239.95	218.56	153.21	10.00	10.00	10.00
7.8	247.35	218.95	149.17	10.31	10.02	9.74

Details of calculations of future value of cash flows in ten years for Bond B:

Interest Rate	Coupon Payments	Interest on Coupon Payments	Price	Total (per bond)
5.8%	$80.00	$26.40	$112.51	$218.91
6.8	80.00	31.96	106.60	218.56
7.8	80.00	37.35	101.06	218.95

Notes: Number of bonds purchased with initial investment of $5,123,765 are 41,675 (Bond A), 45,754 (Bond B), and 65,267 (Bond C). Future value of cash flows equals coupon payments, interest on coupons (reinvested at the rate of interest shown), and the face value of the bonds (Bond A) or the prices of the bonds (Bonds B and C) assuming the interest rates shown and the yields to maturity.

The optimum choice depends on what happens to interest rates. If rates stay exactly the same (6.8 percent), then all three bond alternatives will produce exactly $10 million in ten years. On the other hand, if rates fall from 6.8 percent to 5.8 percent, Bond A fails to produce sufficient cash flows. If rates rise from 6.8 percent to 7.8 percent, Bond C fails to produce sufficient cash flows. The durations of Bonds A and C are either longer or shorter than ten years. Only Bond B, which has a duration close to the horizon date of ten years, produces around $10 million regardless of whether interest rates rise or fall. Table 17.9 details the calculation of the future value of Bond B's cash flows. If rates fall, the decline in interest on coupon income is exactly offset by a higher price in Year 10, and rising interest on interest compensates exactly for a lower price if rates rise.

To summarize, then, if interest rates fall, and the average duration of the bond portfolio fails to reach the target date, the portfolio will fail to produce the needed cash flow. On the other hand, if interest rates rise, and the average duration of the bond portfolio runs past the target date, the portfolio will fail to produce the needed cash flow. Only if the duration of the portfolio is equal to the period before the target date, will the portfolio produce the needed cash flow.

Two comments should be made about target date immunization. First, buying a zero coupon bond that matures on the horizon date will produce sufficient cash flows regardless of interest rates. Remember, a zero coupon bond has a duration equal to its maturity. In practice, however, such a zero coupon bond may not be available. Second, duration changes as interest rates change, as you may recall from Chapter 16. As a result, if interest rates change significantly, it may be necessary to rebalance the bond portfolio to bring the duration back into line with the horizon date.

Cash Flow Matching and Multiperiod Immunization. Many investors need to fund a series of obligations over a period of time. One multiperiod strategy is to purchase a series of bonds (either zero coupon or coupon bonds) with durations equal to the horizon date of each obligation. In essence, this strategy extends target date immunization.

An alternative strategy is to construct a **dedicated portfolio.** Such a portfolio is designed to generate sufficient cash flow in each period to match the series of obligations faced by the investor. A bond is selected with a maturity that matches the last liability and produces sufficient cash flow at maturity to meet this obligation. The coupons from this bond, paid prior to maturity, reduce the other obligations. Next, a second bond is selected with a maturity equal to the next to last obligation which produces sufficient cash flow at maturity to meet this reduced obligation. The portfolio manager continues to go backward in time until all periodic obligations are fully funded. The steps to set up a dedicated portfolio are outlined in Table 17.10. A numerical example is shown in Table 17.11.

Net Worth Immunization. Many depository institutions, such as commercial banks, must compensate for natural mismatches between the average durations of their assets (loans and securities) and the average durations of their liabilities (mainly deposits). Since the average duration of assets is longer than the average duration of liabilities for the typical bank, when interest rates rise, the market value of its assets will fall by more than the market value of its liabilities. As a result, the bank's net worth will fall.[18]

---

[18]A bank's net worth is also referred to as *capital.* The ratio of capital to assets for the typical bank is between 5 percent and 10 percent.

Table 17.10

Illustration of Cash Flow Matching Process

Assume a portfolio manager must fund a five-year liability stream.

End of Year	Liability
1	L_1
2	L_2
3	L_3
4	L_4
5	L_5

Step 1. Purchase Bond A such that $FV_A + CR_A = L_5$. (Assume that all bonds pay interest annually.) The remaining obligation equals:

End of Year	Remaining Obligation
1	$L_1 - CR_A$
2	$L_2 - CR_A$
3	$L_3 - CR_A$
4	$L_4 - CR_A$

Step 2. Purchase Bond B such that $FV_B + CR_B = L_4 - CR_A$. The remaining obligation equals:

End of Year	Remaining Obligation
1	$L_1 - CR_A - CR_B$
2	$L_2 - CR_A - CR_B$
3	$L_3 - CR_A - CR_B$

Step 3. Purchase Bond C such that $FV_C + CR_C = L_3 - CR_A - CR_B$. The remaining obligation equals:

End of Year	Remaining Obligation
1	$L_1 - CR_A - CR_B - CR_C$
2	$L_2 - CR_A - CR_B - CR_C$

Step 4. Purchase Bond D such that $FV_D + CR_D = L_2 - CR_A - CR_B - CR_C$. The remaining obligation equals:

End of Year	Remaining Obligation
1	$L_1 - CR_A - CR_B - CR_C - CR_D$

Step 5. Purchase Bond E with a cash flow in one year equal to $L_1 - CR_A - CR_B - CR_C - CR_D$.

Note: *CR* is coupon payment and *FV* is face value.
Source: Adapted from Exhibit 22–8 in Frank Fabozzi, *Bond Markets, Analysis & Strategies*, 2nd ed. (Englewood Cliffs, N.J.: Prentice-Hall, 1993), 546.

This is illustrated in Table 17.12 on page 606. The hypothetical bank has total assets of $10 million, total liabilities of $9 million, and a net worth of $1 million. The average duration of the bank's assets is 7.5 years while the average duration of its liabilities is 1.5 years. Notice what happens if interest rates rise by 2 percent; the bank's net worth drops from $1 million to −$153,000.

Net worth immunization is an attempt to narrow the gap between the average duration of a depository institution's assets and the average duration of

Table 17.11

Illustration of a Dedicated Portfolio

	Year	Beginning Obligation	Cash Flow from Bonds	Remaining Obligation
Step 1	1	$ 5,000,000	$ 500,000	$4,500,000
Bond A	2	5,000,000	500,000	4,500,000
	3	10,000,000	500,000	9,500,000
	4	10,000,000	500,000	9,500,000
	5	10,500,000	10,500,000	0
Step 2	1	$ 4,500,000	$ 452,381	$4,047,619
Bond B	2	4,500,000	452,381	4,047,619
	3	9,500,000	452,381	9,047,619
	4	9,500,000	9,500,000	0
Step 3	1	$ 4,047,619	$ 430,839	$3,616,780
Bond C	2	4,047,619	430,839	3,616,780
	3	9,047,619	9,047,619	0
Step 4	1	$ 3,616,780	$ 172,228	$3,444,552
Bond D	2	3,616,780	3,616,780	0
Step 5	1	$ 3,444,552	$ 3,444,552	$0
Bond E				

Summary

Bond	Amount Purchased	Maturity
A	$10,000,000	5 years
B	9,047,619	4 years
C	8,616,780	3 years
D	3,444,552	2 years
E	3,280,526	1 year

Note: All bonds have coupon rates of 5 percent, sell at par, and pay interest annually.

its liabilities. (We'll discuss a way a bank can do this in the next section.) If the average durations of the bank's assets and liabilities could be equated to one another, then the institution's net worth would be immunized from increases in interest rates.[19] This is also illustrated in Table 17.12. Notice that if the average duration of the bank's assets is 4.5 years, and the average duration of its liabilities is 5.0 years, then a 2 percent increase in interest rates has no material effect on the bank's net worth. That's because the decrease in the value of the bank's assets is offset by the decrease in the value of its liabilities.

Interest Rate Swaps

In an **interest rate swap,** two parties agree to exchange a series of interest payments. Interest rate swaps first emerged in the early 1980s as a way of controlling interest rate and foreign exchange risk. While the exact size of

---

[19]Unless the value of the bank's assets equals the value of its liabilities, the average duration of assets should be less than the average duration of liabilities in order for net worth to be immunized. Durations should be equated as follows. Let A be the value of the bank's assets, L be the value of its liabilities, D_A be the duration of its assets, and D_L be the duration of its liabilities. To immunize the bank's net worth let: $AD_A = LD_L$.

Table 17.12

Net Worth Immunization

		Amount ($000)	Average Interest Rate	Duration (years)
Original balance sheet	Assets	$10,000	6.50%	7.5
	Liabilities	9,000	5.50	1.5
	Net worth	1,000		
		New Amount	**Change**	
Rates rise by 2.0 percent	Assets	$8,592	($1,408)	
	Liabilities	8,744	(256)	
	Net worth	(153)	(1,153)	
		Amount ($000)	Average Interest Rate	Duration (years)
Net worth immunization	Assets	$10,000	6.50%	4.5
	Liabilities	9,000	5.50	5.0
	Net worth	1,000		
		New Amount	**Change**	
Rates rise by 2.0 percent	Assets	$9,155	($845)	
	Liabilities	8,147	(853)	
	Net worth	1,008	8	

the swap market is hard to determine precisely, some estimates place the total value of these transactions as high as $2.5 *trillion*. The typical interest rate swap involves two parties that face opposite types of interest rate risk or foreign exchange risk. A third party, a large bank or investment banking firm, usually acts as an intermediary between the two parties. Let's look at an example of a simple interest rate swap.

Example of an Interest Rate Swap

Assume that a bank has $100 million in ten-year loans outstanding that carry an average annual interest rate of 8 percent. The loans charge simple interest only, so the borrowers make annual interest payments of $8 million. The bank finances these loans by issuing one-year certificates of deposit that pay interest equal to the yield on one-year T-bills plus 0.5 percent. On the other side, assume that an insurance company has sold $100 million worth of 6.5 percent annuities. The insurance company pays simple interest on the annuities once a year, and it invests the proceeds from the sale of the annuities in a floating rate security. The security's rate is adjusted annually to equal the yield on one-year T-bills plus 1 percent.

The bank and the insurance company face opposite types of interest rate risk. If rates rise, the bank suffers; if rates fall, the insurance company suffers. As we discussed in the prior section, the duration of the bank's assets is greater than that of its liabilities. Therefore, if rates rise, the value of the bank's assets falls by more than the value of its liabilities.

To manage their respective risks, the bank and the insurance company decide to do an interest rate swap, with a third party acting as the interme-

Table 17.13

Effects of an Interest Rate Swap

Year	One Year T-bill Yield	Bank			Insurance Company		
		Receive	Pay	Net (%)	Receive	Pay	Net (%)
1	4.5%	12.5%	11.6%	0.9%	11.8%	11.0%	0.8%
2	5.0	13.0	12.1	0.9	12.3	11.5	0.8
3	5.5	13.5	12.6	0.9	12.8	12.0	0.8
4	6.0	14.0	13.1	0.9	13.3	12.5	0.8
5	5.0	13.0	12.1	0.9	12.3	11.5	0.8
6	4.0	12.0	11.1	0.9	11.3	10.5	0.8
7	3.0	11.0	10.1	0.9	10.3	9.5	0.8
8	4.0	12.0	11.1	0.9	11.3	10.5	0.8
9	4.0	12.0	11.1	0.9	11.3	10.5	0.8
10	4.0	12.0	11.1	0.9	11.3	10.5	0.8

Note: Each year the bank receives 8 percent and the one-year T-bill yield, and pays the one-year T-bill yield plus 0.5 percent and 6.5 percent. Each year the insurance company receives the one-year T-bill yield plus 1.0 percent and 6.3 percent, and pays 6.5 percent and the one-year T-bill yield.

diary. The bank agrees to pay 6.6 percent annually in exchange for the yield on a one-year T-bill. The insurance company agrees to pay the yield on a one-year T-bill in exchange for a set payment of 6.3 percent. The annual cash flows for both parties are shown below:

	Receives	Pays	Net
Bank	1. 8 percent	1. T-bill yield + 0.5 percent	0.9 percent
	2. One-year T-bill yield	2. 6.6 percent	
Insurance company	1. T-bill yield + 1.0 percent	1. 6.5 percent	0.8 percent
	2. 6.3 percent	2. T-bill yield	

The swap has the effect of paying both parties the same spread each year regardless of whether interest rates rise or fall. This is illustrated in Table 17.13. The table assumes that interest rates first rise, and then fall. Notice that the bank makes 0.9 percent each year and the insurance company makes 0.8 percent each year, regardless of what happens to interest rates.

Chapter Summary

1. Briefly discuss the history of bond price volatility.

Starting 25 years ago, bonds began to lose the image of dull, almost boring, securities that investors bought only for regular income. Interest rates, and thus bond prices, started to vary more from month to month, and year to year. On a long-term, historical basis, the most volatile bond returns have occurred in the last 15 years. In fact, bond market volatility over the past 15 years has approached stock market volatility. Whatever the causes of bond market volatility, and whatever the outlook, volatility influences all bond investors. For one thing, increased volatility creates more opportunities to profit from active bond management strategies. At the same time, however, even passive bond investors should be concerned about increased volatility. Increased volatility in the bond market increases the various risks associated with changes in interest rates, and these risks affect all bond investors.

2. **Analyze the term structure of interest rates.**

   The term structure of interest rates, commonly referred to as the *yield curve,* shows the relationship between yield and maturity for a group of bonds that are similar in every respect other than maturity. Treasury securities are often used to draw the yield curve. The yield curve may contain a great deal of valuable information for all types of bond investors. The yield curve is usually upward sloping, meaning that short-term yields are generally lower than long-term yields. However, both the shape and slope of the yield curve have varied substantially over the years. In the early 1980s, for example, the yield curve actually had a negative slope. Spot rates are prevailing, current yields on bonds with particular maturities. Forward rates are expected rates on bonds with particular maturities at some point in the future. Theorists have explored the possibility that forward rates are implied by current spot rates and the possibility of locking in future returns. Three major theories attempt to explain the yield curve. The pure expectations theory holds that forward rates are unbiased estimates of expected future spot rates. Thus, for example, an upward-sloping yield curve means that investors expect interest rates to rise. The liquidity preference theory states that, while forward rates are good predictors of future rates, their predictions are not unbiased because investors prefer short-term bonds to long-term bonds and will buy long-term bonds only in exchange for a liquidity premium. Finally, the market segmentation theory argues that forward rates have essentially no relationship to future spot rates, but that different supply and demand conditions in each maturity group determine yields. Empirical evidence, both anecdotal and scientific, provides some support for all three yield curve theories.

3. **Discuss active bond portfolio management strategies.**

   Active bond portfolio management strategies require investors to specify their expectations about variables that determine the performance of bonds, including interest rates, yield spreads, and so forth. Most active bond management strategies involve swaps, buying one set of bonds with certain characteristics (e.g., long durations) while selling another set of bonds with different characteristics (e.g., short durations). Active bond management strategies base portfolio composition on market expectations regarding interest rates, the yield curve, yield spreads, foreign exchange rates, and individual bonds. Some of these strategies are interrelated. In a pure yield pick up swap, for example, an investor swaps lower-yielding bonds for higher-yielding bonds with roughly similar maturities based on the expectation that neither yields or yield spreads will change significantly over the expected holding period. For an active bond portfolio management strategy to work, it must consistently produce higher risk-adjusted returns, once differences in transaction costs are taken into account. The evidence for the success of such techniques is quite mixed.

4. **Understand how to passively manage bond portfolios.**

   Passive bond management strategies seek to control the risk of a bond portfolio. Two broad categories of passive bond portfolio strategies are indexing and immunization. Indexing attempts to replicate the performance of a broad market index; it has become popular among bond investors in recent years, in part, due to the difficulty of consistently outperforming the bond market averages. Indexing requires the portfolio manager to choose an index, one of various indexing methodologies, and a method of rebalancing. Assessing an index fund's performance requires measuring how well it replicates the performance of its benchmark index. Immunization strategies seek to reduce the exposure of the portfolio to adverse changes in interest rates. Target date immunization involves making sure an investor has sufficient funds available to fund a future liability. The general idea is to set the duration of the bond portfolio equal to the target or horizon date. A second immunization strategy, cash flow matching, involves funding a series of obligations. One way to do this is through a so-called *dedicated portfolio,* which is designed to generate a cash flow in each period sufficient to match a series of obligations faced by the investor. Finally, net worth immunization seeks to solve a problem faced by many depository institutions, such as commercial banks, that need to equate the durations of their assets with the durations of their liabilities.

5. **Outline the basics of interest rate swaps.**

   Interest rate swaps first emerged in the early 1980s as a way of controlling foreign exchange and interest rate risk. A typical swap involves two parties that face opposite types of interest rate or foreign exchange risk. One party might agree to swap a fixed-rate asset for a variable-rate asset, while the other party agrees to swap a variable-rate asset for a fixed-rate asset. Interest rate swaps allow banks, insurance companies, and other financial institutions to change the durations of their assets or liabilities.

Key Terms

Forward rate	Taxable equivalent yield
Spot rate	Indexing strategy
Pure discount bonds	Immunization
Pure expectations theory	Rebalancing
Liquidity preference theory	Tracking error
Liquidity premium	Target date immunization
Market segmentation theory	Dedicated portfolio
	Net worth immunization
Riding the yield curve	Interest rate swap
Pure yield pick up swap	

Mini Case **1**   OBJECTIVE

To practice computing implied forward rates from actual spot rates and to further understand the various theories of the yield curve. The following yields were quoted on pure-discount U.S. Treasury securities as of November 1, 1993:

Maturity (years)	Yield (%)
1	3.54%
2	3.94
3	4.39
4	4.71
5	4.89
6	5.09
7	5.30

a. Compute as many implied forward rates from these spot rates as you can.

b. How would each of the three theories of the yield curve interpret the relationship between the forward rates calculated in Part a and the current spot rates?

c. Show what is meant by *riding the yield curve.* Show why riding the yield curve wouldn't work if the pure expectations hypothesis were correct.

Mini Case **2**   OBJECTIVE

To construct a dedicated bond portfolio. Use the following information to put together a dedicated bond portfolio. Assume that no zero coupon bonds are available, and that all bonds listed sell at par, pay interest once a year, and are free of default and call risk. Round to the nearest dollar.

Year (Maturity)	Obligation	Coupon Rate on Bond
1	$10,000,000	3.0%
2	20,000,000	3.5
3	20,000,000	4.0
4	30,000,000	4.5
5	31,500,000	5.0

Discussion Questions and Problems

1. Explain why all bond investors should be concerned about increased bond market volatility. Cite some specific examples of how bond investors can respond to increased volatility in the market.

2. Define the *term structure of interest rates*. Why are Treasury securities often used to measure the term structure?

3. Assume that a one-year discount bond currently yields 4.00 percent and a two-year discount bond currently yields 4.25 percent. Find the implied forward rate on a one-year bond, one year from today. Show how to lock in that rate today.

4. Explain the differences between the pure expectations theory, the liquidity preference theory, and the market segmentation theory. What would constitute evidence of market segmentation?

5. What is the basic goal of active bond portfolio management strategies? List several categories of active bond strategies.

6. What is meant by *riding the yield curve?* Would riding the yield curve work if the pure expectations theory of the yield curve were correct?

7. List the three types of changes in the yield curve that have been observed historically. For each kind of shift, what is the optimal yield curve strategy?

8. What is the general idea behind yield spread strategies? Why are yield spread strategies and interest rate strategies often interrelated?

9. Assume the current yield on a BBB 10-year is 8.5 percent and the current yield on a 10-year Treasury bond is 6.5 percent (assume both bonds are pure discount bonds and have face values of $1,000). Also assume you believe that the yield on the T-bond will fall to 6 percent over the next year and the yield spread between the BBB bond and the T-bond will narrow from 2 percent to 1.5 percent. Calculate the one-year holding period return for both bonds assuming your expectations are correct. What type of strategy is this?

10. Assume that Congress has just cut the top marginal tax rate on individuals. What would you expect to happen to the yield spread between taxable and tax-exempt bonds? Why?

11. Give two examples of foreign exchange strategies. Why are foreign exchange strategies so potentially risky?

12. Assume one year ago you purchased a 5-year British government bond (the bond is denominated in British pounds, has a face value of £1,000, and is a pure discount bond). At that time the bond had a yield of 6 percent and the exchange rate ($ per £) was $1.20. Today, one year later, you sold the bond. The yield has fallen to 5.5 percent and the exchange

rate is now $1.10. Compute your one-year holding period return in both pounds and dollars. Why are the two different?

13. Why has bond indexing become so popular? What are some of the important decisions an investor has to make when indexing a bond portfolio?

14. What is rebalancing? Why is rebalancing more difficult with bond portfolios than with stock portfolios?

15. What is target date immunization? Show how zero coupon bonds can solve target date immunization problems.

16. How can an investor solve a multiperiod immunization problem? Explain how a dedicated portfolio works.

17. Assume that a bank currently has $50 million in assets (with an average duration of five years and an average interest rate of 7.5 percent) and $45 million in liabilities (with an average duration of one year and an average interest rate of 5 percent). If interest rates rise by 2 percent, to what risk are the bank's shareholders exposed? How could the bank immunize the shareholders' investment from adverse changes in interest rates?

18. What is an interest rate swap? Why do parties engage in them?

Critical Thinking Exercise

1. This exercise requires computer work. Open file CH17A.XLS on the data disk, which stores yields and prices for pure discount bonds with maturities of 1, 7, and 20 years. Classify the 1-year bond as a short-term bond, the 7-year bond as an intermediate-term bond, and the 20-year bond as a long-term bond. The anticipated holding period is one year. Given the following scenarios, determine which bond is optimal.

   a. All yields remain constant.

   b. All yields rise by 1.0 percent.

   c. All yields fall by 1.0 percent.

   d. Yields on long-term bonds fall by 1.5 percent, yields on intermediate-term bonds fall by 0.75 percent, and yields on short-term bonds fall by 0.25 percent.

   e. Yields on long-term bonds rise by 1.0 percent, yields in intermediate-term bonds rise by 1.25 percent, and yields on short-term bonds rise by 1.5 percent.

   f. Yields on long-term bonds fall by 1.0 percent, yields on intermediate-term bonds fall by 1.5 percent, and yields on short-term bonds fall by 2.0 percent.

2. This exercise requires computer work. Open file CH17B.XLS on the data disk and use the data provided to answer the following questions:

   a. A pension fund will need $10 million in exactly five years. Given current yields, how much will the pension fund have to invest today?

   b. Given the choices available, which bond should the pension fund buy? Why?

   c. Would your answer to Part b change if the fund manager believed that interest rates might rise or fall during the next five years?

   d. Show what would happen if (1) interest rates were to rise immediately by 1.5 percent after the bonds were purchased and remain at that level for the rest of the five-year period, or (2) interest rates were to fall immediately by 1.5 percent after the bonds were purchased and remain at that level for the rest of the five-year period.

   e. Should the pension fund make any changes to the bond portfolio if rates were either to rise or fall during the five-year period?

3. This exercise requires library research. Find five bonds that have been upgraded by the rating agencies recently (either corporate or municipal bonds). Obtain price and yield information for the bonds six months prior to the upgrade and six months following it. In addition, obtain yield information from some relevant index for either corporate or municipal bonds.

a. What happened to the bond prices and yields prior to and following the upgrade announcement? How did the spreads between the yields for your sample bonds and the index yield change? Did they widen or narrow?

b. Had you purchased these bonds six months prior to the upgrade announcement, approximately how much higher would your return have been compared to the performance of the broad market index? (*Hint:* Standard & Poor's monthly *Bond Guide* is a good source of upgrade, price, and yield information.)

4. CFA Level III Examination, 1991

Global Foundation has recently hired Strategic Allocation Associates (SAA) to review and make recommendations concerning allocation of its $5 billion endowment portfolio. Global has indicated an interest in introducing a structured approach (where structured management is broadly defined as indexing, immunization, dedication, etc.) to at least a portion of the fund's fixed-income component.

After analysis of Global's current asset mix, investment objectives, international exposure, and cash flow data, SAA has recommended that the overall asset mix be: 50 percent equity, 5 percent real estate, and 45 percent fixed-income securities. Within the fixed-income component, SAA has further recommended the following allocation:

- 50 percent structured management
- 40 percent specialty active management (20 percent market timing, 10 percent high-yield, 10 percent arbitrage)
- 10 percent nondollar/international active management

Global's investment committee has asked you, as a senior partner in SAA, to address several issues.

A. Compare structured management to active management with specific focus on *each* of the following aspects:

- Predictability of returns
- Level of returns
- Cash flow characteristics

(12 minutes)

B. Explain the potential impact on the active managers' strategies and freedoms of action resulting from the introduction of a structured portfolio component.

(8 minutes)

C. Compare the stratified sampling approach to bond index construction with an optimization approach. **Briefly discuss** the strengths and weaknesses of *each* index construction technique with specific consideration of convexity and changes in yield.

(10 minutes)

5. CFA Level II Examination, 1992

U.S. Treasuries represent a significant holding in Monticello's pension portfolio. You decide to analyze the yield curve for U.S. Treasury notes.

A. Using the data in Table A, **calculate** the five-year spot and forward rates assuming annual compounding. **Show** calculations.

(8 minutes)

Table A

U.S. Treasury Note Yield Curve Data

Years to Maturity	Par Coupon Yield to Maturity	Calculated Spot Rates	Calculated Forward Rates
1	5.0%	5.00%	5.00%
2	5.2	5.21	5.42
3	6.0	6.05	7.75
4	7.0	7.16	10.56
5	7.0	□	□

B. Define and **describe** *each* of the following *three* concepts:

- Yield-to-maturity
- Spot rate
- Forward rate

Explain how these *three* concepts are related.

(9 minutes)

C. You are considering the purchase of a zero coupon U.S. Treasury note with four years to maturity. Based on the above yield curve analysis, **calculate** *both* the expected yield to maturity and the price for the security. **Show** calculations.

(3 minutes)

Mini Case **1**   SOLUTION

a. Implied forward rates are shown in Table 17.14

Table 17.14

Implied Forward Rates

Maturity	0	1	2	3	4	5	6
			Years from Today				
1	3.54%	4.34%	5.30%	5.68%	5.61%	6.10%	6.57%
2	3.94	4.82	5.49	5.64	5.85	6.33	
3	4.39	5.10	5.53	5.80	6.09		
4	4.71	5.23	5.67	5.99			
5	4.89	5.40	5.85				
6	5.09	5.60					
7	5.30						

Riding the Yield Curve

	Cost	No Change in Rates			Expectations Theory Correct		
		Yield in One Year	Value in One Year	HPR	Yield in One Year	Value in One Year	HPR
Buy a one-year bond	$96.58	N/A	$100.00	3.54%	N/A	$100.00	3.54%
Buy a two-year bond	92.56	3.54%	96.58	4.34	4.34%	95.84	3.54

b. The pure expectations theory argues that the implied forward rates are pure estimates of future spot rates. Since the current yield curve is upward sloping, the market must be expecting rates to rise.

The liquidity preference theory argues that, while the market may be expecting rates to rise, the upward-sloping yield curve may just indicate investors' liquidity preference. Therefore, the actual rate on a one-year bond, one year from today, will probably be less than the implied forward rate on a one-year bond, one year from today.

The market segmentation theory argues that supply and demand within each maturity group determines the yield in that maturity. Therefore, implied forward rates are not good predictors of future spot rates. The rate, for example, on a five-year bond, one year from today may be higher or lower than 5.40 percent. It depends solely on supply and demand conditions.

c. Riding the yield curve would be buying a two-year bond today and selling it after one year, as in Table 17.14. Riding the yield curve works only if rates remain constant and therefore will not work if the pure expectations theory is correct. This is also shown in Table 17.14.

2. The dedicated portfolio shown in Table 17.15 follows the procedure outlined in Table 17.10 and is similar to Table 17.11.

Table 17.15

Year	Obligation	Cash Flow	Remaining Obligation
1	$10,000,000	$ 1,500,000	$ 8,500,000
2	20,000,000	1,500,000	18,500,000
3	20,000,000	1,500,000	18,500,000
4	30,000,000	1,500,000	28,500,000
5	31,500,000	31,500,000	0
1	8,500,000	1,221,429	7,278,571
2	18,500,000	1,221,429	17,278,571
3	18,500,000	1,221,429	17,278,571
4	28,500,000	28,500,000	0
1	7,278,571	664,560	6,614,011
2	17,278,571	664,560	16,614,011
3	17,278,571	17,278,571	0
1	6,614,011	561,826	6,052,185
2	16,614,011	16,614,011	0
1	6,052,185	6,052,185	0

Bond	Amount Purchased	Maturity	Coupon
A	$30,000,000	5	5.0%
B	27,142,857	4	4.5
C	16,614,011	3	4.0
D	16,052,185	2	3.5
E	5,875,907	1	3.0

Chapter 18

Fundamentals of Options

Chapter Objectives

1. Understand the basic characteristics of option contracts.
2. Determine the value of an option at expiration.
3. Describe common option trading strategies.
4. Review option pricing models.
5. Discuss other securities that resemble options.

In the fall of 1993, a takeover drama began. On one side was Paramount Communications, one of the last of the old, independent film studios. On the other side were QVC Network and Viacom; both wanted to acquire Paramount. The conflict produced a classic bidding war. One suitor would make a bid only to see the other suitor make a higher offer. Furthermore, since both QVC and Viacom were offering their stock in exchange for shares of Paramount, the value of each offer changed daily. Each company even resorted to legal action to try to stop the other from acquiring Paramount. Needless to say, the price of Paramount stock rose and fell sharply on various public announcements; the general trend, not surprisingly, was upward. Within a few weeks during the fall of 1993, Paramount soared from about $55 per share to over $80 per share.

Speculators sought to profit from the outcome of the Paramount acquisition, but some didn't buy Paramount stock; rather these speculators traded **options** on Paramount stock. These options gave holders the right to buy or sell Paramount shares at fixed prices for short periods of time. Options are **derivative securities,** meaning that their values derive from other assets. The value of the Paramount options derive from the price of Paramount's common stock. As Paramount's stock price rose and fell, so did the value of the options. Options are very different from more traditional investments, such as stocks and bonds, and confront investors with a unique set of risks. At the same time, however, options offer investors unique opportunities. Options aren't for everyone, but they still play an important role in the contemporary investment world.

In this chapter we discuss the fundamentals of options. We begin with a description of the basic characteristics of option contracts, covering what options are, what option contracts obligate investors to do, how options are traded, and what types of securities underlie options. Next, we describe how to determine the value of an option at its expiration. This will help us construct profit and loss statements for basic option positions and illustrate some of the unique risks and rewards of options. Our review of the valuation of options at expiration is followed by a discussion of the most common option trading strategies, such as writing covered calls, bull market spreads, and so forth. Next, we outline two option pricing models. These models attempt to develop more precise estimates of the fundamental value of an option. At the same time, these models help us to understand why one option may be worth more than another. The chapter concludes with a description of other securities that resemble options. These include convertible securities and warrants.

Basic Characteristics of Option Contracts

An option contract gives the buyer, or holder, the right, but not the obligation, to buy or sell a stated number of shares of common stock (usually 100 shares) at a specified price (called the **exercise** or **strike price**) until a specified point in time (called the **expiration date**).[1] An option to buy stock is a **call option;** an option to sell is a **put option.** Let's look at an example of each.

On November 5, 1993, a call option on Paramount stock with an exercise price of 75 that would expire in December 1993 was selling for $7\frac{1}{2}$. On the same day, a put option on Paramount with the same exercise price and expiration date was selling for $3\frac{1}{2}$. Owning the call option gives the holder the right to buy 100 shares of Paramount at $75 per share until December 17, 1993. Owning the put option gives the holder the right to sell 100 shares of Paramount at $75 per share until December 17, 1993. The price of the call option was $750 ($7\frac{1}{2}$ times 100) and the price of the put option was $350 ($3\frac{1}{2}$ times 100). Paramount stock closed on November 5, 1993 at $80\frac{3}{8}$ ($80.375) per share.

If a call option has an exercise price lower than the stock price, it is said to be **in-the-money.** In other words, the owner of the 75 call option could buy Paramount for $75 a share, or $5.375 less than the market price of Paramount. If a call option has an exercise price greater than the stock price, it is said to be **out-of-the-money.** If a put's exercise price is greater than the stock price, the put is in-the-money. The owner of the put option could sell Paramount for more than the current market price. If the put's exercise price is less than the stock price, the put is out-of-the-money. If, by chance, the exercise price of an option, either a call or a put, is equal to the stock price, the option is said to be **at-the-money.**

Since a call is an option to buy at a set price, holding all other factors constant, its price should move in the same direction as the price of the stock; the price of a put, since it is an option to sell, should move in the opposite direction from the price of the stock. Figure 18.1 shows the relationship between the price of Paramount's common stock and the price of the 75 December call option between September and early December 1993. Notice that the two prices move pretty much in tandem.

Call options are generally bought by investors who expect the price of a particular stock, like Paramount, to rise over a short period of time. On the other hand, put options are generally bought by investors who believe that the price of the underlying stock will fall over a short period of time.

Options create some tricky situations. The holder of the option has the right to buy or sell stock at a set price for a set period of time. The holder of the option is said to have a **long position.** If the option is **exercised,** that is, if the holder actually buys or sells the stock, from whom does he or she

---

[1]Almost all options are protected from stock splits and stock dividends. If a stock splits, say, 2 for 1, the exercise price of the options will automatically be halved.

Figure 18.1

Paramount's Stock Price and Call Price: September 20, 1993 to December 10, 1993

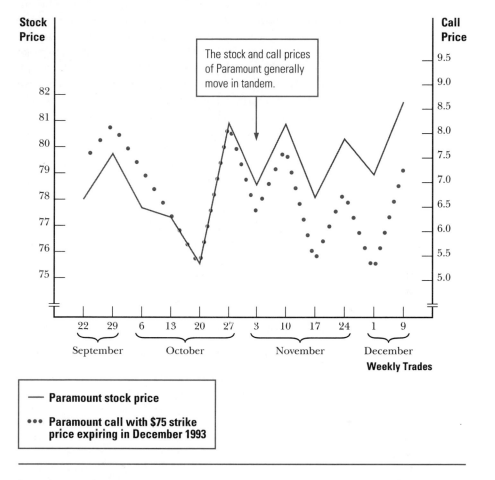

> The stock and call prices of Paramount generally move in tandem.

— **Paramount stock price**

••• **Paramount call with $75 strike price expiring in December 1993**

buy the stock or to whom does he or she sell it? The answer is the person who sold the option the holder bought. In other words, someone who sells a call option agrees to sell stock at a fixed price for a fixed period of time, to someone else at the buyer's discretion. Likewise, someone who sells a put option agrees to buy stock at a fixed price for a fixed period of time from someone else, again at that buyer's discretion. Selling an option is often referred to as **writing an option;** the option writer is said to have a **short position.** It is important to remember that every long position in options *must* have a short position.

Why would anyone write an option and accept an uncertain obligation? The writer does this in exchange for the **premium.** The premium on a call option is defined as the call price minus the stock price plus the exercise price. For the 75 December Paramount call, the premium equals:

$$\$7.500 - \$80.375 + \$75.000 = \$2.125 \text{ or } 2\tfrac{1}{8}$$

The premium on a put option is defined as the put price minus the exercise price plus the stock price. For the 75 December Paramount put, the premium equals:

$$\$3.500 - \$75.000 + \$80.375 = \$8.875 \text{ or } 8\tfrac{7}{8}$$

Notice that if an option is out-of-the-money, its premium will exceed its price.

Options traders often use the terms **intrinsic value** and **time value** when referring to options. The intrinsic value of a call option equals either 0, if the option is out-of-the-money, or the difference between the stock price and exercise price, if the option is in-the-money. The intrinsic value of a put option equals either 0, if the option is out-of-the-money, or the difference between the exercise price and stock price, if the option is in-the-money. The time value of an option is defined as the difference between the price of the option and its intrinsic value. The use of the term *time value* is unfortunate since the difference between an option's price and intrinsic value, like the size of the option's premium, is a function of more than the time until expiration. This issue will be explored in more depth later in the chapter when we discuss option pricing models.

The general reason an investor writes an option is to capture the premium. In other words, someone might write the above call option expecting that Paramount's stock would not rise very much between early November and mid-December. Similarly, someone might write the put option, betting that Paramount's stock wouldn't fall too far between early November and mid-December. In the ideal situation for an option writer, the option expires **unexercised.** The buyer of the Paramount call option would allow it to expire unexercised if Paramount were trading below $75 per share on December 17. The buyer of the Paramount put option would allow it to expire unexercised if the stock were trading above $75 per share on December 17.

The table below summarizes the rights and obligations of the long and short positions for the Paramount call and put option contracts:

Type of Option	Long Position (Buyer)	Short Position (Writer)
75 December call	Has the right, but no obligation to buy 100 shares of Paramount stock at $75 per share until December 17, 1993	Is obligated to sell 100 shares of Paramount stock at $75 per share until December 17, 1993 if option is exercised
75 December put	Has the right, but no obligation, to sell 100 shares of Paramount stock at $75 per share until December 17, 1993	Is obligated to buy 100 shares of Paramount stock at $75 per share until December 17, 1993 if option is exercised

Now that we've defined option contracts and explained the rights and obligations of both parties, let's discuss how option contracts are traded.

Option Trading

An investor can trade options much like stocks and bonds, by giving a market order or a limit order for a specific option to a broker. The broker then transmits the order to the exchange where the option is traded and the order is executed. Note, however, that most brokerage firms have restrictions on option trading by clients. Most, for example, handle option trades only for clients who have large holdings of cash, or other liquid assets, in their accounts.

Prior to 1973, options were traded only on the over the counter (OTC) markets. The OTC markets allowed investors to determine the terms of each contract such as the strike price, expiration date, and number of shares. Transaction costs for these individualized contracts were quite high and trades were infrequent after the initial transaction.

In 1973, the Chicago Board Options Exchange (CBOE) was formed as the first organized option exchange. Since then most options trading has occurred on organized exchanges. By 1989 options were traded on five U.S. exchanges, including the CBOE, American Stock Exchange (AM), Philadelphia Stock Exchange (PB), Pacific Stock Exchange (PC), and New York Stock Exchange (NY).

Options are also actively traded on a number of foreign stock exchanges. Three of the largest option markets outside the United States are located in London, Tokyo, and Toronto.

The organized exchanges provide significant advantages over OTC option trading. Five important ones are listed below:

1. *Standardized Contracts.*   The strike price on a modern option is standardized, as is the expiration date (the close of business on the third Friday of the stated month). Strike prices usually are stated in $5 increments, though larger increments are likely for stocks priced above $100 and increments as low as $2.50 are possible for stocks priced below $30 per share. New call option contracts with new strike prices are written as a stock's price exceeds currently available strike prices.

2. *Increased Liquidity.*   Trading on organized exchanges allows buyers and sellers to exchange option contracts at any time.

3. *More Comprehensive Disclosure and Surveillance Rules.*   Organized exchanges impose relatively strict trading, disclosure, and monitoring procedures. They also keep a market flowing smoothly.

4. *Guaranteed Clearing of Contracts.*   The Option Clearing Corporation (OCC), the clearinghouse for options trading, is jointly owned by the exchanges where options are traded. The OCC basically acts as a guarantor of each options trade to assure that all parties meet their contractual obligations. Because option traders need not be concerned with the creditworthiness of other participants, the OCC helps create liquidity in the options market.

The OCC acts as an agent between the buyer and the seller (or writer) of an option. Once the buyer and seller agree on a price (through orders executed by their brokers), the OCC writes and sells to the option buyer while it buys the contract from the seller. Since all options investors contract with the OCC, it guarantees that all contracts are fulfilled.

Also, the OCC is responsible to fulfill any exercised options contract. If a call option is exercised, the OCC arranges for a member firm to randomly select a client who has written (or sold) a call to deliver 100 shares of the specified common stock at the strike price. If a put option is exercised, the OCC arranges for a member firm to randomly select a client who has written a put to purchase 100 shares of the specified common stock at the strike price.

5. *Lower Transaction Costs.*   Brokerage fees for options traded on organized exchanges are substantially less than fees required for OTC trading. The lower costs reflect increased trading activity (which simplifies making a market) and the OCC relieves brokers of many functions, as discussed above.

Option Price Quotations. Figure 18.2 provides a listing of option price quotes from *The Wall Street Journal* for November 8, 1993. Let's examine Paramount Communications' call and put options. Paramount (ParaCm) has options expiring in November and December 1993, and March 1994. At each expiration date, individual option contracts have several strike prices ranging from $55 to $90, increasing in $5 increments. The strike price of $55 may seem strange. Who was crazy enough to write a call, and accept the obligation to deliver at $55 for a stock with a market price above $80? Apparently the poor soul wrote the option before anyone bid $80 for Paramount! (Why is this option, which is deeply in the money, not exercised? Another good question, which we'll address later.)

In *Wall Street Journal* quotes, the first column provides the company name with its closing stock price for that day under it. The second column lists

Figure 18.2

Option Price Quotes from *The Wall Street Journal*

LISTED OPTIONS QUOTATIONS

Option/Strike	Exp.	Call Vol.	Call Last	Put Vol.	Put Last	Option/Strike	Exp.	Call Vol.	Call Last	Put Vol.	Put Last	Option/Strike	Exp.	Call Vol.	Call Last	Put Vol.	Put Last
PacTel 55	Nov	179	1	25	1 3/8	Pegsus 20	Nov	119	1 1/2	43	1/4	55 1/2 60	Jun	69	2 1/2	...	...
54 7/8 55	Jan	51	2 1/2	...	...	21 1/2 20	Feb	55	2 3/4	10	1 1/4	Phelps 45	Dec	35	1 7/16	...	...
54 7/8 60	Jan	31	3/4	...	...	21 1/2 22 1/2	Dec	30	1 1/4	...	...	PhilEl 25	Dec	40	3 1/8	...	...
54 7/8 60	Apr	44	1	...	...	21 1/2 25	Nov	173	1/16	...	...	PhilPt 35	May	140	1 3/4	...	...
PainWb 25	Nov	30	1 5/8	40	3/8	PennCn 35	Dec	68	7/16	...	...	PhysCp 17 1/2	Nov	60	3 5/8	...	...
26 5/8 25	Jan	10	2	73	15/16	Penney 50	Nov	62	1	55	13/16	21 20	Nov	43	1 1/8	...	...
26 5/8 30	Nov	40	1/16	1	4 3/8	Pennz 60	Nov	35	1/4	10	3 1/8	PicTel 15	Nov	...	...	60	1/8
26 5/8 30	Dec	56	5/16	...	...	Pepsi 35	Jan	51	3 3/4	10	5/8	18 1/4 15	Dec	...	...	100	9/16
26 5/8 30	Jan	...	...	100	4 1/2	38 35	Apr	20	4 1/2	40	1	Placer 20	Mar	70	5 1/4	...	...
Panhdl 20	Dec	60	2 3/8	...	...	38 40	Nov	95	3/16	17	2	24 1/4 22 1/2	Nov	67	2	40	3/8
ParaCm 55	Nov	39	25 3/8	26	3/8	38 40	Dec	293	7/16	5	2 1/2	24 1/4 22 1/2	Dec	253	2 3/8	10	13/16
80 3/8 60	Nov	...	...	190	1/8	38 40	Jan	116	13/16	60	2 3/4	24 1/4 22 1/2	Mar	114	3 1/4	...	...
80 3/8 60	Dec	4	20	472	3/4	38 40	Apr	487	1 5/8	1	3 1/2	24 1/4 25	Nov	418	7/16	95	15/16
80 3/8 65	Nov	...	...	210	1/4	38 45	Apr	550	3/8	10	6 7/8	24 1/4 25	Dec	146	1 1/16	10	2 1/8
80 3/8 65	Dec	420	16 1/2	3404	1 1/4	Perigo 30	Nov	15	1 1/4	31	1/2	24 1/4 25	Mar	145	2	7	3
80 3/8 65	Mar	...	...	70	2 1/2	Pet 17 1/2	Mar	40	1 1/16	...	...	24 1/4 30	Dec	38	1/4	500	5 3/8
80 3/8 70	Nov	294	10 1/2	1878	7/16	Pfizer 60	Nov	30	3 5/8	441	5/16	24 1/4 30	Mar	76	1	...	...
80 3/8 70	Dec	980	11 1/2	5350	2	63 3/8 60	Dec	110	4	110	1 1/8	24 1/4 30	Nov	38	9/16	...	...
80 3/8 70	Mar	...	...	64	4 1/4	63 3/8 65	Nov	195	13/16	...	...	PlatTc 10	Nov	...	...	100	2
80 3/8 75	Nov	6454	6 1/4	1856	1	63 3/8 65	Dec	1421	11/16	12	3 3/4	Players 20	Apr	30	7/16	26	2 1/8
80 3/8 75	Dec	7133	7 1/2	10275	3 1/2	63 3/8 65	Mar	253	3 1/2	10	5	23 3/4 25	Nov	62	1/4	...	...
80 3/8 75	Mar	2	8 7/8	105	6 1/4	Ph Mor 45	Nov	70	8 3/8	15	1/16	PogoPd 17 1/2	Nov	50	5/8	50	1 3/4
80 3/8 80	Nov	8918	2 1/2	795	2 1/8	55 1/2 45	Dec	35	10 1/4	137	1/8	Polar 35	Nov	41	1/2	...	...
80 3/8 80	Dec	2245	4	2334	6 1/2	55 1/2 45	Mar	18	10 3/4	32	5/8	PrceCo 17 1/2	Nov	100	1 1/4	30	11/16
80 3/8 80	Mar	30	5 1/2	150	10 1/4	55 1/2 50	Nov	300	5 3/8	141	1/8	17 7/8 17 1/2	Jan	138	3/8	...	...
80 3/8 85	Nov	4103	11/16	20	5 3/4	55 1/2 50	Dec	986	5 7/8	5221	3/8	17 7/8 20	Jan	...	...	110	6 7/8
80 3/8 85	Dec	2012	1 7/8	...	...	55 1/2 50	Mar	6619	7	280	15/16	Premrk 80	Dec	77	4 3/8	103	1/4
80 3/8 90	Nov	115	1/4	9	9 3/8	55 1/2 55	Nov	6555	1 3/4	1080	1 1/8	PresRv 30	Nov	921	11/16	517	19/16
80 3/8 90	Dec	1461	3/4	108	14 3/4	55 1/2 55	Dec	2845	2 1/2	36	2 1/8	35 5/8 35	Dec	12	2 7/8	80	3 1/8
ParmTc 35	Nov	30	3 3/8	23	3/8	55 1/2 55	Mar	819	3 7/8	34	3 7/8	35 5/8 35	Feb	...	...	578	3 7/8
38 40	Nov	36	7/8	13	2 5/16	55 1/2 60	Nov	52	1/4	...	...	35 5/8 40	Nov	53	1/4	59	5
38 45	Dec	50	1/4	...	...	55 1/2 60	Dec	730	3/4	36	5 7/8	35 5/8 40	Dec	50	1 1/8	15	6
38 50	May	40	2 1/8	...	...	55 1/2 60	Mar	681	2	...	...	35 5/8 45	Nov	40	1/8	53	9 3/4
												Primca 40	Dec	435	2	100	1 3/8

Friday, November 5, 1993

Composite volume and close for actively traded equity and LEAPS, or long-term options, with results for the corresponding put or call contract. Volume figures are unofficial. Open interest is total outstanding for all exchanges and reflects previous trading day. Close when possible is shown for the underlying stock on primary market. **CB**-Chicago Board Options Exchange. **AM**-American Stock Exchange. **PB**-Philadelphia Stock Exchange. **PC**-Pacific Stock Exchange. **NY**-New York Stock Exchange. **XC**-Composite. **p**-Put.

MOST ACTIVE CONTRACTS

Option/Strike	Vol	Exch	Last	Net Chg	a-Close	Open Int	Option/Strike	Vol	Exch	Last	Net Chg	a-Close	Open Int
ParaCm Dec 75	p 10,275	CB	3 1/2	+ 3/4	80 3/8	7,401	Compaq Nov 65	p 2,877	XC	9/16	− 1	67 3/8	5,485
TelMex Dec 60	8,931	XC	13/16	− 5/16	51 7/8	14,704	Ph Mor Dec 55	2,845	AM	2 1/2	+ 1 11/16	55 1/2	16,719
ParaCm Nov 80	8,918	CB	2 1/2	+ 7/8	80 3/8	34,374	Disney Dec 40	p 2,803	XC	1 1/4	+ 3/8	41 5/8	1,800
ParaCm Dec 75	7,133	CB	7 1/2	+ 1 1/8	80 3/8	11,682	Merck Nov 30	2,744	CB	2 1/4	− 1/8	32 1/4	11,729
Ph Mor Mar 50	6,619	AM	7	+ 2 1/4	55 1/2	13,869	MedcoC Nov 35	p 2,616	PC	13/16	− 5/8	37	6,592
Ph Mor Nov 55	6,555	AM	1 3/4	+ 17/16	55 1/2	13,928	Intel Apr 50	2,534	AM	1 7/8	...	60 3/4	
ParaCm Nov 75	6,454	CB	6 1/4	+ 1 1/4	80 3/8	46,004	Motrla Nov 105	2,401	AM	5/8	...	98 7/8	6,407
I B M Nov 50	6,068	CB	7/8	...	49 3/4	18,576	Tex In Nov 65	2,369	CB	5/8	+ 1/8	58 1/4	4,359
TelMex Dec 50	6,027	XC	2 3/4	+ 3/4	51 7/8	22,315	AT&T Jan 60	2,357	CB	7/8	...	56	16,551
ParaCm Dec 70	p 5,350	CB	2	+ 3/8	80 3/8	7,999	ParaCm Dec 80	p 2,334	CB	6 1/2	+ 1 1/4	80 3/8	3,975
TelMex Dec 55	5,225	XC	2 5/16	− 3/8	51 7/8	16,758	StoTch Dec 30	2,313	CB	13/16	+ 5/16	26 5/8	5,262
Ph Mor Dec 50	p 5,221	AM	3/8	− 1/2	55 1/2	11,385	Citicp Jan 35	2,310	CB	2 7/8	+ 7/8	36 1/2	15,075
TelMex Nov 55	4,389	XC	7/8	− 7/16	51 7/8	21,812	ParaCm Dec 80	2,245	CB	4	+ 1 11/16	80 3/8	18,474
Compaq Nov 65	4,107	XC	3	+ 1 1/8	67 3/8	4,581	Intel Nov 55	2,150	AM	1/2	+ 1/8	60 3/4	11,743
ParaCm Nov 85	4,103	CB	11/16	+ 3/16	80 3/8	21,960	D S C Nov 65	2,114	AM	1 3/8	+ 7/16	61 1/8	3,283
Cisco Nov 55	3,983	XC	4 1/4	+ 1 3/4	53 1/2	12,603	Chryslr Nov 55	2,095	CB	1	...	54 1/4	3,360
ParaCm Dec 65	p 3,404	CB	1 1/4	+ 1/4	80 3/8	6,900	Merck Jan 40	2,021	CB	3/16	− 1/16	32 1/4	8,530
TelMex Nov 50	p 3,007	XC	1 3/8	+ 1/2	51 7/8	13,623	ParaCm Dec 85	2,012	CB	1 7/8	+ 5/8	80 3/8	11,305
Intel Nov 60	2,961	AM	2 1/4	+ 3/4	60 3/4	4,942	Salomn Nov 45	p 2,005	PB	2 7/16	− 13/16	42 5/8	812
I B M Nov 50	p 2,918	CB	1	− 1/16	49 3/4	6,314	Salomn Dec 45	p 2,000	PB	3 3/8	+ 1/8	42 5/8	10

Source: *The Wall Street Journal*, November 8, 1993, p. C13.

options' strike prices and the third column lists expiration months. (Remember, virtually all options expire on the third Friday of the month.) The next two columns list the volume of call options traded and the last transacted price per share. (Multiply by 100 to get the dollar price of the option contract.) The last two columns list the volume of put options traded and the last transacted price for the put. A dotted line means that no such option contract exists or none was traded.

As you look through option price quotations in *The Wall Street Journal*, or other financial publications, two questions may come to mind. First, why do some stocks underlie more options with different strike prices and expiration dates than others? Second, why do some option prices seem out of line, either too high or too low? The answer to the first question is rather simple. The exchange, such as the CBOE, determines the number of option contracts available. Its decision is based on investor interest and the volatility of the stock. In general, more investor interest in a stock, and a more volatile price, lead the exchange to create more options.

To answer the question about the relationship of the option price to the underlying stock price, remember that each price printed reflects the price of the last transaction; it is not a current bid or ask price. The fact that a call option last traded for $5\frac{1}{2}$, doesn't mean that anyone could buy or sell for $5\frac{1}{2}$ now, if the stock price has changed substantially. Also, keep in mind that many options listed are not actively traded. (Look at the volume figures.)

Options on Other Securities

During the 1980s, many exchanges began to offer options on stock indexes such as the Standard & Poor's 100 and Value Line Index. Options on industry indexes, foreign currencies, and commodity and financial futures also became available. We will discuss the index options and foreign currency options here, leaving options on financial futures for Chapter 19.

Index Options. An **index option** is a call or put based on a stock market index such as the S&P 100, S&P 500, Value Line Index, or Major Market Index. The S&P 100 index is a value-weighted average of the 100 largest stocks in the S&P 500. The Major Market Index is an average, weighted by price, of 20 large-firm stocks, most of which are also included in the Dow Jones Industrial Average sample. The Value Line Index is an arithmetic (equally weighted) average of approximately 1,700 stocks. Examples of index option price quotations appear in Figure 18.3.

Unlike stock options, exercise of an index option does not require the writer to deliver the securities that comprise the index; instead, a cash settlement takes place. The writer pays, in cash, the difference between the strike price of the option and the value of the index at the time of exercise, multiplied by a fixed number. The multiplier for S&P 100 options is 100. For example, suppose someone were to write a call option on the S&P 100 index with a December 1993 expiration and a strike price of 410. Now, assume that the buyer exercised the option when the index equaled 423. The writer would owe the buyer of the option $1,300, composed of 423 (the index value when the option was exercised) minus 410 (the option's exercise price) multiplied by 100.

More recently, foreign stock index options have been introduced into U.S. options markets. Options are available on such foreign stock indexes as the Financial Times 100 and the Japan Index (a composite index of most major Japanese stocks).

Foreign Currency Options. A currency option gives the holder the right to buy or sell a specified quantity of foreign currency for a specified amount of U.S. dollars. Contracts are quoted in cents or fractions of a cent per unit of foreign currency. Foreign currency options are traded on the Philadelphia Stock Exchange and the Chicago Board Options Exchange.

Option Value at Expiration

In this section, we discuss how to find the values of call and put options at expiration. This allows the investor to determine the profit or loss, at expiration, from the four basic option trades (buying a call option, writing a call

Figure 18.3

Price Quotes for Index Options

INDEX OPTIONS TRADING

Friday, November 5, 1993

Volume, last, net change and open interest for all contracts. Volume figures are unofficial. Open interest reflects previous trading day. p-Put c–Call

CHICAGO

FINTIMES-SE100(FSX)

Strike		Vol.	Last	Net Chg.	Open Int.
Dec	290p	3	1 13/16	+ 9/16	425
Jan	295p	5	3 3/4	+ 1 3/8	5
Nov	305c	5	5 1/8	− 3 1/2	...
Nov	305p	10	2 3/8	+ 3/16	20
Nov	310c	100	2 1/4	− 2 7/8	21
Nov	310p	50	4 5/8	+ 3	60
Nov	315p	10	8	+ 4 5/8	10
Dec	315p	3	9 3/4	+ 5 1/4	3

Call vol.......... 105 Open Int............ 490
Put vol............. 86 Open Int............ 767

RUSSELL 2000(RUT)

Strike		Vol.	Last	Net Chg.	Open Int.
Nov	65p	200	16 5/8	+ 2 7/8	601
Dec	65c	15	3/8	− 9/16	417
Dec	65p	2	15 5/8	...	20
Nov	225p	10	3/16	...	660
Dec	235c	75	15 1/4	− 9 1/2	500
Dec	235p	30	1	+ 3/8	755
Nov	240c	15	10 3/8	...	...
Nov	240p	20	1	+ 7/16	1,352
Dec	240c	25	12 1/8	− 4 3/4	1,657
Dec	240p	60	1 1/2	+ 3/4	3,060
Nov	245c	315	7 7/8	− 1 5/8	258
Nov	245p	115	1 1/16	− 3/16	403
Jan	250p	2,500	5 7/8	+ 2 1/8	3
Nov	250c	670	4 3/8	+ 1	407
Nov	250p	273	2 3/16	− 3/8	498
Dec	250c	1	4 1/8	− 4 3/8	310
Dec	250p	186	4 1/2	+ 1/8	1,481
Jan	255c	2	4 3/8	− 5 5/8	780
Jan	255p	5	9 1/4	+ 4	1
Nov	255c	391	1 1/16	− 5/16	795
Nov	255p	557	5	...	2,071
Dec	255c	10	3 3/8	− 3 3/8	606
Dec	255p	765	8 1/4	+ 1 3/4	396
Nov	260c	202	1/4	...	612
Nov	260p	763	8 3/4	− 3/8	1,179
Dec	260c	5	1 7/16	− 15/16	3,257
Dec	260p	7	10 1/4	+ 3/4	1,982

Call vol......... 1,821 Open Int......... 15,351
Put vol......... 5,547 Open Int......... 21,629

S & P 100 INDEX(OEX)

Strike		Vol.	Last	Net Chg.	Open Int.
Jan	380p	1,214	1 11/16	+ 5/16	2,242
Feb	380p	388	2 1/2	+ 1/8	1,971
Nov	380p	3,961	1/4	...	16,843
Dec	380p	1,234	7/8	...	6,943
Jan	385c	2	40 1/2	− 5 1/8	1
Jan	385p	225	1 15/16	+ 1/8	1,357
Nov	385p	1,269	1/4	− 1/16	7,206
Dec	385p	583	1 1/16	− 1/16	3,505
Jan	390p	289	2 9/16	+ 3/8	1,376
Feb	390c	5	33	...	...
Feb	390p	33	3 1/2	− 1/8	778
Nov	390p	2,115	3/8	− 1/16	16,075
Dec	390p	460	1 3/8	...	6,119
Jan	395p	233	3	+ 7/16	1,442
Nov	395p	5,565	1/2	− 1/16	25,219
Dec	395p	1,233	1 11/16	...	7,946
Jan	400c	1	25 3/4	− 3 1/2	7
Jan	400p	1,417	3 3/4	+ 3/8	4,556
Feb	400p	126	5 1/2	+ 5/8	1,354
Nov	400c	20	21 1/4	− 1 3/4	115
Nov	400p	13,094	3/4	...	40,036
Dec	400p	3,895	2 3/16	− 1/8	18,248
Jan	405p	96	4 3/8	− 1/8	787
Nov	405c	250	18 1/2	− 1/2	533
Nov	405p	18,614	1 1/16	+ 1/16	35,220
Dec	405c	4	20 1/4	− 6 7/8	33
Dec	405p	2,123	2 7/8	− 1/8	11,190
Jan	410c	10	17 1/2	− 1 3/4	74
Jan	410p	1,719	5 1/2	− 1/2	5,513
Feb	410c	10	19 1/2	− 1 5/8	73
Feb	410p	27	8 1/4	+ 7/8	3,587
Nov	410c	425	13 3/4	− 1/4	3,015
Nov	410p	24,520	1 7/16	− 1/16	46,905
Dec	410c	50	15	− 1 1/2	1,377
Dec	410p	3,333	3 3/4	− 1/8	23,995
Jan	415p	1,257	7	− 1/8	3,122
Nov	415c	7,785	9 5/8	+ 5/8	10,604
Nov	415p	32,156	2 3/8	+ 1/16	45,002
Dec	415c	2,130	11 7/8	− 4 1/8	845
Dec	415p	7,093	4 7/8	− 1/4	11,673
Jan	420c	3,397	11 1/2	+ 1/4	6,727
Jan	420p	1,649	8 3/4	− 1/4	7,888
Feb	420c	10	12 3/4	− 1 1/4	262
Feb	420p	154	10	+ 1/4	4,693
Nov	420c	38,481	5 7/8	+ 1/4	30,232
Nov	420p	62,759	3 3/8	− 1/4	59,139
Dec	420c	2,767	8 7/8	+ 1/2	7,164
Dec	420p	12,325	6 3/8	− 1/4	27,905
Jan	425c	1,190	8 1/4	− 1/2	1,780
Jan	425p	1,079	11 1/2	+ 1/4	2,170
Nov	425c	47,296	2 7/8	...	52,058
Nov	425p	40,129	5 3/8	− 1/2	52,338
Dec	425c	5,231	5 7/8	+ 1/2	11,452
Dec	425p	7,927	8 1/4	− 5/8	17,473
Jan	430c	146	6	+ 1/8	6,468
Jan	430p	71	14	...	3,222
Feb	430c	226	6 3/4	− 3/4	1,135
Feb	430p	3	17 1/4	+ 2 1/4	275
Nov	430c	36,600	1	...	51,589
Nov	430p	13,576	8 3/4	− 5/8	25,921
Dec	430c	4,009	3 5/8	+ 1/4	16,044
Dec	430p	1,518	11	− 1	11,685
Jan	435c	181	4	+ 1/4	4,673
Jan	435p	34	16 1/4	− 3/4	1,716
Nov	435c	18,946	3/8	+ 1/16	54,366
Nov	435p	452	13 1/8	− 7/8	2,547
Dec	435c	7,066	1 15/16	+ 3/16	13,950
Dec	435p	75	14 5/8	− 3/8	665
Jan	440c	493	2 9/16	+ 1/16	5,804
Feb	440c	134	3 5/8	− 1/8	3,846
Nov	440c	4,191	1/8	+ 1/16	54,378
Nov	440p	33	18	− 1	202
Dec	440c	3,129	15/16	...	18,871
Dec	440p	37	19 1/4	...	366
Jan	445c	378	1 3/8	− 1/16	2,718
Jan	445p	1	24 3/8	+ 4 7/8	3
Nov	445c	1,864	1/16	...	36,634
Nov	445p	7	24	+ 3 1/2	3
Dec	445c	4,028	7/16	+ 1/16	23,404
Dec	445p	5	22 5/8	− 1 3/4	12
Jan	450c	822	3/4	...	3,841
Jan	450p	2	28 1/2	+ 2 1/4	6
Feb	450c	295	1 3/8	− 1/8	3,825
Feb	450p	2	29 1/4	+ 4 3/4	29
Nov	450p	1	28 1/4	+ 4 1/2	1
Dec	450c	283	1/8	− 1/16	9,734
Jan	455c	100	3/8	− 1/8	516
Dec	455c	400	1/8	+ 1/16	2,679

Call vol..... 192,355 Open Int....... 455,263
Put vol...... 270,111 Open Int....... 568,780

S & P 500 INDEX-AM(SPX)

Strike		Vol.	Last	Net Chg.	Open Int.
Dec	395p	100	5/16	− 1/16	2,202
Jan	400p	21	1 3/8	+ 9/16	144
Nov	400c	1	57	− 11 3/8	601
Nov	400p	40	1/8	+ 1/16	5,065
Dec	400p	174	7/16	...	36,546
Dec	410p	342	11/16	+ 3/16	7,167
Dec	415p	34	1	− 1/16	7,365
Nov	420p	1,315	5/16	...	10,645
Dec	420c	5	40 1/8	− 9 5/8	23
Dec	420p	541	1 1/8	− 1/8	9,140
Nov	425p	291	3/8	− 1/16	2,456
Dec	425c	2	32 1/4	− 9	10,286
Dec	425p	72	1 5/8	+ 3/8	40,351
Jan	430p	29	3 1/2	+ 1/4	377
Nov	430c	50	28	− 9 1/4	4,435
Nov	430p	260	1/2	− 1/16	15,491
Dec	430c	3	27 1/4	− 9 1/2	25

INSTITUTIONAL-AM(XII)

Strike		Vol.	Last	Net Chg.	Open Int.
Nov	425p	7	7/16	+ 1/8	50
Nov	430p	5	9/16	+ 1/4	...
Nov	435p	30	1	+ 1/2	220
Nov	440p	65	1	+ 1/4	100
Nov	445p	5	1 3/4	+ 1/4	45
Jan	450c	50	15 5/8	...	...
Nov	450c	50	10 1/4	− 2 7/8	25
Nov	450p	69	1 7/8	+ 5/8	35
Jan	455c	75	11 7/8	− 7/8	150
Nov	455p	45	3 3/8	− 5/8	390
Jan	460c	50	9 3/4	− 1 1/4	150
Jan	460p	80	11 1/2	+ 3 5/8	100
Nov	460c	33	3 7/8	+ 5/8	541
Nov	460p	81	4 3/4	− 1	25
Jan	465c	2	7 1/8	− 1	145
Nov	465c	45	1 1/2	+ 1/4	413
Nov	470p	1	12 1/4	− 3/4	103
Nov	475p	25	17 1/8	+ 6 7/8	25

Call vol.......... 305 Open Int......... 27,083
Put vol.......... 438 Open Int......... 19,016

INSTITUTIONAL - P.M. (PXP)

Call vol.............. 7 Open Int......... 27,716
Put vol.......... 109 Open Int......... 28,581

JAPAN INDEX(JPN)

Strike		Vol.	Last	Net Chg.	Open Int.
Dec	150p	50	1/4	+ 1/8	1,883
Jan	175p	7	2 1/4	...	...
Dec	175p	72	1 1/2	+ 7/16	2,256
Jan	180p	8	3 7/8	+ 1 3/8	23
Nov	180p	340	7/8	...	...
Dec	180p	804	2 7/16	+ 11/16	1,079
Jan	185p	8	5	...	...
Nov	185c	10	5 3/8	...	...
Nov	185p	418	1 3/4	...	...
Dec	185p	284	3 3/8	+ 3/4	1,009
Jan	190c	5	6 3/4	− 6 1/4	2
Jan	190p	37	7 1/2	+ 2 1/8	16
Nov	190c	36	3 1/4	− 3/4	171
Nov	190p	563	3 3/8	+ 3/4	1,493
Dec	190c	104	5 1/2	− 1	258
Dec	190p	201	5 1/2	+ 1 1/4	5,813
Jan	195c	26	4 5/8	− 3/8	...
Jan	195p	2	9 7/8	+ 4 5/8	900
Nov	195c	508	1 1/8	− 11/16	203
Nov	195p	464	6 1/8	+ 1 1/8	808
Dec	195c	39	3 3/8	− 1/2	392
Dec	195p	68	7 7/8	+ 1 3/8	1,012
Jan	200c	10	3 3/8	...	119
Jan	200p	20	12 1/4	+ 2	578
Nov	200c	18	1/2	...	933
Nov	200p	34	10 5/8	+ 1 7/8	488
Dec	200c	12	1 3/4	− 7/16	2,320
Dec	200p	9	11 1/8	+ 1 7/8	1,304
Nov	205c	24	1/8	− 1/8	1,030
Nov	205p	37	15 7/8	+ 2 5/8	283
Dec	205p	2	16 1/2	+ 3 1/8	1,319
Jan	210c	17	1 3/8	+ 3/16	167
Nov	210c	19	1/16	− 1/16	1,696
Dec	210c	52	1/2	− 1/8	920
Jan	215c	20	1/2	− 3/16	162
Dec	215c	2	1/4	...	2,605
Jan	220c	3	1/2	− 1/4	46
Dec	220c	20	1/8	− 1/16	1,305
Dec	220p	13	29 1/4	+ 2	14

Call vol........ 1,025 Open Int......... 31,619
Put vol......... 4,582 Open Int......... 43,449

MAJOR MARKET(XMI)

Strike		Vol.	Last	Net Chg.	Open Int.
Dec	300p	10	1/4	+ 3/16	5,947
Dec	310p	3	3/16	+ 1/8	1,026
Nov	320p	395	3/16	+ 1/8	327
Jan	325p	1	15/16	...	64
Nov	325c	1,000	44	− 1	4,000
Nov	325p	25	1/16	...	813
Dec	325p	30	9/16	− 1/8	3,570
Dec	330p	80	5/8	+ 3/8	181
Nov	335p	15	1/8	...	1,035
Dec	335p	17	1 1/8	+ 1/2	58
Jan	340p	13	2 1/8	...	35
Nov	340p	10	1/4	+ 1/16	970
Dec	340p	66	1 3/16	+ 5/8	115
Nov	345p	2	7/16	+ 1/8	837
Dec	345p	60	1 7/8	+ 7/16	352
Nov	350p	222	3/4	+ 1/16	1,300
Dec	350p	450	2 3/16	+ 3/16	2,610
Nov	355p	391	1	...	1,328
Dec	355p	75	2 7/8	+ 11/16	114
Jan	360p	16	5 5/8	+ 5/8	61
Nov	360c	125	9 7/8	− 1 1/8	533
Nov	360p	863	1 1/4	− 1/2	1,470
Dec	360c	6	11	− 4	131
Dec	360p	35	4	− 1/4	224
Jan	365p	38	7	+ 1/8	85
Nov	365c	234	7 5/8	+ 1 3/4	837
Nov	365p	890	2 1/16	− 13/16	2,695
Dec	365c	46	7 5/8	− 3/4	65
Dec	365p	22	5 1/4	...	566
Jan	370p	10	9 1/8	+ 1 1/8	138
Nov	370c	986	3 3/4	+ 1 1/8	1,403
Nov	370p	1,118	3 1/2	− 1 1/8	1,722
Dec	370c	159	6	+ 1/4	194
Dec	370p	80	7	− 1/4	373
Nov	375c	821	1 3/8	+ 5/16	2,218
Nov	375p	31	7 1/8	− 1 1/8	670
Dec	375c	101	3 3/8	+ 1/4	1,789
Dec	375p	31	9 3/8	+ 3/8	220
Nov	380c	430	3/8	+ 1/8	1,088
Nov	380p	45	11 1/2	+ 1/4	114
Dec	380c	27	1 15/16	+ 3/8	4,794
Dec	380p	12	14 1/2	+ 1 1/2	95
Nov	385p	4	16 5/8	+ 5 1/4	11
Dec	385c	2	13/16	− 5/16	254

Call vol........ 3,937 Open Int........ 27,408
Put vol......... 5,239 Open Int........ 37,910

RANGES FOR UNDERLYING INDEXES

Friday, November 5, 1993

	High	Low	Close	Net Chg.	From Dec. 31	% Chg.
S&P 100 (OEX)	423.11	418.64	422.37	+ 1.26	+ 25.73	+ 6.5
S&P 500-A.M.(SPX)	459.63	454.36	459.57	+ 2.09	+ 23.86	+ 5.5
S&P 500-P.M.(NSX)	459.63	454.36	459.57	+ 2.09	+ 23.86	+ 5.5
FT-SE 100 (FSX)	310.17	308.33	308.56	− 6.34	+ 23.91	+ 8.4
Russell 2000 (RUT)	253.11	249.96	253.11	.00	+ 32.11	+ 14.5
Lps S&P 100 (OEX)	42.31	41.86	42.24	+ 0.13	+ 2.58	+ 6.5
Lps S&P 500 (SPX)	45.96	45.44	45.96	+ 0.21	+ 2.39	+ 5.5
S&P Midcap (MID)	171.37	168.79	171.37	+ 0.78	+ 10.82	+ 6.7
Major Mkt (XMI)	370.71	366.19	370.54	+ 2.82	+ 23.74	+ 6.8
Leaps MMkt (XLT)	37.07	36.62	37.05	+ 0.28	+ 2.37	+ 6.8
Institut'l-A.M.(XII)	459.88	454.72	459.82	+ 2.39	+ 16.12	+ 3.6
Institut'l-P.M.(PXP)	459.88	454.72	459.82	+ 2.39	+ 16.12	+ 3.6
Eurotop 100 (EUR)	113.72	113.22	113.38	− 2.73	+ 25.82	+ 29.5
Japan (JPN)			189.26	− 3.58	+ 18.03	+ 10.5
MS Cyclical (CYC)	286.06	282.28	285.63	− 0.31	+ 39.32	+ 16.0
MS Consumr (CMR)	191.72	189.49	191.62	+ 1.32	− 16.39	− 7.9
Pharma (DRG)	171.01	169.06	170.59	− 0.42	− 27.25	− 13.8
Biotech (BTK)	125.76	121.01	125.34	− 0.06	− 45.30	− 26.5
NYSE (NYA)	279.76	251.65	254.20	+ 0.73	+ 13.99	+ 5.8
Wilshire S-C (WSX)	321.38	316.26	321.36	+ 1.75	+ 31.05	+ 10.7
Gold/Silver (XAU)	128.50	123.73	125.30	− 0.61	+ 54.00	+ 75.7
OTC (XOC)	573.81	558.55	573.45	+ 8.93	+ 42.70	+ 8.0
Utility (UTY)	274.20	269.80	273.91	+ 1.37	+ 8.77	+ 3.3
Value Line (VLE)	439.25	434.86	439.25	+ 0.18	+ 53.17	+ 13.8
Bank (BKX)	262.05	255.07	261.97	+ 6.62	+ 8.51	+ 3.4

Source: *The Wall Street Journal,* November 9, 1993, p. C17.

option, buying a put option, and writing a put option). Before we get to this, however, we need to define some symbols.

The value, or price, of a call option at a point in time will be denoted by C_T. The value of a put option will be denoted by P_T. The value of the underlying stock will be denoted by S. We will define the exercise price of the option as E and the time left until the option's expiration as T. At the expiration date, T equals 0.

Valuing Calls and Puts at Expiration

Let's assume that a time traveler can return to a point in time right before the December 1993 Paramount options expired. This would be a few minutes before the markets closed on December 17, 1993. How much would this person expect the December call and put options to be worth? (Remember, both have exercise prices of 75, so E equals 75.) The answer, of course, depends on the price of Paramount's stock. Let's start with the call option.

Call Option Value at Expiration. Assume Paramount's common stock was trading for $85 per share moments before the market closed on December 17, 1993. How much would the 75 December call be worth? The answer is $10. To see why, consider what would happen if the option were selling for $7. One could then buy the option contract for $700, exercise it immediately to buy Paramount for $75 per share, and then sell the Paramount shares on the NYSE for $85 per share. The profit, ignoring commissions, would be $300, and this return would be risk free. This is an example of **arbitrage,** the simultaneous purchase and sale of two different securities to make a guaranteed profit.

Now, what would happen if Paramount's stock were trading for $60 per share moments before the 75 December call was about to expire? The call would be worthless ($C = 0$). After all, who would pay *anything* for an option to immediately buy a stock at $75 per share when it was selling on the NYSE for only $60. No rational investor would do this.

These examples illustrate that valuing a call option at expiration is fairly simple. It is equal to zero if the option is about to expire out-of-the-money ($S < E$); the value of the call is equal to the stock price minus the exercise price ($S - E$) if the call is about to expire in-the-money. More formally, the value of a call option at expiration equals:

$$
\begin{aligned}
&C_T = \text{MAX } (0, \ S - E\ ), \text{ where } T = 0 \\
&C_T = 0, \text{ if } S \leq E \\
&C_T = S - E, \text{ if } S > E
\end{aligned}
\tag{18.1}
$$

Put Option Value at Expiration. Similar logic leads to a value for a put option at expiration. Let's use the 75 December Paramount put option. Right before the put option expires on December 17, 1993, suppose that Paramount's common stock is selling for either $85 per share or $60 per share.

If Paramount were selling for $85 per share, the put option would be worthless; it would be about to expire out-of-the-money. No one would pay anything for an option that would allow the holder to immediately sell Paramount at $75 per share, when one could get $85 per share on the NYSE.

On the other hand, if Paramount were trading at $60 per share, right before the put option expired, it would have a value of $15. If it were selling for less than $15, arbitragers could buy the option, buy the stock, and then exercise the option (in essence selling the stock at $85 when its market price was $60).

Putting the example into a more general form, the value of a put option at expiration is equal to zero if the option is about to expire out-of-the-money ($S \geq E$), or $E - S$, if the put option is about to expire in-the-money ($S < E$). More formally, the value of a put option at expiration equals:

$$
\begin{aligned}
&P_T = MAX(0, \ E - S\ ), \text{ where } T = 0 \\
&P_T = 0, \text{ if } S \geq E \\
&P_T = E - S, \text{ if } S < E
\end{aligned}
\tag{18.2}
$$

Table 18.1

Profit (Loss) from Buying or Writing a
75 December Paramount Call Option

Stock Price at Expiration ($T = 0$)	Value of Call Option	Profit (Loss)[a]	
		Buyer	**Writer**
$ 50	$ 0	$ (750)	$ 750
55	0	(750)	750
60	0	(750)	750
65	0	(750)	750
70	0	(750)	750
75	0	(750)	750
80	5	(250)	250
85	10	250	(250)
90	15	750	(750)
95	20	1,250	(1,250)
100	25	1,750	(1,750)

[a] Initial price of call equals $750 and the exercise price equals $75.

Calculating the Profit and Loss from an Option

Knowing the value of call and put options at expiration allows one to calculate the profit or loss from the four basic option trades (buying a call, writing a call, buying a put, and writing a put). Example calculations will use the two familiar Paramount options; the 75 December call was selling for $7\frac{1}{2}$ (the buyer paid $750 to the writer) about seven weeks prior to expiration, and the 75 December put was selling for $3\frac{1}{2}$ (the buyer paid $350 to the writer) seven weeks prior to expiration in December 1993.

Buying a Call Option. The profit from buying the call option depends, of course, on the price of Paramount's stock at expiration. Table 18.1 shows the profit or loss from buying the 75 December call, with a purchase price of $750, for various stock prices. The data are shown graphically in Figure 18.4. At a stock price of 75 or below, the call expires out-of-the-money and worthless; the buyer loses $750. On the other hand, at a stock price above 75, the buyer's profit or loss equals:

$$[(S - E) \times 100] - 750$$

For example, at a stock price of 85, the buyer's profit equals:

$$[(85 - 75) \times 100] - 750 = \$250$$

In general, then, the profit or loss from buying a call option is:[2]

$$\text{Profit (Loss)} = -C, \text{ if } S \leq E \text{ when } T = 0$$
$$= [(S - E) \times 100] - C, \text{ if } S > E \text{ when } T = 0$$
where C is the price paid for call option.

---

[2] The breakeven price occurs where profit equals zero. For the call, it would be a stock price equal to the initial price of the call plus the exercise price. In the above example, the breakeven price is:

$$82.5 = 7.5 + 75$$

Figure 18.4

Profit (Loss) from Buying or Writing a 75 December Paramount Call Option at Expiration[a]

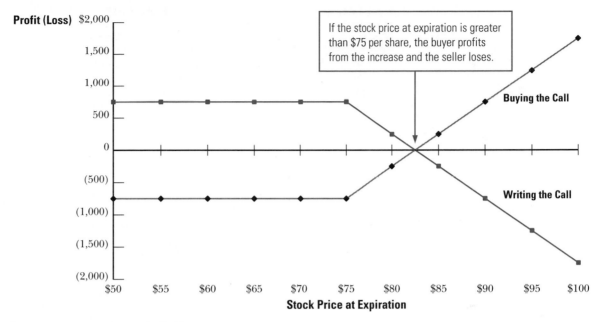

> If the stock price at expiration is greater than $75 per share, the buyer profits from the increase and the seller loses.

[a]Initial price of call equals $750.

Before we go any further, we should make two additional points. First, in reality, most option buyers don't exercise their options when they decide to take profits in cash, unless they actually want to buy or sell the underlying stock. Buyers simply sell their options on the appropriate markets. Exercising an option entails additional transactions, and thus additional transaction costs. For example, exercising a call to cash in option profits requires the holder to sell the shares of stock acquired by exercising the option. The profit from selling the option will be the same, before transaction costs, as that from exercising the option and then selling the stock. This is simply because many investors in the market pay virtually no transaction costs. Their low-cost trades help to eliminate any arbitrage profits.

Second, the example shown in Table 18.1 helps illustrate the derivative nature of options. Options derive their values from the values of the underlying stocks, Paramount in the example. Notice how the value of the call option at expiration increases exactly as much as the stock price, once the call option is in-the-money ($S > E$).

Writing a Call Option. The profit or loss from writing the 75 December Paramount call is also shown in Table 18.1 for various stock prices. Figure 18.4 shows clearly that the profit or loss for the option writer is the exact opposite of the profit or loss for the option buyer. This illustrates an important characteristic of option trading: it is a **zero sum game**—for someone to make a dollar, someone else must lose a dollar. In the example, at a stock price of 85, the option buyer makes $250, while the writer of the option loses $250.

Buying a Put Option. Table 18.2 shows the profit or loss from buying the 75 Paramount December put at $350 for various stock prices at expiration. (The

Table 18.2

Profit (Loss) from Buying or Writing a
75 December Paramount Put Option

Stock Price at Expiration ($T = 0$)	Value of Put Option	Profit (Loss)[a]	
		Buyer	**Writer**
$ 50	$25	$2,150	($2,150)
55	20	1,650	(1,650)
60	15	1,150	(1,150)
65	10	650	(650)
70	5	150	(150)
75	0	(350)	350
80	0	(350)	350
85	0	(350)	350
90	0	(350)	350
95	0	(350)	350
100	0	(350)	350

Source: Reprinted by permission of The Wall Street Journal,
© 1993 Dow Jones & Company, Inc. All Rights Reserved
Worldwide

[a] Initial price of put equals $350 and the exercise price equals
$75.

data are shown graphically in Figure 18.5.) If Paramount stock is selling for 75 or higher just before the put option expires, the option is worthless. (It is about to expire out-of-the-money.) The buyer of the option loses $350. On the other hand, if Paramount is selling for less than 75 just before the put option expires, it is about to expire in-the-money. The profit or loss equals the difference between the exercise price ($E = 75$) and the stock price, multiplied by 100, minus $350. For example, at a stock price of 60, the profit from the put option is:

$$[(75 - 60) \times 100] - \$350 = \$1,150$$

In general then, the profit or loss from buying a put equals:[3]

$$\text{Profit (loss)} = -P, \text{ if } S \geq E \text{ when } T = 0$$
$$= [(E - S) \times 100] - P, \text{ if } E > S \text{ when } T = 0$$
where P is the price paid for the put option.

Writing a Put Option. The profit or loss from writing the 75 December Paramount put for $350 is also shown in Table 18.2 for various stock prices at expiration. Figure 18.5 illustrates that the profit or loss from writing the put is the exact opposite of the profit or loss from buying the same put option. Put option trading is also a zero sum game. If Paramount is trading for $65 per share right before the 75 December put option expires, the buyer of the option has made $650 and the writer of the option has lost $650.

---

[3] The breakeven stock price on a put option is equal to the exercise price minus the initial price of the put. In the example, the breakeven stock price is:

$$71.5 = 75 - 3.5$$

Figure 18.5

Profit (Loss) from Buying or Writing a 75 December Paramount Put Option at Expiration[a]

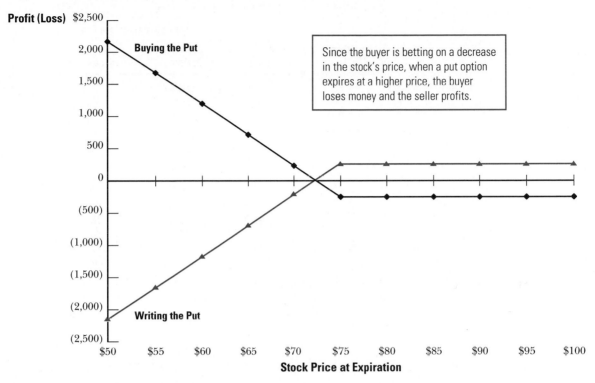

> Since the buyer is betting on a decrease in the stock's price, when a put option expires at a higher price, the buyer loses money and the seller profits.

[a]Initial price of put equals $350.

Common Option Trading Strategies

In this section we review some of the unique risks and opportunities of options along with common option trading strategies.[4] Some of these strategies involve positions in options alone (either calls or puts), while others combine option positions with positions in the underlying stocks. Throughout this discussion, we'll be illustrating these strategies using various December 1993 Paramount options and Paramount's common stock. The options, their prices, and the stock price are shown below:

Security	Price[a]
Paramount common stock	$80\frac{3}{8}$
75 December call option	$7\frac{1}{2}$
75 December put option	$3\frac{1}{2}$
80 December call option	4
80 December put option	$6\frac{1}{2}$
85 December call option	$1\frac{7}{8}$

[a]On November 5, 1993.

---

[4]Traders employ many more option strategies than we discuss in this section. See, for example, Don Chance, *An Introduction to Options & Futures,* 2nd ed. (Fort Worth, TX: Dryden Press, 1991), 197–236.

Table 18.3

Holding Period Return of Paramount
Stock and a 75 December Call Option at
the Date of Option Expiration

Stock Price (T = 0)	Value of Call Option	Holding Period Return	
		Call Option	Stock
$ 50	$ 0	−100.0%	−37.8%
55	0	−100.0	−31.6
60	0	−100.0	−25.3
65	0	−100.0	−19.1
70	0	−100.0	−12.9
75	0	−100.0	−6.7
80	5	−33.3	−0.5
85	10	33.3	5.8
90	15	100.0	12.0
95	20	166.7	18.2
100	25	233.3	24.4

Note: The price of the call option is assumed to be $7\frac{1}{2}$ and the price of the stock is assumed to be $80\frac{3}{8}$.

Source: Reprinted by permission of The Wall Street Journal, © 1993 Dow Jones & Company, Inc. All Rights Reserved Worldwide

Some Unique Risks and Opportunities of Options

Option trading offers investors some unique opportunities. Options, as we'll see in the next section, can be used to **hedge,** or reduce the risk of, stock positions. At the same time, however, option trading exposes investors to substantial, unique risks. An obvious risk of options is the need to be right not only about the direction of a move in a stock's price, but also about its timing. Someone who believes the S&P 100 is going to decline by a certain percentage over the next few months may buy a put option that expires in three months. Even if that person is right and stocks do decline, he or she may still be wrong about when. The decline may begin in four months, after the three-month put option expires. Another risk unique to options is the fact that options trading is a zero sum game; for someone to make money, someone else has to lose the same amount. Still, options do offer investors attractive features.

One of the most potentially attractive features of call options is their **inherent leverage.** Buying a call option is similar to buying a stock on margin. To illustrate this inherent leverage, compare the holding period returns from buying Paramount stock and buying the 75 December call. The returns, assuming various stock prices at the call option's expiration date, are shown in Table 18.3 and Figure 18.6. Someone who guessed right about the outcome of the Paramount acquisition, and the upward direction of Paramount's stock between November and mid-December 1993, would have been better off buying the call option rather than the stock itself. For example, had Paramount moved from around 80 in early November 1993 to 90 in mid-December, the return from owning the stock would have been 12 percent (ignoring transaction costs). On the other hand, owning the 75 December call option would have given a return of 100 percent.

As an aside, many cases of insider trading have involved options rather than stocks. In Chapter 3, we briefly discussed some famous insider trading cases from the 1980s. More often than not, those convicted of violating

Figure 18.6

Holding Period Return of Paramount Common Stock and a 75 December Call Option

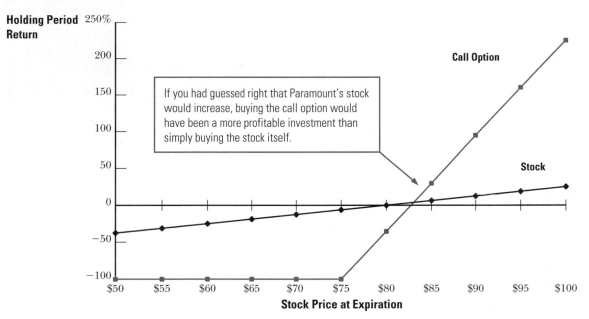

Note: Purchase price of option equals $7\frac{1}{2}$ and purchase price of common stock equals $80\frac{3}{8}$.

insider trading laws were buying call options. The reason comes from the inherent leverage of call options. Those who knew that the price of a stock was going to rise could generate far higher profits from the same dollar investment in the options market than in the stock market.

The trouble with leverage, of course, is that it is a double-edged sword. Take another look at Table 18.3 and Figure 18.6. Had Paramount's stock stayed around 80 or even fallen, the call option owner would have been worse off than the stockholder. For example, had Paramount's stock declined from around 80 in November 1993 to 75 in mid-December, the stock's return would have been around minus 7 percent. On the other hand, the option's return would have been minus 100 percent. The option would have expired out-of-the-money and been worthless.

Put options offer investors unique opportunities, as well. They give investors the opportunity to speculate on the prices of specific stocks, or on specific stock indexes, declining over short periods of time. Remember, as we discussed in Chapter 3, investors can sell a stock short (selling borrowed shares and buying them back later, hopefully at a lower price). Short sellers often face restrictions, however, as we discussed in Chapter 3, as well. An investor may find it easier to speculate on price declines using put options rather than short sales.

Finally, consider the unique risk associated with writing options; the potential gain is limited while the potential loss is almost unlimited.[5] Recall Figure 18.4 for a moment. The maximum gain from writing the 75 December call would have been the premium on the option, $750. On the other hand, if Paramount's stock had soared over the next seven weeks, the potential loss would have been much higher. Had Paramount been trading at $100 per

---

[5]As we'll see in the next section, some strategies involve writing options in combination with other positions. The potential gain and losses of such strategies are quite different from those of writing options by themselves.

Paramount Confusion

Buying options in the hope of profiting on a pending takeover can be a tricky business, and never more so than in the current bidding for Paramount Communications. Besides the usual uncertainties surrounding any takeover, the Paramount deal could surprise option investors in a variety of nasty ways.

First, because Paramount's two suitors own broadcast properties, the deal requires the approval of the Federal Communications Commission. If that approval is denied, Paramount's stock would slump steeply and quickly from its recent price of 81. Likewise, if the Paramount bids were to collapse for lack of financing, the effect on the stock would be disastrous. In either case, those short now out-of-the-money puts, like the Paramount 75s, would get mauled as the stock slid downward.

A second, quite different, danger to option holders could arise if Paramount were acquired in a contested two-step deal. Under this scenario, it is possible that the Paramount shares exchanged for stock in Step 2 could actually fetch more than the cash price paid in Step 1. That would be a nasty surprise for investors shorting Paramount calls.

In the current battle for Paramount, both QVC Network and rival suitor Viacom have proposed two-step tender offers, with $80 cash to be paid for 51 percent of the shares, followed by what is represented as a similar value of stock or convertible shares for the balance.

In any two-step tender, the usual advice warns against being short apparently out-of-the-money puts, meaning the option to deliver Paramount shares at a price of, say, 75. Why the warning? Because after the first step in a two-part takeover, the shares of the target company often drop. Thus, although Paramount's 75-strike puts may look worthless today, they could have real value after the first step of a tender.

But if the Paramount deal is hard-fought until the end, there is another interesting twist to watch for: As mentioned above, the *calls* could rise in price after the first step of a Paramount takeover. This possibility is scarcely appreciated on the street because it hasn't often—if ever—cropped up in the takeover of an option stock.

What events would conspire to make this happen? Viacom and QVC could each fail to gain 51 percent of the shares for $80 and then compete with subsequent, higher bids. Those bids would likely be in the form of more shares, with the cash left at $80 for 51 percent.

INVESTMENT INSIGHTS

It may happen. "This one could get punch at the back end," says Sharon Kalin, who specializes in takeover arbitrage at Athene-Coronado Management. Kalin sees that scenario as possible because both QVC and Viacom are "having trouble coming up with the cash" to do the deal, but they can print all the stock they wish.

After studying the tender documents for the two bids, which were circulated last week, Kalin comments that "this is a stranger deal than people realize," with each bid having unusual escape clauses.

There is another important factor to be considered in evaluating the bids for Paramount: Neither bidder has more than half the $4 billion of cash on hand needed to complete the tender. Bankers' enthusiasm to finance either bid seems lukewarm at best, judging by the unusual caveats placed in the offering documents.

Also disclosed in the documents is what could be an important lapse in QVC's bid. While QVC itself has filed as required under the Hart-Scott-Rodino Act, neither of its partners—NYNEX and Blockbuster Entertainment—had done so as of October 26. This could give Viacom an edge because its deal has already met the 30-day waiting period required by the act.

Given all the uncertainties, investors in Paramount shares, or those with option positions, should consider the risk that both the QVC and Viacom bids might fail. If that were to happen, the shares could well fall back below 60, where they traded prior to the disclosure of acquisition talks. Such a slide isn't impossible, and it would surely create huge swings in option values. Calls now trading at close to 20 might go closer to zero, for example, while apparently worthless puts might prove to have value after all.

There is no question that QVC and Viacom would each like to buy Paramount. But what if they don't?

Source: Thomas N. Cochran, "Paramount Confusion," *Barron's*, November 1, 1993, p. 70.

share in mid-December the call option writer would have lost $1,750. Only experienced option traders who can afford to risk substantial capital should consider writing options.

Some of the unique risks and opportunities of options are discussed in the *Barron's* article reprinted in the Investment Insights feature. While the article deals specifically with the risks and rewards associated with the Paramount acquisition, much of what the author has to say applies to all option trades.

Strategies Involving Just One Option Contract

We've already seen the profit and loss associated with buying and writing call and put options. (Review Table 18.1 and Figure 18.4 for call options, and Table 18.2 and Figure 18.5 for put options.) By now you should have a pretty good idea what investors are expecting when they buy and write call and put options; they buy call options to speculate on the price of a stock rising over a short period of time, and they buy put options to speculate on the price of a stock falling over a short period of time. An investor who writes an option attempts to capture the option's price, hoping that it expires out-of-the-money.

Buying and writing call and put options involves more than just choosing an underlying stock on which to trade options. One must also decide which call or put to buy or write. Go back to Figures 18.2 and 18.3 for a moment; take a look at all the options available for specific stocks or indexes. Deciding which option to buy or write often depends on a tradeoff between risk and return. Generally, an option further out-of-the-money, and/or with a shorter time until expiration, has a greater potential return and greater risk for the option buyer. The option writer takes more risk on an option with a strike price close to the stock's price, and/or with a longer time until expiration. Let's illustrate this with an example.

Someone may have believed that Paramount's stock price would rise sharply between early November and mid-December 1993. This would support a decision to buy a December call option. The next question is, which strike price should the option have? The inherent risk/return tradeoff is shown in Figure 18.7. The figure shows the holding period return for the 85 December call and the 75 December call between early November and the options' expiration date in mid-December.

The call option with the higher exercise price would cost less ($1\frac{7}{8}$ versus $7\frac{1}{2}$) and its leverage potential would be greater. For example, if the price of Paramount were to rise to 95 around the options' expiration date, the 85 call would produce a return in excess of 400 percent while the 75 call would produce a return of around 167 percent. (This, and all the examples that follow, ignores transaction costs.) At the same time, however, the 85 call is riskier than the 75 call. Assume that Paramount's stock rises only slightly between early November and mid-December from 80 to 85. The 75 call would produce a return of 33 percent. The 85 call, however, would expire out-of-the-money, returning −100 percent.

Straddles

A **straddle** involves buying both a call and a put with the same exercise price, and the same expiration date. A straddle is essentially a bet on the volatility of the underlying stock. On the other hand, a **reverse straddle** involves writing both a call and a put with the same exercise price and the same expiration date. Not surprisingly, a reverse straddle is a bet against volatility in the underlying stock.

Figure 18.7

Holding Period Returns for Paramount Call Options to Date of Option Expiration

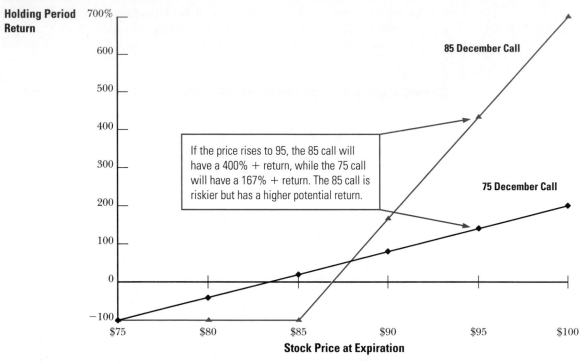

Holding Period Return

If the price rises to 95, the 85 call will have a 400% + return, while the 75 call will have a 167% + return. The 85 call is riskier but has a higher potential return.

85 December Call

75 December Call

Stock Price at Expiration

Note: The initial price of the 75 December call option was $7\frac{1}{2}$ and the initial price of the 85 December call option was $1\frac{7}{8}$.

Assume that someone believed in early November 1993 that one of two things was going to happen to Paramount by mid-December; either the deal would fall apart or the bidding war would continue. This would lead to the conclusion that the price of Paramount's stock would either fall sharply (if the deals were to fall apart) or rise sharply (if the bidding war were to continue). In a straddle, the trader would buy both the 80 December call (for 4) and the 80 December put (for $6\frac{1}{2}$). The profit or loss from this straddle is illustrated in Figure 18.8.

In order for the straddle to be profitable, the stock price would have to move substantially in one direction or the other. At an expiration date stock price of about 70 and below, or about 90 and above, the straddle is profitable. The straddle buyer would have suffered if Paramount had remained at around 80 through mid-December.

Figure 18.8 also illustrates the profit and loss from a reverse straddle. This trade combined writing the 80 December call and 80 December put. The strategy works if Paramount's common stock remains around 80 until mid-December. Like writing a call or a put alone, a wrong guess exposes the option writer to an almost unlimited potential loss.

Spreads

A **spread** involves purchasing one option and writing another on the same underlying stock. The options differ only in terms of one parameter, usually either exercise price or expiration date. The most common type of spread is a money spread.[6]

---

[6]In addition to money spreads option traders construct calendar spreads, butterfly spreads, and box spreads. See Chance, *Introduction to Options,* 208–217.

Figure 18.8

Profit (Loss) from Buying or Writing an Option Straddle

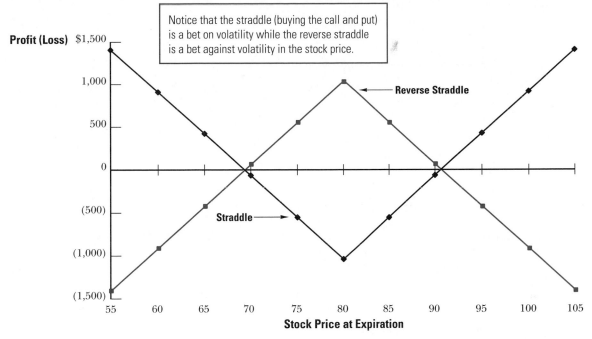

> Notice that the straddle (buying the call and put) is a bet on volatility while the reverse straddle is a bet against volatility in the stock price.

Note: Options used are the 80 December Paramount call (initial price of 4) and 80 December Paramount put (initial price of $6\frac{1}{2}$).

Money Spreads. A **money spread** involves the purchase of one call or put option and the sale of another. The options have the same expiration date, but different exercise prices. Money spreads are often referred to as either **bull spreads** or **bear spreads,** because they constitute bets on whether underlying stocks' prices will rise or fall over a short period of time.

Figure 18.9 illustrates both a bull spread and a bear spread. In the bull spread, one buys the 75 December call and writes the 85 December call. In general, a bull spread involves buying the call with the lower exercise price, while writing the call with the higher exercise price. In the bear spread, one writes the 75 December call and buys the 85 December call. Notice the limits on how much one can make or lose with either spread. The bear spread, for example, has a maximum profit of $562.50 and a maximum loss of $437.50.

Bull and bear spreads can also be constructed with put options. A bear spread would involve buying the put with the higher exercise price, while writing the put with the lower exercise price. A bull spread would combine writing the put with the higher exercise price while buying the put with the lower exercise price.

Why Trade Spreads? As you probably have already guessed, a bull spread using call options is a substitute for simply buying a call option, while a bear spread using call options is a substitute for writing a call option. The advantage of a bull spread over buying a call option is that smaller upward movements in the price of the underlying stock will produce higher profits. For example, if Paramount had moved from about 80 in early November to 85 in mid-December, the bull spread shown in Figure 18.9 would have produced a profit of $437.50. By contrast, simply buying the 75 December call would have produced a profit of $250.00. The disadvantage of the bull spread is that it would limit the maximum profit to $437.50, regardless of how high Paramount's stock price were to climb.

Figure 18.9

Profit (Loss) from a Bull Market or Bear Market Spread

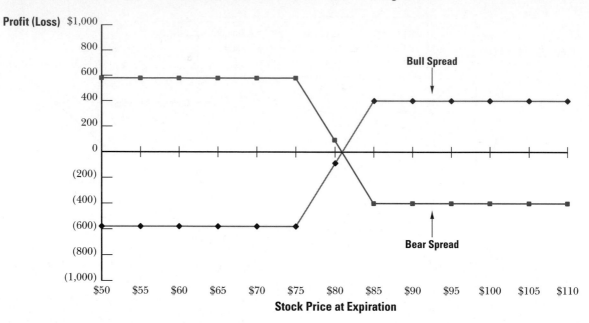

Note: These spreads use the 75 Paramount December call (with an initial price of $7\frac{1}{2}$) and the 85 Paramount December call (with an initial price of $1\frac{7}{8}$).

The advantage of a bear spread over simply writing a call option is very obvious: limited downside risk. Remember, simply writing a call option exposes one to unlimited potential loss. The bear spread shown in Figure 18.9 would limit the potential loss to $437.50, regardless of how high Paramount's stock price were to climb. While a bear spread does sacrifice some upside potential, most experienced option traders speculate on price declines using spreads rather than simply writing individual call options.

Combining Option and Stock Positions

Another common use of options is to combine them with positions in underlying stocks. These combined positions are often called *hedges;* the option is used to reduce the risk of the stock position. Let's look at three common techniques that combine options and stock: writing covered calls, buying protective puts, and covering short sales.

Writing Covered Calls. Writing a **covered call** involves writing a call option on a stock already owned by the investor. Investors write covered calls for two basic reasons: to increase income from the stock (since the writer of an option receives the option premium) and reducing the downside risk of the stock. Optimism about a stock's long-term prospects doesn't eliminate worry about it in the short term.

Assume someone bought Paramount at $80\frac{3}{8}$, and, at the same time, wrote an 80 December call option, perhaps thinking that Paramount's stock price should increase in the long term, despite concern that it may not rise over the short term. The profit and loss from this combination is shown in Table 18.4. Note that this is an unusual position. In reality, few investors would buy a stock and immediately write a call option on it. They are more likely to write call options on stocks they've owned for some time.

Table 18.4

Profit (Loss) from a Covered Call on Paramount Stock

Stock Price at Expiration	Profit (Loss)		
	Option	Stock	Total
$ 60	$ 400	($2,038)	($1,638)
65	400	(1,538)	(1,138)
70	400	(1,038)	(638)
75	400	(538)	(138)
80	400	(38)	363
85	(100)	463	363
90	(600)	963	363
95	(1,100)	1,463	363
100	(1,600)	1,963	363

Note: The option written is the 80 December call (with an initial price of 4). The purchase price of the stock is assumed to be $80\frac{3}{8}$.

As shown in Table 18.4, if Paramount's stock had remained unchanged between early November and mid-December 1993, the covered call would have been more profitable than simply owning the stock. At the same time, had Paramount declined in price, the profit from writing the call would have offset some of the loss from the stock position. (The losses in the stock are only *paper* losses, of course; they become real, cash losses only if the stock is actually sold.)

Protective Puts. A **protective put** is another common combined stock/option position in which an investor buys put options on stock he or she already owns. The rationale for a protective put is straightforward: it reduces some of the downside risk associated with owning stocks, either by guaranteeing a sale price or offsetting losses on the stock with profits on the put. Protective puts can be thought of as a kind of insurance.

Table 18.5 assumes that an investor purchased 100 shares of Paramount stock for $50 a share, just as the takeover frenzy was starting. He or she then watched Paramount soar to over $80 a share. While the investor believes that Paramount could go higher, he or she is starting to worry about the takeover bid falling apart. If that happens, the price of Paramount would drop sharply,

Table 18.5

Profit (Loss) from a Protective Put on Paramount Stock

Stock Price at Expiration	Profit (Loss)		
	Stock	Put	Total
$ 40	($1,000)	$3,150	$2,150
50	0	2,150	2,150
60	1,000	1,150	2,150
70	2,000	150	2,150
80	3,000	(350)	2,650
90	4,000	(350)	3,650
100	5,000	(350)	4,650

Note: The stock was purchased at a price of 50. The put is the 75 December put with an initial price of $3\frac{1}{2}$.

Table 18.6

Profit (Loss) from a Covered Short Sale
on Paramount Stock

Stock Price at Expiration	Profit (Loss)		
	Stock	**Call**	**Total**
$ 50	$3,038	($ 400)	$2,638
55	2,538	(400)	2,138
60	2,038	(400)	1,638
65	1,538	(400)	1,138
70	1,038	(400)	638
75	538	(400)	138
80	38	(400)	(363)
85	(463)	100	(363)
90	(963)	600	(363)
95	(1,463)	1,100	(363)
100	(1,963)	1,600	(363)

Notes: The stock is sold short at $80\frac{3}{8}$. The call is the 85 December call with an initial price of $1\frac{7}{8}$.

wiping out most, if not all, of his or her profit. So, the investor decides to protect some of the profit by buying a 75 December put for $3\frac{1}{2}$. Notice that even if Paramount's stock price collapses, the investor has "locked in" a profit of $2,150.

Buying a protective put requires careful attention to the strike price of the option. A higher strike price lowers the risk, but at the same time, a higher strike price also increases the cost of the put. This decision resembles the choice of a deductible on auto insurance: a higher deductible reduces the cost of the auto insurance, but it increases the loss from an accident.

Covered Short Sales. A **covered short sale** is similar to a protective put: the option provides insurance. In a covered short sale, the investor combines a short position in a stock with a long position in a call option. Remember, a short sale represents a bet on a drop in the price of a stock, allowing the investor to buy back borrowed shares at a lower price. The risk of a short sale is the potential loss if the stock price doesn't drop. The call option reduces some of this risk.

For example, assume that in early November 1993 someone believed that the various acquisition offers for Paramount would fall apart, dropping the price of Paramount's stock sharply. To profit from this drop, the person might short the stock. To cover the position, in case the expectations are wrong, the short seller might also buy an 85 December call option. Table 18.6 shows the profit and loss from this covered short sale.

The table shows clearly how owning the call option greatly reduces the risk of the short sale. For example, if Paramount were to soar to $100 per share by mid-December, the combined position would lose only $363, compared to almost $2,000 for a simple short sale without the call option. Of course, like all insurance, buying the call would reduce some of the short sale's profits if Paramount were to fall in price.

Option Pricing Models

Up to now we've discussed how to determine the value of an option at expiration, and we've used this knowledge to examine the profit and loss potentials of several common option trading strategies. This section will explore the factors that affect the value of an option prior to expiration. These factors help explain why some options are worth more than others, and why option prices rise and fall. We will then use these factors to build models to determine estimates of the functional value of an option prior to its expiration.

Determinants of Option Values

The fundamental value of an option prior to expiration is affected by six factors: (1) the price of the underlying stock, (2) the exercise price, (3) the length of time until expiration, (4) the volatility of the underlying stock, (5) the level of interest rates, and (6) the amount of dividends the underlying stock pays between now and the expiration date. Let's discuss each of these factors.

Price of the Underlying Stock. As we've already seen, as the price of the underlying stock rises (or falls) the value of a call option rises (or falls). The reverse is true for a put option; the value of a put rises (or falls) as the stock falls (or rises) in price.

Exercise Price. Since a call is an option to buy, a higher exercise price implies a lower value. A put is an option to sell, so a higher exercise price implies a higher value. To verify these relationships, go back to Figure 18.2 for a moment. Notice that the 70 December call on Paramount sold for $11\frac{1}{2}$ while the 80 December call sold for 4. The 70 December put sold for 2 while the 80 December put sold for $6\frac{1}{2}$.

Time until Expiration. Referring again to Figure 18.2, what relationship do you see between the value of Paramount options and their times until expiration? The relationship, for both calls and puts, is positive; a longer time until expiration implies a higher price. Let's look at some examples of Paramount options, all with the same exercise price, but different expiration dates:

Call Option	Price	Put Option	Price
80 November	$2\frac{1}{2}$	80 November	$2\frac{1}{8}$
80 December	4	80 December	$6\frac{1}{2}$
80 March	$5\frac{1}{2}$	80 March	$10\frac{1}{4}$

Why do we see this positive relationship between option price and time until expiration? The answer is simply that a longer time until expiration increases the probability that an option will become in-the-money before it expires.

Earlier in this chapter we defined an option's premium. For a call, the premium is equal to the price of the option plus the exercise price minus the current stock price. For a put, the premium equals the price of the option plus the current stock price minus the exercise price. If the price of the underlying stock were to remain constant, the option's premium should diminish as the expiration date gets closer.

Volatility of the Underlying Stock. An option buyer's loss is limited to the price of the option. On the other hand, the potential profit is almost unlimited. As a result, the stock price at expiration is irrelevant if the option expires out-of-the-money. For example, someone who bought the 80 December Paramount call for 4 wouldn't have cared whether Paramount sold for

$30 a share or $80 a share in mid-December. In both cases, the option would have expired out-of-the-money and the owner would have lost $400. On the other hand, Paramount's stock price would become critical if the option were about to expire in-the-money.

This means that more volatility in the underlying stock makes an option more valuable. Increased volatility increases the odds that the option will expire in-the-money. This is true for both call and put options.

The frenzy surrounding the Paramount acquisition made its common stock quite volatile in the fall of 1993. As a result investors were willing to pay large premiums for rights to buy or sell Paramount stock at fixed prices for short periods of time. For example, the 80 December put option had a premium of $6\frac{7}{8}$ in early November 1993 ($6\frac{1}{2} + 80\frac{3}{8} - 80$). Compare that to a 50 December put option selling for $1\frac{13}{16}$ on IBM, a much more stable stock at the time. This option had a premium of only $1\frac{9}{16}$ ($1\frac{13}{16} + 49\frac{3}{4} - 50$).

Level of Interest Rates. As interest rates rise, the value of a call option increases, while the value of a put option decreases. This may initially seem puzzling, but the reason is quite straightforward. As interest rates rise, the present value of the exercise price falls. To exercise a call option, the owner must pay something (the exercise price); therefore, as the present value of this price falls, the value of the call option should rise. The reverse, of course, is true for a put option.

Dividends. We mentioned earlier that options are protected from stock splits and stock dividends. If a stock splits two for one, for example, the exercise price of all options will automatically be halved. Options are not, however, protected from cash dividends. Now, you may also remember that when a stock goes **ex-dividend,** its price falls because the buyer is no longer entitled to the current dividend. A larger cash dividend (as a percentage of the stock price) implies a greater price decline. What does this mean for the price of an option?

If the underlying stock pays dividends between the option's purchase and its expiration date, the dividend payment, and the resulting price drop on the ex-dividend date, will tend to decrease the value of a call option and increase the value of a put option. A larger dividend causes a greater price decrease (or increase) in a call (or put) option.

Table 18.7 summarizes the relationships between these six factors and the value of an option prior to expiration. While the material that follows is somewhat more difficult than what we've covered up to this point, even if you read no further in this section, understanding the relationships summarized in Table 18.7 will help you understand why some options are worth more than others, and why option prices increase or decrease over time. This is important knowledge if you wish to successfully trade options.

Binomial Option Pricing Model[7]

Before we go on, we need to distinguish between **European options** and **American options.** A European option can be exercised only on its expiration date, whereas an American option can be exercised at any time between its creation and its expiration date. All options traded today, throughout the world, are American options. European options are, however, much simpler instruments than American options. Consequently, it is easier to develop pricing models for European options. However, it can be shown that Amer-

---

[7]This section can be skipped without any loss of continuity.

Table 18.7

Six Factors that Affect the Value of an Option Prior to
Expiration

		Impact on Value of	
Variable	Direction	Call Option	Put Option
1. Price of underlying stock	Higher	Increases	Decreases
2. Exercise price	Higher	Decreases	Increases
3. Time until expiration	Longer	Increases	Increases
4. Volatility of underlying stock	Greater	Increases	Increases
5. Interest rates	Higher	Increases	Decreases
6. Dividend yield	Larger	Decreases	Increases

ican options are rarely exercised early.[8] Therefore, the fundamental value of
a European option is often a decent proxy for the fundamental value of a
similar American option.

Let's begin our development of the binomial option pricing model by
describing the security's environment. A stock has a current price of S, which
will either rise or fall by the end of one period. Therefore:

$$Su = S(1 + u)$$
$$Sd = S(1 + d)$$

where u is the percentage gain in price, and d is the percentage decline.
Putting some numbers of this, assume that S equals 100, u equals 10 percent,
and d equals 5 percent. Therefore, Su equals 110 and $Sd = 95$.

Now, assume that a European call option has an exercise price of 100 and
it expires at the end of one period. The value of the call option at expiration
is:

$$Cu = \text{MAX}(0, Su - E)$$
$$Cd = \text{MAX}(0, Sd - E)$$

Using the numbers in the example, Cu equals 10 and Cd equals 0.

Now, assume a riskless portfolio consisting of a long position in the stock
and a short position in the option that earns the risk-free rate of return
between now and the end of the period, when the option expires. The riskless portfolio's value will remain the same regardless of what happens to the
price of the stock. Let Vu be the value of the portfolio if the stock price rises
and Vd be the value of the portfolio if it falls:

$$Vu = hS(1 + u) - Cu \qquad (18.3)$$
$$Vd = hS(1 + d) - Cd$$

where h is the hedge ratio (the number of shares purchased for each call
written). Since Vu must equal Vd, if the portfolio is truly risk free, then:

$$hS(1 + u) - Cu = hS(1 + d) - Cd \qquad (18.4)$$

Solving for h:

$$h = (Cu - Cd)/(Su - Sd) \qquad (18.5)$$

---

[8]See, for example, Chance, *Introduction to Options*, 80–83 and 94–95.

In the example, h equals:

$$(10 - 0)/(110 - 95) = 0.67$$

The riskless portfolio would consist of 0.67 shares for every call option written (assuming that one call option will buy one share). In round numbers, the equation suggests buying three shares and selling two calls.

If the portfolio's current value, $hS - C$, grows at the risk-free rate, denoted by r (which it should, since the portfolio is risk free), the following relationship must be true:[9]

$$(hS - C)(1 + r) = hS(1 + u) - Cu \qquad (18.6)$$

Substituting the formula for h and solving the equation for C gives the binomial option pricing formula:

$$C = [pCu + (1 - p)Cd]/(1 + r) \qquad (18.7)$$

where p is defined as $(r - d)/(u - d)$.

Using the example values ($S = 100$, $Su = 110$, $Sd = 95$, $Cu = 10$, $Cd = 0$, $h = 0.67$, and $r = 5$ percent), first find the value of p:

$$= [0.05 - (-0.05)]/[0.10 - (-0.05)] = 0.67$$

Then find the value of C using Equation 18.7:

$$C = [0.67(10) + 0]/(1.05) = \$6.35$$

Therefore, the binomial option pricing model gives a fundamental value for each call option of $6.35.

Arbitraging Mispriced Calls. Assume, instead, that the call option is selling for $8.00, well above its fundamental value of $6.35. How could an arbitrager profit from this mispricing? Suppose someone were to buy 200 shares of stock at $100 and sell 300 options at $8. The initial investment would be:

$$(200 \times \$100) - (300 \times \$8) = \$20,000 - \$2,400 = \$17,600$$

How much would the portfolio be worth when the options expired?

	Su = 95	*Su* = 110
200 shares of stock	$19,000	$22,000
300 call options	0	− 3,000
Total	$19,000	$19,000

The portfolio would be worth the same amount regardless of what happens to the stock price; the arbitrager would earn a risk-free return of:

$$(\$19,000 - \$17,400)/\$17,400 = 9.2 \text{ percent}$$

This is much higher than the risk-free rate of 5 percent.

Arbitrage could also generate profits from an underpriced call. Assume that the call discussed above was selling for $5.00 rather than $6.35. Someone could sell 200 shares short at $100, buy 300 calls at $5.00, and invest the proceeds in a risk-free asset earning 5 percent that would mature when the

[9]Since *Vu* equals *Vd*, one could choose either the value of the portfolio if the stock were to rise, or its value if the stock were to fall.

options expired. When the options expire, the arbitrager collects the bond repayment, buys the stock (at either 95 or 110), and sells the options.

Even a quick look at the real-world market makes the binomial option pricing model seem very unrealistic. We can't think of a realistic situation in which the change in price of a stock, even over a very short period of time, has only two possibilities. The well-known Black–Scholes option pricing model, which we discuss next, builds on the simple binomial option pricing model to develop a far more realistic, but far more complicated option valuation model.

Black–Scholes Option Pricing Model[10]

An option pricing model developed by Fischer Black and Myron Scholes incorporates the hedging strategy described by the binomial pricing model, but it also allows for infinite possible future stock prices.[11] Mathematically, the Black–Scholes option pricing model is an extension of the simple, one-period binomial pricing model we just discussed.

Black–Scholes Pricing Model for European Calls. The Black–Scholes model makes several important assumptions. It assumes that the risk-free rate and the underlying stock's price volatility remain constant over the life of the option, and that the underlying stock pays no dividends. Given these assumptions, the fundamental value of a European call is:

$$
\begin{aligned}
C &= S[N(d_1)] - Ee^{-rT}N(d_2) \\
d_1 &= [\ln(S/E) + (r + \sigma^2/2)T]/\sigma\sqrt{T} \\
d_2 &= d_1 - \sigma\sqrt{T},
\end{aligned}
\tag{18.8}
$$

where C is the fundamental value of the option, S is the current price of the underlying stock, E is the exercise price, T is the time until expiration stated in years (for an option that expires in six months, $T = 0.5$), r is the risk-free rate of interest, σ is the standard deviation of the underlying stock (a measure of volatility), in (S/E) is the natural log of S/E, e equals 2.71828 (the base of the natural log function), and $N(d)$ is the probability that a random draw from a standard normal distribution function will be less than d. The term Ee^{-rT} is the present value of the exercise price, assuming continuous compounding.

With a little math, the Black–Scholes model, Equation 18.8, can be modified to price European put options.

Loose Interpretation of the Black–Scholes Model. Though the formula looks horrendous, it's not as bad as you think, if you take it step by step. If the price of the stock when the option expires is known pretty much with certainty, assuming that $S > E$, the two $N(d)$ terms will be close to 1. This makes Equation 18.8 approach:

$$
C = S - Ee^{-rT}
$$

In English, the call price equals the current stock price minus the present value of the exercise price.

[10]This section can be skipped without any loss of continuity.

[11]Fischer Black and Myron Scholes, "The Pricing of Options and Corporate Liabilities," *Journal of Political Economy* (May–June 1973): 637–659.

At the other extreme, if there is virtually no chance of the option expiring in-the-money, the two $N(d)$ terms approach 0. The value of the option also approaches 0.

For all the probabilities in between, the Black–Scholes option pricing model can be loosely interpreted as saying that the value of a call is equal to the expected stock price at expiration minus the present value of the exercise price, both weighted by the probability of the option expiring in the money.

Determinants of the Fundamental Value of an Option. Table 18.7 listed the six variables that appear to affect the value of an option. The Black–Scholes model incorporates five of the six. (Remember that it assumes that the underlying stock pays no dividends.) Adjusting the values of these five factors individually in the model increases or decreases the value of the call, exactly as shown in Table 18.7.

For example, increasing the underlying stock's standard deviation, σ in Equation 18.8, while holding all the other variables constant, increases the value of the call option. Familiar information about the intrinsic value of a call option confirms the validity of the Black–Scholes model. (That's always a good feeling.)

Applying the Black–Scholes Formula. Let's apply the Black–Scholes model to a call option on Toys "Я" Us stock (TOY) with a strike price of $35 expiring in March 1994. One appealing characteristic of the model is that all of its variables but one are easily available from a financial newspaper such as *The Wall Street Journal*. The current stock price (S), the exercise price (E), the risk-free rate (r), and the time to expiration (T) can be obtained from the financial press. The only variable that must be estimated is the standard deviation of the underlying stock. Usually historical stock returns (continuously compounded) are used to estimate the standard deviation. Annualizing monthly return data between 1989 and 1992 gives a standard deviation for Toys "Я" Us of 0.3176.

Price quotes for November 5, 1993 give the following estimates of input variables:

$$S = 38$$
$$E = 35$$
$$T = 19 \text{ weeks (or } 0.3654 \text{ years), } \sqrt{T} = 0.6045$$
$$r = 3.11 \text{ percent (yield on three-month T-bills)}$$
$$\sigma = 0.3176 \ (\sigma^2 = 0.1008)$$

Equation 18.8 can give the value of the Toys "Я" Us call option, but it requires values for d_1 and d_2:

$$d_1 = [\ln(38/35) + 0.3654(0.0311 + 0.1008/2)]/[0.3176(0.6045)]$$
$$= 0.5836$$
$$d_2 = 0.5836 - 0.3176(0.6045) = 0.3917$$

The next step is to find the probability that a random draw from a standard normal distribution $N(d_1)$ and (one with a mean of 0 and a standard deviation of 1) will be less than 0.5836 and 0.3917 $N(d_2)$ respectively. The cumulative normal distribution table from Appendix 18A gives N(0.5836) and N(0.3917) as 0.7203 and 0.6523, respectively.

The final step is to fill in the values in Equation 18.8:

$$C = 38(0.7203) - 35e^{-.0311(0.3654)}(0.6523) = \$4.80$$

Note that we've rounded these numbers, so you may get an answer that's a penny or two different.

The Black–Scholes model gives a price for the call option of $4.80. Its actual market price, as of November 5, 1993, was $4.625. The Black–Scholes model's estimate is pretty close to the market price of the 35 TOY March call. Remember, though, that the prices quoted in the press are past trade prices, not current bid or ask prices.

Arbitrage Strategy Using the Black–Scholes Model. Someone who believes the Black–Scholes model's estimate of the fundamental value of a call option may be able to employ a simple arbitrage trading strategy. The Black–Scholes model gave a fundamental value for the Toys "Я" Us call of $4.80. Assume its market price is not $4.625 (the actual market price on November 5, 1993), but rather $5.50. According to the Black–Scholes model, the call is overpriced.

Remember the hedge ratio from the binomial option pricing model? It stated the number of shares to buy for every call option written. Since the Black–Scholes model is a mathematical extension of the binomial option pricing model, it includes a hedge ratio, too. The hedge ratio is equal to $-N(d_1)$. The hedge ratio for the TOY option is -0.7203, let's round it off to -0.72. An arbitrager could profit from the overpriced call by buying 720 shares of Toys "Я" Us stock and writing 1,000 of the 35 March call options. (This still assumes that one option buys one share.) If the Black–Scholes model's price is correct, the call is overpriced and, when the market corrects this mistake, the arbitrager makes money regardless of whether the stock price rises or falls.

In the example trade, buying 720 shares at $38 costs $27,360; writing 1,000 calls at $5.50 generates income of $5,500. The net investment is $21,860. Now, assume that the price of TOY either rises to 39 or falls to 37.

If the price rises to 39, the position makes $720 on the stock (720 shares times $1); if the price falls to 37, the stock's value falls by $720. What about the option? The term $N(d_1)$ indicates the change in the price of the option, given a $1 change in the price of the stock. This isn't a change in the market price, but only a change in the option's fundamental value. Given that $N(d_1)$ is 0.72, if TOY rises to 39, the price of the option should be 5.52 ($4.80 + $0.72). Therefore, the option will lose only $20 in value (1,000 times $0.02). If the stock falls to 37, the new option price should be $4.08, giving profit on the option of $1,420 (1,000 times $1.42). The net profit, should TOY decline in price, amounts to $700, the same profit as the price increase. Remember, this assumes that the market eventually recognizes the fact that the option is priced above its fundamental value and corrects this overpricing.

Alternative Strategy Using the Black–Scholes Model. Another way to use the model is to take the current market price of a call option and find the standard deviation implied by the model. (This can be done by many computer programs including Investment Wizard.) The result, called the **implied standard deviation,** indicates the standard deviation necessary to make the call price conform to the Black–Scholes model. If a reliable estimate of the stock's real standard deviation is less than the implied standard deviation, then the call appears overpriced, a lower standard deviation of the underlying stock gives lower value for a call option. To take advantage of this, an option trader could write the call, buy the stock, and wait for the market to correct the price of the call option.

Another strategy is to calculate the implied standard deviation for two call options with the same expiration date, but different strike prices. The option with the higher implied standard deviation seems more overpriced because increases in the standard deviation increase the value of the call. This strategy could be used to devise a money spread by buying the cheaper call option (the one with the lower implied standard deviation) and selling the more expensive call (the one with the higher implied standard deviation).

Before investing your tuition money for next year based on the Black–Scholes model, note a few caveats about the model:

1. The Black–Scholes model does not consider dividend payments that accrue while the hedged position remains outstanding. Recall from the previous section that a dividend payout decreases a call's price.
2. The model assumes that the risk-free rate, r, and the standard deviation of the stock return are constant over time; they may well vary.
3. The model also assumes that stock prices are continuous and no sudden extreme jumps occur. From the Paramount example, we know that the market can give no guarantee of continuous pricing as new information becomes available.
4. The model also assumes that the hedging process is continuously managed so that hedges remain continuously perfect. Unfortunately, the trades necessary to guarantee this would quickly erode any profits through commission costs.

Like all mathematical models, the Black–Scholes formula approximates the real world and it requires caution. Nevertheless, the model has opened a way to price options and other securities that resemble them. The model is widely used by option traders to identify potentially overpriced and underpriced options.

Other Securities That Resemble Options

Several securities have features like those of options, allowing investors to buy or sell something at fixed prices for fixed periods of time. Many of the same pricing rules we have discussed up to this point apply to these securities, as well. The most common securities with option-like features are convertibles and warrants.

Convertible Securities

A **convertible security,** either a bond or a preferred stock issue, gives the holder the right to convert the security for a specified number of shares of common stock in the same company that issued the convertible. The prescribed number of shares obtained when the bond or preferred share is tendered for conversion, referred to as the **conversion ratio,** is normally fixed for the life of the convertible. For example, a conversion ratio of 20 says that a convertible bond can be exchanged for 20 shares of the company's common stock.

To see how a convertible security resembles a call option, let's look at an example. Home Depot, the home improvement retailer, currently has a convertible bond issue outstanding. The convertible has a conversion ratio of 25.81 (meaning that each bond can be exchanged for 25.81 shares of Home Depot common stock), a face value of $1,000, a coupon rate of 4.5 percent, and a maturity date of 1997. This bond gives its owner the right to buy 25.81 shares of Home Depot stock (by exchanging the bond) at a **conversion price** of $38.75 per share ($1,000 divided by the conversion ratio) until the bond matures in 1997. Until the owner exercises the option and converts the bond, it pays $45 per year in coupon interest.

Figure 18.10

Valuing a Convertible Bond

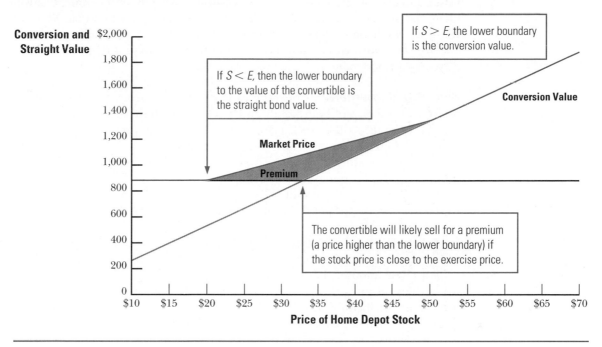

Valuing a Convertible Security. In early November 1993, the Home Depot convertible bond had a market price of $1,200. At the same time, Home Depot's common stock was trading at $40 per share. Multiplying the current stock price (40) by the conversion ratio (25.81) gives the **conversion value** of the bond, $1,032 (rounded to the nearest dollar). In other words, the owner could exchange the bond for common stock worth around $1,032.

In option terminology, the Home Depot convertible bond is in-the-money since the stock price, $40.00, exceeds the conversion price, equivalent to an option's exercise price, of $38.75. Further, the convertible is selling at a premium above its conversion value ($1,200 versus $1,032). Why? As we've discussed, one factor that makes some call options more valuable is the volatility of their underlying stocks. Home Depot has been a volatile stock historically.

The conversion value, of course, has a linear relationship with the stock price, as Figure 18.10 illustrates. Will the conversion value always form the lower boundary to the value of a convertible, regardless of the stock price? The answer is *no*. If the Home Depot convertible didn't have the conversion option, it would simply be a corporate bond with a maturity in 1997 and a coupon rate of 4.5 percent. Presumably it would be valued as such. This is referred to as the convertible's **straight bond value,** the value of the convertible without the conversion feature.

To estimate the straight bond value, find the price of the bond at the same yield to maturity common for straight bonds with similar maturity and quality characteristics. Straight bonds similar to the Home Depot convertible had yields to maturity of around 7.8 percent in early November 1993. Therefore, the bond pricing equation developed in Chapter 16 gives the Home Depot convertible a straight bond value of around $875 per $1,000 of par value. The straight bond value is also plotted on Figure 18.10.

To summarize, the straight bond value is the lower boundary for the value of a convertible if $S < E$. If $S > E$, the lower boundary becomes the conversion value. Will the convertible always sell for a premium over its straight bond value? The answer is *not necessarily;* it depends on the relationship between the stock price and bond's conversion price. If the convertible is deeply out-of-the-money, then it will likely sell for close to its straight bond value. On the other hand, if the convertible is deeply in-the-money, it will likely sell for close to its conversion value. For values in between, like the value of the Home Depot convertible (remember, $S = \$40.00$ and $E = \$38.75$), the convertible will sell for a premium, perhaps a large one, above its straight bond value.

Why Buy Convertibles? Convertibles can offer investors attractive combinations of the best of both bonds and stocks. They have more upside potential than bonds; as the stock price increases, so does the value of the convertible. However, at the same time, convertibles provide more downside protection than stocks; they can always be valued as straight bonds. Furthermore, the coupon rate on a convertible usually exceeds the stock's dividend yield by a substantial amount. The Home Depot convertible has a coupon rate of 4.5 percent; Home Depot's common stock pays an annual dividend of only $0.12 per share, a dividend yield of 0.3 percent.

Convertibles are not perfect securities, however. For one thing, they tend to be rated lower than straight bonds. (The Home Depot convertible is rated A/Baa.) For another, because of the conversion feature, convertibles have lower coupon rates than similar straight bonds. The investor must give up some current income in exchange for the conversion feature. As a result, when considering a convertible, an investor needs to evaluate the prospects for the company's common stock.

Another risk is unique to convertibles: almost all convertibles are callable. Issuers may use the call provision to **force conversion.**[12] Would you, assuming you're a rational investor—and we hope at this point that you are—ever exercise the conversion feature prior to maturity? No! You'd exercise the conversion option only if the convertible were in-the-money. If it is in-the-money, its value will increase dollar for dollar as the stock price increases, while still offering the downside protection of a bond and the higher current income from the coupon payments. When the issuing company wants the convertible bond converted into common stock, if it is deeply in-the-money and the call price is well below the market price, the firm will call the bond. Rather than allowing the company to call the bond in exchange for its par value, you would either convert the bond into common stock or sell the bond to someone else who would.

Warrants

A **warrant** is simply a long-term call option issued by a company. It allows the holder to buy a fixed number of shares of stock (usually one warrant buys one share) from the issuing company at a fixed price for a fixed period of time.[13] Warrants usually have lives between five and ten years when issued. They are often attached to other securities, such as bonds. Most warrants can be detached and sold in the secondary market. Warrants typically trade, along the company's stock, on one of the major stock exchanges.

As an example, the biotechnology company, Genzyme, currently has two warrant issues outstanding. One warrant, issued in 1991 to expire in 1996,

---

[12]The call provision on a bond can be thought of as another sort of call option. In this case, however, the investor has essentially sold a call option to the issuer of the bond; this gives the issuer the right to buy the bond at a fixed price for a fixed period of time.

[13]Some warrants have what is known as a *step up feature*. This means that the exercise price of the warrant rises, or steps up, at predetermined intervals. For example, Intel Corporation has a warrant that expires in 1998. The exercise price steps up each year, from its starting point at $71.50 up to $83.50 about a year before the warrant expires.

allows the holder to buy one share of Genzyme common stock for $38.25. In early November 1993, the warrant was trading for $9 while Genzyme's common stock was trading at $31.50.

Valuing a warrant is similar to valuing a call option. The Genzyme warrant is out-of-the-money ($S < E$) and is selling for a premium of $15.75 ($9.00 + $38.25 − $31.50). That may seem high, but remember that the warrant, unlike a short-term call option, doesn't expire until 1996, and Genzyme is a very volatile stock. (The volatility of biotech stocks was illustrated in Chapter 5, you may remember.)

Trading strategies for warrants are similar to those for call options. Warrants, like call options, have inherent leverage that allows people speculating on the price of a specific stock moving up over the next few months or years. Warrants can also be used to cover, or hedge, a short sale. The downside of warrants is that they are available on only a limited number of stocks and they are often not actively traded.

Chapter Summary

1. **Understand the basic characteristics of option contracts.**

   An option contract gives the buyer the right, but no obligation, to buy or sell a stated number of shares of common stock (usually 100 shares per option) at a specified price, called the *exercise or strike price,* up until a specified point in time, called the *expiration date.* Calls are options to buy and puts are options to sell. Options are considered to be derivative securities—their values derive from those of their underlying stocks. For every option buyer, there must be a seller, or writer. The writer accepts the obligation to buy or sell stock at a specified price up until a specified point in time, at the option buyer's discretion. Options today are traded on organized exchanges, much like stocks and bonds, throughout the world. The largest option market is the Chicago Board Options Exchange. One important feature of the options market is the Options Clearing Corporation. It acts as an agent between the buyer and seller and guarantees that all parties will meet their contractual obligations. In addition to options on individual stocks, options are traded on well-known stock indexes and on foreign currencies. Stock index option positions are settled in cash.

2. **Determine the value of an option at expiration.**

   The value of a call option at expiration is equal to zero if the option is about to expire out-of-the-money (with the stock price less than the exercise price), or the difference between the stock price and the exercise price, if the option is about to expire in-the-money. The value of a put option at expiration is the maximum of zero, if the option is about to expire out-of-the-money, or the difference between the exercise price and the stock price, if the put is about to expire in-the-money. Calculating the profit or loss, at expiration, for both the buyer and writer of calls and puts reveals that options are a zero sum game; if the buyer of an option makes a dollar, the writer of the same option must lose a dollar.

3. **Describe common option trading strategies.**

   Options offer investors unique opportunities, but at the same time, expose them to unique risks. One opportunity comes from options' inherent leverage. Buying a call option produces a much higher return from an increase in a stock's price than simply buying the stock. Leverage, however, is a double-edged sword. The option trader must accurately predict both the direction of a stock's price change, and its timing, as well. Also, the option writer faces potentially unlimited loses. Common option strategies can be divided into two general groups. The first group consists of option positions alone, with no position in the underlying stock. An option buyer must choose both an exercise price and a time until expiration. The buyer of a call takes a greater risk as the exercise price increases and the time until expiration diminishes, but the potential reward increases, as well. A straddle consists of buying both a call and a put on the same underlying stock with the same exercise price and the same time until expiration. Straddles generate higher profits as the volatility of the underlying stock increases. In a spread, a trader buys one option and writes another. The most common type of spread is a money spread. The only difference between the option bought and the option written is the exercise price. Spreads expose investors to less risk than simply buying or writing single options, but offer lower potential returns. The second major group of common option strategies combine option positions with positions in the underlying stocks. In these strategies, options reduce the risk of the stock position, or hedge it. For example, an investor might buy a call option to cover a short sale in the stock.

4. **Review option pricing models.**

   Six factors affect the value of an option prior to expiration. These factors help to explain why some options are worth more than others, and why option prices rise and fall. The factors are: the price of the underlying stock, the exercise price, the time until expiration, the volatility of the underlying stock, the level of interest rates, and the dividends the stock pays between the option's purchase and the expiration date. Option pricing models incorporate these factors to come up with estimates of the intrinsic value of an option. The binomial option pricing model is a simple model that describes a simple world in which the price of a stock at the end of one period must be one of two values. The Black–Scholes option pricing model, widely used by option traders, is a mathematical extension of the binomial option pricing model. It is more complex, and more realistic. The Black–Scholes model incorporates five of the six factors that affect the value of an option prior to expiration.

5. **Discuss other securities that resemble options.**

   Corporations issue two securities that resemble options: convertibles and warrants. A convertible security is a bond or preferred stock issue that can be exchanged for a fixed number of shares of the same company's common stock. This amounts to a call option on the stock. A convertible sells for at least its straight bond value, if it is out-of-the-money, or its conversion value, if it is in-the-money. Convertibles offer investors a number of advantages, including more upside potential than a straight bond, more downside protection than common stock, and higher current income than common stock. Warrants are essentially long-term call options issued by corporations, often attached to other securities. Warrants can be valued like call options, and they can support some of the same investment strategies as call options.

Key Terms

Option	Exercised
Derivative security	Writing an option
Exercise or strike price	Short position
Expiration date	Premium
Call option	Intrinsic value
Put option	Time value
In-the-money	Unexercised
Out-of-the-money	Index options
At-the-money	Arbitrage

Long position	Zero sum game
Hedge	Ex-dividend
Inherent leverage	European option
Straddle	American option
Reverse straddle	Implied standard deviation
Spread	Convertible security
Money spread	Conversion ratio
Bull spread	Conversion price
Bear spread	Conversion value
Covered call	Straight bond value
Protective put	Forcing conversion
Covered short sale	Warrant

Mini Case 1

OBJECTIVES

To find prices, premiums, values at expiration, and profits (losses) for QVC options. (QVC was one of the other parties in the Paramount saga.)

Figure 18.2 listed the following price data for QVC stock and options:

QVC stock: $53\frac{1}{4}$
55 January call option: $4\frac{1}{4}$
55 January put option: $5\frac{3}{4}$

Use this information to answer the following questions:

a. When do the options expire? What rights do they give their buyers?
b. Which option is in-the-money? Find the options' premiums. What does *premium* mean?
c. What will the call and put options be worth when they expire?
d. Construct profit and loss graphs for the call option's buyer and writer.
e. Construct profit and loss graphs for the put option's buyer and writer.

Mini Case 2

OBJECTIVE

Apply the Black–Scholes option pricing model.

a. Using the following data, find the Black–Scholes model's estimate of the intrinsic value of the 25 Wal-Mart December call option. Data are from November 5, 1993.

Stock price: $27\frac{1}{4}$
Exercise price: 25
Risk-free rate of interest: 3.11 percent
Expiration: December 1993 (six weeks hence)
Standard deviation of stock returns: 0.2704
Market price of call = 3.125

b. If the intrinsic value of the option differs from its market price, explain how to arbitrage the mispriced option.

Discussion Questions and Problems

1. What is a derivative security? Why are options considered to be derivative securities?
2. What rights and obligations does the buyer of an option have? How do these differ from the rights and obligations of the writer of the option?

3. Explain cash settlement of index options. Give a numerical example.
4. If a put option has a price of $5 and an exercise price of $50, while the underlying stock is selling for $48, is the put option in-the-money? What is its premium?
5. For the put option described in Question 4, calculate the profit and loss from holding the option to expiration. How much would the price of the stock have to change for the option buyer to break even?
6. What does it mean when we say call options have inherent leverage? What other risks are unique to options?
7. From the option prices shown in Figure 18.2, create a straddle using Pepsi options and find the profit or loss at expiration. Why might a trader create a straddle? What expectations would it imply for Pepsi's common stock?
8. Using the option prices shown in Figure 18.2, create two money spreads using Philip Morris (PhMor) options, one using calls and one using puts, to reflect the expectation that the price of Philip Morris stock should rise. Find the profit and loss of each spread at expiration. Why are spreads considered to be less risky than simply buying or selling individual options?
9. What is a protective put? Illustrate, using the Paramount options listed in Figure 18.2, that the choice of an exercise price is equivalent to choosing a deductible on insurance.
10. Discuss the six factors that affect the value of a call option prior to expiration. How do these relationships change for the value of a put option prior to expiration?
11. The current price of a stock is $50 per share. Next period it will either rise by 20 percent or fall by 10 percent. If the risk-free rate of interest were 5 percent, how much would a call option with an exercise price of $50 be worth now?
12. Give a loose interpretation of the Black–Scholes option pricing model. How realistic are the assumptions made by the model?
13. Assume a convertible bond with a $1,000 face value is convertible into 25 shares of stock. What is the conversion price? If the stock price is currently $50, how much is the conversion value?
14. What are the major investment advantages of convertibles? What are their drawbacks?
15. Why is a warrant just a long-term call option? Why might an investor buy a warrant as opposed to the underlying stock?

Critical Thinking Exercises

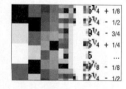

1. This exercise requires computer work. Contained in file OPTION1.XLS on the data disk are recent prices for S&P 100 (OEX) index options. Using the information contained in the file, perform the following calculations and answer the following questions:
   a. Calculate each option's premium. Why are some premiums larger than others?
   b. Construct a straddle and a reverse straddle using the options that are closest to being at the money. Calculate the profit and loss from both at expiration.
   c. Assume that someone believes that the S&P 100 index will rise over the next few weeks. Describe some option trades that would take advantage of this anticipated rise in prices. Which would be the most risky? The least risky?

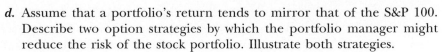

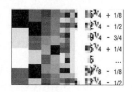

d. Assume that a portfolio's return tends to mirror that of the S&P 100. Describe two option strategies by which the portfolio manager might reduce the risk of the stock portfolio. Illustrate both strategies.

2. This exercise requires both computer work and library research. In file BS1.XLS on the data disk are quarterly returns for the S&P 500 and General Electric. Use these returns to compute standard deviations for both series. Using a recent issue of *The Wall Street Journal* or *Barron's* find the S&P 500 call option and a GE call option with the highest trading volumes and shortest times until expiration.

a. Using the standard computed deviations, along with the other input variables from the financial press, calculate the Black–Scholes model's intrinsic value for the S&P 500 option and the GE option.

b. Comparing the Black–Scholes values to the options' market prices, is either option correctly valued? What could explain differences between the Black–Scholes prices and the market prices?

c. Assume that the calculated standard deviation for GE seems too high, that is, that the implied standard deviation based on the call option price is less than the calculated value. What would this do to the value of the GE call calculated in Part a? Is there an arbitrage possibility here?

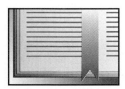

3. This exercise requires library research. Potomac Electric Power has a convertible bond issue outstanding that matures in 2018 and has a coupon rate of 7 percent. Answer the following questions about this bond:

a. What are the bond's conversion ratio and conversion price?

b. What is the bond's current conversion value? Is the convertible currently in the money or out of the money?

c. If this bond were not convertible, for what price would it sell? (What is its straight bond value?)

d. What is the bond's current market price?

e. How much of a premium is included in the bond's current price? Why does this premium seem relatively small?

Mini Case **1**   SOLUTION

a. Options generally expire at the close of trading on the third Friday of the month indicated. The January QVC options expired at the close of trading on January 21, 1994. The buyer of the January call would have had the right to buy 100 shares of QVC stock at $55 per share until January 21, 1994. The buyer of the January put would have had the right to sell 100 shares of QVC stock at $55 per share until January 21, 1994.

b. The call option is out of the money ($S < E$) and the put option is in the money. The call's premium is equal to its price plus the exercise price minus the stock price:

$$\$4.25 + \$55.00 - \$53.25 = \$6.00$$

The put's premium is equal to its price plus the stock price minus the exercise price.

$$\$5.75 + \$53.25 - \$55.00 = \$4.00$$

The premium measures how much the stock price must change (increase in the case of the call, decrease in the case of the put) before the buyer of the option will break even.

c. The value of a call option at expiration = MAX(0, $S - E$). The value of

a put option at expiration = MAX$(0, E - S)$.
d. The profit/loss graphs are shown in Figure 18.11.
e. The profit/loss graphs are shown in Figure 18.12.

Mini Case **2**   SOLUTION

a. Using Equation 18.8, and the information given, finding the value of the Wal-Mart option is matter of several steps. First, find the time until expiration (T). If the option expires in six weeks, $T = 0.1154$ (6 divided by 52). Then find the square root of T: $\sqrt{T} = 0.3397$. Now, find the variance of the underlying stock returns: $(0.2704)^2 = 0.0731$. Next, find d_1 and d_2:

$$d_1 = [in(27.25/25) + 0.1154(0.0311 + 0.0731/2)]/[0.2704(0.3397)]$$
$$= 1.0232$$
$$d_2 = 1.0232 - 0.2704(0.3397) = 0.9313$$

Fourth, find $N(d_1)$ and $N(d_2)$ using the table from Appendix 18A: $N(d_1) = 0.8469$, $N(d_2) = 0.8242$.
Finally, find the value of the call option:

$$C = 27.25(0.8469) - 25e^{-0.0311(0.1154)}(0.8242) = 2.55$$

The option appears to be overpriced.

b. Since the call is overpriced, one might short the call and buy the stock. Since $N(d_1) = 0.8469$, this would require buying 850 shares and writing 1,000 calls (assuming that one call buys one share).

Figure 18.11

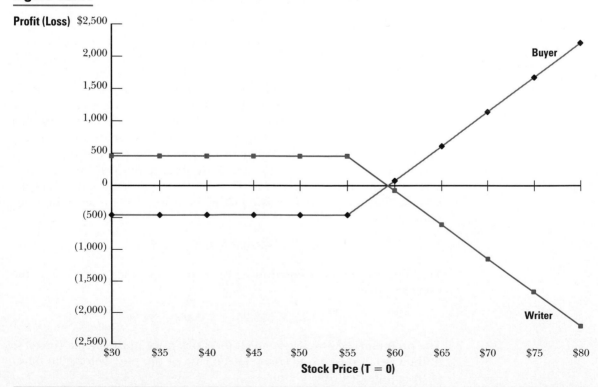

Figure 18.12

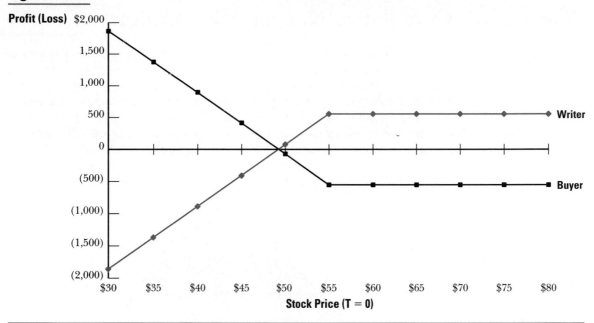

APPENDIX 18A   Cumulative Normal Distribution

The d values are listed from -3.00 to $+3.00$. The table provides the probability for a cumulative normal distribution and it measures the probability that the standard normal value is less than d. Graphically, it measures the area under the curve (or the probability) up to d. For example, if d equals $+1.5$, the number $N(d) = N(+1.5)$. It represents the shaded area up to d (on the horizontal axis) equal to $+1.5$. (See the figure below.) In statistical terms, it measures the probability of a random draw of being less than or equal to $+1.5$. Instead of using calculus and calculating that probability, the table provides the calculated probability for a normal distribution.

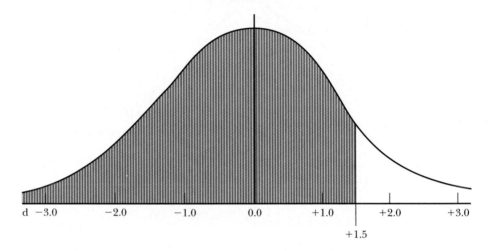

Using the table, if $d = +1.5$, find $+1.5$ in the d column and then find the corresponding $N(d)$ value in the next column to the right. For example, $N(+1.5) = 0.9332$.

d	N(d)	d	N(d)	d	N(d)	d	N(d)
−3.00	.0013	−1.18	.1190	0.02	.5080	1.22	.8888
−2.95	.0016	−1.16	.1230	0.04	.5160	1.24	.8925
−2.90	.0019	−1.14	.1271	0.06	.5239	1.26	.8962
−2.85	.0022	−1.12	.1314	0.08	.5319	1.28	.8997
−2.80	.0026	−1.10	.1357	0.10	.5398	1.30	.9032
−2.75	.0030	−1.08	.1401	0.12	.5478	1.32	.9066
−2.70	.0035	−1.06	.1446	0.14	.5557	1.34	.9099
−2.65	.0040	−1.04	.1492	0.16	.5636	1.36	.9131
−2.60	.0047	−1.02	.1539	0.18	.5714	1.38	.9162
−2.55	.0054	−1.00	.1587	0.20	.5793	1.40	.9192
−2.50	.0062	−0.98	.1635	0.22	.5871	1.42	.9222
−2.45	.0071	−0.96	.1685	0.24	.5948	1.44	.9251
−2.40	.0082	−0.94	.1736	0.26	.6026	1.46	.9279
−2.35	.0094	−0.92	.1788	0.28	.6103	1.48	.9306
−2.30	.0107	−0.90	.1841	0.30	.6179	1.50	.9332
−2.25	.0122	−0.88	.1894	0.32	.6255	1.52	.9357
−2.20	.0139	−0.86	.1949	0.34	.6331	1.54	.9382
−2.15	.0158	−0.84	.2005	0.36	.6406	1.56	.9406
−2.10	.0179	−0.82	.2061	0.38	.6480	1.58	.9429
−2.05	.0202	−0.80	.2119	0.40	.6554	1.60	.9452
−2.00	.0228	−0.78	.2177	0.42	.6628	1.62	.9474
−1.98	.0239	−0.76	.2236	0.44	.6700	1.64	.9495
−1.96	.0250	−0.74	.2297	0.46	.6773	1.66	.9515
−1.94	.0262	−0.72	.2358	0.48	.6844	1.68	.9535
−1.92	.0274	−0.70	.2420	0.50	.6915	1.70	.9554
−1.90	.0287	−0.68	.2483	0.52	.6985	1.72	.9573
−1.88	.0301	−0.66	.2546	0.54	.7054	1.74	.9591
−1.86	.0314	−0.64	.2611	0.56	.7123	1.76	.9608
−1.84	.0329	−0.62	.2676	0.58	.7191	1.78	.9625
−1.82	.0344	−0.60	.2743	0.60	.7258	1.80	.9641
−1.80	.0359	−0.58	.2810	0.62	.7324	1.82	.9656
−1.78	.0375	−0.56	.2877	0.64	.7389	1.84	.9671
−1.76	.0392	−0.54	.2946	0.66	.7454	1.86	.9686
−1.74	.0409	−0.52	.3015	0.68	.7518	1.88	.9699
−1.72	.0427	−0.50	.3085	0.70	.7580	1.90	.9713
−1.70	.0446	−0.48	.3156	0.72	.7642	1.92	.9726
−1.68	.0465	−0.46	.3228	0.74	.7704	1.94	.9738
−1.66	.0485	−0.44	.3300	0.76	.7764	1.96	.9750
−1.64	.0505	−0.42	.3373	0.78	.7823	1.98	.9761
−1.62	.0526	−0.40	.3446	0.80	.7882	2.00	.9772
−1.60	.0548	−0.38	.3520	0.82	.7939	2.05	.9798
−1.58	.0571	−0.36	.3594	0.84	.7996	2.10	.9821
−1.56	.0594	−0.34	.3669	0.86	.8051	2.15	.9842
−1.54	.0618	−0.32	.3745	0.88	.8106	2.20	.9861
−1.52	.0643	−0.30	.3821	0.90	.8159	2.25	.9878
−1.50	.0668	−0.28	.3897	0.92	.8212	2.30	.9893
−1.48	.0694	−0.26	.3974	0.94	.8264	2.35	.9906
−1.46	.0721	−0.24	.4052	0.96	.8315	2.40	.9918
−1.44	.0749	−0.22	.4129	0.98	.8365	2.45	.9929
−1.42	.0778	−0.20	.4207	1.00	.8414	2.50	.9938
−1.40	.0808	−0.18	.4286	1.02	.8461	2.55	.9946
−1.38	.0838	−0.16	.4365	1.04	.8508	2.60	.9953
−1.36	.0869	−0.14	.4443	1.06	.8554	2.65	.9960
−1.34	.0901	−0.12	.4523	1.08	.8599	2.70	.9965
−1.32	.0934	−0.10	.4602	1.10	.8643	2.75	.9970
−1.30	.0968	−0.08	.4681	1.12	.8686	2.80	.9974
−1.28	.1003	−0.06	.4761	1.14	.8729	2.85	.9978
−1.26	.1038	−0.04	.4841	1.16	.8770	2.90	.9981
−1.24	.1075	−0.02	.4920	1.18	.8810	2.95	.9984
−1.22	.1112	0.00	.5000	1.20	.8849	3.00	.9986
−1.20	.1151						

Chapter 19

Futures Contracts

Chapter Objectives

1. Describe futures contracts and the mechanics of futures trading.
2. Provide a primer on the pricing of futures contracts.
3. Discuss the uses of futures contracts.
4. Take a closer look at financial futures.
5. Understand options on futures.

Suppose you're in the market for a new car, so you visit the local dealer who is selling this year's hottest new model. At the dealership, the dealer doesn't have a car to sell you right now. The dealer will have the model you want in one month. Waiting a month for delivery is actually better for you, since you'd like to be able to sell your old car to raise money for the down payment. You and the dealer might enter into a binding contract in which you agree to take delivery of the car in one month at a specified price and the dealer agrees to deliver the car in one month at the same price. This kind of agreement is commonly called a **forward contract.**

Most economic transactions occur in the spot, or cash, market, however, where the buyer takes delivery of the asset from the seller immediately. As the above example illustrates, the buyer, and/or the seller, may not desire to complete the transaction immediately, but rather at some future date. For these individuals, forward contracts offer a way of locking in the price of the asset today and, further, guaranteeing that the transaction will be completed at a future date.

If a forward contract is an agreement between a buyer and seller that stipulates the future delivery of some asset, at a specified price, what is a futures contract? A **futures contract** is simply a highly standardized version of a forward contract. Futures contracts specify standard amounts, delivery dates, and so forth. Unlike forward contracts, futures contracts are marketable and trade on organized exchanges, subject to specific rules.

In this chapter we will examine futures contracts, through which people take positions in such assets as Treasury bonds, Japanese yen, soybeans, pork bellies, orange juice, gold, and crude oil. Like options, which we discussed in Chapter 18, futures are considered to be derivative securities, which means, as you may recall, that their values derive from underlying assets. Also like options, futures are considered to be speculative in nature; options and futures are inherently more risky than more traditional financial assets such as stocks and bonds. However, as we also saw in Chapter 18, and as we will discuss in this chapter, both options and futures can be used to *reduce* the risks associated with stock and bond positions.

We begin Chapter 19 with a description of futures contracts and a discussion of the mechanics of futures trading. We'll discuss the types of contracts available, how trading is conducted, and the role of the clearing corporation. Next, we provide a primer on the pricing of futures. We focus on the relationship between current spot prices of assets, expected future spot prices, and futures contract prices. Are futures prices, for example, related to expected future spot prices? We then discuss the uses of futures contracts, covering both hedging and speculative trading strategies. Our next topic is a closer look at financial futures, including interest rate futures and stock index futures. Finally, we'll take a brief look at options on futures.

What Are Futures?

A futures contract is a binding, legal contract that calls for the future delivery of an asset. The contract specifies the asset to be delivered, the delivery location, the amount to be delivered, the delivery date, and the price. A futures contract has two parties, or positions: the long position and the short position. The person who holds the **long position** agrees to accept delivery of the asset, at the terms specified by the contract, while the person who holds the **short position** agrees to deliver the asset, again at the terms specified by the contract. Someone who goes long in July corn at $2.50 per bushel agrees to accept delivery of 5,000 bushels (the size of one corn contract) in July at a price of $2.50 per bushel. It's important to note that there *must* be a short position for every long position.

Trading in futures, like that in options, is considered to be a zero sum game. If someone makes a dollar in a futures position, the person who holds the opposite position must lose a dollar. If the price of a futures contract rises by a certain amount, the wealth of the long position increases by that amount, while the short position's wealth declines by that amount.

Does the holder of the long position have to take delivery of the corn? The answer is *yes,* if the position remains open until the delivery date. However, prior to the actual delivery date he or she can close out the position merely by taking the opposite position in the same contract. For example, someone who is long in July corn can close out the position by going short in July corn. Most futures traders have no intention of taking delivery, or delivering, the assets they trade; the large majority close out their positions prior to their delivery dates.

An example of a futures contract summary appears in Figure 19.1. The figure shows the highlights of the futures contract on U.S. Treasury bonds. The contract sets pretty specific terms for such things as size ($100,000 face value), deliverable grade (any Treasury bond with at least 15 years remaining to call), delivery months (March, June, September, and December) and delivery method (Federal Reserve book entry wire transfer system).

Evolution of Modern Futures Markets

The historical origins of forward and futures contracts go back to ancient civilizations. There is evidence that the Greeks and Romans actively traded instruments that we would recognize today as forward contracts. Roman emperors are said to have engaged in active forward contracting to ensure that grain was available during winter.

The origins of modern futures exchanges can be traced to the establishment, in 1848, of the Chicago Board of Trade (CBOT). In the mid-1800s, Chicago was rapidly becoming a major transportation and distribution center

Figure 19.1

Contract Highlights: U.S. Treasury Bond Futures

Size	$100,000 face value U.S. Treasury bonds.
Deliverable Grade	U.S. Treasury bonds maturing at least 15 years from date of delivery, if not callable; if callable, not so for at least 15 years from the first day of the delivery month. Coupon based on an 8 percent standard.
Price Quotation	In points ($1,000) and thirty-seconds of a point; for example, 92-16 equals $92\frac{16}{32}$.
Minimum Price Fluctuation	One thirty-second of a point, or $31.25 (one tick) per contract.
Daily Trading Limits	3 points ($3,000) per contract above or below the previous day's settlement price.
Months Traded	March, June, September, and December.
Trading Hours	8 a.m. to 2 p.m. (Chicago time), Monday through Friday. Evening trading hours are from 5 to 8:30 p.m. (Central Standard time) or 6 to 9 p.m. (Daylight Saving time), Sunday through Thursday.[a]
Ticker Symbol	US
Last Trading Day	Seven business days prior to the last business day of the month.
Last Delivery Day	Last business day of the month.
Delivery Method	Federal Reserve book entry wire transfer system.

[a] Subject to change

Source: *CBOT Financial Instruments Guide,* Chicago Board of Trade (1987), 37. Courtesy of the Chicago Board of Trade.

for agricultural products, especially grains such as corn and wheat. Farmers shipped their grain to Chicago for sale and distribution eastward along rail and water shipping channels. The problem, of course, is that grain production in the Midwest is seasonal in nature. At harvest time, supplies would soar, often overwhelming the city's storage facilities, and prices would plunge. Then as supplies were used up through the winter and spring, prices would soar.

To alleviate some of the problems associated with the seasonal nature of grain production, the newly formed CBOT began to offer farmers what were known as *to arrive contracts*.[1] These contracts allowed farmers to deliver their grain at predetermined future dates at prices set in advance of delivery. Financiers soon discovered that these contracts allowed them to speculate on grain prices without having to worry about taking delivery of the grain and storing it.[2] Modern futures trading had begun.

In late 1874, a second futures exchange was established in Chicago. Initially named the Chicago Produce Exchange, it concentrated on futures contracts in meat and livestock. In 1898, the exchange was renamed the Chicago Mercantile Exchange. Also in the late 1800s, the Coffee, Sugar & Cocoa Exchange and the New York Cotton Exchange were formed in New York. Other futures exchanges, both in the United States and the rest of the world, soon followed.

[1]The CBOT was formed initially to standardize both the quantity and quality of grains bought and sold in the city of Chicago.

[2]In the futures markets, *hedgers* are classified as traders with cash positions in assets, such as farmers. By contrast, *speculators* are traders who have no cash positions in the assets they trade.

Development of Financial Futures. Prior to 1972, futures trading was limited to physical commodities such as grains, cotton, and metals. In 1972, the International Monetary Market (IMM), a subsidiary of the Chicago Mercantile Exchange, was created in response to the 1971 decision by most western nations to allow their currency exchange rates to fluctuate. The IMM began offering futures contracts on foreign currencies; these were the first **financial futures.** This was followed in 1975 by the introduction at the CBOT of the first futures contract on an interest-bearing financial instrument, the GNMA mortgage pass-through security. In 1976, the IMM introduced a futures contract on 90-day Treasury bills and in 1977, the CBOT introduced a futures contract on long-term Treasury bonds. It soon became the most successful new contract of all time.

The early 1980s saw the emergence of stock index futures contracts. In 1982, the Kansas City Board of Trade launched a futures contract based on the Value Line Index. This was followed a few months later by the Chicago Mercantile Exchange's introduction of a futures contract based on the S&P 500. By the mid-1980s, trading in financial futures exceeded trading in commodity futures.

Today's Futures Exchanges. Approximately 14 exchanges handle futures trading in the United States today. In addition, another 11 major futures exchanges operate in other parts of the world. The two largest futures exchanges are still the two oldest: the Chicago Board of Trade and the Chicago Mercantile Exchange. In 1992, these two exchanges accounted for approximately 40 percent of all futures trading worldwide. Several of the fastest growing futures exchanges, however, are located outside the United States. The Singapore International Monetary Exchange, established only in 1984, has emerged as a major trading center for financial futures, especially currency futures, in recent years.

One characteristic of today's futures exchanges, especially those in the United States, is exchange specialization. One exchange tends to dominate trading in a specific asset. Virtually all trading in Treasury bond and note futures, for example, takes place on the Chicago Board of Trade. Trading in petroleum futures is dominated by the New York Mercantile Exchange. The exchanges compete intensely to introduce new contracts. Once a successful new contract is introduced, the exchange that introduced it will likely develop a near monopoly in trading in that contract.

In the United States, futures trading is regulated by the Commodity Futures Trading Commission (CFTC), rather than the Securities and Exchange Commission. Even futures on stocks and bonds are regulated by the CFTC. Several bills have been introduced in Congress that would eliminate the CFTC and give regulatory power over futures trading to the SEC.

Types of Contracts

We can initially divide futures contracts into those based on physical commodities and those based on financial instruments. We can divide physical commodities contracts into those based on agricultural products (grains and oilseeds, livestock and meat, and food and fiber) and those based on non-agricultural products (lumber, metals, and petroleum). Financial futures can be divided into three, more specific categories (currency futures, stock index futures, and interest rate futures). The major futures contracts traded on U.S. futures exchanges, along with the dominant exchange for each, are listed in Table 19.1.

Requirements for a Viable Futures Market. In order for an asset to develop a viable futures market, it must have five characteristics: (1) the ability to be

Table 19.1

Major Futures Contracts Listed on U.S. Exchanges

Contract	Exchange	Contract	Exchange	Contract	Exchange
Grains and Oilseeds		**Metals & Petroleum**		**Stock Index**	
Corn	CBOT	Copper	COMEX	Nikkei 225	CME
Oats	CBOT	Crude oil	NYMEX	Major Market Index	CBOT
Soybeans	CBOT	Gold	COMEX	NYSE Index	NYFE
Soybean meal	CBOT	Heating oil	NYMEX	S&P 500	CME
Soybean oil	CBOT	Natural gas	NYMEX	**Interest Rate**	
Wheat	CBOT	Palladium	NYMEX	Eurodollar	CME
Livestock and Meat		Platinum	NYMEX	Municipal bond index	CBOT
Feeder Cattle	CME	Propane	NYMEX	Treasury bills	CME
Hogs	CME	Silver	COMEX	Treasury bonds	CBOT
Live cattle	CME	Unleaded gasoline	NYMEX	Treasury notes (10 year)	CBOT
Pork bellies	CME	**Foreign Currency**		Treasury notes (5 year)	CBOT
Food and Fiber		Australian dollar	CME	Treasury notes (2 year)	CBOT
Cocoa	CSCE	British pound	CME		
Coffee	CSCE	Canadian dollar	CME		
Cotton	NYCTN	German mark	CME		
Domestic sugar	CSCE	Japanese yen	CME		
Orange juice	NYCTN	Swiss franc	CME		
Rice	CRCE				
World sugar	CSCE				

Notes: CBOT is the Chicago Board of Trade; CME is the Chicago Mercantile Exchange (or a one of its subsidiaries); COMEX is the Commodity Exchange; CRCE is the Chicago Rice and Coffee Exchange; CSCE is the Coffee, Sugar & Cocoa Exchange; NYCTN is the New York Cotton Exchange; NYFE is the New York Futures Exchange; and NYMEX is the New York Mercantile Exchange.

standardized, (2) active demand, (3) the ability to be stored for a period of time, (4) relatively high value in proportion to bulk, and (5) relatively high value in proportion to storage and other carrying costs. As an example, consider gold. Gold can be standardized (by purity grades, for example). It is subject to active demand; some 20 million ounces of gold are bought and sold each year. Gold can be stored; it doesn't deteriorate over time. It is valuable in proportion to its bulk; one pound of gold is worth approximately $5,600. Finally, the cost of storing and carrying gold for a period of time is probably less than 5 percent of its value.

Mechanics of Futures Trading

As with the world's stock exchanges, futures exchanges have become more and more automated in recent years. Some foreign futures markets conduct all trading via computer systems; in some cases, no trading takes place on the floor of the exchange (similar to trading on the NASDAQ system or the London Stock Exchange).

In the United States, futures markets, particularly the two largest, the Chicago Board of Trade and the Chicago Mercantile Exchange, still retain much of the traditional futures trading system.[3] In this **open outcry system,** trading takes place on the floor of the exchange, where traders stand in **trading pits** (each contract is assigned to one pit) and bid against one another. They shout out buy and sell bids and use hand signals to communicate to other

---

[3]While it is possible to trade electronically on both the CBOT and the CME, it's hard to believe that either exchange would ever totally abandon the trading floor and the open outcry trading system.

traders. Every trader standing in the pit has, at least in theory, an equal chance of trading. Unlike the NYSE or NASDAQ, futures exchanges do not have specialists or market makers as such. Generally, all traders are allowed to trade all contracts listed on the exchange, though many traders choose to specialize in particular futures contracts.

Who Are the Traders? All traders must be either members of the exchange or employees of members. Some people trade on the floor by leasing trading privileges from a member. The CBOT, for example, currently has about 3,600 members. Like NYSE seats, memberships are bought and sold. Recently, a CBOT membership was sold for around $450,000.

Traders can be grouped into three general categories. **Commission brokers** trade strictly for others. **Local traders** trade strictly for their own, or their firms', accounts. **Dual traders** perform both functions, sometimes acting as brokers and sometimes trading for their own accounts.

Local and dual traders can also be classified in terms of trading style. **Scalpers** attempt to profit from small changes in the contract prices; they rarely hold positions open for more than a few minutes. **Day traders** also attempt to profit from short-term market movements; while holding positions much longer than scalpers, they do not hold positions overnight. Finally, **position traders** hold positions open over much longer periods of time and attempt to profit from longer-term market movements.

Controversy over Dual Trading. Some argue that dual trading is an open invitation to fraud. Traders, they argue, will be tempted to take advantage of their customers by trading in advance of big customer orders (e.g., slipping in their own buy orders prior to executing big customer orders). In August 1989, 48 traders from the CBOT and CME were indicted on 600 counts of fraud, many of them involving dual trading; 34 of the 48 were convicted in early 1991. In response to pressure from various sources, the Chicago Mercantile Exchange banned most forms of dual trading, though the Chicago Board of Trade did not. The controversy over dual trading continues, as the commentary by David Greising, reprinted in the Investment Insights feature on pages 664–665, suggests.

Placing an Order. Placing an order to buy or sell a futures contract (go long or go short) is similar to placing an order to buy or sell stocks or bonds. In response to the order, the broker contacts the firm's trading desk on the floor of the exchange. The order is relayed to the firm's floor broker, or a dual trader that handles the firm's orders, for execution. After execution, the same chain returns confirmation of the trade. Futures traders can place the same types of orders we discussed in Chapter 3 (market orders, stop-loss orders, limit orders, good until canceled orders, and day orders). Commissions on futures trades vary widely from firm to firm. Some brokerage firms do not offer futures trading services for their customers.

Role of the Clearinghouse. A feature unique to the options and futures markets is the clearinghouse, or clearing corporation. Each futures market operates a clearinghouse as a nonprofit corporation owned by members of the exchange. The clearinghouse acts as both an intermediary and guarantor to every trade.[4] The first clearinghouse was organized by the Chicago Board of Trade in 1925.

---

[4]Each trader must have an account with a so-called *clearing firm* and the clearing firms, technically, own the exchange's clearinghouse. All clearing firms must meet minimum standards of financial responsibility.

Table 19.2

Daily Resettlement Example

On October 29, the account went long in December T-bonds at 115 and the position remained open until November 12. The initial value of the contract is $115,000 (1.15 × $100,000). This amount requires a $5,000 initial margin and a $4,000 maintenance margin.

Date	Settlement Price	Daily Mark to Market	Initial Account Balance	Deposit (Withdrawal)	Ending Account Balance
Oct. 29	$115,000		$ 0	$5,000	$5,000
Nov. 1	114,500	($ 500)	4,500	0	4,500
Nov. 2	113,000	(1,500)	3,000	2,000	5,000
Nov. 3	112,500	(500)	4,500	0	4,500
Nov. 4	111,750	(750)	3,750	1,250	5,000
Nov. 5	112,500	750	5,750	0	5,750
Nov. 8	113,000	500	6,250	0	6,250
Nov. 9	113,000	0	6,250	0	6,250
Nov. 10	112,500	(500)	5,750	0	5,750
Nov. 11	114,500	2,000	7,750	0	7,750
Nov. 12	116,500	2,000	9,750	(9,750)	0

In a futures trade, as we've noted, there must be a short position for every long position, and vice versa. Both parties have promised to fulfill certain contractual obligations (deliver, or take delivery, of the asset at the agreed upon price at the agreed upon time). Without a clearinghouse, each party would have to depend on the other party to fulfill his or her contractual obligations. If one party failed to meet his or her obligations, the other party would be left with a worthless claim.

The clearinghouse guarantees that both parties fulfill their contractual obligations by acting as a counterparty in each trade. Let's say a trader decides to go long in July corn. In order to do this, the trader must find someone to go short. (We'll call that person Trader X.) The clearinghouse would establish a short position in July corn with the first trader, who wants to go long in July corn, and, at the same time, it would establish a long position in July corn with Trader X.

Margins and Daily Price Limits. In a futures transaction, both parties must post margin deposits (either in cash or, in some cases, Treasury bills). After satisfying this initial margin requirement, they must also meet maintenance margin requirements. The margin, a percentage of the contract's value, acts as a good faith security deposit.[5] At the end of each trading day, a committee of traders and clearinghouse officials meet to establish a **settlement price** for each contract. Based on that settlement price, each open account is **marked to market** daily. Depending on whether a trader is long or short, and whether the current settlement price is higher or lower than the previous day's settlement price, that trader's margin will either rise or fall. Margin transactions are best illustrated with an example.

Assume someone takes a long position in December T-bonds at 115 on October 29, 1993. This trader must post an initial margin of $5,000 and maintain a margin of $4,000. Suppose the position remains open until November 12, 1993. Table 19.2 shows the settlement prices and transactions

---

[5]In stock trading, remember, margin is the amount of your money the investor must put up to buy a stock. The rest is borrowed (the margin loan). Futures traders do not borrow money.

One Taboo the Chicago Merc Should Maintain

Remember dual trading? That's the practice, commonplace in the capital markets, whereby brokers trade for their own accounts while also handling customer orders. It's also either: (a) an invitation for traders to make a nefarious buck by trading in advance of customer orders or (b) a vital contributor to liquidity in the marketplace. Hint: it does help liquidity—in the bank accounts of rogue traders.

It's not that dual trading is inherently wrong but rather that dual traders may be too easily tempted to take advantage of their customers. And it wasn't too long ago that the Chicago Mercantile Exchange agreed. The Merc banned the practice just this past May, in the wake of a government sting operation in Chicago's commodities pits. Bowing before the political firestorm that followed the indictment of 48 commodities traders in mid-1989, and with 34 of them found guilty by early 1991, the Merc prohibited most

forms of dual trading even as the rival Chicago Board of Trade did nothing. This move was often cited by Merc officials as proof of their fealty to ethics and fair dealing.

Restless. And the Merc was justified in congratulating itself for the ban, because dual trading can spawn a host of abuses. Some brokers can't resist the temptation to illicitly make money by slipping in a personal trade just before executing a big customer order. Others illegally tip off nearby traders to their incoming order flow and, in return, get a favorable price on a subsequent trade. And dual trading enables unscrupulous brokers to steal profits from their customers by diverting the most lucrative trades to their own accounts, leaving their customers with less profitable transactions. Such activities were revealed in the government's four-year investigation of the commodities markets.

Now, less than a year after the ban took effect, some Merc brokers are agitating for a return to the old days.

Some 500, of a total of 2,700 floor traders, have signed a petition requesting that the Merc lift the ban on dual trading. The Merc's board is

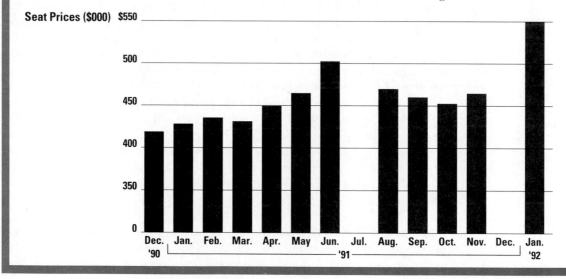

Seat Prices ($000)

for the margin account during the two-week period. After the initial margin deposit of $5,000 on October 29, over the next two trading days (November 1 and 2), the price of December T-bonds falls from 115 to 113, a loss of $2,000 on the contract. At the end of trading on November 2, only $3,000 remains in the margin account. Since the account must maintain $4,000, the trader is subject to a $2,000 **margin call.** In order to keep the position open, he or she must deposit another $2,000 into the account, bring the margin back up to the *initial* amount, $5,000.[6] The table shows another margin call of $1,250 on November 4.

---

[6]Depending on the brokerage firm, the trader may not have to deposit the entire $2,000 immediately in order to keep the position open. After bringing the margin back up to $4,000 immediately, the trader may be allowed a few days to deposit the other $1,000. The table assumes a deposit of the entire $2,000 on November 2.

set to deliberate the matter at a February meeting.

This is no mere intramural squabble but rather a test of the adequacy of self-regulation in the commodities business. The dual-trading prohibition was put into place to appease Congress, which was displeased by the investigation's findings. But Capitol Hill has moved on to other crises, leaving the Merc to police itself. Indeed, reviving dual trading may well arouse the suspicions of legislators and regulators who believe the Chicago exchanges never took to heart the main lesson of the trading scandal: that the pits are vulnerable to a variety of trading abuses.

The Merc's chairman, John F. Sandner, is neutral in the latest debate on the issue, but he feels that the exchange is being held to a too lofty standard. After all, he notes, dual trading is commonplace on stock exchanges, in the over-the-counter market-maker system, and in almost all capital markets. "Our institution is being measured against utopia," Sandner complains. "When you're measured against utopia, you fall short."

The "nobody's perfect" justification offers little solace to victims of unscrupulous brokers. And the claim that "everybody does it" is unconvincing in light of dual-trading chicanery in other markets, such as the Milken/Drexel manipulation of the junk-bond markets or Salomon Brothers Inc.'s overbidding for government securities. And let's not forget the penny-stock ripoffs that are another manifestation of dual trading run amok.

'Two Masters.' From the customer standpoint, the value of the dual-trading ban has never been in doubt. "You can't serve two masters," says William Rafter, a former floor trader, now a futures-fund manager with Prism Asset Management of New York. Others note that the open-outcry system in the pits makes dual-trading abuses hard to detect. Says John A. Wing,

chairman of Chicago Corp.: "They would have to have a lot better audit-trail system before I would be satisfied with dual trading."

INVESTMENT INSIGHTS

In fact, the Merc points out that a better audit system is under development, one that would catch any abuse of dual trading if the practice is reinstated. The Chicago exchanges are putting the finishing touches on handheld, computerized trading cards that would track trades on a real-time basis. The new audit system is indeed promising, but it should be put into operation and proven effective before a revival of dual trading is considered.

Putting aside the issue of whether dual-trading abuses exist or can be detected, there is one overriding concern: Why do it? Why lift the ban? Brokers argue that dual trading makes markets more liquid by making everybody in the pits a potential trader. But despite the dual-trading ban, the Merc last year turned in record volume. Customers have no problem getting orders filled. And seat prices of $550,000 are near the high point set just before the 1987 stock market crash. The market has assessed the dual-trading ban—and decided that the new system works. If the Merc fails to reach the same conclusion, it will be a triumph of greed over not only ethics but just plain common sense.

Source: David Greising, "One Taboo the Chicago Merc Should Maintain," *Business Week*, February 3, 1992, 71. Reprinted from February 3, 1992 issue of *Business Week* by special permission, copyright © 1992 by McGraw-Hill, Inc.

Over the next few days, the price of December T-bonds moves up and down, and the margin follows. The trader faces no additional margin calls because the margin remains above $4,000.[7] Finally, after closing out the position on November 12 at 116.5, $9,750 remains in the margin account. How much did the trade make? The answer is $1,500 ($9,750 − $5,000 − $2,000 − $1,250), about a 23 percent return ($1,500/$6,500).

Partly because a trader must post only a small percentage of the contract's value as margin, many contracts limit the maximum daily price change (for T-bonds, as Figure 19.1 shows, the daily price limit is plus or minus 3 points, ± $3,000 per contract). If the contract price moves up or down by the

---

[7]Notice that between November 5 and November 11, the margin account holds more than $5,000. Some brokerage firms would allow the trader to withdraw the excess amount to bring the margin down to $5,000. The table assumes that he or she doesn't do this, however.

maximum amount, the contract is said to be **limit up** or **limit down**. Normally, no trading can take place at prices outside the daily price limits. However, the exchanges can, under certain circumstances, increase daily price limits to help ensure orderly markets.

Delivery Procedure. As we noted earlier, most traders have no intention of taking delivery, or delivering, the asset in which they trade futures. The major exceptions to this are Treasury bond and note futures. According to some estimates, delivery actually takes place on as many as 10 percent of all Treasury bond and note contracts. The delivery procedure used by the Chicago Board of Trade for Treasury bonds and notes is detailed in Figure 19.2. In addition, the figure shows the relevant dates for the March 1994 contract. Notice that the short position initiates the delivery sequence. Also note the role of the clearinghouse (called the Board of Trade Clearing Corporation, BOTCC) in the delivery procedure. Among other things, the BOTCC assigns the specific long position to take delivery for each open short position.

Futures Pricing Primer

In this section we review the pricing of futures contracts, covering two theories of futures pricing. One theory suggests that futures prices and expected spot prices are related, while the other theory denies any relationship between futures prices and expected spot prices. Before we discuss these two theories, we must introduce several important pricing concepts. We begin with a discussion of how to read futures price quotations in the financial press.

Futures Price Quotations

Figure 19.3 reproduces a sample set of futures price quotations for one trading day. For example, the first quote refers to a contract on corn traded on the Chicago Board of Trade in amounts of 5,000 bushels per contract, with prices stated in cents per bushel. Delivery dates for these contracts run from March 1994 to July 1995. The March 1994 contract opened on January 13, 1994 at 310.00 cents per bushel; it traded as high as 311.75, and as low as 307.50, settling at 310.00. The settlement price represented an increase of 5.25 cents from the prior day's settlement price. Over its life, the March 1994 corn contract had traded as high as 311.75 and as low as 232.75 as of the day of the quote. Open interest was 134,635 contracts. (We'll define *open interest* shortly.) On January 13, approximately 85,000 corn contracts, summing all delivery dates, were traded and open interest decreased by about 1,990 contracts. (Almost 45,000 contracts had been traded the prior day.)

Open Interest. **Open interest** refers to the number of contracts outstanding at any point in time. Remember, each contract must have both a long and a short position. As of January 13, 1994, traders had taken approximately 135,000 long positions and 135,000 short positions in March 1994 corn. Open interest changes constantly as contracts are traded. To see how transactions affect open interest, take a look at the hypothetical example shown in Table 19.3.

The table's hypothetical futures market has five trading days and five participants. During the first day, A goes long in 10 contracts; B takes the short position. Open interest increases by 10 contracts. During the second trading day, C goes long in 10 contracts; D takes the short position. Open interest increases again by 10 contracts.

Figure 19.2

Delivery Procedures for Treasury Bonds and Notes: March 1994 Contract

Date	Long Position	Clearing Corporation	Short Position
The process begins two business days prior to the named delivery month.			
First position day (Friday, February 25)	By 8:00 p.m., two business days before the first day allowed for deliveries in the month, the long and short report all open positions to the Clearing Corporation by origin, house, or customer. They also must report any changes each day as they occur.		
Day 1: Position Day (as early as February 25)			By 8:00 p.m., the short notifies a clearing member of the intention to make delivery. The clearing member then files a Delivery Notice with the Board of Trade Clearing Corporation. This cannot be canceled.
Day 2: Notice of Intention Day[a] (as early as February 28)	By 4:00 p.m., the long provides the short with the name and location of his or her bank.	By 8:30 a.m., the Clearing Corporation matches the oldest long to the short and then notifies both clearing members.	By 2:00 p.m., using calculations based on the Position Day settlement price, the short invoices the long through the BOTCC.
Day 3: Delivery Day (as early as March 1, last delivery date March 31)	By 1:00 p.m., the long clearing member's bank has accepted Treasury bonds or notes by book entry and, at the same time, paid the invoice amount via the Fed system to the short clearing member's account.		Short and long have until 9:30 a.m. to resolve invoice differences. By 10:00 a.m., the short deposits the bonds or notes to be delivered and instructs the bank to wire them to the long's account versus payment.

The process ends on the final business day of the named delivery month.
All times refer to Central Standard time

[a]On the second to last business day of the delivery month, or the last Notice of Intention Day, invoicing must occur by 3:00 p.m.

Source: *The Delivery Process in Brief,* Chicago Board of Trade (1990), p. 14. Courtesy of the Chicago Board of Trade.

Notice what happens, however, on Days 3 and 4. Trader B, who went short on Day 1, closes out the position by going long in 10 contracts; E takes the short position. This is considered to be a trade of existing contracts (E replaces B) and has no affect on open interest. The same thing is true on Day 4 when D, who went short on Day 2, closes out the position (F replaces D). On the last day, E closes out a short position by going long. In the same trade, A also closes out a long position by going short. This trade *decreases* open interest by 10 contracts. At the end of the five-day trading period, only C and F still have open positions, so total open interest equals 10 contracts.

Figure 19.3

Price Quotes for Futures

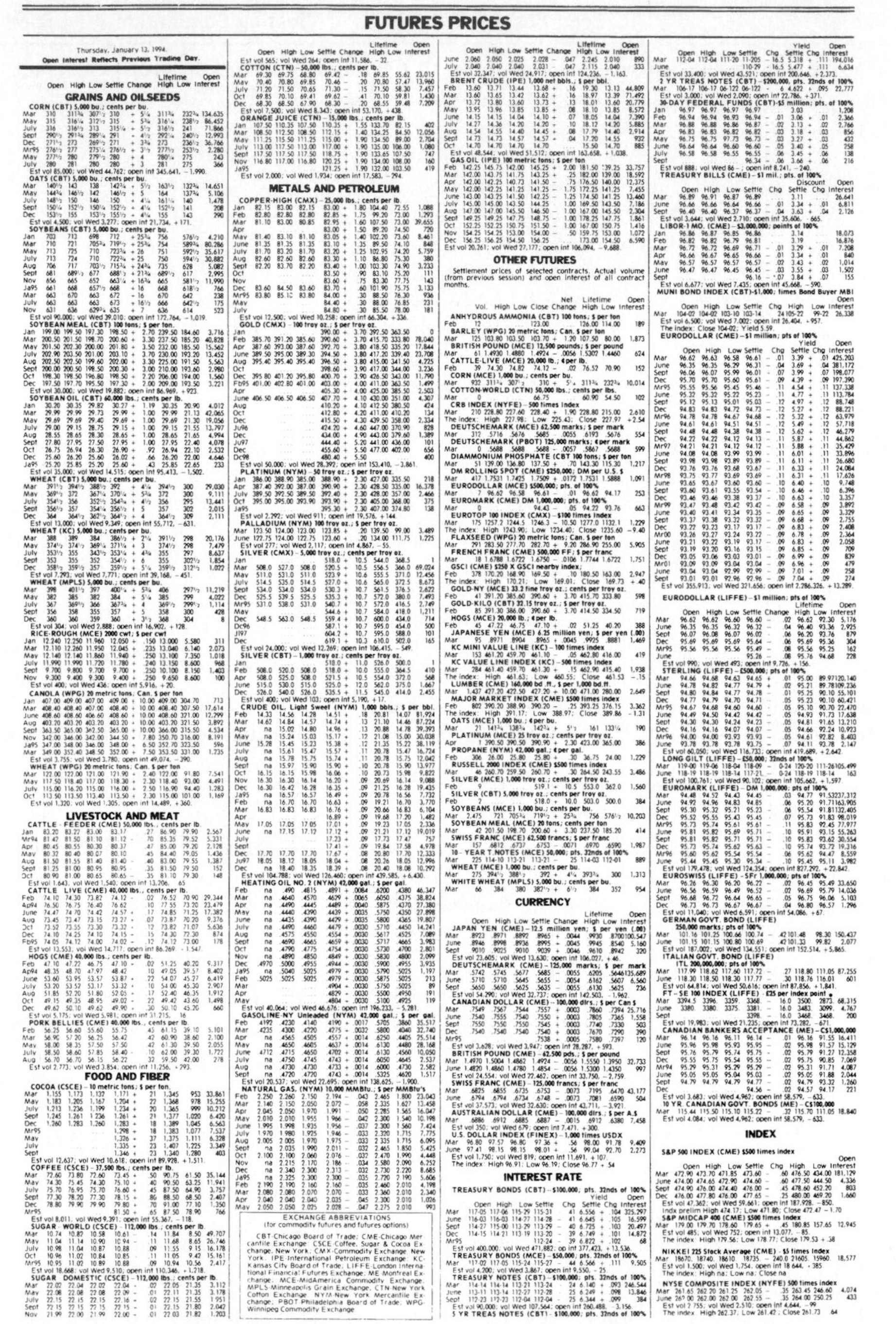

FUTURES PRICES

As you'd expect, open interest increases as the time until delivery gets shorter. Open interest typically peaks a few weeks prior to the first delivery date and then declines sharply. By the time the first delivery date arrives, open interest is close to zero for some contracts.

Basis and Spreads

The terms *basis* and *spread* receive a great deal of attention in the futures markets. Both are important concepts for understanding futures pricing. In

Table 19.3

How Trading Affects Open Interest

Trading Day	Number of Contracts Traded	Long Position	Short Position	Change in Open Interest
Day 1	10	Trader A	Trader B	+10
Day 2	10	Trader C	Trader D	+10
Day 3	10	Trader B	Trader E	None
Day 4	10	Trader D	Trader F	None
Day 5	10	Trader E	Trader A	−10

Open interest after Day 5:

	Long Positions	Short Positions
Trader A	0	0
Trader B	0	0
Trader C	10	0
Trader D	0	0
Trader E	0	0
Trader F	0	10

Total open interest = 10 contracts

addition, many trading strategies, which we'll discuss later in the chapter, are based on expected changes to basis and/or spread. Let's discuss basis first.

Basis is merely the difference between the cash price, or **spot price,** of an asset and the futures contract price. Basis can be either negative or positive. Basis also can change for futures contracts with different delivery dates. The cash price of an asset can differ depending on location and grade. A properly measured basis should compare the cash price of an asset that matches the specific delivery characteristics of the futures contract as closely as possible.

Figure 19.4 shows an example of basis for two futures contracts (crude oil and Treasury bonds). The cash and futures prices are quoted as of November 17, 1993. The cash price of crude oil is the spot price of West Texas Intermediate Crude, which closely matches the delivery characteristics of the crude oil futures contract. The cash price of Treasury bonds is the price of the 8 percent bond that matures in November 2021. This bond can be delivered in any of the contracts shown in Figure 19.4.

Notice that the crude oil basis gets smaller (more negative) as the time until delivery lengthens. This shows that the futures price is higher than the current spot price of crude oil. For T-bond futures, the pattern of the basis is reversed; the bond basis gets larger (more positive) as the time until delivery lengthens. This indicates that the spot price of T-bonds is higher than the futures price. Does this mean that the futures market expects the price of crude oil to rise and the prices of T-bonds to fall? As we'll see when we discuss the two general theories of futures pricing a little later, the answer to this question could be either *yes* or *no.*

Convergence. As the delivery date approaches, it seems natural to expect basis to approach zero. In other words, spot prices and futures prices should show **convergence** as the time until delivery approaches zero. Will basis always equal zero on the delivery date? The answer is technically *yes,* with a couple of qualifications: if the spot and futures prices are for *exactly* the same grade of asset, the same delivery location, and the same delivery size, then the basis should be zero on the delivery date.

Figure 19.4

Basis of Crude Oil and T-Bond Futures:
November 17, 1993

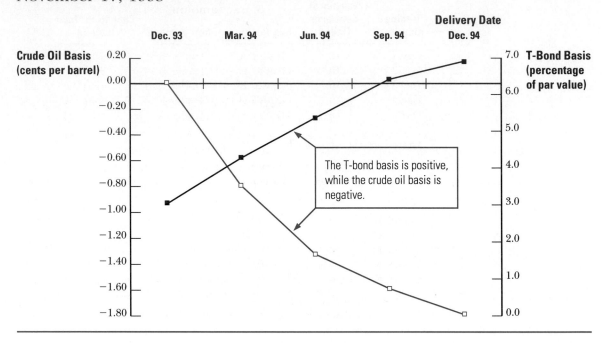

Spreads. A **spread** is the difference between the prices of two different futures contracts. Traders watch two major types of spreads. An **intracommodity spread** measures the difference in price between two futures contracts on the same asset, but with different delivery dates; an example would be the spread between December crude oil and March crude oil contracts. An **intercommodity spread** measures the difference in price between two futures contracts on different assets, but with the same delivery date. Traders are most interested in intercommodity spreads that involve similar, though still different, assets. Examples of similar assets include corn and soybeans, gold and silver, and T-bills and T-bonds.

Spreads are important because there should be strong economic relationships between spreads. Spreads that become either too narrow or too large may create some profitable trading opportunities. Many of the speculative trading strategies we'll review later in the chapter involve trading spreads (i.e., buying one contract while selling another).

Futures Prices and Expected Future Spot Prices

With terms defined and a foundation established, we can build two models of futures contract prices. The first general theory of futures pricing argues that there is a strong relationship between futures prices and expected future spot prices. The presence of speculators in the futures market may seem to guarantee at least a general relationship between the two. For example, assume that 30-day corn futures are selling for $2.50 per bushel while the expected spot price of corn in 30 days is $2.25 per bushel. The speculator could go short in the futures contract, planning to buy corn in the spot market in 30 days at $2.25 and deliver the corn via the futures contract, collecting $2.50 per bushel. In the process, the trader would make $0.25 per bushel.

Should the futures price, with delivery at a specific point in time, merely equal the future spot price expected at the same future point in time? Even if the assets' characteristics in the spot market are identical to those specified in the futures contract, there are several good reasons why the futures price may only approximate the expected future spot price.

One reason is transaction costs. In the example above, say that transaction costs to go short in the futures contract amount to $0.35 per bushel. Now the speculative trade no longer appears profitable since the speculator can net only $2.15 per bushel while paying $2.25 per bushel.

Risk Bearing Services of Speculators. A more important reason why the futures price may only approximate the expected future spot price comes from the fact that both hedgers and speculators trade in the futures market. A hedger has a position in the asset's cash market and uses futures to reduce the risks associated with this cash position. A speculator has no position in the cash market and seeks merely to profit from anticipated changes in prices. Therefore, hedgers are more risk averse than speculators. In fact, speculators may be willing to assume some of the risk that hedgers are trying to avoid, if they can expect appropriate returns. This effect on the relationship between futures prices and expected future spot prices is best illustrated graphically.

Figure 19.5 illustrates a hypothetical futures market that includes both hedgers and speculators. The figure assumes that hedgers are net short. In other words, the sum of all of the positions held by hedgers shows more short positions than long positions. In order for the market to function, therefore, speculators have to be net long. As a futures contract's price declines, speculators should be willing to hold more long positions. At the same time, however, hedgers should be willing to hold fewer short positions.

Now, assume that $S(n)$ is the expected future spot price of some asset, n periods from today. If the futures price were to equal $S(n)$, speculators would be willing to hold no position in the futures contract, since their goal is to make money by taking risk. In order to induce them to hold long positions in the futures, the futures price calling for delivery n periods from today, $F(n)$, has to be below the expected spot price. The futures price has to clear the market, so the number of short positions desired by hedgers equals the number of long positions desired by speculators. The figure shows where

Figure 19.5

Futures Market with Both Hedgers and Speculators

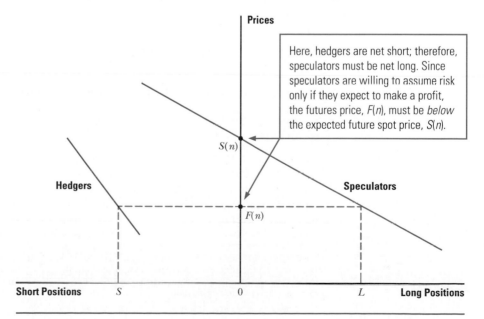

Here, hedgers are net short; therefore, speculators must be net long. Since speculators are willing to assume risk only if they expect to make a profit, the futures price, $F(n)$, must be *below* the expected future spot price, $S(n)$.

Figure 19.6

Theory of Normal Backwardation

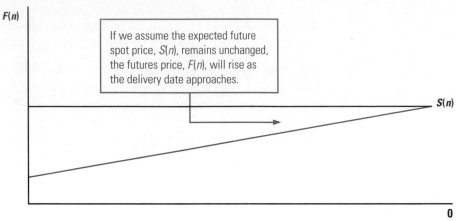

F(n)

> If we assume the expected future spot price, *S(n)*, remains unchanged, the futures price, *F(n)*, will rise as the delivery date approaches.

S(n)

0

Time to Delivery

Notes: $F(n)$ is the futures price; $S(n)$ is the expected future spot price; 0 is the delivery date, at which time to delivery equals 0.

$F(n)$ falls in the hypothetical market, relative to $S(n)$. S is the number of short positions and L is the number of long positions; S must equal L in order for the market to clear.

What will happen over time as the delivery date approaches? If the expected future spot price remains unchanged, the futures price must rise, as shown in Figure 19.6. This rise in the futures price can be considered the expected return to speculators for assuming some of the risk that hedgers want to avoid. The tendency of futures prices to rise as the delivery date approaches was referred to by the legendary economist John Maynard Keynes as **normal backwardation.**[8]

The reverse can also be true. If hedgers are net long, then speculators must be net short. Therefore, in order for the market to clear, the futures price must be above the expected spot price [i.e., $F(n) > S(n)$]. If expected spot prices don't change, the futures price should decline as the delivery date approaches. This is sometimes referred to as **contango.**

Futures Prices and the Cost of Carry

The other major theory of futures pricing argues that the price of a futures contract is merely the current spot price plus the **cost of carry,** the cost associated with storing the asset until the delivery date. In other words:

$$F(n) = S(1 + c) \qquad (19.1)$$

where $F(n)$ is the futures price, S is the spot price, and c is the net cost of carry (expressed as a percentage of the asset's value). The notion of cost of carry can also help to relate the price of a futures contract with a distant delivery date to the price of a contract on the same asset with a nearby deliv-

[8]See John Maynard Keynes, *A Treatise on Money* (London: MacMillan, 1930). Some empirical evidence supports the theory of normal backwardation in the grain futures market. See, for example, Eric Chang, "Returns to Speculators and the Theory of Normal Backwardation," *Journal of Finance* (March 1985): 193–208.

ery date. The price of the distant futures contract must equal the price of the nearby contract plus the cost of carrying the asset between the two delivery dates.

At first glance this formula appears to establish a relationship between the futures price, the spot price, and the cost of carry; otherwise, arbitrage opportunities would exist. For example, assume that the current spot price of gold is $360 per ounce and a three-month gold futures contract specifies a price of $390 per ounce. If the cost of carry for gold, for three months, is 5 percent (including storage, insurance, financing, etc.), an arbitrager could profit from these prices, as shown below:

Time	Transaction	Cash Flow
Today	1. Buy gold in the spot market for $360 per ounce.	−$360 per ounce
	2. Short three-month gold futures.	
Three months hence	1. Pay storage costs (5 percent of $360, per ounce)	−$18 per ounce
	2. Deliver gold to satisfy the futures contract. Collect $390 per ounce.	+$390 per ounce
		Net profit = $12 per ounce

This string of transactions would generate a risk-free profit of $12. Of course, other traders can do the same thing. As a result, these prices won't last very long. Think about it this way: Who'd be willing to sell gold today at $360 per ounce? Who'd be willing to go long in a three-month futures contract at $390? Demand should push the spot price of gold upward and/or the three-month futures price downward.

If futures prices are determined by the cost of carry, basis should be negative (the cash price should be less than the futures price) and the basis should get more negative as the time until delivery gets longer. Return to Figure 19.4 for a moment and take another look at the basis of crude oil futures. If the cost of carry theory is correct, then the basis merely reflects the cost of carrying crude oil between points in time. This implies that futures prices say nothing about whether or not the market expects oil prices to rise or fall.

What about the basis of Treasury bond futures, also shown in Figure 19.4? The cost of carry for T-bonds is negative if short-term rates are lower than long-term rates. Treasury bonds pay coupon interest, even if they are held for only a short period of time. If long-term rates exceed short-term rates, which they generally do, the amount of coupon income from T-bonds should exceed the cost of financing the bonds for a short period of time. Let's look at a simple example.

Assume that the price of a six-month T-bond futures contract and the spot price of an 8 percent T-bond are both 100 (100 percent of par). If the cost of financing T-bonds for six months equals 4 percent annually, one could profit by buying the bonds and shorting the six-month futures. In six months, the trader would deliver the bonds to satisfy the futures contract. The financing cost is 2 percent (4 percent of 100 divided by 2) so the effective cost is 102 percent (100 + 2). However, besides the 100 percent for the bonds at delivery, the trader also gets six months of coupon interest, 4 percent (8 percent divided by 2). This amounts to a riskless profit of 2 percent per bond (100 + 4 − 100 − 2). As in the prior gold example, this arbitrage situation shouldn't last very long.

In the real marketplace, there are several reasons why the price of any futures contract is not simply the current spot price plus the cost of carry.

For one thing, real-market trades impose transaction costs, which the examples have ignored. For another, characteristics of some assets may limit their storage. Some assets, for example, may not last indefinitely in storage (e.g., orange juice).

Restrictions on Short Sales. Perhaps the most important complication to the cost of carry theory is that restrictions on short sales often limit spot market transactions. Think about the gold transaction we discussed earlier. In that example, the following relationship created an arbitrage opportunity:

$$F(n) > S(1 + c)$$

What would happen if the reverse were true: $F(n) < S(1 + c)$. In order to profit, the arbitrager would have to go short in the cash market, go long in the futures market, collect the storage cost, take delivery, and cover the short position in the cash market. Could someone really go short in the spot market for gold and collect the storage cost? It's hard to conceive of such a transaction for gold, or any physical commodity.

Therefore, perhaps Equation 19.1 should be modified to state:

$$F(n) \leq S(1 + c)$$

In other words, perhaps $S(1 + c)$ should be considered an upper boundary to the price of a futures contract.

Consider futures on other assets, however, like Treasury bonds. Some traders can go short in T-bonds in the cash market; in fact, government bond dealers can go short almost as easily as they can go long. Even if it is possible to go short in the cash market, however, other restrictions limit short sales. The most common restriction is the need to keep some of the proceeds of a short position in a margin account. (We discussed this in Chapter 3.) Consequently, a trader cannot earn a market rate of return on the entire proceeds.

Which Theory of Futures Pricing Is Correct?

In our view, both theories are correct, in the sense that both help to understand the relationship between current spot prices, expected future spot prices, and futures prices. Expected future spot prices clearly influence futures prices. At the same time, however, cost of carry relationships limit futures prices, in relation to spot prices.

We argue that which theory gives the most accurate price for a futures contract may depend on the asset. If trading in a contract faces few restrictions on short sales, and hedgers are neither net short nor net long, then futures prices are probably more closely related to costs of carry. Treasury note and bond futures probably fit in this group. On the other hand, if short sales face major restrictions, and if hedgers are clearly net short or net long, then futures prices are probably more closely related to expected future spot prices. Cost of carry, however, still restricts futures prices. Most physical assets probably fit more easily into this group.

Uses of Futures Contracts

Having described the basic characteristics of futures contracts and their pricing, we now turn to a discussion of the general uses of futures contracts. We will examine both speculative and hedging positions. Let's begin with several speculative positions.

Speculating with Futures

As we've discussed, a speculator is a trader who doesn't have a cash position in the asset. He or she is attempting to profit from expected price changes. The most basic speculative position is an **outright position** in a futures contract. The choice of the position, long or short, depends on the trader's expectations for future movements in the asset's price.

For example, suppose that a speculator decides that gold is currently overvalued since there are no signs of inflation in most countries, the political situation is stable, the production of gold is well above consumption, and several countries appear to be selling some of their gold reserves. The speculator may decide to go short in June gold at $395 per ounce. The size of the contract (traded on the COMEX) is 100 ounces so the initial value of one contract is $39,500. This requires a $3,000 margin deposit per contract.

Assume that the expectation turns out to be right. In two months, June gold is down to $375 per ounce. The speculator closes out the position by going long in June gold. In essence this trader sold gold for $395 per ounce ($39,500 per contract) and bought it back at $375 per ounce ($37,500 per contract). This generated a profit of $20 per ounce ($2,000 per contract). On a $3,000 investment (assuming price changes while the position was open required no margin calls), the return is a rather healthy 67 percent ($2,000/ $3,000).

What can go wrong? Lots of things, of course. The expectation about gold prices may simply turn out to be wrong. Gold prices might defy reason and continue to rise. The trader may correctly perceive gold as overvalued, but misjudge the timing of the price correction. If the market doesn't recognize that gold is overvalued until July, after the trader closes out the position, the move comes too late. Another potential risk is that gold might rise sharply after the trader goes short, causing a margin call. If the trader is unwilling, or unable, to deposit more cash, the position will be closed out. If gold then starts to fall, as expected, it's too late.

All of this demonstrates that outright positions in futures are *very* risky. Also, the potential loss is almost unlimited; one can easily lose much more than the initial margin deposit. Experienced futures traders understand that outright positions are very risky and, as a result, most speculate using intracommodity and intercommodity spreads. Because spreads are unlikely to change dramatically, they are far less risky than outright positions. Let's look at some examples of both.

Intracommodity Spreads. As we've discussed, an intracommodity spread is a combination of a long position in one contract with a simultaneous short position in another contract on the same asset with a different delivery date. As an example, assume that today is November 1, 1993 and December 1993 crude oil is selling for $17.00 a barrel, while June 1994 crude oil is selling for $18.00 a barrel. A speculator believes that oil prices are headed lower over the next couple of weeks and this will have a more substantial impact on the distant contract than the near-term contract. In other words, the spread between the June and December crude contracts should narrow. This trader would go short in the June contract and go long in the December contract. Suppose that the position closes out on November 30 with December crude at $16.80 and June crude at $17.50. Details of the trade are shown in Table 19.4.

Table 19.4

Example of an Intracommodity Spread

Date	Transaction
November 1	1. Go long in December crude oil at $17.00 per barrel (1,000 bbl. per contract)
	2. Go short in June 94 crude oil at $18.00 per barrel (1,000 bbl. per contract)
November 30	1. Go short in December crude oil at $16.80 per barrel
	2. Go long in June crude oil at $17.50 per barrel
Profit (loss)	1. December crude oil: Loss of $0.20 per bbl. × 1,000 bbl. = $200 loss
	2. June crude oil: Profit of $0.50 per bbl. × 1,000 bbl. = $500 profit
	Total profit = $300

Notice that even though the trader loses money on the December contract, the profit on the June contract more than offsets that loss. This is because the spread between June and December contract narrowed, as expected. Note that oil prices don't have to fall in order for this trade to be profitable. The only requirement is that the spread changes as expected.

Intercommodity Spread. An intercommodity spread combines a purchase of one contract with a sale of another; the contracts have the same delivery date, but different, though related, assets underlie them. As in an intracommodity spread, the speculator hopes to profit from a change in the spread.

As an example, assume that today is February 1 and July corn is trading at $3.00 per bushel while July soybeans are trading for $7.00 per bushel. Thus, July corn is currently selling for about 43 percent of July soybeans ($3.00/$7.00). Suppose that a trader believes that this percentage is too low. Even though corn and soybeans are closely related commodities (both are grown in the same parts of the country, for example), they are still subject to somewhat different supply and demand factors. A trader may believe that the soybean crop will be larger than expected as farmers plant more beans relative to corn, leading to a decision to buy July corn and sell July beans. Since one bean contract is approximately twice as valuable as one corn contract, the trader buys two corn contracts for every bean contract sold (the size of each contract is 5,000 bushels). Suppose that the position closes out on March 1 with July corn at $2.80 per bushel and July beans at $5.80 per bushel. Details of the transaction are shown in Table 19.5.

Again, even though the trader loses money on the two corn contracts, the spread narrowed, as expected, so the profit on the bean contract more than offsets the loss on the two corn contracts. As long as the spread between beans and corn narrows, the transaction is profitable; whether corn and bean prices rise or fall has no effect.

Hedging with Futures

As we've discussed generally already, futures can help traders to hedge cash positions. Ideally, the hedge should be constructed in such a way that:

$$\Delta C + \Delta F = 0 \qquad (19.2)$$

where ΔC is the change in the value of the cash position and ΔF is the change in the value of the futures position. No matter what happens to the price of

Table 19.5

Example of an Intercommodity Spread

Date	Transaction
February 1	1. Go long in two July corn contracts at $3.00 per bu. 2. Go short in one July soybean contract at $7.00 per bu.
March 1	1. Go short in two July corn contracts at $2.80 per bu. 2. Go long in one July bean contract at $5.80 per bu.
Profit (loss)	1. July corn: Loss of $0.20 per bu. × 10,000 bu. = $2,000 loss. 2. July soybeans: Profit of $1.20 bu. × 5,000 bu. = $6,000 profit Total profit = $4,000

the asset, the overall wealth remains unchanged. In reality, it is very hard to construct an ideal hedge, but a careful trader may be able to get pretty close.

Essentially, constructing a hedge requires a decision about what position to take in the futures market and in what contract (asset, delivery date, and number). The first decision is easy. The position in the futures market should be the *opposite* of the position in the cash market. In other words, if an increase in price in the cash market decreases the trader's wealth, this is a short position in the cash market. Consequently, the trader should go long in the futures market.

Deciding what contract to trade can be very straightforward or something of a problem, depending on what asset the hedge must protect. Let's look at an example of both a short hedge and a long hedge.

Short Hedge. A farmer may need a classic **short hedge.** Let's say it is springtime and an Iowa corn farmer has just planted a crop to be harvested in late September. The farmer worries that the price of corn will fall between planting and harvest time. Since the farmer is long in the cash market, the hedge requires a short position in the futures market.

The hedge turned out pretty well, as Table 19.6 illustrates. The market justified the farmer's worries, as corn fell in price between May and September. Because of the hedge, however, the losses in the cash market were almost totally offset by profits from the futures position. Of course, few actual hedges turn out quite this well, but this example illustrates the logic behind the short hedge.[9]

What happens to the farmer if corn prices rise rather than fall between now and harvest? Assume that on September 20, the farmer can sell the corn in the local spot market for $2.65 per bushel. At the same time, the price of September futures has risen to $3.10 per bushel. The farmer makes $10,200 in the cash market (20 cents times 51,000 bushels) but loses $5,000 in the futures market. In retrospect, the farmer would have been better off by not hedging but that's in retrospect. The purpose of hedging with futures is not to increase expected returns, however, but to reduce the risk of a position in the cash market.

Long Hedge. Now assume that today is March 1, and in two months a corporate treasurer must make a regular payment of DM100 million to a European

[9]You may be wondering why the farmer doesn't just go ahead and deliver corn to satisfy the futures contracts and collect $2.55 per bushel. The major reason is the cost of shipping the corn from the farm in Iowa to the delivery location at a major export terminal (such as New Orleans). The cost of shipping might be more than the difference in price.

Table 19.6

Example of a Short Hedge

Input data: Current local spot price: $2.45 bu.
Anticipated harvest: 51,000 bu.
Futures contract: Corn
Delivery: September (close to harvest)
Number of contracts: 10 (51,000/5,000 ≈ 10)
September futures price: $3.00 bu.

Date	Transaction
May 1	Sell 10 September corn contracts at $3.00 per bu.
September 20	1. Harvest corn and sell 51,000 bu. in the local cash market for $2.10 bu. 2. Buy 10 September corn contracts at $2.55 bu.
Profit (loss)	1. Cash market: Loss of $0.35 per bu. × 51,000 bu. = $17,850 loss 2. Futures market: Profit of $0.35 per bu. × 50,000 bu. = $17,500 profit Overall loss = $350

supplier. Currently the exchange rate between the dollar and the mark is DM0.60 per dollar, DM100 million is worth about $60 million. The treasurer worries that the value of the dollar will fall relative to the mark, meaning that the DM/dollar exchange rate will rise.

In essence, the firm is short in the cash market. The appropriate hedge, therefore, is a **long hedge:** go long in DM in the foreign exchange futures market. The relevant information on the long hedge is shown in Table 19.7.

Had the treasurer not hedged, the rise in the value of the DM relative to the dollar would have cost the company an additional $6 million to meet its

Table 19.7

Example of a Long Hedge

Input data: Spot FX rate: $0.6000/DM
Amount due: DM100 million
Date due: May 1
Futures contract: DM
Delivery: June (closest to due date)
Number of contracts: 800 (DM100 m/DM125k per contract)
June DM futures: $0.5789 per DM

Date	Transaction
March 1	Go long in 800 June DM futures at $0.5789
May 1	1. Buy DM100 million at a spot rate of $0.66 per DM, cost = $66 million 2. Go short in 800 June DM futures at $0.6350
Profit (loss)	1. Cash market: Loss of $0.06 per DM × 100 million = $6 million loss 2. Futures market: Profit of $0.0561 per DM × 100 million = $5.61 million profit Total loss = $0.39 million

May DM100 million obligation. The profits from the long hedge in DM futures reduced this loss to less than $400,000. As in the farmer's example, if the dollar had risen in value relative to the DM, the futures position would have lost money, offsetting some of the cash market profits.

Financial Futures: A Closer Look

We've already noted that trading in financial futures currently exceeds, by a wide margin, trading in futures on physical assets. Now, let's take a closer look at financial futures. First, we'll examine in more detail futures on money market instruments (Treasury bills and Eurodollars), coupon bearing instruments (Treasury bonds and notes), and stock indexes. We will also look at several ways to use financial futures both to speculate and to hedge.

Treasury Bill and Eurodollar Futures

Treasury bill and Eurodollar futures are traded on the International Monetary Market (IMM), which is part of the Chicago Mercantile Exchange. Both contracts are similar in design, and futures on both T-bills and Eurodollars can be used to speculate on or hedge against short-term movements in interest rates. However, traders must recognize some important differences between the two contracts. In recent years, trading in Eurodollar futures has substantially exceeded trading in T-bill futures.

Treasury Bill Futures. Treasury bill futures have delivery dates in March, June, September, and December. Any T-bill with a maturity of 90, 91, or 92 days, at the time of delivery can satisfy the contract. All bills delivered, however, must have the same maturity. The face value of T-bills delivered, per contract, is $1 million. Price quotations are based on the IMM index:

$$100.00\% - DY \tag{19.3}$$

where DY is the discount yield on 90-day T-bills. (We discussed how to find the discount yield in Chapter 2.) The value of one T-bill contract equals:

$$\$1,000,000 \times \frac{100 - (100 - IMM)(360/90)}{100} \tag{19.4}$$

where IMM is the IMM index value.

If the discount yield on T-bills were equal to 3 percent, the IMM index would equal 97. The value of one T-bill contract, with an IMM index of 97, would be:

$$\$1,000,000 \times \frac{100-(100-97)(90/360)}{100} = \$992,500$$

The minimum price fluctuation in T-bill futures is one basis point (0.01 percent) in the discount yield, which translates to $25 per contract. If 91-day or 92-day bills are delivered, the price of the contract would be adjusted slightly by substituting the correct number of days into Equation 19.4.

Eurodollar Futures. Eurodollar futures are based on Eurodollar bank deposits. As we described in Chapter 2, Eurodollar deposits are time deposits held in foreign banks or their U.S. branches. Even though federal law no longer limits the rates offered by U.S. banks, Eurodollar rates are still higher than comparable U.S. interest rates. This is due, in part, to the lack of deposit insurance on Eurodollar deposits.

The Eurodollar futures contract has a face value of $1 million and its price is based on the three-month LIBOR (London Interbank Offered Rate), the average interest rate offered by large London banks on Eurodollar deposits. The value of a Eurodollar futures contract is found in the same way as the value of a T-bill futures contract (Equations 19.3 and 19.4), with one major exception. Unlike T-bills, Eurodollars are not discount securities; rather, they are add-on instruments. Like most bank deposits, they pay interest on the amount deposited.

The add-on yield is calculated as follows:

$$(\text{Interest/Purchase price}) \times (360/\text{Days to maturity})$$

The IMM index for Eurodollars equals:

$$100\% - \text{Add-on yield}$$

The value of one Eurodollar contract is then found using Equation 19.4.

The other major difference between T-bill and Eurodollar futures is that Eurodollar futures are **cash settled.** This means that, instead of allowing the short position to deliver an asset, all accounts that remain open on the last trading day are settled in cash at a LIBOR-based rate determined by the CME clearinghouse.

Treasury Bond and Note Futures

Futures contracts on Treasury bonds and notes, all of which are traded on the Chicago Board of Trade, are virtually identical to each other, except for the deliverable instruments they specify. Treasury bond futures are the most actively traded futures contracts in the U.S. today by a wide margin. Ten-year Treasury note futures are also actively traded, ranking in the top ten. Recently introduced futures on five-year and two-year Treasury notes have established only modest trading volume so far.

All Treasury bond and note contracts, with the exception of the two-year note contract, are based on securities with $100,000 in par value. (The two-year note's contract size is $200,000.) The prices of all bond and note contracts assume a coupon rate of 8 percent and prices are stated in thirty-seconds of a percent. If the price of June bond future is stated as 115–08, the decimal price is 115.25 ($115\frac{8}{32}$), or $115,250 per contract.[10] The minimum price fluctuation is $\frac{1}{32}$, or $31.25 per contract. Treasury note and bond futures have delivery dates in March, June, September, and December.

Conversion Factors and Invoice Amount. As we just noted, all Treasury bond and note contracts are priced assuming an 8 percent coupon rate. Since the short position can deliver any Treasury security that meets the maturity requirements specified by the contract, regardless of the coupon rate, invoice amounts are adjusted by so-called **conversion factors.**[11] The con-

---

[10]These prices can be treated as percentages of the bond's par values at which the bonds are trading. A price of 115.25 means that the bond is selling for 115.25 percent of its par value.

[11]While any Treasury security that meets the maturity requirements specified by the contract can be delivered, all the securities delivered in one contract must be the same.

version factor is the price of the bond delivered, assuming a par value of $1 and a yield to maturity of 8 percent. Generally, bonds with coupon rates greater than 8 percent have conversion factors greater than 1 while bonds with coupon rates less than 8 percent have conversion factors less than 1.[12]

If the short actually delivers securities to the long to fulfill the futures contract (by the delivery procedure shown in Figure 19.2), the invoice amount equals:

(Settlement price as a percentage of par × Number of contracts
× $100,000 × Conversion factor) + Accrued interest

Assume that a short decides to deliver ten T-bond contracts. The settlement price when the short established the position was 117–16 (117.5 percent of par). The short decides to deliver bonds with a coupon rate of 9 percent and a maturity of exactly 17 years, 3 months. The conversion factor for these bonds is 1.0925 and accrued interest equals $22,500 (three months of interest, at 9 percent per year, on $1 million worth of bonds). The invoice equals:

$$(1.175 \times 10 \times \$100,000 \times 1.0925) + \$22,500 = \$1,306,187.50$$

Cheapest to Deliver. One feature unique to Treasury bond and note futures is the fact that some bonds and notes are cheaper to deliver than others due to the way in which conversion factors are computed. Essentially, the method of computing and using conversion factors assumes that all deliverable securities have the same yield to maturity. In reality, of course, they don't. Remember, the short initiates delivery and also chooses the instruments to deliver, assuming that they meet the conditions of the contract. Logically, the short should choose the most advantageous instrument. The instrument that is **cheapest to deliver** is the one that costs the short the least compared to the invoice amount. Let's illustrate this with an example.

Suppose that today is December 1. On August 1, a trader went short in one December T-bond contract at 118. To begin the delivery process, this trader must select which of the two instruments detailed below to deliver:

	Bond A	Bond B
Cash price (per $100,000)	$154,312.50	$110,625.00
Coupon	$11\frac{3}{4}\%$	$7\frac{1}{2}\%$
Maturity	16 years	23 years
Conversion factor	1.3351	0.9478
Accrued interest	None	None
Invoice amount[a]	$157,541.80	$111,840.40
Invoice/Cash price	1.0209	1.0110

[a]The invoice amount for Bond A equals: 1.18 × 1.3351 × $100,000 = $157,541.80. The invoice amount for Bond B equals: 1.18 × 0.9478 × $100,000 = $111,840.40.

It is clearly more advantageous for the short to deliver Bond A rather than Bond B. The security that is cheapest to deliver is the one with the highest ratio between the invoice amount and the cash price. Determining which instrument(s) is the cheapest to deliver is not difficult. As a result, a futures contract's price should closely match the price of the instrument that is cheapest to deliver as the first delivery date approaches.

---

[12]To a lesser extent, conversion factors are also a function of the maturity of the bond or note being delivered.

Stock Index Futures

Stock index futures are contracts based on well-known indexes of common stocks. Today, the most actively traded stock index futures contract, based on the S&P 500, is traded on the CME. (We discussed how the S&P 500 is calculated back in Chapter 4.) Delivery dates are December, March, June, and September. The futures price is quoted in the same manner as the index. The value of one futures contract is the index value multiplied by $500. (An index value of 450 would give one contract a value of $225,000.) Like Eurodollar futures, S&P 500 futures are cash settled.

One feature unique to stock index futures is the lack of any daily limits on price fluctuations, either upward or downward. In theory, a trader could lose an entire margin deposit during one trading day. However, in the wake of the 1987 market break, the futures markets instituted a set of procedures called *circuit breakers*. In periods of extreme stock market volatility, when the index rises or falls by a certain amount, the circuit breakers kick in and trading in stock index futures is suspended.[13]

Program Trading. Stock index futures have faced criticism due to the controversial practice of **program trading,** computer-assisted trading of large blocks of stock simultaneously with stock index futures.[14] Program trading attempts to take advantage of perceived pricing errors between the stock index (the cash market) and the stock index futures. Let's illustrate program trading with a hypothetical example.

Table 19.8 presents an example of program trading. The current index value is 450, and the index futures contract is trading for 465. Between now and the settlement date, the short-term rate of interest is 5 percent and the dividend yield is 2.5 percent. On the settlement date, the futures price and stock index will converge to the same value.

At $t = 0$, the trader borrows $225,000 ($450 \times 500) and buys the stocks in the index. Simultaneously, the trader goes short in the futures at 475. At $t = 1$, the trader sells the index stocks (collecting $220,000), repays the loan (for $236,250), and collects the cash dividends ($5,625, or 2.5 percent of $225,000). The trader also closes out the futures position, buying the con-

Table 19.8

Hypothetical Example of Program Trading

Assumptions: Index value = 450 ($t = 0$)
Index value = 440 ($t = 1$)
Futures price = 465
Short-term interest rate = 5 percent (between $t = 0$ and $t = 1$)
Dividend yield = 2.5 percent (between $t = 0$ and $t = 1$)

Time	Stock Market	Futures Market
$t = 0$	Buy index (cost = $225,000) by borrowing money at 5 percent	Go short on futures at 465
$t = 1$	Sell stock for $220,000 Pay loan of $236,250 Receive dividend of $5,625.	Go long on futures at 440 for a profit of $12,500
Overall profit	$1,875	

---

[13]Whether or not circuit breakers really work is the subject of some controversy.

[14]The term *program trading* is used loosely on Wall Street. Often it refers to any type of computer-assisted trading in which large blocks of stock are bought or sold based on predetermined conditions.

tract at 440. The profit from the futures trade is \$12,500 [(465 − 440 × \$500]. Overall, the trader makes \$1,875. The example assumes that the index is "cheap" relative to the futures. By buying the index and, at the same time, going short in futures, the trader locked in a profit. The position would make money regardless of whether the stock index were to rise or fall in value.[15]

Note two points about the hypothetical example of program trading. First, transaction costs, which Table 19.8 ignored, would be considerable for all but large, institutional investors. Second, the trader need not actually borrow the money at $t = 0$ in order to purchase the index stocks. The short-term interest rate of 5 percent could also be considered the opportunity cost associated with tying up \$225,000 in capital for a period of time.

As we noted, program trading is controversial. Some critics have blamed the technique for increasing volatility in the stock market. Some have even laid much of the blame for the 1987 market break (Meltdown Monday) on program trading. The evidence that program trading has contributed to stock market volatility or the 1987 market break is, however, ambiguous at best.

Speculating and Hedging with Financial Futures

Financial futures create numerous opportunities to speculate on stock prices, interest rates, changes in the shape of the yield curve, and other market moves. As with all futures, most speculative trades in financial futures involve trading spreads. Financial futures can also be used to create both long and short hedges. A pension fund manager can use financial futures, for example, to hedge against declines in the portfolio's stock or bond prices.

In this section we'll look at an example of a speculative trade in financial futures (an intracommodity spread using T-bond futures), an example of a short hedge using T-bond futures, and an example of a long hedge using S&P 500 futures. These are two of dozens of examples of speculative and hedging positions using financial futures.[16]

Intracommodity Spread Example. Assume that today is April 1. Based on some economic data from the first quarter, a trader believes that weak economic growth and very modest inflation should force interest rates downward in the near future. As interest rates fall, of course, bond prices rise. While a general decline in interest rates would affect all T-bond futures prices, the prices of futures for near-term delivery should rise more than the prices of futures for distant delivery.[17] The trader decides to buy five June T-bond futures contracts and, at the same time, sell five December T-bond futures. If interest rates were to decline as expected, with the position remaining open until May 1, the results would resemble those in Table 19.9.

The initial spread between the June and December bond contracts was $\frac{47}{32}$ (\$1,468.75 per contract). Even though the prices of both contracts rose as rates declined, the June contract rose more in price than the December contract. As a result, the spread between the two contracts widened to $\frac{63}{32}$ (\$1,968.75). The speculation made $\frac{16}{32}$ (\$500) per contract, for a total profit of \$2,500.

[15]This example shows an artificially high profit in order to illustrate index arbitrage. Any futures price above 462.5 in the example would be sufficient to trigger arbitrage.

[16]Hedging and speculating using Treasury bond and note futures are described in detail in *Treasury Futures for Institutional Investors* (Chicago: Chicago Board of Trade, 1990). Hedging and speculating with Treasury bill, Eurodollar, and stock index futures are discussed in Robert Kolb, *Understanding Futures Markets*, 3rd ed. (Miami: Kolb Publishing, 1991).

[17]The reason for this is related to the relationship between bond futures and the cost of carry, which is negative if short-term rates are below long-term rates. See, *Treasury Futures for Institutional Investors*, 70–72.

Table 19.9

Intracommodity Spread Using T-Bond
Futures

Date	June T-Bonds (32nds)	December T-Bonds (32nds)	Spread (32nds)
April 1	114–28	113–13	47
May 1	118–28	116–29	63
Profit (loss)	4–00	(3–16)	16

Overall profit (loss): 1. Profit on five June T-bond
   contracts = $20,000
   2. Loss on five December T-bond
   contracts = $17,500

   Overall profit = $2,500

Example of a Short Hedge. On October, 3, 1993 a pension fund held $10 million worth (measured by face value) of $11\frac{3}{4}$ percent, 2009 T-bonds priced at $160\frac{25}{32}$, or $16,078, 125. The fund manager is concerned about interest rates rising, and thus bond prices falling, over the next few weeks. To protect the portfolio, the manager constructs a short hedge using December 1993 T-bond futures. Since each T-bond futures contract has a face value of $100,000, the fund manager shorts 100 contracts at $119\frac{13}{32}$. The market fulfills the fund manager's expectation, and interest rates rise over the next six weeks. By November 22, the value of the fund's bonds declines by $700,000. The December futures, however, also fall; the short position produces a profit of $478,125, reducing the overall loss to $221,875. The details are shown in Table 19.10.

While the futures contracts reduced the fund's cash market loss by more than $478,000, the fund manager did not construct an optimal hedge. A better tactic would consider that, as rates rise, the cash market instrument would show a greater dollar price change than the dollar change in price in the

Table 19.10

Example of a Short Hedge Using T-Bond Futures

A. Unweighted Hedge

	Futures	Cash
October 3	Go short 100 December T-bond futures at 119–13	Hold $10 million (measured by face value) of $11\frac{3}{4}$ percent, 2009 bonds priced at 160–25, or $16,078,125
November 22	Go long 100 December T-bond futures at 114–20	Hold $10 million of $11\frac{3}{4}$ percent, 2009 bonds priced at 153–25, or $15,378,125
Profit (loss)	$478,125	($700,000)

Net loss = ($221,875)

B. Weighted Hedge

Face amount of bond/Contract size × Conversion factor = Number of futures
$10,000,000/$100,000 × 1.3351 ≈ 134 contracts
Profit on futures = 134 × $4,781.25 = $640,687.50
Loss in cash market = ($700,000)
Net loss = ($59,312.50)

Table 19.11

Example of a Weighted Long Hedge Using
S&P 500 Futures

	Futures	**Cash**
January 13	Go long 42 March S&P 500 futures at 450	Will have $10 million for investment in March; current price = $50 per share
March 15	Go short 42 March S&P 500 futures at 472.50	Invest $10 million at $52.50 per share
Profit (loss)	$472,500	($500,000)
Net loss = ($27,500)		

futures. Consequently, weighting the hedge by the conversion factor would have produced a better result. This is illustrated in Table 19.10, as well. Had the fund manager sold 134 December contracts, rather than 100, the net loss would have been reduced to less than $60,000.[18]

Example of a Long Hedge. On January 13, a corporate treasurer is reviewing investment plans for the pension fund contribution the company plans to make in March. The $10 million contribution will be invested in a pension fund at the fund's net asset value on the day of the contribution. Currently, the fund's net asset value is $50.00 per share, so the $10 million contribution would buy 200,000 shares. The treasurer is concerned about stock prices rising before March and decides to construct a long hedge using S&P 500 futures.

After deciding on a March delivery date, the treasurer must determine the number of contracts to buy. Assume the current price of March S&P 500 futures is 450. This gives a current dollar value of $225,000 per contract (450 × 500). Dividing $225,000 into $10 million (the amount to be invested in March) gives 44.44. This isn't the final answer, however. Assume that the pension fund has a beta of 0.95 meaning that, historically at least, the pension fund is about 95 percent as volatile as the overall market. Weighting the hedge by the pension fund's beta gives 42.22 (44.44 × 0.95). Rounding off, the treasurer should buy 42 March S&P 500 futures at 450.

Details of this long hedge are shown in Table 19.11. The table shows the results if stock prices were to rise, as the treasurer feared, between January and March. This would boost March S&P 500 futures by 5 percent, to 472.50. The price per share of the pension fund would also rise by 5 percent, to $52.50. The loss in the cash market would amount to $500,000 ($2.50 times 200,000) while the profit in the futures market would amount to $472,500 (22.50 times 500 times 42). Therefore, the net loss would equal $27,500.

Of course, if stock prices were to fall rather than rise, the treasurer would lose money in the futures market and make money in the cash market. Remember, however, that the idea behind hedging is not to make money, but rather to reduce the risk associated with a position in the cash market.

Options on Futures

In 1982, the Commodity Futures Trading Commission allowed each futures market to begin trading options on one futures contract. The pilot program

---

[18]Weighting strategies can get quite sophisticated, depending on the instrument being hedged. See *Treasury Futures for Institutional Investors*, 37–48.

Figure 19.7

Contract Highlights: Options on Treasury Bond and
Treasury Note Futures

Trading Unit	$100,000 face value CBOT U.S. Treasury bond/note futures contract of a specified delivery month.
Price Quotations	In points and sixty-fourths of a point. For example, 3-37 equals 3-37/64.
Minimum Price Fluctuation	One sixty-fourth of a point, or $15.625 (one tick) per contract.
Daily Trading Limits	Same as daily limit for T-bond/T-note futures, 3 points ($3,000) per contract above or below the previous day's settlement price.
Strike Prices	Strike or exercise prices are set in integral multiples of 2 points per T-bond/T-note futures contract to bracket the current T-bond/T-note futures price. For example, if T-bond/T-note futures are at 86–00, strike prices may be set at 80, 82, 84, 86, 88, 90, etc. However, beginning with the June 1988 expiration series, strike prices are set in integrals of 1 point per *T-note* futures contract (i.e., if T-note futures are at 86–00, strike prices may be set at 80, 81, 82, 83, 84, 85, 86, 87, 88, etc.).
Months Traded	Same as CBOT T-bond/T-note futures; currently, March, June, September, and December.
Trading Hours	8 a.m. to 2 p.m. (Chicago time), Monday through Friday. Evening trading hours are from 5 to 8:30 p.m. (Central Standard time), or from 6 to 9 p.m. (Daylight Saving time) Sunday through Thursday.[a]
Last Trading Day	Options cease trading prior to the delivery month of the underlying T-bond/T-note futures contract. For example, the last trading day for December 1988 bond/note options is November 18, 1988. Options cease trading at noon on the last Friday, preceding by at least five business days the first notice day for the corresponding Treasury bond/Treasury note futures contract.
Exercise	The buyer of a futures option may exercise the option on any business day prior to expiration by giving notice to the Board of Trade Clearing Corporation by 8 p.m. (Chicago time). Such notice is then randomly assigned to an option seller.
Expiration	Unexercised options expire at 10 a.m. (Chicago time) on the first Saturday following the last day of trading.
Ticker Symbols	CG—Treasury bond futures call option PG—Treasury bond futures put option TC—Treasury note futures call option TP—Treasury note futures put option

[a]Subject to change.
Source: *CBOT Financial Instruments Guide,* Chicago Board of Trade, (1987) 61–62.

proved so successful that options on futures were permanently authorized in 1987. Today, options, both calls and puts, are available on most actively traded futures contracts.

Characteristics of Options on Futures

By now you should be familiar with the characteristics of futures contracts. From Chapter 18, you should be familiar with the characteristics of call and put options. This should lead to an understanding of options on futures. An option on a futures contract gives the holder the right, but not the obligation, to go long (with a call) or short (with a put) in a specific futures contract, at a specific price (the stated exercise price), until some point in the future (the option's expiration date). An option on a futures contract expires the month prior to the delivery month of the underlying futures contract. Figure 19.7 describes the characteristics of options on T-bond and T-note futures.

Figure 19.8

Profit (Loss) from Buying a Call Option on a Futures Contract

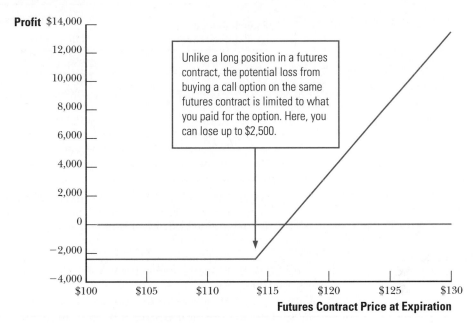

Note box text: Unlike a long position in a futures contract, the potential loss from buying a call option on the same futures contract is limited to what you paid for the option. Here, you can lose up to $2,500.

Note: The option's exercise price is 114; its price is $2\frac{1}{2}$.

As with all options, an option on a futures contract requires a seller (writer) for every buyer. The writer of a call option can be obligated to establish a short position in the futures while the writer of a put option can be obligated to establish a long position in the futures. The most the buyer of an option on a futures contract can lose is the price he or she paid for the option. On the other hand, the option writer faces potentially unlimited losses. (We discussed this in Chapter 18.)

Using Options on Futures

Almost all trading strategies using stock options (whether for speculation or hedging) can be done with options on futures, as well. Much of the discussion in Chapter 18 transfers directly to options on futures. However, it would be useful to examine two basic strategies for options on futures: buying a call option instead of the futures contract, and using a call to protect a short position in the futures contract.

Buying a Call. From Chapter 18 we know that the profit (or loss) from holding a call option on a futures contract until expiration is:

$$\text{Profit (loss)} = \text{MAX}(0, F - E) - C$$

where F is the price of the futures contract at expiration, E is the exercise price, and C is the price paid for the call option. Assume that someone buys a 114 March T-bond call at 2–32 ($2\frac{32}{64}$, or $2,500). The profit or loss from buying one call, at various futures prices, is shown in Figure 19.8.

Buying the call can substitute for establishing a long position in the futures. Assume that a trader expects interest rates to decline before the end of February. This person could go long in March futures at 114–16, or buy the call option on the March futures contract mentioned earlier ($E = 114$,

Table 19.12

Call Option on a Futures Contract versus
a Long Position in the Futures Contract

Futures Contract Price (at expiration)	Profit (Loss)	
	Call	**Futures**
95	($2,500)	($19,500)
100	(2,500)	(14,500)
105	(2,500)	(9,500)
110	(2,500)	(4,500)
115	(1,500)	500
120	3,500	5,500
125	8,500	10,500
130	13,500	15,500

Notes: The price of the futures contract, when the position is established, is $114\frac{1}{2}$ ($114,500). The price of the call when the position is established is $2\frac{1}{2}$ ($2,500).

$C = 2\frac{1}{2}$). The profits and losses from both strategies, at various prices, are shown in Table 19.12.

If the price of March T-bonds were to fall from $114\frac{1}{2}$ to 100, the loss from holding the long position in the futures contract would be $14,500, compared to $2,500 from holding the option on the futures contract. The advantage of buying the call, as opposed to the futures contract, is the limit on the loss to the cost of the option ($2,500 in the example). The loss from a futures position is, at least technically, unlimited. Of course, the disadvantage of the call option is that it sacrifices some of the profit should T-bond prices rise as expected.

Using a Call Option to Protect a Short Futures Position. As we've seen, outright futures positions are very risky. Consequently, most traders use spreads. An alternative to a spread is to combine an option on a futures contract with a futures position. For example, one could combine a call option with a short futures position. Let's look at an example.

Assume that someone shorts March T-bonds at $114\frac{1}{2}$, in expectation of falling bond prices. In order to protect the position, should prices rise, the trader also buys a 116 March call at $1\frac{1}{2}$. The profit and loss from the combination is shown in Table 19.13. The loss is limited to $3,000, regardless of

Table 19.13

Shorting a Futures Contract and Buying a Call Option

Futures Price at Expiration	Profit (Loss)		
	Futures	**Call**	**Total**
95	$19,500	($1,500)	$18,000
100	14,500	(1,500)	13,000
105	9,500	(1,500)	8,000
110	4,500	(1,500)	3,000
115	(500)	(1,500)	(2,000)
120	(5,500)	2,500	(3,000)
125	(10,500)	7,500	(3,000)
130	(15,500)	12,500	(3,000)
135	(20,500)	17,500	(3,000)

how high T-bond prices go. On the other hand, the combination sacrifices profit should prices fall. The cost of the protection is $1,500, the price of the call option.

Chapter Summary

1. **Describe futures contracts and the mechanics of futures trading.**

    A futures contract is a legally binding contract that calls for the future delivery of an asset. The contract specifies the asset to be delivered, the delivery location, the delivery date, and the price. All futures contracts have two positions, the long position (which takes delivery of the asset) and the short position (which delivers the asset). Traders can avoid delivering commodities to satisfy futures by reversing their initial positions prior to the delivery date. The long position will make money if the price of the asset rises while the short position will make money if the price of the asset falls. Futures are considered to be a zero sum game; if the long position makes a dollar, the short position must lose a dollar. Futures markets started by trading contracts for agricultural commodities; they expanded into nonagricultural assets during the last 20 years. Today, futures markets operate worldwide. The most actively traded futures are in financial instruments. Many futures markets still rely on the open outcry system of trading in which traders shout out orders while standing in a trading pit. Each futures market has a clearinghouse that acts as both an intermediary and guarantor to every trade. Both the long position and short position are required to post margin deposits. Futures margins are not loans, but rather security deposits. At the end of each trading day, every account is marked to market. Virtually all futures contracts limit daily maximum price changes (the exception is stock index futures).

2. **Provide a primer on the pricing of futures contracts.**

    The financial press provides daily futures price quotations, including open interest data. *Open interest* refers to the number of contracts outstanding at any point in time. Open interest normally rises as a contract's delivery date approaches, peaks, and then falls sharply. *Basis* refers to the difference between the cash, or spot, price of an asset and its futures price. The basis can be either positive or negative. As the delivery date approaches, basis should approach zero. (This is called *convergence.*) Spreads are differences, or ratios, between the prices of two different futures contracts. An intracommodity spread measures the difference in price between two futures contracts on the same asset, but with different delivery dates. An intercommodity spread measures the difference in price between two futures contracts on different, but related, assets, that have the same delivery date. Two general theories seek to explain futures pricing. The first theory relates futures prices to expected spot prices. The risk-bearing function of speculators implies that, if hedgers are net short, the futures price will be below the expected spot price, and it will rise as the delivery date approaches (normal backwardation). The second general theory of futures pricing relates futures prices to current spot prices and the cost of carry. If the cost of carry is positive (or negative), then the basis will be negative (or positive). Which theory gives the most accurate price may depend on the asset. The cost of carry theory appears to be more accurate for Treasury note and bond futures, for example.

3. **Discuss the uses of futures contracts.**

    Futures can be used both to speculate on price changes of assets and to hedge cash positions. In an outright speculative position, the trader goes either long or short, speculating on the price of an asset either rising or falling. Outright positions are very risky, however, since the trader's loss is potentially unlimited. As a result, most experienced traders speculate using spreads. An intracommodity spread involves buying one contract while selling another, on the same asset with different delivery dates. An intercommodity spread involves buying one contract, while selling another on different, but related, assets; both contracts have the same delivery date. Futures can also be used to hedge cash positions. The general idea is to establish a futures position opposite to a position in the cash market; if a rise in price hurts the cash position, the price increase should benefit the futures position. A short hedger wants to hedge against the price of an asset falling, while a long hedger wants to hedge against the price of an asset rising. In addition to deciding whether to establish a long or short futures position, the hedger must also decide which contract to use, including the delivery date, and the number of contracts to trade.

4. **Take a closer look at financial futures.**

Futures exchanges offer contracts on Treasury bills and Eurodollars. Eurodollars are dollar-denominated time deposits held in foreign banks, or in their U.S. branches. The contracts are very similar; both have face values of $1 million. Interest is computed somewhat differently, however, and the Eurodollar contract is cash settled, meaning that no asset is actually delivered; all open accounts on the last trading day are settled in cash. Traders can also use Treasury note and bond contracts. T-bond futures contracts are by far the most actively traded futures contracts today. All bond and note contracts are very similar. Since all contracts assume that the underlying instrument has a coupon rate of 8 percent, invoice amounts are adjusted by a conversion factor if the instruments delivered don't have an 8 percent coupon. Because conversion factors assume that all deliverable instruments have the same yield, some instruments turn out to be cheaper to deliver. Stock index futures are based on several well-known indexes of common stocks (such as the S&P 500). Stock index futures trading imposes no daily price change limits and the contracts are cash settled. They figure in program trading, which is a strategy designed to take advantage of perceived pricing errors between the stock index and the futures contract. Traders have developed several techniques for speculating and hedging using financial futures.

5. **Understand options on futures.**

Options on futures are similar to stock options. They give the holder the right, but no obligation, to establish a long position (for a call) or a short position (for a put) in a specific futures contract, at a specific price, until some point in time. Options on futures expire in the month prior to the delivery month of the underlying futures contract. As with all options, the contract requires a seller (or writer) of an option for every buyer. Almost all trading strategies for stock options work with options on futures as well. An option on a futures contract is a substitute for an outright futures position. The advantage of the option is that it limits the potential loss to the price of the option, as opposed to the unlimited loss possible with the futures contract. Options on futures can be used to protect outright futures positions (for example, buying a call to protect a short futures position). In this case, the option resembles insurance since it will limit the loss should prices move opposite to the expected direction.

Key Terms

Forward contract	Short position
Futures contract	Financial futures
Long position	Open outcry system

Trading pits	Convergence
Commission broker	Spread
Local trader	Intracommodity spread
Dual trader	Intercommodity spread
Scalper	Normal backwardation
Day trader	Contango
Position trader	Cost of carry
Settlement price	Outright position
Marked to market	Short hedge
Margin call	Long hedge
Limit up/limit down	Cash settled
Open interest	Conversion factor
Basis	Cheapest to deliver
Spot price	

Mini Case 1   OBJECTIVE

To construct an intercommodity spread using futures on Treasury bonds and five-year Treasury notes. Assume that today is December 1. Between now and early next year, interest rates should fall. Further, the slope of the yield curve should remain essentially unchanged. Today, T-bond and five-year note futures are priced as follows:

March Futures	Price	Yield
Five-year notes	11–12[a]	5.375%
Bonds	115–30	6.558
Spread (bonds–notes)	146	1.183

[a]In thirty-seconds.

a. If interest rates do decline, what will happen to bond and note prices? What should happen to the spread between bonds and notes (both price and yield)?

b. What is the appropriate intercommodity spread if rates should decline and the slope of the yield curve does not change?

c. Assume that rates fall, as expected, and the position closes out with March notes selling for 113–04 and March bonds selling for 120–22. How much did the intercommodity spread make?

Mini Case 2   OBJECTIVE

To set up a hedge using a futures contract. Assume that today is January 5. A company will receive a regular payment from its Japanese customers on February 25. The payment will be denominated in Japanese yen and will be equal to ¥10 billion. The current yen–dollar exchange rate is (¥0.0092/$). The March yen futures contract (¥12.5 million per contract) is currently trading at 0.0094.

a. What change to the value of the dollar relative to the yen should the company be concerned about between now and late February? Explain.

b. What is the proper hedge using yen futures?

c. Assume that the spot exchange rate equals ¥0.0080/$ on February 25. On the same day, March yen futures are selling for ¥0.0083/$. How much did the company lose in the cash market and how much did it make in the futures market? How well did the hedge work out?

Discussion Questions and Problems

1. Describe the characteristics of a futures contract. How does a futures contract differ from a forward contract?

2. Why is futures trading considered to be a zero sum game? Who makes money and who loses money if futures decline in price?

3. Who begins the delivery process? Does a long position have to take delivery of the asset?

4. What are the necessary characteristics for an asset to have a viable futures market? Why has an active futures market developed in Treasury securities?

5. Describe the role of the clearinghouse. Why is the clearinghouse so important to the orderly functioning of a futures market?

6. What is margin in futures trading? What happens at the end of each trading day to a futures margin account?

7. Assume that someone goes long in March T-bonds at 114–00 ($114\frac{0}{32}$). The trader must post $4,000 in initial margin and maintain $3,000 in margin. What would happen to the account if March T-bonds were to settle the next day at 113–16? Would the trader face a margin call?

8. Describe open interest. Assume that A went short in 10 March T-bonds two weeks ago (B went long). Today, A went long in 5 March T-bonds (C went short). How much would open interest change?

9. What is basis? Does basis have to equal zero on the delivery date?

10. Explain the differences between intracommodity and intercommodity spreads. Why are spreads important?

11. What is normal backwardation? What does normal backwardation assume about the net position of hedgers?

12. Explain cost of carry. Why is the cost of carry generally negative for T-bond futures?

13. Assume that the spot price of gold is $350 per ounce and the price of a three-month futures contract is $380. What do these prices imply about the cost of carry for gold? If the actual cost of carry were $5 per ounce per month, show how one could profit from these spot and futures prices.

14. What is an outright futures position? Why are outright positions considered to be so risky?

15. If someone buys March corn and, at the same time, sells March wheat, what type of spread is traded? What does the trader expect to happen to the prices of corn and wheat between now and March?

16. What is the general idea behind hedging? What decisions about futures does the hedger have to make?

 17. What are Eurodollars? Explain the differences between T-bill and Eurodollar futures.

18. What is the conversion factor in T-note and T-bond futures? Why does the conversion factor lead to the notion of the cheapest security to deliver?

19. Use the following information to find the invoice amount on a T-bond futures contract.
Settlement price 108–00
Conversion factor .9000
Size of contract $100,000
Number of contracts 5
Accrued interest $1.75 p/$100

20. What is program trading? If someone believes that futures are overpriced, relative to the current index, how could he or she take advantage of this?

21. Assume that a trader is long in T-bonds in the cash market. What is this person concerned about in the near term? What position should this person establish in the futures market?

22. What are options on futures? Why would someone buy a put option as opposed to establishing a short position in the futures contract?

23. 1991 CFA Exam, Level II

Robert Chen, CFA, is reviewing the characteristics of derivative securities and their use in portfolios.

   A. Chen is considering the addition of either a short position in stock index futures or a long position in stock index options to an existing well-diversified portfolio of equity securities. **Contrast** the way in which *each* of these *two* alternatives would affect the risk and return of the resulting combined portfolios.

   (15 minutes)

   B. Four factors affect the value of a futures contract on a stock index. Three of these factors are: the current price of the stock index, the time remaining until the contract maturity (delivery) date, and the dividends on the stock index. **Identify** the *fourth* factor and **explain** *how and why* changes in this factor affect the value of the futures contract.

   (5 minutes)

   C. Six factors affect the value of call options on stocks. Three of these factors are: the current price of the stock, the time remaining until the option expires, and the dividend on the stock. **Identify** the other *three* factors and **explain** *how and why* changes in *each* of these three factors affect the value of call options.

   (15 minutes)

Critical Thinking Exercises

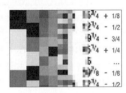

1. The following exercise requires computer work. Open file CTD.XLS on the data disk. The file lists all the T-bonds that could be delivered for the December 1993 bond contract, along with their prices and conversion factors (as of November 15, 1993). Use this information to answer the following questions:

   a. Determine which of the bonds is cheapest to deliver. What does *cheapest to deliver* mean?

   b. Calculate the basis for each bond. Why should the basis be smallest for the bond that is cheapest to deliver? Assume delivery occurs on December 15, 1993.

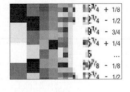

2. The following exercise requires computer work. Open file OOF.XLS on the data disk. It lists prices of call and put options for December 1993 T-bond futures. Use this information to answer the following questions:

   a. Assume that a trader believes that bond prices will rise before December. What position would this person establish in the futures market?

   b. What position in the option on futures market could function as an alternative to the futures position? What are the advantages and disadvantages of the options position, compared to the futures position?

   c. Assume that the trader has established a position in December T-bond futures based on the expectation of rising bond prices. What positions in the options on futures market could protect the futures position in the event that bond prices decline?

d. Calculate the profits and losses from all the positions listed in Parts a, b, and c, at the options' expiration dates, assuming T-bond futures are at the prices listed in the file. Explain the differences in profit/loss between the various positions.

Mini Case **1**   SOLUTION

a. If interest rates fall, both bond and note prices should rise. Since bonds have longer durations than notes (with their longer maturities), bond prices should rise more than note prices. Therefore, the price spread between bonds and notes should get wider. The yield spread, on the other hand, may remain the same because the slope of the yield curve didn't change.

b. Since bond prices will rise more than note prices, one would buy bonds and sell notes. Since both contracts have the same size ($100,000 par value), one would buy one bond contract for every note contract sold.

c. The profit (loss) from the spread would be:

	Initial Price	Closing Price	Profit (Loss)[a]
Five-year notes	111–12	113–04	(56)
Bonds	115–30	120–22	152
Spread	146[a]	242[a]	96

[a] In thirty-seconds.

In dollar terms, the intercommodity spread produces a profit of $3,000 per spread (one note contract sold and one bond contract bought).

Mini Case **2**   SOLUTION

a. The company should be concerned about a rise in the value of the dollar relative to the yen. If, for example, the exchange rate between yen and dollars falls from 0.0092 to 0.0082, the value of ¥10 billion falls from $92 million to $82 million.

b. Since the company is long in yen, it should go short in yen futures. Since each yen futures contract is for ¥12.5 million, the company should sell 800 March yen futures (¥10 billion divided by ¥12.5 million) at 0.0094.

c. At those prices, the company lost $12 million in the cash market ($92 million − $80 million), but made $11 million in the futures market ($13,750 per contract × 800 contracts). In an ideal hedge, any loss in the cash market is exactly offset by profits in the futures market. This hedge came pretty close, reducing the company's loss from $12 million to $1 million.

Chapter 20

Investment Companies

Chapter Objectives

1. Describe the general characteristics of investment companies.
2. Examine the investment characteristics of unit investment trusts.
3. Outline the essentials of closed-end investment companies.
4. Review the historical background and growth of mutual funds.
5. Describe the types of mutual funds and the services they offer to investors.
6. Understand how to select and evaluate investment companies.

As we've seen in the prior chapters, investors today must choose among a staggering number of investment alternatives. The stock market in the United States alone offers over 6,000 different stock issues. Throughout the international markets, the number of stock issues worldwide is closer to 10,000. Add to that the thousands of money market, government, municipal, and corporate debt issues available, and investors face a bewildering task in choosing the right investments for their particular needs.

Many investors find that the best way to select securities intelligently in today's environment is to buy them indirectly by purchasing shares of **investment companies.** There are three types of investment companies: unit investment trusts, closed-end funds, and mutual funds. All investment companies pool funds from many investors and use these funds to purchase securities. Owning shares of an investment company means owning a small piece of a diversified portfolio; dividends (or interest income) and capital gains (or losses) flow through to the investor in proportion to the number of shares he or she owns. Most investment companies hire professional portfolio managers for which they pay management fees. The fund manager seeks securities that provide the best return given the goals and objectives of the investment company.

Investment companies are essentially creatures of the 20th century, and they have become extremely popular in recent years. For example, net assets of U.S.-based mutual funds increased at an annual rate of over 20 percent between the end of 1987 and the end of 1993 to total almost $2 trillion. At the end of 1993, mutual fund assets exceeded, by a wide margin, the total deposits of U.S. savings banks, and approached the total assets of U.S. life insurance companies. Investment companies played a key role in the transition during the last 30 years of so many individuals from simple savers to investors. The fact that record numbers of Americans own stock today is due, in large part, to the existence and growth of investment companies.

In this chapter, we take a detailed look at investment companies. First, we review what investment companies are, how they work, what advantages they offer investors, and so forth. Next, we examine each type of investment company in more depth. For example, we discuss the types of mutual funds and the services they offer investors. Finally, we consider how investors should evaluate and select investment companies, focusing on expenses and performance. Given their popularity and potential benefits, a thorough understanding of investment companies is critical for all contemporary investors who want to make intelligent decisions.

Understanding Investment Companies

The ancestors of today's investment companies can be traced back to 19th-century Britain. Money invested in English and Scottish investment trusts (as these companies were known) contributed substantial financing to the U.S. economy following the Civil War. British investment trusts, for example provided much of the financing to build the railroads that opened up America's western frontier.

Today's investment companies are fairly simple organizations. They raise money by selling shares of their own to the investing public. They use these funds to purchase various types of securities that help them achieve their stated investment objectives. For example, a **money market mutual fund** purchases only money market instruments such as commercial paper and Treasury bills.

As the securities owned by the investment company pay interest or dividends, it passes this income along to its shareholders. If the securities become more or less valuable, these capital gains or losses are also passed along to the investment company's shareholders. Investment companies work in a straightforward fashion, as the simple example in Table 20.1 illustrates.

The investment company (let's call it The Fund) sells 1 million shares, at $10 per share, to the investing public, raising a total of $10 million. (Assume that The Fund charges no fees or expenses to investors.) The Fund uses the $10 million to purchase equal dollar amounts of five stocks with the initial purchase prices, annual dividends, and numbers of shares purchased shown in Table 20.1. Someone who buys 1,000 shares of The Fund, a total investment of $10,000, owns 0.1 percent of its equally weighted portfolio of five stocks.[1] Assume that in six months, the total value of The Fund's portfolio rises to $11.6 million, even though only two of the five stocks in the portfolio actually rise in price. The value of 1,000 shares in The Fund also rises, to $11,600. If, at the end of one year, the total value of The Fund's portfolio rises to $12.6 million, the value of 1,000 shares becomes $12,600.

Now assume that The Fund decides to liquidate at the end of one year. The investor receives $12,600 for 1,000 shares (the $10,000 initial investment plus $2,600 in capital gains) and $220 in dividends. The owner of 0.1 percent of The Fund receives 0.1 percent of its capital gains and 0.1 percent of the

---

[1]Recognize several simplifying assumptions in Table 20.1: It assumes that investors pay no management fees or commissions, the portfolio undergoes no changes during the year, the number of shares issued by The Fund stays constant at 1 million, and all dividends are paid, in cash, to its shareholders.

Table 20.1

Illustration of a Hypothetical Investment Company

The Fund initially sells 1 million shares priced at $10.00 per share. It buys equal dollar amounts of five stocks with the proceeds.

Stock	Purchase Price	Annual Dividend	Number of Shares Purchased	After Six Months		After One Year		
				Price	Total Value	Price	Total Value	Total Dividends
A	$ 20	$0.50	100,000	$ 30.00	$ 3,000,000	$ 34.00	$ 3,400,000	$ 50,000
B	25	0.50	80,000	24.75	1,980,000	22.50	1,800,000	40,000
C	50	1.00	40,000	67.50	2,700,000	80.00	3,200,000	40,000
D	50	1.25	40,000	48.00	1,920,000	45.00	1,800,000	50,000
E	100	2.00	20,000	100.00	2,000,000	120.00	2,400,000	40,000
Total portfolio value					$11,600,000		$12,600,000	$220,000
Per-share value					$11.60		$12.60	$0.22

dividends produced by its portfolio. (Remember, this example assumes no transaction costs.) The investor's return for the year equals:[2]

$$(\$12,600 - \$10,000 + \$220)/\$10,000 = 28.2 \text{ percent}$$

Not a bad return for one year! Obviously, the operations of real investment companies are more complicated than the example, but they all work in basically the same way.

The example emphasized the investment company's **net asset value (NAV).** Net asset value is simply the market value of the investment company's assets minus its liabilities (if any) divided by the number of outstanding shares. The Fund's NAV equals $10.00 when it begins operations, $11.60 in six months, and $12.60 in one year. (Remember, the number of outstanding shares stays constant at 1 million.)[3]

Advantages of Investment Companies

The popularity of investment companies is no fluke. They offer some clear advantages to investors which more than justify their costs. (We'll talk more about the costs associated with investment companies later.) We'll look at the three most obvious advantages of investment companies here.

Diversification. Perhaps the most important advantage of investment companies is diversification. Time and time again, the markets confirm the value of diversification. We've seen how diversification can improve the risk/return tradeoff associated with investing (e.g., reducing an investor's risk without sacrificing too much expected return). Even simple, naive diversification (owning multiple, randomly chosen securities) can produce substantial benefits for investors.

Since investment companies own multiple securities, they offer investors naive diversification at a minimum. (Whether or not they offer efficient

---

[2]This example ignores taxes, of course. We'll take a look at how investment companies, and their shareholders, are taxed later in the chapter.

[3]Calculating the NAV of a mutual fund can be slightly more difficult, as we'll see later in the chapter.

diversification is a question we'll try to answer later.) For example, Fidelity's Magellan Fund (the world's largest mutual fund) owns approximately 600 different stocks. To see the potential benefits of this kind of diversification, take another look at the hypothetical investment company shown in Table 20.1. At the end of six months, two of the five stocks owned by The Fund have risen in price, two have fallen in price, and one is unchanged. Overall, the NAV of The Fund rises by $1.60 since the gain from stocks that rise in price more than offsets the loss from stocks that fall in price. At the end of one year, three stocks rise in price and two fall in price; the NAV rises another dollar. The Fund offers the advantage of diversification, as do all investment companies.

Smaller Minimum Investments. Another advantage of investment companies is their need for smaller minimum investments. Consider The Fund again; to create this portfolio independently, buying equal dollar amounts of all five stocks in round lots (multiples of 100 shares), an investor would have to spend $50,000.[4] The investment company can give the investor some of the benefits of diversification while making a much smaller investment.

Of course, The Fund is hypothetical, but real investment companies also offer the benefit of smaller minimum investments. For example, the Magellan mutual fund has a minimum investment of $2,500; for this relatively small investment, one can obtain a piece, albeit a small one, of a portfolio of several hundred different stocks. Another example is a money market mutual fund. As you may recall from Chapter 2, many money market instruments (such as commercial paper and banker's acceptances) are sold in very large denominations ($1 million or more). Obviously, few individual investors can directly buy any of these instruments. Small investors who put up as little as $1,000 can buy these instruments indirectly, however, by purchasing shares of a money market fund. Simply put, investment companies allow small investors access to large, diversified portfolios and securities they couldn't purchase on their own.

Professional Management. All investment companies provide some management services to their shareholders, for instance, basic clerical services including the preparation of some relevant tax forms. Managing even a small investment portfolio can involve a substantial amount of time-consuming clerical work. Investment companies relieve the individual investor of much of that work.

In addition to the clerical function, most investment companies have professional portfolio managers who decide what securities to buy, when to buy them, and when to sell them. This relieves the investor of the sometimes arduous task of security analysis and selection, right? The answer is both *yes* and *no*. The investor still has to select the right investment company for his or her objectives, no easy job given the number of investment companies today; also, a fund owner should always monitor its performance. (We'll look at some investment strategies using investment companies later in the chapter.)

Some proponents of investment companies claim that, since portfolio managers are professional investors and therefore have greater knowledge of the markets, investment companies can produce superior returns for their shareholders compared to what they would earn investing directly on their own. This issue will be examined in depth later in the chapter; at this point,

---

[4]The portfolio would consist of 500 shares of Stock A, 400 shares of Stock B, 200 shares of Stock C, 200 shares of Stock D, and 100 shares of Stock E.

note simply that the evidence of superior returns from investment companies is not conclusive.

Regulation and Taxation

As with most investments, federal agencies impose the most significant regulation on investment companies in the United States.[5] Many of the federal securities laws discussed in Chapter 3 apply to investment companies. For example, the Securities Act of 1933 requires that every mutual fund provide potential investors with a current prospectus (the official offering document for the investment company) and the act limits the types of advertisements that investment companies may use. Under the Securities Exchange Act of 1934, distributors of mutual fund shares are subject to regulation by the SEC and the National Association of Securities Dealers (NASD).

The more important Investment Company Act of 1940 regulates much of the operation of every investment company. The act contains numerous provisions designed to protect the integrity of investment company assets and prevent funds from charging shareholders excessive fees, among other provisions. For example, the act sets the maximum sales charge a fund can impose at 8.5 percent of the net asset value. The SEC is responsible for administering all aspects of the Investment Company Act.

In 1992, the SEC proposed a number of major changes to the regulation of investment companies.[6] These proposed changes include the deregulation of sales charges, allowing so-called **off the page sales** (which would allow investors to purchase shares of a mutual fund before they see the entire prospectus), and creating **interval funds** (hybrid closed-end and open-end investment companies). Many of these changes will require congressional approval, over opposition from the industry. Their future is uncertain.

Recently, news reports have revealed disturbing facts about a few mutual fund managers' practices. Some managers are permitted to trade for their own accounts, for example; the rules vary widely from fund to fund. Some practices are illegal; managers may not purchase stock for their own accounts, and then buy shares for the fund, thus pushing up the stock's price. Still, many gray areas remain. Some argue that mutual funds need new rules and regulations. A *Business Week* editorial on this subject appears in the Investment Insights feature.

Taxation. Virtually all investment companies choose to be taxed as regulated investment companies under Subchapter M of the IRS code. To qualify, an investment company must meet a number of requirements on asset diversification, sources of income, short-term gains, and distribution of income. The last requirement has the most significant impact on investors; to qualify under Subchapter M, an investment company must distribute virtually all investment income to its shareholders each year.

Regulated investment companies pay no taxes on investment income or capital gains; rather, income and capital gains pass through to individual shareholders, who assume the tax liability. Generally, for taxable individual investors, investment income (interest and dividends) is taxed as ordinary income, and increases in the value of the fund's portfolio are taxed as either short-term or long-term capital gains. Distributions of these capital gains, which are called *dividends,* are taxable for individual investors. Investment

[5]In addition to federal regulation, most states regulate sales of mutual fund shares to their residents. State regulations vary widely.

[6]See, for example, "SEC to Propose Most Sweeping Changes in a Decade for Mutual Fund Industry," *The Wall Street Journal,* May 18, 1992, C1.

Mutual Funds Need Tighter Rules

It doesn't get much better than this. Mutual-fund investors, who plunked down $128.2 billion last year for equity portfolios, racked up an average of 20 percent total return—doubling the Standard & Poor's 500 stock index and far surpassing what they could earn with certificates of deposit. So happy are customers that they now entrust $2 trillion of their money to funds. With the Dow heading toward 4000 and interest rates remaining low, that figure is sure to soar.

But there have been some disquieting revelations about how some mutual-fund managers behave. To the surprise of many new investors, it turns out that fund managers are permitted to trade for their own accounts while managing publicly owned portfolios. In at least one case, it appears that a fund manager got into a private placement, thanks to the favors of a stock promoter. The same promoter turned out to be offering stock to the manager's fund.

That mutual-fund manager was accused of violating the fund's rules on personal trading. Another resigned to move to another fund after an internal investigation cleared him. It is now clear that what is permitted varies from one fund group to another. Worse, very little information is made available to the investor.

The issue is not a legal one. Such trading practices as front running, whereby managers buy stock for their own accounts and then buy it

for the fund, pushing up the prices of their own equities, are illegal. But the gray areas abound and beg for both transparency and close monitoring.

One way for the mutual-fund industry to retain its squeaky-clean image is to forbid its managers from trading for themselves. Tie their compensation to the performance of their portfolios. If they want to participate personally in the market, let them buy the same funds as their customers do—on the same terms.

A number of mutual-fund groups actively encourage their managers to trade for themselves. They want them to have a good "feel" for the markets. For these funds, full disclosure and close monitoring by a third party of all personal trades and investments is in order. Indeed, personal trades by managers that overlap with the fund's investments should be disclosed to the public owners of the mutual fund in a timely fashion.

The mutual-fund industry has been a glorious financial success story for millions. It should strive to keep their trust by taking immediate steps to retain its Mr. Clean image.

Source: "Mutual Funds Need Tighter Rules," *Business Week,* February 14, 1994, 134. Reprinted from February 14, 1994 issue of *Business Week* by special permission, copyright © 1994 by McGraw-Hill, Inc.

companies are allowed to pass through the federal tax exemption on interest from municipal securities to shareholders.

To illustrate this kind of pass through, let's look at two actual examples. During the 1993 fiscal year (October 31, 1992 through October 31, 1993), the Janus Fund (a mutual fund) distributed $1.19 per share to its shareholders. This was broken down into investment income of $0.29 per share and long-term capital gains of $0.90 per share. An owner of 1,000 shares of the fund would have reported $290 in dividend income and long-term capital gains of $900 on his or her 1993 federal tax return. The Vanguard Intermediate Maturity municipal bond fund distributed income of $0.696 per share and long-term capital gains of $0.076 per share during 1993. An owner of 1,000 shares of this fund would have received $696 in income during 1993 and capital gains of $76. The capital gain is fully taxable, but the income is exempt from federal income taxes since it derives from municipal bonds.

The above examples don't consider the change in each fund's net asset value (NAV) during the year. (As we'll see, the change in NAV, along with the amount distributed, determines a fund's total return during a specific time period.) The Janus Fund's NAV, for example, increased from $18.86 to $20.82 between the beginning and end of the 1993 fiscal year. Not surprisingly, much of the change in NAV was due to the change in the market value of the fund's assets; put another way, this change came from capital gains and losses not yet realized by the fund. If shares are not redeemed, a fund shareholder has no tax consequence due to a change in NAV. The change in NAV is treated just like any unrealized capital gain or loss. If shares are redeemed, then the increase (or decrease) in NAV during the holding period becomes a capital gain (or loss) for tax purposes.[7]

Types of Investment Companies

As we've mentioned, investment companies can be divided into three types or groups: unit investment trusts, closed-end investment companies, and mutual funds. Of the three, mutual funds are, by far, the most significant. At the end of 1993, for example, mutual funds held more than 85 percent of total investment company assets. The differences between the three are straightforward. Let's start with a discussion of perhaps the least known, and in many ways simplest, type of investment company, the unit investment trust.

Unit Investment Trusts

A **unit investment trust** is typically an unmanaged portfolio of fixed income securities put together by a sponsor and run by an independent trustee. The sponsor sells a fixed number of shares, called *units,* and uses the proceeds, less a sales charge, to purchase a portfolio of securities. All income from the securities held by the trust is distributed to the owners of the units, along with any principal repayments. The major advantages of unit investment trusts, compared to other investment companies, are generally lower annual fees and the routine return of principal.

The securities that make up a unit investment trust's portfolio almost always remain unchanged. Unit investment trusts are usually unmanaged, passive investments. A unit investment trust with a portfolio of bonds ceases to exist when the last of the bonds in the portfolio mature. An investor can usually sell units prior to maturity. The sponsor typically makes a market in the units, buying and selling them at their current net asset value, though sponsors aren't obligated to do so. Shares of unit investment trusts are generally the least liquid of any investment company. In addition to the initial sales charge (typically 3 to 4 percent), some unit investment trusts charge small annual management fees. Some sponsors also charge commissions if units are sold early.

The first unit investment trust was created in 1961; since then, over $200 billion worth of units have been sold. Only municipal bond unit investment trusts were available until 1972 when the first corporate bond trust was created; government bond trusts became available in 1978. In spite of these developments, municipal bond trusts have remained the most popular. Municipal bond trusts have accounted for more than 65 percent of the total amount of unit investment trusts sold since 1961.

A very recent development is the stock trust, a unit investment trust that purchases a fixed portfolio of between 10 and 40 stocks with the intention

---

[7]The tax consequences associated with the redemption of mutual fund shares, especially if they've been purchased at several different points in time, can get quite complicated and are beyond the scope of this text.

of liquidating the portfolio at some set point in time (usually after one to five years). The purpose is to offer small investors a way of purchasing a diversified portfolio of common stocks.[8] (Units are initially sold for as little as $1,000 each.)

Closed-End Investment Companies

Like all investment companies, **closed-end investment companies** (or *closed-end funds*) raise money by selling shares to the investing public. They invest this money in a variety of securities consistent with their stated investment objectives. A closed-end fund usually does not sell additional shares after the initial public offering, however, and thus the number of outstanding shares is usually fixed.[9] In addition, a closed-end fund will not redeem shares unless it liquidates. Shares of closed-end funds trade on various stock exchanges. (About 80 percent of closed-end fund shares are listed on the NYSE.) Investors can buy or sell shares of closed-end funds just like ordinary shares of common stock.

Some see advantages in the limits on the number of shares that closed-end investment companies have outstanding. For one thing, this limits how large a closed-end investment company can get, unlike the potentially unlimited growth of a mutual fund. Some argue that performance can suffer if an investment company gets too large. (We'll consider this issue later in the chapter.) Another potential advantage of a closed-end investment company, with its limited number of shares, is potential to buy shares at a discount. We'll discuss this issue shortly.

Unlike unit investment trusts, virtually all closed-end funds are actively managed. Each fund has a portfolio manager, or advisor, who buys and sells securities in an attempt to maximize return for what the advisor believes is an acceptable level of risk. For example, the manager of a closed-end fund that invests in government securities might increase the average duration of the portfolio if interest rates seem likely to decline. The manager of a closed-end fund that invests primarily in common stocks might increase the percentage of the portfolio held in money market instruments if common stocks appear temporarily overvalued, making price declines likely in the near future.

Approximately 377 closed-end funds trade in the United States with total net assets exceeding $85 billion. Once considered to be an investment backwater, closed-end investment companies have experienced explosive growth in recent years. Over 300 new closed-end funds were formed between 1985 and 1993, causing total net assets of all closed-end funds to grow at an annual rate of over 40 percent during that period.

More than half of all closed-end funds invest in debt securities (either municipal or corporate bonds). However, the most rapidly growing type of closed-end funds is the single-country equity fund. Such a fund limits its investments to equity securities issued in a specific country. Two examples are the France Fund and the Korea Fund.

Example of a Closed-End Fund. A report on the Zweig Fund, an example of a closed-end fund, appears in Figure 20.1. (Perhaps you remember Martin Zweig from Chapter 6.) The Zweig Fund invests primarily in U.S. common stocks (which currently make up about 52 percent of the portfolio); it has

---

[8]See, "Asking $1,000 a Pop, Stock Trusts Aim to Lure Small Investors," *The Wall Street Journal,* January 30, 1990, p. C1.

[9]This is not always the case, however. Restrictions on issues of new shares vary from company to company. Occasionally closed-end funds sell new shares by rights offerings. Further, some companies offer dividend reinvestment plans. Instead of receiving dividends in cash, the shareholder receives additional shares.

about $500 million in net assets. Since the Zweig Fund is actively managed, based on Martin Zweig's market timing and stock selection techniques, the percentage of the portfolio held in common stocks varies from year to year; it has been as low as about 50 percent and as high as 80 percent. Its annual portfolio turnover can be quite high (173 percent in 1992 and 202 percent in 1990).

Clearly, the Zweig Fund has a fairly generous distribution policy. In 1992, for example, it paid out $1.14 per share, or about 9 percent of the year-end net asset value. The fund has an investment advisory and management agreement with Zweig Advisors, Inc. (that's a big surprise!) for which the annual fee equals 0.85 percent of the average daily net asset value. This fee is paid out of investment income (dividends and interest) before any distribution to the fund's shareholders.

Net Asset Value Discount. Because the shares of closed-end funds trade on stock exchanges like ordinary common stocks, market prices are set by the sometimes mysterious interaction of supply and demand. In fact, the market prices of closed-end fund shares rarely equal their respective net asset values. Take another look at Figure 20.1; notice that the year-end share price of the Zweig Fund has never been equal to its year-end NAV since its inception (though it was close in 1988). At the end of 1987, the share price was about 7.5 percent less than the NAV ($9.00 versus $9.73). On the other hand, at the end of 1992, the share price was about 14 percent higher than the fund's NAV ($13.00 versus $11.36).

The Zweig Fund is not unusual. Figure 20.2 shows the ratio of share price to NAV for three closed-end funds (Zweig Fund, Nuveen Municipal Value Fund, and Tri-Continental Corporation) from 1989 to 1993. The Nuveen Fund invests in municipal securities, while Tri-Continental Corporation invests primarily in common stocks. Each fund has more than $1.5 billion in net assets. Over a recent five-year period, none of the three have sold, at year-end, for their NAVs. In fact, Tri-Continental sold at a discount from its NAV at the end of each of the five years.

Historically, closed-end funds have generally sold at discounts from their respective NAVs. In recent years the typical discount has narrowed and some funds (such as the Zweig Fund) currently sell at premiums (i.e., their share prices exceed their NAVs). In 1979, for example, equity closed-end funds sold at an average discount of 28 percent; by 1992 the average discount was only about 4 percent. This raises a number of interesting questions. Why would a closed-end fund sell at a discount? Why does the discount vary from fund to fund? Why has the average discount narrowed in recent years?

There are no definitive answers to these questions, but several reasonable explanations have been offered. Some suggest that the discount is due, in part, to thin secondary markets. (Remember, shares of closed-end funds are traded on stock exchanges.) As the secondary markets for the shares of these funds have improved in recent years, the average discount has diminished. Others suggest that the discount is due to poor average historical performance; since the funds have exhibited better performance in recent years, the discount has shrunk. Other factors may help to explain the variation in the NAV discount, including distribution policies, taxes, management fees, and relative performance.[10]

---

[10]The relationship between relative performance and NAV discount is far from conclusive. Funds with more generous distribution policies and/or lower annual management fees typically have smaller NAV discounts. The tax argument is based on the observation that many older funds have substantial positions in some of the great historic growth stocks. If the funds were to sell these stocks and distribute the proceeds to the shareholders as capital gains, all shareholders would have to pay taxes, regardless of whether or not they owned the shares in time to enjoy the profits.

Figure 20.1

Example Closed-End Fund: The Zweig Fund

Zweig Fund

2526

NYSE Symbol ZF

NAV	Price	%Difference	Dividend	Yield	S&P Ranking	Beta
May 6'94	May 6'94					
10.70	12½	+16.8	¹0.87	¹7.0%	NR	0.66

Summary

This closed-end investment company seeks to achieve capital appreciation primarily through investment in equity securities, although a substantial portion of assets may be held in cash or equivalents when a defensive position is deemed advisable. Short-term instruments accounted for 35% of net assets at December 31, 1993. The fund's distribution policy is to provide a stable cash flow of at least 2.5% of net asset value per quarter.

Business Summary

The Zweig Fund, Inc. is a closed-end, diversified management investment company. The fund's investment objective is capital appreciation, primarily through investment in equity securities. Debt securities that present opportunities for capital appreciation may also be purchased. Dividends and current income are incidental to the objective of capital appreciation.

As of December 31, 1993, investments aggregated $505.0 million (at market; 94.4% of net assets). Net assets at December 31, 1993 and 1992, were divided as follows:

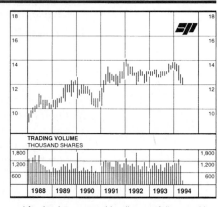

	12/93	12/92
Common stock	56.7%	52.1%
Short–term investments	35.0%	29.0%
U.S. Gov't obligations	5.8%	16.1%
Short sales	–3.1%	–2.9%
Cash & other (net)	5.6%	5.7%

The 10 largest common stock holdings at December 31, 1993 (17.1% of net assets) were EMC Corp., Oracle Systems, Southwest Airlines, Tele-Communications Inc. (Class A), Wells Fargo & Co., Green Tree Financial Corp., Deere & Co., Cirrus Logic, Homestake Mining and Hasbro, Inc.

The fund will attempt to achieve its objectives by using the following investment methods, some of which will subject it to greater-than-average risks and costs: writing covered listed put and call equity options, including options on stock indexes, and purchasing such options; under certain circumstances, writing call options that are not covered or put options that are not secured; short sales of securities; purchasing and selling, for hedging purposes, stock index, interest rate and other futures contracts and purchasing options on such futures; borrowing from banks to purchase securities; investing in securities of special-situation companies

and foreign issuers; and lending portfolio securities to institutional borrowers.

The fund expects that at least 65% of its net assets will consist of equity securities, including convertible securities and warrants. However, when a defensive position is warranted, a substantial percentage of the fund's assets may be held in cash or invested in money-market instruments. The fund expects that its annual portfolio turnover rate will be between 100% and 200%—higher than that of most other funds.

The fund's investment adviser is Zweig Advisors Inc. The adviser receives a monthly fee at an annual rate of 0.85 of 1% of the fund's average daily net assets during the previous month. The advisory fee for 1993 amounted to $4,388,821, compared with $4,176,697 the year before. Zweig/Glaser Advisers administers the fund.

Per Share Data ($)

Yr. End Dec. 31	1993	1992	1991	1990	1989	1988	1987	²1986
Net Asset Value	**11.68**	11.36	12.40	10.48	11.43	10.35	9.73	9.31
Yr. End Prices	**13⅝**	13	13¾	11⅛	12%	10⅜	9	9⅛
% Difference	**+16.7%**	+14.4%	+10.9%	+6.2%	+8.3%	NM	–7.5%	–2.0%
Dividends—								
Invest. Inc.	**0.22**	0.10	0.30	0.49	0.52	0.25	0.28	Nil
Capital Gains	**1.00**	1.04	0.82	0.69	0.60	0.79	0.64	Nil
Portfolio Turned	**236%**	173%	144%	202% ·	184%	206%	281%	56%

Data as orig. reptd. **1.** Paid in the past 12 mos. from invest. inc.: excl. 0.31 from long-term capital gains. **2.** From Oct. 2, 1986 (date of inception) - Dec. 31, 1986.

Dual Purpose Funds. A special type of closed-end fund is a **dual purpose fund.** Unlike the typical investment company, a dual purpose fund sells two types of shares and has a predetermined life span (typically 10 to 20 years). Investors who buy the fund's *income shares* receive all income (interest and dividends) from its assets plus a fixed redemption value when the fund liquidates. Investors who purchase the fund's *capital shares* receive everything else. Both sets of shares trade on the secondary markets. Only a handful of

Figure 20.1 continued

2526

The Zweig Fund, Inc.

Income Data (Million $)

Year Ended Dec. 31	Total Invest Inc.	-Net Invest Income- Total	Per Share	Realized Cap. Gains Total	Per Sh.	²% Net Inv. Inc./ Net Assets	—% Expenses To— ²Net Assets	Invest. Inc.	Price Ranges Com. Stk. HI LO
1993	12.5	6.1	0.13	47.1	1.03	1.2	1.2	51.0	13⅞–12⅝
1992	14.7	8.5	0.20	43.2	0.98	1.7	1.3	42.1	14⅛–12
1991	16.0	10.4	0.26	35.7	0.84	2.4	1.3	35.2	13⅞–10¼
1990	22.0	17.1	0.47	21.9	0.59	4.4	1.3	22.5	12⅝–10⅛
1989	23.4	18.3	0.52	24.2	0.68	4.7	1.3	21.9	12⅜–10
1988	16.2	11.5	0.33	28.8	0.84	3.4	1.4	29.2	11¼–8⅞
1987	12.9	7.7	0.22	30.7	0.91	2.2	1.5	40.6	10⅝–7⅝
¹1986	4.3	3.3	0.10	d6.0	d0.18	4.2	1.2	21.9	10⅜–8¾

Balance Sheet Data (Million $)

Dec. 31	Net Assets	% Change NAV	³S&P 500	Bonds AAA	Investments Cost	Market	Net Cash	% Net Asset Distribution ST Oblig.	Bonds & Pfd.	Com. Stk.	Other Invest.
1993	535	+11.4	+7.1	+13.2	456	522	2.5	35.0	5.8	56.7	Nil
1992	500	–0.2	+4.5	+0.1	434	486	2.8	29.0	16.1	52.1	Nil
1991	526	+25.5	+26.3	+10.0	458	560	d6.3	19.5	15.0	71.8	Nil
1990	390	–2.4	–6.6	–2.9	360	390	d0.1	27.0	19.8	53.2	0.1
1989	409	+16.0	+27.3	+8.1	342	401	1.9	29.7	18.0	50.1	0.3
1988	357	+14.4	+12.4	–0.3	324	345	3.2	40.2	6.3	50.3	Nil
1987	329	+6.7	+2.0	–8.9	313	316	4.0	9.6	3.6	82.8	Nil
1986	317	NA	+14.6	+8.9	315	316	2.9	27.2	15.8	54.1	Nil

Data as orig. reptd. **1.** From Oct. 2, 1986 (date of inception) - Dec. 31, 1986. **2.** As reptd. by Co. (annualized in 1986) **3.** Bef. reinvestment of divs. d-Deficit. NA-Not Available.

Net Asset Value Per Share ($)

As of:	1993	1992	1991	1990
Mar. 31............	11.47	11.49	11.82	10.82
Jun. 30	11.65	11.31	11.14	11.15
Sep. 30............	---	---	11.57	10.38
Dec. 31............	11.68	11.36	12.40	10.48

In the 12 months ended December 31, 1993, net asset value per share (adjusted for capital gains distributions) was up 11.4%. For the same period, the Standard & Poor's 500 Stock Index rose 7.1%.

Total investment income for 1993 fell 15% from that of 1992, on a 23% decline in interest income and a 1.2% drop in dividend income. With a 2.7% increase in total expenses, net investment income declined 28%, to $0.13 a share, from $0.20. There was a net realized and unrealized gain on investments of $1.41 a share, versus a loss of $0.10.

Net Invest. Income Per Share ($)

Quarter:	1993	1992	1991	1990
Mar.	0.04	0.04	0.08	0.11
Jun.	0.03	0.06	0.06	0.11
Sep.	0.03	0.05	0.07	0.12
Dec.	0.03	0.05	0.05	0.13
	0.13	0.20	0.26	0.47

Dividend Data

The fund's policy is to distribute to shareholders at least 2.5% of net asset value per quarter. The fund will pay out all investment income and any short-term capital gains each year (paying any excess over the 10% annual payment rate in the final quarter) and will thereby be relieved of any federal income taxes thereon. Dividends paid from net investment income are taxable to shareholders as dividend income whether or not they are reinvested in fund shares. The fund may retain for reinvestment net long-term capital gains in excess of net short-term capital losses, requiring federal income taxes to be paid thereon by the fund, and such capital gains will be treated as having been distributed to shareholders. As a result, such amounts will be taxed to shareholders as long-term capital gains, and shareholders will be able to claim their proportionate share of the federal income taxes paid by the fund on such gains as a credit against their own federal income tax liabilities and will be entitled to increase the adjusted tax basis of their shares by the difference between their pro rata share of such gains and their tax credit. A dividend reinvestment plan is available.

Amt. of Divd. $	Date Decl.	Ex-divd. Date	Stock of Record	Payment Date
0.28	Jun. 21	Jul. 6	Jul. 12	Jul. 26'93
0.30	Sep. 20	Oct. 6	Oct. 13	Oct. 26'93
0.31*	Dec. 14	Jan. 5	Dec. 31	Jan. 10'94
0.29	Mar. 21	Apr. 6	Apr. 12	Apr. 26'94

*Long-term capital gains.

Capitalization

Long Term Debt: None.

Common Stock: 45,777,783 shs. ($0.10 par).

Office—900 Third Ave., New York, NY 10022. **Tel**—(212) 755-9860. **Chrmn & Pres**—M. E. Zweig. **VP-Treas & Investor Contact**—Jeffrey Lazar. **Secy**—R. E. Smith. **Dirs**—E. S. Babbitt Jr., W. M. Batten, J. A. DiMenna, E. J. Glaser, E. S. Jaffe, J. B. Rogers Jr., A. M. Santomero, R. E. Smith, M. E. Zweig. **Transfer Agent**—Bank of New York, NYC. **Incorporated** in Maryland in 1986.

Information has been obtained from sources believed to be reliable, but its accuracy and completeness are not guaranteed.   Helene K. Phillips

Source: *Standard & Poor's Stock Reports* 61, no. 95, sec. 0 (May 17, 1994). Reprinted with permission of Standard & Poor's, a division of Hill, Inc.

new dual purpose funds have been formed in the last few years; currently the market offers about six dual purpose funds.

Mutual Funds

As we noted earlier, **mutual funds** are, by far, the most popular type of investment company; their assets dwarf those of unit investment trusts and closed-

Figure 20.2

Net Asset Value (NAV) versus Market Price for Three Closed-End Funds: 1989–1993

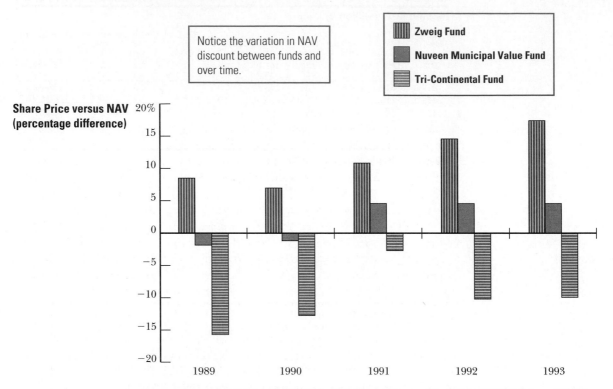

Source: Standard & Poor's, *NYSE Stock Reports*, February 1, 1994, 1708, 2256, and 2526.

end funds. Like closed-end funds, the vast majority of mutual funds are actively managed. (Index funds are an exception.) Unlike closed-end funds, however, mutual funds continually sell new shares and they also directly redeem shares.[11] As a result, the number of outstanding shares for a mutual fund can vary from day to day. Since an investor can buy and sell directly with the fund, there is no need for mutual fund shares to trade on a secondary market. Therefore, in addition to offering the general advantages of investment companies (diversification, smaller minimum investments, and professional management), mutual funds often provide better liquidity for investors than other types of investment companies.

Growth and Development. The Massachusetts Investment Trust, founded in 1924, is considered to be the first mutual fund organized in the United States.[12] At the time, the idea of continuously offering and immediately redeeming shares was considered to be a radical departure in the financial community. In spite of this, the idea took hold and other newly organized mutual funds soon followed. Most of the early mutual funds survived the 1929 stock market crash and the Great Depression.

[11]Because of this feature, mutual funds are sometimes called *open-end investment companies*.

[12]The Massachusetts Investment Trust is still in operation; it is one of the mutual funds managed by the Massachusetts Financial Services (MFS) Group. At the end of 1993, it had about $1.6 billion in net assets.

The growth of the mutual fund industry accelerated following the end of World War II. At the end of 1940, mutual funds had net assets of $448 million; the net assets of mutual funds exceeded $2 billion by 1950, $17 billion by 1960, and $47 billion by 1970. At the end of 1970, 361 U.S. mutual funds served some 10.5 million shareholders.

Mutual funds continued to grow throughout the 1970s aided by two new types of mutual funds: money market funds and tax-exempt municipal bond funds.[13] Money market funds became especially popular during the 1970s as small savers, who were used to earning $5\frac{1}{2}$ percent on their savings, were given the opportunity to earn market yields. In 1974, 16 money market funds had net assets of slightly more than $1.7 billion; by 1980 96 money market funds had net assets in excess of $74.4 billion. By the end of the end of 1980, 564 U.S. mutual funds had net assets of $138.4 billion.

The 1980s saw extraordinary growth in the mutual fund industry, no doubt fueled in part by the historic bull market in paper assets. Between 1980 and 1984 the number of mutual funds and shareholder accounts almost tripled; the net assets of mutual funds increased by over 200 percent. During the last few years, the growth in the mutual fund industry has not abated. Between 1984 and the end of 1993, for example, the net assets of mutual funds increased from less than $400 billion to almost $2,000 billion (an increase of more than 385 percent). At the end of 1993, almost 4,000 mutual funds operated in the United States. The recent growth of mutual fund net assets is shown in Figure 20.3.

Mutual funds have also played an important role in the burgeoning business of tax-deferred retirement savings (IRAs, Keogh plans, etc.). For example, at the end of 1993, mutual funds held more than $200 billion of individual retirement account (IRA) assets. The percentage of IRA assets held by mutual funds has increased steadily since 1986, from 19.4 percent to more than 30.0 percent today.

International Perspective. Mutual funds are also popular in other parts of the world. The worldwide distribution of mutual fund assets in 1988 and 1992 are shown in Figure 20.4. At the end of 1992, for example, non-U.S. mutual funds had net assets of about $1.5 billion, compared to $1.6 billion for U.S. funds. France, with net assets of $432.5 million, and Japan, with net assets of $342.7 million, had the largest mutual funds, measured by assets, outside the United States at the end of 1992. Like their U.S. counterparts, non-U.S. mutual funds have grown very rapidly in recent years. The net assets of French mutual funds, for example, more than doubled between the end of 1987 and the end of 1992.

Types of Mutual Funds. Mutual funds can be classified on the basis of their overall investment objectives and the types of securities that they purchase to obtain that objective. Along with the rapid growth in mutual fund assets, the number of different categories of mutual funds has also expanded in recent years to meet changing investment needs. In 1975, all mutual funds fit neatly into seven categories; the number of different categories of mutual funds expanded to 16 by 1985 and to the current number of 22 by 1987. Today mutual funds invest in junk bonds, GNMAs, variable-rate mortgages, stocks in specific industries (such as utilities and biotech companies), small-capitalization stocks, the entire S&P 500 (index funds), and so forth. Some

---

[13]The 1976 Tax Reform Act allowed mutual funds to pass through the tax exemption on interest from municipal securities to shareholders. Prior to 1976, only unit investment trusts had the authority to pass through tax exempt interest.

Figure 20.3

Net Asset Growth of U.S. Mutual Funds: 1984–1993

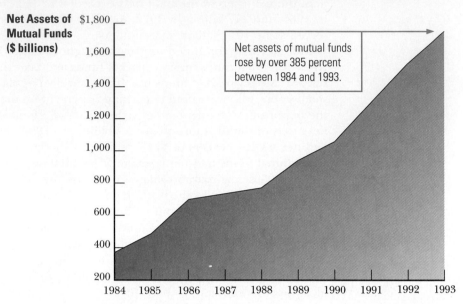

Net Assets of Mutual Funds ($ billions)

Net assets of mutual funds rose by over 385 percent between 1984 and 1993.

Source: *1994 Yearbook* (Washington, D.C.: Investment Company Institute, 1994), 101.

mutual funds shift their portfolios drastically between money market instruments, bonds, and stocks as market conditions change.[14] The 22 different categories of mutual funds are briefly described in Figure 20.5. More generally, most mutual funds can be classified as one of four types: equity funds, bond and income funds, money market funds, and tax-exempt money market funds.[15]

Figure 20.6 on page 712 illustrates the distribution of mutual fund assets by type of fund for 1982 and 1992. Not surprisingly, given the high level of interest rates at the time, the net assets of taxable money market funds made up almost 70 percent of total mutual fund assets at the end of 1982. While all types of mutual funds grew rapidly during this ten-year period, bond and income funds grew the fastest; the net assets of these funds increased by close to 2,000 percent between 1982 and 1992. At the end of 1992 the net assets of bond and income funds exceeded those of taxable money market funds and equity funds.

International funds, which invest primarily outside the United States, have grown very rapidly during the last few years. In 1993, international funds more than doubled in size; by the end of the year, they had over $113 billion in net assets.

Load Funds versus No Load Funds. Mutual funds can also be classified based on whether or not they charge sales charges, referred to as **load charges,** to buy and/or redeem shares. The load charge can be as high as 8.5 percent. We'll discuss load charges, along with other mutual fund expenses, in detail

---

[14]An example of this type of mutual fund is Fidelity's Asset Manager. At the end of 1993, 60 percent of the fund's assets were invested in common stocks, 20 percent were invested in money market instruments, and 20 percent were invested in long-term bonds.

[15]There are two exceptions: precious metals funds and option/income funds. At the end of 1991 these two types of funds had net assets of approximately $4.5 billion, or less than 0.5 percent of total mutual fund net assets.

Figure 20.4

Worldwide Distribution of Mutual Fund Assets: 1988 and 1992

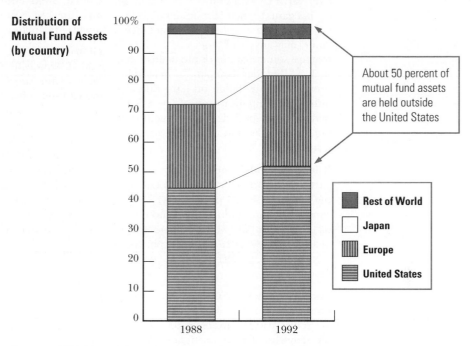

Source: *1993 Mutual Fund Factbook* (Washington, D.C.: Investment Company Institute, 1993) 66.

later in the chapter. At this point, note that the trend in the mutual fund industry in recent years has been toward no-load funds.

Services Offered. Mutual funds offer a variety of services to shareholders, though the actual services offered vary from fund to fund. Five services are the most common:

1. *Automatic reinvestment of distributions.* Instead of paying distributions (dividends and capital gains) to the shareholder in cash, the fund automatically reinvests the distributions, increasing the number of shares the shareholder owns.
2. *Automatic investment plans.* The shareholder can elect to have a specific dollar amount transferred periodically (usually either monthly or quarterly) from a bank account to the fund to purchase additional shares.[16]
3. *Check writing.* All money market funds, and many bond and income funds, allow shareholders to write checks (usually for at least $500). These checks can be used just like bank checks. Sufficient shares of the fund are redeemed in order to cover the check. Very few equity funds offer check writing services.
4. *Exchange privileges.* Many funds are part of **mutual fund families.** The same management company may offer several different mutual funds. Fidelity Investments, for example, offers over 75 different mutual funds. Exchange privileges allow shareholders to transfer money from one fund

---

[16]Sometimes referred to as *dollar cost averaging,* this is a form of diversification across time. We discussed this concept briefly back in Chapter 14.

Figure 20.5

Types of Mutual Funds

Aggressive Growth Funds seek maximum capital gains as their investment objective. Current income is not a significant factor. Some may invest in stocks of businesses that are somewhat out of the mainstream, such as fledgling companies, new industries, companies fallen on hard times, or industries temporarily out of favor. Some may also use specialized investment techniques such as option writing or short-term trading.

Balanced Funds generally have a three-part investment objective: (1) to conserve the investors' initial principal, (2) to pay current income, and (3) to promote long-term growth of both principal and income. Balanced funds have portfolios mix of bonds, preferred stocks, and common stocks.

Corporate Bond Funds, like income funds, seek high levels of income. They do so by buying bonds of corporations for the majority of their portfolios. The rest of the portfolios may be in U.S. Treasury bonds or bonds issued by federal agencies.

Flexible Portfolio Funds may be 100 percent invested in stocks OR bonds OR money market instruments, depending on market conditions. These funds give the money managers the greatest flexibility in anticipating or responding to economic changes.

GNMA or Ginnie Mae Funds invest in mortgage securities backed by the Government National Mortgage Association (GNMA). To qualify for this category, the majority of the portfolio must always be invested in mortgage-backed securities.

Global Bond Funds invest in the debt securities of companies and countries worldwide, including the United States.

Global Equity Funds invest in securities traded worldwide, including the United States. Compared to direct investments, global funds offer investors an easier avenue to investing abroad. The funds' professional money managers handle the trading and recordkeeping details and deal with differences in currencies, languages, time zones, laws and regulations, and business customs and practices. In addition to another layer of diversification, global funds add another layer of risk—exchange-rate risk.

Growth Funds invest in the common stock of well-established companies. Their primary aim is to increase the values of their investments (capital gains) rather than flows of dividends. Investors who buy a growth fund are more interested in seeing the fund's share price rise than in receiving income from dividends.

Growth and Income Funds invest mainly in the common stock of companies that have had increasing share values but also solid records of paying dividends. This type of fund attempts to combine long-term capital growth with a steady stream of income.

High-Yield Bond Funds maintain at least two-thirds of their portfolios in lower-rated corporate bonds (Baa or lower by Moody's rating service and BBB or lower by Standard & Poor's rating service). In return for a generally higher yield, investors must bear a greater degree of risk than for higher-rated bonds.

---

to another. Let's say a money market fund shareholder believes that stocks are cheap. The exchange privilege would allow this person to move all, or part, of his or her money from the money market fund to an equity fund managed by the same company. Many funds allow for exchanges by telephone.

5. *Periodic statements.* All funds provide shareholders with periodic statements that show how much their shares have earned (dividends and capital gains), what their shares are currently worth, new shares purchased, shares redeemed, and so forth. All funds also periodically distribute information on their expenses and portfolio compositions. Funds also provide important year-end tax information to shareholders.

Income–Bond Funds seek high levels of current income for their shareholders by investing at all times in mixes of corporate and government bonds.

Income–Equity Funds seek high levels of current income for their shareholders by investing primarily in equity securities of companies with good dividend-paying records.

Income–Mixed Funds seek high levels of current income for their shareholders by investing in income-producing securities, including both equities and debt instruments.

International Funds invest in equity securities of companies located outside the United States. Two-thirds of their portfolios must be so invested at all times to be categorized here.

Long-Term Municipal Bond Funds invest in bonds issued by states and municipalities to finance schools, highways, hospitals, airports, bridges, water and sewer works, and other public projects. In most cases, income earned on these securities is not taxed by the federal government, but may be taxed under state and local laws. For some taxpayers, portions of income earned on these securities may be subject to the federal alternative minimum tax.

Precious Metals/Gold Funds maintain two-thirds of their portfolios invested in securities associated with gold, silver, and other precious metals.

State Municipal Bond Funds—Long-Term work just like other long-term municipal bond funds except their portfolios contain the issues of only one state. A resident of that state has the advantage of receiving income free of both federal and state tax. For some taxpayers, portions of income from these securities may be subject to the federal alternative minimum tax.

State Tax-Exempt Money Market Funds work just like other tax-exempt money market funds except their portfolios contain the issues of only one state. A resident of that state has the advantage of receiving income free of both federal and state tax. For some taxpayers, portions of income from these securities may be subject to the federal alternative minimum tax.

Taxable Money Market Funds seek to maintain stable net asset values by investing in the short-term, high-grade securities sold in the money market, such as Treasury bills, bank certificates of deposit, and commercial paper (the short-term IOUs of large U.S. corporations). Money market funds limit the average maturities of their portfolios to 90 days or less.

Tax-Exempt Money Market Funds—National invest in municipal securities with relatively short maturities. Investors who use these funds seek investments with minimum risk. For some taxpayers, portions of income from certain of these securities may be subject to the federal alternative minimum tax.

U.S. Government Income Funds invest in a variety of government securities. These include U.S. Treasury bonds, federally guaranteed mortgage-backed securities, and other government notes.

Source: *1993 Mutual Fund Fact Book* (Washington, D.C.: Investment Company Institute, 1993), 19–20. 1993 Mutual Fund Fact Book, Investment Company Institute, DC. Reprinted with permission.

Mutual Fund Example: The Janus Fund. As an example of an actual mutual fund, we take a brief look at the Janus Fund. The Janus Fund is a no-load fund that has as its primary investment objective: ". . . [the] growth of capital in a manner consistent with the preservation of capital. Realization of income is not a significant investment consideration."[17] Based on that investment objective the Janus Fund is classified as a growth equity fund; it normally invests virtually all of its assets in common stocks. However, if the

---

[17]Janus Fund prospectus, December 18, 1991.

Figure 20.6

Distribution of Mutual Fund Assets by Type of Fund: 1982 and 1992

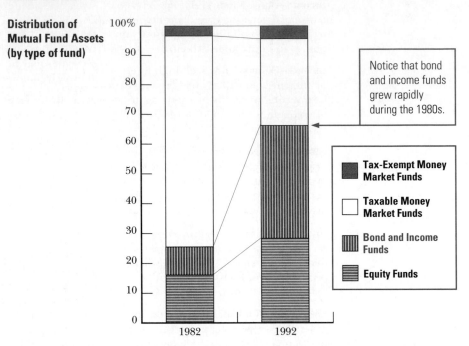

Distribution of Mutual Fund Assets (by type of fund)

Notice that bond and income funds grew rapidly during the 1980s.

■ Tax-Exempt Money Market Funds

□ Taxable Money Market Funds

▦ Bond and Income Funds

▤ Equity Funds

Source: *1992 Mutual Fund Factbook* (Washington, D. C.: Investment Company Institute, 1992), 24.

fund manager believes that prevailing market conditions dictate a defensive position, then the Janus Fund may invest its assets in short-term, interest-bearing securities (e.g., Treasury bills and notes). As of October 31, 1993, the Janus Fund had net assets of approximately $9.0 billion, 79 percent of which consisted of common stocks.

As of October 31, 1993, the Janus Fund's stock portfolio included 78 different common stock issues. Its top five holdings are listed in Table 20.2. These five stocks made up about 16 percent of the fund's total portfolio. The largest single holding, Wal-Mart, made up slightly less than 4 percent of the portfolio.

The Janus Fund offers most of the usual services of equity funds (automatic reinvestment of cash distributions, an automatic investment program, exchange privileges, and so forth). The Janus Fund mirrors the industry's rapid growth in recent years. Its net assets more than doubled between Octo-

Table 20.2

Five Largest Holdings of the Janus Fund: October 31, 1993

Stock	Market Value (millions)	Percentage of Portfolio
1. Wal-Mart Stores	$ 359.9	3.96%
2. Roche Holdings	325.1	3.57
3. Gillette	280.7	3.09
4. MCI	260.8	2.87
5. Swiss Bank	253.6	2.79
Total	$1,480.1	16.27%

ber 31, 1992 and October 31, 1993 as over $4 billion in new money flowed into the Janus Fund.

Calculating a Mutual Fund's NAV. As we discussed earlier, a fund's net asset value (NAV) equals the market value of its assets (minus any liabilities) divided by the number of outstanding shares. Since mutual funds constantly sell and redeem shares and virtually all allow shareholders to reinvest cash distributions, the number of outstanding shares varies from day to day. For example, assume that a mutual fund starts the day with 50 million outstanding shares and net assets of $500 million (NAV = $10.00). At the beginning of the day it receives $20 million in new investments and redeems shares worth $5 million. At the end of the day, the market value of its assets rises to $515 million. Its NAV at the end of the day is $10.29:

	$ Millions	Shares (millions)
Beginning balance	$500.0	50.0
Sales of shares	20.0	2.0
Redemptions	(5.0)	(0.5)
Unrealized gains	15.0	N/A
Ending balance	$530.0	51.5

NAV (per share): $530/51.5 = $10.29

Table 20.3 provides a statement of changes in net assets for the Janus Fund for the 1993 fiscal year (October 31, 1992 through October 31, 1993).

Selecting and Evaluating Investment Companies

Having developed a basic understanding of investment companies (how they work, the types, etc.), we now explore the techniques used to evaluate and select investment companies. Given their preeminent position, much of our discussion will center around mutual funds, though much of what we say is applicable to all investment companies. Selecting the right investment company is no easy task since almost 4,000 operate in the United States. Even a simple investment in a taxable money market mutual fund requires a choice among over 550 alternatives!

Some of the criteria by which investors should select investment companies are fairly straightforward. For example, a fund's investment objectives should be consistent with those of the investor. Someone who has a primary objective of, say, long-term capital gains, with only secondary concern for current income, should probably limit the search to growth-oriented stock funds. The decision should also depend on the contents of the fund's portfolio and how well they match its stated objectives. For example, if a fund advertises itself as an intermediate government income fund, most of its portfolio should consist of government securities with maturities shorter than ten years.

In addition to looking for funds consistent with one's investment objectives, the decision depends on how much risk one can tolerate. Someone who can't tolerate a lot of risk should avoid aggressive growth funds—they might cause too many sleepless nights. Another criterion an investor should consider is the services offered by the fund. Some investors may be interested,

Table 20.3

Statement of Changes in Net Assets for the Janus Fund:
Fiscal year ending October 31, 1993

Transaction	Dollars (thousands)	Shares (thousands)
Operations		
Net investment income	$ 113,392	
Net realized gain	461,479	
Net change in unrealized gain	556,612	
Total from operations	$1,131,483	
Dividends to shareholders		
Net investment income	(86,066)	
Capital gains	(266,234)	
Net decrease from dividends	($352,300)	
Capital share transactions		
Shares sold	4,452,281	229,413
Reinvested distributions	340,828	18,246
Shares repurchased	(1,463,591)	(74,887)
Net increase from capital share transactions	$3,329,518	172,772
Increase in net assets	4,108,701	
Net assets (shares) beginning of period	4,989,299	264,514
Net assets (shares) end of period	9,098,000	437,286

Source: *1993 Annual Report,* Janus Fund, 36.

for instance, in automatic investment plans or check writing. Some investors may prefer mutual funds that are part of a large family of funds.

Beyond these simple criteria, two factors need to be examined in detail: (1) fees and expenses, and (2) performance. All investors, of course, want superior performance and low fees, but evaluating investment companies on the basis of performance and cost is not always easy, nor is it totally objective. We will consider fees and expenses first.

Fees and Expenses

One important criterion for evaluating and selecting an investment company is the amount it charges its shareholders for management and other costs. Some, even some industry participants, argue that mutual funds charge too much for the services they provide, a conclusion hotly contested by others both within and outside the mutual fund industry. The article reprinted from *The Wall Street Journal* in the Investment Insights feature effectively summarizes the arguments made by both sides. While we're not prepared to resolve the controversy over mutual fund fees, it is important for investors to understand and evaluate the fees charged by all investment companies. Fees and expenses charged by mutual funds can be divided into two rough categories: load charges and annual operating expenses.

Load Charges. A load charge is a fee associated with buying or redeeming shares of a mutual fund. Some mutual funds charge **front-end loads,** in which the investor pays the load charge when purchasing shares initially.[18] By law a front-end load cannot exceed 8.5 percent of the fund's net asset value. For example, Fidelity's Magellan Fund had the following recent price quotations:

---

[18]A few funds also assess load charges for distributions reinvested in the fund.

NAV	Offering Price
$73.13	$75.39

Magellan charges about a 3 percent front-end load (the difference between the NAV and the offering price).[19] To purchase 100 shares of Magellan at these prices, one would pay $7,539 ($75.39 × 100). The value of the shares, NAV, would amount to $7,313 (73.13 × 100).

A **back-end load** refers to a fee assessed when an investor redeems shares of a mutual fund. Like a front-end load, a back-end load charge is stated as a percentage of NAV. If, for example, to redeem 1,000 shares of a fund with an NAV of $8.50 and a 3 percent back-end load, one would receive $8,245 for the shares [0.97 × (1,000 × 8.50)].

One type of back-end load, known as a **contingent deferred sales charge** (CDSC), is assessed, usually on a declining scale, only if shares are redeemed during the first few years of ownership. For example, the Eaton Vance National Limited Maturity Tax Free Fund has a CDSC that starts at 3 percent for shares redeemed less than one year after purchase; the charge declines to zero for shares held for at least four years. To determine whether a fund has a CDSC or other back-end load, look for an *r* following the name of the fund in a newspaper's listing of mutual funds. Of course, information on all fees and expenses is outlined in the fund's prospectus.

Front-end loads are often designated, in part, as compensation for the brokers or dealers who sell investment company shares to investors. Back-end loads, especially CDSCs, are designed to discourage short-term trading by investors who might otherwise move money in and out of the fund frequently. Traditionally, all mutual funds had load charges, especially front-end loads. However, no-load funds have become increasingly popular in recent years. Excluding money market funds, which are all no-load funds, approximately 30 percent of mutual fund assets today are held by no-load funds, up from about 20 percent ten years ago.

Operating Expenses. All mutual funds assess management or advisory fees, along with fees to cover other operating expenses, to shareholders each year. These expenses are paid out of investment income, before it is distributed to shareholders. Instead of measuring operating expenses as a percentage of investment income, or in total dollars, a fund measures this charge as a percentage of NAV (or dollars per share). For example, shareholders of the Janus Fund paid $0.18 a share (or 0.92 percent of NAV) in operating expenses for the fiscal year ending October 31, 1993. The majority of this amount, about $0.10 per share or about 0.65 percent of NAV, covered the investment advisory fee paid to the fund's portfolio managers. The balance went to pay for such things as postage, registration fees, audit fees, and so forth. Operating expenses can, of course, vary from year to year. However, most mutual funds set their advisory fees at fixed percentages of net assets. Details on operating expenses are provided in a fund's prospectus.

Some mutual funds now assess **12b–1 fees** (named after the 1980 SEC rule that allowed them). A 12b–1 fee can range up to 1.25 percent of NAV annually. It covers distribution costs, such as advertising, or commissions to brokers or dealers who sell the fund, in lieu of an initial load charge. Details on the 12b–1 fee, if a fund charges one, can be found in the prospectus. The Janus Fund does not currently charge a 12b–1 fee, though the fund's manager reserves the right to begin doing so.

---

[19]Of course, a no-load mutual fund's offering price equals its NAV. Most papers simply print *N.L.* under the offering price column in a price quote for a no-load fund.

Debate Rages over Whether Funds Charge Too Much

Are mutual fund companies charging investors too much?

"Some fees are substantially out of line," contends Vanguard Group's John Bogle, outspoken chairman of the fund industry's third largest mutual fund company.

"In general, the fees are fair and reasonable for the services provided," counters Charles Dornbush, chief financial officer for Fidelity Investments' mutual funds, the largest U.S. fund complex.

The Securities and Exchange Commission is about to throw itself into the fracas over mutual fund fees. The agency, which regulates the mutual fund industry, is planning this week to announce proposed changes in the rules governing funds, including some affecting costs.

Adding a Charge

How do mutual funds make money? Some funds charge a sales commission (or "load"), either when you buy a fund or when you cash out. In addition, all funds charge annual expenses. In the past decade, many have added a new annual charge known as a "12b–1" fee, named after the applicable SEC rule. For fund companies, the 12b–1 fee has become an alternative way to compensate brokers who sell mutual funds.

The controversy over mutual fund fees centers on stock funds. The debate kicked into high gear in October, when Vanguard's Mr. Bogle gave a scathing speech about the fund industry to a convention of state securities regulators. In the speech, Mr. Bogle said that annual stock fund expenses had risen to 1.45 percent of assets in 1991 from 1.04 percent a decade earlier, despite huge growth in fund assets that should have generated some economies of scale. He noted that it is costing investors $3.5 billion a year to be in stock funds—and that figure doesn't include fund sales commissions.

Mr. Bogle also criticized recent increases in mutual fund management fees. And he charged that 12b–1 fees aren't producing their purported benefits. These fees are supposed to help funds bring in more assets, allowing funds to reap benefits from bigness and thus hold down expenses. That just hasn't happened, argued Mr. Bogle.

In response to Mr. Bogle's speech and to media criticism about rising fees, Fidelity's Mr. Dornbush conducted a study of mutual fund expenses. "I'm just trying to offer an alternative view of the facts," says Mr. Dornbush. "I'm not trying to get into a war with Jack."

Mr. Dornbush came up with his own figures for average stock-fund expenses. His calculations show that average stock fund expenses rose to 1.01 percent in 1991, from 0.72 percent in 1981. Mr. Dornbush's averages are weighted, depending on the size of different funds. That has the effect of muting the influence of smaller funds, which typically have higher expenses.

Mr. Dornbush believes there are good reasons for the past decade's 0.29 percentage-point expense increase. He notes that because of the

Evaluating Fees and Expenses. Some professional investment advisors recommend against ever buying a mutual fund with any kind of load charge or 12b–1 fee.[20] All things being equal, that's probably sound advice. Certainly, a front-end load automatically reduces the rate of return on the investment (though the amount of the reduction depends, of course, on the investor's holding period). Also, a back-end load could be very costly if one were to move money into and out of the fund frequently.

The trouble is all things are rarely equal; buying one fund over another, simply on the basis of low fees and/or no load charge, may not always be a wise decision. Obviously, an investor must examine the fund's performance in relation to its costs. Perhaps the fund that charges higher fees also exhibits consistently superior performance. Another factor to consider is the services

---

[20]Examples include William Donoghue and Thomas Tilling, *Donoghue's No-Load Mutual Fund Guide* (New York: Harper & Row, 1983), 8–17; and Charles J. Givens, *More Wealth without Risk* (New York: Simon & Schuster, 1991), 432–435. Givens backs off this position a little, saying that investors should occasionally consider low-load mutual funds (with initial loads of 3 percent or less).

huge growth in the number of stock funds, the average stock fund today is barely larger than in 1981, adjusted for inflation. Moreover, he found that, on an inflation-adjusted basis, the average investor has less money invested in stock funds today than ten years ago.

Stock funds "need to have raised the fees on average, because funds weren't growing in size and the average account size is smaller," says Mr. Dornbush.

Role of 12b–1 Fees

In addition, Mr. Dornbush found that half of the 0.29 percentage-point increase was due to imposition of 12b–1 fees. In many cases, the introductions of 12b–1 fees were accompanied by cuts in upfront sales commissions, so that, overall, investors were better off.

Mr. Bogle counters that 12b–1 fees are getting imposed on investors who bought into stock funds before the upfront sales charges were cut. As a result, these investors have ended up paying both high upfront sales commissions and 12b–1 fees. "The customary expression for this is double-dipping," says Mr. Bogle.

Moreover, Mr. Bogle argues, the combination of sales charges and 12b–1 fees is proving even more expensive for long-term stock fund investors than the older sales-commission structure, where investors paid steep upfront sales charges.

Mr. Bogle also asserts that economies of scale aren't evident at the country's largest fund, $20 billion Fidelity Magellan Fund. Magellan's expense ratio today is the same as seven years ago, when the fund was a tenth of the current size.

INVESTMENT INSIGHTS

Which side does the SEC favor? A recent memorandum sent from the SEC Division of Investment Management to Rep. John Dingell, chairman of the House Committee on Energy and Commerce, provides some solace for both camps. In the memorandum, the division said it believes mutual-fund fee levels "are not necessarily cause for concern."

Nonetheless, in its memorandum, the division laid out three proposed changes. First, the division wants to make fund sales commissions negotiable, which could make it cheaper for investors to get into load funds. Secondly, to make it easier for investors to shop for funds based on expenses, the division wants to give funds the option of using a simplified fee structure. Finally, the division supports a proposal from the National Association of Securities Dealers that would limit the combined amount of sales commissions and 12b–1 fees that a fund can charge.

Would these changes satisfy Jack Bogle? "I'll probably never be satisfied," says Vanguard's chairman. "Competition will only do so much in providing lower prices to investors. It's up to the fund directors to make sure that fees are at the right level."

the fund provides shareholders. Funds that offer more shareholder services may charge more.[21]

Perhaps the single most important question concerning fees and expenses is whether or not the fund's charges are reasonable, given its performance, services, and so forth, taking into account one's specific investment objectives (e.g., anticipated holding period). How should one define *reasonable?* This can be a difficult question to answer. It requires some sort of standardized measure by which to compare load and no-load funds. For example, assume that two mutual funds, both of similar size, have the same overall investment objective and roughly similar performance. Assume that Fund A charges a 2.5 percent load and has annual operating expenses of 0.90 percent (of net assets) while Fund B has no load charge and annual operating expenses of 1.8 percent (of net assets). Which fund is really cheaper? Which has lower expenses? To answer this question, take a look at Table 20.4.

---

[21]Some mutual fund companies have recently established low fee, low service funds for investors willing to exchange fewer services for lower fees. The best example of these types of funds are the so-called *Spartan mutual funds* managed by Fidelity.

Table 20.4

Comparing Fees and Expenses for Two
Hypothetical Mutual Funds

Year	Fund A		Fund B	
	Ending Balance	Fees	Ending Balance	Fees
0	$ 975	$25	$1,000	$ 0
1	1,073	10	1,100	20
2	1,180	11	1,210	22
3	1,298	12	1,331	24
4	1,427	13	1,464	26
5	1,570	14	1,611	29
Total fees paid		$84		$121
Net ending balance	$1,486		$1,490	

Year	Fund A		Fund B	
	Ending Balance	Fees	Ending Balance	Fees
0	$ 975	$ 25	$1,000	$ 0
1	1,073	10	1,100	20
2	1,180	11	1,210	22
3	1,298	12	1,331	24
4	1,427	13	1,464	26
5	1,570	14	1,611	29
6	1,727	16	1,772	32
7	1,900	17	1,949	35
8	2,090	19	2,144	39
9	2,299	21	2,358	42
10	2,529	23	2,594	47
Total fees paid		$179		$316
Net ending balance	$2,350		$2,278	

Notes: Fund A has a 2.5 percent initial load and an annual
expense ratio of 0.9 percent. Fund B has no initial load and a
1.8 percent annual expense ratio. Both funds assume an initial
investment (before load charges) of $1,000 and earn 10 per-
cent (compounded annually).

The table assumes a $1,000 investment in both funds. (Remember, since
Fund A has a 2.5 percent initial load, this buys shares worth $975). It also
assumes that both funds earn 10 percent a year, compounded annually. Over
a five-year holding period, the investor would pay a total of $84 in fees
(including the $25 initial load charge) for Fund A and $121 for Fund B. Over
a ten-year holding period, Fund A would cost $179 in fees while Fund B
would cost $316. Even though Fund B charges less initially, since it has no
load charge, in the end the investor pays more in higher annual operating
expenses.[22] Most publications that evaluate mutual funds provide similar,
standardized measures of expenses. The SEC requires that a fund include a
standardized measure of expenses in its prospectus.

Aside from a standardized measure, some sort of benchmark is needed to
fully evaluate mutual fund fees. For example, during its 1993 fiscal year

---

[22]This example ignores the time value of money and the fact that a larger effective investment
in Fund B earns more income. The net ending balances after five or ten years minus the total
fees paid for Fund A amount to $1,486 and $2,350, respectively, versus $1,490 and $2,278,
respectively, for Fund B.

(October 31, 1992 through October 31, 1993), the Janus Fund had operating expenses equal to 0.92 percent of net assets. Using the SEC standardized measure of five-year expenses (starting with $1,000 and an annual return of 5 percent), the Janus Fund would cost about $54. Is this high or low? One way of answering that is to look at the expenses paid by similar mutual funds. According to a survey by *Money* magazine (reported in February 1994), growth funds had five-year expenses that ranged from $17 to $207, with a median of $107. Considering the performance of the Janus Fund, its expenses look reasonable.

A final factor to consider when evaluating mutual fund fees is any trend in fees that may become evident over time. There is some evidence that annual fees tend to decline as funds get larger, due to economies of scale. Indeed, Janus' annual operating fee dropped from 1.31 percent of net assets in 1982 to 0.92 percent of net assets in 1993 as its net assets soared from $76.5 million to about $9.0 billion.

Finally, as a marketing tool, a mutual fund company may subsidize, or even waive, annual management fees for new mutual funds for the first few years of operation. Investors should be aware of this tactic (it will be outlined in the prospectus) and should expect to see annual expenses increase eventually for such a fund.

Evaluating Historical Performance

How well an investment company performs is perhaps the single most important criterion for choosing between investment companies. Investors need to consider several factors when assessing performance. Absolute performance is obviously very important, but so is relative performance (how well the fund's performance compares to some benchmark). Also, the consistency of the fund's performance and its risk level need to be considered.

Many of the performance evaluation techniques we discussed in Chapter 15 can be applied to the evaluation of mutual funds. However, the investor still must remember that all objective measures of performance are based on ex-post, or historical, data. While the past is no guarantee of the future, a careful examination of historical performance can give some very important insight.

As an example, we will evaluate the historical performance of the Janus Fund. While the Janus Fund has a good track record, we're not recommending it to you or anyone else. We use the Janus Fund merely to illustrate how to go about evaluating the performance of an actual mutual fund. With these caveats in mind, let's look first at how to measure mutual fund returns.

Measuring Returns. Mutual fund returns can be measured the same way as the returns from any investment. Using the standard holding period return formula, the one-period return from a mutual fund (for a single day, month, quarter, etc.) is:

$$(NAV_t - NAV_{t-1} + \text{DIV}_t)/NAV_{t-1} \tag{20.1}$$

where NAV_{t-1} is the net asset value at the beginning of the period, NAV_t is the net asset value at the end of the period, and DIV_t is the amount of cash (capital gains and investment income) distributed during the period.[23]

---

[23]For a closed-end fund, the beginning and ending market prices would be substituted for NAV. For a load fund, in the first period of ownership, the sales price would be substituted for the beginning NAV. Since mutual funds pay operating expenses out of investment income prior to distribution, the holding period return shown in Equation 20.1 reflects the return after expenses, though before taxes.

At the beginning of the 1993 fiscal year, the Janus Fund had an NAV of $18.86 per share; at the end of the fiscal year its NAV had risen to $20.81 per share and it had distributed $1.19 per share. The Janus Fund's total return for the 1993 fiscal year (not the calendar year) was 16.7 percent [($20.81 − $18.86 + $1.19)/$18.86].

Measuring performance over longer periods of time provides more valuable information to investors than performance over just one year. After all, one year's return may be an aberration. Even the best funds have occasional bad quarters, or even years, and mediocre funds have rare days in the sun. For example, for the five-year period ending December 31, 1993, the Janus Fund had an average annualized total return of 19.7 percent.

Another way of measuring performance over longer periods is to construct a total return index. (We discussed how to do this in earlier chapters.) Figure 20.7 shows such an index for the Janus Fund from 1972 (its first year of operation) through the end of 1993. Remember, the total return index can be interpreted as the current value of an initial investment of $1,000 in the Janus Fund at the beginning of 1972; this investment would have been worth approximately $26,735 by the end of 1993. Of course, this assumes reinvestment of all cash distributions. Annualized, the Janus Fund had a total return of about 16.1 percent per year during this 22-year period.

Performance Benchmark. The Janus Fund returned, on average, over 19.5 percent between the beginning of 1989 and the end of 1993. While that sounds pretty impressive, without a standard for comparison, it really doesn't say very much about how well it performed relative to other alternatives. Two benchmarks are commonly used to evaluate mutual fund performance. One is a broad market index such as the Standard & Poor's 500 for a stock fund; the other is the average return for the group of mutual funds to which a given fund belongs (growth equity funds in the case of Janus). Let's see how well Janus did relative to the S&P 500 and the average for all growth funds. (At the end of 1993, 513 mutual funds were classified as growth funds.)

Figure 20.7

Performance of the Janus Fund: 1972–1993

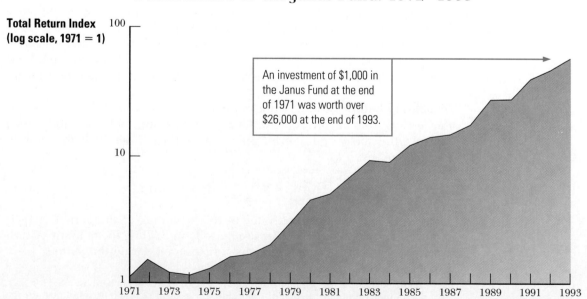

Source: *Annual Report,* Janus Fund, various years.

Figure 20.8 compares the average annual returns for the Janus Fund, the S&P 500, and the average growth fund over varying periods ending December 31, 1993. In each of the periods, the Janus Fund outperformed the S&P 500. For example, over the ten years ending on December 31, 1993, the Janus Fund produced an average annual return of 15.2 percent compared to 14.9 percent for the S&P 500. The difference has been more pronounced in recent years. Over the three-year period, the Janus Fund produced an average annual return of 19.2 percent compared to 15.6 percent for the S&P 500.

Some argue that even ten years is too short a time to measure the relative performance of a mutual fund. During the 22 years from 1972 to 1993, which covers the entire operating life of the Janus Fund, it outperformed the S&P 500 by a wide margin, 16.1 percent versus 11.6 percent. Put another way, while $1,000 invested in the Janus Fund at the beginning of 1972 would have been worth more than $26,000 at the end of 1993, the same $1,000 invested in the S&P 500 would have been worth $11,255 at the end of 1993.

The Janus Fund also compares favorably with the growth fund average, as shown in Figure 20.8. Over the five years ending on December 31, 1993, the Janus Fund produced an average annual total return of 19.7 percent compared to 14.3 percent for the average growth fund. However, notice that during 1993, the Janus Fund did underperform the average growth fund slightly (10.9 percent versus 11.5 percent).

Figure 20.8

Performance of the Janus Fund versus the Growth Fund Average and S&P 500

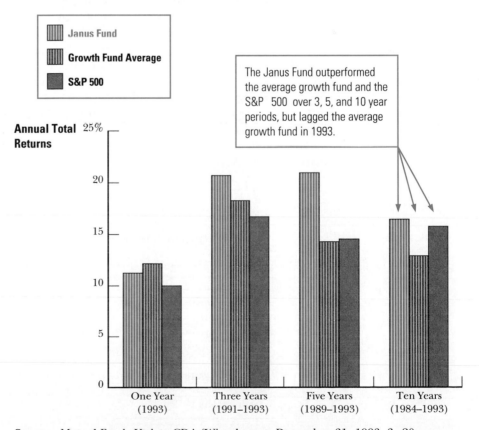

Source: *Mutual Funds Update,* CDA/Wisenberger, December 31, 1993, 3–20.

Consistency of Performance and Risk. Perhaps the Janus Fund beat the market over the last 20-plus years solely because it's riskier than the market. Maybe Janus outperformed a rising market, but underperformed a falling market. How can an investor measure and evaluate the consistency of performance and the risk of mutual funds?

One method of assessing mutual fund risk, and its relationship to return, is to examine modern portfolio theory statistics. We discussed how to calculate and interpret MPT statistics in prior chapters. Based on annual returns for the Janus Fund and the S&P 500 between 1972 and 1993, Table 20.5 lists several MPT statistics.

By comparison to the S&P 500, besides earning a higher return, the Janus Fund also appears to have been less risky over the 1972 to 1993 time period. For example, even though the Janus Fund has a slightly higher standard deviation than the S&P 500 (17.2 percent versus 16.4 percent), its arithmetic average return is much higher (17.4 percent versus 12.9 percent). Consequently, the Janus Fund's coefficient of variation is smaller than the S&P 500's (0.99 versus 1.28). Notice also that the Janus Fund's beta is less than 1.

The table also lists the three measures of risk-adjusted performance first discussed in Chapter 15, the Treynor, Sharpe, and Jensen measures. By any of the three measures of risk-adjusted performance, the Janus Fund compares favorably with the S&P 500. For example, the fund's Sharpe measure is almost twice that of the market (0.5817 versus 0.3406).

Using MPT statistics to assess mutual fund risk and return raises the same methodological issues we first discussed in Chapter 14. Recall, for example, the debate concerning whether beta is an appropriate risk measure. In addition, some critics, especially practitioners, argue that, methodological issues aside, statistical measures of risk give little help to most investors, since the investors don't really understand the numbers. Can you imagine a mutual fund advertising that it's a low beta fund, or that its Treynor measure is higher than that of the market?

As an alternative, many publications track mutual fund performance by providing information on how well mutual funds perform in various market environments. The argument is that a superior fund will post superior relative performance in both up and down markets. Table 20.6 compares the performance of the Janus Fund to that of the S&P 500 during the five worst years for the market and its five best years between 1972 and 1993.

These data confirm that the Janus Fund appears to have performed well, relative to the overall market, in both up and down markets. For example, 1974 was one of the worst years for stocks since the end of World War II; the

Table 20.5

MPT Statistics for the Janus Fund and the S&P 500

	Janus Fund	S&P 500
Arithmetic mean	17.4%	12.9%
Geometric mean	16.1%	11.6%
Standard deviation	17.2%	16.4%
Coefficient of variation	0.99	1.27
Beta	0.8246	1.0000
Treynor measure	0.1178	0.0558
Sharpe measure	0.5817	0.3406
Jensen's alpha	0.0543	0.0000

Note: Statistics are computed for annual returns between 1972 (the first year of operation for the Janus Fund) and 1993.

Source: *Annual Report,* Janus Fund, various issues.

Table 20.6

Performance of the Janus Fund during the Five Best and Five Worst Years for the S&P 500: 1972–1993

	S&P 500	Janus Fund Return	+/− S&P 500
Best			
1975	37.2%	13.4%	−23.8%
1991	32.5	42.8	10.3
1980	32.4	51.6	19.2
1985	32.2	24.6	−7.6
1989	30.3	42.6	12.3
Average	32.9	35.0	2.1
Worst			
1974	−26.5%	−6.7%	19.8%
1973	−14.7	−16.0	−1.3
1977	−7.2	3.5	10.7
1981	−4.9	7.1	12.0
1990	−3.2	−0.7	2.5
Average	−11.3	−2.6	8.7

Source: *Annual Report*, Janus Fund, various years.

S&P 500 produced a total return of −26.5 percent. The Janus Fund also lost ground during 1974 at −6.7 percent, but not nearly as much. Overall, the Janus Fund beat the market by an average of 8.7 percent during the market's five worst years. It also beat the market, on average, during the market's five best years between 1972 and 1993 by a little more than 2 percent, though the fund trailed the market in both 1975 and 1985.

Assessing Future Performance

Past performance is attractive, but it doesn't help today's investor. Future performance is much more interesting. Investors don't buy mutual funds because of what they did yesterday, but how well they seem likely to do tomorrow. A key question, therefore, is how much investors should rely on the historical performance of mutual funds to assess future performance.

A school of thought, which is especially popular in the academic community, argues that past performance is a very poor predictor of future performance.[24] Backed by some statistical evidence, the argument holds that individual mutual funds do not consistently, over long periods of time, post better risk-adjusted performance than the broad market averages.[25] Some funds beat the averages some years, while others beat the averages in other years, but trying to predict which fund will beat the averages next year, or during the next five years, is a waste of time—random selection would do just as well. Too many investors have made the mistake of buying last year's hot fund, only to see it cool off this year, so these critics claim that they are better off simply buying and holding shares of a well-diversified mutual fund

---

[24]The evidence of whether past performance is a guide to future performance has been discussed in several prior chapters, most notably Chapter 7 and Chapter 15. This issue is also part of the broader issue of whether investors should manage their investment portfolios actively or passively.

[25]Over the ten-year period ending on December 31, 1993, the average growth fund underperformed the S&P 500 by over 2 percent per year (12.6 percent versus 14.9 percent).

that has investment objectives consistent with individual objectives and tolerance for risk. According to this school of thought, if a fund lags behind the averages for a couple of years, shareholders are still better off holding onto the fund instead of looking for a new fund. Past performance is simply no guarantee of future performance.

Others argue that this view is nonsense. They cite evidence, discussed in prior chapters, that past performance is a reasonable, though not perfect, predictor of future performance. For example, one can point to the performance records of a number of mutual funds that have consistently beaten the averages in both up and down markets. These funds may not beat the averages *every* year, but over 5-year, 10-year, or 20-year periods, they have posted superior performance. This school of thought argues that past records have to reflect more than just luck. A good track record, they argue, at the very least tilts the odds of success in the investor's favor.

By extension, this school of thought argues, if a fund lags behind the averages for three or four years, an investor may be wise to look elsewhere. The drop in performance may very well indicate that the fund manager's investment philosophy or security selection process isn't working.

While we're in no position to resolve the controversy over how much investors should rely on past performance to gauge future performance, let's look at some anecdotal evidence. In 1992, international stock funds performed poorly, on average. The average international equity fund had a total return of −3.1 percent compared to about 8 percent for the average domestic stock fund. However, in 1993, international stock funds soared, producing an average return of more than 37 percent, three times the average return produced by domestic stock funds. Those who relied only on 1992 performance would probably have overlooked most international stock funds and missed the rally in 1993.

Table 20.7 compares the performance between 1987 and 1993 of the ten top-ranked mutual funds for 1986. The table ranks the funds on the basis of their five-year performance for the period ending on December 31, 1986. The top-ranked mutual fund, Fidelity's Magellan Fund, had an average annual return of 29.4 percent between the end of 1981 and the end of 1986. How did these funds do between the beginning of 1987 and the end of 1993? The record is mixed.

Some of the top-ranked funds of 1986 struggled during the next seven years. The Eaton Vance Stock fund, for example, lagged behind both the S&P 500 and its group average (for growth and income funds) between 1987 and 1993. The fund produced an average annual return of 8.5 percent compared to 11.4 percent for the average growth and income fund and 13.6 percent for the S&P 500. In 1993, the Eaton Vance Stock fund ranked in the 22nd percentile of all growth and income funds, meaning that 78 percent of all growth and income funds outperformed it.

Other top-ranked funds of 1986 have done somewhat better. Magellan, the Linder Dividend fund, and the Vanguard Windsor fund all outperformed their respective group averages between the end of 1986 and the end of 1993. Magellan, for example, beat its group average by over 3 percent per year over this seven-year period. Even these funds, however, had some poor years. Magellan, for example, ranked in the bottom half of its group in both 1991 and 1992. The data in Table 20.7 show just how tough it can be for a top-ranked mutual fund to remain on top year after year.

Can a Mutual Fund Get Too Large?

Not surprisingly, mutual funds that establish good performance records tend to grow rapidly. The Janus Fund, as we've noted, more than doubled in size

Table 20.7

Performance of Top-Ranked Mutual Funds for 1986: 1987–1993

Fund Name	Group	Five-Year Return (ending 12/31/86)	Seven-Year Return (ending 12/31/93)		Annual Percentile Ranking within Group		
			Fund	Group Average	1993	1992	1991
Fidelity Magellan	MAX	29.4%	17.0%	13.9%	70	30	41
Vanguard Preferred Stock	EI	29.0	9.3	10.0	52	23	24
Strong Total Return	GI	25.5	9.8	11.4	66	23	50
Eaton Vance Stock	GI	25.2	8.5	11.4	22	39	31
Lindner Dividend	FI	25.1	12.0	9.7	60	66	41
Strong Investment	BAL	24.4	8.4	10.4	23	48	36
Quest for Value	MAX	24.4	11.5	13.9	33	49	32
Putnam Global Growth	INT	24.1	10.8	11.2	30	56	45
Evergreen Total Return	GI	23.9	8.6	11.4	21	68	43
Vanguard Windsor	GI	23.8	12.4	11.4	58	63	42
S&P 500	—	15.3	13.6	—			

Notes: All returns are annualized total returns. MAX is maximum capital gain; EI is equity–income; GI is growth and income; FI is flexible income; BAL is balanced; INT is international equity. Percentile rankings show what percentage of funds in the same group the specific fund outperformed.

Sources: *Money*, February 1994, 82–96; *Mutual Fund Report*, CDA/Wisenberger, various issues.

during 1993. This may lead investors to wonder, can a mutual fund get too large?

Some professionals argue that investors should avoid large mutual funds that hold stock, especially those that have grown rapidly over short periods of time. Even Thomas Bailey, the chairman of Janus Capital which runs the Janus Fund, has been quoted as saying, "Too much money can ruin a good mutual fund."[26] Charles J. Givens recommends avoiding any mutual fund with more than $3 billion in assets.[27] He argues that once a fund gets too large, the manager loses flexibility. Much of the success of a typical stock fund is due to portfolio turnover—moving money into and out of stocks in anticipation of gains or losses; this becomes more cumbersome if the fund is too large. Some also argue that large funds cannot buy or sell without artificially pushing stock prices upward or downward. Further, if cash pours in too quickly, the manager may run out of good stocks, at good prices, to buy. Either the fund will pay too much for stocks, or cash reserves will accumulate. Both actions can hurt fund performance.

These arguments may have some validity. In fact, some rapidly growing mutual funds have gone as far as to stop accepting new accounts. However, no conclusive, scientific evidence confirms that performance suffers once a mutual fund reaches a certain size. Indeed, some evidence suggests that size and performance are totally unrelated. Let's look at some anecdotal evidence on the relationship between size and performance.

Table 20.8 reports on the performance of the ten largest mutual funds as of December 31, 1993. Performance of each fund, over one-year and three-

---

[26]*Forbes*, July 6, 1992, 112.

[27]Givens, *More Wealth without Risk*, p. 467. Givens also recommends avoiding mutual funds with less than $25 million in assets; these funds are just too small to hire the best professional managers, in his opinion.

Table 20.8

Performance of the Ten Largest Mutual Funds

| Fund | Net Assets, 12/31/93 ($ billions) | Group | Performance for Period Ending 12/31/93 | | | |
			One Year	Group Average	Three Years	Group Average
Fidelity Magellan	$30.5	MAX	24.7%	15.5%	23.5%	21.8%
INVESCO	18.4	GI	11.6	11.4	14.8	15.9
Washington Mutual	12.4	GI	13.1	11.4	15.0	15.9
Vanguard Windsor	10.5	GI	19.4	11.4	21.4	15.9
Income Fund of America	9.7	EI	14.1	12.9	16.5	16.6
Janus Fund	9.0	GRO	10.9	11.5	19.2	18.1
Fidelity Puritan	8.3	EI	21.5	12.9	20.4	16.6
20th Century Ultra	7.9	MAX	21.8	15.5	32.0	21.8
Vanguard Windsor II	7.3	GI	13.6	11.4	17.9	15.9
Fidelity Growth & Income	7.1	GI	19.5	11.4	23.7	15.9

Notes: All returns are annualized total returns. MAX is maximum capital gains; GRO is long-term growth; GI is growth and income; EI is equity–income.

Sources: *Mutual Fund Report,* CDA/Wisenberger, Rockville, Md., December 31, 1993, p. 3; *Money,* February 1994, 76–96; *USA Today,* January 5, 1994, p. 5B.

year periods, is compared to group averages. With only a couple of exceptions, these big funds beat at least their respective group averages, sometimes by substantial amounts. The Fidelity Puritan fund, an equity–income fund, beat its group average by almost 4 percent per year over the three-year period ending December 31, 1993. For most of the funds listed in Table 20.8, size appears not to have hindered performance.

Chapter Summary

1. Describe the general characteristics of investment companies.

Investment companies (unit investment trusts, closed-end funds, and mutual funds) all raise funds by selling shares to the public and then investing the proceeds in portfolios of securities. Any interest or dividends earned on securities owned by an investment company pass through to its shareholders. Further, as the market value of those securities increases (or decreases), the net asset value of the investment company's shares increases (or decreases). Investment companies offer a number of advantages to investors, including diversification, smaller minimum investments, and professional management. Investment companies are regulated primarily by the U.S. Securities and Exchange Commission. Virtually all investment companies choose to be taxed as regulated investment companies, which allows them to avoid federal income taxes on investment income or capital gains and losses. Like the investment income, all tax consequences pass through to investment company shareholders.

2. Examine the investment characteristics of unit investment trusts.

Unit investment trusts are unmanaged portfolios of securities, with shares divided among fixed numbers of shares, or units, outstanding. Unit investment trusts are designed to have finite lives; if a trust's portfolio consists of bonds, the trust ceases to exist when all bonds in the portfolio mature. Most sponsors of unit investment trusts make secondary markets in the units, buying and selling them at their current net asset values. Unit investment trusts started by investing in municipal bonds, and municipal bond trusts still make up the largest percentage of unit investment trusts sold since 1961. Corporate and government bond trusts are also available. A recent development has been the creation of stock trusts.

3. **Outline the essentials of closed-end investment companies.**

   Closed-end investment companies, or funds, are similar to unit investment trusts in that they have fixed numbers of shares outstanding. However, unlike unit investment trusts, almost all closed-end funds are actively managed, so the contents of their portfolios change over time. Shares of closed-end funds trade on the various stock exchanges. (Most U.S. funds trade on the NYSE.) Once considered to be rather an investment backwater, closed-end funds have grown rapidly in recent years to hold approximately $76 billion in total assets. Closed-end funds invest in bonds (municipal, corporate, and government issues), international securities (mainly single-country equity funds), and common stocks. It is interesting that closed-end funds rarely sell for their respective net asset values; most sell at discounts to their NAVs. A special type of closed-end fund, the dual-purpose fund, offers two classes of shares, one that receives all interest and dividends plus a fixed redemption value when the fund liquidates, and another that receives anything above the redemption value when the fund liquidates.

4. **Review the historical background and growth of mutual funds.**

   Mutual funds resemble closed-end funds in that their portfolios are actively managed. However, unlike closed-end funds, mutual funds continually offer and redeem shares. Since their origins in the 1920s, mutual funds have come to hold about 85 percent of total investment company assets. They have become especially popular in recent years. Mutual fund assets grew by over 385 percent between 1984 and 1993 to almost $2 trillion. Mutual funds are also popular in other parts of the world (especially in France and Japan).

5. **Describe the types of mutual funds and the services they offer to investors.**

   The first mutual funds invested primarily in common stocks; bond (income) mutual funds started soon after. The 1970s saw the creation of the first money market and municipal bond mutual funds. Today, mutual funds span 22 different categories. In 1982, the assets of money market funds made up about 70 percent of total mutual fund assets. By the end of 1993, bond and income funds made up the largest single group of mutual funds, followed by equity funds and money market funds. Mutual funds offer a variety of services to investors including automatic reinvestment of dividends, automatic investment plans, check writing, and exchange privileges.

6. **Understand how to select and evaluate investment companies.**

   An investor should select a mutual fund or other investment company on the basis of such obvious factors as the type of securities it purchases and the services it offers. Beyond that, the two most important criteria are fees and performance. Investment companies charge two types of fees: loads (or sales charges) and annual operating expenses. Loads are assessed at either the front end (when the shares are purchased) or the back end (when shares are redeemed). Many mutual funds today impose no load charges, and the trend in the industry has been toward no-load funds. All mutual funds assess annual operating expenses and some charge so-called *12b–1 fees*. Operating expenses are paid out of investment income prior to distribution to shareholders. Wise investors don't buy one mutual fund over another simply on the basis of lower fees; they ask whether or not a fund's charges are reasonable given its performance and the services it offers, and compared to similar funds' charges. Mutual fund performance should be measured over long periods of time and compared to market and group averages. The consistency of performance (in both up and down markets) and the fund's overall risk should also be assessed. While historical performance and risk are important, future performance is critical. The key issue of how reliably historical performance predicts future performance is unresolved. Some argue that mutual funds do not achieve consistently higher risk-adjusted returns than market or group average returns in the long run. Therefore, switching between funds on the basis of historical performance will not produce superior returns. Others argue that some funds do consistently beat market or group averages due to portfolio managers' superior investment skills. Thus a good track record can tilt the odds of success in the investor's favor. Finally, evidence is inconclusive so the question of whether mutual funds can get too large remains unresolved.

Key Terms

Investment company	Mutual fund
Money market mutual fund	Load charge
Net asset value (NAV)	Mutual fund family
Off the page sale	Front-end load
Interval fund	Back-end load
Unit investment trust	Contingent deferred sales charge
Closed-end investment company	12b–1 fee
Dual purpose fund	

Mini Case 1

OBJECTIVE:

To determine which of three mutual funds impose lower costs over a specific period of time.

Your aunt has asked you to help her solve an investment problem. She wants to invest $10,000 in one of three mutual funds. All have similar investment objectives and historical performance, but they charge different fees. She would like to know how to go about determining which fund is cheapest. Your aunt plans to invest for five years and will reinvest all cash distributions.

Fund	Sales Load	Management Fee	12b–1 Fee	Back-End Load
A	1%	1.5%	0.0%	0.0%
B	0	1.0	0.5	0.5 in five years
C	3	0.5	0.0	0.5 in five years

Use the above data to find the cheapest fund. Clearly state your assumptions.

Mini Case 2

OBJECTIVE:

To compute and interpret holding period returns and expense data for an actual mutual fund.

Reprinted in Table 20.9 is per share information from the Fidelity Magellan fund for the 1989 through 1993 fiscal years. Use the data to answer the following questions:

a. Fill in the missing information.
b. Compute the annual total return. How much of this return came from distributions and how much came from changes in net asset value?

Table 20.9

	Years Ended March 31				
	1993	**1992**	**1991**	**1990**	**1989**
Investment income	$ 1.77	$ 1.35	$ 1.98		$ 1.64
Expenses	0.57		0.59	$0.55	0.55
Net investment income	1.20	0.81	1.39	1.35	
Distributions from net income	(1.25)		(0.83)	(1.24)	(0.90)
Net gain on investments	9.18	9.21		9.39	8.63
Distributions from net gain		(5.43)	(2.42)	(3.82)	0.00
Change in net asset value		3.29	6.24	5.68	
NAV beginning of period	68.13	64.84			44.10
NAV end of period	$68.44	$68.13	$64.84		$52.92

c. Compute the annual expense ratio.

d. Do you notice any significant trends over this five-year period?

Discussion Questions and Problems

1. List the advantages of investing through investment companies. Elaborate on one.

2. How are most investment companies regulated and taxed? How are individual cash distributions to shareholders taxed?

3. Compare and contrast a unit investment trust and closed-end fund. What types of securities do most unit investment trusts purchase?

4. Define *net asset value discount*. Why do many closed-end funds trade at prices other than their respective net asset values?

5. During the 1970s, two new types of mutual funds appeared. What were they? Why were they so popular with investors almost immediately?

6. List some of the common services offered by mutual funds. What is a family of mutual funds?

7. Define *net asset value*. List the data you would need to compute the change in a mutual fund's net asset value over a specified period of time.

8. List the criteria investors should use when selecting between investment companies. What two should be examined in detail?

9. Define *sales load*. What is a contingent deferred sales charge (CDSC), or back-end load?

10. When evaluating mutual fund expenses, what is the meaning of *standardization?* Once mutual fund expenses have been standardized, what key question must an investor answer?

11. How should total returns for a mutual fund be measured? Explain the purposes and assumptions behind the construction of a total return index.

12. Assume that the total index on a stock fund rose from 1.6469 to 6.1403 between the end of 1984 and the end of 1994. Calculate the annual compound total rate of return. What other information would you need to fully assess this fund's relative performance?

13. What is the meaning of *consistency of performance* for a mutual fund?

14. Is past performance a good predictor of future performance for a mutual fund? Should you examine other factors to predict future performance?

15. Explain the differences between passive and active mutual fund strategies. What common problem is associated with any system to indicate when to switch between mutual funds?

Critical Thinking Exercises

1. This exercise requires library research. Using a well-known source of mutual fund information (such as February issues of *Money* magazine or recent issues of Morningstar), review data for the five-year period 1989 through 1993. Measured in terms of total performance, find the five best-performing stock (or equity) mutual funds each year. Remember, in one year the best-performing funds may be small stock funds while in another year they may be equity–income funds. Record each fund's name and its total one-year return. Also record the average total return for all stock funds, as well as the total return for the S&P 500 or some other market benchmark.

   a. How did each fund on your list do the following year? For example, how did the top-performing stock fund in 1989 do in 1990?
   b. Do these one-year returns show any consistent patterns? In other words, do one year's top-performing funds perform well the next year? Discuss your findings.
   c. Assume you buy the best-performing fund from the prior year on January 1 and hold it for 12 months, so you would own 1988's best-performing fund during 1989, for example. How well would this strategy have worked? Does this tell you anything about active versus passive mutual fund strategies?

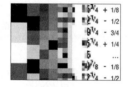

2. This exercise requires computer work. Open file FUND2.XLS on the data disk. It contains several years' worth of quarterly return data for the Dreyfus Third Century mutual fund, along with quarterly returns for the S&P 500. Use the data to perform the following calculations and answer the following questions:

   a. Compute the arithmetic and geometric average returns for both the fund and the S&P 500. Annualize the returns.
   b. Compute the MPT statistics for both the fund and the S&P 500. (This should produce something similar to the Janus Fund data in Table 20.5.)
   c. Using the information you computed in Parts a and b, evaluate the performance of the Dreyfus Third Century fund.

Mini Case **1**   SOLUTION

Even though Fund C has the highest initial load and charges a back-end load, it is the least expensive fund for your aunt to own over the five-year period. She ends up with more money at the end of five years. Data are shown in Table 20.10, which assumes an annual total return of 10 percent (before expenses) for each fund. A 12b–1 fee is just an additional annual management fee, so Fund B's annual expense ratio is 1.5 percent.

Mini Case **2**   SOLUTION

The completed table is shown in Table 20.11.

   a. Remember, distributions, whether from capital gains or investment income, reduce a mutual fund's net asset value.

Table 20.10

Year End	Fund A Balance	Loads	Annual Charges	Fund B Balance	Loads	Annual Charges	Fund C Balance	Loads	Annual Charges
0	$ 9,900	$100	—	$10,000	$ 0	—	$ 9,700	$300	—
1	10,727	—	$163	10,835	—	$165	10,617	—	$53
2	11,622	—	177	11,740	—	179	11,620	—	58
3	12,593	—	192	12,720	—	194	12,718	—	64
4	13,644	—	208	13,782	—	210	13,920	—	70
5	14,784	—	225	14,933	75	227	15,235	76	77

Fund	Total Fees	Balance (after back-end load)
A	$1,065	$14,784
B	1,049	14,858
C	698	15,159

Assumptions
1. Each fund earns 10 percent per year.
2. Include 12b–1 fee with annual expenses.
3. Yearly balances are calculated after annual expenses, but before back-end loads.

b. Total returns are shown in Table 20.11. The formula is: Total return = (Distributions + Change in net asset value)/Beginning net asset value. In addition, the breakdown between distributions and net asset value changes is also shown.

c. The annual expense ratio for each fiscal year is also shown in Table 20.11. The formula is: Expenses/[(Beginning *NAV* + Ending *NAV*)/2].

d. Some interesting trends are evident. First, there is a downward trend in fiscal year total returns. Magellan, which was among the best-performing mutual funds during the 1980s, may have lost some of its luster. Seond, the amount of the fund's total return from distributions (mostly from capital gains) relative to increases in NAV has increased sharply. In 1989, most of the 22.00 percent total return came from an increase in NAV. By contrast, in 1993, virtually all of the fund's 15.24 percent total return came from distributions. One could conclude that Magellan realized some substantial capital gains on investments during 1993.

Table 20.11

	Years Ended March 31				
	1993	1992	1991	1990	1989
Investment income	$ 1.77	$ 1.35	$ 1.98	$ 1.90	$ 1.64
Expenses	0.57	0.54	0.59	0.55	0.55
Net investment income	1.20	0.81	1.39	1.35	1.09
Distributions from net income	(1.25)	(1.30)	(0.83)	(1.24)	(0.90)
Net gain on investments	9.18	9.21	8.10	9.39	8.63
Distributions from net gain	(8.82)	(5.43)	(2.42)	(3.82)	0.00
Change in net asset value	0.31	3.29	6.24	5.68	8.82
NAV beginning of period	68.13	64.84	58.60	52.92	44.10
NAV end of period	$68.44	$68.13	$64.84	$58.60	$52.92
Total return	15.24%	15.45%	16.19%	20.29%	22.04%
Return from distributions	14.78	10.38	5.55	9.56	2.04
Return from change in NAV	0.46	5.07	10.65	10.73	20.00
Ratio of expenses to NAV	0.83	0.81	0.96	0.99	1.13

Another explanation for the large distributions of capital gains is that the fund's portfolio underwent substantial changes in 1992. This appears to have happened. Magellan was taken over by a new manager, Jeff Vink, in July 1992. He has made a number of changes to Magellan. One has been a reduction in the number of stocks owned by the fund, from about 1,500 when Vink took over to around 600 as of March 1993. Obviously any changes in the fund's investment philosophy should be monitored carefully by current and potential Magellan shareholders.

Careers in Investments

Many readers may be interested in working in the investments field; it can be a very rewarding career. While it is difficult to estimate exactly how many full-time investment professionals there are, a good guess would be several hundred thousand, at least. For example, Merrill Lynch, the nation's largest brokerage and investment company, has around 40,000 employees. As another example, Fidelity Investments, the world's largest mutual fund company, which also operates a large discount brokerage firm, employs more than 7,500 people. Of course, not all of these workers are engaged in investment management, but a majority probably are.

In this appendix, we take a brief look at some of the career opportunities in the investments field. Before we begin, however, there are a couple of things to consider. First, competition for most jobs in the investments field is intense. Institutions have many high-quality applicants from whom to choose. Second, the number of investment professionals is not growing especially rapidly; in some job categories, the number of workers may actually be declining. Several well-known investment firms have cut staff in recent years. As a result, you must be flexible in your job search. You must be willing to relocate, be willing to start at the bottom, and be prepared to work very hard. Finally, you should be aware of the fact that many positions in the investments field require federal and/or state licenses.

Who Employs Investment Professionals?

The obvious employers of investment professionals are brokerage firms, investment banking firms, life insurance companies, pension funds, and mutual funds. Ask your librarian for sources that list the addresses and phone numbers of these organizations. Also, don't forget about banks. Many investment professionals begin work in bank trust departments. Also, many large banks have active bond trading operations, especially for municipal bonds. Even large, nonfinancial corporations employ investment professionals to manage such things as investor relations and pension plans.

Brokerage and Sales Positions

The first job that probably comes to mind in the investments field is that of a stockbroker (now called an *account executive* in most brokerage firms). Account executives work mainly with individual investors, though some may handle accounts for small, institutional investors, as well. Account executives provide advice, execute orders, and help maintain records. Account executives who work for full-service firms (such as Merrill Lynch) earn most of their compensation through commissions on trades. Successful account executives can do quite well financially, earning six-figure annual incomes. Brokers at discount brokerage firms, on the other hand, are salaried employees. They are responsible for maintaining records, providing price quotations, and executing orders; these are, of course, very important services. The distinction between full-service and discount brokerage firms was described in Chapter 3.

Large investment firms also employ salespeople who deal mainly with institutional investors and other workers who execute orders (traders). In any case, the most important skills to be a successful account executive or investment salesperson are effective selling skills, along with some interest in finance. New account executives often have prior sales or business experience.

Analysts and Portfolio Managers

Security analysts work for a variety of organizations studying stocks, bonds, options, futures, and so forth. Analysts then write research reports for distribution to their organizations' clients. Most analysts specialize in particular securities. Stock analysts, for example, specialize in specific industries and companies, following the pattern described in Chapters 8 to 11. Analysts are employed by large banks, brokerage firms, life insurance companies, mutual funds, and pension funds. The analyst whose name appears on a research report usually has a staff to assist him or her. Many analysts begin their careers by doing tedious grunt work for the senior analyst. Top analysts can easily command six-figure salaries.

Portfolio, or money managers, in the view of many, represent the pinnacle of the investments field. Portfolio managers are responsible for managing large pools of funds and work for mutual funds and other large, institutional investors. Most managers have staffs of assistant managers and analysts. The compensation of a top portfolio manager can exceed $1 million annually.

Investment Bankers

As we discussed in Chapter 3, investment bankers act as intermediaries between issuers of securities and investors. They also advise corporate and government clients on financial strategies. Investment bankers often lead large staffs and are well-compensated.

Financial Planners

In order to help them deal with personal finance issues, including estate planning, taxes, insurance, and investments, many individuals turn to financial planners. Financial planners come from a variety of backgrounds, including accounting and insurance sales. Some work for firms, others work independently. *Financial planner* is still a very loosely defined term, however. Almost anyone, regardless of qualifications, can call himself or herself a financial planner. Recently there has been an attempt to develop some sort of professional designation for financial planners. The Certified Financial Planner designation means that an individual has met education and experience requirements, and has demonstrated a minimum level of knowledge and competence about subjects such as life insurance and estate planning. For more information, contact the College of Financial Planning, 4695 South Monaco Street, Denver, CO 80237-3403; (303) 220-1200.

Chartered Financial Analysts

There are approximately 17,000 Chartered Financial Analysts (CFAs) in the United States. Obtaining a CFA designation enhances the prestige of an investment professional, such as a security analyst or portfolio manager, much as a CPA designation enhances the prestige of an accounting professional. In order to obtain a CFA designation, you must pass a series of three comprehensive examinations (Levels I, II, and III) over a three-year period. You must also meet certain educational and experience requirements to reach each level.

Throughout the text we've included sample questions from past CFA exams. These sample questions will give you a good feel for the types of subjects and information a CFA candidate at each level is expected to know.

While a CFA designation is not necessarily a requirement to get into the investments field, there is little question that the designation is valued by most investment organizations. It is rare today to find a top analyst or portfolio manager that isn't a CFA. For more information, we suggest you contact the Association for Investment Management and Research, Department of Candidate Programs, P.O. Box 3668, Charlottesville, VA 22903-0668; (804) 980-3668.

We wish you the best of luck on whatever career path you decide to take.

Glossary

accrued interest interest that builds up between coupon payment dates; most bonds accrue interest daily and pay every six months (p. 545).

active investor investors who look for specific investment instruments that offer superior risk/return characteristics (p. 10).

activity ratios measure of how effectively company uses its assets to generate sales; help determine stock value (p. 358).

actual rate of return return if reinvested coupon payments earn rate other than yield to maturity which assumes reinvestment of coupon payments at yield to maturity (p. 548).

ADR. *See* American Depository Receipt

American Depository Receipt (ADR) claims to shares of foreign stocks; denominated in U.S. dollars and traded on U.S. stock exchanges to eliminate some risk and complication of foreign investing (p. 50).

American option option that can be exercised at any time between its creation and its expiration date (p. 638).

anomaly financial market situations that seem to violate the concept of market efficiency (p. 203).

anticipation survey qualitative economic forecasting method examining surveys that attempt to measure future economic behavior of businesses, consumers, and government agencies (p. 282).

arbitrage simultaneous purchase and sale of two different securities to make a guaranteed profit (p. 25, 623).

arbitrage principle statement that two identical securities (or goods) will sell at identical prices; if one invests nothing, one should get nothing in return (p. 484).

arithmetic mean the simple average of all observations in a series (p. 12).

ask price price at which market maker (dealer willing to buy and sell securities traded on that market) is willing to sell a security (p. 73).

asset utilization ratio measure of how effectively company utilizes assets (p. 348).

at-the-money option whose exercise price, at a call or a put, is equal to the stock price (p. 616).

auction market stock exchange, such as a NYSE, at which all trading takes place on the exchange floor (p. 75).

average collection period measure of number of days taken to collect on receivables (p. 359).

Babson Break stock market drop on September 5, 1929, forecast by financial advisor Roger Babson (p. 139).

back-end load load charge assessed when investor redeems shares of mutual fund (p. 715).

balance sheet statement giving overview of company's asset holdings on left-hand side and sources of funding for those assets on right-hand side (p. 349).

bank discount basis Standard quotation of Treasury bill prices (p. 35).

bank discount yield quotation of T-bill prices based on bank discount basis; understates actual return on investor (p. 35).

banker's acceptance instruments that facilitate commercial trade transactions; banks accept ultimate responsibility for paying off all parties (p. 38).

Barron's Confidence Index measure of investor sentiment; ratio of average yield on small sample of high-quality corporate bonds divided by average yield on small sample of medium-quality corporate bonds (p. 168).

basis in futures pricing, difference between cash price and futures contract price; can be negative or positive (p. 669).

bear market stock market movement toward falling prices (p. 159).

bear spread transaction involving purchase of one call or put option and sale of another which constitutes a bet that the underlying stocks' prices will fall over a short period of time (p. 633).

beta measure of relative risk of a stock; beta of market equals 1 (p. 449).

beta risk Systematic or non-diversifiable risk of a stock (p. 500).

bid price price at which market maker (dealer willing to buy and sell securities traded on that market) is willing to buy a security (p. 73).

biotech companies that develop new drugs through genetic engineering (p. 144).

block trade NYSE-defined trade of at least 10,000 shares with minimum market value of $200,000; these trades have increased as a result of greater institutional investing in stocks (p. 89).

blue chip description of stocks of largest, most consistently profitable companies (based on poker in which blue chips are most valuable) (p. 47).

blue sky law state securities laws; some states are lax and defer regulatory power to the SEC, others are strict (p. 94).

bond equivalent yield yield on a T-bill, a truer estimate than the bank discount yield of the return an investor would actually earn from owning a T-bill (p. 36).

bond rating rating assigned by agency such as Standard & Poor's or Moody's to help investors assess credit risk (p. 44, 561).

bonds Treasury securities with original maturities in excess of 10 years; often callable starting five years prior to maturity (p. 43).

bootstrap game technique through which conglomerate could report higher earnings because it had acquired another earnings stream, regardless of efficiency or profitability (p. 141).

borrowing-lending line capital market line (p. 445).

bourse. *See* stock exchange

Bubble Act act passed in 1720 in England which forbade stock issues by companies that lacked royal charters (p. 136).

bulldog bond foreign bonds issued in United Kingdom (p. 46).

bull market stock market movement toward rising prices (p. 159).

bull spread transaction involving purchase of one call or put option and sale of another which constitutes a bet that the underlying stocks' prices will rise over a short period of time (p. 633).

business cycle sequences of long-term economic growth that exhibit nonperiodic but recurrent sequences of expansions and contractions (p. 268).

business risk variability of company's operating profits over time (p. 326).

buy-and-hold strategy passsive management process in which investor buys and holds well-diversified portfolio of securities (p. 193).

CAAR. *See* cumulative average abnormal return (CAAR)

callable bond call provision gives issuer the option of buying the bond back from the investor at a specified price during a specified period of time, prior to maturity (p. 543).

call option option to buy (p. 50, 616).

call protection period during which a bond is not callable (p. 543).

call provision provision of fixed-income securities that allow issuers to buy back securities from their owners, at prespecified prices, prior to maturity (p. 43).

call risk option available to bond issuer of buying bond back from investor at specified price during specified period of time, prior to maturity (p. 543).

Capital Asset Pricing Model (CAPM) objective method of determining risk and return for each security in context of portfolio diversification (p. 439).

capital market line (CML) tangent line that touches efficient frontier; identifies all efficient portfolios and has highest expected return for given risk (p. 443).

CAPM. *See* Capital Asset Pricing Model

cash flow statement financial statement integrating information provided in balance sheet and income statement to report cash inflows and outflows (p. 353).

cash settled in Eurodollar futures, all accounts that remain open on last trading day are settled in cash at LIBOR-based rate determined by CME clearinghouse (p. 680).

certificate of deposit interest-bearing time deposits issued by financial institutions such as banks and credit unions; mature between a few weeks and a few years from date of issue (p. 39).

charting technical analysis involving plotting past price history of security or index and then examining chart for patterns that suggest shifts in underlying supply and demand relationship, indicating shifts in investor attitudes (p. 159).

cheapest to deliver Treasury bond or note future that costs the least compared to the invoice amount (p. 681).

closed-end fund actively managed investment company, with a fixed number of shares outstanding (p. 52).

closed-end investment company company that raises money by selling shares to investing public; also called closed-end fund (p. 702).

CML. *See* capital market line

coefficient of variation (CV) statistical standardized measure of risk/return tradeoff; standard deviation divided by the mean (p. 23, 374, 406).

commercial paper corporate equivalent of Treasury bill; short-term IOU issued by a corporation to provide working capital (p. 38).

commission broker traders who trade strictly for others and are paid for the service (p. 662).

company analysis report report containing description of company's business and properties, financial material, past stock price history and volume data, and company prospects (p. 310).

competitive position company position within an industry relative to other companies in the industry (p. 311).

conglomerate diversified companies enlarged by acquisitions of other businesses (p. 141).

consumer confidence index survey measuring consumer confidence (p. 282)

consumer expectations index anticipation survey measuring consumer attitudes; closely related to leading indicators (p. 283).

consumer price index (CPI)   inflation measure designed to measure monthly change in retail price to consumers of a selection (basket) of goods and services (p. 275).

contango   decline in futures price as delivery date approaches if expected spot prices do not change (p. 672).

contingent deferred sales charge   type of back-end load, assessed on declining scale if shares are redeemed during first few years of ownership (p. 715).

contrarian   approach to investing based on market overreaction (p. 205).

contrary opinion theory   theory that as market approaches a peak, consensus among investors tends to be bullish; as market approaches trough, consensus among investors tends to be bearish (p. 163).

controlling   management function concerned with monitoring performance, keeping organization moving toward goals, and correcting deficiencies (p. 318).

convergence   process in which spot prices and futures prices approach zero as time to delivery approaches zero (p. 669).

conversion factor   in Treasury bond and note futures, the price of bond delivered (p. 680).

conversion price   effective price paid per share of common stock if conversion option is exercised (p. 644).

conversion ratio   prescribed number of shares obtained when bond or preferred share is tendered for conversion (p. 644).

conversion value   multiple of current stock price by conversion ratio (p. 645).

convertible security   security such as regular corporate bond or preferred stock issue with added feature of option to exchange the convertible for a fixed number of shares of the issuing company's common stock (p. 51, 644).

corporate governance   issue of whether corporate managers run their companies in best interests of stockholders (p. 331).

correlation   degree of interrelationship between two variables (p. 408).

correlation analysis   statistical technique for analyzing demand and other industry data (p. 299).

correlation coefficient   measures the strength of the correlation between two variables; ranges from -1 to $+1$ (p. 409).

cost of carry   cost associated with storing an asset until delivery date (p. 672).

coupon rate   regular interest payments paid at fixed rates by fixed-income securities; computed and paid at regular intervals as percentage of security's par (face) value (p. 42, 544).

covariance   interrelationship between probability distributions (p. 409).

coverage ratios   measure of number of times firm can repay fixed charges with generated income (p. 365).

covered call   writing a call option on stock already owned by the investor (p. 634).

covered short sale   combined short position in a stock with long position in a call option (p. 636).

CPI.   *See* consumer price index

credit risk   possibility that bond's issuer will not make interest and principal payments when due (p. 542).

cross-sectional regression   in second step of test of CAPM, estimated beta values serve as independent variables (p. 479).

cumulative average abnormal return (CAAR)   return in response to jump in stock prices after takeover announcement (p. 200).

cumulative wealth index   indexes showing how much wealth investments in stocks or bills would produce at end of given period (p. 21).

current ratio   measure of how much liquid (current) assets a firm has available to repay current liabilities (p. 357).

current yield   coupon rate divided by price (p. 113, 547).

CV.   *See* coefficient of variation

cyclical company   company whose earnings increase by more than economy's aggregate earnings when economy is in expansionary phase; earnings fall more during recessionary phase (p. 373).

cyclical industry   industry whose performance tends to be positively related to economic activity (p. 289).

D.   *See* duration

day trader   traders who attempt to profit from short-term market movements; while holding positions much longer than scalpers, they do not hold positions overnight (p. 662).

DDM.   *See* Dividend Discount Model

debenture   unsecured corporate bonds; holders are considered to be general creditors of the issuers (p. 45).

debt-equity ratio   total long-term debt divided by total equity (p. 363).

dedicated portfolio   portfolio designed to generate sufficient cash flow in each period to match series of obligations faced by investor (p. 603).

default   bond's issuer does not make interest and principal payments when due (p. 542).

defensive industry   industry whose performance tends to be relatively insensitive to economic activity despite cyclical ups and downs (p. 289).

derivative security   security whose value depends on value of another asset such as agricultural commodity, individual common stock, stock index, or Treasury bond; speculative security (p. 50, 615).

diffusion index   number of advancing stocks plus one-half the number of unchanged stocks divided by the total number of stocks trading (p. 165).

discount a bill   to buy a promissory note at less than its face value (p. 130).

discount brokerage firms   firms providing mainly order execution and record-keeping services; customers usually deal with many individual brokers; firms charge lower commissions and fees than full-service firms (p. 83).

discount security   money market instruments that are sold for less than face (par) values and do not pay periodic interest payments (p. 34).

diversifiable risk   firm-specific risk that can be eliminated by diversifying (p. 420).

diversification   distribution of available funds among several investments to reduce risk (p. 23, 413).

Dividend Discount Model (DDM)   model by investors can evaluate the intrinsic value of a stock based on the present value of expected dividends (p. 226).

dividend payout ratio   portion of earnings paid as dividends (p. 230).

dividend yield   stock dividend divided by current price (p. 113).

Dollar Cost Averaging   buying equal dollar amounts of mutual fund at regular intervals (p. 422).

dominant or leading company   company producing higher and more consistent future earnings than company in weak competitive position (p. 311).

Dow theory   assumption that demonstrated trend in stock prices will continue until a reversal in investor attitudes occurs (p. 159).

dual purpose fund   special type of closed-end fund that sells two types of shares and has predetermined life span (p. 704).

dual trader   traders who sometimes trade as brokers and sometimes trade for their own accounts (p. 662).

DuPont Chart   flow chart summarizing effects of operating and financial activities of a company (p. 370).

duration (D)   measure that allows comparison and measure of price sensitivity of various bonds, regardless of coupons and maturities (p. 554).

Earnings Model (EM)   method for estimating intrinsic value of common stock by dividing earnings generated by firm's future investment opportunities into earnings firm pays out as cash dividends and earnings it rein-

vests to fund future investment opportunities (p. 229).

earnings per share   profits after taxes divided by number of common shares outstanding (p. 352).

econometric model   application of mathematical and statistical techniques to economic forecasting; principal tools of quantitative economist (p. 283).

economic analysis   effort by analyst to determine where the domestic and international economies are headed and outlook for important economic variables such as inflation and interest rates (p. 265).

efficient diversification   finding portfolio combinations that produce the best risk/return profiles (p. 425).

Efficient frontier   portfolios that maximize return for a given level or risk and minimize risk for a given level of return (p. 426).

efficient market   market in which security prices reflect all relevant information **(p. 65.)**

efficient markets hypothesis   belief that securities' prices fluctuate randomly around respective intrinsic values; random walk theory (p. 187).

Elliot wave   principle that stock prices exhibit basic wave characteristics common to all natural forces (p. 171)

EM.   *See* Earnings Model

emergency fund   investor-established fund available before investing, consisting of low-risk, short-term investments such as money market instruments (p. 8).

end-use analysis   tool though which analyst attempts to identify source of demand for industry's product and uncover relationships that help to explain demand; also called product-demand analysis (p. 297).

Eurobond   bond denominated in U.S. dollars but issued outside the United States (p. 46).

Eurodollar   foreign money market bank deposits denominated in U.S. dollars but issued and held outside the U.S., or in U.S. branches of foreign banks (p. 41).

European option   option that can be exercised only on the expiration date (p. 638).

event study   scientific studies of semistrong-form market efficiency examining market reactions to specific kinds of announcements (p. 200).

ex-ante return   future returns (p. 400).

excess return   difference between risk-free rate and return on security (p. 479).

ex-dividend   stock whose price falls because buyer is no longer entitled to the current dividend (p. 638).

executive compensation   amount paid to senior executives (p. 331).

exercised   option whose stock has actually been bought or sold by holder of option (p. 616)

exercise or strike price   right given to buyer, or holder, to buy or sell stated number of shares of common stock at specified price until specified point in time (p. 616).

expected return   future return (p. 8).

expiration date   time at which option contract buyer, or holder, can buy or sell a stated number of shares of common stock (p. 616).

ex post return   actual, historical return (p. 400).

face (par) value   bond value fixed at issue; determiner of cash flows associated with bond (p. 544).

federal agency security   debt securites issued by federal and quasifedral government agencies (p. 37).

filter rule   trading rule stating that if stock rises certain percent from most recent low (support level), buy it because it has defined an up trend (p. 199).

financial asset   nonmarketable assets such as bank deposits and U.S. savings bonds and marketable securities such as money market instruments, capital market instruments, and derivative securities (p. 32).

financial futures   futures contracts on foreign currencies, on interest-bearing financial instruments, on Treasury bills and bonds, and on stock indexes (p. 660).

financial information services   investment advisory services such as Standard & Poor's, brokerage firms like Merrill Lynch, and investment newsletters (p. 115).

financial leverage   concept that company with more debt will find that any changes in operating earnings will result in greater change in firm's EPS (p. 362).

financial risk   caused by the use of financial leverage (p. 326).

firm-specific risk   returns on stocks whose firm-specific factors differ (p. 419).

first pass regression   first of two regressions in CAPM empirical testing procedure (p. 479).

fixed asset turnover   sales divided by average net fixed assets (p. 362).

fixed charge coverage ratio   measure of number of times firm can cover its fixed obligations, including debt charges, lease payments, and pretax preferred dividend payments (p. 365).

flow figure   accounts on income statements that receive additions over time as information flows in; revenues and sales are examples (p. 351).

forcing conversion   forcing exercise of conversion option by calling convertible (p. 646).

foreign exchange risk   foreign bond returns depend on both interest rates and foreign exchange rates; changing currency strengths changes bond yields (p. 544).

forward contract   binding contract in which buyer agrees to take delivery of contract at specified time and place in future and dealer agrees to deliver contract at same price (p. 657).

forward rate   expected rate on a bond with a particular maturity at some point in the future; tomorrow's projected spot rate (p. 582).

fourth market   market trading stocks listed on NYSE or AMEX over the counter, between institutions without the intervention of market makers; private deals between buyers and sellers (p. 80).

front-end load   load charge paid by investor when purchasing shares initially (p. 714).

full and fair disclosure   SEC requirement that in security registration process, issuer gives investors enough information to make informed decisions **(p. 92).**

full faith and credit   government guarantee that purchase of government security investment (such as Treasury bill) is secure (p. 35).

full-service brokerage firm   firms offering investment advice to customers in addition to order execution and record keeping; usually specific broker assigned to each individual customer **(p. 83).**

fundamental analysis   examining securities based on the assumption that every security has an intrinsic value (p. 158).

futures contract   contract between parties for future delivery of commodity at agreed price, usually within one year (p. 51, 657).

GDP.   *See* gross domestic product

general obligation bond   municipal bonds backed by the full faith and credit of the government unit that issues them; can only be issued by government units that have independent taxing authority (p. 43).

geometric mean   alternative measure of average over several periods of time; geometric mean of return series is also the average compound rate of return **(p. 130).**

good market   financial market in which trading is conducted in fair, open, and orderly manner; market with liquidity, price continuity, and low transaction costs (p. 64).

government bond dealer   primary dealer designated by Federal Reserve to submit competitive bids at U.S. Treasury security open auctions (p. 67).

Graham and Dodd approach   traditional common stock valuation (p. 26).

Great 1929 Stock Market Crash   speculative bubble in United States in which frantic trading, margin buying, and growth of investment trusts were followed by economic slowdown, rising interest rates, and tightening credit, leading to stock market collapse and worst depression experienced in U.S. (p. 136).

gross domestic product (GDP) total production of goods and services by a nation in a given year (p. 105).

gross profit margin measure of gross profits, or sales minus cost of goods sold, relative to sales (p. 367).

Group 1 MPT investor investors who believe that markets are so efficient that any well-diversified portfolio will provide just return relative to risk (p. 515).

Group 2 MPT investor investors who believe market is essentially efficient but who believe that some securities are always temporarily mispriced (p. 515).

growth company company with undervalued stocks which can produce abnormal profits (p. 233).

growth industry industry characterized by rapid growth in sales and earnings, often independent of the business cycle (p. 289).

growth stock stock that is currently undervalued enough to drive its return above those of other stocks at the same risk level (p. 235).

"Heard on the Street" *Wall Street Journal* column covering price quotations, earnings announcements, dividend declarations, new product information, and management changes (p. 114).

hedge reducing risk of an investment position often involving use of options or futures (p. 50, 628).

herd instinct analysts behavior in the face of uncertainty, in which forecasts are issued that have little variation (p. 182).

historical information information from past about security performances, trading volume, trading patterns, and short interest (p. 190).

holding period amount of time security is owned (p. 8).

holding period return measure of total return from investment over specific period of time; (p. 11).

homogeneous expectations assumption that other market participants agree with assessment (p. 241).

hybrid security preferred stock issued by corporations; shares characteristics of both common stock and bonds (p. 47).

immunization attempt by bond investor to reduce portfolio's exposure to risks associated with changing interest rates (p. 599).

implied standard deviation result of taking current market price of call option and finding standard deviation implied by the model (p. 643).

income bond corporate equivalent of municipal revenue bonds; finance purchase of income-producing assets (p. 45).

income statement document providing information about a company's sales cost, and profits during a specified period of time (p. 351).

index arbitrage use of program trading which attempts to gain risk-free returns by exploiting differences between prices of stock index futures and prices of underlying stocks (p. 90).

index fund mutual funds that match their portfolios to compositions of market indexes (p. 194).

indexing strategy effort to replicate performance of broad market indexes (p. 599).

index of leading indicators U.S. Department of Commerce combination of several specific variables (indicators) of future economic activity (p. 277).

index options call or put based on stock market index such as Standard & Poor's 100 or 500, Value Line Index, or Major Market Index (p. 621).

indirect investment investment giving ownership of entity that owns actual securities; includes mutual funds, closed-end funds, and unit investment trusts (p. 32).

industry analysis analysis of company's industry (growth or mature), speed of technological change, demographic trends, production costs, and government regulation (p. 265).

industry life cycle theory theory stating that every industry goes through a four-stage life cycle consisting of birth, growth, mature growth, and stabilization/decline (p. 294).

inherent leverage call option buying process similar to buying stock on margin (p. 628).

initial public offering (IPO) primary market transaction; company's first sale of common stock to the investing public when it initially goes public (p. 71).

insider trading use of nonpublic information to make investment profits (p. 91, 191).

intercommodity spread measure of difference in price between two futures contacts on different assets, but with same edelivery date (p. 670).

interest coverage ratio income before interest and taxes divided by debt interest charges (p. 365).

interest rate risk possibility that one will need to sell bond when interest rates rise and bond prices fall (p. 542).

interest rate swap agreement between two parties to exchange a series of interest payments; method of controlling interest rate and foreign exchange risk (p. 605).

inter market trading system system developed by eight markets (NYSE, AMEX, NASDAQ, and some regional exchanges) to allow brokers, specialists, and market makers to interact with their counterparts on any other markets (p. 96).

interval fund hybrid closed-end and open-end investment companies (p. 699).

in-the-money call option with exercise price lower than stock price (p. 616).

intracommodity spread measure of difference in price between two futures contracts on same asset, but with different delivery dates (p. 670).

intrinsic value fundamental economic value of issuing company's equity; rationally reflects all relevant publicly available information and perhaps privately available information (p. 159, 224, 618).

inventory turnover measure of how efficiently company uses its inventory to generate sales (p. 360).

investment advisory service. *See* financial information services

investment banker banker who originates, bears risk, and distributes nongovernment security issues; investment bankers underwrite (purchase) issues and accept responsibilty for reselling to other investors (p. 68).

investment company company that pools funds from many investors and purchases securities with these funds; investor purchases fund shares which represent piece of diversified portfolio; unit investment trusts, closed-end funds, and mutual funds are types of investment companies (p. 695).

investment grade bond bond with Moody's and Standard & Poor ratings of Baa/BBB or above (p. 562).

investment newsletter subscription information sources such as *The Zweig Forecast, The Prudent Speculator, The Chartist,* and *Elliott Wave Theorist* (p. 120).

investment opportunity set possible combinations of securities (p. 412).

investor sentiment optimistic (bullish) or pessimistic (bearish) investment attitudes (p. 163).

IPO. *See* initial public offering

January effect seasonal return pattern of stocks in which returns are higher in January for all stocks (p. 209).

Jensen's alpha measure of risk-adjusted return using characteristic line estimated by market model (p. 510).

joint-stock association capital pool to jointly finance and own a business venture (p. 130).

junk bond speculative bond rated Ba/BB or below by Moody's and Standard & Poor's (p. 562).

leading motivating employees to achieve organizational goals (p. 318).

leading company company in industry that should produce higher and more consistent future earnings than company in weak competitive position (p. 311).

leverage ratio measure of how much of firm's total assets are financed by equity as opposed to debt (p. 348)

LIBOR. *See* London Interbank Offered Rate

limited partnership general partner and several limited partners who invest funds in return for equity in property purchased by the partnership; partners have limited liability (p. 54).

limit order order instructing broker to buy security for no more than specific price or to sell for no less than specific price (p. 86).

limit up/limit down in futures trading, situation in which contract price moves up or down by maximum amount (p. 666).

liquidity ability to quickly buy or sell an asset at a price justified by its underlying supply and demand conditions (p. 64).

liquidity preference theory theory that forward rates are good predictors of future rates (p. 586).

liquidity premium premium that will encourage investors to hold longer-term bonds (p. 586).

liquidity ratios measure of how much of current liabilities company could pay off with its current assets if it were to liquidate at book value (p. 356).

liquidity risk difficulty for investors to sell certain bonds prior to maturity for anything approaching their true values; special problem for small municipal bond issues (p. 543).

load charge mutual fund sales charges (p. 708).

local trader trader who trades strictly for his/her own or firm's, account (p. 662).

London Interbank Offered Rate (LIBOR) rate at which five large London banks are willing to lend dollar-denominated funds to one another in interbank market (p. 42).

long hedge long position in future market used to hedge against a rise in prices in the cash market (p. 678).

long position position in which holder of option has right to buy or sell stock at set price for set period of time (p. 616, 658).

low-cost producer company that can produce the same quality good or service more cheaply than competitors (p. 315)

margin call deposit required by trader to keep position open to bring margin back up to initial amount (p. 87, 664).

marked to market open account pricing based on settlement price for each contract;

trader's margin will rise or fall depending on whether trader is long or short, and whether current settlement price is higher or lower than previous day's settlement price (p. 663).

marketable security   money market instruments such as Treasury bills and commercial paper, capital market instruments such as Treasury bonds and common stocks, and derivative securities such as options and futures contracts (p. 32).

marketing strategy   plan for satisfying demands of consumers; basic components are target market and marketing mix variables (p. 323).

market maker   dealer in small-firm stocks traded over-the-counter; buyers and sellers of such stocks from their own inventories **(p. 78).**

market model   linear regression model showing relationship between return on market portfolio and security return (p. 459).

market momentum   belief that the market for securities takes a long time to get going and a long time to stop; trendlines can be considered measure of momentum (p. 164).

market order   instruction to broker to buy or sell a security at the best currently prevailing price (p. 84).

market overreaction   systematic and predictable errors in security prices based on receipt of new information (p. 203).

market portfolio   portfolio that contains all traded assets (p. 446).

market risk   stock return based on economic factors such as business cycles, inflation rate, and interest rates, and firm-specific factors such as labor contracts, mangerial policies, and new product development (p. 419).

market segmentation theory   theory that forward rates have essentially no relationship with future spot rates; bonds with different maturities are not substitutes for each other (p. 586).

market-to-book ratio (MV/BV)   valuation method for finding undervalued stocks (p. 246).

MD.   *See* modified duration

mean-variance efficient   investment that maximizes expected return for a given level of risk (p. 405).

mean-variance efficient portfolios   portfolios that lie along the efficient frontier and offer investors optimal risk/return combinations (p. 426).

meltdown Monday   stock market break in 1987 when stocks suffered worst one-day decline in history (p. 143).

minimum risk portfolio   portfolio with the lowest standard deviation that lies along the efficient frontier (p. 415).

minor movement   small advances or declines in stock prices that last only a few days (p. 160).

Mississippi Company   Company of the West; French royal monopoly organized by John Law to trade with territories of Louisiana and Canada; speculative bubble that crumbled by end of 1720 (p. 134).

MNC.   *See* multinational corporation

modern portfolio theory (MPT)   theory proposed by Harry Markowitz in which investor can produce optimal allocation of securities within portfolio that will achieve the best possible risk/return tradeoff (p. 426, 499).

modified duration (MD)   measure reflecting approximate percentage change in price for a given change in yield to maturity (p. 555).

money market mutual fund   fund that purchases only money market instruments such as commercial paper and Treasury bills (p. 696).

money spread   transaction involving purchase of one call or put option and sale of another (p. 633).

mortgage bond   corporate bond secured by a lien on real assets, such as property or machinery (p. 45).

mortgage pass-through   security issued by Ginnie Mae (Government National Mortgage Association) which pledges interest payments backed by self-liquidating pool of mortgages, all with same term and interest rate (p. 46).

moving average   average of prices over specified period which move over time; used in charting trends (p. 162).

MPT.   *See* modern portfolio theory

multifactor APT model   extension of security pricing based on arbitrage to more than one factor (p. 496).

multinational corporation (MNC)   company that generates more than 25 percent of its revenues outside its home country (p. 322).

mutual fund   actively managed investment company that continually issues new shares and redeems existing shares; can be divided into categories depending on types of securities purchased and investment objectives; also called open-end funds (p. 52, 705).

mutual fund family   umbrella organization with several different mutual funds (p. 709).

MV/BV.   *See* market-to-book ratio

naive diversification   random stock selection (p. 425).

naive strategy   portfolio strategy that assumes markets are so efficient that any well-diversified portfolio will provide just return relative to risk; belief that all securities are correctly valued (p. 515).

National Association of Securities Dealers Automated Quotation (NASDAQ) system   computer-based communications network linking member firms to serve over-the-counter market for stocks (p. 77).

national market system system set up by Securities Act Amendments (1975) to promote fully competitive market for trading of securities (p. 96).

NAV. *See* net asset value

net asset value (NAV) measurement of investment company shareholders' costs and changes in wealth; found by subtracting fund's liabilities from market value of its assets and dividing this figure by number of outstanding shares (p. 53).

net asset value (NAV) market value of investment company's assets minus liabilities divided by number of outstanding shares (p. 53, 697).

net profit margin measure of net profits after taxes relative to sales (p. 368).

net worth immunization effort to narrow the gap between average duration of depository institution's assets and average duration of its liabilities (p. 604).

new issue initial public offerings of stock (p. 140).

nifty fifty 1970s bubble in stocks of well known growth companies such as Disney and Xerox (p. 142)

nominal rate of return risk-free return (p. 18).

nondiversifiable risk market risk that exists with diversification (p. 420).

nonsystematic risk firm-specific risk that can be eliminated by diversifying (p. 420).

normal backwardation tendency of futures prices to rise as delivery date approaches (p. 672).

notes Treasury securities issued with maturities between 2 and 10 years; not usually callable (p. 43).

objective information source government or private organization that compiles and publishes economic and industry data (p. 105).

off the page sale transaction that allows investors to purchase shares of mutual fund before they see entire prospectus (p. 699).

open auction auction in which investors bid on the basis of price or yield (p. 67).

open interest number of contracts outstanding at any point in time (p. 666).

open outcry system trading system on floor of exchange where traders stand in trading pits and bid out loud against one another (p. 661).

operating leverage effect of fixed costs increasing variablility in operating profits (p. 374).

operating profit margin measure of operating profits relative to sales (p. 367).

option provision that gives holder right to buy or sell shares at fixed prices for short periods of time (p. 615).

organizational objective company goal of applying resources effectively and efficiently to accomplish company's goals (p. 318).

organizing basic management function of assigning tasks to various organization parts and allocating resources within organization (p. 318).

out-of-the-money call option with exercise price greater than stock price (p. 616).

outright position basic speculative position in futures contract (p. 675).

over-the-counter market market where trading doesn't take place on a trading floor; NASDAQ is an over-the-counter market (p. 78).

overvalued stock that is priced too high (p. 228).

overvalued security security whose price is out of line with its intrinsic value (p. 159, 228).

passive investor investor who tries to "buy the market," usually in form of mutual fund that tries to replicate performance of broad market without many changes in portfolio composition (p. 9).

passive (naive) strategy portfolio strategy that assumes markets are so efficient that any well-diversified portfolio will provide a just return relative to its risk; believes all securities are correctly valued (p. 515).

P/E. *See* price/earnings ratio

perfect market frictionless market with no transaction costs, taxes, or constraining regulations (p. 57).

planning management function involving setting organizational goals and identifying tasks and resources necessary to obtain those goals (p. 318).

portfolio separation theorem individuals choose risky portfolio independently of their utility functions (p. 446).

position trader trader who holds positions over longer periods of time and attempt to profit from longer-term market movements (p. 662).

preemptive rights rights to retain proportionate ownership in company if company decides to sell additional shares of common stock (p. 49).

premium on call option, call price minus stock price plus exercise price; on put option, put price minus exercise price plus stock price (p. 617).

price continuity assumption that no new information has entered market and that one can buy or sell at price close to that of most recent, similar trade (p. 65).

price discovery secondary market information informing investor of what security is currently worth (p. 72).

price/earnings ratio (P/E) stock sales price times its earnings; measure used by investors when searching for potential investments (p. 113, 248).

price leader   company holding dominant competitive position in an industry (p. 315).

price sensitivity   bond price change if market yield to maturity falls (p. 550).

primary financial market   market in which investors buy newly issued securities and security issuers receive proceeds from sales (p. 66).

primary movement   major, or overall, trend in stock prices (p. 159).

private information   information not generally available to public; confidential inside information (p. 191).

private placement   sale of security issues to small, select group of large, institutional investors (such as pension funds and life insurance companies); most private placements involve corporate debt issues (p. 72).

probability   assumption that all possible returns are known and will occur (p. 14).

product line   goods and services; indicative of company's competitive position (p. 314).

profitability ratio   gross profits, operating profits, and net profits as percentages of sales revenues (p. 367).

profit margin   measurement of how much of sales pass through to become net profits for stockholders (p. 348).

program trading   trading via sophisticated computer programs which can make automatic decisions to buy or sell (p. 90).

promised return   bond's required rate of return; interest rate used to discount its cash flows to determine its present value (p. 544).

proprietary technology   patented technology that can give company dominant position in an industry (p. 315).

prospectus   document prepared and filed with the SEC by issuer of securities before securities can be offered for sale (p. 91).

protective put   combined stock/option position in which investor buys put options on stock he or she already owns (p. 635).

public information   historical information and all public information on a company's product lines, financial policies, and management quality (p. 191).

purchasing power risk   impact of future rates of inflation on cash flows (p. 543).

pure discount bonds   zero coupon bonds (p. 583).

pure expectations theory   theory that forward rates are unbiased estimates of expected future spot rates (p. 585).

pure yield pick up swap   simple yield spread strategy in which investor swaps lower-yielding bonds for higher-yielding bonds with roughly similar maturities to earn higher return (p. 594).

put option   option to sell (p. 50, 616).

qualitative forecasting   process in which economist looks at variety of economic data and makes subjective assessment about economic outlook (p. 277).

quality and quantity of future earnings   level and predictability of future earnings; considered to be the single most important determinant of the intrinsic value of a stock (p. 310).

quality conscious   investment behavior showing concern that corporations are more likely to default on bonds during economic contractions (p. 272).

quality of management   success of management in attaining organizational goals in effective and efficient manner through planning, organizing, leading, and controlling organizational resources (p. 311).

quantitative forecasting   process in which economist assesses economic outlook by using econometric models (p. 277).

quick ratio   measure of cash, receivables, and marketable securities divided by current liabilities; also called acid test ratio (p. 358).

random walk   time series behavior of stock prices; stochastic time series in which each successive change in a variable is drawn independently from probability distribution with constant mean and variance (p. 188).

range   difference between highest return and lowest return (p. 15).

ratio analysis   process of dividing industry data by aggregate economic data over period of time (p. 299).

real asset   real estate, precious metals, gems, art works, and other real property (p. 32).

real estate investment trust (REIT)   corporations that invest in real estate by pooling funds from many investors and using proceeds to purchase property, mortgages, or both (p. 54).

real rate of interest   actual interest rate; risk factor in determining bond returns (p. 568).

real rate of return   required (expected) return that assumes no inflation or risk (p. 18).

rebalancing   bond portfolio indexing methodology in which each individual bond is purchased in proportion to its market value (p. 600).

regression analysis   statistical technique for analyzing relationship between two, or more, variables where one variable is said to be a function of another variable (p. 299).

reinvestment risk   actual rate of return may not equal promised return of bond because part of actual return comes from reinvesting intermediate cash flows (coupon payments); reinvesting coupon payments could raise actual rate of return (p. 543).

REIT.   *See* real estate investment trust

relationship investing strategy in which investors agree to take long-term stake in company; in exchange, company agrees to talk with investor group regularly, possibly giving group seat on board (p. 336).

relative strength indicator measure that divides the price of stock by broad market average and examines the trend over time (p. 165).

repurchase agreement short-term loans with securities as collateral; also called repos (p. 40).

residual claimant common stockholders, individuals with ownership claim in corporation; in case of liquidation, claims paid after all creditors have been paid (p. 47).

resistance level stock price level above which prices tend not to rise (p. 160).

retention rate portion of earnings retained for reinvestment (p. 230).

return profit from investing (p. 4).

return on stockholders' equity (ROE) measure of firm's operating and financing activities; includes overall company performance and return of money that stockholders have invested; factor in determining stock's intrinsic value (p. 369).

return on total capital measure of rate of return on all long-term capital invested in company (p. 369).

revenue bond municipal bond used to finance revenue-producing projects; only revenues generated by the project may be used to pay bondholders (p. 43).

reversal market overreaction to new information (p. 203).

reverse straddle writing both call and put with same exercise price and same expiration date; bet against volatility in underlying stock (p. 631).

riding the yield curve strategy in which yield curve is upward sloping and expectations predict that neither the shape nor the slope of the yield curve will change over the investment horizon; yields on specific bonds will fall as they approach maturity (ride the yield curve downward) (p. 590).

risk danger of possible loss (p. 8, 392).

risk aversion effort to avoid risk without promise of reward (p. 22, 393).

risk neutral investor investor whose utility function increases at a constant rate as wealth increases (p. 395).

risk premium premium that reflects compensation for the amount of risk for a particular security (p. 19).

risk structure of interest rates risk that takes into account differences in bond yields across bonds with different degrees of credit risk (p. 571).

risk taker investor whose utility function increases at increasing rate as wealth increases (p. 395).

risky portfolio investment portfolio with a standard deviation greater than zero (p. 442).

ROE. *See* return on stockholders' equity

runs test count of number of times that price changes, each one designated positive or negative (p. 197).

scalper traders who attempt to profit from small changes in contract prices; rarely hold positions open for more than a few minutes (p. 662).

seasonally adjusted data method of presenting data with adjustments for seasonal differences; adjusted data considered to present better picture of underlying trend of economic series (p. 275).

secondary movement large changes in trend in prices in opposite direction from primary movement (p. 159).

second pass regression second set of regressions run to test the CAPM (p. 479).

Securities Investor Protection Corporation (SIPC) organization insuring brokerage accounts up to $500,000 to reimburse investors in event brokerage firm fails (p. 83).

security characteristic line graphic representation of relationship between return on market portfolio and security return (p. 459).

security market index investment information source such as Standard & Poor's 500 (p. 105).

security market line (SML) graphic display of capital asset pricing model (p. 453).

semiannual coupons bond coupon interest paid twice a year; annual coupon divided by two (p. 545).

semistrong-form market efficiency statement that security prices reflect all public information and react almost instantaneously to new public information (p. 191).

serial bond municipal bond issue in which predetermined number of bonds mature each year until final maturity (p. 44).

serial correlation measurement of strength of relationship between current value of time series and past share values (p. 197).

settlement price price set by committee of traders and clearinghouse officials at end of each trading day (p. 663).

Sharpe measure performance measure that adjusts portfolio performance by total risk rather than beta risk (p. 504).

short hedge short position in futures market (p. 677).

short position position of option writer (seller of option) (p. 617, 658).

short sale selling borrowed stock with the expectation of buying back shares at lower price to return to the owner at some point in future (p. 88).

SIC. *See* Standard Industry Classification

single-factor APT model security pricing model based on arbitrage with one factor (p. 485).

SIPC. *See* Securities Investor Protection Corporation

small-firm effect abnormal profits what can be earned by investing in shares of small companies (p. 212).

smart money investors who are more astute than average and lead bull and bear markets (p. 164).

SML. *See* security market line

South Sea Company speculative bubble in which English joint-stock company was given monopoly of trade between England and New World; shares sold throughout England, peaked in 1720, and burst after insiders disposed of their shares (p. 135).

specialist NYSE member assigned responsibility of maintaining an orderly and liquid market in each security assigned to member; specialists have roles as auctioneers, catalysts, agents for limit orders, and providers of liquidity (p. 76).

speculative bubble rapid increase in price of something with no apparent justification except belief that price will go still higher; as bubble rises, trading volume explodes; when bubble bursts, prices collapse (p. 129).

speculative grade bond bond with Moody's or Standard & Poor rating of Ba/BB or below; commonly called junk bond (p. 562).

speculative security derivative security; security dependent on value of another asset such as agricultural commodity, individual common stock, stock index, or Treasury bond (p. 50).

spot price cash price of asset (p. 669).

spot rate today's prevailing yield on a bond with a particular maturity (p. 582).

spread purchasing one option and writing another on the same undryling stock (p. 632, 670).

standard deviation statistical measure of risk as the dispersion around the mean, or average, return (p. 15, 374, 403).

Standard Industry Classification (SIC) federal government-developed classification covering all organizations, organized from general to specific by dividing all organizations into 11 divisions identified by SIC codes; updated every ten years (p. 290).

stock exchange or bourse financial market in which dealings in commodities, bills of exchange, and insurance take place (p. 130).

stock figure balance of each account in balance sheet on specific date (p. 349).

stop order market order entered to take effect at specified price; often referred to as stop-loss orders (p. 86).

straddle bet on volatility of underlying stock (p. 631).

straight bond value value of convertible without conversion feature (p. 645).

strategic planning set of decisions and actions used to formulate and implement strategies that will provide competitively superior fit between organization and its environment to achieve organizational goals (p. 322)

strike price. *See* exercise or strike price

strong-form market efficiency statement that security prices reflect all public and all private information (p. 191).

subjective information source nongovernment information sources such as fact books, newspapers, and periodicals (p. 105).

subordinated debenture corporate bond with lower claims to assets than regular debenture in event of corporate bankruptcy (p. 45).

SuperDot system NYSE electronic order-routing system that carries members' orders directly to appropriate trading posts and returns trade confirmations (p. 84).

supply and demand notion that security prices are determined by the number of buyers and sellers bidding against on another (p. 159).

support level price level below which prices tend not to fall (p. 160).

syndicate group of investment banking firms, each of which purchases portion of an issue, accepting responsibility for reselling only that portion (p. 71).

synergy belief that company could acquire another company, even if in different industry, and increase earnings potential of combined enterprise (p. 141).

systematic risk market risk that exists with diversification (p. 420).

target date immunization effort to ensure that investor has sufficient funds available at point in time to meet single liability; sets duration of bond portfolio equal to horizon date (p. 602).

taxable equivalent yield computation used by taxable investors when comparing municipals to other securities (p. 41, 595).

tax-deferred income account income on which the owner pays no taxes until the money is withdrawn at retirement (p. 9).

technical analysis broad group of indicators based on belief that past patterns in security can reliably predict future price patterns; applied to stock indexes, individual stocks, bonds, and foreign currencies (p. 158).

term bond municipal bonds in which all bonds in single issue mature on same date (p. 44).

term structure of interest rates relationship betgween bond yields and maturity; also called yield curve (p. 569).

third market trading of NYSE-listed stocks off the exchange floor; over-the-counter market in which non-NYSE firms act as market makers for institutional investors (p. 78).

time diversification phenonmenon in which annualized standard deviation declines as time horizon increases (p. 421).

time series regression regression comparing time-based data for a single variable (p. 479).

time to maturity factor in price of noncallable, default-free bond fixed at issue; determiner of cash flows associated with bond (p. 544).

time value difference between option's price and its intrinsic value (p. 618).

total asset turnover measure of how effectively company utilizes assets (p. 348, 362).

total debt-total assets ratio measure of how much of company's assets are financed by total debt (p. 364).

total risk risk measure using standard deviation instead of beta (p. 504).

tracking error way of assessing how well index fund replicates performance of its benchmark index (p. 601).

trading pits areas in exchanges where traders stand and bid against one another (p. 661).

trading range values showing no primary trend; some technicians see trading range as bullish indicator, others as bearish indicator (p. 161).

transaction costs costs of buying or selling securities (p. 65).

Treasury bill IOU issued by the United States Treasury backed by full faith and credit of U.S. government; Treasury bill has effectivcly no default risk; also called T-bill (p. 35).

trendline charted line showing price patterns over specific period of time (p. 162).

Treynor-Black portfolio combination model method by which portfolio managers can naively select well-diversified portfolios and enhance their performance by investing in more selected stocks found through securities analysis (p. 523).

Treynor measure measure of reward relative to risk; states reward (return minus risk-free rate) in relation to portfolio's basis risk; equation stems from security market line (p. 500).

'tronics boom speculative bubble in postwar U.S., centered on new issues of companies associated with glamorous technologies such as electronics and space exploration (p. 140).

tulipomania speculative bubble in mid-17th century Holland in which demand for tulip bulbs drove prices upward until tulips were seen as investments; by early 1637, prices fell,

dealers went bankrupt, and Holland's economy entered a severe recession (p. 133).

12b-1 fee mutual fund assessment to cover distribution costs or commissions (p. 715).

undervalued security security whose price is out of line with intrinsic value (p. 159, 228).

underwriting purchase of issue by investment banker who accepts reponsibility for selling issue to other investors (p. 68).

underwriting discount service charge imposed by investment bankers for process of purchasing securities from users below the prices at which the securities will be resold **(p. 68)**.

unexercised allowing option to expire without it being exercised (p. 618).

unit investment trust unmanagcd invcstmcnt company with fixed numbers of shares outstanding that hold set portfolios over time (p. 52, 701).

uptick NYSE-allowed short sale at last trade price if that price exceeds the last different price before it (p. 89).

utility of wealth desiredness, capacity to satisfy want; used in explaining investment behavior (p. 393).

Value Line enigma predictive value of Value Line ranking system showing that investor who bought stocks with Value Line rankings of 1, while avoiding or selling stocks with rankings of 5, would have earned abnormal risk-adjusted profits (p. 213).

voting rights rights conveyed to owners of common stock shares in which stock owners are given one vote in election of company's board of directors and on other significant issues facing the company (p. 48).

Wall Street walk sale of shares by investors who did not like how company was doing or how company was performing (p. 336).

warrant long-term call options issued by companies; redeemed with issuing corporation for specified number of common stock shares at preset price (p. 51, 646).

weak-form market efficiency statement that current security prices fully reflect all historical information (p. 190).

weekend effect explanation of why returns for Monday differ from other day-of-the-week returns (p. 208).

writing an option selling an option (p. 617).

Yankee bond foreign bonds issued in the United States (p. 46).

yield curve relationship between yield and maturity for group of bonds that are similar in other respects (p. 569).

yield spread difference in yield between any two securities (p. 272, 570).

yield to call   measure of return in which expected return is based on bond being called at some future time, prior to maturity (p. 548).

yield to maturity   return on a bond held to maturity (p. 546).

zero-beta portfolio   portfolio consisting of combination of securities with beta equal to zero or which has zero correlation to chosen risky portfolio (p. 476).

zero sum game   market in which for someone to make a dollar, someone else must loose a dollar (p. 625).

Name and Organization Index

Subject Index